DIRECTORY OF U.S. LABOR
ORGANIZATIONS

DIRECTORY OF U.S. LABOR ORGANIZATIONS

2003 Edition

Court Gifford
Editor

The Bureau of National Affairs, Inc. Washington, D.C. 20037

Published by BNA Books
1231 25th St., NW, Washington, DC 20037

http://www.bnabooks.com

International Standard Serial Number: 0734-6786
International Standard Book Number: 1-57018-392-9

Printed in the United States of America

Preface

The aim of this directory is to provide the user with a comprehensive compilation of a wide range of vital information about labor organizations in the United States and to give a basic overview of organized labor's structure, composition, and leadership. Approximately 30,000 local, intermediate, state, national, and international labor organizations, representing millions of workers in the private and public sectors, are identified in this edition. By law, unions representing even one worker in the private sector are required to file annual financial and membership reports with the U.S. Department of Labor. The union membership figures for "parent" unions listed in Part III are taken directly from the annual reports filed by the individual unions. Part IV identifies unions at the state and local levels that are independent or subgroups of national or international unions. Local and intermediate union bodies identified in Part IV are arranged alphabetically by state and by union within each state, the District of Columbia, and several territories and possessions. The location shown for each union indicates the state (or other jurisdiction) and the city where that union operates. A chart explaining the abbreviations used in Part IV is included at the beginning of that part. Some independent unions that represent municipal or state public employees exclusively are not required to file reports with the federal government and, therefore, may not be included.

Unions are complex and diverse organizations that serve millions and millions of workers.

Increasingly, members and the public are linked to union offices by way of the Internet. Union web sites make it easier for users to keep up with developments such as mergers, changes in leadership, legislation, strikes, and conventions. AFL-CIO and union web sites are included in Parts II and III. Researchers also may find it valuable to examine the more detailed data found in the appendixes covering average membership of unions affiliated with the AFL-CIO, BLS data on union membership and earnings, BLS data on state union membership, and a listing of the union financial reporting requirements under the Labor-Management Reporting and Disclosure Act and the Civil Service Reform Act.

The Directory of U.S. Labor Organizations is now available on the web. The web version includes all the material available in the print version, plus union financial data and membership figures from the LM forms filed with the U.S. Department of Labor for approximately 30,000 local, national, and international unions. The web version of the Directory also includes links to national and international union web sites; connections to dozens of key government and union Internet sites; extensive background information, including links to news about current labor union developments; resource material on national and international labor union issues, and more. For information about how you can have single-user, multi-user, and/or multi-location access to the web Directory, go to http://online.bnabooks.com.

Contents

Part I. Introduction

Union Membership

Union membership in the United States in 2002 fell by 280,000 to 16.1 million (see Appendix A) or 13.2 percent of the wage and salary workforce, as the U.S. economy struggled to recover from the recession following the terrorist attacks on September 11, 2001.

Union membership has hovered around 16 million for the last decade, according to figures released annually by the U.S. Bureau of Labor Statistics.

Nearly 4 in 10 (37.5 percent) of public workers belonged to unions, compared with less than 1 in 10 (8.5 percent) of workers in the private sector (see Chart 3). The unionization rate for government workers has held steady since 1983, the first year for which comparable union data are available, while the rate for private industry workers has fallen by nearly one-half over the same time period. The overall union membership rate recorded by BLS in 1983 was 20.1 percent. No comparable figures for the years prior to 1983 are available.

Local government workers had the highest rate of unionization within the public sector—42.8 percent. In the private sector, transportation workers had the highest union membership rate, at 23.8 percent. Among occupational groups, protective service workers had the highest unionization rate, at 37.0 percent.

Union workers' pay continued to be higher than non-union workers in 2002. The median usual weekly earnings of full-time wage and salary workers who belonged to unions in 2002 was $740, compared to $587 for non-union workers, according to the government survey.

About 1.7 million workers were entitled to union benefits at their workplace, but were not dues-paying union members. More than half of them were employed by the government and about 20 percent worked in the service industry, BLS said.

The membership gap between men and women narrowed again in 2002. The membership rate for men fell slightly to 14.7 percent for men, while the

Chart 1. Union Membership, Ranked by State, 2002

New York	25.3%
Hawaii	24.4%
Alaska	24.3%
Michigan	21.1%
Illinois	19.6%
New Jersey	19.4%
Washington	18.4%
Minnesota	17.6%
California	17.5%
Rhode Island	17.2%
Connecticut	16.7%
Ohio	16.7%
Wisconsin	15.6%
Oregon	15.5%
Pennsylvania	15.5%
Nevada	15.2%
Massachusetts	14.2%
Maryland	14.1%
Montana	14.1%
District of Columbia	13.8%
Indiana	13.3%
West Virginia	13.3%
Missouri	13.2%
Maine	12.9%
Delaware	11.1%
Iowa	11.1%
Kentucky	10.0%
New Hampshire	9.7%
Vermont	9.5%
Tennessee	9.0%
Alabama	8.9%
Oklahoma	8.9%
Kansas	8.2%
Louisiana	8.1%
North Dakota	8.1%
Nebraska	7.9%
Colorado	7.8%
Wyoming	7.8%
Idaho	7.1%
Mississippi	6.6%
New Mexico	6.6%
Utah	6.2%
Georgia	6.0%
Arkansas	5.9%
Virginia	5.9%
Florida	5.7%
South Dakota	5.6%
Arizona	5.5%
Texas	5.1%
South Carolina	4.9%
North Carolina	3.2%

Source: U.S. Bureau of Labor Statistics

Chart 2. Unions With 100,000 Members or More, 2002

2,668,925	National Education Association
1,398,412	International Brotherhood of Teamsters
1,385,043	United Food and Commercial Workers International Union
1,376,292	Service Employees International Union
1,300,000	American Federation of State, County and Municipal Employees
795,335	Laborers' International Union of North America
741,270	American Federation of Teachers
722,987	International Association of Machinists and Aerospace Workers
701,818	International Union, United Automobile, Aerospace and Agricultural Implement Workers of America
589,143	Communications Workers of America
588,790	United Steelworkers of America
538,431	United Brotherhood of Carpenters and Joiners of America
389,173	National Postal Mail Handlers Union
388,526	International Union of Operating Engineers
324,349	United Association of Journeymen and Apprentices of the Plumbing and Pipe Fitting Industry of the United States and Canada
297,150	National Association of Letter Carriers
294,127	American Postal Workers Union
292,395	Paper, Allied-Industrial, Chemical and Engineering Workers International Union
255,137	Hotel Employees and Restaurant Employees International Union
217,604	Union of Needletrades, Industrial and Textile Employees
198,453	American Federation of Government Employees
179,861	Amalgamated Transit Union
153,090	American Nurses' Association
151,257	Sheet Metal Workers International Association
136,586	Office and Professional Employees International Union
135,072	International Association of Bridge, Structural, Ornamental and Reinforcing Iron Workers
115,218	Bakery, Confectionery, Tobacco Workers and Grain Millers International Union
109,105	United Mine Workers of America
104,827	Transportation Communications International Union
104,000	American Federation of Musicians of the United States and Canada
103,506	International Alliance of Theatrical Stage Employes, Moving Picture Technicians, Artists and Allied Crafts of the United States and Canada
102,402	International Union of Painters and Allied Trades
101,823	International Union of Bricklayers and Allied Craftworkers
100,652	National Rural Letter Carriers' Association

Source: U.S. Department of Labor

rate for women remained unchanged, at 11.6 percent. In 1983, the rate for men was 10 points higher than for women.

Blacks had the highest overall rate of union membership, at 16.9 percent of the wage and salary workforce, compared to 12.8 percent for whites and 10.5 percent for Hispanics. Black men had the highest unionization rate among the major demographic groups, at 18.2 percent.

In the manufacturing sector, the proportion of workers belonging to unions declined from 14.6 percent in 2001 to 14.3 percent in 2002. However, union membership grew in the durable goods manufacturing sector from 15.0 percent of all workers in 2001 to 15.6 percent in 2002.

About 900,000 jobs were lost during the year after the 9/11 attacks in the United States. Many of the jobs lost were in traditionally unionized sectors, such as airlines, hotels, construction, and manufacturing.

Membership by State

In 2002, 33 states and the District of Columbia reported lower membership and 15 states registered increases. Two states reported no change in their membership rates from 2001 to 2002. All states in the East North Central, Middle Atlantic, and Pacific divisions had union membership rates above the national average of 13.2 percent, while all states in the East South Central and West South Central divisions had rates below it.

Four states had union membership rates over 20 percent in 2002 (see Chart 1): New York (25.3 percent), Hawaii (24.4 percent), Alaska (24.3 percent), and Michigan (21.1 percent). North Carolina and South Carolina continued to report the lowest union membership rates, 3.2 percent and 4.9 percent, respectively.

California had the largest number of union members (2.5 million), followed by New York (2.0 million), and Illinois (1.1 million). Over one-half (8.1 million) of the 16.1 million union members in the U.S. lived in California, Illinois, Michigan, New York, Ohio, and Pennsylvania.

The BLS union membership estimates are obtained from the Current Population Survey con-

ducted by the U.S. Census Bureau. The survey of approximately 60,000 households provides basic information on the labor force, employment, and unemployment.

Largest Unions

Five unions reported membership in excess of 1 million members in 2002 (see Chart 2). The National Education Association remained the largest union in the U.S. with 2.6 million members, followed by the International Brotherhood of Teamsters (1.4 million), United Food and Commercial Workers International Union (1.4 million), Service Employees International Union (1.4 million), and the American Federation of State, County and Municipal Employees (1.3 million).

AFL-CIO Structure

The majority of national and international unions in the U.S. are affiliated with the American Federation of Labor-Congress of Industrial Organizations, commonly referred to as the AFL-CIO. The federation serves as labor's lobbying representative before the U.S. Congress and state legislatures, reinforcing the lobbying activities of individual unions. It also acts as a watchdog over state and federal regulatory activities, and as American labor's representative in national and international forums. The federation also disseminates labor policy developed by leaders of its affiliated unions, assists in coordinating organizing among its affiliates, and provides research and other assistance through its various departments.

Some affiliated unions are called "international" unions because they have members in both the United States and Canada. But Canada has a labor federation of its own, the Canadian Labour Congress (CLC). Unions affiliated with the AFL-CIO pay per capita dues to support its activities (see Appendix C). The AFL-CIO network (see Part II) is composed of its national headquarters in Washington, D.C., and four regional divisions (see Chart 4). Within the regions are 50 state federations and the Puerto Rico Federation of Labor that function in much the same manner as the national headquarters by lobbying for labor's interests in the state legisla-

---

Chart 3. Union Membership, Employed Wage and Salary Workers, 2002

Occupation

Precision Production, Craft and Repair—20.7%
Operators, Fabricators, and Laborers—19.1%
Managerial and Professional Specialty—13.0%
Service Occupations—12.6%
Technical, Sales, and Administrative Support—8.9%
Farming, Forestry, and Fishing—4.3%

Industry

Government Workers—37.5%
Private Wage and Salary Workers—8.5%
    Transportation and Public Utilities—23.0%
    Manufacturing—14.3%
    Wholesale and Retail Trade—4.5%
    Agriculture—2.3%
    Finance, Insurance, and Real Estate—1.9%

Source: U.S. Bureau of Labor Statistics

---

tures and serving as centers to coordinate activities of affiliates. There also are hundreds of central councils to coordinate activities at the local level.

AFL-CIO policy between conventions is set by the Executive Council (see Chart 5). The responsibilities of the council include proposing and evaluating legislation of interest to the labor movement, developing positions for labor on major national and international issues, assisting unions in organizing and other activities, and resolving jurisdictional disputes among unions.

Another AFL-CIO policy-making body between conventions is the General Board. It consists of the members of the Executive Council and a principal officer of each affiliated international union and department. The General Board acts on matters referred to it by the executive officers or the Executive Council. It meets upon the call of the AFL-CIO president. Unlike members of the Executive Council, General Board members vote as representatives of their unions. Voting strength is based on union membership.

AFL-CIO President John J. Sweeney was elected to office on October 25, 1995, at the federation's

---

Chart 4. AFL-CIO Structure

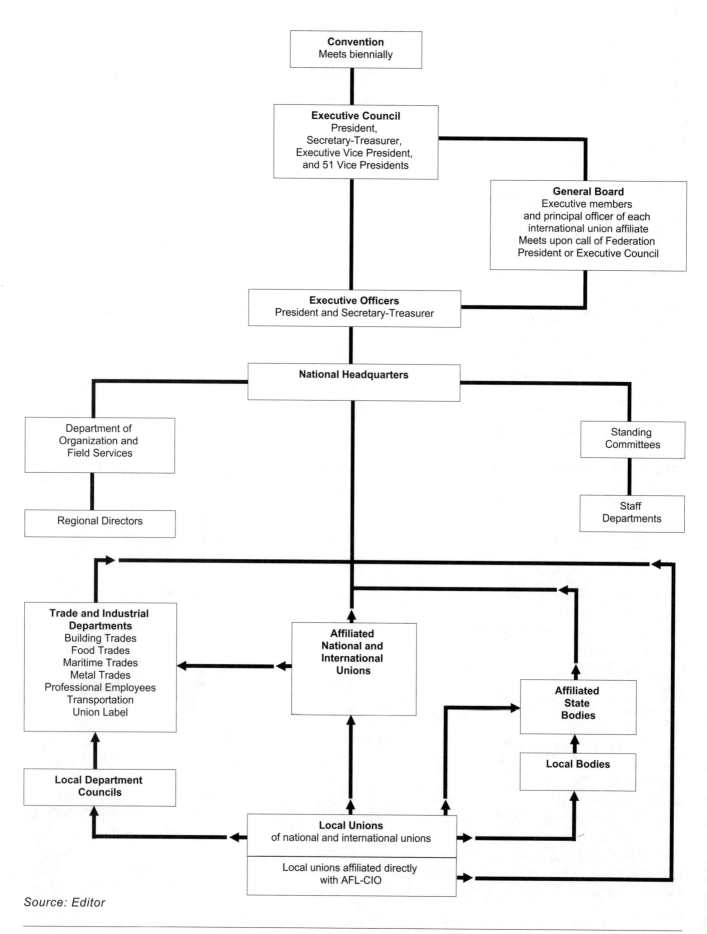

Source: Editor

Chart 5. AFL-CIO Executive Council

President
John J. Sweeney
Secretary-Treasurer
Richard L. Trumka
Executive Vice President
Linda Chavez-Thompson

Vice Presidents
(for address and telephone numbers of unions listed below, and names of other officers, see Part III)

Stuart Appelbaum
President: Retail, Wholesale and Department Store Union

Morton Bahr
President: Communications Workers of America

John M. Bowers
President: International Longshoremen's Association

Clayola Brown
Vice President: Union of Needletrades, Industrial and Textile Employees

R. Thomas Buffenbarger
President: International Association of Machinists and Aerospace Workers

Elizabeth Bunn
Secretary-Treasurer: International Union, United Automobile, Aerospace and Agricultural Implement Workers of America

Sonny Hall
President: Transport Workers Union of America

William Burrus
President: American Postal Workers Union

Sandra Feldman
President: American Federation of Teachers

Edward L. Fire
President: International Union of Electronic, Electrical, Salaried, Machine and Furniture Workers- Communication Wrokers of America

Mac A. Fleming
President: Brotherhood of Maintenance of Way Employes

Patricia A. Friend
President: Association of Flight Attendants

Leo W. Gerard
President: United Steelworkers of America

Ron Gettelfinger
President: International Union, United Automobile, Aerospace and Agricultural Implement Workers of America

Melissa Gilbert
President: Screen Actors Guild

Michael Goodwin
President: Office and Professional Employees International Union

Joe L. Greene
President: American Federation of School Administrators

Sonny Hall
President: Transport Workers Union of America

Frank Hanley
President: International Union of Operating Engineers

Bobby L. Harnage
President: American Federation of Government Employees

Carl Haynes
Vice President: International Brotherhood of Teamsters

Edwin D. Hill
President: International Brotherhood of Electrical Workers

James P. Hoffa
President: International Brotherhood of Teamsters

Joseph J. Hunt
President: International Association of Bridge, Structural, Ornamental and Reinforcing Iron Workers

Frank Hurt
President: Bakery, Confectionery, Tobacco Workers and Grain Millers International Union

Cheryl L. Johnson
Chairperson: United American Nurses

Gloria T. Johnson
President: Coalition of Labor Union Women

James La Sala
President: Amalgamated Transit Union

William Lucy
Secretary-Treasurer: American Federation of State, County and Municipal Employees

Leon Lynch
Vice President: United Steelworkers of America

Martin J. Maddaloni
President: United Association of Journeymen and Apprentices of the Plumbing and Pipe Fitting Industry of the United States and Canada

Edward J. McElroy
Secretary-Treasurer: American Federation of Teachers

Gerald W. McEntee
President: American Federation of State, County and Municipal Employees

Terence M. O'Sullivan
President: Laborers' International Union of North America

Bruce Raynor
President: Union of Needletrades, Industrial and Textile Employees

Dennis Rivera
President: 1199, National Health and Human Service Employee Union

Clyde Rivers
State President: California School Employees Association

Cecil E. Roberts
President: United Mine Workers of America

Arturo S. Rodriguez
President: United Farm Workers of America

Michael Sacco
President: Seafarers International Union of North America

Robert A. Scardelletti
President: Transportation Communications International Union

Harold A. Schaitberger
President: International Association of Fire Fighters

Vincent R. Sombrotto
President: National Association of Letter Carriers

Andrew L. Stern
President: Service Employees International Union

Edward C. Sullivan
President: AFL-CIO Building and Construction Trades Department

Michael J. Sullivan
President: Sheet Metal Workers International Association

Gene Upshaw
Executive Director: Federation of Professional Athletes

John W. Wilhelm
President: Hotel Employees and Restaurant Employees International Union

James A. Williams
President: International Union of Painters and Allied Trades

Capt. Duane Woerth
President: Air Line Pilots Association International

Boyd Young
President: Paper, Allied-Industrial, Chemical Employees International Union

Source: Editor

biennial convention in New York. Sweeney previously was president of the Service Employees International Union.

Reporting Requirements

Under the Labor-Management Reporting and Disclosure Act of 1959, unions that represent workers in the private sector and the U.S. Postal Service are required to submit annual financial reports to the U.S. Department of Labor's Office of Labor-Management Standards (OLMS). Organizations that represent federal workers must file reports in accordance with the Civil Service Reform Act of 1978 (see Appendix D for the types of reports and requirements). Unions that exclusively represent public employees whose employers are states or political subdivisions of states such as counties or municipalities are not required to file reports with OLMS.

All reports, plus copies of the organization's constitution and bylaws, are public information and may be examined at most of the 31 OLMS field offices located in major U.S. cities or at the OLMS headquarters in Washington, D.C. (See Chart 6). Copies of reports for the year 2000 and subsequent years may be viewed at the following site:

http://www.union-reports.dol.gov

Union Member Rights

The law guarantees certain rights to union members and imposes certain responsibilities on union officers (see Chart 7). Title I of the Labor-Management Reporting and Disclosure Act (LMRDA) states that union members have equal rights to participate in union activities; freedom of speech and assembly; a voice in setting rates of dues, fees, and assessments; protection of the right to sue; and safeguards against improper discipline. Union members may enforce these rights through private suit in federal court.

Members also are guaranteed the right to receive or inspect copies of collective bargaining agreements, constitutions, bylaws, and financial reports; nominate candidates for union office, run for office, cast a secret ballot, and protect the conduct of an election; and remove an elected officer guilty of serious misconduct. Members also may not be threatened, fined, expelled, or otherwise disciplined for exercising any LMRDA right.

Chart 6. Financial Reports

Copies of reports for the years 2000 and later may be viewed at the following site:

http://www.union-reports.dol.gov

Reports also may be obtained in person at OLMS field offices in the following cities:

Atlanta	Miami
Boston	Milwaukee
Buffalo	Minneapolis
Chicago	Nashville
Cincinnati	New Orleans
Cleveland	New York
Dallas	Philadelphia
Denver	Pittsburgh
Detroit	St. Louis
Hato Rey, PR	San Francisco
Honolulu	Seattle
Los Angeles	

Information about OLMS, how to obtain reports, the text of the LMRDA, and related information is also available on-line at:

http://www.dol.gov/esa/olms_org.htm

Source: U.S. Department of Labor

Chart 7. Union Member Rights and Officer Responsibilities

The Labor-Management Reporting and Disclosure Act (LMRDA) guarantees certain rights to union members and imposes certain responsibilities on union officers. The law's "Bill of Rights" may only be enforced by union members through private suit in federal court, while other provisions are enforced by the U.S. Labor Department's Office of Labor-Management Standards (OLMS).

Union Member Rights

Under the "Bill of Rights" union members are guaranteed equal rights to participate in union activities, freedom of speech and assembly, a voice in setting rates of dues, fees, and assessments, protection of the right to sue, and safeguards against improper discipline.

Union members and nonunion employees represented by the union have the right to receive or inspect copies of collective bargaining agreements.

Unions are required to file an initial information report (Form LM-1), copies of constitutions and bylaws, and an annual financial report (LM-2/3/4) with OLMS. Unions must make the reports available to members and permit members to examine supporting records. The reports are public information and copies are available from OLMS.

Union members have the right to nominate candidates for union office, run for office, cast a secret ballot, and protest the conduct of an election.

Local union members have the right to an adequate procedure for the removal of an elected officer guilty of serious misconduct.

Unions may only be placed in trusteeship by a parent body for the reasons specified in the law.

A union or any of its officials may not fine, expel, or otherwise discipline a member for exercising any LMRDA right.

No one may use or threaten to use force or violence to interfere with a union member in the exercise of LMRDA rights.

Union Officer Responsibilities

Union officers have a duty to manage the funds and property of the union solely for the benefit of the union and its members in accordance with the union's constitution and bylaws. Union officers or employees who embezzle or steal union funds or other assets commit a federal crime punishable by a fine and/or imprisonment.

Union officers or employees who handle union funds or property must be bonded to provide protection against losses if their union has property and annual financial receipts which exceed $5,000.

Union officers must file an initial information report (LM-1) and annual financial reports (Forms LM-2/3/4) with OLMS, and retain the records necessary to verity the reports for at least five years.

Union officers and employees must file reports concerning any loans and benefits received from, or certain financial interests in, employers whose employees their unions represent and businesses that deal with their unions.

Unions must hold elections of officers of local unions by secret ballot at least every three years, conduct regular elections in accordance with their constitution and bylaws and preserve all records for one year, mail a notice of election to every member at least 15 days prior to the election, comply with a candidate's request to distribute campaign material, not use union funds or resources to promote any candidate (nor may employer funds or resources be used), permit candidates to have election observers, and allow candidates to inspect the union's membership list once within 30 days prior to the election.

A person convicted of certain crimes may not serve as a union officer, employee, or other representative of a union for up to 13 years.

A union may not have outstanding loans to any one officer or employee that in total exceed $2,000 at any time.

A union may not pay the fine of any officer or employee convicted of any willful violation of the LMRDA.

Source: U.S. Department of Labor

PART II. AFL-CIO

This Part lists AFL-CIO officers, executive staff, Trade and Industrial Departments and Staff Departments located in Washington, D.C., and regional and state federations and central labor councils located throughout the United States. For a list of AFL-CIO affiliates and their paid membership, see Appendix C. For further information on affiliates, see the appropriate listing in Part III.

American Federation of Labor-Congress of Industrial Organizations

Web: www.aflcio.org

815 16th St., N.W., Washington, DC 20006
Phone: (202) 637-5000
Fax: (202) 637-5058
Convention: Odd-numbered years
Publication: *America@work*

President: John J. Sweeney
Phone: (202) 637-5231
Administrative Assistant to the President:
Liz Maiorany
Phone: (202) 637-5221
Executive Assistant to the President and
Chief of Staff: Robert W. Welsh
Phone: (202) 637-5298
Secretary to the Executive Assistant and
Chief of Staff: Linda Hall
Phone: (202) 637-5299
Assistant to the President for Government
Affairs: Gerald M. Shea
Phone: (202) 637-5237
Assistant to the President for Public
Affairs: Denise Mitchell
Phone: (202) 637-5340
Assistant to the President: Arleen Gilliam
Phone: (202) 637-5235
Assistant to the President: Arlene
Holt-Baker
Phone: (202) 637-5180
Assistant to the President: Karen Nussbaum
Phone: (202) 637-5064
Assistant to the President: Janet Shenk
Phone: (202) 637-5007
Assistant to the President: John Welsh
Phone: (202) 637-6266
Scheduling Director: Pat Lleras
Phone: (202) 637-3910

Secretary-Treasurer: Richard L.
Trumka
Phone: (202) 637-5300
Executive Assistant to the
Secretary-Treasurer: Brad Burton
Phone: (202) 637-5296
Assistant to the Secretary-Treasurer: Joe
Jurczak
Phone: (202) 637-5330
Administrative Assistant to the
Secretary-Treasurer: Norma Itz
Phone: (202) 637-5229

Executive Vice President: Linda
Chavez-Thompson
Phone: (202) 637-5233
Executive Assistant to the Executive Vice
President: Susan Washington
Phone: (202) 637-5156
Administrative Assistant to the Executive
Vice President: Carmen M. Perez
Phone: (202) 637-5305

Trade and Industrial Departments

Building and Construction Trades Department
815 16th St., N.W., Washington, DC 20006
Phone: (202) 347-1461
Fax: (202) 628-0724
Web: www.buildingtrades.org
President: Edward C. Sullivan
Secretary-Treasurer: Joseph Maloney

Food and Allied Service Trades Department
1925 K St., N.W., Suite 400, Washington, DC 20006-1132
Phone: (202) 737-7200
Fax: (202) 737-7208
Web: www.fastaflcio.org
President: Jeffrey P. Fiedler
Secretary-Treasurer: Gene Bruskin

Industrial Union Council
815 16th St., N.W., Washington, DC 20006
Phone: (202) 637-3966
Fax: (202) 508-6902
Web: www.aflcio.org/manufacturing
Chair: Richard L. Trumka
Director: Bob Baugh

Maritime Trades Department
815 16th St., N.W., Washington, DC 20006
Phone: (202) 628-6300
Fax: (202) 637-3989
President: Michael Sacco
Executive Secretary-Treasurer: Frank Pecquex

Metal Trades Department
888 16th St., N.W., Suite 690, Washington, DC 20006
Phone: (202) 974-8030
Fax: (202) 974-8035
Web: www.metaltrades.org
President: Ronald Ault

Professional Employees, Department for
1025 Vermont Ave., N.W., Suite 1030, Washington, DC 20005
Phone: (202) 638-0320
Fax: (202) 628-4379
President: Paul E. Almeida
Treasurer: Linda Foley

Transportation Trades Department
888 16th St., N.W., Suite 650, Washington, DC 20006
Phone: (202) 628-9262
Fax: (202) 628-0391
Web: www.ttd.org
President: Sonny Hall
Secretary-Treasurer: Patricia A. Friend
Executive Director: Ed Wytkind

Union Label and Service Trades Department
888 16th St., N.W., Washington, DC 20006
Phone: (202) 628-2131
Fax: (202) 638-1602
Web: www.unionlabel.org
President: Charles E. Mercer
Secretary-Treasurer: Matthew C. Bates

Staff Departments

Accounting Department
815 16th St., N.W., Washington, DC 20006
Phone: (202) 637-5250
Controller: Thomas Salvetti

Civil, Human Rights and Women's Rights Department
815 16th St., N.W., Washington, DC 20006
Phone: (202) 637-5270
Director: Richard Womack

Corporate Affairs Department
815 16th St., N.W., Washington, DC 20006
Phone: (202) 637-5160
Director: Ron Blackwell

Facility Management Department
815 16th St., N.W., Washington, DC 20006
Phone: (202) 637-3976
Facility Manager: Mark Zobrisky

Field Mobilization Department
815 16th St., N.W., Washington, DC 20006
Phone: (202) 637-5356
Director: Marilyn Sneiderman
Community Services Office:
Phone: (202) 637-5191

General Counsel Office
815 16th St., N.W., Washington, DC 20006
Phone: (202) 637-5053
General Counsel: Jon Hiatt

Human Resources Department
815 16th St., N.W., Washington, DC 20006
Phone: (202) 637-5026
Director: Karla Garland

Information Technology Department
815 16th St., N.W., Washington, DC 20006
Phone: (202) 637-5268
Director: Bill Mountjoy

International Affairs Department
815 16th St., N.W., Washington, DC 20006
Phone: (202) 637-5050
Director: Barbara Shailor
European Representative: Jerry Zellhoefer
23 Rue de Rome, Paris 75008 France
Phone: 011-331-4-387-7457
Fax: 011-331-4-387-7460

Legislation Department
815 16th St., N.W., Washington, DC 20006
Phone: (202) 637-5320
Director: William Samuel

Meetings and Travel Department
815 16th St., N.W., Washington, DC 20006
Phone: (202) 637-5225
Director: Sam Whalen

Organizing Department
815 16th St., N.W., Washington, DC 20006
Phone: (202) 639-6200
Director: Stewart Acuff

Politics Department
815 16th St., N.W., Washington, DC 20006
Phone: (202) 637-5101
Director: Karen Ackerman

Public Affairs Department
815 16th St., N.W., Washington, DC 20006
Phone: (202) 637-5340
Assistant to the President for Public Affairs: Denise Mitchell
Deputy Director, Publications, Web, Broadcast Division: Donna Jablonski
Phone: (202) 637-5034
Deputy Director, Media Outreach Division: Lane Windham
Phone: (202) 637-3962
Speechwriting Division
Phone: (202) 637-5378

Public Policy Department
815 16th St., N.W., Washington, DC 20006
Phone: (202) 637-5178
Director: Chris Owens

Safety and Health Department
815 16th St., N.W., Washington, DC 20006
Phone: (202) 637-5366
Director: Peg Seminario

Support Services Department
815 16th St., N.W., Washington, DC 20006
Phone: (202) 637-5327
Director: Larry Anderson

Other Organizations

A. Philip Randolph Institute
1444 Eye St., N.W., 3rd Floor,
Washington, DC 20005
Phone: (202) 289-2774
Fax: (202) 289-5289
Web: www.apri.org
President: Norman Hill

AFL-CIO Employees Federal Credit Union
1750 New York Ave., N.W.,
Washington, DC 20006
Phone: (202) 661-7711
Fax: (202) 661-7756
Web: www.aflciocreditunion.com
General Manager: Gavin D. Cochran

AFL-CIO Retirees Association
7720 Bellington Ct., Springfield, VA
22151
Phone: (703) 451-7008
Fax: (703) 451-4042
President: Edwin M. Schmidt

AFL-CIO Working for America Institute
888 16th St., N.W., Washington, DC
20006
Phone: (202) 974-8100; (800)
842-4734
Fax: (202) 974-8101
Web: www.workingforamerica.org
President: John J. Sweeney
Executive Director: Nancy Mills

Alliance for Retired Americans
888 16th St., N.W., Suite 520,
Washington, DC 20006
Phone: (202) 974-8222
Fax: (202) 974-6497
Web: www.retiredamericans.org
President: George J. Kourpias
Executive Director: Edward F. Coyle

American Center for International Labor Solidarity
1925 K St., N.W., Suite 300,
Washington, DC 20006
Phone: (202) 778-4500
Fax: (202) 778-4525
Director: Harry G. Kamberis

Asian Pacific American Labor Alliance
888 16th St., N.W., Washington, DC
20006
Phone: (202) 974-8051
Fax: (202) 974-8056
Web: www.apalanet.org
President: Luisa Blue
Executive Director: Gloria T. Caoile

Center for Working Capital
888 16th St., N.W., Washington, DC
20006
Phone: (202) 974-8020
Fax: (202) 974-8029
Web: www.centerforworkingcapital.
org
President: Robert J. Pleasure

Coalition of Black Trade Unionists
P.O. Box 66268, Washington, DC
20035
Phone: (202) 429-1203
Fax: (202) 429-1102
Web: www.cbtu.org
President: William Lucy
Special Assistant to the President: Wil
Duncan

Coalition of Labor Union Women
1925 K St., N.W., Suite 402,
Washington, DC 20006
Phone: (202) 223-8360
Fax: (202) 776-0537
Web: www.cluw.org
President: Gloria T. Johnson

George Meany Center for Labor Studies
10000 New Hampshire Ave., Silver
Spring, MD 20903
Phone: (301) 431-6400
Fax: (301) 434-0371
Web: www.georgemeany.org
President: Susan J. Schurman

George Meany Memorial Archives
10000 New Hampshire Ave., Silver
Spring, MD 20903
Phone: (301) 431-5451
Fax: (301) 431-0385
Web: www.georgemeany.org
Director: Mike Merrill
Librarian: Ruby Tyson
Phone: (301) 431-5445

Housing Investment Trust
1717 K St., N.W., Suite 707,
Washington, DC 20036
Phone: (202) 331-8055
Fax: (202) 331-8190
Web: www.aflcio-hit.com
Chief Executive Officer: Stephen Coyle

International Labor Communications Association AFL-CIO/CLC
888 16th St., N.W., Suite 630,
Washington, DC 20006
Phone: (202) 637-5068
Fax: (202) 508-6973
Web: www.ilcaonline.org
President: Martin Fishgold
Secretary-Treasurer: Anthony Carobine
Phone: (906) 774-9599
Fax: (906) 774-6829
Executive Director: Lynn D. Clark

Jewish Labor Committee
25 E. 21st St., 2nd Floor, New York,
NY 10010
Phone: (212) 477-0707
Fax: (212) 477-1918
Executive Director: Avram Lyon

Labor Council for Latin American Advancement
888 16th St., N.W., Suite 640,
Washington, DC 20006
Phone: (202) 347-4223
Fax: (202) 347-5095
Web: www.lclaa.org
President: Milton Rosado
Executive Director: Oscar Sanchez

Pride at Work
815 16th St., N.W., Room 5019,
Washington, DC 20006
Phone: (202) 637-5085
Fax: (202) 508-6923
Web: www.prideatwork.org
Co-President: Nancy F. Wohlforth
Co-President: Vacant
Executive Director: Marta Ames

Union Community Fund
888 16th St., N.W., Suite 570,
Washington, DC 20006
Phone: (202) 974-8389
Fax: (202) 974-8393
Web: www.unioncommunityfund.org
Executive Director: Rosalyn W. Pelles

Union Privilege
1125 15th St., N.W., Suite 300,
Washington, DC 20005
Phone: (202) 293-5330
Fax: (202) 293-5311
Web: www.unionprivilege.org
President: Leslie A. Tolf

Field Mobilization and Community Services Regional Offices

Midwest Region
940 W. Adams St., Suite 404, Chicago, IL 60607
Phone: (312) 492-6569
Fax: (312) 492-6610
Area: Illinois, Indiana, Iowa, Kansas, Michigan, Minnesota, Missouri, Nebraska, North Dakota, Ohio, Oklahoma, South Dakota, Wisconsin
Acting Director: Teresa Ball
Community Services Liaison: Nancy I. McCormick
6551 S. Base Rd., Lynn, IN 47355
Phone: (765) 874-1989
Fax: (765) 874-2710

Northeast Region
211 E. 43rd St., Room 304, New York, NY 10017
Phone: (212) 661-1555
Fax: (212) 661-5213
Area: Connecticut, Delaware, District of Columbia, Maine, Maryland, Massachusetts, New Hampshire, New Jersey, New York, Pennsylvania, Puerto Rico, Rhode Island, Vermont, West Virginia
Director: José Alvarez
Deputy Director: Merrilee Milstein
56 Town Line Rd., Rocky Hill, CT 06067
Phone: (860) 571-8467
Fax: (860) 529-2548
Community Services Liaison: William R. Hauenstein
2311 E. Tilden Rd., Harrisburg, PA 17112
Phone: (717) 657-9116
Fax: (717) 657-9747

Southern Region
2314 Sullivan Rd., Suite 100, College Park, GA 30337
Phone: (404) 766-5050
Fax: (404) 766-2049
Area: Alabama, Arkansas, Florida, Georgia, Kentucky, Louisiana, Mississippi, North Carolina, South Carolina, Tennessee, Texas, Virginia
Director: Ken Johnson
Deputy Director: Vacant
Community Services Liaison: J. Robert Miller
3005 Cody St., Irving, TX 75062
Phone: (972) 256-3389
Fax: (972) 594-8912

Western Region
2800 First Ave., Suite 206, Seattle, WA 98121
Phone: (206) 448-4888
Fax: (206) 448-9250
Area: Alaska, Arizona, California, Colorado, Hawaii, Idaho, Montana, Nevada, New Mexico, Oregon, Utah, Washington, Wyoming
Director: Ron Judd
Deputy Director: Jerry Acosta
2761 Geary Blvd., San Francisco, CA 94118
Phone: (415) 292-1400
Fax: (415) 292-1413
Community Services Liaison: Armando Olivas
10395 Palm Desert Dr., Sparks, NV 89436
Phone: (213) 387-1974
Fax: (213) 387-3525

State Federations

Alabama AFL-CIO
435 S. McDonough St., Montgomery, AL 36104
Phone: (334) 834-1061
Fax: (334) 834-1065
Web: www.alaflcio.org
President: D. Stewart Burkhalter
Secretary-Treasurer: Billy J. Tindle

Alaska State AFL-CIO
2501 Commercial Dr., Anchorage, AK 99501
Phone: (907) 258-6284
Fax: (907) 274-0570
Executive President: Jim Sampson
Secretary-Treasurer: Bruce Ludwig

Arizona State AFL-CIO
5818 N. 7th St., Suite 200, Phoenix, AZ 85014
Phone: (602) 631-4488
Fax: (602) 631-4490
Web: www.azaflcio.org
President: Rebekah Friend
Secretary-Treasurer: Micahel McGrath

Arkansas AFL-CIO
1115 Bishop St., Little Rock, AR 72202
Phone: (501) 375-9101
Fax: (501) 375-8217
President: Alan B. Hughes
Secretary-Treasurer: Jean Lee

California Labor Federation, AFL-CIO
600 Grand Ave., Suite 410, Oakland, CA 94610
Phone: (510) 663-4000
Fax: (510) 663-4099
Web: www.calaborfed.org
President: Tom Rankin
Executive Secretary-Treasurer: Art Pulaski

Colorado AFL-CIO
10 Lakeside Ln., Suite 1-A, Denver, CO 80212
Phone: (303) 433-2100
Fax: (303) 433-1260
Web: www.coaflcio.org
President: Steve Adams
Secretary-Treasurer: Estevan M. Trujillo

Connecticut AFL-CIO
56 Town Line Rd., Rocky Hill, CT 06067
Phone: (860) 571-6191
Fax: (860) 571-6190
Web: www.ctaflcio.org
President: John W. Olsen
Secretary-Treasurer: Lori Pelletier

Delaware State AFL-CIO
922 New Rd., Wilmington, DE 19805
Phone: (302) 999-9886
Fax: (302) 999-9840
President: Michael A. Begatto
296 Churchmans Rd., New Castle, DE 19720
Phone: (302) 323-2121
Fax: (302) 323-2119
Secretary-Treasurer: James P. Ciliberto
1501 Casho Mill Rd., Suite 11, Newark, DE 19711
Phone: (302) 292-6670
Fax: (302) 292-6674

Florida AFL-CIO
135 S. Monroe St., Tallahassee, FL 32301
Phone: (850) 224-6926
Fax: (850) 224-2266
Web: www.flaflcio.org
President: Cindy Hall
Secretary-Treasurer: Dwayne Sealy

Georgia State AFL-CIO
501 Pulliam St., S.W., Suite 549, Atlanta, GA 30312
Phone: (404) 525-2793
Fax: (404) 525-5983
Web: www.gaaflcio.org
President: Richard Ray
Secretary-Treasurer: Charlie Key

Hawaii State AFL-CIO
320 Ward Ave., Suite 209, Honolulu, HI 96814
Phone: (808) 597-1441
Fax: (808) 593-2149
Web: www.hawaflcio.org
President: Harold J. Dias, Jr.

Idaho State AFL-CIO
412 E. 41st St., Suite 5, Boise, ID 83714
Phone: (208) 321-4814
Fax: (208) 321-4827
Web: www.idaflcio.unions-america. com
President: David D. Whaley
Secretary-Treasurer: Cindy Hedge

Illinois AFL-CIO
55 W. Wacker Dr., Suite 716, Chicago, IL 60601
Phone: (312) 251-1414
Fax: (312) 251-1420
Web: www.ilafl-cio.org
President: Margaret Blackshere
Secretary-Treasurer: Michael Carrigan
534 S. 2nd St., Springfield, IL 62701
Phone: (217) 544-4014
Fax: (217) 544-0225

Indiana State AFL-CIO
1701 W. 18th St., Indianapolis, IN 46202
Phone: (317) 632-9147
Fax: (317) 638-1217
Web: www.aflcio.gen.in.us
President: Ken Zeller
Acting Secretary-Treasurer: Ben Ramsey

Iowa Federation of Labor, AFL-CIO
2000 Walker St., Suite A, Des Moines, IA 50317
Phone: (515) 262-9571
Fax: (515) 262-9573
Web: www.iowaaflcio.org
President: Mark L. Smith
Secretary-Treasurer: Ken Sagar

Kansas AFL-CIO
2131 S.W. 36th St., Topeka, KS 66611
Phone: (785) 267-0100
Fax: (785) 267-0919
Web: www.kansasaflcio.org
President: Ron Eldridge
Executive Secretary-Treasurer: Jim DeHoff

Kentucky State AFL-CIO
340-1 Democrat Dr., Frankfort, KY 40601
Phone: (502) 695-6172
Fax: (502) 695-6176
Web: www.kyaflcio.org
President: William J. Londrigan
Secretary-Treasurer: Chris Sanders

Louisiana AFL-CIO
P.O. Box 3477, Baton Rouge, LA 70821 (mailing address)
429 Government St., Baton Rouge, LA 70802 (street address)
Phone: (225) 383-5741
Fax: (225) 383-8847
President: John R. Bourg
Secretary-Treasurer: Sibal S. Holt

Maine AFL-CIO
P.O. Box 2669, Bangor, ME 04402 (mailing address)
157 Park St., Suite 1, Bangor, ME 04401 (street address)
Phone: (207) 947-0006
Fax: (207) 945-9984
Web: www.mainepage.com/maineafl-cio
President: Edward F. Gorham
Secretary-Treasurer: Ned McCann

Maryland State and D.C. AFL-CIO
7 School St., Annapolis, MD 21401
Phone: (410) 269-1940; (301) 261-1400 (DC Metro Area)
Fax: (410) 280-2956
President: Fred Mason
Secretary-Treasurer: Donna Edwards

Massachusetts AFL-CIO
389 Main St., Malden, MA 02148
Phone: (718) 324-8230
Fax: (718) 324-8225
Web: www.massaflcio.org
President: Robert J. Haynes
Secretary-Treasurer: Kathleen A. Casavant

Michigan State AFL-CIO
419 Washington Sq. S., Suite 200, Lansing, MI 48933
Phone: (517) 487-5966
Fax: (517) 487-5213
Web: www.miaflcio.org
President: Mark T. Gaffney
Secretary-Treasurer: Tina Abbott

Minnesota AFL-CIO
175 Aurora Ave., St. Paul, MN 55103
Phone: (651) 227-7647
Fax: (651) 227-3801
Web: www.mnaflcio.org
President: Ray Waldron
Secretary-Treasurer: Steve Hunter

Mississippi AFL-CIO
P.O. Box 3379, Jackson, MS 39207 (mailing address)
760 N. West St., Jackson, MS 39202 (street address)
Phone: (601) 948-0517
Fax: (601) 948-8588
President and Secretary-Treasurer: Robert Shaffer

Missouri AFL-CIO
227 Jefferson St., Jefferson City, MO 65101
Phone: (573) 634-2115
Fax: (573) 634-5618
Web: www.moaflcio.org
President: Hugh M. McVey
Secretary-Treasurer: Herb Johnson

Montana State AFL-CIO
P.O. Box 1176, Helena, MT 59624 (mailing address)
110 W. 13th St., Helena, MT 59601 (street address)
Phone: (406) 442-1708
Fax: (406) 449-3324
Web: www.mtaflcio.com
President: Jim McGarvey
Executive Secretary: Jerry Driscoll

Nebraska State AFL-CIO
5418 S. 27th St., Suite 1, Omaha, NE 68107
Phone: (402) 734-1300
Fax: (402) 734-1205
President: Ken E. Mass
Secretary-Treasurer: James M. Tylski

Nevada State AFL-CIO
3005 Ripon Dr., Las Vegas, NV 89134
Phone: (775) 882-7490
Fax: (775) 882-1701
Web: www.nvaflcio.org
President: Walt Elliot
Executive Secretary-Treasurer: Danny L. Thompson
602 E. John St., Carson City, NV 89706

New Hampshire AFL-CIO
161 Londonderry Tpke., Hookset, NH 03106
Phone: (603) 623-7302
Fax: (603) 623-7304
Web: www.nhaflcio.org
President: Mark S. MacKenzie
Secretary-Treasurer: William Stetson

New Jersey State AFL-CIO
106 W. State St., Trenton, NJ 08608
Phone: (609) 989-8730
Fax: (609) 989-8734
Web: www.njaflcio.org
President: Charles Wowkanech
Secretary-Treasurer: Laurel Brennan

New Mexico Federation of Labor, AFL-CIO
130 Alvarado Dr., N.W., Suite 200, Albuquerque, NM 87108
Phone: (505) 262-2629
Fax: (505) 266-7155
President: Christine Trujillo
Secretary-Treasurer: James Beaty
Executive Director: Dan Rivera

New York State AFL-CIO
48 E. 21st St., 12th Floor, New York, NY 10010
Phone: (212) 777-6040
Fax: (212) 777-8422
Web: www.nysaflcio.org
President: Denis M. Hughes
Secretary-Treasurer: Paul F. Cole
100 S. Swan St., Albany, NY 12210
Phone: (518) 436-8516
Fax: (518) 436-8470

North Carolina State AFL-CIO
P.O. Box 10805, Raleigh, NC 27605 (mailing address)
1408 Hillsborough St., Raleigh, NC 27605 (street address)
Phone: (919) 833-6678
Fax: (919) 828-2102
Web: www.aflcionc.org
President: James Andrews
Secretary-Treasurer: Ray Riffe

North Dakota AFL-CIO
1323 E. Front St., Bismarck, ND 58504
Phone: (701) 223-0784
Fax: (701) 223-9387
Web: www.ndaflcio.org
President: David L. Kemnitz
Secretary-Treasurer: Chris Y. Runge
Phone: (701) 223-1964
Fax: (701) 223-1755

Ohio AFL-CIO
395 E. Broad St., Suite 300, Columbus, OH 43215
Phone: (614) 224-8271
Fax: (614) 224-2671
Web: www.ohaflcio.org
President: William A. Burga
Secretary-Treasurer: Petee Talley

Oklahoma State AFL-CIO
501 N.E. 27th St., Oklahoma City, OK 73105
Phone: (405) 528-2409
Fax: (405) 525-2810
Web: www.okaflcio.org
President and Secretary-Treasurer: Jim C. Curry

Oregon AFL-CIO
2110 State St., Salem, OR 97301
Phone: (503) 585-6320; (503)
224-3169 (Portland Area)
Fax: (503) 585-1668
Web: www.oraflcio.unions-america.
com
President: Tim Nesbitt
Secretary-Treasurer: Brad Witt

Pennsylvania AFL-CIO
231 State St., 7th Floor, Harrisburg, PA
17101
Phone: (717) 238-9351
Fax: (717) 238-8541
Web: www.paaflcio.org
President: William M. George
Secretary-Treasurer: Richard W.
Bloomingdale
Phone: (717) 231-2840
Fax: (717) 231-2850

**Puerto Rico Federation of Labor,
AFL-CIO**
P.O. Box 19689, Fernandez Juncos
Sta., Santurce, PR 00910 (mailing
address)
1704 Ponce de Leon Ave., Stop 24 1/2,
Santurce, PR 00922 (street address)
Phone: (787) 728-0320
Fax: (787) 728-0470
President: José Rodriquez Baez
Secretary-Treasurer: Renan Soto

Rhode Island AFL-CIO
194 Smith St., Providence, RI 02908
Phone: (401) 751-7100
Fax: (401) 331-8533
President: Frank J. Montanaro
Secretary-Treasurer: George H. Nee

South Carolina AFL-CIO
254 LaTonea Rd., Columbia, SC 29210
Phone: (803) 798-8300
Fax: (803) 798-2231
President: Donna DeWitt
Secretary-Treasurer: Mike Godfrey
80 Persimmon Rd., Great Falls, SC
24075

**South Dakota State Federation of Labor,
AFL-CIO**
P.O. Box 1445, Sioux Falls, SD
57101 (mailing address)
738 S. First Ave., Sioux Falls, SD
57104 (street address)
Phone: (605) 339-7284
Fax: (605) 339-7285
President and Financial Secretary: Gil
Koetzle

Tennessee AFL-CIO Labor Council
1901 Lindell Ave., Nashville, TN
37203
Phone: (615) 269-7111
Fax: (615) 269-8534
Web: www.tnaflcio.org
President: Harold G. Woods
Secretary-Treasurer: Eddie L. Bryan

Texas AFL-CIO
P.O. Box 12727, Austin, TX
78711 (mailing address)
1106 Lavaca St., Suite 200, Austin, TX
78701 (street address)
Phone: (512) 477-6195
Fax: (512) 477-2962
Web: www.texasaflcio.org
President: Joe D. Gunn
Secretary-Treasurer: Emmett Sheppard

Utah State AFL-CIO
2261 S. Redwood Rd., Suite M, Salt
Lake City, UT 84119
Phone: (801) 972-2771
Fax: (801) 972-9344
President and Secretary-Treasurer: Ed P.
Mayne

Vermont State Labor Council, AFL-CIO
P.O. Box 858, Montpelier, VT
05601 (mailing address)
7 Court St., 4th Floor, Montpelier, VT
05602 (street address)
Phone: (802) 223-5229
Fax: (802) 223-1123
Web: www.vtafl-cio.org
President: Ron Pickering
Secretary-Treasurer: Florence Stancliffe

Virginia State AFL-CIO
3315 W. Broad St., Richmond, VA
23230
Phone: (804) 355-7444
Fax: (804) 353-0442
Web: www.va-aflcio.org
President: Daniel G. LeBlanc
Secretary-Treasurer: James R. Leaman

**Washington State Labor Council,
AFL-CIO**
314 First Ave., W., Seattle, WA 98119
Phone: (206) 281-8901
Fax: (206) 285-5805
Web: www.wslc.org
President: Rick Bender
Secretary-Treasurer: Alan O. Link

West Virginia AFL-CIO
501 Leon Sullivan Way, Suite 304,
Charleston, WV 25301
Phone: (304) 344-3557
Fax: (304) 344-3550
Web: www.wvaflcio.org
President: Jim L. Bowen
Secretary-Treasurer: Kenneth M. Perdue

Wisconsin State AFL-CIO
6333 W. Blue Mound Rd., Milwaukee,
WI 53213
Phone: (414) 771-0700
Fax: (414) 771-1715
Web: www.wisaflcio.org
President: David Newby
Secretary-Treasurer: Phillip L. Neuenfeldt

Wyoming State AFL-CIO
1021 W. 23rd St., Suite A, Cheyenne,
WY 82001
Phone: (307) 635-2823
Fax: (307) 635-8516
President: Dale Hill
Executive Secretary: John M. Faunce

Central Labor Councils

Alabama

Jefferson County Labor Council, AFL-CIO
2522 Mikell Rd., Hayden, AL 35079
Phone: (205) 738-2912
Fax: (205) 647-6715
President: Richard W. Jones

Mid-State Labor Council, AFL-CIO
200 Fulton Gap Cir., Sylacauga, AL 35150
Phone: (256) 245-2551
President: Scott Williams

Montgomery Central Labor Council, AFL-CIO
P.O. Box 241883, Montgomery, AL 36124
Phone: (334) 242-2891
President: Pete Wethington

North Alabama Area Labor Council, AFL-CIO
218 Lime-Quarry Rd., Madison, AL 35758
Phone: (256) 461-8476
Fax: (256) 772-0617
President: Charlie Jones

Northeast Alabama Labor Council, AFL-CIO
5077 Pinewood Dr., Gadsden, AL 35903
Phone: (256) 236-2506
Fax: (256) 236-0272
President: Charlotte Flowers

Shoals Area Central Labor Council
P.O. Box 831, Sheffield, AL 35660
Phone: (256) 383-2758
Fax: (256) 383-2758
President: Gene Tackett

Southwest Alabama Labor Council, AFL-CIO
P.O. Box 7688, Mobile, AL 36670
Phone: (334) 478-9060
Fax: (334) 476-0606
President: Byron Vice

West Alabama Labor Council, AFL-CIO
7801 Lake Judson Rd., Cottondale, AL 35453
Phone: (205) 752-9433
Fax: (205) 752-7707
President: Ann Skelton

West Central Alabama Labor Council, AFL-CIO
P.O. Box 362, Oakman, AL 35579
Phone: (205) 622-3206
President: Jackie Peoples

Wiregrass Labor Council, AFL-CIO
116 Blackhawk Dr., Daleville, AL 36322
Phone: (334) 598-6308
Fax: (334) 503-9503
Secretary-Treasurer: Don Shaw

Alaska

Anchorage Central Labor Council, AFL-CIO
P.O. Box 91136, Anchorage, AK 99509
Phone: (907) 274-0827
Fax: (907) 272-0292
President: Valerie Baffone

Fairbanks Central Labor Council, AFL-CIO
819 First Ave., Fairbanks, AK 99701
Phone: (907) 452-8131
Fax: (907) 452-1434
President: John Brown

Juneau Central Labor Council, AFL-CIO
723 W. 10th St., Juneau, AK 99801
Phone: (907) 586-2874
Fax: (907) 463-5116
President: Max Mielke

Kenai Peninsula Central Labor Council, AFL-CIO
2501 Commercial Dr., Anchorage, AK 99502
Phone: (907) 272-4571
Fax: (907) 274-0570
Business Agent: Blake Johnson

Ketchikan Central Labor Council, AFL-CIO
2204 Tongass Ave., Ketchikan, AK 99901
Phone: (907) 225-4010
Fax: (907) 225-3924
President: Roe Thomas

Arizona

Central Arizona Labor Council, AFL-CIO
5818 N. 7th St., No. 208, Phoenix, AZ 85014
Phone: (602) 263-5460
Fax: (602) 263-9252
President: William T. Murphree

Coconino and Navajo Counties Central Labor Body, AFL-CIO
P.O. Box 30996, Flagstaff, AZ 86003
Phone: (928) 699-2352
President: Paulette H. Meyers

Eastern Arizona Labor Council, AFL-CIO
1650 N. 26th St., Phoenix, AZ 85008
Phone: (602) 275-6222
Fax: (602) 244-2402
President: Walter Goodman

Nal-Nishii Federation of Labor, AFL-CIO
P.O. Box 1001, Window Rock, AZ 86515
Phone: (520) 871-5323
President: Lawrence Oliver

Southern Arizona Central Labor Council, AFL-CIO
606 S. Plumer Ave., Tucson, AZ 85719
Phone: (520) 882-8168
Fax: (520) 670-1735
President: Ian Robertson

Yavapai County Central Labor Council, AFL-CIO
P.O. Box 1162, Prescott, AZ 86301
Phone: (520) 445-0292
President: Merle Langfeldt

Arkansas

Camden Central Trades and Labor Council, AFL-CIO
2724 Cherokee Ave., Camden, AR 71701
Phone: (870) 231-5839
President: Danny Launius

Central Arkansas Labor Council, AFL-CIO
7804-A Delray Dr., Little Rock, AR 72227
Phone: (501) 833-1200
Fax: (501) 664-5420
President: Nancy T. Eddy

Crossett Labor Council, AFL-CIO
3207 Prairie Rd., Hamburg, AR 71646
Phone: (870) 364-4530
Fax: (870) 364-4530
President: Jerry Cruce

East Central Arkansas Labor Council, AFL-CIO
622 Mann St., Forrest City, AR 72335
President: Louise Fields

Hot Spring and Saline Counties Labor Council, AFL-CIO
2303 Cherry Xing, Benton, AR 72015
Phone: (501) 315-2054
President: Raymond F. Myers

Hot Springs Labor Union Council, AFL-CIO
154 Morphew Rd., Hot Springs, AR 71913
Phone: (501) 767-5979
President: Brian Perrine

Jefferson County Trades and Labor Council, AFL-CIO
1504 Dansing Rapid Dr., Pine Bluff, AR 71603
Phone: (870) 541-3772
Fax: (870) 247-9635
President: Dallas C. Ford

Northeast Arkansas Central Trades and Labor Council, AFL-CIO
2227 C.C. 353, Bono, AR 72416
President: Robert Lloyd

Northwest Arkansas Joint Labor Council, AFL-CIO
P.O. Box 49, Fayetteville, AR 72701
Phone: (479) 521-3021
President: Steve Ritchie

Sebastian-Crawford Counties AFL-CIO Labor Council
2237 Hwy. 348, Rudy, AR 72952
Phone: (501) 646-6143
President: Tom Clemmons

Texarkana Central Trades and Labor Council, AFL-CIO
221 Marguerite Dr., Texarkana, AR 71854
President: Gloria Lynn

Union County Labor Council, AFL-CIO
604 S. Nelson Ave., El Dorado, AR 71730
Phone: (870) 862-1111
President: David Ross

White River Valley Labor Council, AFL-CIO
Status Pending

California

Alameda County AFL-CIO, Central Labor Council
7992 Capwell Dr., Oakland, CA 94621
Phone: (510) 632-4242
Fax: (510) 632-3993
Executive Secretary-Treasurer: Judith M. Goff

Butte and Glenn Counties AFL-CIO, Central Labor Council of
P.O. Box 840, Magalia, CA 95954
Phone: (530) 343-9474
Fax: (530) 873-3680
President: Mickey Harrington

Contra Costa County AFL-CIO, Central Labor Council of
1333 Pine St., No. E, Martinez, CA 94553
Phone: (925) 228-0161
Fax: (925) 228-0224
Executive Director: John Dalrymple

Five Counties Central Labor Council, AFL-CIO
2865 Churn Creek Rd., Redding, CA 96002
Phone: (503) 241-0319
Secretary-Treasurer: Gary Sharette

Fresno-Madera-Tulare-Kings Central Labor Council
3485 W. Shaw Ave., No. 101, Fresno, CA 93711
Phone: (559) 275-1151
Fax: (559) 276-2150
Executive Secretary-Treasurer: Randy C. Ghan

Humboldt and Del Norte Counties AFL-CIO, Central Labor Council of
840 E St., Suite 9, Eureka, CA 95501
Phone: (707) 443-7371
Fax: (707) 443-0819
President: Jim Smith

Kern, Inyo and Mono Counties Central Labor Council, AFL-CIO
200 W. Jeffrey St., Bakersfield, CA 93305
Phone: (805) 324-6451
Fax: (805) 327-8379
President: Ward Wollesen

Los Angeles County Federation of Labor, AFL-CIO
2130 W. James M. Wood Blvd., Los Angeles, CA 90006
Phone: (213) 381-5611
Fax: (213) 383-0772
Executive Secretary-Treasurer: Miguel Contreras

Marysville Central Labor Council, AFL-CIO
468 Century Park Dr., Yuba City, CA 95991
Phone: (530) 671-6228
Fax: (530) 671-4689
President: A.C. Steelman

Merced-Mariposa County Central Labor Council, AFL-CIO
625 W. Olive Ave., Suite 103, Merced, CA 95348
Phone: (209) 722-3636
Fax: (209) 722-9640
President: Jerry Martin

Monterey Bay Central Labor Council, AFL-CIO
10353 Merritt St., Castroville, CA 95012
Phone: (831) 633-1869
Fax: (831) 633-1859
Secretary-Treasurer: Ed Brown

Napa and Solano Counties AFL-CIO, Central Labor Council of
945 Empire St., Fairfield, CA 94533
Phone: (707) 428-1055
Fax: (707) 428-1393
Acting President: Linda Russell

North Bay Labor Council, AFL-CIO
1700-C Corby Ave., Santa Rosa, CA 95407
Phone: (707) 545-6970
Fax: (707) 544-6336
Secretary-Treasurer: Alex Mallonee

Orange County AFL-CIO, Central Labor Council of
1010 W. Chapman Ave., Suite 210, Orange, CA 92868
Phone: (714) 532-1570
Fax: (714) 953-3086
Executive Secretary-Treasurer: Al Ybarra

Sacramento Central Labor Council, AFL-CIO
2840 El Centro Rd., Suite 111, Sacramento, CA 95833
Phone: (916) 927-9772
Fax: (916) 927-1643
Executive Secretary: Bill Camp

San Bernardino and Riverside Counties, Central Labor Council of
1074 E. La Cadena Dr., No. 1, Riverside, CA 92501
Phone: (909) 825-7871
Fax: (909) 825-0110
Executive Secretary-Treasurer: Laurie Stalnaker

San Diego-Imperial Counties Labor Council, AFL-CIO
3717 Camino del Rio, San Diego, CA 92108
Phone: (619) 283-5411
Fax: (619) 283-2782
Secretary-Treasurer: Jerry Butkiewicz

San Francisco Labor Council, AFL-CIO
1188 Franklin St., Suite 203, San Francisco, CA 94109
Phone: (415) 440-4809
Fax: (415) 440-9297
Secretary-Treasurer: Walter L. Johnson

San Joaquin and Calaveras Counties, Central Labor Council of
121 E. Vine St., Stockton, CA 95202
Phone: (209) 948-5526
Fax: (209) 948-2652
Secretary-Treasurer: Sandra Carter

San Mateo County Central Labor Council, AFL-CIO
1153 Chess Dr., Suite 200, Foster City, CA 94404
Phone: (650) 572-8848
Fax: (650) 572-2481
Executive Secretary-Treasurer: Shelley Kessler

South Bay AFL-CIO, Labor Council of
2102 Almaden Rd., Suite 107, San Jose, CA 95125
Phone: (408) 266-3790
Fax: (408) 266-2653
Web: www.atwork.org
Executive Officer: Amy B. Dean

Stanislaus and Tuolumne Counties, Central Labor Council of
1125 Kansas Ave., Modesto, CA 95351
Phone: (209) 523-8079
Fax: (209) 523-2619
Secretary-Treasurer: Lucille Palmer-Byrd

Tri-Counties Central Labor Council of Ventura, Santa Barbara, Santa Maria and San Luis Obispo, AFL-CIO
21 S. Dos Caminos St., Ventura, CA 93003
Phone: (805) 641-3712
Fax: (805) 643-9426
Executive Secretary-Treasurer: Marilyn Valenzuela

Colorado

Boulder Area Labor Council, AFL-CIO
P.O. Box 957, Boulder, CO 80306
Phone: (303) 544-0166
President: Herman Romero

Colorado Springs Area Labor Council, AFL-CIO
2150 Naegele Rd., Colorado Springs, CO 80904
Phone: (719) 633-3872
Fax: (719) 633-2553
President: Marshall Johnson

Denver Area Labor Federation, AFL-CIO
10 Lakeside Ln., Suite 1B, Denver, CO 80212
Phone: (303) 477-6111
Fax: (303) 477-6123
President: Leslie Moody

Northern Colorado Central Labor Council, AFL-CIO
1308 Meadowridge Ct., Loveland, CO 80537
Phone: (970) 490-5931
President: Randall W. Chestnut

Pueblo Area Labor Council, AFL-CIO
108 Broadway, Pueblo, CO 81005
Phone: (719) 543-6053
Fax: (719) 542-7064
President: Don Difatta

Western Colorado Trades and Labor Assembly, AFL-CIO
60815 Hwy. 50, Montrose, CO 81401
Phone: (970) 209-4507
Fax: (970) 323-9476
President: Tammy Theis

Connecticut

Bristol Labor Council, AFL-CIO (Greater)
30 Walnut St., Bristol, CT 06010
Phone: (860) 493-1570
Fax: (860) 953-1777
President: Mike Petosa

Danbury Central Labor Council, AFL-CIO
P.O. Box 121, Danbury, CT 06813
Phone: (877) 777-2666
Fax: (203) 317-4759
President: James Juliano

Fairfield County Labor Council, AFL-CIO
290 Post Rd. W., Westport, CT 06880
Phone: (203) 226-4751
President: Thomas Wilkinson

Hartford Labor Council, AFL-CIO (Greater)
77 Huyshope Ave., Suite 210, Hartford, CT 06106
Phone: (860) 757-8785
Fax: (860) 547-1979
President: Judy D. Warfield

Meriden Labor Council, AFL-CIO
35 Pleasant St., Suite 1A, Meriden, CT 06450
Phone: (203) 634-8830
President: Thomas Bruenn

Middletown Labor Council, AFL-CIO
93 Doral Ln., Southington, CT 06489
Phone: (860) 257-9782
Fax: (860) 257-8214
President: Stefan Ozga

New Britain Central Labor Council, AFL-CIO
29 Wellington St., New Britain, CT 06053
Phone: (860) 332-8587
President: Francis Zicardi

New Haven Central Labor Council, AFL-CIO (Greater)
267 Chapel St., New Haven, CT 06513
Phone: (203) 865-3259
Fax: (203) 776-6438
President: Robert J. Proto

Northeastern Connecticut Central Labor Council, AFL-CIO
P.O. Box 448, Willimantic, CT 06226
Phone: (860) 456-1644
Fax: (860) 456-1232
President: Fletcher Fischer

Southeastern Connecticut Central Labor Council, AFL-CIO
P.O. Box 7275, Groton, CT 06340
Phone: (860) 448-0552
Fax: (860) 448-3721
President: Wayne J. Burgess

Western Connecticut Central Labor Council
P.O. Box 1027, Waterbury, CT 06721
Phone: (860) 263-6623
Fax: (203) 755-2120
President: Blair F. Bertaccini

District of Columbia

Metropolitan Washington Council, AFL-CIO
1925 K St., N.W., Suite 410, Washington, DC 20006
Phone: (202) 857-3410
Fax: (202) 857-3420
President: Joslyn N. Williams

Florida

Broward County AFL-CIO
1700 N.W. 66th Ave., Suite 100C, Plantation, FL 33313
Phone: (954) 327-9007
Fax: (954) 327-9081
President: Daniel Reynolds

Central Florida AFL-CIO
P.O. Box 560779, Orlando, FL 32856
Phone: (407) 492-0168
Fax: (407) 654-3811
President: Debra M. Booth

North Central Florida AFL-CIO, Central Labor Council of
P.O. Box 140420, Gainesville, FL 32614
Phone: (352) 372-6888
Fax: (352) 335-2587
President: Tom Summers

North Florida Central Labor Council
966 Liberty St., Jacksonville, FL 32206
Phone: (904) 634-1217
President: Eddie Dedmon

Northwest Florida Federation of Labor, AFL-CIO
8233 Lifair Dr., Pensacola, FL 32506
Phone: (850) 455-2000
Fax: (850) 455-9672
President: Cecilia Gentry

Palm Beach-Treasure Coast, AFL-CIO
1003 Belvedere Rd., Suite 1, West Palm Beach, FL 33405
Phone: (561) 833-8571
Fax: (561) 434-0455
President: Michele Nemo

South Florida AFL-CIO
7910 N.W. 25th St., No. 201, Miami, FL 33122
Phone: (305) 593-8886
Fax: (305) 593-7806
President: Fred Frost

Southwest Florida Central Labor Council, AFL-CIO
6300 S. Pointe Blvd., Apt. 314, Fort Myers, FL 33919
Phone: (941) 267-4483
Fax: (941) 267-0341
President: William Sunday

Space Coast AFL-CIO Labor Council
P.O. Box 3787, Cocoa, FL 32924
Phone: (407) 631-0110
Fax: (407) 631-0103
President: Barry L. Beattie

West Central Florida Federation of Labor, AFL-CIO
10108 U.S. Hwy. 92 E., Tampa, FL 33610
Phone: (813) 740-2233
Fax: (813) 740-2234
President: R. Floyd Suggs

Georgia

Albany/Southwest Georgia Labor Council, AFL-CIO
2319 White Hall Ln., Albany, GA 31707
Phone: (912) 432-0799
Fax: (912) 435-3273
President: Edward J. Tynes

Athens Area Central Labor Council, AFL-CIO
230 Gilleland Dr., Athens, GA 30606
Phone: (706) 540-9756
Fax: (770) 621-4110
President: Kenneth Hembre

Atlanta Labor Council, AFL-CIO
501 Pulliam St., S.W., Atlanta, GA 30312
Phone: (404) 525-3559
Fax: (404) 525-3550
President: Charles Flemming

Augusta Federation of Trades, AFL-CIO
1250 Reynolds St., Augusta, GA 30901
Phone: (706) 722-6357
President: Dennis G. Rocque

Central Georgia Federation of Trades and Labor Council
P.O. Box 5263, Macon, GA 31208
Phone: (912) 743-7017
Fax: (912) 743-4482
President: Michael H. Gardner

Chattahoochee Valley Labor Council, AFL-CIO
P.O. Box 477, Midland, GA 31820
Phone: (706) 561-1338
Fax: (706) 718-5579
President: Raymond Taylor

Northwest Georgia Labor Council, AFL-CIO
P.O. Box 408, Buchanan, GA 30013
President: Rick Pettit

Savannah and Vicinity, AFL-CIO Trades and Labor Assembly, AFL-CIO
P.O. Box 22654, Savannah, GA 31403
Phone: (912) 921-7873
Fax: (912) 921-7802
President: Brett Hulme

South Georgia Labor Council, AFL-CIO
603 4-H Club Rd., Lake Park, GA 31636
Phone: (229) 559-7109
President: Linda A. Ray

Southeast Georgia Central Labor Council, AFL-CIO
P.O. Box 5772, St. Mary's, GA 31558
Phone: (912) 673-3012
Fax: (912) 673-4412
President: Gary Dondero

Idaho

Boise Central Trades and Labor Council, AFL-CIO
225 N. 16th St., Boise, ID 83702
Phone: (208) 343-1561
President: Mark Briggs

East Idaho Central Labor Council, AFL-CIO
445 6th St., Idaho Falls, ID 83401
Phone: (208) 529-0191
President: Chuck Vogel

Lewiston, Idaho-Clarkston, Washington Central Labor Council, AFL-CIO
1618 Idaho St., Suite 102, Lewiston, ID 83501
Phone: (208) 746-7357
Fax: (208) 746-7968
President: Mike Naccarato

Magic Valley Central Labor Council, AFL-CIO
41 E. 700 N., Rupert, ID 83350
Phone: (208) 532-4376
President: Dan Maloney

Northern Idaho Central Labor Council, AFL-CIO
P.O. Box 698, Coeur d'Alene, ID 83816
Phone: (208) 667-6947
President: Barbara Harris

Pocatello Central Labor Union, AFL-CIO
P.O. Box 1574, Pocatello, ID 83204
Phone: (208) 232-3201
Fax: (208) 232-8493
President: Gene McAfee

Western Idaho Central Labor Council
P.O. Box 73, Nampa, ID 83653
Phone: (208) 467-4539
President: Ron Stewart

Illinois

Bloomington-Normal Trades and Labor Assembly, AFL-CIO of McLean County
Rural Rte. 20, P.O. Box 3248, Bloomington, IL 61702
Phone: (309) 828-8813
Fax: (309) 829-0377
President: Ronald C. Morehead

Champaign County AFL-CIO
404 W. Church St., Champaign, IL 61820
Phone: (217) 352-6533
Fax: (217) 351-4904
President: Kevin Sandefur

Chicago Federation of Labor and Industrial Union Council, AFL-CIO
130 E. Randolph Dr., Suite 2600, Chicago, IL 60601
Phone: (312) 222-1000
Fax: (312) 565-6769
President: Dennis J. Gannon

Decatur Trades and Labor Assembly, AFL-CIO of Macon County
P.O. Box 2847, Decatur, IL 62524
Phone: (217) 422-8953
Fax: (217) 422-8955
President: Michael Shampine

Elgin Trades Council, AFL-CIO
450 Shepard Dr., Unit 17A, Elgin, IL 60123
Phone: (847) 695-8130
President: Pete Culver

Galesburg Trades and Labor Assembly, AFL-CIO
2243 Grand Ave., Galesburg, IL 61401
Phone: (309) 342-7015
President: Vacant

Kankakee Federation of Labor, AFL-CIO
220 W. Court St., Kankakee, IL 60901
Phone: (815) 932-6915
Fax: (815) 932-6930
President: Michael W. Smith

Madison County Federation of Labor, AFL-CIO (Greater)
132 S. Thorngate Dr., Granite City, IL 62040
Phone: (618) 931-1068
Fax: (618) 931-7657
Secretary-Treasurer: Norma Gaines

Mideastern Illinois Labor Council, AFL-CIO
P.O. Box 774, Atwood, IL 61913
President: Kyle Wierman

North Central Illinois Labor Council
2900 Ogden Ave., Suite 105, Lisle, IL 60532
Phone: (708) 416-1400
Fax: (708) 416-6973
President: George Holtschlag

Northeastern Illinois, AFL-CIO
248 Ambrogio Dr., Gurnee, IL 60031
Phone: (224) 628-2223
Fax: (847) 263-8120
President: Lee M. Schillinger

Northern LaSalle, Bureau and Putnam County Labor Council, AFL-CIO
P.O. Box 17, LaSalle, IL 61301
Phone: (312) 729-6263
Fax: (815) 434-1240
President: Kelly Reffett

Northwest Illinois Central Labor Council
214 W. Main St., Freeport, IL 61032
Phone: (815) 235-4030
President: Steven R. Jennings

Quad City, Illinois and Iowa Federation of Labor, AFL-CIO
311 1/2 21st St., Rock Island, IL 61201
Phone: (309) 788-1303
Fax: (309) 788-6433
President: Gerald Messer

Rockford United Labor, AFL-CIO
212 S. 1st St., Rockford, IL 61104
Phone: (815) 968-1411
Fax: (815) 968-1438
President: Amedeo Giorgi

South Central Illinois Trades and Labor Council, AFL-CIO
3150 Deadmond Rd., Odin, IL 62870
Phone: (618) 548-5425
President: Evan Deadmond

Southern Illinois Central Labor Council
106 N. Monroe St., West Frankfort, IL 62896
Phone: (618) 932-2102
Fax: (618) 932-2311
President: Paul Noble

Southwestern Illinois Central Labor Council, AFL-CIO
1605 Mascoutah Ave., Belleville, IL 62220
Phone: (618) 235-1905
Fax: (618) 235-6898
President: William E. Thurston

Springfield and Central Illinois Trades and Labor Council, AFL-CIO
P.O. Box 6128, Springfield, IL 62708
Phone: (217) 522-0014
Fax: (217) 522-0090
President: Al Pieper

Streator Trades and Labor Council, AFL-CIO, of Southern LaSalle County
113 11th St., Streator, IL 61364
Phone: (815) 672-3807
Fax: (815) 672-6801
President: Daniel Lanning

Vermilion County Federation of Labor, AFL-CIO
P.O. Box 1575, Danville, IL 61834
Phone: (217) 443-0493
President: Maurice W. Arbuckle

West Central Illinois Labor Council, AFL-CIO
400 N.E. Jefferson Ave., No. 408, Peoria, IL 61603
Phone: (309) 673-3961
Fax: (309) 673-4747
President: Michael Everett

Western Trades and Labor Assembly, AFL-CIO
2929 N. 5th St., Quincy, IL 62301
Phone: (217) 222-0497
Fax: (217) 222-1094
President: Daniel Doellman

Will-Grundy Counties Central Trades and Labor Council, AFL-CIO
113 Republic Ave., Suite 104, Joliet, IL 60435
Phone: (815) 846-6450
Fax: (815) 846-6459
President: Edward L. Breen

Indiana

Cass and White Counties Central Labor Body, AFL-CIO
P.O. Box 181, Logansport, IN 46947
Phone: (574) 732-0065
President: Liz Troxell

Central Indiana Labor Council, AFL-CIO
1701 W. 18th St., Indianapolis, IN 46202
Phone: (317) 638-3455
Fax: (317) 638-1053
President: Robert H. Voorhies

East Central Indiana AFL-CIO Council
2412 Briar Rd., Anderson, IN 46011
Phone: (765) 707-2038
Fax: (765) 643-3731
President: Anthony Coppock

Grant County, AFL-CIO Central Labor Union of
P.O. Box 1496, Marion, IN 46952
Phone: (765) 651-0407
Fax: (765) 651-0410
President: Terri Lahr

Howard and Tipton Counties, Indiana, AFL-CIO, Central Labor Council of
P.O. Box 2796, Kokomo, IN 46904
Phone: (765) 457-5371
Fax: (765) 459-3951
President: Artie Scruggs

North Central Indiana AFL-CIO Council
209 Marycrest Bldg., 2015 Western Ave., South Bend, IN 46629
Phone: (574) 289-6414
Fax: (574) 233-5543
President: Robert Warnock, Jr.

Northeast Indiana Central Labor Council, AFL-CIO
1520 Profit Dr., Fort Wayne, IN 46808
Phone: (260) 482-5588
Fax: (260) 471-3957
President: Tom Lewandowski

Northwest Central Labor Council, AFL-CIO
2535 S. 30th St., Suite 8A, Lafayette, IN 47909
Phone: (765) 742-5757
Fax: (765) 742-5792
President: Richard Emery

Northwest Indiana Federation of Labor, AFL-CIO
63 W. 68th Pl., Merrillville, IN 46410
Phone: (219) 769-4811
Fax: (219) 762-4836
President: Jerome Davison

Peru Labor Trades Council, AFL-CIO
357 W. Main St., Peru, IN 46970
Phone: (765) 473-9214
Fax: (765) 473-7657
President: Ron Butler

South Central Indiana Central Labor Council, AFL-CIO
2209 Glen Abbey, Jeffersonville, IN 47130
Phone: (812) 282-2733
Fax: (812) 282-4493
President: Ken Ogden

Southern Indiana AFL-CIO, Central Labor Council of
210 N. Fulton Ave., Evansville, IN 47710
Phone: (812) 422-2552
Fax: (812) 425-9797
President: Jack McNeely

Wabash County Central Labor Council, AFL-CIO
489 Bond St., Wabash, IN 46992
Phone: (260) 563-4197
Fax: (260) 563-6596
President: Jane Long

Wabash Valley Central Labor Council, AFL-CIO
31 S. 13th St., Terre Haute, IN 47807
Phone: (812) 466-9481
Fax: (812) 235-9559
President: Bill Treash

White River Central Labor Council, AFL-CIO
840 W. 17th St., Suite 9, Bloomington, IN 47404
Phone: (812) 333-8494
Fax: (812) 333-6229
President: Jackie Yenna

Whitewater Valley Indiana AFL-CIO Council
813 W. 6th St., Connersville, IN 47331
Phone: (765) 825-0859
President: Melvin Merz

Iowa

Black Hawk Union Council, AFL-CIO
1695 Burton Ave., Waterloo, IA 50703
Phone: (319) 232-2484
Fax: (319) 232-6845
President: Carol Eckhoff

Clinton Labor Congress, AFL-CIO
1410 Becknan Ln., Clinton, IA 52732
Phone: (563) 242-4298
President: Robert J. Krajnovich

Des Moines/Henry County Labor Council
315 Broadway, West Burlington, IA 52655
Phone: (319) 752-2723
Fax: (319) 752-0549
President: Sherri Riney

Dubuque Federation of Labor, AFL-CIO
1610 Garfield Ave., Dubuque, IA 52001
Phone: (319) 583-0122
Fax: (319) 583-9399
President: Wayne Laufenberg

Hawkeye Labor Council, AFL-CIO
1211 Wiley Blvd., S.W., Cedar Rapids, IA 52404
Phone: (319) 396-8461
Fax: (319) 396-4964
Executive Director: Doug Peters

Iowa City Federation of Labor, AFL-CIO
705 S. Clinton St., Iowa City, IA 52240
Phone: (319) 398-5372
Fax: (319) 398-5381
President: Patrick Hughes

Lee County Labor Council, AFL-CIO
301 Blondeau St., Keokuk, IA 52632
Phone: (319) 524-9861
Fax: (319) 524-8028
President: Tom Cale

North Central Federation of Labor, AFL-CIO
P.O. Box 387, 621 East St., Fort Dodge, IA 50501
Phone: (515) 573-4139
President: Dale Struecker

**North Iowa Nine Labor Council,
AFL-CIO**
   503 18th St., S.E., Mason City, IA
   50401
   Phone: (641) 423-1733
   President: Michael Herman

**Northwest Iowa Central Labor Council,
AFL-CIO**
   3038 S. Lakeport Rd., Suite 100, Sioux
   City, IA 51106
   Phone: (712) 276-0473
   President: Jim Marshall

**South Central Iowa Federation of Labor,
AFL-CIO**
   2000 Walker St., Suite L, Des Moines,
   IA 50317
   Phone: (515) 265-1862
   Fax: (515) 263-2670
   President: Dan Albritton

Southern Iowa Labor Council, AFL-CIO
   411 North Ct., Ottumwa, IA 52501
   Phone: (641) 683-4630
   Fax: (641) 682-3754
   President: Steve Siegel

Southwest Iowa Labor Council, AFL-CIO
   425 N. 10th St., Council Bluffs, IA
   51503
   Phone: (712) 328-4641
   President: Rodney D. Klein

Kansas

**Lawrence Central Labor Council,
AFL-CIO**
   P.O. Box 4041, 930 E. 28th St.,
   Lawrence, KS 66046
   Phone: (785) 843-5242
   Fax: (785) 843-3421
   President: Dwayne Peaslee

Salina Central Labor Union, AFL-CIO
   201 Hawkes St., Gypsum, KS 67448
   Phone: (785) 536-4321
   President: Don Dooley

Topeka Federation of Labor, AFL-CIO
   P.O. Box 8630, Topeka, KS 66608
   Phone: (785) 276-9078
   Fax: (785) 276-9077
   President: Clyde A. Bracken

**Tri-County Labor Council of Eastern
Kansas, AFL-CIO**
   7540 Leavenworth Rd., Kansas City,
   KS 66109
   Phone: (913) 334-3505
   Fax: (913) 334-6660
   President: James A. Hadel

**Wichita/Hutchinson Labor Federation of
Central Kansas, AFL-CIO**
   3219 W. Central Ave., Wichita, KS
   67203
   Phone: (316) 941-4061
   Fax: (316) 942-9840
   President: Mark Love

Kentucky

Ashland Area Labor Council, AFL-CIO
   P.O. Box 932, Ashland, KY 41105
   Phone: (606) 324-8701
   Fax: (606) 324-8701
   Secretary-Treasurer: Stephen Payton

**Bluegrass Central Labor Council,
AFL-CIO**
   P.O. Box 54728, Lexington, KY 40555
   Phone: (859) 533-5851
   President: Bob McNulty

**Bowling Green Area Central Labor
Union, AFL-CIO**
   3330 Pinecroft Dr., Louisville, KY
   40219
   Phone: (502) 582-3508
   Fax: (502) 582-9152
   President: Irv Conely

**Central Kentucky Central Labor Council,
AFL-CIO**
   7902 Old Minors Ln., Louisville, KY
   40219
   Phone: (800) 443-5191
   Fax: (502) 582-9152
   President: Dave Riggs

**Danville Central Labor Union Council,
AFL-CIO**
   515 Upper Saltriver Rd., Danville, KY
   40422
   Phone: (606) 236-3100
   President: James L. Duncan

**Frankfort Central Labor Council,
AFL-CIO**
   P.O. Box 4054, Frankfort, KY 40604
   Phone: (502) 875-2273
   Fax: (502) 875-3597
   President: Charles Walls

**Lake Cumberland Area Central Labor
Council, AFL-CIO**
   1611 Tandy Way, Somerset, KY 42503
   Phone: (606) 677-6921
   Fax: (606) 451-1712
   Executive Secretary: Brenda Steele

**Louisville Central Labor Council,
AFL-CIO (Greater)**
   1224 S. 4th St., Louisville, KY 40202
   Phone: (502) 635-2867
   Fax: (502) 635-2842
   President: Charles Clephas

**Northern Kentucky AFL-CIO Labor
Council**
   1450 Crittenden Mount Zion Rd., Dry
   Ridge, KY 41035
   Phone: (513) 559-0200
   Fax: (513) 559-0734
   President: Wayne J. Whalen

Owensboro Council of Labor, AFL-CIO
   Box 620, 530 Yale Pl., Owensboro,
   KY 42301
   Phone: (270) 275-9016
   Fax: (270) 926-3167
   President: Truman Burden

**Pennyrile Area Central Labor Council,
AFL-CIO**
   433 Linda Dr., Hopkinsville, KY
   42240
   Phone: (270) 886-5756
   Fax: (775) 306-7901
   Treasurer: Betty Robertson

Tri-County Council of Labor, AFL-CIO
   230 S. Alvasia St., Henderson, KY
   42420
   Phone: (270) 827-2511
   Fax: (270) 831-1768
   President: Ray Horton

**Western Kentucky AFL-CIO Area
Council**
   300 Hathaway Trail, Paducah, KY
   42003
   Phone: (270) 898-2558
   President: Jeff Wiggins

Louisiana

Acadian Central Labor Council, AFL-CIO
   P.O. Box 804, Lafayette, LA 70583
   Phone: (318) 235-4370
   Fax: (318) 234-1030
   President: Dale Brasseaux

**Alexandria Central Labor Union,
AFL-CIO**
    1211 Rapides Ave., Alexandria, LA
    71301
    Phone: (318) 442-9923
    President: Johnny Gypin

**Bastrop Central Trades and Labor
Council**
    Status Pending

Baton Rouge AFL-CIO (Greater)
    P.O. Box 267, Baton Rouge, LA 70821
    Phone: (225) 927-4066
    Fax: (225) 687-3961
    Secretary-Treasurer: Eddie H.
    Schoonmaker, Sr.

**Jonesboro-Hodge Central Trades and
Labor Council, AFL-CIO**
    1008 Maple St., Jonesboro, LA 71251
    Phone: (318) 259-8918
    President: James Taylor

New Orleans AFL-CIO (Greater)
    837 N. Carrollton Ave., New Orleans,
    LA 70119
    Phone: (504) 488-6544
    Fax: (504) 482-6958
    President: Robert F. Hammond

**Ouachita Parish Central Trades and
Labor Council, AFL-CIO**
    P.O. Box 555, West Monroe, LA
    71294
    Phone: (318) 322-1886
    President: Leslie Hamilton

**Ruston and Vicinity, AFL-CIO, Central
Trades and Labor Council of**
    P.O. Box 653, Ruston, LA 71273
    Phone: (318) 257-2603
    Fax: (318) 257-2562
    President: Ronald H. Thompson

**Shreveport and Vicinity Central Trades
and Labor Council, AFL-CIO**
    3924 Greenwood Rd., Shreveport, LA
    71109
    Phone: (318) 635-8139
    Fax: (318) 635-8141
    President: Roosevelt Smalley

**Southwest Louisiana Central Trades and
Labor Council, AFL-CIO**
    223 Stagecoach Ln., Sulpher, LA
    70663
    Phone: (318) 528-2553
    Fax: (337) 433-2014
    President: Robert Moss

**St. Tammany, Tangipahoa and
Washington, Parishes of**
    P.O. Box 8428, Metairie, LA 70011
    Phone: (504) 885-3054
    Fax: (504) 454-2584
    President: Lance Albin

**Thibodaux Central Labor Council,
AFL-CIO**
    21030 Hwy. 20, Vacherie, LA 70090
    Phone: (225) 869-2535
    Fax: (225) 869-2172
    President: Stanley C. Folse

Maine

**Bangor Labor Council, AFL-CIO
(Greater)**
    20 Ayer St., Brewer, ME 04412
    Phone: (207) 621-8160
    Fax: (207) 621-8170
    President: Jack McKay

Central Maine Labor Council, AFL-CIO
    P.O. Box 561, Oakland, ME 04963
    Phone: (207) 465-3279
    Fax: (207) 465-8289
    President: Neena Quirion

Katahdin Labor Council, AFL-CIO
    92 Canyon Dr., Millinocket, ME 04462
    Phone: (207) 723-5746
    Fax: (207) 723-9262
    Financial and Recording Secretary:
    Herbert Clark

Southern Maine Labor Council
    28 Tryon Rd., Pownal, ME 04069
    Phone: (207) 838-6329
    Fax: (207) 797-9443
    President: Dennis Norton

Maryland

**Baltimore Council of AFL-CIO Unions,
Metropolitan**
    2701 W. Patapsco Ave., Suite 110,
    Baltimore, MD 21230
    Phone: (410) 242-1300
    Fax: (410) 247-3197
    President: Ernest R. Grecco

Central Maryland AFL-CIO Council
    511 E. Franklin St., Hagerstown, MD
    21740
    Phone: (301) 739-9500
    Fax: (301) 739-6936
    President: Charles W. McNemar

**Del-Mar-Va Peninsula Central Labor
Council, AFL-CIO**
    P.O. Box 3095, Salisbury, MD 21802
    Phone: (302) 934-5389
    Fax: (302) 934-7868
    President: Gil Cephas

**Western Maryland Central Labor
Council, AFL-CIO**
    152-154 N. Mechanic St., Cumberland,
    MD 21501
    Phone: (301) 777-1820
    Fax: (301) 777-0121
    President: Randy Appel

Massachusetts

**Berkshire Central Labor Council,
AFL-CIO**
    290 Merrill Rd., Pittsfield, MA 01201
    Phone: (413) 442-1970
    Fax: (413) 442-4892
    President: Alfred L. Shogry

**Boston Labor Council, AFL-CIO
(Greater)**
    25 Colgate Rd., Roslindale, MA 02131
    Phone: (617) 524-2717
    Fax: (617) 524-2623
    Executive Secretary-Treasurer: Anthony
    B. Romano

Central Massachusetts AFL-CIO
    400 Washington St., Auburn, MA
    01501
    Phone: (508) 832-4218
    Fax: (508) 832-4219
    President: Joe Carlson

**Hampshire/Franklin Labor Council,
AFL-CIO**
    20 Maple St., Springfield, MA 01103
    Phone: (413) 732-5122
    Fax: (413) 732-1035
    President: Jonathan Tuttle

**Merrimack Valley Central Labor Council,
AFL-CIO**
    169 Merrimack St., Lowell, MA 01852
    Phone: (781) 937-9991
    Fax: (781) 937-9310
    President: George Noel

Norfolk County Labor Council, AFL-CIO
    P.O. Box 690429, Quincy, MA 02269
    Phone: (617) 228-5730
    Fax: (617) 825-5128
    President: Robert Rizzi

North Shore Labor Council, AFL-CIO
112 Exchange St., Lynn, MA 01901
Phone: (781) 595-2538
Fax: (781) 595-8770
President: Jeffrey C. Crosby

North Worcester County Central Labor Council, AFL-CIO
149 Mechanic St., Leominster, MA 01453
Phone: (978) 534-6534
Fax: (978) 537-7060
President: Charles F. Ferreira

Pioneer Valley Labor Council, AFL-CIO
640 Page Blvd., Springfield, MA 01104
Phone: (413) 732-7970
Fax: (413) 732-1881
President: Rick Brown

Plymouth-Bristol Central Labor Council, AFL-CIO
P.O. Box 265, Dennis, MA 02638
Phone: (508) 385-3163
Fax: (508) 385-6685
President: William Johansen

Southeastern Massachusetts Labor Council (Greater)
867 State Rd., North Dartmouth, MA 02747
Phone: (508) 997-2931
Fax: (508) 997-6069
President: Cynthia Rodrigues

Michigan

Bay County Labor Council, AFL-CIO
1300 W. Thomas St., Bay City, MI 48706
Phone: (517) 684-5480
Fax: (517) 372-9137
President: James Davison

Delta County Trades and Labor Council, AFL-CIO
P.O. Box 411, Gladstone, MI 49837
Phone: (906) 786-1660
Fax: (906) 789-3222
President: Maria Maniaci

Detroit AFL-CIO, Metropolitan
600 W. Lafayette Blvd., Suite 200, Detroit, MI 48226
Phone: (313) 961-0800
Fax: (313) 961-9776
President: Donald Boggs

Dickinson-Iron Counties Labor Council, AFL-CIO
P.O. Box 863, Iron Mountain, MI 49801
Phone: (906) 774-6070
Fax: (906) 774-1199
President: Joe Gallino

Eastern Upper Peninsula Central Labor Council, AFL-CIO
2 Forest Lodge Rd., Kincheloe, MI 49788
Phone: (906) 495-7343
Fax: (906) 495-2723
Recording Secretary: Paul Warrick

Flint AFL-CIO Council (Greater)
P.O. Box 310864, Flint, MI 48531
Phone: (810) 732-1590
President: Paul Long

Huron Valley Central Labor Council, AFL-CIO
1612 W. Cross St., Ypsilanti, MI 48197
Phone: (734) 482-1824
Fax: (734) 485-7255
President: Fred Veigel

Jackson/Hillsdale Counties Central Labor Council, AFL-CIO
1983 S. Dearing Rd., Parma, MI 49269
Phone: (517) 782-4771
Fax: (517) 750-4289
President: Gerald Emmons

Kent-Ionia Labor Council, AFL-CIO
918 Benjamin Ave., N.E., Grand Rapids, MI 49503
Phone: (616) 456-8233
Fax: (616) 456-0574
President: Mark Davis

Lansing Labor Council, AFL-CIO (Greater)
419 S. Washington Sq., Suite 302, Lansing, MI 48933
Phone: (517) 485-5169
Fax: (517) 485-5322
President: Paul Hufnagel

Manistee County Labor Federation, AFL-CIO
93 Spruce St., Manistee, MI 49660
Phone: (616) 723-7113
Financial Secretary: Joe Showalter

Marquette County Labor Council, AFL-CIO
710 Chippewa Sq., Marquette, MI 49855
Phone: (906) 225-1122
Fax: (906) 225-1530
President: Shana Harvala

Mid-Michigan Labor Council, AFL-CIO
5533 Swede Ave., Midland, MI 48642
Phone: (517) 839-9194
Secretary-Treasurer: George Yost

Midland County Labor Council, AFL-CIO
321 S. Saginaw Rd., Midland, MI 48640
Phone: (517) 835-7161
Fax: (517) 835-6944
President: William L. Laney, Jr.

Monroe/Lenawee County AFL-CIO Council
15583 S. Dixie Hwy., No. 44, Monroe, MI 48161
Phone: (734) 832-3887
Fax: (734) 242-2646
President: Bill Conner

Northwest Upper Peninsula Labor Council, AFL-CIO
410 Diamond St., Ontonagon, MI 49953
Phone: (906) 884-4798
President: John Hamm

Saginaw Labor Council, AFL-CIO
6165 Bay Rd., Suite A, Saginaw, MI 48603
Phone: (989) 797-6000
Fax: (989) 797-3866
President: Joseph F. Smith

South Central Michigan AFL-CIO Labor Council
5906 E. Morgan Rd., Battle Creek, MI 49017
Phone: (616) 968-0993
President: Richard G. Frantz

Southwestern Michigan Labor Council, AFL-CIO
P.O. Box 1503, Benton Harbor, MI 49023
Phone: (269) 925-8090
Fax: (269) 925-8940
President: John Godush

St. Clair County Labor Council, AFL-CIO
1723 Military St., Port Huron, MI 48060
Phone: (810) 985-8169
Fax: (810) 982-7202
President: Richard Cummings

Thumb Area Michigan AFL-CIO Labor Council
1700 W. Atwater Rd., Bad Axe, MI 48413
Phone: (989) 375-2772
Fax: (989) 375-4506
President: Harold Conley

Thunder Bay AFL-CIO Council
P.O. Box 55, Alpena, MI 49707
Phone: (517) 356-9741
President: Craig Zelazny

Traverse Bay Area Central Labor Council, AFL-CIO
P.O. Box 5547, Traverse City, MI 49696
Phone: (231) 943-3537
Fax: (231) 943-3537
Web: www.tbaclc.org
President: John Toth

West Michigan Labor Council, AFL-CIO
1336 W. Summit Ave., Muskegon, MI 49441
Phone: (231) 733-7735
Fax: (231) 733-8343
President: Florence Shriver

Minnesota

Albert Lea Trades and Labor Assembly, AFL-CIO
404 E. Main St., Albert Lea, MN 56007
Phone: (507) 373-5938
Fax: (507) 373-4471
President: Richard Hagen

Austin Central Labor Union, AFL-CIO
316 4th Ave., N.E., Austin, MN 55912
Phone: (507) 437-8647
Fax: (507) 437-3767
President: Gary Morgan

Bemidji Central Labor Union, AFL-CIO
P.O. Box 1715, Bemidji, MN 56601
President: James P. Walinski

Brainerd AFL-CIO Trades and Labor Assembly
2438 Country Rd. 25, N.E., Brainerd, MN 56401
Phone: (218) 829-0222
President: Kenneth Zelinske

Carlton County Central Labor Body
1217 28th St., Cloquet, MN 55720
Phone: (218) 879-9242
President: Robert Oswold

Central Minnesota AFL-CIO Trades and Labor Assembly
1903 4th St., N., St. Cloud, MN 56303
Phone: (320) 252-4654
Fax: (320) 252-1002
President: Roger Juaire

Duluth AFL-CIO Central Body
2002 London Rd., Duluth, MN 55812
Phone: (218) 724-1413
President: Alan Netland

Iron Range Labor Assembly, AFL-CIO
P.O. Box 211, Mount Iron, MN 55768
Phone: (218) 728-5174
President: Tom Cvar

Mankato South Central Labor Union, AFL-CIO
310 McKenzie St. S., Mankato, MN 56001
Phone: (507) 388-6031
Fax: (507) 388-1226
President: Vacant

Minneapolis Central Labor Union Council, AFL-CIO
10923 Nassau Cir., Blaine, MN 55449
Phone: (612) 379-4206
Fax: (612) 379-1307
President: William McCarthy

Red Wing Area AFL-CIO Council
319 1/2 W. 3rd St., Red Wing, MN 55066
Phone: (651) 388-3785
Fax: (651) 388-9469
President: Carol McNary

Southeast Central Labor Council, AFL-CIO
405 1/2 S. Broadway, Rochester, MN 55904
Phone: (507) 252-0145
President: Connie Dammen

Southern Dakota County Labor Council, AFL-CIO
14443 Glenda Dr., Apple Valley, MN 55124
Phone: (612) 891-1251
Fax: (612) 891-3718
President: Steven T. Boice

Southwest Central Labor Council, AFL-CIO
500 W. Hatting St., Luverne, MN 56156
Phone: (507) 376-4234
President: Dale E. Moerke

St. Croix Valley AFL-CIO Central Labor Union
1746 Ramada Ave., St. Croix Beach, MN 55043
Phone: (612) 330-1959
Fax: (651) 647-1556
President: Rick Magler

St. Paul AFL-CIO Trades and Labor Assembly
411 Main St., Suite 202, St. Paul, MN 55102
Phone: (651) 222-3787
Fax: (651) 293-1989
President: Shar Knutson

Willmar AFL-CIO Trades and Labor Assembly
601 18th St., S.W., Willmar, MN 56201
President: Jacque Collins

Mississippi

Central Mississippi Central Labor Union, AFL-CIO
6664 Presidential Dr., Jackson, MS 39213
Phone: (601) 362-5175
President: Robert Gooden

Columbus and Vicinity AFL-CIO, Central Labor Union
P.O. Box 561, West Point, MS 39773
Phone: (662) 494-6173
Fax: (662) 494-0275
Vice President: J.R. Sims

Jackson County AFL-CIO, Central Labor Union
P.O. Box 1247, Pascagoula, MS 39568
Phone: (228) 762-2155
Fax: (601) 762-3642
President: William McGill

McComb Central Labor Council, AFL-CIO
10 Kenny Boyd Rd., Tylertown, MS 39667
Phone: (601) 876-3142
President: David Boyd

Mississippi Pine Belt Central Labor Council, AFL-CIO
P.O. Box 17006, Hattiesburg, MS 39404
Phone: (601) 543-0861
President: Terrell Pickett

Natchez Central Labor Council, AFL-CIO
1002 Kenwood Ln., Natchez, MS 39120
Phone: (601) 442-1773
President: Vacant

North Delta Central Labor Council
Status Pending

South Central Labor Union, AFL-CIO
221 N. Lang Ave., Long Beach, MS 39560
Phone: (228) 214-9886
Fax: (228) 914-9828
President: Ed Hatem

Tupelo Central Labor Union, AFL-CIO
P.O. Box 234, Amory, MS 38821
Phone: (662) 256-8489
Fax: (662) 257-4007
President: Ronnie Turner

Missouri

Cape Girardeau Central Trades and Labor Council, AFL-CIO
P.O. Box 1242, Cape Girardeau, MO 63702
Phone: (573) 334-9987
Fax: (573) 334-9987
President: Roy Gunter

Central Missouri Labor Council, AFL-CIO
2650 S. Roby Farm Rd., Rocheport, MO 65279
Phone: (573) 449-5723
President: Phyllis Fugit

Jefferson City Central Labor Union, AFL-CIO
230 W. Dunklin St., Suite 206, Jefferson City, MO 65101
Phone: (573) 635-8282
President: Guy Otto

Kansas City Labor Council, AFL-CIO (Greater)
1012 Pennsylvania Ave., Kansas City, MO 64105
Phone: (816) 221-6163
Fax: (816) 221-6165
President: Bridgette Williams

Northeast Missouri Trades and Labor Council, AFL-CIO
P.O. Box 571, Palmyra, MO 63461
Phone: (573) 592-0201
Fax: (573) 592-6610
President: Emmett Garner

Northwest Missouri Central Labor Council, AFL-CIO
1222 S. 10th St., St. Joseph, MO 64503
Phone: (816) 232-9517
Fax: (816) 232-4500
President: Gary Grubb

Sedalia Federation of Labor, AFL-CIO
P.O. Box 397, Smithton, MO 65350
Phone: (660) 343-5511
Fax: (660) 343-5540
President: Marke E. Franken

Springfield Labor Council, AFL-CIO
2902 E. Division St., Springfield, MO 65803
Phone: (417) 866-2236
Fax: (417) 869-1814
President: Russell Strunk

St. Louis Labor Council, AFL-CIO (Greater)
P.O. Box 411544, St. Louis, MO 63141
Phone: (314) 439-5001
Fax: (314) 439-9903
Chief Executive Officer/Secretary-Treasurer: Robert Soutier

Montana

Big Sky Central Labor Council, AFL-CIO
P.O. Box 466, Helena, MT 59624
Phone: (406) 442-1708
President: Sandi Curriero

Central Montana Central Labor Council, AFL-CIO
P.O. Box 1593, Great Falls, MT 59403
Phone: (406) 452-1973
Fax: (406) 453-9556
President: John Pejko

Eastern Montana Central Labor Council, AFL-CIO
P.O. Box 703, Sidney, MT 59270
Phone: (406) 482-2364
President: Karlon Schmitt

Flathead Area Central Labor Council, AFL-CIO
650 Birch Grove Rd., Kalispell, MT 59901
Phone: (406) 775-1538
Fax: (406) 857-3710
President: Terry Leishman

Missoula Area Central Labor Council, AFL-CIO
208 E. Main St., Missoula, MT 59802
Phone: (406) 722-4575
President: Mark Hanson

North Central Montana Central Labor Council, AFL-CIO
Inactive; Status Pending

Northwestern Montana Central Labor Council, AFL-CIO
653 Flower Creek Rd., Libby, MT 59923
Phone: (406) 293-9240
President: Barry L. Brown

South Central Montana Central Labor Council, AFL-CIO
P.O. Box 4056, Bozeman, MT 59772
Phone: (406) 585-8979
Secretary-Treasurer: Kathleen Callahan

Southeastern Montana Central Labor Council, AFL-CIO
P.O. Box 1019, Forsyth, MT 59327
Phone: (406) 356-2757
Fax: (406) 356-2757
President: Ken Treib

Southwestern Montana Central Labor Council, AFL-CIO
P.O. Box 3173, Butte, MT 59702
Phone: (406) 494-3051
Fax: (406) 494-5790
President: Teresa Wilson

Yellowstone Central Labor Council, AFL-CIO (Greater)
1238 Yale Ave., Billings, MT 59102
Phone: (406) 252-8973
Fax: (406) 252-8973
President: Tom Curry

Nebraska

Central Nebraska Central Labor Council
1707 Central Ave., Kearney, NE 68847
Phone: (308) 237-2292
President: Mary E. Hakanson

Lincoln Central Labor Union, AFL-CIO
4625 Y St., Lincoln, NE 68503
Phone: (402) 466-5444
Fax: (402) 466-5444
President: Jim Willis

Midwest Nebraska Central Labor Council, AFL-CIO
306 S. Ash St., North Platte, NE 69101
Phone: (308) 534-3017
President: Floyd Houser

Northeast Nebraska Central Labor Council, AFL-CIO
2410 Colorado Ave., Fremont, NE 68025
Phone: (402) 721-0429
President: Richard Woita

Omaha Federation of Labor, AFL-CIO
Twin Towers, 3000 Farnam St., Suite 5E, Omaha, NE 68131
Phone: (402) 346-4800
Fax: (402) 346-6669
President: Terry Moore

Western Nebraska Central Labor Council, AFL-CIO
19 E. 15th St., Scotts Bluff, NE 69361
Phone: (308) 630-9777
President: Curt Magelky

Nevada

North Eastern Nevada Central Labor Council, AFL-CIO
P.O. Box 1868, Elko, NV 89803
Secretary-Treasurer: Mike McDonald

Northern Nevada Central Labor Council, AFL-CIO
1819 Hymer Ave., Suite 105, Sparks, NV 89431
Phone: (775) 355-9200
Fax: (775) 355-9934
President: Richard Houts, Jr.

Southern Nevada Central Labor Council, AFL-CIO
1701 Whitney Mesa Dr., Suite 101, Henderson, NV 89014
Phone: (702) 452-8799
Fax: (702) 452-9357
Secretary-Treasurer: Robert Nard

New Hampshire

Manchester AFL-CIO, Central Labor Council
161 Londonderry Tpke., Hooksett, NH 03106
Phone: (603) 622-3955
Fax: (603) 895-0474
President: Arthur Beaudry

Nashua Labor Council, AFL-CIO
7C Taggard Dr., Nashua, NH 03060
Phone: (603) 888-7544
President: Brad Schott

New Jersey

Atlantic and Cape May Counties Central Labor Council, AFL-CIO
P.O. Box 1118, Hammondton, NJ 08037
Phone: (609) 704-8351
Fax: (609) 704-0621
President: Roy Foster

Bergen County Central Trades and Labor Council, AFL-CIO
205 Robin Rd., Mailbox 4, Paramus, NJ 07652
Phone: (201) 967-5953
Fax: (201) 967-1547
Web: www.bergenclc.org
President: Charles Mattson

Burlington County Central Labor Union, AFL-CIO
510 8th St., Riverside, NJ 08075
Phone: (732) 287-4011
Fax: (732) 248-0353
President: John E. Shinn

Essex-West Hudson Labor Council, AFL-CIO
14 Fairfield Pl., West Caldwell, NJ 07006
Phone: (973) 227-6426
Fax: (973) 227-3785
President: Thomas P. Giblin

Hudson County Central Labor Council, AFL-CIO
P.O. Box 17328, Jersey City, NJ 07307
Phone: (201) 432-7080
Fax: (201) 653-7050
President: Peter Busacca

Mercer County Labor Union Council, AFL-CIO
2 Iron Ore Rd. at Rte. 33, Englishtown, NJ 07726
Phone: (732) 792-0999
Fax: (732) 792-1999
President: Michael Maloney

Middlesex County AFL-CIO Labor Council
15 Debonis Dr., Milltown, NJ 08850
Phone: (609) 989-8730
Fax: (609) 989-8734
President: John Bicsko, Jr.

Monmouth and Ocean Counties Central Labor Union, AFL-CIO
846 Paul Dr., Suite U, Toms River, NJ 08753
Phone: (732) 349-1779
Fax: (732) 349-1789
President: Wyatt Earp

Passaic County Labor Council, AFL-CIO
1389 Broad St., Clifton, NJ 07013
Phone: (973) 777-3700
Fax: (973) 777-3430
President: Michael Kinsora

Somerset County Central Labor Council, AFL-CIO
61 Woodhill St., Somerset, NJ 08873
Phone: (732) 828-6908
President: Helen Verhage

Southern New Jersey Central Labor Council, AFL-CIO
4212 Beacon Ave., Pennsauken, NJ 08109
Phone: (856) 663-1555
Fax: (856) 663-1511
President: Donald Norcross

Union County AFL-CIO Council
35 Fadem Rd., Springfield, NJ 07081
Phone: (973) 258-1900
Fax: (973) 258-1240
President: Edward Zarnock

Warren-Hunterdon Counties Central Labor Union, AFL-CIO
792 Chimney Rock Rd., Suite H, Martinsville, NJ 08836
Phone: (732) 748-2008
Fax: (732) 748-2016
President: Andrew Sona

New Mexico

Central New Mexico Central Labor Council, AFL-CIO
1209 Hall Ct., S.W., Albuquerque, NM 87105
Phone: (505) 877-5986
President: Jon Thomas-Weger

Four Corners Central Labor Council, AFL-CIO
2005 E. 11th St., Farmington, NM 87401
Phone: (505) 327-5420
Fax: (505) 327-9448
President: Lonnie Dame

Northern New Mexico Central Labor Council, AFL-CIO
533 Todd Loop S., Los Alamos, NM 87544
Phone: (505) 672-1730
President: Sidney McDermitt

Southwestern New Mexico Central Labor Council, AFL-CIO
P.O. Box 1807, Las Cruces, NM 88004
Phone: (505) 382-5140
Fax: (505) 382-8044
President: Chuck Shuman

New York

Albany Central Federation of Labor, AFL-CIO
890 Third St., Albany, NY 12206
Phone: (518) 489-5791
President: Jeff Stark

Broome County Federation of Labor, AFL-CIO
58 Meadow Ln., Kirkwood, NY 13795
Phone: (607) 763-3662
President: Ken Smith

Buffalo AFL-CIO Council
295 Main St., Room 532, Buffalo, NY 14203
Phone: (716) 852-0375
Fax: (716) 855-1802
President: John J. Kaczorowski

Cattaraugus-Allegany Counties Central Labor Council, AFL-CIO
67 Waverly St., Cattaraugus, NY 14719
Phone: (716) 257-3610
President: Hobart Rhinehart

Cayuga County Labor Council
18 Asbury Ln., Lansing, NY 14882
Phone: (607) 256-9398
President: Baschki Leo

Central New York Labor Council, AFL-CIO
270 Genesee St., Utica, NY 13502
Phone: (315) 433-0050
President: Jim Moore

Chemung County AFL-CIO Assembly
459 E. Church St., Elmira, NY 14901
Phone: (607) 734-8290
Fax: (607) 734-8219
President: Penny Weston

Dunkirk Area Labor Council, AFL-CIO
133 S. Martin St., Dunkirk, NY 14048
Phone: (716) 565-1720
Fax: (716) 565-1727
President: James Bickhart

Dutchess County Central Labor Council, AFL-CIO
157 Van Wagner Rd., Poughkeepsie, NY 12603
Phone: (914) 451-6065
Fax: (914) 485-6501
President: Dona Lansing

Glens Falls Central Labor Council, AFL-CIO (Greater)
28 Thompson Ave., Glens Falls, NY 12801
Phone: (518) 798-0670
President: Tom Capone

Hudson-Catskill Central Labor Council of New York, AFL-CIO
P.O. Box 1299, 37 North St., Newburgh, NY 12550
Phone: (845) 563-7394
Fax: (845) 563-7650
President: John F. Wolner

Jamestown Area AFL-CIO Council
6460 Charlotte Center Rd., Sinclairville, NY 14782
Phone: (716) 962-5024
Fax: (716) 962-4747
President: Jack Rudy

Jefferson, Lewis and St. Lawrence Counties Central Trades and Labor Council, AFL-CIO
32 Andrews St., Massena, NY 13662
Phone: (315) 764-2293
Fax: (315) 769-5839
President: Ron McDougall

Long Island Federation of Labor, AFL-CIO
1111 Rte. 110, Suite 320, Farmingdale, NY 11735
Phone: (631) 396-1170
Fax: (631) 396-1174
President: Jack Caffey

Mid-State Central Labor Council, AFL-CIO
265 Merrill Creek Rd., Marathon, NY 13803
Phone: (607) 849-3420
President: Linda Smith

New York City Central Labor Council, AFL-CIO
31 W. 15th St., New York, NY 10011
Phone: (212) 604-9552
Fax: (212) 604-9550
Web: www.nycclc.org
President: Brian McLaughlin

Niagara-Orleans Labor Council, AFL-CIO
684 Walnut St., Lockport, NY 14094
Phone: (716) 433-6747
President: James Gugliuzza

Northeast Central Labor Council, AFL-CIO
73 Lafayette St., Plattsburgh, NY 12901
Phone: (518) 561-6135
President: Betty Lennon

Oswego County Labor Council, AFL-CIO
182 Creamery Rd., Oswego, NY 13126
Phone: (315) 343-3903
President: Dan Dougherty

Rochester and Vicinity Labor Council, AFL-CIO
30 N. Union St., Suite 100, Rochester, NY 14607
Phone: (585) 263-2650
Fax: (585) 263-4671
President: Jim Bertolone

Rockland County Central Labor Union, AFL-CIO
9 Johnsons Ln., New City, NY 10956
Phone: (845) 634-4601
Fax: (845) 634-4924
President: Joseph Maraia

Saratoga County Central Labor Council, AFL-CIO
36 Briarhurst Dr., Gansevoort, NY 12831
Phone: (518) 587-1596
President: Cliff Brosnan

Schenectady Area Central Labor Council, AFL-CIO
　　4 Wimberly Ct., Albany, NY 12205
　　Phone: (518) 399-7970
　　President: Neal Truesdale

Steuben County Central Labor Council, AFL-CIO
　　P.O. Box 561, Bath, NY 14810
　　President: Gary Ostrander

Syracuse Labor Council, AFL-CIO (Greater)
　　404 Oak St., Suite 130, Syracuse, NY 13203
　　Phone: (315) 422-3363
　　Fax: (315) 422-2260
　　President: Marshall Blake

Tri-County Labor Council
　　P.O. Box 187, Mount Upton, NY 13809
　　Phone: (607) 764-8524
　　President: Mary Twitchell

Troy Area Labor Council, AFL-CIO
　　43 Madonna Lake Rd., Cropseyville, NY 12052
　　Phone: (518) 279-3749
　　President: Mike Keenan

Upper Hudson Valley Labor Council, AFL-CIO
　　822 Neighborhood Rd., Lake Katrine, NY 12449
　　Phone: (845) 883-3351
　　President: John Kaiser

Westchester/Putnam Counties AFL-CIO Central Labor Body
　　595 W. Hartsdale Ave., White Plains, NY 10607
　　Phone: (914) 328-7988
　　Fax: (914) 328-7993
　　President: Tony Pagano

North Carolina

Eastern North Carolina Central Labor Council, AFL-CIO
　　P.O. Box 716, Havelock, NC 28532
　　Phone: (252) 447-2115
　　Fax: (252) 447-2296
　　President: Joseph Greaser

Eastern Piedmont Central Labor Body, AFL-CIO
　　P.O. Box 2, Seaboard, NC 27876
　　Phone: (252) 537-1009
　　President: Bennett Taylor

Sandhills Central Labor Council, AFL-CIO (Greater)
　　P.O. Box 87029, Fayetteville, NC 28311
　　Phone: (910) 630-2118
　　Fax: (910) 485-7909
　　Web: www. greatersandhillscentrallaborcouncil. org
　　President: Marina West

Southeastern North Carolina Central Labor Council, AFL-CIO
　　P.O. Box 12609, Wilmington, NC 28405
　　Phone: (910) 772-5501
　　President: Melvin Simpson

Southern Piedmont Central Labor Council, AFL-CIO
　　P.O. Box 19103, Charlotte, NC 28219
　　Phone: (704) 953-3033
　　President: Will Cashion

Tri-Ad Central Labor Body Union, AFL-CIO
　　325 W. J.J. Dr., Suite 210, Greensboro, NC 27406
　　Phone: (336) 274-2722
　　President: Randy Conrad

Triangle Labor Council, AFL-CIO
　　P.O. Box 90112, Raleigh, NC 27675
　　Phone: (919) 785-7945
　　President: Ann Deese

Western North Carolina Central Labor Council, AFL-CIO
　　45 Sardis Rd., Asheville, NC 28806
　　Phone: (828) 665-2198
　　Fax: (828) 665-1889
　　President: Laura Gordon

North Dakota

Missouri Slope Central Labor Council, AFL-CIO
　　1323 E. Front Ave., Bismarck, ND 58504
　　Phone: (701) 224-9053
　　President: Rick Pfenning

Northern Plains United Labor Council
　　3002 1st Ave. N., Fargo, ND 58102
　　Phone: (701) 235-2341
　　Fax: (701) 235-2341
　　President: Barbara May

Northern Valley Labor Council, AFL-CIO
　　1714 1/2 N. Washington St., Grand Forks, ND 58203
　　Phone: (701) 772-7404
　　Fax: (701) 772-7404
　　Secretary-Treasurer: Wayne Burlog

Northwest Labor Council, AFL-CIO (Greater)
　　P.O. Box 9, Minot, ND 58702
　　Phone: (701) 527-0886
　　Fax: (701) 852-3026
　　President: Mark Hager

Ohio

Akron-Medina County Labor Council, AFL-CIO (Greater)
　　720 Wolf Ledges Pkwy., No. 207, Akron, OH 44311
　　Phone: (330) 253-2111
　　Fax: (330) 253-4447
　　Executive Secretary-Treasurer: James Frost

Ashland County Ohio Central Labor Council, AFL-CIO
　　6570 Adario N. Rd., Shiloh, OH 44878
　　President: Allen Clark

Ashtabula County AFL-CIO Labor Council
　　5928 Hillcrest Ave., Ashtabula, OH 44404
　　Phone: (216) 993-3082
　　Fax: (216) 576-2758
　　President: Richard Charles

Barberton Council of Labor, AFL-CIO
　　173 E. Tuscarawas Ave., Barberton, OH 44203
　　Phone: (330) 848-6744
　　Fax: (330) 745-2764
　　President: Tom Miller

Bay Area Labor Council AFL-CIO
　　P.O. Box 1365, Sandusky, OH 44871
　　President: Robert Warner

Belmont and Monroe Counties AFL-CIO Trades and Labor Council
　　46010 Liddle Rd., Jacobsburg, OH 43933
　　Phone: (740) 686-9813
　　President: Nada Hanes

Butler-Warren-Clinton Counties AFL-CIO Labor Council
11794 Hamilton-Cleves Rd., Hamilton, OH 45013
Phone: (513) 738-8893
Fax: (513) 738-8894
President: Herbert Jacobs

Cincinnati AFL-CIO Labor Council
1014 Vine St., Suite 2575, Cincinnati, OH 45202
Phone: (513) 421-1846
Fax: (513) 345-8833
Web: www.cincinnatiaflcio.org
Executive Secretary-Treasurer: V. Daniel Radford

Cleveland AFL-CIO Federation of Labor
3250 Euclid Ave., Room 250, Cleveland, OH 44115
Phone: (216) 881-7200
Fax: (216) 881-9025
Executive Secretary: John W. Ryan

Columbiana County AFL-CIO Labor Council
P.O. Box 69, Salem, OH 44460
Phone: (330) 332-9032
Fax: (330) 332-8071
President: Ken Hogue

Columbus-Franklin County AFL-CIO
1545 Alum Creek Dr., 2nd Floor, Columbus, OH 43209
Phone: (614) 257-1920
Fax: (614) 257-1929
Executive Secretary-Treasurer: Walter L. Workman

Coshocton County Trades and Labor Council, AFL-CIO
219 Jackson St., Coshocton, OH 43812
Phone: (614) 622-6997
President: Kent F. Arnold

Crawford County AFL-CIO Council
607 Lee St., Marion, OH 43302
Phone: (740) 383-5917
President: Phil Hatch

Dayton, Springfield, Sidney, Miami Valley AFL-CIO Regional Labor Council
4127 E. 2nd St., Dayton, OH 45403
Phone: (937) 259-9814
Fax: (937) 259-9815
Executive Secretary-Director: Wesley Wells

Grand Lake Ohio Central Labor Council, AFL-CIO
625 E. Ervin Rd., Van Wert, OH 45891
President: Steven B. Dalley

Guernsey County Central Labor Union, AFL-CIO
P.O. Box 1254, Cambridge, OH 43725
Phone: (740) 432-2351
Financial Secretary: Darryl Hughes

Hancock County AFL-CIO Council
530 Monroe Ave., Findlay, OH 45840
Phone: (419) 424-4056
President: Ken Ludwig

Jefferson County Trades and Labor Assembly, AFL-CIO
7037 Scio Rd., Carrollton, OH 44615
Phone: (740) 283-4165
Fax: (330) 627-7382
Executive Secretary-Treasurer: Kathy Derheimer

Knox County Labor Council, AFL-CIO
14180 Beckley Rd., Mount Vernon, OH 43050
Phone: (740) 452-4553
President: Andy Campbell

Lake County AFL-CIO Central Labor Council
9437 Hamilton Dr., Mentor, OH 44060
Phone: (440) 354-8009
Fax: (440) 352-6664
President: Robert G. Schiebli

Lancaster Federation of Labor
2149 Lendale Dr., Lancaster, OH 43130
Phone: (740) 654-7820
Fax: (740) 689-0601
President: Everette Kness

Lima Regional AFL-CIO Federation of Labor
637 Ilata Ave., Lima, OH 45805
Phone: (419) 222-6803
Fax: (419) 222-4966
President: Charles D. Fuller

Lorain County AFL-CIO Federation of Labor
52818 Trinter Rd., Vermilion, OH 44089
Phone: (440) 967-2031
Treasurer: Donald Ferres

Mid-Ohio AFL-CIO Council
974 Woodrow Ave., Marion, OH 43302
Phone: (740) 383-6047
Fax: (740) 387-1914
President: Mike Thomas

Muskingum County AFL-CIO Central Labor Council
1016 Wabash Ave., P.O. Box 8108, Zanesville, OH 43701
Phone: (740) 453-3612
President: Mary Corder

Newark Area AFL-CIO Council
P.O. Box 977, Newark, OH 43058
Phone: (740) 345-1765
Fax: (740) 345-7037
President: Gary Sites

Portage County AFL-CIO Labor Council
844 Manchester St., Kent, OH 44240
Phone: (330) 677-3295
Fax: (330) 678-6843
President: Michael DeLuke

Richland County (Ohio) Council, AFL-CIO
P.O. Box 1234, Mansfield, OH 44901
Phone: (419) 892-3913
Fax: (419) 892-1927
President: Dan Martin

Ross County AFL-CIO Council
319 E. 8th St., Wellston, OH 45692
Phone: (740) 384-6903
President: Harold Hollingshead

Sandusky County Labor Council, AFL-CIO
1223 Hamlin St., Fremont, OH 43420
Phone: (419) 332-3854
Financial Secretary: Paul Wagner

Shawnee District AFL-CIO Council
P.O. Box 577, Portsmouth, OH 45662
Phone: (740) 353-5869
Fax: (740) 353-5770
President: Kenny Ruggles

Southeastern Ohio AFL-CIO Council
P.O. Box 571, Marietta, OH 45750
Phone: (740) 585-2100
President: Troy Farrell

Stark County AFL-CIO Council (Greater)
618 High Ave., N.W., Room 4, Canton, OH 44703
Phone: (330) 453-3624
Fax: (330) 453-3688
President: Daniel F. Sciury

Tiffin Central Labor Union, AFL-CIO
182 Melmore St., Tiffin, OH 44883
Phone: (419) 447-2171
Financial Secretary: Randy Smith

Toledo Area AFL-CIO Council
2300 Ashland Ave., Toledo, OH 43620
Phone: (419) 241-1851
Fax: (419) 241-1823
Executive Secretary-Treasurer: Ronald E. Coughenour

Trumbull County Federation of Labor, AFL-CIO
116 Pine Ave., N.E., Warren, OH 44481
Phone: (330) 399-1541
Fax: (330) 399-1541
Financial Secretary: Roy Billion

Tuscarawas County AFL-CIO
P.O. Box 40, New Philadelphia, OH 44663
Phone: (330) 343-2456
President: Todd E. Beegle

Wayne-Holmes Labor Council, AFL-CIO
9786 Sterling Rd., Rittman, OH 44270
Phone: (330) 925-2180
President: Don Lance

Williams County Labor Council, AFL-CIO
15100 Country Rd. 15, Pioneer, OH 43554
Phone: (419) 737-2267
President: Alan LaCombe

Youngstown AFL-CIO Council (Greater)
25 N. Canfield-Niles Rd., Suite 80, Youngstown, OH 44515
Phone: (330) 792-0861
Fax: (330) 793-0611
President: Larry Fauver

Oklahoma

Central Oklahoma Labor Federation, AFL-CIO
5315 S. Shartel Ave., Oklahoma City, OK 73109
Phone: (405) 634-4030
Fax: (405) 634-3732
President: Tim O'Connor

Northeastern Oklahoma Labor Council, AFL-CIO
4620 E. 11th St., Suite 202, Tulsa, OK 74112
Phone: (918) 832-8128
Fax: (918) 838-8485
President: Roger Nelson

Oregon

Central Oregon Labor Council, AFL-CIO
2161 S.E. 1st St., Redmond, OR 97756
Phone: (541) 548-2642
Fax: (541) 548-8002
President: Jerry Fletcher

Clatsop County Central Labor Council, AFL-CIO
P.O. Box 55, Astoria, OR 97103
Phone: (503) 325-7874
Secretary-Treasurer: George Kiepke

Douglas County Labor Council, AFL-CIO
P.O. Box 788, Roseburg, OR 97470
Phone: (541) 664-4605
Fax: (541) 664-4713
President: John Hilkey

Eastern Oregon Central Labor Council, AFL-CIO
1902 3rd St., No. 102, La Grande, OR 97805
Phone: (541) 963-3203
President: Anthony Marks

Lane County Labor Council, AFL-CIO
317 S. A St., Springfield, OR 97477
Phone: (541) 741-4771
Fax: (541) 736-1786
Executive Secretary-Treasurer: Pat Riggs-Henson

Linn-Benton-Lincoln Labor Council, AFL-CIO
14514 S.E. Helen St., Jefferson, OR 97352
Phone: (541) 327-3638
President: Lee King

Marion, Polk and Yamhill Counties Central Labor Council, AFL-CIO
38517 Groshong Rd., N.E., Albany, OR 97321
President: Garner Pool

Mid-Columbia Labor Council, AFL-CIO
3313 W. 2nd St., The Dalles, OR 97058
Phone: (541) 296-6161
President: Gil Hayes

Northwest Oregon Labor Council, AFL-CIO
1125 S.E. Madison St., Suite 103-A, Portland, OR 97214
Phone: (503) 235-9444
Fax: (503) 233-8259
Executive Secretary-Treasurer: Judy O'Connor

Southeastern Oregon Central Labor Council, AFL-CIO
3836 Altamont Dr., Klamath Falls, OR 97603
Phone: (541) 884-8106
Fax: (541) 884-3471
President: Marty Demaris

Southern Oregon Central Labor Council, AFL-CIO
4480 Rogue Valley Hwy., No. 3, Central Point, OR 97502
Phone: (541) 664-0800
Fax: (541) 664-0806
Secretary-Treasurer: Carol Bennett

Southwestern Oregon Central Labor Council, AFL-CIO
3427 Ash St., North Bend, OR 97459
Phone: (541) 756-2559
Fax: (541) 756-5612
President: Gary Marconi

Umatilla-Morrow Central Labor Council, AFL-CIO
308 S.W. Dorion Ave., Pendleton, OR 97801
Phone: (541) 278-0209
President: Becky Marks

Pennsylvania

Allegheny County Labor Council, AFL-CIO
Arrott Bldg., 401 Wood St., Suite 501, Pittsburgh, PA 15222
Phone: (412) 281-7450
Fax: (412) 765-2673
President: Jack Shea

Beaver County AFL-CIO, Labor Council of
P.O. Box A, Beaver, PA 15009
Phone: (724) 770-0606
Web: www.beavercountyaflcio.org
President: Jeff Davis

Blair-Bedford Central Labor Council, AFL-CIO
302 E. Wopsononock Ave., Altoona, PA 16601
Phone: (814) 944-4081
Fax: (814) 944-7809
President: Robert K. Kutz, Jr.

Bucks County Federation of Trade and Industrial Council of Pennsylvania, AFL-CIO
    1811 Farragut Ave., Bristol, PA 19007
    Phone: (215) 788-8155
    Fax: (215) 785-3934
    President: Mike Peterpaul

Butler County United Labor Council, AFL-CIO
    237 Sixth St., Pittsburgh, PA 15238
    Phone: (412) 828-5100
    Fax: (412) 828-2607
    President: Ed Grystar

Centre County Central Labor Council, AFL-CIO
    2782 Zion Rd., Bellefonte, PA 16823
    Phone: (814) 383-4112
    President: Jerry Emerick

Chester County AFL-CIO Council
    750 Charles St., Coatesville, PA 19320
    Phone: (610) 384-9180
    Fax: (610) 384-9187
    President: David L. McLimas

Clearfield, Elk, Cameron, Jefferson Central Labor Council, AFL-CIO
    Rural Delivery No. 1, Box 5800, Olanta, PA 16863
    Phone: (814) 236-0205
    President: Thomas Tozer

Crawford County Labor Union Council, AFL-CIO
    287 1/2 Chestnut St., Meadville, PA 16335
    Phone: (814) 337-4133
    President: Larry Harvey

Delaware County AFL-CIO Council
    400 N. Springfield Rd., Clifton Heights, PA 19018
    Phone: (610) 623-0555
    Fax: (610) 623-8957
    President: Randy Canale

Erie County, Central Labor Union and Industrial Union Council, AFL-CIO
    1701 State St., Erie, PA 16501
    Phone: (814) 455-4752
    Fax: (814) 455-4752
    President: Matthew Gress

Fayette County Central Labor Union, AFL-CIO
    268 Duff Rd., McClellandtown, PA 15458
    Phone: (724) 439-0582
    Fax: (724) 439-0757
    President: Terry Janosek

Five County United Labor Council
    50 Country Rd., Lewisburg, PA 17837
    Phone: (570) 523-3361
    President: Freeman Snyder

Harrisburg Region Central Labor Council, AFL-CIO
    200 Gibson St., Steelton, PA 17113
    Phone: (717) 939-9366
    Fax: (717) 939-1452
    President: Ike Gittlen

Huntingdon County, AFL-CIO, United Labor Council of
    Rural Rte. 1, Box 356A, Huntingdon, PA 16652
    Phone: (814) 643-1490
    President: K.D. Kurtz

Indiana-Armstrong-Clarion Central Labor Council, AFL-CIO
    P.O. Box 200, Lucerne Mines, PA 15754
    Phone: (724) 479-8692
    Fax: (724) 479-4010
    President: Ron Airhart

Johnstown Regional Central Labor Council, AFL-CIO
    1730 Linwood Ave., Johnstown, PA 15902
    Phone: (814) 535-7621
    Fax: (814) 535-7624
    President: Ernest J. Esposito

Lancaster United Labor Council, AFL-CIO
    675 Manor St., Lancaster, PA 17603
    Phone: (717) 392-2518
    Fax: (717) 392-7594
    President: Jean Martin

Lawrence County, AFL-CIO Council of
    2504 Marie Dr., Suite 2, New Castle, PA 16105
    Phone: (724) 652-8981
    Fax: (412) 652-0840
    President: Ted Scardefield

Lehigh Valley Labor Council
    124 N. 6th St., Allentown, PA 18101
    Phone: (610) 432-3757
    Fax: (610) 520-4255
    President: John Werkheiser

Lower Luzerne and Carbon Counties, AFL-CIO United Labor Council of
    31 N. Broad St., West Hazleton, PA 18101
    Phone: (570) 455-3876
    President: Keith Kocher

McKean and Potter Counties Federation of Labor, AFL-CIO
    10 N. Third St., Bradford, PA 16701
    Phone: (814) 887-3200
    Fax: (814) 887-2242
    President: James M. Weaver

Mercer County Central Labor Council, AFL-CIO
    825 Sharon-New Castle Rd., Farrell, PA 16121
    Phone: (724) 346-3537
    President: Dominic Vadala

Mifflin-Juniata Counties United Labor Council, AFL-CIO
    7 Park Pl., Lewistown, PA 17044
    Phone: (717) 248-3919
    President: Wayne Hackett

Monongahela Valley Central Labor Council, AFL-CIO
    P.O. Box 143, Allenport, PA 15412
    Phone: (724) 326-4546
    President: Don Shephard

Monroe and Pike Counties AFL-CIO, Central Labor Union of
    Rural Delivery No. 7, Box 7762, Stonehedge Rd., Stroudsburg, PA 18360
    Phone: (717) 421-7827
    President: Edward B. McMaster

Montgomery County AFL-CIO Union Council
    5416 Rising Sun Ave., Philadelphia, PA 19120
    Phone: (215) 329-8833
    Fax: (215) 329-8668
    President: John Cairns

Northern Tier Central Labor Council, AFL-CIO
    1183 Rte. 189 Hwy., Trout Run, PA 17771
    Phone: (570) 998-8609
    Fax: (570) 998-8609
    President: Tim Bowen

Philadelphia Council of the AFL-CIO
    22 S. 22nd St., 2nd Floor, Philadelphia, PA 19103
    Phone: (215) 665-9800
    Fax: (215) 665-1973
    President: Patrick Eiding

Reading and Berks County AFL-CIO, United Labor Council of
116 N. 5th St., Reading, PA 19601
Phone: (610) 374-2725
Fax: (610) 374-6521
Web: www.berkslabor.org
President: G. Fred Shaeff, Jr.

Schuylkill County, United Labor Council of
1066 Deep Creek Rd., Ashland, PA 17921
Phone: (570) 682-9440
President: Keith Yoder

Scranton Central Labor Union, AFL-CIO (Greater)
AFSCME Bldg., 1258 O'Neill Hwy., Dunmore, PA 18512
Phone: (570) 346-9440
Fax: (570) 969-2977
President: James Byrnes

Somerset County Central Labor Council, AFL-CIO
2926 E. Mudpike Rd., Berlin, PA 15530
Phone: (814) 267-4212
President: Lana J. Foor

Venango County Labor Council, AFL-CIO
1276 Liberty St., Franklin, PA 16323
Phone: (814) 437-7654
Fax: (814) 432-8393
President: Edward L. Scurry

Warren County Central Labor Council, AFL-CIO
5 Wilson St., Warren, PA 16365
Phone: (814) 723-0709
President: Charles Davidson

Washington/Greene County Central Labor Council, AFL-CIO
5 Wilson St., Washington, PA 15301
Phone: (724) 229-7080
Fax: (724) 229-7198
President: Frederick J. Ricker

Westmoreland County Labor Union Council, AFL-CIO (Greater)
1 Northgate Sq., Greensburg, PA 15601
Phone: (724) 837-6312
Fax: (724) 837-2583
President: Charles Datz

Wilkes-Barre Labor Council, AFL-CIO (Greater)
501 E. Main St., Wilkes-Barre, PA 18702
Phone: (570) 823-6716
Fax: (570) 825-2219
President: Samuel Bianco

York/Adams County Central Labor Council, AFL-CIO
1490 Hametown Rd., Glen Rock, PA 17327
Phone: (717) 235-1777
Fax: (717) 235-1777
Web: www.yorkadamslabor.org
President: Richard L. Boyd

Rhode Island

Pawtucket and Central Falls Central Labor Council, AFL-CIO
129 Rosemont Ave., Pawtucket, RI 02861
Phone: (401) 722-7181
Fax: (401) 728-5588
Secretary: Mary A. Kaveny

Providence Central Federated Council, AFL-CIO
514 Colwell Rd., Harrisville, RI 02830
Phone: (401) 467-3323
Fax: (401) 467-9480
President: Paul A. MacDonald

Woonsocket Labor Council, AFL-CIO (Greater)
P.O. Box 1584, Woonsocket, RI 02895
Phone: (401) 487-0612
President: Thomas L. Papa

South Carolina

Catawba Central Labor Union, AFL-CIO
1582 S. Hwy. 161, York, SC 29745
Phone: (803) 222-4574
President: Bill Wise

Charleston Labor Council, AFL-CIO (Greater)
P.O. Box 60850, Charleston, SC 29419
Phone: (843) 881-6134
Fax: (775) 871-2866
President: Erin McKee

Columbia Central Labor Union, AFL-CIO (Greater)
5411 Bamberg Rd., Cope, SC 29038
Phone: (803) 343-1650
Fax: (803) 252-4151
President: Cindy Rickards

Pee Dee Central Labor Union, AFL-CIO
P.O. Box 1456, Hartsville, SC 29551
Phone: (843) 332-4540
President: Carolyn Ladd

Piedmont Central Labor Union, AFL-CIO (Greater)
245 Brookmere Rd., Simpsonville, SC 29681
Phone: (864) 963-9568
President: Darrell E. Curry

South Dakota

Aberdeen Central Labor Union, AFL-CIO
1323 N. Pennsylvania St., Aberdeen, SD 57401
Phone: (605) 229-5965
Treasurer: James Kraft

Rapid City Central Labor Council, AFL-CIO
4702 Baldwin St., Rapid City, SD 57702
Phone: (605) 394-5253
President: Michael Richardson

Sioux Falls Trades and Labor Assembly, AFL-CIO
101 S. Fairfax Ave., Sioux Falls, SD 57103
Phone: (605) 338-3091
President: James Larson

Watertown AFL-CIO Trades and Labor Assembly
106 2nd St., S.E., Watertown, SD 57201
President: Dan Bendel

Tennessee

Chattanooga Area Labor Council, AFL-CIO
3922 Volunteer Dr., Chattanooga, TN 37416
Phone: (423) 899-0134
President: Gary Watkins

Jackson Central Labor Council, AFL-CIO
P.O. Box 223, 175 Adams St., McLemoresville, TN 38235
Phone: (731) 986-5975
President: Tony Poole

Knoxville-Oak Ridge Area Central Labor Council, AFL-CIO
311 Morgan St., Knoxville, TN 37917
Phone: (865) 523-9752
Fax: (865) 523-9478
President: Harold G. Woods

Memphis AFL-CIO Labor Council
3035 Director Row, Bldg. B, Suite
1207, Memphis, TN 38131
Phone: (901) 332-3531
Fax: (901) 332-3532
President: Fred Ashwill

**Nashville and Middle Tennessee AFL-CIO
Central Labor Council**
P.O. Box 290153, Nashville, TN 37229
Phone: (615) 885-7778
Fax: (615) 885-7776
President: Patrick Saltkill

**Upper East Tennessee Central Labor
Council, AFL-CIO**
924 Old Stage Rd., Rogersville, TN
37857
Phone: (423) 345-2810
Fax: (423) 345-4463
President: Bill Givens

Texas

**Abilene/Big Country Central Labor
Council, AFL-CIO**
P.O. Box 3161, Abilene, TX 79604
Phone: (915) 677-3585
Fax: (915) 692-4820
President: Michael J. Armstrong

**Amarillo Central Labor Council,
AFL-CIO**
P.O. Box 387, Amarillo, TX 79105
Phone: (806) 373-4574
Fax: (806) 374-4437
Secretary-Treasurer: James N. Brookes

**Anderson County Area Central Labor
Council, AFL-CIO**
P.O. Box 4174, Palestine, TX 75802
Phone: (903) 723-3020
Fax: (903) 723-3483
President: Sam Merrell

Austin Area AFL-CIO Council
P.O. Box 87, Austin, TX 78711
Phone: (512) 472-2850
Fax: (512) 472-1190
President: David Brown

**Bell County Central Labor Council,
AFL-CIO**
P.O. Box 10277, Killeen, TX 76547
Phone: (254) 200-4578
President: Phyllis Jones

**Brazos Valley Central Labor Council,
AFL-CIO**
P.O. Box 1355, Bryan, TX 77806-1355
Phone: (979) 779-1028
Fax: (979) 775-8460
President: Alfred Bolla

Central Texas Labor Council, AFL-CIO
4029 Old Marlin Rd., Waco, TX 76705
Phone: (254) 755-7111
President: Nolene Sykora

Coastal Bend Labor Council, AFL-CIO
2301 Saratoga Blvd., Corpus Christi,
TX 78415
Phone: (361) 855-1084
Fax: (361) 854-7453
President: Robert Shake

Dallas AFL-CIO Council
1408 N. Washington Ave., Suite 240,
Dallas, TX 75204
Phone: (214) 826-4808
Fax: (214) 826-0570
Secretary-Treasurer: Jim McCasland

**Deep East Texas Council of Labor,
AFL-CIO**
P.O. Box 153, Lufkin, TX 75902
Phone: (936) 632-3958
Fax: (936) 824-3524
President: Jimmy Horton

**East Texas Central Labor Council,
AFL-CIO (Greater)**
P.O. Box 1842, Longview, TX 75606
Phone: (903) 753-7646
Fax: (903) 758-7222
President: Billie D. Payne

El Paso Central Labor Union, AFL-CIO
6967 Commerce St., P.O. Box 971365,
El Paso, TX 79997
Phone: (915) 781-0242
Fax: (915) 781-0540
President: David Aranda

Ellis County Labor Council, AFL-CIO
112 Auburn Dr., Waxahachie, TX
75165
Phone: (972) 937-2664
President: Billy Roberts

Galveston County AFL-CIO
7912 Larkspur Dr., Texas City, TX
77591
Phone: (409) 256-9706
Fax: (409) 938-3418
President: Sam Munn

**Harris County Central Labor Council,
AFL-CIO**
2506 Sutherland St., Houston, TX
77023
Phone: (713) 923-9473
Fax: (713) 923-5010
Secretary-Treasurer: Richard C. Shaw

**Henderson-Navarro Central Labor
Council, AFL-CIO**
16480 State Hwy. 31 E., Brownsboro,
TX 75756
Phone: (903) 852-6580
President: Lloyd Starr

**Lubbock Central Labor Council,
AFL-CIO**
405 50th St., Lubbock, TX 79404
Phone: (806) 747-5287
President: Billy Martinez

Montgomery County AFL-CIO
P.O. Box 7694, The Woodlands, TX
77387
Phone: (713) 853-4911
Fax: (713) 853-4913
Vice President: Robert Mahle

Paris Central Labor Council, AFL-CIO
2285 N.W. 19th St., Paris, TX 75460
Phone: (903) 785-3686
President: Gary Cunningham

**Permian Basin Central Labor Union,
AFL-CIO**
1406 S. Terrell St., Midland, TX 79701
Phone: (915) 563-0583
Fax: (915) 563-0583
President: D.L. Dally Willis

**Rio Grande Valley Central Labor Council,
AFL-CIO**
P.O. Box 359, Donna, TX 78537
Phone: (956) 464-5556
President: Gene Hanson

**Sabine Area Central Labor Council,
AFL-CIO**
1500 Jefferson Dr., Port Arthur, TX
77642
Phone: (409) 982-8180
Fax: (409) 985-3519
President: William Ruelle Parker

San Antonio AFL-CIO Council
311 S. St. Mary's St., No. 15E, San
Antonio, TX 78205
Phone: (210) 226-8447
Fax: (210) 226-6285
President: Bob Salvatore

Smith County Central Labor Council, AFL-CIO
19968 F.M. 3079, Chandler, TX 75758
Phone: (903) 535-1673
President: John Nash

Tarrant County Central Labor Council, AFL-CIO
4025 Rufe Snow Dr., Fort Worth, TX 76180
Phone: (817) 284-1461
Fax: (817) 595-4894
President: Tim Smith

Texoma AFL-CIO Council
Status Pending

Tideland Central Labor Council, AFL-CIO
211 Persimmon St., Lake Jackson, TX 77566
Phone: (409) 297-1399
President: O.D. Kenemore

Victoria Area Central Labor Council, AFL-CIO
1415 Westpark Ave., Victoria, TX 77905
Phone: (361) 576-0376
President: Lummie Peterson

Webb County AFL-CIO, Central Labor Council
Status Pending

Wichita Falls Trades and Labor Council, AFL-CIO
613 W. Texas Ave., Iowa Park, TX 76367
Phone: (940) 676-4217
President: Walter Beeman

Utah

Central Utah Federation of Labor, AFL-CIO
2261 S. Redwood Rd., Suite M, Salt Lake City, UT 84116
Phone: (801) 972-2771
Fax: (801) 972-9344
President: Calvin J. Noyce

Northern Utah Central Labor Council, AFL-CIO
900 N. 400 W., Suite 4, North Salt Lake, UT 84054
Phone: (801) 295-6198
President: Thomas Lewis

Southern Utah Labor Council, AFL-CIO
1847 S. Columbia Ln., Orem, UT 84097
Phone: (801) 225-8533
President: Lionel Camara

Vermont

Champlain Valley Labor Council, AFL-CIO
P.O. Box 5841, Burlington, VT 05402
Phone: (802) 860-4376
President: Mark Nolan

Northeast Kingdom Labor Council, AFL-CIO
145 Mountain St., St. Johnsbury, VT 05819
Phone: (802) 626-9995
President: Dick Gammell

Rutland-Addison Central Labor Council, AFL-CIO
170 Cedar Dr., Addison, VT 05491
Phone: (802) 388-2681
President: Jill Charbonneau

Washington and Orange Counties Labor Council, AFL-CIO
38 State St., 2nd Floor, Montpelier, VT 05601
Phone: (802) 229-0009
Web: home.workingfamilies.com/ ~wovtclc
President: Hal Layshon

Windham County Labor Council, AFL-CIO
104 Forest St., Brattleboro, VT 05301
Phone: (802) 257-2366
President: Kevin McAvoy

Virginia

Central Virginia Labor Council, AFL-CIO
P.O. Box 2853, Lynchburg, VA 24501
Phone: (434) 846-4204
President: Walter Fore

Mountain Empire Labor Council, AFL-CIO
P.O. Box 1094, Abingdon, VA 24212
President: Geneva Miller

New River Valley Central Labor Council, AFL-CIO
270 White Pine Dr., Christianburg, VA 24073
Phone: (540) 674-5130
Fax: (540) 674-2534
President: Robbie Wyrick

Northern Virginia Central Labor Council, AFL-CIO
P.O. Box 565, Annandale, VA 22003
Phone: (703) 750-3633
Fax: (703) 941-6210
President: Lou Cernak

Portsmouth Central Labor Council, AFL-CIO
4415 County St., Portsmouth, VA 23707
Phone: (757) 485-4144
Fax: (757) 485-4144
President: Stephen L. Whitehead

Richmond Regional Labor Council, AFL-CIO
231 E. Belt Blvd., Richmond, VA 23224
Phone: (804) 232-2955
Fax: (804) 233-2965
President: John Gregory

Roanoke United Central Labor Union, AFL-CIO
1202 Jamison Ave., S.E., Roanoke, VA 24013
Phone: (540) 345-4561
Fax: (540) 345-1300
President: Rick Howard

Shenandoah Valley Central Labor Council, AFL-CIO
P.O. Box 871, Verona, VA 24482
Phone: (540) 886-4750
Fax: (540) 885-8380
President: Harry L. Dull

Tidewater Central Labor Council, AFL-CIO (Greater)
5307 Virginia Beach Blvd., Norfolk, VA 23502
Phone: (757) 623-1246
Fax: (757) 640-8467
President: Marian Flickinger

Virginia Peninsula Central Labor Union, AFL-CIO
2013 Cunningham Dr., Suite 331, Hampton, VA 23666
Phone: (757) 825-8660
Fax: (757) 825-8783
President: Russ Axsom

Washington

Clark, Skamania and West Klickitat Counties AFL-CIO, Central Labor Council of
P.O. Box 61929, Vancouver, WA 98666
Phone: (360) 921-7484
Fax: (360) 673-3584
Secretary-Treasurer: Mike Phillips

Cowlitz-Wahkiakum Counties Labor Council, AFL-CIO
P.O. Box 430, Longview, WA 98632
Phone: (360) 425-3550
Fax: (360) 425-8137
President: Jeff Smith

Grays Harbor County Labor Council, AFL-CIO
P.O. Box 1109, Aberdeen, WA 98520
Phone: (360) 532-2643
Fax: (360) 532-7596
President: John Warring

King County Labor Council, AFL-CIO
2800 First Ave., Suite 206, Seattle, WA 98121
Phone: (206) 441-8510
Fax: (206) 441-7103
Web: www.kclc.org
Executive Secretary-Treasurer: Steve Williamson

Kitsap County Central Labor Council, AFL-CIO
632 5th St., Suite 5, Bremerton, WA 98337
Phone: (360) 373-5800
Fax: (360) 373-5800
President: John S. Arena

Mason County Labor Council, AFL-CIO
P.O. Box 268, Shelton, WA 98584
Phone: (360) 426-5541
Fax: (360) 427-4472
Recording Secretary: Dale Whinery

North Central Washington Central Labor Council, AFL-CIO
27 N. Chelan Ave., Wenatchee, WA 98801
Phone: (509) 662-7192
Fax: (509) 662-9762
President: Robert Abbott

Northwest Washington Central Labor Council
1700 N. State St., Suite 202, Bellingham, WA 98225
Phone: (360) 676-0099
Fax: (360) 733-8840
President: David F. Warren

Olympic Labor Council, AFL-CIO
P.O. Box 688, Port Angeles, WA 98362
Phone: (360) 565-2198
Fax: (360) 417-5160
President: Bob Zindel

Pacific County Central Labor Council, AFL-CIO
1610 Fowler St., Raymond, WA 98577
Phone: (360) 942-3316
Treasurer: Judy Jones

Pierce County Central Labor Council, AFL-CIO
3049 S. 36th St., No. 201, Tacoma, WA 98409
Phone: (253) 473-3810
Fax: (253) 472-6050
Secretary-Treasurer: Patty Rose

Snohomish County Labor Council, AFL-CIO
2812 Lombard Ave., Suite 207, Everett, WA 98201
Phone: (425) 259-7922
Fax: (425) 339-9173
Web: www.snolabor.org
Secretary-Treasurer: Mike Sells

Southeastern Washington Labor Council
P.O. Box 1324, Pasco, WA 99301
Phone: (509) 547-7553
Fax: (509) 547-4313
President: Mark Reavis

Spokane Labor Council, AFL-CIO
1522 N. Washington St., Suite 103, Spokane, WA 99201
Phone: (509) 327-7637
Fax: (509) 327-2331
Executive Secretary-Treasurer: Beth Thew

Thurston-Lewis Counties Labor Council, AFL-CIO
P.O. Box 66, Olympia, WA 98507
Phone: (360) 736-9901
President: Bob Guenther

Yakima South Central Counties Central Labor Council, AFL-CIO
507 S. 3rd St., Yakima, WA 98901
Phone: (509) 248-3894
Fax: (509) 248-3894
President: Dale Palmer

West Virginia

Brooke-Hancock Labor Council, AFL-CIO
P.O. Box 307, Newell, WV 26050
Phone: (330) 385-2301
President: Linda Dickey

Kanawha Valley Labor Council, AFL-CIO
600 Leon Sullivan Way, Charleston, WV 25301
Phone: (304) 343-6952
Fax: (304) 346-3862
President: Charles Matthews

Marion County AFL-CIO
P.O. Box 96, Kingmont, WV 26578
Phone: (304) 367-0195
Fax: (304) 367-0195
President: Vernon Swisher

Marshall, Wetzel, Tyler Central Labor Council, AFL-CIO
P.O. Box 416, New Martinsville, WV 26155
Phone: (304) 455-5500
Fax: (304) 455-5500
President: Raymond Smith

Mason-Jackson-Roane Labor Council, AFL-CIO
112 Hall St., Ripley, WV 25271
Phone: (304) 372-5361
President: Jim Picarella

Monongalia-Preston Labor Council, AFL-CIO
P.O. Box 551, Morgantown, WV 26505
Phone: (304) 296-4631
Fax: (304) 291-3849
President: Rita McCrobie

North Central West Virginia Labor Council, AFL-CIO
518 Kuhl Ave., Clarksburg, WV 26301
Phone: (304) 622-6125
Fax: (304) 623-5997
President: Tony Blidgette

Ohio Valley Trades and Labor Assembly of Wheeling, AFL-CIO
P.O. Box 4047, Wheeling, WV 26003
Phone: (304) 232-4411
Secretary-Treasurer: Evan S. Cundiff

Parkersburg Area Labor Council, AFL-CIO
P.O. Box 102, Parkersburg, WV 26102
Phone: (304) 863-0379
President: Richard Schaffer

South Central AFL-CIO
P.O. Box 416, Oak Hill, WV 25901
Phone: (304) 469-9815
President: Nancy Law

Southwestern District Labor Council, AFL-CIO
P.O. Box 2142, Huntington, WV 25721
Phone: (304) 523-2353
Fax: (304) 523-0756
Secretary-Treasurer: Tim Millne

Tri-County Central Labor Council, AFL-CIO
P.O. Box 1258, Shepherdstown, WV 25443
Phone: (304) 876-2104
Fax: (304) 876-1757
President: Sheila Hamilton

Wisconsin

Ashland Area Trades and Labor Council, AFL-CIO
Rte. 1, Box 262, Ashland, WI 54806
Phone: (715) 682-5669
President: John Nuutinen

Chippewa County Central Labor Council, AFL-CIO
647 W. Canal St., Chippewa Falls, WI 54729
Phone: (715) 723-9613
President: Melanie Schaller

Dodge County Central Labor Council, AFL-CIO
108 Winn Terr., Beaver Dam, WI 53916
Phone: (414) 887-8871
Fax: (414) 887-0105
President: Jim Giedd

Eau Claire Area Council, AFL-CIO
2233 Birch St., Eau Claire, WI 54703
Phone: (715) 723-2894
Secretary: Patrick Cumming

Fond du Lac County Labor Council, AFL-CIO
50 E. Bank St., Fond du Lac, WI 54935
Phone: (920) 924-0779
Fax: (920) 924-0758
Recording Secretary: Laurie Gruber

Fox Valley Area Labor Council, AFL-CIO
P.O. Box 186, Menasha, WI 54952
Phone: (920) 727-1790
Fax: (920) 727-1794
President: Mark Westphal

Green Bay Labor Council, AFL-CIO (Greater)
W. 1820 Mile Dr., Pulaski, WI 54162
President: Matt Zernicke

Jefferson County Central Labor Council, AFL-CIO
829 McCoy Park Rd., Fort Atkinson, WI 53538
Phone: (920) 563-6888
Fax: (920) 648-8000
Acting President: Roger Kluver

Kenosha AFL-CIO
4817 60th St., Kenosha, WI 53144
Phone: (262) 697-4681
Fax: (262) 657-5242
President: Ronald J. Frederick

La Crosse AFL-CIO Council
2020 Winnebago St., La Crosse, WI 54601
Phone: (608) 782-5851
Fax: (608) 782-8015
President: Terry L. Hicks

Lakes Regional Labor Council, AFL-CIO
411 E. Reed Ave., Manitowoc, WI 54220
Phone: (920) 684-3842
Fax: (920) 684-3150
Vice President: Myron Halla

Marathon County Labor Council, AFL-CIO
318 S. 3rd Ave., Wausau, WI 54401
Phone: (715) 848-3320
President: Bob Andringa

Marinette, Wisconsin and Menominee, Michigan Labor Council, AFL-CIO
71 Hosmer St., Marinette, WI 54143
Phone: (715) 789-2466
President: Dale Carlson

Marshfield Central Labor Council, AFL-CIO
1503 S. Locust Ave., No. 2, Marshfield, WI 54449
Phone: (715) 389-1253
Recording Secretary: Bruce Stargardt

Milwaukee County Labor Council, AFL-CIO
633 S. Hawley Rd., Suite 110, Milwaukee, WI 53214
Phone: (414) 771-7070
Fax: (414) 771-0509
President: John Goldstein

North Central Labor Council
P.O. Box 172, Tomahawk, WI 54487
Phone: (715) 453-1130
Fax: (715) 453-8620
President: Steven Heikkinen

Northern Area Wisconsin Labor Council, AFL-CIO
N-15873 Hwy. 13 N., Park Falls, WI 54552
Recording Secretary: Jim Shepherd

Ozaukee County Trades and Labor Council, AFL-CIO
124 E. Pierron St., Port Washington, WI 53074
President: Robert Klein

Racine AFL-CIO Council
5425 Vliet St., Milwaukee, WI 53208
Phone: (800) 242-5822
President: Marc A. DeJarlais

Rock County Central Labor Council, AFL-CIO
1620 Shore Dr., Beloit, WI 53511
Phone: (608) 221-1401
Fax: (608) 362-1028
President: Geoff Upperton

Sheboygan County Labor Council, AFL-CIO
1104 Wisconsin Ave., Sheboygan, WI 53081
Phone: (920) 452-0321
Fax: (920) 452-0347
President: Bennett Kunert

South Central Federation of Labor, AFL-CIO
1602 S. Park St., No. 228, Madison, WI 53715
Phone: (608) 256-5111
Fax: (608) 256-6661
President: Jim Cavanaugh

Stevens Point, Portage County Central Labor Council, AFL-CIO
    400 Indiana Ave., Stevens Point, WI 54481
    Phone: (715) 341-1413
    President: Joe Wanta

Superior Federation of Labor, AFL-CIO
    1701 E. 7th St., Superior, WI 54880
    Phone: (715) 398-7270
    President: James Mattson

Walworth County Central Labor Council, AFL-CIO
    W5433 Schmidt Rd., Elkhorn, WI 53121
    Phone: (262) 723-3571
    President: Kathy Franklin

Washington County Central Labor Council, AFL-CIO
    8735 Hwy. 45, Kewaskum, WI 53040
    Phone: (262) 626-2805
    President: Harold P. Schladweiler

Waukesha County Labor Council, AFL-CIO
    1726 S. West Ave., Waukesha, WI 53189
    Phone: (262) 691-7348
    Fax: (262) 542-3819
    President: George Urban

Waupun Central Labor Council, AFL-CIO
    635 Maxon St., Waupun, WI 53963
    Phone: (920) 324-3379
    President: Harvey Austin

West Central Wisconsin Labor Council, AFL-CIO
    855 Hopwood Ave., Menomonie, WI 54751
    Phone: (715) 235-4368
    President: Mark Amthor

Winnebago County Labor Council, AFL-CIO
    3100 Fond du Lac Rd., Oshkosh, WI 54902
    Phone: (920) 233-9767
    Fax: (920) 688-1407
    President: Stephen DeDow

Wisconsin Rapids Central Labor Council, AFL-CIO
    220 Johnson St., Wisconsin Rapids, WI 54495
    Phone: (715) 423-4202
    Fax: (715) 424-1407
    President: Wayne Wesenberg

Wyoming

Casper Area Trades and Labor Assembly, AFL-CIO
    P.O. Box 369, Casper, WY 82602
    Phone: (307) 237-9556
    President: Rick Martinez

Northeast Wyoming Central Labor Council, AFL-CIO
    P.O. Box 2668, Gillette, WY 82717
    Phone: (307) 680-9395
    President: J.C. Calhoun

Sheridan Area Central Labor Union, AFL-CIO
    443 E. College Ave., Sheridan, WY 82801
    Phone: (307) 672-0894
    Fax: (307) 672-9478
    President: Mel Logan

Southeast Wyoming Central Labor Council, AFL-CIO
    P.O. Box 813, Cheyenne, WY 82003
    Phone: (307) 638-3428
    President: Will Cox

Southwestern Wyoming Central Labor Council, AFL-CIO
    P.O. Box 1452, Rock Springs, WY 82901
    Phone: (307) 382-2484
    Fax: (307) 362-4156
    President: John Hastert

PART III. International, National, and State Unions

Union membership figures are from the latest Labor Organization Information Reports submitted by the unions to the U.S. Department of Labor's Office of Labor-Management Standards. Membership information was not available from state employee organizations, which are not covered by federal law.

Union affiliations are in parentheses and acronyms are in brackets.

Actors and Artistes (AFL-CIO)
Associated Actors and Artistes of America [AAAA]
165 W. 46th St., 16th Floor, New York, NY 10036
Phone: (212) 869-0358
Fax: (212) 869-1746
E-mail: actors1919@aol.com
Founded: 1919
Membership: 69,000
Executive Director: John H. Sucke
President: Theodore Bikel
Note: AAAA is comprised of seven autonomous branches: Actors' Equity Association; American Federation of Television and Radio Artists; American Guild of Musical Artists, Inc.; American Guild of Variety Artists; Hebrew Actors' Union, Inc.; Italian Actors Union; and Screen Actors Guild.

Actors' Equity (AAAA)
Actors' Equity Association [AEA]
165 W. 46th St., 15th Floor, New York, NY 10036
Phone: (212) 869-8530
Fax: (212) 719-9815
E-mail: info@actorsequity.org
Web site: www.actorsequity.org
Founded: 1913
Membership: 45,000
Publications: *Equity News* (9 times a year)
President: Patrick Quinn
Executive Director: Alan Eisenberg

Agricultural Employees
National Association of Agricultural Employees [NAAE]
P.O. Box 31143, Hononlulu, HI 96820-1143
Phone: (808) 861-8449
Founded: 1998
Membership: 951
Publications: *Infested*
President: Mike Randall

Vice Presidents:
Willis Gentry
Mike Greenberg
Bill Johnson
John Keck
Eileen Thrift
Secretary: Sarah Clore

Air Traffic Controllers
National Air Traffic Controllers Association [NATCA]
1325 Massachusetts Ave., NW, Washington, DC 20005
Phone: (202) 628-5451
Fax: (202) 628-5767
E-mail: webstaff@natca.org
Web site: www.natca.org
Founded: 1987
Membership: 12,645
Publications: *The Air Traffic Controller* (monthly)
President: John S. Carr
Executive Vice President: Ruth E. Marlin
Vice Presidents:
Mike Blake
Carol Branaman
Jim D'Agati
Pat Forrey
Joseph Fruscella
Bob Marks
Mark Pallone
Ricky Thompson
John Tune
Rodney Turner

Air Traffic Specialists
National Association of Air Traffic Specialists [NAATS]
11303 Amherst Ave., Suite 4, Wheaton, MD 20902
Phone: (301) 933-6228
Fax: (301) 933-3902
Web site: www.naats.org
Founded: 1959
Membership: 1,405
Publications: *NAATS News* (monthly)
President: Walter W. Pike
Treasurer: Marc Lackman

Aircraft Mechanics
Aircraft Mechanics Fraternal Association [AMFA]
67 Water St., Suite 208A, Laconia, NH 03246
Phone: (603) 527-9212
Fax: (603) 527-9151
E-mail: admin@amfanatl.org
Web site: www.amfanatl.org
Membership: 10,294
Director: O.V. Delle-Femine
Secretary: Steve Lanier
Treasurer: Ken Wagers, Jr.

Asbestos Workers (AFL-CIO) (CLC)
International Association of Heat and Frost Insulators and Asbestos Workers [HFIA]
9602 Martin Luther King, Jr. Hwy., Lanham, MD 20706
Phone: (301) 731-9101
Fax: (301) 731-5058
Web site: www.insulators.org
Founded: 1904
Membership: 21,380
Publications: *The Journal* (quarterly)
President: James A. Grogan
Secretary-Treasurer: James (Bud) McCourt

Atlantic Independent Union
Atlantic Independent Union [AIU]
520 Cinnaminson Ave., Palmyra, NJ 08065
Phone: (856) 303-0076
Fax: (856) 346-0803
Web site: www.aiuunion.com
Founded: 1937
Publications: *A.I.U. News* (annually)
President: John W. Kerr
Vice President: Anthony J. Dellaratta
Secretary: Daniel Kalai
Treasurer: William Mehler

Automobile, Aerospace Workers
(AFL-CIO)

International Union, United Automobile, Aerospace and Agricultural Implement Workers of America [UAW]

8000 E. Jefferson Ave., Detroit, MI 48214

Phone: (313) 926-5000

Fax: (313) 823-6016

Web site: www.uaw.org

Washington, DC office: 1757 N St., NW, Washington, DC 20036

Phone: (202) 828-8500

Fax: (202) 293-3457

Founded: 1935

Membership: 701,818

Publications: *Solidarity* (monthly)

President: Ron Gettelfinger

Secretary-Treasurer: Elizabeth Bunn

Vice Presidents:
Gerald Bantom
Nate Gooden
Bob King
Cal Rapson
Richard Shoemaker

Bakery, Confectionery, Tobacco Workers and Grain Millers (AFL-CIO)

Bakery, Confectionery, Tobacco Workers and Grain Millers International Union [BCTGM]

10401 Connecticut Ave., Kensington, MD 20895-3961

Phone: (301) 933-8600

Fax: (301) 946-8452

Web site: www.bctgm.org

Founded: 1886

Membership: 115,218

Publications: *BCTGM News* (bimonthly)

President: Frank Hurt

Secretary-Treasurer: David B. Durkee

International Executive Vice Presidents:
Larry Barber
Joseph Thibodeau

Baseball Players

Major League Baseball Players Association [MLBPA]

12 E. 49th St., 24th Floor, New York, NY 10017

Phone: (212) 826-0808

Fax: (212) 752-4378

E-mail: feedback@mlbpa.org

Web site: www.bigleaguers.com

Founded: 1966

Membership: 1,350

Executive Director and General Counsel:
Donald M. Fehr

Basketball Players

National Basketball Players Association [NBPA]

2 Penn Plaza, Suite 2430, New York, NY 10121

Phone: (212) 655-0880

Fax: (212) 655-0881

E-mail: info@nbpa.com

Web site: www.nbpa.com

Founded: 1954

Membership: 406

Publications: *Time Out* (quarterly)

President: Michael Curry

First Vice President: Greg Anthony

Vice Presidents:
Ray Allen
Antonio Davis
Sam Mitchell
Alonzo Mourning
Theo Ratliff
Jerome Williams

Secretary-Treasurer: Pat Garrity

Executive Director: G. William Hunter

Boilermakers (AFL-CIO)

International Brotherhood of Boilermakers, Iron Ship Builders, Blacksmiths, Forgers and Helpers [IBB]

753 State Ave., Kansas City, KS 66101

Phone: (913) 371-2640

Fax: (913) 281-8101

Web site: www.boilermakers.org

Washington, DC office: 2722 Merrilee Dr., #360, Fairfax, VA 22031

Phone: (703) 560-1493

Fax: (703) 560-2584

Founded: 1880

Membership: 79,892

Publications: *The Boilermaker Reporter* (6 times a year) and *The Boilermaker Bulletin for Local Lodge Editors* (bimonthly)

President: Charles W. Jones

Secretary-Treasurer: Jerry Z. Willburn

Vice Presidents:
Richard C. Albright
James Hickenbotham
Newton B. Jones
Don Lacefield
Alexander C. MacDonald
Lawrence J. McManamon
Michael S. Murphy
George Rogers
Othal Smith

Bricklayers (AFL-CIO)

International Union of Bricklayers and Allied Craftworkers [BAC]

1776 I St., NW, Washington, DC 20006

Phone: (202) 783-3788

Fax: (202) 393-0219

E-mail: askbac@bacweb.org

Web site: www.bacweb.org

Founded: 1865

Membership: 101,823

Publications: *Journal* (monthly)

President: John J. Flynn

Secretary-Treasurer: James Boland

Executive Vice Presidents:
Kenneth Lambert
Gerald O'Malley
Dominic Spano

California School Employees
(AFL-CIO)

California School Employees Association [CSEA]

2045 Lundy Ave., San Jose, CA 95131

Phone: (408) 263-8000

Fax: (408) 954-0948

Web site: www.csea.com

President: Clyde Rivers

Vice President: John Coffee

Secretary: Rosemary Willoughby

Executive Director: Bud Dougherty

Carpenters

United Brotherhood of Carpenters and Joiners of America [UBC]

101 Constitution Ave., NW, Washington, DC 20001

Phone: (202) 546-6206

Fax: (202) 543-5724

Web site: www.carpenters.org

Founded: 1881

Membership: 538,431

Publications: *Carpenter* (bimonthly)

President: Douglas J. McCarron

Vice President: Douglas Banes

Secretary-Treasurer: Andris J. Silins

Catholic School Teachers

National Association of Catholic School Teachers [NACST]

1700 Sansom St., Suite 903, Philadelphia, PA 19103

Phone: (800) 99-NACST

Fax: (215) 568-8270

E-mail: nacst.nacst@verizon.net

Web site: www.nacst.com

Founded: 1978

Publications: *Newsworthy*

President: Rita C. Schwartz

Secretary-Treasurer: William Blumenstein

Executive Vice President: Michael A.
  Milz
Vice Presidents:
  Patrick Cassidy
  Stephen Lieb
  Catherine Sue Manzella
  George Rudolph

Christian Labor Association
Christian Labor Association [CLA]
  405 Centerstone Ct., P.O. Box 65,
    Zeeland, MI 49464
  Phone: (616) 772-9164
  Fax: (616) 772-9830
  E-mail: chrlabor@egl.net
  Founded: 1931
  Membership: 1,729
  Publications: *Christian Labor Herald*
President: Doug Reese
Secretary: Willis Van Dorp
Vice President: Mike Koppenol
Treasurer: Duane Zwagerman

Civilian Technicians
**Association of Civilian
  Technicians** [ACT]
  12510-B Lake Ridge Dr., Lake Ridge,
    VA 22192
  Phone: (703) 494-4845
  Fax: (703) 494-0961
  Web site: www.actnat.com
  Founded: 1960
  Membership: 6,346
  Publications: *The Technician* (monthly)
President: Thomas G. Bastas
Executive Vice President: Leon J. Cich
Secretary: Theresa Allen
Treasurer: Richard A. Richie
Vice Presidents:
  William Brown
  Julie Curtis
  Leslie Hackett
  G. Dwain Reynolds

Classified School Employees
**American Association of Classified
  School Employees** [AACSE]
  7140 S.W. Childs Rd., Lake Oswego,
    OR 97035
  Phone: (503) 620-5663
  Fax: (503) 684-4597
  Web site: www.aacse.org
  Founded: 1958
President: Wayne Scott
Vice President: Joe Brantley
Secretary: Ron Rogers

Communications Workers (AFL-CIO)
**Communications Workers of
  America** [CWA]
  501 Third St., NW, Washington, DC
    20001
  Phone: (202) 434-1100
  Fax: (202) 434-1279
  E-mail: cwaweb@cwa-union.org
  Web site: www.cwa-union.org
  Membership: 589,143
  Publications: *CWA News*
President: Morton Bahr
Secretary-Treasurer: Barbara J. Easterling
Executive Vice President: Larry Cohen
  Note: CWA-affiliated unions include
    The Newspaper Guild (TNG-CWA),
    International Union of Electronic,
    Electrical, Salaried, Machine and
    Furniture Workers (IUE-CWA), and
    the National Association of
    Broadcast Employees and
    Technicians (NABET-CWA).

Commuter Rail Employees
**Association of Commuter Rail
  Employees** [ACRE]
  420 Lexington Ave., Suite 215, New
    York, NY 10017
  Phone: (212) 599-5856
  Fax: (212) 599-2029
  Web site: members.aol.com/acrelocal1/
    new.html
  Membership: 1,204
Contact: Mark Amorello

Congreso Uniones Industriales
**Congreso de Uniones Industriales de
  Puerto Rico** [PRCUI]
  Barbosa #154, Esquina Progreso,
    Catano, PR 00963
  Phone: (787) 788-0160
  Membership: 1,000
President: Jose Figueroa

Directors Guild
Directors Guild of America [DGA]
  7920 Sunset Blvd., Hollywood, CA
    90046
  Phone: (310) 289-2000
  Fax: (310) 289-2029
  E-mail: dga@dga.org
  Web site: www.dga.org
  Chicago office: 400 N. Michigan Ave.,
    Suite 307, Chicago, IL 60611
  Phone: (312) 644-5050
  Fax: (312) 644-5776
  New York office: 110 W. 57th St.,
    New York, NY 10019
  Phone: (212) 581-0370
  Fax: (212) 581-1441
  Founded: 1936
  Membership: 12,460
  Publications: *DGA* (bimonthly)
President: Martha Coolidge
Secretary-Treasurer: Gilbert Cates
Vice Presidents:
  Michael Apted
  Larry Auerbach
  Paris Barclay
  William Brady
  Casey Childs
  Ed Sherin
  Steven Soderbergh
National Executive Director: Jay D. Roth

DuPont Workers
**International Brotherhood of DuPont
  Workers** [IBDW]
  P.O. Box 16333, Louisville, KY
    40256-0333
  Phone: (502) 569-3232
  Web site: www.dupontworkers.com
  Publications: *Voice of the IBDW*
    (monthly)
President: Carl J. Goodman
Secretary-Treasurer: Dave Gibson
Vice Presidents:
  Jim Flickinger
  Greg Lowman

Education
National Education Association [NEA]
  1201 16th St., NW, Washington, DC
    20036
  Phone: (202) 833-4000
  Fax: (202) 822-7974
  Web site: www.nea.org
  Founded: 1857
  Membership: 2,668,925
  Publications: *NEA Today* (eight issues
    annually)
President: Reg Weaver
Vice President: Dennis Van Roekel
Secretary-Treasurer: Lily Eskelsen
Executive Director: John I. Wilson

Electrical Workers (AFL-CIO)
International Brotherhood of Electrical Workers [IBEW]
1125 15th St., NW, Washington, DC 20005
Phone: (202) 833-7000
Fax: (202) 467-6316
Web site: www.ibew.org
Founded: 1891
Publications: *IBEW Journal*
President: Edwin D. Hill
Vice Presidents:
Frank J. Carroll
Lawrence P. (Pat) Curley
William C. Eads
Melvin W. Horton
Carl Lansden
Donald Lounds
Michael S. Mowrey
Lawrence E. Rossa
Orville A. Tate, Jr.
Jon F. Walters
Paul J. Witte
Secretary-Treasurer: Jeremiah J. O'Connor

Electrical, Radio and Machine Workers
United Electrical, Radio and Machine Workers of America [UE]
One Gateway Center, Suite 1400, Pittsburgh, PA 15222-1416
Phone: (412) 471-8919
Fax: (412) 471-8999
E-mail: ue@ranknfile-ue.org
Web site: www.ranknfile-ue.org
Washington, DC office: 1800 Diagonal Rd., Suite 600, Alexandria, VA 22314
Phone: (703) 684-3123
Fax: (703) 548-9446
Founded: 1936
Membership: 35,000
Publications: *UE News* (monthly)
President: John H. Hovis, Jr.
Secretary-Treasurer: Bruce J. Klipple

Electronic Workers (CWA)
International Union of Electronic, Electrical, Salaried, Machine and Furniture Workers [IUE-CWA]
1275 K St., NW, Suite 600, Washington, DC 20005
Phone: (202) 513-6300
Fax: (202) 513-6357
Web site: www.iue-cwa.org
Founded: 1949
Membership: 160,000
Publications: *IUE News* (six issues a year)
President: Edward L. Fire

Elevator Constructors (AFL-CIO)
International Union of Elevator Constructors [IUEC]
7154 Columbia Gateway Dr., Columbia, MD 21046
Phone: (410) 953-6150
Fax: (410) 953-6169
E-mail: contact@iuec.org
Web site: www.iuec.org
Founded: 1901
Membership: 26,693
Publications: *Elevator Constructor* (monthly)
President: Dana A. Brigham
Secretary-Treasurer: Kevin P. Stringer
Vice Presidents:
Rick Baxter
Ernie Brown
John Davenport
John G. Green
George Miller
Donald Mitchell
Steve Sampson
Thaddeus Tomei

Farm Labor Committee (AFL-CIO)
Farm Labor Organizing Committee [FLOC]
1221 Broadway, Toledo, OH 43609
Phone: (419) 243-3456
Fax: (419) 243-5655
E-mail: info@floc.com
Web site: www.floc.com
Founded: 1968
Membership: 7,366
Publications: *Nuestra Lucha*
President: Baldemar Velasquez
Secretary-Treasurer: Jerry Ceille

Farm Workers (AFL-CIO)
United Farm Workers of America [UFW]
P.O. Box 62, Keene, CA 93531-0062
Phone: (661) 822-5571
Web site: www.ufw.org
Founded: 1962
Membership: 5,945
President: Arturo S. Rodriguez
Secretary-Treasurer: Dolores Huerta

Federacion Puertorriqueno
Federacion Puertorriqueno de Trabajadores [PRFPT]
Calle Dresde #516, Puerto Nuevo, PR 00920
Phone: (787) 781-5376
Membership: 900
President: Ramon Fuentes
Secretary-Treasurer: Antonia Quinoses

Federal Education Association (NEA)
Federal Education Association [FEA]
1201 16th St., NW, Suite 117, Washington, DC 20036
Phone: (202) 822-7850
Fax: (202) 822-7867
E-mail: fea@feaonline.org
Web site: www.feaonline.org
Founded: 1956
Membership: 5,700
Publications: *FEA Journal* (bimonthly)
President: Sheridan Pearce
Vice President: Edward (Ted) Carlin
Secretary-Treasurer: Laura Bauernfeind
Executive Director: H.T. Nguyen

Federal Employees (IAMAW) (AFL-CIO) (CLC)
National Federation of Federal Employees [NFFE]
1016 16th St., NW, Washington, DC 20036
Phone: (202) 862-4400
Fax: (202) 862-4432
Web site: www.nffe.org
Founded: 1917
Membership: 7,528
Publications: *The Federal Employee* (monthly)
President: Richard N. Brown
Secretary-Treasurer: John Paolino
Vice Presidents:
Betty Crocker
Jozef Drozdowski
Janette Lambert
Kolleen McGrath
John R. Obst
Lorraine Payton
Gloria Porter

Federal Firefighters (AFGE) (AFL-CIO)
Federal Firefighters Association [FFA]
P.O. Box 8459, Washington, DC 20336-8459
Phone: (202) 433-3334
Web site: www.hellointer.net/afgefederal firefighters
Founded: 1986

Fire Fighters (AFL-CIO)
International Association of Fire
Fighters [IAFF]
1750 New York Ave., NW,
Washington, DC 20006
Phone: (202) 737-8484
Fax: (202) 737-8418
E-mail: pr@iaff.org
Web site: www.iaff.org
Founded: 1918
Publications: *International Fire*
Fighter (bimonthly)
President: Harold A. Schaitberger
Secretary-Treasurer: Vincent J. Bollon
Vice Presidents:
Dominick F. Barbera
Bruce Carpenter
Joseph M. Conway, Jr.
Michael Crouse
Nick Davila
James A. Fennell
James T. Ferguson
Kevin Gallagher
Paul Harvey
Ernest Mass
Michael D. McNeill
Thomas H. Miller
Michael Mullane
Terry A, Ritchie
William V. Taylor
Danny Todd
Louie A. Wright

Fire/Security Officers
United Technologies Corporation
Independent Fire/Security Officers
Association [IFSOA]
357 Main St., East Hartford, CT 06118
Phone: (860) 568-7640
Membership: 98
Contact: Winfred Dailey

Flight Attendants (AFL-CIO)
Association of Flight Attendants [AFA]
1275 K St., NW, Suite 500,
Washington, DC 20005
Phone: (202) 712-9799
Fax: (202) 712-9797
E-mail: afatalk@afanet.org
Web site: www.flightattendant-afa.org
and www.afanet.org
Founded: 1973
Membership: 53,040
Publications: *Flightlog* (quarterly)
President: Patricia A. Friend
Secretary-Treasurer: Paul MacKinnon
Vice President: George Donahue

Flint Glass Workers (AFL-CIO)
American Flint Glass Workers
Union [AFGWU]
1440 S. Byrne Rd., Toledo, OH 43614
Phone: (419) 385-6687
Fax: (419) 385-8839
Web site: www.afgwu.org
Founded: 1878
Membership: 14,576
Publications: *Flint Magazine*
(bimonthly) and *Circular*
(bimonthly)
President: Joseph Coccho
Secretary-Treasurer: David Lusetti

Food and Commercial Workers
(AFL-CIO)
United Food and Commercial Workers
International Union [UFCW]
1775 K St., NW, Washington, DC
20006
Phone: (202) 223-3111
Fax: (202) 466-1562
Web site: www.ufcw.org
Founded: 1979
Membership: 1,385,043
Publications: *Working America*
(quarterly)
President: Douglas H. Dority
Secretary-Treasurer: Joseph Hansen
Executive Vice Presidents:
Sarah Palmer Amos
Michael E. Leonard
Anthony M. Perrone

Football Players
National Football League Players
Association [NFLPA]
2021 L St., NW, Suite 600,
Washington, DC 20036
Phone: (202) 463-2200
Fax: (202) 857-0380
E-mail: nflpaexecutivedept@
nflplayers.com
Web site: www.nflpa.org
Western Office: 423 Washington St.,
Suite 700, San Francisco, CA 94111
Phone: (800) 900-9404
Fax: (415) 438-3808
Founded: 1956
Publications: *Audible* (quarterly)
Executive Director: Gene Upshaw

Foreign Service Association
American Foreign Service
Association [AFSA]
2101 E St., NW, Washington, DC
20037
Phone: (202) 338-4045
Fax: (202) 338-6820
E-mail: afsa@afsa.org
Web site: www.afsa.org
Founded: 1924
Membership: 1,204
Publications: *Foreign Service Journal*
(monthly) and *Retiree Newsletter*
(quarterly)
President: John K. Naland
Vice Presidents:
Louis K. Crane
Robert W. Farrand
Peter Frederick
Joe Pastic
Ed Porter
Secretary: Tex Harris
Treasurer: Tom Boyatt

Glass, Molders, Pottery and Plastics
Workers (AFL-CIO)
Glass, Molders, Pottery, Plastics and
Allied Workers International
Union [GMP]
608 E. Baltimore Pike, P.O. Box 607,
Media, PA 19063
Phone: (610) 565-5051
Fax: (610) 565-0983
E-mail: gmpiu@ix.netcom.com
Web site: www.gmpiu.org
Founded: 1842
Publications: *Horizons* (monthly)
President: James H. Rankin
Secretary-Treasurer: Joseph Mitchell, Sr.
Vice Presidents:
David Doyle
Jesse J. Garcia
Ralph Sidebottom
Bruce Smith

Government Employees (AFL-CIO)
American Federation of Government
Employees [AFGE]
80 F St., NW, Washington, DC
20001-1583
Phone: (202) 737-8700
Fax: (202) 639-6441
E-mail: comments@afge.org
Web site: www.afge.org
Founded: 1932
Membership: 198,453
Publications: *The Government*
Standard (bimonthly) and *The*
Bulletin (semi-monthly)
President: Bobby L. Harnage
Secretary-Treasurer: Jim Davis

Government Employees Association
(SEIU)
**National Association of Government
Employees** [NAGE]
159 Burgin Pkwy., Quincy, MA 02169
Phone: (617) 376-0220
Fax: (617) 376-0285
Web site: www.nage.org
Founded: 1961
Publications: *Federal News Update*
President: David Holoway
Secretary: David Bernard
Treasurer: James Farley

Government Security Officers
**United Government Security Officers of
America** [UGSOA]
7230 Meade St., Westminster, CO
80030
Phone: (303) 650-8515
Fax: (303) 650-8510
E-mail: ugsoaint@qwest.net
Web site: www.ugsoa.com
Membership: 6,000
President: James A. Vissar
Secretary-Treasurer: Richard Ward
Executive Vice President: Steven Giller
Vice Presidents:
James D. Carney
Lance Lucius

Graphic Artists
Graphic Artists Guild, Inc. [GAG]
90 John St., #403, New York, NY
10038
Phone: (212) 791-3400
Fax: (212) 791-0333
E-mail: execdir@gag.org
Web site: www.gag.org
Publications: *Guild News* (bimonthly)
and *Handbook, Pricing & Ethical
Guidelines* (biannually)
President: Lloyd Dangle
Secretary-Treasurer: Mark Monlux
Vice Presidents:
Lauri Baram
Molly Knappen
Sarah Love
Bud Peen
Lauren Rabinowitz
John Schmelzer
Peleg Top
Executive Director: Steven R. Schubert

Graphic Communications (AFL-CIO)
**Graphic Communications International
Union** [GCIU]
1900 L St., NW, Washington, DC
20036
Phone: (202) 462-1400
Fax: (202) 721-0600
Web site: www.gciu.org
Canadian Office: 21 St. Clair Ave. E.,
Suite 901, Toronto, ON M4T 1L9
Canada
Membership: 84,554
Publications: *Graphic Communicator*
(8 times a year)
President: George Tedeschi
Secretary-Treasurer: Gerald H. Deneau
Vice Presidents:
Leonard E. Adams
Duncan K. Brown
David A. Grabhorn
Lawrence Martinez
Edward J. Toff

Hockey Players
**National Hockey League Players
Association** [NHLPA]
777 Bay St., Suite 2400, Toronto, ON
M5G 2C8 Canada
Phone: (416) 313-2300
Fax: (416) 313-2301
Web site: www.nhlpa.com
Founded: 1967
Membership: 1,400
President: Trevor Linden
Executive Director and General Counsel:
Bob Goodenow
Vice Presidents:
Daniel Alfredsson
Bill Boughner
Vincent Demphouse
Adam Graves
Bill Guerin
Arturs Irbe

Horseshoers (AFL-CIO)
**International Union of Journeymen
Horseshoers of United States and
Canada** [IUJH]
2070 Jericho Tpke., Commack, NY
11725
Founded: 1874
Membership: 55
Contact: William Sweeney

Hotel and Restaurant Employees
(AFL-CIO)
**Hotel Employees and Restaurant
Employees International Union**
[HERE]
1219 28th St., NW, Washington, DC
20007
Phone: (202) 393-4373
Fax: (202) 333-0468
Web site: www.hereunion.org
Founded: 1891
Membership: 255,137
Publications: *CIE (Catering Industry
Employee)*
President: John W. Wilhelm
Secretary-Treasurer: Sherri Chiesa
Executive Vice President: Ron Richardson

Independent Unions Congress
Congress of Independent Unions
[COIU]
303 Ridge St., Alton, IL 62002
Phone: (618) 462-2447
Founded: 1958
Contact: Richard Davis

Independent Unions Federation
(LIUNA) (AFL-CIO)
**National Federation of Independent
Unions** [NFIU]
1166 S. 11th St., Philadelphia, PA
19147
Phone: (215) 336-3300
Web site: www.nfiu.org
Founded: 1963
Membership: 6,975
President: Francis J. Chiappardi
Secretary/Treasurer: Alonzo Wheeler

Industrial Trade Unions
**National Organization of Industrial
Trade Unions** [NOITU]
148-06 Hillside Ave., Jamaica, NY
11435
Phone: (718) 291-3434
Fax: (718) 526-2920
Web site: www.noitu.org
Membership: 4,504
Publications: *NOITU Reporter*
(quarterly)
President: Gerard Jones
Executive Vice President: Gerald Hustick,
Jr.

Industrial Workers (NFIU)
National Industrial Workers Union [NIW]
1045 Jefferson Ave., Defiance, OH 43512
Membership: 64
Contact: Charles Hillman

Industrial Workers United (SIUNA) (AFL-CIO)
United Industrial, Service, Transportation, Professional and Government Workers of North America [UISTPGW]
501 Auth Way, Camp Springs, MD 20746
Phone: (301) 899-0675
Fax: (301) 899-7355
Membership: 8,130
Contact: David Heindel

Inlandboatmen (ILWU) (AFL-CIO)
Inlandboatmen's Union of the Pacific [IBU]
1711 W. Nickerson St., Suite D, Seattle, WA 98119
Phone: (206) 284-6001
Fax: (206) 284-5043
Web site: www.ibu.org
Founded: 1918
Publications: *Waterfront Warrior*
President: David Freiboth
Secretary-Treasurer: Terri Mast

Interns and Residents (SEIU)
Committee of Interns and Residents [CIR]
520 Eighth Ave., 12th Floor, New York, NY 10018
Phone: (212) 356-8100
Fax: (212) 356-8111
E-mail: info@cirseiu.org
Web site: www.cirseiu.org
Founded: 1957
Membership: 2,022
Publications: *CIR News* (quarterly)
President: Ruth Potee, M.D.
Executive Vice President: Angela Dee Nossett, M.D.
Secretary-Treasurer: Stella Nelson-Twakor, M.D.
Vice Presidents:
Srinivas Bonthu, M.D.
Sunil Pandya, M.D.
Paulo Pinho, M.D.
Nina Raoof, M.D.
Sonya Rasminsky, M.D.
Dan Schaefer, M.D.
Vicky Seelall, M.D.
Scott Selco, M.D.
Amit Tailor, M.D.
Cynthia Wang, M.D.

Iron Workers (AFL-CIO)
International Association of Bridge, Structural, Ornamental and Reinforcing Iron Workers [BSORIW]
1750 New York Ave., NW, Suite 400, Washington, DC 20006
Phone: (202) 383-4800
Fax: (202) 638-4856
Web site: www.ironworkers.org
Founded: 1896
Membership: 135,072
Publications: *The Ironworker* (monthly)
President: Joseph J. Hunt
Secretary: Michael Fitzpatrick
Treasurer: Dennis Toney

Laborers (AFL-CIO)
Laborers' International Union of North America [LIUNA]
905 16th St., NW, Washington, DC 20006
Phone: (202) 737-8320
Fax: (202) 737-2754
Web site: www.liuna.org
Founded: 1903
Membership: 795,335
Publications: *The Laborer* (quarterly) and *LIUNA Faxline* (biweekly)
President: Terence M. O'Sullivan
Secretary-Treasurer: Armand E. Sabitoni
Vice Presidents:
Chuck Barnes
Rocco Davis
George R. Gudger
James C. Hale
Steve Hammond
Vere O. Haynes
Terrence M. Healy
Joseph S. Mancinelli
Dennis Martire
Vincent Masino
Raymond M. Pocino
Mike Quevedo, Jr.
William H. Quinn
Edward M. Smith

Laborista de Puerto Rico
Confederacion Laborista de Puerto Rico [PRCL]
Ave. Gonzalez Clemente #225, Mayaguez, PR 00680
Phone: (787) 833-5820
Membership: 300
Contact: Roman Velez Mangua

Laundry and Dry Cleaning (AFL-CIO) (UNITE)
Laundry and Dry Cleaning International Union [LDCIU]
307 4th Ave., Suite 405, Pittsburgh, PA 15222
Phone: (412) 471-4829
Membership: 7,860
Contact: Sam Begler

Letter Carriers (AFL-CIO)
National Association of Letter Carriers [NALC]
100 Indiana Ave., NW, Washington, DC 20001
Phone: (202) 393-4695
Fax: (202) 737-1540
E-mail: nalcinf@nalc.org
Web site: www.nalc.org
Founded: 1889
Membership: 297,150
Publications: *The Postal Record* (monthly), *NALC Activist* (quarterly), and *NALC Retiree* (quarterly)
President: William H. Young
Executive Vice President: Jim Williams
Vice President: Gary H. Mullins
Secretary-Treasurer: Jane E. Broendel

Locomotive Engineers (AFL-CIO) (CLC)
Brotherhood of Locomotive Engineers [BLE]
Standard Bldg., 1370 Ontario St., Cleveland, OH 44113-1702
Phone: (216) 241-2630
Fax: (216) 241-6516
E-mail: webmaster@ble.org
Web site: www.ble.org
Washington, DC office: 10 G St., NE, Suite 480, Washington, DC 20002
Phone: (202) 347-7936
Founded: 1863
Membership: 57,621
Publications: *Locomotive Engineers Journal*
President: Don M. Hahs
First Vice President: Ed Rodzwicz
Secretary-Treasurer: William C. Walpert
Vice Presidents:
Merle W. Geiger, Jr.
Gilles Hallé
Raymond Holmes
Thomas G. Hucker
Dale L. McPherson
Lee Pruitt
Rick Radek
Paul Sorrow
Stephen D. Speagle
Paul L. Wingo, Jr.

Longshore and Warehouse (AFL-CIO)
International Longshore and Warehouse Union [ILWU]
1188 Franklin St., San Francisco, CA 94109
Phone: (415) 775-0533
Fax: (415) 775-1302
E-mail: ilwu@patriot.net
Web site: www.ilwu.org
Washington, DC office: 1775 K St., NW, Suite 200, Washington, DC 20006
Phone: (202) 463-6265
Fax: (202) 467-4875
Founded: 1937
Membership: 37,373
Publications: *The Dispatcher* (monthly)
President: James Spinosa
Vice Presidents:
Wesley Furtado
Robert McEllrath
Secretary-Treasurer: Joe Ibarra

Longshoremen (AFL-CIO)
International Longshoremen's Association [ILA]
17 Battery Pl., Suite 930, New York, NY 10004
Phone: (212) 425-1200
Fax: (212) 425-2928
Web site: www.ilaunion.org
Founded: 1892
Membership: 47,000
Publications: *ILA Newsletter*
President: John M. Bowers
Secretary-Treasurer: Robert Gleason
Executive Vice President: Albert Cernadas
Vice President: Benny Holland, Jr.

Machine Printers and Engravers
Machine Printers and Engravers Association of the United States [MPEA]
690 Warren Ave., East Providence, RI 02914
Phone: (401) 438-5849
Fax: (401) 438-5849
E-mail: mpea74@aol.com
Founded: 1874
Membership: 75
President: Albert A. Poitras
Secretary-Treasurer: William Aniszewski

Machinists (AFL-CIO)
International Association of Machinists and Aerospace Workers [IAMAW]
9000 Machinists Pl., Upper Marlboro, MD 20772-2687
Phone: (301) 967-4500
Fax: (301) 967-4588
Web site: www.iamaw.org
Founded: 1888
Membership: 722,987
Publications: *IAM Journal* (quarterly)
President: R. Thomas Buffenbarger
Secretary-Treasurer: Donald E. Wharton
Vice Presidents:
Alex M. Bay
George Hooper
Warren L. Mart
Lee Pearson
Dave Ritchie
Robert Roach, Jr.
Robert V. Thayer

Maintenance of Way Employes (AFL-CIO)
Brotherhood of Maintenance of Way Employes [BMWE]
26555 Evergreen Rd., Suite 200, Southfield, MI 48076-4225
Phone: (248) 948-1010
Fax: (248) 948-7150
Web site: www.bmwe.org
Washington, DC office: 10 G St., NE, Suite 460, Washington, DC 20002
Phone: (202) 638-2135
Founded: 1887
Membership: 39,254
Publications: *BMWE Journal* (monthly)
President: Mac A. Fleming
Secretary-Treasurer: Freddie N. Simpson

Marine Engineers (AFL-CIO)
Marine Engineers' Beneficial Association [MEBA]
444 North Capitol St., NW, Suite 800, Washington, DC 20001
Phone: (202) 638-5355
Fax: (202) 638-5369
Web site: www.d1meba.org
Founded: 1875
Membership: 29,026
Publications: *The Marine Officer* (bimonthly) and *The Telex Times* (weekly)
President: Ron Davis
Secretary-Treasurer: Cecil A. McIntyre

Maritime Union (AFL-CIO)
National Maritime Union [NMU]
1150 17th St., NW, Suite 700, Washington, DC 20036
Phone: (202) 466-7060
Fax: (202) 872-0912
Web site: www.nmuhou.org
President: Rene Lioeanjie
Executive Vice President and Treasurer: Kathleen Hunt
Vice Presidents:
John Cameron
Charles Stewart

Masters, Mates and Pilots (ILA)
International Organization of Masters, Mates and Pilots [IOMM&P]
700 Maritime Blvd., Linthicum Heights, MD 21090-1941
Phone: (410) 850-8700
Fax: (410) 850-0973
Web site: www.bridgedeck.org
Washington, DC office: 1775 K St., NW, Suite 200, Washington, DC 20006
Phone: (202) 463-6505
Fax: (202) 223-9093
Founded: 1880
Membership: 5,171
Publications: *The Master, Mate & Pilot* (bimonthly)
President: Timothy A. Brown
Secretary-Treasurer: Glen P. Banks
Vice Presidents:
Steven Demeroutis
Robert Groh
Donald Marcus
Richard W. May
George A. Quick
William Rabatsky
Luis Ramirez

Mine Workers
United Mine Workers of America [UMWA]
8315 Lee Hwy., Fairfax, VA 22031
Phone: (703) 208-7200
Fax: (703) 208-7227
Web site: www.umwa.org
Founded: 1890
Membership: 109,105
Publications: *UMWA Journal* (bimonthly)
President: Cecil E. Roberts
Vice President: Jerry D. Jones
Secretary-Treasurer: Carlo Tarley
Executive Director: Don Barnett

Musical Artists (AAAA)
**American Guild of Musical
Artists** [AGMA]
1430 Broadway, 14th Floor, New
York, NY 10018
Phone: (212) 265-3687
Fax: (212) 262-9088
E-mail: agma@musicalartists.org
Web site: www.musicalartists.org
Founded: 1936
Membership: 7,000
Publications: *AGMagazine* (quarterly)
President: Linda Mays
Vice Presidents:
John Coleman
Donna Marie Covert
Joseph Evans
Jimmy Odom
Colby Roberts
Secretary: Candace Stow
Treasurer: Lynn Lundgren
Executive Director: Alan S. Gordon

Musicians (AFL-CIO)
**American Federation of Musicians of
the United States and Canada** [AFM]
1501 Broadway, Suite 600, New York,
NY 10036
Phone: (212) 869-1330
Fax: (212) 764-6134
E-mail: info@afm.org
Web site: www.afm.org
Founded: 1896
Membership: 104,000
Publications: *International Musician*
(monthly) and *Officers Edge*
(usually quarterly)
President: Thomas Lee
Secretary-Treasurer: Florence Nelson

National Staff Organization
National Staff Organization [NSO]
302 S. State St., P.O. Box 405, Gobles,
MI 49055
Web site: www.nationalstaff.org
Founded: 1969
Membership: 4,922
President: Chuck Agerstrand
Vice Presidents:
Lynn Adler
Marius Ambrose
Secretary: Mary Henson
Treasurer: Vera Stafford

Needletrades (AFL-CIO)
**Union of Needletrades, Industrial and
Textile Employees** [UNITE]
1710 Broadway, New York, NY
10019-5299
Phone: (212) 265-7000
Fax: (212) 265-3415
Web site: www.uniteunion.org
Founded: 1900
Membership: 217,604
Publications: *UNITE!*
President: Bruce Raynor
Secretary-Treasurer: Edgar Romney
Executive Vice President: William Lee
Vice President: Clayola Brown

Newspaper and Mail Deliverers' Union
**Newspaper and Mail Deliverers' Union
of New York and Vicinity** [NMDU]
41-18 27th St., Long Island City, NY
11101
Phone: (718) 392-8367
Fax: (718) 392-9810
Membership: 1,631
President: Ronald O'Keefe
Vice President: James DeMarzo
Secretary-Treasurer: Brian Wittenberg

NLRB Professional Association
**National Labor Relations Board
Professional Association** [PA]
1099 14th St., NW, Suite 9120,
Washington, DC 20570
Phone: (202) 273-1749
Fax: (202) 273-4286
Web site: www.nlrb.gov
Founded: 1963
Membership: 1,230
President: Leslie Rossen
Vice President: Eric C. Marx
Secretary: Ann Marie Scarpino
Treasurer: Tom Clark

Novelty and Production Workers
(AFL-CIO)
**International Union of Allied Novelty
and Production Workers** [NPW]
1950 W. Erie St., Chicago, IL 60622
Phone: (312) 738-0822
Fax: (312) 738-3553
Membership: 20,978
President: Hermes Ruiz
Vice Presidents:
Jeff Keating
Johnnie Miranti
Antonio Patino
Steve Torello
Secretary-Treasurer: Mark Spano

Nurses (AFL-CIO)
United American Nurses [UAN]
600 Maryland Ave., SW, Suite 100 W.,
Washington, DC 20024
Phone: (202) 651-7000
Fax: (202) 651-7347
Web site: www.uannurse.org
Membership: 81,986
President: Cheryl L. Johnson
Vice President: Ann Converso
Secretary-Treasurer: Jeanne Surdo

Nurses and Health Professionals (AFT)
**Federation of Nurses and Health
Professionals** [FNHP]
555 New Jersey Ave., NW,
Washington, DC 20001
Phone: (202) 879-4491
Fax: (202) 879-4597
E-mail: healthcare@aft.org
Web site: www.aft.org/healthcare/
index.html
Founded: 1978
Membership: 60,000
Publications: *Healthwire* (bimonthly)
President: Sandra Feldman
Secretary-Treasurer: Edward J. McElroy
Executive Vice President: Nat LaCour
Executive Director: Mary Lehman
MacDonald

Nurses Associations of California
(AFSCME)
**United Nurses Associations of
California/Union of Health Care
Professionals** [UNAC]
300 S. Park Ave., Suite 840, Pomona,
CA 91766
Phone: (909) 620-7749
Fax: (909) 620-9119
E-mail: info@unac-ca.org
Web site: www.unac-ca.org
President: Kathy J. Sackman, R.N.
Executive Vice President: Sonia E.
Moseley, R.N.P.
Secretary: Barbara L. Blake, R.N.
Treasurer: Delima M. MacDonald, R.N.

Nurses, Practical
**National Federation of Licensed
Practical Nurses** [NFLPN]
605 Poole Dr., Garner, NC 27529
Phone: (919) 779-0046
Fax: (919) 779-5642
Web site: www.nflpn.org
Publications: *Practical Nursing Journal*
President: Gregory Howard
Secretary: Peggy Fishburn
Treasurer: Mary Barbour
Executive Director: Charlene Barbour

Nurses, Professional
United Professional Nurses Association [UPNA]
Bewley Bldg., Suite 318, Lockport, NY 14094
Phone: (716) 433-1477
Membership: 183
President: James Huff

Obreros Unidos
Sindicato de Obreros Unidos del Sur de Puerto Rico [PRSPT]
Supermercado Grande-Altos, Salinas, PR 00751
Phone: (787) 824-2850
Contact: Jose Luis Caraballo

Office and Professional Employees (AFL-CIO)
Office and Professional Employees International Union [OPEIU]
265 W. 14th St., 6th Floor, New York, NY 10011
Phone: (212) 675-3210
Fax: (212) 727-3466
E-mail: opeiu@opeiu.org
Web site: www.opeiu.org
Washington, DC office: 1660 L St., NW, Suite 801, Washington, DC 20036
Phone: (202) 393-4464
Fax: (202) 347-0649
Founded: 1945
Membership: 136,586
Publications: *White Collar* (quarterly)
President: Michael Goodwin
Secretary-Treasurer: Nancy Wohlforth

Operating Engineers (AFL-CIO)
International Union of Operating Engineers [IUOE]
1125 17th St., NW, Washington, DC 20036
Phone: (202) 429-9100
Fax: (202) 778-2616
E-mail: iuoe@access.digex.net
Web site: www.iuoe.org
Founded: 1896
Membership: 388,526
Publications: *The International Operating Engineer* (bimonthly)
President: Frank Hanley
Secretary-Treasurer: Vincent J. Giblin

Vice Presidents:
Peter Babin, III
Vergil L. Belfi, Jr.
Fred P. Dereschuk
Don Doser
William E. Dugan
James H. Gardner
Sam T. Hart
Brian E. Hickey
Gary W. Kroeker
Thomas P. Maguire
James McLaughlin
Jan Pelroy
William P. Ryan
William Waggoner

Painters (AFL-CIO)
International Union of Painters and Allied Trades [IUPAT]
1750 New York Ave., NW, Washington, DC 20006
Phone: (202) 637-0700
Fax: (202) 637-0771
E-mail: webmaster@iupat.org
Web site: www.iupat.org
Founded: 1887
Membership: 102,402
President: James A. Williams
Secretary-Treasurer: George Galis
Vice Presidents:
William D. Candelori, Jr.
Armando Colafrancheschi
Sean McGarvey
Alfred Monroe, Jr.
Gary Monroe
Raymond J. Price, III
Kenneth E. Rigmaiden
Raymond Sesma

Paper, Allied-Industrial, Chemical Employees (AFL-CIO)
Paper, Allied-Industrial, Chemical and Engineering Workers International Union [PACE]
3340 Perimeter Hill Dr., Nashville, TN 37211
Phone: (615) 834-8590
Fax: (615) 831-6791
Web site: www.paceunion.org
Mailing address: P.O. Box 1475, Nashville, TN 37202
Founded: 1884
Membership: 292,395
President: Boyd Young
Secretary/Treasurer: James Dunn
Vice President-at-Large: James (Kip) Phillips
Administrative Vice President: James Pannell

Vice Presidents:
Jim Byrd
Gary Cook
William Gibbons
Roger Heiser
Gerald Johnston
Donald Langham
Lewis Peacock
Robert Smith
Kenneth O. Test
Leon Towne
Lloyd Waters

Petroleum and Industrial Workers
International Union of Petroleum and Industrial Workers [UPIW]
8131 E. Rosecrans Ave., Paramount, CA 90723
Phone: (562) 630-6232
Fax: (562) 408-1073
Membership: 2,178
President: George Beltz
Secretary-Treasurer: Pamela Barlow

Physicians and Dentists (AFSCME)
Union of American Physicians and Dentists [UAPD]
1330 Broadway, Suite 730, Oakland, CA 94612
Phone: (510) 839-0193
Fax: (510) 763-8756
E-mail: uapd@uapd.com
Web site: www.uapd.com
Sacramento office: 1225 Eighth St., Suite 340, Sacramento, CA 95814
Phone: (916) 442-6977
Fax: (916) 446-3827
Southern California Office: 5777 W. Century Blvd., Suite 880, Los Angeles, CA 90045
Phone: (310) 398-4038
Fax: (310) 398-6427
Founded: 1972
Membership: 6,000
Publications: *The UAPD Report* (quarterly)
President: Robert L. Weinmann, M.D.
Secretary: Deane Hillsman, M.D.
Treasurer: Peter A. Statti, M.D.
Executive Director: Gary R. Robinson

Pilots, Air Line (AFL-CIO)
Air Line Pilots Association International [ALPA]
535 Herndon Pkwy., Herndon, VA 20170
Phone: (703) 689-2270
Fax: (703) 689-4370
Web site: www.alpa.org
Washington, DC office: 1625 Massachusetts Ave., NW, Washington, DC 20036
Phone: (202) 797-4037
Fax: (202) 797-4052
Founded: 1931
Membership: 54,513
Publications: *Air Line Pilot* (6 times a year) and *Point-to-Point* (four times a year)
President: Capt. Duane Woerth
First Vice President: Capt. Dennis J. Dolan
Secretary: Capt. Jerry Mugerditchian
Treasurer: Capt. John Feldvary
Executive Vice Presidents:
Capt. Crass Bernard
Capt. Dan Brennan
Capt. Kevin Dillon
Capt. John Eckert
Capt. Doug Hahn
Capt. Matt Kernan
Capt. Bill Kientz
Capt. Dave Morrow

Pilots, Independent
Independent Pilots Association [IPA]
3607 Fern Valley Rd., Louisville, KY 40219-1916
Phone: (502) 968-0341
Fax: (502) 968-0470
E-mail: comments@ipapilot.org
Web site: www.ipapilot.org
Founded: 1990
Membership: 2,530
Publications: *Flight Times* and *Home Front*
President: Robert M. Miller
Vice President: Richard Halsall
Secretary: Herbert Hurst
Treasurer: John Andersen

Plant Protection
Plant Protection Association National Union [PPA]
302 N. Heron St., Ypsilanti, MI 48917-2947
Phone: (734) 487-5522
Fax: (734) 487-5588
President: Larry Daniel
Secretary-Treasurer: John Hessian

Plant Protection Employees
Independent Union of Plant Protection Employees [PPE]
12 Austin Ave., Pittsfield, MA 01201
Contact: Barry McMahon

Plasterers and Cement Masons (AFL-CIO)
Operative Plasterers' and Cement Masons' International Association of the United States and Canada [OP&CMIA]
14405 Laurel Pl., Suite 300, Laurel, MD 20707
Phone: (301) 470-4200
Fax: (301) 470-2502
Web site: www.opcmia.org
Founded: 1864
Membership: 40,396
Publications: *Plasterer and Cement Mason* (quarterly)
President: John J. Dougherty
Secretary-Treasurer: Patrick D. Finley
Executive Vice President: William J. Schell, Jr.
Vice Presidents:
Ronald K. Bowser
Dell French
Thomas Mora
David Robinson
Mary Thompson

Plate Printers, Die Stampers and Engravers (AFL-CIO)
International Plate Printers, Die Stampers and Engravers Union of North America [PPDSE]
14th and C Sts., SW, Room 213-5A, Washington, DC 20228
Phone: (202) 874-2693
Fax: (202) 874-1187
Founded: 1893
Membership: 200
President: Daniel J. Bradley
Secretary-Treasurer: James L. Kopernick
Vice President: William Brabitz

Plumbing and Pipe Fitting (AFL-CIO)
United Association of Journeymen and Apprentices of the Plumbing and Pipe Fitting Industry of the United States and Canada [UA]
901 Massachusetts Ave., NW, Washington, DC 20001
Phone: (202) 628-5823
Fax: (202) 628-5024
Web site: www.ua.org
Founded: 1889
Membership: 324,349
Publications: *UA Journal* (monthly)

President: Martin J. Maddaloni
Secretary-Treasurer: Thomas H. Patchell

Police
National Fraternal Order of Police [FOP]
1410 Donelson Pike, Suite A-17, Nashville, TN 37217
Phone: (615) 399-0900
Fax: (615) 399-0400
E-mail: glfop@grandlodgefop.org
Web site: www.grandlodgefop.org
Founded: 1915
Membership: 299,000
President: Chuck Canterbury
Secretary: Jerry Atnip
Treasurer: Tom Penoza

Police Associations (AFL-CIO)
International Union of Police Associations [IUPA]
1421 Prince St., Suite 400, Alexandria, VA 22314
Phone: (703) 549-7473
Fax: (703) 683-9048
E-mail: iupa@iupa.org
Web site: www.iupa.org
Founded: 1978
Membership: 49,838
Publications: *Police Union News* (monthly)
President: Sam A. Cabral
Secretary-Treasurer: Richard A. Estes
Vice President: Dennis J. Slocumb

Postal and Federal Employees
National Alliance of Postal and Federal Employees [NAPFE]
1628 11th St., NW, Washington, DC 20001
Phone: (202) 939-6325
Fax: (202) 939-6389
E-mail: headquarters@napfe.com
Web site: www.napfe.com
Founded: 1913
Membership: 11,894
Publications: *National Alliance* (monthly)
President: James M. McGee
Vice Presidents:
Comer Cash
Charles J. Denson, Jr.
Secretary: Wilbur Duncan
Treasurer: Warren E. Powell

Postal Mail Handlers (LIUNA)

National Postal Mail Handlers Union [NPMHU]
1101 Connecticut Ave., NW, Suite 500, Washington, DC 20036
Phone: (202) 833-9095
Fax: (202) 833-0008
Web site: www.npmhu.org
Membership: 389,173
Publications: *Mail Handler Magazine*
President: John F. Hegarty
Secretary-Treasurer: Mark A. Gardner
Vice Presidents:
Samuel C. D'Ambrosio
Efraim Daniel
James C. Terrell
Arthur S. Vallone
Hardy Williams

Postal Workers (AFL-CIO)

American Postal Workers Union [APWU]
1300 L St., NW, Washington, DC 20005
Phone: (202) 842-4200
Fax: (202) 842-4297
Web site: www.apwu.org
Founded: 1971
Membership: 294,127
President: William Burrus
Executive Vice President: C.J. (Cliff) Guffey
Secretary-Treasurer: Robert L. Tunstall

Production Workers

National Production Workers Union [NPWU]
2210 Midwest Rd., Suite 310, Oak Brook, IL 60521
Phone: (630) 575-0560
Membership: 228
Contact: Joseph Senese

Professional and Technical Engineers (AFL-CIO)

International Federation of Professional and Technical Engineers [IFPTE]
8630 Fenton St., Suite 400, Silver Spring, MD 20910
Phone: (301) 565-9016
Fax: (301) 565-0018
Web site: www.ifpte.org
Founded: 1918
Membership: 51,694
Publications: *The Outlook* (bimonthly)
President: Gregory J. Junemann
Secretary-Treasurer: Dolores A. Gorczyca

Professional Athletes (AFL-CIO)

Federation of Professional Athletes [FPA]
2021 L St., NW, Washington, DC 20036
Phone: (202) 463-2200
Membership: 1,680
President: Gene Upshaw
Secretary-Treasurer: Doug Allen

Pulp and Paper Workers (AFL-CIO)

Association of Western Pulp and Paper Workers [AWPPW]
1430 S.W. Clay St., P.O. Box 4566, Portland, OR 97208-4566
Phone: (503) 228-7486
Fax: (503) 228-1346
E-mail: info@awppw.org
Web site: www.awppw.org
Founded: 1964
Membership: 9,551
Publications: *The Rebel* (monthly)
President: John Rhodes
Secretary-Treasurer: James L. Hassey
Vice President: Greg Pallesen

Railroad Signalmen (AFL-CIO)

Brotherhood of Railroad Signalmen [BRS]
601 Golf Rd., Mount Prospect, IL 60056-4276
Phone: (847) 439-3732
Fax: (847) 439-3743
E-mail: signalman@brs.org
Web site: www.brs.org
Washington, DC office: 10 G St., NE, Suite 440, Washington, DC 20002
Phone: (202) 628-5935
Fax: (202) 347-3548
Founded: 1901
Membership: 10,117
President: W. Dan Pickett
Secretary-Treasurer: W.A. Barrows
Vice Presidents:
J.C. Boles
D.M. Boston
G.E. Jones
F.E. Mason
J.L. Mattingly
C.A. McGraw

Retail, Wholesale and Department Store (UFCW)

Retail, Wholesale and Department Store Union [RWDSU]
30 E. 29th St., 4th Floor, New York, NY 10016
Phone: (212) 684-5300
Fax: (212) 779-2809
Web site: www.rwdsu.org
Founded: 1937
Publications: *The Record* (bimonthly)
President: Stuart Appelbaum
Secretary-Treasurer: Jack Wurm

Roofers, Waterproofers and Allied Workers (AFL-CIO)

United Union of Roofers, Waterproofers and Allied Workers [RWAW]
1660 L St., NW, Suite 800, Washington, DC 20036
Phone: (202) 463-7663
Fax: (202) 463-6906
E-mail: roofers@unionroofers.com
Web site: www.unionroofers.com
Founded: 1919
Membership: 21,777
Publications: *Journeyman Roofer and Waterproofer* (quarterly)
President: John C. Martini
Secretary-Treasurer: Kinsey M. Robinson
Vice Presidents:
Paul F. Bickford
Alex Bodnariuk
Don Cardwell
Robert J. Danley
James A. Hadel
Robert J. Lloyd
Donald A. O'Blenis
Thomas Pedrick
Douglas Ziegler

Rural Letter Carriers

National Rural Letter Carriers' Association [NRLCA]
1630 Duke St., 4th Floor, Alexandria, VA 22314-3465
Phone: (703) 684-5545
Fax: (703) 548-8735
Web site: www.nrlca.org
Founded: 1903
Membership: 100,652
President: Gus Baffa
Vice President: Dale A. Horton
Secretary-Treasurer: Clifford D. Dailing

School Administrators (AFL-CIO)

American Federation of School Administrators [AFSA]
1729 21st St., NW, Washington, DC 20009-1101
Phone: (202) 986-4209
Fax: (202) 986-4211
Web site: www.admin.org
Founded: 1976
Publications: *AFSAnews* (10 times a year)
President: Joe L. Greene
Executive Vice President: Beverly Tunney
Treasurer: Jill Levy
Secretary: Roch Girard

Screen Actors (AAAA)
Screen Actors Guild [SAG]
5757 Wilshire Blvd., Los Angeles, CA 90036-3600
Phone: (323) 954-1600
Fax: (323) 549-6603
Web site: www.sag.com
New York office: 1515 Broadway, 44th Floor, New York, NY 10036
Phone: (212) 944-1030
Fax: (212) 944-6774
Founded: 1933
Membership: 73,759
Publications: *Screen Actor Magazine* (quarterly)
President: Melissa Gilbert
Recording Secretary: Elliott Gould
Treasurer: Kent McCord
First Vice President: Mike Farrell
National Executive Director/Chief Executive Officer: A. Robert Pisano

Seafarers (AFL-CIO)
Seafarers International Union of North America [SIUNA]
5201 Auth Way, Camp Springs, MD 20746
Phone: (301) 899-0675
Fax: (301) 899-7355
Web site: www.seafarers.org
Founded: 1938
Membership: 32,000
Publications: *Seafarers Log* (monthly)
President: Michael Sacco
Executive Vice President: John Fay
Secretary-Treasurer: David Heindel
Vice Presidents:
Dean Corgey
René Lioeanjie
Kermett Mangram
Nicholas J. Marrone
Tom Orzechowski
Joseph T. Soresi
Charles Stewart
Augustine Tellez
Note: Seafarers' is a federation of 17 autonomous unions: Alaska Fish Cannery Workers Union of the Pacific; Alaska Fishermen's Union; Canadian Marine Officers Union; Chauffeurs and Industrial Workers Local 5; Fishermen's Union of America, Pacific and Caribbean; Industrial Professional and Technical Workers; Marine Firemen's Union; Marine Staff Officers, Pacific District; Professional Security Officers Association; Sailors' Union of the Pacific; Seafarers-Atlantic, Gulf, Lakes and Inland Waters District; Seafarers Entertainment and Allied Trades Union; Seafarers International Union of Canada; Seafarers of Puerto Rico, Caribe and Latin America; Seafarers Maritime Union; Sugar Workers Union No. 1; and United Industrial Service, Transportation, Professional and Government Workers of North America.

Security Officers
International Union of Security Officers [IUSO]
2404 Merced St., San Leandro, CA 94577
Phone: (510) 895-9905
Fax: (510) 895-6974
Founded: 1945
Membership: 4,331
President: Alan Welch
Secretary-Treasurer: Ed Pena

Security Officers, Police and Guards
International Security Officers', Police and Guards' Union [ISOPGU]
321 86th St., Brooklyn, NY 11209
Phone: (718) 836-3508
Membership: 3,690
Contact: Salvatore Melluso

Security, Police and Fire Professionals
International Union, Security, Police and Fire Professionals of America [SPFPA]
25510 Kelly Rd., Roseville, MI 48066
Phone: (800) 228-7492
E-mail: spfpa@aol.com
Web site: www.spfpa.org
Founded: 1948
Membership: 10,000
Publications: *The Security Link* (semiannually)
President: David L. Hickey
Secretary-Treasurer: Dennis Eck
Vice Presidents:
Jim Allen
Terry Fowler
Gary Hartlage
Bobby Jenkins
Kerry Lacey
Daniel Payne

Service Employees (AFL-CIO)
Service Employees International Union [SEIU]
1313 L St., NW, Washington, DC 20005
Phone: (202) 898-3200
Fax: (202) 898-3491
E-mail: info@seiu.org
Web site: www.seiu.org
Founded: 1921
Membership: 1,376,292
Publications: *SEIU Action* (bimonthly)
President: Andrew L. Stern
Executive Vice Presidents:
Patricia Ann Ford
Eliseo Medina
Tom Woodruff
Secretary-Treasurer: Anna Burger

Sheet Metal Workers (AFL-CIO)
Sheet Metal Workers International Association [SMW]
United Unions Bldg., 1750 New York Ave., NW, Washington, DC 20006
Phone: (202) 783-5880
Fax: (202) 662-0894
E-mail: info@smwia.org
Web site: www.smwia.org
Founded: 1888
Membership: 151,257
Publications: *SMWIA Journal* (bimonthly) and *Focus on Funds* (bimonthly)
President: Michael J. Sullivan
Secretary-Treasurer: Thomas J. Kelly
Vice Presidents:
Thomas Blankman
John D. Churuvia, Jr.
John Harrington
Stanley F. Karczynski
Richard R. Lloyd
James M. Long
James E. Marshall
William A. Moyer
Jay K. Potesta
George B. Slater
Joseph L. Wall

Shoe and Allied Craftsmen
Brotherhood of Shoe and Allied Craftsmen [BSAC]
P.O. Box 390, East Bridgewater, MA 02333
Phone: (508) 378-9300
Contact: Albert Hamlen

Sindicato Puertorriqueno
Sindicato Puertorriqueno de Trabajadores [PRSPT]
Urbanization Altamesa, 1387 Ave. San Ignacio, Rio Piedras, PR 00921
Membership: 13,000
Contact: Roberto Pagan

Solidarity of Labor
Solidarity of Labor Organization [SOLO]
34 Industrial St., Bronx, NY 10461
Contact: William Fagello

State, County and Municipal Employees (AFL-CIO)
American Federation of State, County and Municipal Employees [AFSCME]
1625 L St., NW, Washington, DC 20036-5687
Phone: (202) 429-1000
Fax: (202) 429-1293
E-mail: organize@afscme.org
Web site: www.afscme.org
Founded: 1936
Membership: 1,300,000
Publications: *The Public Employee Magazine* (six issues annually) and *Leader* (weekly)
President: Gerald W. McEntee
Secretary-Treasurer: William Lucy
Vice Presidents:
Ronald C. Alexander
Linda Ard
Henry L. Bayer
Peter J. Benner
George Boncoraglio
Anthony Caso
Jan Corderman
Danny Donohue
Christopher Dugovich
Charles Ensley
David Fillman
Albert Garrett
Raglan George
Sherryl A. Gordon
Edward J. Keller
Salvatore Luciano
Roberta Lynch
Glenard S. Middleton
Patricia Moss
Michael D. Murphy
Henry Nicholas
Russell K. Okata
George E. Popyack
Greg Powell
Lawrence Roehrig
Joseph P. Rugola
Kathy J. Sackman
Mary Sullivan
Garland W. Webb
Jeanette Wynn

Steelworkers (AFL-CIO)
United Steelworkers of America [USWA]
Five Gateway Ctr., Pittsburgh, PA 15222
Phone: (412) 562-2400
Fax: (412) 562-2484
E-mail: webmaster@uswa.org
Web site: www.uswa.org
Washington, DC office: 1150 17th St., NW, Suite 300, Washington, DC 20036
Phone: (202) 778-4384
Fax: (202) 293-5308
Founded: 1942
Membership: 588,790
Publications: *Steelabor* (six times yearly)
President: Leo W. Gerard
Secretary-Treasurer: James D. English
Vice Presidents:
Leon Lynch
Andrew V. Palm

Teachers (AFL-CIO)
American Federation of Teachers [AFT]
555 New Jersey Ave., NW, Washington, DC 20001
Phone: (202) 879-4400
Fax: (202) 879-4545
E-mail: online@aft.org
Web site: www.aft.org
Founded: 1916
Membership: 741,270
Publications: *Action* (twice a month); *American Teacher* and *On Campus* (monthly from Sept. to June); *Healthwire* and *Public Service Reporter* (6 times a year); *Lifetimes* and *Reporter* (4 times a year)
President: Sandra Feldman
Secretary-Treasurer: Edward J. McElroy
Executive Vice President: Nat LaCour

Teamsters (AFL-CIO)
International Brotherhood of Teamsters [IBT]
25 Louisiana Ave., NW, Washington, DC 20001
Phone: (202) 624-6800
Fax: (202) 624-6918
E-mail: feedback@teamster.org
Web site: www.teamster.org
Founded: 1903
Membership: 1,398,412
Publications: *The Teamster* (monthly)
President: James P. Hoffa
Secretary-Treasurer: C. Thomas Keegel
Vice Presidents:
Randy Cammack
Fred Gegare
Carl Haynes
Thomas O'Donnell
Ralph Taurone

Television and Radio Artists (AAAA)
American Federation of Television and Radio Artists [AFTRA]
260 Madison Ave., 7th Floor, New York, NY 10016-2402
Phone: (212) 532-0800
Fax: (212) 532-2242
E-mail: aftra@aftra.com
Web site: www.aftra.com
Los Angeles office: 5757 Wilshire Blvd., 9th Floor, Los Angeles, CA 90036-3689
Phone: (323) 634-8100
Fax: (323) 634-8194
Founded: 1937
Membership: 63,212
Publications: *AFTRA Magazine* (three times a year)
President: John Connolly
Secretary: Bernie Alan
Treasurer: Mitch McGuire
Vice Presidents:
Susan Boyd
Dave Corey
Belva Davis
Bob Edwards
Anne Gartlan
David Hartley
Dick Kay
Shelby Scott
Jimmie Wright
Executive Director: Greg Hessinger

Texas Unions
Federated Independent Texas Unions [FITU]
P.O. Box 151005, Fort Worth, TX 76108
Membership: 272
Contact: Randy Donelson

Theatrical Stage Employees (AFL-CIO)
International Alliance of Theatrical Stage Employes, Moving Picture Technicians, Artists and Allied Crafts of the United States and Canada [IATSE]
1430 Broadway, 20th Floor, New York, NY 10018
Phone: (212) 730-1770
Fax: (212) 730-7809
Web site: www.iatse.lm.com
Founded: 1893
Membership: 103,506
Publications: *The Official Bulletin* (quarterly)
President: Thomas C. Short
Secretary-Treasurer: James B. Wood

Vice Presidents:
  Michael Barnes
  J. Walter Cahill
  Thom Davis
  Anthony DePaulo
  Jean Fox
  Daniel Kerins
  Matthew D. Loeb
  Timothy Magee
  Rudy N. Napoleone
  Damian Petri
  Edward Powell
  Michael J. Sullivan
  Mimi Wolch

Tool Craftsmen (NFIU)
International Association of Tool Craftsmen [IATC]
3718 Wright Ave., Racine, WI 53405
Phone: (309) 782-5776
Membership: 103
Contact: Michael Loomis

Trabajadores de Puerto Rico
Confederacion General de Trabajadores (Autentica) de Puerto Rico [PRCGT]
516 Calle Dresde, Puerto Nuevo, PR 00920
Phone: (787) 751-2987
Membership: 300
Contact: Ramon L. Fuentes

Trabajadores Industriales de Puerto Rico
Union Trabajadores Industriales de Puerto Rico [TIPR]
1006 Vallejo St., San Juan, PR 00928
Membership: 939
Contact: Angel Del Valle

Train Dispatchers (AFL-CIO)
American Train Dispatchers Association [ATDA]
1370 Ontario St., Suite 1040, Cleveland, OH 44113
Phone: (216) 241-2770
Fax: (216) 241-6286
E-mail: atddflm@aol.com
Web site: www.atdd.org
Founded: 1917
Membership: 2,491
Publications: *The Train Dispatcher* (quarterly)
President: F. Leo McCann
Secretary-Treasurer: Gary L. Melton
Vice Presidents:
  C.R. Mundy
  J.W. Parker
  A.M. Snyder
  D.W. Volz

Transit Union (AFL-CIO)
Amalgamated Transit Union [ATU]
5025 Wisconsin Ave., NW, Washington, DC 20016-4139
Phone: (202) 537-1645
Fax: (202) 244-7824
Web site: www.atu.org
Founded: 1892
Membership: 179,861
Publications: *In Transit* (bimonthly)
President: James La Sala
International Executive Vice President:
  Warren S. George
Secretary-Treasurer: Oscar Owens
International Vice Presidents:
  Robert H. Baker
  Jackie B. Breckenridge
  Charles Cook
  Randy Graham
  Donald T. Hansen
  Bob M. Hykaway
  Larry R. Kinnear
  William D. McLean
  Karen S. Moore
  Tommy Mullins
  Richard M. Murphy
  Javier Perez, Jr.
  Charles Pettus
  J.C. Reynolds
  Rodney Richmond
  Melvin W. Schoppert
  Michael J. Siano
  Joseph Welch

Transport Workers (AFL-CIO)
Transport Workers Union of America [TWU]
1700 Broadway, New York, NY 10019
Phone: (212) 259-4900
Fax: (212) 265-4537
E-mail: mailbox@twu.org
Web site: www.twu.org
Founded: 1934
Publications: *TWU Express* (11 months a year)
President: Sonny Hall
Secretary-Treasurer: John J. Kerrigan
Executive Vice President: Frank McCann
Administrative Vice Presidents:
  James Little
  Larry Martin

Transportation Communications Union (AFL-CIO)
Transportation Communications International Union [TCU]
3 Research Place, Rockville, MD 20850
Phone: (301) 948-4910
Fax: (301) 948-1369
Web site: www.tcunion.org
Founded: 1899
Membership: 104,827
Publications: *Interchange* (six times annually) and *Telling It Like It Is* (six times annually)
President: Robert A. Scardelletti
Secretary-Treasurer: L. Earl Bosher
Vice Presidents:
  Lori Ann Ames
  Carl H. Brockett
  Joseph P. Condo
  Robert F. Davis
  Steve Elliott
  Richard A. Johnson
  Joel M. Parker
  James L. Quilty
  Howard W. Randolph, Jr.

Transportation Union (AFL-CIO)
United Transportation Union [UTU]
14600 Detroit Ave., Cleveland, OH 44107-4250
Phone: (216) 228-9400
Fax: (216) 228-5755
E-mail: utunews@utu.org
Web site: www.utu.org
Washington, DC office: 304 Pennsylvania Ave., S.E., Washington, DC 20003-1130
Phone: (202) 543-7714
Fax: (202) 543-0015
Founded: 1969
Membership: 65,752
Publications: *UTU News* (monthly)
President: Byron A. Boyd, Jr.
Secretary-Treasurer: Daniel E. Johnson, III
Vice Presidents:
  Dan Carver
  D.L. Hackey
  B.J. McNelis

Treasury Employees

National Treasury Employees Union
[NTEU]
1750 H St., N.W., Washington, DC 20006
Phone: (202) 572-5500
Fax: (202) 572-5641
E-mail: nteu-info@nteu.org
Web site: www.nteu.org
Founded: 1938
Publications: *NTEU Bulletin* (monthly), *Steward Update* (monthly), and *Capital Report* (monthly)
President: Colleen M. Kelley
Executive Vice President: Frank D. Ferris

University Professors

American Association of University Professors [AAUP]
1012 14th St., NW, Suite 500, Washington, DC 20005
Phone: (202) 737-5900
Fax: (202) 737-5526
E-mail: aaup@aaup.org
Web site: www.aaup.org
Founded: 1915
Membership: 45,000
Publications: *Academe* (six issues annually)
President: Jane Buck
Vice Presidents:
Cary Nelson
Janet M. West
Secretary-Treasurer: Kerry E. Grant

Utility Co-Workers

Utility Co-Workers' Association [UCA]
55 Washington St., Suite 200, Bloomfield, NJ 07003-2483
Phone: (973) 748-0233
Membership: 1,447
Contact: Ed Dickert

Utility Workers (AFL-CIO)

Utility Workers Union of America [UWUA]
815 16th St., NW, Washington, DC 20006
Phone: (202) 974-8200
Fax: (202) 974-8201
Web site: www.uwua.org
Founded: 1944
Membership: 44,280
Publications: *Light* (bimonthly)
President: Donald E. Wightman
Executive Vice President: James P. Keller
Vice President: Joseph F. Flaherty
Secretary-Treasurer: Gary M. Ruffner

Variety Artists (AAAA) (AFL-CIO)

American Guild of Variety Artists [AGVA]
184 Fifth Ave., 6th Floor, New York, NY 10010
Phone: (212) 675-1003
Membership: 3,900
Executive President: Rod McKuen

Weather Service Employees

National Weather Service Employees Organization [NWSEO]
601 Pennsylvania Ave., NW, Suite 900, Washington, DC 20004
Phone: (703) 293-9651
Fax: (703) 293-9653
Web site: www.nwseo.org
Membership: 1,220
Publications: *The Four Winds* (monthly)
President: Paul Greaves
Secretary-Treasurer: Marguerite Matera

Westinghouse Salaried Employees

Association of Westinghouse Salaried Employees [AWSE]
820 East Pittsburgh Plaza, Pittsburgh, PA 15112
Phone: (412) 823-9333
Fax: (412) 823-9299
Membership: 1,852
President: Peter Sullivan
Secretary-Treasurer: Tony Bozik

Writers (UAW)

National Writers Union [NWU]
113 University Place, 6th Floor, New York, NY 10003-1209
Phone: (212) 254-0279
Fax: (212) 254-0673
E-mail: nwu@nwu.org
Web site: www.nwu.org
Founded: 1981
Membership: 6,500
Publications: *American Writer* (quarterly)
President: Marybeth Menaker
Secretary-Treasurer: Gail Kinney
Vice Presidents:
Barbara Beckwith
Dennis DeMaio
Sara Forth
Sue Grieger
Leslie Millenson
Dan Moldea
Joel Washington
Miryam Williamson
Executive Director: Chris Zic

Writers, East (AFL-CIO)

Writers Guild of America, East, Inc. [WGAE]
555 W. 57th St., New York, NY 10019
Phone: (212) 767-7800
Fax: (212) 582-1909
Web site: www.wgaeast.org
Founded: 1954
Membership: 4,173
Publications: *WGAE Newsletter* (bimonthly)
President: Herb Sargent
Secretary-Treasurer: Gail Lee
Vice President: Warren Leight
Executive Director: Mona Mangan
Note: Affiliated with Writers Guild of America, West, Inc.

Writers, West

Writers Guild of America, West, Inc. [WGA, W]
7000 W. Third St., Los Angeles, CA 90048
Phone: (323) 951-4000
Fax: (323) 782-4801
Web site: www.wga.org
Founded: 1933
Membership: 7,646
Publications: *Journal* (monthly)
President: Victoria Riskin
Secretary-Treasurer: Patrick Verrone
Vice President: Charles Holland
Executive Director: John McLean
Note: Affiliated with Writers Guild of America, East, Inc.

PART IV. Local, Intermediate, and Independent Unions

The abbreviations used in Part IV are shown below:

AREA	Area	**LCH**	Local Chapter
ASSN	Association	**LDIV**	Local Division
BCTC	Building and Construction Trades Council	**LEC**	Local Executive Council
		LG	Lodge
BD	Board	**LJEB**	Local Joint Executive Board
BR	Branch	**LLG**	Local Lodge
C	Council	**LSC**	Local Staff Council
CH	Chapter	**LU**	Local Union
COM	Committee	**MEC**	Master Executive Council
CONBD	Conference Board	**MTC**	Metal Trades Council
CONF	Conference	**NC**	National Council
D	District	**NHQ**	National Headquarters
DALU	Directly Affiliated Local Union	**PC**	Port Council
DC	District Council	**R**	Region
DIV	Division	**RB**	Regional Board
DJC	District Joint Council	**RC**	Regional Council
DLG	District Lodge	**SA**	State Association, State Affiliate
FASTC	Food and Allied Service Trade Council	**SBA**	System Board of Adjustment
FED	Federation	**SC**	System Council
GC	General Committee	**SCOM**	System Committee
GCA	General Committee of Adjustment	**SD**	System Division
IUDTC	Industrial Union Department Trades Council	**SF**	System Federation
		SFED	State Federation
JB	Joint Board	**SLB**	State Legislative Board
JC	Joint Council	**SLG**	Sub-Lodge, Subordinate Lodge
JCONF	Joint Conference	**STC**	State Council
JPB	Joint Protective Board	**STCON**	State Conference
LBR	Local Branch	**ULSTC**	Union Label Service Trades Council
LC	Local Council	**UNIT**	Unit

Alabama

AFL-CIO Trade and Industrial Departments

Building and Construction Trades Department
BCTC Alabama . . . . . . Mobile
BCTC Central
Alabama . . . . . . Birmingham
BCTC Coosa Valley . . . Gadsden
BCTC Mobile Alabama-Pensacola
Florida . . . . Mobile
BCTC North Alabama . . . Sheffield
BCTC Shoals Area Central Labor
Union . . . . Sheffield
BCTC Tuscaloosa . . . . Tuscaloosa

Maritime Trades Department
PC Mobile Area . . . . . . Mobile

Metal Trades Department
MTC Wiregrass Trades . Fort Rucker

Other Councils and Committees
C Northeast Alabama Labor
Council . . . . Gadsden

AFL-CIO Directly Affiliated Locals
C Montgomery Central
Labor . . . . Montgomery

Affiliated Labor Organizations

Air Traffic Controllers
LU . . . . Dothan
LU BHM . . . . Birmingham
LU HSV . . . . Madison
LU MGM . . . . Hope Hull
LU MOB . . . . Mobile

Asbestos Workers
CONF 12 Southeastern
States . . . . Birmingham
LU 55. . . . . Mobile
LU 78. . . . . Birmingham

Automobile, Aerospace Workers
C Alabama CAP . . . . Birmingham
LU 759. . . . . Fayette
LU 1155 . . . . Birmingham
LU 1413. . . . . Huntsville
LU 1639 . . . . Theodore
LU 1929 . . . . . . Union Grove
LU 1990 . . . . Hamilton
LU 2083 . . . . Tuscaloosa
LU 2195 . . . . Tanner
LU 2222 . . . . Birmingham
LU 2276 . . . . . . Union Grove
LU 2281 . . . . Birmingham
LU 4927 . . . . Jasper

Bakery, Confectionery, Tobacco Workers and Grain Millers
LU 611 . . . . Fort Payne
LU 09-150-G . . . . . . Attalla
LU 09-173-G . . . . . . Attalla

Boilermakers
LG 56-S . . . . Stevenson
LG 79-D Cement
Workers . . . . . . Demopolis
LG 108 . . . . Birmingham

LG 112 . . . . Mobile
LG 455 . . . . . Muscle Shoals
LG 583 . . . . Quinton
LG 584. . . . . . . Moundville

Bricklayers
LU 1 . . . . Birmingham
LU 3 . . . . Montgomery
LU 4 . . . . Tuscaloosa
LU 8 . . . . Sheffield
LU 11 . . . . Arab
LU 15 . . . . Athens

Carpenters
LU 89. . . . . Mobile
LU 109 . . . . Sheffield
LU 127 . . . . Birmingham
LU 1192 . . . . Birmingham
LU 1274 . . . . Decatur
LU 2401 . . . . Birmingham
LU 4001 Alabama Carpenters
Regional Council . . . . . Irondale

Civilian Technicians
CH 67 Northern Alabama . Cullman
CH 68 Southern Alabama . . . . Fort
Deposit
CH 123 Alabama Air . . Birmingham

Communications Workers
COM Alabama Political &
Legislative . . . . Decatur
LU 3901 . . . . Anniston
LU 3902 . . . . Birmingham
LU 3903 . . . . Decatur
LU 3904 . . . . Gadsden
LU 3905. . . . . . . Huntsville
LU 3906 . . . . Jasper
LU 3907 . . . . Mobile
LU 3908 . . . . Montgomery
LU 3909 . . . . Sylacauga
LU 3910. . . . . Selma
LU 3911 . . . . . Muscle Shoals
LU 3912 . . . . Tuscaloosa
LU 3950 . . . . Birmingham
LU 3971 . . . . Andalusia
LU 3972 . . . . Dothan
LU 3974 . . . . Tallassee
LU 3990 . . . . Prattville
LU 14300. . . . . . . Birmingham
LU 14307. . . . . . . Birmingham
LU 83777 IUE . . . . . . Foley

Electrical Workers
LU 136 . . . . Birmingham
LU 253 . . . . Birmingham
LU 345 . . . . Mobile
LU 391 . . . . Hokes Bluff
LU 443 . . . . Montgomery
LU 505 . . . . Mobile
LU 558 . . . . Sheffield
LU 656 . . . . . . Pleasant Grove
LU 765 . . . . Athens
LU 780. . . . . Eufaula
LU 796 . . . . Columbia
LU 801 . . . . Tallassee
LU 833 . . . . Jasper
LU 841 . . . . Trussville
LU 904 . . . . Greenville
LU 1053 . . . . Demopolis
LU 1629 . . . . Sylacauga
LU 1642 . . . . Lineville
LU 1871 . . . . Birmingham
LU 1980. . . . . Ashford
LU 2040 . . . . Brewton

LU 2048 . . . . Pennington
LU 2077. . . . . . . Sylacauga
LU 2129. . . . . . . Satsuma
LU 2152. . . . . . . Enterprise
LU 2251. . . . . . . Andalusia
LU 2298 . . . . Leroy
LU 2362 . . . . Selma
SC 19-U . . . . . . Birmingham

Electronic Workers
LU 693 . . . . Selma
LU 711 . . . . Gadsden
LU 783 . . . . Huntsville
LU 793 . . . . Selma

Elevator Constructors
LU 24. . . . . Birmingham
LU 124 . . . . Lillian

Federal Employees
LU 131 . . . . Tuscaloosa

Food and Commercial Workers
LU 88-T . . . . Decatur
LU 125-C . . . . Anniston
LU 191-T . . . . Trinity
LU 223-C . . . . Florence
LU 488-C . . . . Mobile
LU 504-T . . . . Dutton
LU 683-T . . . . Falkville
LU 1657 . . . . Birmingham
LU 1999-G . . . . Florence
RC 3 . . . . Birmingham

Glass, Molders, Pottery and Plastics Workers
LU 62 . . . . Birmingham
LU 65-B . . . . Boaz
LU 85-B . . . . Leeds
LU 214 . . . . Madison
LU 248 . . . . . . Dearmanville
LU 255 . . . . Birmingham
LU 256-B . . . . Tarrant
LU 324 . . . . Anniston
LU 338 . . . . Mobile
LU 413-A . . . . Piedmont

Government Employees
C 27 Alabama State . . . . . Coker
C 45 Food Inspection Councils
National Joint . . . . . . Remlap
C 67 Food Inspection Locals,
Southern. . . . . Opelika
LU 110 VA . . . . . . Tuskegee
LU 131 VA . . . . . Tuscaloosa
LU 503 . . . . Montgomery
LU 522 Montgomery . Montgomery
LU 997 DoD . . . . . Montgomery
LU 1815 DoD . . . . Fort Rucker
LU 1858 DoD . . . Redstone Arsenal
LU 1941 DoD . . . . Fort McClellan
LU 1945 DoD . . . . . . Bynum
LU 2206 HHS . . . . . Birmingham
LU 2207 VA . . . . . Birmingham
LU 2357 USDA . . . . . Opelika
LU 3024 DoD . . . . Birmingham
LU 3384 DoL . . . . . Hueytown
LU 3434 NASA . . Marshall Space
Flight Center
LU 3438 HHS . . . . Birmingham
LU 3844 . . . . . . Childersburg
LU 4058
COP . . . Maxwell Air Force Base

Government Security Officers
LU 22 Browns Ferry Nuclear Plant
. . . . Madison

Graphic Communications
LU 100-C . . . . Mobile
LU 121-C . . . . Vincient
LU 540-M . . . . . . Bessemer

Guards
LU 33 . . . . Toney

Hotel and Restaurant Employees
LU 719 . . . . Madison

Iron Workers
DC Southeastern States. Birmingham
LU 92. . . . . Birmingham
LU 477 . . . . Sheffield
LU 798 . . . . Semmes

Laborers
DC Alabama . . . . . . Birmingham
LU 70. . . . . Mobile
LU 366 . . . . Sheffield
LU 559 . . . . Birmingham
LU 784. . . . . Webb
LU 1317 Public
Employees . . . . . Birmingham
LU 1370 State
Employees . . . . . Birmingham

Letter Carriers
BR 106 . . . . Montgomery
BR 448 . . . . Anniston
BR 462 . . . . Huntsville
BR 469 . . . . Mobile
BR 530 . . . . Birmingham
BR 892 . . . . Florence
BR 937. . . . . Bessemer
BR 1047 . . . . Gadsden
BR 1096 . . . . Tuscaloosa
BR 1210 Talladega,
Alabama. . . . . . . Talladega
BR 1314 . . . . Decatur
BR 1630 . . . . Dothan
BR 2119. . . . . . . Andalusia
BR 2270 . . . . Hanceville
BR 2547. . . . . . . Sylacauga
BR 3077 . . . . . Alexander City
BR 3099 Jasper, Alabama. . . Jasper
BR 3122 . . . . Phenix City
BR 3135 Oneonta,
Alabama . . . . Oneonta
BR 3266 Lanett, Alabama . . Lanett
BR 3344 . . . . . . Jacksonville
BR 3359 . . . . . . Fort Payne
BR 3372 Heflin, Alabama . . Heflin
BR 3386 Roanoke,
Alabama . . . . Roanoke
BR 3457 Clanton, Alabama . Clanton
BR 3588 Eutaw, Alabama . . Eutaw
BR 3589 Marion, Alabama . Marion
BR 3590 Montevallo,
Alabama . . . . Montevallo
BR 3852 Haleyville,
Alabama . . . . Haleyville
BR 4030 Luverne,
Alabama . . . . Luverne
BR 4309 Citronelle,
Alabama . . . . Citronelle
BR 4352 Childersburg,
Alabama . . . . . . Childersburg
BR 4564 Warrior, Alabama . Warrior
BR 4626 . . . . Aliceville

BR 4671 Monroeville,
  Alabama . . . . . . Monroeville
BR 5007 Winfield,
  Alabama . . . . Winfield
BR 5130. . . . . Valley
BR 6118 Foley, Alabama . . . Foley
BR 6194 Moulton,
  Alabama . . . . Moulton
BR 6375 Brundidge,
  Alabama . . . . Brundidge
BR 6494 . . . . Lafayette
SA Alabama . . . . Laceys Spring

Locomotive Engineers
DIV 73 . . . . Moody
DIV 140 . . . . . . Chunchula
DIV 150 . . . . . . Birmingham
DIV 156 . . . . . . Birmingham
DIV 223 . . . . Selma
DIV 280 . . . . Tuscumbia
DIV 332 . . . . Deatsville
DIV 386 . . . . Empire
DIV 409 . . . . . . Phenix City
DIV 423 . . . . Muscle Shoals
DIV 495 . . . . . Montgomery
DIV 684 . . . . . . Birmingham
DIV 899 . . . . Bynum
SLB Alabama. . . . . Birmingham

Longshoremen
LU 1410 . . . . Mobile
LU 1410-1 . . . . Mobile
LU 1459 . . . . Mobile
LU 1985 . . . . Mobile

Machinists
DLG 75. . . . . Daleville
DLG 92. . . . . Sheffield
LG 7 . . . . Fultondale
LG 65. . . . . Sheffield
LG 271 . . . . Birmingham
LG 291 . . . . Jacksonville
LG 359 . . . . Hueytown
LG 985 . . . . Sylacauga
LG 1189 . . . . Sheffield
LG 1632 . . . . . . Napier Field
LG 2003 . . . . Daleville
LG 2452 . . . . Grove Hill
LG 2766 . . . . Madison
LG 2802-PM . . . . . . Anniston
LLG 44 . . . . Folrence
STC Alabama . . . . . Newmarket

Maintenance of Way Employes
LG 546 . . . . Boaz
LG 645 . . . . Boaz
LG 682 . . . . Repton
SLG 529. . . . . Selma
SLG 585 . . . . Oxford
SLG 992 . . . . Hanceville
SLG 1600 . . . . Carrollton
SLG 1857. . . . . . . Brundidge
SLG 2033 . . . . Aliceville
SLG 2154 . . . . Mobile

Mine Workers
D 20 . . . . Birmingham
LU 1288. . . . . Jasper
LU 1553 . . . . . . Holly Pond
LU 1554 . . . . Dora
LU 1867. . . . . . . Hueytown
LU 1876. . . . . Vance
LU 1881. . . . . . . Goodspring
LU 1926 . . . . Northport
LU 1928 . . . . Hatchechubbee
LU 1947 . . . . Joppa
LU 1948 . . . . Adger
LU 1987 . . . . . Carbon Hill

LU 2042. . . . . Jasper
LU 2133. . . . . . . Hueytown
LU 2245 . . . . . . Tuscaloosa
LU 2368 . . . . Brookwood
LU 2397 . . . . Brookwood
LU 2427 . . . . Adger
LU 5841 . . . . Winfield
LU 5932 . . . . Guin
LU 5986 . . . . Mulga
LU 6255. . . . . . . Graysville
LU 6855 . . . . Nauvoo
LU 7154 . . . . Double Springs
LU 7813 . . . . Parrish
LU 7918 . . . . . . Adamsville
LU 7930 . . . . Jasper
LU 8460 . . . . . . West Blocton
LU 8982 . . . . Midfield
LU 9511 . . . . Winfield
LU 9984 . . . . Cordora

Musicians
LU 256-733 Birmingham
  Musicians Protective
  Association. . . . . Birmingham

National Staff Organization
LU Staff Organization, Association,
  Alabama Education
  Association . . . . Montgomery
LU Staff Organization, Professional,
  Alabama . . . . . . Montgomery

Needletrades
LU 1021-C. . . . . . Montgomery
LU 1465. . . . . . . Andalusia
LU 1882 . . . . . . Montgomery

Nurses
SA Alabama State Nurses
  Association . . . . Montgomery

Office and Professional Employees
LU 102 . . . . Daleville

Operating Engineers
LU 312 . . . . Birmingham
LU 320 . . . . Florence
LU 653 . . . . Mobile

Painters
LU 57. . . . . Birmingham
LU 779 . . . . Mobile
LU 1293 Sheffield-Florence-
  Tuscumbia Local. . Muscle Shoals

**Paper, Allied-Industrial, Chemical
Employees**
C Alabama . . . . Prattville
LU 501 . . . . Huntsville
LU 03-44 . . . . Ragland
LU 03-108 . . . . Leeds
LU 03-193 . . . . . . Courtland
LU 03-229 . . . . Mobile
LU 03-265 . . . . . . Saraland
LU 03-297 . . . . . . Moundville
LU 03-300 . . . . . Montgomery
LU 03-328 . . . . . Thomasville
LU 03-336 . . . . . Pennington
LU 03-339 . . . . . Thomasville
LU 03-361 . . . . . . Jackson
LU 03-462 . . . . . . Prattville
LU 03-488 . . . . . . Maytown
LU 03-516 . . . . . . Hollins
LU 03-524 Bayou La
  Batree Community
  Center . . . . Bayou La Batree
LU 03-525 . . . . . Tuscaloosa
LU 03-537 . . . . Calera

LU 03-541 . . . . . . Mobile
LU 03-542 . . . . Leeds
LU 03-543 . . . . Leeds
LU 03-546 . . . . Bay Minette
LU 03-562 . . . . . . McIntosh
LU 03-563 . . . . Calera
LU 03-592 . . . . Mobile
LU 03-593 . . . . Axis
LU 03-594 . . . . . . Northpot
LU 03-675 . . . . Guin
LU 03-692 . . . . . Childersburg
LU 03-719 . . . . . . Demopolis
LU 03-881 . . . . . . Huntsville
LU 03-888 . . . . . . Brewton
LU 03-906 . . . . . . Decatur
LU 03-923 . . . Pleasant Grove
LU 03-941 . . . . Wing
LU 03-950 . . . . Linden
LU 03-952 . . . . . Dixon Mills
LU 03-966 . . . . Linden
LU 03-971 . . . . . . Cottonton
LU 03-1083 . . . . . . Jackson
LU 03-1137 . . . . . Courtland
LU 03-1140 . . . . . Fairfield
LU 03-1161 . . . . . . Florence
LU 03-1286 . . . . . . Mobile
LU 03-1368 . . . . . Thomasville
LU 03-1394 . . . . . . Atmore
LU 03-1406 . . . . . . Georgiana
LU 03-1421 . . . . . . Saraland
LU 03-1441 . . . . . . Selma
LU 03-1444 . . . . . . Clanton
LU 03-1458 . . . . . . Prattville
LU 03-1486 . . . . . Birmingham
LU 03-1514 . . . . . . Crossville
LU 03-1522 . . . . . . Talladega
LU 03-1575 . . . . . Chickasaw
LU 03-1595 . . . . . Sylacauga
LU 03-1684 . . . . . . Munford
LU 03-1693 . . . . Childersburg
LU 03-1704. . . . . . Birmingham
LU 03-1835 . . . . . Demopolis
LU 03-1865 . . . . . . Columbia
LU 03-1873 . . . . . . Mobile
LU 03-1972 . . . . Fort Mitchell
LU 03-1978 . . . . . . Prattville
LU 03-1995 . . . . . Grove Hill
LU 05-919 . . . . . . Flat Rock
LU 05-965 . . . . . . Flat Rock
LU 50-113 . . . . . . Mobile

Plasterers and Cement Masons
LU 62 . . . . Birmingham

Plumbing and Pipe Fitting
LU 52 . . . . Montgomery
LU 91 . . . . Birmingham
LU 119 . . . . Mobile
LU 372 . . . . Tuscaloosa
LU 377 . . . . Huntsville
LU 498 . . . . Gadsden
LU 548 . . . . Deatsville
LU 760 . . . . . Muscle Shoals

Postal and Federal Employees
LU 401 . . . . Bessemer
LU 402 . . . . Birmingham
LU 408 . . . . Eight Mile

Postal Mail Handlers
LU 317 . . . . Birmingham

Postal Workers
LU 303 Birmingham . . Birmingham
LU 323 Montgomery
  Area . . . . . . Montgomery
LU 332 Dothan. . . . . . . Dothan

LU 359 North Alabama
  Area . . . . Madison
LU 399 West Alabama
  Area . . . . . . Tuscaloosa
LU 501 Jasper . . . . . . Jasper
LU 525 Anniston. . . . . Anniston
LU 537 Gadsden . . . . . Gadsden
LU 714 Evergreen Local . Evergreen
LU 715 South Alabama
  Area . . . . Mobile
LU 805 Athens Local . . . . Athens
LU 810 Florence . . . . . Florence
LU 895 Brewton Local . . . Brewton
LU 1105 Haleyville
  Local . . . . Haleyville
LU 1515 Montevallo
  Local . . . . . . Montevallo
LU 1705 Guntersville
  Local . . . . . . Guntersville
LU 1800 Albertville
  Local . . . . Albertville
LU 2634 Fayette Local. . . . Fayette
LU 2635 Clanton Local . . Clanton
LU 2660 Scottsboro . . . Scottsboro
LU 2675 Alexander City
  Local . . . . . . Alexander City
LU 2708 Enterprise
  Local . . . . Enterprise
LU 2709 Opp Local . . . . . . Opp
LU 2827 Fort Payne . . . Fort Payne
LU 2870 Boaz Local . . . . . Boaz
LU 3511 Pell City Local . . Pell City
LU 3513 Leeds Local . . . . Leeds
LU 5515 Hamilton Local . Hamilton
SA Alabama . . . . Madison

**Professional and Technical
Engineers**
LU 27. . . . . Huntsville
LU 561 . . . . Mobile

Railroad Signalmen
LLG 137 . . . . . . Bay Minette
LLG 178 . . . . Pinson

**Retail, Wholesale and Department
Store**
JC 932 Alabama
  Mid-South . . . . . Birmingham
LU 102-A. . . . . . Birmingham
LU 103 United Dairy
  Workers . . . . . Birmingham
LU 105 . . . . . . Birmingham
LU 107 . . . . . . Birmingham
LU 180-C. . . . . . Birmingham
LU 201-A. . . . . . Birmingham
LU 261 . . . . . . Birmingham
LU 405 . . . . . . Birmingham
LU 441 . . . . . . Birmingham
LU 451 . . . . . . Birmingham
LU 506 . . . . Gadsden
LU 555 . . . . . . Birmingham
LU 590 . . . . . . Birmingham
LU 615 . . . . . . Birmingham
LU 620 . . . . Waterloo
LU 645 . . . . . . Birmingham
LU 761 . . . . Athens
LU 928 Alabama ABC
  Employees . . . . . Birmingham
LU 1095 . . . . . . Birmingham

Rural Letter Carriers
SA Alabama . . . . . Guntersville

**Security, Police and Fire
Professionals**
LU 599 . . . . Mobile
LU 600 . . . . Trinity

LU 601 . . . . Killen

Sheet Metal Workers
DC Southeast. . . . . Mobile
LU 48. . . . . Birmingham
LU 441 . . . . Mobile

Steelworkers
LU 844 . . . . Birmingham
LU 09-12-L. . . . . Gadsden
LU 09-81-S . . . . Saginaw
LU 09-127-S . . . . Gurley
LU 09-200-ABG . . . Muscle Shoals
LU 09-203-A . . . . Decatur
LU 09-207-A . . . . Moulton
LU 09-217 . . . . Florence
LU 09-223 . . . . Leighton
LU 09-276. . . . . Jasper
LU 09-295 . . . . Winfield
LU 09-351-L. . . . . . Tuscaloosa
LU 09-417 . . . . Cherokee
LU 09-481-G . . . . Florence
LU 09-553-S . . . . . . Bessermer
LU 09-753-L . . . . Opelika
LU 09-759-L. . . . . . . Cherokee
LU 09-896-L . . . . Lineville
LU 09-915-L . . . . Madison
LU 09-936-L . . . . . . Scottsboro
LU 09-976-L . . . . Eutaw
LU 09-1013-S. . . . . . . Fairfield
LU 09-1057-S . . . . Birmingham
LU 09-2122-S . . . Pleasant Grove

LU 09-2140-S . . . . Birmingham
LU 09-2176-S . . . . . . Gadsden
LU 09-2210-S. . . . . . . Fairfield
LU 09-2528-S . . . . . Bridgeport
LU 09-3768-S . . . . Birmingham
LU 09-4754-S. . . . . . Whistler
LU 09-4841-S . . . . West Blocton
LU 09-5190-S. . . . . . . Calera
LU 09-7436-S . . . . Birmingham
LU 09-7468-S . . . . . Scottsboro
LU 09-7564-S. . . . . . Semmes
LU 09-7700-S. . . . . . Cullman
LU 09-7740-S . . . . . . Warrior
LU 09-7750-S . . . . Montgomery
LU 09-8235-S . . . . . . Warrior
LU 09-8285-S . . . . Birmingham
LU 09-8309-S. . . . . . Centre
LU 09-8538-S . . . . Pike Road
LU 09-8542-S . . . . . . Moody
LU 09-8767-S . . . Mount Vernon
LU 09-8855-S . . . . Valley Head
LU 09-9201-S. . . . . Hueytown
LU 09-9226-S . . . . Birmingham
LU 09-9282-S. . . . . . Glencoe
LU 09-9287-S. . . . . . Huntsville
LU 09-9361-S. . . . Duncunville
LU 09-12014-S . . . . . . Pinson
LU 09-12019-S . . . . Birmingham
LU 09-12030-S . . . . Birmingham
LU 09-12136-S . . . . . Warrior
LU 09-12768-S. . . . . Cottondale
LU 09-13140-S. . . . Birmingham

LU 09-13350-S . . . . Montgomery
LU 09-13358-S . . . . . . Warrior
LU 09-13679-S . . . . . . Bryant
LU 09-14530-S . . . . . . Centre
LU 09-15329-S . . . . . Flat Rock

Teamsters
LU 402 . . . . . . Muscle Shoals
LU 612 . . . . Birmingham
LU 991 . . . . Mobile

Theatrical Stage Employees
LU 78 . . . . Birmingham
LU 142 . . . . Mobile
LU 900 . . . . Huntsville

Transit Union
LDIV 725 . . . . . . Birmingham
LDIV 765 . . . . . . Montgomery

Transportation Communications Union
D 376. . . . . Hanceville
D 691. . . . . Birmingham
D 1081. . . . . Theodore
D 1409 Southeastern System Board
96. . . . . Birmingham
LG 6060 Iron City. . . . Trussville
LG 6385 Birmingham . . . . Pinson

Transportation Union
LU 598 . . . . Loxley

LU 622 . . . . Birmingham
LU 762 . . . . Coosada
LU 772 . . . . Leighton
LU 847 . . . . Dora
LU 1053 . . . . Jones
LU 1291 . . . . . . Birmingham
LU 1887 . . . . . . Pleasant Grove
LU 1912 . . . . Spanish Fort
SLB LO-1 Alabama . . Montgomery

Treasury Employees
CH 12. . . . . Birmingham
CH 220 . . . . McCalla

Weather Service Employees
BR 02-12 . . . . Huntsville
BR 02-18. . . . . Alabaster
BR 02-29. . . . . Mobile

Unaffiliated Labor Organizations
Alabama Organized Labor Awards
Foundation . . . . Decatur
Alabama Pipe Trades
Association. . . . . Birmingham
Alabama Plant Police Association
Birmingham LG 1 . . Birmingham
Court Security Officers Benevolent
Association . . . . Mobile
Workers Association
Independent . . . . . Birmingham

Alaska

AFL-CIO Trade and Industrial Departments

Building and Construction Trades Department
BCTC Juneau. . . . . Juneau
BCTC Ketchikan . . . . . Ketchikan
BCTC Western Alaska. . Anchorage

Other Councils and Committees
C Fairbanks Joint Crafts . Anchorage

Affiliated Labor Organizations

Agricultural Employees
BR 54. . . . . Anchorage

Air Traffic Controllers
LU A11. . . . . Anchorage
LU ANC . . . . Anchorage
LU FAI . . . . Fairbanks
LU JNU. . . . . Juneau
LU MRI . . . . Anchorage
LU NATCA Engineers
  Architects . . . . . . Anchorage
LU ZAN . . . . Anchorage

Aircraft Mechanics
LU 34. . . . . Anchorage

Asbestos Workers
LU 97. . . . . Anchorage

Bricklayers
LU 1 . . . . Anchorage

Carpenters
C Alaska. . . . . Fairbanks
LU 1243 . . . . Fairbanks
LU 1281 . . . . Anchorage
LU 2247 . . . . Juneau
LU 2520 . . . . Anchorage

Civilian Technicians
CH 84 Alaska. . . . Fort Richardson

Electrical Workers
LU 1547 . . . . Anchorage

Food and Commercial Workers
LU 1496 . . . . Anchorage

Government Employees
LU 183 DoT . . . . Anchorage
LU 1101 Elmendorf Air Force
  Base . . Elmendorf Air Force Base
LU 1668 DoD . . . . . Anchorage
LU 1712 DoD. . . . Fort Richardson
LU 1834 DoD . . . Fort Wainwright
LU 1836
  DoD. . . . Eielson Air Force Base
LU 1949 DoD . . . . Delta Junction
LU 3028 DoT . . . . . Anchorage
LU 3937 SSA . . . . . Anchorage

Government Security Officers
LU 67. . . . . Anchorage

Graphic Communications
LU 327-C. . . . . Anchorage
LU 704-C . . . . Fairbanks

Hotel and Restaurant Employees
LU 878 . . . . Anchorage

Iron Workers
LU 751 . . . . Anchorage

Laborers
DC Alaska . . . . . . Anchorage
LU 341 . . . . Anchorage
LU 942 . . . . Fairbanks

Laundry and Dry Cleaning
LU 333 . . . . Anchorage

Letter Carriers
BR 4319 . . . . Anchorage
BR 4368 Ketchikan,
  Alaska . . . . Ketchikan
BR 4491 . . . . Fairbanks
BR 4985 . . . . Juneau
BR 5275 . . . . Kodiak
BR 5893 Sitka, Alaska . . . . Sitka

Longshore and Warehouse
LU 16. . . . . Juneau
LU 62 Alaska. . . . . . Metlakatla
LU 200 Alaska Division . . . Kodiak
LU 200 Dutch Harbor Unit
  201 . . . . Dutch Harbor
LU 200 Unit 2201 . . . . . Juneau
LU 200 Unit 222 . . . . . . Kodiak
LU 200 Unit 223 . . . Dutch Harbor
LU 200 Unit 60 . . . . . . Seward
LU 200 Unit 61 . . . . . Ketchikan
LU 200 Unit 62 . . . . . Ketchikan

LU 200 Unit 62-B . . . . . Klawock
LU 200 Unit 65 . . . . Haines
LU 200 Unit 66. . . . . . Cordova
LU 200 Unit 87 . . . . . . Wrangell

Machinists
LG 601 . . . . Anchorage
LG 1735 . . . . Anchorage
LG 2263 . . . . Juneau
LLG 1690 . . . . Anchorage
LLG FL-251 . . . . Sitka

Musicians
LU 650 . . . . Anchorage

National Staff Organization
LU Alaska . . . . Juneau

Nurses
SA Alaska . . . . Anchorage

Painters
LU 1140 . . . . Anchorage
LU 1555 . . . . Fairbanks

Plasterers and Cement Masons
LU 867 . . . . Anchorage

Plumbing and Pipe Fitting
LU 262 . . . . Juneau
LU 367 . . . . Anchorage
LU 375 . . . . Fairbanks
SA Alaska Pipe Trades . . Fairbanks

Postal Workers
LU 1416 Fairbanks . . . . Fairbanks
LU 2756 Anchorage . . . Anchorage
LU 3323 Juneau . . . . . . Juneau
LU 3667 Ketchikan. . . . Ketchikan
LU 6991 Sitka . . . . Sitka
SA Alaska . . . . Juneau

Roofers, Waterproofers and Allied Workers
LU 190 . . . . Anchorage

Sheet Metal Workers
LU 23 . . . . Anchorage

Teachers
LU 5200 Alaska Public Employees
  Association. . . . . Juneau

Teamsters
LU 959 . . . . Anchorage

Theatrical Stage Employees
LU 918 . . . . Anchorage

Train Dispatchers
SCOM Alaska Railroad . Anchorage

Transportation Communications Union
LG 6067 Far North. . . . Anchorage

Transportation Union
LU 1626 . . . . Anchorage

Treasury Employees
CH 69 . . . . Anchorage
CH 176 . . . . Anchorage

Weather Service Employees
BR 05-8-A . . . . . . Anchorage
BR 05-9. . . . . Juneau
BR 05-10 . . . . Nome
BR 05-11 . . . . Fairbanks
BR 05-12 . . . . Yakutat
BR 05-14. . . . . Cold Bay
BR 05-15 . . . . Valdez
BR 05-16 . . . . Bethel
BR 05-17. . . . . Barrow
BR 05-20. . . . . King Salmon
BR 05-21. . . . . Kodiak
BR 05-23 . . . . . St. Paul Island
BR 05-24 . . . . McGrath
BR 05-25. . . . . . . Kotzebue
BR 05-29 . . . . . . Anchorage
BR 05-30 . . . . . . Anchorage
BR 05-31 . . . . . . Anchorage
BR 05-33 . . . . . . Anchorage
BR 08-10 . . . . Juneau

Unaffiliated Labor Organizations
Alaska Independent Carpenters &
  Millwrights LU 1 . . . . Fairbanks
Alaska Petroleum Joint Crafts
  Council. . . . . Anchorage
Anchorage Independent
  Longshoremen LU 1 . . Anchorage
Denali National Park Professional
  Drivers Association . . Anchorage
Fairbanks Building and Construction
  Trades Council . . . . Fairbanks
Professional Labor Organization
  Alaska . . . . Juneau

American Samoa

Affiliated Labor Organizations

Air Traffic Controllers
LU TUT . . . . Pago Pago

Weather Service Employees
BR 07-4. . . . . Pago Pago

Arizona

AFL-CIO Trade and Industrial Departments

Building and Construction Trades Department
BCTC Phoenix . . . . Phoenix
BCTC Southern Arizona . . . Tucson

Affiliated Labor Organizations

Air Traffic Controllers
LU DVT . . . . Phoenix
LU FFZ . . . . Mesa
LU GCN . . . . . . Grand Canyon
LU P50 . . . . Phoenix
LU PHX . . . . Phoenix
LU PRC . . . . Prescott
LU SDL . . . . Scottsdale
LU TUS . . . . Tucson
LU U90 . . . . Tucson

Asbestos Workers
LU 73 . . . . Phoenix

Bakery, Confectionery, Tobacco Workers and Grain Millers
LU 232 . . . . Phoenix

Boilermakers
LG 4 . . . . Page
LG 361-D Cement Workers . . . . Kingman
LG 627 . . . . Phoenix

Bricklayers
LU 3 . . . . Phoenix

Carpenters
DC Arizona . . . . Phoenix
LU 408 . . . . Phoenix
LU 897 . . . . Bullhead City
LU 1914 . . . . Phoenix
LU 2093 . . . . Phoenix

Civilian Technicians
CH 61 Arizona Army . . . . Marana
CH 71 Phoenix Air . . . . . Phoenix

Communications Workers
LU 4277 . . . . Surprise
LU 7019 . . . . Phoenix
LU 7026 . . . . Tucson
LU 7032 . . . . Yuma
LU 7050 . . . . Tempe
LU 7060 . . . . Phoenix
LU 7090 . . . . Tempe
LU 7096 . . . . Tempe
STC Arizona . . . . Phoenix

Electrical Workers
C GCC-1 Government Coordinating . . . . . . Phoenix
LU 266 . . . . Phoenix
LU 387 . . . . Phoenix
LU 518 . . . . Globe
LU 570 . . . . Tucson
LU 640 . . . . Phoenix
LU 769 . . . . Phoenix
LU 893 . . . . Tucson
LU 1116 . . . . Tucson
LU 2223 . . . . Oracle

Electronic Workers
LU 1124 . . . . Tucson

Elevator Constructors
LU 140 . . . . Phoenix

Federal Employees
LU 81 . . . . Tucson
LU 232 . . . . Sacaton
LU 267 . . . . Whiteriver
LU 291 . . . . Chinle
LU 376 . . . . Peoria
LU 422 . . . . Parker
LU 520 . . . . Sells
LU 526 . . . . Coolidge
LU 1487 . . . . Yuma
LU 2094 . . . . Yuma
LU 2104 . . . . Yuma
LU 2112 Coconino National Forest . . . . Flagstaff

Fire Fighters
LU 142-F . . . . Yuma

Food and Commercial Workers
LU 99-R . . . . Phoenix
LU 184-C . . . . Benson

Government Employees
C 117 National INS . . . . . Yuma
C 159 Arizona State . . . . . Mesa
LU 495 VA . . . . Tucson
LU 1305 . . . . . . Grand Canyon
LU 1547 DoD . Luke Air Force Base
LU 1662 DoD . . . . Fort Huachuca
LU 2313 DoJ . . . . Safford
LU 2382 VA . . . . Phoenix
LU 2401 VA . . . . Prescott
LU 2544 DoJ . . . . Ajo
LU 2595 DoJ . . . . Yuma
LU 2846 DoD . . . . Phoenix
LU 2859 DoJ . . . . Phoenix
LU 2894 USDA . . . . . . Glendale
LU 2924 DoD . . . . Tucson
LU 3694 . . . . Mesa
LU 3954 Federal Correctional Institution . . . . . . Glendale
LU 3955 . . . . Tucson
LU 3973 . . . . Tucson

Government Employees Association
LU 14-142 . . . . Yuma
LU 14-143 . . . . Yuma

Government Security Officers
LU 54 . . . . Phoenix

Graphic Communications
LU 58-M . . . . Phoenix
LU 212-C . . . . Tucson
LU 512-M . . . . . Apache Junction

Hotel and Restaurant Employees
LU 631 . . . . Phoenix

Iron Workers
LU 75 . . . . Phoenix

Laborers
LU 383 . . . . Phoenix
LU 1386 SWNA Health Care Employees . . . . . . Phoenix

Letter Carriers
BR 576 . . . . Phoenix
BR 704 Carl J. Kennedy . . . Tucson
BR 859 . . . . Prescott
BR 1642 . . . . Yuma
BR 1902 . . . . Mesa
BR 2417 . . . . Nogales
BR 3238 . . . . Payson
BR 4761 Ajo, Arizona . . . . . Ajo
BR 5850 . . . . Lake Havasu City
BR 6156 . . . . Sun City
BR 6320 Holbrook, Arizona . . . . Holbrook
SA Arizona . . . . Sun City

Locomotive Engineers
DIV 28 . . . . Tucson
DIV 123 . . . . Goodyear
DIV 134 . . . . Winslow
DIV 647 . . . . Phoenix
SLB Arizona . . . . Tucson

Machinists
LG 519 . . . . Phoenix
LG 933 . . . . Tucson
LG 2181 . . . . San Manuel
LG 2282 . . . . Yuma
LG 2559 . . . . Phoenix
STC Arizona . . . . Goodyear

Maintenance of Way Employes
LG 508 . . . . Tucson
LG 2921 . . . . . Indian Wells
SLG 2417 . . . . . Prescott Valley

Mine Workers
LU 1332 . . . . . . Window Rock
LU 1620 . . . . Kayenta
LU 1924 . . . . Kayenta
LU 2483 . . . . Kayenta

Musicians
LU 586 . . . . Phoenix

National Staff Organization
LU Staff Organization, Arizona Education Association . . . . Mesa

NLRB Professional Association
LU 28 . . . . Phoenix

Office and Professional Employees
LU 56 . . . . Phoenix
LU 319 . . . . Tucson

Operating Engineers
LU 428 . . . . Phoenix

Painters
LU 86 . . . . Phoenix
LU 1610 . . . . Phoenix

Paper, Allied-Industrial, Chemical Employees
LU 08-296 . . . . Tucson
LU 08-869 . . . . Snowflake
LU 08-968 . . . . Phoenix
LU 08-978 . . . . Peoria

Plasterers and Cement Masons
LU 394 . . . . Phoenix
STCON Rocky Mountain Multi-States OP CMIA . . Phoenix

Plumbing and Pipe Fitting
LU 469 . . . . Phoenix
LU 741 . . . . Tucson

Postal and Federal Employees
LU 910 . . . . Phoenix

Postal Mail Handlers
LU 320 . . . . Tempe

Postal Workers
LU . . . . Page
LU 93 Valley of the Sun . . Phoenix
LU 255 Tucson . . . . Tucson
LU 397 Globe . . . . Globe
LU 425 Douglas . . . . . . Douglas
LU 530 Yuma . . . . Yuma
LU 611 Kingman . . . . Kingman
LU 704 Holbrook . . . . Holbrook
LU 1459 Prescott . . . . . Prescott
LU 2367 Ajo Local . . . . . . Ajo
LU 3992 Safford Local . . . Safford
LU 6852 Lake Havasu City . . . . . . Lake Havasu City
LU 7001 Verde Valley Area . . . . . . Cottonwood
LU 7008 Show Low . . . Show Low
LU 7071 Parker Local . . . . Parker
LU 7083 Bullhead City Local . . . . . . Bullhead City
LU 7087 Sedona . . . . . . Sedona
SA Arizona . . . . Phoenix

Railroad Signalmen
LLG 126 . . . . Mesa
LLG 172 . . . . Williams

Roofers, Waterproofers and Allied Workers
LU 135 . . . . Phoenix

Rural Letter Carriers
D 2 . . . . Flagstaff
D 3 Arizona . . . . Scottsdale
D 4 Arizona . . . . Tucson
D 5 . . . . Mesa
D 6 . . . . Yuma
SA Arizona . . . . . Chino Valley

Security, Police and Fire Professionals
LU 823 . . . . Mesa
LU 824 . . . . Fort Mohave

Sheet Metal Workers
LU 359 . . . . Phoenix

State, County and Municipal Employees
C 97 Arizona Public Employees Association . . . . Phoenix
LU 449 Tucson-Pima County . . . . Cortaro

Steelworkers
LU 12-470-S . . . . Douglas
LU 12-586-S . . . . Kearny
LU 12-886-S . . . . . . Winkelman
LU 12-915-S . . . . Kearny
LU 12-937-S . . . . Tucson
LU 12-3937-S . . . . Phoenix
LU 12-5252-S . . . Apache Junction

Teachers
SFED 8002 Arizona . . . . . Phoenix

Teamsters
LU 104 . . . . Phoenix
LU 752 Phoenix Mailers
  Union . . . . Phoenix

Television and Radio Artists
LU Phoenix . . . . Phoenix

Theatrical Stage Employees
LU 294 . . . . Phoenix
LU 336 . . . . Phoenix
LU 415 . . . . Tucson

LU 485 . . . . Tucson
LU 875 . . . . Tempe

Transit Union
LDIV 1433 . . . . Phoenix

Transport Workers
LU 580 . . . . Tempe

Transportation Communications Union
D 715 Southern Pacific . . . Phoenix

Transportation Union
LU 113 . . . . Winslow
LU 807 . . . . Tucson
LU 1081 . . . . Mesa
LU 1629 . . . . Mesa
LU 1800 . . . . Tucson
SLB LO-3 Arizona . . . . . Phoenix

Treasury Employees
CH 33 . . . . Phoenix
CH 116 . . . . Tucson

Weather Service Employees
BR 04-15 . . . . Phoenix
BR 04-16 . . . . Tucson
BR 04-74 . . . . Bellemont

Unaffiliated Labor Organizations

Engineers & Associate Employees of
  KTVK . . . . Phoenix
International Employees Welfare
  Union . . . . Gold Canyon

Arkansas

AFL-CIO Trade and Industrial Departments

Building and Construction Trades Department
BCTC Arkansas . . . . . Little Rock
BCTC Central Arkansas . Little Rock
BCTC Northwestern
  Arkansas . . . . Van Buren

Other Councils and Committees
C Hot Springs Labor . . Hot Springs

Affiliated Labor Organizations

Air Traffic Controllers
LU . . . . Texarkana
LU FSM . . . . Fort Smith
LU LIT . . . . Little Rock

Asbestos Workers
LU 10 . . . . Little Rock

Automobile, Aerospace Workers
C Arkansas CAP . . . . . Little Rock
LU 415 . . . . Malvern
LU 716 . . . . Fort Smith
LU 1000 . . . . Searcy
LU 1107 . . . . Cedarville
LU 1482 . . . . Melbourne
LU 1550 . . . . Mariana
LU 1762 . . . . Conway

Boilermakers
DLG 1241 . . . . Benton
LG 66 . . . . Conway
LG 69 . . . . Little Rock
LG 397-D Cement
  Workers . . . . Wintnrop
LG 1241-S . . . . . . Hot Springs
LG 1510 . . . . Atkins

Carpenters
DC Arkansas/Southeast Missouri
  #4004 . . . . Russellville
LU 71 . . . . Fort Smith
LU 497 . . . . Warren
LU 576 . . . . Little Rock
LU 690 . . . . Little Rock
LU 891 . . . . Hot Springs
LU 1225 . . . . Russellville
LU 1683 . . . . El Dorado
LU 1836 . . . . Russellville
LU 2019 . . . . Prescott
LU 2186 . . . . Hot Springs
LU 2271 . . . . Waldo
LU 2345 . . . . Emerson
LU 2346 . . . . Huttig
LU 2385 . . . . Greenbrier
LU 2661 . . . . Fordyce
LU 2697 . . . . Emerson
LU 2892 . . . . Tyrowza

Civilian Technicians
CH 117 Arkansas Air National
  Guard (Razorback) . . Jacksonville

Communications Workers
C Arkansas State . . . . . Little Rock
LU 341-FW . . . . Swifton
LU 747 . . . . Jonesboro
LU 1106 . . . . Forrest City
LU 1113 . . . . Little Rock

LU 1146 . . . . Bald Knob
LU 1147 . . . . Jonesboro
LU 6500 . . . . Van Buren
LU 6502 . . . . Charleston
LU 6503 . . . . Magnolia
LU 6505 . . . . West Memphis
LU 6507 . . . . Little Rock
LU 6508 . . . . Little Rock
LU 14600 . . . . Fort Smith

Electrical Workers
LU 295 . . . . Little Rock
LU 386 . . . . Texarkana
LU 436 . . . . El Dorado
LU 647 . . . . Little Rock
LU 700 . . . . Fort Smith
LU 750 . . . . Pine Bluff
LU 807 . . . . Cabot
LU 1516 . . . . Jonesboro
LU 1658 . . . . Pine Bluff
LU 1703 . . . . El Dorado
LU 1758 . . . . Pine Bluff
LU 2022 . . . . Little Rock
LU 2033 . . . . Sheridan
LU 2037 . . . . El Dorado
LU 2219 . . . . Conway
LU 2284 . . . . El Dorado

Elevator Constructors
LU 79 . . . . Little Rock

Federal Employees
LU 1079 . . . . Royal
LU 1669 . . . . Fort Smith
LU 2045 . . . . . North Little Rock

Fire Fighters
LU 99-F . . . . . North Little Rock

Flint Glass Workers
LU 74 . . . . Bond
LU 717 . . . . Van Buren

Food and Commercial Workers
LU 526-T . . . . Little Rock
LU 740-C . . . . Walnut Ridge
LU 2008 . . . . Little Rock

Glass, Molders, Pottery and Plastics Workers
LU 131 . . . . Bono
LU 282 . . . . West Memphis

Government Employees
C 17 Food Inspection Locals,
  Southwest . . . . . . Van Buren
LU 108 . . . . Mountain View
LU 922 . . . . Forrest City
LU 953 DoD . . . . . Pine Bluff
LU 2054 VA . . . North Little Rock
LU 2066 DoD . . . . . Jacksonville
LU 2201 VA . . . . . . Fayetteville
LU 2650 USDA . . . . Booneville
LU 3253 USDA . . . . Bonnerdale
LU 3291 HHS . . . . . Jonesboro

Graphic Communications
LU 502-M . . . . Little Rock
LU 527-M . . . . Jonesboro
LU 630-S . . . . Benton
LU 673-S . . . . Greenland

Iron Workers
LU 321 . . . . Little Rock

Laborers
DC Federal
  Guards . . . . North Little Rock
LU 1282 . . . . Little Rock
LU 1671 . . . . . North Little Rock

Letter Carriers
BR 35 . . . . Denison
BR 240 . . . . Pine Bluff
BR 399 . . . . Fort Smith
BR 543 . . . . Hot Springs
BR 569 . . . . Texarkana
BR 1004 . . . . Fayetteville
BR 1094 Helena, Arkansas . . Helena
BR 1131 . . . . Jonesboro
BR 1293 Paragould,
  Arkansas . . . . Paragould
BR 1334 Eureka Springs,
  Arkansas . . . . . Eureka Springs
BR 1514 . . . . Rogers
BR 1592 . . . . Vilonia
BR 1684 . . . . Batesville
BR 1802 . . . . Warren
BR 1820 . . . . Forrest City
BR 1873 De Queen,
  Arkansas . . . . De Queen
BR 1922 . . . . Blytheville
BR 1946 . . . . Russellville
BR 2277 Harrison,
  Arkansas . . . . Harrison
BR 2353 . . . . Bentonville
BR 2357 Prescott, Arkansas . Prescott
BR 2527 Wynne, Arkansas . Wynne
BR 2642 Marianna,
  Arkansas . . . . Marianna
BR 2733 Harrisburg,
  Arkansas . . . . Harrisburg
BR 2755 Fordyce,
  Arkansas . . . . Fordyce
BR 2756 . . . . Keiser
BR 2959 . . . . Eudora
BR 3191 Piggott, Arkansas . Piggott
BR 3329 Pocahontas,
  Arkansas . . . . Pocahontas
BR 3360 McGehee,
  Arkansas . . . . McGehee
BR 3418 Booneville,
  Arkansas . . . . Booneville
BR 3612 Gurdon, Arkansas . Gurdon
BR 3642 Brinkley,
  Arkansas . . . . Brinkley
BR 3671 . . . . Springdale
BR 3692 Clarksville,
  Arkansas . . . . Clarksville
BR 3693 Ozark, Arkansas . . Ozark
BR 3706 . . . . Benton
BR 3719 . . . . Magnolia
BR 3730 Warren, Arkansas . Warren
BR 3733 Stamps, Arkansas . Stamps
BR 3745 . . . . . North Little Rock
BR 3754 Monticello,
  Arkansas . . . . Monticello
BR 3802 . . . . Nashville
BR 4189 . . . . . . West Memphis
BR 4294 Waldron,
  Arkansas . . . . Waldron
BR 4382 Corning,
  Arkansas . . . . Corning
BR 4726 Lake Village,
  Arkansas . . . . . . Lake Village
BR 4932 Heber Springs,
  Arkansas . . . . . . Heber Springs
BR 5141 . . . . Dumas
BR 5207 Hamburg,
  Arkansas . . . . Hamburg

BR 5217 Dermott,
  Arkansas . . . . Dermott
BR 5383 De Witt, Arkansas . De Witt
BR 5557 . . . . Ashdown
BR 5574 England,
  Arkansas . . . . England
BR 5707 Berryville,
  Arkansas . . . . Berryville
BR 5876 Marked Tree,
  Arkansas . . . . . . Marked Tree
BR 5877 Wilson, Arkansas . Wilson
BR 6069 West Helena,
  Arkansas . . . . . . West Helena
BR 6075 . . . . Mountain Home
BR 6437 Clarendon,
  Arkansas . . . . Clarendon
BR 6467 Smachover,
  Arkansas . . . . Smackover
BR 6478 Earle, Arkansas . . . Earle
BR 6522 Marion, Arkansas . Marion
SA Arkansas . . . . . Hot Springs

Locomotive Engineers
DIV 116 . . . . . Mountain Home
DIV 170 . . . . White Hall
DIV 182 . . . . . North Little Rock
DIV 278 . . . . . . Heber Springs
DIV 496 . . . . Texarkana
DIV 524 . . . . Van Buren
DIV 585 . . . . Sherwood
DIV 858 . . . . Pine Bluff
SLB Arkansas . . . . . . Sherwood

Machinists
CONF South Central
  States . . . . Little Rock
DLG 156 . . . . Little Rock
LG 51 . . . . Pine Bluff
LG 224 . . . . El Dorado
LG 260 . . . . Fort Smith
LG 325 . . . . . North Little Rock
LG 463 Hercules . . . . . . Beebe
LG 502 . . . . Little Rock
LG 911 . . . . Brookland
LG 921 . . . . Little Rock
LG 1093 . . . . Harrison
LG 1362 . . . . Crossett
LG 1775 . . . . Little Rock
LG 1948 . . . . Newport
LG 2091 . . . . El Dorado
LG 2248 . . . . Batesville
LG 2907 . . . . Little Rock
LLG W-15 Woodworkers . De Queen
LLG W-298
  Woodworkers . . North Little Rock
LLG W-332 Woodworkers . . Waldo
LLG W-475 Woodworkers . Crossett
LLG W-484 Woodworkers . Warren
STC Arkansas . . . . . Little Rock

Maintenance of Way Employes
LG 852 . . . . Morrilton
LG 1427 . . . . Cabot
LG 1549 . . . . Pine Bluff
LG 2729 . . . . Oil Trough
SLG 601 . . . . . North Little Rock
SLG 617 . . . . Crossett
SLG 780 . . . . Searcy
SLG 1009 . . . . Cabot
SLG 1127 . . . . Malvern

National Staff Organization
LU Staff Organization,
  Arkansas . . . . Little Rock

Office and Professional Employees
LU 105 . . . . Little Rock
LU 303 . . . . Foreman
LU 420 . . . . White Hall

Operating Engineers
LU 323 . . . . Smackover
LU 381 . . . . El Dorado
LU 382 . . . . Little Rock

Painters
LU 424 . . . . Little Rock

Paper, Allied-Industrial, Chemical Employees
LU 379 . . . . Alexander
LU 1741 . . . . . North Little Rock
LU 05-355 . . . . Camden
LU 05-368 . . . . Kingsland
LU 05-369 . . . . Crossett
LU 05-370 . . . . . Fort Smith
LU 05-434 . . . . . . El Dorado
LU 05-496 . . . . . Fort Smith
LU 05-517 . . . . England
LU 05-577 . . . . . . El Dorado
LU 05-589 . . . . Crossett
LU 05-591 . . . . Magazine
LU 05-606 . . . . . . Greenwood
LU 05-619 . . . . . . Pine Bluff
LU 05-656 . . . . . . Fort Smith
LU 05-735 . . . . . . Grapevine
LU 05-796 . . . . Crossett
LU 05-833 . . . . . . White Hall
LU 05-844 . . . . . . White Hall
LU 05-898 . . . . . . Pine Bluff
LU 05-935 . . . . . . Pine Bluff
LU 05-936 . . . . . . Pine Bluff
LU 05-986 . . . . . . Van Buren
LU 05-1053 . . . . Rogers
LU 05-1253 . . . . . Jacksonville
LU 05-1288 . . . . . Little Rock
LU 05-1327 . . . . . . Ashdown
LU 05-1329 . . . . . . Ashdown
LU 05-1422 . . . . . Little Rock
LU 05-1532 . . . . . . McGehee
LU 05-1533 . . . . Arkansas City
LU 05-1671 Wire Workers. Star City
LU 05-1731 . . . . . Pine Bluff
LU 05-1965 . . . . . Russellville
LU 50-929 . . . . . West Helena

Plumbing and Pipe Fitting
LU 29 . . . . Van Buren
LU 155 . . . . Little Rock
LU 706 . . . . El Dorado
SA Arkansas . . . . . . El Dorado

Postal and Federal Employees
D 9 . . . . Little Rock
LU 907 . . . . Little Rock
LU 909 . . . . Little Rock
LU 913 Texarkana . . . Texarkana

Postal Workers
LU 122 Hot Springs . . . Hot Springs
LU 189 Central Arkansas
  Area . . . . Little Rock
LU 217 Newport . . . . . Newport
LU 532 Arkadelphia . . Arkadelphia
LU 574 Blytheville . . . Blytheville
LU 632 Camden . . . . . . Camden
LU 637 Nashville Local . Nashville
LU 642 Pine Bluff . . . Pine Bluff
LU 660 Batesville . . . . Batesville
LU 667 Fayetteville . . . Fayetteville
LU 1211 Western
  Arkansas . . . . . . Fort Smith
LU 1415 Springdale . . . Springdale
LU 1434 McGehee Local . McGehee
LU 1670 Hope Local . . . . . Hope
LU 1675 Benton . . . . . . Benton
LU 1802 Mena Local . . . . Mena
LU 1843 Jonesboro . . . Jonesboro
LU 2922 Marianna Local . Marianna
LU 2982 Magnolia . . . . Magnolia
LU 3083 Stuttgart Local . . Stuttgart
LU 3187 Heber Springs
  Local . . . . . . Heber Springs
LU 3688 El Dorado . . . El Dorado
LU 3727 Rogers . . . . . Rogers
LU 3728 Bentonville . . Bentonville
LU 3915 Crossett . . . . Crossett
LU 3930 Harrison Area . . . Omaha
LU 4022 Monticello
  Local . . . . Monticello
LU 5008 Mountain
  Home . . . . . . Mountain Home
LU 5817 Jacksonville . . Jacksonville
LU 6003 Osceola Local . . Osceola
SA Arkansas . . . . . . Pine Bluff

Railroad Signalmen
LLG 72 . . . . Jonesboro

Rural Letter Carriers
D 1 . . . . Cherry
D 2 . . . . Alpena
D 3 . . . . Altus
D 4 . . . . Bismarck
D 5 Arkansas Rural Letter Carriers
  Association . . . . Bradford
D 6 . . . . Sheridan
LU 91 Roughriders
  Association . . . . . . Texarkana
SA Arkansas . . . . Batesville

Security, Police and Fire Professionals
LU 726 . . . . Little Rock
LU 730 . . . . Little Rock
LU 737 . . . . Lamar
LU 739 . . . . Pine Bluff

Service Employees
LU 616 Firemen & Oilers . . . Rison
LU 718 Firemen & Oilers . . Benton

Sheet Metal Workers
LU 78 . . . . Conway
LU 428 . . . . Benton

State, County and Municipal Employees
LU 966 Pine Bluff Municipal
  Employees . . . . Atheimer

Steelworkers
LU . . . . Pinebluff
LU 9452 . . . . Fort Smith
LU 12-230-A . . . . Newport
LU 12-558-L . . . . Searcy
LU 12-602-B . . . . . . Malvern
LU 12-607-L . . . . . . Magnolia
LU 12-752-L . . . . . . Texarkana
LU 12-769-L . . . . . . Calion
LU 12-883-L . . . . . Little Rock
LU 12-884-L . . . . . Russellville
LU 12-970-L . . . . . . Delight
LU 12-4880-S . . . . . . Benton
LU 12-5073-S . . . . . . Gurdon
LU 12-5681-S . . . . . . Palestine

LU 12-6357-S . . . . Conway
LU 12-6433-S . . . . Benton
LU 12-6606-S . . . . . Forrest City
LU 12-6794-S . . . . . . Little Rock
LU 12-6904-S . . . . . . Little Rock
LU 12-7366-S . . . . . . Malvern
LU 12-7612-S . . . . . Malvern
LU 12-7893-S . . . . Fort Smith
LU 12-7972-S . . . . . Malvern
LU 12-9285-S . . . . . Monticello
LU 12-9308-S . . . . . Texarkana

Teamsters
JC 88 . . . . Little Rock
LU 373 . . . . Fort Smith
LU 878 . . . . Little Rock

Theatrical Stage Employees
LU 204 . . . . Mabelvale

Transit Union
LDIV 704 . . . . Little Rock

Transportation Communications Union
D 31 Southern Pacific . . . Pine Bluff
D 5512 . . . . Sheridan
LG 288 . . . . Lonoke
LG 6007 Cotton Belt . . . Sheridan
LG 6114 Harmony . . . . . Benton

Transportation Union
GCA GO-569 Missouri Pacific
  Railroad . . . . . North Little Rock
LU 221 . . . . Ward
LU 462 . . . . Pine Bluff
LU 507 . . . . Van Buren
LU 656 . . . . . North Little Rock
LU 950 . . . . Paragould
SLB LO-4 Arkansas . . . Little Rock

Treasury Employees
CH 59 . . . . Little Rock

Weather Service Employees
BR 02-1 . . . . . . North Little Rock

Unaffiliated Labor Organizations
Fordyce and Princeton Railroad
  Employees Union . . . . . . Rison

California

AFL-CIO Trade and Industrial Departments

Building and Construction Trades Department
BCTC Alameda County . . Oakland
BCTC California . . . . Sacramento
BCTC Contra Costa
County . . . . Martinez
BCTC Fresno-Madera-Kings-Tulare
Counties . . . . Fresno
BCTC Humboldt & Del Norte
Counties . . . . Eureka
BCTC Imperial County . . El Centro
BCTC Kern-Inyo & Mono
Counties . . . . Bakersfield
BCTC Los Angeles
County . . . . Los Angeles
BCTC Marin County . . San Rafael
BCTC Mid-Valley . . . . Yuba City
BCTC Napa-Solano
Counties . . . . Fairfield
BCTC Northeastern
California . . . . Redding
BCTC Sacramento-
Sierras . . . . Sacramento
BCTC San Bernardino & Riverside
Counties . . . . Riverside
BCTC San Diego . . . . San Diego
BCTC San Francisco . San Francisco
BCTC San Joaquin County. Stockton
BCTC San Mateo
County . . . . Foster City
BCTC Santa Barbara-San Louis
Obispo Counties . . Santa Barbara
BCTC Santa Clara-San Benito-Santa
Cruz Counties . . . . San Jose
BCTC Santa Cruz & Monterey
Counties . . . . Castroville
BCTC Sonoma & Mendocino
Counties . . . . Santa Rosa
BCTC Stanislaus-Merced-
Tuolumne . . . . Modesto
BCTC Ventura County . . . Oxnard

Maritime Trades Department
PC San Francisco . . . San Francisco
PC Southern California . Wilmington

Metal Trades Department
MTC Bay Cities. . . . . . Oakland
MTC Indian Wells
Valley . . . . Ridgecrest
MTC Pacific Coast . . . . Oakland
MTC Southern California . El Monte

Other Councils and Committees
COM Los Angeles-Orange Counties
Organizing . . . . . Los Angeles

Affiliated Labor Organizations

Aeronautical Examiners
LU 5 . . . . San Diego

Agricultural Employees
BR 23 . . . . . South San Francisco
BR 28 . . . . Los Angeles

Air Traffic Controllers
LU 090 . . . . Oakland
LU APC . . . . Napa
LU BFL . . . . Bakersfield

LU BUR . . . . Burbank
LU CCR . . . . Concord
LU CMA . . . . Camarillo
LU CNO. . . . . Chino
LU CRQ Palomar . . . . . Carlsbad
LU E10. . . Edwards Air Force Base
LU EMT . . . . El Monte
LU Engineers of Western Pacific
Region . . . . . Redondo Beach
LU FAT. . . . . Fresno
LU HWD . . . . Hayward
LU LAX . . . . Los Angeles
LU LGB. . . . . Long Beach
LU LVK . . . . Livermore
LU MCC . . . . Rio Linda
LU MRY . . . . Monterey
LU MYF . . . . San Diego
LU OAK . . . . Oakland
LU ONT . . . . Ontario
LU Palo Alto Tower . . . . Palo Alto
LU POC . . . . La Verne
LU PSP . . . . Palm Springs
LU RDD . . . . Redding
LU RHV . . . . San Jose
LU SAN . . . . San Diego
LU SBA . . . . Goleta
LU SCK . . . . Stockton
LU SCT. . . . . San Diego
LU SDM . . . . San Diego
LU SEE . . . . El Cajon
LU SFO . . . . San Francisco
LU SJC . . . . Santa Clara
LU SMF . . . . Sacramento
LU SMO . . . . Santa Monica
LU SNA . . . . Costa Mesa
LU STS . . . . Santa Rosa
LU TOA . . . . Torrance
LU VNY . . . . Van Nuys
LU ZLA . . . . Palmdale
LU ZOA . . . . Fremont

Aircraft Mechanics
LU 37 . . . . Oakland

Asbestos Workers
CONF Western States . . . . Azusa
LU 5 . . . . Azusa
LU 16. . . . . Alameda

Automobile, Aerospace Workers
C Northern California. . . . Fremont
C Southern California
CAP . . . . Pico Rivera
C 5 Western States . . Pico Rivera
LU 76 Emeryville-San Leandro
Local . . . . Fremont
LU 148 . . . . Lakewood
LU 179 . . . . . North Hollywood
LU 230 . . . . Alta Loma
LU 506 . . . . San Diego
LU 509 . . . . Pico Rivera
LU 805 . . . . Long Beach
LU 887 . . . . Paramount
LU 1519 . . . . Chatsworth
LU 1797 . . . . Visalia
LU 2103. . . . . . . San Francisco
LU 2244. . . . . Fremont
LU 2350 Headquarters Staff
Organization . . . . Sacramento
LU 6645 . . . . La Mirada

Bakery, Confectionery, Tobacco Workers and Grain Millers
C Pacific Coast States . . . Carson
LU 24 . . . . Redwood City

LU 31. . . . . Carson
LU 37. . . . . Commerce
LU 59-G . . . . . . Woodbridge
LU 71-G . . . . Fairfield
LU 83 . . . . Buena Park
LU 85 . . . . Sacramento
LU 102-G . . . . . . San Diego
LU 119 . . . . . . San Leandro
LU 125 . . . . . . San Leandro
LU 315 . . . . San Diego

Boilermakers
LG 6. . . . . Oakland
LG 46-D Cement
Workers . . . . . . Santa Cruz
LG 54-S . . . . Maywood
LG 67-M . . . . Fontana
LG 92 . . . . Bloomington
LG 99-D . . . . Hollister
LG 100-D Cement
Workers . . . . . . San Jose
LG 106-S Stove
Division . . . . . Long Beach
LG 125-S . . . . Huntington Park
LG 128-M. . . . . San Francisco
LG 228-S . . . Huntington Beach
LG 232 . . . . Sylmar
LG 343 . . . . Ventura
LG 344 . . . . Ridgecrest
LG 549 . . . . Pittsburg
LG 583-D Cement
Workers . . . . . . Concord

Bricklayers
LU 3. . . . . Oakland
LU 4 California . . . . . El Monte
LU 18 Tile, Marble &
Terrazzo. . . . . . Diamond Bar
STCON 99 California . . Bakersfield

Carpenters
C . . . . Oakland
C Industrial Coalition . . . . Whittier
CONF 46 Northern California
Counties . . . . Oakland
CONF California
Conference . . . . . . Oakland
CONF Eighth District
Organization & Education
Program . . . . . . Los Angeles
DC Golden Gate-
Lathers . . . . . . Sacramento
DC Los Angeles County
#4008. . . . . . . Los Angeles
LU 22 . . . . San Francisco
LU 25 . . . . Manteca
LU 34 . . . . Oakland
LU 35 . . . . San Rafael
LU 46 . . . . Sacramento
LU 68-L . . . . Oakland
LU 83-L . . . . Fresno
LU 102 . . . . Sacramento
LU 109-L . . . . . . Sacramento
LU 144-L . . . . San Jose
LU 150 . . . . Camarillo
LU 152 . . . . Martinez
LU 180 . . . . Vallejo
LU 209 . . . . Sylmar
LU 217 . . . . Foster City
LU 262 . . . . San Jose
LU 405 . . . . San Jose
LU 409 . . . . Los Angeles
LU 440-L . . . . . . Santa Ana
LU 505. . . . . Aptos
LU 547 . . . . San Diego

LU 605 . . . . Marina
LU 630 . . . . . . Long Beach
LU 701 . . . . Fresno
LU 713 . . . . Hayward
LU 721 . . . . Whittier
LU 743 . . . . Bakersfield
LU 751 . . . . Santa Rosa
LU 803 . . . . Orange
LU 944 . . . . . San Bernardino
LU 1062. . . . . Santa Barbara
LU 1109 . . . . Visalia
LU 1240 . . . . Chico
LU 1496 . . . . Fresno
LU 1506 . . . . . Los Angeles
LU 1553 . . . . . . Hawthorne
LU 1599 . . . . Redding
LU 1607 . . . . . Los Angeles
LU 1618 . . . . . Sacramento
LU 1789 . . . South Lake Tahoe
LU 1800 . . . . Arroyo Grande
LU 1861 . . . . . Foster City
LU 2007 . . . . Orange
LU 2035 . . . . . Kings Beach
LU 2236. . . . . . . Oakland
LU 2361 . . . . Orange
LU 2375 . . . . . Wilmington
LU 2652 . . . . . . Standard
LU 2687 . . . . . Marysville
LU 2728 . . . . Sutter Creek
LU 2749 . . . . Camind
LU 2927 . . . . . Suttercreek
LU 3074 . . . . . . Chester
LU 3088 . . . . . . Stockton

Christian Labor Association
LU 17 Dairy Employees
Union . . . . Chino
LU 25 Poultry Workers
Union . . . . Chino

Civilian Technicians
CH 105 Channel Islands . . . Oxnard
CH 109 Moffett
Air . . . Moffett Federal Airfield
CH 118 Fresno Grizzlies . . . Fresno

Communications Workers
C Coastal Valley . . . . Bakersfield
C Northern California-
Nevada. . . . . . . Foster City
C Southern California . . . Pasadena
LU 262-FW . . . . . San Leandro
LU 1111 . . . . Anaheim
LU 1201 . . . . San Jose
LU 9000 . . . . . . Los Angeles
LU 9400 . . . . . . Paramount
LU 9404 . . . . . . San Rafael
LU 9407 . . . . Merced
LU 9408 . . . . Fresno
LU 9410. . . . . . San Francisco
LU 9412 . . . . . . Hayward
LU 9414 . . . . Chico
LU 9415 . . . . . . Oakland
LU 9416 . . . . . . Bakersfield
LU 9417 . . . . . . Stockton
LU 9418 . . . . . . Modesto
LU 9419 . . . . . . Redding
LU 9421 . . . . . Sacramento
LU 9423 . . . . . . San Jose
LU 9426 . . . . . . Marina
LU 9430 . . . . . Foster City
LU 9431 . . . . . . Auburn
LU 9432 . . . . . . Camino
LU 9477 . . . . Taft
LU 9490 . . . . . . Salinas

LU 9503 . . . . . North Hollywood
LU 9504 . . . . Ventura
LU 9505 . . . . Pasadena
LU 9509 . . . . San Diego
LU 9510 . . . . Orange
LU 9511 . . . . Escondido
LU 9573 . . . . . San Bernardino
LU 9575 . . . . Camarillo
LU 9576 . . . . Santa Ynez
LU 9583 . . . . Rancho Cordova
LU 9586 . . . . Norwalk
LU 9587 . . . . . San Fernando
LU 9588 . . . . Colton
LU 9590 . . . . Riverside
LU 14900 . . . . . . Bakersfield
LU 14903 . . . . Chico
LU 14904 . . . . . . Long Beach
LU 14908 . . . . Lodi
LU 14910 . . . . Salinas
LU 14916 . . . . Santa Cruz
LU 39052 San Francisco-
Oakland . . . . . . San Francisco
LU 39095 . . . . San Diego
LU 39098 . . . . San Jose
LU 39202 . . . . . . Bakersfield
LU 59051 . . . . San Francisco
LU 59053 NABET Local
53 . . . . Burbank
LU 59054 . . . . . Chula Vista
LU 59057 NABET Local
57 . . . . Burbank
LU 89511 . . . . Bell Gardens
LU 89850 . . . . Ontario

Directors Guild
NHQ . . . . Los Angeles

Electrical Workers
LU. . . . . Romoland
LU 6 . . . . San Francisco
LU 11 . . . . Pasadena
LU 40 . . . . North Hollywood
LU 45 . . . . Hollywood
LU 47 . . . . . . Diamond Bar
LU 100 . . . . Fresno
LU 180 . . . . Napa
LU 234 . . . . Castroville
LU 302 . . . . Martinez
LU 332 . . . . San Jose
LU 340 . . . . . . Sacramento
LU 360 . . . . Berkeley
LU 413 . . . . Buellton
LU 428 . . . . Bakersfield
LU 440 . . . . Riverside
LU 441 . . . . Orange
LU 465 . . . . San Diego
LU 477 . . . . San Bernardino
LU 543 . . . . Victorville
LU 551 . . . . . . Santa Rosa
LU 569 . . . . San Diego
LU 595 . . . . Dublin
LU 617 . . . . San Mateo
LU 639 . . . . San Luis Obispo
LU 684 . . . . Modesto
LU 800 . . . . Roseville
LU 889 . . . . . Redondo Beach
LU 946 . . . . Yucaipa
LU 952 . . . . Ventura
LU 1011 . . . . . Grover Beach
LU 1023 . . . . Victorville
LU 1245 . . . . . Walnut Creek
LU 1269 . . . . . San Francisco
LU 1682 . . . . Roseville
LU 1710 . . . . El Monte
LU 2016 . . . . . Suisun City
LU 2131 . . . . Antioch
LU 2139 . . . . Santa Ana
LU 2295 . . . . El Monte

LU 2343 . . . . Colusa

Electrical, Radio and Machine Workers
DC 10 . . . . Quartz Hill
LU . . . . Valencia
LU 99 . . . . . . Sacramento
LU 1009 . . . . Anaheim
LU 1010 . . . . Ontario
LU 1014 . . . . Parlier
LU 1412 . . . . . Walnut Creek
LU 1421 . . . . Compton
LU 1422 . . . . Norwalk

Elevator Constructors
LU 8 . . . . San Francisco
LU 18 . . . . Pasadena

Farm Workers
NHQ . . . . Keene

Federal Employees
C Forest Service . . . Mount Shasta
LU 1 . . . . . . San Francisco
LU 119 Sherman Indian High
School . . . . Riverside
LU 721 . . . . Strathmore
LU 777 . . . . . . Los Angeles
LU 919 . . . . . Camp Pendleton
LU 951 . . . . . . Sacramento
LU 1001 . . . . Vandenberg Air
Force Base
LU 1263 . . . . Monterey
LU 1450 . . . . San Francisco
LU 1558 . . . . Mentone
LU 1650 . . . . . . La Canada
LU 1690 . . . . Monterey
LU 1771 . . . . Platina
LU 1781 . . . . . . Placerville
LU 1836 . . . . Alturas
LU 1865 . . . . Yreka
LU 1891 . . . Point Reyes Station
LU 1937 . . . . Eureka
LU 1979 . . . . . . San Dimas
LU 1981 . . . . Vallejo
LU 1995 . . . . Quincy
LU 2023 . . . . . Santa Maria
LU 2035 . . . . Barstow
LU 2066 . . . . . . Placerville
LU 2080 . . . . . . Santa Rosa
LU 2081 . . . . Bishop
LU 2090 . . . . . . Sunnyvale
LU 2091 . . . . . Crescent City
LU 2096 . . . . San Diego
LU 2135 . . . . . . Upper Lake
LU 2152 . . . . Moreno Valley
LU 2153 . . . . Susanville
LU 2163 California National
Guard . . . . . . Atascadero
SFED California . . . . . Lompoc

Fire Fighters
LU . . . . San Diego
LU 25-I . . . . Lancaster
LU 33-F . . . . San Diego
LU 53-F . . Edwards Air Force Base
LU 85-F Camp Pendleton
Local . . . . Fallbrook
LU 102-F . . . . Lemoore
LU 116-F . . . . . Santa Maria
LU 166-F . . . . . . Monterey

Flint Glass Workers
LU 18 . . . . Hughson
LU 19 . . . . Chowchilla
LU 139 . . . . San Dimas
LU 705 . . . . Chino

Food and Commercial Workers
C United Sugar Workers of
California . . . . Fresno
LU 1-C . . . . Norwalk
LU 25-C . . . . Martinez
LU 30-I . . . . Antioch
LU 45-D . . . . Fresno
LU 47-C . . . . . . Bakersfield
LU 58-C . . . . La Verne
LU 75 Textile Workers . Sacramento
LU 78-C . . . . La Verne
LU 97-C . . . . . . Tranquility
LU 101 . . . . South San Francisco
LU 120 . . . . Oakland
LU 135 . . . . San Diego
LU 146-C . . . . Lompoc
LU 151-D . . . . Glendale
LU 174-D . . . . Brawley
LU 179-D . . . . . . Woodland
LU 181-D . . . . Lathrop
LU 186-D . . . . Modesto
LU 188-D . . . . Fresno
LU 193-I . . . . Fresno
LU 194-I . . . . . . Santa Cruz
LU 294-C . . . . Milpitas
LU 324 . . . . Buena Park
LU 350-C . . . . . . Pico Rivera
LU 373-R . . . . Vallejo
LU 428 . . . . San Jose
LU 588-R . . . . Roseville
LU 648 . . . . . . San Francisco
LU 770 . . . . . . Los Angeles
LU 839 . . . . Salinas
LU 870 . . . . Hayward
LU 995-C . . . . . Buena Park
LU 1036 . . . . Camarillo
LU 1096 . . . . Salinas
LU 1167 . . . . . Bloomington
LU 1179 . . . . Martinez
LU 1288 . . . . Fresno
LU 1428 . . . . . . Claremont
LU 1442 . . . . . Santa Monica
RC 8 . . . . Buena Park

Glass, Molders, Pottery and Plastics Workers
LU 2 . . . . Livermore
LU 17 . . . . Modesto
LU 19 . . . . . . Los Angeles
LU 39 . . . . Rosemead
LU 47 . . . . Canyon Country
LU 52 . . . . San Jose
LU 81 . . . . Orange
LU 137 . . . . Maywood
LU 141 . . . . San Pablo
LU 142 . . . . Martinez
LU 164-B . . . . Oakland
LU 167 . . . . Fremont
LU 177 . . . . Lathrop
LU 254 . . . . Madera
LU 279 . . . . Jackson
LU 307-A . . . . Covina
LU 354-A . . . . Carson
LU 374-B . . . . . Long Beach

Government Employees
C 5 Northern California . . Richmond
C 31 Western Food Inspection
Locals . . . . Castro Valley
C 109 National SS Payment Center
Locals . . . . Oakland
C 147 Regional SS Field Operations
Locals . . . . Fresno
C 236 National GSA
Locals . . . . Stockton
C 263 VA 12th District . Seal Beach
LU . . . . Atwater
LU 51 DoD . . . . . San Francisco

LU 52 Independent . . . . Fremont
LU 63 . . . . Imperial Beach
LU 490 VA . . . Los Angeles
LU 505 DoT . . . . Los Angeles
LU 511 . . . . . . Chatsworth
LU 926 USDA . . . . . Cypress
LU 988 USDA . . . . . Tracy
LU 1061 VA . . . Los Angeles
LU 1122 HHS . . . . Richmond
LU 1157 DoD . . . . . Oakland
LU 1159 VA . . . . . Oakland
LU 1200 . . . . Laguna Niguel
LU 1202 . . . . San Francisco
LU 1203 VAMC . . . . Seal Beach
LU 1206 Department of Veterans
Affairs . . . . Oakland
LU 1216 . . . . . San Francisco
LU 1227 Defense Finance &
Accounting
Services . . . San Bernardino
LU 1233 . . . . . San Francisco
LU 1399 DoD . . . . . Coronado
LU 1406 . . Edwards Air Force Base
LU 1482 DoD . . . . . Barstow
LU 1533 DoD . . . . . Oakland
LU 1546 DoD . . . . . Stockton
LU 1613 DoJ . . . . . San Diego
LU 1616 DoJ . . . . Bakersfield
LU 1620 VA . . . . Livermore
LU 1657 USDA . . . . Albany
LU 1680 DoJ . . Terminal Island
LU 1697 VA . . . . North Hills
LU 1764
DoD . . . Travis Air Force Base
LU 1808 DoD . . . . . Herlong
LU 1857 DoD . . . North Highlands
LU 1881 DoD . . . . . San Diego
LU 1918 USDA . . . . El Cajon
LU 2003 SSA . . . . . Salinas
LU 2018 DoD . . Twentynine Palms
LU 2025 DoD . Beale Air Force Base
LU 2029 DoD . . . . . Stockton
LU 2060 . . . . . Canoga Park
LU 2110 VA . . . . Palo Alto
LU 2111 DoD . . . . . Lemoore
LU 2136 DoD . . . . San Diego
LU 2161 DoD . . . . . Seal Beach
LU 2275 GSA . . . San Francisco
LU 2297 VA . . . Los Angeles
LU 2391 DoL . . . San Francisco
LU 2403 HUD . . . Long Beach
LU 2429 DoD . . . . Hawthorne
LU 2433 DoD . . Hacienda Heights
LU 2452 HHS . . . . Lynwood
LU 2554 DoJ . . . . El Centro
LU 2654 VA . . . . . Fresno
LU 2723 DoD . . . . . Elverta
LU 2730 DoJ . . . . Bakersfield
LU 2776
DoD . . . March Air Force Base
LU 2805 DoJ . . . . San Diego
LU 2879 HHS . . . National City
LU 2947 GSA . . . . . Carson
LU 3048 DoJ . . . . . Lompoc
LU 3172 HHS . . . . Sacramento
LU 3584 DoJ . . . . . Dublin
LU 3619 DoJ . . . . San Diego
LU 3723 DoD . . . . . San Diego
LU 3854 ID . March Air Force Base
LU 3899 DoE . . . San Francisco
LU 3943 VA, Hospitals Professional
Unit . . . . Los Angeles
LU 3969 . . . . Adelanto
LU 4038 BOP, MDC, Los
Angeles . . . . . . Los Angeles
LU 4048 BOP, FPC,
Lompoc . . . . Lompoc

Government Employees Association

LU 69 . . . . Oakland
LU 186 . . . . San Diego
LU 337 Police Officers . . Ridgecrest
LU 12-28 . . . . . . Port Hueneme
LU 12-29 . . . . . . Port Hueneme
LU 12-33 . . . . . . Port Hueneme
LU 12-35 . . . . . . National City
LU 12-40 . . . . . Port Hueneme
LU 12-44 . . . . . . Long Beach
LU 12-120 . . . . North Highlands
LU 12-188 Army Air Techician
  Union . . . . Los Alamitos
LU 12-196 Federal Union of
  Scientists & Engineers . . Oxnard
LU 12-198 Federal Union
  of Scientists &
  Engineers. . . . . . Port Hueneme
LU 12-200 EMT's and
  Paramedics . . . . Eureka
LU R-12-90 Fort Hunter Liggett
  Labor Union . . . . Jolon

Government Security Officers

LU 52 . . . . San Diego
LU 57 . . . . Sacramento
LU 64 . . . . San Diego
LU 74 . . . . Tustin

Graphic Communications

DC 2 Southern California Printing
  Specialists . . . . Fullerton
LU 4-N . . . . San Francisco
LU 24-H . . . . . . San Francisco
LU 28-N . . . . Fullerton
LU 388-M . . . . Fullerton
LU 404-M. . . . . Monrovia
LU 432-M. . . . . . . San Diego
LU 468-S . . . . . . San Francisco
LU 583 . . . . San Francisco
LU 625-S . . . . Fullerton

Hotel and Restaurant Employees

LU 2. . . . . San Francisco
LU 11 . . . . Los Angeles
LU 19 . . . . San Jose
LU 30 . . . . San Diego
LU 49 . . . . Sacramento
LU 309. . . . . . . Palm Springs
LU 340 . . . . Burlingame
LU 483 . . . . . . Pacific Grove
LU 535 . . . . . . San Bernardino
LU 681 . . . . Anaheim
LU 2850. . . . . Oakland
STC California . . . . Sacramento

Iron Workers

DC California & Vicinity . . . Pinole
LU 118 . . . . Sacramento
LU 155 . . . . Fresno
LU 229 . . . . San Diego
LU 377 . . . . . . San Francisco
LU 378. . . . . Benicia
LU 416 . . . . Norwalk
LU 433 . . . . Los Angeles
LU 509 . . . . Los Angeles
LU 624 . . . . Fresno
LU 627 . . . . San Diego
LU 790 . . . . Oakland
LU 844 Shoremen's Local . . Pinole

Laborers

DC Northern California . Suisun City
DC San Francisco Region Public
  Employees . . . . . . Sacramento
DC Southern California . . El Monte
LU 36 . . . . Daly City

LU 67 . . . . Oakland
LU 73. . . . . Stockton
LU 89. . . . . San Diego
LU 139 . . . . Santa Rosa
LU 166 . . . . Oakland
LU 185 . . . . Sacramento
LU 220. . . . . Bakersfield
LU 261 . . . . San Francisco
LU 270 . . . . San Jose
LU 291 . . . . San Rafael
LU 294 . . . . Fresno
LU 297 . . . . Salinas
LU 300 . . . . Los Angeles
LU 304 . . . . Hayward
LU 324 . . . . Martinez
LU 326 . . . . Vallejo
LU 345 . . . . Burbank
LU 389 . . . . San Mateo
LU 402 . . . . Nipomo
LU 507 . . . . Lakewood
LU 550 San Joaquin Valley Packing
  & Miscellaneous . . . . Parlier
LU 585 . . . . Ventura
LU 591 . . . . Santa Barbara
LU 652 . . . . Santa Ana
LU 724 . . . . Hollywood
LU 783 . . . . . . San Bernardino
LU 792 United Public Employees of
  California . . . . Redding
LU 802 . . . . Wilmington
LU 882 . . . . Pomona
LU 886 . . . . Oakland
LU 1082 . . . . El Monte
LU 1130 . . . . Modesto
LU 1141 National Parks & Public
  Employees . . . . San Francisco
LU 1184 . . . . Riverside

Laundry and Dry Cleaning

LU 3 . . . . San Leandro
LU 52 . . . . Los Angeles

Letter Carriers

BR 24. . . . . Los Angeles
BR 52 Central California
  Coast. . . . . . San Luis Obispo
BR 70 . . . . San Diego
BR 133 . . . . . . North Highlands
BR 183 Northcoast. . . . Santa Rosa
BR 193 . . . . San Jose
BR 213 . . . . Stockton
BR 214 . . . . San Francisco
BR 231 . . . . Fresno
BR 269 . . . . Castroville
BR 290 . . . . Goleta
BR 348 . . . . Eureka
BR 411 . . . . San Bernardino
BR 627 . . . . Napa
BR 737 . . . . Santa Ana
BR 782. . . . . Bakersfield
BR 857 . . . . Watsonville
BR 866 . . . . Visalia
BR 1100. . . . . Santa Ana
BR 1111. . . . . Richmond
BR 1184 . . . . Pacific Grove
BR 1280 . . . . Burlingame
BR 1291 . . . . Modesto
BR 1310 . . . . Monterey
BR 1340 . . . . Merced
BR 1427 . . . . . . Mountain View
BR 1432. . . . . Lodi
BR 1439 . . . . Ontario
BR 1465 Coalinga,
  California . . . . Coalinga
BR 1469 . . . . Porterville
BR 1563 . . . . Ukiah
BR 1650 . . . . Culver City
BR 1707 . . . . Hayward

BR 1726 . . . . El Centro
BR 1742 . . . . Turlock
BR 1810 . . . . Tulare
BR 2009 Corning,
  California . . . . Corning
BR 2086 . . . . Burbank
BR 2152 Exeter, California . . Exeter
BR 2168 . . . . Upland
BR 2200 . . . . Pasadena
BR 2207 . . . . Torrance
BR 2293 . . . . Beverly Hills
BR 2462 . . . . Van Nuys
BR 2472 Willows,
  California. . . . . . . Willows
BR 2525 . . . . Escondido
BR 2605 . . . . El Centro
BR 2608. . . . . Susanville
BR 2614 . . . . Hawthorne
BR 2704. . . . . Brawley
BR 2757 Dunsmuir,
  California . . . . Dunsmuir
BR 2854 . . . . Tracy
BR 2901 . . . . Hemet
BR 2902 . . . . Chatsworth
BR 3060 . . . . Auburn
BR 3217 . . . . Crescent City
BR 3223 Yreka, California . . Yreka
BR 3275 . . . . Lemoore
BR 3347 . . . . La Mesa
BR 3656 . . . . Fort Bragg
BR 3768 . . . . Los Banos
BR 3982 . . . . Rialto
BR 4006 . . . . Canoga Park
BR 4114 . . . . Camarillo
BR 4149 . . . . Palm Springs
BR 4249 . . . . Manteca
BR 4430 . . . . Lancaster
BR 4494 . . . . Carmichael
BR 4625 Sonora, California . Sonora
BR 4724 . . . . . Rancho Cordova
BR 4735 Ripon, California . . Ripon
BR 4748 Atwater,
  California . . . . Atwater
BR 4850 . . . . Modesto
BR 4868 . . . . Oakdale
BR 4899 Cambria,
  California . . . . Cambria
BR 4941 . . . . . Santa Fe Springs
BR 5190 Cloverdale,
  California . . . . . . Cloverdale
BR 5502 Rio Vista,
  California . . . . . . Rio Vista
BR 5576 Gustine,
  California . . . . Gustine
BR 5583 Corcoran,
  California . . . . . . Corcoran
BR 6201 Bishop, California . Bishop
BR 6242 Firebaugh,
  California . . . . . . Firebaugh
BR 6264 Brisbane,
  California . . . . Brisbane
BR 6354 Orange Cove,
  California . . . . . Orange Cove
BR 6385 Marina . . . . . Marina
BR 6416 Farmersville,
  California . . . . . Farmersville
BR 6446 Newman,
  California . . . . Newman
BR 6458 Mount Shasta,
  California . . . . . Mount Shasta
BR 6550 Idyllwild,
  California . . . . . . Winchester
BR 6667 Alturas, California . Alturas
SA California . . . . . Sacramento

Locomotive Engineers

DIV 5 . . . . Long Beach
DIV 20 . . . . Lakewood

DIV 56 . . . . Yucaipa
DIV 65 San Jose . . . . Brisbane
DIV 126 . . . . Bakersfield
DIV 144 . . . . Berkeley
DIV 214 . . . . Long Beach
DIV 283 . . . . Brentwood
DIV 383 . . . . Needles
DIV 398. . . . . Colton
DIV 415 . . . . Roseville
DIV 425 . . . . Dunsmuir
DIV 553. . . . . Clovis
DIV 660 . . . . Cerritos
DIV 662 . . . . Palmdale
DIV 664 . . . . Atascadero
DIV 692 . . . . Rocklin
DIV 739 . . . . Bakersfield
DIV 839 . . . . Stockton

Longshore and Warehouse

DC Coast Pro Rata
  Committee . . . . . San Francisco
DC Northern
  California. . . . . . San Francisco
DC Southern
  California. . . . . . Los Angeles
LU 6. . . . . Oakland
LU 10 . . . . San Francisco
LU 13 . . . . Wilmington
LU 14 . . . . Eureka
LU 17 . . . . . West Sacramento
LU 18 . . . . . West Sacramento
LU 20-A. . . . . . . Wilmington
LU 26 . . . . Los Angeles
LU 29 . . . . National City
LU 30 Mine Mineral & Processing
  Workers. . . . . Boron
LU 34 . . . . San Francisco
LU 46 . . . . Port Hueneme
LU 54. . . . . Stockton
LU 56 Ship Scalers &
  Painters . . . . San Pedro
LU 63 . . . . San Pedro
LU 63 Marine Clerks
  Association . . . . . Long Beach
LU 75 . . . . San Francisco
LU 91 . . . . Oakland
LU 94 . . . . San Pedro
NHQ . . . . San Francisco

Machinists

DLG 93 . . . . San Jose
DLG 141. . . . . Redwood
DLG 190 . . . . Oakland
DLG 725 . . . . Huntington Beach
DLG 947 . . . . Long Beach
LG 25 . . . . Ontario
LG 102 . . . . Long Beach
LG 201 Newspaper
  Lodge. . . . . . . Los Angeles
LG 286 . . . . Elverta
LG 311 . . . . Bell
LG 389 . . . . San Diego
LG 504 . . . . San Jose
LG 536 . . . . Rocklin
LG 547 . . . . San Jose
LG 565 . . . . San Jose
LG 575 . . . . Ontario
LG 620 . . . . Los Angeles
LG 653 . . . . Fresno
LG 706 . . . . Barstow
LG 720-E. . . . . Huntington Beach
LG 720-G. . . . . El Monte
LG 720-J. . . . . Huntington Beach
LG 726 . . . . San Diego
LG 727-N. . . . . Palmdale
LG 727-P. . . . . Palmdale
LG 755 . . . . Chula Vista
LG 801 . . . . Oakland

LG 812 Security
Lodge . . . . . Rancho Cordova
LG 821 . . . . Ontario
LG 906 . . . . Anaheim
LG 946 . . . . . . Rancho Cordova
LG 964 . . . . Riverside
LG 1101 . . . . San Jose
LG 1125 . . . . San Diego
LG 1173 . . . . Concord
LG 1186 . . . . El Monte
LG 1209 . . . . Roseville
LG 1414 . . . . San Mateo
LG 1484 . . . . Wilmington
LG 1528 . . . . Modesto
LG 1546 . . . . Oakland
LG 1584 . . . . Oakland
LG 1596 . . . . Petaluma
LG 1781 . . . . Burlingame
LG 1782 . . . . . . San Francisco
LG 1824 . . . . San Jose
LG 1910 . . . . . . City of Industry
LG 1932 Los Angeles Air
Transport . . . . Hawthorne
LG 1980 . . . . Ontario
LG 2023 . . . . Hawthorne
LG 2024 . . . . Westminster
LG 2182 . . . . Sacramento
LG 2225 . . . . Sunnyvale
LG 2226 . . . . Sunnyvale
LG 2227 . . . . Sunnyvale
LG 2228 . . . . Sunnyvale
LG 2230 . . . . Felton
LG 2231 . . . . Sunnyvale
LG 2765 . . . . San Diego
LG 2785 . . . . Hawthorne
LG 2786 . . . . Santa Maria
LLG W-98 Woodworkers . . Arcata
LLG W-469
Woodworkers . . . . . Fort Bragg
STC California . . . . Sacramento

Maintenance of Way Employes
FED Pacific . . . . . . Sacramento
LG 875 . . . . Norwalk
LG 914 . . . . Dunsmuir
LG 922 . . . . Roseville
LG 1246 . . . . Storrie
LG 1834 . . . . San Jose
LG 2418 . . . . Los Angeles
SLG 134 . . . . Fontana
SLG 407 . . . . Suisun City
SLG 621 . . . . Cawesville
SLG 1002 . . . . Mineral
SLG 1096 . . . . Visalia
SLG 1196 . . . . Dunsmuir
SLG 2419 . . . . Clovis

Marine Engineers
ASSN Engineers & Scientists of
California . . . . Oakland

Musicians
CONF California
Conference . . . . . San Francisco
CONF Western . . . . San Francisco
LU 6 . . . . San Francisco
LU 7 . . . . Santa Ana
LU 12 . . . . Sacramento
LU 47 . . . . Los Angeles
LU 153 . . . . San Jose
LU 189 . . . . Stockton
LU 292 . . . . Santa Rosa
LU 308 . . . . Santa Barbara
LU 325 . . . . San Diego
LU 353 . . . . Long Beach
LU 367 . . . . Vallejo
LU 424 . . . . Pinole
LU 581 . . . . Ventura

National Staff Organization
LU Staff Organization of California
Professionals . . . . . . Anaheim
LU Staff Union, California Higher
Education . . . . . . Los Angeles

Needletrades
JB Western Joint
Board . . . . Los Angeles
JB Western Regional . . . San Diego
LU 8 . . . . Los Angeles
LU 14-T . . . . San Diego
LU 14-Y . . . . San Diego
LU 44 . . . . Los Angeles
LU 55-D . . . . San Diego
LU 71-JT . . . . San Diego
LU 74-JT . . . . San Diego
LU 99-A . . . . San Diego
LU 101 . . . . Los Angeles
LU 107 . . . . San Diego
LU 188-T . . . . San Diego
LU 213-I . . . . Los Angeles
LU 214 . . . . Los Angeles
LU 215-I . . . . Los Angeles
LU 277 . . . . Los Angeles
LU 288 . . . . San Diego
LU 289 . . . . Los Angeles
LU 294 . . . . Los Angeles
LU 311 . . . . Los Angeles
LU 482-I . . . . . . Los Angeles
LU 512-I . . . . . . Los Angeles
LU 711 . . . . San Diego
LU 818-A . . . . San Diego
LU 1007 . . . . San Diego
LU 1089 . . . . San Diego
LU 1108-T . . . . San Diego
LU 1291 . . . . San Diego

NLRB Professional Association
LU 20 . . . . San Francisco
LU 21 . . . . Los Angeles
LU 31 . . . . Los Angeles
LU 32 . . . . Oakland

Nurses
SA California Nurses
Association . . . . Oakland

Nurses Associations of California
LU . . . . Pomona
LU . . . . Pomona
LU Balboa Registered Nurses
Association . . . . Pomona
LU Garden Grove Registered Nurses
Association . . . . Pomona
LU Kaiser San Gabriel
Valley . . . . Pomona
LU Kaiser Sunset Registered Nurses
Association . . . . Pomona
LU Kpasco . . . . Pomona
LU Registered Nurses Association
Kaiser Bellflower . . . . Pomona
LU Registered Nurses Association
Kaiser Fontana . . . . . Pomona
LU Registered Nurses Association
Kaiser San Diego . . . . Pomona
LU Registered Nurses Association
Kaiser West Los Angeles . Pomona
LU Registered Nurses Association St.
Francis . . . . Pomona
LU 31-14 Registered Nurses
Association Kaiser Woodland
Hills . . . . Pomona
LU 31-23 Kaiser Panorama Register
Nurses Association . . . . Pomona
LU 31-24 Kaiser Harbor County
Register Nurses . . . . . Pomona

LU 31-27 Pettis Memorial Registered
Nurses . . . . Pomona
LU 31-32 Kaiser Riverside
Registered Nurses . . . . Pomona
LU 31-36 Bear Valley . . . Pomona
LU 31-39 Kaiser Orange County
Professional Association . Pomona
NHQ . . . . Pomona

Office and Professional Employees
LU 3 . . . . Daly City
LU 29 . . . . Oakland
LU 30 . . . . Ontario
LU 62 . . . . Walnut
LU 140 . . . . Burbank
LU 174 . . . . Burbank
LU 472 . . . . Tarzana
LU 537 . . . . Monrovia

Operating Engineers
CONF California-
Nevada . . . . Sacramento
CONF Western . . . . Sacramento
LU 3 . . . . Alameda
LU 12 . . . . Pasadena
LU 39 . . . . San Francisco
LU 82 . . . . Lemon Grove
LU 501 . . . . Los Angeles

Painters
CONF Fourth District
Western . . . . Sacramento
DC 16 . . . . Livermore
DC 36 . . . . Pasadena
LU 3 . . . . Oakland
LU 4 . . . . San Francisco
LU 12 Carpet, Linoleum, Soft Tile
Workers . . . . San Jose
LU 52 . . . . Bakersfield
LU 83 . . . . San Rafael
LU 95 . . . . Downey
LU 169 . . . . Oakland
LU 256 . . . . Buena Park
LU 272 . . . . Castroville
LU 294 . . . . Fresno
LU 333 . . . . San Diego
LU 376 . . . . Vallejo
LU 487 . . . . Sacramento
LU 507 . . . . San Jose
LU 510 . . . . San Francisco
LU 636 . . . . Pasadena
LU 718 . . . . San Francisco
LU 741 . . . . Martinez
LU 767 . . . . Sacramento
LU 775 . . . . San Bernardino
LU 831 . . . . . . City of Commerce
LU 913 . . . . Redwood City
LU 1034 . . . . Dublin
LU 1053 . . . . Oakland
LU 1176 . . . . Oakland
LU 1237 . . . . Sacramento
LU 1247 . . . . Whittier
LU 1399 . . . . San Diego
LU 1595 . . . . Pasadena
LU 1621 . . . . San Jose
LU 1798 . . . . Pasadena
LU 2345 . . . . Inglewood

**Paper, Allied-Industrial, Chemical
Employees**
C Tosco Nationwide . Arroyo Grande
DC 1 . . . . Bakersfield
DC 3 . . . . Oak Hills
LU 8-326 . . . . Rodeo
LU 08-5 . . . . Martinez
LU 08-6 . . . . Taft
LU 08-49 . . . . Victorville
LU 08-52 . . . . Mojave

LU 08-192 . . . . Ore Grande
LU 08-208 . . . . Downey
LU 08-219 Kern River Coalinga
Avenal . . . . Bakersfield
LU 08-307 . . . . Bell
LU 08-329 . . . . Pittsburg
LU 08-427 . . . . . . Palo Cedro
LU 08-471 . . . . Bakersfield
LU 08-519 . . . . Oak Hills
LU 08-534 . . . . . Arroyo Grande
LU 08-535 . . . . Newberry Springs
LU 08-675 . . . . Carson
LU 08-682 . . . . Oxnard
LU 08-810 . . . . Riverside
LU 08-819 . . . . . . Sacramento
LU 08-846 . . . . Seal Beach
LU 08-854 . . . . Turlock
LU 08-961 . . . . La Habra
LU 08-976 . . . . Fillmore
LU 08-1876 . . . . . . Red Bluff
LU 08-1979 . . . . Upland
LU 08-7601 . . . . . . La Puente
LU 30-89 . . . . Colton

Petroleum and Industrial Workers
LCH 6 . . . . Paramount
LCH 9 . . . . Paramount
LCH 22 . . . . Richmond
LCH 25 . . . . Paramount
LU 12 . . . . Paramount
LU 13 . . . . Paramount
LU 34 . . . . Paramount
LU 35 . . . . Paramount
LU 36 . . . . Paramount
NHQ . . . . Paramount

Plasterers and Cement Masons
DC Northern
California . . . . . San Francisco
DC Southern California . . Santa Ana
LU 66 . . . . San Francisco
LU 200 . . . . Pomona
LU 300 . . . . San Mateo
LU 400 . . . . Sacramento
LU 500 . . . . Santa Ana
LU 600 . . . . Bell Gardens
LU 755 . . . . Sherman Oaks
STCON California . . . . San Mateo

Plumbing and Pipe Fitting
C California State Pipe
Trades . . . . Sacramento
DC 16 . . . . Los Angeles
DC 36 Pipe Trades . . . . Fresno
LU 38 . . . . San Francisco
LU 62 . . . . Castroville
LU 78 . . . . Los Angeles
LU 114 . . . . Buellton
LU 159 . . . . Martinez
LU 228 . . . . Yuba City
LU 230 Labor Hall
Association . . . . . . San Diego
LU 246 . . . . Fresno
LU 250 . . . . Gardena
LU 342 . . . . Concord
LU 343 . . . . Vallejo
LU 345 . . . . Monrovia
LU 355 . . . . Vallejo
LU 393 . . . . San Jose
LU 398 . . . . Montclair
LU 442 . . . . Stockton
LU 447 . . . . Sacramento
LU 460 . . . . . . San Luis Obispo
LU 467 . . . . Burlingame
LU 483 . . . . Hayward
LU 484 . . . . Ventura
LU 494 . . . . Long Beach
LU 582 . . . . Santa Ana

LU 709 . . . . Whittier
LU 761 . . . . Burbank

Police
LU 2 U.S.P.S.. . . . . Los Angeles

Postal and Federal Employees
D 10 . . . . Culver City
LU 1002 . . . . Culver City
LU 1003 . . . . Los Angeles
LU 1004. . . . . Oakland
LU 1008 . . . . Culver City
LU 1014. . . . . Rialto
LU 1016 Glendale (Foothills)
 Local . . . . Verdugo

Postal Mail Handlers
LU 302 . . . . San Francisco
LU 303 . . . . Los Angeles

Postal Workers
LU 2 San Francisco. . San Francisco
LU 47 East Bay Area . Walnut Creek
LU 64 Los Angeles. . . Los Angeles
LU 66 Sacramento
 Area. . . . . . . West Sacramento
LU 71 Bernard Skip Whalen
 Area. . . . . Mountain View
LU 73 San Jose . . . . . . San Jose
LU 78 Oakland Area . . . . Oakland
LU 115 Long Beach
 Area. . . . . Long Beach
LU 159 Salmont Area . . . Monterey
LU 197 San Diego County
 Area . . . . San Diego
LU 211 Marysville . . . Marysville
LU 264 Santa Barbara . . . Goleta
LU 320 Stockton . . . . . Stockton
LU 339 Fresno . . . . Fresno
LU 401 Calexico . . . . . Calexico
LU 423 Tri County
 Area . . . . Palm Springs
LU 472 Bakersfield . . . Bakersfield
LU 589 Channel Islands
 Area . . . . Oxnard
LU 614 Visalia . . . . Visalia
LU 635 Modesto . . . . . . Modesto
LU 731 Pasadena . . . . . Pasadena
LU 837 Brawley . . . . . . Brawley
LU 885 Bishop Local . . . Bishop
LU 891 Susanville Local . Susanville
LU 917 Southwest Coastal
 Area . . . . Anaheim
LU 926 Wilmington. . . Wilmington
LU 960 Redding . . . . . Redding
LU 1053 Tulare . . . . Tulare
LU 1056 Eureka . . . . . . Eureka
LU 1071 Merced. . . . . . Merced
LU 1099 Inglewood . . . Culver City
LU 1159 San Fernando Valley
 Area. . . . . Van Nuys
LU 1174 Crescent
 City . . . . Crescent City
LU 1199 Paso Robles
 Local . . . . Paso Robles
LU 1250 Escondido . . . Escondido
LU 1253 Delano . . . . . . Delano
LU 1256 North
 Hollywood . . . North Hollywood
LU 1291 Redwood Empire
 Area. . . . . Petaluma
LU 1465 Sonora Local . . . Sonora
LU 1702 Fort Bragg . . . Fort Bragg
LU 1938 Yreka . . . . Yreka
LU 1977 La Mesa . . . . La Mesa
LU 2025 Yuba City . . . Yuba City
LU 2052 Alturas Local. . . Alturas
LU 2587 Lancaster . . . . Lancaster

LU 2875 El Cajon . . . . . El Cajon
LU 4604 Arcata. . . . . . . Arcata
LU 4635 California Area . . Whittier
LU 5715 Cloverdale
 Local . . . . Cloverdale
LU 5765 Lemoore . . . . . Lemoore
LU 5864 Chatsworth . . Chatsworth
LU 6074 High Desert Area . Mojave
LU 6135 South Lake
 Tahoe. . . . . . South Lake Tahoe
LU 6154 Folsom. . . . . . Folsom
LU 6159 Daly City . . . . Daly City
LU 6212 Thousand
 Oaks. . . . . Thousand Oaks
LU 6669 San Mateo Postal Data
 Center . . . . San Mateo
LU 6792 Tahoe City
 Local . . . . Tahoe City
LU 6916 Altadena Local . . Altadena
LU 7060 Truckee . . . . . Truckee
SA California . . . . . . Santa Ana

Professional and Technical
Engineers
LU . . . . San Diego
LU 16 NAPEP Council . . Coronado
LU 26 . . . . San Jose
LU 30 Ames Federal Employees
 Union . . . . Moffett Field
LU 49 . . . . San Francisco
LU 86 . . . . San Francisco
LU 103 California . . . . . Campbell

Pulp and Paper Workers
LU 49 . . . . Samoa
LU 83. . . . . Stockton
LU 249 . . . . Antioch
LU 318 . . . . Pomona
LU 320 . . . . Lodi
LU 657. . . . . Santa Clara
LU 672 . . . . Anaheim
LU 850 . . . . Antioch
LU 863 . . . . Ripon

Railroad Signalmen
LLG 19 . . . . Brea
LLG 92 . . . . Hayward
LLG 104 . . . . Loma
LLG 153 . . . . . San Francisco
LLG 156. . . . . Hinkley
LLG 173 . . . . Wasco
LLG 229 . . . . Roseville
LLG 233 Arte. . . . . . . Concord

Roofers, Waterproofers and Allied
Workers
DC California-Hawaii-Nevada
 Roofers . . . . Santa Clara
LU 27. . . . . Fresno
LU 36. . . . . Los Angeles
LU 40 . . . . San Francisco
LU 45 . . . . San Diego
LU 81 . . . . Oakland
LU 95 . . . . Santa Clara
LU 220 . . . . Orange

Rural Letter Carriers
LU California Unit 15 . . . . Atwater
LU California Unit 18 . . . . Arcata
LU Fresno-Madera Counties . Clovis
LU Riverside-San Bernardino
 Counties . . . . Mentone
LU San Joaquin County Unit
 01. . . . . Stockton
LU Unit 02 . . . . Folsom
LU Unit 04. . . . . El Centro
LU Unit 05. . . . . . . Bakersfield
LU Unit 06 . . . . Encino

LU Unit 08. . . . . Anderson
LU Unit 09 . . . . . Redwood Valley
LU Unit 11 . . . . Ramona
LU Unit 16 . . . . Visalia
LU Unit 17 . . . . . . Santa Paula
LU 13 San Luis Obispo
 County . . . . Nipomo
LU 14 California . . . . Castroville
SA California . . . . Chino
UNIT 7 California . . . . Live Oak
UNIT 12 California . . . . Vacaville

Screen Actors
LBR Arizona . . . . . Los Angeles
LBR Atlanta . . . . . . Los Angeles
LBR Boston . . . . . . Los Angeles
LBR Chicago. . . . . . Los Angeles
LBR Colorado . . . . . Los Angeles
LBR Dallas. . . . . . Los Angeles
LBR Detroit . . . . . . Los Angeles
LBR Florida . . . . . . Los Angeles
LBR Hawaii . . . . . . Los Angeles
LBR Houston Branch. . Los Angeles
LBR Nashville . . . . Los Angeles
LBR Nevada . . . . . . Los Angeles
LBR New Mexico . . . Los Angeles
LBR New York. . . . . Los Angeles
LBR Philadelphia. . . . Los Angeles
LBR San Diego. . . . . Los Angeles
LBR San Francisco. . . Los Angeles
LBR Seattle. . . . . . Los Angeles
LBR Utah. . . . . . . Los Angeles
LBR Washington DC. . Los Angeles
NHQ . . . . Los Angeles

Seafarers
LU Fishermen's Union Pacific &
 Caribbean. . . . . . . San Diego
LU Industrial Professional &
 Technical Workers . . . Downey
LU Marine Firemen's
 Union . . . . San Francisco
LU Mortuary Employees'
 Union . . . . South San Francisco
LU Sailors' Union of the
 Pacific . . . . San Francisco
LU 1 Industrial, Professional &
 Technical Workers . . . Downey
LU 1 Sugar Workers
 Union . . . . Crockett
LU 2 Industrial, Professional &
 Technical Workers . . . Downey

Security Officers
LU . . . . Fresno
LU 2160. . . . . Oakland
NHQ . . . . San Leandro

Security, Police and Fire
Professionals
LU 100 . . . . Los Angeles
LU 153 . . . . Avila Beach
LU 158 . . . . Oceanside
LU 159 . . . . Fountain Valley
LU 160 . . . . Los Angeles
LU 165 . . . . Imperial
LU 2001 . . . . Norwalk

Service Employees
C California State . . . Sacramento
CONF Western . . . . . Los Angeles
JC 2 . . . . Oakland
JC 9 North Bay-Central
 Counties . . . . Fairfield
LU . . . . Los Angeles
LU . . . . San Rafael

LU 31 International Leather Goods,
 Plastics, Novelty and Service
 Union. . . . . San Francisco
LU 87 . . . . San Francisco
LU 101 . . . . . . San Bernardino
LU 250 Health Care Workers
 Union. . . . . Oakland
LU 265 . . . . Tiburon
LU 280 . . . . Duarte
LU 399 . . . . Los Angeles
LU 415 . . . . Santa Cruz
LU 504 Firemen & Oilers . Arlington
LU 535 . . . . Oakland
LU 616 . . . . Oakland
LU 660 Los Angeles
 County Employees
 Association. . . . . Los Angeles
LU 707 Sonoma County
 Public/Private
 Employees. . . . . . Santa Rosa
LU 715 . . . . San Jose
LU 758 Firemen &
 Oilers . . . . . . San Bernardino
LU 782 Firemen & Oilers . Foresthill
LU 790 . . . . Oakland
LU 812 Firemen &
 Oilers . . . . Union City
LU 817 . . . . Salinas
LU 998 . . . . Ventura
LU 1186 Firemen & Oilers . Barstow
LU 1292. . . . . Redding
LU 1401 Firemen &
 Oilers . . . . Granite Bay
LU 1877 . . . . Los Angeles
LU 2028 San Diego County
 Service . . . . San Diego
LU 4988 . . . . Jackson

Sheet Metal Workers
C Mid-Western States Production
 Workers. . . . . Mississagua
LU 104 . . . . San Francisco
LU 162 . . . . Sacramento
LU 170 . . . . Pico Rivera
LU 206 . . . . San Diego
LU 273 . . . . Santa Barbara
LU 371 . . . . Hayward
LU 376 . . . . La Verne
LU 434 . . . . . . Rowland Heights
LU 461 . . . . Walnut
LU 476 . . . . Barstow

State, County and Municipal
Employees
DC 57 Northern California . Oakland
LU 31-037 Sharp Professional Nurses
 Network. . . . . Pomona
LU 35 Fountain Valley Professional
 Association . . . . Pomona
LU 101 . . . . San Jose
LU 146 . . . . Sacramento
LU 800 Community & Social Agency
 Employees . . . . . Los Angeles
LU 829 San Mateo County
 Workers . . . South San Francisco
LU 1108 Social Service Agency
 Employees . . . . . . Los Angeles
LU 1684 Humboldt County Public
 Employees Union . . . . Eureka

Steelworkers
LU 64. . . . . Concord
LU 9440 . . . . Caruthers
LU 12-44-L . . . . Los Angeles
LU 12-171-L . . . . Downey
LU 12-418. . . . . Lathrop
LU 12-458-L . . . . . . El Segundo
LU 12-474-G . . . . Fresno

LU 12-515-U . . . . Bell
LU 12-555 . . . . Fresno
LU 12-560-L . . . . Los Alamitos
LU 12-565-S . . . . Folsom
LU 12-657-L . . . . Riverside
LU 12-703-L . . . . Hanford
LU 12-766-L . . . . . La Puente
LU 12-843 . . . . Selma
LU 12-1304-S . . . . San Leandro
LU 12-1440-S . . . . . Pittsburg
LU 12-1981-S . . . Huntington Park
LU 12-2018-S . . . . . Maywood
LU 12-2571-S . . . . . Pittsburg
LU 12-4997-S . . . . . Maywood
LU 12-5632-S . . . . . . Fontana
LU 12-5726-S . . . . San Gabriel
LU 12-6703-S . . . . . Riverside
LU 12-7524-S . . . . Lodi
LU 12-7600-S . . . . . . Fontana
LU 12-8049-S . . . Valley Springs
LU 12-8065-S . . . . . . Fontana
LU 12-8433-S . . . Santa Clarita
LU 12-8599-S . . . . . . Fontana
LU 12-8844 . . . . Fontana
LU 12-8957-S . . . . . Maywood
LU 39-6966-S . . . . . . Stockton

Teachers

LU 1475 Early Childhood
  Federation . . . . Burbank
LU 4128 Oakwood . . . . Burbank
LU 4163 Buckley Faculty
  Association . . . . Burbank
LU 4269 USF Faculty
  Association . . . . San Francisco
LU 4886 Westridge . . . . Monrovia
SFED California . . . . . Burbank

Teamsters

C California Cannery & Food
  Processing Unions . . . . Modesto
JC 7 . . . . San Francisco
JC 38 . . . . Modesto
JC 42 . . . . El Monte
LU 15 Northern California Mailers
  Union . . . . Union City
LU 36 . . . . San Diego
LU 63 . . . . Covina
LU 70 . . . . Oakland
LU 78 . . . . Hayward
LU 85 . . . . San Francisco
LU 87 . . . . Bakersfield
LU 94 . . . . Visalia
LU 137 . . . . Redding
LU 150 . . . . Sacramento
LU 166 . . . . Bloomington
LU 186 . . . . Ventura
LU 228 . . . . Sacramento
LU 278 . . . . . . San Francisco
LU 287 . . . . San Jose
LU 315 . . . . Martinez
LU 350 Sanitary Truck Drivers &
  Helpers Union . . . . . Daly City
LU 381 . . . . Santa Maria
LU 386 . . . . Modesto
LU 396 . . . . Covina
LU 399 . . . . . North Hollywood
LU 431 . . . . Fresno
LU 439 . . . . Stockton
LU 481 . . . . San Diego
LU 484 . . . . . . San Francisco
LU 490 . . . . Vallejo
LU 495 . . . . Pico Rivera
LU 517 . . . . Visalia
LU 542 . . . . San Diego
LU 572 . . . . Carson
LU 578 . . . . Orange
LU 601 . . . . Stockton

LU 616 . . . . Fresno
LU 624 . . . . Santa Rosa
LU 630 . . . . Los Angeles
LU 665 . . . . Daly City
LU 683 . . . . San Diego
LU 692 . . . . Long Beach
LU 746 . . . . Kingsburg
LU 748 . . . . Modesto
LU 848 . . . . El Monte
LU 853 . . . . San Leandro
LU 856 . . . . San Bruno
LU 857 . . . . Oroville
LU 890 . . . . Salinas
LU 896 . . . . Los Angeles
LU 911 . . . . Long Beach
LU 912 . . . . Watsonville
LU 952 . . . . Orange
LU 986 . . . . . South El Monte

Television and Radio Artists

LU Los Angeles . . . . Los Angeles
LU San Diego . . . . . San Diego
LU San Francisco . . . San Francisco
LU 224 Sacramento-
  Stockton . . . . . . Sacramento

Theatrical Stage Employees

ASSN District 2 Locals . Bakersfield
LU 16 . . . . San Francisco
LU 18-B . . . . . . San Francisco
LU 33 . . . . Burbank
LU 44 . . . . . North Hollywood
LU 50 . . . . Sacramento
LU 66-B . . . . Sacramento
LU 80 . . . . Burbank
LU 107 . . . . Oakland
LU 122 . . . . San Diego
LU 134 . . . . San Jose
LU 150 . . . . Los Angeles
LU 158 . . . . Fresno
LU 166 . . . . Santa Rosa
LU 169 . . . . Oakland
LU 192-B . . . . North Hollywood
LU 215 . . . . Bakersfield
LU 252 . . . . Sacramento
LU 297 . . . . La Mesa
LU 442 . . . . Santa Barbara
LU 504 . . . . Anaheim
LU 521 . . . . Long Beach
LU 564 . . . . Merced
LU 577 . . . . Upland
LU 600 . . . . Hollywood
LU 611 . . . . Santa Cruz
LU 614 . . . . . San Bernardino
LU 683 . . . . Burbank
LU 695 . . . . . North Hollywood
LU 700 Motion Picture Editors
  Guild . . . . Los Angeles
LU 705 Motion Picture
  Costumers . . . . . Los Angeles
LU 706 . . . . Burbank
LU 707 . . . . Palm Desert
LU 728 . . . . . Panorama City
LU 729 . . . . Burbank
LU 767 . . . . Burbank
LU 768 Theatrical Wardrobe
  Union . . . . Sherman Oaks
LU 784 . . . . . . San Francisco
LU 790 . . . . Sherman Oaks
LU 795 Television Broadcast Studio
  Employees . . . . La Mesa
LU 816 . . . . Sherman Oaks
LU 839 . . . . . North Hollywood
LU 847 . . . . Sherman Oaks
LU 854 . . . . Los Angeles
LU 857 . . . . Sherman Oaks
LU 871 . . . . . North Hollywood
LU 874 . . . . Sacramento

LU 876 . . . . Studio City
LU 884 . . . . Los Angeles
LU 892 . . . . Sherman Oaks
LU 905 . . . . San Diego
LU 914 Burlingame
  Local . . . . . . San Francisco
LU 916 . . . . El Segundo
LU 923 . . . . Anaheim

Transit Union

LDIV 1225 . . . . Vallejo
LDIV 1309 . . . . San Diego
LU 192 . . . . Oakland
LU 1027 . . . . Fresno
LU 1574 . . . . Foster City
LU 1700 . . . . Los Angeles

Transport Workers

LU 250-A . . . . . . San Francisco
LU 502 . . . . El Segundo
LU 505 . . . . Burlingame
LU 564 . . . . Inglewood

Transportation Communications Union

D 666 Santa Fe . . . . . . Stockton
D 674 Union Pacific-Eastern Lines
  SB 106 . . . . Tustin
D 802 Southern Pacific . . . Fairfield
D 1227 Union Pacific-Eastern Lines
  SB 106 . . . . Rico Rivera
D 2507 . . . . Long Beach
D 2508 . . . . Los Angeles
D 2511 . . . . Riverside
D 5504 WRSA . . . . . . Lincoln
D 5514 . . . . . . Panorama City
LG 2506 . . . . Richmond
LG 5050 Southern
  Pacific . . . . . . Santa Clara
LG 6250 Richmond . . . . Stockton
LG 6357 Covina . . . . . Covina
LG 6510 Woodbridge . . . Roseville
LG 6601 Los Angeles . . . Encino
LG 6713 Barstow . . . . . Barstow
LG 6721 Mission
  Bay . . . . San Francisco

Transportation Union

GCA GO-17 Atchison Topeka Santa
  Fe . . . . Santa Ana
GCA GO-20 Atchison Topeka Santa
  Fe-Coast . . . . . . Huntington
GCA GO-887 Southern Pacific
  Transportation Company-Western
  Lines-Railroad . . . Burlingame
GCA GO-888 Southern Pacific
  Transportation Company-Western
  Lines-Railroad . . . . . Aptos
LU 23 . . . . Watsonville
LU 31 . . . . Fremont
LU 32 . . . . Arcadia
LU 84 . . . . San Diego
LU 98 . . . . . San Luis Obispo
LU 100 . . . . Pleasant Hill
LU 239 . . . . San Ramon
LU 240 . . . . Alta Loma
LU 492 . . . . Rocklin
LU 694 . . . . Dunsmuir
LU 771 . . . . Needles
LU 811 . . . . . San Bernardino
LU 835 . . . . Bakersfield
LU 1200 . . . . Portola
LU 1201 . . . . Acampo
LU 1241 . . . . Fairfield
LU 1252 . . . . Fresno
LU 1422 . . . . Anaheim
LU 1469 . . . . Piedmont
LU 1544 . . . . Tustin

LU 1570 . . . . Auburn
LU 1581 . . . . Bakersfield
LU 1674 . . . . Alta Loma
LU 1694 . . . . Barstow
LU 1730 . . . . Fairfield
LU 1732 . . . . Hayward
LU 1741 . . . . . San Francisco
LU 1770 . . . . . . Los Angeles
LU 1801 . . . . . . Pleasant Hill
LU 1813 . . . . Colton
LU 1846 . . . . Redlands
LU 1915 . . . . Manteca
SLB LO-5 California . . Sacramento

Treasury Employees

CH 15 . . . . Los Angeles
CH 20 . . . . Oakland
CH 81 . . . . San Jose
CH 92 . . . . San Diego
CH 97 . . . . Fresno
CH 103 . . . . Long Beach
CH 105 . . . . San Ysidro
CH 107 . . . . El Monte
CH 108 . . . . . . Laguna Niguel
CH 111 . . . . Los Angeles
CH 117 . . . . Long Beach
CH 118 . . . . Bakersfield
CH 123 . . . . Calexico
CH 165 . . . . . . San Francisco
CH 198 . . . . El Segundo
CH 212 . . . . . . San Francisco
CH 227 . . . . . . San Francisco
CH 233 . . . . Van Nuys
CH 234 . . . . Riverside
CH 238 . . . . San Jose
CH 239 . . . . . North Highlands
CH 267 . . . . Los Angeles
CH 283 . . . . Venice

Utility Workers

C California Water Utility . Torrance
LU 132 . . . . Whittier
LU 160 . . . . Stockton
LU 160-C . . . . Brentwood
LU 160-D . . . . Chico
LU 170 . . . . Bakersfield
LU 205 . . . . Bakersfield
LU 246 . . . . Los Alamitos
LU 259 . . . . San Jose
LU 283 . . . . Whittier
LU 483 . . . . Goleta
LU 484 . . . . San Pedro
LU 508-A . . . . . . Newbury Park
LU 511 . . . . Pacific Grove
LU 522 . . . . Los Angeles
LU 570 . . . . Gardena

Weather Service Employees

BR 04-17 . . . . Sacramento
BR 04-29 . . . . Fremont
BR 04-35 . . . . Hanford
BR 04-36 . . . . Oxnard
BR 04-37 . . . . Palmdale
BR 04-45 . . . . Eureka
BR 04-61 . . . . San Diego
BR 04-80 . . . . Monterey
BR 08-8 . . . . Long Beach

Writers, West

NHQ . . . . Los Angeles

Unaffiliated Labor Organizations

Aerospace Professional Staff
  Association . . . . . Hawthorne

Allied Service Workers Union of the Thirteen Western States LU 1 . . . . Grand Terrace

Amalgamated Industrial Workers Union. . . . . Colton

Amalgamated Industrial Workers Union LU 14406 . . . . . Lompoc

American Federation of Guards LU 1 . . . . Los Angeles

APW Union of Southern California . . . . Cudahy

Association Employees Union . . . . San Jose

Atlantic Maritime Officers Association Independent. . . . . Long Beach

Bet Tzedek Legal Services Union . . . . Los Angeles

Buck Knives Employees Association. . . . . . . El Cajon

California Associate Staff . . . . Burlingame

California Log Scalers Association . . . . Trinidad

Canyon Manor Employees Association . . . . Novato

Caregivers and Healthcare . Glendale

Coastal Berry of California Farm Workers Committee . Watsonville

Coca Cola Bottlers Employees Union . . . . Sacramento

Committee for Recognition of Nursing Achievement-Stanford University . . . . Redwood City

Community Workers Union California . . . . Salinas

Dameron Hospital Employees Association. . . . . . . Stockton

Department of Defense Police Officers Association (IBPO) . . . . San Diego

Depot Employees Association Independent . . . . Tracy

Douglas Association of Security Officers Independent. . . Torrance

Employee Action Representatives . . . . Anaheim

Employees of Professional Organizations Labor Union . . . . La Jolla

Engineering Technicians & Technical Inspectors . . . . . . Sacramento

Engineers & Architects Association Independent General Dynamics Electronics Technology CH . . . . San Diego

Engineers & Architects Association Independent Technical Engineering Division . . . . San Diego

Engineers & Scientists Guild Lockheed Section . . . . Palmdale

Exxon Employees Federation Western Division. . . . . Goleta

Federation of Agents and International Representatives . . . . Sacramento

Field Representatives Union, California Federation of Teachers . . . . Oakland

Friedman Brothers Employees Association . . . . Rohnert Park

Grocery Employees Association Independent. . . . . Galt

Independent Employees of Merced County. . . . . Merced

Independent Employees Service Association . . . . Anaheim

Independent Oil & Chemical Workers. . . . . . . Sacramento

Independent Pharmacists Association . . . . . . Sacramento

Inland Empire Security Handlers Association LU 1 . San Bernardino

International Association of EMT's Paramedics AFL-CIO LU R1-187 . . . . Covina

International Union for the Natural Health Complement & Alternative Medicine Professions . West Hills

Kaiser Permanente Nurse Anesthetists Association of Southern California . . . . Orange

Labor Workers Union . . . Berkeley

Latin-American Musicians Union . . . . South Gate

Law Professors of the University of San Francisco School of Law, Associated . . . . San Francisco

Local 399 Staff Union . Los Angeles

Lumber & Moulding Handlers Union . . . . Orangevale

Marin Medical Laboratories Employees Association . Petaluma

Motion Picture Industry Basic Crafts . . . . . North Hollywood

National Electronics Systems Technician's Union . . . San Jose

Nor-Cal Beverage Company Employees Union . . . . . West Sacramento

Peacekeepers Security Officers Union National Association . . Vacaville

Pepsi People Employees Association. . . . . . . Redding

Physical Therapists-United California State Federation . . . . . Berkeley

Pipe Trades Association . . . Vallejo

Port Stockton Food Distributors Employee Association . . . . Galt

Private Duty Security Officers Association . . . . . Sacramento

Professional Automobile Sales Consultants Organization. . . . . Agoura Hills

Professional Pharmacists Guild . . . . . . Woodland Hills

Professional Resource Federation of Nurses . . . . San Jose

Public & Industrial Workers LU 1 . . . . Paramount

Public & Industrial Workers International Union . . Paramount

Representatives of Los Angeles United Union. . . . . Los Angeles

Royal Service Warehouse Employees Association . . . . . Sacramento

Santa Clara County Public Safety Officers Association . San Leandro

Security Police Employees Service Union . . . . Long Beach

Shipyard Workers Union. . . . . . . Chula Vista

Southern California Professional Engineering Association, Huntington Beach UNIT. . . . . Huntington Beach

Southern California Professional Engineering Association, Long Beach UNIT . . Huntington Beach

Sport Air Traffic Controllers Organization SATCO. . Lancaster

Staff and Office Employees Union International Federation . Ventura

Stanford Deputy Sheriffs Association . . . . Stanford

Studio Security & Fire Association Warner Brothers . . . . . Burbank

Tile Setters & Finishers Union of North Carolina . . . . Sacramento

Trainers & Recruiters Unity Council . . . . Orangevale

Union of Union Representatives . . . Los Angeles

United Domestic Workers of America . . . . San Diego

United Packinghouse Workers LU 5183. . . . . Coachella

United Police & Security Association . . . . Tracy

United Security Workers of America . . . . . . Long Beach

United Service Workers for Democracy . . . . . San Francisco

United Waterfront Council of San Diego. . . . . San Diego

United Wholesalers and Retailers Union . . . . Hickman

West Coast Employees Union . . . . Bakersfield

Western Region Wildlife Specialist Association . . . . . Penn Valley

Western States Pipe Trades Council. . . . . San Jose

Yuba City Plant Employees . . . . Marysville

Colorado

AFL-CIO Trade and Industrial Departments

Building and Construction Trades Department
BCTC Colorado . . . . . Lakewood

Food and Allied Service Trades Department
C Colorado Food & Beverage
Trades . . . . Denver

Metal Trades Department
MTC Western Slope . . . . Palisade

Affiliated Labor Organizations

Air Traffic Controllers
LU APA . . . . Englewood
LU ASE . . . . Aspen
LU BJC . . . . Broomfield
LU COS . . Peterson Air Force Base
LU D-01 . . . . Denver
LU DEN . . . . Denver
LU GJT . . . . . . Grand Junction
LU PUB . . . . Pueblo
LU ZDV . . . . Longmont

Asbestos Workers
LU 28 . . . . Denver

Automobile, Aerospace Workers
C Colorado . . . . Aurora
LU 186 . . . . Thornton
LU 431 . . . . Morrison
LU 766 . . . . Englewood
LU 1415 . . . . Aurora

Bakery, Confectionery, Tobacco Workers and Grain Millers
LU 26 . . . . Denver

Boilermakers
LG 1-P Denver Pep . . . . Denver
LG 101 . . . . Denver

Bricklayers
LU 7 Colorado . . . . Denver

Carpenters
LU 244 . . . . Denver
LU 510 . . . . Denver
LU 515 . . . . . Colorado Springs
LU 1068 . . . . Denver
LU 2834 . . . . Denver

Civilian Technicians
CH 48 Mile High Chapter . . Aurora

Communications Workers
C Colorado State . . . . . Englewood
LU 7702 . . . . Pueblo
LU 7707 . . . . Fort Collins
LU 7708 . . . . . . Colorado Springs
LU 7716 . . . . . . Pagosa Springs
LU 7717 . . . . Boulder
LU 7743 . . . . . . Grand Junction
LU 7750 . . . . Northglenn
LU 7755 . . . . Greenwood Village
LU 7774 . . . . Pueblo
LU 7777 . . . . Englewood
LU 7790 . . . . Denver
LU 7855 . . . . Greenwood Village

LU 14705 . . . . Denver
LU 14708 . . . . . Colorado Springs
LU 37074 . . . . Denver
LU 37174 Pueblo Newspaper
Guild . . . . Pueblo
LU 57052 . . . . Denver

Electrical Workers
LU 12 . . . . Pueblo
LU 68 . . . . Denver
LU 111 . . . . Denver
LU 113 . . . . . Colorado Springs
LU 667 . . . . Pueblo
LU 708 . . . . Denver
LU 969 . . . . Clifton
LU 2159 . . . . Montrose
LU 2300 . . . . Northglenn

Electronic Workers
LU 1020 . . . . Denver

Elevator Constructors
LU 25 . . . . Lakewood

Federal Employees
LU 1678 . . . . Aurora
LU 1945 . . . . Denver
LU 1950 . . . . Fort Collins
LU 2004 . . . . Monte Vista
LU 2074 . . . . Fort Collins
SFED Colorado . . . . . Lakewood

Food and Commercial Workers
LU 7-R . . . . Wheat Ridge
LU 990 . . . . Greeley

Government Employees
C 157 National Mint . . . . Denver
C 200 National Meat
Graders . . . . Greeley
LU 695 ID . . . . Denver
LU 709 DoJ . . . . Littleton
LU 898 DoL . . . . Denver
LU 925 USDA . . . . . Fort Morgan
LU 1103 Rocky Flats Field
Office . . . . Golden
LU 1105 . . . . Lakewood
LU 1248 GPO . . . . . . Lakewood
LU 1301 . . . . Florence
LU 1302 DoJ . . . . Florence
LU 1303 Council of Prisons . Aurora
LU 1345 DoD . . . . . Fort Carson
LU 1557 VA . . . . Lakewood
LU 1802 HHS . . . . Denver
LU 1867 DoD . . Colorado Springs
LU 2040 DoD . . . . Denver
LU 2186 DoC . . . . Boulder
LU 2197 DoD . . . . Commerce City
LU 2241 VA . . . . Denver
LU 2430 VA . . . . Swink
LU 2477 DoD . . . . Pueblo
LU 3230 EEOC . . . . . . Denver
LU 3275 GSA . . . . Denver
LU 3373 USDA . . . . . . Greeley
LU 3392 GPO . . . . Pueblo
LU 3416 DoL . . . . . Broomfield
LU 3499 USDA . . . . . Springfield
LU 3540 DoD . . Colorado Springs
LU 3607 EPA . . . . Denver
LU 3806 ID . . . . Denver
LU 3824 DoE . . . . . . Loveland
LU 3898 DoE . . . . Denver
LU 3939 DoI . . . . Craig
LU 3942 . . . . Denver
LU 3972 HUD . . . . Denver

Government Employees Association
LU 14-5 . . . . Pueblo
LU 14-77 . . . . . Grand Junction

Government Security Officers
LU 1 . . . . Arvada
LU 21 . . . . Westminister
LU 34 U.S. Department of
Agriculture . . . . . Westminister
LU 43 . . . . Denver
LU 53 . . . . Denver
NHQ . . . . Westminister

Graphic Communications
LU 22-N . . . . Denver
LU 440-M . . . . Denver

Guards
LU 65 . . . . Grand Junction
LU 66 . . . . Commerce City

Hotel and Restaurant Employees
LU 14 . . . . Denver

Iron Workers
DC Rocky Mountain
Area . . . . Englewood
LU 24 . . . . Denver

Laborers
DC Colorado . . . . Denver
LU 578 . . . . . Colorado Springs
LU 720 . . . . Lakewood

Letter Carriers
BR 47 . . . . Denver
BR 179 . . . . Trinidad
BR 204 . . . . . Colorado Springs
BR 229 . . . . Pueblo
BR 324 . . . . Greeley
BR 508 Leadville,
Colorado . . . . Leadville
BR 642 . . . . Boulder
BR 792 . . . . Durango
BR 849 . . . . Fort Collins
BR 913 . . . . . . Grand Junction
BR 1105 . . . . Longmont
BR 1178 . . . . La Junta
BR 1207 . . . . Loveland
BR 1426 . . . . Delta
BR 1511 . . . . Sterling
BR 1517 . . . . Montrose
BR 1861 Las Animas,
Colorado . . . . . . Las Animas
BR 1960 Brush, Colorado . . . Brush
BR 2139 Walsenburg,
Colorado . . . . . . Walsenburg
BR 3631 . . . . Akron
BR 3681 Fowler, Colorado . . Fowler
BR 4259 . . . . Wheat Ridge
BR 4405 . . . . Arvada
BR 4459 Springfield,
Colorado . . . . Springfield
BR 4902 Fort Lupton,
Colorado . . . . . . Fort Lupton
BR 5225 Cortez, Colorado . . Cortez
BR 5236 . . . . Craig
BR 5301 Gunnison,
Colorado . . . . Gunnison
BR 5996 . . . . Denver
BR 6202 . . . . Aspen
SA Colorado . . . . Denver

Locomotive Engineers
DIV 29 . . . . Pueblo
DIV 47 . . . . Lakewood
DIV 133 . . . . Aurora
DIV 186 . . . . Aurora
DIV 215 . . . . . Grand Junction
DIV 256 . . . . Littleton
DIV 430 . . . . Trinidad
DIV 488 . . . . . Grand Junction
DIV 505 . . . . La Junta
DIV 727 . . . . Sterling
DIV 940 . . . . Littleton
GCA C&S, FWD & JTD BNSF
Railway . . . . Hoehne
GCA Santa Fe Railroad . . . La Junta
SLB Colorado SLB . . . . Arvada

Machinists
LG . . . . Aurora
LG 13 . . . . Rocky Ford
LG 47 . . . . . . Commerce City
LG 606 . . . . . . Commerce City
LG 1338 . . . . Arvada
LG 1886 . . . . . Commerce City
LG 1910-FL . . . . . . Frederick
R 9 . . . . Lakewood
STC Colorado . . . . Commerce City

Maintenance of Way Employes
FED Mountain &
Plains . . . . . Colorado Springs
LG 1351 . . . . Thornton
LG 1517 . . . . Pueblo
SLG 14 . . . . Lakewood
SLG 204 . . . . Trinidad
SLG 779 . . . . . Grand Junction
SLG 833 . . . . Salida
SLG 925 . . . . . . Pueblo West
SLG 941 . . . . Lakewood
SLG 1501 . . . . Walsenburg
SLG 1516 . . . . Phippsburg

Mine Workers
LU 1281 . . . . Nucia
LU 1385 . . . . Hayden
LU 1799 . . . . Craig
LU 1984 . . . . Rangely
LU 5909 . . . . Longmont
LU 6417 . . . . Somerset
LU 6778 . . . . Oak Creek
LU 8431 . . . . Denver
LU 8935 . . . . Trinidad
LU 9856 . . . . Trinidad

Musicians
LU 20-623 . . . . Denver
LU 154 . . . . . . Colorado Springs

National Staff Organization
LU Staff Organization, Colorado
Education Association . . . Denver

NLRB Professional Association
LU 27 . . . . Denver

Nurses
SA Colorado . . . . Denver

Office and Professional Employees
LU 5 . . . . Denver

Operating Engineers
LU 1 . . . . Northglenn
LU 9 . . . . Denver

Painters
LU 79 . . . . Denver
LU 419. . . . . Englewood
LU 930. . . . . Englewood

Paper, Allied-Industrial, Chemical Employees
LU 655. . . . . . . Grand Junction
LU 742 . . . . Lakewood
LU 05-477 . . . . Arvada
LU 05-710 . . . . Brighton
LU 05-844. . . . . Canon City
LU 05-920 . . . . Centennial
LU 05-1396 . . . . Commerce City
LU 08-594. . . . . . Williamsburg

Plasterers and Cement Masons
LU 577 . . . . Denver

Plumbing and Pipe Fitting
LU 3 . . . . Denver
LU 20. . . . . Pueblo
LU 58 . . . . . . Colorado Springs
LU 145. . . . . . Grand Junction
LU 208 . . . . Denver
SA Colorado Pipe Trades . . Denver

Postal and Federal Employees
LU 903 . . . . Denver

Postal Mail Handlers
LU 321 . . . . Denver

Postal Workers
LU 229 Denver. . . . . . . Aurora
LU 247 Colorado Springs
  Area. . . . . . Colorado Springs
LU 345 La Junta . . . . . . Pueblo
LU 382 Loveland . . . . . Loveland
LU 436 Pueblo . . . . . . Pueblo
LU 441 Fort Morgan . . Fort Morgan
LU 539 Fort Collins. . . Fort Collins
LU 600 Western Colorado
  Area. . . . . . . Grand Junction
LU 706 Alamosa . . . . . Alamosa
LU 918 Sterling . . . . . . Sterling

LU 1337 Steamboat Spring
  Local. . . . . Steamboat Springs
LU 3477 Littleton. . . . . Littleton
LU 4503 Gunnison . . . . Gunnison
LU 6315 Aurora . . . . . . Aurora
LU 7029 Denver Bulk Mail
  Center . . . . Denver
SA Colorado . . . . Eastlake

Professional and Technical Engineers
LU 128 . . . . Lakewood

Roofers, Waterproofers and Allied Workers
DC Southwest Roofers. . . . Denver
LU 41 . . . . Denver
LU 58 . . . . . . Colorado Springs

Rural Letter Carriers
D 1 . . . . Evans
D 2 . . . . Merino
D 3 . . . . Aurora
D 4 . . . . Fowler
D 5 . . . . Pueblo
D 6 . . . . Bayfield
D 7 . . . . Olathe
SA Colorado . . . . Clifton

Security, Police and Fire Professionals
LU 265. . . . . Englewood

Service Employees
LU 105 . . . . Denver
LU 540 Firemen &
  Oilers . . . . . . Grand Junction
LU 543 Firemen & Oilers . . Pueblo
LU 607 Firemen & Oilers . Thornton

Sheet Metal Workers
LU 9 . . . . Denver
LU 253 . . . . Arvada

State, County and Municipal Employees
C 76 Colorado . . . . Pueblo
LU 1572 University of Denver
  Employees. . . . . Denver

Steelworkers
LU 12-154-L . . . . Denver
LU 12-724-L . . . . Denver
LU 12-2102-S . . . . Pueblo
LU 12-3267-S . . . . Pueblo
LU 12-3405-S . . . . Pueblo
LU 12-8031-S . . . . Arvada
LU 12-14457-S . . . Grand Junction
LU 12-14482-S . . . . . . Florence

Teachers
LU 5016 Denver Federation of
  Nurses and Health . . . . Denver
SFED Colorado . . . . . . Denver

Teamsters
JC 3. . . . . Denver
LU 17 . . . . Denver
LU 267 . . . . Laporte
LU 435 . . . . Lakewood
LU 537. . . . . Denver
LU 961 Line Drivers . . . . Denver

Television and Radio Artists
LU 208 Denver. . . . . . . Denver

Theatrical Stage Employees
LU 7 . . . . Denver
LU 30-B . . . . Denver
LU 47. . . . . Pueblo
LU 62 . . . . . . Colorado Springs
LU 229 . . . . Fort Collins
LU 230. . . . . Frederick
LU 719 . . . . Wheat Ridge

Transit Union
LDIV 19. . . . . Colorado Springs

Transportation Communications Union
D 5516 WRSA. . . . Grand Junction
LG 270 . . . . Johnstown
LG 6146 Main Line . . . . . Arvada

Transportation Union
GCA GO-245 Burlington
  Northern . . . . Arvada
GCA GO-291 Burlington
  Northern . . . . Littleton
GCA GO-306. . . . . . . Lakewood
LU 49. . . . . Pueblo
LU 201 . . . . Trinidad
LU 202 . . . . Brighton
LU 204 . . . . Pueblo
LU 500 . . . . Clifton
LU 945 . . . . La Junta
LU 1136 . . . . Sterling
SLB LO-7 Colorado . . . Lakewood

Treasury Employees
CH 32 . . . . Arvada
CH 235 . . . . Denver
CH 275 FDIC . . . . . . Elizabeth

University Professors
CH Regis College . . . . . Denver

Weather Service Employees
BR 03-16 . . . . Boulder
BR 03-56 . . . . . Grand Junction
BR 03-95 . . . . Pueblo

Unaffiliated Labor Organizations

Association of Professional Taxi-Cab
  Drivers of Colorado . . Lakewood
Denver Police Protective
  Association . . . . Denver
Frontier Airline Pilots
  Association. . . . . Aurora
Ski Patrol Association, Aspen
  Professional. . . . . Aspen
United Local Seven Staff
  Union . . . . Wheat Ridge

Connecticut

AFL-CIO Trade and Industrial Departments

Building and Construction Trades Department
BCTC Connecticut State . Harwinton
BCTC Fairfield County, Greenwich
  & Vicinity . . . . Norwalk
BCTC Hartford &
  Vicinity . . . . . . East Hartford
BCTC New Haven &
  Vicinity . . . . Rocky Hill
BCTC New
  London-Norwich . . East Hartford
BCTC Waterbury . . . . . . Berlin

Metal Trades Department
MTC New London County. . Groton

Affiliated Labor Organizations

Air Traffic Controllers
LU BDL . . . . . . Windsor Locks
LU DXR . . . . Danbury
LU Y90 . . . . East Hartland

Asbestos Workers
LU 33 . . . . Wallingford

Automobile, Aerospace Workers
C Connecticut . . . . . Farmington
C Massachusetts . . . . Farmington
C New Hampshire CAP . Farmington
C New York Regional
  CAP . . . . . . Farmington
C Puerto Rico CAP . . . Farmington
C Rhode Island Community Action
  (CAP) . . . . Farmington
C Vermont-CAP . . . . . Farmington
LU 376 Elmwood-Hartford
  Local . . . . Newington
LU 379 . . . . Hartford
LU 405 . . . . West Hartford
LU 571 Marine Draftmen's
  Association . . . . Groton
LU 712 . . . . Bristol
LU 1187 . . . . Newington
LU 1645 . . . . Torrington
LU 1699 . . . . Torrington
LU 8868 . . . . . South Windsor

Boilermakers
LG 237 . . . . East Hartford
LG 558 . . . . Glastonbury
LG 614 . . . . Groton

Bricklayers
LU 1 Connecticut . . . . New Haven

Carpenters
LU 24 . . . . Yalesville
LU 43 . . . . Hartford
LU 210 . . . . Norwalk
LU 1302 . . . . Groton

Catholic School Teachers
LU Greater Hartford. . . Manchester

Civilian Technicians
CH 97 Flying Yankees . East Granby
CH 98 Connecticut Army . . Groton

Communications Workers
LU Connecticut Union of Telephone
  Workers. . . . . Hamden
LU Connecticut Union of Telephone
  Workers Plant 7 . . . . . Hamden
LU 143-FW . . . . Stevenson
LU 238 . . . . Bridgeport
LU 266 . . . . Newington
LU 1250 . . . . Cheshire
LU 1290 . . . . Northford
LU 14101 Bridgeport Typographical
  Union . . . . Stratford
LU 14102 . . . . Marlborough
LU 14105 . . . . North Haven
LU 14106 . . . . Quaker Hill
LU 14109 . . . . Darien
LU 14110 . . . . Torrington
LU 51014 . . . . . . North Haven
LU 51017 NABET Local
  17 . . . . Newington
LU 81203 . . . . Bridgeport
LU 81215 . . . . Newington
LU 81227 . . . . Enfield
LU 81237 . . . . Trubull
LU 81244 . . . . Trumbull
LU 81247 . . . . Torrington
LU 81249 . . . . . . East Hartford
LU 81281 . . . . Bloomfield
LU 81287 . . . . Bridgeport
LU 81295 . . . . Newington

Electrical Workers
LU 35 . . . . Hartford
LU 42 . . . . Manchester
LU 90 . . . . New Haven
LU 208 . . . . Norwalk
LU 261 . . . . Groton
LU 420 . . . . Waterbury
LU 457 . . . . Meriden
LU 488 . . . . Monroe
LU 747 . . . . Hamden
LU 1040 . . . . Hartford
LU 2015 . . . . Danbury
SA 04-Connecticut State
  Association. . . . . Groton

Electrical, Radio and Machine Workers
LU 211 . . . . Milford
LU 243 . . . . New Haven
LU 275 . . . . Colchester
LU 299 . . . . North Haven

Elevator Constructors
LU 91 . . . . North Haven

Fire/Security Officers
LU . . . . Oakville
LU East Hartford . . . East Hartford
LU Middletown . . . . Middletown
LU North Haven . . . . East Hartford
LU Southington . . . . . Waterbury
NHQ . . . . East Hartford

Food and Commercial Workers
C Insurance Workers Area
  1 . . . . Wilsonville
LU 23 . . . . Enfield
LU 197-B . . . . Stratford
LU 215 . . . . North Haven
LU 315-C . . . . Norwalk
LU 371 . . . . Westport
LU 436-C . . . . Wallingford
LU 560-C . . . . Danbury
LU 919 . . . . Farmington

Glass, Molders, Pottery and Plastics Workers
LU 39-B . . . . Bethel

Government Employees
C 163 New England DCAA
  Locals . . . . . . South Windsor
C 258 Veteran Affairs
  Department . . . . . . Durham
LU 1661 DoJ . . . New Fairfield
LU 1674 VA . . . . West Haven
LU 2105 DoD . . . . . Groton
LU 2538 DoJ . . . . . Hartford
LU 2749 USDA . . . Torrington
LU 3237 DoD . . . . Guilford
LU 3244 DCAA . . . East Hartford
LU 3655 DoT . . . . New London

Government Employees Association
LU 01-76 . . . . . . East Hartford
LU 01-100 . . . . Groton
LU 01-109 . . . . . . Newington
LU 01-143 . . . . . . New Haven
LU 01-145 . . . . . New London
LU 01-181 . . . . Stratford

Graphic Communications
LU 74-M . . . . Meriden
LU 488-S . . . . . . South Windsor

Hotel and Restaurant Employees
LU 34 . . . . New Haven
LU 35 . . . . New Haven
LU 217 . . . . New Haven

Iron Workers
LU 15 . . . . Hartford
LU 424 . . . . New Haven
LU 832 . . . . Newington

Laborers
DC Connecticut. . . . . . Hartford
LU 146 . . . . Norwalk
LU 230 . . . . Hartford
LU 390 . . . . Waterbury
LU 455 . . . . East Haven
LU 547 . . . . Groton
LU 611 . . . . New Britain
LU 665 . . . . Bridgeport
LU 675 . . . . Danbury
LU 1224 . . . . Hartford

Letter Carriers
BR 19 . . . . North Haven
BR 20 . . . . Meriden
BR 32 . . . . Stratford
BR 60 . . . . Stamford
BR 86 . . . . East Hartford
BR 109 . . . . Derby
BR 147 . . . . Norwalk
BR 363 . . . . Danbury
BR 746 . . . . Naugatuck
BR 759 . . . . Greenwich
BR 2313 . . . . Fairfield
BR 5016 Essex, Connecticut . Essex
BR 5427 Plainfield,
  Connecticut . . . . . . Plainfield
BR 6374 Moosup,
  Connecticut . . . . Moosup
BR 6582 . . . . Madison
SA Connecticut . . . . North Haven

Locomotive Engineers
DIV 77 . . . . Bethany

Longshoremen
LU 1398 . . . . Wallingford
LU 1411 . . . . Oakdale

Machinists
CONF New England . . Southington
DLG 91 . . . . East Hartford
DLG 170 . . . . Kensington
LG 354 . . . . East Hartford
LG 609 . . . . New Haven
LG 700 Canel . . . . Middletown
LG 707 . . . . North Haven
LG 743 . . . . Windsor Locks
LG 782 . . . . Middletown
LG 983 . . . . Oakville
LG 1112 . . . . North Haven
LG 1137 . . . . Kensington
LG 1249 . . . . Plainville
LG 1396 . . . . Branford
LG 1433 . . . . Kensington
LG 1746 . . . . East Hartford
LG 1746-A . . . . Marion
LG 1871 . . . . Groton
STC Connecticut . . . . Kensington

Maintenance of Way Employes
LG 90 . . . . Groton
SLG 1718 . . . . . . West Haven

Musicians
LU 52-626 . . . . Norwalk
LU 87 . . . . Danbury
LU 186 . . . . Waterbury
LU 234-486 . . . . . New Haven
LU 285 . . . . Gales Ferry
LU 400 . . . . Rocky Hill
LU 499 . . . . Rockfall
LU 514 . . . . Torrington
STCON Connecticut . . . Waterbury

National Staff Organization
LU Staff Organization, Association,
  Connecticut Education
  Association . . . . Hartford
LU Staff Organization, Professional,
  Connecticut Education
  Association . . . . . . Trumbull

Needletrades
JB Greater New England
  Regional . . . . . . Willimantic
JB Greater
  Northeastern . . . . . Willimantic
LU 31 . . . . Willimantic
LU 121-H . . . . Willimantic
LU 431-T . . . . Willimantic
LU 468-E . . . . Willimantic
LU 469-A . . . . Willimantic
LU 471-A . . . . Willimantic
LU 477-A . . . . Willimantic
LU 652-T . . . . Willimantic
LU 687-T . . . . Willimantic
LU 808-A . . . . Willimantic
LU 841-T . . . . Willimantic
LU 939-A . . . . Willimantic
LU 1016-A . . . . Willimantic
LU 1036-T . . . . Willimantic
LU 1156-T . . . . Willimantic
LU 1198-T . . . . Willimantic
LU 1201-T . . . . Willimantic
LU 1208-T . . . . Willimantic
LU 1226 . . . . Willimantic
LU 1296 . . . . Willimantic
LU 1321 . . . . Willimantic
LU 1362 . . . . Willimantic

LU 1371. . . . . Willimantic
LU 1460. . . . . Willimantic
LU 1468-T . . . . Willimantic
LU 1483 . . . . Willimantic
LU 1554. . . . . Willimantic
LU 1560. . . . . Willimantic
LU 1569. . . . . Willimantic
LU 1657. . . . . Willimantic
LU 1712-T . . . . Willimantic
LU 1723. . . . . Willimantic
LU 1751. . . . . Willimantic
LU 1832. . . . . Willimantic
LU 1834-T . . . . Willimantic
LU 2527. . . . . Willimantic
LU 2687-T . . . . Willimantic
LU 2688-T . . . . Willimantic

NLRB Professional Association
LU 34 . . . . Hartford

Office and Professional Employees
LU 106 . . . . Groton
LU 376 . . . . North Haven

Operating Engineers
LU 478 . . . . Hamden

Painters
DC 11 . . . . Berlin
LU 186 . . . . New Haven
LU 481 . . . . Windsor
LU 1122 . . . . New London
LU 1274. . . . . West Haven
LU 1719. . . . . New Haven

Paper, Allied-Industrial, Chemical Employees
LU 01-46. . . . . Rogers
LU 01-457. . . . . . New Haven
LU 01-655. . . . . . . Versailles
LU 01-683 . . . . Norwich
LU 01-745 . . . . . . Middletown
LU 01-753 . . . . Meriden
LU 01-845 . . . . Danbury
LU 01-859 . . . . Meriden
LU 01-902 . . . . . . Southbury
LU 01-1554 . . . . . . Manchester
LU 01-1840 . . . . . . Versailles
LU 01-5370 . . . . . . Wallingford

Plumbing and Pipe Fitting
LU 676 . . . . Wallingford
LU 777 . . . . Meriden

Police Associations
LU 1178 Waterbury Emergency
   Services Union . . . . . Prospect

Postal and Federal Employees
LU 808 . . . . Stratford
LU 811 . . . . New Haven
LU 815. . . . . Stamford

Postal Workers
LU 147 Hartford. . . . East Hartford
LU 237 Greater Connecticut
   Area . . . . North Haven
LU 240 Stamford . . . . Stamford
LU 549 Bridgeport . . . . Bridgeport
LU 646 New London . New London
LU 832 Willimantic . . . Willimantic
LU 1097 Fairfield. . . . . Fairfield
LU 2468 Danielson . . . . Danielson
LU 2921 Waterbury . . . Waterbury
LU 3093 Norwalk . . . . Norwalk
LU 3151 Meriden . . . . Meriden
LU 4865 West Connecticut
   Area . . . . Danbury

LU 5892 Kensington . . Kensington
SA Connecticut. . . . . Bridgeport

Railroad Signalmen
GC 56 Southern New
   England. . . . . Guilford
LLG 5. . . . . Guilford
LLG 7 . . . . Branford
LLG 62 . . . . Danielson
LLG 160 . . . . Meriden

Roofers, Waterproofers and Allied Workers
LU 9 . . . . Rocky Hill
LU 12 . . . . New Haven

Rural Letter Carriers
BR 29 . . . . Thomaston
LU 1 Litchfield County. . . Roxbury
LU 2 Hartford County . . East Berlin
LU 3 Tolland County . . . . Vernon
LU 4 Windham County . Woodstock
LU 5 Fairfield County . . . Norwalk
LU 6 New Haven County . Waterbury
LU 7 Middlesex County . Old Lyme
LU 29-8 New London
   County . . . . Colchester

Security, Police and Fire Professionals
LU 537 . . . . Oakdale
LU 538 . . . . . . Middle Haddam
LU 690 . . . . Stratford

Service Employees
D 1199 New England Health Care
   Employees Union . . . . Hartford
LU 25 International Leather Goods,
   Plastics, Novelty and Service
   Union. . . . . Bridgeport
LU 760 . . . . Hartford
LU 760 Connecticut Service
   Council . . . . New Britain

Sheet Metal Workers
C Nuclear & Hazardous
   Material . . . . Rocky Hill
LU 40. . . . . Rocky Hill
LU 328 . . . . North Haven

State, County and Municipal Employees
C 4. . . . . New Brintain
D 1199 NUHHCE,
   CHCA . . . . Wallingford
DC 4 Connecticut & Special District
   Employees . . . . . New Britain
LU 184 Hartford, Connecticut, Metro
   District Employees . West Hartford
LU 1026 Metro District Supervisors
   Union . . . . Manchester
LU 1303 State of Connecticut
   Municipal Employees
   Union . . . . East Windsor
LU 1522 . . . . Bridgeport
LU 3145 Red Cross
   Employees . . . . . Farmington
UNIT 10 NUHHCE, CHCA,
   Waterbury Hospital RN . Waterbury
UNIT 23 Connecticut Health Care
   Associates . . . . Norwalk
UNIT 45-46 NUHHCE, CHCA,
   Wallingford Hospital . Wallingford
UNIT 53 Connecticut Health Care
   Associates . . . . . Wallingford
UNIT 61 NUHHCE, CHCA, Bradley
   Memorial Hospital . . Southington

UNIT 75 NUHHCE, CHCA, Milford
   Hospital Nurses . . . . . Oxford

Steelworkers
LU 12000 . . . . . . Beacon Falls
LU 04-134-L. . . . . Orange
LU 04-218-L. . . . . . Naugatuck
LU 04-826-B . . . . Hartford
LU 04-837-L. . . . . . . Milford
LU 04-895-L . . . . . . Waterbury
LU 04-2242-S. . . . . Wallingford
LU 04-6445-S. . . . . . . Ansonia
LU 04-8831-S. . . . . . . Milford
LU 04-9411-S . . . . . . Norwich
LU 04-12000-S . . . . . . Shelton
LU 04-12160-S . . . . . . Hamden
LU 04-14323-A . . . . Watertown
LU 04-15536-S . . . . . Norwalk

Teachers
LU 933 New Haven Federation of
   Teachers . . . . . . New Haven
LU 3249 Mitchell College Faculty
   Federation . . . . . New London
LU 3394 Quinnipiac Faculty
   Federation . . . . Hamden
LU 3949 West Hartford Dormitory
   Supervisors. . . . . West Hartford
LU 4230 American School for the
   Deaf . . . . West Hartford
LU 5041 Windham Hospital
   Registered Nurses . . . . Putnam
LU 5046 Johnson Memorial
   Registered Nurses. Stafford Springs
LU 5047 Danbury Hospital
   Professional Nurses
   Association . . . . Danbury
LU 5048 Nurses Association,
   Visiting, Professional
   Nurses . . . . Norwalk
LU 5049 Lawrence & Memorial
   Hospitals Registered
   Nurses . . . . New London
LU 5051 Lawrence &
   Memorial Hospitals LPN &
   Technicians . . . . . New London
LU 5052 Natchaug Federation of
   Registered Nurses . . . Colchester
LU 5055 Manchester Memorial
   Hospital Professional
   Nurse . . . . Ellington
LU 5063 Nurses & Health
   Professionals . . . . . Willimantic
LU 5099 Windham Community
   Memorial Hospital
   Employees . . . . Columbia
LU 5101 New Milford Hospital Fed.
   of Registered . . . . New Milford
SFED Connecticut State . Rocky Hill

Teamsters
LU 145 . . . . Stratford
LU 191 . . . . Bridgeport
LU 443 . . . . New Haven
LU 493 . . . . Uncasville
LU 559 . . . . South Windsor
LU 671 . . . . Bloomfield
LU 677 . . . . Waterbury
LU 1035 . . . . South Windsor
LU 1040 . . . . Bridgeport
LU 1150 . . . . Stratford

Theatrical Stage Employees
LU 74 . . . . East Haven
LU 84 . . . . West Hartford
LU 109 . . . . Stratford
LU 133 . . . . Norwalk
LU 486 . . . . Hartford

LU 538 . . . . Danielson

Transit Union
CONBD Connecticut . East Hartford
LDIV 281 . . . . New Haven
LDIV 443 . . . . Stamford
LU 425. . . . . East Hartford
LU 1336 . . . . Bridgeport
LU 1348 . . . . Norwich
LU 1588 . . . . . . South Windsor
LU 1734 . . . . Milford

Transport Workers
LU 2055 . . . . Branford

Transportation Communications Union
D 227 Conrail . . . . . East Haven
D 1402 . . . . Killingworth

Transportation Union
GCA GO-663 Conrail-PC-NHR-
   NYNH&H . . . . . . Woodbridge
LU 277 . . . . Prospect
LU 328. . . . . East Haven
LU 1361 . . . . Woodbridge
SLB LO-8 Connecticut . Woodbridge

Treasury Employees
CH 18 . . . . Broad Brook
CH 124. . . . . Beacon Falls

University Professors
CH Post College Faculty
   Association. . . . . . Waterbury

Utility Workers
LU 380 . . . . Norwalk
LU 384 . . . . Norwalk
LU 470-001 . . . . . New Haven

Unaffiliated Labor Organizations

Association of Court
   Security Officers-
   Connecticut . . . . North Branford
Clerks Secretaries & Bookkeepers
   Unlimited LG 1 . . . Old Saybrook
Connecticut Independent Utility
   Workers LU 12924. . . Hartford
Environmental Workers
   Association. . . . . . Bridgeport
Graduate Employees & Students
   Organization . . . . New Haven
Greater Hartford Emergency Medical
   Technicians Association. . Enfield
Hamilton Standard Independent
   Security Officers
   Association . . . . . Windsor Locks
New Milford Employees
   Association . . . . New Milford
Plant Protection Employees
   Independent Union of, General
   Electric Company . . . Bridgeport
Regional Emergency
   Medical Technician
   Association . . . . . North Haven
Security Department Membership
   LU 001 . . . . Hamden
St. Bernard Education
   Association. . . . . . Uncasville
Staff Union of Connecticut
   Independent . . . . . Rocky Hill
Stamford Paramedic
   Association . . . . Stamford
Yale Police Benevolent
   Association . . . . . Killingworth

Delaware

AFL-CIO Trade and Industrial Departments

Building and Construction Trades Department
BCTC Delaware . . . . Wilmington

Affiliated Labor Organizations

Air Traffic Controllers
LU ILG . . . . New Castle

Automobile, Aerospace Workers
C Delaware . . . . Newark
LU 404. . . . . Newark
LU 435 . . . . Wilmington
LU 498. . . . . Smyrna
LU 1183 . . . . Newark
LU 1212 . . . . Newark
LU 1516. . . . . Middletown
LU 1542. . . . . Wilmington
LU 1756 . . . . Newark

Bricklayers
LU 2. . . . . Hockessin

Carpenters
LU 626. . . . . New Castle
LU 1545 . . . . New Castle
LU 2001 Milford Manor. . . Milford
LU 2006 Rehabilitation & Retirement
    Center. . . . . Laurel

Civilian Technicians
CH 24 Delaware . . . . Wilmington

Communications Workers
LU 13100 Diamond State Telephone
    Commercial. . . . . Wilmington
LU 13101 United Telephone Workers
    of Delaware . . . . Newark
LU 14801 . . . . Hockessin

Electrical Workers
LU 313. . . . . New Castle
LU 1238 . . . . New Castle

LU 2201 . . . . Georgetown
LU 2270. . . . . Wilmington

Fire Fighters
LU 135-F. . . . . Bridgeville

Food and Commercial Workers
LU 987-C. . . . . Georgetown

Glass, Molders, Pottery and Plastics Workers
LU 118 . . . . Selbyville

Government Employees
LU 1709 DoD . . . . Dover

Graphic Communications
LU 690-S . . . . Wilmington

Iron Workers
LU 451 . . . . Wilmington

Laborers
LU 199 . . . . Wilmington
LU 847. . . . . Lincoln
LU 1029 . . . . Georgetown
LU 1154. . . . . Wilmington

Letter Carriers
BR 191 . . . . Wilmington
BR 906 . . . . Dover
BR 1977 . . . . Newark
BR 3846 Lewes, Delaware . . Lewes
BR 4015 . . . . New Castle
SA Delaware . . . . . Wilmington

Locomotive Engineers
DIV 484 . . . . Seaford

Longshoremen
LU 1694. . . . . Wilmington
LU 1694-001 . . . . . Wilmington
LU 1883 Clerks &
    Checkers . . . . . . Wilmington
LU 1884. . . . . Wilmington

Machinists
LG 1284 . . . . Newark

Maintenance of Way Employes
SLG 3052 . . . . New Castle
SLG 3077 . . . . Felton
SLG 3095 . . . . Newark

Musicians
CONF Pennsylvania
    Maryland Delaware & DC
    Areas . . . . Wilmington
LU 21 . . . . Wilmington

National Staff Organization
LU Staff Organization,
    Delaware State Education
    Association . . . . Dover

Painters
LU 100 . . . . Wilmington

Paper, Allied-Industrial, Chemical Employees
C . . . . Bear
LU 02-770. . . . . . . Marshallton
LU 02-786 . . . . Edgemoor
LU 02-898 . . . . Bear
LU 02-1134. . . . . . Middletown

Plumbing and Pipe Fitting
LU 74 . . . . Wilmington
LU 782. . . . . Seaford

Postal Workers
LU 152 Wilmington
    Delaware/Malcolm T. Smith
    Area . . . . New Castle
LU 1742 Newark . . . . . Newark
LU 5885 Dover . . . . Dover

Rural Letter Carriers
SA Delaware . . . . . . Hockessin

Security, Police and Fire Professionals
LU 410. . . . . Newark

Sheet Metal Workers
LU 526 . . . . Wilmington

State, County and Municipal Employees
C 81 Delaware Public
    Employees. . . . . . New Castle
LU 3898 Kent Convalescent . Dover

Steelworkers
LU 04-6628-S . . . . . New Castle
LU 04-8184-S. . . . . . Wilmington
LU 04-8936-S . . . . . . Claymont
LU 04-12886-S . . . . . . Newark
LU 04-13028-S . . . . Bear
LU 04-13788-S . . . . . Magnolia

Teamsters
LU 326. . . . . New Castle

Theatrical Stage Employees
LU 284 . . . . Wilmington

Transport Workers
LU 2015. . . . . Wilmington

Transportation Communications Union
D 584 . . . . Wilmington
D 812 . . . . Wilmington
LG 5087 Amtrak . . . . Willmington
SBA 86 Conrail. . . . . Wilmington

Transportation Union
GCA GO-743 National Railroad
    Passenger Corporation . . . Felton
LU 1378. . . . . Seaford
SLB LO-9 Delaware. . . New Castle

Treasury Employees
CH 56 . . . . Wilmington

Unaffiliated Labor Organizations

Dupont Systems Unions Independent
    Seaford Nylon Employees
    Council . . . . Seaford
Flight Attendants for Independent
    Representation (FAIR) . Hockessin
Texaco Employees Association South
    Jersey Employees . . . New Castle

District of Columbia

AFL-CIO Trade and Industrial Departments

Building and Construction Trades Department
NHQ. . . . . Washington

Food and Allied Service Trades Department
FASTC Food & Allied
Services. . . . . . Washington
NHQ. . . . . Washington

Maritime Trades Department
NHQ. . . . . Washington

Metal Trades Department
MTC Washington DC
Area. . . . . Washington
NHQ. . . . . Washington

Union Label and Service Trades Department
NHQ. . . . . Washington

AFL-CIO Directly Affiliated Locals
NHQ. . . . . Washington

Affiliated Labor Organizations

Agricultural Employees
BR 30 . . . . Washington

Air Traffic Controllers
LU DCA . . . . Washington
LU IAD . . . . Washington
NHQ. . . . . Washington

Asbestos Workers
NHQ. . . . . Washington

Bakery, Confectionery, Tobacco Workers and Grain Millers
LU 118 . . . . Washington

Bricklayers
NHQ. . . . . Washington

Carpenters
LU 1110. . . . . Washington
NHQ. . . . . Washington

Communications Workers
LU 2300. . . . . Washington
LU 2336. . . . . Washington
LU 2381. . . . . Washington
LU 2382. . . . . Washington
LU 2385 Federation of National
Representatives . . . . Washington
LU 14200 . . . . Washington
LU 32035 Washington-
Baltimore . . . . Washington
NHQ. . . . . Washington

Education
NHQ. . . . . Washington
SA Federal Education
Association . . . . . . Washington

Electrical Workers
LU 26 . . . . Washington

NHQ. . . . . Washington

Federal Employees
LU 2. . . . . Washington
LU 1418. . . . . Washington
LU 1461. . . . . Washington
LU 1800 . . . . Washington
LU 1919. . . . . Washington
LU 2008. . . . . Washington
LU 2015. . . . . Washington
NHQ. . . . . Washington

Fire Fighters
NHQ. . . . . Washington

Flight Attendants
LEC 5 United Airlines . Washington
LEC 6 United Airlines . Washington
LEC 7 United Airlines . Washington
LEC 8 United Airlines . Washington
LEC 9 United Airlines . Washington
LEC 10 United Airlines . Washington
LEC 11 United Airlines. Washington
LEC 12 United Airlines . Washington
LEC 14 United Airlines. Washington
LEC 15 United Airlines. Washington
LEC 16 United Airlines. Washington
LEC 17 Horizon
Airlines . . . . Washington
LEC 18 Alaska Airlines. Washington
LEC 19 Alaska Airlines. Washington
LEC 20 United Airlines. Washington
LEC 21 United Airlines . Washington
LEC 22 United Airlines. Washington
LEC 23 United Airlines. Washington
LEC 24 United Airlines. Washington
LEC 25 United Airlines. Washington
LEC 26 United Airlines. Washington
LEC 27 United Airlines. Washington
LEC 28 Air Wisconsin . Washington
LEC 29 Air Wisconsin . Washington
LEC 31 American Trans
Air . . . . Washington
LEC 32 American Trans
Air . . . . Washington
LEC 33 American Trans
Air . . . . Washington
LEC 34 American Trans
Air . . . . Washington
LEC 35 American Trans
Air . . . . Washington
LEC 36 American Trans
Air . . . . Washington
LEC 37 American Trans
Air . . . . Washington
LEC 38 United Airlines. Washington
LEC 39 Alaska Airlines. Washington
LEC 40 U.S. Airways. . Washington
LEC 41 USAir . . . . . Washington
LEC 42 Pro Air . . . . . Washington
LEC 43 Hawaiian
Airlines . . . . Washington
LEC 44 Midwest Express
Airlines . . . . Washington
LEC 45 Mesaba
Airlines . . . . Washington
LEC 46 Mesaba
Airlines . . . . Washington
LEC 47 Hawaiian
Airlines . . . . Washington
LEC 48 Mesaba
Airlines . . . . Washington
LEC 49 Executive
Airlines . . . . Washington

LEC 50 Atlantic Coast
Airlines . . . . Washington
LEC 51 Simmons
Airlines . . . . Washington
LEC 52 Simmons
Airlines . . . . Washington
LEC 53 Wings West
Airlines . . . . Washington
LEC 54 Aloha Airlines . Washington
LEC 55 American Eagle
Airlines . . . . Washington
LEC 56 Mesa . . . . . Washington
LEC 57 Air Tran . . . . Washington
LEC 58 Flagship
Airlines . . . . Washington
LEC 59 Flagship
Airlines . . . . Washington
LEC 60 Southeast
Airlines . . . . Washington
LEC 61 Piedmont
Airlines . . . . Washington
LEC 62 C C Air. . . . . Washington
LEC 63 Midway
Airlines . . . . Washington
LEC 65 Allegheny . . Washington
LEC 66 America West . Washington
LEC 68 Pan Am. . . . Washington
LEC 69 USAirways. . . Washington
LEC 70 USAirways. . . Washington
LEC 71 Tower Airlines . Washington
LEC 73 Atlantic Coast
Jet . . . . Washington
LEC 74 Spirit Airlines . Washington
LEC 75 PSA . . . . . Washington
LEC 76 Spirit Airlines . Washington
LEC 77 Iberia Airlines . Washington
LEC 78 Spirit Airlines . Washington
LEC 82 USAirways. . . Washington
LEC 87 USAir . . . . . Washington
LEC 89 U.S. Airways . Washington
MEC Air Wisconsin . . Washington
MEC Alaska Airlines . . Washington
MEC Aloha Airlines . . Washington
MEC America West. . Washington
MEC American Eagle
Airlines . . . . Washington
MEC American Trans
Air . . . . Washington
MEC Eastern Region . . Washington
MEC Hawaiian
Airlines . . . . Washington
MEC Mesaba Airlines . Washington
MEC Midwest Express
Airlines . . . . Washington
MEC Spirit Airlines. . . Washington
MEC Tower Airlines . . Washington
MEC United Airlines . . Washington
MEC USAirways . . . Washington
MEC Western Region . . Washington
NHQ. . . . . Washington

Food and Commercial Workers
NHQ. . . . . Washington

Football Players
NHQ. . . . . Washington

Government Employees
C 252 Department of Education
Locals. . . . . Washington
JC Printing Crafts U.S. Government
Printing Office . . . . Washington
LU 12 DoL . . . . . . Washington
LU 17 VA, Central
Office . . . . Washington

LU 25 VA. . . . . . . Washington
LU 32 MSPB-OPM . . . Washington
LU 421 DoE. . . . . . Washington
LU 476 HUD . . . . . Washington
LU 1118 DoT . . . . . Washington
LU 1534 DoS . . . . . Washington
LU 1733 GSA. . . . . Washington
LU 1812 USIA . . . . . Washington
LU 1831 NGA . . . . . Washington
LU 1935 . . . . Washington
LU 2151 GSA. . . . . Washington
LU 2211 USITC . . . . Washington
LU 2272 DoJ . . . . . Washington
LU 2303 DoT . . . . . Washington
LU 2463 SI . . . . . . Washington
LU 2532 SBA. . . . . Washington
LU 2607 DoE . . . . . Washington
LU 2640 DoC. . . . . Washington
LU 2667 EEOC. . . . . Washington
LU 2798 VA . . . . . . Washington
LU 2876 GPO. . . . . Washington
LU 3295 FHLBB . . . . Washington
LU 3313 DoT . . . . . Washington
LU 3653 DoT . . . . . Washington
LU 3810 DoC. . . . . Washington
LU 4060 . . . . Washington
NHQ. . . . . Washington

Government Employees Association
LU 3-77-R. . . . . . . Washington

Government Security Officers
LU 21 . . . . Washington
LU 44 . . . . Washington
LU 80 . . . . Washington

Graphic Communications
CONF Commercial
Unions . . . . Washington
LU 285-M. . . . . . . Washington
LU 449-S . . . . Washington
LU 713-S . . . . Washington
NHQ. . . . . Washington

Hotel and Restaurant Employees
LU 25 . . . . Washington
LU 27 Parking & Service
Workers. . . . . . . Washington
LU 2000. . . . . Washington
NHQ. . . . . Washington

Iron Workers
LU 201 . . . . Washington
NHQ. . . . . Washington

Laborers
LU 74 . . . . Washington
LU 456 . . . . Washington
NHQ. . . . . Washington

Letter Carriers
BR 142 Capitol . . . . Washington
NHQ. . . . . Washington

Machinists
LG. . . . . Washington
LG 174 . . . . Washington
LLG 1 National Professional
Employees . . . . . Washington

Marine Engineers
D 1 Pacific Coast
District . . . . Washington

D 6 Professional Airways Systems
 Specialists . . . . . Washington
NHQ. . . . . Washington

Musicians
LU 161-710 . . . . . . Washington

National Staff Organization
ASSN NEA Staff
 Organization . . . . . Washington
LU NEA Association of Field Service
 Employees . . . . . Washington

Nurses
NHQ. . . . . Washington
SA DC Nurses
 Association . . . . . Washington

Office and Professional Employees
NHQ. . . . . Washington

Operating Engineers
LU 5 . . . . Washington
LU 99 . . . . Washington
NHQ. . . . . Washington

Painters
LU 1997 . . . . Washington
NHQ. . . . . Washington

Plasterers and Cement Masons
LU 891 . . . . Washington

**Plate Printers, Die Stampers and
 Engravers**
LU 32 . . . . Washington

Plumbing and Pipe Fitting
LU 602 . . . . Washington
LU 652 . . . . Washington
NHQ. . . . . Washington

Police
LG 1 BEP Labor
 Committee . . . . . Washington
LG 1 Defense Protective Labor
 Committee . . . . . Washington
LG 1 Library of Congress Labor
 Committee . . . . . Washington
LG 1 U.S. Capitol Police Labor
 Committee . . . . . Washington
LG 1-F WRAMC/DoD Police Labor
 Committee . . . . . Washington

Police Associations
LU 122 Metropolitan Special
 Police . . . . Washington
LU 1991 . . . . Washington

Postal and Federal Employees
LU 206 . . . . Washington
LU 209 . . . . Washington
NHQ. . . . . Washington

Postal Mail Handlers
NHQ. . . . . Washington

Postal Workers
LU 140 Nation's Capital Southern
 Maryland . . . . . . Washington
LU 7002 Washington Mail
 Equipment Shops . . . Washington
NHQ. . . . . Washington
SA Rhode Island . . . . Washington

**Professional and Technical
 Engineers**
LU 9 . . . . Washington
LU 75 Congressional
 Research Employees
 Association . . . . . Washington

Professional Athletes
NHQ. . . . . Washington

**Roofers, Waterproofers and Allied
 Workers**
NHQ. . . . . Washington

Service Employees
CONF National Conference of
 Firemen & Oilers . . . Washington
LU 64 Firemen &
 Oilers . . . . Washington
LU 82 . . . . Washington
LU 722 . . . . Washington
LU 1199 NUHHCE D 1199 Strategic
 & Defense Fund . . . Washington
NHQ. . . . . Washington

Sheet Metal Workers
NHQ. . . . . Washington

**State, County and Municipal
 Employees**
C 20 District of
 Columbia . . . . . . Washington
C 26 Capital Area . . . . Washington

D 1199 Hospital and Healthcare
 Employees . . . . . Washington
LU 2477 Library of Congress
 Employees . . . . . Washington
LU 2478 Commission on Civil Rights
 Employees . . . . . Washington
LU 2830. . . . . Washington
LU 2910. . . . . Washington
LU 3097 DoJ . . . . . Washington
LU 3548. . . . . Washington
NHQ. . . . . Washington

Teachers
LU 6 Washington Teachers
 Union . . . . Washington
NHQ. . . . . Washington

Teamsters
CONF Brewery & Soft Drink
 Workers . . . . . . Washington
JC 55 . . . . Washington
LU 67 . . . . Washington
LU 96 Public Utility
 Workers . . . . . . Washington
LU 246 . . . . Washington
LU 639 . . . . Washington
LU 730 . . . . Washington
LU 922 . . . . Washington
NHQ. . . . . Washington

Theatrical Stage Employees
LU 224 . . . . Washington
LU 815 . . . . Washington
LU 819 . . . . Washington
LU 868 . . . . Washington
LU 868-B . . . . Washington

Transit Union
NHQ. . . . . Washington

**Transportation Communications
 Union**
LG 6364 Capitol . . . . Washington

Treasury Employees
CH 65 . . . . Washington
CH 83 . . . . Washington
CH 86 . . . . Washington
CH 101 . . . . Washington
CH 159 . . . . Washington
CH 201 . . . . Washington
CH 204 . . . . Washington
CH 207 . . . . Washington
CH 208 . . . . Washington
CH 209 . . . . Washington
CH 213 . . . . Washington

CH 229 . . . . Washington
CH 250 . . . . Washington
CH 251 . . . . Washington
CH 280 . . . . Washington
CH 293 . . . . Washington
NHQ. . . . . Washington

University Professors
NHQ. . . . . Washington

Utility Workers
NHQ. . . . . Washington

Weather Service Employees
BR 01-74 . . . . . . Washington
BR 01-88 . . . . . . Washington
BR 08-1 . . . . Washington
NHQ. . . . . Washington

Unaffiliated Labor
Organizations
Communications Workers of
 America Guild . . . . Washington
English Language Institute Faculty
 Association . . . . . Washington
Executive Staff Association of B'nai
 B'rith/Jewish Women
 International . . . . . Washington
Foreign Service Association
 American . . . . . . Washington
House Staff Association, Childrens
 Hospital National Medical
 Center. . . . . Washington
Interstate Commerce
 Commission Professional
 Association . . . . . Washington
Joint Council of Unions Government
 Printing Office . . . . Washington
National Association of Special
 Police and Security
 Officers . . . . Washington
Organized NATCA Employees
 Union . . . . Washington
Police Association of
 DC . . . . Washington
Professional Association,
 National Labor Relations
 Board . . . . Washington
Rosemount Center Workers
 Association . . . . . Washington
Staff Unions of Congress
 International . . . . . Washington
UMWA Welfare & Retirement Fund
 Employees Union. . . Washington
United Staff Union . . . Washington
United States National Soccer Team
 Players Association. . Washington
Washington International School
 Staff Association . . . Washington

Florida

AFL-CIO Trade and Industrial Departments

Building and Construction Trades Department
BCTC Broward
County . . . . . Fort Lauderdale
BCTC Central Florida. . . . Orlando
BCTC Florida State . . . Tallahassee
BCTC Miami . . . . Miami Lakes
BCTC Northeastern
Florida . . . . Jacksonville
BCTC Palm
Coast . . . . . West Palm Beach
BCTC Tampa Area. . . . . Mango

Maritime Trades Department
PC Greater South
Florida . . . . Dania Beach
PC South Atlantic Area. Jacksonville

Metal Trades Department
MTC Tampa . . . . Tampa

Other Councils and Committees
C Brevard County Central
Labor . . . . Cocoa
C Service Trades . . . . . Orlando

Affiliated Labor Organizations

Aeronautical Examiners
LU 3 . . . . Jacksonville

Agricultural Employees
BR 8. . . . . Miami
BR 26 . . . . . . Fort Lauderdale
BR 29 . . . . Jacksonville
BR 36 . . . . Orlando

Air Traffic Controllers
LU DAB. . . . . . . Daytona Beach
LU FLL . . . . . . Fort Lauderdale
LU FPR . . . . Fort Pierce
LU FXE. . . . . . Fort Lauderdale
LU JAX. . . . . Jacksonville
LU MCO . . . . Orlando
LU MIA. . . . . Miami
LU MLB . . . . Melbourne
LU ORL. . . . . Orlando
LU P31 . . . . Pensacola
LU PBI . . . . . West Palm Beach
LU PIE . . . . Clearwater
LU PMP . . . . . . Pompano Beach
LU PNS . . . . Pensacola
LU RSW . . . . Fort Myers
LU SFB . . . . Sanford
LU SRQ . . . . Tallevast
LU TLH . . . . Tallahassee
LU TMB . . . . Miami
LU TPA. . . . . Tampa
LU VRB . . . . Vero Beach
LU ZJX . . . . Hilliard
LU ZMA . . . . Miami

Asbestos Workers
LU 13 . . . . Jacksonville
LU 60. . . . . Opa Locka
LU 67 . . . . Tampa
LU 302 Heat & Frost
Insulators . . . . Orlando

Automobile, Aerospace Workers
C Florida . . . . Orlando
LU 298 . . . . Clearwater
LU 323 . . . . Jacksonville
LU 788 . . . . Orlando
LU 1124 . . . . . . Pinellas Park
LU 1522 . . . . Kissimmee
LU 1649 . . . . Orlando
LU 1707. . . . . Orlando
LU 1821 . . . . Ocala
LU 6520 . . . . Jacksonville

Bakery, Confectionery, Tobacco Workers and Grain Millers
LU 103 . . . . Orlando
LU 361 . . . . Tampa
LU 482 . . . . Jacksonville

Boilermakers
LG 199 . . . . Jacksonville
LG 433 . . . . Tampa

Bricklayers
LU 1 . . . . Pembroke Park

Carpenters
C Florida Industrial & Public
Employees. . . . . Winter Garden
C South Florida Region . . . Hialeah
DC Central/North Florida DC
4032 . . . . Tampa
LU 75 . . . . Gainesville
LU 115. . . . . Hialeah
LU 123 . . . . . Fort Lauderdale
LU 125 . . . . Miami
LU 130 . . . . . West Palm Beach
LU 140 . . . . Tampa
LU 627 . . . . Jacksonville
LU 1000 . . . . Tampa
LU 1026 . . . . Hallandale
LU 1554 . . . . Hialeah
LU 1641 . . . . Naples
LU 1765 . . . . Orlando
LU 1820 . . . . . . Winter Garden
LU 2357 . . . . Cross City
LU 2411 . . . . Jacksonville
LU 2471 . . . . Pensacola

Civilian Technicians
CH 86 Florida Air . . . Jacksonville
CH 87 Florida Army . . Jacksonville

Communications Workers
LU 3101 . . . . Cocoa
LU 3102 . . . . Port Orange
LU 3103 . . . . Chipley
LU 3104 . . . . . Pompano Beach
LU 3105 . . . . Gainesville
LU 3106 . . . . Jacksonville
LU 3108 . . . . Orlando
LU 3109 . . . . Pensacola
LU 3110. . . . . . . St. Augustine
LU 3111 . . . . Fort Pierce
LU 3112. . . . . West Palm Beach
LU 3113 . . . . Debary
LU 3114 . . . . . Panama City
LU 3115 . . . . Brooksville
LU 3120 . . . . Hollywood
LU 3121. . . . . Miami
LU 3122. . . . . Miami
LU 3140. . . . . Orlando
LU 3151 . . . . Jacksonville
LU 3171 . . . . . . Newahitchka
LU 3174 . . . . Wellborn
LU 3175. . . . . Miami

LU 3176 . . . . Ocala
LU 3177 . . . . Key West
LU 3190. . . . . Fort Lauderdale
LU 14309. . . New Smyrna Beach
LU 14310 . . . . Lakeland
LU 14315. . . . . Tampa
LU 14318. . . . . . San Antonio
LU 53033 . . . . . . Hollywood
LU 83-712. . . . . . Lake Worth
STC Florida State . . . Panama City

Education
LU United Faculty of
Florida. . . . . . . Tallahassee

Electrical Workers
LU 108 . . . . Tampa
LU 177 . . . . Jacksonville
LU 199 . . . . Fort Myers
LU 222 . . . . Reddick
LU 308 . . . . . . St. Petersburg
LU 349 . . . . Miami
LU 359 . . . . Miami
LU 433 . . . . Homosassa
LU 606 . . . . Orlando
LU 622 . . . . Sanderson
LU 624 . . . . Panama City
LU 626 . . . . Winter Haven
LU 627 . . . . Port St. Lucie
LU 641 . . . . Fort Myers
LU 676 . . . . Pensacola
LU 682 . . . . . . St. Petersburg
LU 728 . . . . . Fort Lauderdale
LU 756 . . . . Daytona Beach
LU 759 . . . . . . Pompano Beach
LU 820 . . . . Ellenton
LU 824 . . . . Tampa
LU 862 . . . . Jacksonville
LU 915 . . . . Tampa
LU 1042 . . . . . . Lake Monroe
LU 1055. . . . . . . Cantonment
LU 1066. . . . . . . Port Orange
LU 1191. . . . . West Palm Beach
LU 1205 . . . . Gainesville
LU 1263 . . . . . . Pomona Park
LU 1346 . . . . . Pembroke Pines
LU 1412 . . . . . Mount Plymouth
LU 1491 . . . . Deland
LU 1496 . . . . Monticello
LU 1583 . . . . Palatka
LU 1908 . . . . Titusville
LU 1924 . . . . . Fernandina Beach
LU 1933. . . . . North Fort Myers
LU 1937 . . . . Molino
LU 2000. . . . . Orlando
LU 2072 . . . . Umatilla
LU 2088 . . . . Cocoa
LU 2156 . . . . Alachua
SC U-4 Florida Power &
Light . . . . Bradenton
SC 8-U . . . . Dunnellon

Electronic Workers
LU 736 . . . . Miami
LU 740 . . . . Jacksonville
LU 751 . . . . Jacksonville

Elevator Constructors
LU 49 . . . . Jacksonville
LU 71 . . . . Miami
LU 74 . . . . Tampa
LU 139 . . . . Orlando

Federal Employees
LU 153 . . . MacDill Air Force Base

LU 1485 . . . . Homestead
LU 1608 . . . . . Miami Springs
LU 2147 . . . . Green Cove Springs
LU 2154 . . . . . . Orange Park

Flint Glass Workers
LU 38 . . . . Jacksonville
LU 46 . . . . Bradenton

Food and Commercial Workers
LU . . . . Lakeland
LU 35-C . . . . Mulberry
LU 39-C . . . . Mulberry
LU 328-C . . . . . . Panama City
LU 359-C . . . . Orlando
LU 377-C . . . . . . Fort Meade
LU 428-C . . . Palm Beach Gardens
LU 439-C . . . . Gibsonton
LU 753-C . . . . Lakeland
LU 784-C . . . . . . White Springs
LU 814-C . . . . . Bowling Green
LU 836-C . . . . . . Port St. Joe
LU 1625 . . . . Orlando

Glass, Molders, Pottery and Plastics Workers
LU 91 . . . . Jacksonville
LU 184 . . . . Casselberry
LU 208 . . . . Grove City
LU 211 . . . . Eustis
LU 268. . . . . Sanford
LU 310 . . . . Lakeland

Government Employees
C 41 Florida State . . . Gainesville
LU 192 ID . . . Jacksonville
LU 501 FBOP. . . . . . Miami
LU 507 . . . . . . Riveria Beach
LU 508 DFAS. . . . . Orlando
LU 509 . . . . Lake Buena Vista
LU 513. . . . Kennedy Space Center
LU 515 Miami VAMC . . . . Miami
LU 547 VA . . . . Tampa
LU 548 . . . . Bay Pines
LU 696 DoD . . . . . Orange Park
LU 1113 . . . . . . Panama City
LU 1167 . . . . . . Homestead Air
Reserve Station
LU 1380 . . . . . Panama City
LU 1458 DoJ . . . . . Orlando
LU 1566 DoD . . . . Key West
LU 1570 DoJ . . . . . Tallahassee
LU 1594 WCFB . . . St. Petersburg
LU 1897 DoD . Eglin Air Force Base
LU 1940 . . . Eglin Air Force Base
LU 1943 . . . . . Jacksonville
LU 1960 DoD . . . . . Pensacola
LU 1976 VA. . . . . . Lake City
LU 2010 DoD . . . . Mayport
LU 2014 DoD . . . . Margate
LU 2113 . . . . Orlando
LU 2447 DoD. . . . . . Miami
LU 2453 DoD. . . . Jacksonville
LU 2519 DoL . . . Jacksonville
LU 2568
DoD . . . Patrick Air Force Base
LU 2779 VA. . . . . Gainesville
LU 2875 DoC. . . . . . Miami
LU 3168 USDA . . . . . Sunrise
LU 3240
DoD . . . Tyndall Air Force Base
LU 3412 DoJ . . . . Jacksonville
LU 3690 DoJ . . . . . . Miami
LU 3725 DoJ . . . . . Jacksonville

LU 3953 DLA, Florida
Employees . . . . Orlando
LU 4035 BOP, FPC, Eglin Air Force
Base . . . . . Eglin Air Force Base
LU 4036 FCI . . . . Bonifay
LU 4037 FPCP . . . . . . Pensacola
LU 4056 SSA . . . . . Fort Myers

Government Employees Association
LU 05-45 . . . . . . St. Petersburg
LU 05-82 . . . . . . Atlantic Beach
LU 05-95 . . . . Gulf Breeze

Government Security Officers
LU 131 . . . . Miami
LU 132 . . . . Tampa

Graphic Communications
LU 61-N. . . . . West Palm Beach
LU 180-C . . . . . . St. Petersburg
LU 193-C . . . . Tallahassee
LU 444-C . . . . . Ormond Beach
LU 628-S . . . . . Miami Springs

Hotel and Restaurant Employees
LU . . . . Fort Lauderdale
LU 55 . . . . Orlando
LU 104 . . . . Tampa
LU 355 . . . . Miami
LU 362 . . . . Orlando
LU 737 . . . . Orlando

Iron Workers
LU 272 . . . . Fort Lauderdale
LU 397 . . . . Mango
LU 402 . . . . Riviera Beach
LU 597 . . . . Jacksonville
LU 698 . . . . Jacksonville
LU 808 . . . . Orlando

Laborers
DC North & Central
Florida . . . . Jacksonville
DC 53 Southeast
Florida . . . . Miami Beach
LU 478 . . . . Miami
LU 517 . . . . Orlando
LU 630 . . . . Jacksonville
LU 767 . . . . . West Palm Beach
LU 800 . . . . Miami
LU 1240 . . . . Lakeland

Letter Carriers
BR 53 . . . . Jacksonville
BR 321 . . . . Pensacola
BR 599 . . . . Tampa
BR 689 . . . . St. Augustine
BR 818 . . . . Key West
BR 1025 . . . . Gainesville
BR 1071 . . . . Miami
BR 1091 . . . . Orlando
BR 1103 . . . . Ocala
BR 1172 . . . . Tallahassee
BR 1477 . . . . Pinellas Park
BR 1690 . . . . . West Palm Beach
BR 1721 Arcadia, Florida . . Arcadia
BR 1753 . . . . Bradenton
BR 1779 . . . . Lakeland
BR 2008 Springtime
City . . . . Clearwater
BR 2072 . . . . Fort Myers
BR 2088 . . . . Winter Haven
BR 2148 . . . . Sarasota
BR 2325 MacClenny, Florida
. . . . MacClenny
BR 2550 . . . . Fort Lauderdale
BR 2591 . . . . Deland

BR 2689 . . . . Melbourne
BR 2744 . . . . Sebring
BR 2750 . . . . Lake Wales
BR 2776 Quincy, Florida . . Quincy
BR 2796 Madison, Florida . Madison
BR 2889 . . . . Perry
BR 3018 Williston,
Florida . . . . Williston
BR 3129 . . . . New Smyrna Beach
BR 3348 . . . . De Funiak Springs
BR 3367 . . . . Panama City
BR 3641 Monticello,
Florida . . . . Monticello
BR 3663 Apalachicola,
Florida . . . . . . Apalachicola
BR 3667 Chipley, Florida . . Chipley
BR 3761 . . . . Cocoa
BR 3765 Bonifay, Florida . . Bonifay
BR 3847 . . . . Vero Beach
BR 4000 . . . . Avon Park
BR 4559 . . . . . Fort Walton Beach
BR 4669 Chattahoochee,
Florida . . . . . . Chattahooche
BR 4716 . . . . Naples
BR 4997 Frostproof,
Florida . . . . Frostproof
BR 5002 . . . . . Fort Walton Beach
BR 5192 . . . . Apopka
BR 5201 Port St. Joe,
Florida . . . . Overstreet
BR 5480 . . . . Venice
BR 5561 . . . . Casselberry
BR 5951 . . . . Edgewater
BR 5955 . . . . Altamonte Springs
BR 5957 . . . . . Lake Hamilton
BR 6013 Inverness,
Florida . . . . Inverness
BR 6200 Blountstown,
Florida . . . . . . Blountstown
BR 6491 . . . . Crystal River
BR 6551 Havana, Florida . . Havana
BR 8008 Tampa,
Florida . . . . . . St. Petersburg
SA Florida . . . . Miami

Locomotive Engineers
DIV 35 . . . . Jacksonville
DIV 49 . . . . . . Pembroke Pines
DIV 92 . . . . Polk City
DIV 216 . . . . Valrico
DIV 275 . . . . Cantonment
DIV 309 . . . . Orange Park
DIV 769 . . . . Sanford
GCA CSX Transportation . Chulvota
GCA CSXT Northern Railroad
Lines . . . . . . Ponte Vedra Beach
GCA CSXT Western Railroad
Lines . . . . . Jacksonville Beach
SLB Florida . . . . Deland

Longshoremen
C Southeastern Dock &
Marine . . . . Jacksonville
LU 1359 . . . . Fort Pierce
LU 1402 . . . . Tampa
LU 1408 . . . . Jacksonville
LU 1416 . . . . Miami
LU 1526 . . . . Fort Lauderdale
LU 1569 . . . . Tampa
LU 1593 . . . . Jacksonville
LU 1691 . . . . Tampa
LU 1713 . . . . Port St. Joe
LU 1759 . . . . Tampa
LU 1922 . . . . Miami
LU 1922-1 . . . . Miami
LU 1988 . . . . Pensacola
LU 2062 . . . . Miami

Machinists
DLG 112 . . . . Jacksonville
DLG 166 . . . . . Cape Canaveral
LG 40 . . . . Yulee
LG 57 . . . . South Bay
LG 192 . . . . Pensacola
LG 257 . . . . Jacksonville
LG 368 . . . . Miami
LG 458-FL . . . . Bristol
LG 501 . . . . Daytona Beach
LG 570 . . . . Pinellas Park
LG 610 . . . . Cocoa
LG 676 . . . . Milton
LG 731 . . . . Jacksonville
LG 759 . . . . Jacksonville
LG 773 . . . . Titusville
LG 815 . . . . Merritt Island
LG 971 . . . . Jupiter
LG 1003 . . . . Jacksonville
LG 1098 . . . . Interlachen
LG 1106 . . . . Panama City
LG 1163 . . . . Merritt Island
LG 1852 . . . . Fort Lauderdale
LG 2061 Banana River . . . . Cocoa
LG 2152 . . . . South Bay
LG 2319 . . . . Seminole
LG 2460 . . . . Pensacola
LG 2508 . . . . Orlando
LG 2777 . . . . Milton
LG 2902 . . . . Gulf Breeze
LU 1453 . . . . Miami
STC Florida . . . . . . Melbourne

Maintenance of Way Employes
FED Seaboard . . . . . Riverview
LG . . . . Fort Pierce
LG 540 . . . . St. Cloud
LG 2655 . . . . Seffner
LG 2912 . . . . Sebring
LG 2914 . . . . St. Augustine
SLG 539 . . . . Jacksonville
SLG 547 . . . . Lakeland
SLG 702 . . . . Century
SLG 739 . . . . Avon Park
SLG 2057 . . . . Greenville
SLG 2162 . . . . Lawtey

Marine Engineers
D 1 Federation of Private Employees,
Division of NFOPAE . . Plantation
D 1 National Federation of Public &
Private Employees . . . Plantation

Musicians
LU 283 . . . . Pensacola
LU 389 . . . . Orlando
LU 427-721 . . . . Clearwater
LU 444 . . . . Jacksonville
LU 655 . . . . Hollywood
STCON Florida
Georgia . . . . Jacksonville

National Staff Organization
LU Staff Organization,
Florida . . . . Orange Park

NLRB Professional Association
LU 12 . . . . Tampa

Nurses
LU Florida Nurses Association of
Shands Hospital . . . . . Orlando
LU Florida Nurses-Wuesthoff
Unit . . . . Orlando
SA Florida Nurses
Association . . . . Orlando

Nurses, Practical
SA Licensed Practical Nurses
Association of
Florida . . . . St. Petersburg

Office and Professional Employees
LU 46 . . . . Riverview
LU 55 . . . . Palm City
LU 73 . . . . Jacksonville
LU 80 . . . . Panama City
LU 100 . . . . Miami
LU 337 . . . . Palatka

Operating Engineers
LU 487 . . . . Miami
LU 673-ABC . . . . Orlando
LU 925 . . . . Mango

Painters
DC 78 . . . . Orlando
LU 88 . . . . Tampa
LU 164 . . . . Jacksonville
LU 365 . . . . Miami
LU 452 . . . . . West Palm Beach
LU 1010 . . . . Orlando
LU 1175 . . . . Miami

Paper, Allied-Industrial, Chemical Employees
ASSN Southern Pulp & Paper
Industry . . . . Palatka
LU 991-003 . . . . . Palm Harbor
LU 3-585 . . . . Perry
LU 03-30 . . . . Palatka
LU 03-392 . . . . Miami
LU 03-395 . . . . Fernandina Beach
LU 03-415 . . . . Fernandina Beach
LU 03-426 . . . . . . Jacksonville
LU 03-444 . . . . . . Cantonment
LU 03-447 . . . . . . Cantonment
LU 03-450 . . . . Fernandina Beach
LU 03-458 . . . . Lutz
LU 03-475 . . . . . Winter Haven
LU 03-530 . . . . Palatka
LU 03-547 . . . . . . Cantonment
LU 03-606 . . . . Riverview
LU 03-622 . . . . . . Lake Wales
LU 03-720 . . . . Riverview
LU 03-766 . . . . Fernandina Beach
LU 03-802 . . . . Fernandina Beach
LU 03-834 . . . . Orlando
LU 03-835 . . . . . Winter Haven
LU 03-874 . . . . . . Jacksonville
LU 03-984 . . . . Tampa
LU 03-996 . . . . . . Jacksonville
LU 03-1138 . . . . . Lake Placid
LU 03-1192 . . . . Perry
LU 03-1342 . . . . . Panama City
LU 03-1466 . . . . . Middleburg
LU 03-1561 . . . . . Cantonment
LU 03-1649 . . . . . Jacksonville
LU 03-1717 . . . . . . Palatka
LU 05-130 . . . . Riverview

Plasterers and Cement Masons
LU 401 . . . . Jacksonville

Plumbing and Pipe Fitting
DC Florida Pipe Trades . Tallahassee
LU 123 . . . . Dover
LU 234 . . . . Jacksonville
LU 295 . . . . Daytona Beach
LU 366 . . . . Pensacola
LU 519 . . . . Miami Lakes
LU 592 . . . . Tallahassee
LU 630 . . . . . West Palm Beach
LU 719 . . . . Fort Lauderdale
LU 725 . . . . Opa Locka

LU 803 . . . . Orlando
LU 821 . . . . Hollywood

Postal and Federal Employees
LU 320 . . . . Jacksonville
LU 322 . . . . Miami
LU 323 . . . . Pensacola
LU 327 . . . . Tampa
LU 329 . . . . Lake Mary
LU 333 . . . . Fort Pierce
LU 334 . . . . . . Fort Lauderdale

Postal Mail Handlers
LU 318 . . . . Orlando

Postal Workers
LU 138 Northeast Florida
  Area . . . . Jacksonville
LU 172 Miami Area . . . . Miami
LU 259 Tampa Area . . . . Tampa
LU 551 Pensacola . . . . Pensacola
LU 620 Florida Keys
  Area . . . . Key West
LU 749 Palm Beach
  Area . . . . Lake Worth
LU 1073 Sarasota . . . . . Sarasota
LU 1201 Broward County
  Area . . . . Fort Lauderdale
LU 1209 Melbourne
  Area . . . . Melbourne
LU 1213 Fort Pierce . . . Fort Pierce
LU 1228 Suncoast
  Area . . . . Pinellas Park
LU 1279 Fort Myers . . . Fort Myers
LU 1414 Panama City . Panama City
LU 1462 Central Florida
  Area . . . . Orlando
LU 1519 Tallahassee . . Tallahassee
LU 1672 Daytona
  Beach . . . . . . Daytona Beach
LU 1684 New Smyrna
  Beach . . . . . New Smyrna Beach
LU 2502 Titusville . . . . Titusville
LU 2503 Madison Local . . Madison
LU 2510 Perry Local . . . . . Perry
LU 2664 Cocoa . . . . . Cocoa Beach
LU 3057 Manatee Area . . Bradenton
LU 3399 Clearwater . . . Clearwater
LU 3450 Vero Beach . . Vero Beach
LU 3525 Gainesville . . . Gainesville
LU 3537 Plant City . . . . Plant City
LU 3732 Marianna . . . . Marianna
LU 3796 St. Cloud . . . . . St. Cloud
LU 3799 Citrus Center
  Area . . . . Lakeland
LU 3803 Venice . . . . . . Venice
LU 3804 Jasper . . . . . . Jasper
LU 3858 Bonifay . . . . . Bonifay
LU 3936 Crestview Local . Crestview
LU 4158 De Land . . . . . Deland
LU 4613 Dunnellon
  Local . . . . Dunnellon
LU 5643 Play Ground Area
  Local . . . . Fort Walton Beach
LU 5661 Orange City . . . Deltona
LU 6676 Lake Placid
  Local . . . . Lake Placid
LU 7041 Jacksonville Bulk Mail
  Center . . . . Jacksonville
LU 7136 Manasota . . . . Tallevast
LU 7138 Mid-Florida . . Lake Mary
LU 8002 First Coast
  Local . . . . Jacksonville
SA Florida . . . . Tallahassee

**Professional and Technical
  Engineers**
LU 22 NAPEP Council . Jacksonville

Railroad Signalmen
GC 3690 Seaboard Coastline
  Railroad . . . . . . Jacksonville
LLG 16 . . . . Jacksonville

**Retail, Wholesale and Department
  Store**
LU 43 . . . . Dade City
LU 531 . . . . Jacksonville

**Roofers, Waterproofers and Allied
  Workers**
LU 103 . . . . . West Palm Beach
LU 181 . . . . Jacksonville

Rural Letter Carriers
D 1 . . . . Port St. Lucie
D 2 . . . . Lehigh Acres
D 3 . . . . Chuluota
D 4 . . . . Brooksville
D 5 . . . . Citra
D 6 . . . . Gainesville
D 7 . . . . Leesburg
D 8 . . . . Live Oak
D 9 . . . . Chipley
D 10 . . . . Baker
D 11 . . . . Jacksonville
D 12 . . . . Lake Wales
D 13 . . . . St. Augustine
D 14 Florida . . . . Fort Lauderdale
D 15 Florida . . . . . . Venice
D 16 Florida . . . . . Palm Bay
D 17 Florida . . . . . Bradenton
D 18 Florida . . . . . Springhill
SA Florida . . . . . . Floral City

**Security, Police and Fire
  Professionals**
LU . . . . Homestead
LU 127 . . . . . . Merritt Island
LU 129 . . . . Fort Pierce
LU 602 . . . . Orlando
LU 603 . . . . . Lake Buena Vista
LU 604 . . . . Lecanto
LU 607 . . . . Oviedo
LU 611 . . . . Miramar

Service Employees
LU . . . . Miami
LU 1991 . . . . Miami

Sheet Metal Workers
LU 15 . . . . Tampa
LU 32 . . . . . North Miami Beach
LU 435 . . . . Jacksonville
LU 490 . . . . Deltona

**State, County and Municipal
  Employees**
C 79 Florida Public
  Employees . . . . . Tallahassee
LU 1781 University Medical Center
  Employees . . . . . Jacksonville
LU 2897 Shands Teaching Hospital
  & Clinics Employees . Gainesville

Steelworkers
LU 4987 . . . . Jacksonville
LU 8018 . . . . Crawfordville
LU 09-174-S . . . . Havana
LU 09-425-U . . . . . Jacksonville
LU 09-775-L . . . . . High Springs
LU 09-7609-S . . . . . . Miami
LU 09-7752-S . . . . . Wildwood
LU 09-7858-S . . . . . Plant City
LU 09-8461-S . . . . . Jacksonville
LU 09-9292-S . . . . . Jacksonville

LU 09-12130-S . . . . . Pensacola
LU 09-14963-S . . . . Port St. Joe
LU 09-15431-S . . . . . Jacksonville

Teachers
LU 3842 De Soto County Teachers
  Association . . . . Arcadia

Teamsters
CONF Georgia-Florida . Auburndale
LU 79 . . . . Tampa
LU 173 . . . . Bradenton
LU 385 . . . . Orlando
LU 390 . . . . Miami
LU 512 . . . . Jacksonville
LU 769 . . . . Miami
LU 947 . . . . Jacksonville

Television and Radio Artists
LU Miami . . . . Miami

Theatrical Stage Employees
LU 60 . . . . Pensacola
LU 115 . . . . Jacksonville
LU 321 . . . . Tampa
LU 412 . . . . Tallevast
LU 477 . . . . North Miami
LU 545 . . . . North Miami
LU 552 . . . . . . St. Petersburg
LU 558 . . . . Daytona Beach
LU 623 . . . . . West Palm Beach
LU 631 . . . . Orlando
LU 646 . . . . Fort Lauderdale
LU 647 . . . . Estero
LU 835 Exhibition
  Employees . . . . Orlando
LU 843 . . . . Orlando
LU 938-AE . . . . . . Jacksonville

Train Dispatchers
SCOM CSX . . . . . . Jacksonville

Transit Union
LDIV . . . . Tampa
LDIV 1197 . . . . . . Jacksonville
LDIV 1395 . . . . . . Pensacola
LDIV 1593 . . . . Tampa

Transport Workers
LU 500 . . . . . Miami Springs
LU 525 . . . . . . Cocoa Beach
LU 561 . . . . Miami
LU 568 . . . . Miami
LU 570 . . . . . Miami Springs

**Transportation Communications
  Union**
D 229 . . . . Jacksonville
D 697 . . . . Jacksonville
D 724 . . . . . . Jacksonville Beach
D 1220 . . . . Riverview
D 1523 . . . . Jacksonville
D 1908 Allied Services
  Division . . . . . Winter Garden
D 2501 . . . . . North Miami Beach
D 2502 System Division 250 . Ocala
LG 125 United Service
  Workers . . . . . Juno Beach
LG 5093 Amtrak . . . . . Seminole
LG 6021 Brandon . . . . . Seffner
LG 6046 Carmen
  Division . . . . . Orange City
LG 6199 Jax Local . . . . Hilliard
LG 6335 Sibert . . . . . Pensacola
LG 6553 Moncrief . . . Jacksonville
LG 6633 Lakeland . . . . Lakeland
LG 6649 Sun Queen . . . . Sunrise

SBA 3 SCL-L&N
  Southeastern . . . . Jacksonville

Transportation Union
GCA GO-49 Baltimore & Ohio
  Railroad . . . . . . Jacksonville
GCA GO-513 Louisville & Nashville
  Railroad . . . . . . Jacksonville
GCA GO-851 Seaboard Coast Line
  Railroad . . . . . . Jacksonville
LU 903 . . . . Jacksonville
LU 1035 . . . . Lakeland
LU 1138 . . . . Fort Pierce
LU 1221 . . . . Valrico
LU 1312 . . . . Pensacola
LU 1502 . . . . Wildwood
LU 1900 . . . . . . Fort Lauderdale
SLB LO-11 Florida . . . . . Hialeah

Treasury Employees
CH 16 . . . . Jacksonville
CH 77 . . . . Miami
CH 84 . . . . Maitland
CH 87 . . . . Tampa
CH 93 . . . . Plantation
CH 137 . . . . Miami
CH 171 . . . . Jacksonville
CH 174 . . . . Tampa
CH 249 . . . . Sarasota

University Professors
CH Edward Waters
  College . . . . Jacksonville

Utility Workers
LU 551 . . . . Palatka

Weather Service Employees
BR 02-19 . . . . Tallahassee
BR 02-21 . . . . Jacksonville
BR 02-25 . . . . Key West
BR 02-62 . . . . Ruskin
BR 02-65 . . . . Miami
BR 02-72 . . . . Melbourne
BR 02-77 . . . . Hilliard
BR 02-84 . . . . Miami
BR 08-7 . . . . St. Petersburg

Unaffiliated Labor
Organizations
American Longshoremens
  Association of West Florida LU
  1482 . . . . Panama City
Florida Education
  Association . . . . . . Tallahassee
Florida Marble Polishers,
  Independent Tile, Marble and
  Stone Workers . . Fort Lauderdale
Florida Rural Legal Services Workers
  Union . . . . Lakeland
Hospitality Workers Union LU
  10 . . . . Fort Lauderdale
International Organization of
  Professionals International Models
  Guild LU 2000 . . . . . Jupiter
Jacksonville Symphony Players
  Association . . . . . Jacksonville
Jewish Women International Staff
  Association . Palm Beach Gardens
National Association of Government
  Inspectors UNIT 1 . . Jacksonville
Pari-Mutuel Employees Florida
  Independent Association . . Miami
Plastic Workers Organization LU
  1 . . . . Lakeland
Professional Pharmacists
  Association . . . . Lutz

Restaurant Hotel Motel Nightclub . . . . . Fort Lauderdale

Staff Union, Florida AFSCME C 79 . . . . Jacksonville

Sun Marine Licensed Officers Association . . . . . Englewood

United Government Security of America LU 202 . . . . . Miami

World Umpires Association . Cocoa

Georgia

AFL-CIO Trade and Industrial Departments

Building and Construction Trades Department
BCTC Augusta . . . . . . Augusta
BCTC North Georgia . . . . Atlanta
BCTC Savannah . . . . . Savannah

Metal Trades Department
MTC Columbus . . . . Fort Benning

AFL-CIO Directly Affiliated Locals
DALU 461 . . . . Macon

Affiliated Labor Organizations

Agricultural Employees
BR . . . . Savannah
BR 37 . . . . Atlanta

Air Traffic Controllers
LU . . . . Albany
LU AGS . . . . Augusta
LU ATL . . . . Peachtree City
LU CSG . . . . Columbus
LU ESO . . . . College Park
LU M87 . . . . Peachtree City
LU MCN . . . . Macon
LU PDK . . . . Chamblee
LU SAV . . . . Savannah
LU ZTL . . . . Hampton

Aircraft Mechanics
LU 19 . . . . College Park

Asbestos Workers
LU 48 . . . . Atlanta
LU 96 . . . . Pooler

Automobile, Aerospace Workers
C Georgia . . . . Smyrna
LU 10 . . . . Doraville
LU 472 . . . . Covington
LU 868 . . . . Morrow
LU 882 . . . . Hapeville
LU 1103 . . . . Armuchee
LU 1726 . . . . Covington
LU 2188 . . . . Fitzgerald
LU 2378 . . . . Suwanee

Bakery, Confectionery, Tobacco Workers and Grain Millers
LU 42 . . . . Atlanta
LU 362-T . . . . Macon
LU 434 . . . . Macon
LU 600 . . . . Columbus

Boilermakers
LG 23-D Cement Workers . . . . . Hawkinsville
LG 26 . . . . Savannah
LG 100-M . . . . Albany
LG 425 . . . . Waycross
LG 523-D Cement Workers . . . . . Sandersville
LG 545-D Cement Workers . . . . . Montrose

Bricklayers
LU 3 . . . . Forest Park

LU 7 . . . . Athens
LU 22 . . . . Jesup
LU 33 Georgia/North Carolina/South Carolina . . . . Forest Park

Carpenters
LU 144 . . . . Macon
LU 225 . . . . Jonesboro
LU 256 . . . . Savannah
LU 283 . . . . Augusta
LU 865 . . . . Brunswick
LU 1263 . . . . Kennesaw
LU 1723 . . . . Columbus
LU 2268 . . . . Gray
LU 3078 . . . . Danielsville
LU 4043 Southeastern . . . Augusta

Civilian Technicians
CH 36 Aaron B. Roberts . . . . . . Locust Grove
CH 38 Savannah Act . . . Savannah
CH 55 North Georgia Armact . . . . Clarkton
CH 56 South Georgia . . . Hinesville
STC Georgia . . . . . Lawrenceville

Communications Workers
C Georgia Political Council . Macon
LU 3201 . . . . Albany
LU 3203 . . . . Athens
LU 3204 . . . . Atlanta
LU 3205 . . . . Covington
LU 3207 . . . . Martinez
LU 3209 . . . . Brunswick
LU 3212 . . . . Columbus
LU 3215 . . . . Griffin
LU 3217 . . . . Macon
LU 3218 . . . . Marietta
LU 3220 . . . . Savannah
LU 3250 . . . . Norcross
LU 3263 . . . . Norcross
LU 3290 . . . . Canton
LU 14320 . . . . Atlanta
LU 14322 . . . . Atlanta

Education
LU Fort Stewart Association of Educators . . . . . . Fort Stewart

Electrical Workers
LU 84 . . . . Smyrna
LU 508 . . . . Savannah
LU 511 . . . . Valdosta
LU 613 . . . . Atlanta
LU 632 . . . . Cumming
LU 741 . . . . St. Marys
LU 779 . . . . Columbus
LU 1132 . . . . Cochran
LU 1193 . . . . Conyers
LU 1208 . . . . Richmond Hill
LU 1316 . . . . Macon
LU 1391 . . . . Savannah
LU 1531 . . . . Albany
LU 1545 . . . . Jesup
LU 1579 . . . . Augusta
LU 1947 . . . . Valdosta
LU 1984 . . . . Waycross
LU 2064 . . . . Valdosta
LU 2109 . . . . Athens
LU 2127 . . . . Lithonia
LU 2194 . . . . Americus
SC 6 Railroad . . . . . . Cumming

Electronic Workers
LU 190 . . . . Lindale

LU 195 . . . . Atlanta

Elevator Constructors
LU 32 . . . . Atlanta

Federal Employees
LU 122 . . . . Decatur
LU 1329 . . . . Chatsworth
LU 1766 . . . . Atlanta
LU 1788 . . . . Marietta
LU 2047 . . . . Atlanta
LU 2102 . . . . Atlanta

Fire Fighters
LU 107-F Robins Air Force Base . . . . . . Warner Robins
LU 118-F Moody Air Force Base Local . . . . Adel
LU 152-F Dobbins Air Force Base Local . . . . Woodstock

Flint Glass Workers
LU 3 . . . . Warner Robins
LU 6 . . . . Newnan

Food and Commercial Workers
LU 90-T . . . . Rockmart
LU 218 Textile Workers . . . Atlanta
LU 340-T . . . . Cartersville
LU 354 . . . . Cedartown
LU 609-C . . . . Camilla
LU 722 . . . . Atlanta
LU 736-C . . . . Brunswick
LU 832-C . . . . Woodbine
LU 1016-C . . . . Hinesville
LU 1996 . . . . College Park
LU 2600 . . . . Union City

Glass, Molders, Pottery and Plastics Workers
LU 25 . . . . Griffin
LU 53 . . . . Ringgold
LU 63 . . . . Newnan
LU 98 . . . . Midland
LU 101 . . . . Morrow
LU 204 . . . . Austell
LU 234 . . . . Warner Robins
LU 236 . . . . Palmetto
LU 251 . . . . Atlanta
LU 260 . . . . Athens
LU 377-A . . . . Winder
LU 393-A . . . . . . Union Point
LU 395 . . . . Social Circle

Government Employees
C 19 Fifth District . . . . Riverdale
C 39 Georgia State . . . . . Albany
C 228 National SBA Locals . Atlanta
C 240 National U.S. Marine Corps Locals . . . . Albany
LU 54 DoD . . . . . Fort Benning
LU 81 DoD . . . . Stone Mountain
LU 217 VA . . . . Augusta
LU 500 Council of Prisons 33 . . . . Glynco
LU 504 . . . . Fort Benning
LU 517 . . . . Atlanta
LU 518 . . . . Atlanta
LU 987 DoD . . . . Warner Robins
LU 1011 USDA . . . . . . Rome
LU 1145 DoJ . . . . . . Atlanta
LU 1568 DoC . . . . . . Atlanta
LU 1759 DoD . . . . . . Atlanta
LU 1845 DoD . . . . . Kings Bay
LU 1922 DoD . . . . Fort Stewart

LU 1985 VA . . . . Dublin
LU 2002 HHS . . . . . . Glynco
LU 2017 DoD . . . . Fort Gordon
LU 2067 GSA . . . . . Palmetto
LU 2069 DoD . . . . . . Marietta
LU 2252 USDA . . . . Gainesville
LU 2317 DoD . . . . . . Albany
LU 2778 VA . . . . Decatur
LU 2883 DoD . . . . . Decatur
LU 3123 INS . . . . . . Atlanta
LU 3152 USDA . . . Thomasville
LU 3627 HHS . . . . . Savannah
LU 3836 FEMA . . . . Ellenwood
LU 3855 CPSC . . . . . Conyers
LU 3887 DE . . . . . . Atlanta
LU 3981 FCI . . . . Jesup

Government Employees Association
LU 5-120-R Army & Airforce Exchange Service . . . . . Smyrna

Government Security Officers
LU 62 . . . . Fayetteville
LU 135 . . . . Augusta

Graphic Communications
CONF Southern Specialty Unions . . . . Fairburn
DC 7-S Southeastern Printing Specialists . . . . . . Mableton
LU 8-M . . . . Atlanta
LU 96-B . . . . Smyrna
LU 527-S . . . . Mableton
LU 641-S . . . . Newnan

Hotel and Restaurant Employees
LU 151 . . . . Marietta
LU 804 . . . . Columbus

Iron Workers
LU 387 . . . . Atlanta
LU 709 . . . . . . Port Wentworth

Laborers
DC Georgia-South Carolina . Atlanta
LU 438 . . . . Atlanta
LU 752 . . . . Rome
LU 1073 . . . . Columbus
LU 1137 . . . . Augusta

Letter Carriers
BR 73 . . . . Decatur
BR 263 . . . . Augusta
BR 270 . . . . Macon
BR 313 . . . . Brunswick
BR 420 . . . . Leesburg
BR 536 . . . . Rome
BR 546 . . . . Columbus
BR 578 . . . . Savannah
BR 588 . . . . Athens
BR 958 . . . . Waycross
BR 972 . . . . Pitts
BR 998 . . . . Valdosta
BR 1026 . . . . Thomasville
BR 1068 . . . . Dublin
BR 1119 . . . . Marietta
BR 1150 . . . . Tifton
BR 1200 . . . . Bainbridge
BR 1230 . . . . Griffin
BR 1269 . . . . . . Milledgeville
BR 1342 . . . . Lagrange
BR 1393 Fitzgerald, Georgia . . . . Fitzgerald
BR 1421 . . . . Newnan

BR 1441 . . . . Gainesville
BR 1478 Quitman,
  Georgia. . . . . Quitman
BR 1537 . . . . Lilburn
BR 1565 Carrollton,
  Georgia. . . . . Carrollton
BR 1585 . . . . Moultrie
BR 1751 . . . . Statesboro
BR 1833 . . . . Dalton
BR 1919 West Point,
  Georgia . . . . West Point
BR 2225 . . . . Decatur
BR 2389 Eastman, Georgia. Eastman
BR 2390 Washington,
  Georgia . . . . Thomson
BR 2476 Vienna, Georgia . . Vienna
BR 2480 Dawson, Georgia . Dawson
BR 2567 Ashburn, Georgia. Ashburn
BR 2584 . . . . Toccoa
BR 2660 . . . . Cedartown
BR 2758 Cuthbert,
  Georgia. . . . . Cuthbert
BR 2761 Tallapoosa,
  Georgia. . . . . . . Tallapoosa
BR 2808 . . . . Cohutta
BR 2809 . . . . Thomaston
BR 2853 Canton, Georgia . . Canton
BR 2882 Vidalia, Georgia. . Vidalia
BR 2894 Sandersville,
  Georgia. . . . . . . Sandersville
BR 2987 . . . . Lafayette
BR 3006 Baxley, Georgia. . Baxley
BR 3025 Trion, Georgia. . . Trion
BR 3070 Abbeville,
  Georgia . . . . Abbeville
BR 3076 Ocilla, Georgia . . Ocilla
BR 3091 Hogansville,
  Georgia. . . . . . . Hogansville
BR 3203 Commerce,
  Georgia . . . . Commerce
BR 3224 Thomson,
  Georgia . . . . Thomson
BR 3227 Louisville,
  Georgia. . . . . Louisville
BR 3245 . . . . Glennville
BR 3248 Sparta, Georgia . . Sparta
BR 3249 Hawkinsville,
  Georgia . . . . . . Hawkinsville
BR 3254 Waynesboro,
  Georgia. . . . . . . Waynesboro
BR 3261 Blakely, Georgia . Blakely
BR 3269 Pelham, Georgia. . Pelham
BR 3299 Sylvania,
  Georgia. . . . . Sylvania
BR 3353 Barnesville,
  Georgia . . . . Barnesville
BR 3354 Manchester,
  Georgia . . . . Manchester
BR 3361 Tennille, Georgia . Tennille
BR 3364. . . . . Douglas
BR 3365 McRae, Georgia . . McRae
BR 3369 Lyons, Georgia . . . Lyons
BR 3370 Swainsboro,
  Georgia. . . . . . . Swainsboro
BR 3371 Warrenton,
  Georgia. . . . . Warrenton
BR 3445 Forsyth, Georgia. . Forsyth
BR 3458 . . . . Monroe
BR 3504 Cochran, Georgia. Cochran
BR 3511 Rockmart,
  Georgia . . . . Rockmart
BR 3514 . . . . Jesup
BR 3539. . . . . Metter
BR 3547 Donalsonville,
  Georgia. . . . . . . Donalsonville
BR 3578 Monticello,
  Georgia . . . . Monticello
BR 3580 Adel, Georgia. . . . Adel

BR 3581 Blackshear,
  Georgia . . . . Blackshear
BR 3582 Cairo, Georgia . . . Cairo
BR 3583 Camilla, Georgia . Camilla
BR 3584 Hartwell, Georgia Hartwell
BR 3585 Millen, Georgia. . . Millen
BR 3598 Lavonia, Georgia . Lavonia
BR 3637 Alma, Georgia . . . . Alma
BR 3654 Greensboro,
  Georgia . . . . Greensboro
BR 3722 Claxton, Georgia . Claxton
BR 3723 Wrightsville,
  Georgia. . . . . . . Wrightsville
BR 3793 . . . . Buford
BR 3960 Juniper, Georgia . . Juniper
BR 4040 . . . . Leesburg
BR 4057 . . . . Warner Robins
BR 4060 . . . . Summerville
BR 4135 Bremen, Georgia . Bremen
BR 4191 Hazlehurst,
  Georgia. . . . . Hazlehurst
BR 4557 Eatonton,
  Georgia. . . . . Eatonton
BR 4558 Cornelia, Georgia. Cornelia
BR 4568 . . . . Forest Park
BR 4572 Montezuma,
  Georgia . . . . Montezuma
BR 4831 Union Point,
  Georgia. . . . . . . Union Point
BR 4847 Colquitt, Georgia . Colquitt
BR 4854 Homerville,
  Georgia . . . . Homerville
BR 4862. . . . . Roswell
BR 4871 Jackson, Georgia . Jackson
BR 4944. . . . . Hinesville
BR 4946 Perry, Georgia . . . . Perry
BR 5020 Lakeland,
  Georgia . . . . Lakeland
BR 5177 Ellijay, Georgia. . . Ellijay
BR 5756 Soperton,
  Georgia. . . . . Soperton
BR 5795 St. Marys,
  Georgia . . . . St. Marys
BR 5891 Royston, Georgia . Royston
BR 6030 Scottdale,
  Georgia . . . . Scottdale
BR 6070 . . . . Tucker
BR 6275 Cumming,
  Georgia. . . . . . . Cumming
BR 6277. . . . . . . Powder Springs
BR 6278 Villa Rica,
  Georgia. . . . . . . Villa Rica
BR 6425 Folkston,
  Georgia. . . . . Folkston
BR 6578 Chatsworth,
  Georgia. . . . . . . Chatsworth
SA Georgia . . . . Macon

Locomotive Engineers

DIV 30 . . . . Dallas
DIV 59 . . . . Valdosta
DIV 210 . . . . Leary
DIV 316 . . . . Douglasville
DIV 323 . . . . Evans
DIV 328 . . . . Powder Springs
DIV 503 . . . . Dacula
DIV 646. . . . . Statesboro
DIV 648. . . . . Waycross
DIV 696 Currahee . . . . . Suwanee
DIV 706 . . . . Fitzgerald
DIV 779 . . . . Plains
DIV 786 . . . . Macon
DIV 803 . . . . Savannah
SLB Georgia . . . . . . Pembroke

Longshoremen

LU 1414 . . . . Savannah
LU 1423 . . . . Brunswick

LU 1475 . . . . Savannah
LU 1863 . . . . Brunswick
LU 2046. . . . . . . Garden City

Machinists

DLG 96 . . . . Savannah
DLG 131. . . . . Cordele
LG 1 . . . . Conyers
LG 2 . . . . Palmetto
LG 23 . . . . Savannah
LG 204 . . . . Valdosta
LG 272 . . . . Jesup
LG 414. . . . . Rome
LG 615 . . . . Marietta
LG 625 . . . . Hoboken
LG 650 . . . . Savannah
LG 709 . . . . Marietta
LG 713 . . . . Evans
LG 1034 . . . . Macon
LG 1128 . . . . St. Marys
LG 1141. . . . . McDorough
LG 2204 . . . . Waycross
LG 2451 . . . . Naylor
LG 2519 . . . . Folkston
LG 2590 . . . . Gray
LG 2665 . . . . College Park
LG 2699 . . . . Albany
LG 2731 . . . . Griffin
LG 2772 Kings Bay . . . . St. Marys
LG 2783 . . . . St. Marys
LG 2789 . . . . Grovetown
LG 2901 . . . . Conley
LLG W-176
  Woodworkers . . . . . Bainbridge
LLG W-356 Woodworkers. . . Adel
STC Georgia . . . . . . Savannah

Maintenance of Way Employes

LG 806 . . . . Swainsboro
LG 808. . . . . Warner Robins
LG 1643 . . . . Manchester
SLG 56 . . . . Cherrylog
SLG 536 . . . . Lithonia
SLG 619 . . . . Valdosta
SLG 627 . . . . Warthen
SLG 665 . . . . Adairsville
SLG 673 . . . . Clarkesville
SLG 804. . . . . Columbus
SLG 2060 . . . . Americus
SLG 2067 . . . . Bloomingdale
SLG 2163 . . . . Blackshear
SLG 2167 . . . . Tybee Island

Marine Engineers

D 5 Industrial Technical &
  Professional Employees. Savannah

Musicians

CONF International Symphony &
  Opera . . . . Atlanta
LU 148-462 . . . . Atlanta
LU 447-704 . . . . . Savannah

National Staff Organization

LU Georgia Staff . . . . . Decatur

Needletrades

JB South Florida
  Council . . . . Union City
JB Southern Regional . . Union City
LU . . . . Union City
LU . . . . Union City
LU 14-L . . . . Union City
LU 50-11 . . . . Union City
LU 50-13 . . . . Union City
LU 50-14 . . . . Union City
LU 50-15 . . . . Union City
LU 50-16 . . . . Union City

LU 50-17. . . . . . . Union City
LU 50-18. . . . . . . Union City
LU 50-19. . . . . . . Union City
LU 50-20 . . . . . . Union City
LU 50-21 . . . . . . Union City
LU 50-22 . . . . . . Union City
LU 50-23 . . . . . . Union City
LU 50-24 . . . . . . Union City
LU 50-25 . . . . . . Union City
LU 50-27 . . . . . . Union City
LU 50-28 . . . . . . Union City
LU 50-30 . . . . . . Union City
LU 50-31 . . . . . . Union City
LU 50-012 . . . . . . Union City
LU 50-029 . . . . . . Union City
LU 50-032 . . . . . . Union City
LU 116 . . . . Union City
LU 121 . . . . Union City
LU 122 . . . . Union City
LU 147-G . . . . . . Union City
LU 302 . . . . Union City
LU 308 . . . . Union City
LU 310 . . . . Union City
LU 357 . . . . Union City
LU 360 . . . . Union City
LU 365 . . . . Union City
LU 415-475 . . . . . Union City
LU 457 . . . . Union City
LU 478 . . . . Union City
LU 479-I . . . . . . Union City
LU 501-I . . . . . . Union City
LU 515 . . . . Union City
LU 516 . . . . Union City
LU 551-I . . . . . . Union City
LU 565 . . . . Union City
LU 570-I . . . . . . Union City
LU 574-I . . . . . . Union City
LU 576-I . . . . . . Union City
LU 586 . . . . Union City
LU 588-I . . . . . . Union City
LU 599 . . . . Union City
LU 829-A . . . . . . Union City
LU 903-A . . . . . . Union City
LU 913-C . . . . . . Union City
LU 963-A . . . . . . Union City
LU 1113-T . . . . . . Union City
LU 1501 . . . . . . Union City
LU 1504 . . . . . . Union City
LU 1506 . . . . . . Union City
LU 1516 . . . . . . Union City
LU 1633 . . . . . . Union City
LU 1716 . . . . . . Union City
LU 1752 . . . . . . Union City
LU 1781 . . . . . . Union City
LU 1807 . . . . . . Union City
LU 1833 . . . . . . Union City
LU 1836 . . . . . . Union City
LU 1855. . . . . . . Columbus
LU 1855-B . . . . . . Columbus
LU 1876 . . . . . . Union City
LU 1922 . . . . . . Union City
LU 1997 . . . . . . Union City
LU 2000 . . . . . . Union City
LU 2031 . . . . . . Union City
LU 2295 . . . . . . Union City
LU 2341 . . . . . . Union City
LU 2351 . . . . . . Union City
LU 2376 . . . . . . Union City
LU 2386 . . . . . . Union City
LU 2395 . . . . . . Union City
LU 2420 . . . . . . Union City
LU 2423 . . . . . . Union City
LU 2448 . . . . . . Union City
LU 2490 . . . . . . Union City
LU 2496 . . . . . . Union City
LU 2500 . . . . . . Union City
LU 2524 . . . . . . Union City
LU 2526 . . . . . . Union City

LU 2534 . . . . Union City
LU 2544 . . . . Union City
LU 2558 . . . . Union City
LU 2566 . . . . Union City
LU 2570 . . . . Union City
LU 2603 . . . . Union City
LU 2609 . . . . Union City
LU 2610 . . . . Union City
LU 2618 . . . . Union City
LU 2619 . . . . Union City
LU 2620 . . . . Union City
LU 2625 . . . . Union City
LU 2648 . . . . Union City
LU 2653 . . . . Union City
LU 2679 . . . . Union City
LU 2690 . . . . Union City
LU 2691 . . . . Union City
LU 2692 . . . . Union City
LU 2695 . . . . Union City
LU 2696 . . . . Union City

NLRB Professional Association
LU 10 . . . . Atlanta

Nurses
SA Georgia Nurses
 Association . . . . Atlanta

Office and Professional Employees
LU 179 . . . . Rossville
LU 455 . . . . Eden

Operating Engineers
LU 329 . . . . Columbus
LU 443 . . . . Fort Benning
LU 474 . . . . Savannah
LU 926 . . . . Atlanta

Painters
LU 193 . . . . Forest Park
LU 1169 . . . . Brunswick
LU 1940 . . . . Forest Park
LU 1961 . . . . Forest Park

Paper, Allied-Industrial, Chemical Employees
C Merck Sharpe & Dohme . . Albany
DC 5 . . . . Cartersville
LU 1993 . . . . Savannah
LU 03-116 . . . . Snellville
LU 03-232 . . . . Macon
LU 03-233 . . . . Gordon
LU 03-238 . . . . Oconee
LU 03-346 . . . . Savannah
LU 03-353 . . . . . Warner Robins
LU 03-388 . . . . . Port Wentworth
LU 03-400 . . . . Brunswick
LU 03-407 . . . . Savannah
LU 03-446 . . . . St. Marys
LU 03-510 . . . . Macon
LU 03-518 . . . . Rome
LU 03-527 . . . . Brunswick
LU 03-531 . . . . . . Jeffersonville
LU 03-572 . . . . Macon
LU 03-573 . . . . . . Sandersville
LU 03-613 . . . . . . Rising Fawn
LU 03-643 . . . . Savannah
LU 03-646 . . . . Valdosta
LU 03-673 . . . . Savannah
LU 03-700 . . . . . Lawrenceville
LU 03-703 . . . . Alpharetta
LU 03-734 . . . . Savannah
LU 03-777 . . . . Lake Park
LU 03-787 . . . . Screven
LU 03-794 . . . . Colbert
LU 03-804 . . . . Rome
LU 03-816 . . . . Augusta
LU 03-838 . . . . Coosa

LU 03-958 Georgia State . St. Marys
LU 03-983 . . . . Augusta
LU 03-1086 . . . . Riceboro
LU 03-1087 . . . . Riceboro
LU 03-1354 . . . . Midway
LU 03-1465 . . . . . . Blackshear
LU 03-1471 . . . . . . Columbus
LU 03-1496 . . . . Eden
LU 03-1503 . . . . . . Cartersville
LU 03-1504 . . . . Martinez
LU 03-1648 . . . . Valdosta
LU 03-1703 . . . . . Cedar Springs
LU 03-1755 . . . . . College Park
LU 03-1762 . . . . Albany
LU 03-1803 . . . . Augusta
LU 03-1864 . . . . . Donalsonville
LU 03-1958 . . . . Augusta
LU 03-1994 . . . . . . Monticello
LU 05-219 . . . . . Chickamauga
LU 05-237 . . . . . . East Dublin
LU 50-26 Southern Regional Joint
 Board . . . . Union City
LU 50-33 . . . . . Union City

Plant Protection
LU 109 Atlanta Unit . . . . Fairburn

Plasterers and Cement Masons
LU 15 . . . . Savannah
LU 148 . . . . Atlanta

Plumbing and Pipe Fitting
C Georgia Pipe Trades . . Savannah
LU 72 . . . . Atlanta
LU 150 . . . . Augusta
LU 177 . . . . Brunswick
LU 188 . . . . Savannah
LU 473 . . . . Jesup

Postal and Federal Employees
LU 301 . . . . Albany
LU 305 . . . . Atlanta
LU 306 . . . . Decatur
LU 307 . . . . Augusta
LU 310 . . . . Atlanta
LU 314 . . . . Columbus
LU 321 . . . . Marietta

Postal Mail Handlers
LU 310 . . . . Atlanta

Postal Workers
LU . . . . Suwanee
LU 12 Athens . . . . Athens
LU 29 Savannah . . . . . Savannah
LU 32 Atlanta Metro Area . . Atlanta
LU 35 Americus Local . . Americus
LU 118 Columbus . . . . Columbus
LU 124 Brunswick . . . . Brunswick
LU 290 Augusta . . . . . Augusta
LU 322 Valdosta . . . . . Valdosta
LU 538 Thomasville . . Thomasville
LU 569 Waycross . . . . Waycross
LU 717 Rome . . . . Rome
LU 979 Gainesville . . Gainesville
LU 1002 Dalton . . . . . Dalton
LU 1054 Bainbridge . . . Bainbridge
LU 1061 La Grange . . . . Lagrange
LU 1075 Cordele Local . . . Cordele
LU 1090 Washington
 Local . . . . Washington
LU 1338 Dublin . . . . . Dublin
LU 1340 Macon . . . . . . Macon
LU 1346 Newnan . . . . . Newnan
LU 1377 Albany . . . . . . Albany
LU 1586 Elberton Local . . Elberton
LU 1676 Marietta . . . . . Marietta
LU 1687 Winder Local . . . Winder

LU 1689 Statesboro
 Local . . . . Statesboro
LU 2074 McRae Local . . . . McRae
LU 2237 Tifton . . . . Tifton
LU 2314 Swainsboro
 Local . . . . Swainsboro
LU 2319 Cedartown
 Local . . . . Cedartown
LU 2427 Vidalia Local . . . Vidalia
LU 2472 Baxley Local . . . . Baxley
LU 2534 Fitzgerald Local . Fitzgerald
LU 2535 Toccoa Local . . . Toccoa
LU 2582 Thomaston
 Local . . . . Thomaston
LU 2637 Buford . . . . . . Buford
LU 2678 Griffin . . . . . . Griffin
LU 2694 Cornelia Local . Cornelia
LU 2695 Calhoun . . . . . Calhoun
LU 2997 Eastman Local . Eastman
LU 3434 Decatur . . . . . Decatur
LU 3499 Hinesville . . . . Allenhurst
LU 3655 Dallas . . . . . . Dallas
LU 3684 Warner
 Robins . . . . . Warner Robins
LU 3908 Bremen . . . . . Bremen
LU 3927 Dahlonega
 Local . . . . Dahlonega
LU 4349 Moultrie . . . . . Moultrie
LU 5215 Hampton Local . Hampton
LU 5281 Cartersville
 Local . . . . Cartersville
LU 5923 Forest Park . . Forest Park
LU 6088 Adairsville
 Local . . . . Adairsville
LU 6089 Norcross . . . . Norcross
LU 6221 Hartwell Local . Hartwell
LU 6394 Conyers Local . . Conyers
LU 7063 Cleveland . . . . Cleveland
LU 7131 Powder
 Springs . . . . . Powder Springs
SA Georgia . . . . Augusta

Railroad Signalmen
GC 44 Louisville &
 Nashville . . . . . . Silver Creek
GC 78 Southern Railway System
 Lines . . . . Macon
LLG 11 . . . . Macon
LLG 49 . . . . Macon
LLG 208 . . . . Jonesboro

Retail, Wholesale and Department Store
C Southeast . . . . Atlanta
LU 315 . . . . Atlanta
LU 586 . . . . Atlanta
LU 595 . . . . Atlanta

Roofers, Waterproofers and Allied Workers
LU 136 . . . . Atlanta

Rural Letter Carriers
D 1 . . . . Midway
D 2 . . . . Albany
D 3 . . . . Warner Robins
D 4 . . . . Duluth
D 5 . . . . Jasper
D 6 . . . . Bowdon
D 7 . . . . Chatsworth
D 8 . . . . Denton
D 9 . . . . Royston
D 10 . . . . Hephzibah
SA Georgia . . . . Moultrie

Security, Police and Fire Professionals
LU 572 . . . . Austell

LU 574 . . . . Kingsland
LU 575 . . . . . Stone Mountain
LU 576 . . . . Vidalia

Service Employees
LU 358 International Leather Goods,
 Plastics, Novelty and Service
 Union . . . . Atlanta
LU 413 Firemen & Oilers . Waycross
LU 679 Firemen &
 Oilers . . . . College Park
LU 1985 Georgia State . . . Atlanta

Sheet Metal Workers
LU 85 . . . . Atlanta
LU 260 . . . . Acworth
LU 422 . . . . Waycross

Steelworkers
LU 09-170-S . . . . . . Attapulgus
LU 09-188-U . . . . . . Cornelia
LU 09-190-A . . . . . Savannah
LU 09-254 . . . . Atlanta
LU 09-486 . . . . Winder
LU 09-871-L . . . . . . Athens
LU 09-1070-L . . . . . Waycross
LU 09-1158-S . . . . . . Atlanta
LU 09-2401-S . . . . . . Atlanta
LU 09-2948-S . . . . . Columbus
LU 09-3944-S . . . . McDonough
LU 09-5812-S . . . . . Daycross
LU 09-7834-S . . . . . Moultrie
LU 09-8074-S . . . . . Tallapoosa
LU 09-9326-S . . . Milledgeville
LU 09-14087-S . . . . . Flintstone
LU 09-14102-S . . . . . Newnan
LU 09-14981-S . . . . . Americus

Teamsters
LU 528 . . . . Atlanta
LU 728 . . . . Atlanta
LU 1129 . . . . Cartersville

Television and Radio Artists
LU Atlanta . . . . Atlanta

Theatrical Stage Employees
LU 479 . . . . Conyers
LU 834 . . . . Atlanta
LU 859 . . . . Red Oak
LU 927 . . . . Atlanta

Transit Union
LDIV 732 . . . . Decatur
LDIV 898 . . . . Macon
LDIV 1324 . . . . Savannah

Transport Workers
LU . . . . College Park
LU 526 . . . . St. Marys
LU 527 . . . . Grovetown

Transportation Communications Union
D 102 Southeastern System Board
 #96 . . . . Austell
D 146 . . . . Macon
D 324 . . . . Waycross
D 550 Southeastern System Board
 96 . . . . Augusta
D 892 . . . . Villa Rica
D 943 Southeastern System Board
 96 . . . . Newnan
D 1295 . . . . Dallas
JPB 410 Seaboard Coast
 Line-Georgia Railroad . Waycross
LG 6045 Georgia . . . . Adairsville
LG 6354 Atlanta . . . . . . Atlanta

LG 6489 Seaboard. . . . . Savannah
LG 6508 Waycross. . . . . Patterson

Transportation Union
GCA GO-25 Atlanta & West Point
   Railway . . . . Dallas
GCA GO-169 Central of Georgia
   Railroad . . . . Gordon
LU 30 . . . . Folkston
LU 511 . . . . . . Powder Springs
LU 535 . . . . Gray
LU 674 . . . . Augusta
LU 941 . . . . Columbus
LU 998 . . . . Waycross
LU 1031 . . . . Savannah
LU 1033 . . . . . . Powder Springs
LU 1245 . . . . Lawrenceville
LU 1261 . . . . Lithonia

LU 1263 . . . . Valdosta
LU 1598 . . . . Senoia
LU 1790 . . . . Fitzgerald
LU 1910 . . . . Gordon
SLB LO-12 Georgia . . . . Snellville

Treasury Employees
CH 26 . . . . Atlanta
CH 70 . . . . Chamblee
CH 104 . . . . Atlanta
CH 150 . . . . Tybee Island
CH 177 . . . . Atlanta
CH 210 . . . . Atlanta
CH 268 . . . . Atlanta
CH 281 EPA Region 4 . . . . Atlanta
CH 284 . . . . Chamblee

Utility Workers
LU 121 . . . . Ringgold
LU 461 . . . . Chickamauga

Weather Service Employees
BR 02-46 . . . . . . Peachtree City
BR 02-64 . . . . Atlanta
BR 02-71 . . . . Hampton

Westinghouse Salaried Employees
ASSN Athens Employee's . . Athens

Unaffiliated Labor Organizations

Dixie Pipeline Union Oil
   Industry . . . . Kennesaw

IBT & HERE Employee
   Representatives Council . . Atlanta
Independent Staff Union . . . Atlanta
International Union of Industrial and
   Independent Workers . Alpharetta
National Basketball Trainers
   Association . . . . Atlanta
National Laborers, Crafts & Office
   Workers' Union . . . . . Palmetto
National Pilots Association . Atlanta
Professional Airline Flight Control
   Association . . . . Atlanta
Professional Airline Flight Control
   Association PAFCA-ASA . Atlanta
Professional Airline Flight Control
   Association PAFCA-
   Delta . . . . Atlanta
Veteran Affairs Police Officers
   Association . . . . Stone Mountain
Wholesale Sales Representatives,
   Bureau of . . . . Atlanta

Guam

**Affiliated Labor
Organizations**

Air Traffic Controllers
LU ZUA . . . . Yigo

Fire Fighters
LU 150-F . . . . Barrigada

Government Employees
LU 1689 DoD . . . . Hagatna

Letter Carriers
BR 4093 . . . . Barrigada

Machinists
LU . . . . Dededo

Postal Workers
LU 6255 Agana . . . . . . Barrigada

Weather Service Employees
BR 07-2 . . . . Barrigada

Hawaii

AFL-CIO Trade and Industrial Departments

Building and Construction Trades Department
BCTC Honolulu . . . . . . Honolulu

Maritime Trades Department
PC Honolulu . . . . Honolulu

Metal Trades Department
MTC Hawaii . . . . Aiea

Affiliated Labor Organizations

Agricultural Employees
BR 11 . . . . Honolulu
NHQ . . . . Honolulu

Air Traffic Controllers
LU HCF . . . . Honolulu
LU ITO . . . . Hilo
LU KOA . . . . Kailua-Kona
LU OGG . . . . Puunene

Asbestos Workers
LU 132 . . . . Honolulu

Boilermakers
LG 90 . . . . Aiea

Bricklayers
LU 1 . . . . Honolulu

Carpenters
LU 745 . . . . Honolulu

Communications Workers
LU 14921 . . . . Honolulu
LU 39117 Hawaii . . . . Honolulu

Electrical Workers
C Citizens Utilities
  Coordinating . . . . . . Honolulu
LU 1186 . . . . Honolulu
LU 1260 . . . . Honolulu
LU 1357 . . . . Honolulu

Elevator Constructors
LU 126 . . . . Honolulu

Fire Fighters
LU 263-F . . . . Pearl City

Food and Commercial Workers
LU 480 . . . . Honolulu

Government Employees
LU 1209 . . . . Kailua
LU 1229 . . . . Aiea
LU 2886 DoJ . . . . Honolulu

Government Security Officers
LU 81 . . . . Honolulu

Graphic Communications
LU 413-N . . . . Honolulu
LU 501-M . . . . Honolulu

Hotel and Restaurant Employees
LU 5 . . . . Honolulu

Iron Workers
LU 625 . . . . Waipahu
LU 742 . . . . Kaneohe
LU 803 . . . . Waipahu

Laborers
LU 368 . . . . Honolulu
LU 368 . . . . Honolulu

Letter Carriers
BR 860 . . . . Honolulu
BR 2932 . . . . Hilo
BR 4372 . . . . Wailuku
BR 4454 . . . . Kailua
BR 4644 . . . . Kahului
BR 4682 Aiea-Pearl City . Pearl City
BR 4683 . . . . Waipahu
BR 4836 . . . . Kaneohe
BR 4837 . . . . Mililani
BR 5206 . . . . Ewa Beach
BR 5306 . . . . Lahaina
BR 5316 Waimanalo,
  Hawaii . . . . Waimanalo
BR 5516 . . . . . . Kailua-Kona
BR 5579 . . . . Waianae
BR 6241 . . . . Lihue
BR 6254 . . . . Koloa
BR 6312 Haleiwa, Hawaii . Haleiwa
SA Hawaii . . . . Honolulu

Longshore and Warehouse
LU 142 . . . . Honolulu
LU 142 2420 . . . . Wailuku
LU 142 2507 . . . . Wailuku
LU 142 3405 . . . . Lihue
LU 142 4428 . . . . Honolulu
LU 142 4521 . . . . Honolulu
LU 142 Unit 1201 . . . . . . Hilo
LU 142 Unit 1401 . . . . . . Hilo
LU 142 Unit 1402 . . . . . . Hilo
LU 142 Unit 1403 . . . . . . Hilo
LU 142 Unit 1409
  Area . . . . Hilo
LU 142 Unit 1410 . . . . . . Hilo
LU 142 Unit 1412 . . . . . . Hilo
LU 142 Unit 1414 . . . . . . Hilo
LU 142 Unit 1416 . . . . . . Hilo
LU 142 Unit 1417 . . . . . . Hilo
LU 142 Unit 1418 . . . . . . Hilo
LU 142 Unit 1419 . . . . . . Hilo
LU 142 Unit 1421 . . . . . . Hilo
LU 142 Unit 1426 . . . . . . Hilo
LU 142 Unit 1501 . . . . . . Hilo
LU 142 Unit 1503 . . . . . . Hilo
LU 142 Unit 1505 . . . . . . Hilo
LU 142 Unit 1506 . . . . . . Hilo
LU 142 Unit 1510 . . . . . . Hilo
LU 142 Unit 1513 . . . . . . Hilo
LU 142 Unit 1515 . . . . . . Hilo
LU 142 Unit 1516 . . . . . . Hilo
LU 142 Unit 1517 . . . . . . Hilo
LU 142 Unit 1209 . . . . . . Hilo
LU 142 Unit 2101 . . . . . Wailuku
LU 142 Unit 2107 . . . . . Wailuku
LU 142 Unit 2201 . . . . . Wailuku
LU 142 Unit 2305 . . . . . Wailuku
LU 142 Unit 2306 . . . . . Wailuku
LU 142 Unit 2307 . . . . . Wailuku
LU 142 Unit 2401 . . . . . Wailuku
LU 142 Unit 2403 . . . . . Wailuku
LU 142 Unit 2404 . . . . . Wailuku
LU 142 Unit 2405 . . . . . Wailuku
LU 142 Unit 2406 . . . . . Wailuku
LU 142 Unit 2408 . . . . . Wailuku
LU 142 Unit 2409 . . . . . Wailuku
LU 142 Unit 2411 . . . . . Wailuku

LU 142 Unit 2417 . . . . . Wailuku
LU 142 Unit 2419 . . . . . Wailuku
LU 142 Unit 2501 . . . . . Wailuku
LU 142 Unit 2502 . . . . . Wailuku
LU 142 Unit 2505 . . . . . Wailuku
LU 142 Unit 2506 . . . . . Wailuku
LU 142 Unit 2508 . . . . . Wailuku
LU 142 Unit 2509 . . . . Honolulu
LU 142 Unit 2511 . . . . . Wailuku
LU 142 Unit 2512 . . . . . Wailuku
LU 142 Unit 2514 . . . . . Wailuku
LU 142 Unit 2515 . . . . . Wailuku
LU 142 Unit 2516 . . . . . Wailuku
LU 142 Unit 2518 . . . . . Wailuku
LU 142 Unit 2520 . . . . . Wailuku
LU 142 Unit 2522 . . . . . Wailuku
LU 142 Unit 2523 . . . . . Wailuku
LU 142 Unit 2526 . . . . . Wailuku
LU 142 Unit 3102 . . . . . . Lihue
LU 142 Unit 3105 . . . . . . Lihue
LU 142 Unit 3109 . . . . . . Lihue
LU 142 Unit 3201 . . . . . . Lihue
LU 142 Unit 3401 . . . . . . Lihue
LU 142 Unit 3402 . . . . . . Lihue
LU 142 Unit 3403 . . . . . . Lihue
LU 142 Unit 3404 . . . . . . Lihue
LU 142 Unit 3406 . . . . . . Lihue
LU 142 Unit 3407 . . . . . . Lihue
LU 142 Unit 3408 . . . . . . Lihue
LU 142 Unit 3410 . . . . . . Lihue
LU 142 Unit 3411 . . . . . . Lihue
LU 142 Unit 3503 . . . . . . Lihue
LU 142 Unit 3504 . . . . . . Lihue
LU 142 Unit 3505 . . . . . . Lihue
LU 142 Unit 3510 . . . . . . Lihue
LU 142 Unit 3511 . . . . . . Lihue
LU 142 Unit 3514 . . . . . . Lihue
LU 142 Unit 4106 . . . . . Honolulu
LU 142 Unit 4201 . . . . . Honolulu
LU 142 Unit 4202 . . . . . Honolulu
LU 142 Unit 4203 . . . . . Honolulu
LU 142 Unit 4204 . . . . . Honolulu
LU 142 Unit 4207 . . . . . Honolulu
LU 142 Unit 4209 . . . . . Honolulu
LU 142 Unit 4301 . . . . . Honolulu
LU 142 Unit 4303 . . . . . Honolulu
LU 142 Unit 4304 . . . . . Honolulu
LU 142 Unit 4305 . . . . . Honolulu
LU 142 Unit 4306 . . . . . Honolulu
LU 142 Unit 4402 . . . . . Honolulu
LU 142 Unit 4403 . . . . . Honolulu
LU 142 Unit 4404 . . . . . Honolulu
LU 142 Unit 4405 . . . . . Honolulu
LU 142 Unit 4406 . . . . . Honolulu
LU 142 Unit 4407 . . . . . Honolulu
LU 142 Unit 4408 . . . . . Honolulu
LU 142 Unit 4409 . . . . . Honolulu
LU 142 Unit 4410 . . . . . Honolulu
LU 142 Unit 4411 . . . . . Honolulu
LU 142 Unit 4412 . . . . . Honolulu
LU 142 Unit 4414 . . . . . Honolulu
LU 142 Unit 4415 . . . . . Honolulu
LU 142 Unit 4418 . . . . . Honolulu
LU 142 Unit 4419 . . . . . Honolulu
LU 142 Unit 4420 . . . . . Honolulu
LU 142 Unit 4421 . . . . . Honolulu
LU 142 Unit 4422 . . . . . Honolulu
LU 142 Unit 4427 . . . . . Honolulu
LU 142 Unit 4435 . . . . . Honolulu
LU 160 . . . . Wailuku
LU 4524 Unit 4424 . . . . Honolulu

Machinists
LG 1245 . . . . Honolulu
LG 1979 . . . . Honolulu

LG 1998 . . . . Honolulu
STC Hawaii . . . . Honolulu

Musicians
LU 677 . . . . Honolulu

National Staff Organization
LU Hawaii State Teachers Staff
  Organization . . . . . . Honolulu

Nurses
SA Hawaii Nurses
  Association . . . . Honolulu

Painters
DC 50 . . . . Honolulu
LU 1791 . . . . Honolulu
LU 1889 . . . . Honolulu
LU 1903 . . . . Honolulu
LU 1926 . . . . Honolulu
LU 1944 . . . . Honolulu

Plasterers and Cement Masons
LU 630 . . . . Honolulu

Plumbing and Pipe Fitting
LU 675 . . . . Honolulu
LU 811 . . . . Aiea

Postal Mail Handlers
LU 299 . . . . Honolulu

Postal Workers
LU 162 Honolulu . . . . . Honolulu
LU 664 Big Island
  Area . . . . Kailua Kona
LU 5434 Kauai Area . . . . . Lihue
LU 5528 Maui Area . . . . . Kihii
LU 5918 Windward Area . . . Kailua
LU 6044 Wahiawa . . . . . Mililani
LU 6069 Leeward Oahu
  Area . . . . Kapolei
SA Hawaii . . . . Pearl City

Professional and Technical Engineers
LU 121 . . . . Aiea

Roofers, Waterproofers and Allied Workers
LU 221 . . . . Honolulu

Security, Police and Fire Professionals
LU 650 . . . . Honolulu

Sheet Metal Workers
LU 293 . . . . Honolulu

State, County and Municipal Employees
LU 646 Division 075 Hospital
  Workers . . . . Honolulu
LU 646 Unit #515 Kahuku
  Hospital . . . . Honolulu
LU 646 UPW #527 Kuakini Geriatric
  Care . . . . Honolulu
LU 646 UPW Unit #503 Nuuanu
  Hale . . . . Honolulu
LU 646 UPW Unit #504 Kuakini
  Hospital . . . . Honolulu
LU 646 UPW Unit #505 Molokai
  Hospital . . . . Honolulu
LU 646 UPW Unit #509 Wahiawa
  Hospital . . . . Honolulu

LU 646 UPW Unit #531
  Intercontinental . . . . . Honolulu
LU 646 UPW Unit #532 Aloha
  United Way . . . . Honolulu
LU 646 UPW Unit 512-Convalescent
  Center . . . . Honolulu
LU 646 UPW Unit 513-Beverly
  Manor . . . . Honolulu
LU 646 UPW Unit 516-Hale
  Makua . . . . Honolulu
LU 646 UPW Unit 520-
  Rehabilitation Center . . Honolulu
LU 646 UPW Unit 523-Kapiolani
  Medical Center . . . . Honolulu
LU 928 East West Center . Honolulu

Teamsters
LU 681 . . . . Honolulu
LU 996 . . . . Honolulu

Theatrical Stage Employees
LU 665 . . . . Honolulu

Treasury Employees
CH 35 . . . . Honolulu
CH 151 . . . . Honolulu

Weather Service Employees
BR 07-1 . . . . Lihue
BR 07-5 . . . . Honolulu

BR 07-6 . . . . Hilo
BR 07-7 . . . . Honolulu
BR 07-9 . . . . Ewa Beach

Unaffiliated Labor Organizations

Allied Crafts & Employees LU
  1 . . . . Kaneohe
Clerical, Professional, & Technical
  Employees Bargaining
  Committee . . . . Honolulu
Handivan Drivers
  Association . . . . Waipanu

Hawaii Association of Security
  Officers . . . . Honolulu
Hawaii Association of Union
  Agents . . . . Honolulu
Hawaii Council of Defense
  Commissary Unions . . . Honolulu
Hawaii Office Workers
  Union . . . . Honolulu
Kamehameha Schools Faculty
  Association . . . . Mililani
Maui County Paramedics
  Association . . . . Puunene
Mid-Pacific Teachers
  Association . . . . . . Honolulu
Security Officers Union International
  LU 1 . . . . Kamuela

Idaho

AFL-CIO Trade and Industrial Departments

Building and Construction Trades Department
BCTC Idaho . . . . Pocatello
BCTC Southwest Idaho, Southeast Oregon. . . . . Boise

Metal Trades Department
MTC Eastern Idaho . . . Idaho Falls

Affiliated Labor Organizations

Air Traffic Controllers
LU BOI . . . . Boise
LU SUN. . . . . Hailey
LU TWF . . . . Twin Falls

Bakery, Confectionery, Tobacco Workers and Grain Millers
LU 282-G . . . . Burley
LU 283-G . . . . Jerome
LU 284-G. . . . . Caldwell
LU 290-G . . . . Payette
LU 296-G . . . . Burley

Boilermakers
LG 234-D Cement Workers . Inkom

Carpenters
LU 313 . . . . Moscow
LU 398 . . . . Lewiston
LU 808 . . . . Idaho Falls
LU 1691 . . . . Coeur d'Alene
LU 2816 . . . . Emmett

Communications Workers
C Idaho State. . . . . Boise
LU 7603 . . . . Boise
LU 7610 . . . . Twin Falls
LU 7621 . . . . Pocatello
LU 7670 . . . . . . Coeur d'Alene
LU 14709 . . . . Boise

Electrical Workers
LU 283. . . . . Emmett
LU 291. . . . . Boise
LU 449 . . . . Pocatello
LU 582. . . . . Pocatello

Federal Employees
LU 181 . . . . Coeur d'Alene
LU 1436. . . . . Grangeville
LU 1818 . . . . . . Coeur d'Alene
LU 2030 . . . . Idaho Falls

Food and Commercial Workers
LU 330 Textile Workers. . . . Boise
LU 368-A . . . . Boise

Government Employees
LU 1273 VA . . . . Boise

LU 2233 USDA . . . . Eagle
LU 3006 DoD . . . . Boise
LU 3872 USAF. . . Mountain Home Air Force Base
LU 3923 INS. . . . . Boise

Graphic Communications
LU 278-C . . . . Rigby

Iron Workers
LU 732 . . . . Pocatello

Laborers
LU 155 . . . . Idaho Falls

Letter Carriers
BR 331 . . . . Boise
BR 927 . . . . Pocatello
BR 1039 Wallace, Idaho . . Wallace
BR 1192 . . . . Lewiston
BR 1260 . . . . . . Coeur d'Alene
BR 1364 . . . . Idaho Falls
BR 1386 . . . . Caldwell
BR 1392 . . . . Twin Falls
BR 1409 . . . . Nampa
BR 1411 . . . . Blackfoot
BR 1481 . . . . Moscow
BR 1602 Sandpoint, Idaho . . . . Sandpoint
BR 1703 Weiser, Idaho . . . Weiser
BR 1837 St. Maries, Idaho . . . . St. Maries
BR 1857 . . . . Burley
BR 1979 Payette, Idaho . . . Payette
BR 2095 Rexburg, Idaho . . Rexburg
BR 2097 Rupert, Idaho . . . Rupert
BR 2208 Kellogg, Idaho . . Kellogg
BR 2616 Preston, Idaho . . . Preston
BR 2777 American Falls, Idaho . . . . . . American Falls
BR 3011 St. Anthony, Idaho . . . . St. Anthony
BR 3277 Grangeville, Idaho . . . . Grangeville
BR 3838 Emmett, Idaho. . . Emmett
BR 4420 . . . . Gooding
BR 4745 Meridian, Idaho . Meridian
BR 4822 . . . . . Mountain Home
BR 5297 Montpelier, Idaho. . . . . Montpelier
BR 5580 Malad City, Idaho. . . . . Malad City
BR 5581 . . . . Jerome
SA Idaho . . . . Pocatello

Locomotive Engineers
DIV 113 . . . . Heyburn
DIV 228 . . . . Pocatello
DIV 676 . . . . Nampa
DIV 840 . . . . Peru
GCA Union Pacific Western Region . . . . Pocatello
SLB Idaho 5051 . . . . . . Nampa

Machinists
LG 364-W . . . . Lewiston
LG 1295. . . . . St. Maries
LG 1402-FL. . . . . . . Sandpoint
LG 1452-FL . . . . . Bonners Ferry
LG 1753 . . . . . Mountain Home
LG 1933 . . . . Pocatello
LG 2052-FL . . . . . . Meridian
STC STC . . . . Pocatello

Maintenance of Way Employes
SLG 124 . . . . Peck
SLG 1402 . . . . Pocatello

National Staff Organization
LU Staff Organization, Idaho Education Association. . Lewiston

Nurses
SA Idaho Nurses Association . Boise

Painters
LU 477 . . . . Boise
LU 764 . . . . Pocatello

Paper, Allied-Industrial, Chemical Employees
C . . . . Rexburg
LU 02-632 . . . . Pocatello
LU 08-608 . . . . Lewiston
LU 08-652 . . . . Idaho Falls
LU 08-712 . . . . Lewiston

Plasterers and Cement Masons
LU 219 . . . . Meridian
LU 629 . . . . Pocatello

Plumbing and Pipe Fitting
LU 296 . . . . Meridian
LU 648 . . . . Pocatello
SA Idaho . . . . Pocatello

Postal Mail Handlers
LU 330 . . . . Boise

Postal Workers
LU Idaho Panhandle Area . . . . Coeur d'Alene
LU 129 Nampa . . . . Nampa
LU 179 Twin Falls . . . . Twin Falls
LU 479 Caldwell . . . . . Caldwell
LU 627 Burley . . . . Burley
LU 650 Boise . . . . Boise
LU 703 Pocatello . . . . . Pocatello
LU 1001 Lewiston . . . . Lewiston
LU 1104 Idaho Falls . . . Idaho Falls
LU 1262 Moscow. . . . . Moscow
LU 1327 Blackfoot Local . Blackfoot
LU 4724 Orofino Local . . . Orofino
LU 6412 McCall Local . . . McCall
SA Idaho . . . . Boise

Professional and Technical Engineers
LU 94 . . . . Idaho Falls

Pulp and Paper Workers
LU 747 . . . . Nampa

Railroad Signalmen
LLG 111 . . . . Pocatello

Roofers, Waterproofers and Allied Workers
LU 200 . . . . Pocatello

Rural Letter Carriers
D 1 . . . . Nampa
D 2 . . . . Gooding
D 3 . . . . American Falls
D 5 North Idaho . . . Coeur d'Alene
SA Idaho . . . . Coeur d'Alene

Security, Police and Fire Professionals
LU 3 . . . . Rigby
LU 6 . . . . Boise
LU 14 . . . . Boise

Sheet Metal Workers
LU 60 . . . . Pocatello
LU 213 . . . . Boise

Steelworkers
LU 9052. . . . . Smelterville
LU 11-5089-S . . . . Kellogg
LU 11-5114-S . . . . . . Kingston

Teamsters
LU 483 . . . . Boise
LU 983 . . . . Pocatello

Transit Union
LDIV 398 . . . . Boise
LDIV 1517. . . . . . . Idaho Falls

Transportation Communications Union
LG 6094 Bannock . . . . . Pocatello

Transportation Union
LU 78 . . . . Bloomington
LU 265 . . . . Pocatello
LU 1058 . . . . Nampa
SLB LO-15 Idaho . . . . Pocatello

Treasury Employees
CH 5 . . . . Boise

Weather Service Employees
BR 04-23. . . . . Boise
BR 04-38. . . . . Pocatello

Unaffiliated Labor Organizations
Heavy & Highway Committee Five Basic Crafts AREA 10 . Pocatello
United Power Trades Organization Association-Pacific Northwest . . . . Pierce

Illinois

AFL-CIO Trade and Industrial Departments

Building and Construction Trades Department
BCTC Central Illinois . . Springfield
BCTC Chicago & Cook
  County . . . . Chicago
BCTC Danville . . . . . . Danville
BCTC De Kalb County . . . Dekalb
BCTC Decatur. . . . . . . Decatur
BCTC Du Page County. . . . Lisle
BCTC East Central
  Illinois . . . . Champaign
BCTC Egyptian . . . West Frankfort
BCTC Fox Valley . . . . . . Elgin
BCTC Illinois Valley . . . . Utica
BCTC Kankakee . . . . Kankakee
BCTC Lake County . . . Waukegan
BCTC Livingston-McLean
  Counties . . . . Bloomington
BCTC McHenry
  County . . . . Crystal Lake
BCTC Northwestern
  Illinois . . . . Rockford
BCTC Southwestern
  Illinois . . . . Collinsville
BCTC Tri-City . . . . . Rock Island
BCTC West Central Illinois . . Peoria
BCTC Will & Grundy
  Counties . . . . Joliet

Maritime Trades Department
PC Greater Chicago Area . Hinsdale

Other Councils and Committees
C Western Employees . . East Alton

Affiliated Labor Organizations

Agricultural Employees
BR 17 . . . . Chicago

Air Line Employees
LC 91 ALEA Staff . . . . . Chicago
NHQ. . . . . Chicago

Air Traffic Controllers
LU ALN . . . . East Alton
LU ARR . . . . Somonauk
LU BMI . . . . Bloomington
LU C90. . . . . Elgin
LU CMI . . . . Savoy
LU CPS . . . . Cahokia
LU DPA . . . . . . West Chicago
LU MDW . . . . Chicago
LU MLI . . . . Milan
LU MWA . . . . Marion
LU ORD . . . . Chicago
LU PIA . . . . Peoria
LU PWK. . . . . Wheeling
LU RFD . . . . Rockford
LU SPI . . . . Springfield
LU ZAU . . . . Aurora

Asbestos Workers
LU 17 . . . . Chicago
LU 56. . . . . Jerseyville

Automobile, Aerospace Workers
C Central Illinois CAP . East Peoria
C Chicago Area CAP . . Des Plaines
C Fox River Valley . . Montgomery

C Illinois State CAP . . . Des Plaines
C Iowa. . . . . Des Plaines
C Quad Cities Area . . . East Moline
C R.L. Kelly/Downstate Illinois
  CAP . . . . Bloomington
C Wisconsin CAP . . . Des Plaines
LU 6 . . . . Stone Park
LU 79 . . . . East Moline
LU 145 . . . . Montgomery
LU 152 . . . . Plano
LU 285 . . . . La Salle
LU 333 . . . . Calumet Park
LU 419 . . . . Chicago
LU 434 . . . . East Moline
LU 477 . . . . Chicago
LU 543 . . . . Fairfield
LU 551 . . . . Chicago
LU 565 . . . . Peoria
LU 579 . . . . Danville
LU 588 . . . . Chicago Heights
LU 592 . . . . Rockford
LU 622 . . . . Rockford
LU 694 Chicago-La Grange
  Local . . . . Westmont
LU 718 . . . . Rockford
LU 719 La Grange-Chicago
  Local . . . . Countryside
LU 751 . . . . Decatur
LU 803 . . . . Rockford
LU 844 . . . . Vermont
LU 865 . . . . East Moline
LU 890 . . . . Morton Grove
LU 904 . . . . Sublette
LU 916 . . . . Mattoon
LU 974 . . . . East Peoria
LU 1023 . . . . Rockford
LU 1066 . . . . Chicago
LU 1088 . . . . Mendota
LU 1178 . . . . Sugar Grove
LU 1235 . . . . Springfield
LU 1268 . . . . Belvidere
LU 1271 . . . . Georgetown
LU 1277 . . . . Moline
LU 1304 . . . . East Moline
LU 1306 . . . . East Moline
LU 1356 . . . . Silvis
LU 1414 . . . . Rock Island
LU 1494 . . . . Washington
LU 1509 . . . . Washington
LU 1576 . . . . Rockford
LU 1615 . . . . Aurora
LU 1720 . . . . Rockford
LU 1761 . . . . Rockford
LU 1766 . . . . Centralia
LU 1948 . . . . Rock Island
LU 2030 . . . . Havana
LU 2056 . . . . Rockford
LU 2059. . . . . . . Spring Valley
LU 2096 . . . . Pontiac
LU 2114. . . . . Westchester
LU 2127. . . . . Freeport
LU 2128 . . . . Danville
LU 2152 . . . . Batavia
LU 2201 . . . . Freeport
LU 2263 . . . . Lewistown
LU 2272 . . . . Pontiac
LU 2282 . . . . Rock Island
LU 2283 . . . . Manito
LU 2293 . . . . Stone Park
LU 2323 . . . . Ottawa
LU 2343 . . . . Paris
LU 2390 . . . . Bushnell
LU 2488 . . . . Bloomington
LU 2592 . . . . Rockford
LU 2840 . . . . Rockford

LU 3206 . . . . Granite City

Bakery, Confectionery, Tobacco Workers and Grain Millers
C Biscuit . . . . Chicago
LU 1 . . . . Lyons
LU 7-G . . . . Hamilton
LU 40-G. . . . . Galesburg
LU 69-G. . . . . Chicago
LU 81-G . . . . East Alton
LU 103-G . . . . Decatur
LU 115-G. . . . . Paris
LU 300 . . . . Chicago
LU 303-G . . . . Armington
LU 316-G . . . . Geneva
LU 325-G . . . . . . Gibson City
LU 342. . . . . Bloomington
LU 343-G . . . . Eola
LU 347-G . . . . Danville
LU 392-G. . . . . Millstadt
LU 399-G . . . . Rossville

Boilermakers
C Great Lakes Area
  Industrial. . . . . Hoffman Estates
C Southern Illinois
  Industrial. . . . . . East Alton
LG 1 . . . . Chicago
LG 3-S . . . . Quincy
LG 4-S . . . . Belleville
LG 6-M Metal Polishers . . Chicago
LG 7-S. . . . . Belleville
LG 8-S Willow Lake
  Mine . . . . Harrisburg
LG 12-D Cement Workers. Granville
LG 16-S . . . . Belleville
LG 60 . . . . Morton
LG 60-S . . . . O'Fallon
LG 81-D Cement Workers . . Dixon
LG 105-S. . . . . Dieterich
LG 114-M . . . . Leland
LG 158 . . . . Peoria
LG 185-S. . . . . O'Fallon
LG 363. . . . . Belleville
LG 480 . . . . Murrayville
LG 482 . . . . East Alton
LG 483 . . . . East Alton
LG 484 . . . . Meredosia
LG 486 . . . . East Alton
LG 499. . . . . Carman
LG 1234 . . . . Des Plaines
LG 1239 . . . . Hoffman
LG 1247 . . . . Chicago
LG 1255 . . . . Spring Grove
LG 1600 . . . . Aurora
LG 1626. . . . . St. Joseph
LG 1994-S . . . . Harrisburg

Bricklayers
DC 1 Illinois . . . . Chicago
LU. . . . . Chicago
LU 6 . . . . Rockford
LU 8 . . . . Champaign
LU 20 . . . . Waukegan
LU 21 . . . . Chicago
LU 27 . . . . Elgin
LU 52 . . . . Chicago
LU 56. . . . . Winfield
LU 67 . . . . Chicago
LU 74 . . . . Westmont

Carpenters
DC Chicago & Northeast
  Illinois . . . . Chicago

DC Mid-Central Illinois
  #4281 . . . . Springfield
DC Northwest Illinois. . . . Sterling
LU 1. . . . . Chicago
LU 10 . . . . Bridgeview
LU 13 . . . . Chicago
LU 16 . . . . Springfield
LU 44 . . . . Champaign
LU 54 . . . . Bridgeview
LU 58 . . . . Chicago
LU 62 . . . . Chicago Heights
LU 63 . . . . Bloomington
LU 74-L . . . . Hinsdale
LU 80 . . . . Elmwood Park
LU 141. . . . . Bridgeview
LU 166 . . . . Rock Island
LU 169. . . . . Belleville
LU 174 . . . . Joliet
LU 181 . . . . Elmwood Park
LU 183 . . . . East Peoria
LU 189 . . . . Quincy
LU 195 . . . . Ottawa
LU 250 . . . . Waukegan
LU 269 . . . . Westville
LU 272 . . . . Chicago Heights
LU 295 . . . . Wood River
LU 347 . . . . Mattoon
LU 363 . . . . St. Charles
LU 377 . . . . Wood River
LU 433 . . . . Belleville
LU 434 . . . . Chicago Heights
LU 480 . . . . Belleville
LU 496 . . . . Kankakee
LU 558 . . . . Glen Ellyn
LU 578 . . . . Hinsdale
LU 633 . . . . Belleville
LU 634 . . . . Salem
LU 636 . . . . Mount Vernon
LU 638 . . . . Marion
LU 640 . . . . Metropolis
LU 644 . . . . Pekin
LU 725 . . . . Litchfield
LU 742 . . . . Decatur
LU 790 . . . . Rock Falls
LU 792 . . . . Rockford
LU 839 . . . . Hoffman Estates
LU 904 . . . . Jacksonville
LU 916 . . . . St. Charles
LU 1027 . . . . . . River Forest
LU 1051 . . . . Lincoln
LU 1185 . . . . Hinsdale
LU 1186 . . . . Brighton
LU 1307 . . . . Lisle
LU 1361 . . . . Chester
LU 1535. . . . . . . Wood River
LU 1539 . . . . . . Des Plaines
LU 1693 . . . . Hinsdale
LU 1889 . . . . Lisle
LU 1997 . . . . Columbia
LU 2087 . . . . St. Charles
STC Illinois . . . . Rockford

Civilian Technicians
CH 34 Illinois Air . . . . Bartonville
CH 106 Springfield Air . Springfield
CH 111 Windy City . . . Maryville
LU 1-120 Land of
  Lincoln . . . . Springfield

Communications Workers
LU 71 Chicago Newspaper
  Guild . . . . Chicago
LU 906 . . . . Benton
LU 4202 . . . . Lombard
LU 4209 . . . . Springfield

LU 4214 . . . . Peoria
LU 4215 . . . . Danville
LU 4216 . . . . Chicago
LU 4217 . . . . Belleville
LU 4250 . . . . Chicago
LU 4252 . . . . Marseilles
LU 4260 . . . . Warrenville
LU 4270 . . . . Rantoul
LU 4290 . . . . Lemont
LU 4711 . . . . Olney
LU 4998 . . . . . . Clarendon Hills
LU 14404 Bloomington
  Typographical . . . . Bloomington
LU 14405 . . . . Carlinville
LU 14406 Central Illinois
  Typographical . . . . . Springfield
LU 14407 . . . . Savoy
LU 14408 . . . . Chicago
LU 14411 . . . . Highland
LU 14413 Jacksonville
  Typographical . . . . . . Virginia
LU 14420 Mascoutah Typographical
  Union . . . . . . New Baden
LU 14423
  Murphysboro . . . . Murphysboro
LU 14424 Pana Typographical
  Union . . . . Pana
LU 14426 . . . . . . East Peoria
LU 14427 . . . . Rockford
LU 14430 Chicago Mailers
  Union . . . . Hinsdale
LU 14431 Peoria Mailers
  Union . . . . Peoria
LU 14434 . . . . Springfield
LU 34086 . . . . Peoria
LU 54041 . . . . Chicago

Education
SA Illinois Education
  Association . . . . . Springfield

Electrical Workers
C Central Illinois
  Coordinating . . . . . . Decatur
LU 9 . . . . Hillside
LU 15 . . . . Naperville
LU 19 . . . . Aurora
LU 21 . . . . Downers Grove
LU 34 . . . . Peoria
LU 51 . . . . Springfield
LU 109 . . . . Moline
LU 117 . . . . Elgin
LU 134 . . . . Chicago
LU 145 . . . . Moline
LU 146 . . . . Decatur
LU 150 . . . . Libertyville
LU 176 . . . . Joliet
LU 186 . . . . Steger
LU 193 . . . . Springfield
LU 196 . . . . Elgin
LU 197 . . . . Bloomington
LU 214 . . . . Romeoville
LU 309 . . . . Collinsville
LU 364 . . . . Rockford
LU 461 . . . . Aurora
LU 513 . . . . Decatur
LU 533 . . . . Brookfield
LU 538 . . . . Danville
LU 601 . . . . Champaign
LU 633 . . . . Belleville
LU 649 . . . . Alton
LU 701 . . . . Lisle
LU 702 . . . . . West Frankfort
LU 794 . . . . . . South Holland
LU 885 . . . . . . Richton Park
LU 963 . . . . Kankakee
LU 1031 . . . . Lombard
LU 1220 . . . . Chicago

LU 1306 . . . . Decatur
LU 1475 . . . . Walnut Hill
STCON Illinois . . . . . Springfield

Electrical, Radio and Machine
  Workers
DC 11 . . . . Chicago
LU 151 . . . . Chicago
LU 189 . . . . Hedgkins
LU 1114 . . . . Chicago
LU 1160 . . . . Rock Island
LU 1174 . . . . Moline

Electronic Workers
LU 840 . . . . Highland
LU 1060 . . . . Henning
LU 1078 . . . . Lombard
LU 1081 . . . . Dekalb
LU 1110 . . . . Rock Island
LU 1199 . . . . Hinsdale

Elevator Constructors
LU 2 . . . . Chicago
LU 55 . . . . Peoria

Federal Employees
LU 739 . . . . Chicago
LU 1840 . . . . Golconda
LU 2119 . . . . Moline
LU 2144 Shawnee National
  Forest . . . . Murphysboro

Fire Fighters
LU 21-I . . . . Batavia
LU 37-F . . . . Great Lakes
LU 125-F . . . . Hines
LU 292-F Rock Island
  Arsenal . . . . Moline
LU 1889 Mehlville . . . . Mascoutah
LU 3234 Downers Grove
  Professional . . . Downers Grove

Flint Glass Workers
LU 77 . . . . Godfrey
LU 85 . . . . Streator
LU 87 . . . . Richton Park
LU 96 . . . . Lincoln
LU 702 . . . . Ottawa

Food and Commercial Workers
BR 24-A Illinois State . . . Chicago
C Insurance Workers Area
  X . . . . Oak Brook
LU . . . . Chicago
LU 4-D . . . . Pekin
LU 5-C . . . . Lansing
LU 6-C . . . . Godfrey
LU 12-C . . . . Collinsville
LU 16-C . . . . Marion
LU 50-C . . . . Granite City
LU 68-C . . . . Edwardsville
LU 79-C . . . . Ladd
LU 79-I . . . . Carbon Cliff
LU 126 Textile Workers . . Danville
LU 142 Textile Workers . . Chicago
LU 200-T . . . . Addison
LU 203-C . . . . Utica
LU 498-C . . . . St. Anne
LU 524-C . . . . Brookfield
LU 534 . . . . Belleville
LU 536 . . . . Peoria
LU 580-T . . . . Chicago
LU 617-C . . . . Oakwood
LU 678-T . . . . Woodstock
LU 686 . . . . Westville
LU 758-C . . . . Polo
LU 763-C . . . . Plainfield
LU 764-C . . . . Bethalto

LU 862-C . . . . Bourbonnais
LU 871-C . . . . Granite City
LU 872-C . . . . Kankakee
LU 881 . . . . Oak Brook
LU 894-C . . . . Morris
LU 1015-C . . . . Ottawa
LU 1281-P . . . . . . Bourbonnais
RC 6 . . . . Schaumburg

General Workers
NHQ . . . . Chicago

Glass, Molders, Pottery and
  Plastics Workers
LU 3 . . . . Streator
LU 70 . . . . Park Forest
LU 71 . . . . Beason
LU 117 . . . . Lincoln
LU 138 . . . . Chicago
LU 140 . . . . Toluca
LU 171 . . . . Belleville
LU 174 . . . . Streator
LU 182-B . . . . Belleville
LU 221 . . . . Wheeling
LU 233-B . . . . Chicago
LU 267 . . . . Centralia
LU 290 . . . . Aurora
LU 340 . . . . Macomb
LU 468 . . . . Kewanee

Government Employees
C 57 Railroad Retirement
  Board . . . . Chicago
C 59 VA, Seventh District . . Ozark
C 224 National SS Field Assessment
  Locals . . . . Chicago
C 245 St. Louis Area . . . . Venice
LU 15 . . . . Rock Island
LU 44 USDA . . . . . Schaumburg
LU 57 . . . . Chicago
LU 375 RRB . . . . Chicago
LU 584 . . . . Rushville
LU 603 . . . . Chicago
LU 701 . . . . Pekin
LU 704 . . . . Forest Park
LU 741 USDA . . . . . Beardstown
LU 808 RRB . . . . Chicago
LU 911 HUD . . . . Chicago
LU 914 DoL . . . . Rockford
LU 1304 Council of Prisons
  C-33 . . . . Greenville
LU 1346 HHS . . . . . . Rockford
LU 1395 HHS . . . . . . Chicago
LU 1765 VA . . . . . . Chicago
LU 1963 VA . . . . . . Danville
LU 2086 DoI . . . . . . Marion
LU 2107 VA . . . North Chicago
LU 2121 DoD . . . . . Chicago
LU 2134 . . . . Moline
LU 2326 DoD . . . . Great Lakes
LU 2343 DoJ . . . . . Carterville
LU 2461 DoL . . . . . . Benton
LU 2483 VA . . . . . . Marion
LU 2718 . . . . Chicago
LU 2925 USDA . . . . . . Galva
LU 3247 USDA . . . . . . Peoria
LU 3356 USDA . . . Lawrenceville
LU 3415 . . . . . Fairview Heights
LU 3504 EEOC . . . . . . Chicago
LU 3531 DLA . . . . . . Chicago
LU 3652 DoJ . . . . Chicago
LU 3896 DoE . . . . . . Chicago

Government Employees
  Association
LU 72 . . . . Belleville
LU 07-23 . . . Scott Air Force Base
LU 07-51 . . . . Great Lakes

LU 07-68 . . . . Rock Island

Government Security Officers
LU 63 . . . . Collinsville
LU 79 . . . . New Lenox
LU 112 . . . . Champaign
LU 117 . . . . Peoria

Graphic Communications
C Mount Morris Allied Printing
  Trades . . . . . . Mount Morris
CONF Specialty Unions . . Chicago
LU 7-N . . . . Chicago
LU 8-IW . . . . Hazel Crest
LU 32-M . . . . Springfield
LU 39-B . . . . Effingham
LU 65-B . . . . Mount Morris
LU 68-C . . . . Princeville
LU 91-P . . . . Forreston
LU 98-C . . . . East Moline
LU 111-C . . . . Joliet
LU 124-C . . . . . . Mount Morris
LU 171-C . . . . Quincy
LU 219-M . . . . Decatur
LU 240-B . . . . Batavia
LU 391-C . . . . Effingham
LU 415-S . . . . Chicago
LU 418-C . . . . Murphysboro
LU 458-3M . . . . . . Carol Stream
LU 467-S . . . . Forreston
LU 471-M . . . . Joliet
LU 523-S . . . . Peoria
LU 680-S . . . . Marseilles
LU 787-C . . . . Salem

Guards
LU 25 . . . . Channahon

Hotel and Restaurant Employees
LJEB Chicago . . . . Chicago
LU 1 . . . . Chicago
LU 16 . . . . Peoria
LU 43 . . . . Chicago
LU 310 . . . . East Moline
LU 450 . . . . Forest Park
STC Illinois . . . . . Springfield
STC Midwest Organizing
  Council . . . . Chicago

Independent Unions Congress
NHQ . . . . Alton

Iron Workers
DC Chicago & Vicinity . . . La Salle
LU 1 . . . . Forest Park
LU 46 . . . . Springfield
LU 63 . . . . Broadview
LU 111 . . . . Rock Island
LU 112 . . . . East Peoria
LU 136 . . . . River Grove
LU 380 . . . . Urbana
LU 386 . . . . La Salle
LU 392 . . . . . East St. Louis
LU 393 . . . . Aurora
LU 444 . . . . Joliet
LU 465 . . . . Kankakee
LU 473 . . . . Berkeley
LU 498 . . . . Rockford
LU 514 . . . . East Peoria
LU 590 . . . . Naperville
LU 827 . . . . Tilton

Laborers
DC Chicago . . . . . . Burr Ridge
DC North Central Illinois . . . Peoria
DC Southern Illinois . . . . Marion
DC 8 Southwestern
  Illinois . . . . Collinsville

LU 1. . . . . Chicago
LU 2. . . . . Chicago
LU 4. . . . . Chicago
LU 5. . . . . . . Chicago Heights
LU 6. . . . . Chicago
LU 25 . . . . Westchester
LU 32 . . . . Rockford
LU 44 . . . . Collinsville
LU 75 . . . . Joliet
LU 76 . . . . Chicago
LU 96 . . . . Glen Ellyn
LU 100 . . . . Caseyville
LU 118 . . . . Mount Prospect
LU 149 . . . . Aurora
LU 152 . . . . Highland Park
LU 159 . . . . Decatur
LU 165 . . . . Peoria
LU 171 . . . . Mattoon
LU 179 . . . . Edwardsville
LU 196 . . . . Waterloo
LU 197 . . . . Belleville
LU 218 . . . . Godfrey
LU 225 . . . . Des Plaines
LU 227 . . . . Carbondale
LU 231 . . . . Pekin
LU 253 . . . . Jacksonville
LU 269 . . . . Chicago
LU 288 . . . . Westmont
LU 309 . . . . Rock Island
LU 338 . . . . Wood River
LU 362 . . . . Bloomington
LU 393 . . . . Marseilles
LU 397 . . . . Granite City
LU 414 . . . . Glen Carbon
LU 454 . . . . . . East St. Louis
LU 459 . . . . Belleville
LU 474 . . . . Glen Carbon
LU 477 . . . . Springfield
LU 508 . . . . Carterville
LU 528 . . . . Salem
LU 529 . . . . Benton
LU 538 . . . . Wataga
LU 577 . . . . Marion
LU 581 . . . . Carlyle
LU 582 . . . . Elgin
LU 622 . . . . Greenville
LU 624 . . . . Danville
LU 670 . . . . O'Fallon
LU 674 . . . . St. Jacob
LU 677 . . . . Pocahontas
LU 680 . . . . Pocahontas
LU 681 . . . . Westmont
LU 703 . . . . Urbana
LU 727 . . . . Dixon
LU 738 . . . . Du Quoin
LU 742 . . . . Mascoutah
LU 751 . . . . Kankakee
LU 773 . . . . Cairo
LU 803 . . . . Eddyville
LU 911 . . . . Ottawa
LU 925 . . . . Ellis Grove
LU 950 . . . . Mount Olive
LU 962 . . . . Carterville
LU 996 . . . . Roanoke
LU 1001 . . . . Chicago
LU 1006 . . . . Chicago
LU 1035 . . . . Marengo
LU 1048 . . . . . . Brownstown
LU 1083 . . . . Collinsville
LU 1084 . . . . Hillsboro
LU 1092 . . . . Chicago
LU 1197 . . . . . . McLeansboro
LU 1244 . . . . Waterloo
LU 1280 . . . . Robinson
LU 1330 . . . . Anna
LU 1655 . . . . . . North Riverside

Letter Carriers
BR 11 . . . . Chicago
BR 31 . . . . Peoria
BR 80 . . . . Springfield
BR 88 . . . . Galesburg
BR 155 . . . . Belleville
BR 206 . . . . Sterling
BR 209 . . . . Delavan
BR 216 . . . . Clayton
BR 219 . . . . Sandwich
BR 223 . . . . Freeport
BR 245 John H.
    Swanson . . . . Stillman Valley
BR 287 . . . . Streator
BR 292 . . . . Rock Island
BR 305 . . . . Joliet
BR 309 . . . . Alton
BR 311 . . . . Danville
BR 316 . . . . Ottawa
BR 317 . . . . Decatur
BR 318 . . . . Moline
BR 319 . . . . . . East St. Louis
BR 384 . . . . Mattoon
BR 406 . . . . La Salle
BR 407 . . . . Kankakee
BR 409 . . . . Grayslake
BR 522 . . . . Bloomington
BR 561 . . . . Dixon
BR 608 . . . . Oak Park
BR 658 . . . . Macomb
BR 671 . . . . Champaign
BR 688 . . . . Toulon
BR 706 . . . . Dekalb
BR 738 . . . . Centralia
BR 784 . . . . Urbana
BR 825 . . . . Elmhurst
BR 843 . . . . Wheaton
BR 861 . . . . Clinton
BR 942 Mendota, Illinois . Mendota
BR 953 Princeton, Illinois . Princeton
BR 964 . . . . Galena
BR 977 Hoopeston,
    Illinois . . . . . . Hoopeston
BR 1063 Sycamore,
    Illinois . . . . Sycamore
BR 1107 . . . . Wilmette
BR 1132 . . . . . . Granite City
BR 1151 . . . . . . Naperville
BR 1197 . . . . . . Carterville
BR 1235 Shelbyville,
    Illinois . . . . . . Shelbyville
BR 1316 . . . . Peru
BR 1396 Monticello,
    Illinois . . . . . . Monticello
BR 1496 Galva, Illinois . . . Galva
BR 1498 . . . . Winnetka
BR 1499 Morrison,
    Illinois . . . . Morrison
BR 1505 Sullivan, Illinois . Sullivan
BR 1516 Geneseo, Illinois . Geneseo
BR 1539 Du Quoin,
    Illinois . . . . Du Quoin
BR 1555 Tuscola, Illinois . Tuscola
BR 1627 Savanna, Illinois . Savanna
BR 1649 Dundee, Illinois . . Dundee
BR 1672 . . . . Carthage
BR 1762 Spring Valley,
    Illinois . . . . . . Spring Valley
BR 1830 . . . . . . Rock Falls
BR 1859 Abingdon,
    Illinois . . . . Abingdon
BR 1870 . . . . . Downers Grove
BR 2076 . . . . . . Des Plaines
BR 2083 Virden, Illinois . . . Virden
BR 2093 Gibson City,
    Illinois . . . . . . Gibson City
BR 2107 Nokomis, Illinois . Nokomis

BR 2131 Assumption,
    Illinois . . . . . . Assumption
BR 2183 . . . . . Melrose Park
BR 2210 Roodhouse,
    Illinois . . . . . . Roodhouse
BR 2340 Pittsfield, Illinois . Pittsfield
BR 2392 Greenfield,
    Illinois . . . . . . Greenfield
BR 2411 Farmer City,
    Illinois . . . . . . Farmer City
BR 2439 . . . . . Mount Sterling
BR 2517 . . . . Rantoul
BR 2603 Carrollton,
    Illinois . . . . . . Carrollton
BR 2624 Winchester,
    Illinois . . . . . . Winchester
BR 2790 Girard, Illinois . . . Girard
BR 2799 Fulton, Illinois . . . Fulton
BR 2810 . . . . Arlington Heights
BR 3071 . . . . Skokie
BR 3072 Stockton, Illinois . Stockton
BR 3092 . . . . Lockport
BR 3107 Lebanon, Illinois . Lebanon
BR 3148 Amboy, Illinois . . Amboy
BR 3172 Sandwich,
    Illinois . . . . . . Sandwich
BR 3178 Lyons, Illinois . . . . Lyons
BR 3232 Chenoa, Illinois . . Chenoa
BR 3350 Lexington,
    Illinois . . . . . . Lexington
BR 3352 Windsor, Illinois . Windsor
BR 3398 Bement, Illinois . . Bement
BR 3470 . . . . Highwood
BR 3536 Prophetstown,
    Illinois . . . . . . Prophetstown
BR 3542 Knoxville,
    Illinois . . . . . . Knoxville
BR 3555 Palestine, Illinois . Palestine
BR 3558 . . . . Oglesby
BR 3592 . . . . . . Morton Grove
BR 3652 Moweaqua,
    Illinois . . . . . . Moweaqua
BR 3736 Barry, Illinois . . . . Barry
BR 3770 Aledo, Illinois . . . . Aledo
BR 3980 . . . . Morton
BR 4007 . . . . Glenview
BR 4016 . . . . Flossmoor
BR 4065 . . . . Plano
BR 4073 Mount Carroll,
    Illinois . . . . . . Mount Carroll
BR 4099 . . . . . Mount Prospect
BR 4180 Wilmington,
    Illinois . . . . . . Wilmington
BR 4268 . . . . Palatine
BR 4364 . . . . Mundelein
BR 4380 Minonk, Illinois . . Minonk
BR 4739 . . . . Wheeling
BR 4741 . . . . . . Mount Olive
BR 4799 Arcola, Illinois . . . Arcola
BR 4955 Red Bud, Illinois . Red Bud
BR 4958 Warsaw, Illinois . Warsaw
BR 4961 Hamilton,
    Illinois . . . . . . Hamilton
BR 4962 Benld, Illinois . . . . Benld
BR 5143 Wyoming,
    Illinois . . . . . . Wyoming
BR 5168 Rockton, Illinois . Rockton
BR 5369 Genoa, Illinois . . . Genoa
BR 5783 Milan, Illinois . . . . Milan
BR 5933 Hartford, Illinois . Hartford
BR 6171 . . . . Montgomery
BR 6237 East Dubuque,
    Illinois . . . . . . East Dubuque
SA Illinois . . . . Chicago

Locomotive Engineers
DIV 10 . . . . Plainfield
DIV 24 . . . . Salem

DIV 32 . . . . Oswego
DIV 40 . . . . . West Chicago
DIV 45 . . . . Ava
DIV 96 . . . . Lombard
DIV 100 . . . . Westville
DIV 109 . . . . Collinsville
DIV 118 . . . . . . Edwardsville
DIV 135 . . . . Rushville
DIV 152 . . . . . . East Moline
DIV 155 . . . . Decatur
DIV 184 . . . . Gilberts
DIV 200 . . . . Silvis
DIV 251 . . . . Urbana
DIV 294 . . . . Algonquin
DIV 302 . . . . . Evergreen Park
DIV 315 . . . . . . Cerro Gordo
DIV 354 . . . . Bradley
DIV 394 . . . . Chicago
DIV 404 . . . . Aurora
DIV 444 . . . . . . Glen Carbon
DIV 458 . . . . Chicago
DIV 512 . . . . . . Edwardsville
DIV 551 . . . . Steger
DIV 575 . . . . Fox Lake
DIV 577 . . . . Centralia
DIV 582 . . . . Plainfield
DIV 602 . . . . Champaign
DIV 644 . . . . Galesburg
DIV 665 . . . . Centralia
DIV 682 . . . . . . Sauk Village
DIV 683 . . . . Plainfield
DIV 724 . . . . Salem
DIV 790 . . . . Streamwood
DIV 815 . . . . . Calumet Park
DIV 848 . . . . Pekin
GCA Burlington
    Northern . . . . . . Galesburg
GCA Canadian Central-Illinois
    Central . . . . Salem
GCA Norfolk & Western
    Railway . . . . Decatur
GCA Terminal Railroad . . Waterloo
GCA The Belt Railway Company of
    Chicago . . . . Chicago
GCA W C . . . . St. Charles
SLB Illinois . . . . Fairview Heights

Longshoremen
LU 19 . . . . Chicago
LU 101 . . . . Chicago
LU 1427 . . . . . . East Peoria
LU 1652 . . . . . . Wood River

Machinists
DLG 8 . . . . Forest Park
DLG 55 . . . . Channahon
DLG 101 . . . . Belvidere
DLG 102 . . . . Galesburg
DLG 111 . . . . Herrin
LG 48 . . . . Hickory Hills
LG 49 . . . . Crete
LG 124 . . . . Channahon
LG 126 . . . . Hinsdale
LG 213 . . . . Galesburg
LG 266 . . . . Centralia
LG 308 . . . . Collinsville
LG 313 . . . . Caseyville
LG 353 . . . . Freeburg
LG 360 . . . . Peoria
LG 377 . . . . . Chicago Heights
LG 401 . . . . Channahon
LG 431 . . . . Champaign
LG 478 . . . . Chicago
LG 492 . . . . Midlothian
LG 524 . . . . Countryside
LG 554 . . . . Herrin
LG 628 . . . . Springfield
LG 660 Bluff City . . . . East Alton

LG 701 . . . . Countryside	SLG 788 . . . . Virginia	LU 798 . . . . Taylorville	LU 399 . . . . Chicago
LG 710 Vermilion . . . . . Danville	SLG 798 . . . . Galesburg	STCON Illinois . . . . . Schaumburg	LU 428-A . . . . Chicago
LG 742 . . . . Argonne	SLG 965 . . . . Coulterville		LU 428-I . . . . Chicago
LG 746 . . . . Sheridan	SLG 1003 . . . . Texico	**National Staff Organization**	LU 463 . . . . Chicago
LG 822 . . . . Quincy	SLG 1046 . . . . Elburn	LU Staff Organization, Illinois	LU 465-C . . . . Chicago
LG 833 . . . . Mount Zion	SLG 1069 . . . . Champaign	Education Association. Springfield	LU 479-A . . . . Chicago
LG 851 . . . . Channahon	SLG 1152 . . . . Rockfall		LU 488-I . . . . Chicago
LG 930 . . . . Dekalb	SLG 1162 . . . . Breese	**Needletrades**	LU 496-A . . . . Chicago
LG 1000 . . . . Bloomington	SLG 1302 . . . . Streator	JB Central . . . . Chicago	LU 501-A . . . . Chicago
LG 1052 . . . . Dixon	SLG 1599 . . . . Chapin	JB Chicago & Central	LU 502-A . . . . Chicago
LG 1165 . . . . Lincoln	SLG 1867 . . . . Ottawa	States . . . . Chicago	LU 504-A . . . . Chicago
LG 1191 . . . . Silvis	SLG 1983 . . . . Lerna	JB Cincinnati . . . . Chicago	LU 512-A . . . . Chicago
LG 1197 . . . . South Beloit	SLG 2401 . . . . Cicero	JB Cincinnati Regional . . . Chicago	LU 517 . . . . Chicago
LG 1202 . . . . Aurora	SLG 2618 . . . . East Peoria	JB Eastern District . . . . Chicago	LU 529-I . . . . Chicago
LG 1239 . . . . Streator	SLG 2677 . . . . Ivesdale	JB Kentuckiana . . . . . . Chicago	LU 546-I . . . . Chicago
LG 1242 . . . . Carbondale	SLG 2703 . . . . Fithian	JB Midwest Regional . . . . Chicago	LU 562-A . . . . Chicago
LG 1269 . . . . Genoa	SLG 2834 . . . . Effingham	JB Northern . . . . Chicago	LU 593 . . . . Chicago
LG 1487 . . . . Des Plaines	SLG 3045 . . . . Chicago	LU . . . . Chicago	LU 617-A . . . . Chicago
LG 1553 . . . . Rockford		LU . . . . Chicago	LU 724-A . . . . Chicago
LG 1557 . . . . South Elgin	**Mine Workers**	LU 5 . . . . Chicago	LU 768-A . . . . Chicago
LG 1613 . . . . Vandalia	D 12 . . . . Springfield	LU 5-H . . . . Chicago	LU 777-I . . . . Chicago
LG 1623 . . . . Morrison	LU 12 . . . . Hillsboro	LU 14-M . . . . Chicago	LU 782-A . . . . Chicago
LG 1659 . . . . Knoxville	LU 15 District 12 . . . . . Tamaroa	LU 17 . . . . Chicago	LU 839-A . . . . Chicago
LG 1749 . . . . Channahon	LU 1131 . . . . Galesburg	LU 17-56H . . . . Chicago	LU 840-A . . . . Chicago
LG 1815 . . . . Springfield	LU 1148 . . . . Freeburg	LU 36-A. . . . . Chicago	LU 851-T . . . . Chicago
LG 1832 . . . . Marengo	LU 1392 . . . . Pinckneyville	LU 39-C. . . . . Chicago	LU 870-A . . . . Chicago
LG 1856 . . . . Mount Carmel	LU 1393 . . . . Hillsboro	LU 48 . . . . Chicago	LU 871-A . . . . Chicago
LG 1880 . . . . Streator	LU 1458 . . . . Red Bud	LU 50-010. . . . . Chicago	LU 872-A . . . . Chicago
LG 2063 . . . . Galesburg	LU 1474 . . . . Marion	LU 56 . . . . Chicago	LU 874-A . . . . Chicago
LG 2068 . . . . Rochelle	LU 1487 . . . . Thompsonville	LU 56-ASW. . . . . Chicago	LU 888-A . . . . Chicago
LG 2125 . . . . Wheeling	LU 1523 . . . . Fairview	LU 61 . . . . Chicago	LU 920-A . . . . Chicago
LG 2268 . . . . Lawrenceville	LU 1545 . . . . Herrin	LU 62 . . . . Chicago	LU 940-A . . . . Chicago
LG 2293 Lincoln Trail . . . Robinson	LU 1602 . . . . Ridgway	LU 63-H. . . . . Chicago	LU 958-A . . . . Chicago
LG 2421 . . . . Justice	LU 1613 . . . . Gillespie	LU 64-H. . . . . Chicago	LU 969-A . . . . Chicago
LG 2458 . . . . Argonne	LU 1820 . . . . Baldwin	LU 66 . . . . Chicago	LU 978-A . . . . Chicago
LG 2600 . . . . Oak Forest	LU 1825 . . . . Tamaroa	LU 73-A. . . . . Chicago	LU 981-A . . . . Chicago
LG 2806-PM . . . . La Grange Park	LU 1969 . . . . Coulinville	LU 76 . . . . Chicago	LU 1008-A . . . . Chicago
LG 2825-PM . . . . . East Moline	LU 2117 . . . . Thompsonville	LU 81-R. . . . . Chicago	LU 1050. . . . . Chicago
LG 2832-PM . . . . . . Lewistown	LU 2161 . . . . Coulterville	LU 86-C. . . . . Chicago	LU 1051. . . . . Chicago
STC Illinois . . . . Herrin	LU 2216 . . . . Vergennes	LU 90-I . . . . Chicago	LU 1094-T . . . . Chicago
	LU 2295 . . . . Germantown	LU 91 . . . . Chicago	LU 1106. . . . . Chicago
Maintenance of Way Employes	LU 2382 . . . . Cave in Rock	LU 99-H. . . . . Chicago	LU 1107. . . . . Chicago
LG 122 . . . . Pittsfield	LU 2412 . . . . Marissa	LU 104 . . . . Chicago	LU 1110. . . . . Chicago
LG 276 . . . . Shorewood	LU 2414 . . . . Woodlawn	LU 108-A . . . . Chicago	LU 1164. . . . . Chicago
LG 377 . . . . Lombard	LU 2420 . . . . Johnston City	LU 112 . . . . Chicago	LU 1166-C . . . . Chicago
LG 409 . . . . Chicago	LU 2452 . . . . Belleville	LU 120 . . . . Chicago	LU 1170. . . . . Chicago
LG 591 . . . . Chicago	LU 2463 . . . . Metropolis	LU 144-JTU. . . . . Chicago	LU 1259. . . . . Chicago
LG 783 . . . . Colchester	LU 2488 . . . . Rushville	LU 146-SW. . . . . Chicago	LU 1385. . . . . Chicago
LG 1063 . . . . Bridgeport	LU 5134 . . . . Du Quoin	LU 151-A . . . . Chicago	LU 1406. . . . . Chicago
LG 1081 . . . . O'Fallon	LU 7031 . . . . Omaha	LU 168-AC . . . . Chicago	LU 1422. . . . . Chicago
LG 1107 . . . . Butler	LU 7110 . . . . Dunfermline	LU 183 . . . . Chicago	LU 1426. . . . . Chicago
LG 1259 . . . . Kankakee	LU 7333 . . . . Duquoin	LU 187-I . . . . Chicago	LU 1448. . . . . Chicago
LG 1514 . . . . Homewood	LU 8317 . . . . West Frankfort	LU 188-I . . . . Chicago	LU 1481. . . . . Chicago
LG 1698 . . . . Edwardsville	LU 9111 . . . . West Frankfort	LU 189-T . . . . Chicago	LU 1490. . . . . Chicago
LG 2853 . . . . . Arlington Heights	LU 9746 . . . . Girard	LU 193 . . . . Chicago	LU 1495. . . . . Chicago
LG 2854 . . . . Creve Coeur	LU 9819 . . . . Taylorville	LU 195 . . . . Chicago	LU 1525-T . . . . Chicago
LG 2856 . . . . East Peoria	LU 9878 . . . . West Frankfort	LU 199 . . . . Chicago	LU 1538. . . . . Chicago
LG 3086 . . . . Chicago	LU 9905 . . . . Du Quoin	LU 205-ASW . . . . Chicago	LU 1557. . . . . Chicago
SD Chicago & Eastern	LU 9939 . . . . Stonefort	LU 208-A . . . . Chicago	LU 1558. . . . . Chicago
Illinois . . . . Salem		LU 210-T . . . . Chicago	LU 1737. . . . . Chicago
SD Elgin Joliet & Eastern	**Musicians**	LU 223-SW . . . . Chicago	LU 1749. . . . . Chicago
Railroad . . . . Joliet	LU 10-208. . . . . Chicago	LU 224-T . . . . Chicago	LU 1758. . . . . Chicago
SLG 17 . . . . Creal Springs	LU 26 . . . . Peoria	LU 252-M. . . . . Chicago	LU 1812. . . . . Chicago
SLG 41 . . . . Chrisman	LU 29 . . . . Collinsville	LU 255 . . . . Chicago	LU 1818. . . . . Chicago
SLG 42 . . . . Addison	LU 37 . . . . Joliet	LU 261 . . . . Chicago	LU 1820. . . . . Chicago
SLG 46 . . . . Atwood	LU 48 . . . . Schaumburg	LU 270-A . . . . Chicago	LU 1828. . . . . Chicago
SLG 55 . . . . Savanna	LU 88 . . . . Benld	LU 272-A . . . . Chicago	LU 1863. . . . . Chicago
SLG 97 . . . . Marion	LU 98 . . . . Edwardsville	LU 284-SW . . . . Chicago	LU 1871. . . . . Chicago
SLG 212 . . . . Maeystown	LU 100 Kewanec . . . . . . Galva	LU 295-C . . . . Chicago	LU 1872. . . . . Chicago
SLG 226 . . . . Decatur	LU 175 . . . . Highland	LU 304 . . . . Chicago	LU 1899. . . . . Chicago
SLG 299 . . . . Nashville	LU 178 . . . . Galesburg	LU 319-C . . . . Chicago	LU 1901. . . . . Chicago
SLG 358 . . . . Crest Hill	LU 196 . . . . Champaign	LU 322 . . . . Chicago	LU 1902. . . . . Chicago
SLG 436 . . . . Cicero	LU 240 . . . . Rockford	LU 323 . . . . Chicago	LU 1923. . . . . Chicago
SLG 469 . . . . New Lenox	LU 265 Quincy. . . . . . . Quincy	LU 335-T . . . . Chicago	LU 2299. . . . . Chicago
SLG 505 . . . . Marshall	LU 301 . . . . Morton	LU 379 . . . . Chicago	LU 2302. . . . . Chicago
SLG 510 . . . . Milledgeville	LU 307 . . . . Spring Valley	LU 383 . . . . Chicago	LU 2352. . . . . Chicago
SLG 565 . . . . McLeansboro	LU 717 . . . . Granite City	LU 393-T . . . . Chicago	LU 2375. . . . . Chicago
SLG 694 . . . . Bradley	LU 759 . . . . Streator	LU 398 . . . . Chicago	LU 2378. . . . . Chicago

LU 2403 . . . . Chicago
LU 2405 . . . . Chicago
LU 2430 . . . . Chicago
LU 2440 . . . . Chicago
LU 2458 . . . . Chicago
LU 2483 . . . . Chicago
LU 2484 . . . . Chicago
LU 2497 . . . . Chicago
LU 2512 . . . . Chicago
LU 2543 . . . . Chicago
LU 2565 . . . . Chicago
LU 2568 . . . . Chicago
LU 2573 . . . . Chicago
LU 2577 . . . . Chicago
LU 2580 . . . . Chicago
LU 2590 . . . . Chicago
LU 2615 . . . . Chicago
LU 2616 . . . . Chicago
LU 2634 . . . . Chicago
LU 2635 . . . . Chicago
LU 2636 . . . . Chicago
LU 2646 . . . . Chicago
LU 2656 . . . . Chicago
LU 2668 . . . . Chicago
LU 2675 . . . . Chicago
LU 2685 . . . . Chicago
LU 2686 . . . . Chicago

NLRB Professional Association
LU 13 . . . . Chicago
LU 33 . . . . Peoria

Novelty and Production Workers
JB Central States . . . . . Chicago
LU 10 Production Workers . Chicago
LU 12 Production Workers . Chicago
LU 16 Metal Processors . . Chicago
LU 18 Plastic Workers . . . Chicago
LU 20 Brushmakers . . . . Chicago
LU 24 Toy & Novelty
   Workers . . . . Chicago
NHQ . . . . Chicago

Nurses
LU Hines VA INA . . Elmwood Park
LU Illinois . . . . Chicago
LU North Chicago VA
   INA . . . . Chicago
LU Reynolds Unit INA . . . Chicago
LU St. Joseph Hospital Nurses
   Association . . . . Joliet
LU Union Health Service
   Unit . . . . Chicago
SA Illinois Nurses
   Association . . . . Chicago
UNIT INA University of Chicago
   Local . . . . Chicago

Nurses, Practical
DIV 1 Licensed Practical Nurses
   Association of Illinois . Chicago
SA Licensed Practical Nurses
   Association of Illinois . Springfield

Office and Professional Employees
LU 28 . . . . Chicago
LU 391 . . . . Chicago
LU 444 . . . . Galesburg

Operating Engineers
LU 148 . . . . Maryville
LU 150 . . . . Countryside
LU 318 . . . . Marion
LU 399 . . . . Chicago
LU 520 . . . . Granite City
LU 649 . . . . Peoria
LU 965 . . . . Springfield

Painters
CONF Central Region . . St. Charles
DC 14 . . . . Chicago
DC 30 . . . . St. Charles
DC 58 . . . . Collinsville
LU 27 . . . . Brookfield
LU 32 . . . . Carterville
LU 33 . . . . Joliet
LU 35 . . . . Benld
LU 85 . . . . Mascoutah
LU 90 . . . . Springfield
LU 97 . . . . St. Charles
LU 101 . . . . Chicago
LU 120 . . . . Granite
LU 124 . . . . Centralia
LU 147 . . . . Chicago
LU 154 . . . . Elgin
LU 157 . . . . Peoria
LU 180 . . . . Darien
LU 184 . . . . Chicago Ridge
LU 191 . . . . Oak Forest
LU 194 . . . . Chicago
LU 209 . . . . Bloomington
LU 215 . . . . Belleville
LU 265 . . . . Crestwood
LU 273 . . . . Palos Hills
LU 275 . . . . Round Lake
LU 288 . . . . Decatur
LU 363 . . . . Champaign
LU 448 . . . . Aurora
LU 455 . . . . Hanover Park
LU 465 . . . . Streator
LU 467 . . . . Clifton
LU 471 . . . . Hardin
LU 502 . . . . Rock Island
LU 521 . . . . Buffalo Grove
LU 581 . . . . Rock Island
LU 607 . . . . Rockford
LU 611 Wood Finishers . . . Niles
LU 830 . . . . Hickory Hills
LU 849 . . . . Breese
LU 863 . . . . Crystal Lake
LU 910 . . . . Hillsboro
LU 1164 . . . . Peoria
LU 1168 . . . . Niantic
LU 1285 . . . . St. Chatles
LU 1299 . . . . Caseyville
LU 1332 . . . . Chicago
LU 1705 . . . . Willow Hill
LU 1850 . . . . East St. Louis
LU 2007 . . . . Jacksonville

**Paper, Allied-Industrial, Chemical
   Employees**
C Illinois Council of
   Locals . . . . West Peoria
C Region VI Council . . West Peoria
LU 923 . . . . Freeport
LU 1345 . . . . Plainfield
LU 7821 . . . . Illiopolis
LU 06-91 . . . . Westchester
LU 06-188 . . . . Delavan
LU 06-189 . . . . Illiopolis
LU 06-194 . . . . Peoria
LU 06-198 . . . . Quincy
LU 06-268 . . . . Chicago
LU 06-325 . . . . Dolton
LU 06-347 . . . . Cahokia
LU 06-362 . . . . Moweaqua
LU 06-368 . . . . . . Lawrenceville
LU 06-429 . . . . Ashkum
LU 06-455 . . . . Chicago
LU 06-507 . . . . Summit
LU 06-517 . . . . Oak Lawn
LU 06-626 . . . . Morris
LU 06-643 . . . . Galesburg
LU 06-647 . . . . La Grange
LU 06-657 . . . . Oglesby

LU 06-662 . . . . Pekin
LU 06-717 . . . . Burbank
LU 06-728 . . . . Decatur
LU 06-765 . . . . . Chicago Heights
LU 06-807 . . . . Delavan
LU 06-837 . . . . Decatur
LU 06-838 . . . . Decatur
LU 06-839 . . . . Decatur
LU 06-865 . . . . . . Bolingbrook
LU 06-876 . . . . Decatur
LU 06-904 . . . . Joliet
LU 06-960 . . . . . . West Peoria
LU 06-972 . . . . Danville
LU 06-975 . . . . Fairmount
LU 06-985 . . . . Hoopeston
LU 06-1085 . . . . Frankfort
LU 06-1208 . . . . Chicago
LU 06-1210 . . . . Chicago
LU 06-1211 . . . . Plainfield
LU 06-1215 . . . . Highland
LU 06-1216 . . . . Worth
LU 06-7591 . . . . Charleston
LU 07-898 . . . . Stonington
LU 07-1201 . . . . Beach Park
LU 07-1651 . . . . Morrison

Plasterers and Cement Masons
DC Northern Illinois . . . Villa Park
LU 5 . . . . Alsip
LU 11 . . . . McHenry
LU 18 . . . . Peoria
LU 90 . . . . Troy
LU 143 . . . . Champaign
LU 502 . . . . Bellwood
LU 803 . . . . Villa Park
STCON Illinois . . . . . . Troy

Plumbing and Pipe Fitting
DC 34 Pipe Trades . . . . . Peoria
LU 23 . . . . Rockford
LU 25 . . . . Rock Island
LU 63 . . . . East Peoria
LU 65 . . . . Decatur
LU 93 . . . . Waukegan
LU 99 . . . . Bloomington
LU 101 . . . . Belleville
LU 130 . . . . Chicago
LU 137 . . . . Springfield
LU 149 . . . . Savoy
LU 160 . . . . Murphysboro
LU 281 . . . . Alsip
LU 353 . . . . Peoria
LU 360 . . . . Collinsville
LU 422 . . . . Joliet
LU 439 . . . . East St. Louis
LU 501 . . . . Aurora
LU 551 . . . . West Frankfort
LU 553 . . . . East Alton
LU 597 . . . . Chicago
LU 649 . . . . East St. Louis
LU 653 . . . . Centralia
SA Illinois Pipe Trades . . . Chicago

Police
LG 1-F Federal Police Officers,
   Illinois . . . . Tinley Park

Police Associations
LU 7 Illinois Council of Police &
   Sheriffs . . . . Elmhurst

Postal and Federal Employees
D 7 . . . . Chicago
LU 701 Chicago Illinois . . Chicago
LU 703 . . . . St. Louis
LU 704
   Evanston . . . Country Club Hills

Postal Mail Handlers
LU 306 . . . . Chicago

Postal Workers
LU 1 Chicago . . . . Chicago
LU 39 Matton . . . . Mattoon
LU 74 East St. Louis . East St. Louis
LU 77 Quincy Area . . . . . Quincy
LU 79 Rockford . . . . . Rockford
LU 97 Lake Country
   Area . . . . Waukegan
LU 105 Ottawa . . . . . . Ottawa
LU 109 Bi-State Area . . Rock Island
LU 117 Freeport . . . . . Freeport
LU 182 Gem Area . . . . Maryville
LU 228 Bloomington . Bloomington
LU 239 Lincoln Land
   Area . . . . Springfield
LU 243 Danville . . . . . Danville
LU 279 Streator Local . . . Streator
LU 324 Joliet . . . . Joliet
LU 337 Mount Carmel
   Local . . . . Mount Carmel
LU 351 Aurora . . . . . . Aurora
LU 407 Belleville . . . . Belleville
LU 563 Elgin . . . . Elgin
LU 594 Blue Island
   Local . . . . Blue Island
LU 604-605 . . . . . . Countryside
LU 671 Galesburg . . . . Galesburg
LU 686 Jacksonville . . Jacksonville
LU 692 Champaign . . Champaign
LU 734 Olney Local . . . . Olney
LU 854 Heart of Illinois Area . Peoria
LU 920 Oak Park . . . . River Forest
LU 944 Carbondale . . . Carbondale
LU 1021 Illinois Valley . . La Salle
LU 1050 Cairo . . . . Cairo
LU 1051 Metropolis
   Local . . . . Metropolis
LU 1152 Marion . . . . . . Marion
LU 1208 Rantoul Local . . . Rantoul
LU 1222 Effingham . . . Effingham
LU 1224 Evanston . . . . Evanston
LU 1258 De Kalb . . . . . Dekalb
LU 1306 Harvey . . . . . . Harvey
LU 1343 Elmhurst . . . . Elmhurst
LU 1621 Salem . . . . . . Salem
LU 1679 West Frankfort
   Local . . . . . West Frankfort
LU 1701 . . . . Peru
LU 1730 Des Plaines . . Des Plaines
LU 1788 Park Ridge . . . Park Ridge
LU 1879 Crystal Lake . East Dundee
LU 1884 Flora Local . . . . Flora
LU 2072 Benton Local . . . Benton
LU 2088 Wheaton . . . . Wheaton
LU 2250 Macomb . . . . Macomb
LU 2257 Marengo Local . Marengo
LU 2536 Paris Local . . . . Paris
LU 2583 Harrisburg
   Local . . . . . . Harrisburg
LU 3090 Sparta Local . . . . Sparta
LU 3092 O'Fallon . . . . . O'Fallon
LU 3226 Belvidere Local . Belvidere
LU 3417 Urbana . . . . . Urbana
LU 3455 Centralia . . . . Centralia
LU 3558 Grayslake . . . Grayslake
LU 3987 Sandwich Local . Sandwich
LU 4319 Skokie . . . . . . Skokie
LU 4408 Anna Local . . . . Anna
LU 4545 Arlington
   Heights . . . . Arlington Heights
LU 4726 Decatur . . . . . Decatur
LU 4733 Bellwood . . . Bellwood
LU 4779 Kewanee . . . Kewanee
LU 4803 Morton
   Grove . . . . Morton Grove

LU 4871 Schaumburg . . Schaumburg
LU 5007 Kankakee . . . . Kankakee
LU 5154 Mendota Local . . Mendota
LU 5924 Charleston
　Local . . . . Charleston
LU 6111 Carlinville
　Local . . . . Carlinville
LU 6479 Monmouth . . . Monmouth
LU 6591 South Suburban
　Facility . . . . Bedford Park
LU 6993 Wheeling . . Buffalo Grove
LU 7011 O'Hare-Midway
　Terminals . . . . Chicago
LU 7033 Chicago Bulk Mail
　Center . . . . Forest Park
LU 7081 . . . . Bartlett
LU 7139 Fox Valley . . . . . Aurora
LU 7140 Northwest Illinois
　Area . . . . Elmhurst
SA Illinois . . . . . . Bourbonnais

Production Workers

LU 707 Chicago &
　Vicinity . . . . Oak Brook
LU 707 Cleveland and
　Vicinity . . . . Oak Brook
LU 707 Professional Technical &
　Clerical Employees . . Oak Brook
LU 707 Truck Drivers Chauffeurs
　Warehousemen . . . . Oak Brook
NHQ . . . . Oak Brook

**Professional and Technical
　Engineers**

C Central States. . . . . Lisle
LU 81. . . . . Lisle
LU 777 . . . . Chicago

Railroad Signalmen

GC 12 Burlington
　Northern . . . . Galesburg
GC 24 Soo Line . . Mount Prospect
GC 36 Illinois Central
　Railroad. . . . . Mount Prospect
LLG 3 . . . . Chicago
LLG 15 . . . . Mount Prospect
LLG 20 . . . . Dahinda
LLG 25 . . . . . . Mount Carmel
LLG 29 . . . . Lena
LLG 34 . . . . . . Mount Prospect
LLG 55 . . . . Champaign
LLG 81 . . . . Tuscola
LLG 85 . . . . Carlinville
LLG 99 Gulf Coast Local
　99 . . . . Mount Prospect
LLG 103 . . . . Knoxville
LLG 108 . . . . Rock Falls
LLG 130 . . . . Gilberts
LLG 143 . . . . Oak Forest
LLG 163 . . . . . . Mount Prospect
LLG 174 . . . . . . Mount Vernon
LLG 183 . . . . Manteno
LLG 191. . . . . . . Pinckneyville
LLG 194 . . . . . . Mount Prospect
NHQ . . . . Mount Prospect

**Retail, Wholesale and Department
　Store**

JB Chicago . . . . Chicago
LU 15 . . . . Chicago
LU 17. . . . . Mendota
LU 20 . . . . Chicago
LU 200 Cook County Pharmacy
　Association . . . . Chicago
LU 239 . . . . Chicago
LU 291 . . . . Chicago
LU 317 . . . . Chicago
LU 578 . . . . Rochelle

LU 853 . . . . Chicago

**Roofers, Waterproofers and Allied
　Workers**

DC Illinois Roofers . . . Westchester
LU 11 . . . . Westchester
LU 32 . . . . Rock Island
LU 69 . . . . Peoria
LU 92 . . . . Decatur
LU 97 . . . . Champaign
LU 112 . . . . Springfield

Rural Letter Carriers

D 16 Cumberland County . . Mattoon
D 17 De Kalb County . . Somonauk
D 46 Lawrence County West Liberty
LU Bond County . . . . Smithboro
LU Champaign County. . . . Sidney
LU Clinton County . . . . Trenton
LU Edgar County. . . . . . . Paris
LU Effingham County . . Shumway
LU Gallatin County . . . . Omaha
LU Hamilton County . McLeansboro
LU Iroquois County . . . Martinton
LU Jasper County . . . Willow Hill
LU Jo Daviess County . Orangeville
LU Johnson County . . . . Vienna
LU Kane, Du Page, & North Cook
　Counties . . . . Yorkville
LU Kankakee County . . Herscher
LU Kendall County . . . . . Plano
LU Knox County . . . . Galesburg
LU Lee County . . . . Dixon
LU Livingston-Ford
　Counties . . . . Menonk
LU Macon County. . . . . Decatur
LU Madison County . . Granite City
LU McDonough County . . Macomb
LU McLean County . . Bloomington
LU Mercer County . . . . . Aledo
LU Montgomery County . Litchfield
LU Peoria County . . . . Hopedale
LU Perry-Jackson County. Du Quoin
LU Piatt County . . . White Heath
LU Pike County. . . . . . Baylis
LU Rock Island County . . . Milan
LU Sangamon County. . . Cantrall
LU Stark County . . . . Bradford
LU Vermilion County . . . Danville
LU Whiteside County . . Rock Falls
LU 1 Adams County. . . . . Quincy
LU 4 Boone-Winnebago
　Counties . . . . Rockford
LU 6 Bureau-Putnam
　Counties . . . . Granville
LU 8 Carroll County . Mount Carroll
LU 11 Christian County . . . . Pana
LU 11 Clark County . . Martinsville
LU 12 Clay County
　Association. . . . . Flora
LU 21 Edwards County. West Salem
LU 23 Fayette County . . . Farina
LU 25 Franklin
　County. . . . . . West Frankfort
LU 26 Fulton County . . . . Avon
LU 31 Henderson-Warren
　Counties . . . . Seaton
LU 44 Lake County . . . . Russell
LU 45 Lasalle County. . . . Oglesby
LU 52 Crawford County . Flat Rock
LU 53 Jersey-Macoupin
　Counties . . . . Jerseyville
LU 55 Marion County . . . . Odin
LU 56 Mason-Logan-Menard
　Counties . . . . Manito
LU 60 Monroe County . . . Millstadt
LU 62 Morgan-Scott-Cass-Green
　Counties . . . . Arenzville

LU 63 Moultrie County. . . Sullivan
LU 64 Ogle County . . Lindenwood
LU 70 Randolph County . . . Sparta
LU 71 Richland County. . . . Olney
LU 73 St. Clair County . . . Marissa
LU 74 Saline County . . . . Galatia
LU 77 Shelby County. . Assumption
LU 80 Alexander, Pulaski & Union
　Counties . . . . Anna
LU 83 Washington County . . Venedy
LU 84 Wayne County . . Fairfield
LU 87 Will-South Cook
　Counties . . . . Minooka
LU 108 Pope-Hardin
　Counties . . . . Golconda
SA Illinois . . . . Illiopolis

Security Officers

LU 1 . . . . Vernon Hills

**Security, Police and Fire
　Professionals**

LU 225 . . . . Chicago
LU 226 . . . . Oneida
LU 227 . . . . . . East Hazelcrest
LU 228 . . . . Martinton
LU 235 . . . . East Peoria
LU 236 . . . . Morrison
LU 237 . . . . Rockford
LU 238 . . . . Hillsdale

Service Employees

C Illinois . . . . Chicago
LU 1 . . . . Chicago
LU 4 . . . . Chicago
LU 7 Firemen & Oilers . . . Chicago
LU 8 Firemen & Oilers . . . Peoria
LU 15 . . . . Springfield
LU 19 Firemen & Oilers. Springfield
LU 34-Z . . . . Lombard
LU 73 . . . . Chicago
LU 73-HC. . . . . Chicago
LU 116 . . . . Belleville
LU 352 International Leather Goods,
　Plastics, Novelty and Service
　Union . . . . Pinckneyville
LU 570 Firemen & Oilers. . Chicago
LU 660 Firemen &
　Oilers . . . . Sauk Village
LU 728 Firemen &
　Oilers . . . . Taylorville
LU 865 Firemen & Oilers. Galesburg
LU 944 Firemen & Oilers . . Harvey
LU 18007 . . . . Chicago

Sheet Metal Workers

LU 1 . . . . Peoria Heights
LU 73 . . . . Chicago
LU 91 . . . . Rock Island
LU 218 . . . . Springfield
LU 219 . . . . Rockford
LU 256 . . . . Bourbonnais
LU 265 . . . . Carol Stream
LU 268 . . . . Caseyville
LU 367 . . . . Chicago
LU 450. . . . . Bradley
LU 484 . . . . Orland Hills
STC Illinois . . . . Peoria Heights

**State, County and Municipal
　Employees**

C 31 Illinois Public
　Employees. . . . . . . Springfield
LU . . . . Broadview
LU . . . . Hoyleton
LU . . . . Springfield
LU 1514 Aurora Area Public
　Employees . . . . Aurora

LU 3237 United Cerebral Palsy of
　Will County . . . . . Romeoville
LU 3280 Anna Veterans' Home
　Employees . . . . . . Buncombe
LU 3513 Family Counseling
　Center . . . . Simpson
LU 3538 Heritage 53 Employees
　Council 31 . . . . . Rock Island
LU 3784 Beverly Farm Foundation
　Inc. . . . . Bethalto

Steelworkers

LU 2-19-G . . . . Ottawa
LU 07-16-S . . . . . Granite City
LU 07-17-U . . . . Chicago
LU 07-30-S . . . . . Granite City
LU 07-31-G . . . . Ottawa
LU 07-63-S . . . . Sterling
LU 07-67-S . . . . . Granite City
LU 07-68-S . . . . . Granite City
LU 07-86-G . . . . Bushhell
LU 07-193-S . . . . . Mount Zion
LU 07-215-L . . . . . Rock Island
LU 07-436-S . . . . . . La Salle
LU 07-442 . . . . Ladd
LU 07-685-L . . . . . Galesburg
LU 07-704-L . . . . Dekalb
LU 07-706-A . . . . . Georgetown
LU 07-713-L . . . . . . Decatur
LU 07-745-L . . . . . . Freeport
LU 07-787-L . . . . Normal
LU 07-960-L . . . . . South Beloit
LU 07-1033-S . . . . Chicago
LU 07-1053-S . . . . . Bridgeview
LU 07-1063-S . . . . . Granite City
LU 07-1636-S . . . . . . Aurora
LU 07-1744-S . . . . . Hainesville
LU 07-2154-S . . . . Chicago
LU 07-2629-S . . . . . Galesburg
LU 07-3510-S . . . . . Bardolph
LU 07-3643-S . . . . Alton
LU 07-4063-S . . . . . Granite City
LU 07-4268-S . . . . . . Oglesby
LU 07-4294-S . . . . . . Cahokia
LU 07-4804-S . . . . . Granite City
LU 07-5109-S . . . . . Mount Olive
LU 07-5544-S . . . . . . Pocahontas
LU 07-5574-S . . . . . Edwardsville
LU 07-6063-S . . . . . Edwardsville
LU 07-6496-S . . . . . . O'Fallon
LU 07-7234-S . . . . Harvey
LU 07-7252-S . . . . . Pinckneyville
LU 07-7367-S . . . . . Hennepin
LU 07-7495-S . . . . . South Elgin
LU 07-7773-S . . . . . Bolingbrook
LU 07-7999-S . . . . . . Oswego
LU 07-9189-S . . . . . Wood River
LU 07-9325-S . . . . . Granite City
LU 07-9777 . . . . . . Bridgeview
LU 07-13605-S . . . . . . Tamaroa
LU 07-13748-S . . . . Pekin
LU 07-13881-S . . . . . New Lenox
LU 07-14676-S . . . . . Cartervinlle
LU 07-14728-S . . . . . Bradley
LU 07-15009-S . . . Johnston City
LU 34-8390. . . . . . . Charleston

Teachers

LU 2063 Faculty-University of
　Chicago Lab Schools . . . Chicago
SFED 310 Illinois . . . . Oak Brook

Teamsters

CONF Illinois Conference of
　Teamsters . . . . . Springfield
JC 25 . . . . Chicago
JC 65 . . . . Springfield
LU 26 . . . . Danville

LU 50 . . . . Belleville
LU 179 . . . . Joliet
LU 279 . . . . Decatur
LU 301 . . . . Waukegan
LU 325 . . . . Rockford
LU 330 . . . . Elgin
LU 347 . . . . . . West Frankfort
LU 371 . . . . Rock Island
LU 525 . . . . Alton
LU 627 . . . . Peoria
LU 673 . . . . . . West Chicago
LU 703 . . . . Chicago
LU 705 . . . . Chicago
LU 706 . . . . Chicago
LU 710 . . . . Chicago
LU 714 . . . . Berwyn
LU 722 . . . . La Salle
LU 727 . . . . Chicago
LU 731 . . . . . La Grange Park
LU 734 . . . . Chicago
LU 738 . . . . Chicago
LU 743 . . . . Chicago
LU 744 . . . . Chicago
LU 754 . . . . Elmhurst
LU 777 . . . . Brookfield
LU 781 . . . . Des Plaines
LU 786 . . . . Chicago
LU 916 . . . . Springfield

Television and Radio Artists
LU Chicago . . . . Chicago
LU 1080 Peoria Area . . East Peoria

Theatrical Stage Employees
CONF Illinois State . . . . Sidney
D 9 Wisconsin-Iowa-Illinois-
  Missouri-Minnesota-North
  Dakota-South Dakota-
  Nebraska . . . . Sidney
LU 2 . . . . Chicago
LU 46-B . . . . Chicago
LU 110 . . . . Chicago
LU 124 . . . . Joliet
LU 138 . . . . Springfield
LU 193 . . . . Bloomington
LU 217 . . . . Rockford
LU 374 . . . . New Lenox
LU 421 . . . . Metropolis
LU 433 . . . . Cleveland
LU 476 . . . . Chicago
LU 482 . . . . Urbana
LU 750 Treasurers &
  Ticketsellers . . . La Grange Park
LU 769 . . . . Hoffman Estates
LU 780 . . . . Chicago

Train Dispatchers
SCOM Belt Railroad of
  Chicago . . . . Tinley Park
SCOM Norfolk & Western
  Railway . . . . Mount Zion
SCOM Northeast Illinois Regional
  Commute . . . . Minooka
SCOM Peoria & Pekin Union
  Railroad . . . . Delavan
SCOM Terminal Railroad
  Association of St.
  Louis . . . . Caseyville

Transit Union
LDIV 313 . . . . Rock Island
LDIV 416 . . . . Glasford
LDIV 752 . . . . Bloomington
LDIV 859 . . . . Decatur
LDIV 1333 . . . . Rockford
LU 1028 . . . . Elk Grove Village
LU 1702 . . . . Richton Park
LU 1711 . . . . Rockford

Transport Workers
LU 512 . . . . . Elk Grove Village
LU 540 . . . . Palatine
LU 563 . . . . Des Plaines
LU 571 . . . . Chicago
LU 572 . . . . Tinley Park
LU 2014 . . . . Chicago
LU 2037 . . . . Alhambra

Transportation Communications Union
D 245 Great Lakes System Board
  118 . . . . Joliet
D 439 . . . . Decatur
D 521 Southeastern System Board
  96 . . . . Alton
D 679 . . . . Lisle
D 782 . . . . Chicago
D 829 Allied Services
  Division . . . . Arlington Heights
D 1068 . . . . Desoto
D 1266 . . . . Tinley Park
D 1505 Great Lakes System Board
  118 . . . . Chicago
D 1960 Allied Services
  Division . . . . Arlington Heights
D 2500 . . . . Hometown
D 2503 . . . . Springfield
D 2509 . . . . Chicago
JPB 240 Illinois Central
  System . . . . Joliet
JPB 600 Chicago Milwaukee St. Paul
  & Pacific . . . . Chicago
LG 512 . . . . Collinsville
LG 549 . . . . Addison
LG 574 . . . . Troy
LG 695 . . . . Crestwood
LG 781 . . . . Willow Springs
LG 867 . . . . Galesburg
LG 5098 American Rail & Airway
  Supervisors . . . . . Homewood
LG 6024 Midwest . . . . . Beason
LG 6034 Violet . . . . . . Swansea
LG 6100 Fellowship . . . . Manteno
LG 6176 Proviso . . . . . Chicago
LG 6266 Cook County . . . Palatine
LG 6277 Decatur . . . . . Decatur
LG 6297 Surprise . . . . . Worth
LG 6324 New Hope . . . . Mokena
LG 6560 Stony Island . . . Lansing
LG 6591 Purple . . . . . . Chicago
LG 6608 Chesterfield . . Beaverville
LG 6787 Galesburg . . . . Wataga
LG 6861 Beacon . . . . . Bluford
SBA 155 Allied Services
  Division . . . . Arlington Heights

Transportation Union
GCA GO-65 Belt Railroad of
  Chicago . . . . . . Palos Heights
GCA GO-209 Chicago & Eastern
  Railway . . . . . . Grant Park
GCA GO-217 Chicago Illinois
  Midland Railroad . . . . . Easton
GCA GO-330 Elgin Joliet Eastern
  Railway . . . . . . Wilmington
GCA GO-401 SPCSL-GWWR-IC
  Railroad . . . . . . Bloomington
GCA GO-449 Indiana Harbor Belt
  Railroad . . . . Matteson
GCA GO-919 Terminal
  Railroad Association-St.
  Louis . . . . Granite City
LLG 1973 LLG . . . Palos Heights
LU 171 . . . . Aurora
LU 195 . . . . Galesburg
LU 196 . . . . Beardstown
LU 198 . . . . . Marquette Heights

LU 234 . . . . Bloomington
LU 281 . . . . Spring Grove
LU 432 . . . . Urbana
LU 453 . . . . Clinton
LU 469 . . . . Granite City
LU 528 . . . . Chicago
LU 565 . . . . Dix
LU 577 . . . . Elmwood Park
LU 597 . . . . Carol Stream
LU 653 . . . . Mokena
LU 740 . . . . Mokena
LU 768 . . . . Decatur
LU 979 . . . . Salem
LU 1003 . . . . Bourbonnais
LU 1083 . . . . Allerton
LU 1258 . . . . Schaumburg
LU 1290 . . . . Chicago
LU 1358 . . . . Danville
LU 1402 . . . . Millstadt
LU 1405 . . . . Smithton
LU 1421 . . . . Tinley Park
LU 1423 . . . . Galesburg
LU 1433 . . . . Franklin Park
LU 1534 . . . . Mokena
LU 1538 . . . . Beecher
LU 1597 . . . . Midlothian
LU 1895 . . . . New Lenox
LU 1929 . . . . Belleville
SLB LO-16 Illinois . . . . . Chicago

Treasury Employees
CH 10 . . . . Chicago
CH 43 . . . . Champaign
CH 172 . . . . Chicago
CH 230 . . . . Chicago
CH 237 . . . . Chicago
CH 242 . . . . Dunlap

Utility Workers
LU 405 . . . . Belleville
LU 467 . . . . Bourbonnais
LU 500 . . . . Urbana

Weather Service Employees
BR 03-44 . . . . Romeoville
BR 03-46 . . . . Chicago
BR 03-84 . . . . Aurora
BR 03-94 . . . . Lincoln

Unaffiliated Labor Organizations
Amalgamated Workers Union
  Independent LU
  711 . . . . Franklin Park
American Allied Workers
  Information . . . . . Richton Park
American Allied Workers
  Laborers . . . . . . Richton Park
American Allied Workers Laborers
  International Union LU
  101 . . . . Chicago
American Allied Workers Laborers
  Union LU 120 . . . . . Chicago
Chicago Barbers Hairdressers
  Cosmetologists Union LU
  939 . . . . Chicago
Contract Mail Drivers Association
  Independent . . . . . Franklin Park
Employees Independent Association
  JC . . . . Vernon
Faculty Association Francis W.
  Parker School . . . . . Chicago
Faculty Association of DeVry
  Chicago Inc. . . . . . . Chicago
Food Clerks Union
  Independent . . . Highland Park

Guards & Watchmen of America
  Independent . . . . . Homewood
Highlands Supply Corporation
  Workers Union . . . . . Highland
Hospital Employees Labor Program
  of Metropolitan Chicago
  Independent . . . . . . Chicago
Illinois Central Train Dispatchers
  Association . . . . . . Matteson
Illinois State Security Service
  Association . . . . . . Chicago
Independent Installation Workers
  Union . . . . Romeoville
Industrial Construction Equipment
  Builders Union Employees
  Association of Kewanee . Kewanee
International Brotherhood of Service
  Employees LU 33 . . River Grove
International Federation of
  Independent Labor Unions . Sidell
International Union of Industrial and
  Independent Workers LU
  11 . . . . Chicago
Lift Truck Builders
  Independent . . . . . . Danville
Lincoln Land Building &
  Construction . . . . . . Robinson
Lincolnshire Local . . . Lincolnshire
Liquor & Wine Sales Representatives
  Tire Plastic & Allied Workers LU
  3 . . . . Chicago
Marine & Machinists Association
  Independent Johnson Division
  Outboard Marine
  Corporation . . . . . Waukegan
Medical Staff of the Union Health
  Service of Chicago . . . . Chicago
Metal Workers Union
  Independent . . . . . Sandwich
Metropolitan Alliance of Police
  Illinois Institute of Technology CH
  99 . . . . Chicago
Modern Metal Products Employee
  Benefit Association . . Loves Park
Mosstype Employees Association
  Illinois . . . . . Elk Grove Village
MPC Employees Representative
  Union . . . . Niles
National Alliance of Business
  and Professionals LU
  100 . . . . Palos Heights
National Allied Workers
  Union . . . . Cicero
National Allied Workers Union LU
  831 . . . . Berwyn
National Association of Bus
  Drivers . . . . . . Vernon Hills
National Pharmacists
  Association . . . . Darien
NTN Organization of Workers NTN
  Inside Union . . . Des Plaines
Oil & Chemical Workers
  Independent Procter &
  Gamble-Texas . . . . . Waterloo
Petroleum Marketing Employees
  Union . . . . Joliet
Physicians for Responsible
  Negotiation . . . . . . Chicago
Private Sector Police Benevolent
  Labor Council . . . . . Springfield
Procter & Gamble Employees
  Association St. Louis
  Plant . . . . New Douglas
Production & Maintenance Union
  Production & Maintenance LU
  101 . . . . Chicago

Professional Airline Flight Control
  Association PAFCA-
  United . . . . . Elk Grove Village
Roosevelt Adjunct Faculty
  Organization. . . . . . . Oak Park
Socony Mobile Boatmen's Union
  DIV B . . . . Tamms

Steel Workers Alliance
  Independent . . . . . Bartonville
Stockton Employees Independent
  Union. . . . . Stockton
United Health Care
  Association . . . . . Broadview

United Highway Workers
  Union. . . . . Fairfield
United Independent Workers
  International Union. . . . Chicago
United Professional Workers and
  Affiliates. . . . . Elmhurst

United Security Services
  Union . . . . Oregon
United Steel Fabricators LU
  101. . . . . Pontiac
Weatherstrip Workers Union,
  Independent. . . . . . . Lansing
Workers Security League
  Union . . . . Blue Island

Indiana

AFL-CIO Trade and Industrial Departments

Building and Construction Trades Department

BCTC Central Indiana . Indianapolis
BCTC Central Wabash
  Valley . . . . Terre Haute
BCTC Dearborn & Ripley
  Counties . . . . . Lawrenceburg
BCTC Floyd & Clark
  Counties . . . . . . Charlestown
BCTC Indiana State . . Indianapolis
BCTC La Porte-Satarke-Pulaski
  Counties . . . . La Porte
BCTC Lower Ohio
  Valley . . . . Evansville
BCTC North Central . . . Kokomo
BCTC Northeastern
  Indiana . . . . . . Fort Wayne
BCTC Northwest Indiana. Hammond
BCTC Richmond . . . . Richmond
BCTC South Central
  Indiana . . . . . Indianapolis
BCTC St. Joseph
  Valley . . . . South Bend
BCTC Tippecanoe County. Lafayette
BCTC United East Central . Muncie

Metal Trades Department

MTC Atomic Trades &
  Labor . . . . Aurora

Other Councils and Committees

C Council of Industrial
  Organizers . . . . . . Newburgh

AFL-CIO Directly Affiliated Locals

JC Wabash Valley Central
  Labor . . . . Terre Haute

Affiliated Labor Organizations

Air Traffic Controllers

LU EVV . . . . Evansville
LU FWA . . . . Fort Wayne
LU HUF . . . . Terre Haute
LU IND . . . . Indianapolis
LU LAF . . . . . West Lafayette
LU SBN . . . . South Bend
LU ZID . . . . Indianapolis

Asbestos Workers

CONF Central States . . Fort Wayne
LU 18 . . . . Indianapolis
LU 37 . . . . Evansville
LU 41 . . . . Fort Wayne
LU 75 . . . . South Bend

Automobile, Aerospace Workers

C Adams Allen Wells Joint
  CAP . . . . Fort Wayne
C Bartholomew Decatur Rush-
  Shelby . . . . . . Connersville
C Cass-Carroll-Fulton-
  Pulaski . . . . Winamac
C Clinton Tippecanoe County
  CAP . . . . Lafayette
C Dekalb County . . . . . Auburn
C Elkhart County. . . . . . Elkhart

C Fayette Union-Franklin
  Counties . . . . . Connersville
C Grant-Wabash Counties . . Marion
C Greater Marion
  County . . . . . . Indianapolis
C Henry CAP . . . . . New Castle
C Howard County . . . . Kokomo
C Huntington-Noble-
  Whitley . . . . Marion
C Lagrange-Steuben . . . . Angola
C Lawrence-Orange-
  Washington . . . . . . Bedford
C Madison-Hamilton
  Counties . . . . . . Anderson
C Region 3 CAP . . . . Indianapolis
C St. Joseph County . . . South Bend
C Starke-Marshall-Kosciusko. Argos
C Vanderburch County UAW CAP
  Council . . . . Evansville
C Wayne-Randolph. . . . Richmond
LU . . . . Gary
LU 5 . . . . South Bend
LU 9 . . . . South Bend
LU 23 . . . . Indianapolis
LU 52 . . . . Bourbon
LU 98 . . . . Indianapolis
LU 151 . . . . Connersville
LU 164 . . . . Auburn
LU 194 . . . . North Liberty
LU 226 . . . . Indianapolis
LU 279 . . . . . . Williamsburg
LU 287 . . . . Muncie
LU 292 . . . . Kokomo
LU 295 . . . . Elkhart
LU 321 . . . . Muncie
LU 358 . . . . Silver Lake
LU 361 . . . . Avon
LU 364 . . . . Elkhart
LU 371 . . . . . . New Castle
LU 428 . . . . Elkhart
LU 440 . . . . Bedford
LU 494 . . . . Union City
LU 499 . . . . Muncie
LU 499 Delaware County
  CAP . . . . Muncie
LU 530 . . . . Kingsbury
LU 531 . . . . Attica
LU 550 . . . . Indianapolis
LU 607 . . . . Plymouth
LU 612 . . . . Goshen
LU 661 . . . . Pendleton
LU 662 . . . . Anderson
LU 663 . . . . Anderson
LU 685 . . . . Kokomo
LU 729 . . . . . . New Castle
LU 761 . . . . Anderson
LU 825 . . . . . . Fort Wayne
LU 871 . . . . Albion
LU 914 . . . . Delphi
LU 933 . . . . Indianapolis
LU 941 . . . . Elkhart
LU 947 . . . . Rochester
LU 957 . . . . Anderson
LU 977 . . . . Marion
LU 1073 . . . . . . Richmond
LU 1101 . . . . Ossian
LU 1111 . . . . . . Indianapolis
LU 1118 . . . . . . Connersville
LU 1123 . . . . Bedford
LU 1166 . . . . Kokomo
LU 1168 . . . . . . Greensburg
LU 1172 . . . . . Rolling Prairie
LU 1244 . . . . . . Richmond
LU 1302 . . . . . . Kokomo
LU 1317 . . . . Butler

LU 1363 . . . . Richmond
LU 1368 . . . . Bremen
LU 1373 . . . . . . Kendallville
LU 1389 . . . . . . Fort Wayne
LU 1395 . . . . Fremont
LU 1404 . . . . . Columbia City
LU 1405 . . . . Warsaw
LU 1417 . . . . Orland
LU 1420 . . . . Hanover
LU 1448 . . . . . . Kewanna
LU 1457 . . . . . . Connersville
LU 1497 . . . . Lafayette
LU 1518 . . . . . . Connersville
LU 1539 . . . . . . Fort Wayne
LU 1571 . . . . Arcadia
LU 1763 . . . . . . Greencastle
LU 1793 . . . . . . Shelbyville
LU 1888 . . . . Bluffton
LU 1904 . . . . . . Connersville
LU 1942 . . . . . . Huntington
LU 1949 . . . . . . Frankfort
LU 1954 . . . . . . Logansport
LU 1969 . . . . . . Garrett
LU 1983 . . . . Fishers
LU 2046 . . . . . . Noblesville
LU 2049 . . . . . Columbia City
LU 2050 . . . . . . Brookville
LU 2052 . . . . . . Rushville
LU 2074 . . . . . . Evansville
LU 2119 . . . . . . New Castle
LU 2140 . . . . Shirley
LU 2158 . . . . Oolitic
LU 2209 . . . . . . Roanoke
LU 2242 . . . . . Columbia City
LU 2274 . . . . . . Indianapolis
LU 2277 . . . . Angola
LU 2289 . . . . . . Corydon
LU 2317 . . . . . . Lafayette
LU 2335 . . . . . . Hammond
LU 2339 . . . . . . Rushville
LU 2345 . . . . . Pleasant Lake
LU 2347 . . . . . . Corydon
LU 2357 . . . . . . Fort Wayne
LU 2371 . . . . . . Jonesboro
LU 2374 . . . . . . Richmond
LU 2382 . . . . . . Greencastle
LU 2401 . . . . . . Edinburgh
LU 2408 . . . . . . Indianapolis
LU 2414 . . . . . . New Castle
LU 2620 . . . . . . Kendallville
LU 2911 Society of Engineer
  Employees . . . . . . Fort Wayne

Bakery, Confectionery, Tobacco Workers and Grain Millers

LU 33-G . . . . Greenville
LU 102-G . . . . Oxford
LU 104-G . . . . . . Frankfort
LU 132 . . . . Columbus
LU 184-G . . . . . . Whiteland
LU 205-G . . . . . . Indianapolis
LU 280 . . . . Evansville
LU 315-G . . . . . . Mount Vernon
LU 372-A . . . . . . Indianapolis
LU 372-B . . . . . . Indianapolis
LU 394-G . . . . . . Frankfort

Boilermakers

LG National Cement
  Lodge . . . . Cloverdale
LG 16-M . . . . . . Fountain City
LG 24-M . . . . Kokomo
LG 39-D Cement
  Workers . . . . . . Greencastle
LG 50-M . . . . Pierceton

LG 51 . . . . Indianapolis
LG 68-M . . . . . . Connersville
LG 209-D Cement
  Workers . . . . . . Sellersburg
LG 300-M . . . . . . Aurora
LG 357 . . . . Denver
LG 374 . . . . Hammond
LG 524 . . . . Hammond
LG 1240 . . . . Lagro
LG 1620 . . . . Portland

Bricklayers

LU 4 Indiana and
  Kentucky . . . . Anderson

Carpenters

DC State of Indiana . . . Indianapolis
LU 60 . . . . Indianapolis
LU 90 . . . . Evansville
LU 133 . . . . Terre Haute
LU 215 . . . . Lafayette
LU 232 . . . . Warsaw
LU 364 . . . . Indianapolis
LU 413 . . . . Warsaw
LU 546 . . . . Vincennes
LU 599 . . . . Hammond
LU 615 . . . . Warsaw
LU 631 . . . . Charlestown
LU 758 . . . . Indianapolis
LU 859 . . . . Greencastle
LU 912 . . . . Richmond
LU 1003 . . . . . . Indianapolis
LU 1005 . . . . Hobart
LU 1016 . . . . Muncie
LU 1029 . . . . Warsaw
LU 1043 . . . . Hobart
LU 1142 . . . . . . Lawrenceburg
LU 1155 . . . . . . Columbus
LU 1406 . . . . Hobart
LU 1481 Great Lakes Regional
  Industrial . . . . . . South Bend
LU 1485 . . . . La Porte
LU 1664 . . . . . . Bloomington
LU 1775 . . . . . . Columbus
LU 1788 . . . . . . Hartford City
LU 2133 . . . . . . Corydon
LU 2177 . . . . . . Martinsville
LU 2323 . . . . Monon
LU 2489 . . . . Salem
LU 2577 . . . . Salem
LU 2690 . . . . . . Fort Wayne
LU 2930 . . . . Jasper
LU 2993 . . . . . . Franklin
LU 3055 . . . . Goshen
LU 3056 . . . . La Porte
LU 8093-T . . . . . . Williams

Civilian Technicians

CH 72 Fort Wayne . . . Fort Wayne

Communications Workers

C Indiana State . . . . . Evansville
LU 907 . . . . Mitchell
LU 999 IUE-CWA Industrial
  Division . . . . . . Fort Wayne
LU 4700 . . . . Evansville
LU 4703 . . . . Clarksville
LU 4770 . . . . . . Connersville
LU 4773 . . . . La Porte
LU 4780 . . . . Richmond
LU 4800 . . . . . . Indianapolis
LU 4818 . . . . . . Bloomington
LU 4900 . . . . . . Indianapolis
LU 14438 . . . . . . Michigan City

LU 14441 La Porte Typographical
Union. . . . . La Porte
LU 14442 . . . . Linton
LU 14445 South Bend Typographical
Union . . . . South Bend
LU 14446 Terre Haute Typographical
Union . . . . Clinton
LU 14448 Evansville Mailers
Union. . . . . Evansville
LU 14449 Indianapolis Mailers
Union . . . . Terre Haute
LU 34014 . . . . Gary
LU 34046 . . . . Terre Haute
LU 34070 . . . . Indianapolis
LU 84863 . . . . Auburn
LU 84865 . . . . . . Terre Haute
LU 84888 . . . . Angola
LU 84901 . . . . Fort Wayne
LU 84903 . . . . Garrett
LU 84911 . . . . Mishawaka
LU 84913 . . . . South Bend
LU 84919 . . . . . . Connersville

Electrical Workers
CONF Indiana State . . Indianapolis
LU 16 . . . . Evansville
LU 153 . . . . South Bend
LU 281 . . . . Anderson
LU 305 . . . . Fort Wayne
LU 481 . . . . Indianapolis
LU 531 . . . . La Porte
LU 651 . . . . Crown Point
LU 668 . . . . Lafayette
LU 697 . . . . Hammond
LU 723 . . . . Fort Wayne
LU 725 . . . . . Terre Haute
LU 757 . . . . Crown Point
LU 784 . . . . Indianapolis
LU 855 . . . . Muncie
LU 873 . . . . Kokomo
LU 983 . . . . Huntington
LU 1000 . . . . Marion
LU 1048 . . . . Indianapolis
LU 1109 . . . . Goshen
LU 1160 . . . . Marion
LU 1225 . . . . Indianapolis
LU 1392 . . . . South Bend
LU 1393 . . . . Indianapolis
LU 1395 . . . . Indianapolis
LU 1400 . . . . Indianapolis
LU 1424 . . . . Columbus
LU 1865 . . . . Elkhart
LU 1976 . . . . Argos
LU 2043 . . . . Richmond
LU 2214 . . . . Oolitic
LU 2249 . . . . Bloomington
LU 2344 . . . . Lafayette
LU 2355 . . . . . Michigan City
SC EM-4 BICC/General
Cable . . . . Gas City

**Electrical, Radio and Machine
Workers**
LU 770 . . . . Kendallville
LU 1177 . . . . . . Merrillville

Electronic Workers
LU 155-FW . . . . . South Bend
LU 302-FW . . . . . Indianapolis
LU 303-FW . . . . . Rensselaer
LU 320-FW . . . . . Portland
LU 802 . . . . Bluffton
LU 803 . . . . Indianapolis
LU 805 . . . . Tell City
LU 807 . . . . Jeffersonville
LU 808 . . . . Evansville
LU 809 . . . . South Bend
LU 812 . . . . Lafayette

LU 826 . . . . Bloomington
LU 845 . . . . Evansville
LU 848 . . . . Evansville
LU 855 . . . . Clinton
LU 859 . . . . Evansville
LU 924 . . . . Fort Wayne
LU 950 . . . . Attica
LU 963 . . . . Fort Wayne
LU 998 . . . . Fort Wayne
LU 1001 . . . . Clayton

Elevator Constructors
LU 34 . . . . Indianapolis

Fire Fighters
LU 1348 . . . . Muncie

Flint Glass Workers
LU 81 . . . . Lapel
LU 89 . . . . Highland
LU 104 . . . . Winchester
LU 106 . . . . Winchester
LU 112 . . . . Winchester
LU 115 . . . . Hartford City
LU 138 . . . . Milan
LU 501 . . . . Dunkirk
LU 513 . . . . Hartford City
LU 518 . . . . Modoc
LU 607 . . . . Rochester
LU 614 . . . . Etna Green
LU 726 . . . . Winchester

Food and Commercial Workers
C Indiana-Kentucky
State . . . . Indianapolis
LU 13-D . . . . . Lawrenceburg
LU 15-C . . . . Clarksville
LU 84-D . . . . . . New Albany
LU 157-C . . . . Whiting
LU 157-I . . . . Merrillville
LU 493-C . . . . La Porte
LU 557-T . . . . Goshen
LU 663-C . . . . . New Albany
LU 692-C . . . . Jeffersonville
LU 700 . . . . Indianapolis
LU 833-C . . . . . . Evansville
LU 988-C . . . . . Charlestown

**Glass, Molders, Pottery and
Plastics Workers**
CONF Indiana Educational . Redkey
LU 14 . . . . Muncie
LU 32 . . . . Shelbyville
LU 37 . . . . Fairmount
LU 38 . . . . Marion
LU 65 . . . . Winchester
LU 66 . . . . Sullivan
LU 86 . . . . Columbus
LU 96 . . . . Dunkirk
LU 121 . . . . Dunkirk
LU 127-B . . . . . Terre Haute
LU 166 . . . . Griffith
LU 189 . . . . Marion
LU 207 . . . . Lapel
LU 229 . . . . Ligonier
LU 238 . . . . Kokomo
LU 242 . . . . Winchester
LU 262 . . . . La Grange
LU 285 . . . . Fort Wayne
LU 316-B . . . . La Porte
LU 322 . . . . Auburn
LU 349 . . . . Grandview
LU 447 . . . . Lagrange
LU 455 . . . . Bluffton

Government Employees
C 3 Sixth District . . . . New Albany
LU 516 USDA . . . . . Rochester

LU 609 . . . . Indianapolis
LU 720 DoJ . . . . . Terre Haute
LU 1016 . . . . Indianapolis
LU 1020 VA . . . . Marion
LU 1384 VA . . . . . Fort Wayne
LU 1411 DoD . . . . . Indianapolis
LU 1415 DoD . . . . . . Crane
LU 1438 . . . . . . Jeffersonville
LU 1744 DoD . . . . . Indianapolis
LU 2150 USDA . . . New Salisbury
LU 3098 DoD . . . . Terre Haute
LU 3254 DoD . . . . Bunker Hill
LU 3571 HHS . . . . Indianapolis
LU 3956 HUD . . . . Indianapolis

Government Security Officers
LU 113 . . . . South Bend

Graphic Communications
LU 17-M . . . . Indianapolis
LU 19-M . . . . Fort Wayne
LU 128-N Midwest Newspaper
Printing Pressmen . . Indianapolis
LU 303-M . . . . Speedway
LU 411-M . . . . Andrews
LU 571-M . . . . . . Evansville
LU 761-S . . . . . Greensburg

Guards
LU 26 . . . . Rising Sun
RC Seventh . . . . . . Dillsboro

Independent Unions Federation
LU 235 Universal Employees
Union . . . . Butler

Iron Workers
LU 22 . . . . Indianapolis
LU 103 . . . . Evansville
LU 147 . . . . Fort Wayne
LU 292 . . . . South Bend
LU 379 . . . . Lafayette
LU 395 . . . . Hammond
LU 439 . . . . Terre Haute
LU 529 . . . . Muncie
LU 585 . . . . Vincennes
LU 726 . . . . Fort Wayne
LU 730 . . . . South Bend
LU 799 . . . . Lafayette

Laborers
DC 57 Indiana . . . . . Terre Haute
LU 41 . . . . Hammond
LU 81 . . . . Valparaiso
LU 120 . . . . Indianapolis
LU 204 . . . . Terre Haute
LU 213 . . . . Fort Wayne
LU 274 . . . . Lafayette
LU 561 . . . . Evansville
LU 645 . . . . South Bend
LU 741 . . . . Bloomington
LU 795 . . . . New Albany
LU 1047 . . . . Richmond
LU 1112 . . . . Muncie
LU 1325 . . . . Rushville

Laundry and Dry Cleaning
LU 3017 . . . . Indianapolis

Letter Carriers
BR 39 . . . . Indianapolis
BR 98 . . . . Muncie
BR 112 . . . . Vincennes
BR 116 . . . . Fort Wayne
BR 160 . . . . Columbus
BR 198 . . . . . Crawfordsville
BR 200 . . . . La Porte
BR 239 . . . . . . Connersville

BR 271 . . . . Richmond
BR 330 . . . . South Bend
BR 367 . . . . New Albany
BR 368 . . . . Frankfort
BR 377 . . . . Evansville
BR 378 . . . . Marion
BR 428 . . . . Columbia City
BR 455 . . . . Michigan City
BR 466 . . . . Lafayette
BR 472 Madison, Indiana . . Madison
BR 479 . . . . Terre Haute
BR 489 . . . . Anderson
BR 533 . . . . Kokomo
BR 547 . . . . Elkhart
BR 553 . . . . Jeffersonville
BR 580 . . . . Hammond
BR 670 . . . . Brazil
BR 748 Attica, Indiana . . . . Attica
BR 753 . . . . Valparaiso
BR 789 . . . . Seymour
BR 790 . . . . North Vernon
BR 799 Winchester,
Indiana . . . . Winchester
BR 801 Greensburg,
Indiana . . . . Greensburg
BR 814 . . . . New Castle
BR 820 . . . . Mishawaka
BR 828 South Central
Indiana . . . . Bloomington
BR 867 Hartford City,
Indiana . . . . Hartford City
BR 868 Portland, Indiana . . Portland
BR 877 Warsaw, Indiana . . Warsaw
BR 878 Rushville, Indiana . Rushville
BR 882 Greencastle,
Indiana . . . . Greencastle
BR 888 . . . . Carmel
BR 918 Franklin, Indiana . . Franklin
BR 952 Kendallville,
Indiana . . . . Kendallville
BR 1011 Union City,
Indiana . . . . Union City
BR 1054 . . . . Columbia City
BR 1060 Decatur, Indiana . . Decatur
BR 1116 . . . . Mitchell
BR 1288 Rochester,
Indiana . . . . Rochester
BR 1319 Tipton, Indiana . . . Tipton
BR 1326 . . . . Lake Station
BR 1382 . . . . Plymouth
BR 1395 Lawrenceburg,
Indiana . . . . Lawrenceburg
BR 1399 . . . . East Chicago
BR 1405 Sullivan, Indiana . Sullivan
BR 1472 North Manchester,
Indiana . . . . . North Manchester
BR 1584 Ligonier, Indiana . Ligonier
BR 1624 . . . . Crown Point
BR 1689 . . . . Whiting
BR 1816 French Lick,
Indiana . . . . French Lick
BR 1834 Aurora, Indiana . . . Aurora
BR 1835 Nappanee,
Indiana . . . . Nappanee
BR 1868 Boonville,
Indiana . . . . Boonville
BR 1899 Delphi, Indiana . . . Delphi
BR 1974 Rensselaer,
Indiana . . . . Rensselaer
BR 2132 Monticello,
Indiana . . . . Monticello
BR 2240 Petersburg,
Indiana . . . . Petersburg
BR 2256 Brookville,
Indiana . . . . Brookville
BR 2298 Butler, Indiana . . . Butler
BR 2343 Knox, Indiana . . . . Knox
BR 2374 Liberty, Indiana . . Liberty

BR 2421 . . . . Greenwood
BR 2448 La Grange,
  Indiana . . . . La Grange
BR 2658 Hagerstown,
  Indiana . . . . Hagerstown
BR 2717 Salem, Indiana . . . Salem
BR 2724 Argos, Indiana . . . Argos
BR 2802 Dunkirk, Indiana . Dunkirk
BR 2919 Loogootee,
  Indiana . . . . Loogootee
BR 2968 Winamac,
  Indiana . . . . Winamac
BR 3032 . . . . Hobart
BR 3146 Cannelton,
  Indiana . . . . Cannelton
BR 3153 Berne, Indiana . . . Berne
BR 3293 Batesville,
  Indiana . . . . Batesville
BR 3323 Edinburg,
  Indiana . . . . Edinburgh
BR 3333 Clay City,
  Indiana . . . . Clay City
BR 3394 Montpelier,
  Indiana . . . . Montpelier
BR 3416 Veedersburg,
  Indiana . . . . Veedersburg
BR 3447 Bremen, Indiana . . Bremen
BR 3448 Thorntown,
  Indiana . . . . Thorntown
BR 3519 Paoli, Indiana . . . . Paoli
BR 3532 Williamsport,
  Indiana . . . . Williamsport
BR 3546 Covington,
  Indiana . . . . Covington
BR 3571 Vevay, Indiana . . . Vevay
BR 3608 Orleans, Indiana . . Orleans
BR 3628 Albion, Indiana . . . Albion
BR 3646 Kentland,
  Indiana . . . . Kentland
BR 3661 Crothersville,
  Indiana . . . . Crothersville
BR 3708 . . . . Ridgeville
BR 4260 Charlestown,
  Indiana . . . . Charlestown
BR 4426 Fowler, Indiana . . . Fowler
BR 4649 Walkerton,
  Indiana . . . . Walkerton
BR 4800 . . . . Chesterton
BR 5251 Sellersburg,
  Indiana . . . . Sellersburg
BR 5276 Austin, Indiana . . . Austin
BR 5568 Brownsburg,
  Indiana . . . . Brownsburg
BR 5652 Flora, Indiana . . . . Flora
BR 5682 Bourbon, Indiana . Bourbon
BR 5684 Odon, Indiana . . . . Odon
BR 5706 Albany, Indiana . . Albany
BR 5967 Winona Lake,
  Indiana . . . . Winona Lake
BR 6318 Churubusco,
  Indiana . . . . Churubusco
BR 6473 Brownstown,
  Indiana . . . . Brownstown
BR 6492 Yorktown,
  Indiana . . . . Yorktown
SA Indiana . . . . . . New Haven

Locomotive Engineers
DIV 7 . . . . Lebanon
DIV 12 Conrail . . . . Kendallville
DIV 25 . . . . Terre Haute
DIV 106 . . . . Fort Wayne
DIV 121 . . . . Mooresville
DIV 153 . . . . Auburn
DIV 154 . . . . Evansville
DIV 165 . . . . Corydon
DIV 204 . . . . Sandborn
DIV 246 . . . . Evansville

DIV 289 . . . . Washington
DIV 343 . . . . Princeton
DIV 348 . . . . Wakarusa
DIV 474 . . . . Walkerton
DIV 520 . . . . Chesterton
DIV 537 . . . . Fort Wayne
DIV 545 . . . . Hebron
DIV 548 . . . . Bunker Hill
DIV 597 . . . . Avon
DIV 613 . . . . Dyer
DIV 722 . . . . Camby
DIV 742 . . . . Evansville
DIV 754 . . . . Clinton
GCA Elgin Joliet & Eastern
  Railroad . . . . . . Chesterton
SLB Indiana . . . . Angola

Longshoremen
LU 1803 . . . . Whiting
LU 1969 . . . . Portage
LU 2038 . . . . Portage
LU 2058 . . . . Portage

Machinists
DLG 90 . . . . Indianapolis
DLG 153 . . . . Evansville
LG . . . . Columbus
LG 70 . . . . Fort Wayne
LG 120-DS . . . . Springport
LG 161 . . . . Indianapolis
LG 229 . . . . Goshen
LG 327 . . . . Hammond
LG 450 . . . . Burnettsville
LG 498 . . . . Hammond
LG 511 . . . . Rockville
LG 1109 . . . . Lexington
LG 1227 . . . . Valparaiso
LG 1315 . . . . Elkhart
LG 1391 . . . . Lawrenceburg
LG 1541 . . . . Kendallville
LG 1595 . . . . Portland
LG 1621 . . . . Fort Wayne
LG 1955 . . . . Evansville
LG 2034 . . . . Churubusco
LG 2040 . . . . Evansville
LG 2069 . . . . Peru
LG 2186 . . . . Evansville
LG 2258 . . . . Evanscille
LG 2294 Hoosier Air
  Transport . . . . . . Indianapolis
LG 2410 . . . . Madison
LG 2520 . . . . Fort Wayne
LG 2532 . . . . Richmond
LG 2543 . . . . La Porte
LG 2569 . . . . Fort Wayne
LG 2574 . . . . Huntington
LG 2717 . . . . Evansville
LG 2723 . . . . Underwood
LG 2819-PM . . . . . . Speedway
LG 2823 . . . . Swayzee
LG 2903 . . . . Westville
LLG W-197
  Woodworkers . . . . Indianapolis
LLG W-2912 River's
  Bend . . . . Evansville
STC Indiana . . . . . Indianapolis

Maintenance of Way Employes
LG 74 . . . . Terre Haute
LG 302 . . . . Floyds Knobs
LG 507 . . . . La Porte
LG 696 . . . . Oaktown
LG 1056 . . . . Kendallville
LG 1355 . . . . Bloomington
LG 1362 . . . . Muncie
LG 1532 . . . . Hammond
LG 1806 . . . . Union Mills
LG 1903 . . . . Valparaiso

LG 3025 . . . . Fort Wayne
SD Chicago South Shore & South
  Bend . . . . Michigan City
SLG 34 . . . . Dale
SLG 63 . . . . Lowell
SLG 287 . . . . Peru
SLG 463 . . . . . . Lake Station
SLG 466 . . . . Nappanee
SLG 498 . . . . Medaryville
SLG 991 . . . . Elkhart
SLG 1035 . . . . Evansville
SLG 1060 . . . . Mitchell
SLG 1297 . . . . Merrillville
SLG 1349 . . . . North Vernon
SLG 1363 . . . . . . Columbia City
SLG 1649 . . . . Liberty
SLG 1916 . . . . Bedford
SLG 1980 . . . . Greenwood
SLG 1984 . . . . Alexandria
SLG 3043 . . . . Logansport
SLG 3060 . . . . Terre Haute
SLG 3097 . . . . Columbus

Mine Workers
LU 11 . . . . Chandler
LU 352 . . . . Winslow
LU 1038 . . . . Boonville
LU 1189 . . . . Boonville
LU 1216 . . . . Staunton
LU 1410 . . . . Linton
LU 1423 . . . . Linton
LU 1791 . . . . Princeton
LU 1851 . . . . Lynnville
LU 1907 . . . . Boonville
LU 4011 . . . . Francisco
LU 4343 . . . . Petersburg
LU 5179 . . . . Oakland City
LU 8682 . . . . Terre Haute
LU 9926 . . . . Boonville

Musicians
LU 3 . . . . Indianapolis
LU 25 . . . . Clinton
LU 58 . . . . Fort Wayne
LU 203 . . . . Hammond
LU 228 . . . . South Bend
LU 232 . . . . South Bend
LU 245 . . . . Muncie
LU 278 . . . . South Bend

National Staff Organization
ASSN Indiana Professional Staff
  Teacher . . . . Bedford
ASSN Indiana State
  Teachers . . . . Greenwood

NLRB Professional Association
LU 25 . . . . Indianapolis

Nurses
SA Indiana State Nurses
  Association . . . . . Indianapolis

Office and Professional Employees
LU 1 . . . . Kokomo
LU 509 . . . . Elkhart

Operating Engineers
LU 103 . . . . Fort Wayne
LU 841 . . . . Terre Haute

Painters
LU . . . . Evansville
LU 47 . . . . Indianapolis
LU 80 . . . . Lafayette
LU 156 . . . . Evansville
LU 197 . . . . Terre Haute
LU 460 . . . . Merrillville

LU 469 . . . . Fort Wayne
LU 669 . . . . Chesterfield
LU 1118 . . . . South Bend
LU 1165 . . . . Indianapolis

Paper, Allied-Industrial, Chemical Employees
C Corn . . . . Indianapolis
C Lehigh Joint Conference . Mitchell
LU 304-007 . . . . . Fort Wayne
LU 6-30 . . . . Mitchell
LU 6-899 . . . . North Manchester
LU 6-945 . . . . Arcadia
LU 05-53 . . . . Mexico
LU 05-814 . . . . Batesville
LU 05-1261 . . . . . . Tell City
LU 06-1 . . . . Whiting
LU 06-7 . . . . Kewanna
LU 06-69 . . . . Carthage
LU 06-103 . . . . Camden
LU 06-113 . . . . Marion
LU 06-154 . . . . . . Mooresville
LU 06-159 . . . . Kokomo
LU 06-164 . . . . . Crawfordsville
LU 06-168 . . . . . . Indianapolis
LU 06-182 . . . . . Hartford City
LU 06-184 . . . . . . Fort Wayne
LU 06-186 . . . . Dunkirk
LU 06-210 . . . . Whiting
LU 06-248 Tulox Plastics . . Marion
LU 06-254 . . . . . . Fort Wayne
LU 06-270 . . . . Peru
LU 06-285 . . . . Wabash
LU 06-307 . . . . Andrews
LU 06-320 . . . . Marion
LU 06-336 . . . . . East Chicago
LU 06-354 . . . . Shoals
LU 06-472 . . . . Camden
LU 06-489 . . . . . . Churubusco
LU 06-509 . . . . Bruceville
LU 06-518 . . . . . . Logansport
LU 06-521 . . . . . . Hammond
LU 06-555 . . . . . . Vincennes
LU 06-563 . . . . Lagro
LU 06-596 . . . . Gary
LU 06-613 . . . . Rosedale
LU 06-645 . . . . Gary
LU 06-652 . . . . Peru
LU 06-706 . . . . . . Indianapolis
LU 06-729 . . . . . . Fort Wayne
LU 06-809 . . . . . . Warsaw
LU 06-822 . . . . . . Freetown
LU 06-903 . . . . . . Fort Wayne
LU 06-1043 . . . . . . Shelbyville
LU 06-1045 . . . . . . Anderson
LU 06-1046 . . . . . . Princeton
LU 06-1047 . . . . . . Whiteland
LU 06-1052 . . . . . . Elkhart
LU 06-1055 . . . . . Fort Wayne
LU 06-1056 . . . . . . Elkhart
LU 06-1057 . . . . . Indianapolis
LU 06-1106 . . . . . . Eaton
LU 06-1107 . . . . . Fort Wayne
LU 06-1109 . . . . . . Freetown
LU 06-1135 . . . . . Terre Haute
LU 06-1159 . . . . . North Vernon
LU 06-1195 . . . . . . Hammond

Plant Protection
LU 123 Visteon Steering
  Systems . . . . Indianapolis

Plasterers and Cement Masons
LU 692 . . . . Indianapolis

Plumbing and Pipe Fitting
LU 136 . . . . Evansville
LU 157 . . . . Terre Haute

LU 166 . . . . Fort Wayne
LU 172 . . . . South Bend
LU 210 . . . . Merrillville
LU 440 . . . . Indianapolis
LU 661 . . . . Muncie
SA Indiana State Pipe
Trades . . . . Muncie

Postal and Federal Employees
LU 608 . . . . Indianapolis

Postal Workers
LU New Albany . . . . New Albany
LU 130 Indianapolis . . Indianapolis
LU 210 Northern Indiana Unified
Area . . . . South Bend
LU 224 La Porte . . . . . . La Porte
LU 266 Gary . . . . Gary
LU 278 Mishawaka . . . Mishawaka
LU 280 Hammond . . . . Hammond
LU 286 Fort Wayne Indiana
Area . . . . Fort Wayne
LU 347 Evansville Area . Evansville
LU 398 Whiting Local . . . Whiting
LU 618 Terre Haute
Area . . . . Terre Haute
LU 753 Jeffersonville . Jeffersonville
LU 774 Vincennes . . . Vincennes
LU 839 Lafayette . . . . . Lafayette
LU 914 . . . . East Chicago
LU 1014 Kokomo Area . . Kokomo
LU 1063 Elwood Local . . Elmwood
LU 1077 Marion . . . . . . Marion
LU 1524 Crown Point . Crown Point
LU 1921 Aurora Local . . . Aurora
LU 2122 Bloomington. Bloomington
LU 2432 Muncie . . . . . . Muncie
LU 2514 Valparaiso . . . Valparaiso
LU 2658 . . . . Frankfort
LU 2668 Noblesville . . Noblesville
LU 2724 Richmond. . . Richmond
LU 2725 Batesville Local . Batesville
LU 2769 Washington . . Washington
LU 2889
Crawfordsville. . . Crawfordsville
LU 3223 Dunes Area . Michigan City
LU 3740 Columbus . . . . Columbus
LU 3980 North
Manchester . . . North Manchester
LU 4166 Bedford . . . . . . Bedford
LU 7159 Fishers . . . . . . Fishers
SA Indiana. . . . . . . South Bend

Professional and Technical Engineers
LU 137 . . . . Fort Wayne

Railroad Signalmen
LLG 42 . . . . Plainfield
LLG 45 . . . . Anderson
LLG 68 . . . . Hammond
LLG 71 . . . . Evansville
LLG 91 . . . . Wheatfield
LLG 97 . . . . Hobart
LLG 228 . . . . Tipton

Retail, Wholesale and Department Store
JB Indiana . . . . . . Fort Wayne
LU 29 John Sexton &
Company . . . . . . Indianapolis
LU 202 . . . . Terre Haute
LU 357 . . . . Alexandria
LU 512 . . . . Indianapolis
LU 810 . . . . Fort Wayne
LU 835 . . . . Fort Wayne
LU 1096 . . . . Indianapolis
LU 1976 . . . . Frankfort

UNIT D-Indiana Joint
Board . . . . Marion

Roofers, Waterproofers and Allied Workers
LU 23 . . . . South Bend
LU 26 . . . . Merrillville
LU 106 . . . . Evansville
LU 119 . . . . Indianapolis
LU 150 . . . . Terre Haute
LU 205 . . . . Chesterfield
LU 233 . . . . Lafayette

Rural Letter Carriers
BR 34 . . . . Tipton
LU Adams-Tri-County
Association . . . . . . Decatur
LU Bartholomew-Brown
Countys. . . . . Columbus
LU Boone County . . . . Lebanon
LU Cass County . . . . Logansport
LU Dubois-Martin-Pike
Counties. . . . . Jasper
LU Fountain-Warren
Counties . . . . . . Veedersburg
LU Grant County . . . . . Swayzee
LU Greene County. . . . Bloomfield
LU Hancock County . . Wilkinson
LU Hendricks County . Martinsville
LU Jefferson-Switzerland
Counties . . . . Vevay
LU Jennings County . North Vernon
LU Johnson County . . Shelbyville
LU Kosciusko County . Silver Lake
LU Lagrange County . . Wolcottville
LU Lawrence Orange County
Chapter . . . . . . West Baden
LU Marshall-St. Joseph-Starke
Counties. . . . . Osceola
LU Monroe County . . . Spencer
LU Montgomery
County . . . . Crawfordsville
LU Morgan County Unit
55 . . . . Martinsville
LU Owen County . . . . Coal City
LU Perry-Spencer
Counties. . . . . . St. Meinrad
LU Porter County . . . Cedar Lake
LU Putnam County . . . Greencastle
LU Randolph County. . Ridgeville
LU Southeastern Indiana. Rising Sun
LU Steuben-De Kalb
Counties . . . . Angola
LU Sullivan County . . . . Dugger
LU Tippecanoe County . . Lafayette
LU Vanderburg-Warrick
Counties . . . . Evansville
LU Wabash County . . . . . Macy
LU Whitley County . Columbia City
LU 7 Fayette-Henry-Rush-Union-
Wayne County . . Cambridge City
LU 18 Delaware Jay
Blackford. . . . . . . Portland
LU 48 Madison County . . . Kirklin
LU 49 Marion
County . . . . . New Palestine
LU 72-88 Scott-Washington
Counties . . . . . . Scottsburg
LU 84 Vigo
County . . . . . West Terre Haute
LU 603 Elkhart County . . . Topeka
SA Allen County . . . . Hoagland
SA Indiana . . . . Galveston

Security, Police and Fire Professionals
LU 4 . . . . Speedway
LU 7 . . . . South Bend

LU 8 . . . . Terre Haute
LU 10 . . . . Bedford
LU 20 . . . . Kokomo
LU 21 . . . . Marion
LU 110 . . . . Clarksville
LU 123 . . . . Muncie
LU 133 . . . . New Castle
LU 205 . . . . Connersville

Service Employees
LU 131 Firemen &
Oilers. . . . . . . Indianapolis
LU 431 Firemen &
Oilers . . . . Greenwood
LU 551 . . . . Indianapolis
LU 571 Firemen & Oilers . . . Dyer

Sheet Metal Workers
C Michigan/Indiana
States . . . . Indianapolis
LU 20 . . . . Indianapolis
LU 179 . . . . Beech Grove
LU 204 . . . . Huntington
LU 237 . . . . Fort Wayne

State, County and Municipal Employees
C 62 Indiana State . . . Indianapolis

Steelworkers
LU . . . . Hudson
LU 3127 . . . . East Chicago
LU 2-201-B. . . . . . . Covington
LU 7-190-A . . . . . . Wanatah
LU 04-6982-S . . . . . . Monon
LU 07-14-S . . . . . Fort Wayne
LU 07-70. . . . . Portage
LU 07-93-G . . . . . . Muncie
LU 07-103-S . . . . . Terre Haute
LU 07-104-S . . . . . Newburgh
LU 07-112-A . . . . . Boonville
LU 07-115 . . . . . . Lafayette
LU 07-119-A . . . . . Mitchell
LU 07-138-L. . . . . Noblesville
LU 07-184 . . . . . . Bourbon
LU 07-188-S . . . . . Wanatah
LU 07-331-U . . . . . . Jasper
LU 07-466-L . . . . . . Marion
LU 07-525-U . . . . . Batesville
LU 07-626-L . . . . . . Wabash
LU 07-634-L . . . . . . Auburn
LU 07-650-L. . . . . . Milford
LU 07-710 . . . . . . Kingman
LU 07-715-L . . . . . Woodburn
LU 07-798-L. . . . . Logansport
LU 07-1010-S . . . . East Chicago
LU 07-1011-S . . . . East Chicago
LU 07-1014-S . . . . . . Gary
LU 07-1015-L . . . . . Angola
LU 07-1066-S . . . . . . Gary
LU 07-1191-S . . . . Mishawaka
LU 07-1999-S. . . . . Indianapolis
LU 07-2695-S . . . . . . Gary
LU 07-2818-S . . . . . Evansville
LU 07-2958-S . . . . . Kokomo
LU 07-3069-S . . . . . . Hobart
LU 07-3261-S . . . . . Rockfield
LU 07-3875-S. . . . . . Tipton
LU 07-4863-S . . . . Logansport
LU 07-5163-S. . . . . Richmond
LU 07-5840-S . . . . . Rochester
LU 07-6103-S . . . . . Portage
LU 07-6743-S . . . . Lawrenceburg
LU 07-6787-S . . . . Chesterton
LU 07-6805-S . . . . . Warsaw
LU 07-7441-S . . . . Terre Haute
LU 07-8017-S . . . . Valparaiso
LU 07-8535-S . . . . New Castle

LU 07-8759-S . . . . Edwardsport
LU 07-8985-S. . . . . . Munster
LU 07-9144-S . . . . Chesterton
LU 07-9231-S . . . . New Carlisle
LU 07-12213. . . . . . Muncie
LU 07-12273-S . . . . Osceola
LU 07-12502-S . . . . . Dyer
LU 07-12775-S . . . . Portage
LU 07-13584-S. . . . Valparaiso
LU 07-13796-S . . . . La Porte
LU 07-14810-S. . . . . Elkhart
LU 07-15173-S . . . . Decatur

Teamsters
JC 69 . . . . Indianapolis
LU 135 . . . . Indianapolis
LU 142 . . . . Gary
LU 215 . . . . Evansville
LU 364 . . . . South Bend
LU 414 . . . . Fort Wayne
LU 716 . . . . Indianapolis
LU 1070 . . . . Lafayette
LU 2001 Indiana Mailers
Union . . . . Noblesville

Theatrical Stage Employees
D 8 Michigan-Indiana-Ohio-
Kentucky . . . . Munster
LU 30 . . . . Indianapolis
LU 49 . . . . Terre Haute
LU 102 . . . . Evansville
LU 125. . . . . Merrillville
LU 146 . . . . Fort Wayne
LU 163 . . . . Clarksville
LU 174 . . . . Lafayette
LU 187 . . . . South Bend
LU 194 . . . . Greenwood
LU 194-B . . . . Greenwood
LU 373 . . . . Terre Haute
LU 618 . . . . Bloomington
LU 836 . . . . Indianapolis
LU 893 . . . . Indianapolis
SA Indiana. . . . . . . Greenwood

Train Dispatchers
SCOM Chicago South Shore-South
Bend . . . . Michigan City
SCOM Indiana Harbor Belt
Railway. . . . . Hammond
SCOM New York Chicago & St.
Louis Railroad . . . . Fort Wayne

Transit Union
LDIV 517 . . . . Gary
LDIV 996 . . . . Osceola
LDIV 1070 . . . . . . Indianapolis
LDIV 1474 . . . . . . Richmond

Transport Workers
LU 2003 . . . . Indianapolis
LU 2053 . . . . Mishawaka

Transportation Communications Union
D 155 . . . . Evansville
D 357 Conrail . . . . . . Portage
D 464 . . . . North Liberty
D 708 Southeastern System Board
96 . . . . Princeton
D 905 . . . . Schererville
D 1229. . . . . Anderson
LG 5001 Chicago &
Northwestern . . . . . Portage
LG 5088 Amtrak . . . Indianapolis
LG 6009 Dixieland . . . Evansville
LG 6011 . . . . Griffith
LG 6295 South Shore. . . La Porte

LG 6720
Determination . . . . Lake Station
LG 6738 Morton Park . . Merrillville
LG 6760 Fort Wayne . . New Haven

Transportation Union
GCA GO-329 Elgin Joliet Eastern
Railway . . . . Portage
GCA GO-623 Conrail-PC-Ill-Div-
NYC-IHB. . . . . . Schererville
LU 6 . . . . New Palestine
LU 168 . . . . Gary
LU 206 . . . . Peru
LU 298. . . . . Auburn
LU 333 . . . . Washington
LU 383 . . . . New Albany
LU 490. . . . . Hazlton
LU 620 . . . . Gary
LU 744. . . . . Lafayette
LU 904 . . . . Evansville
LU 1186 . . . . . Valparaiso

LU 1202. . . . . Craigville
LU 1299 . . . . Gary
LU 1328 . . . . New Albany
LU 1381 . . . . Dyer
LU 1383 . . . . Valparaiso
LU 1399 . . . . Plainfield
LU 1494 . . . . Highland
LU 1518 . . . . Avon
LU 1526 . . . . . . Michigan City
LU 1548 . . . . Indianapolis
LU 1620 . . . . Elkhart
LU 1663 . . . . Greencastle
LU 1883 . . . . Dyer
SLB LO-17 Indiana. . . Indianapolis

Treasury Employees
CH 49. . . . . Indianapolis
CH 246 . . . . Indianapolis

Utility Workers
LU 418 . . . . Lawrenceburg

Weather Service Employees
BR 03-1. . . . . Indianapolis
BR 03-98. . . . . Syracuse

Unaffiliated Labor Organizations
Bertrand Employees LU
7701. . . . . South Bend
Diesel Workers Union
Independent. . . . . . Columbus
Employees Protective Association
Circulation Department-
Indianapolis
Newspapers. . . . . Indianapolis
Fort Wayne Patrolman's Benevolent
Association Inc.. . . . Fort Wayne
Independent Employees Union of
Northwest Indiana Markets
Inc. . . . . Hobart

Independent Wayne Metal Products
Inc. Union . . . . . . Huntington
Lift Workers of Greensburg
United . . . . Greensburg
Midstates Independent
Union . . . . Schererville
Musicians Union of America,
National . . . . Highland
Office Committee Union of Cummins
Engine Company inc.. . Columbus
Plant Protection Employees
Union . . . . Sellersburg
Professional Salesmen American
Federation. . . . . . . Granger
Steel Workers Progressive Union of
Hammond . . . . . . Hammond
Stonecutters Association of Indiana,
Journeymen. . . . . . . Bedford
USWA . . . . Kentland
Ventra Production Workers
Union . . . . Columbus

Iowa

AFL-CIO Trade and Industrial Departments

Building and Construction Trades Department

BCTC Cedar Rapids. . Cedar Rapids
BCTC Central Iowa. . . Des Moines
BCTC Dubuque . . . . . . Dubuque
BCTC Iowa . . . . Bettendorf
BCTC South Central Iowa. Ottumwa
BCTC Southeastern
Iowa . . . . Burlington
BCTC Waterloo . . . . . Waterloo

Metal Trades Department

MTC Dubuque . . . . . . Dubuque

Affiliated Labor Organizations

Air Traffic Controllers

LU ALO . . . . Waterloo
LU CID . . . . . . Cedar Rapids
LU DSM . . . . . . Des Moines
LU SUX . . . . Sioux City

Asbestos Workers

LU 57 . . . . Sioux City
LU 74 . . . . Des Monies
LU 81 . . . . Cedar Rapids

Automobile, Aerospace Workers

C Iowa-Second Area CAP . Dubuque
C Iowa-UAW North Central CAP
Council . . . . Marshalltown
C Southeast Iowa UAW CAP
Council . . . . Burlington
C West Central CAP . . . Newton
LU 13 . . . . Dubuque
LU 74 . . . . Ottumwa
LU 94 . . . . Dubuque
LU 120 . . . . Cresco
LU 242 . . . . . . Cedar Rapids
LU 270 . . . . . West Des Moines
LU 281 . . . . Davenport
LU 411 . . . . Waverly
LU 442 . . . . . . Webster City
LU 450 . . . . Des Moines
LU 616 . . . . . . Cedar Rapids
LU 807 . . . . Burlington
LU 838 . . . . Waterloo
LU 893 . . . . . . Marshalltown
LU 997 . . . . Newton
LU 1024 . . . . . . Cedar Rapids
LU 1201 . . . . Grinnell
LU 1237 . . . . Burlington
LU 1349 . . . . . . Cedar Rapids
LU 1391 . . . . Dubuque
LU 1540 . . . . Jefferson
LU 1551 . . . . . . Fort Madison
LU 1613 . . . . . . Monticello
LU 1672 . . . . . . Des Moines
LU 1740 . . . . Waterloo
LU 1896 . . . . Davenport
LU 1946 . . . . Creston
LU 1982 . . . . Dyersville
LU 2310 . . . . Pulaski

Bakery, Confectionery, Tobacco Workers and Grain Millers

LU 10-G . . . . . . Cedar Rapids
LU 36 . . . . Davenport
LU 48-G . . . . Keokuk
LU 49-G . . . . Iowa Falls

LU 100-G . . . . . . Cedar Rapids
LU 269-G . . . . Mason City
LU 349-G . . . . Atlantic
LU 389-G . . . . Indianola

Boilermakers

LG 6-D Cement Workers . . Buffalo
LG 66-D Cement
Workers . . . . . . Fort Dodge
LG 106-D Cement
Workers . . . . . . Mason City
LG 584-D . . . . . . Davenport

Bricklayers

LU 3 Iowa . . . . . . Des Moines

Carpenters

LU 4 . . . . Davenport
LU 106 . . . . Des Moines
LU 308 . . . . . . Cedar Rapids
LU 410 . . . . . . Fort Madison
LU 678 . . . . Dubuque
LU 767 . . . . Ottumwa
LU 772 . . . . Clinton
LU 948 . . . . Sioux City
LU 1039 . . . . Palo
LU 1260 . . . . Iowa City
LU 1313 . . . . Mason City
LU 1835 . . . . Waterloo
LU 2158 . . . . Bettendorf
LU 2704 . . . . Epworth
LU 2831 . . . . Decorah

Civilian Technicians

CH 75 Hawkeye . . . Sergeant Bluff
CH 101 Heartland . . . . Johnston

Communications Workers

C State of Iowa . . . . . Waterloo
LU 7101 . . . . Marion
LU 7102 . . . . Des Moines
LU 7103 . . . . Sioux City
LU 7107 . . . . Humboldt
LU 7108 . . . . Waterloo
LU 7109 . . . . Oelwein
LU 7110 . . . . Dubuque
LU 7115 . . . . Ottumwa
LU 7117 . . . . Davenport
LU 7171 . . . . . . Fort Dodge
LU 7172 . . . . Le Grand
LU 7175 . . . . Waterloo
LU 7181 . . . . Burlington
LU 14712 . . . . Burlington
LU 14719 . . . . . . Cedar Falls
LU 37123 . . . . Sioux City

Electrical Workers

LU 13 . . . . Burlington
LU 55 . . . . Des Moines
LU 204 . . . . Cedar Rapids
LU 231 . . . . Sioux City
LU 288 . . . . Waterloo
LU 347 . . . . Des Moines
LU 405-D . . . . . . Cedar Rapids
LU 452 . . . . Burlington
LU 499 . . . . Clive
LU 618 . . . . . . Missouri Valley
LU 704 . . . . Dubuque
LU 825 . . . . Davenport
LU 939 . . . . Hudson
LU 1362 . . . . . . Cedar Rapids
LU 1379 . . . . Bettendorf
LU 1429 . . . . . . Cedar Rapids
LU 1634 . . . . . . North Liberty
SC 2 Railroad . . . . . Mondamin

Electrical, Radio and Machine Workers

LU 793 . . . . Tama
LU 811 . . . . Lawton
LU 869 . . . . Decorah
LU 888 . . . . Des Moines

Elevator Constructors

LU 33 . . . . Des Moines

Fire Fighters

LU 1672 . . . . Muscatine

Food and Commercial Workers

C Insurance Workers Area
IX . . . . Dubuque
LU 79 . . . . Estherville
LU 86-D . . . . Muscatine
LU 166-G . . . . Waterloo
LU 179 . . . . Cherokee
LU 222 . . . . Sioux City
LU 230 . . . . Ottumwa
LU 431 . . . . Davenport
LU 440 . . . . Denison
LU 617 . . . . Fort Madison
LU 1009-C . . . . Muscatine
LU 1142 . . . . Sioux City
LU 1149 . . . . Perry
SA Iowa Barbers,
Beauticians . . . . . . Sioux City

Glass, Molders, Pottery and Plastics Workers

CONBD Iowa Area . . . . Kellogg
LU 9-B . . . . Argyle
LU 17-B . . . . Creston
LU 74-B . . . . Kellogg
LU 263-B . . . . . . East Dubuque
LU 359 . . . . Ratauia
LU 388-A . . . . Eddyville
LU 459 . . . . Waterloo

Government Employees

C 202 Food Inspection Locals, Mid
West . . . . Lone Tree
LU 744 USDA . . . . . . Dubuque
LU 766 USDA . . . . Marshalltown
LU 769 USDA . . . . . Sioux City
LU 836 . . . . Des Moines
LU 1226 VA . . . . . . Knoxville
LU 1228 VA . . . . . Des Moines
LU 2071 USDA . . . . . Waukee
LU 2315 USDA . . . . . Ames
LU 2547 VA . . . . . . Iowa City
LU 2752 DoD . . . . . Hiawatha
LU 2773 USDA . . . . Washington
LU 2814 DoT . . . . Council Bluffs
LU 2826 DoD . . . . Middletown
LU 2955 DoD . . . . . Des Moines
LU 3390 USDA . . . . Storm Lake
LU 3452 HUD . . . . . Des Moines
LU 3722 HHS . . . . . Dubuque
LU 3738 HHS . . . . . Davenport
LU 3886 SSA . . . . Cedar Rapids
LU 52-2323 USDA . . . . Denison

Graphic Communications

LU 157-M . . . . . . Des Moines
LU 256-C . . . . . . Fort Madison
LU 518-M . . . . . . Davenport
LU 591-C . . . . . . Washington
LU 711-S . . . . . . Camanche
LU 727-S . . . . . . Des Moines

Guards

LU 22 . . . . Burlington
RC Third . . . . Burlington

Hotel and Restaurant Employees

LU 146 . . . . Waterloo
LU 497 . . . . Cedar Rapids

Industrial Workers

LU 860 . . . . Des Moines

Iron Workers

LU 67 . . . . Des Moines
LU 89 . . . . Cedar Rapids
LU 184 . . . . Sioux City
LU 493 . . . . Des Moines
LU 553 . . . . Council Bluffs
LU 577 . . . . . . West Burlington
LU 691 . . . . Clinton

Laborers

DC Iowa . . . . Des Moines
LU 43 . . . . Cedar Rapids
LU 177 . . . . Des Moines
LU 353 . . . . Des Moines
LU 427 . . . . Sioux City
LU 566 . . . . Ottumwa
LU 659 . . . . Dubuque
LU 1238 . . . . Iowa City

Laundry and Dry Cleaning

LU 180 . . . . Dubuque

Letter Carriers

BR 69 . . . . Sioux City
BR 126 . . . . Clinton
BR 222 . . . . Burlington
BR 257 . . . . Dubuque
BR 314 . . . . . . Council Bluffs
BR 352 . . . . Des Moines
BR 371 . . . . Keokuk
BR 373 . . . . . . Cedar Rapids
BR 403 . . . . West Point
BR 445 Decorah, Iowa . . Decorah
BR 447 . . . . Ottumwa
BR 471 . . . . Mason City
BR 483 . . . . Iowa City
BR 506 . . . . Davenport
BR 512 . . . . Waterloo
BR 611 . . . . Boone
BR 644 . . . . Muscatine
BR 645 . . . . Fort Dodge
BR 655 . . . . Boxholm
BR 660 Mount Pleasant,
Iowa . . . . . . Mount Pleasant
BR 665 Grinnell, Iowa . . . Grinnell
BR 719 . . . . Cedar Falls
BR 726 . . . . Fairfield
BR 741 . . . . Independence
BR 787 . . . . Reasnor
BR 805 Charles City,
Iowa . . . . Charles City
BR 851 Shenandoah,
Iowa . . . . Shenandoah
BR 925 . . . . Centerville
BR 967 . . . . Osage
BR 1010 . . . . Estherville
BR 1036 Iowa Falls,
Iowa . . . . Iowa Falls
BR 1040 Le Mars, Iowa . . Le Mars
BR 1070 Cherokee, Iowa . Cherokee
BR 1075 Sheldon, Iowa . . . Sheldon
BR 1081 . . . . Ames
BR 1268 Albia, Iowa . . . Albia
BR 1284 Chariton, Iowa . . Chariton

BR 1312 . . . . Indianola
BR 1318 Clarinda, Iowa . . Clarinda
BR 1373 Waverly, Iowa . . Waverly
BR 1534 . . . . Hampton
BR 1559 Eagle Grove,
   Iowa . . . . Eagle Grove
BR 1626 Storm Lake,
   Iowa . . . . Storm Lake
BR 1686 Jefferson, Iowa . . Jefferson
BR 1704 Harlan, Iowa . . . . Harlan
BR 1791 Cresco, Iowa . . . . Cresco
BR 1805 Eldora, Iowa . . . . Eldora
BR 1808 Emmetsburg,
   Iowa . . . . Emmetsburg
BR 1839 Lamoni, Iowa . . . Lamoni
BR 1920 Pella, Iowa . . . . . Pella
BR 1931 New Hampton,
   Iowa . . . . New Hampton
BR 2034 Nevada, Iowa . . . Nevada
BR 2035 Rockwell City,
   Iowa . . . . Rockwell City
BR 2192 Bloomfield,
   Iowa . . . . Bloomfield
BR 2193 Corning, Iowa . . . Corning
BR 2195 Osceola, Iowa . . . Murray
BR 2196 Seymour, Iowa . . Seymour
BR 2197 Sigourney,
   Iowa . . . . Sigourney
BR 2198 Woodbine,
   Iowa . . . . Woodbine
BR 2227 Belle Plaine,
   Iowa . . . . Belle Plaine
BR 2231 Forest City,
   Iowa . . . . Forest City
BR 2243 . . . . Manchester
BR 2334 Ida Grove, Iowa. Ida Grove
BR 2409 Waukon, Iowa . . Waukon
BR 2413 Audubon, Iowa . Audubon
BR 2483 Clarion, Iowa . . . Clarion
BR 2507 Manning, Iowa . . Manning
BR 2508 Moulton, Iowa . . Moulton
BR 2513 Hamburg, Iowa . Hamburg
BR 2634 Rock Rapids,
   Iowa . . . . Rock Rapids
BR 2725 Dunlap, Iowa . . . Dunlap
BR 2903 Greenfield,
   Iowa . . . . Greenfield
BR 2953 West Union,
   Iowa. . . . . West Union
BR 2989 Villisca, Iowa . . . Villisca
BR 3043 Monticello,
   Iowa . . . . Monticello
BR 3054 Sibley, Iowa. . . . . Sibley
BR 3142 Logan, Iowa. . . . . Logan
BR 3149 Onawa, Iowa . . . Onawa
BR 3181 Tipton, Iowa . . . . Tipton
BR 3429 Belmond, Iowa . . Belmond
BR 3463 Spirit Lake,
   Iowa . . . . Spirit Lake
BR 3803 Rolfe, Iowa . . . . . Rolfe
BR 3811 . . . . Bettendorf
BR 4140 Bellevue, Iowa . . Bellevue
BR 4196 Rock Valley,
   Iowa . . . . Rock Valley
BR 4375 Garner, Iowa . . . . Garner
BR 4643 Orange City,
   Iowa . . . . Orange City
BR 5026 Columbus Junction,
   Iowa. . . . . Columbus Junction
BR 5028 Lake City, Iowa . Lake City
BR 5181 Lake Mills,
   Iowa. . . . . Lake Mills
BR 5182 Ackley, Iowa . . . Ackley
BR 5218 Laurens, Iowa . . . Laurens
BR 5221 Britt, Iowa. . . . . . Britt
BR 5222 Pocahontas,
   Iowa . . . . Pocahontas
BR 5258 Sumner, Iowa . . . Sumner

BR 5341 Milford, Iowa . . . Milford
BR 5392 . . . . Reinbeck
BR 5603 . . . . Traer
BR 5636 Wapello, Iowa . . Wapello
BR 5667 Lenox, Iowa. . . . . Lenox
BR 5669 Mount Ayr,
   Iowa . . . . Mount Ayr
BR 5670 Story City,
   Iowa . . . . Story City
BR 5975 Underwood,
   Iowa. . . . . Underwood
BR 6004 Rockwell, Iowa . Rockwell
BR 6265 . . . . Norwalk
BR 6294 Coon Rapids,
   Iowa . . . . Coon Rapids
SA Iowa . . . . Mediapolis

Locomotive Engineers
DIV 6 . . . . Boone
DIV 114 . . . . Cedar Falls
DIV 125 . . . . Clinton
DIV 391 . . . . Fort Madison
DIV 642 . . . . Creston
DIV 656 . . . . Rockwell
DIV 687 . . . . . . Sergeant Bluff
DIV 778 . . . . Des Moines
SLB Iowa . . . . Boone

Machinists
CONF Midwest States. Cedar Rapids
DLG 7 . . . . Des Moines
DLG 105 . . . . Oskaloosa
DLG 134 . . . . Waterloo
DLG 201 . . . . Algona
LG 254 . . . . Des Moines
LG 388 Tri City. . . . . Davenport
LG 531 . . . . Burlington
LG 831. . . . . Cedar Rapids
LG 1010 . . . . Fort Madison
LG 1045 . . . . Algona
LG 1215 Quad City Tool &
   Diemakers . . . . Eldridge
LG 1238 . . . . Dubuque
LG 1293 . . . . Packwood
LG 1300 . . . . Clarinda
LG 1426 . . . . Sioux City
LG 1498 . . . . Eddyville
LG 1499. . . . . Muscatine
LG 1526 . . . . Palo
LG 1728 . . . . Waterloo
LG 2548 . . . . Pocahontas
LG 2850-PM . . . . Waterloo
LLG W-2908
   Woodworkers. . . . . McGregor
STC Iowa . . . . . Des Moines

Maintenance of Way Employes
LG 36 . . . . Wilton
LG 67 . . . . Cedar Rapids
LG 342 . . . . Des Moines
LG 381 . . . . Marshalltown
LG 437 . . . . Ogden
LG 626 . . . . Clare
LG 1393 . . . . Fairbank
LG 1533 . . . . Burlington
LG 1757 . . . . Mason City
LG 1935 . . . . Oelwein
LG 2920 . . . . Stuart
SLG 412. . . . . Britt
SLG 416 . . . . Carpenter
SLG 692 . . . . Deloit
SLG 1148 . . . . Ames
SLG 1788 . . . . . Council Bluffs
SLG 1832 . . . . . Mount Pleasant
SLG 1847 . . . . . . Cedar Rapids
SLG 1888 . . . . Creston
SLG 1902 . . . . Ottumwa

Musicians
CONF Midwest. . . . . . . Gilbert
LU 67 . . . . Davenport
LU 75 . . . . Des Moines
LU 137 . . . . Mount Vernon
LU 450 . . . . Iowa City

National Staff Organization
LU Staff Association, Support, Iowa
   Education Association . Davenport
LU Staff Union-NSO,
   Iowa . . . . Hampton

Nurses
LSC United Nurses
   Caring. . . . . . . Marshalltown
LU Professional Security Unit
   J E M H . . . . . . Council Bluffs
SA Iowa Nurses
   Association . . . West Des Moines
UNIT Iana-Des Moines
   VA . . . . Des Moines

Operating Engineers
LU 234 . . . . Des Moines
LU 275. . . . . Cedar Rapids
LU 758 . . . . Dubuque

Painters
DC 81 . . . . Ankeny
LU 214 . . . . Sioux City
LU 246. . . . . Ankeny
LU 447. . . . . Cedar Rapids
LU 676 . . . . Davenport
LU 1075 Glaziers and Glass
   Workers . . . . Ankeny
LU 2003 . . . . Alburnett

**Paper, Allied-Industrial, Chemical
Employees**
LU 07-249 . . . . Keokuk
LU 07-436 . . . . Marion
LU 07-502 . . . . Fort Dodge
LU 07-503 . . . . Fort Dodge
LU 07-604 . . . . Rockwell
LU 07-709 . . . . Waterloo
LU 07-743 . . . . Tama
LU 07-761 . . . . Clinton
LU 07-795 . . . . . . Council Bluffs
LU 07-827 . . . . . . Cedar Rapids
LU 07-1257. . . . . . . Sioux City
LU 07-1774 . . . . . Marshalltown

Plasterers and Cement Masons
LU 21 . . . . Des Moines
LU 561 . . . . Robins

Plumbing and Pipe Fitting
LU 33 . . . . Des Moines
LU 125. . . . . Cedar Rapids

Postal Mail Handlers
LU 333 . . . . . West Des Moines

Postal Workers
LU Iowa. . . . . . . Des Moines
LU 38 Keokuk Local . . . Keokuk
LU 44 Des Moines . . Des Moines
LU 91 Davenport . . . . Davenport
LU 153 Marshalltown
   Area. . . . . . . Marshalltown
LU 166 Rapid Area . . Cedar Rapids
LU 186 Sioux City . . . Sioux City
LU 213 Iowa Falls Local . Iowa Falls
LU 306 Mason City . . Mason City
LU 317 Fort Dodge . . Fort Dodge
LU 383 Red Oak Local . . Red Oak

LU 394 Mount Pleasant
   Local . . . . . . Mount Pleasant
LU 411 Burlington . . . . Burlington
LU 426 Carroll . . . . Carroll
LU 451 Waterloo . . . . Waterloo
LU 454 Newton . . . . . Newton
LU 510 Council
   Bluffs . . . . . . Council Bluffs
LU 528 Hawkeye . . . Iowa City
LU 725 Clinton . . . . . Clinton
LU 738 Charles City
   Local . . . . . . Charles City
LU 758 Maquoketa
   Local. . . . . Maquoketa
LU 813 Creston . . . . . Creston
LU 881 Ottumwa . . . . Ottumwa
LU 904 Sheldon Local . . . Sheldon
LU 1023 Centerville
   Local. . . . . Centerville
LU 1065 Shenandoah . . Shenandoah
LU 1445 Fort
   Madison. . . . . . Fort Madison
LU 1949 Grinnell Local . . Grinnell
LU 1997 Muscatine. . . Muscatine
LU 2166 Oelwein Local . . Oelwein
LU 2339 Dubuque . . . . Dubuque
LU 3121 Ames. . . . . . . Ames
LU 3685 Nevada. . . . . . Nevada
LU 3962 Decorah Local . . Decorah
LU 4082 Boone Local . . . Boone
LU 4122 Cedar Falls
   Local . . . . . . Cedar Falls
LU 4266 Oskaloosa
   Local. . . . . Oskaloosa
LU 4274 Fairfield . . . . . Faifield
LU 7027 Des Moines Bulk Mail
   Center. . . . . Des Moines

Railroad Signalmen
GC 88 Union Pacific. . Nora Springs
LLG 43. . . . . Lake View
LLG 98. . . . . Desoto

**Retail, Wholesale and Department
Store**
LU 110. . . . . Cedar Rapids

**Roofers, Waterproofers and Allied
Workers**
LU 142 . . . . Des Moines
LU 182 . . . . Marion

Rural Letter Carriers
D North Central Iowa . . . Sheffield
D Northeast Iowa . . . . . Marion
D Southeast Iowa . . . . Preston
D 63 South Central. . . . . Collins
D 65 Southwest Iowa . . . Lenox
D 97 Northwest Iowa . . . Dickens
LU Benton County . Mount Auburn
LU Bremer County . . . . Sumner
LU Butler County . . . . . Allison
LU Calhoun County . Rockwell City
LU Cass County . . . . . Griswold
LU Cherokee County . . Cherokee
LU Clayton County . . Guttenberg
LU Clinton County . . . Charlotte
LU Crawford County . . . Manning
LU Humboldt County . . Humboldt
LU Iowa County . . . . Marengo
LU Jackson County . . Maquoketa
LU Jasper County . . . . Newton
LU Marshall County . . . Laurel
LU Muscatine County . . Muscatine
LU Palo Alto County . . Havelock
LU Plymouth County . . Le Mars
LU Story County . . . . Huxley
LU Tama County . . . . Gladbrook

LU Wayne County . . . . . Allerton
LU Woodbury County . . . . Anthon
LU 10 Buchanan County . . Hazleton
LU 14 Carroll County . . . Manning
LU 16 Cedar County . . . . Clarence
LU 19 Chickasaw
   County . . . . . . New Hampton
LU 30 Hancock County . . . Keokuk
LU 33 Fayette County . West Union
LU 66 Mitchell County . . . Osage
LU 83 Shelby County . . . . Shelby
LU 96 Winneshiek
   County . . . . . . Fort Atkinson
SA Iowa . . . . Drakesville

Security, Police and Fire
  Professionals
LU 214 . . . . Palo
LU 215 . . . . Newton
LU 218 . . . . Dubuque
LU 777 . . . . Council Bluffs

Service Employees
LU 199 . . . . Coralville

Sheet Metal Workers
DC Great Plains . . . . Des Moines
LU 45 . . . . Des Moines
LU 263 . . . . Cedar Rapids
LU 369 . . . . Burlington

State, County and Municipal
  Employees
C 61 Iowa Public
   Employees . . . . . . Des Moines
LU 1547 University of
   Osteopathic Medicine &
   Health Sciences . . . . Des Moines
LU 3746 Iowa Council
   61 . . . . Marshalltown

Steelworkers
LU 11-105-A . . . . . . Bettendorf
LU 11-142-G . . . . Adel
LU 11-164-L . . . . . Des Moines
LU 11-310-L . . . . . Des Moines
LU 11-444-L . . . . . . Keokuk
LU 11-932-L . . . . Argyle
LU 11-1860-U . . . . . Danville
LU 11-1861-U . . . . . . Dubuque
LU 11-3141-S . . . Council Bluffs
LU 11-3311-S . . . . . Keokuk
LU 11-8581-S . . . . . . Wilton
LU 11-9310-S . . . . . Mason City
LU 11-9317-S . . . . . Mason City

Teamsters
CONF Iowa . . . . . . Des Moines
JC 45 . . . . Des Moines
LU 90 . . . . Des Moines
LU 147 . . . . Des Moines
LU 238 . . . . Cedar Rapids

LU 358 Des Moines Mailers
   Union . . . . Des Moines
LU 387 . . . . Des Moines
LU 421 . . . . Dubuque
LU 650 . . . . Waterloo
LU 828 . . . . Mason City

Theatrical Stage Employees
LU 67 . . . . Des Moines
LU 85 . . . . Bettendorf
LU 690 . . . . Iowa City

Tool Craftsmen
LU 1 . . . . Bettendorf

Transit Union
LDIV 1192 . . . . Waterloo

Transportation Communications
  Union
LG 713 . . . . Burlington
LG 6069 Trans United . . . Oelwein
LG 6091 Hawkeye . . . . Cedar Falls
LG 6577 Kenneth . . Council Bluffs

Transportation Union
LU 17 . . . . Marshalltown
LU 199 . . . . Creston
LU 228 . . . . Hiawatha
LU 258 . . . . Davenport
LU 306 . . . . Goldfield

LU 316 . . . . Clinton
LU 329 . . . . Boone
LU 493 . . . . Waterloo
LU 643 . . . . West Point
LU 867 . . . . Ames
LU 872 . . . . Council Bluffs
SLB LO-18 Iowa . . . . Clive

Treasury Employees
CH 4 . . . . Des Moines

Utility Workers
LU 525 . . . . Bettendorf
LU 526 . . . . Clinton

Weather Service Employees
BR 03-49 . . . . Johnston
BR 03-96 . . . . Davenport

Unaffiliated Labor
Organizations
Drug Products Employees
   Association Iowa City . . . . Hills
Representatives Union,
   International Chemical Workers
   Union . . . . Muscatine
Transparent Film Workers
   Inc. . . . . Camanche
Umthun Trucking Employees
   Association . . . . . Eagle Grove
United Staff Union of
   Iowa . . . . Des Moines

Kansas

AFL-CIO Trade and Industrial Departments

Building and Construction Trades Department
BCTC Central & Western Kansas. . . . . Wichita
BCTC Kansas . . . . Topeka
BCTC Lawrence. . . . . Lawrence
BCTC Riley & Geary Counties . . . . Manhattan
BCTC Southeast Kansas. . Parsons
BCTC Topeka . . . . Topeka

Metal Trades Department
MTC Coffeyville . . . . Edna

Affiliated Labor Organizations

Air Traffic Controllers
LU ICT . . . . Wichita
LU ZKC. . . . . Olathe

Asbestos Workers
LU 1 Production Workers. . . . . . Kansas City
LU 15 . . . . Haysville

Automobile, Aerospace Workers
LU 31 . . . . Kansas City
LU 31 Kansas State Community Action Program. . . Kansas City
LU 1021. . . . . Olathe
LU 2366 . . . . Coffeyville

Bakery, Confectionery, Tobacco Workers and Grain Millers
LU 57-G . . . . Topeka
LU 73-G . . . . Topeka
LU 99-G . . . . Wichita
LU 107-G . . . . Salina
LU 158-G . . . . Dodge City
LU 200-G . . . . . . Whitewater
LU 218-A. . . . . . Overland Park
LU 245. . . . . Wichita
LU 335-G . . . . Leavenworth
LU 402-G. . . . . Atchison

Boilermakers
LG 34 . . . . Topeka
LG 73-D Cement Workers . . . . Medicine Lodge
LG 75-D Cement Workers . Fredonia
LG 76-D Cement Workers . Sun City
LG 84 . . . . Paola
LG 93-D Cement Workers. . . . . Humboldt
LG 109-D Cement Workers. . . . . . Independence
LG 194-D Cement Workers. . . . . Chanute
LG 1256. . . . . Moran
NHQ . . . . Kansas City

Carpenters
LU 168 . . . . Kansas City
LU 201. . . . . Wichita
LU 714 . . . . Olathe
LU 918 . . . . Manhattan
LU 1445 . . . . Topeka

Civilian Technicians
CH 74 Wichita Air Capitol . Wichita

CH 104 Jayhawk. . . . . . Topeka
CH 129 Kansas Coyotes . . . Topeka

Communications Workers
LU 6395 . . . . Merriam
LU 6401 . . . . Topeka
LU 6402 . . . . Wichita
LU 6406 . . . . Colby
LU 6407 . . . . Lawrence
LU 6409 . . . . Lansing
LU 6410 . . . . Parsons
LU 6411 . . . . Abilene
LU 6412 . . . . Dodge City
LU 14607 . . . . Peck

Electrical Workers
LU 226 . . . . Topeka
LU 271. . . . . Wichita
LU 304. . . . . Topeka
LU 661. . . . . Hutchinson
LU 959 . . . . Horton
LU 1523 . . . . Wichita
LU 1832-M . . . . . . Kansas City

Electronic Workers
LU 1004 . . . . . . Arkansas City

Federal Employees
LU 1205. . . . . . . Kansas City
LU 1765 . . . . . . Leavenworth
LU 1807 . . . . Iola

Food and Commercial Workers
LU 74-D . . . . Atchison
LU 109-I . . . . Kansas City
LU 188-C . . . . Hutchinson
LU 210-C . . . . Fredonia
LU 278-C . . . . Lyons
LU 409-G . . . . . Baxter Springs
LU 431-G . . . . . Bonner Springs
LU 509-G . . . . Paola
LU 605-C . . . . Lawrence

Glass, Molders, Pottery and Plastics Workers
LU 198. . . . . Buffalo
LU 233 . . . . Olathe

Government Employees
C 131 Ninth District. . . . . Mission
LU 9 At-Large. . . . . Erie
LU 85 VA . . . . . Leavenworth
LU 477 VA . . . . Wichita
LU 482 USDA . . . . . . Emporia
LU 738 DoD . . . Fort Leavenworth
LU 834 USDA . . . . Derby
LU 919 DoJ . . . . . Leavenworth
LU 1737 DoD . . . . . . Wichita
LU 1748 DoL . . . . . . Kansas City
LU 2324 DoD . . . . . . Fort Riley
LU 3960 HUD . . . Kansas City

Government Employees Association
LU 14-8 . . . . Topeka

Government Security Officers
LU 154. . . . . Topeka

Graphic Communications
LU 49-C. . . . . Tecumseh
LU 147-C . . . . Wichita
LU 560-S. . . . . Topeka
LU 575-M . . . . Wichita

Hotel and Restaurant Employees
LU 803. . . . . Junction City

Independent Unions Federation
LU 228 Hesston Corporation Workers Association . . . Hesston

Iron Workers
LU 606. . . . . Wichita

Laborers
LU 142 . . . . Topeka
LU 1290. . . . . . . Kansas City

Letter Carriers
BR 10 . . . . Topeka
BR 104 . . . . Lawrence
BR 141 . . . . Atchison
BR 185 . . . . Emporia
BR 194 Arkansas City, Kansas . . . . . Arkansas City
BR 201. . . . . Wichita
BR 412 Winfield, Kansas . Winfield
BR 477. . . . . Erie
BR 485. . . . . Hutchinson
BR 486 . . . . Salina
BR 499 . . . . Kansas City
BR 582 . . . . Ottawa
BR 695 . . . . Pittsburg
BR 766 . . . . Coffeyville
BR 834 . . . . Iola
BR 1018 . . . . Manhattan
BR 1035. . . . . . Independence
BR 1055 Chanute, Kansas . Chanute
BR 1122 . . . . Great Bend
BR 1157 Concordia, Kansas . . . . Concordia
BR 1171 . . . . McPherson
BR 1190 Girard, Kansas . . . Girard
BR 1205 Beloit, Kansas. . . . Beloit
BR 1344 . . . . Fredonia
BR 1412. . . . . . . Garden City
BR 1560 Columbus, Kansas . . . . . . Columbus
BR 1573 Anthony, Kansas . Anthony
BR 1579 . . . . Dodge City
BR 1679 Pratt, Kansas . . . Pratt
BR 1735 Herington, Kansas . . . . . . Herington
BR 2046 Lyons, Kansas. . . Lyons
BR 2115 . . . . Liberal
BR 2161 . . . . Hays
BR 2275 Goodland, Kansas. . . . . . . Goodland
BR 2276 Norton, Kansas. . Norton
BR 2338 Osborne, Kansas . Osborne
BR 2451 Horton, Kansas. . Horton
BR 2519 Sterling, Kansas . Sterling
BR 2564 Phillipsburg, Kansas . . . . . . Phillipsburg
BR 2630 Marion, Kansas . Marion
BR 2774 Seneca, Kansas. . . Seneca
BR 2787 Washington, Kansas . . . . . . Washington
BR 2895 Baxter Springs, Kansas . . . . . Baxter Springs
BR 3197 Frankfort, Kansas . . . . . . Frankfort
BR 3313 Oswego, Kansas . Oswego
BR 4036 Oberlin, Kansas . Oberlin
BR 4170 Hillsboro, Kansas. . . . . . . Hillsboro
BR 4288 Mankato, Kansas. Mankato
BR 4289 Ellinwood, Kansas . . . . . . Ellinwood

BR 4306 Kiowa, Kansas . . . Kiowa
BR 4341 Scott City, Kansas. . . . . . . Scott City
BR 4635 . . . . Colby
BR 4720 Haysville, Kansas. . . . . . . Haysville
BR 4727 Peabody, Kansas . Peabody
BR 4746 Plainville, Kansas. . . . . . . Plainville
BR 4824 Valley Center, Kansas . . . . . Valley Center
BR 4832 Oakley, Kansas. . . Oakley
BR 4840 Ness City, Kansas. . . . . . . Ness City
BR 4983 Halstead, Kansas . Halstead
BR 5034 Harper, Kansas. . . Harper
BR 5035 Wakefield, Kansas. . . . . . . Wakefield
BR 5336 Hill City, Kansas . Hill City
BR 5418 St. Marys, Kansas. . . . . . . St. Marys
BR 5521 . . . . . . Shawnee Mission
BR 5587 Wakeeney, Kansas. . . . . . . Wakeeney
BR 5884 Atwood, Kansas. . Atwood
BR 6031 Greensburg, Kansas. . . . . . Greensburg
SA Kansas . . . . Colby

Locomotive Engineers
DIV 64. . . . . Wichita
DIV 81 . . . . Shawnee
DIV 90 . . . . . Council Grove
DIV 130 . . . . Lenexa
DIV 179 . . . . Altamont
DIV 224 . . . . Marysville
DIV 237 . . . . Fort Scott
DIV 261 . . . . Herington
DIV 344 . . . . Wellington
DIV 364 . . . . Wichita
DIV 393 . . . . Olathe
DIV 462. . . . . Arkansas City
DIV 527 . . . . Pittsburg
DIV 587 . . . . Salina
DIV 740 . . . . Iuka
GCA Union Pacific Railroad-Central Region . . . . . Marysville
GCA Union Pacific Railroad-Eastern Region . . . . . . Osawatomie
SLB Kansas . . . . . . Hoisington

Machinists
DLG 70 . . . . Wichita
LG 293. . . . . Parsons
LG 356 . . . . Olathe
LG 378 . . . . Topeka
LG 639. . . . . Wichita
LG 693 . . . . Cherryvale
LG 708. . . . . Wichita
LG 733. . . . . Wichita
LG 774. . . . . Wichita
LG 834. . . . . Wichita
LG 1989 . . . . Wichita
LG 1992 . . . . Wichita
LG 1994 . . . . Wichita
LG 2328 . . . . Wichita
LG 2799 . . . . Wichita
STC Kansas . . . . Wichita

Maintenance of Way Employes
FED Southwestern . . Mound Valley
LG 455 . . . . Paola
LG 1333 . . . . Hoisington
LG 2400 . . . . Newton
LG 2404 . . . . Ottawa

LG 2407 . . . . Hutchinson
SF Atchison Topeka & Santa
  Fe . . . . Newton
SLG 376 . . . . Herington
SLG 487 . . . . Atchison
SLG 518 . . . . Cherokee
SLG 934 . . . . Marion
SLG 1175 . . . . Conway Springs
SLG 1216 . . . . Topeka
SLG 2405 . . . . Salina
SLG 2406 . . . . Newton
SLG 2412 . . . . Newton

Mine Workers
LU 14 . . . . Pittsburg

Musicians
CONF Regional Orchestra Players'
  Association . . . . Wichita
LU 169 Manhattan . . . . Manhattan
LU 297 . . . . Wichita

National Staff Organization
LU Staff Organization,
  Kansas . . . . Pittsburg

NLRB Professional Association
LU 17 . . . . Overland Park

Nurses
SA Kansas State Nurses
  Association . . . . Topeka

Operating Engineers
LU 119 . . . . Wichita
LU 123 . . . . Coffeyville
LU 126 . . . . Parsons
LU 418 . . . . Russell
LU 647 . . . . Allen

Painters
LU 76 . . . . Wichita
LU 96 . . . . Topeka
LU 229 . . . . Kansas City

Paper, Allied-Industrial, Chemical Employees
DC 5 . . . . El Dorado
LU 510 . . . . Bonner Springs
LU 05-114 . . . . Tonganoxie
LU 05-241 . . . . El Dorado
LU 05-348 . . . . Kansas City
LU 05-495 . . . . Pittsburg
LU 05-508 . . . . Parsons
LU 05-558 . . . . McPherson
LU 05-571 . . . . Blue Rapids
LU 05-613 . . . . Eudora
LU 05-765 . . . . Kansas City
LU 05-813 . . . . . Edwardsville

LU 05-1146 . . . . Shawnee
LU 05-1350 . . . . . . Hutchinson

Plumbing and Pipe Fitting
LU 165 . . . . Topeka
LU 171 . . . . Wichita
LU 664 . . . . Frontenac
LU 763 . . . . Lawrence

Postal Workers
LU 194 Dodge City . . . Dodge City
LU 238 Kansas Kaw Valley
  Area . . . . Kansas City
LU 265 Pittsburg . . . . . Pittsburg
LU 270 Topeka . . . . Topeka
LU 393 Lawrence . . . . . Lawrence
LU 439 Hutchinson . . . Hutchinson
LU 447 Coffeyville
  Local . . . . Coffeyville
LU 506 Atchison Local . . Atchison
LU 576 Parsons Local . . . Parsons
LU 582 Arkansas City
  Local . . . . Arkansas City
LU 588 Manhattan . . . Manhattan
LU 617 Chanute Local . . Chanute
LU 639 Great Bend . . . Great Bend
LU 735 Wichita . . . . . . Wichita
LU 743 Fort Scott . . . . Fort Scott
LU 886 Salina . . . . Salina
LU 890 Olathe . . . . Olathe
LU 959 . . . . Independence
LU 1145 Garden City . . Garden City
LU 1274 Leavenworth . Leavenworth
LU 2009 Northwest Kansas
  Area . . . . Hays
LU 2021 Liberal . . . . . . Liberal
LU 2094 McPherson . . . McPherson
LU 2132 Concordia . . . . Concordia
LU 2665 Colby . . . . Colby
LU 4117 Ottawa Local . . . Ottawa
LU 4458 Junction City . . Fort Riley
LU 4990 Newton . . . . . Newton
LU 5706 Paola Local . . . . Paola
LU 6862 Western Area Supply
  Center . . . . Topeka
SA Kansas . . . . Topeka

Professional and Technical Engineers
LU 1 Administrative Law Judges
  Judicial Council . . . . Leawood

Railroad Signalmen
LLG 157 . . . . Herington

Rural Letter Carriers
D 1 . . . . Wamego
D 2 . . . . Emporia
D 3 . . . . Beloit

D 4 . . . . Lewis
LU Clay County . . . . Clay Center
LU Cowley County . . . . Burden
LU Marshall County . . Marysville
LU 21 Brown County . . . Seneca
LU 23 Cloud County . . Miltonvale
LU 52 Chase County . . Strong City
LU 81 Jackson-Nemaha
  Counties . . . . Goff
LU 113 Mitchell County . Glen Elder
LU 133 Osborne County . Natoma
LU 141 Pottowatomie
  County . . . . Onago
LU 172 Lyon County . . . . Emporia
LU 181 Washington
  County . . . . Washington
LU 203 Saline County . . . Salina
SA Kansas . . . . McPherson

Security, Police and Fire Professionals
LU 252 . . . . Burlington
LU 253 . . . . Galesburg
LU 255 . . . . Wichita

Service Employees
LU 513 . . . . Wichita
LU 1086 Firemen & Oilers . Topeka
LU 1099 Firemen & Oilers . Newton

Sheet Metal Workers
LU 29 . . . . Wichita
LU 77 . . . . Topeka
LU 165 . . . . Kansas City
LU 472 . . . . St. Marys

Steelworkers
LU 11-307-L . . . . Topeka
LU 11-2351-S . . . . . Kansas City
LU 11-3092-S . . . . . . Atchison
LU 11-6943-S . . . . . . Atchison
LU 11-12458-S . . . . . Hutchinson
LU 11-12561-S . . . . . Kansas City
LU 11-12606-S . . . . . Hutchinson
LU 11-12788-S . . . . . Ellsworth
LU 11-13417-S . . . . . . Wichita
LU 11-15312-S . . . . . . Neodesha

Teamsters
LU 696 . . . . Topeka
LU 795 . . . . Wichita

Theatrical Stage Employees
LU 190 . . . . Wichita
LU 464 . . . . Salina
LU 910 TWA . . . . Wichita
SA Kansas . . . . Benton

Transportation Communications Union
LG 121 . . . . Tonganoxie
LG 427 . . . . Topeka
LG 843 . . . . Topeka
LG 846 . . . . Topeka
LG 6026 Berwind . . . Independence
LG 6054 Coffeyville . . . . Wichita
LG 6762 Armstrong . Kansas City
LG 6850 Argentine . . . Kansas City
LG 6887 Shawnee . . . . . Topeka
SBA 92 Santa Fe Railroad . . Topeka

Transportation Union
GCA GO-9 Atchison Topeka Santa
  Fe-P-E & W . . . . Overland Park
GCA GO-953 Union Pacific Railroad
  Eastern . . . . Topeka
LU 44 . . . . Agra
LU 445 . . . . Overland Park
LU 464 . . . . Arkansas City
LU 477 . . . . Hutchinson
LU 495 . . . . Lindsborg
LU 506 . . . . Herington
LU 527 . . . . Coffeyville
LU 533 . . . . Osawatomie
LU 707 . . . . Marysville
LU 763 . . . . Pittsburg
LU 774 . . . . Leavenworth
LU 1126 . . . . Pratt
LU 1227 . . . . Wichita
LU 1409 . . . . Shawnee
LU 1532 . . . . Kansas City
SLB LO-19 Kansas . . . Osawatomie

Treasury Employees
CH . . . . Kansas City
CH 51 . . . . Mission
CH 254 . . . . Lenexa

Weather Service Employees
BR 03-12 . . . . Topeka
BR 03-17 . . . . Wichita
BR 03-55 . . . . Goodland
BR 03-61 . . . . Olathe
BR 03-91 . . . . Dodge City

Unaffiliated Labor Organizations
Contech Construction Products,
  Topeka Shop Committee . Topeka
Dillons Employees
  Association . . . . . . Hutchinson
Independent Union of Graphic
  Industry International
  Personnel . . . . Wichita
Kansas State Union Label & Service
  Trades Council of the Kansas
  AFL-CIO . . . . Topeka

Kentucky

AFL-CIO Trade and Industrial Departments

Building and Construction Trades Department
BCTC Central Kentucky . Lexington
BCTC Greater Louisville . Louisville
BCTC Kentucky . . . . . Frankfort
BCTC Tri-State . . . . . . Ashland
BCTC Western Kentucky. . Paducah

AFL-CIO Directly Affiliated Locals
DALU 3039 Billposters &
  Billers . . . . Florence

Affiliated Labor Organizations

Air Traffic Controllers
LU . . . . Owensboro
LU LEX . . . . Lexington
LU LOU . . . . Louisville
LU SDF . . . . Louisville

Asbestos Workers
LU 51 . . . . Louisville

Automobile, Aerospace Workers
C 5th & 6th Districts of
  Kentucky . . . . Livingston
C Clark-Floyd-Harrison-Jennings-
  Scott . . . . Louisville
C Kentucky-First Area . Fancy Farm
C South Central
  Kentucky . . . . Bowling Green
C Third & Fourth Areas-
  Kentucky . . . . Louisville
LU . . . . Bloomfield
LU 43 . . . . Louisville
LU 178 . . . . Henderson
LU 523 . . . . Calvert City
LU 862 . . . . Louisville
LU 912 . . . . Georgetown
LU 1153 . . . . Shepherdsville
LU 1584 . . . . Carrollton
LU 1608 . . . . Winchester
LU 1772 . . . . Lexington
LU 1813 . . . . Warsaw
LU 1937 . . . . Cynthiana
LU 2012 . . . . Buffalo
LU 2164 . . . . . . Bowling Green
LU 2302 . . . . Bardstown
LU 2306 . . . . . Summer Shade
LU 2309 . . . . Fairdale
LU 2336 . . . . Fancy Farm
LU 2370 . . . . Franklin
LU 2383 . . . . Frankfort
LU 2386 . . . . Providence
LU 2407 . . . . Auburn

Bakery, Confectionery, Tobacco Workers and Grain Millers
LU 16-T . . . . Louisville
LU 196-T . . . . Owensboro
LU 201-T . . . . Louisville
LU 365-T . . . . Mayfield

Boilermakers
LG . . . . Owensboro
LG 20-S . . . . Louisville
LG 40 . . . . Elizabethtown
LG 595-D . . . . . Brandenburg

LG 726 . . . . Owensboro
LG 727 . . . . Whitesville

Bricklayers
LU 2 . . . . Southgate
LU 17 . . . . Lexington

Carpenters
DC Kentucky . . . . . . Frankfort
LU 64 . . . . Louisville
LU 96-T . . . . Frankfort
LU 357 . . . . Paducah
LU 472 . . . . Ashland
LU 549 . . . . Owensboro
LU 1031 . . . . Louisville
LU 1080 . . . . Owensboro
LU 1299 . . . . Covington
LU 1650 . . . . Lexington
LU 2184 . . . . . Shepherdsville
LU 2501 . . . . Louisville
LU 3191 . . . . . . Beaver Dam
LU 3223 . . . . . Elizabethtown

Civilian Technicians
CH 69 Bluegrass . . . . Louisville
CH 83 Kentucky Longrifle
  Association . . . . . . Radcliff

Communications Workers
LU 229 . . . . Lexington
LU 761 . . . . Louisville
LU 762 . . . . . . Elizabethtown
LU 3301 . . . . . Bowling Green
LU 3304 . . . . Danville
LU 3305 . . . . Shelbyville
LU 3309 . . . . . . Hopkinsville
LU 3310 . . . . Louisville
LU 3312 . . . . . . Madisonville
LU 3313 . . . . Pineville
LU 3314 . . . . Owensboro
LU 3315 . . . . Paducah
LU 3317 . . . . Pikeville
LU 3321 . . . . Winchester
LU 3371 . . . . Flatwoods
LU 3372 . . . . Lexington
LU 54044 . . . . . Independence

Education
LU Fort Knox Teachers'
  Association . . . . . . Fort Knox

Electrical Workers
LU 369 . . . . Louisville
LU 463 . . . . . . Campbellsville
LU 475 . . . . Hardin
LU 816 . . . . Paducah
LU 940 . . . . Worthington
LU 1353 . . . . London
LU 1625 . . . . Corbin
LU 1627 . . . . Lexington
LU 1701 . . . . Owensboro
LU 2100 . . . . Louisville
LU 2220 . . . . Lexington
LU 2246 . . . . . Mount Sterling
LU 2356 . . . . Richmond
LU 2360 . . . . Somerset
SC 9 Railroad . . . . . London

Electronic Workers
LU 697 . . . . Lebanon
LU 701 . . . . . . Madisonville
LU 743 . . . . Leitchfield
LU 766 . . . . . . Elizabethtown
LU 767 . . . . Somerset
LU 795 . . . . Taylor Mill

Elevator Constructors
LU 20 . . . . Louisville

Federal Employees
LU 466 . . . . Winchester
LU 852 . . . . Louisville
LU 1579 . . . . Louisville

Fire Fighters
LU 27 Lexington Blue Grass Army
  Depot . . . . Richmond
LU 45 Newport . . . . . Newport
LU 927 . . . . . Bowling Green

Flint Glass Workers
LU 1009 . . . . Danville
LU 1016 . . . . . . Harrodsburg

Food and Commercial Workers
LU 10-D . . . . . Lawrenceburg
LU 23-D . . . . Bardstown
LU 24-D . . . . Frankfort
LU 28-D . . . . Guston
LU 31-D . . . . Owensboro
LU 38-D . . . . Frankfort
LU 72-D . . . . Louisville
LU 111-D . . . . . . Bardstown
LU 227 . . . . Louisville
LU 561-C . . . . Hebron
LU 664-C . . . . Elsemere
LU 970-C . . . . . Elizabethtown

Glass, Molders, Pottery and Plastics Workers
LU 176 . . . . Glencoe
LU 303 . . . . Louisville
LU 334-A . . . . Somerset

Government Employees
C 61 Tennessee . . . . Fort Campbell
LU 608 . . . . Fort Knox
LU 817 HHS . . . . . Lexington
LU 1123 USDA . . . . . Louisville
LU 1133 VA . . . . . Louisville
LU 1160 DoL . . . . . Louisville
LU 1286 DoJ . . . . . Ashland
LU 1938 DoD . . . . . Greenup
LU 2022 DoD . . . Fort Campbell
LU 2302 DoD . . . . Fort Knox
LU 3228 USDA . . . . . Padvcah
LU 3431 DoL . . . . Middlesboro
LU 3984 . . . . . . Frankfort
LU 4051 . . . . . . Manchester

Government Security Officers
LU 137 Cincinnati . . . California

Graphic Communications
LU 619-M . . . . Louisville

Guards
LU 8 . . . . . Crescent Springs
LU 15 . . . . . . Brandenburg
LU 78 . . . . Owenton

Hotel and Restaurant Employees
LU 181 . . . . Louisville

Iron Workers
LU 70 . . . . Louisville
LU 682 . . . . Louisville
LU 769 . . . . Ashland
LU 782 . . . . Paducah

Laborers
DC Kentucky . . . . . Lawrenceburg
LU 189 . . . . Lexington
LU 575 . . . . Louisville
LU 576 . . . . Louisville
LU 1214 . . . . Paducah
LU 1392 . . . . Owensboro
LU 1445 . . . . Catlettsburg

Letter Carriers
BR 14 . . . . Louisville
BR 234 . . . . Owensboro
BR 361 . . . . Lexington
BR 374 . . . . . Highland Heights
BR 383 . . . . Paducah
BR 410 . . . . Henderson
BR 468 . . . . . Bowling Green
BR 745 . . . . Ashland
BR 836 . . . . Hopkinsville
BR 1106 . . . . Mayfield
BR 1265 Mount Sterling,
  Kentucky . . . . Mount Sterling
BR 1408 . . . . . . Madisonville
BR 1616 Middlesboro,
  Kentucky . . . . Middlesboro
BR 1701 . . . . Shelbyville
BR 1827 Fulton, Kentucky . . Fulton
BR 1909 Lebanon,
  Kentucky . . . . Lebanon
BR 1988 Russellville,
  Kentucky . . . . . . Russellville
BR 2010 Morganfield,
  Kentucky . . . . . . Morganfield
BR 2014 Dawson Springs,
  Kentucky . . . . Dawson Springs
BR 2039 . . . . Somerset
BR 2156 . . . . Murray
BR 2188 Princeton,
  Kentucky . . . . Princeton
BR 2226 Pineville,
  Kentucky . . . . Pineville
BR 2242 . . . . London
BR 2306 Providence,
  Kentucky . . . . . . Providence
BR 2444 Earlington,
  Kentucky . . . . . . Earlington
BR 2648 Carlisle, Kentucky. Carlisle
BR 2668 Harlan, Kentucky. . Harlan
BR 2773 Campbellsville,
  Kentucky . . . . Campbellsville
BR 2856 Barbourville,
  Kentucky . . . . . Barbourville
BR 2883 Carrollton,
  Kentucky . . . . . . Carrollton
BR 2891 Clinton, Kentucky . Clinton
BR 2892 Pikeville,
  Kentucky . . . . Pikeville
BR 2933 Hickman,
  Kentucky . . . . Hickman
BR 2973 Paintsville,
  Kentucky . . . . . . Paintsville
BR 3199 Central City,
  Kentucky . . . . . Central City
BR 3226 Louisa, Kentucky. . Louisa
BR 3308 Marion, Kentucky . Marion
BR 3438 La Grange,
  Kentucky . . . . . . La Grange
BR 3484 Franklin,
  Kentucky . . . . Franklin
BR 3486 . . . . Eminence
BR 3494 Flemingsburg,
  Kentucky . . . . . Flemingsburg
BR 3515 . . . . Sonora
BR 3554 Williamstown,
  Kentucky . . . . . Williamstown

BR 3569 Irvine, Kentucky. . . Irvine
BR 3623 Augusta,
    Kentucky . . . . Augusta
BR 3624 Lawrenceburg,
    Kentucky . . . . Lawrenceburg
BR 3640 Sturgis, Kentucky . Sturgis
BR 3660 Walton, Kentucky . Walton
BR 3666 Morehead,
    Kentucky . . . . Morehead
BR 3753 . . . . Bardstown
BR 3857 Hazard, Kentucky . Hazard
BR 4391 Prestonburg,
    Kentucky . . . . . . Prestonburg
BR 5355 Columbia,
    Kentucky . . . . Columbia
BR 5492 Scottsville,
    Kentucky . . . . . . Scottsville
BR 5799 Leitchfield,
    Kentucky . . . . . . Leitchfield
BR 5815 Beaver Dam,
    Kentucky . . . . . . Beaver Dam
BR 5882 Monticello,
    Kentucky . . . . . . Monticello
BR 5883 Tompkinsville,
    Kentucky . . . . . Tompkinsville
BR 6067 Springfield,
    Kentucky . . . . . . Springfield
BR 6094 Greensburg,
    Kentucky . . . . . . Greensburg
BR 6192 Greenup,
    Kentucky . . . . Greenup
BR 6288 Manchester,
    Kentucky . . . . . . Manchester
BR 6531 Brandenburg,
    Kentucky . . . . . . Brandenburg
BR 6537 Cumberland,
    Kentucky . . . . . . Cumberland
BR 6538 . . . . West Liberty
BR 6547 West Point,
    Kentucky. . . . . . . West Point
BR 6554 Radcliff,
    Kentucky. . . . . Radcliff
BR 6609 Whitesburg,
    Kentucky . . . . . . Whitesburg
SA Kentucky . . . Highland Heights

Locomotive Engineers
DIV 39 . . . . Independence
DIV 78 . . . . Louisville
DIV 110 . . . . Edgewood
DIV 199 . . . . Mount Vernon
DIV 211 . . . . Cold Spring
DIV 271. . . . . Flatwoods
DIV 365 . . . . Shepherdsville
DIV 463 Corbin . . . . . Corbin
DIV 489 . . . . Burlington
DIV 698 . . . . Pikeville
DIV 804. . . . . Covington
DIV 829 . . . . Irvine
DIV 830 . . . . Sassafras

Machinists
DLG 19 . . . . Paducah
DLG 27 . . . . Louisville
DLG 154 . . . . Calvert City
LG 123 . . . . Paducah
LG 249 . . . . Worthington
LG 376 . . . . Erlanger
LG 619. . . . . Winchester
LG 681 . . . . Louisville
LG 804 . . . . Florence
LG 830 . . . . Louisville
LG 859 . . . . Richmond
LG 1073 . . . . London
LG 1157 . . . . West Paducah
LG 1294 . . . . Boaz
LG 1404 . . . . Lexington
LG 1720. . . . . Calvert City

LG 1969. . . . . Paducah
LG 2244 . . . . Graham
LG 2396. . . . . Elkton
LG 2409. . . . . Louisville
LG 2423 . . . . Louisville
LG 2507 . . . . Fredonia
LG 2781 . . . . Eddyville
LLG 19 PVC . . . . Paducah
LLG W-366 Woodworkers . Lebanon
STC Kentucky . . . . . Calvert City

Maintenance of Way Employes
FED Illinois Central Gulf . Mayfield
LG 8 . . . . Vanceburg
LG 225 . . . . Prestonburg
LG 666. . . . . London
LG 1038. . . . . Flatwoods
LG 1210 . . . . Princeton
LG 2388 . . . . Bee Spring
LG 2619 . . . . Walton
SF Affiliated System
    Federation . . . . . . Ashland
SLG 542 . . . . . . Harrodsburg
SLG 636 . . . . Erlanger
SLG 671 . . . . Brodhead
SLG 818 . . . . Henderson
SLG 1155 . . . . Fern Creek
SLG 1464 . . . . Louisa
SLG 1674 . . . . Irvine
SLG 1745 . . . . Jackson
SLG 2606. . . . . Pineville

Marine Engineers
LU 310 Professional Airways
    Systems Specialists . . . Louisville

Mine Workers
LU 30. . . . . Pikeville
LU 105 . . . . Virgie
LU 621 District 17 . . . . . Phelps
LU 1071 . . . . Henderson
LU 1092. . . . . Central City
LU 1178. . . . . Central City
LU 1440. . . . . Forest Hills
LU 1464. . . . . Powerly
LU 1468 . . . . Elkhorn City
LU 1511. . . . . Phelps
LU 1569. . . . . Middlesboro
LU 1605. . . . . Central City
LU 1623 . . . Dawson Springs
LU 1740 . . . . Uniontown
LU 1741 . . . . Wayland
LU 1793 . . . . Morganfield
LU 1802 . . . . Sturgis
LU 1812. . . . . Whitesburg
LU 1830 . . . . Madisonville
LU 1905 . . . . Uniontown
LU 2001 School Employees . Lynue
LU 2264 . . . . Pikeville
LU 2305 . . . . Sturgis
LU 2360 . . . . Lewisburg
LU 2390 . . . . Greenville
LU 2395 . . . . Drakesboro
LU 2470 . . . . Beaver Dam
LU 3000 . . . . Beaver Dam
LU 5138 . . . . Princeton
LU 5737 . . . . Pinsonfork
LU 5741 . . . . Jenkins
LU 5890 . . . . Scuddy
LU 5899 . . . . Berinsville
LU 5967 . . . . Hi Hat
LU 6492 . . . . Beaver Dam
LU 6660 . . . . Cawood
LU 7093 . . . . Lovely
LU 7425 . . . . Cumberland
LU 8198 . . . . Marion
LU 8588 . . . . Elkhorn City
LU 8790 . . . . Beechmont

LU 8941 . . . . Caneyville
LU 9653 . . . . Madisonville
LU 9800 . . . . Hartford
LU 9845 . . . . Langley

Musicians
LU 11-637. . . . . Louisville
LU 554-635 . . . . . . Lexington

National Staff Organization
LU KESPA/NEA Field
    Representatives . . . . . Jackson
LU Staff Organization, Kentucky
    Education Association . . Calhoun

Nurses
LSC Hazard ARH Unit, KNA LU
    104 . . . . Hazard
LSC McDowell ARH-KNA-Unit LU
    112 . . . . McDowell
LSC Middlesboro ARH KNA Unit
    LU106 . . . . Middlesboro
LSC Whiteburg-ARH Unit KNA LU
    111 . . . . Eolia
LU 102 Kentucky . . . . . Louisville
LU 103 Williamson Appalachian
    Regional . . . . McCarr
LU 114 Harlan ARH-KNA Unit
    114 . . . . Cawood
SA Kentucky Nurses
    Association . . . . . . Louisville

Office and Professional Employees
LU 172 . . . . Paducah

Operating Engineers
LU 181 . . . . Henderson

Painters
LU 118 . . . . Louisville
LU 238 . . . . Alexandria
LU 500 . . . . Paducah
LU 1072 . . . . Ashland

Paper, Allied-Industrial, Chemical Employees
ASSN Mid-Valley Pipeline
    Group. . . . . Elizabethtown
LU 5-518 . . . . Fort Thomas
LU 02-512. . . . . Bypro
LU 03-505 . . . . Russell
LU 03-744 Langley. . . . . Martin
LU 05-214. . . . . Ashland
LU 05-367 . . . . . . Brandenburg
LU 05-372. . . . . . . Prestonburg
LU 05-511 . . . . Dayton
LU 05-523 . . . . Paintsville
LU 05-550 . . . . Paducah
LU 05-556 . . . . Benton
LU 05-680 . . . . Mayfield
LU 05-727 . . . . . . Calvert City
LU 05-775 . . . . Wickliffe
LU 05-783 . . . . Owensboro
LU 05-805 . . . . Walton
LU 05-832 . . . . Newport
LU 05-848. . . . . Louisville
LU 05-861. . . . . Louisville
LU 05-879 . . . . Murray
LU 05-897. . . . . . Sharon Grove
LU 05-931 . . . . Alexandria
LU 05-943 . . . . Springfield
LU 05-998 . . . . Benton
LU 05-1048 . . . . . . Lovisville
LU 05-1241 . . . . Fairfield
LU 05-1506 . . . . . Elizabethtown
LU 05-1538 . . . . Barlow
LU 05-1737 . . . . Louisville
LU 06-669 . . . . Paducah

LU 07-399 . . . . Berea
LU 07-532 . . . . . Lawrenceburg

Pilots, Independent
NHQ. . . . . Louisville

Plasterers and Cement Masons
LU 135 . . . . Paducah

Plumbing and Pipe Fitting
LU 107 . . . . Louisville
LU 184 . . . . Paducah
LU 248 . . . . Ashland
LU 452 . . . . Lexington
LU 522 . . . . Louisville
LU 633 . . . . Owensboro

Postal Workers
LU 4 Louisville . . . . . Louisville
LU 343 Russellville
    Local . . . . Russellville
LU 350 Owensboro . . . Owensboro
LU 453 Bowling Green
    Area . . . . Bowling Green
LU 1318 Lebanon Local . . Lebanon
LU 1370 Covington . . . Covington
LU 1412 Mayfield . . . . Mayfield
LU 1425 Danville Local . . Danville
LU 1552 Madisonville
    Local. . . . . Madisonville
LU 2275
    Elizabethtown . . . Elizabethtown
LU 2278 Murray Local . . . Murray
LU 2307 Central Kentucky
    Area. . . . . Lexington
LU 2324 Pikeville . . . . . Pikeville
LU 2325 Somerset . . . . . Somerset
LU 2326 Campbellsville
    Local. . . . . Campbellsville
LU 2500 Paducah. . . . . . Paducah
LU 2608 Southeastern Kentucky
    Area . . . . London
LU 3298 La Grange
    Local . . . . La Grange
LU 3332 Whitesburg
    Local . . . . Whitesburg
LU 3944 Frankfort. . . . . Frankfort
LU 4551 Louisa. . . . . Catlettsburg
LU 4741 Grayson. . . . Catlettsburg
LU 4900 West Liberty
    Local. . . . . West Liberty
LU 5529 Maysville Local. Maysville
LU 5546 Fort Knox. . . . Fort Knox
LU 6314 Fairdale Local. . . Fairdale
LU 6593 Campton Local. . Campton
LU 6605 Salyersville
    Local. . . . . Salyersville
LU 6662 Radcliff Local. . . Radcliff
LU 6696 Shepherdsville
    Local. . . . . Shepherdsville
SA Kentucky . . . . . . Louisville

Railroad Signalmen
LLG 13 . . . . Louisville
LLG 46 . . . . . Beaver Dam
LLG 51 . . . . Princeton
LLG 176 . . . . Walton
LLG 215 . . . . Irvine
LLG 234 Safetran . . . . . Louisville

Roofers, Waterproofers and Allied Workers
LU 147 . . . . Louisville

Rural Letter Carriers
D 1 . . . . Louisa
D 1 District A. . . . . Gilbertsville
D 2 District B . . . . . Leitchfield

D 3 District C . . . . Bowling Green
D 4 District D . . . . . Hodgenville
D 5 District E . . . . . . Louisville
D 6 District F . . . . Bedford
D 7 District G . . . . . Georgetown
D 8 District H . . . . . . Somerset
LU Grant County. . . . . . Verona
LU Obion-Lake Counties . . Hickman
LU Warren County . Bowling Green
SA Kentucky . . . . . . Louisville

**Security, Police and Fire
   Professionals**
LU 111 . . . . Paducah

Service Employees
LU 5 National Conference of
   Firemen & Oilers . . . Olive Hill
LU 70 Firemen & Oilers. . . . Berea
LU 77 Firemen & Oilers. . . . Berea
LU 320 Firemen & Oilers. Louisville
LU 350 International Leather Goods,
   Plastics, Novelty and Service
   Union . . . . Hopkinsville
LU 362 Firemen & Oilers . . Corbin
LU 541 Racetrack Employees
   Union . . . . Louisville
LU 578 Firemen & Oilers . . Walton
LU 593 Firemen & Oilers . Russell
LU 754 Firemen & Oilers . Greenup

Sheet Metal Workers
LU 110 . . . . Louisville
LU 226 . . . . Florence
LU 261 . . . . Flatwoods
LU 354. . . . . London
LU 433. . . . . . . Bowling Green
LU 462 . . . . Ashland

**State, County and Municipal
   Employees**
LU 3911 Nurses
   Professional. . . . . . Louisville

Steelworkers
LU 01-5541-S . . . . Independence
LU 01-14340-S . . . . . Edgewood
LU 08-106. . . . . Louisville
LU 08-124-A . . . . . . Louisville
LU 08-133-S . . . . . South Shore
LU 08-152-S . . . . Clarkson
LU 08-153 . . . . . Elizabethtown
LU 08-155. . . . . . . Louisville
LU 08-162-S . . . . . . Maysville
LU 08-180-A . . . . . Shelbyville
LU 08-665-L . . . . Mayfield
LU 08-780-L . . . . . Elizabethtown
LU 08-857-G . . . . . . Olive Hill
LU 08-1693-S . . . . . . Louisville
LU 08-1865-S . . . . . . Ashland
LU 08-1870-S . . . . Dayton
LU 08-7054-S . . . . . . Ashland
LU 08-7153-S . . . . . Catlettsburg
LU 08-7461-S . . . . Tompkinsville
LU 08-7926-S . . . . . . Van Lear
LU 08-8118-S . . Lebanon Junction
LU 08-8158-S . . . . Grand Rivers
LU 08-8411-S . . . . . Barbourville
LU 08-8998-S . . . . . . Pikeville
LU 08-9120-S . . . . . East Point
LU 08-9148-S . . . . West Liberty
LU 08-9345-S . . . . Virgie
LU 08-9423 . . . . . . Lewisport
LU 08-9443 . . . . Robards
LU 08-9447 . . . . . . Eddyville
LU 08-12593-S . . . . Dana
LU 08-13675-S . . . . Beechmont
LU 08-14002-S . . . . Nicholasville
LU 08-14269-S . . . . Grand Rivers
LU 08-14300-S . . . . . Hinkle
LU 08-14398-S. . . . . . . Toler
LU 08-14491-S . . . . Cumberland
LU 08-14568-S . . . . . Whitesburg
LU 08-14581-S . . . . Elkhorn City
LU 08-14628-S . . . . Middlesboro
LU 08-14636-S . . . . . McDowell
LU 08-14637-S . . . . . . Bulan
LU 08-14746-S . . . . Central City

Teamsters
CONF Kentucky-West
   Virginia Conference of
   Teamsters . . . . Louisville
JC 94 . . . . Louisville
LU 89 . . . . Louisville
LU 236 . . . . Paducah
LU 651 . . . . Lexington
LU 783 . . . . Louisville
LU 2727 . . . . Louisville

Theatrical Stage Employees
LU 17 . . . . Louisville
LU 38-B . . . . Ludlow
LU 346 . . . . Lexington
LU 897 Theatrical Wardrobe
   Union . . . . Louisville

Transit Union
LDIV 628 . . . . Taylor Mill

**Transportation Communications
Union**
D 359. . . . . Raceland
D 611 . . . . Keavy
LG 6088 Southwind. . . . Louisville
LG 6104 Whitney . . . . . . Gray
LG 6344 Raceland . . . Worthington
LG 6401 Cincinnati . . . . . Hebron

Transportation Union
GCA GO-347 UTU. . . . Flatwoods
LU 376 . . . . Louisville
LU 496 . . . . South Shore
LU 573 . . . . . Kings Mountain
LU 630 . . . . Louisa
LU 785 . . . . Paducah
LU 1062. . . . . Flatwoods
LU 1190 . . . . Burlington
LU 1310 . . . . Corbin
LU 1315. . . . . . . Independence
LU 1316 . . . . Irvine
LU 1389. . . . . Ashland
LU 1517 . . . . Florence
LU 1567 . . . . Corbin

LU 1869. . . . . . . Turkey Creek
LU 1917. . . . . Park Hills
LU 1963 . . . . Henderson
SLB LO-20 Kentucky. . . Louisville

Treasury Employees
CH 25 . . . . Louisville
CH 73 . . . . Covington

Weather Service Employees
BR 03-4 . . . . Louisville
BR 03-7 . . . . Jackson
BR 03-63 . . . . . . West Paducah

Unaffiliated Labor
Organizations

Allied Mechanical
   Workers Independent LU
   714 . . . . Independence
American Sign & Marketing Services
   Inc. Independent Union . Florence
Chemical Protection Employees
   LU 1 . . . . Louisville
Falcon Coal Company Employees
   Association . . . . Jackson
Federal Employees Tobacco
   Organization. . . . . Shelbyville
Florence Steelworkers LU
   1 . . . . Florence
Independent Factory Workers
   Union . . . . Louisville
Jockeys' Guild, Inc. National
   Organization . . . . . Lexington
Kentucky State Pipe Trades
   Association . . . . . . Ashland
Neoprene Clerical Workers
   Independent. . . . . . Louisville
Neoprene Craftsmen Union
   Independent LU 788 . . Louisville
Plant Protection Association,
   National Ford's Louisville
   Assembly Plant LU
   118 . . . . Louisville
Scotia Employee
   Association . . . . . . Bledsoe
Utilities Union
   Independent . . . . . . Newport

Louisiana

AFL-CIO Trade and Industrial Departments

Building and Construction Trades Department
BCTC Baton Rouge . . Baton Rouge
BCTC Lafayette . . . . Lake Charles
BCTC Louisiana . . . . . Metairie
BCTC Northeastern
Louisiana . . . . Monroe
BCTC Shreveport . . . Shreveport
BCTC Southeast
Louisiana . . . . . New Orleans
BCTC Southwest
Louisiana . . . . . Lake Charles

Maritime Trades Department
PC New Orleans Area . . . . Harvey

Metal Trades Department
MTC Lake Charles . . Lake Charles
MTC New Orleans . . . Bridge City

Affiliated Labor Organizations

Agricultural Employees
BR 3 . . . . New Orleans

Air Traffic Controllers
LU BTR . . . . Baton Rouge
LU LCH . . . . Lake Charles
LU LFT . . . . Lafayette
LU MLU . . . . Monroe
LU MSY . . . . . . New Orleans
LU NEW . . . . . . New Orleans
LU SHV . Barksdale Air Force Base

Asbestos Workers
CONF Southwestern States . Kenner
LU 53 . . . . Kenner
LU 112 . . . . Lake Charles

Automobile, Aerospace Workers
C Louisiana State . . . . Shreveport
LU 1532 . . . . Shreveport
LU 1805 . . . . . . New Orleans
LU 1921 . . . . . . New Orleans
LU 1977 . . . . Monroe
LU 2166 . . . . . . Shreveport
LU 2297 . . . . . . Shreveport

Bakery, Confectionery, Tobacco Workers and Grain Millers
LU 235-G . . . . Port Allen
LU 238-G . . . . . . Shreveport
LU 369 . . . . Keithville

Boilermakers
LG 37 . . . . Slidell
LG 79 . . . . Lake Charles
LG 582 . . . . Baton Rouge
LG 1814 . . . . Bridge City

Bricklayers
LU 6 . . . . New Orleans

Carpenters
DC Louisiana . . . . . . Chalmette
LU 584 Industrial and Shipyard
Workers . . . . . . Bridge City
LU 720 . . . . . . Baton Rouge
LU 764 . . . . Shreveport
LU 953 . . . . Lake Charles

LU 1098 . . . . Baton Rouge
LU 1846 . . . . . . New Orleans
LU 1897 . . . . Lafayette
LU 1931 . . . . . . New Orleans
LU 2091 . . . . Jonesboro
LU 3094 . . . . Belmont
LU 3101 . . . . Oakdale
LU 3172 . . . . Jonesboro

Communications Workers
LU 1105 IUE-CWA . . New Orleans
LU 3402 . . . . Alexandria
LU 3403 . . . . . . Baton Rouge
LU 3404 . . . . Covington
LU 3406 . . . . Lafayette
LU 3407 . . . . . . Lake Charles
LU 3410 . . . . . . New Orleans
LU 3411 . . . . . . Shreveport
LU 3412 . . . . Houma
LU 3414 . . . . Monroe
LU 3450 . . . . . . New Orleans

Electrical Workers
LU 130 . . . . Metairie
LU 194 . . . . Shreveport
LU 329 . . . . Shreveport
LU 446 . . . . Monroe
LU 576 . . . . Alexandria
LU 767 . . . . . . Baton Rouge
LU 861 . . . . . . Lake Charles
LU 895 . . . . Monroe
LU 995 . . . . . . Baton Rouge
LU 1077 . . . . Bogalusa
LU 1139 . . . . . . New Orleans
LU 1700 . . . . . . Waggaman
LU 1829 . . . . . . Bossier City
LU 2149 . . . . . . New Orleans

Elevator Constructors
LU 16 . . . . Metairie

Federal Employees
C Veterans Administration
Locals . . . . . . New Orleans
LU 95 . . . . New Orleans
LU 1124 . . . . . . New Orleans
LU 1593 . . . . Slidell
LU 1707 . . . . . . Belle Chasse
LU 1708 . . . . Fort Polk
LU 1737 . . . . Natalbany
LU 1904 . . . . . . New Orleans
LU 1953 . Barksdale Air Force Base
LU 1956 . . . . . . Shreveport

Fire Fighters
LU 189-F Naval Air Station
Local . . . . Harvey

Flint Glass Workers
LU 70 . . . . Ruston
LU 711 . . . . Shreveport

Food and Commercial Workers
LU 27-C . . . . . . Avery Island
LU 29-C . . . . New Iberia
LU 67-I . . . . Westwego
LU 88-C . . . . Bastrop
LU 187-C . . . . Dubach
LU 273-C . . . . . . Ville Platte
LU 458-C . . . . Lydia
LU 483-C . . . . Franklin
LU 496 . . . . Metairie
LU 638-C . . . . Franklin
LU 883-C . . . . . . Lafayette
LU 1101 . . . . Arabi

LU 1167-P . . . . . . Gramercy

Glass, Molders, Pottery and Plastics Workers
LU 253 . . . . Simsboro

Government Employees
C 222 National HUD
Locals . . . . . New Orleans
C 237 Federal Grain Inspection
Locals . . . . La Place
LU 1972 VA . . . . Tioga
LU 2000 DoD . . . . . Shreveport
LU 2038 DoJ . . . . . . Oakdale
LU 2062 VA . . . . . New Orleans
LU 2341 USDA . . . . New Orleans
LU 2525 VA . . . . . Shreveport
LU 2528 . . . . Pineville
LU 2867 SBA . . . . . New Orleans
LU 2873 USDA . . . . Spearsville
LU 3157 USDA . . . . . La Place
LU 3457 DoI . . . . . New Orleans
LU 3475 HUD . . . . New Orleans
LU 3501 USDA . . . . Hammond
LU 3553 VA . . . . . New Orleans
LU 3957 BOP, FDC,
Oakdale . . . . Oberlin

Government Employees Association
LU 05-87 . . . . . . New Orleans
LU 05-89 . . . . . . New Orleans
LU 05-168 . . . . . Fort Polk
LU 05-169 . . . . . Fort Polk
LU 05-190 . . . . . New Orleans

Government Security Officers
LU 109 . . . . Monroe
LU 110 . . . . Tickfaw
LU 111 . . . . Slidell

Graphic Communications
LU 260-C . . . . . Lake Charles
LU 537-M . . . . . . Metairie

Guards
LU 81 . . . . Minden

Hotel and Restaurant Employees
LU 166 . . . . . . New Orleans

Iron Workers
DC Mid South . . . Denham Springs
LU 58 . . . . New Orleans
LU 591 . . . . Shreveport
LU 623 . . . . . . Baton Rouge
LU 710 . . . . Monroe

Laborers
DC Louisiana . . . Baton Rouge
LU 207 . . . . . . Lake Charles
LU 689 . . . . . . New Orleans
LU 692 . . . . . . Baton Rouge
LU 762 . . . . Lafayette
LU 1016 . . . . . . Baton Rouge
LU 1177 . . . . . . Baton Rouge

Letter Carriers
BR 124 . . . . . . New Orleans
BR 129 . . . . . . Baton Rouge
BR 136 . . . . Monroe
BR 197 Queen City . . . . Haughton
BR 914 . . . . . . Lake Charles
BR 932 . . . . . . Alexandria
BR 988 . . . . . . New Iberia

BR 1659 . . . . Bogalusa
BR 1760 . . . . Lafayette
BR 2223 . . . . . . Hammond
BR 2464 Houma-
Thibodaux . . . . . Thibodaux
BR 2730 . . . . Gretna
BR 2993 . . . . Baldwin
BR 3063 Bunkie,
Louisiana . . . . Bunkie
BR 3295 Rayne, Louisiana . . Rayne
BR 3632 Arabi, Louisiana . . Arabi
BR 3696 Donaldsonville,
Louisiana . . . . Donaldsonville
BR 3713 Winnfield,
Louisiana . . . . . . Winnfield
BR 3769 . . . . St. Martinville
BR 3815 . . . . . Morgan City
BR 3861 Westwego,
Louisiana . . . . . Westwego
BR 3868 . . . . . . Harvey
BR 3940 . . . . . . Tallulah
BR 4218 Homer, Louisiana . Homer
BR 4323 . . . . . . Marrero
BR 4342 . . . . . . Kenner
BR 4413 . . . . . . Slidell
BR 4489 Ponchatoula,
Louisiana . . . . Ponchatoula
BR 4517 Oakdale,
Louisiana . . . . . . Oakdale
BR 4521 . . . . . . Amite
BR 4591 Rayville,
Louisiana . . . . . . Rayville
BR 4617 . . . . . Bossier City
BR 4622 Springhill,
Louisiana . . . . . Springhill
BR 5318 . . . . . . Eunice
BR 5604 Ville Platte,
Louisiana . . . . . Ville Platte
BR 5605 New Roads,
Louisiana . . . . . New Roads
BR 5607 Norco, Louisiana . . Norco
BR 5608 Golden Meadow,
Louisiana . . . . Golden Meadow
BR 5609 Breaux Bridge,
Louisiana . . . . . Breaux Bridge
BR 5611 Berwick,
Louisiana . . . . . . Berwick
BR 5614 Many, Louisiana . . . Many
BR 5856 Church Point,
Louisiana . . . . . Church Point
BR 6102 Erath, Louisiana . . . Erath
BR 6119 . . . . . . Metairie
BR 6160 Lake Providence,
Louisiana . . . . Lake Providence
BR 6268 Kentwood,
Louisiana . . . . . Kentwood
BR 6377 . . . . . . Mandeville
BR 6379 Vidalia, Louisiana . Vidalia
BR 6461 Delcambre,
Louisiana . . . . . Delcambre
BR 6462 Jonesville,
Louisiana . . . . . Jonesville
BR 6601 Ferriday,
Louisiana . . . . . . Ferriday
SA Louisiana . . . . . . Metairie

Locomotive Engineers
DIV 18 . . . . . . New Orleans
DIV 193 . . . . Kenner
DIV 219 . . . . . . Greenwood
DIV 326 . . . . Benton
DIV 426 . . . . . . Baton Rouge
DIV 531 . . . . . . Baton Rouge
DIV 599 . . . . Vivian
DIV 632 . . . . Heflin

DIV 755 . . . . De Quincy
DIV 765 . . . . Monroe
DIV 914 . . . . Baton Rouge
DIV 915. . . . . Dry Prong
SLB Louisiana . . . . . Sterlington

Longshoremen
LU 854 . . . . New Orleans
LU 1349 . . . . . . Lake Charles
LU 1497 . . . . . . New Orleans
LU 1998 . . . . Westlake
LU 2036 . . . . Chalmette
LU 2047 . . . . . . Lake Charles
LU 3000 . . . . . . New Orleans
LU 3033 . . . . Port Allen

Machinists
DLG 161 . . . . . . Lake Charles
LG 37 . . . . Gretna
LG 69 . . . . Breaux Bridge
LG 281 . . Barksdale Air Force Base
LG 470 . . . . Lake Charles
LG 855 . . . . Ferriday
LG 1036 . . . . Sarepta
LG 1317 . . . . . . Lake Charles
LG 1366 . . . . . . Baton Rouge
LG 1905 . . . . Metairie
LG 2518 . . . . Tioga
STC Louisiana . . . . . . Tulles

Maintenance of Way Employes
LG 564 . . . . Shreveport
LG 944 . . . . Winnsboro
LG 1048 . . . . Carencro
LG 1176 . . . . Opelousas
LG 1193 . . . . Shreveport
LG 1539 . . . . Hammond
SLG 655 . . . . Bridge City
SLG 1100 . . . . . . New Orleans
SLG 1165 . . . . Reserve
SLG 1404 . . . . Plaquemine
SLG 1630 . . . . Harvey

Musicians
CONF Southern . . . . Shreveport
LU 116 . . . . Shreveport
LU 174-496 . . . . . New Orleans

National Staff Organization
LU Staff Organization, Louisiana
   State . . . . Baton Rouge

NLRB Professional Association
LU 15 . . . . New Orleans

Office and Professional Employees
LU 87 . . . . Sulphur
LU 89 . . . . Bogalusa
LU 107 . . . . New Iberia
LU 108 . . . . New Iberia
LU 383 . . . . Baton Rouge
LU 411 . . . . Springhill
LU 428 . . . . Baton Rouge
LU 465 . . . . Alexandria

Operating Engineers
LU 216 . . . . Baton Rouge
LU 406 . . . . New Orleans
LU 407 . . . . Lake Charles

Painters
DC 80 . . . . Kenner
LU 728 . . . . Baton Rouge
LU 1192 . . . . Kenner
LU 1244 . . . . Kenner
LU 2350 . . . . Kenner

Paper, Allied-Industrial, Chemical Employees
DC 4 . . . . De Quincy
LU 3-584 . . . . Baker
LU 4-500 Citgo Nationwide
   Council . . . . Sulphur
LU 04-189 . . . . Bogalusa
LU 04-245 . . . . Keithville
LU 04-269 . . . . Lockport
LU 04-272 . . . . Bastrop
LU 04-335 . . . . Zachary
LU 04-351 . . . . Pineville
LU 04-360 . . . . Bastrop
LU 04-364 . . . . . West Monroe
LU 04-382 . . . . Bastrop
LU 04-398 . . . . Cullen
LU 04-447 . . . . Westwego
LU 04-500 . . . . Sulfur
LU 04-522 . . . . Chalmette
LU 04-554 . . . . Springhill
LU 04-555 . . . . Sulphur
LU 04-618 . . . . Tallulah
LU 04-620 . . . . Gonzales
LU 04-654 . . . . . West Monroe
LU 04-677 . . . . Minden
LU 04-725 . . . . Deridder
LU 04-750 . . . . Norco
LU 04-752 . . . . . St. Francisville
LU 04-786 . . . . . . Sterlington
LU 04-840 . . . . . . New Orleans
LU 04-928 . . . . . St. Francisville
LU 04-1081 . . . . Simsboro
LU 04-1226 . . . . Deridder
LU 04-1331 . . . . . . Coushatta
LU 04-1334 . . . St. Francisville
LU 04-1362 . . . . Bogalusa
LU 04-1505 . . . . Hodge
LU 04-1685 . . . . . . Shreveport
LU 04-1749 . . . . Lillie

Plasterers and Cement Masons
LU 487 . . . . Lake Charles
LU 567 . . . . New Orleans
LU 812 . . . . Baton Rouge

Plumbing and Pipe Fitting
LU 60 . . . . Metairie
LU 106 . . . . Lake Charles
LU 141 . . . . Shreveport
LU 198 . . . . Baton Rouge
LU 247 . . . . Alexandria
LU 659 . . . . Monroe
SA Louisiana . . . . . Alexandria

Postal and Federal Employees
D 1 . . . . New Orleans
LU 102 . . . . Baton Rouge
LU 108 . . . . Lake Charles
LU 110 . . . . New Orleans

Postal Mail Handlers
LU 312 . . . . New Orleans

Postal Workers
LU Covington . . . . . Covington
LU 83 New Orleans . . New Orleans
LU 174 Baton Rouge . Baton Rouge
LU 205 Alexandria . . . Alexandria
LU 223 Southwest Louisiana
   Area . . . . Lake Charles
LU 418 Northwest Louisiana
   Area . . . . Shreveport
LU 792 Monroe . . . . . Monroe
LU 1171 Plaquemine
   Local . . . . Plaquemine
LU 1182 Winnfield Local . Winnfield
LU 1278 Hammond . . . Hammond
LU 1430 Rayville Local . . Rayville

LU 2102 Houma . . . . . . Houma
LU 2103 Thibodaux . . . Thibodaux
LU 2106 Morgan City . Morgan City
LU 2802 Eunice . . . . . . Eunice
LU 2803 Lafayette . . . . Lafayette
LU 2848 Leesville . . . . . Leesville
LU 2871 Tri-Parish Area . . . Gretna
LU 3036 Ville Platte
   Local . . . . Ville Platte
LU 3037 Springhill Local . Springhill
LU 3049 Bogalusa . . . . Bogalusa
LU 3067 New Iberia . . New Iberia
LU 3234 Many Local . . . . Many
LU 3815 Jena Local . . . . . Jena
LU 3900 Lockport Local . . Lockport
LU 3902 Slidell . . . . . . Slidell
LU 4300 Denham Springs
   Local . . . . . . Denham Springs
LU 4653 Opelousas
   Local . . . . Opelousas
LU 5283 Napoleonville
   Local . . . . Napoleonville
LU 5903 Gonzales Local . Gonzales
LU 5959 Metairie Area . . . Metairie
LU 6101 Vidalia . . . . . . Vidalia
LU 6190 Mandeville . . Mandeville
LU 6347 Chalmette
   Local . . . . Chalmette
LU 6598 Baker Local . . . . Baker
LU 6665 St. Francisville
   Local . . . . St. Francisville
SA Louisiana . . . . . New Orleans

Roofers, Waterproofers and Allied Workers
DC Southern Roofers . Baton Rouge
LU 59 . . . . Shreveport
LU 317 . . . . Baton Rouge

Rural Letter Carriers
D 1 Deep South . . . . . . Meraux
D 4 . . . . Heflin
D 5 . . . . Sterlington
D 6 Southeast . . . . . Ponchatoula
D 7 Southwest District . . . . Vinton
D 8 Central District . . . . Pineville
SA Louisiana . . . . Noble

Security, Police and Fire Professionals
LU 268 . . . . Sulphur
LU 700 . . . . Lake Charles
LU 704 . . . . New Orleans
LU 707 . . . . St. Francisville
LU 709 . . . . Houma
LU 710 . . . . New Orleans

Service Employees
LU 22 International Leather Goods,
   Plastics, Novelty and Service
   Union . . . . New Orleans
LU 100 . . . . New Orleans
LU 880 . . . . New Orleans

Sheet Metal Workers
LU 11 . . . . Metairie
LU 21 . . . . Baton Rouge
LU 361 . . . . Shreveport

State, County and Municipal Employees
C 17 Louisiana Public
   Employees . . . . . Baton Rouge

Steelworkers
LU 09-211-A . . . . Lake Charles
LU 09-275-A . . . Denham Springs
LU 09-5651 . . . . Kenner

LU 09-5702-S . . . . . . Vacherie
LU 09-6296-S . . . . . Zachary
LU 09-8363-S . . . . . Chalmette
LU 09-8373-S . . . . Belle Chasse
LU 09-8394-S . . . . . Zachary
LU 09-9059-S . . . . . Ventress
LU 09-9121-S . . . . . Laplace
LU 09-13000-S . . . . . Chalmette
LU 09-13314-S . . . . . Elizabeth
LU 09-13841-S . . . Ville Platte
LU 09-14425-S . . . New Iberia
LU 09-14465-S . . Baton Rouge

Teamsters
JC 93 . . . . New Orleans
LU 5 . . . . Baton Rouge
LU 270 . . . . New Orleans
LU 568 . . . . Shreveport
LU 969 . . . . Lake Charles

Theatrical Stage Employees
LU 39 . . . . New Orleans
LU 260 . . . . Lake Charles
LU 298 . . . . Shreveport
LU 478 Studio
   Mechanics . . . . . New Orleans
LU 540 . . . . Baton Rouge
LU 668 . . . . Monroe
LU 840 . . . . Hammond

Train Dispatchers
SCOM Louisiana & Arkansas
   Railroad . . . . Shreveport

Transit Union
CONBD Louisiana
   Legislative . . . . New Orleans
LDIV 558 . . . . . . Shreveport
LDIV 1400 . . . . Gretna
LDIV 1546 . . . . . Baton Rouge
LDIV 1560 . . . . . New Orleans
LU 1535 . . . . . . New Orleans

Transportation Communications Union
D 1461 Southwestern . . Shreveport
D 5513 . . . . Gretna
LG 6136 True Blue . . . Alexandria
LG 6461 Crescent . . . . . Avondale
LG 6825 Red Stick . . Baton Rouge
LG 6872 New
   Orleans . . . . Greenwell Springs

Transportation Union
LU 659 . . . . Sulphur
LU 781 . . . . Blanchard
LU 976 . . . . Stonewall
LU 1066 . . . . New Orleans
LU 1337 . . . . Hammond
LU 1501 . . . . Baton Rouge
LU 1545 . . . . Bastrop
LU 1678 . . . . Shreveport
LU 1836 . . . . Belle Chasse
LU 1947 . . . . Lake Charles
SLB LO-21 Louisiana . Baton Rouge

Treasury Employees
CH 6 . . . . New Orleans
CH 168 . . . . New Orleans

Weather Service Employees
BR 02-7 . . . . Lake Charles
BR 02-10 . . . . Shreveport
BR 02-15 . . . . Slidell
BR 02-81 . . . . Slidell

Unaffiliated Labor Organizations

Allied Oil Workers Union of Baton Rouge, Louisiana . . . . Fordoche

American Federation of Unions LU 102 . . . . Prairieville
Baton Rouge Oil & Chemical Workers Union . . . Baton Rouge
Exxon Employees Federation Southeastern Division . . Crowley

Hospitality Hotels and Restaurants Organizing Council (HOTROC) . . . . New Orleans
Industrial Guards Association Independent . . . . . Baton Rouge

Norco Chemical Workers' Union . . . . Norco
Southern Association of Nurse Anesthetists . . . . Metairie
Southern Pipe Liners Union-Exxon . . . . Houma
Texas Gulf Federation Shell Pipe Line . . . . Prairieville
United Security Workers of America . . . . . . New Orleans

Maine

AFL-CIO Trade and Industrial Departments

Building and Construction Trades Department
BCTC Maine. . . . . Clinton

Affiliated Labor Organizations

Air Traffic Controllers
LU BGR . . . . Bangor
LU PWM . . . . Portland

Asbestos Workers
LU 134 . . . . South Berwick

Automobile, Aerospace Workers
LU 3999 . . . . Bath

Bakery, Confectionery, Tobacco Workers and Grain Millers
LU 234-G . . . . Island Falls
LU 334 . . . . Portland

Carpenters
LU 658 . . . . Lincoln
LU 1612 . . . . . East Millinocket
LU 1996 . . . . Augusta
LU 2400 . . . . Baileyville
LU 3196 . . . . . . South Portland

Civilian Technicians
CH 79 Pine Tree . . . . . Freedom
CH 128 Maine Acts . . . . Bangor

Communications Workers
LU 14112 . . . . Bangor
LU 14113 . . . . Gorham
LU 14115 . . . . Winslow
LU 14116 . . . . Brewer
LU 31128 . . . . Portland
LU 81077 . . . . Greenwood

Education
SA Maine Education Association . . . . . . Augusta

Electrical Workers
LU 119 . . . . Lewiston
LU 567 . . . . Lewiston
LU 1057 . . . . Baileyville
LU 1253 . . . . Augusta
LU 1750 . . . . Sidney
LU 1768 . . . . Hinkley
LU 1777 . . . . Sorrento
LU 1837 . . . . Manchester
LU 2071 . . . . Eliot
LU 2144 . . . . Rumford
LU 2233 . . . . Buxton
LU 2327 . . . . Augusta
SC T-6 New England Telephone Company . . . . Augusta

Fire Fighters
LU 123-F . . . . Kittery

Food and Commercial Workers
LU 650-C . . . . Hampden

Government Employees
C 137 Food Inspection Locals, Northeast . . . . Albion
LU 294 . . . . Limestone

LU 2610 VA . . . . Augusta
LU 2635 DoD . . . . Cutler
LU 2711 DoJ . . . . Bangor
LU 2906 DoD . . . . Bath
LU 3728 USDA . . . . . . China

Government Employees Association
LU 01-77 . . . . Brunswick

Graphic Communications
LU 22-C . . . . Windham
LU 558-C . . . . Orrington

Iron Workers
LU 496 . . . . Clinton
LU 807 . . . . Smithfield

Laborers
LU 327 . . . . Augusta
LU 1284 . . . . Skowhegan
LU 1377 . . . . Brewer

Letter Carriers
BR 92 . . . . Westbrook
BR 241 . . . . Lewiston
BR 345 . . . . Auburn
BR 391 Trans-Maine Merged . . . . Hampden
BR 774 . . . . Litchfield
BR 1448 . . . . Sanford
BR 2394 . . . . Presque Isle
BR 5484 East Holden, Maine . . . . East Holden
BR 6115 Chebeague Island, Maine . . . . . Chebeague Island
SA Maine . . . . Westbrook

Locomotive Engineers
DIV 72 . . . . Fairfield
DIV 191 . . . . Raymond

Longshoremen
LU 861 . . . . Portland
LU 1519 . . . . Swanville

Machinists
DLG 4 . . . . Topsham
DLG 99 . . . . Bucksport
LG 5 Mid Coast United Health Care Employees . . . . Bath
LG 6-S . . . . Bath
LG 7-S . . . . Bath
LG 89-S . . . . Bath
LG 156 . . . . Benedicta
LG 362 . . . . Enfield
LG 409 . . . . Waterville
LG 559 . . . . Madison
LG 836 . . . . Sanford
LG 1482 . . . . Milford
LG 1490 Border . . . . . Alexander
LG 1696 . . . . Corinna
LG 1821 . . . . Bucksport
LG 2287 . . . . Westbrook
LG 2740 . . . . Fairfield

Maintenance of Way Employes
LG 602 . . . . Saco
LG 633 . . . . Benton
LG 1085 . . . . Glenburn
LG 1159 . . . . Houlton
LG 1318 . . . . Caribou
SLG 32 . . . . Oxford

National Staff Organization
LU Staff Organization of the Maine Teachers Association . . . Augusta

Nurses
LU 1 Maine State Nurses Association . . . . Augusta
LU 116 Maine State Nurses Association . . . . Augusta
LU 124 Maine State Nurses Association . . . . Augusta
LU 188 Maine State Nurses Association . . . . Augusta
LU 210 Maine State . . . . Augusta
LU 296 Maine State Nurses Association . . . . Augusta
LU 384 Maine State Nurses Association . . . . Augusta
LU 911 Maine State Nurses . Augusta
LU 982 Maine State Nurses . Augusta
LU 1082 Maine State Nurses . . . . Augusta
LU 5050 Maine State . . . . Augusta
LU 7631 Aroostook Medical Center . . . . Augusta
SA Maine State Nurses Association . . . . Augusta

Office and Professional Employees
LU 192 . . . . Millinocket
LU 232 . . . . Madawaska
LU 295 . . . . Charlotte
LU 442 . . . . . . Livermore Falls
LU 555 . . . . Bucksport

Painters
LU 1468 . . . . Oakland
LU 1915 . . . . Springvale

Paper, Allied-Industrial, Chemical Employees
LU 01-9 . . . . Skowhegan
LU 01-11 . . . . Kents Hill
LU 01-12 . . . . Millinocket
LU 01-14 . . . . Jay
LU 01-24 . . . . Millinocket
LU 01-27 . . . . Calais
LU 01-36 . . . . Madison
LU 01-37 . . . . . East Millinocket
LU 01-80 . . . . Stillwater
LU 01-152 . . . . East Millinocket
LU 01-261 . . . . Bucksport
LU 01-291 . . . . Frenchville
LU 01-365 . . . . Grand Isle
LU 01-396 . . . . Lincoln
LU 01-403 . . . . Brewer
LU 01-449 . . . . Waterville
LU 01-900 . . . . Rumford
LU 01-1069 . . . . Westbrook
LU 01-1188 . . . . Bucksport
LU 01-1247 . . . . Frenchville
LU 01-1310 . . . . Ashland
LU 01-1363 . . . . Patten
LU 01-1367 . . . . Princeton
LU 01-1977 . . . . . . Madawaska

Plumbing and Pipe Fitting
LU 485 . . . . Millinocket
LU 716 . . . . Bangor

Postal Workers
LU 289 Biddeford . . . . Biddeford
LU 458 Portland . . . . Portland
LU 461 Augusta . . . . . . Augusta
LU 509 Lewiston . . . . . Lewiston

LU 536 Bangor . . . . Bangor
LU 1353 Farmington Local . . . . Farmington
LU 2767 Caribou Local . . . Caribou
LU 3185 Calais Local . . . . Calais
LU 3437 Gardiner . . . . Gardiner
LU 4910 Houlton . . . . . Houlton
LU 5435 Ellsworth Local . Ellsworth
LU 5622 Armand Rowe Area Local . . . . Auburn
LU 5729 Waterville Area . Waterville
LU 5947 Millinocket Local . . . . Millinocket
LU 5998 Presque Isle . . Presque Isle
LU 6484 Freeport Local . . Freeport
SA Maine . . . . . Cape Elizabeth

Rural Letter Carriers
LU Aroostook County . . . Houlton
LU Cumberland County . Westbrook
LU Hancock County . . . . Lamoine
LU Kennebec County . Farmingdale
LU Mid-Coast Association . Bowdoin
LU Oxford-Androscoggin-Franklin Counties . . . . Kingfield
LU Penobscott County . . . . Mild
LU Somerset County . . . Cambridge
LU Washington County . Harrington
LU York County . . . South Berwick
SA Maine . . . . . . Edgecomb

Security, Police and Fire Professionals
LU 501 . . . . Sanford
LU 549 . . . . Patten
LU 550 . . . . Waterville

Service Employees
LU . . . . Augusta
LU 247 Firemen & Oilers . . . . . . East Livermore
LU 398 Green Valley . . . . Patten
LU 1030 Firemen & Oilers . Gorham
LU 1989 B.A. Green Maine State Employees Association 697 . . . . Bangor
LU 1989 Maine State Employees Association . . . . Augusta

Teachers
LU 5059 Health Professionals, Lubec Federation of . . . . . . Lubec
LU 5073 Health Care Professionals, Downeast Federation of . Jonesport

Teamsters
LU 340 . . . . . . South Portland

Theatrical Stage Employees
LU 114 . . . . Portland
LU 926 . . . . Auburn

Transportation Communications Union
LG 6923 Kennebec . . . . Waterville

Transportation Union
GCA GO-57 Banger & Aroostook Railroad . . . . Millinocket
LU 663 . . . . Orrington
LU 752 . . . . Eddington
LU 856 . . . . Millinocket
LU 1400 . . . . . . South Portland
SLB LO-22 Maine . . . . West Paris

Treasury Employees
CH 7 . . . . South Portland
CH 141 . . . . St. David

Utility Workers
LU 341 . . . . Portland

LU 497 . . . . Wiscasset

Weather Service Employees
BR 01-24 . . . . Caribou
BR 01-37 . . . . Grey

Unaffiliated Labor Organizations

Consolidated Railway Supervisors Association . . . . Freeport

Independent Guards
  Association . . . . Bath
Plant Protection Quarantine Office
  Support Employees . . Winterport
S A P P I Council . . . . Skowhegan
Staff Organization of Maine State
  Employees Association . . Augusta

Maryland

AFL-CIO Trade and Industrial Departments

Building and Construction Trades Department
BCTC Baltimore . . . . . Baltimore
BCTC Maryland State & District of
Columbia . . . . Baltimore
BCTC Washington
DC . . . . Camp Springs
BCTC Western
Maryland . . . . . . Cumberland

Maritime Trades Department
PC Baltimore . . . . . . Baltimore

Metal Trades Department
MTC Baltimore Area. . . Curtis Bay
MTC East Coast . . . . . . Crofton

Affiliated Labor Organizations

Agricultural Employees
BR 6 . . . . Baltimore

Air Traffic Controllers
LU ABA . . . . Arnold
LU ADW . . . . Camp Springs
LU BWI . . . . Baltimore

Air Traffic Specialists
NHQ . . . . Wheaton

Asbestos Workers
LU 24 . . . . Laurel
LU 42 . . . . Elkton

Automobile, Aerospace Workers
C Community Action Program
Council . . . . Baltimore
C Maryland . . . . Baltimore
C South Central Pennsylvania CAP
Steering Committee. . . Baltimore
C Virginia State CAP . . . Baltimore
LU 66 . . . . Baltimore
LU 171 . . . . Hagerstown
LU 239 . . . . Baltimore
LU 738 . . . . Baltimore
LU 1247 . . . . Maugansville
LU 1338 . . . . . . Havre de Grace
LU 1590 . . . . Williamsport
LU 2212 . . . . Baltimore
LU 2301 . . . . Elkridge
LU 2372 . . . . Baltimore
LU 2388 . . . . Baltimore

Bakery, Confectionery, Tobacco Workers and Grain Millers
LU 68 . . . . Baltimore
NHQ . . . . Kensington

Boilermakers
LG 50-S . . . . Baltimore
LG 193 . . . . Baltimore
LG 533-D Cement
Workers . . . . . . Williamsport

Bricklayers
LU 1 Maryland Virginia & District of
Columbia . . . . . . Camp Springs

Carpenters
C Mid-Atlantic Regional . Forestville

LU 101 . . . . Baltimore
LU 132 . . . . Forestville
LU 340 . . . . Hagerstown
LU 974 . . . . Baltimore
LU 1024 . . . . Cumberland
LU 1145 . . . . Glen Burnie
LU 1354 . . . . Aberdeen
LU 1548 . . . . Baltimore
LU 1590 . . . . Harwood
LU 1694 . . . . . . Upper Marlboro
LU 2311 . . . . Huntington

Civilian Technicians
CH Chesapeake 122 . . . . . . Joppa
CH 125 Chesapeake Air. . Baltimore

Communications Workers
LU 2000 . . . . Silver Spring
LU 2100 . . . . Chase
LU 2101 . . . . Baltimore
LU 2105 . . . . Williamsport
LU 2106 . . . . Salisbury
LU 2107 . . . . Annapolis
LU 2108 . . . . Landover
LU 2109 . . . . Cumberland
LU 2150 . . . . Baltimore
LU 2390 . . . . Finksburg
LU 14201 . . . . . Upper Marlboro
LU 14203 . . . . Cumberland
LU 14620 St. Louis Mailers
Union . . . . Florissant
LU 32100 The Translators
Guild. . . . . Silver Spring
LU 52031 NABET Local
31 . . . . Silver Spring
STC Maryland . . . . . Annapolis

Electrical Workers
LU 24 . . . . Baltimore
LU 70 . . . . Forestville
LU 307 . . . . Cumberland
LU 362 . . . . Glen Burnie
LU 865 . . . . Glen Burnie
LU 870 . . . . Rawlings
LU 1200 . . . . . . Upper Marlboro
LU 1307 . . . . Delmar
LU 1383 . . . . Baltimore
LU 1501 . . . . Cockeysville
LU 1718 . . . . Chaptico
LU 1805 . . . . Glen Burnie
LU 1900 . . . . Largo

Electrical, Radio and Machine Workers
LU 120 . . . . Baltimore
LU 121 . . . . Baltimore

Electronic Workers
LU 75-FW . . . . Baltimore
LU 109 . . . . Baltimore
LU 130 . . . . Baltimore
LU 472-FW . . . . . . Hagerstown

Elevator Constructors
LU 7 . . . . Baltimore
LU 10 . . . . Suitland
NHQ . . . . Columbia

Federal Employees
LU 178 . Aberdeen Proving Grounds
LU 262 . . . . Silver Spring
LU 639 . . . . Baltimore
LU 1153 . . . . Cascade
LU 1658 . . . . Welcome
LU 1692 . . . . . . Havre de Grace

LU 1705 . . . . Temple Hills
LU 2058 . . . . Edgewood

Fire Fighters
LU 121-F . . . . Indian Head
LU 254-F U.S. Naval
Academy . . . . Annapolis
LU 267-F . . . . Perryville
LU 271-F National Institutes of
Health . . . . Walkersville
LU 297-F . . . . Suitland

Flint Glass Workers
LU 90 . . . . Baltimore

Food and Commercial Workers
C Mid-Atlantic Regional . Landover
LU 27 . . . . Baltimore
LU 34-D . . . . Baltimore
LU 217-C . . . . Baltimore
LU 261-C . . . . . . Cumberland
LU 266-T . . . . Elkton
LU 392 . . . . Baltimore
LU 400 . . . . Landover
LU 853-C . . . . Belcamp
LU 976-C . . . . Baltimore

Glass, Molders, Pottery and Plastics Workers
LU 19-B . . . . Baltimore
LU 113 . . . . Baltimore
LU 200 . . . . Baltimore
LU 218 . . . . Baltimore
LU 375 . . . . Rising Sun

Government Employees
C 143 Food Inspection Locals,
Midatlantic . . . . . . Salisbury
C 220 National SSA Field Operations
Local . . . . Towson
C 260 NARA . . . . . College Park
LU 331 VA . . . . . . Perry Point
LU 361 DoD . . . . Bethesda
LU 896 DoD . . . . . . Annapolis
LU 902 DoD . . . . Chesapeake City
LU 966 USDA . . . . . Manchester
LU 1041 DoD . . . . Gaithersburg
LU 1092 DoD . . . Upper Marlboro
LU 1401 . . . . Owings
LU 1603 DoD . . . Patuxent River
LU 1622 DoD. . . . . . . Odenton
LU 1923 HHS . . . . . . Baltimore
LU 1983 . . . . Emmitsburg
LU 2146 VA . . . . . Fort Howard
LU 2371 USCG . . . . . Baltimore
LU 2419 HHS . . . . . . Bethesda
LU 2422 USDA . . . . . Quantico
LU 2484 DoD . . . . . Frederick
LU 2578 GSA . . . . College Park
LU 2756 INS . . . . . . Salisbury
LU 2782 DoC . . . . . . Suitland
LU 3090 DoD . . . Mount Rainier
LU 3122 HUD . . . . St. Leonard
LU 3147 USDA . . . . . Beltsville
LU 3176 DoD . . . . . . Bel Air
LU 3302 HHS . . . . . Baltimore
LU 3331 EPA . . . Mount Rainier
LU 3407 DoD . . . . . Glen Echo
LU 3546 BOP, Headquarters Office
Staff . . . . Clinton
LU 3579 CPSC . . . . . Bethesda
LU 3614 EEOC . . . Davidsonville
LU 4010 . . . . Cumberland

Government Employees Association
LU 03-84 . Andrews Air Force Base
LU 03-112 . . . . Baltimore
LU 04-93 Arlington National
Cemetery . . . . Suitland
LU 04-102 . . . . Camp Springs

Government Security Officers
LU 98 . . . . Silver Spring

Graphic Communications
LU 1 . . . . Temple Hills
LU 4-B . . . . College Park
LU 31-N . . . . Baltimore
LU 61-C . . . . Baltimore
LU 72-C . . . . Riverdale
LU 98-L . . . . Boyds
LU 144-B . . . . Greenbelt
LU 481-S . . . . Baltimore
LU 582-M . . . . Baltimore
LU 754-S . . . . . . Hagerstown

Horseshoers
LU 7 . . . . Woodburne

Hotel and Restaurant Employees
LU 7 . . . . Baltimore

Industrial Workers United
NHQ . . . . Camp Springs

Iron Workers
LU 5 . . . . Upper Marlboro
LU 16 . . . . Baltimore
LU 568 . . . . Cumberland

Laborers
DC Baltimore County . . . . Towson
DC Washington DC &
Vicinity . . . . Camp Springs
LU 194 . . . . Baltimore
LU 481 . . . . Baltimore
LU 516 . . . . Baltimore
LU 616 . . . . Cumberland
LU 912 Material Yard & Residential
Construction . . . . . Baltimore
LU 1231 . . . . Towson
LU 1273 . . . . Towson
LU 1396 . . . . Rockville

Letter Carriers
BR 176 . . . . Baltimore
BR 638 . . . . Cumberland
BR 651 . . . . Annapolis
BR 664 . . . . Frederick
BR 902 . . . . Salisbury
BR 1050 . . . . . East New Market
BR 1052 Easton, Maryland . . Easton
BR 1718 Crisfield,
Maryland . . . . . . Crisfield
BR 1749 Havre de Grace,
Maryland . . . . Havre de Grace
BR 1869 Chestertown,
Maryland . . . . . Chestertown
BR 2069 Elkton, Maryland . . Elkton
BR 2611 . . . . Woodbine
BR 2820 Federalsburg,
Maryland . . . . . Federalsburg
BR 2961 . . . Mount Lake Park
BR 3325 Snow Hill,
Maryland . . . . . . Snow Hill
BR 3338 Denton, Maryland . Denton
BR 3755 . . . . Laurel
BR 3825 . . . . Rockville

BR 3939 . . . . Gaithersburg
BR 4266 . . . . Kensington
BR 4422 . . . . Glen Burnie
BR 4444 Indian Head,
    Maryland . . . . Indian Head
BR 5203 Hancock,
    Maryland . . . . Hancock
BR 5394 Centreville,
    Maryland . . . . Centreville
BR 6076 North East,
    Maryland . . . . North East
BR 6079 Lexington Park,
    Maryland . . . . . Lexington Park
BR 6080 Patuxent River,
    Maryland . . . . . Patuxent River
BR 6273 Damascus,
    Maryland . . . . Damascus
BR 6545 . . . . . . Upper Marlboro
SA Maryland-District of
    Columbia . . . . . . Cumberland

Locomotive Engineers
DIV 97 . . . . Ellicott City
DIV 181 . . . . Brunswick
DIV 482 . . . . . . Charlotte Hall
DIV 934 . . . . . . Mount Savage

Longshoremen
DC Baltimore . . . . . . Baltimore
LU 333 . . . . Baltimore
LU 921 . . . . Baltimore
LU 953 . . . . Baltimore
LU 1429 . . . . Baltimore
LU 2004 . . . . Baltimore
LU 2066 . . . . Baltimore

Machinists
DLG 12 . . . . Baltimore
LG 33-S . . . . Baltimore
LG 43-S . . . . Baltimore
LG 186 . . . . Baltimore
LG 193 . . . . Waldorf
LG 212 . . . . Cumberland
LG 486 . . . . Perry Hall
LG 605 . . . . Baltimore
LG 846 . . . . Baltimore
LG 1299 . . . . Silver Spring
LG 1561 . . . . Baltimore
LG 1784 . . . . Baltimore
LG 2135 . . . . Lanham
LG 2424 . . . . Aberdeen
LG 2795 . . . . Salisbury
NHQ . . . . Upper Marlboro

Maintenance of Way Employes
LG 3041 . . . . Owings Mills
SLG 695 . . . . Baltimore
SLG 711 . . . . Hagerstown
SLG 993 . . . . Brunswick
SLG 1028 . . . . . . Bloomington
SLG 3005 . . . . . . Rising Sun
SLG 3028 . . . . . . Brentwood
SLG 3075 . . . . Baltimore

Masters, Mates and Pilots
NHQ . . . . Linthicum

Musicians
LU 40-543 . . . . Baltimore
LU 770 . . . . Hagerstown

National Staff Organization
ASSN Tabco Staff Association
    . . . . Towson
LU Staff Organization, Maryland
    State Teachers
    Association . . . . . . Annapolis

Needletrades
JB Baltimore Regional . . Baltimore
JB Mid Atlantic
    Regional . . . . . . Gaithersburg
LU 4-I . . . . Gaithersburg
LU 9 . . . . Gaithersburg
LU 14-R . . . . Baltimore
LU 15 . . . . Baltimore
LU 35 . . . . Gaithersburg
LU 50-7 . . . . Gaithersburg
LU 50-8 . . . . Gaithersburg
LU 50-9 . . . . Gaithersburg
LU 51 . . . . Baltimore
LU 70 . . . . Baltimore
LU 86 . . . . Gaithersburg
LU 106 . . . . Gaithersburg
LU 118-C . . . . . . Gaithersburg
LU 128-C . . . . . . Gaithersburg
LU 131 . . . . Gaithersburg
LU 131-A . . . . . . Gaithersburg
LU 132 . . . . Gaithersburg
LU 133-A . . . . . . Gaithersburg
LU 133-H . . . . . . Gaithersburg
LU 137 . . . . Gaithersburg
LU 138-C . . . . . . Gaithersburg
LU 188-A . . . . . . Baltimore
LU 208-C . . . . . . Baltimore
LU 224 . . . . Gaithersburg
LU 239-I . . . . Gaithersburg
LU 262 . . . . Frederick
LU 317-C . . . . . . Gaithersburg
LU 393-C . . . . . . Gaithersburg
LU 402 . . . . Gaithersburg
LU 402-C . . . . . . Baltimore
LU 420 . . . . Baltimore
LU 426-A . . . . . . Baltimore
LU 427-A . . . . . . Baltimore
LU 429 . . . . Gaithersburg
LU 464 . . . . Gaithersburg
LU 472 . . . . Gaithersburg
LU 528-A . . . . . . Gaithersburg
LU 584-A . . . . . . Gaithersburg
LU 604-A . . . . . . Baltimore
LU 622-A . . . . . . Gaithersburg
LU 658-T . . . . . . Gaithersburg
LU 673-A . . . . . . Gaithersburg
LU 713-A . . . . . . Gaithersburg
LU 730-T . . . . . . Gaithersburg
LU 744-A . . . . . . Baltimore
LU 745-A . . . . . . Baltimore
LU 747-A . . . . . . Gaithersburg
LU 806-A . . . . . . Baltimore
LU 844-T . . . . . . Gaithersburg
LU 879-A . . . . . . Gaithersburg
LU 976-C . . . . . . Gaithersburg
LU 998-T . . . . . . Gaithersburg
LU 1044 . . . . Gaithersburg
LU 1049 . . . . Gaithersburg
LU 1099 . . . . Gaithersburg
LU 1118 . . . . Gaithersburg
LU 1335 . . . . Gaithersburg
LU 1436 . . . . Gaithersburg
LU 1493 . . . . Gaithersburg
LU 1566 . . . . Gaithersburg
LU 1598 . . . . Gaithersburg
LU 1607 . . . . Gaithersburg
LU 1645 . . . . Gaithersburg
LU 1678 . . . . Gaithersburg
LU 1701 . . . . Gaithersburg
LU 1706 . . . . Gaithersburg
LU 1710 . . . . Gaithersburg
LU 1739 . . . . Gaithersburg
LU 1785 . . . . Gaithersburg
LU 1808 . . . . Gaithersburg
LU 1853-T . . . . . . Gaithersburg
LU 1934 . . . . Gaithersburg
LU 2247 . . . . Gaithersburg
LU 2278 . . . . Baltimore

LU 2326 . . . . Gaithersburg
LU 2331 . . . . Gaithersburg
LU 2475 . . . . Gaithersburg
LU 2567 . . . . Gaithersburg

NLRB Professional Association
LU 5 . . . . Baltimore

Office and Professional Employees
LU 2 . . . . Silver Spring

Operating Engineers
LU 37 . . . . Baltimore
LU 77 . . . . Suitland

Painters
CONF Eastern Region . . . Suitland
DC 51 . . . . Suitland
LU 1 . . . . Baltimore
LU 368 . . . . Suitland
LU 963 . . . . Suitland
LU 1773 Montgomery County
    Local . . . . St. Leonard
LU 1937 . . . . . . Upper Marlboro

Paper, Allied-Industrial, Chemical Employees
LU 744 . . . . Dundalk
LU 02-20 . . . . Baltimore
LU 02-31 . . . . Frederick
LU 02-33 . . . . . . Hagerstown
LU 02-111 . . . . . . Baltimore
LU 02-388 . . . . . . Thurmont
LU 02-482 . . . . . . Thurmont
LU 02-652 . . . . . . Baltimore
LU 02-676 . . . . . . Westernport
LU 02-741 . . . . . . Freeland
LU 02-743 . . . . . . Elkton
LU 02-798 . . . . . . Baltimore
LU 02-822 . . . . . . Baltimore
LU 02-1038 . . . . . Baltimore
LU 02-1165 . . . . . Baltimore

Plasterers and Cement Masons
NHQ . . . . Laurel

Plate Printers, Die Stampers and Engravers
LU 2 . . . . Baltimore
LU 24 Electrolytic Plate Makers
    Washington DC . . . . . Frederick

Plumbing and Pipe Fitting
C Multistate Pipe
    Trades . . . . . . Camp Springs
LU 5 . . . . Camp Springs
LU 486 . . . . Baltimore
LU 489 . . . . Cumberland
LU 536 . . . . Baltimore
LU 669 . . . . Columbia
SA Maryland Pipe
    Trades . . . . . . Camp Springs

Postal and Federal Employees
LU 202 . . . . Baltimore

Postal Workers
LU 181 Baltimore Francis 'Stu
    Filbey' Area . . . . . . Baltimore
LU 512 Southwest Maryland Bay
    Area . . . . Cockeysville
LU 513 Cumberland . . Cumberland
LU 2315 Frederick . . . . Frederick
LU 2574 Hagerstown . . Hagerstown
LU 3630 Silver Spring . Gaithersburg
LU 4321 Salisbury . . . . Salisbury
LU 5744 Patuxent
    River . . . . Patuxent River

LU 5932 Lexington Park
    Local . . . . . . Lexington Park
LU 6743 Germantown . Germantown
SA Maryland-District of
    Columbia . . . . . Capitol Heights

Professional and Technical Engineers
LU 29 Goddard Scientists . Greenbelt
NHQ . . . . Silver Spring

Railroad Signalmen
LLG 31 . . . . Cresaptown
LLG 48 . . . . Rising Sun
LLG 65 . . . . Baltimore
LLG 114 . . . . Ellicott City

Rural Letter Carriers
LU Allegany-Garrett
    Counties . . . . Oakland
LU Delaware-Maryland-Virginia
    Association . . . . Berlin
LU Macon County . . . . . Callao
LU Mid-Shore Group . . Centreville
LU Mid-State Group . . Jarrettsville
LU Southern Maryland County
    Association . . . . Laurel
LU Tri-County . . . . . Hagerstown
LU 35 Putnam-Sullivan
    Counties . . . . Mercer
SA Maryland . . . . . Windsor Mill

Seafarers
ASSN Professional Security
    Officers . . . . Camp Springs
D Atlantic Gulf Lakes & Inland
    Waters . . . . . . Camp Springs
LU Entertainment & Allied Trades
    Union . . . . Camp Springs
LU Seafarers Maritime
    Union . . . . Camp Springs
NHQ . . . . Camp Springs

Security Officers, Police and Guards
LU 1852 . . . . Baltimore

Security, Police and Fire Professionals
LU . . . . Fort Washington
LU 120 . . . . Hagerstown
LU 270 . . . . Baltimore
LU 275 . . . . Waldorf

Service Employees
JC 54 . . . . Gaithersburg
LU 63 Firemen & Oilers . . Landover
LU 439 Firemen &
    Oilers . . . . Cumberland
LU 1199 NUHHCE, Maryland-DC
    Health Care Workers . . Baltimore
LU 1998 PSNA of
    Maryland . . . . Columbia

Sheet Metal Workers
LU 100 . . . . Suitland

State, County and Municipal Employees
C 67 Maryland . . . . . Baltimore
C 92 Maryland State
    Employees . . . . . . Baltimore
LU 1104 . . . . Baltimore
LU 2751 . . . . Baltimore
LU 3374 John's Hopkins Bay View
    Medical Center . . . . Baltimore

Steelworkers

LU. . . . . Baltimore
LU 649 . . . . Baltimore
LU 13128 . . . . Annapolis Junction
LU 08-581-L . . . . Baltimore
LU 08-679-L . . . . . Glen Burnie
LU 08-2609-S . . . . . . Baltimore
LU 08-2610-S . . . . . . Baltimore
LU 08-2819-S . . . . . . Baltimore
LU 08-4727-S . . . . Joppa
LU 08-5054-S . . . . . . Dundalk
LU 08-5861-S . . . . . . Baltimore
LU 08-6221-S . . . . . . Baltimore
LU 08-6759-S . . . . . . Baltimore
LU 08-6967-S . . . . . . Baltimore
LU 08-7212-S . . . . . Fruitland
LU 08-7886-S . . . . . Hagerstown
LU 08-8034-S . . . . . . Dundalk
LU 08-8094-S . . . . Arnold
LU 08-8678-S . . . . . Cambridge
LU 08-9016-S . . . . . . Baltimore
LU 08-9084-S . . . . . Edgewood
LU 08-9116-S . . . . . . Baltimore
LU 08-9386-S . . . . . Hagerstown
LU 08-12200-S . . . . . Baltimore
LU 08-12328-S . . . . . Hyattsville
LU 08-12517-S . . . . . Baltimore
LU 08-12978-S . . . . . Baltimore
LU 08-12993-S . . . . . Baltimore
LU 08-14019-S . . . . . Baltimore
LU 08-14600-S . . . . . Rising Sun
LU 08-14638-S . . . . . Frostburg
LU 08-15338-S . . . . Middle River

Teamsters

JC 62 . . . . Baltimore
LU 311 . . . . Baltimore
LU 355 . . . . Baltimore
LU 453 . . . . Cumberland
LU 557 . . . . Baltimore
LU 570 . . . . Baltimore

LU 888 Baltimore Mailers
Union . . . . Baltimore
LU 992 . . . . Hagerstown

Television and Radio Artists

LU Washington . . . . . Bethesda

Theatrical Stage Employees

LU 19 . . . . Baltimore
LU 22 . . . . Silver Spring
LU 181 . . . . Baltimore
LU 487 Mid Atlantic Studio
Mechanic . . . . Baltimore
LU 591 . . . . Damascus
LU 772 . . . . Cheverly
LU 833 . . . . Baltimore
LU 913 . . . . Catonsville

Transit Union

JC Del-Mar-Va . . . . . Forestville
LU 1708 . . . . Forestville

Transport Workers

LU 2025 . . . . Baltimore

Transportation Communications Union

D 511 . . . . Catonsville
D 514 Conrail . . . . . . Pasadena
D 570 . . . . Capitol Heights
D 2512 . . . . Baltimore
LG 5058 Washington Terminal
Company . . . . . . Ellicott City
LG 5092 Amtrak . . . . . Fallston
LG 6195 Silver Star . . . . Baltimore
LG 6656 Maryland . . . Cumberland
NHQ . . . . Rockville
SBA 250 Amtrak . . . . Rockville

Transportation Union

LU 454 . . . . Aberdeen

LU 600 . . . . Frostburg
LU 610 . . . . Baltimore
LU 631 . . . . Knoxville
LU 1470 . . . . Baltimore
LU 1591 . . . . Essex
LU 1881 . . . . Hanover
LU 1949 . . . . Baltimore
SLB LO-23 Maryland . . . Frostburg

Treasury Employees

CH 62 . . . . Baltimore
CH 132 . . . . Baltimore
CH 202 . . . . Hyattsville
CH 228 . . . . Germantown
CH 282 . . . . Bethesda
CH 287 . . . . Hyattsville

Utility Workers

LU 102-Q Frederick . . . . Jefferosn
LU 102-R Cumberland,
Oakland . . . . Oakland
LU 102-S . . . . Hagerstown
LU 459 . . . . Port Deposit
LU 584 . . . . . Havre de Grace

Weather Service Employees

BR 01-73 . . . . Suitland
BR 01-76 . . . . . . Silver Spring
BR 01-77 . . . . . . Silver Spring
BR 08-2 . . . . Silver Spring
BR 08-3 . . . . Silver Spring
BR 08-4 . . . . Silver Spring
BR 08-5 . . . . Silver Spring

Westinghouse Salaried Employees

ASSN Baltimore Division . Hanover

Unaffiliated Labor Organizations

Aluminum Racing Plate Workers
Union . . . . Baltimore
Broadcast Employees Staff
Team . . . . Gaithersburg
Certified Registered Nurses
Anesthetists-Washington Hospital
Center . . . . Burtonsville
Certified Registered Nurses
Association of Fairfax
(CRNA) . . . . Bethesda
Exxon Employees Association of
Pennsylvania . . . . Elkton
Faculty Association of the French
International School . . Bethesda
French International School of
Washington Association of
Administration &
Maintenance . . . . . Bethesda
German School-Washington DC
Employees Association . Potomac
I A M Representatives Association
Independent . . . . Owings
Maryland Professional Staff
Association Staff Organization,
Professional, Maryland
Sta . . . . Annapolis
National Association of Basketball
Referees . . . . Severn
National Postal Professional
Nurses . . . . Temple Hills
Petroleum Transport
Workers . . . . Severn
Registered Nurses & Physical
Therapists-Group Health
Association Inc. . . . . . Landover
Staff Union Independent,
Communications Workers
of America
AFL-CIO . . . Washington Grove
United Union of Security
Guards . . . . Baltimore

Massachusetts

AFL-CIO Trade and Industrial Departments

Building and Construction Trades Department

BCTC Boston . . . . Boston
BCTC Brockton . . . . . Lakeville
BCTC Framingham-
 Newton. . . . . Dorchester
BCTC Merrimack Valley . . Lowell
BCTC North Shore . . . . Danvers
BCTC Pioneer Valley . Northampton
BCTC Quincy-South Shore-
 Norfolk . . . . Quincy
BCTC Southeast
 Massachusetts. . . . . Fairhaven
BCTC Worcester . . . . Worcester

Maritime Trades Department

PC Boston-New England
 Area . . . . Gloucester

Other Councils and Committees

C Lawrence Printing
 Trades . . . . Bradford

Affiliated Labor Organizations

Air Traffic Controllers

LU A90 . . . . East Boston
LU ACK . . . . Nantucket
LU BED. . . . . Bedford
LU BOS . . . . Boston
LU K90 . . . . . . Otis Air National
 Guard Base
LU NATCA Engineers. . Burlington
LU NE/HYA . . . . Dennis

Aircraft Mechanics

LU 2. . . . . East Boston

Asbestos Workers

LU 6 . . . . Boston

Automobile, Aerospace Workers

LU 168 . . . . Mattapoisett
LU 422 . . . . Framingham
LU 470. . . . . Avon
LU 899 Fairhaven-New Bedford
 Local. . . . . Acushnet
LU 1596. . . . . Dedham
LU 2322 . . . . Northampton
LU 2324 . . . . Boston

Bakery, Confectionery, Tobacco Workers and Grain Millers

LU 45 . . . . Stoughton
LU 348 . . . . Framingham

Boilermakers

LG 29 . . . . North Quincy
LG 132-D Cement Workers . Dalton
LG 651 . . . . Cambridge
LG 698. . . . . Leominster
LG 725. . . . . Ludlow
LG 748. . . . . Oxford
LG 1570 . . . . Feeding Hills
LG 1851 . . . . Chicopee

Bricklayers

LU 1 Massachusetts . . . Springfield
LU 3 Eastern
 Massachusetts . . . . Charlestown

Carpenters

C New England Regional . . Boston
LU 26 . . . . Wilmington
LU 33. . . . . Boston
LU 40 . . . . Cambridge
LU 51. . . . . Dorchester
LU 56. . . . . Boston
LU 67. . . . . Dorchester
LU 107 . . . . Worcester
LU 108 . . . . Springfield
LU 111 . . . . Methuen
LU 218 . . . . Medford
LU 275. . . . . Newton
LU 424. . . . . Randolph
LU 475 . . . . Ashland
LU 535. . . . . Randolph
LU 624. . . . . Randolph
LU 723 . . . . Boston
LU 1121 . . . . Allston
LU 1305 . . . . Fall River
LU 2168 . . . . Dorchester

Catholic School Teachers

LU Boston Archdiocesan Teachers
 Association . . . . . Watertown

Civilian Technicians

CH 39 Western
 Massachusetts. . . . . Westfield

Communications Workers

LU 217 . . . . Ayer
LU 221 . . . . . East Longmeadow
LU 254 . . . . Pittsfield
LU 257 . . . . Saugus
LU 259 IUE . . . . Taunton
LU 261 . . . . Lynn
LU 1051 . . . . Fairhaven
LU 1301 . . . . Cambridge
LU 1302 . . . . Lynn
LU 1365 . . . . . . North Andover
LU 1370 . . . . Clinton
LU 1371 . . . . Dorchester
LU 1395. . . . . Fayville
LU 14117 ITU LU 13 . South Boston
LU 14119 . . . . Fall River
LU 14122 Lawrence Typographical
 Union. . . . . Methuen
LU 14123 . . . . Chelmsford
LU 14125 . . . . Fairhaven
LU 14127 . . . . Chicopee
LU 14128 . . . . . . Mattapoisett
LU 14173 . . . . Somerset
LU 31027 . . . . Whitman
LU 31032. . . . . Boston
LU 31055. . . . . Lynn
LU 31245. . . . . Boston
LU 51018 . . . . . . Swampscott
LU 51019 . . . . Chicopee
LU 81154 . . . . Gardner
LU 81200 . . . . . . North Adams
LU 81201. . . . . Lynn
LU 81204 . . . . Dracut
LU 81211 . . . . Springfield
LU 81214 . . . . Marblehead
LU 81225. . . . . Pittsfield
LU 81228 Moore Drop Forging
 Employees. . . . . . Ludlow
LU 81231 . . . . . . North Adams
LU 81232. . . . . Boston
LU 81250 . . . . Warren
LU 81251 . . . . Wilmington
LU 81255. . . . . Pittsfield
LU 81263. . . . . Saugus
LU 81274. . . . . Waltham

LU 81284 . . . . Chicopee
LU 81288 . . . . . . Indian Orchard
LU 81298 . . . . East Boston

Education

LU Endicott College Faculty
 Association . . . . Beverly
LU Laboure College Staff
 Association. . . . . . . Boston

Electrical Workers

C TCC-1 National Bell
 Coordinating . . . . North Quincy
LU 7 . . . . Springfield
LU 96 . . . . Worcester
LU 103 . . . . Boston
LU 104 . . . . Walpole
LU 123 . . . . Belmont
LU 223 . . . . Lakeville
LU 326 . . . . Lawrence
LU 455 . . . . Hadley
LU 486 . . . . Worcester
LU 674 . . . . Melrose
LU 791 . . . . Somerville
LU 1014 . . . . Medford
LU 1228 . . . . Newton Highlands
LU 1386 . . . . Newburyport
LU 1465 . . . . Fall River
LU 1499 . . . . Fall River
LU 1505 . . . . Worburn
LU 2222 . . . . Quincy
LU 2313 . . . . Hanover
LU 2321 . . . . . . North Andover
LU 2322 . . . . . . Middleborough
LU 2324 . . . . Springfield
LU 2325. . . . . Northborough

Electrical, Radio and Machine Workers

DC 2. . . . . Taunton
LU 204 . . . . Taunton
LU 223 . . . . Taunton
LU 226 . . . . Taunton
LU 240 Looseleaf Book Binder
 Workers Union . . . . Somerset
LU 248 . . . . Mattapoisett
LU 259 . . . . Holyoke
LU 262. . . . . . . South Boston
LU 264 . . . . Holyoke
LU 269 . . . . Athol
LU 270 . . . . Holyoke
LU 271 . . . . . . South Hamilton
LU 274 . . . . Greenfield
LU 279 . . . . Salem

Electronic Workers

LU 206. . . . . Chicopee
LU 216 . . . . Hyannis

Elevator Constructors

LU 4 . . . . Allston
LU 41 . . . . Sterling

Federal Employees

LU 1164 . . . . Concord
LU 1384 . . . . New Bedford
LU 1884 . . . . Boston

Fire Fighters

LU 264-F Otis Air National
 Guard. . . . . East Falmouth

Flint Glass Workers

LU 94 . . . . Milford

Food and Commercial Workers

LU 8-D . . . . Boston
LU 36-I Professional Division
 Insurance. . . . West Hyannisport
LU 138 . . . . Canton
LU 414-C . . . . Belchertown
LU 791 Warehouse Employees
 Union. . . . . West Bridgewater
LU 1445. . . . . Dedham
LU 1459 . . . . Springfield

Glass, Molders, Pottery and Plastics Workers

LU 95 . . . . Westfield
LU 169. . . . . Milford
LU 190. . . . . Salisbury
LU 317 . . . . Billerica
LU 399 . . . . Hanover

Government Employees

LU 38 U.S.I.N.S. . . . . East Boston
LU 221 Boston VA Medical
 Center . . . . Boston
LU 829 USDA. . . . . Beverly
LU 948 DoL . . . . . Swampscott
LU 1164 HHS . . . . Brewster
LU 1900 DoD . . . . . Roslindale
LU 1906 DoD . . . . Norton
LU 2073 SBA . . . . Boston
LU 2143 VA . . . . Mattapan
LU 2264 GSA . . . . Boston
LU 2363 DoD. . . . . . . Natick
LU 2682 DoD . . . . Buzzards Bay
LU 2772 VA . . . . Boston
LU 3004 DoD . . . Otis Air National
 Guard Base
LU 3033 USDA . . . . . . Holden
LU 3258 HUD . . . . Boston
LU 3428 EPA . . . . Boston
LU 3707 DoD . . . . Chicopee
LU 3760 HHS . . . . Boston
LU 3789 DoI . . . . South Wellfleet
LU 3830 DoD . . . . Pittsfield
LU 3893 DE . . . . Boston

Government Employees Association

LU 1 EMT & Paramedics . . Quincy
LU 34 . . . . Natick
LU 86. . . . . . . West Roxbury
LU 132 . . . . Stoneham
LU 184 . . . . Quincy
LU 195 . . . . Cambridge
LU 235 . . . . Quincy
LU 556 Police Officers . Springfield
LU 01-4 . . . . Devens
LU 01-8 . . . . Bedford
LU 01-9. . . . . Brockton
LU 01-25 . . . . Brockton
LU 01-32 . . . . Woburn
LU 01-54 . . . . Otis Air National
 Guard Base
LU 01-110 . . . . Malden
LU 01-127 . . . . Bourne
LU 01-187 . . . . Brockton
LU 01-210 . . . . Boston
LU 01-211 . . . . Newton
LU 01-274 . . . . Leeds
LU 01-529 . . . . Boston
LU LU-347 IBPO Boston University
 Police Patrolman. . . . Boston
LU O1-112 General Electric
 Company. . . . . Lynn
LU R1-107 . . . . Shelburne Falls
NHQ . . . . Quincy

Government Security Officers
LU 15 . . . . Cheshire

Graphic Communications
CONF North American
   Newspaper . . . . Quincy
LU 3-N . . . . Quincy
LU 67-C . . . . Quincy
LU 264-M Springfield-Hartford
   Local . . . . Springfield
LU 600-M . . . . Revere

Horseshoers
LU 9 . . . . Boston
LU 15 . . . . East Boston

Hotel and Restaurant Employees
LU 26 . . . . Boston
LU 29 . . . . Lowell

Iron Workers
DC New England
   States . . . . South Boston
LU 7 . . . . South Boston
LU 57 . . . . Worcester
LU 357 . . . . Chicopee Falls
LU 501 . . . . Braintree

Laborers
DC Massachusetts . . . . Hopkinton
LU 14 . . . . Salem
LU 22 . . . . Malden
LU 39 . . . . Fitchburg
LU 88 Compressed Air
   Workers . . . . Quincy
LU 133 . . . . Quincy
LU 138 . . . . Norwood
LU 151 . . . . Cambridge
LU 175 . . . . Lawrence
LU 223 . . . . Dorchester
LU 243 . . . . Auburn
LU 290 . . . . Lynn
LU 367 . . . . Scituate
LU 380 . . . . Cambridge
LU 381 . . . . Arlington
LU 385 . . . . Fairhaven
LU 429 . . . . Lowell
LU 473 . . . . Pittsfield
LU 560 . . . . Waltham
LU 596 . . . . Holyoke
LU 609 . . . . Framingham
LU 610 . . . . Fall River
LU 721 . . . . . East Bridgewater
LU 876 . . . . Taunton
LU 999 . . . . . East Longmeadow
LU 1144 . . . . Taunton
LU 1162 . . . . Brockton
LU 1249 . . . . Falmouth
LU 1285 . . . . Beverly
LU 1421 Building Wreckers . Boston

Letter Carriers
BR 7 . . . . Lynn
BR 12 . . . . Worcester
BR 18 . . . . New Bedford
BR 25 . . . . Tewksbury
BR 33 . . . . Beverly
BR 34 . . . . South Boston
BR 46 . . . . Springfield
BR 51 . . . . Fall River
BR 64 . . . . Northampton
BR 71 . . . . Taunton
BR 152 . . . . Manchester
BR 156 . . . . . . Middleborough
BR 212 . . . . Lawrence
BR 286 . . . . Pittsfield
BR 308 . . . . Milford
BR 334 . . . . Framingham

BR 362 . . . . Natick
BR 539 . . . . . North Attleboro
BR 742 . . . . Norwood
BR 747 . . . . Gardner
BR 764 . . . . Dedham
BR 1614 Turners Falls,
   Massachusetts . . . Turners Falls
BR 1661 Nantucket,
   Massachusetts . . . . Nantucket
BR 1708 . . . . Fairhaven
BR 1798 Shelburne Falls,
   Massachusetts . . . Shelburne Falls
BR 1800 . . . . Walpole
BR 1978 . . . . . West Springfield
BR 2124 Ayer, Massachusetts . Ayer
BR 2512 . . . . Bridgewater
BR 3240 Merrimac,
   Massachusetts . . . . . Merrimac
BR 4497 East Walpole,
   Massachusetts . . . East Walpole
BR 5525 . . . . Seekonk
SA Massachusetts . . . . Brockton

Locomotive Engineers
DIV 57 . . . . Northfield
DIV 63 . . . . . West Springfield
DIV 112 . . . . Greenfield
DIV 312 . . . . . East Weymouth
DIV 439 . . . . Blackstone
SLB Massachusetts . . . . Northfield

Longshoremen
DC New England Dock &
   Marine . . . . Braintree
LU 799 . . . . . Charlestown
LU 800 . . . . Wrentham
LU 805 . . . . Hanover
LU 809 . . . . Boston
LU 1066 . . . . Raynham
LU 1413 . . . . . New Bedford
LU 1572-2 . . . . Malden
LU 1604 . . . . Stoneham
LU 1749 . . . . . New Bedford
LU 1908 . . . . Everett

Machinists
DLG 38 . . . . Quincy
LG 25-S . . . . Winthrop
LG 264 . . . . Quincy
LG 318 . . . . Westford
LG 481 . . . . Erving
LG 1271 . . . . . South Lawrence
LG 1376 . . . . Fitchburg
LG 1420 . . . . Chicopee
LG 1451 . . . . Halifax
LG 1726 . . . . . . East Boston
LG 1803 . . . . . Lake Pleasant
LG 1836 . . . . Billerica
LG 1973 . . . . . Framingham
LG 2175 . . . . . Northampton
LG 2654 . . . . . . Gloucester
STC Massachusetts . . . . . Norton

Maintenance of Way Employes
LG 160 . . . . Phillipston
LG 347 . . . . Greenfield
LG 987 . . . . Danvers
SF Northeastern . . . . Mansfield
SLG 201 . . . . Beverly
SLG 612 . . . . Granby

Musicians
CONF New England . . . Taunton
LU 9-535 . . . . Belmont
LU 126 . . . . Salem
LU 138 . . . . Holbrook
LU 143 . . . . Worcester
LU 171 . . . . Springfield

LU 173 . . . . Lunenburg
LU 216 . . . . Fall River
LU 231 . . . . Taunton
LU 281 . . . . Kingston
LU 302 . . . . Haverhill
LU 393 Framingham-
   Marlboro . . . . Maynard

National Staff Organization
LU Field Services
   Organization . . . . Auburn
LU Staff Association, Massachusetts
   Teachers Association . . . Boston
LU Teacher Attorneys,
   Massachusetts Association
   of . . . . Boston

Needletrades
JB New England . . . . . . Boston
LU 1 . . . . North Dartmouth
LU 12 . . . . Boston
LU 12-ASW . . . . North Dartmouth
LU 24 . . . . Boston
LU 33-I . . . . Boston
LU 73-I . . . . Boston
LU 75 . . . . Boston
LU 80-I . . . . Boston
LU 141 . . . . Boston
LU 151-I . . . . Boston
LU 164 . . . . Boston
LU 177 . . . . . . North Dartmouth
LU 178 . . . . Boston
LU 187-A . . . . . North Dartmouth
LU 223 . . . . Boston
LU 226 . . . . Boston
LU 229 . . . . Taunton
LU 242 . . . . Boston
LU 257 . . . . Boston
LU 281 . . . . Boston
LU 301 . . . . Boston
LU 305-T . . . . . North Dartmouth
LU 311 . . . . Boston
LU 313 . . . . Boston
LU 324 . . . . Boston
LU 341 . . . . Boston
LU 359-I . . . . Boston
LU 361 . . . . Boston
LU 371-C . . . . . North Dartmouth
LU 377-C . . . . . North Dartmouth
LU 406-A . . . . . North Dartmouth
LU 438 . . . . . . North Dartmouth
LU 484-I . . . . Boston
LU 486-C . . . . . North Dartmouth
LU 513 . . . . Boston
LU 533-I . . . . Boston
LU 554-I . . . . Boston
LU 580 . . . . Boston
LU 616-T . . . . . North Dartmouth
LU 624 . . . . Boston
LU 667 . . . . . . North Dartmouth
LU 911 . . . . . . North Dartmouth
LU 1856 . . . . . North Dartmouth
LU 1999 . . . . Boston
LU 2001 . . . . Boston
LU 2370-T . . . . North Dartmouth
LU 2624 . . . . . North Dartmouth
LU 2661 . . . . . North Dartmouth

NLRB Professional Association
LU 1 . . . . Boston

Nurses
D 2 Massachusetts Nurses
   Association . . . . Webster
D 3 Massachusetts . . . . Mashpee
D 4 Massachusetts . . . . Gloucester
D 5 Massachusetts . . . . Norwood

SA Massachusetts Nurses
   Association . . . . Canton

Office and Professional Employees
LU . . . . South Boston
LU 6 . . . . Quincy
LU 1021 . . . . Peabody
LU 1295 . . . . Woburn

Operating Engineers
LU 4 . . . . Roslindale
LU 98 . . . . . East Longmeadow
LU 877 . . . . Norwood

Painters
DC 35 . . . . Roslindale
LU 48 . . . . Worcester
LU 257 . . . . Springfield
LU 258 . . . . Randolph
LU 391 . . . . Roslindale
LU 402 . . . . East Boston
LU 577 . . . . Randolph
LU 691 . . . . New Bedford
LU 939 . . . . Dorchester
LU 1138 . . . . Dorchester
LU 1280 . . . . Revere
LU 1333 . . . . . North Dartmouth

Paper, Allied-Industrial, Chemical
Employees
LU 01-3 . . . . Lawrence
LU 01-78 . . . . Lee
LU 01-197 . . . . West Springfield
LU 01-204 . . . . Bradford
LU 01-366 . . . . Waltham
LU 01-383 . . . . Chicopee
LU 01-434 . . . . . Baldwinville
LU 01-453 . . . . Attleboro
LU 01-513 . . . . . . Springfield
LU 01-516 . . . . . Framingham
LU 01-521 . . . . East Templrton
LU 01-534 . . . . Ashby
LU 01-579 . . . . . Longmeadow
LU 01-594 . . . . Orange
LU 01-599 . . . . . . Norwood
LU 01-651 . . . . North Andover
LU 01-708 . . . . Ware
LU 01-818 . . . . Gardner
LU 01-836 . . . . . . Worcester
LU 01-837 . . . . Lynn
LU 01-880 . . . . Groton
LU 01-916 . . . . Quincy
LU 01-917 . . . . . Leominster
LU 01-992 . . . . . . Methuen
LU 01-995 . . . . . . Medford
LU 01-1102 . . . . . Westminster
LU 01-1360 . . . . . . Fitchburg
LU 01-1395 . . . . . . Chicopee
LU 01-1409 . . . . South Boston
LU 01-1487 . . . . South Hadley
LU 01-1584 . . . . . Housatonic
LU 01-1702 . . . . Marlborough
LU 01-1772 . . . . Lowell
LU 01-1832 . . . . North Adams
LU 01-1847 . . . . . Thorndike
LU 01-1889 . . . . . Brockton
LU 01-1952 . . . . . Randolph
LU 07-905 . . . . . Tewksbury

Plant Protection Employees
LU 1 . . . . Pittsfield
LU 2 . . . . Lynn
NHQ . . . . Pittsfield

Plasterers and Cement Masons
LU 534 . . . . Boston

Plumbing and Pipe Fitting
LU 4 . . . . Worcester
LU 12 . . . . Boston
LU 104 . . . . Chicopee
LU 138 . . . . Danvers
LU 537 . . . . Allston
LU 550 . . . . Boston

Police Associations
LU 364 Police Officers . Springfield

Postal Mail Handlers
LU 301 . . . . Natick

Postal Workers
LU 100 Boston . . . . Boston
LU 219 North
  Attleboro . . . . North Attleboro
LU 366 Northeast Area . Tewksbury
LU 485 Peabody . . . . . . Peabody
LU 497 Springfield . . . Springfield
LU 511 Fall River . . . . Fall River
LU 575 Southeastern
  Area . . . . New Bedford
LU 638 North Adams . North Adams
LU 755 Western Mass
  Area . . . . Easthampton
LU 756 Framingham . . Framingham
LU 2461 Lynn . . . . Lynn
LU 3451 Pittsfield . . . . Pittsfield
LU 3844 South Shore
  Area . . . . Brockton
LU 4553 Central Massachusetts
  Area . . . . Worcester
LU 4631
  Williamstown . . . Williamstown
LU 4692 Attleboro . . . . Attleboro
LU 4930 Hyannis
  Area . . . . South Dennis
LU 4952 Randolph . . . Randolph
LU 5015 Taunton . . . . Taunton
LU 5345 Whitinsville
  Local . . . . Whitinsville
LU 6005 Cape Cod
  Area . . . . West Wareham
LU 6021 Athol . . . . Athol
LU 6492 Gloucester . . . Rockport
LU 6592 Whitman Local . Whitman
LU 6758 Sharon . . . . . . Sharon
SA Massachusetts . . . . Waltham

**Professional and Technical
  Engineers**
LU 15 . . . . Boston
LU 101 . . . . Adams
LU 105 . . . . Boston
LU 140 . . . . Pittsfield
LU 142 . . . . Lynn
LU 149 . . . . Lynn

Railroad Signalmen
LLG 120 . . . . Woburn
LLG 213 . . . . . . West Brookfield

**Retail, Wholesale and Department
  Store**
JB New England . . . . . Leominster
LU 60 . . . . Leominster
LU 173 New England Joint
  Board . . . . Leominster
LU 224 . . . . . . East Longmeadow
LU 444 . . . . Leominster
LU 513 . . . . Leominster
LU 515 . . . . Leominster
LU 566 . . . . Leominster
LU 584 . . . . Leominster
LU 588 . . . . Leominster
LU 593 . . . . Leominster

LU 599 . . . . Leominster
LU 875 . . . . Leominster
LU 965 . . . . Leominster

**Roofers, Waterproofers and Allied
  Workers**
LU 33 . . . . Boston
LU 248 . . . . Chicopee

Rural Letter Carriers
D 1 . . . . Granby
D 2 . . . . Middleborough
D 3 . . . . North Reading
D 4 . . . . Westborough
SA Massachusetts . . North Hatfield
SA Rhode Island . . North Attleboro

**Security, Police and Fire
  Professionals**
LU . . . . Oxford
LU 540 . . . . Plymouth

Service Employees
C Massachusetts State
  Council . . . . Boston
LU Committee of Interns &
  Residents . . . . Boston
LU 3 Firemen & Oilers . Charlestown
LU 46 International Leather Goods,
  Plastics, Novelty and Service
  Union . . . . Chicopee
LU 80 International Leather Goods,
  Plastics, Novelty and Service
  Union . . . . New Bedford
LU 88 International Leather Goods,
  Plastics, Novelty and Service
  Union . . . . New Bedford
LU 143 Firemen &
  Oilers . . . . Northampton
LU 211 . . . . Hadley
LU 254 . . . . Boston
LU 263 Smith College
  Employees . . . . Florence
LU 285 . . . . Roxbury
LU 509 . . . . Cambridge
LU 767 Hospital Workers
  Union . . . . Hyannis

Sheet Metal Workers
DC New England . . . . Waltham
LU 17 . . . . Dorchester
LU 63 . . . . Springfield
LU 139 . . . . Hyde Park
LU 377 . . . . Lawrence

Shoe and Allied Craftsmen
LU Cutters . . . . . East Bridgewater
LU Dressers & Packers . Bridgewater
LU Edgetrimmers . East Bridgewater
LU Finishers . . . . East Bridgewater
LU Goodyear
  Operators . . . . East Bridgewater
LU Heelers . . . . East Bridgewater
LU Lasters . . . . . East Bridgewater
LU Mixed Local . . Middleborough
LU Stitchers . . . . East Bridgewater
LU Treers . . . . Brockton
LU Vampers . . . . East Bridgewater
NHQ . . . . East Bridgewater

**State, County and Municipal
  Employees**
C 93 AFSCME . . . . . . Boston
LU 683 Salem Hospital
  RN's . . . . Peabody
LU 851 Southern Bristol
  County Municipal
  Employees . . . . New Bedford

LU 1809 Springfield Library
  & Museums
  Professionals . . . . . Springfield
LU 2824 . . . . Plymouth
LU 3650 Harvard Clerical &
  Technical Workers . . . Cambridge

Steelworkers
LU 1051 . . . . Easthampton
LU 9431 . . . . Rockland
LU 7-9432 . . . . Woburn
LU 04-421-U . . . . Brockton
LU 04-506-L . . . . Shirley
LU 04-562-L . . . . Brockton
LU 04-2285-S . . . . Auburn
LU 04-2431-S . . . . Everett
LU 04-2782-S . . . . Wareham
LU 04-2936-S . . . . Auburn
LU 04-3623-S . . . . . . Wrentham
LU 04-3637-S . . . Attleboro Falls
LU 04-5989-S . . . . Three Rivers
LU 04-7896-S . . . . . Fitchburg
LU 04-7912-S . . . . . . Chicopee
LU 04-8672-S . . . . . Sturbridge
LU 04-8751-S . . . . . Roslindale
LU 04-9358-S . . . . Boston
LU 04-9360-S . . . . Boston
LU 04-12003-s . . . . . Dorchester
LU 04-12004-S . . . . . . Ashland
LU 04-12008-S . . . . . . Lowell
LU 04-12012-s . . . . . . Peabody
LU 04-12026-S . . . . . Springfield
LU 04-12266-S . . . . Lynn
LU 04-12282-S . . . . . . Dracut
LU 04-12325-S . . . . . Pittsfield
LU 04-12431-S . . . . . Rehoboth
LU 04-13492-S . . . . . Norwell
LU 04-13507-S . . . . . Pocasset
LU 04-13585-S . . . . . Dedham
LU 23-1357 . . . . New Bedford

Teachers
LU 2403 Wentworth Faculty
  Federation . . . . Salem
LU 3359 Becker Junior College
  Federation of Teachers . Worcester
LU 4412 Berklee Federation of
  Teachers . . . . Boston
LU 5018 Nurses & Health
  Professionals, St.
  Josephs . . . . Swansea
LU 5023 Nurses & Health
  Professionals, Fairview . Mill River
SFED Massachusetts . . . . Boston

Teamsters
JC 10 . . . . Boston
LU 1 Boston Mailers Union . Quincy
LU 25 . . . . Boston
LU 42 . . . . Lynn
LU 49 . . . . Dracut
LU 59 . . . . New Bedford
LU 82 . . . . South Boston
LU 122 Metro Boston Auto Salesman
  Union . . . . Worcester
LU 170 . . . . Worcester
LU 259 . . . . South Boston
LU 379 . . . . South Boston
LU 404 . . . . Springfield
LU 653 . . . . South Easton

Television and Radio Artists
LU Boston . . . . Boston

Theatrical Stage Employees
D 3 Maine-New
  Hampshire-Vermont-
  Massachusetts-Rhode
  Island-Connecticut . . . . Boston
LU 4-B . . . . Lynnfield
LU 11 . . . . Boston
LU 53 . . . . Springfield
LU 83 . . . . North Adams
LU 96 . . . . Barre
LU 182 . . . . Boston
LU 186 . . . . Ludlow
LU 232 . . . . Shutesbury
LU 381 . . . . Haverhill
LU 437 . . . . . . East Weymouth
LU 481 . . . . Woburn
LU 505 . . . . Revere
LU 753 . . . . Boston
LU 775 . . . . Plymouth
LU 792 . . . . Plymouth

Train Dispatchers
SCOM Amtrak . . . . . . Franklin

Transit Union
LDIV 22 . . . . Worcester
LDIV 448 . . . . Springfield
LDIV 690 . . . . Fitchburg
LDIV 1037 . . . . . New Bedford
LDIV 1363 . . . . . . Rehoboth
LDIV 1512 . . . . . . Springfield
LDIV 1547 . . . . . . Brockton
LDIV 1548 . . . . . . Plymouth

Transport Workers
LU 507 . . . . East Boston

**Transportation Communications
  Union**
D 1089 . . . . Hanover
D 1374 Conrail . . . . . Woburn
LG 6315 Prospect . . . . Tewksbury

Transportation Union
GCA GO-81 Conrail-PC-SP Div-
  B & A . . . . Framingham
LU 254 . . . . Fitchburg
LU 262 . . . . Manomet
LU 352 . . . . Agawam
LU 587 . . . . Gill
LU 679 . . . . Swansea
LU 898 . . . . Attleboro
LU 1462 . . . . Weymouth
LU 1473 . . . . Framingham
SLB LO-24 Massachusetts . . Natick

Treasury Employees
CH . . . . Stoneham
CH 23 . . . . Boston
CH 68 . . . . Andover
CH 102 BATF . . . . . . Boston
CH 133 . . . . Boston
CH 236 . . . . Boston
CH 241 . . . . Waltham
CH 253 . . . . Boston

University Professors
CH Curry College . . . . . Milton
CH Emerson College . . . . Boston

Utility Workers
LU . . . . Berlin
LU . . . . Malden
LU 273 . . . . Taunton
LU 355-B . . . . Berlin
LU 362 . . . . Nantucket
LU 369 . . . . Braintree
LU 396 . . . . Somerset

LU 431 . . . . Swansea
LU 446 . . . . Swampscott
LU 464 . . . . Somerset
LU 472 . . . . . . South Attleboro
LU 480 . . . . Sandwich

Weather Service Employees
BR 01-11 . . . . Taunton
BR 01-62 . . . . Taunton
BR 08-6. . . . . Gloucester

Unaffiliated Labor Organizations

American General Workers
  Union . . . . Walpole
Berkshire Transportation Association
  LU 2 . . . . Pittsfield
Boston College Police
  Association Union of Campus
  Police . . . . Chestnut Hill
Brandeis University Police
  Association . . . . . . Waltham
Brotherhood of Utility Workers of
  New England LU 317 . . . Beverly
Brotherhood of Utility Workers of
  New England LU 318 . . . Beverly

Brotherhood of Utility Workers of
  New England LU 322. . . Monson
Brotherhood of Utility Workers of
  New England LU 329 . . Mendon
Brotherhood of Utility Workers of
  New England LU 330 . Worcester
Brotherhood of Utility Workers of
  New England LU
  340 . . . . Hubbardston
Brotherhood of Utility Workers of
  New England LU 343 . . . Dudley
Brotherhood of Utility Workers of
  New England LU
  345 . . . . Westborough
Brotherhood of Utility Workers of
  New England LU 350 . Leominster
Court Security Officers
  Association. . . . . Boston
Educational Foundation Employees
  Association . . . . . Cambridge
Exxon Workers Union Inc.. . Everett
Guild of Massachusetts Nurses
  Association Employees . . Canton
Harvard University Police
  Association . . . . . . Whitman
Harvard University Security, Parking
  and Museum Guards
  Union . . . . Cambridge

Jewish Family & Children
  Service Employees
  Association . . . Newton Centre
Ken's Food's Employee
  Union . . . . Marlborough
Laundry Workers Union Independent
  LU 66-L . . . . Somerville
Maintenance & Service Employees
  Union of America. . . . Wellesley
Major Indoor Lacrosse League Players
  Association . . . . Sudbury
Massachusetts Institute of
  Technology Campus Police
  Association
  Independent . . . . . Cambridge
Merrimack Valley Legal Services
  Staff Association . . . . Lawrence
Museum of Fine Arts Independent
  Security Union (MISU) . . Boston
New England Social Security
  Management
  Association . . . . . . Attleboro
Northeastern University Police
  Association NUPA. . . . . Boston
Patriot Ledger Associates . . Quincy
Petroleum Workers Association
  Middlesex . . . . Arlington

Raytheon Guards
  Association . . . . . Foxborough
Raytheon Guards Association LU
  2 . . . . Haverhill
Research Development & Technical
  Employees Union . . . . Arlington
Security & Watchmens Amalgamated
  Union . . . . Readville
Service Maintenance & Mechanics
  Association Inc. . . . . . Revere
Springfield Newspapers Employees
  Association Inc.. . . . Springfield
Staff Association of AJCC Greater
  Boston . . . . Brighton
Suffolk University Police
  Association. . . . . Boston
Sun Oil Company Employees
  Association Reverse Terminal
  Operating Employees . . . Revere
Sunburst Employees Association
  Independent. . . . . Salem
Tanker Officers American
  Association . . Great Bar Rington
Union Employees, American
  Federation, Independent. . Holden
Union of Campus Police Wellesley
  College Campus Police . Wellesley
Union Workers Union Staff Union of
  SEIU LU 285. . . . . . . Roxbury
Virgin Atlanta Airways Employees
  Association . . . . . . East Boston

Michigan

AFL-CIO Trade and Industrial Departments

Building and Construction Trades Department

Trades Council Inc. . . . Ann Arbor
BCTC Detroit-Wayne
County . . . . Detroit
BCTC Flint-Genesee-Shiawassee &
Lapeer . . . . Flint
BCTC Michigan. . . . . . Lansing
BCTC Northern
Michigan . . . . . . Traverse City
BCTC Southeastern
Michigan . . . . Jackson
BCTC Southwestern
Michigan . . . . Kalamazoo
BCTC Tri-County . . . . Bay City
BCTC Upper Peninsula . . Escanaba
BCTC Washtenaw
County . . . . Ann Arbor

Maritime Trades Department

PC Michigan . . . . Algonac

AFL-CIO Directly Affiliated Locals

DALU 3064 Billposters &
Billers . . . . Warren
DALU 23409 Protection
Employees . . . . . . Muskegon

Affiliated Labor Organizations

Agricultural Employees

BR 20 . . . . . Commerce Township

Air Traffic Controllers

LU ARB . . . . Ann Arbor
LU AZO . . . . Kalamazoo
LU D21. . . . . Detroit
LU DTW . . . . Detroit
LU FNT. . . . . Flint
LU GRR. . . . . . . Grand Rapids
LU LAN. . . . . Lansing
LU MBS . . . . Freeland
LU MKG . . . . Muskegon
LU PTK . . . . Waterford
LU TVC . . . . Traverse City
LU YIP . . . . Belleville

Aircraft Mechanics

LU 5 . . . . Romulus

Asbestos Workers

LU 25 . . . . Farmington
LU 47 . . . . Saginaw
LU 127 . . . . Gwinn
LU 207 . . . . Taylor

Automobile, Aerospace Workers

C Allegan/Ottawa Counties CAP . .
Grand Rapids
C Barry County . . . . Grand Rapids
C Bay County. . . . . . . Saginaw
C Berrien-Cass-Van
Buren . . . . Kalamazoo
C Central U.P. UAW CAP
Council . . . . Escanaba
C Ionia-Montcalm
Counties. . . . . . . Grand Rapids

C Kalamazoo County
CAP . . . . Kalamazoo
C Kent County CAP . Grand Rapids
C Menominee County . . . Escanaba
C Michigan CAP. . . . . . Detroit
C Muskegon County . Grand Rapids
C National CAP . . . . . . Detroit
C Northern Michigan . Traverse City
C Quad County CAP . . . . Saginaw
C Region 1 CAP . . . . . . Detroit
C Region 1-A CAP. . . . . Detroit
C Region 1-C CAP. . . . . Detroit
C Region 1-D C.A.P. . . . . Detroit
C Region 1-D CAP . . Grand Rapids
C Saginaw County CAP . . Saginaw
C St. Clair County . . . Port Huron
C St. Joseph County . . . Kalamazoo
C Wexford-Osceola
Counties. . . . . . Traverse City
LU. . . . . Dowagiac
LU . . . . Grand Haven
LU . . . . Howell
LU . . . . Traverse City
LU 1 . . . . Watervliet
LU 4 . . . . Orleans
LU 7 . . . . Detroit
LU 8 . . . . Newaygo
LU 19 . . . . Wyoming
LU 21 . . . . Thompsonville
LU 22 . . . . Detroit
LU 36 . . . . Wixom
LU 38 . . . . Ann Arbor
LU 44 . . . . Port Huron
LU 51 . . . . Centerline
LU 62 . . . . Jackson
LU 67 . . . . Alma
LU 113 . . . . Muskegon
LU 135 . . . . Grand Rapids
LU 137 . . . . Greenville
LU 138 . . . . Hastings
LU 140 Detroit-Warren
Local. . . . . Warren
LU 147 . . . . Webberville
LU 155 Warren-Detroit
Local. . . . . Warren
LU 160 . . . . Warren
LU 163 . . . . Detroit
LU 167 . . . . Wyoming
LU 174 New West Side Local
174. . . . . Romulus
LU 182. . . . . Livonia
LU 212 . . . . . . Sterling Heights
LU 220 . . . . Marshall
LU 227 . . . . Detroit
LU 228 . . . . . . Sterling Heights
LU 235 . . . . Hamtramck
LU 245 . . . . Dearborn
LU 246 . . . . Detroit
LU 247 . . . . . . Sterling Heights
LU 262 . . . . Hamtramck
LU 284 . . . . Zeeland
LU 306 . . . . Detroit
LU 308 . . . . Sheridan
LU 318 . . . . Alpena
LU 330 . . . . Wyoming
LU 334 . . . . Adrian
LU 362 . . . . Bay City
LU 369 . . . . . . St. Clair Shores
LU 372. . . . . Trenton
LU 375 St. Clair . . . Marysville
LU 382 . . . . Sturgis
LU 383 . . . . Benton Harbor
LU 387 . . . . Flat Rock
LU 388 . . . . Gaylord
LU 389 . . . . Big Rapids

LU 400 Mount Clemens-Highland
Park Local . . . . Utica
LU 412. . . . . Warren
LU 437. . . . . Chelsea
LU 455 . . . . Saginaw
LU 467 . . . . Saginaw
LU 474 . . . . Albion
LU 475. . . . . Jackson
LU 488. . . . . Kalamazoo
LU 496 . . . . Bay City
LU 503 . . . . Mendon
LU 504 . . . . Jackson
LU 524 Fenton-Holly Local . . Flint
LU 537 . . . . Saginaw
LU 539 . . . . Muskegon
LU 566 . . . . Menominee
LU 572 . . . . Detroit
LU 594 . . . . Pontiac
LU 598 . . . . Flint
LU 599 . . . . Flint
LU 600 . . . . Dearborn
LU 602 . . . . Lansing
LU 637 . . . . Muskegon
LU 649 . . . . Watervliet
LU 651 . . . . Flint
LU 652 . . . . Lansing
LU 653 Pontiac Local . . . . Pontiac
LU 659 . . . . Flint
LU 660 . . . . Jackson
LU 668 . . . . Saginaw
LU 670 . . . . Litchfield
LU 690 . . . . Ihkster
LU 699 . . . . Saginaw
LU 704 . . . . Galesburg
LU 708 Corunna-Flint Local . Burton
LU 723 . . . . Monroe
LU 724 . . . . Lansing
LU 730 . . . . Wyoming
LU 735 . . . . Canton
LU 743 . . . . Owosso
LU 771 Warren-Detroit Local . Troy
LU 783 . . . . Ludington
LU 810 . . . . Coldwater
LU 811 . . . . Ludington
LU 812 . . . . Harbor Beach
LU 822 . . . . Bronson
LU 828 . . . . Grandville
LU 845 . . . . Canton
LU 849 . . . . Ypsilanti
LU 869 . . . . Warren
LU 878 . . . . Monroe
LU 889 Detroit-Warren
Local. . . . . Warren
LU 892 . . . . Saline
LU 898 . . . . Ypsilanti
LU 900 . . . . Wayne
LU 909 . . . . Warren
LU 925 . . . . St. Johns
LU 931 . . . . Dearborn
LU 961 . . . . Detroit
LU 963 . . . . Adrian
LU 983 . . . . Warren
LU 985 Detroit-Dearborn
Local . . . . Redford
LU 1002 . . . . Middleville
LU 1009 . . . . Battle Creek
LU 1071 . . . . . Muskegon Heights
LU 1131 . . . . Frankenmuth
LU 1134 . . . . Pinconning
LU 1135 . . . . Bay City
LU 1149 . . . . Marysville
LU 1150 . . . . Homer
LU 1158 . . . . Greenville
LU 1176 . . . . Albion
LU 1210 . . . . South Haven

LU 1218 . . . . Dowagiac
LU 1223 . . . . Bronson
LU 1230 . . . . Watervliet
LU 1231 . . . . . . Comstock Park
LU 1243 . . . . Whitehall
LU 1248 Allen Park-Warren
Local. . . . . Warren
LU 1253 . . . . Three Rivers
LU 1264 . . . . . Sterling Heights
LU 1279 . . . . Muskegon
LU 1284 . . . . Chelsea
LU 1289 . . . . Quincy
LU 1292 . . . . Grand Blanc
LU 1294 . . . . Marshall
LU 1313 . . . . Plymouth
LU 1320 . . . . . . Byron Center
LU 1330 . . . . Jackson
LU 1348 . . . . Petersburg
LU 1374 . . . . Detroit
LU 1386 . . . . Coldwater
LU 1402 . . . . Holland
LU 1403 . . . . Boyne
LU 1433 . . . . Copemish
LU 1436 . . . . Edmore
LU 1440 . . . . Plymouth
LU 1441 . . . . Muskegon
LU 1464 . . . . Ludington
LU 1485 . . . . . . Grand Rapids
LU 1488 . . . . Lansing
LU 1503 . . . . Ellsworth
LU 1511 . . . . Mancelona
LU 1554 . . . . Greenville
LU 1586 . . . . Reed City
LU 1618 . . . . Lansing
LU 1637 . . . . West Branch
LU 1660 . . . . Elsie
LU 1666 . . . . Kalamazoo
LU 1669 . . . . Cheboygan
LU 1700 . . . . Detroit
LU 1703 . . . . Muskegon
LU 1753 . . . . Lansing
LU 1781 . . . . . Farmington Hills
LU 1810 . . . . Goodrich
LU 1811 . . . . . . Swartz Creek
LU 1819 . . . . Roscommon
LU 1869 . . . . Warren
LU 1898. . . . . Coldwater
LU 1966 . . . . Jackson
LU 1970 . . . . Dearborn
LU 1972 . . . . . Benton Harbor
LU 1996 . . . . Three Rivers
LU 2017 . . . . Greenville
LU 2031 . . . . Adrian
LU 2064 . . . . Allegan
LU 2076 . . . . New Buffalo
LU 2093 . . . . Three Rivers
LU 2101 . . . . Leroy
LU 2107 . . . . Kalamazoo
LU 2117 . . . . Hudson
LU 2122. . . . . Dowagiac
LU 2145 . . . . . . Grand Rapids
LU 2151 . . . . Coopersville
LU 2183 . . . . Wallace
LU 2214 . . . . St. Helen
LU 2228 . . . . Parchment
LU 2229 . . . . Menominee
LU 2256 . . . . Lansing
LU 2270 . . . . Evart
LU 2275 . . . . Sainaw
LU 2280 . . . . Utica
LU 2304 . . . . . . Grand Rapids
LU 2344 . . . . . . Grand Rapids
LU 2362 . . . . Cheboygan
LU 2363 Mesa . . . . Adrian
LU 2392. . . . . . . Grand Rapids

LU 2403 . . . . Traverse City
LU 2416 . . . . Hillsdale
LU 2500 . . . . Detroit
LU 2600 . . . . Wyoming
LU 3000 . . . . Woodhaven
LU 3500 . . . . Westland
LU 3803 . . . . Sault Ste. Marie
LU 3911 . . . . Pontiac
LU 4911 . . . . Lansing
LU 5960 . . . . Lake Orion
LU 6911 Pontiac General Hospital
  Nurses . . . . Pontiac
LU 7777 . . . . Detroit
LU 9699 . . . . Marlette
NHQ . . . . Detroit

**Bakery, Confectionery, Tobacco
Workers and Grain Millers**
LU 3-G . . . . Battle Creek
LU 66-G . . . . Dowling
LU 70 . . . . Grand Rapids
LU 77 . . . . . Grosse Points Park
LU 81 . . . . Traverse City
LU 120-G. . . . . Hillsdale
LU 207 . . . . Galien
LU 259-G . . . . Chesaning
LU 260-G . . . . Cass City
LU 261-G . . . . Sebewaing
LU 262-G . . . . Melvin
LU 263-G . . . . Essexville
LU 326 . . . . Allen Park
LU 365-G . . . . . . Battle Creek
LU 397-G. . . . . Delton

Barbers
LU 55. . . . . Royal Oak
LU 90 . . . . Holland
LU 5040. . . . . Rochester
NHQ . . . . Flint

Boilermakers
LG 7-M. . . . . Mesick
LG 169. . . . . Dearborn
LG 335-D Cement
  Workers. . . . . Essexville
LG 351-D Cement Workers . Alpena
LG 408-D Cement
  Workers . . . . Petersburg
LG 472-D Cement Workers. . Posen
LG 480-D Cement
  Workers . . . . Charlevoix
LG 500-D Cement
  Workers. . . . . Rogers City
LG 699 . . . . Menominee

Bricklayers
LU 1 Michigan. . . . . . Warren
LU 6 Michigan . . . . . Marquette
LU 9 . . . . Lansing
LU 32 . . . . Warren

Carpenters
C Great Lakes Region Industrial
  4291 . . . . Luna Pier
C Michigan Regional #4085 . Detroit
LU 100 . . . . Coopersville
LU 202 . . . . Bay City
LU 525 . . . . Kalamazoo
LU 687 . . . . Detroit
LU 706 . . . . Saginaw
LU 1004 . . . . Lansing
LU 1033 . . . . Luna Pier
LU 1045 . . . . Warren
LU 1102 . . . . Warren
LU 1395 . . . . Muskegon
LU 1510 . . . . Escanaba
LU 1615 . . . . Alto
LU 1701 . . . . Kentwood

LU 2535 . . . . Grant
LU 2776 . . . . Kalamazoo
LU 2815 . . . . Bellevue

Christian Labor Association
LU 10 United Construction
  Workers . . . . Zeeland
LU 12 Service Employees. . Zeeland
LU 18 United Construction
  Workers . . . . Zeeland
LU 55 United Metal
  Workers . . . . Zeeland
NHQ. . . . . Zeeland

Civilian Technicians
CH 13 Detroit Area . . Selfridge Air
  National Guard
CH 15 Battle Creek. . . Battle Creek
STC . . Selfridge Air National Guard

Communications Workers
C Metro Area . . . . . . Southfield
JB Unified Council of
  Michigan . . . . Flint
LU 4004 . . . . Detroit
LU 4008 . . . . Eastpointe
LU 4009. . . . . Southfield
LU 4011 . . . . Ann Arbor
LU 4013 . . . . Pontiac
LU 4017 . . . . Wayne
LU 4018 . . . . Wyandotte
LU 4024. . . . . Chassell
LU 4025 . . . . Kincheloe
LU 4032 . . . . Lawrence
LU 4034 . . . . Wyoming
LU 4035 . . . . Holland
LU 4039 . . . . Kalamazoo
LU 4040 . . . . Lansing
LU 4050 . . . . Detroit
LU 4070 . . . . Warren
LU 4090 . . . . Royal Oak
LU 4100 . . . . Detroit
LU 4101 . . . . Bay City
LU 4103. . . . . Flint
LU 4104 . . . . Manistee
LU 4107 . . . . Port Huron
LU 4108 . . . . Saginaw
LU 4109 . . . . Traverse City
LU 14501. . . . . Alpena
LU 14503. . . . . Detroit
LU 14504. . . . . Carney
LU 14508 . . . . Lake Ann
LU 14510 . . . . Jackson
LU 34022. . . . . Detroit
LU 54043 NABET Local
  43 . . . . Southfield
LU 54046 . . . . Flint
LU 54048 . . . . Bay City
LU 54410 . . . . Cadillac
LU 54412 . . . . . Mount Pleasant
LU 84419 . . . . Petoskey
LU 84422 . . . . Flint
LU 84436. . . . . Ionia

Education
ASSN Detroit College Business
  Faculty. . . . . Dearborn
LU Adrian College Association of
  Professors . . . . Adrian
LU Baker College Education
  Association . . . . Flint
LU University of Detroit Professors'
  Union . . . . Redford
LU University of Detroit Support
  Staff . . . . Detroit
SA Michigan Education
  Association . . . . East Lansing

Electrical Workers
LU 17. . . . . Southfield
LU 58. . . . . Detroit
LU 131. . . . . Kalamazoo
LU 205. . . . . Livonia
LU 219 . . . . Iron Mountain
LU 252 . . . . Ann Arbor
LU 275 . . . . Coopersville
LU 352 . . . . Lansing
LU 445 . . . . Battle Creek
LU 498 . . . . Traverse City
LU 510 . . . . Marquette
LU 557 . . . . Saginaw
LU 665 . . . . Lansing
LU 692 . . . . Bay City
LU 876. . . . . . . Comstock Park
LU 948 . . . . Flint
LU 979 . . . . Escanaba
LU 1070 . . . . Marquette
LU 1106 . . . . Lansing
LU 1672 . . . . . . Benton Harbor

Electronic Workers
DC 8-FW Michigan . . Grand Rapids
LU 415 . . . . Grand Rapids
LU 438-FW . . . . Greenville
LU 444-FW. . . . . Ionia
LU 932 . . . . Oak Park
LU 934 . . . . Oak Park
LU 981 . . . . Grand Rapids

Elevator Constructors
LU 36 . . . . Detroit
LU 85 . . . . Lansing

Federal Employees
LU 1804 . . . . Detroit
LU 1928 . . . . . Bruce Crossing
LU 2083 . . . . Gladstone
LU 2086 . . . . . . East Tawas
LU 2132 . . . . . . Grand Ledge

Fire Fighters
LU 35-I . . . . Dearborn

Flint Glass Workers
LU 110 . . . . Olivet

Food and Commercial Workers
C Insurance Workers Area
  VIII . . . . Lansing
C United Local
  Unions. . . . . Madison Heights
LU 16 . . . . Saginaw
LU 42-D . . . . Roseville
LU 70-C . . . . Muskegon
LU 132-C . . . . Zeeland
LU 169-B . . . . Kalamazoo
LU 232 . . . . Battle Creek
LU 360-I . . . . Eastpointe
LU 600-A . . . . Rockford
LU 613-B . . . . Monroe
LU 689 . . . . Ann Arbor
LU 799-C . . . . . Sault Ste. Marie
LU 867-C . . . . . . Smiths Creek
LU 876. . . . . . Madison Heights
LU 951 . . . . Grand Rapids
LU 1039-C . . . . . . Roscommon
LU 1044-C. . . . . . Tawas City
LU 1058-AB . . . . . . Eastpointe

**Glass, Molders, Pottery and
Plastics Workers**
CONBD Michigan L
  Vicinity. . . . . Coldwater
LU 120-B . . . . Quincy
LU 202 . . . . Grand Ledge
LU 265 . . . . Constantine

LU 401 . . . . Menominee
LU 408 . . . . Watervliet
LU 412 . . . . Kalamazoo
LU 421 . . . . Cedar Springs

Government Employees
C 175 Food Inspection Locals, North
  Central . . . . Saginaw
LU 46 DoJ . . . . Detroit
LU 138 VA . . . . Inkster
LU 722 USDA . . . . Detroit
LU 830 DoD . . . . Sault Ste. Marie
LU 933 VA . . . . Detroit
LU 1626 DoD . . . . . Battle Creek
LU 1629 VA . . . . . Battle Creek
LU 1658 DoD . . . . . . Warren
LU 1741 DoJ . . . . Milan
LU 2075 GSA . . . . Detroit
LU 2077 DoD . . . . . Selfridge Air
  National Guard
LU 2092 VA . . . . . . Ann Arbor
LU 2130 DoD . . . . Detroit
LU 2274 VA . . . . Saginaw
LU 2280 VA . . . . Iron Mountain
LU 2499 INS, Border
  Patrol . . . . . Dearborn Heights
LU 2795 DoD . . . . . Center Line
LU 3239 HHS . . . . . . Dearborn
LU 3265 USDA . . . . . . Athens
LU 3272 HHS. . . . . Grand Rapids
LU 3604 HHS. . . . . Marquette
LU 3907 EPA . . . . . Ann Arbor
LU 3908 DoC . . . . . Ann Arbor

Graphic Communications
LU 2-C . . . . Ferndale
LU 13-N . . . . Canton
LU 27-N . . . . Blissfield
LU 135-C . . . . . . Battle Creek
LU 282-C . . . . Birch Run
LU 507-S . . . . Kalamazoo
LU 550-M . . . . . . Grand Rapids
LU 555-S . . . . Belmont
LU 663-S . . . . Vulcan
LU 692-C . . . . Negaunee
LU 705-S . . . . . . Battle Creek

Horseshoers
LU 2 . . . . White Lake

Hotel and Restaurant Employees
LU 24 . . . . Southfield
LU 688 . . . . Bay City

Independent Unions Federation
LU 373 Litchfield Independent
  Workers Union . . . . . Litchfield

Iron Workers
DC Great Lakes and
  Vicinity . . Chesterfield Township
LU 25 . . . . Novi
LU 340 . . . . Battle Creek
LU 499 . . . . Temperance
LU 508 . . . . Wayne
LU 831 . . . . Garden City

Laborers
DC Michigan . . . . Lansing
LU 334 . . . . Detroit
LU 355 . . . . Battle Creek
LU 463 . . . . Port Huron
LU 465 . . . . Monroe
LU 959 . . . . Ann Arbor
LU 998 . . . . Lansing
LU 1075 . . . . Flint
LU 1076 . . . . Pontiac
LU 1098 . . . . Saginaw

LU 1191 . . . . Detroit
LU 1329 . . . . . . Iron Mountain
LU 2132 . . . . Grand Ledge

Laundry and Dry Cleaning
LU 151 . . . . Kalamazoo

Letter Carriers
BR 1 . . . . Detroit
BR 13 . . . . Muskegon
BR 49 . . . . Manistee
BR 56 . . . . Grand Rapids
BR 74 . . . . Saginaw
BR 83 . . . . Albion
BR 95 . . . . Marquette
BR 122 . . . . Lansing
BR 187 . . . . Bay City
BR 232 . . . . Jackson
BR 249 . . . . Menominee
BR 256 . . . . Flint
BR 259 . . . . Alpena
BR 262 . . . . Battle Creek
BR 320 North Oakland
   County . . . . Waterford
BR 386 Ishpeming,
   Michigan . . . . Ishpeming
BR 395 . . . . Iron Mountain
BR 414 . . . . Ypsilanti
BR 434 . . . . Ann Arbor
BR 437 . . . . Ironwood
BR 438 . . . . Escanaba
BR 523 . . . . Petoskey
BR 529 . . . . Port Huron
BR 560 . . . . Benton Harbor
BR 568 . . . . Calumet
BR 579 . . . . Adrian
BR 601 . . . . Holland
BR 618 . . . . Traverse City
BR 653 . . . . St. Joseph
BR 654 . . . . . Mount Clemens
BR 669 . . . . Ludington
BR 672 Big Rapids,
   Michigan . . . . Big Rapids
BR 707 . . . . . Sault Ste. Marie
BR 750 . . . . Newport
BR 758 . . . . Riverview
BR 775 . . . . Niles
BR 788 Charlotte,
   Michigan . . . . Charlotte
BR 794 . . . . Cadillac
BR 919 Hancock,
   Michigan . . . . Hancock
BR 1056 . . . . . . Mount Pleasant
BR 1147 . . . . . . Grand Haven
BR 1282 Caro, Michigan . . . . Caro
BR 1466 Belding, Michigan . Belding
BR 1580 . . . . Alma
BR 1640 Hudson, Michigan . Hudson
BR 1691 . . . . Gladstone
BR 1817 Bad Axe,
   Michigan . . . . Bad Axe
BR 2006 Negaunee,
   Michigan . . . . . . Negaunee
BR 2178 Zeeland,
   Michigan . . . . Zeeland
BR 2184 Western Wayne County,
   Michigan . . . . Taylor
BR 2317 . . . . Midland
BR 2347 Otsego, Michigan . Otsego
BR 2469 Quincy, Michigan . Quincy
BR 2555 . . . . . . East Lansing
BR 2672 Crystal Falls,
   Michigan . . . . . . Crystal Fall
BR 2701 St. Louis,
   Michigan . . . . St. Louis
BR 2768 Lowell, Michigan . Lowell
BR 2845 Munising,
   Michigan . . . . . . Munising

BR 2846 Iron River,
   Michigan . . . . . . Iron River
BR 2952 Hart, Michigan . . . . Hart
BR 2958 Cassopolis,
   Michigan . . . . . . Cassopolis
BR 2975 Harbor Beach,
   Michigan . . . . . Harbor Beach
BR 3023 Reed City,
   Michigan . . . . Reed City
BR 3106 Rogers City,
   Michigan . . . . . . Rogers City
BR 3126 . . . . . Madison Heights
BR 3476 Homer, Michigan . . Homer
BR 3477 Bronson,
   Michigan . . . . Bronson
BR 3478 Constantine,
   Michigan . . . . . . Constantine
BR 3479 Dundee, Michigan . Dundee
BR 3480 Croswell,
   Michigan . . . . Croswell
BR 3481 Shelby, Michigan . . . Hart
BR 3785 Newberry,
   Michigan . . . . Newberry
BR 3786 West Branch,
   Michigan . . . . . . West Branch
BR 3804 . . . . Vassar
BR 3810 Bessemer,
   Michigan . . . . Bessemer
BR 3860 Norway,
   Michigan . . . . . Iron Mountain
BR 3876 Bangor, Michigan . Bangor
BR 3908 Lake Odessa,
   Michigan . . . . . . Lake Odessa
BR 4227 Milford, Michigan . Milford
BR 4314 Wakefield,
   Michigan . . . . Wakefield
BR 4345 Lanse, Michigan . . L'Anse
BR 4366 Ithaca, Michigan . . Ithaca
BR 4374 . . . . Roseville
BR 4417 Grandville,
   Michigan . . . . Grandville
BR 4439 Lake Linden,
   Michigan . . . . . . Lake Linden
BR 4547 Gaylord,
   Michigan . . . . Gaylord
BR 4642 Stevensville,
   Michigan . . . . . . Stevensville
BR 4709 . . . . Lake Orion
BR 4772 East Tawas,
   Michigan . . . . . . East Tawas
BR 4779 . . . . Allen Park
BR 4851 Marlette,
   Michigan . . . . Marlette
BR 4926 Sandusky,
   Michigan . . . . Sandusky
BR 5041 Ontonagon,
   Michigan . . . . . . Ontonagon
BR 5145 Fruitport,
   Michigan . . . . Fruitport
BR 5175 St. Charles,
   Michigan . . . . . . St. Charles
BR 5179 Spring Lake,
   Michigan . . . . . . Spring Lake
BR 5233 Cass City,
   Michigan . . . . Cass City
BR 5239 Union City,
   Michigan . . . . . . Union City
BR 5270 Hudsonville,
   Michigan . . . . . . Hudsonville
BR 5284 Montague,
   Michigan . . . . . . Montague
BR 5380 Rockford,
   Michigan . . . . Rockford
BR 5530 St. Ignace,
   Michigan . . . . . . St. Ignace
BR 5591 Richmond,
   Michigan . . . . . . Richmond

BR 5764 Conklin,
   Michigan . . . . Conklin
BR 5785 . . . . Houghton
BR 6002 Oscoda, Michigan . Oscoda
BR 6530 Sebewaing,
   Michigan . . . . . . Sebewaing
BR 11246 . . . . . . Kalamazoo
SA Michigan . . . . Detroit

Locomotive Engineers
DIV . . . . Battle Creek
DIV 1 . . . . Livonia
DIV 2 . . . . Holt
DIV 19 . . . . Eastpointe
DIV 33 . . . . Athens
DIV 122 . . . . Port Huron
DIV 185 . . . . Gladstone
DIV 286 . . . . . . Grand Rapids
DIV 304 . . . . Saginaw
DIV 385 . . . . Sand Creek
DIV 542 . . . . Westland
DIV 650 . . . . Durand
DIV 812 . . . . Eastpointe
DIV 831 . . . . . . Brownstown
DIV 850 . . . . Trenton
DIV 920 . . . . Holly
GCA Grand Trunk Western
   Railroad . . . . . . Battle Creek

Longshoremen
LU 1608 . . . . Traverse City

Machinists
DLG 60 . . . . Detroit
DLG 97 . . . . Battle Creek
LG 46 . . . . Battle Creek
LG 46-S . . . . River Rouge
LG 82 . . . . Detroit
LG 110-DS . . . . Warren
LG 117 . . . . Marysville
LG 141 . . . . Romulus
LG 194 . . . . Marquette
LG 218 . . . . Burtchville
LG 435 . . . . Jackson
LG 475 . . . . Coopersville
LG 600 . . . . Bridgman
LG 670 . . . . Muskegon
LG 698 . . . . Detroit
LG 1113 . . . . Bellevue
LG 1118 . . . . Three Rivers
LG 1275 . . . . Niles
LG 1418 . . . . Holland
LG 1424 . . . . Sturgis
LG 1813 . . . . Muskegon
LG 1918 . . . . . . Benton Harbor
LG 2140 . . . . Eau Claire
LG 2184 . . . . Lansing
LG 2259 . . . . St. Clair
LG 2434 . . . . Galesburg
LG 2449 . . . . Albion
LG 2584 . . . . Marshall
LG 2597 . . . . Muskegon
LG 2839-PM . . . . . . Saginaw
LG 2848-PM . . . . Warren
LLG W-166
   Woodworkers . . . . . Grayling
LLG W-260
   Woodworkers . . . . . Ossineke
LLG W-268
   Woodworkers . . . Lake Linden
LLG W-283 Woodworkers . Barara
LLG W-303
   Woodworkers . . . . . Munising
STC Michigan . . . . . . Livonia

Maintenance of Way Employes
LG 25 . . . . Millington
LG 109 . . . . Gaines

LG 427 . . . . Detroit
LG 721 . . . . Escanaba
LG 1629 . . . . Mattawan
LG 2225 . . . . Niles
LG 2725 . . . . Lincoln Park
NHQ . . . . Southfield
SF Allied Eastern
   Federation . . . . . . Manistee
SLG 28 . . . . Gowen
SLG 166 . . . . Battle Creek
SLG 176 . . . . Detroit
SLG 460 . . . . Kentwood
SLG 583 . . . . Breedsville
SLG 1012 . . . . Southfield
SLG 1388 . . . . Balwin
SLG 1489 . . . . Marquette
SLG 1504 . . . . Munith

Musicians
LU 5 . . . . Southfield
LU 56 . . . . Grand Rapids
LU 57 . . . . Pinckney
LU 218 . . . . Marquette
LU 387 . . . . Jackson
LU 542 . . . . Flint
LU 625 . . . . Ann Arbor
LU 784 Pontiac Federation of
   Musicians . . . . Bloomfield Hills

National Staff Organization
LU Financial Service Marketing
   Representatives Michigan
   Education Association . . Jackson
LU Staff Association Michigan
   Educators Financial Service
   Association . . . . . East Lansing
LU Staff Organization, Association,
   Michigan Education
   Association . . . . Gobles
LU Staff Organization, Professional,
   Michigan Education
   Association . . . . . East Lansing
LU Staff Organization, Professional,
   Michigan Education
   Association . . . . . East Lansing
LU Staff Organization, Professional,
   Michigan Education Special
   Service . . . . . . Traverse City
NHQ . . . . Gobles
STC Staff Organization/NSO, United,
   (Michigan) . . . . Gobles

Needletrades
LU 57-A . . . . Detroit
LU 124-A . . . . Detroit
LU 748-A . . . . Detroit
LU 2402 . . . . Detroit
LU 2411 . . . . Detroit
LU 2562 . . . . Detroit
LU 2563 . . . . Detroit

NLRB Professional Association
LU 7 . . . . Detroit

Nurses
C Borgess Medical Center
   Staff . . . . Kalamazoo
LSC Borgess Pipp Health
   Center . . . . Plainwell
LSC Lansing Community Health
   Nurses . . . . Lansing
LSC Professional Nurses
   Association, Bixby . . . . Adrian
LSC Professional Nurses, Portage
   View Hospital . . . . . Hancock
LSC Registered Nurses, Allegan
   General Hospital . . . . . Gobles

LSC Registered Nurses, Community Memorial Hospital . . Cheboygan
LSC Registered Nurses, Marquette General Hospital . . . Marquette
LSC Sparrow Hospital Professional Employees . . . . Lansing
LSC Visiting Nurse Association of Metro Detroit. . . . . Garden City
LSC Visiting Nurse Association of St. Clair County . . North Street
LSC Visiting Nurse Services. . . . . . Grand Rapids
SA Michigan Nurses Association . . . . Okemos

Office and Professional Employees
LU 40 . . . . Chesterfield Township
LU 42 . . . . St. Clair Shores
LU 393 . . . . Flint
LU 459 . . . . Lansing
LU 494. . . . . Warren
LU 512 . . . . Okemos

Operating Engineers
CONF North Central States . Livonia
LU 324. . . . . Livonia
LU 547 . . . . Detroit

Painters
DC 22 . . . . Hazel Park
LU 37. . . . . Hazel Park
LU 42 . . . . Garden City
LU 213 . . . . . . St. Clair Shores
LU 312 . . . . Potage
LU 357 . . . . Hazel Park
LU 514. . . . . Belleville
LU 591 . . . . Hazel Park
LU 675 . . . . Temperance
LU 826 . . . . Grand Blanc
LU 845 . . . . Lansing
LU 1011 . . . . Escanaba
LU 1052. . . . . Flint
LU 1396 . . . . Benton Harbor
LU 1401 . . . . Livonia
LU 1474 . . . . Port Huron
LU 1803 . . . . Freeland

Paper, Allied-Industrial, Chemical Employees
LU . . . . Coloma
LU 126. . . . . Pontiac
LU 6-4 . . . . Avoca
LU 6-513 . . . . Ypsilanti
LU 6-921 . . . . Fenton
LU 6-1999 . . . . St. Louis
LU 6-2000 . . . . Paw Paw
LU G-165 . . . . Lansing
LU 06-10 . . . . Lincoln Park
LU 06-51 . . . . Applegate
LU 06-100. . . . . Onaway
LU 06-111 . . . . Unionville
LU 06-127. . . . . Jackson
LU 06-196. . . . . Trenton
LU 06-220 . . . . Portage
LU 06-238 . . . . Kalamazoo
LU 06-239 . . . . Tawas City
LU 06-252 . . . . Grand Haven
LU 06-255. . . . . Hart
LU 06-274 . . . . Manistee
LU 06-278 . . . . Grand Haven
LU 06-286 . . . . Muskegon
LU 06-293 . . . . Kalamazoo
LU 06-314 . . . . Detroit
LU 06-323 . . . . Parchment
LU 06-332 . . . . Battle Creek
LU 06-358 . . . . Vassar
LU 06-363 . . . . Decatur
LU 06-389 . . . . Taylor

LU 06-396 . . . . . . Spring Lake
LU 06-402 . . . . Dorr
LU 06-403 . . . . Auburn
LU 06-410 . . . . . . Grand Haven
LU 06-414 . . . . Lansing
LU 06-416 . . . . Kalamazoo
LU 06-421 . . . . Flint
LU 06-430 . . . . Niles
LU 06-431 . . . . Brighton
LU 06-433 . . . . Saginaw
LU 06-479 . . . . Kalamazoo
LU 06-495 . . . . Pontiac
LU 06-502 . . . . Jackson
LU 06-540 . . . . Alma
LU 06-544 . . . . . . Grand Haven
LU 06-547. . . . . Bridgman
LU 06-561 . . . . Bellevue
LU 06-564 . . . . Reese
LU 06-568 . . . . Roseville
LU 06-585 . . . . Shepherd
LU 06-591 . . . . Southgate
LU 06-628 . . . . Bad Axe
LU 06-636 . . . . Boyne City
LU 06-639 . . . . Detroit
LU 06-644 . . . . Muskegon
LU 06-667 . . . . Manistee
LU 06-668 . . . . Ludington
LU 06-670 . . . . Jackson
LU 06-672 . . . . Grand Haven
LU 06-673 . . . . Tecumseh
LU 06-677 . . . . Grand Haven
LU 06-682 . . . . Kalamazoo
LU 06-720 . . . . Hart
LU 06-814 World Wide Employees Association . . . . Shepherd
LU 06-816 . . . . Union Pier
LU 06-824 . . . . Holland
LU 06-825 . . . . Flat Rock
LU 06-829 . . . . Corunna
LU 06-842 . . . . Detroit
LU 06-910 . . . . Newport
LU 06-946 . . . . Kalamazoo
LU 06-987 . . . . Muskegon
LU 06-1001 . . . . . . Lincoln Park
LU 06-1005 . . . . Westland
LU 06-1007 . . . . Lansing
LU 06-1008 . . . . . . White Pigeon
LU 06-1010 . . . . Kalamazoo
LU 06-1011 . . . . Paw Paw
LU 06-1012 . . . . Niles
LU 06-1015. . . . . Fruitport
LU 06-1017 . . . . Fargo
LU 06-1019 . . . . Paw Paw
LU 06-1021 . . . . Battle Creek
LU 06-1023 . . . . Ray
LU 06-1025 . . . . Otsego
LU 06-1026. . . . . Adrian
LU 06-1029 . . . . Coloma
LU 06-1031 . . . . Monroe
LU 06-1033 . . . . . . Three Rivers
LU 06-1034 . . . . . . White Pigeon
LU 06-1035 . . . . Wayne
LU 06-1044 . . . . Monroe
LU 06-1050 . . . . Wyoming
LU 06-1063 . . . . Clare
LU 06-1077 . . . . Monroe
LU 06-1082 . . . . Canton
LU 06-1117 . . . . Buchanan
LU 07-21 . . . . Escanaba
LU 07-44. . . . . Manistique
LU 07-87 . . . . Limestone
LU 07-96. . . . . Munising
LU 07-172. . . . . Menominee
LU 07-176 . . . . Warren
LU 07-354 . . . . Ontonagon
LU 07-569 . . . . Grand Haven
LU 07-762. . . . . Owosso
LU 07-979 . . . . Merritt

LU 07-1018 . . . . Kingsford

Plant Protection
LU 100 Rouge Unit . . . . Detroit
LU 101 Wayne Plant Unit . Westland
LU 103 World Headquarters Unit . . . . Farmington Hills
LU 104 Branch Plant Unit . . . Milan
LU 105 Automotive Assembly Plant Unit . . . . . . Dearborn Heights
LU 106 Detroit Parts Unit . Belleville
NHQ . . . . Ypsilanti

Plant Protection Employees
LU 136. . . . . Fowlerville

Plasterers and Cement Masons
LU 16 . . . . Lansing
LU 67 . . . . Dearborn
LU 514 . . . . Detroit
STCON Michigan . . . . . . Lasing

Plumbing and Pipe Fitting
LU 85 . . . . Saginaw
LU 98 . . . . . Madison Heights
LU 174 West Michigan . . . . Coopersville
LU 190 . . . . Ann Arbor
LU 333 . . . . Lansing
LU 357 Kalamazoo Pipefitters & HVAC Service . . . . Kalamazoo
LU 370 . . . . Flushing
LU 506 . . . . Escanaba
LU 636. . . . . . Farmington Hills
LU 671. . . . . Monroe
LU 704. . . . . Farmington
SA Michigan . . . . . . Ann Arbor

Postal and Federal Employees
LU 702 . . . . Oak Park
LU 706 . . . . Kalamazoo
LU 711 . . . . Saginaw

Postal Mail Handlers
LU 307 . . . . Detroit

Postal Workers
LU 143 Greater Southwestern Area . . . . Kalamazoo
LU 235 Battle Creek . . Battle Creek
LU 271 Flint Michigan Area . . Flint
LU 273 Jackson . . . . . . Jackson
LU 281 Western Michigan Area . . . . Grand Rapids
LU 282 Saginaw 486/487 Area . . . . Saginaw
LU 293 Charlotte Local . . Charlotte
LU 295 Detroit Area . . . . Detroit
LU 307 Cheboygan . . . Cheboygan
LU 329 Manistee. . . . . Manistee
LU 424 Muskegon . . Muskegon
LU 467 Hillsdale . . . . Hillsdale
LU 480-481 480-481 Area . Ferndale
LU 488-489 Central Michigan Area. . . . . Lansing
LU 498-499 Iron Mountain. . . . . Iron Mountain
LU 519 Petoskey. . . . . Petoskey
LU 531 Traverse City . Traverse City
LU 1766 Pontiac Area . . Pontiac
LU 3307 St. Ignace Local . St. Ignace
LU 3466 Ludington. . . . Ludington
LU 3529 Fenton Local . . . Fenton
LU 3971 Sault Ste. Marie . . . . . Sault Ste. Marie
LU 4752 Rogers City . Rogers City
LU 4881 Gaylord . . . . . Gaylord
LU 5024 Alpena . . . . . Alpena

LU 5858 Farmington . . . Farmington Hills
LU 6178 Stevensville Local . . . . Stevensville
LU 6723 Troy. . . . . Troy
LU 6818 Tecumseh Local Tecumseh
SA Michigan . . . . Flint

Railroad Signalmen
LLG 14. . . . . Durand
LLG 28 . . . . Taylor
LLG 123 . . . . Bay City
LLG 214 . . . . Dundee

Retail, Wholesale and Department Store
C 30 United Distributive Workers . . . . Warren
LU 83 . . . . Southfield
LU 86 . . . . Bannister
LU 87 . . . . Saginaw
LU 93 . . . . Lansing
LU 374 . . . . Battle Creek
LU 383 . . . . Burton
LU 386 . . . . Grand Rapids
LU 530 . . . . Fremont
LU 602 . . . . Burton
LU 665 . . . . Marquette
LU 705 . . . . Holland
LU 822 . . . . Holland
LU 825. . . . . Lawton
LU 1064. . . . . Southfield

Roofers, Waterproofers and Allied Workers
LU 70 . . . . Howell
LU 149 . . . . Detroit

Rural Letter Carriers
LU Berrien County . . . . Eau Claire
LU Clare-Gladwin-Isabella Counties . . . . Rosebush
LU 1 Allegan County . . . . . Dorr
LU 2 Barry County . . . . . Delton
LU 5 Branch County . . . Union City
LU 6 Calhoun County . . . Bellevue
LU 7 Cass-St. Joseph Counties . . . . . . Edwardsburg
LU 9 Clinton-Shiawassee Counties . . . . St. Johns
LU 10 Eaton County . . . . Charlotte
LU 11 Genesee County . . Birch Run
LU 12 Northwest Michigan . . . . Fife Lake
LU 13 Gratiot County . . . . Ashley
LU 14 Hillsdale County . . Clarklake
LU 15 Huron County . . . Owendale
LU 16 Ingham-Livingston Counties. . . . . Jackson
LU 17 Ionia County . . . Greenville
LU 19 Jackson County . . . Jackson
LU 20 Kalamazoo County . . . . Vicksburg
LU 21 Kent County . . . . . . Dorr
LU 22 Lake-Osceola Counties. . . . . Reed City
LU 23 Lenawee County . . Pittsford
LU 24 Lapeer County . North Branch
LU 27 Mecosta County. . . . Remus
LU 29 Monroe County . Ottawa Lake
LU 31 Muskegon County . Whitehall
LU 32 Newaygo County. . . . Grant
LU 33 Northeastern Area . Rose City
LU 34 Oakland County . . Clarkston
LU 36 Ottawa County . Hudsonville
LU 37 Tri-County Association . . . . Alpena

LU 38 Saginaw-Bay-Midland
Counties . . . . Chesaning
LU 39 Macomb-St. Clair
Counties . . . . Marine City
LU 42 Top-O-Michigan
RLCA . . . . Cheboygan
LU 43 Tuscola-Sanilac
Counties . . . . Fostoria
LU 44 Upper Peninsula
Association . . . . . . Bark River
LU 45 Van Buren
County . . . . South Haven
LU 46 Washtenaw
County . . . . Ann Arbor
LU 47 Wayne County . . . Dearborn
Heights
LU 26 Mason County . . . Ludington
LU 30 Montcalm County . . Stanton
SA Michigan . . . . . . Bark River

Security, Police and Fire
Professionals
LU. . . . . Flint
LU 32 . . . . Tapinabee
LU 35 . . . . Chelsea
LU 40 . . . . South Haven
LU 41 . . . . Roseville
LU 114 . . . . Centerline
LU 116. . . . . Pontiac
LU 117 . . . . Flint
LU 124 . . . . Roseville
LU 149 . . . . Lansing
LU 168 . . . . Saginaw
LU 349. . . . . Boyne City
LU 525 . . . . Adrian
LU 564 . . . . Republic
LU 1212 . . . . Detroit
NHQ . . . . Roseville

Service Employees
JC 35 . . . . Detroit
LU 32 Firemen & Oilers. . . Livonia
LU 78 Firemen & Oilers . . . Otsego
LU 79. . . . . Detroit
LU 79 Hackley Hospital . Muskegon
LU 79 Professional Registered
Nurses . . . . Bay City
LU 99-A Firemen & Oilers . Otsego
LU 1219 Firemen & Oilers . Owosso

Sheet Metal Workers
LU 7. . . . . Lansing
LU 80 . . . . Southfield
LU 292 . . . . Troy

State, County and Municipal
Employees
C 25 Michigan. . . . . . . Lansing
LU 139 Jackson Medical Center
Employees . . . . Jackson
LU 140 Hospital & Nursing Home
Employees. . . . . . . Oak Park
LU 181 Detroit Receiving
Hospital . . . . Detroit
LU 226 Houghton County Public
Employees Union . . . . Hancock
LU 249 Lenawee County Hospital &
Medical Care. . . . . . . Adrian
LU 825 Hurley Medical Center
LPN. . . . . Flint
LU 825-C . . . . Lansing
LU 867 Kelsey Memorial
Hospital . . . . Lakeview
LU 875 . . . . Flint
LU 992 Gogebic County Public
Employees. . . . . . . Ironwood
LU 1106 Olivet College
Employees . . . . Olivet

LU 1511 Gratiot County Public &
Hospital Employees . . . Elm Hall
LU 1640 Community Social Agency
Employees. . . . . Detroit
LU 1820 St. Joseph Mercy Hospital
Employees Union . . . . Pontiac
LU 1855 Public & Hospital
Employees, 3 Counties . Rosebush
LU 1923 Ontonagon County Public
Employees Union . . . Ontonagon
LU 2372 Greenery Nursing Home
Employees. . . . . Howell
LU 2568 Oakwood
Employees. . . . . . Lincoln Park
LU 2635 St. Joseph Hospital
Employees . . . . . Columbiaville
LU 2642 Hills & Dales General
Hospital Employees. . . Cass City
LU 2653 St. Francis Hospital
Employees. . . . . . . Escanaba
LU 2793 Oakland County
Private Sector
Employees. . . . Bloomfield Hills
LU 3069 Michigan Legal Services
Plan Attorneys . . . . . Saginaw
LU 3082 Metropolitan Hospital
Employees . . . . . . Hamtramck
LU 3110 Genesee County Michigan
Convalescent . . . . Flint
LU 3579 Bay Medical
Center . . . . Auburn
LU 3582 Grand Valley State
University Food
Service . . . . Allendale
LU 3695 . . . . Detroit

Steelworkers
LU 5266 . . . . Kawkawlin
LU 15203 . . . . Saginaw
LU 02-49-L . . . Grand Rapids
LU 02-84-S . . . . Owosso
LU 02-139-S . . . . . . Lachine
LU 02-182-S . . . . . . Pickford
LU 02-199-S . . . . . . Alpena
LU 02-204-S . . . . . . Alpena
LU 02-206-A. . . . . . . Alpena
LU 02-207-S . . . . . . Alpena
LU 02-209-S . . . . . . Alpena
LU 02-210-L . . . . Benton Harbor
LU 02-211-SA . . . . . Alpena
LU 02-431-L . . . . Covert
LU 02-609-L . . . . . Kalamazoo
LU 02-690-L . . . . Detroit
LU 02-882-L . . . . Port Sanilac
LU 02-1018-L . . . . Caro
LU 02-1279-S . . . Sterling Heights
LU 02-1299-S . . . . River Rouge
LU 02-1358-S. . . . . . Southfield
LU 02-1900-S . . . . South Lyon
LU 02-2167-S . . . . . Plainwell
LU 02-2395 . . . . . . Tecumseh
LU 02-2511-S . . . . . . Monroe
LU 02-2659-S . . . . . Southgate
LU 02-3056-S. . . . . . . Galien
LU 02-3135-S. . . . . Marquette
LU
02-4933-S . Chesterfield Township
LU 02-4950-S . . . . . Ishpeming
LU 02-4974-S. . . . . Marquette
LU 02-5024-S . . . . . White Pine
LU 02-5187-S . . . . Kawkawlin
LU 02-5965-S . . . . . Hastings
LU 02-6119-S . . . . . . Augusta
LU 02-6222-S. . . . . . . Caro
LU 02-6277-S . . . . . . Delton
LU 02-6747-S . . . . Battle Creek
LU 02-6811-S . . . . . Allegan
LU 02-7237-S . . . . . . Adrian

LU 02-7380-S . . . . . Bay City
LU 02-7489-S . . . . . . Macomb
LU 02-7652-S . . . . Pinconning
LU 02-7720-S . . Sterling Heights
LU 02-7798-S . . . . . Mohawk
LU 02-7948-S . . . . Rogers City
LU 02-8058-S . . . . . Charlotte
LU 02-8082-S . . . . . Plainwell
LU 02-8086-S . . . . Niles
LU 02-8140-S. . . . . . Rudyard
LU 02-8220-S . . . . Port Huron
LU 02-8287-S . . . . . Kalkaska
LU 02-8293-S . . . . Ishpeming
LU 02-8339-S . . . . . Concord
LU 02-8384-S . . . . . Conway
LU 02-8410-S . . . . Bridgeport
LU 02-8422-S . . . . . Bay City
LU 02-8569-S . . . West Branch
LU 02-8874-S . . . . . . Adrian
LU 02-8986-S. . . . . . . Hart
LU 02-9036-S . . . . . Saginaw
LU 02-9162-S . . . . . Berkley
LU 02-9264-S . . . River Rouge
LU 02-9442. . . . . . . Pigeon
LU 02-12075-S . . . . Midland
LU 02-12295-S . . . . Bridgman
LU 02-12585-S. . . . . Manistee
LU 02-12760-S . . . . . Pigeon
LU 02-12773-S . . . . Ludington
LU 02-12934-S . . . . Midland
LU 02-13569-S . . Sault Ste. Marie
LU 02-13635-S . . Sault Ste. Marie
LU 02-13685-S . . Sault Ste. Marie
LU 02-13702-A. . Clinton Township
LU 02-13729-S. . . . . . . Niles
LU 02-14009-S. . . . . . Merrill
LU 02-14178-S . . . . Coldwater
LU 02-14317-S . . . . . Cadillac
LU 02-14449-S . . . . . Manton
LU 02-14450-S. . . . . Manistee
LU 02-14540-S . . . . . . Mio
LU 02-14557-S . . . . . Frankfort
LU 02-14723-S . . . . . . Adrian
LU 02-14758-S. . . . . Manistee
LU 02-14913-S . . . . Rogers City
LU 02-14965-S . . . . Essexville
LU 02-15095-S . . . West Branch
LU 02-15100-S. . . . . Coleman
LU 02-15157-S . . . . . Bay City
LU 02-15301-S . . . . Essexville
LU 02-15528-S. . . . West Branch
LU 02-16201-S. . . . . . Niles
LU 11-13547-S . . . Sault Ste. Marie

Teachers
LU 1899 Hebrew Teachers
Association, Shaarez
Zedek . . . . . . West Bloomfield
LU 1899 Hillel Day School Teachers
Association . . . . West Bloomfield
LU 4437 Federation of Credit Union
Employees . . . . Taylor
SFED Michigan . . . . . Detroit

Teamsters
JC 43 . . . . Detroit
LU 7 . . . . Kalamazoo
LU 51 . . . . Detroit
LU 164. . . . . Jackson
LU 243 . . . . Detroit
LU 247 . . . . Detroit
LU 283 . . . . Wyandotte
LU 299 . . . . Detroit
LU 328 . . . . Escanaba
LU 332 . . . . Flint
LU 337 . . . . Detroit
LU 339 . . . . Port Huron
LU 372 . . . . Detroit

LU 406 . . . . Grand Rapids
LU 486 . . . . Saginaw
LU 580 . . . . Lansing
LU 614 . . . . Pontiac
LU 1038 . . . . Detroit
LU 1620 . . . . Canton
LU 2040 Detroit Mailers
Union. . . . . Detroit

Television and Radio Artists
LU 202 Detroit . . . . . Southfield

Theatrical Stage Employees
LU 26 . . . . Grand Rapids
LU 38. . . . . Detroit
LU 179-B . . . . Warren
LU 199 . . . . Hazel Park
LU 201 . . . . Flint
LU 274 . . . . Lansing
LU 395 . . . . Ann Arbor
LU 472 . . . . Burton
LU 757 . . . . . St. Clair Shores
LU 786. . . . . Roseville
LU 812 . . . . Detroit
SA Michigan
Alliance. . . . . St. Clair Shores

Tool Craftsmen
LU 6 . . . . Charlotte
LU 8 . . . . Belding

Train Dispatchers
SCOM Grand Trunk Western
Railroad. . . . . . . Waterford

Transit Union
LU 1564 . . . . . Madison Heights
LU 1639 . . . . Kalamazoo

Transport Workers
LU 521 . . . . Romulus
LU 574 . . . . Ishpeming
LU 2051 . . . . Allen Park

Transportation Communications
Union
D 289 Southeastern . . . . Southgate
D 354 Grand Trunk
Railway. . . . . . . Grosse Pointe
D 493 . . . . Newport
D 706 . . . . Bay City
D 1950 Allied Services
Division . . . . Taylor
LG 187 . . . . Marquette
LG 669. . . . . Westland
LG 5004 Grand Trunk . . . Lennon
LG 6318 Pontiac . . . . . Burton
LG 6327 Flint . . . . . Bay City
LG 6334 Detroit . . . . Lincoln Park
LG 6638 Junior. . . . Battle Creek
LG 6641 Huron . . . Port Huron
LG 6789 Valley City . . . Allendale
SBA 45 Grand Trunk . . White Lake

Transportation Union
GCA GO-377 Grand Trunk Western
Railroad . . . . Pontiac
GCA GO-627 Conrail-PC-ND-
NYC. . . . . Warren
GCA GO-630 Conrail-Western
Region. . . . . Dearborn
LU 72 . . . . Battle Creek
LU 194. . . . . . . Edwardsburg
LU 278 . . . . Perry
LU 313 . . . . Wyomins
LU 320 . . . . Saginaw
LU 734 . . . . Battle Creek
LU 881 . . . . Milan

LU 886 . . . . Marquette
LU 927. . . . . Warren
LU 1183 . . . . Fort Gratiot
LU 1438 . . . . Melvindale
LU 1477 . . . . Carleton
LU 1709 . . . . White Lake
LU 1736. . . . . Davison
LU 1760 . . . . Livonia
LU 1765 . . . . Grand Rapids
SLB LO-25 Michigan . . . . Lansing

Treasury Employees
CH 24. . . . . Detroit
CH 78. . . . . Detroit
CH 152. . . . . Port Huron
CH 173 . . . . Detroit
CH 187 . . . . . Sault Ste. Marie

Utility Workers
LU 101 . . . . Rives Junction
LU 103 . . . . Muskegon
LU 104 . . . . Reese
LU 105 . . . . Fenton
LU 106 . . . . Battle Creek
LU 107. . . . . Byron Center
LU 119 . . . . Burton
LU 123 . . . . Eagle
LU 124 . . . . Ludington
LU 129 . . . . Ithaca
LU 144 . . . . Bay City
LU 150. . . . . Kalamazoo
LU 154 . . . . Bitely
LU 223 . . . . Dearborn
LU 223 Buildings & Properties
    Division . . . . Detroit
LU 223 Enrico Fermi Division . Erie
LU 223 Maintenance
    Division . . . . Dearborn
LU 223 Meter Department
    Division . . . . Riverview
LU 223 Motor Transportation
    Division . . . . Plymouth
LU 223 Office, Professional &
    Technical Division . . . Dearborn
LU 223 Stores & Transportation
    Division . . . . Detroit
LU 223 Substation
    Division . . . . Dearborn
LU 223 Underground Lines
    Division . . . . Dearborn

LU 223 Warren Service Shops
    Division. . . . . Northville
LU 253 . . . . Owosso
LU 254 . . . . Roseville
LU 257 . . . . Hastings
LU 258 . . . . Newport
LU 261 . . . . Howard City
LU 286 . . . . Alpena
LU 295 . . . . Traverse City
LU 315 . . . . Midland
LU 337 . . . . Hesperia
LU 346 . . . . Cheboygan
LU 347 . . . . Kingsley
LU 358 . . . . Saginaw
LU 388. . . . . . . Grand Haven
LU 417. . . . . Monroe
LU 445 . . . . Battle Creek
LU 473 . . . . Port Huron
LU 517 . . . . Erie
LU 521 . . . . Interlochen
LU 543. . . . . Monroe
LU 564 . . . . Midland
LU 911. . . . . Monroe
STC Michigan. . . . . . . Lansing

Weather Service Employees
BR 03-19 . . . . . . Grand Rapids
BR 03-33 . . . . . . White Lake
BR 03-57 . . . . Gaylord
BR 03-69 . . . . Negaunee

Westinghouse Salaried Employees
ASSN Detroit . . . . . . Southfield

Unaffiliated Labor Organizations
Altec Employees Union . . . Howell
Bay County Public Health Registered
    Nurses . . . . Bay City
Central Office Staff
    Association . . . . Lansing
Citation Tool Employees Bargaining
    Committee . . . . Fraser
Clerical Association LU 214 . Detroit
Dean Transportation Employees
    Association . . . . Lansing
Executone of Northeastern Employee
    Association . . . . . Frankenmuth

Executone of Northeastern Michigan
    Employee Association
    International. . . . . Frankenmuth
Grand Rapids Employee
    Association . . . . Grand Rapids
Gratiot Community Hospital
    Registered Nurse
    Association . . . . . Mount Pleasant
Great Lakes Licensed Officers
    Organization . . . . Detroit
Greektown Casino Police
    Officers. . . . . Southfield
Licensed Practical Nurse
    Association . . . . Canton
Licensed Practical Nurses
    Association of Hutzel
    Hospital . . . . Detroit
Maghielse Employee Labor
    Organization . . . . Grand Rapids
Magline Standish Employees
    Association . . . . Standish
Manchester Plastics Independent
    Union . . . . Manchester
McClain Hourly Employees
    Union . . . Chesterfield Township
Metropolitan Council of Newspaper
    Workers Justice
    Committee . . . . Detroit
Michigan Association of Police
    911 . . . . Southfield
Michigan Association of Police 911
    Mount Clemens General Security
    Office . . . . Detroit
Michigan Association of Police
    Cranbrook Public Safety
    Officers . . . . Waterford
Michigan Association of Police
    Henry Ford Health System
    Police. . . . . Detroit
Michigan Association of Police
    Loomis Armored Guards
    Association . . . . Holly
Michigan Association of Police St.
    Joseph Mercy-Oakland
    Public . . . . Pontiac
Michigan Executive Directors
    Association . . . . Auburn Hills
Michigan Nurses Association Lapeer
    Registered Nurse Staff
    Council . . . . Lapeer

Monroe Federation of School
    Administrators . . . . . Monroe
North Ottawa Community Hospital
    Employees Association
    (NOCHEA) . . . . Grand Haven
Nucraft Committee Nucraft
    Furniture Company
    Employees. . . . Comstock Park
Paper Products Workers Association
    LU 1 . . . . Livonia
Pico Employees
    Association . . . . . . Wyandotte
Pine Knoll Convalescent Center Inc.
    Employees Association. . . Taylor
Plant Protection Independent Ford
    Sterling Plant LU
    598 . . . . Grosse Pointe
Plant Protection Independent
    National LU
    255 . . . . Browstown Township
Precase Concrete Products Union LU
    14 . . . . Waterford
Professional Representatives
    Organization. . . . . . . Warren
Rapid Engineering Employees
    Association . . . . Belmont
Registered Nurses Staff Council
    Spectrum Health-Kent Community
    Camp . . . . Grand Rapids
Renaissance Police Officers
    Association. . . . . Detroit
Rochester Crittenton Medical Lab
    Employees Association . Rochester
Rochester Crittenton
    Radiologic Employees
    Association . . . Rochester Hills
Starr Commonwealth Employees
    Association. . . . . . . Albion
UAW Staff Council . . . . . Detroit
United Protective Workers of
    America LU 1 . . . . . Dearborn
University of Detroit Police Officers
    Association Inc. . . . . . Detroit
Westland Convalescent Center
    Employees Association . Westland
Wire Drawers United Inc. . . Comins
Wisne Automation Employees . Novi
Wolverine Products Pipe Line
    Union . . . . Manchester

Minnesota

AFL-CIO Trade and Industrial Departments

Building and Construction Trades Department
BCTC Brainerd. . . . . . . Brainerd
BCTC Duluth. . . . . Duluth
BCTC Iron Range. . . . . Virginia
BCTC Mankato-Minnesota
Valley . . . . Mankato
BCTC Minneapolis . . . Minneapolis
BCTC Minnesota State . . . St. Paul
BCTC Northwest
Minnesota. . . . . Detroit Lakes
BCTC Southeastern
Minnesota. . . . . Rochester
BCTC St. Cloud . . . . . . St. Cloud
BCTC St. Paul. . . . . . . St. Paul
BCTC Willmar . . . . . . Willmar

Affiliated Labor Organizations

Agricultural Employees
BR 38 . . . . St. Paul

Air Traffic Controllers
LU DLH . . . . Duluth
LU FCM . . . . Eden Prairie
LU M98. . . . . Minneapolis
LU MIC . . . . Crystal
LU MSP . . . . Minneapolis
LU RST . . . . Rochester
LU STP . . . . St. Paul
LU ZMP . . . . Farmington

Aircraft Mechanics
LU 33 MSP . . . . . Bloomington
LU 35. . . . . Duluth

Asbestos Workers
LU 34. . . . . Minneapolis
LU 49. . . . . Duluth
LU 133 . . . . Crookston
LU 205 Asbestos & Hazardous Waste
Abatement . . . . . Minneapolis

Automobile, Aerospace Workers
C Minnesota CAP . . . Bloomington
LU 125. . . . . St. Paul
LU 241 . . . . Knife River
LU 316 . . . . Caledonia
LU 349 . . . . Hibbing
LU 683 . . . . Minneapolis
LU 722 St. Paul-Minneapolis
Local . . . . Cologne
LU 763 . . . . . . South St. Paul
LU 867 Albert Lea-Austin
Local . . . . Austin
LU 879. . . . . St. Paul
LU 958 . . . . Lacrescent
LU 1016 . . . . Fairmont
LU 2125. . . . . Rochester
LU 2340 . . . . Winona

Bakery, Confectionery, Tobacco Workers and Grain Millers
C -G District 2-Sugar
Council . . . . Olivia
LU 1-G. . . . . Cannon Falls
LU 13-G . . . . . . Cannon Falls
LU 22 . . . . Minneapolis
LU 27-G . . . . Minneapolis
LU 55-G . . . . Burnsville

LU 62-G . . . . Lake Crystal
LU 133-G . . . . Winona
LU 264-G . . . . East Grand Forks
LU 265-G . . . . Shakopee
LU 266-G . . . . Moorhead
LU 267-G . . . . Crookston
LU 360-G. . . . . . . Worthington
LU 369-G . . . . Bird Island
LU 403-G . . . . Minneapolis

Boilermakers
LG 3 . . . . Coon Rapids
LG 647 . . . . Ramsey
LG 650 . . . . Lake City

Bricklayers
LU 1. . . . . Moorhead
LU 1 Minnesota . . . Minneapolis

Carpenters
C North Central
Regional . . . . . Hermantown
DC Minnesota Statewide . . St. Paul
LU 87 . . . . St. Paul
LU 190-L . . . . Minneapolis
LU 361. . . . . Hermantown
LU 548 . . . . . . New Brighton
LU 587. . . . . St. Paul
LU 596. . . . . Roseville
LU 606 . . . . Virginia
LU 766 . . . . Albert Lea
LU 851 . . . . Anoka
LU 930 . . . . St. Cloud
LU 1348. . . . . Virginia
LU 1382. . . . . Rochester
LU 1644 . . . . Minneapolis
LU 1847 . . . . Richfield
LU 1865 Twin City Cabinetmakers
and Millmen . . . . Minneapolis

Christian Labor Association
LU 78 Highway Construction
Workers. . . . . Willmar
LU 84 United Construction
Workers. . . . . Willmar

Civilian Technicians
CH 21 Tony Kempenich
Memorial. . . . . . Little Falls
CH 73 Duluth. . . . . . . Duluth

Communications Workers
LU 7200 . . . . Minneapolis
LU 7201 . . . . St. Paul
LU 7202. . . . . Virginia
LU 7203. . . . . Rochester
LU 7204 . . . . Windom
LU 7205 . . . . Spicer
LU 7206 . . . . Winona
LU 7212 . . . . St. Cloud
LU 7214 . . . . Duluth
LU 7219 . . . . Wadena
LU 7220. . . . . Crookston
LU 7250 . . . . Minneapolis
LU 7270 . . . . Farmington
LU 7272 . . . . Erskine
LU 7290 . . . . Minneapolis
LU 14723 Albert Lea-Austin
Typo . . . . Austin
LU 14725 Duluth Typographical
Union. . . . . Duluth
LU 14726 . . . . Hibbing
LU 14727 . . . . International Falls
LU 14728 . . . . Mankato
LU 14731 . . . . Sauk Rapids

LU 14733. . . . . Duluth
LU 37002 Twin Cities . St. Anthony
LU 37008 Lake Superior . . . Duluth
LU 57411 . . . . . . St. Louis Park
STC Minnesota . . . . Minneapolis

Electrical Workers
LU 23 . . . . St. Paul
LU 31. . . . . Duluth
LU 110. . . . . St. Paul
LU 160 . . . . Minneapolis
LU 242 . . . . Duluth
LU 292 . . . . Minneapolis
LU 294 . . . . Hibbing
LU 343 . . . . Rochester
LU 366 . . . . Esko
LU 506 . . . . Fridley
LU 731 . . . . . . International Falls
LU 783. . . . . St. Paul
LU 886 . . . . Mora
LU 949 . . . . Burnsville
LU 1999 . . . . . . North Mankato
LU 2047 . . . . . . South St. Paul
STC 16 Minnesota. . . . . St. Paul

Electrical, Radio and Machine Workers
LU 1139 . . . . Minneapolis

Electronic Workers
LU 1042 . . . . St. Paul
LU 1140 . . . . Minneapolis
LU 1160 . . . . . . Mountain Iron

Elevator Constructors
LU 9 . . . . Minneapolis

Federal Employees
LU 14 . . . . Burnsville
LU 2138 . . . . Silver Bay

Flint Glass Workers
LU 133 . . . . Shakopee

Food and Commercial Workers
LU 6 . . . . Albert Lea
LU 6 . . . . Chaska
LU 9. . . . . Austin
LU 12. . . . . Duluth
LU 134. . . . . Plymouth
LU 199 . . . . Rochester
LU 228-C . . . . Winona
LU 335. . . . . Red Wing
LU 442-P . . . . Owatonna
LU 527 . . . . Red Wing
LU 653. . . . . Plymouth
LU 789 . . . . . . South St. Paul
LU 1116 . . . . Duluth
LU 1161 . . . . Worthington

Glass, Molders, Pottery and Plastics Workers
CONBD Midwest. . . . Minneapolis
CONBD Twin Cities . . Minneapolis
LU 21-B. . . . . Hibbing
LU 37-B. . . . . Virginia
LU 63-B . . . . Minneapolis
LU 129. . . . . Chaska
LU 142-B. . . . . Mankato

Government Employees
C 259 VA, Eighth
District . . . . Minneapolis
LU 169 USDA . . . . Austin
LU 368 USDA . . . . . Albert Lea

LU 390 VA. . . . . . Sauk Rapids
LU 488 USDA . . . . Long Prairie
LU 683 DoJ. . . . . Duluth
LU 800 . . . . Minneapolis
LU 801 Council of Prison . . Waseca
LU 1106 OGC/USDA . . . St. Paul
LU 1969 VA . . . . Fort Snelling
LU 1997 DoD . . . . Minneapolis
LU 2265 DoD . Inver Grove Heights
LU 2999 DoD . . . . . . St. Paul
LU 3015 USDA . . . Worthington
LU 3105 DoJ . . . . Apple Valley
LU 3129 SSA. . . . . Minneapolis
LU 3381 HHS . . . . Minneapolis
LU 3419 HUD . . . . Minneapolis
LU 3669 VA . . . . . Minneapolis
LU 3935 DoJ . . . . Duluth
LU 3947 Council of
Prison . . . . Rochester

Government Security Officers
LU . . . . St. Paul
LU 24 . . . . Red Wing
LU 28. . . . . Monticello

Graphic Communications
LU 1-B . . . . Minneapolis
LU 1-M Upper Midwest. . . St. Paul
LU 6-A Twin Cities . . . . St. Paul
LU 29-C . . . . St. Paul
LU 76-C . . . . Duluth
LU 379-C Mankato Pressman's
Union . . . . . North Mankato

Guards
LU 32 . . . . Eagan
LU 51 . . . . Andover
RC Fifth. . . . . Blaine

Hotel and Restaurant Employees
LU 17. . . . . Minneapolis
LU 21 . . . . Rochester
LU 99 . . . . Duluth
STC Minnesota . . . . Minneapolis

Independent Unions Federation
LU 220 American Musicians Union
of Minnesota . . . . . Rochester
LU 440 American Musicians Union
of Minnesota . . . . . Zimmerman

Iron Workers
DC North Central
Minnesota . . . . . . Woodbury
LU 512. . . . . St. Paul
LU 535. . . . . St. Paul
LU 563 . . . . Duluth

Laborers
DC Minnesota-North
Dakota. . . . . Lino Lakes
LU 68 . . . . Wells
LU 132. . . . . St. Paul
LU 405 . . . . Rochester
LU 563 . . . . Minneapolis
LU 1091 . . . . Duluth
LU 1097 . . . . Virginia

Letter Carriers
BR 9 . . . . Minneapolis
BR 28 . . . . St. Paul
BR 90. . . . . Mankato
BR 114 . . . . Duluth
BR 350 Faribault,
Minnesota . . . . . . Faribault

BR 388 . . . . St. Cloud
BR 401 . . . . Red Wing
BR 440 . . . . Rochester
BR 679 . . . . Crookston
BR 717 . . . . Austin
BR 718 . . . . Albert Lea
BR 776 . . . . Owatonna
BR 806 . . . . Fergus Falls
BR 864 . . . . Brainerd
BR 911 Northfield,
    Minnesota . . . . . . Northfield
BR 956 . . . . New Ulm
BR 1051 . . . . Moorhead
BR 1058 . . . . Hibbing
BR 1092 . . . . Bemidji
BR 1109 Lake City,
    Minnesota . . . . . . Lake City
BR 1113 . . . . Sleepy Eye
BR 1117 . . . . Willmar
BR 1243 . . . . Cloquet
BR 1246 . . . . Virginia
BR 1317 . . . . . . Detroit Lakes
BR 1418 . . . . . Thief River Falls
BR 1446 Montevideo,
    Minnesota . . . . . Montevideo
BR 1447 . . . . Waseca
BR 1451 Eveleth,
    Minnesota . . . . . . Eveleth
BR 1532 . . . Inver Grove Heights
BR 1581 . . . . Marshall
BR 1722 Pipestone,
    Minnesota . . . . . . Pipestone
BR 1927 Morris, Minnesota . Morris
BR 1959 Warren,
    Minnesota . . . . . . Warren
BR 2013 Redwood Falls,
    Minnesota . . . . Redwood Falls
BR 2065 . . . . Worthington
BR 2121 Breckenridge,
    Minnesota . . . . . Breckenridge
BR 2149 International Falls,
    Minnesota . . . International Falls
BR 2166 Tracy, Minnesota . . Tracy
BR 2377 . . . . St. James
BR 2415 Ada, Minnesota . . . . Ada
BR 2548 Hutchinson,
    Minnesota . . . . . . Hutchinson
BR 2590 Springfield,
    Minnesota . . . . . . Springfield
BR 2637 Le Sueur,
    Minnesota . . . . . . Le Sueur
BR 2869 Ely, Minnesota . . . . . Ely
BR 2870 Staples, Minnesota . Staples
BR 2937 Blue Earth,
    Minnesota . . . . . . Blue Earth
BR 2938 Spring Valley,
    Minnesota . . . . . Spring Valley
BR 2939 . . . . Luverne
BR 2942 . . . . Hopkins
BR 3140 . . . . . East Grand Forks
BR 3193 Waterville,
    Minnesota . . . . . . Waterville
BR 3196 New Prague,
    Minnesota . . . . . New Prague
BR 3263 Montgomery,
    Minnesota . . . . . Montgomery
BR 3270 Park Rapids,
    Minnesota . . . . . . Park Rapids
BR 3283 Melrose,
    Minnesota . . . . . . Melrose
BR 3304 Madison,
    Minnesota . . . . . . Madison
BR 3522 Caledonia,
    Minnesota . . . . . . Caledonia
BR 3531 . . . . Litchfield
BR 3610 . . . . . . Grand Rapids
BR 3697 . . . . Le Center

BR 3776 Benson,
    Minnesota . . . . Benson
BR 4095 Glencoe,
    Minnesota . . . . . . Glencoe
BR 4096 Ortonville,
    Minnesota . . . . . . Ortonville
BR 4185 Granite Falls,
    Minnesota . . . . . Granite Fall
BR 4545 Aitkin, Minnesota . . Aitkin
BR 4833 Olivia, Minnesota . . Olivia
BR 4967 Kenyon,
    Minnesota . . . . . . Kenyon
BR 5204 . . . . Babbitt
BR 5213 Hoyt Lakes,
    Minnesota . . . . . Hoyt Lakes
BR 5228 Princeton,
    Minnesota . . . . . . Princeton
BR 5237 . . . . Silver Bay
BR 5249 Waconia,
    Minnesota . . . . . . Waconia
BR 5370 Aurora, Minnesota . Aurora
BR 5519 Appleton,
    Minnesota . . . . . . Appleton
BR 5545 Perham,
    Minnesota . . . . . . Perham
BR 5556 . . . . La Cresent
BR 5626 Canby, Minnesota . Canby
BR 5692 Plainview,
    Minnesota . . . . . . Plainview
BR 5776 Cannon Falls,
    Minnesota . . . . Cannon Falls
BR 5945 Bayport,
    Minnesota . . . . . . Bayport
BR 5946 Pine City,
    Minnesota . . . . . . Pine City
BR 6090 Stewartville,
    Minnesota . . . . . Stewartville
BR 6141 . . . . Warroad
BR 6172 . . . . St. Charles
BR 6182 Kasson,
    Minnesota . . . . . . Kasson
BR 6183 Chatfield,
    Minnesota . . . . . . Chatfield
BR 6228 Fosston,
    Minnesota . . . . . . Fosston
BR 6229 Wheaton,
    Minnesota . . . . . . Wheaton
SA Minnesota . . . . . . Northrop

Locomotive Engineers
DIV 9 . . . . Elysian
DIV 27 . . . . St. Cloud
DIV 117 . . . . Albert Lea
DIV 163 . . . . Duluth
DIV 164 . . . . Duluth
DIV 290 . . . . Duluth
DIV 333 . . . . Minneapolis
DIV 357 . . . . Eagan
DIV 369 . . . . St. Paul
DIV 494 . . . . West St. Paul
DIV 517 . . . . Oakdale
DIV 549 . . . . Spicer
DIV 768 . . . . Middle River
DIV 861 . . . . Duluth
GCA Chicago & Northwestern
    Railroad. . . . . Blaine
SLB Minnesota . . . . . . Blaine

Longshoremen
LU 1279 . . . . Duluth

Machinists
DLG 77 . . . . St. Paul
DLG 143 . . . . St. Paul
DLG 165 . . . . St. Cloud
LG 112 . . . . Burnsville
LG 149 . . . . Eagan
LG 197 . . . . Brainerd

LG 459 Capitol City & Minneapolis
    Metal Workers . . . . . St. Paul
LG 623 . . . . St. Cloud
LG 672 . . . . Proctor
LG 737 . . . . St. Paul
LG 760 . . . . Ranier
LG 924 . . . . Madison Lake
LG 1030 . . . . Winona
LG 1037 . . . . St. Paul
LG 1416 . . . . Owatonna
LG 1502 . . . . Esko
LG 1575 . . . . Duluth
LG 1833 . . . . Bloomington
LG 1956 . . . . Bingham Lake
LG 1996 . . . . Mora
LG 2036 . . . . Hastings
LLG W-33
    Woodworkers . International Falls
LLG W-62
    Woodworkers . . . Detroit Lakes
LLG W-150
    Woodworkers . . . . Shoreview
STC Minnesota . . . . . St. Paul

Maintenance of Way Employes
LG 91 . . . . Aitkin
LG 364 . . . . Crookston
LG 397 . . . . Aldrich
LG 519 . . . . Heron Lake
LG 1296 . . . . St. Cloud
LG 1488 . . . . Eden Valley
SD Duluth Missabe Iron
    Range . . . . Proctor
SD Soo Line . . . . Richfield
SF Burlington
    Northern . . . . . . Minneapolis
SF Chicago-Milwaukee-St.
    Paul-Pacific . . . . . . Elk River
SLG 57 . . . . Brownsville
SLG 144 . . . . Maplewood
SLG 182 . . . . Fertile
SLG 278 . . . . Waseca
SLG 322 . . . . Baudette
SLG 331 . . . . Wabasha
SLG 343 . . . . Savage
SLG 420 . . . . Glencoe
SLG 706 . . . . Hibbing
SLG 928 . . . . Minneapolis
SLG 1055 . . . . Willmar
SLG 1132 . . . . Bemidji
SLG 1490 . . . . Gully
SLG 1662 . . . . Barnum
SLG 1710 . . . . Duluth
SLG 1879 . . . . Burnsville
SLG 1906 . . . . Hastings

Musicians
LU 18 . . . . Duluth
LU 30-73 Twin Cities . . . . St. Paul
LU 382 . . . . Moorhead
LU 536 . . . . St. Joseph
LU 567 . . . . Faribault

National Staff Organization
ASSN Minnesota Professional
    Staff . . . . Duluth

Needletrades
LU 150 . . . . St. Paul

NLRB Professional Association
LU 18 . . . . Minneapolis
NHQ . . . . Minneapolis

Nurses
SA Minnesota . . . . . . St. Paul

Office and Professional Employees
LU 12 . . . . Minneapolis

Operating Engineers
LU 49 . . . . Minneapolis
LU 50 . . . . . . International Falls
LU 70 . . . . St. Paul
LU 756 . . . . Rochester

Painters
DC 82 . . . . St. Paul
LU 61 . . . . St. Paul
LU 106 . . . . Duluth
LU 259 . . . . Rochester
LU 386 . . . . Minneapolis
LU 681 . . . . Rochester
LU 880 . . . . St. Paul
LU 884 . . . . Milaca
LU 1324 . . . . Fridley
LU 2002 . . . . Stewartville

**Paper, Allied-Industrial, Chemical
Employees**
LU 7-75 . . . . St. Paul
LU 07-49 . . . . International Falls
LU 07-63 . . . . Cloquet
LU 07-79 Brainerd . . . . Brainerd
LU 07-118 . . . . New Ulm
LU 07-159 . . . . International Falls
LU 07-164 . . . . Pierz
LU 07-264 . . . . St. Paul
LU 07-274 . . . . St. Cloud
LU 07-409 . . . . Stillwater
LU 07-418 . . . . . Cottage Grove
LU 07-505 . . . . Fairmont
LU 07-528 . . . . Hastings
LU 07-578 . . . . Austin
LU 07-662 Pine Bend . . . Hastings
LU 07-717 . . . . Hastings
LU 07-776 . . . . Duluth
LU 07-970 . . . . Wrenshall
LU 07-1095 . . . . Grand Rapids
LU 07-1259 Minneapolis . . Ramsey
LU 07-1417 . . . . . . Belle Plaine
LU 07-1976 . . . . Sartell

Plasterers and Cement Masons
LU 265 . . . . Minneapolis
LU 633 . . . . Minneapolis
STCON Midwest Multi-State
    Conference . . . . . New Brighton

Plumbing and Pipe Fitting
DC 3 Twin City Pipe
    Trades . . . . Minneapolis
LU 6 . . . . Rochester
LU 11 . . . . Duluth
LU 15 . . . . Minneapolis
LU 34 . . . . St. Paul
LU 126 . . . . Detroit Lakes
LU 340 . . . . New Hope
LU 417 . . . . Minneapolis
LU 455 . . . . St. Paul
LU 539 . . . . Minneapolis
LU 589 . . . . Virginia
SA Minnesota Pipe Trades . St. Paul

Postal and Federal Employees
LU 709 . . . . Minneapolis

Postal Mail Handlers
LU 323 . . . . St. Paul

Postal Workers
LU Twin Cities Postal Data
    Center . . . . Eagan
LU 65 St. Paul . . . . . . St. Paul
LU 125 Minneapolis . . Minneapolis

LU 142 Duluth Area . . . . Duluth
LU 207 International Falls
   Local . . . . . International Falls
LU 597 Morris Local . . . . Morris
LU 606 Moorhead . . . Moorhead
LU 631 Willmar. . . . . . Willmar
LU 647 St. Cloud Area . . St. Cloud
LU 798 Brainerd . . . . . Brainerd
LU 897 Rochester . . . . Rochester
LU 933 Worthington . . Worthington
LU 1006 Mankato . . . . Mankato
LU 1036 Winona . . . . . Winona
LU 1080 Austin. . . . . . . Austin
LU 1130 Thief River
   Falls . . . . . . Thief River Falls
LU 1333 Detroit
   Lakes . . . . Detroit Lakes
LU 1544 Litchfield Local . Litchfield
LU 2321 Marshall . . . . Marshall
LU 2364 St. Peter Local . . St. Peter
LU 2885 Windom . . . . Windom
LU 3142 Fergus Falls . . Fergus Falls
LU 3890 Hutchinson
   Local . . . . Hutchinson
LU 5425 Wayzata Local . . Wayzata
SA Minnesota . . . . Sartell

Railroad Signalmen
LLG 154 . . . . Hawley
LLG 168 . . . . Jackson
LLG 226 . . . . Paynesville

Roofers, Waterproofers and Allied
  Workers
LU 96 . . . . Minneapolis

Rural Letter Carriers
AREA 1 South and Southeast
  Minnesota . . . . Rochester
AREA 2 South and Southwest
  Minnesota . . . . Lakefield
AREA 3 East and Central
  Minnesota . . . . . Bloomington
AREA 4 Minnesota . . . . Melrose
AREA 5 North and Northwest
  Minnesota. . . . . Fertile
AREA 6 North and Central
  Minnesota. . . . . Ogilivie
LU Aitkin County . . . . . . Esko
LU Anoka-Sherburn-Isanti
  Counties . . . . Anoka
LU Beltrami County. . . . Bemidji
LU Benton County. . . . . . Foley
LU Big Stone-Traverse
  Counties. . . . . Dumont
LU Blue Earth-Nicollet
  Counties. . . . . Nicollet
LU Carver County . . . . . Waconia
LU Clay County . . . . . Moorhead
LU Clearwater County . . . Bagley
LU Dakota-Scott
  Counties . . . . Northfield
LU Dodge-Olmsted
  Counties. . . . . Rochester
LU Douglas & Pope County . Villard
LU Fillmore County . Spring Valley
LU Freeborn County . New Richland
LU Goodhue County . . . Red Wing
LU Houston County . . . Caledonia
LU Hubbard County . . Park Rapids
LU Jackson-Nobles-Rock
  Counties . . . . Rushmore
LU Kandiyohi County. . . . Atwater
LU Le Sueur County . . . Lonsdale
LU Lyon-Lincoln Counties . Tyler
LU McLeod County . . . . Stewart
LU Meeker County . . . . . Dassel

LU Morrison-Crow Wing
  Counties . . . . Bertha
LU Mower County . . . . . Austin
LU Norman-Mahnomen
  Counties . . . . Gary
LU Northeastern Minnesota . Aurora
LU Northern Minnesota
  Counties . . . . Viking
LU Ottertail County . . . Underwood
LU Polk County. . . . . . . Fertile
LU Redwood County . Walnut Grove
LU Rice County . . . . . . Kenyon
LU Sibley County . . . . Henderson
LU Stearns County . . . . . . Avon
LU Swift County . . . . . . Benson
LU Todd County . . . . Eagle Bend
LU Wadena County . . . . . Sebeka
LU Western Minnesota . Montevideo
LU Winona County . . . . Winona
LU 3 Chisago County . . . . Stacy
LU 5-B Becker
  County . . . . Detroit Lakes
LU 17 Fairbault-Martin
  Counties . . . . Sherburn
LU 22 Hennepin County . Plymouth
LU 26 Kanabec-Pine-Mille Lacs
  Counties . . . . Milaca
LU 53 Washington-Ramsey
  Counties . . . . Stacy
LU 61 Cass County . . . Pine River
LU 58 Wright County . . . . Buffalo
LU 60 Murray-Pipestone
  Counties . . . . Fulda
SA Minnesota . . . . Freeport

Service Employees
JC 7 . . . . Minneapolis
LU 26 . . . . Minneapolis
LU 113 . . . . Minneapolis
LU 259 Firemen & Oilers . . Duluth
LU 284 School Service . Eden Prairie
LU 292 Firemen & Oilers . . Isanti
LU 532 Firemen & Oilers . Andover
LU 937 Firemen &
  Oilers . . . . . . International Falls
LU 939 Firemen & Oilers . Cloquet
LU 970 Firemen & Oilers . . Canyon

Sheet Metal Workers
LU 10 . . . . St. Paul
LU 209 . . . . Shoreview
LU 403 . . . . Cloquet
LU 480 . . . . Faribault

State, County and Municipal
  Employees
C 6 Minnesota State Employees
  Union . . . . . South St. Paul
C 14 Twin Cities
  AFSCME . . . . . . South St. Paul
C 65 Minnesota . . . . . Nashwauk
DC 96 Minnesota
  Arrowhead . . . . Duluth
LU 8 St. Paul City & Ramsey County
  Employees . . . . . Apple Valley
LU 9 . . . . Minneapolis
LU 105 MLPNA . . . . . . Sawyer
LU 395 Ely-Bloomenson Community
  Hospital Employees . . . Embarrass
LU 722 St. Paul Ramsey Hospital
  Employees . . . . St. Paul
LU 730 . . . . Buhl
LU 753 St. Cloud State University
  Employees . . . . Rice
LU 791 City of Hibbing. . . Hibbing
LU 1119 Hibbing-Big Fork Hospital
  Employees. . . . . . . Keewatin

LU 1149 Lake Region Hospital
  Employees . . . . . Fergus Falls
LU 1949 Bemidji State University
  Employees . . . . Bemidji
LU 2385 Southwest Minnesota State
  College Employees . . . Marshall
LU 3481 . . . . . . South St. Paul
LU 3558 Arrowhead Region
  Non-Profit Employees . . . Duluth
LU 3931 North Central Blood
  Services . . . . . . West St. Paul

Steelworkers
LU 11-31-L . . . . Red Wing
LU 11-61-U. . . . . . Minneapolis
LU 11-460-G . . . . Kasota
LU 11-1028-S . . . . Duluth
LU 11-1938-S . . . . . . Virginia
LU 11-2127-S . . Vadnais Heights
LU 11-2175-S . . . . . Farmington
LU 11-2660-S . . . . . . Keewatin
LU 11-2705-S . . . . . . Chisholm
LU 11-4108-S . . . . . Hoyt Lakes
LU 11-6115-S . . . . Virginia
LU 11-6803-S . . . . . . Albert Lea
LU 11-6860-S . . . . . . Eveleth
LU 11-7090-S . . . . . . Eveleth
LU 11-7263-S . . . . Cottage Grove
LU 11-7505-S . . . . . . Crosby
LU 11-7796-S . . White Bear Lake
LU 11-8392-S . . . . . Grey Eagle
LU 11-9115-S . . . . . . Virginia
LU 11-9198-S . . . . . Plymouth
LU 11-9225-S . . . . . . Royalton
LU 11-9230-S . . . . . . Pierz
LU 11-9273-S . . . . . . Hewitt
LU 11-9333-S . . . . . Onamia
LU 11-9349-S . . . . . Chisholm
LU 11-9359-S . . . . . . Pierz
LU 11-9454 . . . . . . Lonsdale
LU 11-9460. . . . . . . Duluth
LU 11-12106-S . . . . Minneapolis
LU 11-12571-S . . . Little Falls
LU 11-13241-S . . North Mankato
LU 11-15199-S . . . . Big Lake
LU 33-5859-S . . . . . . Crosby

Teachers
LU 3468 Breck Federation of
  Teachers . . . . . Minneapolis

Teamsters
CONF Bakery &
  Laundry . . . . . Minneapolis
JC 32 . . . . Minneapolis
LU 4 Minneapolis-St. Paul Mailers
  Union . . . . . Minneapolis
LU 120 . . . . St. Paul
LU 160 . . . . Rochester
LU 221 . . . . Minneapolis
LU 289 . . . . Minneapolis
LU 346 . . . . Duluth
LU 471 . . . . Minneapolis
LU 503 . . . . St. Paul
LU 638 . . . . Minneapolis
LU 792 . . . . Minneapolis
LU 970 . . . . Minneapolis
LU 974 . . . . Minneapolis
LU 1145 . . . . St. Paul
LU 2000 Airline
  Division . . . . . . Bloomington

Television and Radio Artists
LU Minneapolis . . . . Minneapolis

Theatrical Stage Employees
LU 13 . . . . Minneapolis
LU 219 . . . . Minneapolis

LU 416 . . . . Rochester
LU 490 Studio
  Mechanics . . . . . Minneapolis

Train Dispatchers
SCOM Duluth Missabe & Iron
  Range. . . . . Duluth
SCOM Soo Line. . . . . . . Eagan

Transport Workers
LU 543 . . . . Bloomington

Transportation Communications
  Union
LG 319 . . . . Duluth
LG 325 . . . . Shoreview
LG 434 . . . . St. Cloud
LG 593 . . . . Woodbury
LG 838 . . . . Richfield
LG 1085 . . . . Dilworth
LG 6004 Carvers Cave . Coon Rapids
LG 6615 Hiawatha . . . . Woodbury
LG 6811 Lakehead . . . . . Duluth
SBA 46 Consolidated Burlington
  Northern . . . . Fridley

Transportation Union
GCA GO-261 Chicago Milwaukee
  St. Paul-Pac
  Railroad-E . . . . . . Woodbury
GCA GO-270 . . . . . . Mankato
GCA GO-315 Duluth Missabe & Iron
  Range . . . . Two Harbors
GCA GO-321 Duluth Missabe &
  Ironrange-Missabe D. . . . Duluth
GCA GO-325 Duluth Winnipeg &
  Pacific Railway . . . . . Duluth
GCA GO-387 Burlington Northern
  Railroad. . . . . . Forest Lake
GCA GO-859 Soo Line
  Railroad. . . . . . . Wanamingo
LU 525 . . . . . East Grand Forks
LU 650. . . . . Shakopee
LU 911 . . . . Welch
LU 1000 . . . . Woodbury
LU 1067 . . . . Duluth
LU 1177 . . . . Willmar
LU 1292 . . . . Hermantown
LU 1614 . . . . Bloomington
LU 1882 . . . . Minnetonka
LU 1976 . . . . Circle Pines
SLB LO-26
  Minnesota . . . Columbia Heights

Treasury Employees
CH 29 . . . . St. Paul
CH 167 . . . . Duluth
CH 170 . . . . Edina

Weather Service Employees
BR 03-29 . . . . Chanhassen
BR 03-52 . . . . Duluth
BR 03-83 . . . . Chanhassen

Unaffiliated Labor
Organizations

A M P I Employees
  Union . . . . New Ulm
AFSCME Council 14
  Employees Union,
  Independent . . . . South St. Paul
Aircraft Technical Support
  Association . . . . . St. Paul
Diagnostic Imaging
  Technologists . . . . . Andover
Education Minnesota . . . . St. Paul

Faribault Woolen Mill Workers
  Guild . . . . Faribault
Garlook Employees Union
  Independent . . . Young America
Honeywell Plant Protection
  Association Independent
  Honeywell Plant . . . Eden Prairie

Life Link Employee
  Association . . . . St. Paul
Milk Producers Inc.-Association
  Employees. . . . . . Paynesville
Minnesota Arrowhead District Staff
  Employee's Union C 96 . . Duluth

Minnesota Nurses Association Staff
  Organization LU 1 . . . . St. Paul
Northwest Airlines Meteorologists
  Association . . . . St. Paul

Paper Mill Workers Union
  Independent Blandin Paper
  Company Hourly
  Employees . . . . Grand Rapids
Prior Lake Secretary Association LU
  4887 . . . . Prior Lake
Soo Line Locomotive & Car
  Foremen's . . . . . Circle Pines
Technical Employees Association of
  Minnesota . . . . . Minneapolis

Mississippi

AFL-CIO Trade and Industrial Departments

Building and Construction Trades Department

BCTC Central Mississippi . Jackson
BCTC Mississippi Gulf
  Coast . . . . Gulfport
BCTC Northeast
  Mississippi . . . . Brandon

Metal Trades Department

MTC Pascagoula . . . . . Pascagoula
MTC South Central
  Mississippi . . . . Gulfport

Affiliated Labor Organizations

Air Traffic Controllers

LU GPT . . . . Gulfport
LU JAN . . . . Jackson
LU NMM . . . . Lauderdale

Asbestos Workers

LU 114 . . . . Columbus

Automobile, Aerospace Workers

LU 1724 . . . . Clarksdale
LU 1956 . . . . Pearl
LU 2190 . . . . Laurel
LU 2402 . . . . Brandon

Boilermakers

LG 110 . . . . Hattiesburg
LG 693 . . . . Pascagoula
LG 903 . . . . West Point

Carpenters

C Southern Industrial Workers
  #4065 . . . . Jackson
LU 303 Mississippi . . . . Vicksburg
LU 1409 . . . . Coila
LU 2085 . . . . Natchez
LU 2086 . . . . Magee
LU 2116 . . . . Grenada
LU 2147 Southern Council of
  Industrial Workers . . . Vicksburg
LU 2153 . . . . Raleigh
LU 2181 . . . . Canton
LU 2272 . . . . Shuqualak
LU 2280 . . . . Osyka
LU 2285 . . . . Vicksburg
LU 2289 . . . . Jackson
LU 2305 . . . . Columbus
LU 2335 . . . . Columbus
LU 2445 . . . . Columbus
LU 2568 . . . . Grenada
LU 2639 . . . . Bigcreek
LU 3031 . . . . Bentonia
LU 3181 . . . . Louisville
LU 3213 . . . . Bentonia

Communications Workers

LU 3490 . . . . Florence
LU 3504 . . . . Columbus
LU 3505 . . . . Corinth
LU 3509 . . . . Hattiesburg
LU 3510 . . . . Indianola
LU 3511 . . . . Jackson
LU 3513 . . . . Brookhaven
LU 3514 . . . . Meridian
LU 3516 . . . . Thaxton
LU 3517 . . . . Tupelo

LU 3518 . . . . Vicksburg
LU 3519 . . . . D'Iberville
LU 3550 . . . . Jackson
LU 14330 . . . . Gulfport

Electrical Workers

LU . . . . Mendenhall
LU 480 . . . . Jackson
LU 605 . . . . Jackson
LU 733 . . . . Pascagoula
LU 852 . . . . Corinth
LU 903 . . . . Gulfport
LU 917 . . . . Meridian
LU 985 . . . . Boyle
LU 1028 . . . . Tupelo
LU 1204 . . . . Hattiesburg
LU 1209 . . . . Collinsville
LU 1210 . . . . Laurel
LU 1211 . . . . Gulfport
LU 1317 . . . . Laurel
LU 1650 . . . . Natchez
LU 1840 . . . . Natchez
LU 1873 . . . . Vicksburg
LU 2164 . . . . Brandon
LU 2198 . . . . Mendenhall
LU 2265 . . . . Valley Park
SC U-21 Mississippi Power
  Company . . . . Gulfport

Electronic Workers

LU 655 . . . . Jackson
LU 698 . . . . Clinton
LU 718 . . . . Brookhaven
LU 792 . . . . Jackson
LU 794 . . . . Brandon
LU 799 . . . . Crystal Springs
LU 83770 . . . . Caledonia

Federal Employees

LU 589 . . . . Jackson
LU 943 . . . . Biloxi

Fire Fighters

LU 92-F . . . . Biloxi

Food and Commercial Workers

LU 361-g . . . . Hazlehurst
LU 583-C . . . . Sandersville
LU 790-C . . . . Brandon
LU 834-C . . . . Brandon
LU 982-C . . . . Canton
LU 1000-C . . . . Laurel
LU 1191-T . . . . . . Shuqualak
LU 1991 . . . . West Point

Government Employees

LU 1009 HUD . . . . Jackson
LU 1028 DoD . . . . . . Gulfport
LU 1031 . . . . Jackson
LU 1045 . . . . Gulfport
LU 1296 . . . . Columbus
LU 2053 DoD . . . . . . Gulfport
LU 2244 DoD . . . . . . Meridian
LU 2504 USDA . . . . . . Morton
LU 2543 USDA . . . . . Wiggins
LU 2670 DoD . . . . Biloxi
LU 3190 USDA . . . . . Nettleton
LU 3200 Hattiesburg Circuit Food
  Inspectors . . . . . Hattiesburg
LU 3310 DoD . . . . . . Vicksburg

Government Employees Association

LU 5-125-R . . . . Goutier

Graphic Communications

LU 223-M . . . . Walls
LU 734-S . . . . Clinton

Guards

LU 123 . . . . Port Gibson

Iron Workers

LU 469 . . . . Jackson

Laborers

LU 145 . . . . Jackson
LU 693 . . . . Collins

Letter Carriers

BR 94 . . . . Vicksburg
BR 217 Magnolia Capital
  City . . . . Jackson
BR 260 Lucedale,
  Mississippi . . . . . . Lucedale
BR 476 . . . . Natchez
BR 487 . . . . Collinsville
BR 516 . . . . Greenville
BR 938 . . . . Petal
BR 1080 . . . . Greenwood
BR 1195 . . . . Clarksdale
BR 1374 . . . . Gulfport
BR 1437 . . . . Laurel
BR 1593 . . . . Saltillo
BR 1682 . . . . McComb
BR 1692 . . . . Columbus
BR 1963 Okolona,
  Mississippi . . . . . . Okolona
BR 2202 . . . . Corinth
BR 2241 . . . . Pascagoula
BR 2291 . . . . Starkville
BR 2396 Brookhaven,
  Mississippi . . . . Brookhaven
BR 2403 Lumberton,
  Mississippi . . . . . Lumberton
BR 2543 Charleston,
  Mississippi . . . . . Charleston
BR 2832 Leland, Mississippi . Leland
BR 2842 New Albany,
  Mississippi . . . . . New Albany
BR 2896 . . . . Cleveland
BR 2995 Winona,
  Mississippi . . . . . . Winona
BR 3090 Louisville,
  Mississippi . . . . . Louisville
BR 3150 Indianola,
  Mississippi . . . . . Indianola
BR 3152 Aberdeen,
  Mississippi . . . . . Aberdeen
BR 3184 Philadelphia,
  Mississippi . . . . Philadelphia
BR 3548 Macon, Mississippi . Macon
BR 3773 . . . . Hazlehurst
BR 3781 . . . . Oxford
BR 3827 . . . . . . Ocean Springs
BR 4107 Hernando,
  Mississippi . . . . . Hernando
BR 4475 Forest, Mississippi . Forest
BR 4597 Drew, Mississippi . . Drew
BR 4610 Ruleville,
  Mississippi . . . . . Ruleville
BR 4927 Olive Branch,
  Mississippi . . . . Olive Branch
BR 5257 . . . . Mendenhall
BR 5511 . . . . Magee
BR 5842 Marks, Mississippi . Marks
BR 6299 Fulton, Mississippi . Fulton
BR 6362 Tylertown,
  Mississippi . . . . . Tylertown
BR 6441 . . . . Walls

SA Mississippi . . . . . . Natchez

Locomotive Engineers

DIV 23 . . . . Southaven
DIV 99 . . . . Water Valley
DIV 196 . . . . Smithdale
DIV 203 . . . . Lena
DIV 230 . . . . Meridian
DIV 450 . . . . Porterville
DIV 552 . . . . Hattiesburg
DIV 593 . . . . Meridian
DIV 762 . . . . Senatobia
DIV 827 . . . . Hattiesburg
DIV 919 . . . . Amory
SLB Mississippi State Legislative
  Board . . . . Southaven

Longshoremen

D East Gulf Dock & Marine
  Council . . . . Pascagoula
LU 1303 . . . . Gulfport
LU 1752 . . . . Pascagoula
LU 1967 . . . . Pascagoula

Machinists

DLG 73 . . . . Pascagoula
LG 14 . . . . Como
LG 18 . . . . Daleville
LG 261 . . . . Pascagoula
LG 1133 . . . . Pascagoula
LG 1341 . . . . Natchez
LG 1343 . . . . Richton
LG 2008 . . . . Clarksdale
LG 2249 . . . . Sandy Hook
LG 2386 . . . . Marion
LG 2793 . . . . Meridian
LLG 50 . . . . Columbus
LLG W-50 Woodworkers . Meridian
LLG W-349 Woodworkers . Liberty
LLG W-376 Woodworkers . Oxford
LLG W-440 Woodworkers . Natchez
LLG W-443 Woodworkers . . Laurel

Maintenance of Way Employes

LG 616 . . . . Union
LG 657 . . . . Sardis
LG 660 . . . . Purvis
LG 1171 . . . . West Point
SLG 615 . . . . Lucedale
SLG 637 . . . . Kilmichael
SLG 652 . . . . Edwards
SLG 916 . . . . Waveland
SLG 2838 . . . . Iuka

Musicians

LU 579 . . . . Jackson
LU 777 Association of the Gulf
  Coast . . . . Ocean Springs

National Staff Organization

LU Staff Organization, Mississippi
  Educators . . . . . Water Valley

Needletrades

LU 701-C . . . . Jackson
LU 708-A . . . . Jackson
LU 914-A . . . . Jackson
LU 944-C . . . . Jackson
LU 1148-C . . . . Jackson
LU 2550 . . . . Jackson
LU 2554 . . . . Jackson
LU 2576 . . . . Jackson

Office and Professional Employees

LU 204 . . . . Pascagoula

Operating Engineers
LU 624. . . . . Jackson

Painters
LU 1225 . . . . Pascagoula
LU 1967. . . . . Grenada

Paper, Allied-Industrial, Chemical Employees
LU 04-371 . . . . Sontag
LU 04-575 . . . . Brandon
LU 04-602. . . . . Natchez
LU 04-632 . . . . Columbus
LU 04-927 . . . . Woodville
LU 04-1076 . . . . Louisville
LU 04-1080. . . . . . . Vicksburg
LU 04-1113 . . . . Natchez
LU 04-1369 . . . . . . Monticello
LU 04-1384 . . . . McComb
LU 04-1418 . . . . Houston
LU 04-1452. . . . . . . Ackerman
LU 04-1501 . . . . . . Hattiesburg
LU 04-1578 . . . . Marion
LU 04-1699 . . . . Natchez
LU 04-1760 . . . . Hurly
LU 40-313 . . . . Florence

Plasterers and Cement Masons
LU 311. . . . . Jackson

Plumbing and Pipe Fitting
LU 436. . . . . Pascagoula
LU 568 . . . . Gulfport
LU 619 . . . . Vicksburg
LU 714 . . . . Brandon
SA Mississippi . . . . . . Gulfport
SA Tri-States Pipe
  Trades . . . . Vicksburg

Postal and Federal Employees
LU . . . . Pass Christian
D 4. . . . . Jackson
LU 405. . . . . Jackson
LU 414 Tupelo . . . . Saltillo

Postal Mail Handlers
LU 325. . . . . Jackson

Postal Workers
LU 54 Greenville . . . . . Greenville
LU 204 Gulfport . . . . . . Saucier
LU 389 Clarksdale . . . . Clarksdale
LU 440 Meridian. . . . . . Meridian
LU 968 McComb . . . . . McComb
LU 1200 Mississippi Gulf Coast Area
  Local . . . . Pass Christian
LU 1207 Jackson . . . . . Jackson
LU 1280 Tupelo . . . . . . Tupelo
LU 1311 Hattiesburg . . Hattiesburg
LU 1371 Laurel . . . . Laurel
LU 2070 Northeast Mississippi
  Area. . . . . Columbus
LU 2075 Philadelphia
  Local . . . . Philadelphia
LU 2092 Brockhaven . . Brookhaven
LU 2415 Grenada. . . . . Grenada
LU 2424 Greenwood . . Greenwood
LU 2685 Cleveland . . . Cleveland
LU 2772 Carthage Local . . Carthage
LU 2862 Batesville Local . Batesville
LU 2864 Ripley . . . . Ripley
LU 2865 Pontotoc Local . Pontotoc
LU 2867 Houston Local . . Houston
LU 2992 Senatobia Local . Senatobia
LU 4807 University
  Local . . . . University
LU 4924 Louisville Local. Louisville
LU 4961 Calhoun
  City . . . . Calhoun City
LU 5844 Oxford Local. . . . Oxford
SA Mississippi. . . . . . . Clinton

Railroad Signalmen
LLG 107 . . . . McComb

Rural Letter Carriers
D 1 . . . . Gattman
D 2 . . . . Walnut
D 3 . . . . Cleveland
D 4 . . . . Ackerman
D 5 . . . . Decatur
D 6. . . . . Columbia
D 7 . . . . Wesson
D 8 . . . . Florence
SA Mississippi . . . . New Albany

Security, Police and Fire Professionals
LU 711 . . . . . . Bay St. Louis
LU 712. . . . . Clinton

Service Employees
LU 572. . . . . Jackson

Sheet Metal Workers
LU 227 . . . . Southaven
LU 406. . . . . Jackson

Steelworkers
LU 8958 . . . . Jackson
LU 02-206-A . . . . Iuka
LU 09-202-A . . . . Grenada
LU 09-204-A . . . . . . Hernando
LU 09-245 . . . . Gulfport
LU 09-303-L . . . . Natchez
LU 09-363-L . . . . Jackson
LU 09-401 . . . . Terry
LU 09-523-G . . . . . Plantersville
LU 09-556-L . . . . . . Clarksdale
LU 09-748-L . . . . . . Columbus
LU 09-832-L . . . . . . West Point
LU 09-975-L . . . . Ripley
LU 09-1011-L . . . . Ripley
LU 09-1061-L. . . . . . Port Gibson
LU 09-1543-S . . . . . . Amory
LU 09-7256-S . . . . Weir
LU 09-7477-S . . . . . . Amory
LU 09-7772-S . . . . Philadelphia
LU 09-7891-S . . . . . Duck Hill
LU 09-8420-S. . . . . . . Fulton
LU 09-8421-S . . . . . Indianola
LU 09-8630-S . . . . . . Tupelo
LU 09-8789-S . . . . . Itta Bena
LU 09-15198-S . . . . . Aberdeen

Teamsters
JC 87. . . . . Jackson
LU 119 Memphis Mailers
  Union . . . . Southaven
LU 258. . . . . Hattiesburg
LU 891. . . . . Jackson

Theatrical Stage Employees
LU 589 . . . . Madison
LU 616 . . . . Meridian
LU 674 . . . . . . Pass Christian
LU 825 Theater Wardrobe
  Union . . . . . . Holly Springs

Transit Union
LDIV 1208 . . . . Jackson

Transportation Communications Union
D 745 . . . . Jackson
D 1293 . . . . South Haven
LG 1476 . . . . . . Olive Branch
LG 6164 Bulletin. . . . . Southaven
LG 6178 New Year . . . . . Terry
LG 6724 Chickasaw . . Olive Branch

Transportation Union
GCA GO-436 Illinois Central
  Railroad. . . . . Ridgeland
LU 427 . . . . Smithdale
LU 584 . . . . Quitman
LU 853. . . . . Praire
LU 1088 . . . . Richland
LU 1334 . . . . Hattiesburg
LU 1557. . . . . Nesbit
SLB LO-27 Mississippi . . . Jackson

Treasury Employees
CH 13 . . . . Clinton

Weather Service Employees
BR 02-52 . . . . Jackson

Unaffiliated Labor Organizations
Gas Employees Independent
  Union . . . . Jackson
Guards & Watchmen-Mississippi
  Gulf Coast LU 1. . . . Pascagoula
Meridan Association of
  Flight Training
  Instructions . . . . Meridian Naval
                            Air Station

Missouri

AFL-CIO Trade and Industrial Departments

Building and Construction Trades Department
BCTC Columbia . . . . . Westphalia
BCTC Greater Kansas
  City . . . . Independence
BCTC Joplin Area . . . . . . Joplin
BCTC Leavenworth
  County . . . . St. Joseph
BCTC Missouri State . Jefferson City
BCTC Northeastern
  Missouri . . . . Hannibal
BCTC Sedalia . . . . Sedalia
BCTC Springfield . . . . Springfield
BCTC St. Joseph . . . . . St. Joseph
BCTC St. Louis . . . . . . St. Louis

Food and Allied Service Trades Department
FASTC Eastern Missouri . St. Louis

Maritime Trades Department
PC Greater St. Louis Area . St. Louis

AFL-CIO Directly Affiliated Locals
DALU 20711 Advertising Publicity
  & News Representatives . St. Louis

Affiliated Labor Organizations

Air Traffic Controllers
LU ECE . . . . Kansas City
LU MCI . . . . Kansas City
LU MKC . . . . Kansas City
LU SGF . . . . Springfield
LU STL/T75 . . . . Bridgeton
LU SUS . . . . Chesterfield
LU T75 St. Louis Tracon
  Local . . . . Bridgeton

Asbestos Workers
CONF Midwestern
  States . . . . Independence
LU 1 . . . . St. Louis
LU 27 . . . . Independence
LU 63 . . . . Joplin

Automobile, Aerospace Workers
C Greater Kansas City . Kansas City
C Greater St. Louis . . . . Florissant
C Missouri . . . . Hazelwood
LU 25 . . . . St. Louis
LU 110 . . . . Fenton
LU 136 . . . . Fenton
LU 249 . . . . . Pleasant Valley
LU 282 . . . . St. Louis
LU 325 . . . . Hazelwood
LU 597 St. Louis-Fenton
  Local . . . . Catawissa
LU 691 . . . . St. Peters
LU 710 . . . . Kansas City
LU 1070 . . . . Neosho
LU 1760 . . . . Pacific
LU 1887 . . . . St. Louis
LU 1930 . . . . Dexter
LU 2250 . . . . Wentzville
LU 2379 . . . . . Jefferson City

Bakery, Confectionery, Tobacco Workers and Grain Millers
LU 4 . . . . St. Louis
LU 8-G . . . . St. Joseph
LU 16-G . . . . . . Kansas City
LU 51-G . . . . Carthage
LU 108-G . . . . St. Louis
LU 194-G . . . . Trenton
LU 235 . . . . Springfield
LU 348-G . . . . Palmyra

Boilermakers
LG 13-M . . . . St. Louis
LG 27 . . . . St. Louis
LG 27-D Cement
  Workers . . . . . . Kansas City
LG 83 . . . . Kansas City
LG 146-M . . . . Gladstone
LG 229-D Cement Workers . Willard
LG 455-D Cement
  Workers . . . . . . Bloomsdale
LG 469-D Cement
  Workers . . . . Louisiana
LG 1012 . . . . St. Louis

Bricklayers
LU 1 . . . . St. Louis
LU 15 . . . . Kansas City
LU 18 . . . . St. Louis
LU 23 . . . . . . Cape Girardeau

Carpenters
DC Kansas City . . . . Kansas City
DC St. Louis . . . . . . St. Louis
LU 5 . . . . St. Louis
LU 27-L . . . . Oak Grove
LU 47 . . . . St. Louis
LU 61 . . . . Grain Valley
LU 73 . . . . St. Louis
LU 73-L . . . . St. Louis
LU 110 . . . . St. Joseph
LU 185 . . . . St. Louis
LU 311 . . . . Joplin
LU 412 . . . . Wentzville
LU 417 . . . . St. Louis
LU 602 . . . . St. Louis
LU 607 . . . . Palmyra
LU 777 . . . . Harrisonville
LU 795 . . . . St. Louis
LU 938 . . . . . Excelsior Springs
LU 945 . . . . . . Jefferson City
LU 978 . . . . Springfield
LU 1008 . . . . . . Bowling Green
LU 1181 . . . . Grandview
LU 1310 . . . . St. Louis
LU 1312 A C E Educators . St. Louis
LU 1329 . . . . . . Independence
LU 1529 . . . . Kansas City
LU 1596 . . . . St. Louis
LU 1635 . . . . Kansas City
LU 1739 . . . . St. Louis
LU 1770 . . . . . Cape Girardeau
LU 1795 . . . . Park Hills
LU 1839 . . . . Washington
LU 1875 . . . . Elsberry
LU 1904 . . . . Parkville
LU 1925 . . . . Columbia
LU 1987 . . . . St. Charles
LU 2016 . . . . Naylor
LU 2030 . . . . . Ste. Genevieve
LU 2119 . . . . St. Louis
LU 2214 . . . . Festus
LU 2298 . . . . Rolla
LU 2301 . . . . . . Jefferson City
LU 2733 . . . . . Cape Girardeau

LU 3202 . . . . Warrenton

Catholic School Teachers
ASSN St. Louis
  Archiocesan . . . . . Hazelwood

Civilian Technicians
CH 92 Missouri Show Me
  Army . . . . Eldon
CH 93 St. Louis Show Me
  Air . . . . St. Louis
CH 94 Pony Express . . . St. Joseph

Communications Workers
C Greater St. Louis City . . St. Louis
C Kansas City . . . . . Kansas City
CONF Heartland Typographical &
  Mailer . . . . St. Louis
LU 1114 . . . . Washington
LU 6301 . . . . Ladue
LU 6310 . . . . St. Louis
LU 6311 . . . . Brashear
LU 6312 . . . . Springfield
LU 6313 . . . . Joplin
LU 6314 . . . . Marshall
LU 6316 . . . . . Cape Girardeau
LU 6320 . . . . St. Louis
LU 6325 . . . . Kansas City
LU 6326 . . . . Kansas City
LU 6327 . . . . Kansas City
LU 6333 . . . . Kansas City
LU 6350 . . . . St. Louis
LU 6372 . . . . . . Warrensburg
LU 6373 . . . . Cameron
LU 6374 . . . . Princeton
LU 6377 . . . . Bridgeton
LU 6390 . . . . St. Louis
LU 6391 . . . . Kansas City
LU 6450 . . . . Kansas City
LU 6477 . . . . Camdenton
LU 14612 . . . . Webb City
LU 14615 . . . . St. Joseph
LU 14616 . . . . St. Joseph
LU 14618 . . . . Springfield
LU 36047 St. Louis Newspaper
  Guild . . . . St. Louis
LU 86116 . . . . St. Joseph

Electrical Workers
LU 1 . . . . St. Louis
LU 2 . . . . St. Louis
LU 4 . . . . St. Louis
LU 53 . . . . Kansas City
LU 95 . . . . Joplin
LU 124 . . . . Kansas City
LU 257 . . . . Jefferson City
LU 350 . . . . Hannibal
LU 412 . . . . Kansas City
LU 453 . . . . Springfield
LU 545 . . . . St. Joseph
LU 615 . . . . Kansas City
LU 695 . . . . St. Joseph
LU 753 . . . . Springfield
LU 778 . . . . Springfield
LU 814 . . . . Sedalia
LU 866 . . . . Kansas City
LU 1439 . . . . St. Louis
LU 1455 . . . . St. Louis
LU 1464 . . . . Kansas City
LU 1474 . . . . Joplin
LU 1553 . . . . Springfield
LU 1613 . . . . Kansas City

Electronic Workers
LU 818 . . . . High Ridge

LU 820 . . . . Moberly
LU 821 . . . . Centralia
LU 823 . . . . St. Louis
LU 1104 . . . . St. Louis

Elevator Constructors
LU 3 . . . . St. Louis
LU 12 . . . . Kansas City

Federal Employees
LU 29 . . . . Kansas City
LU 405 Independent . . . . Foristel
LU 858 . . . . Kansas City
LU 1763 . . . . St. Louis
LU 2099 . . . . Hazelwood

Fire Fighters
LU 34-I . . . . Kansas City
LU 108-F . . . . Houston

Flint Glass Workers
LU 1004 . . . . Sedalia

Food and Commercial Workers
C View Insurance Workers Area
  XI . . . . St. Charles
LU 2 . . . . Kansas City
LU 74-A . . . . Weston
LU 81-C . . . . St. Louis
LU 88 . . . . St. Louis
LU 211 . . . . Kansas City
LU 344-C . . . . Florissant
LU 432-C . . . . Imperial
LU 655 . . . . Manchester
LU 796-C . . . . . Cape Girardeau
LU 887-C . . . . Hannibal
LU 1026-C . . . . St. Louis

Glass, Molders, Pottery and Plastics Workers
LU 20 . . . . Pleasant Valley
LU 30 . . . . Pevely
LU 43 . . . . Dexter
LU 143 . . . . La Grange
LU 372 . . . . Nevada

Government Employees
C 170 Defense Contact Management
  Agency . . . . Neosho
LU . . . . Kansas City
LU 96 VA . . . . St. Louis
LU 104 NARS . . . . . St. Louis
LU 638 USDA . . . . King City
LU 739 USDA . . . Bowling Green
LU 900 GSA . . . . . . St. Louis
LU 903 . . . . Columbia
LU 905 . . . . St. Louis
LU 908 . . . . . Fort Leonard Wood
LU 910 . . . . Kansas City
LU 1336 HHS . . . . . Kansas City
LU 1612 DoJ . . . . . . Seymour
LU 1711 DLA . . . . . St. Louis
LU 1827 . . . . Arnold
LU 2192 VA . . . . . . St. Louis
LU 2338 VA . . . . . Poplar Bluff
LU 2361
  DoD . . Whiteman Air Force Base
LU 2663 VA . . . . . Kansas City
LU 2754 . . . . Kansas City
LU 2761 DoD . . . . . . Overland
LU 2825 DoD . . . . Independence
LU 2904 DoD . . . . . Kansas City
LU 2936 DLA-DCMAO . . . Neosho
LU 3353 USDA . . . . . Neosho
LU 3354 USDA . . . . . St. Louis

LU 3399 VA . . . . Columbia
LU 3479 . . . . Springfield
LU 3502 USDA . . . . . Marshall
LU 3521 HHS . . . . Poplar Bluff
LU 3529 DoD . . . . . Hazelwood
LU 3629 EEOC . . . . . St. Louis
LU 3838 ACE . . . . . Moure City
LU 3892 DoE . . . . . Kansas City
LU 3934 HUD . . . . . . St. Louis
LU 3949 USDA . . . . . . Liberal
LU 3983 Immigration &
  Naturalization . . . . Kansas City
LU 4059 . . . . Kansas City

Government Employees Association
LU 14-32 . . . . Fort Leonard Wood
LU 14-96 . . . . St. Louis
LU 14-116 . . . . Arnold
LU 14-139 . . . Fort Leonard Wood
LU 14-149 . . . Fort Leonard Wood
LU 14-150 . . . Fort Leonard Wood

Government Security Officers
LU 20 . . . . St. Charles
LU 59 . . . . St. Louis

Graphic Communications
LU 6-M . . . . . Maryland Heights
LU 15-C . . . . St. Joseph
LU 16-C . . . . Kansas City
LU 16-H . . . . St. Louis
LU 38-N St. Louis . . . . . St. Louis
LU 235-M . . . . . . Independence
LU 505-M . . . . Maryland Heights

Guards
LU 36 . . . . St. Louis

Hotel and Restaurant Employees
LU 64 . . . . Kansas City
LU 74 . . . . St. Louis

Independent Unions Congress
LU 10 Fleming Manufacturing
  Company Employees Independent
  Union . . . . Cuba
LU 18 Musicians . . . Jefferson City

Iron Workers
DC St. Louis and Vicinity . St. Louis
LU 10 . . . . Kansas City
LU 396 . . . . St. Louis
LU 518 . . . . St. Louis
LU 520 . . . . Kansas City

Laborers
DC Eastern Missouri . . . Bridgeton
DC Western Missouri-
  Kansas . . . . Kansas City
LU 42 . . . . St. Louis
LU 53 . . . . Bridgeton
LU 110 . . . . St. Louis
LU 264 . . . . Kansas City
LU 319 . . . . Joplin
LU 424 . . . . Hannibal
LU 509 . . . . St. Louis
LU 579 . . . . St. Joseph
LU 660 . . . . St. Charles
LU 662 . . . . . . Jefferson City
LU 663 . . . . Kansas City
LU 676 . . . . Springfield
LU 718 . . . . De Soto
LU 829 . . . . . . Ste. Genevieve
LU 840 . . . . Rolla
LU 916 . . . . Farmington
LU 955 . . . . Columbia
LU 1104 . . . . . . Cape Girardeau

Letter Carriers
BR 30 . . . . Kansas City
BR 127 . . . . Jefferson City
BR 139 . . . . Sedalia
BR 195 . . . . St. Joseph
BR 203 . . . . Springfield
BR 244 . . . . Frankford
BR 291 Tom Sawyer . . . Hannibal
BR 335 . . . . Moberly
BR 343 . . . . St. Louis
BR 366 . . . . Joplin
BR 511 Chillicothe,
  Missouri . . . . Chillicothe
BR 639 . . . . Kirksville
BR 763 . . . . Columbia
BR 827 . . . . . . Independence
BR 984 . . . . St. Peters
BR 1005 Macon, Missouri . . Macon
BR 1015 . . . . . . Cape Girardeau
BR 1016 . . . . Poplar Bluff
BR 1215 Brookfield,
  Missouri . . . . . . Brookfield
BR 1217 Excelsior Springs,
  Missouri . . . . Excelsior Springs
BR 1264 . . . . Liberty
BR 1287 Lexington,
  Missouri . . . . Lexington
BR 1369 Monett, Missouri . . Monett
BR 1675 Caruthersville,
  Missouri . . . . . Caruthersville
BR 1678 Charleston,
  Missouri . . . . . . Charleston
BR 1715 . . . . . . Mountain Grove
BR 1878 Monroe City,
  Missouri . . . . . . Monroe City
BR 1938 . . . . Lebanon
BR 2027 Marceline,
  Missouri . . . . Marceline
BR 2140 Bowling Green,
  Missouri . . . . . Bowling Green
BR 2170 Kennett, Missouri . Kennett
BR 2257 Kahoka, Missouri . Kahoka
BR 2292 Harrisonville,
  Missouri . . . . . . Harrisonville
BR 2302 Savannah,
  Missouri . . . . Savannah
BR 2311 Albany, Missouri . . Albany
BR 2327 Canton, Missouri . Canton
BR 2354 Shelbina,
  Missouri . . . . Shelbina
BR 2362 Memphis,
  Missouri . . . . Memphis
BR 2477 Slater, Missouri . . . Slater
BR 2601 Rich Hill,
  Missouri . . . . Rich Hill
BR 2604 Eldon, Missouri . . . Eldon
BR 2667 Dexter, Missouri . . Dexter
BR 2706 Paris, Missouri . . . . Paris
BR 2741 Windsor,
  Missouri . . . . Windsor
BR 2915 Marshfield,
  Missouri . . . . . . Marshfield
BR 2934 Centralia,
  Missouri . . . . Centralia
BR 2985 Perryville,
  Missouri . . . . Perryville
BR 3014 Appleton City,
  Missouri . . . . . Appleton City
BR 3198 Sweet Springs,
  Missouri . . . . . Sweet Spring
BR 3236 Stanberry,
  Missouri . . . . . . Stanberry
BR 3241 . . . . Gallatin
BR 3242 Milan, Missouri . . . Milan
BR 3351 Norborne,
  Missouri . . . . Norborne
BR 3441 Glasgow,
  Missouri . . . . Glasgow

BR 3442 Montgomery City,
  Missouri . . . Montgomery City
BR 3563 Mound City,
  Missouri . . . . . . Mound City
BR 3566 Edina, Missouri . . . Edina
BR 3567 Salisbury,
  Missouri . . . . Salisbury
BR 3576 Hermann,
  Missouri . . . . Hermann
BR 3606 Vandalia,
  Missouri . . . . Vandalia
BR 3629 La Plata, Missouri . La Plata
BR 3711 Malden, Missouri . Malden
BR 3767 Brunswick,
  Missouri . . . . . . Brunswick
BR 3778 Tarkio, Missouri . . Tarkio
BR 4050 . . . . Farmington
BR 4159 Greenfield,
  Missouri . . . . . . Greenfield
BR 4216 Palmyra,
  Missouri . . . . Palmyra
BR 4472 Huntsville,
  Missouri . . . . . . Huntsville
BR 4474 Elsberry,
  Missouri . . . . Elsberry
BR 4659 Hayti, Missouri . . . Hayti
BR 4839 . . . . Florissant
BR 4940 Belton, Missouri . . Belton
BR 5050 . . . . Manchester
BR 5053 Mountain View,
  Missouri . . . . Mountain View
BR 5056 Versailles,
  Missouri . . . . . . Versailles
BR 5267 . . . . Grandview
BR 5510 Fort Leonard Wood,
  Missouri . . . Fort Leonard Wood
BR 5657 . . . . Owensville
BR 5671 Doniphan,
  Missouri . . . . Doniphan
BR 5743 Keytesville,
  Missouri . . . . . . Keytesville
BR 5847 . . . . Florissant
BR 5903 Portageville,
  Missouri . . . . . Portageville
BR 6039 Rock Port,
  Missouri . . . . Rock Port
BR 6054 Bevier, Missouri . . Bevier
BR 6062 Houston,
  Missouri . . . . Houston
BR 6325 Ironton, Missouri . Ironton
BR 6396 Thayer, Missouri . . Thayer
BR 8010 Clayton,
  Missouri . . . . . . Shrewsbury
D East Central Missouri . Villa Ridge
D Northeast Missouri . . . Shelbina
D Northwest Missouri . . St. Joseph
D Southeast Missouri . . . Kennett
D Southwest Missouri . . Springfield
D West Central Missouri . . Sedalia
SA Missouri . . . . . . Springfield

Locomotive Engineers
DIV 8 . . . . Marshall
DIV 17 . . . . Liberty
DIV 42 . . . . Arnold
DIV 48 . . . . St. Louis
DIV 61 . . . . Kansas City
DIV 75 . . . . Kearney
DIV 80 . . . . Brookfield
DIV 83 . . . . Springfield
DIV 86 . . . . Moberly
DIV 107 . . . . St. Joseph
DIV 120 . . . . Kansas City
DIV 147 . . . . Parkville
DIV 178 . . . . Golden City
DIV 285 . . . . Thayer
DIV 336 . . . . Lawson
DIV 428 . . . . Manchester

DIV 442 . . . . Scott City
DIV 491 . . . . Kansas City
DIV 502 . . . . Gladstone
DIV 507 . . . . Joplin
DIV 567 . . . . Springfield
DIV 595 . . . . Scott City
DIV 609 . . . . Fulton
DIV 629 . . . . Hannibal
DIV 674 . . . . De Soto
DIV 708 . . . . Kansas City
DIV 777 . . . . Galdstone
DIV 930 . . . . . . Lee's Summit
GCA St. Louis-San Francisco
  Railway . . . . Granby
SLB Missouri . . . . . Jefferson City

Longshoremen
DC St. Louis . . . . . . St. Louis
LU 1765 . . . . St. Louis

Machinists
CONF Tool & Die . . . . Bridgeton
DLG 9 . . . . Bridgeton
DLG 142 . . . . Kansas City
DLG 837 . . . . Hazelwood
LG 17 Deer Lake . . . . . Clever
LG 27 . . . . Holden
LG 41 . . . . Bridgeton
LG 176 Harley Davidson . Riverside
LG 232 . . . . Webb City
LG 314 . . . . Kansas City
LG 561 . . . . Kansas City
LG 688 . . . . Hazelwood
LG 777 . . . . Bridgeton
LG 778 . . . . Kansas City
LG 837-A . . . . Hazelwood
LG 837-B . . . . Hazelwood
LG 949 . . . . Bridgeton
LG 1345 . . . . Bridgeton
LG 1745 . . . . Warrenton
LG 1997 TWA Flight
  Attendants . . . . . . St. Louis
LG 2782 . . . . West Plains
STC Missouri . . . . . . Bridgeton

Maintenance of Way Employes
LG 493 . . . . Springfield
LG 745 . . . . Millersville
LG 996 . . . . Bland
LG 1137 . . . . Bernie
LG 1217 . . . . Brunswick
LG 1365 . . . . . . Lee's Summit
LG 1523 . . . . Belle
LG 1659 . . . . . . Independence
LG 1911 . . . . Trenton
LG 2402 . . . . Marceline
LG 2403 . . . . Pleasant Hill
LG 2621 . . . . Hannibal
SD Kansas City
  Terminal . . . . . . Kansas City
SLG 224 . . . . St. Louis
SLG 230 . . . . St. Joseph
SLG 301 . . . . Jacksonville
SLG 344 . . . . St. Joseph
SLG 345 . . . . . . Marthasville
SLG 353 . . . . Smithton
SLG 450 . . . . De Soto
SLG 662 . . . . Orrick
SLG 800 . . . . Kansas City
SLG 1041 . . . . . . Jefferson City
SLG 1067 . . . . . . Martinsburg
SLG 1097 . . . . Dearborn
SLG 1306 . . . . . . Chillicothe
SLG 1353 . . . . . . Lexington
SLG 1700 . . . . . . St. Louis
SLG 1701 . . . . St. Ann

Mine Workers

LU 1122 . . . . Montrose
LU 7688 . . . . Clifton Hill

Musicians

LU 2-197 . . . . St. Louis
LU 34-627 . . . . . . Kansas City
STCON Kansas-
Missouri . . . . . Kansas City

National Staff Organization

LU Staff Organization,
Missouri . . . . . Holts Summit

Needletrades

JB Missouri District . . . . St. Louis
JB Texas . . . . St. Louis
LU 14-K . . . . St. Louis
LU 50-002 . . . . St. Louis
LU 50-003 . . . . St. Louis
LU 50-005 . . . . St. Louis
LU 50-006 . . . . St. Louis
LU 108 . . . . St. Louis
LU 174 . . . . St. Louis
LU 225-A . . . . St. Louis
LU 254-C . . . . St. Louis
LU 371 . . . . St. Louis
LU 373 . . . . St. Louis
LU 848-T . . . . St. Louis
LU 1071-C . . . . St. Louis
LU 1117 . . . . St. Louis
LU 1158 . . . . St. Louis
LU 1798 . . . . St. Louis
LU 2638 . . . . St. Louis
LU 2647 . . . . St. Louis
LU 2684 . . . . St. Louis

NLRB Professional Association

LU 14 . . . . St. Louis

Nurses

SA Missouri . . . . . Jefferson City

Office and Professional Employees

LU 13 . . . . Bridgeton
LU 320 . . . . Blue Springs

Operating Engineers

LU 2 . . . . St. Louis
LU 101 . . . . Kansas City
LU 513 . . . . Bridgeton

Painters

DC 2 . . . . St. Louis
DC 3 . . . . Raytown
LU 9 . . . . Raytown
LU 46 . . . . St. Charles
LU 98 . . . . St. Joseph
LU 115 . . . . Dittmer
LU 137 . . . . Hillsboro
LU 203 . . . . Springfield
LU 513 . . . . St. Louis
LU 558 . . . . Smithville
LU 604 . . . . High Ridge
LU 774 . . . . St. Louis
LU 820 . . . . Raytown
LU 861 . . . . Kansas City
LU 980 . . . . St. Louis
LU 1156 . . . . . . St. Charles
LU 1179 . . . . Raytown
LU 1185 . . . . Columbia
LU 1199 . . . . Hazelwood
LU 1265 . . . . . . Waynesville
LU 1292 . . . . . . Cape Girardeau
LU 1594 . . . . Liberty
LU 1786 . . . . Springfield
LU 2341 . . . . St. Louis

Paper, Allied-Industrial, Chemical Employees

LU 05-6 . . . . Imperial
LU 05-29 . . . . St. Joseph
LU 05-107 . . . . Potosi
LU 05-152 . . . . St. Louis
LU 05-161 . . . . Liberal
LU 05-164 . . . . . . Cape Girardeau
LU 05-179 . . . . . . Kansas City
LU 05-194 . . . . St. Louis
LU 05-205 . . . . Hannibal
LU 05-266 . . . . St. Joseph
LU 05-312 . . . . Gladstone
LU 05-500 . . . . Joplin
LU 05-531 . . . . St. Louis
LU 05-617 . . . . Excelsior Springs
LU 05-713 . . . . Louisiana
LU 05-726 . . . North Kansas City
LU 05-760 . . . . . . Kansas City
LU 05-770 . . . . Nixa
LU 05-856 . . . . . Independence
LU 05-884 . . . . Festus
LU 05-937 . . . . Oran

Pilots, Air Line

LEC Vanguard . . . . Kansas City

Plant Protection

LU 251 1 . . . . Lathrop

Plant Protection Employees

LU 267 . . . . Hazelwood

Plasterers and Cement Masons

LU 3 . . . . St. Louis
LU 518 . . . . Independence
LU 527 . . . . Bridgeton
LU 908 . . . . . . Cape Girardeau
STCON Missouri . . . . Bridgeton

Plumbing and Pipe Fitting

LU 8 . . . . Kansas City
LU 45 . . . . St. Joseph
LU 178 . . . . Springfield
LU 268 . . . . St. Louis
LU 314 . . . . Kansas City
LU 533 . . . . Kansas City
LU 562 . . . . St. Louis
LU 781 . . . . Kansas City

Postal and Federal Employees

LU 912 . . . . St. Louis

Postal Mail Handlers

LU 297 . . . . Kansas City
LU 314 . . . . Berkeley

Postal Workers

LU St. Louis Gateway District
Area . . . . St. Louis
LU 67 Greater Kansas City Metro
Area . . . . Kansas City
LU 221 Hannibal . . . . . Hannibal
LU 248 Joplin . . . . Joplin
LU 249 Lexington Local . Lexington
LU 253 Nevada Local . . Nevada
LU 254 St. Joseph . . . . St. Joseph
LU 333 Sedalia . . . . . . Sedalia
LU 335 Excelsior
Springs . . . . Excelsior Springs
LU 336 Jefferson
City . . . . Jefferson City
LU 697 Moberly Local . . . Moberly
LU 700 Chillicothe . . . . Chillicothe
LU 786 Warrensburg . . Warrensburg
LU 888 Springfield . . . Springfield
LU 1475 Harrisonville . Harrisonville
LU 1487 California Local . California

LU 1841 Poplar . . . . . Poplar Bluff

LU 1888 Kirksville . . . . Kirksville
LU 2082 Rolla . . . . Rolla
LU 2140 Dexter Local . . . . Dexter
LU 2188 Flat River . . . Park Hills
LU 2271 Palmyra Local . . Palmyra
LU 2272 Maryville Local . Maryville
LU 2279 Ste. Genevieve
Local . . . . . . Ste. Genevieve
LU 3454 Savannah Local . Savannah
LU 3698 West Plains
Local . . . . West Plains
LU 4088 Cape
Girardeau . . . . . Cape Girardeau
LU 4110 Boonville Local . Boonville
LU 4783 Belton Local . . . Belton
LU 4853 St. Charles . . . St. Charles
LU 5402 Sikeston . . . . Sikeston
LU 7043 St. Louis Bulk Mail
Center . . . . Hazelwood
LU 7065 Mid Missouri General Mail
Facility . . . . Ashland
SA Missouri . . . . . Jefferson City

Railroad Signalmen

LLG 21 . . . . Lee's Summit
LLG 129 . . . . Chaffee
LLG 132 . . . . Labadie

Retail, Wholesale and Department Store

LU 125 . . . . St. Joseph
LU 184-L . . . . . . Independence

Roofers, Waterproofers and Allied Workers

DC North Central States . . Raytown
LU 2 . . . . St. Louis
LU 20 . . . . Raytown

Rural Letter Carriers

D 1 . . . . Guilford
D 2 . . . . Chillicothe
D 3 . . . . Holliday
D 4 . . . . Bive Springs
D 5 . . . . Berger
D 6 . . . . Mount Vernon
D 7 . . . . Summersville
D 8 . . . . Poplar Bluff
LU Adair County . . . . . Edina
LU Andrew-Buchanan
Counties . . . . . St. Joseph
LU Atchison-Holt-Nodaway
Counties . . . . . . Skidmore
LU Audrain-Callaway
Counties . . . . . . Fulton
LU Barton-Cedar-Vernon
Counties . . . . . . Walker
LU Bates County . . . . . Rich Hill
LU Benton County . . . . Warsaw
LU Boone County . . . . Columbia
LU Butler-Stoddard
Counties . . . . . Poplar Bluff
LU Caldwell-Daviess
Counties . . . . . Gallatin
LU Camden-Dallas-Polk
Counties . . . . . Bolivar
LU Cape-Perry-Scott-Mississippi
Counties . . . . Cape Girardeau
LU Carroll County . . . . Bosworth
LU Carter-Ripley-Reynolds
Counties . . . . . Ellington
LU Cass County . . . . . Leeton
LU Chariton County . . . Salisbury
LU Christian-Taney
Counties . . . . . Springfield
LU Clark-Schuyler-Scotland
Counties . . . . . Queen City

LU Cole County . . . . . Lohman

LU Cooper-Moniteau-Morgan
Counties . . . . . Versailles
LU Dunklin-Pemiscot-New Madrid
Counties . . . . . East Prairie
LU Franklin County . . . . Sullivan
LU Johnson County . . Warrensburg
LU Laclede County . . . . Conway
LU Linn County . . . . New Boston
LU Marion County . . . . Hannibal
LU Miller County . . . . . Eldon
LU Montgomery
County . . . . Montgomery City
LU Newton & McDonald
County . . . . . . Stark City
LU Oregon County . . . Koshkonong
LU Pettis County . . . . Sedalia
LU Randolph County . . Huntsville
LU Ray County . . . . Richmond
LU Saline County . . . . Marshall
LU Shelby County . . . . Holliday
LU St. Charles County . . Wentzville
LU St. Clair County . . . . Osceola
LU St. Francois-Ste. Genevieve
Counties . . . . . Farmington
LU St. Louis County . . . . Labadie
LU Texas-Dent
Counties . . . . . Summersville
LU Webster County . . . . Ava
LU Wright-Douglas-Ozark
Counties . . . . . Mansfield
LU 7 Bollinger-Madison-Wayne
Counties . . . . Fredericktown
LU 20 Clay-Platte
Counties . . . . . Kansas City
LU 32 Gasconade County . . . Cuba
LU 33 Gentry-Worth-Harrison
Counties . . . . . Grant City
LU 34 Greene County . . Springfield
LU 38 Hickory County . . Wheatland
LU 39 Howard County . . . . Fayette
LU 41 Jackson County . Blue Springs
LU 42 Jasper County . . . . Sarcoxie
LU 43 Jefferson
County . . . . . House Springs
LU 45 Knox County . . Knox City
LU 47 Lafayette County . Bates City
LU 48 Barry-Dade-Lawrence-Stone
Counties . . . . . Mount Vernon
LU 50 Lincoln-Pike Counties . Eolia
LU 52 Livingston
County . . . . . Chillicothe
LU 54 Maries-Phelps
Counties . . . . . Belle
LU 64 Osage . . . . Jefferson City
LU 86 Washington-Iron
Counties . . . . . Potosi
SA Missouri . . . . . Fairfax

Seafarers

LU 5 Chauffeurs & Industrial
Workers . . . . . . St. Louis

Security, Police and Fire Professionals

LU . . . . Jackson
LU . . . . Lawson
LU 249 . . . . Kansas City
LU 250 . . . . O'Fallon
LU 251 . . . . Harrisonville

Service Employees

JC 28 . . . . St. Louis
JC 29 . . . . St. Louis
JC 1001 Midwest . . . . St. Louis
LU 50 . . . . St. Louis
LU 96 . . . . Kansas City

LU 359 International Leather Goods, Plastics, Novelty and Service Union . . . . St. Louis
LU 642 Firemen & Oilers . . . . Kansas City
LU 716-A Firemen & Oilers . . . . Kansas City
LU 896 Firemen & Oilers . . . . Bonne Terre
LU 1106 Firemen & Oilers . . . . Springfield
LU 1142 Firemen & Oilers . . . . Kansas City
LU 2000 . . . . St. Louis
SC 19 Firemen & Oilers . Springfield

Sheet Metal Workers
LU 2 . . . . Kansas City
LU 36 . . . . St. Louis
LU 146 . . . . Springfield
LU 202 . . . . St. Louis
LU 208 . . . . Springfield
LU 419 . . . . Springfield

State, County and Municipal Employees
C 72 . . . . Jefferson City
LU 410 Institutional & Public Employees . . . . St. Louis

Steelworkers
LU 01-437 . . . . Bridgeton
LU 07-300-B . . . . . . Bridgeton
LU 10-91-S . . . . Bridgeton
LU 11-13-S . . . . . . Kansas City
LU 11-25-U . . . . St. Louis
LU 11-39-U . . . . St. Louis
LU 11-169-G . . . . Ste. Genevieve
LU 11-400-G . . . . Ste. Genevieve
LU 11-433 . . . . High Hill
LU 11-434 . . . . Bridgeton
LU 11-469-G . . . . . . Bridgeton
LU 11-660 . . . . Mexico
LU 11-662-L . . . . . . Springfield
LU 11-790-S . . . . Mexico
LU 11-812-L . . . . Joplin
LU 11-853-S . . . . . . Curryville
LU 11-891 . . . . Wellsville
LU 11-990 . . . . Braymer
LU 11-1149-L . . . . Kakoke
LU 11-1958-S . . . . Kansas City
LU 11-5783-S . . . . . St. Joseph
LU 11-7033-S . . . . . . Annapolis

LU 11-7450-S . . . . . . Annapolis
LU 11-7686-S . . . . Marston
LU 11-8139 . . . . St. Clair
LU 11-8734-S . . . . . . Park Hills
LU 11-9014-S . . . . . . Bridgeton
LU 11-13558-S . . . . Independence
LU 11-14228-S . . . . . . Joplin
LU 11-14627-S . . . . . . Fulton
LU 11-15485-S . . . . Springfield

Teachers
LU 3576 Park College Faculty, Federation of . . . . . . Parkville
SFED 8023 Missouri . Jefferson City

Teamsters
CONF Mo-Kak Conference of Teamsters . . . . . Springfield
JC 13 . . . . St. Louis
JC 56 . . . . Kansas City
LU 6 . . . . St. Louis
LU 41 . . . . Kansas City
LU 245 . . . . Springfield
LU 303 . . . . St. Louis
LU 460 . . . . St. Joseph
LU 541 . . . . Kansas City
LU 574 . . . . Cape Girardeau
LU 600 . . . . St. Louis
LU 604 . . . . St. Louis
LU 610 . . . . . Maryland Heights
LU 618 . . . . St. Louis
LU 682 . . . . St. Louis
LU 688 . . . . St. Louis
LU 823 . . . . Joplin
LU 833 . . . . Jefferson City
LU 838 . . . . Kansas City
LU 955 . . . . Kansas City

Television and Radio Artists
LU St. Louis . . . . St. Louis
LU 213 Kansas City . . Kansas City

Theatrical Stage Employees
LU . . . . St. Louis
LU 2-B . . . . St. Louis
LU 6 . . . . St. Louis
LU 31 . . . . Kansas City
LU 143 . . . . St. Louis
LU 443 . . . . Jefferson City
LU 498 . . . . Independence
LU 774 . . . . St. Louis
LU 805 . . . . St. Louis
LU 810 . . . . Kingsville

Transit Union
LDIV 788 . . . . St. Louis
LDIV 1498 . . . . . Independence
LU 847 . . . . St. Joseph
LU 1287 . . . . Kansas City

Transport Workers
LU . . . . Kansas City
LU 1647 . . . . St. Louis

Transportation Communications Union
D 126 Allied Services Division . . . . Kansas City
D 326 . . . . Granview
LG 149 . . . . Buffalo
LG 554 . . . . St. Louis
LG 777 . . . . Buffalo
LG 6078 De Soto . . . . . De Soto
LG 6343 Shippers . . . . North Kansas City

Transportation Union
GCA GO-1 . . . . Springfield
LU 5 . . . . Blue Springs
LU 94 . . . . Parkville
LU 185 . . . . Marceline
LU 219 . . . . Hannibal
LU 226 . . . . Moberly
LU 259 . . . . Platte City
LU 303 . . . . Springfield
LU 330 . . . . Poplar Bluff
LU 349 . . . . Blue Springs
LU 412 . . . . Kansas City
LU 607 . . . . Thayer
LU 933 . . . . California
LU 947 . . . . Chaffee
LU 1216 . . . . Blue Springs
LU 1388 . . . . Fenton
LU 1403 . . . . Lee's Summit
LU 1780 . . . . Independence
LU 1823 . . . . St. Louis
LU 1975 . . . . Lee's Summit
SLB LO-28 Missouri . Jefferson City

Treasury Employees
CH 14 . . . . St. Louis
CH 36 . . . . Kansas City
CH 66 . . . . Kansas City
CH 121 . . . . St. Louis
CH 182 . . . . Kansas City
CH 217 . . . . Kansas City
CH 264 . . . . Kansas City

CH 274 . . . . Kansas City

Utility Workers
LU 335 . . . . Florissant
LU 398 . . . . Fredericktown
LU 455 . . . . St. Charles

Weather Service Employees
BR 03-28 . . . . Kansas City
BR 03-35 . . . . Pleasant Hill
BR 03-62 . . . . Pleasant Hill
BR 03-70 . . . . Kansas City
BR 03-71 . . . . Kansas City
BR 03-89 . . . . St. Charles
BR 03-97 . . . . Kansas City

Unaffiliated Labor Organizations

Bowling Lane Resurfacer Installers Associated St. Louis . . . St. Louis
Craftsman Independent Union LU 1 . . . . Cape Girardeau
Craftsman International Union . . . . . . Cape Girardeau
Electric Protective Association Independent . . . . Calverton Park
FMCS Association of Federal Mediators . . . . Ballwin
Fuse Workers Inc. Independent . . . . Ellisville
Independent Store Employees Association . . . . . St. Charles
Mink Pipe Trades Association . . . . Springfield
Missouri Professional Staff Organization . . . . Independence
Nash Missouri Employees Union . . . . St. Peters
Railway Exchange Building Employees Association Independent . . . . St. Louis
Screen Printers United LU 1 . . . . Kansas City
St. Vincents Federation of Day Care Workers . . . . Kansas City
Surgical Instrument Workers Inc. . . . . Villa Ridge
United Health Care Workers of Greater St. Louis LU 1 . . St. Louis
Wehrenberg Alliance of Motion Picture Machine Operation . . . . St. Louis

Montana

AFL-CIO Trade and Industrial Departments

Building and Construction Trades Department
BCTC Helena . . . . Helena
BCTC Montana State . . . . Butte
BCTC North Central
Montana . . . . Great Falls
BCTC Southeastern
Montana . . . . Billings
BCTC Southwestern Montana . Butte
BCTC Western Montana . . Missoula

Affiliated Labor Organizations

Air Traffic Controllers
LU BIL . . . . Billings
LU GTF . . . . Great Falls
LU HLN . . . . Helena

Bakery, Confectionery, Tobacco Workers and Grain Millers
LU 109-G . . . . Belt
LU 193 . . . . Butte
LU 285-G . . . . Sidney
LU 466 . . . . Billings

Boilermakers
LG 11 . . . . East Helena
LG 239-D Cement
Workers . . . . Three Forks
LG 435-D Cement
Workers . . . . East Helena
LG 599 . . . . Edgar

Bricklayers
LU 1 . . . . Butte
LU 3 . . . . Great Falls
LU 5 . . . . Three Forks
LU 6 . . . . Clancy
LU 7 . . . . Missoula
LU 10 . . . . Billings
LU 12 . . . . Havre
STCON 99 Montana . . . . . Butte

Carpenters
LU 28 . . . . Missoula
LU 112 . . . . Butte
LU 153 . . . . Helena
LU 286 . . . . Great Falls
LU 557 . . . . Bozeman
LU 670 . . . . Polson
LU 911 . . . . Kalispell
LU 1172 . . . . Billings
LU 2225 . . . . Libby
LU 2446 . . . . Laurel
LU 2581 . . . . Libby
LU 3038 . . . . Missoula

Civilian Technicians
CH 29 Montana Air . . . Great Falls
CH 57 Treasure State
Chapter . . . . Clancy

Communications Workers
LU 14734 . . . . Billings
LU 14737 . . . . Havre
LU 14740 Missoula Typographical
Union . . . . Missoula

Electrical Workers
LU 44 . . . . Butte

LU 152 . . . . Glendive
LU 206 . . . . Helena
LU 233 . . . . Helena
LU 532 . . . . Billings
LU 653 . . . . Miles City
LU 758 . . . . Peerless
LU 768 . . . . Kalispell
LU 958 . . . . Baker
LU 988 . . . . Sidney
LU 1050 . . . . Glendive
LU 1155 . . . . Roundup
LU 1638 . . . . Colstrip
LU 1856 . . . . Havre
LU 2226 . . . . Saco

Federal Employees
LU 58 Fort Belknap Service
Unit . . . . Harlem
LU 224 . . . . Crow Agency
LU 248 . . . . Browning
LU 478 . . . . Hardin
LU 1150 . . . . Billings
LU 1241 . . . . Kalispell
LU 1398 . . . . Libby
LU 1492 . . . . Conner
LU 2107 . . . . Browning
LU 2171 . . . . Poplar

Food and Commercial Workers
LU 4 . . . . Butte
LU 8 . . . . Great Falls
LU 301 . . . . Butte

Government Employees
C 201 Food Inspection Locals,
Northern . . . . Butte
LU 2609 DoD . . . . . . Great Falls
LU 3355 USDA . . . . . . Billings
LU 3570 VA . . . . . Fort Harrison

Government Employees Association
LU 14-84 . . . . Helena

Government Security Officers
LU 128 . . . . Missoula

Graphic Communications
LU 227-C . . . . Billings
LU 242-C . . . . Missoula

Hotel and Restaurant Employees
LU 427 . . . . Missoula

Iron Workers
LU 841 . . . . Helena

Laborers
DC 43 Montana . . . . . . Helena
LU 98 . . . . Billings
LU 254 . . . . Helena
LU 1334 . . . . Great Falls

Letter Carriers
BR 220 . . . . Helena
BR 621 . . . . Butte
BR 623 Anaconda,
Montana . . . . Anaconda
BR 650 . . . . Great Falls
BR 701 . . . . Missoula
BR 815 . . . . Billings
BR 948 . . . . Kalispell
BR 968 Livingston,
Montana . . . . . . Livingston
BR 1028 . . . . Bozeman

BR 1160 . . . . Lewistown
BR 1281 . . . . Miles City
BR 1425 . . . . Havre
BR 1643 . . . . Glendive
BR 1680 Hamilton,
Montana . . . . Hamilton
BR 1698 Glasgow,
Montana . . . . Glasgow
BR 1778 Dillon, Montana . . . Dillon
BR 2328 Roundup,
Montana . . . . Roundup
BR 2382 . . . . Kalispell
BR 3204 Conrad, Montana . Conrad
BR 3839 . . . . Deer Lodge
BR 4305 Sidney, Montana . . Sidney
BR 4537 Stevensville,
Montana . . . . Stevensville
BR 4890 Cut Bank,
Montana . . . . Cut Bank
BR 4891 Shelby, Montana . . Shelby
BR 4892 Wolf Point,
Montana . . . . Wolf Point
BR 5157 Laurel, Montana . . Laurel
BR 5193 Plentywood,
Montana . . . . Plentywood
BR 5265 Hardin, Montana . . Hardin
BR 5387 Libby, Montana . . . Libby
BR 5533 Corvallis,
Montana . . . . Corvallis
BR 6560 Troy, Montana . . . . Troy
SA Montana . . . . Billings

Locomotive Engineers
DIV 180 . . . . Glendive
DIV 195 . . . . Forsyth
DIV 232 . . . . Billings
DIV 262 . . . . Missoula
DIV 392 . . . . Havre
DIV 499 . . . . Whitefish
DIV 504 . . . . Great Falls
LU MRL . . . . Missoula
SLB Montana . . . . Forsyth

Machinists
DLG 86 . . . . Butte
LG 88 . . . . Butte
LG 169 . . . . Livingston
LG 231 . . . . Helena
LG 430 . . . . Havre
LG 509 . . . . Glendive
LG 622 . . . . Billings
LG 701-FL . . . . Dillow
LG 1760 . . . . Columbia Falls
LG 1801 . . . . Lame Deer
LLG FL-60 . . . . Missoula
LLG FL-1697 . . . . Anaconda
STC Montana . . . . Missoula

Maintenance of Way Employes
LG 16 . . . . Harlem
LG 272 . . . . Missoula
LG 295 . . . . Laurel
LG 297 . . . . Miles City
SLG 158 . . . . Helena
SLG 735 . . . . Great Falls
SLG 1092 . . . . Kalispell
SLG 1189 . . . . Glasgow

Mine Workers
LU 1575 . . . . Forsyth

Musicians
LU 498 . . . . Missoula
LU 642 . . . . Helena
LU 709 . . . . Bozeman

National Staff Organization
LU Staff Organization, Professional,
Montana Education
Association . . . . . . Glendive

Needletrades
LU 25 . . . . Great Falls

Nurses
SA Montana Nurses
Association . . . . Helena

Operating Engineers
LU 400 . . . . Helena

Painters
LU 260 . . . . Great Falls
LU 1922 . . . . Billings

Paper, Allied-Industrial, Chemical Employees
LU 8-443 Pace Pioneer
Local . . . . Laurel
LU 08-1 . . . . Laurel
LU 08-470 . . . . Billings
LU 08-491 . . . . Great Falls
LU 08-493 . . . . Cut Bank
LU 08-885 Hellgate . . . . Missoula
LU 08-1509 . . . . Missoula

Plasterers and Cement Masons
LU 119 . . . . Anaconda
LU 436 . . . . Bigfork

Plumbing and Pipe Fitting
LU 30 . . . . Billings
LU 41 . . . . Butte
LU 459 . . . . Missoula
SA Montana . . . . Billings

Postal Mail Handlers
LU 327 . . . . Billings

Postal Workers
LU 82 Butte . . . . Butte
LU 113 Missoula . . . . . Missoula
LU 119 Miles City . . . Miles City
LU 132 Billings . . . . . . Billings
LU 208 Great Falls . . . . Great Falls
LU 649 Helena . . . . . . Helena
LU 651 Sidney . . . . Sidney
LU 680 Bozeman . . . . . Bozeman
LU 683 Kalispell . . . . . Kalispell
LU 728 Glendive . . . . . Glendive
LU 843 Lewistown . . . . Lewistown
LU 922 Wolf Point . . . . Wolf Point
LU 4679 Dillon Local . . . . . Dillon
LU 6505 Polson . . . . . . Polson
SA Montana . . . . Lewistown

Railroad Signalmen
LLG 87 . . . . Billings

Roofers, Waterproofers and Allied Workers
LU 229 . . . . Billings
LU 250 . . . . Butte

Rural Letter Carriers
D 1 . . . . Hamilton
D 2 . . . . Simms
D 3 . . . . Helena
D 4 . . . . Absarokee
SA Montana . . . . Shepherd

Security, Police and Fire Professionals
LU 15. . . . . Butte

Service Employees
LU 468 Firemen & Oilers . Glendive
LU 840 Firemen & Oilers . . Billings
LU 911 Firemen & Oilers . . . Havre

Sheet Metal Workers
LU 103 . . . . Helena
LU 140 . . . . Glendive

State, County and Municipal Employees
LU 398 Montana Health Care Employees Association . . . . . Stevensville

LU 4016 Eastern Montana Industries, Inc. Employees. . . . . . Helena
STC 9 . . . . Helena

Steelworkers
LU 11-72 . . . . East Helena
LU 11-320-A . . . . Columbia Falls
LU 11-3169-S . . . . Billings

Teachers
LU 5005 Butte Silverbow Federation of LPN . . . . Butte
SFED Montana . . . . Helena

Teamsters
LU 2 . . . . Butte
LU 190. . . . . Billings

Theatrical Stage Employees
LU 240. . . . . Billings

LU 339 . . . . Great Falls

Transportation Communications Union
LG 43. . . . . Missoula
LG 656 . . . . Havre
LG 6476 Laurel . . . . Laurel
LG 6670 Bear Paw . . . . . . Havre

Transportation Union
LU 486 . . . . Glendive
LU 544 . . . . Havre
LU 730 . . . . Great Falls
LU 891 . . . . Whitefish
LU 1840 . . . . Glasgow
SLB LO-29 Montana. . . . Kalispell

Treasury Employees
CH 42 . . . . Missoula
CH 231 . . . . Eureka

Weather Service Employees
BR 04-5 . . . . Missoula
BR 04-6 . . . . Great Falls
BR 04-7 . . . . Billings
BR 04-73 . . . . Glasgow

Unaffiliated Labor Organizations

Aluminum Workers Trades Council . . . . . Columbia Falls
Big Sky Pilots Association . Billings
Continental Company-Wide Union Council . . . . Billings
John Muir LU 100 . . . . . Bozeman
Oil Basin Pipeliners Union . Billings
Rocky Mountain Federation-Equilone Pipeline Corporation . . . . Baker
Rocky Mountain Union-Exxon Pipeline Company . . . . . Bridger

Nebraska

AFL-CIO Trade and Industrial Departments

Building and Construction Trades Department
BCTC Lincoln . . . . Lincoln
BCTC Omaha . . . . Omaha

Affiliated Labor Organizations

Air Traffic Controllers
LU LNK-GRI . . . . Lincoln
LU OMA . . . . Omaha
LU R90 . . . . Bellevue

Asbestos Workers
LU 39 . . . . Blair

Bakery, Confectionery, Tobacco Workers and Grain Millers
LU 31-G . . . . Ceresco
LU 50-G . . . . Omaha
LU 80-G . . . . Crete
LU 178-G . . . . Fremont
LU 433 . . . . . . South Sioux City

Boilermakers
LG 174-D Cement
  Workers . . . . Louisville
LG 561-D Cement Workers . Omaha

Bricklayers
LU 1 . . . . Omaha

Carpenters
LU 444 . . . . Omaha
LU 832 . . . . Liberty
LU 1055 . . . . Lincoln
LU 1463 . . . . Wahoo

Civilian Technicians
CH 88 Cornhusker . . . . . Lincoln

Communications Workers
LU 7150 . . . . Omaha
LU 7400 . . . . Omaha
LU 7401 . . . . Grand Island
LU 7470 . . . . Lincoln
LU 7471 . . . . Kearney
LU 7476 . . . . Hastings
LU 14744 . . . . Omaha
LU 57045 . . . . Omaha

Electrical Workers
C Nebraska . . . . Omaha
LU 22 . . . . Omaha
LU 244 . . . . Seward
LU 265 . . . . Lincoln
LU 843 . . . . Scottsbluff
LU 1022 . . . . Lincoln
LU 1517 . . . . Alliance
LU 1525 . . . . Omaha
LU 1614 . . . . Omaha
LU 1920 . . . . North Platte
LU 1974 . . . . Omaha
LU 2366 . . . . Lincoln

Elevator Constructors
LU 28 . . . . Omaha

Federal Employees
C Bureau of Indian Affairs
  Locals . . . . Rushville

Food and Commercial Workers
LU 22 . . . . Fremont
LU 271 . . . . Omaha
LU 815-C . . . . Beatrice

Government Employees
LU 771 USDA . . . . . . Bellevue
LU 1486
  DoD . . . . Offutt Air Force Base
LU 2200 VA . . . . Lincoln
LU 2219 VA . . . . Lincoln
LU 2223 USDA . . . . . . Omaha
LU 2270 VA . . . . Omaha
LU 2601 VA . . . . . Grand Island
LU 2706 HHS . . . . . . Omaha
LU 3286 HUD . . . . . . Omaha
LU 3363 USDA . . . . . . Chadron
LU 3684 HHS . . . . Grand Island
LU 3717 USDA . . . . . . Dodge
LU 3749 USDA . . . . . . Kenesaw
LU 3928 INS . . . . Lincoln

Graphic Communications
DJC Missouri Kansas Iowa
  Nebraska . . . . Omaha
LU 221-M . . . . Lincoln
LU 543-M . . . . Omaha

Guards
LU 133 . . . . Omaha

Iron Workers
LU 21 . . . . Omaha

Laborers
LU 1140 . . . . Omaha

Letter Carriers
BR 5 . . . . Omaha
BR 8 . . . . Lincoln
BR 89 . . . . Ames
BR 93 . . . . Hastings
BR 312 . . . . Kearney
BR 390 . . . . Grand Island
BR 593 Nebraska City,
  Nebraska . . . . . Nebraska City
BR 896 . . . . York
BR 1014 . . . . Fairbury
BR 1020 . . . . Norfolk
BR 1043 . . . . Columbus
BR 1258 . . . . North Platte
BR 1278 . . . . McCook
BR 1300 Alliance,
  Nebraska . . . . Alliance
BR 1483 Broken Bow,
  Nebraska . . . . . . Broken Bow
BR 1525 Blair, Nebraska . . . . Blair
BR 1582 Falls City,
  Nebraska . . . . . . Falls City
BR 1591 Aurora, Nebraska . Aurora
BR 1774 Minden, Nebraska . Minden
BR 1836 . . . . Scottsbluff
BR 1883 . . . . Seward
BR 1885 . . . . Lexington
BR 1924 Wahoo, Nebraska . Wahoo
BR 1952 Schuyler,
  Nebraska . . . . Schuyler
BR 2061 Superior,
  Nebraska . . . . Superior
BR 2209 Chadron,
  Nebraska . . . . Chadron
BR 2261 Wymore,
  Nebraska . . . . Wymore
BR 2314 . . . . Crete
BR 2499 Wayne, Nebraska . Wayne

BR 2692 St. Paul, Nebraska . St. Paul
BR 2726 South Sioux City,
  Nebraska . . . . South Sioux City
BR 2798 Gothenburg,
  Nebraska . . . . . . Gothenburg
BR 2907 Sidney, Nebraska . . Sidney
BR 2926 Oakland,
  Nebraska . . . . Oakland
BR 2956 Franklin,
  Nebraska . . . . Franklin
BR 2963 Auburn, Nebraska . Auburn
BR 2964 . . . . West Point
BR 2966 Clay Center,
  Nebraska . . . . . . Clay Center
BR 2967 Geneva, Nebraska . Geneva
BR 3101 Ainsworth,
  Nebraska . . . . . . Ainsworth
BR 3141 Ord, Nebraska . . . . . Ord
BR 3171 Gordon, Nebraska . Gordon
BR 3425 Tekamah,
  Nebraska . . . . Tekamah
BR 4017 Ogallala,
  Nebraska . . . . Ogallala
BR 4072 Mitchell,
  Nebraska . . . . Mitchell
BR 4128 . . . . Bellevue
BR 4142 Red Cloud,
  Nebraska . . . . . . Red Cloud
BR 4152 Cozad, Nebraska . . Cozad
BR 4646 Valentine,
  Nebraska . . . . Valentine
BR 4904 O'Neill, Nebraska . O'Neill
BR 5333 Kimball,
  Nebraska . . . . Kimball
SA Nebraska . . . . Lincoln

Locomotive Engineers
DIV 88 . . . . Paxton
DIV 98 . . . . Lincoln
DIV 183 . . . . Lincoln
DIV 303 . . . . Mitchell
DIV 621 . . . . Lincoln
DIV 622 . . . . Alliance
DIV 623 . . . . McCook
DIV 699 . . . . Elkhorn
SLB Nebraska . . . . Alliance

Machinists
LG 31 . . . . Martell
LG 60 . . . . Omaha
LG 180 . . . . Maywood
LG 543 . . . . Beatrice
LG 602 . . . . Alliance
LG 612 . . . . Lincoln
LG 1394 . . . . Red Cloud
LG 1569 . . . . Dwight
LG 1826 . . . . Omaha
STC Nebraska . . . . Beatrice

Maintenance of Way Employes
LG 1214 . . . . Hastings
LG 1316 . . . . Sodell
LG 1320 . . . . Lincoln
SD Burlington Railroad . . Hastings
SLG 216 . . . . Omaha
SLG 473 . . . . Central City
SLG 688 . . . . Rulo
SLG 700 . . . . Fremont
SLG 899 . . . . Sidney
SLG 961 . . . . Bridgeport
SLG 1105 . . . . La Vista
SLG 1108 . . . . Alliance
SLG 1133 . . . . Fairbury

Musicians
LU 70-558 . . . . Omaha
LU 463 . . . . Lincoln

National Staff Organization
LU Staff Association,
  Nebraska . . . . Lincoln

Office and Professional Employees
LU 53 . . . . Omaha

Operating Engineers
LU 571 . . . . Omaha

Painters
LU 109 . . . . Omaha

Paper, Allied-Industrial, Chemical Employees
LU 565 . . . . Omaha
LU 05-309 . . . . Omaha
LU 05-699 . . . . Omaha
LU 05-907 . . . . Lincoln
LU 05-974 . . . . Plattsmouth
LU 05-1473 . . . . Omaha

Plasterers and Cement Masons
LU 538 . . . . Omaha

Plumbing and Pipe Fitting
LU 16 . . . . Omaha
LU 464 Steamfitters . . . . Omaha

Postal Mail Handlers
LU 298 . . . . Omaha

Postal Workers
LU 9 Central Nebraska
  Area . . . . Grand Island
LU 11 Omaha Area . . . . . Omaha
LU 112 Lincoln . . . . . . Lincoln
LU 310 Beatrice Local . . . Beatrice
LU 311 Hastings . . . . . Hastings
LU 313 Columbus Local . Columbus
LU 314 Nebraska
  City . . . . Nebraska City
LU 319 York . . . . York
LU 430 Seward Local . . . . Seward
LU 480 Fremont . . . . . . Fremont
LU 619 North Platte . North Platte
LU 845 Scottsbluff . . . . Scottsbluff
LU 948 Alliance . . . . . Alliance
LU 1148 Valentine Local . Valentine
LU 1187 Norfolk . . . . . Norfolk
LU 2813 O'Neil Local . . . . O'Neill
LU 4040 Ogallala Local . . Ogallala
LU 4048 Blair Local . . . . . Blair
LU 4072 Sidney . . . . . . Sidney
SA Nebraska City . . . . . La Vista

Railroad Signalmen
LLG 8 . . . . Kimball
LLG 119 . . . . Hickman

Retail, Wholesale and Department Store
LU 1771 . . . . Adams
LU 1808 . . . . Lincoln

Roofers, Waterproofers and Allied Workers
LU 19 . . . . Omaha
LU 85 . . . . Bellevue

Rural Letter Carriers
D 1 . . . . Seward
D 2 . . . . Prague
D 3 . . . . St. Edwards
D 4 . . . . Holdrege
D 5 . . . . Gering
SA Nebraska . . . . Firth

Service Employees
LU 226 . . . . Omaha
LU 403 Firemen &
  Oilers . . . . North Platte
LU 736 Firemen & Oilers . . Lincoln
LU 861 Firemen & Oilers . Alliance
LU 1204 Firemen & Oilers . Lincoln

Sheet Metal Workers
DC 1 U.S. Railroads . . . . . Lincoln
LU 3 . . . . Omaha
LU 259 . . . . Alliance
LU 334 . . . . North Platte
LU 402 . . . . Lincoln

Steelworkers
LU 11-286-L . . . . Lincoln
LU 11-815-L . . . . Kearney
LU 11-5427-S . . . . Omaha
LU 11-6257-S . . . . Fremont
LU 11-8612-S . . . . Waverly

Teamsters
LU 554 . . . . Omaha

Television and Radio Artists
LU Omaha . . . . Omaha

Theatrical Stage Employees
LU 42 . . . . Omaha
LU 151 . . . . Lincoln
LU 343 . . . . Omaha
LU 831 . . . . Omaha
SA Nebraska . . . . Lincoln

Transportation Communications Union
JPB 50 Burlington Northern
  Railway . . . . Lincoln
LG 112 . . . . North Platte
LG 471 . . . . Lincoln
LG 763 . . . . Omaha
LG 1288 . . . . Alliance
LG 6743 Box Butte . . . . . Alliance
LG 6799 Cornhusker . . . . Lincoln
LG 6832 Platte Valley . North Platte
SBA 106 Union Pacific Lines-
  East . . . . Omaha

Transportation Union
LU 7 . . . . North Platte
LU 200 . . . . North Platte
LU 257 . . . . Scottsbluff
LU 286 . . . . North Platte
LU 305 . . . . Lincoln
LU 367 . . . . Papillion
LU 418 . . . . . . South Sioux City

LU 626 . . . . McCook
LU 627 . . . . Walton
LU 646 . . . . Omaha
LU 934 . . . . Alliance
LU 962 . . . . Alliance
LU 1503 . . . . Beatrice
SLB LO-30 Nebraska . . . . Lincoln

Treasury Employees
CH 3 . . . . Omaha

University Professors
CH University of Nebraska at
  Omaha . . . . Omaha

Weather Service Employees
BR 03-27 . . . . North Platte
BR 03-73 . . . . Valley
BR 03-92 . . . . Hastings

Unaffiliated Labor Organizations
Contech Inc. Wahoo Plant Shop
  Committee . . . . Wahoo

Nevada

AFL-CIO Trade and Industrial Departments

Building and Construction Trades Department
BCTC Northern Nevada . . . Sparks
BCTC Southern Nevada . Henderson

Affiliated Labor Organizations

Air Traffic Controllers
LU L30 . . . . Las Vegas
LU LAS . . . . Las Vegas
LU RNO . . . . Reno
LU VGT . . . . . North Las Vegas

Asbestos Workers
LU 135 . . . . Las Vegas

Automobile, Aerospace Workers
LU 2162 . . . . Reno

Boilermakers
LG 263-D Cement Workers. . Fallon
LG 381-D Cement
  Workers . . . . Las Vegas

Bricklayers
LU . . . . Las Vegas

Carpenters
LU 971 . . . . Reno
LU 1780 . . . . Las Vegas
LU 1827 . . . . Las Vegas
LU 1977 . . . . Las Vegas

Civilian Technicians
CH 77 Silver Barons . . . . . Reno
CH 78 Silver Sage . . . . . . Reno

Communications Workers
LU 9413 . . . . Sparks
LU 14922 . . . . Las Vegas
LU 87177 . . . . Fallon

Electrical Workers
C TCC-3 Telephone
  Coordinating . . . . . Las Vegas
LU 357 . . . . Las Vegas
LU 396 . . . . Las Vegas
LU 401 . . . . Reno

Electronic Workers
LU 1118. . . . . Fallon

Fire Fighters
LU 268-F . . . . Gardnerville

Food and Commercial Workers
LU 220-I . . . . Las Vegas
LU 711 . . . . Las Vegas

Government Employees
LU 1199 DoD. Nellis Air Force Base
LU 1201. . . . . Fallon
LU 1978 DoI. . . . . Boulder City
LU 2152 VA . . . . Reno
LU 3062 DoI Lake Mead National
  Recreation Center . . Boulder City
LU 4000 AFGE Local 4000
  CPL33 . . . . . North Las Vegas

Government Security Officers
LU 76. . . . . Henderson

Hotel and Restaurant Employees
LJEB Las Vegas . . . . . Las Vegas
LU 86. . . . . Reno
LU 165 . . . . Las Vegas
LU 226 Culinary . . . . . Las Vegas
LU 227 Culinary & Casino Workers
  Union . . . . Las Vegas

Laborers
DC Nevada. . . . . Reno
LU 169 . . . . Reno
LU 872 . . . . Las Vegas

Letter Carriers
BR 709 . . . . Reno
BR 2502 . . . . Las Vegas
BR 2778 . . . . Sparks
BR 2862. . . . . Elko
BR 4515 Battle Mountain,
  Nevada . . . . . Battle Mountain
BR 6390 Winnemucca,
  Nevada. . . . . . . Winnemucca
BR 6496 . . . . Ely
BR 6575 Yerington,
  Nevada . . . . Yerington
SA Nevada . . . . Las Vegas

Locomotive Engineers
DIV 158. . . . . Sparks
DIV 229 . . . . Winnemucca
DIV 766. . . . . Las Vegas
DIV 794. . . . . Elko
DIV 800 . . . . Reno
SLB California . . . . Reno
SLB Nevada State Legislative
  Board . . . . Sparks

Machinists
LG . . . . Las Vegas
LG 845 . . . . Las Vegas

Maintenance of Way Employes
LG 85 . . . . Sparks
LG 107. . . . . Wells
LG 1020 . . . . Henderson

Musicians
LU 368 . . . . Sparks
LU 369 . . . . Las Vegas

National Staff Organization
ASSN Nevada Education . . . Reno
LU Staff Organization Clark
  County . . . . Las Vegas

Nurses
SA Nevada Nurses
  Association. . . . . . Henderson

Painters
LU 159 . . . . Henderson
LU 567 . . . . Sparks
LU 2001 . . . . Las Vegas

Plasterers and Cement Masons
LU 241 . . . . Sparks
LU 797 . . . . Las Vegas

Plumbing and Pipe Fitting
LU 350 . . . . Sparks
LU 525 . . . . Las Vegas
SA Nevada State Pipe
  Trades . . . . Las Vegas

Postal Workers
LU 746 Winnemucca
  Local. . . . . Winnemucca
LU 761 Las Vegas Area . Las Vegas
LU 936 Reno. . . . . Reno
LU 1992 Elko. . . . . Elko
LU 4636 Tonopah . . . . Tonopah
LU 5085 Carson City . . Carson City
LU 5718 Sparks . . . . . Sparks
LU 6668 Ely Local. . . . . . . Ely
LU 6689 Zephyr Cove Area
  Local. . . . . . . Zephyr Cove
LU 6806 Hawthorne
  Local. . . . . Hawthorne
LU 7125 Crystal Bay Incline Village
  Area . . . . . . Incline Village
LU 7156 Pahrump Nevada . Pahrump
SA Nevada . . . . Las Vegas

Railroad Signalmen
LLG 179 . . . . Spring Creek

Roofers, Waterproofers and Allied Workers
LU 162 . . . . Las Vegas

Rural Letter Carriers
SA 48. . . . . Reno

Security, Police and Fire Professionals
LU . . . . Reno
LU 888 . . . . Las Vegas

Service Employees
LU 1107 Nevada Service Employees
  Union. . . . . Las Vegas

Sheet Metal Workers
C Western States . . . . . . Sparks
LU 26 . . . . Sparks
LU 88 . . . . Las Vegas

Steelworkers
LU 12-233-S . . . . Ely
LU 12-711-A . . . . Las Vegas
LU 12-4856-S . . . . . Henderson
LU 12-5282-S . . . . . Henderson
LU 12-7307-S . . . . . Henderson

Teamsters
LU 14 . . . . Las Vegas
LU 533 . . . . Reno
LU 631 . . . . Las Vegas
LU 995 . . . . Las Vegas

Theatrical Stage Employees
D 2 California-Nevada-Arizona-
  Hawaii . . . . Las Vegas
LU 363 . . . . Reno
LU 720 . . . . Las Vegas

Transit Union
LU 1637 . . . . Las Vegas

Transport Workers
LU 721 . . . . Las Vegas

Transportation Union
LU 105 . . . . Las Vegas
LU 1043 . . . . Reno
LU 1117 . . . . Las Vegas
LU 1775. . . . . Elko
SLB LO-31 Nevada. . . . Las Vegas

Treasury Employees
CH 38. . . . . Reno
CH 85 . . . . Las Vegas

Weather Service Employees
BR 04-54 . . . . Las Vegas
BR 04-59 . . . . Reno
BR 04-77 . . . . Elko

Unaffiliated Labor Organizations
Boilermakers Riggers Welders
  Fitters Helpers Brotherhood LG
  777 . . . . Las Vegas
Clark County Associate Staff
  Organization-Teachers
  Staff . . . . Las Vegas
Guard Association of Nevada
  Independent LU 1 . . . Mercury
National Council of Security
  Inspectors. . . . . . . Las Vegas
Nevada Security Inspectors
  Association LU 1 . . . Tonopah
Professional Office Personnel
  Alliance. . . . . Las Vegas
Security Police Association of
  Nevada . . . . Las Vegas

New Hampshire

AFL-CIO Trade and Industrial Departments

Building and Construction Trades Department
BCTC New Hampshire. . . Hooksett

Metal Trades Department
MTC Portsmouth . . . . Portsmouth

Affiliated Labor Organizations

Air Traffic Controllers
LU MHT. . . . . Manchester
LU ZBW. . . . . Nashua

Aircraft Mechanics
NHQ. . . . . Laconia

Automobile, Aerospace Workers
LU 1913 . . . . Seabrook

Boilermakers
LG 752 . . . . Plaistow
LG 920 . . . . Nothwood

Bricklayers
LU 1 Northern New England . . Lee

Carpenters
LU 3073 . . . . Portsmouth

Civilian Technicians
CH 19 Granite State . . . Newington
CH 99 White Mountain . Manchester

Communications Workers
LU 1366 . . . . Plaistow
LU 1400 . . . . Portsmouth
LU 14131 . . . . Manchester
LU 14132 . . . . Auburn
LU 14133 . . . . Manchester
LU 31167 . . . . Manchester
LU 81243 . . . . Dover

Electrical Workers
LU 490 . . . . Dover
LU 2320 . . . . Manchester

Electrical, Radio and Machine Workers
LU 278. . . . . Woodsville
LU 293 . . . . Gonic

Food and Commercial Workers
LU 17-T . . . . Nashua
LU 952-C . . . . Nashua
LU 1046-C . . . . Boscawen

Glass, Molders, Pottery and Plastics Workers
LU 257-B . . . . Hudson

Government Employees
LU 2024 DoD . . . . . Portsmouth
LU 2551 DoD. . . . . Keene
LU 3257 USDA. . . . . . . Bedford
LU 3698 VA. . . . . . Manchester

Government Employees Association
LU 01-17 . . . . Manchester
LU 01-154 . . . . Greenville

Graphic Communications
LU 271-M. . . . . Concord

Iron Workers
LU 474. . . . . Manchester
LU 745 . . . . Dover

Laborers
DC Maine-New Hampshire & Vermont. . . . . . . Portsmouth
LU 668 . . . . Hooksett
LU 976. . . . . Portsmouth

Letter Carriers
BR 44 . . . . Manchester
BR 72 . . . . Concord
BR 161. . . . . Portsmouth
BR 230. . . . . Nashua
BR 570 . . . . Laconia
BR 590 . . . . Keene
BR 777. . . . . . . North Walpole
BR 833 . . . . Claremont
BR 990 . . . . Rochester
BR 1027 Franklin, New Hampshire . . . . Franklin
BR 1536. . . . . Berlin
BR 1597 Littleton, New Hampshire . . . . Littleton
BR 1633 . . . . Lebanon
BR 1738 Lancaster, New Hampshire. . . . . . Lancaster
BR 2002 Plymouth, New Hampshire. . . . . . Plymouth
BR 2007 Newport, New Hampshire . . . . Newport
BR 2053 Tilton, New Hampshire. . . . . Tilton
BR 2247 . . . . . . Peterborough
BR 4516 Pittsfield, New Hampshire . . . . Pittsfield
BR 4519 Suncook, New Hampshire . . . . Suncook
BR 4713 Gorham, New Hampshire . . . . Gorham
BR 4906 Jaffrey, New Hampshire . . . . Jaffrey
BR 4917 . . . . Hudson

BR 5057 Rindge, New Hampshire . . . . Rindge
BR 5174 Groton, New Hampshire. . . . . . . Groveton
BR 5631 Colebrook, New Hampshire . . . . . . Colebrook
BR 5879 Whitefield, New Hampshire . . . . . . Whitefield
SA New Hampshire . . . . Hooksett

Longshoremen
LU 1947 . . . . Portsmouth

Machinists
LG 527. . . . . Raymond
LG 2342 . . . . Jaffrey
LG 2450 . . . . Newmarket
LG 2503. . . . . Bedford

Maintenance of Way Employes
LG 2820. . . . . Dover

Musicians
LU 349. . . . . Manchester
LU 374 . . . . Concord

National Staff Organization
LU Staff Organization, New Hampshire Educational . Concord

Nurses
SA New Hampshire Nurses Association. . . . . . . Concord

Office and Professional Employees
LU 104 . . . . Merrimack

Paper, Allied-Industrial, Chemical Employees
LU 01-61 . . . . Groveton
LU 01-75 . . . . Berlin
LU 01-270 . . . . Merrimack
LU 01-472 . . . . . . Bennington
LU 01-499 . . . . . . Woodsville
LU 01-574 . . . . Tilton
LU 01-979. . . . . . . Rochester
LU 01-1424 . . . . . Rochester

Plumbing and Pipe Fitting
LU 131 . . . . Hooksett
LU 788. . . . . Portsmouth

Postal Workers
LU 230 Manchester . . . Manchester
LU 242 Rochester. . . . Rochester
LU 355 Portsmouth . . . Portsmouth
LU 494 Laconia . . . . . Laconia
LU 1074 Keene . . . . . . Keene
LU 1214 Meredith Local. . Meredith
LU 2619 Littleton Local . . Littleton
LU 2964. . . . . Durham
LU 3157 Woodsville Local . . . . Woodsville
LU 3403 Lancaster Local . Lancaster

LU 3408 Conway . . . . . Conway
LU 3435 Hanover. . . . . Hanover
LU 4504 New Market Local . . . . Newmarket
LU 4890 Peterborough Peterborough
LU 5080 Lebanon . . . . Lebanon
SA New Hampshire . . . Manchester

Professional and Technical Engineers
LU 4 . . . . Portsmouth
LU 4 Chapter 1 . . . . . Hanover
LU 202 . . . . Concord

Rural Letter Carriers
SA New Hampshire. . . . . Plaistow

Security, Police and Fire Professionals
LU 545 . . . . New Boston

Service Employees
LU 560. . . . . Grafton
LU 941 Firemen & Oilers . . Pelham
LU 1984 . . . . Concord

Sheet Metal Workers
LU 546. . . . . Portsmouth

Steelworkers
LU 04-570-L. . . . . Milford
LU 04-8566-S. . . . . . . Laconia
LU 04-8938-S . . . . . Manchester

Teachers
LU 2433 Rindge Faculty Federation . . . . Rindge
LU 8027 New Hampshire. . . Bow

Teamsters
LU 633. . . . . Manchester

Theatrical Stage Employees
LU 195. . . . . Milford

Treasury Employees
CH 11. . . . . Chichester

Utility Workers
LU 555. . . . . Seabrook

Weather Service Employees
BR 01-63. . . . . Nashua

Unaffiliated Labor Organizations
American Independent Cockpit Alliance Inc. . . . . . . Laconia
Guild Representatives Federation . . . . . . Goffstown
Professional Flight Attendants Association . . . . . . Laconia
Seabrook Dog Track Employees Association . . . . . . Seabrook
Security Officers Independent Union . . . . Merrimack

New Jersey

AFL-CIO Trade and Industrial Departments

Building and Construction Trades Department
BCTC Atlantic City . . . . Winslow
BCTC Bergen County . Hackensack
BCTC Camden County . Cherry Hill
BCTC Elizabeth &
 Vicinity . . . . Westfield
BCTC Essex County. . . Bloomfield
BCTC Hudson County . . . . . Lodi
BCTC Mercer County . Robbinsville
BCTC Middlesex County . . Newark
BCTC Monmouth & Ocean
 Counties . . . . Howell
BCTC Morris County . . Parsippany
BCTC New Jersey State . . . . Clark
BCTC Passaic County . . . . Lodi
BCTC Plainfield &
 Vicinity . . . . Westfield
BCTC Somerville . . . . Somerville
BCTC Warren County . Phillipsburg

Other Councils and Committees
C Essex West Hudson Labor
 Council . . . . Newark

AFL-CIO Directly Affiliated Locals
DALU 24356 Engineering
 Employees . . . . Edison

Affiliated Labor Organizations

Agricultural Employees
BR 39 . . . . Elizabeth

Air Traffic Controllers
LU ACY . . . . Atlantic City
LU CDW . . . . Fairfield
LU CXY . . . . Pomona
LU EWR. . . . . Newark
LU MMU. . . . . Lake Stockholm
LU TEB . . . . Teterboro
LU TTN . . . . . West Trenton

Asbestos Workers
CONF Middle Atlantic
 States . . . . Newark
LU 32 . . . . Newark
LU 89 . . . . Columbus

Atlantic Independent Union
NHQ. . . . . Palmyra

Automobile, Aerospace Workers
C New Jersey CAP . . . . . Trenton
LU 153 . . . . Wood Ridge
LU 267 . . . . Perth Amboy
LU 595 . . . . Linden
LU 980 . . . . Edison
LU 1038 . . . . Metuchen
LU 1668 . . . . Spotswood
LU 2210 . . . . Lodi
LU 2315 . . . . Millville
LU 2326 . . . . . . Woodbridge
LU 2327 . . . . Vineland

Bakery, Confectionery, Tobacco Workers and Grain Millers
LU 50 . . . . Spotswood

Boilermakers
LG 28. . . . . Bayonne
LG 194 . . . . Fair Lawn
LG 432-D Cement Workers. . Berlin
LG 661 . . . . Florence

Bricklayers
LU 4 . . . . Morristown
LU 5 . . . . Bordentown

Carpenters
C New Jersey Regional
 Council. . . . . Edison
LU 6 . . . . North Bergen
LU 15 . . . . Hackensack
LU 31 . . . . Trenton
LU 36 . . . . Hackensack
LU 121 . . . . Vineland
LU 124 . . . . Wayne
LU 155 . . . . Plainfield
LU 393 . . . . Gloucester
LU 455 . . . . Somerville
LU 542 . . . . Pennsville
LU 620 . . . . Madison
LU 623 . . . . Atlantic City
LU 715 . . . . Cranford
LU 781 . . . . Princeton
LU 821 . . . . Kenilworth
LU 1006 . . . . Milltown
LU 1107 . . . . Parsippany
LU 1342 . . . . Bloomfield
LU 1489 . . . . Burlington
LU 1578 . . . . Gloucester
LU 1743 . . Cape May Court House
LU 2018 . . . . Red Bank
LU 2098 . . . . Gloucester
LU 2212 . . . . Union
LU 2250 . . . . Red Bank

Catholic School Teachers
LU South Jersey . . . . . Audubon

Civilian Technicians
CH 70 Garden State. . . . Tuckerton
CH 124 New
 Jersey Air . Egg Harbor Township

Communications Workers
C New Jersey Presidents
 Coordinating . . . . West Trenton
LU 110 . . . . Camden
LU 305. . . . . Newark
LU 310. . . . . Hillside
LU 441 . . . . Clark
LU 1001 . . . . Wall
LU 1002 . . . . Rockaway
LU 1006 . . . . Union
LU 1009 . . . . Hillside
LU 1010 . . . . Paramus
LU 1012 . . . . Absecon
LU 1013 . . . . . . Cinnaminson
LU 1020 . . . . Bloomfield
LU 1022 . . . . . . Englishtown
LU 1023 . . . . Cranford
LU 1032 . . . . Trenton
LU 1034 . . . . Trenton
LU 1037 . . . . Newark
LU 1039 . . . . Trenton
LU 1040 . . . . Trenton
LU 1058 . . . . Bridgewater
LU 1060 . . . . North Plainfield
LU 1061 . . . . Bayonne
LU 1062 . . . . Holmdel

LU 1067. . . . . Camden
LU 1090 . . . Egg Harbor Township
LU 14142 . . . . Phillipsburg
LU 14143 . . . . Vineland
LU 14800 . . . . Oaklyn
LU 14826 Philadelphia
 Typographical
 Union . . . . Mount Laurel
LU 34042 Hudson
 County . . . . Jersey City
LU 51209 NABET Local
 209. . . . . Secaucus
LU 81103 . . . . Camden
LU 81134 . . . . Bellmawr
LU 81332 . . . Hasbrouck Heights
LU 81401 . . . . Edison
LU 81427 . . . . Montville
LU 81440 . . . . Blackwood

DuPont Workers
LU Chemical Workers Association
 Inc. . . . . Pennsville

Electrical Workers
LU 94 . . . . Hightstown
LU 102 . . . . Parsippany
LU 164 . . . . Paramus
LU 210 . . . . Absecon
LU 269. . . . . Trenton
LU 327 . . . . Phillipsburg
LU 351 . . . . Hammonton
LU 400 . . . . Wall
LU 454 . . . . Carteret
LU 456. . . . . . North Brunswick
LU 604 . . . . Bayonne
LU 827 . . . . East Windsor
LU 864 . . . . . . Cliffwood Beach
LU 1153 . . . . Elizabeth
LU 1158 . . . . Clifton
LU 1289 . . . . Wall
LU 1293 . . . . Oceanview
LU 1303 . . . . Matawan
LU 1309 . . . . Wall
LU 1470 . . . . Rahway
LU 1684 . . . . . . West Orange
LU 1820 . . . . Toms River
LU 1940 . . . . Milford
LU 2066 . . . . Union City
SA New Jersey . . . . . . Absecon
SA New Jersey State Construction
 Division . . . . Wall
SC U-3 Jersey Central Power & Light
 Company . . . . . Phillipsburg

Electrical, Radio and Machine Workers
LU 404 . . . . Clifton
LU 417 . . . . Parsippany
LU 420. . . . . Trenton

Electronic Workers
DC 3 . . . . . Hasbrouck Heights
LU 106 . . . . Moorestown
LU 414. . . . . Newark
LU 416. . . . . . North Brunswick
LU 439 . . . . Skillman
LU 447 . . . . Clifton
LU 455 . . . . Trenton
LU 467 . . . . Mahwah
LU 491 . . . . Edison
LU 496 Benzol Production Workers
 Organization . . . . . . Edison
LU 498 . . . . Marlboro

Federal Employees
LU 476 . . . . Fort Monmouth
LU 1154. . . . . East Orange
LU 1340 . . . . Atlantic City
LU 1431 . . . . Plainfield
LU 1437. . . . . Picatinny Arsenal
SFED New Jersey . . . . . . Orange

Fire Fighters
LU 26-I Uniformed Fire Patrolmen's
 Association . . . . West Milford
LU 103-F . . . . . . Fort Monmouth
LU 106-F . McGuire Air Force Base
LU 114-F . . . . Lakehurst
LU 115-F . . . . Fort Dix
LU 147-F . . . . Eatontown

Flint Glass Workers
LU 7 . . . . Millville
LU 129 . . . . Pennsville
LU 132 . . . . . . Wildwood Crest
LU 153 . . . . Newfield
LU 154 . . . . Sayreville
LU 591 . . . . Franklinville
LU 701 . . . . Vineland

Food and Commercial Workers
C Insurance Area
 2A. . . . . . Whitehouse Station
C Insurance Workers Area V . Berlin
DC New York and Northern New
 Jersey . . . . Little Falls
LU 9-C. . . . . Summit
LU 56 . . . . Cherry Hill
LU 100-R . . . . . . Green Brook
LU 153-C . . . . Bayonne
LU 167-I . . . . Whitehouse Station
LU 202-I . . . . Oakland
LU 209-D. . . . . Linden
LU 212-D Professional Librarians
 Union. . . . . Linden
LU 220-T. . . . . Clifton
LU 271-C . . . . Sayreville
LU 276-T . . . . Clifton
LU 450-T . . . . Paterson
LU 464-A. . . . . . . Little Falls
LU 527-C . . . . Sayreville
LU 825-C . . . . Totowa
LU 1206-I . . . . . . Cherry Hill
LU 1245 . . . . Little Falls
LU 1262 . . . . Clifton
LU 1358 . . . . Atlantic City
LU 1360. . . . . . . West Berlin

Glass, Molders, Pottery and Plastics Workers
LU 6. . . . . Salem
LU 7 . . . . Millville
LU 21. . . . . Penns Grove
LU 40 . . . . Kearny
LU 103 . . . . . . Mays Landing
LU 111 . . . . Carteret
LU 126 . . . . . . Mays Landing
LU 145 . . . . Sicklerville
LU 157 . . . . . Carneys Point
LU 185-A . . . . Trenton
LU 197. . . . . . . Maple Shade
LU 219 . . . . Bellplain
LU 227. . . . . . . Perth Amboy
LU 236-A . . . . Little Egg Harbor

Government Employees
C 238 . . . . Trenton
LU 42 ID, Second District
 At-Large . . . . New Brunswick

LU 200 . . . . Atlantic City
LU 225 DoD . . . Picatinny Arsenal
LU 371 National Army-Air
  Technicians
  Association . . . . . Maplewood
LU 632 USDA. . . . . . . Milford
LU 1012 VA . . . . Lyons
LU 1659 DoD . . . . Colts Neck
LU 1778 DoD . . . . Wrightstown
LU 1904 DoD . . . . . Eatontown
LU 1999 DoD. . . . . . Fort Dix
LU 2001. . . . . Fort Dix
LU 2041 GSA . . . . . Burlington
LU 2149 DoJ . . . . Newark
LU 2175 DoD . . . . . . Bayonne
LU 2335 DoT . . . . Pomona
LU 2369 HHS . . . . Brick
LU 2442 VA. . . . . Newark
LU 2513 DoL. . . . . Edison
LU 2658 GSA . . . . Newark
LU 2735 USDA . . . . Robbinsville
LU 2855 DoD . . . . . Jersey City
LU 2868 DoD . . . . . Colts Neck
LU 3183 USDA . . . . . . Norma
LU 3451 Non-Professional &
  Professionals . . . . . . Newark
LU 3486
  DoD . . . . Egg Harbor Township
LU 3564 USDA. . . . Bordentown
LU 3588 SBA . . . . . . Newark
LU 3673 DoD . . . Hamilton Square
LU 3975 . . . . Fairton

Government Employees
  Association
LU 560 Police Officers. . . Bayonne
LU R2-84 . . . . Lakehurst

Government Security Officers
LU 14 . . . . Glassboro

Graphic Communications
LU 8-N . . . . Rivervale
LU 31-C . . . . Nutley
LU 70-C . . . . Trenton
LU 196-C . . . . Somerset
LU 447-S. . . . . Jersey City
LU 474-S . . . . . South Plainfield
LU 612-M . . . . . West Caldwell

Hotel and Restaurant Employees
LU 3 . . . . Newark
LU 54 . . . . Atlantic City
LU 69 . . . . Secaucus
STC New Jersey. . . . . . Trenton

Independent Unions Federation
LU 152 American Musicians
  Union . . . . Dumont
LU 229 Sheridan Printing Company
  Employees'
  Association . . . . . Phillipsburg

Iron Workers
DC Northern New Jersey . . . Union
LU 11 . . . . Bloomfield
LU 45 . . . . Jersey City
LU 68 . . . . Trenton
LU 350 . . . . Atlantic City
LU 373. . . . . . . Perth Amboy
LU 399 . . . . Westville
LU 480 . . . . Union
LU 483 . . . . Paterson

Laborers
DC Building Laborers District
  Council . . . . Fort Lee

DC Building Laborers District
  Council. . . . . . Robbinsville
DC Central New Jersey,
  Building. . . . . . East Brunswick
DC NJH & GCL. . . . . . Newark
LU. . . . . Rochelle Park
LU 137. . . . . Cherry Hill
LU 172. . . . . Trenton
LU 222 . . . . Camden
LU 305 . . . . West Orange
LU 325 . . . . Jersey City
LU 394. . . . . Elizabeth
LU 415. . . . . Pleasantville
LU 472. . . . . Newark
LU 592 Building & General
  Construction Craft . . . . Fort Lee
LU 593 . . . . Hillsborough
LU 594 . . . . East Brunswick
LU 595 Building & General
  Construction Craft . . Robbinsville
LU 734 . . . . Rochelle Park
LU 889. . . . . Newark
LU 1030 . . . . North Bergen
LU 1153 . . . . Newark
LU 1412 . . . . Belleville

Laundry and Dry Cleaning
LU 284 . . . . Lyndhurst

Letter Carriers
BR 38 . . . . Springfield
BR 42 . . . . Brick
BR 65 . . . . Passaic
BR 67 . . . . Elizabeth
BR 120 . . . . Paterson
BR 268. . . . . Princeton
BR 272 . . . . Hopatcong
BR 342 . . . . Montclair
BR 370 . . . . Atlantic City
BR 380. . . . . Trenton
BR 396. . . . . Plainfield
BR 425 . . . . Hackensack
BR 444. . . . . North Brunswick
BR 457. . . . . . . Perth Amboy
BR 534 . . . . Vineland
BR 540 . . . . Oaklyn
BR 673 . . . . South Orange
BR 754 . . . . Cranford
BR 768 . . . . Bridgewater
BR 769 . . . . Haddonfield
BR 903 . . . . Northfield
BR 908 . . . . Woodbury
BR 924 . . . . Freehold
BR 1089 . . . . Lakewood
BR 1492 . . . . Westfield
BR 1776 . . . . Atlantic Highland
BR 1904 . . . . . Bradley Beach
BR 1908 . . . . Riverside
BR 1913 . . . . Bordentown
BR 2128 . . . . Toms River
BR 2138. . . . . Fort Lee
BR 2458 Garwood, New
  Jersey . . . . Garwood
BR 2653 Avon by the Sea, New
  Jersey . . . . . Avon by the Sea
BR 2682. . . . . . . Mount Laurel
BR 2876. . . . . Linden
BR 3540. . . . . Bergenfield
BR 4089 Vauxhall, New
  Jersey . . . . Vauxhall
BR 4091 . . . . . New Milford
BR 4102 . . . . Raritan
BR 4212 . . . . Cedar Grove
BR 4307 Frenchtown, New
  Jersey . . . . Frenchtown
BR 4378 Haskell, New
  Jersey . . . . Haskell

BR 4433 Wanaque, New
  Jersey . . . . Wanaque
BR 4556. . . . . Berlin
BR 4623. . . . . . . Pennsauken
BR 4697 Demarest, New
  Jersey . . . . Demarest
BR 5363 . . . . Belford
BR 5420 . . . . Brick
BR 5554 Northvale, New
  Jersey . . . . Northvale
BR 5571 Hopewell, New
  Jersey . . . . Hopewell
BR 5648 . . . . . . Mount Holly
BR 5801. . . . . Willingboro
BR 5818 Norwood, New
  Jersey . . . . Norwood
BR 6311 . . . . Cherry Hill
BR 6339 Oakhurst, New
  Jersey . . . . Oakhurst
BR 6487 Gibbsboro, New
  Jersey . . . . Gibbsboro
SA New Jersey . . . . Westwood

Locomotive Engineers
DIV 11 . . . . Edison
DIV 53 . . . . South Belmar
DIV 157 . . . . Toms River
DIV 171 . . . . . . Hackettstown
DIV 226 . . . . Monroe Township
DIV 231 . . . . . . Maple Shade
DIV 272 . . . . . . Mount Tabor
DIV 353 . . . . Mickleton
DIV 373 . . . . . . Toms River
DIV 387 . . . . Atco
DIV 497. . . . . Sparta
DIV 521. . . . . Hewitt
DIV 601 . . . . Livingston
GCA Amtrak. . . . . Cherry Hill
GCA NJTRO . . . . South Belmar
SLB New Jersey. . . . Toms River

Longshoremen
DC New York . . . . North Bergen
LU 1 . . . . Newark
LU 1233 . . . . Newark
LU 1235 . . . . Newark
LU 1478-2 . . . . Newark
LU 1588 . . . . Bayonne
LU 1804-1 . . . . North Bergin
LU 1964. . . . Ridgefield Park
LU 2049 . . . . Newark

Machinists
DLG 15. . . . . Clifton
LG 15-S . . . . Hoboken
LG 76-S . . . . Classboro
LG 95-S . . . . Pleasantville
LG 315 . . . . Clark
LG 321 Aircrew Training
  Professionals . . . . Burlington
LG 329 . . . . Morganville
LG 367 . . . . Toms River
LG 447 . . . . Clifton
LG 677 . . . . Blairstown
LG 914 . . . . Old Bridge
LG 1041 . . . . . West Long Branch
LG 1445 . . . . Newark
LG 1812 . . . . Vineland
LG 2339 . . . . Newark
STC New
  Jersey. . . . . Upper Saddle River

Maintenance of Way Employes
DIV Commuter Railroad
  System . . . . Clinton
LG 705. . . . . Clark
LG 2627 . . . . . . Franklinville
LG 3082 . . . . Port Reading

SLG 305. . . . . Rahway
SLG 2905 . . . . Hillside
SLG 2906 . . . . . Long Branch
SLG 2907 . . . . Newton
SLG 3012 . . . . . Mount Laurel

Musicians
LU 16 . . . . West Orange
LU 62 . . . . Trenton
LU 151 . . . . Union
LU 204-373. . . . . Edison
LU 248 . . . . Paterson
LU 336 . . . . Riverton
LU 399 Asbury Park
  Local . . . . Toms River
LU 595 . . . . Vineland
LU 661-708 . . . . Ventnor
LU 746. . . . . Plainfield
STCON New Jersey . . . . Edison

National Staff Organization
ASSN New Jersey. . . . . Trenton

Needletrades
JB Central & South Jersey . Somerset
JB Greater New York & New
  Jersey . . . . Union City
LU 2-H . . . . Union City
LU 21 . . . . Union City
LU 24-042 . . . . . . Union City
LU 26-A . . . . Somerset
LU 59 . . . . Union City
LU 75-087 . . . . . . Union City
LU 85-I. . . . . Union City
LU 99-I. . . . . Union City
LU 133-I . . . . Union City
LU 134 . . . . Union City
LU 135-I . . . . Union City
LU 138 . . . . Union City
LU 145 . . . . Union City
LU 148 . . . . Union City
LU 149 . . . . Union City
LU 157. . . . . Union City
LU 158-I . . . . Union City
LU 161 . . . . Union City
LU 162 . . . . Union City
LU 166-I . . . . Union City
LU 180 . . . . Union City
LU 215-T . . . . Union City
LU 222 . . . . Union City
LU 252-T. . . . . . . Union City
LU 292-H . . . . Union City
LU 630-A . . . . Somerset
LU 654 . . . . Union City
LU 696-T. . . . . . . Union City
LU 1166-T . . . . . . Union City
LU 1298 . . . . Somerset
LU 1338 . . . . Union City
LU 1439 . . . . Somerset
LU 1528 . . . . Somerset
LU 1648 . . . . Union City
LU 1733 . . . . Union City
LU 1790 . . . . Union City
LU 1932 . . . . Union City
LU 1939 . . . . Union City
LU 2052 . . . . Union City
LU 13298-102 . . . . Union City

NLRB Professional Association
LU 22 . . . . Newark

Novelty and Production Workers
LU 148 Production
  Workers . . . . Jersey City
LU 246 . . . . Jersey City

Nurses
SA New Jersey. . . . . . Hamilton

SA New Jersey State Nurses Association . . . . Trenton

Office and Professional Employees
LU 20 . . . . Bayonne
LU 32 . . . . Union
LU 153 . . . . Phillipsburg

Operating Engineers
JNESO DC 1 . . . . New Brunswick
CONF Northeastern
State . . . . West Caldwell
LU Arbor Glen Care & Rehabilitation
Center . . . . Caldwell
LU Betty Bacharach Rehabilitation
Hospital . . . . Northfield
LU Irvington Organization of
Nurses . . . . Irvington
LU JNESO Kessler Unit . . Dorothy
LU JNESO St. Marys
Hospital . . . . Bayonne
LU JNESO United Hospitals . Edison
LU Long Branch Public Health
Nursing . . . . Long Branch
LU MCOSS Nursing Services,
JNESO . . . . Red Bank
LU St. Michael's . . . . . . Kearny
LU Zurbrugg Memorial Hospital
JNESO . . . . Bordentown
LU 25 . . . . Millstone
LU 68 . . . . West Caldwell
LU 825 . . . . Springfield

Painters
DC 711 . . . . Egg Harbor Township
LU 277 . . . . Egg Harbor Township
LU 694 . . . . Neptune
LU 1004 . . . . Bloomfield
LU 1005 . . . . Bloomfield
LU 1007 . . . . Bloomfield
LU 1009 State of New Jersey
Glaziers . . . . Toms River
LU 1310 . . . . Bloomfield
LU 1331 . . . . Glassboro
LU 1976 . . . . Bloomfield

Paper, Allied-Industrial, Chemical Employees
LU 284 . . . . Newark
LU 948 . . . . . . North Brunswick
LU 01-292 . . . . . East Rutherford
LU 01-300 . . . . . . Mountainside
LU 01-417 . . . . Bloomfield
LU 01-870 . . . . . . Saddle Brook
LU 01-1275 . . . . Newark
LU 01-1564 . . . . . . South River
LU 02-149 . . . . Rahway
LU 02-380 . . . . Deptford
LU 02-397 . . . . Avenel
LU 02-406 . . . . Bayonne
LU 02-438 . . . . North Brunswick
LU 02-562 . . . . Bayville
LU 02-575 . . . . Rahway
LU 02-716 . . . . . . Mount Holly
LU 02-890 . . . . . Edgewater Park
LU 02-891 . . . . Piscataway
LU 02-991 . . . . Elmer
LU 02-1308 . . . . Frenchtown
LU 02-1426 . . . . Plainsboro
LU 02-1482 . . . . Manalapan
LU 02-1712 . . . . . . Bloomsbury
LU 02-1928 . . . . . Perth Amboy
LU 02-5570 . . . . Cranbury
LU 08-138 . . . . Cranbury

Plasterers and Cement Masons
LU 29 . . . . Jersey City

Plumbing and Pipe Fitting
LU 9 . . . . Englishtown
LU 14 . . . . Lodi
LU 24 . . . . Springfield
LU 274 . . . . Ridgefield
LU 322 . . . . Winslow
LU 475 . . . . Warren
LU 696 . . . . Millburn
LU 855 . . . . Edison
SA New Jersey State Pipe
Trades . . . . Winslow

Police
LU . . . . Fort Monmouth
LU 1 FOP-NLC Conrail . . . . Parlin

Postal and Federal Employees
LU 501 . . . . Atlantic City
LU 513 . . . . Newark

Postal Workers
LU North Jersey Area . . . . Clifton
LU 149 Central Jersey
Area . . . . North Brunswick
LU 361 Elizabeth . . . . . Elizabeth
LU 381 New Jersey Mid-State
Area . . . . Watchung
LU 483 Jersey City . . . Jersey City
LU 526 South New Jersey
Area . . . . Blackwood
LU 750 . . . . Ridgewood
LU 986 Red Bank . . . . Red Bank
LU 1020 Trenton Metropolitan
Area . . . . Trenton
LU 1153 Bloomfield . . . Bloomfield
LU 1270 Passaic . . . . . . Passaic
LU 1593 Egg Harbor City
Local . . . . Egg Harbor City
LU 1629 Clifton . . . . . . Clifton
LU 2434 Linden . . . . . . Linden
LU 2912
Bernardsville . . . Bernardsville
LU 3568 Keansburg
Local . . . . Keansburg
LU 3617 Cape Atlantic
Area . . . . Pomona
LU 3760 Millville . . . . Millville
LU 4884 Rutherford . . . Woodridge
LU 5276 Paramus . . . . . Paramus
LU 6419 New Jersey Shore
Area . . . . Brick
SA New Jersey . . . . . . Watchung

Professional and Technical Engineers
C New Jersey/Pennsylvania Area
Council . . . . Iselin
LU 18 . . . . Audubon
LU 66 . . . . Hackensack
LU 241 . . . . Maple Shade

Railroad Signalmen
LLG 58 . . . . . . Egg Harbor City
LLG 60 . . . . Jersey City
LLG 84 . . . . Howell
LLG 102 . . . . Metuchen

Retail, Wholesale and Department Store
LU 29 Industrial Workers
Union . . . . Paramuss
LU 108 . . . . Maplewood
LU 262 . . . . East Orange

Roofers, Waterproofers and Allied Workers
LU 4 . . . . Parsippany
LU 10 . . . . Haledon

Rural Letter Carriers
D 1 New Jersey . . . . . Blairstown
D 2 New Jersey . . . . Edison
D 3 New Jersey . . . . . . Marlton
SA New Jersey . Monmouth Junction

Security Officers, Police and Guards
LU 1456 . . . . Bayonne

Security, Police and Fire Professionals
LU 125 . . . . Rockaway

Service Employees
C New Jersey . . . . Trenton
LU . . . . Garfield
LU 45 International Leather Goods,
Plastics, Novelty and Service
Union . . . . Gloucester
LU 61 International Leather Goods,
Plastics, Novelty and Service
Union . . . . Camden
LU 76 International Leather Goods,
Plastics, Novelty and Service
Union . . . . . . Ridgefield Park
LU 164 International Leather Goods,
Plastics, Novelty and Service
Union . . . . Lambertville
LU 175 . . . . Trenton
LU 302 Firemen &
Oilers . . . . . . Mount Laurel
LU 338 Firemen &
Oilers . . . . Port Reading
LU 617 . . . . Newark
LU 1050 Firemen &
Oilers . . . . Vineland
SC 2 Firemen &
Oilers . . . . . . Mount Laurel

Sheet Metal Workers
LU 25 . . . . Carlstadt
LU 27 . . . . Farmingdale
LU 396 . . . . Lyndhurst

State, County and Municipal Employees
C Hospital & Health Care
Employees . . . . Newark
C 1 . . . . Trenton
C 52 . . . . Jersey City
C 71 . . . . Williamstown
C 73 Central New Jersey
District . . . . Hamilton
D 1199 United Nurses of
Pennsylvania . . . . . . Newark
D 1199-J New Jersey Health Care
Employees . . . . Newark
LU 956 Princeton University Library
Assistants . . . . Princeton
LU 2252 Eastern Pines
Convalescent . . . . Atlantic City
LU 2254 . . . . Jersey City
LU 2303-b . . . . . . Atlantic City
LU 3043 Rider College Clerical
Union . . . . Lawrenceville
LU 3499 Bergen Regional Medical
Center . . . . Paterson
LU 3666 National Prescription
Administrators . . . . . . Clifton
LU 3965 Central Fill Inc. . Elizabeth
LU 6881 Patco . . . . . . Newark

Steelworkers
LU . . . . South Amboy
LU 04-107-L . . . . Trenton
LU 04-182-L . . . . Carteret
LU 04-396 . . . . Bloomfield

LU 04-420-U . . . . . . Piscataway
LU 04-482 . . . . Roebling
LU 04-493-SB . . . . . . Trenton
LU 04-547-L . . . . Trenton
LU 04-637-L . . . . Stanhope
LU 04-770 . . . . Howell
LU 04-2026-S . . . . . Burlington
LU 04-2040-S . . . . . . Roebling
LU 04-3297-S . . . . Newark
LU 04-3355-S . . . . Trenton
LU 04-5210-S . . . Perth Amboy
LU 04-8228-S . . . . Edison
LU 04-8972-S . . . . Erial
LU 04-12238-S . . . . Birmingham
LU 04-12663-S . . . . Salem
LU 04-13742-S . . . . . . Passaic
LU 04-14756-S . . . . Edison
LU 04-15024-S . . . . . . Edison
LU 04-15540-S . . . . Manalapan

Teachers
LU 2373 . . . . Glassboro
LU 5057 Hospital Professional &
Allied Employees of New
Jersey . . . . Emerson
SFED New Jersey Hospital
Professional & Allied
Employees . . . . Emerson
SFED 8028 New Jersey
State . . . . Edison

Teamsters
JC 73 . . . . Union
LU 11 . . . . North Haledon
LU 35 . . . . Trenton
LU 97 . . . . Union
LU 102 . . . . Fair Lawn
LU 125 . . . . Totowa
LU 177 . . . . Hillside
LU 194 . . . . Vauxhall
LU 331 . . . . Pleasantville
LU 408 . . . . Union
LU 418 . . . . Garfield
LU 469 . . . . Hazlet
LU 478 . . . . Union
LU 560 . . . . Union City
LU 575 . . . . Union
LU 641 . . . . Union
LU 676 . . . . Collingswood
LU 701 . . . . . North Brunswick
LU 723 . . . . Montville
LU 815 . . . . . Englewood Cliffs
LU 843 . . . . Springfield
LU 863 . . . . Mountainside
LU 877 . . . . Linden
LU 945 . . . . Wayne
LU 966 . . . . Cresskill
LU 1100 New Jersey Mailers
Union . . . . Piscataway

Theatrical Stage Employees
LU 21 . . . . Vauxhall
LU 59 . . . . Secaucus
LU 77 . . . . Linwood
LU 534 . . . . New Brunswick
LU 536 . . . . Keyport
LU 632 . . . . Hackensack
LU 645 . . . . Closter
LU 804 . . . . Stratford
LU 917 . . . . Atlantic City

Train Dispatchers
SCOM New Jersey Rail
Transit . . . . Rahway
SCOM New Jersey Transit Power
Supervisors . . . . . . Rockaway
SCOM Trans-Hudson Port
Authority . . . . Red Bank

Transit Union
JC New Jersey State . . . Kenilworth
LDIV 540 . . . . Willingboro
LDIV 819 . . . . Irvington
LDIV 820 . . . . North Bergen
LDIV 821 . . . . Jersey City
LDIV 822 . . . . Bloomfield
LDIV 823 . . . . Irvington
LDIV 824 . . . . Howell
LDIV 825 . . . . Waldwick
LDIV 880 . . . . . Mount Ephraim
LDIV 1317 . . . . . . West Orange
LDIV 1614 . . . . Dover
LU 1626 . . . . Bricktown

Transport Workers
LU 225 . . . . Hackensack
LU 225 Branch #4 . . . . . . Brick
LU 1400 . . . . North Bergen

Transportation Communications Union
D 435 Conrail . . . . Sparta
D 626 . . . . Roselle
D 1218 Conrail . . . . Mount Laurel
LG . . . . Raritan
LG 16 United Service
  Workers . . . . Sparta
LG 5045 New Jersey
  Transit . . . . Middletown
LG 5075 Port Authority Trans
  Hudson . . . . Howell
LG 6053 Hoboken . . . . Keyport
LG 6965 Oak Island . . . . Rahway
LU 306 . . . . Jersey City

Transportation Union
GCA GO-770 Conrail South . Delran
GCA GO-795 Path . . . . . Howell
LU 300 . . . . Turnersville
LU 419 . . . . Mount Laurel
LU 759 . . . . Clifton
LU 838 . . . . Woolwich Township
LU 1370 . . . . Belford
LU 1413 . . . . Montclair
LU 1440 . . . . Hazlet
LU 1445 . . . . Toms River
LU 1447 . . . . Bricktown
LU 1558 . . . . Dumont
LU 1589 . . . . Somerset
SLB LO-33 New Jersey . . . Trenton

Treasury Employees
CH 60 . . . . Springfield
CH 110 . . . . Cherry Hill
CH 161 . . . . Elizabeth

University Professors
CH Bloomfield College . Bloomfield
CH Monmouth College, Faculty
  Association of . West Long Branch
CH Rider College . . . Lawrenceville
CH Union College . . . . Cranford

Utility Co-Workers
C Bridgewater . . . . . Greenbrook

C Claim . . . . Newark
C Cranford . . . . Bloomfield
C Customer Payment
  Processing . . . . . . Bloomfield
C East Gate . . . . . . Bloomfield
C Garrett Mountain . . West Paterson
C Harmon Cove . . . . Bloomfield
C Newark . . . . Bloomfield
C Northern Center . . . . Cranford
C Paramus . . . . Bloomfield
C Princeton . . . . Trenton
C Roseland . . . . . . Middlesex
C Southern Center . . . Bloomfield
NHQ . . . . Bloomfield

Utility Workers
LU 375 . . . . Elmwood Park
LU 391 . . . . Vauxhall
LU 395 . . . . Belmar
LU 409 . . . . Bayville
LU 423 . . . . Middlesex
LU 424 . . . . Elizabeth
LU 503 . . . . Lakehurst

Weather Service Employees
BR 01-14 . . . . Mount Holly

Westinghouse Salaried Employees
ASSN New York Engineering &
  Service . . . . Aberdeen

Unaffiliated Labor Organizations

195 Broadway Corporation
  Employees Council . . . Bayonne
Allied Trades Council . . Englewood
  Cliffs
Ball & Pebble Mill Workers
  Inc. . . . . Little Falls
Bayonne Chemical
  Workers . . . . Bayonne
Bayway Employees Salary
  Union . . . . Linden
Bell Telephone Lab Protective
  Union . . . . Scotchplains
Best Foods Employees Association
  Independent . . . . . . Bayonne
Buckeye Tri-State Pipe Line
  Union . . . . Sewell
Building Service Employees
  Association Westmill Management
  Company . . . . . . West Orange
Building Trades International Union
  LU 777 . . . . Emerson
Catalyst Employees
  Association . . . . . Gibbstown
Chemical & Industrial
  Union . . . . Barnsboro
Chemical Workers Independent
  Union Delaware
  Valley . . . . Monroeville
Colgate Chemical Workers
  Independent Union
  Inc. . . . . Mount Laurel
Comite Organizador de Trabajadores
  Agricolas . . . . Rosenhayn

Dairy Workers Association Inc.
  Cream-O-Land Dairy . Burlington
Electromagnetic Steel Manufacturing
  Employees Union LU
  16 . . . . Moorestown
Exxon Employees Association of
  New Jersey . . . . Linden
Federation of Police Security &
  Correction Officers . . . Rahway
Financial Consultants Guild of
  America Inc. Employees Industrial
  LU 2 . . . . Clifton
Freedmans Bakery Association
  Independent . . . . . . Belmar
Grand Lodge Railway
  Independent . . . . Colonia
Hayward Industrial Employees Union
  Inc. Independent . . . . Elizabeth
Hazardous Materials & Lead
  Abatement Workers Union LU
  1 . . . . Newark
Independent Dock Workers Union
  LU 1 . . . . Gloucester
Independent United Workers Union
  of Leone Industries . . . Bridgeton
International Union of Aides Nurses
  & Professional Employees LU
  1199 . . . . Middletown
International Union of District 55,
  Allied & Industrial Workers of the
  U.S. & Canada . . . . Bergenfield
Laboratory Employees Union
  Independent . . . . Linden
Lay Teachers Association of St.
  Josephs High School . . Metuchen
Licorice & Paper Employees
  Association . . . . . . Pennsauken
Mobilab Union Inc. . . . Clarksboro
Mona Employees
  Association . . . . Paterson
Mosstype Employees Association
  New Jersey . . . . Prospect Park
National Employees Union . Harrison
New Jersey Civil Service Association
  Camden C 10 . . . . . Camden
New Jersey Nurses
  Union . . . . Livingston
New Jersey Paralegal Association
  Inc. Union Number
  One . . . . Farmingdale
New Jersey Regional
  Council . . . . Edison
Oil & Chemical Workers
  Independent Procter &
  Gamble-Staten Island . . . Avenel
Oil Workers of Paulsboro Gibbstown
Parlin Employees Association
  Inc. . . . . Parlin
Paulette Fashions Inc. Union
  Independent . . . . Weehawken
Pfister Chemical Works Employees
  Association . . . . . . Ridgefield
Physicians & Dentists Union,
  Independent State Federation
  Florida . . . . Newark

Presbyterian Hospital Professional
  Dietician's
  Association . . . Englewood Cliffs
President Container Employees
  Association . . . . . Kenilworth
Production Clerical & Public
  Employees International Union LU
  911 . . . . Brick
Professional Employees
  Guild . . . . Hackensack
Professional Health Care Union DC
  JNESO Council Technical
  Unit . . . . Matawan
Professional Industrial and Trade
  Workers Union . . . . Cherry Hill
Publishers Employees
  Independent Association
  Inc. . . . . Princeton Junction
Quaker Independent Union . Newark
Railway Independent Transit Union
  Grand Lodge . . . . . . Colonia
Registered Professional Nurse UNIT
  1 . . . . Sewell
Resilent Floor Layers LU
  29 . . . . Atlantic City
Rutherford Machinery Employees
  Association . . . . East Rutherford
Scientists & Professional
  Engineers Personnel
  Association . . . . Mount Laurel
Service, Healthcare, and Public
  Employees Union . . . Union City
Sheet Metal Workers of New Jersey
  LU 22 . . . . Cranford
Sovac Petroleum Union of South
  Jersey . . . . Clarksboro
Standard Refinery Union Inc.-
  Exxon . . . . Bayonne
Star Manufacturing Employees
  Union . . . . Little Ferry
Stationary Engineers LU
  4 . . . . Glenridge
Sun Oil Company Employees
  Association South Amboy
  District . . . . Piscataway
Tank Truck Workers
  Union . . . . Carneys Point
Tool Die & Mold Makers
  International Union LU
  69984 . . . . Rahway
Trades Independent United LU
  732 . . . . Union
Transoceanic Pursers Association
  International . . . . . Morristown
Tri-States Employee Union . Kearny
Union de Trabajadores Agricolas y
  del Hongo . . . . Glassboro
Union of Heat Stretch
  Ceiling . . . . Upper Saddle River
United Armed Guards of
  America . . . . Lyndhurst
United States Oil and Chemical
  Workers . . . . Linden
United Workers of
  America . . . . . . Morris Plains
Vending Employees Union
  Independent . . . . Kearny
Workers Committee of Campbell's
  Fresh . . . . Glassboro

New Mexico

AFL-CIO Trade and Industrial Departments

Building and Construction Trades Department
BCTC Albuquerque . . Albuquerque

Metal Trades Department
MTC Atomic Projects & Production Workers . . . . Albuquerque

Affiliated Labor Organizations

Air Traffic Controllers
LU ABQ . . . . Albuquerque
LU KFMN. . . . . Farmington
LU ROW . . . . Roswell
LU SAF. . . . . Santa Fe
LU ZAB . . . . Albuquerque

Asbestos Workers
LU 76 . . . . Albuquerque

Bakery, Confectionery, Tobacco Workers and Grain Millers
LU 351 . . . . Albuquerque

Boilermakers
LG 338 . . . . Albuquerque

Carpenters
LU 1245 . . . . Las Cruces
LU 1319 . . . . Albuquerque
LU 1353 . . . . Santa Fe
LU 1385 . . . . . Fairview Station
LU 2088 Nurses . . . Alamogordo
LU 2166 Health Care Workers . . . . Albuquerque
LU 4031 Mountain West Regional . . . . . . Albuquerque

Communications Workers
LU 1314 Associated Press System . . . . Albuquerque
LU 7001 . . . . Las Cruces
LU 7009. . . . . Roswell
LU 7011 . . . . Albuquerque
LU 7037 . . . . Santa Fe
LU 14745 . . . . Albuquerque
LU 57407 NABET. . . Albuquerque

Electrical Workers
LU 496 . . . . Bayard
LU 611. . . . . Albuquerque
LU 1199 . . . . Belen
LU 1988 . . . . Albuquerque

Elevator Constructors
LU 131 . . . . Albuquerque

Federal Employees
C Darcom . . . . Chaparral
LU 40 . . . . Albuquerque
LU 485 . . . . Taos
LU 1031 . . . . Alamogordo
LU 1901 . . . . Albuquerque
LU 2034 . . . . Santa Fe
LU 2044 . . . . Gallup
LU 2049 . . . . White Sands Missile Range
LU 2148 . . . . Albuquerque

Fire Fighters
LU 164-F Holloman Air Force Base Local . . Holloman Air Force Base
LU 294-F White Sands Missile Range Fire Department. . . . . White Sands Missile Range

Food and Commercial Workers
LU 1564 . . . . Albuquerque

Government Employees
C 219 VA, Thirteenth District. . . . . . . Albuquerque
LU 1032 . . . . Albuquerque
LU 1257 DoL . . . . . Albuquerque
LU 2063 VA . . . . . Albuquerque
LU 2263 DoD . . . . . Albuquerque
LU 2308 DoD. . . . . . . Clovis
LU 3137 USDA . . . . . Coyote
LU 3309 IBWC . . . . . . Hatch
LU 4041 Mega-Teleservice Center . . . . . . Albuquerque

Government Employees Association
LU 14-40 . . . . Carlsbad

Guards
LU 69 . . . . Los Alamos
LU 106. . . . . Socorro
LU 122 . . . . Albuquerque
LU 131 . . . . Albuquerque
RC Sixth . . . . Albuquerque

Hotel and Restaurant Employees
LU 436 . . . . Albuquerque

Iron Workers
LU 495 . . . . Albuquerque

Laborers
LU 1376 . . . . Albuquerque
LU 1636 . . . . Santa Fe

Letter Carriers
BR 504 . . . . Albuquerque
BR 823 . . . . Las Vegas
BR 989 . . . . Santa Fe
BR 1069. . . . . Roswell
BR 1142 . . . . Raton
BR 1509 . . . . Silver City
BR 2290 Clayton, New Mexico . . . . Clayton
BR 2691. . . . . Clovis
BR 2905 . . . . Las Cruces
BR 2990 . . . . Gallup
BR 3144 . . . . Deming
BR 3244 . . . . Carlsbad
BR 3556 Tucumcari, New Mexico. . . . . . . Tucumcari
BR 3657 Portales, New Mexico . . . . Portales
BR 3703 . . . . Artesia
BR 3727. . . . . Hobbs
BR 3849 . . . . . . San Antonio
BR 3994 Rocket City. . Alamogordo
BR 4112. . . . . . . Los Alamos
BR 4278 Truth or Consequence, New Mexico . . Truth or Consequences
BR 4347 Santa Rosa, New Mexico. . . . . . Santa Rosa
BR 4377. . . . . Farmington
BR 5331 Grants, New Mexico . . . . Grants

BR 6230 Holloman Air Force Base, New Mexico . . . . Holloman Air Force Base
BR 6504 Lordsburg, New Mexico . . . . Lordsburg
SA New Mexico . . . . Albuquerque

Locomotive Engineers
DIV 15 . . . . Albuquerque
DIV 400 . . . . Edgewood
DIV 446. . . . . Los Lunas
DIV 791 . . . . Belen
DIV 811. . . . . Clovis

Machinists
LG 331 . . . . Belen
LG 794 . . . . Albuquerque
LG 1635 Albuquerque . Albuquerque
LG 1689 . . . . Albuquerque
LG 2515 . . . . Alamogordo
LG 2577. . . . . Roswell
STC New Mexico . . . Alamogordo

Maintenance of Way Employes
LG 2414 . . . . Las Vegas
LG 2415 . . . . Rio Rancho
SLG 2416 . . . . Clovis

Mine Workers
LU 7949 . . . . Raton

Musicians
LU 618 . . . . Albuquerque

National Staff Organization
LU Staff Organization of New Mexico, National. . . . . Santa Fe

Nurses
LSC Holy Cross Professional Performance Association . . . Ranchos de Taos

Office and Professional Employees
LU 251 . . . . Albuquerque

Operating Engineers
LU 953 . . . . Albuquerque

Painters
LU 823 . . . . Albuquerque

Paper, Allied-Industrial, Chemical Employees
LU 04-659 . . . . Ranchos de Taos
LU 04-9477 Wipp Site . . . Carlsbad

Plasterers and Cement Masons
LU 254 . . . . Albuquerque

Plumbing and Pipe Fitting
LU 412 . . . . Albuquerque

Postal Mail Handlers
LU 331 . . . . Albuquerque

Postal Workers
LU 356 Raton Local. . . . . Raton
LU 380 Albuquerque . Albuquerque
LU 402 Las Cruces . . Las Cruces
LU 404 Tucumcari . . Tucumcari
LU 422 Santa Fe . . . Santa Fe
LU 434 Roswell. . . . . Roswell
LU 655 Silver City . . . Silver City
LU 689 Gallup . . . . . . Gallup

LU 1633 Portales Local . . . Portales
LU 2263 Carlsbad . . . . Carlsbad
LU 2270 Las Vegas. . . . Las Vegas
LU 2287 Clovis . . . . Clovis
LU 2342 Hobbs . . . . . . Hobbs
LU 2501 Taos Local . . . . . Taos
LU 2525 Artesia Local. . . . Artesia
LU 2745 Socorro Local . . . Socorro
LU 2882 Belen Local . . . . . Belen
LU 2884 Farmington . . Farmington
LU 5538 Lovington Local . . . . Lovington
LU 6310 Holloman Air Force Base Local . . Holloman Air Force Base
LU 7148. . . . . Ruidoso
SA New Mexico. . . . Farmington

Rural Letter Carriers
SA New Mexico . . . . Las Cruces

Service Employees
LU 1173 Firemen & Oilers . . . . Los Lunas

Sheet Metal Workers
DC Rocky Mountain. . Albuquerque
LU 49 . . . . Albuquerque

State, County and Municipal Employees
D 1199-NM New Mexico Health Care Employees . . . . Santa Fe

Steelworkers
LU 12-187-S . . . . . . Carlsbad
LU 12-188-A . . . . . . Carlsbad
LU 12-890-S . . . . Bayard
LU 12-8507-S . . . . . Carlsbad
LU 12-9424 . . . . . . Las Cruces

Teachers
LU 4524 Bureau of Indian Affairs Educators . . . . . . Albuquerque
SFED New Mexico . . Albuquerque

Teamsters
LU 492 . . . . Albuquerque

Theatrical Stage Employees
D 5 Wyoming-Colorado-Utah-New Mexico. . . . . Albuquerque
LU 423 . . . . Albuquerque
LU 480 . . . . Santa Fe
LU 869 . . . . Albuquerque

Transportation Communications Union
LG 6846 Belen. . . . . . . Belen

Transportation Union
LU 1168. . . . . Portales
LU 1687 . . . . Belen
LU 1745 . . . . Albuquerque
SLB LO-34 New Mexico . . . Belen

Treasury Employees
CH 41 . . . . Albuquerque

Weather Service Employees
BR 02-24 . . . . Santa Teresa
BR 02-31-A . . . . . . Albuquerque
BR 02-66 . . . . Albuquerque

**Unaffiliated Labor
Organizations**

Independent Security Police
Association LU 1 . . Albuquerque

New York

AFL-CIO Trade and Industrial Departments

Building and Construction Trades Department

BCTC Binghamton-Oneonta
Area . . . . Binghamton
BCTC Buffalo and
Vicinity . . . . West Seneca
BCTC Dutchess County . Newburgh
BCTC Elmira . . . . Elmira
BCTC Greater New York. New York
BCTC Ithaca . . . . Ithaca
BCTC Mohawk Valley. . . . Utica
BCTC Nassau & Suffolk
Counties . . . . Hauppauge
BCTC New York State. . . . Albany
BCTC Niagara County . West Seneca
BCTC Orange County . Newburgh
BCTC Plattsburgh . . . . Plattsburgh
BCTC Rochester . . . . . Rochester
BCTC Rockland County . New City
BCTC Southwestern New
York . . . . Jamestown
BCTC Syracuse . . . . . . Syracuse
BCTC Tri-Cities . . . . . . Albany
BCTC Ulster Sullivan Delaware
Green Counties . . . . . Verbank
BCTC Watertown . . . . Watertown
BCTC Westchester
County . . . . Elmsford

Maritime Trades Department

PC Buffalo . . . . Buffalo
PC Greater New York &
Vicinity . . . . Brooklyn

Metal Trades Department

MTC New York . . Long Island City

Other Councils and Committees

C New York Hotel
Trades . . . . New York
C Niagara Orleans . . . Niagara Falls
LU 1 Hotel Maintenance
Carpenters . . . . . . New York

Affiliated Labor Organizations

Actors and Artistes

BR Actors Equity
Association. . . . . . New York
BR Employees (L I F E) Local
890. . . . . Brooklyn
BR Hebrew Actors . . . . New York
BR Italian Actors . . . . New York
NHQ . . . . New York

Agricultural Employees

BR 14 . . . . Jamaica
BR 35 . . . . Jackson Heights

Air Traffic Controllers

LU ALB . . . . Latham
LU BGM . . . . Johnson City
LU BUF . . . . Cheektowaga
LU EEA . . . . Eastchester
LU ELM. . . . . Horseheads
LU FRG . . . . Farmingdale
LU HPN . . . . White Plains
LU ISP. . . . . Ronkonkoma
LU JFK . . . . Jamaica
LU LGA . . . . Flushing

LU N90 . . . . Westbury
LU NATCA ITH Local . . . . Ithaca
LU POU . . . . . Wappingers Falls
LU RME. . . . . Rome
LU ROC . . . . Rochester
LU SYR . . . . . North Syracuse
LU ZNY . . . . Bohemia

Asbestos Workers

CONF New York-New England
States . . . . . Wappingers Falls
LU 4 . . . . South Wales
LU 12 . . . . . . Long Island City
LU 12-A . . . . . Long Island City
LU 30. . . . . Syracuse
LU 40 . . . . Schenectady
LU 91 . . . . Tarrytown
LU 201 . . . . . Wappingers Falls
LU 202 . . . . Rochester

Automobile, Aerospace Workers

C Central New York
CAP. . . . . East Syracuse
C New York State CAP . . . Buffalo
C Western New York CAP . Buffalo
D 65 Distributive
Workers . . . . New York
D 65 Legal Aid Attorneys, New York
City . . . . New York
LU 55 . . . . Buffalo
LU 259 Schenectady-New York
Local . . . . New York
LU 260 . . . . Buffalo
LU 338 . . . . Jamestown
LU 365 Denville-Brooklyn
Local. . . . . . Long Island City
LU 424 . . . . Cheektowaga
LU 465 . . . . Massena
LU 481 . . . . Leroy
LU 508. . . . . Buffalo
LU 604 . . . . Elmira
LU 624 . . . . East Syracuse
LU 629 . . . . Clymer
LU 686 . . . . Lockport
LU 774 . . . . Buffalo
LU 798 . . . . . . North Syracuse
LU 802 . . . . Cortland
LU 846 . . . . Buffalo
LU 850 . . . . Cheektowaga
LU 854 . . . . East Syracuse
LU 897. . . . . Buffalo
LU 936 . . . . Buffalo
LU 1060 . . . . Munnsville
LU 1097 . . . . Rochester
LU 1128 . . . . Liverpool
LU 1326 . . . . Cortland
LU 1337 . . . . Elmira
LU 1416 . . . . West Falls
LU 1508 . . . . . . Green Island
LU 1752 . . . . . Elmira Heights
LU 1774 . . . . Truxton
LU 1826. . . . . Minoa
LU 1981 National Writers
Union . . . . New York
LU 2094 . . . North Tonawanda
LU 2100 . . . . Buffalo
LU 2110 . . . . New York
LU 2110 Association of Ecumenical
Employees . . . . . New York
LU 2149 . . . . Auburn
LU 2179 . . . . New York
LU 2231 . . . . . . Jamestown
LU 2243 . . . . Oriskany
LU 2300 . . . . Ithaca

LU 2320 Legal Services
Workers . . . . . . New York
LU 2367 Mesa. . . . . . . Rome
LU 2571 . . . . . . Niagara Falls

Bakery, Confectionery, Tobacco Workers and Grain Millers

C East Central . . . . . Cheektowaga
LU 3 . . . . . . Long Island City
LU 16 . . . . Cheektowaga
LU 36-G . . . . Buffalo
LU 54-G . . . . West Sand Lake
LU 69 . . . . Port Chester
LU 102 . . . . Ozone Park
LU 110-G . . . . Buffalo
LU 116 . . . . . . North Syracuse
LU 150-G . . . . . . New York
LU 429 . . . . Cheektowaga

Baseball Players

NHQ . . . . New York

Basketball Players

NHQ . . . . New York

Boilermakers

LG 5 . . . . Floral Park
LG 7 . . . . Orchard Park
LG 18-M . . . . Buffalo
LG 50-D Cement Workers. . . Cairo
LG 82-S . . . . Corfu
LG 175 . . . . Oswego
LG 197 . . . . Albany
LG 308-D Cement
Workers . . . . Lancaster
LG 328-D . . . . Alden
LG 342-D Cement
Workers. . . . . . West Chazy
LG 569-D Cement
Workers . . . . Freedom
LG 1916. . . . . Ilion

Bricklayers

LU 1 . . . . . . Long Island City
LU 2 . . . . Albany
LU 3 . . . . Ithaca
LU 5 New York . . . Poughkeepsie
LU 7 . . . . . . Long Island City
LU 52 . . . . Harrison
STCON 99 New
York . . . . . Long Island City

Carpenters

C Suburban New York
Region. . . . . . . Hauppauge
DC New York City & Vicinity
#4112. . . . . . . New York
DC New York City
Industrial . . . . . . Jamaica
LU 7 . . . . Hauppauge
LU 9 . . . . Cheektowaga
LU 11 . . . . Hawthorne
LU 19 . . . . Rock Tavern
LU 20 . . . . . . Staten Island
LU 42 . . . . Stony Point
LU 45 . . . . . Queens Village
LU 66 . . . . Olean
LU 85 . . . . Rochester
LU 157 . . . . New York
LU 229 . . . . South Glens Falls
LU 280 . . . . Lockport
LU 281 . . . . . . Binghamton
LU 370 . . . . Albany
LU 608 . . . . New York
LU 740 . . . . . . Woodhaven

LU 747 . . . . Mattydale
LU 926 . . . . Brooklyn
LU 964 . . . . . . Stony Point
LU 1163 . . . . Syracuse
LU 1456 . . . . New York
LU 1536 . . . . New York
LU 2090 . . . . . . Woodhaven
LU 2287 . . . . New York
LU 2682 . . . . Bronx
LU 2819 . . . . Long Island City
LU 2947 . . . . Jamaica
LU 3127 . . . . New York

Catholic School Teachers

ASSN Deta Diocesan
Elementary . . . . . . Amherst
ASSN Secondary Lay Teachers of
Diocese . . . . . . West Seneca

Civilian Technicians

CH Vincent J. Paterno
Memorial . . . . . Baldwinsville
CH 2 New York City . . . Brooklyn
CH 4 Genesee Valley . . . Ontario
CH 6 Capital District . Stoney Creek
CH 7 Harold E. Brooks
Memorial . . . . . Westhampton
CH 8 Mid Hudson Valley . . Colonie
CH 9 Long Island . . . . . Islandia
CH 10 Western New York . Depew
CH 11 Niagara . . . . . . Sanborn
CH 12 Northern New
York . . . . . . Alexandria Bay
CH 17 Schenectady . . . Alplaus
CH 37 Hancock Field . . . Syracuse
CH 51 Stewart . . . . Middletown
STC New York . . . . Baldwinsville

Communications Workers

C New York State Plant
Coordinating . . . . . Farmingdale
C Western New York . . . . Buffalo
COM Downstate Grievance
Coordinating . . . . Farmingdale
LU 3 . . . . New York
LU 301-AE . . . . . Schenectady
LU 302 . . . . Wayland
LU 327. . . . . Hudson
LU 333 . . . . Eden
LU 342 . . . . Rochester
LU 349 . . . . Fredonia
LU 359 . . . . Waterford
LU 396 . . . . . . West Valley
LU 403. . . . . Buffalo
LU 1100 . . . . . Queens Village
LU 1101 . . . . . . New York
LU 1102 . . . . . Staten Island
LU 1103 . . . . . Port Chester
LU 1104 . . . . . Farmingdale
LU 1105 . . . . Bronx
LU 1106 . . . . Queens
LU 1107 . . . . . . New City
LU 1108 . . . . . . Patchogue
LU 1109 . . . . . . Brooklyn
LU 1110 . . . . . . Jamaica
LU 1111 . . . . Elmira
LU 1113 . . . . Albany
LU 1114 . . . . . Seneca Falls
LU 1115 . . . . Olean
LU 1117 . . . . . . Lockport
LU 1118 . . . . Albany
LU 1120 . . . . . Poughkeepsie
LU 1122 . . . . Buffalo
LU 1123 . . . . . . Syracuse
LU 1124 . . . . . . Watertown

LU 1126 . . . . . . New York Mills
LU 1128 . . . . Potsdam
LU 1133 . . . . Buffalo
LU 1139 . . . . Glens Falls
LU 1141 . . . . Cohoes
LU 1150 . . . . New York
LU 1152 . . . . Syracuse
LU 1153 . . . . Valhalla
LU 1164 . . . . Syracuse
LU 1168 . . . . Buffalo
LU 1170 . . . . Rochester
LU 1171 . . . . . East Syracuse
LU 1177 . . . . Brooklyn
LU 1180 . . . . New York
LU 1190 . . . . New York
LU 1191 . . . . . . Baldwinsville
LU 14146 . . . . Batavia
LU 14147 . . . . . . Binghamton
LU 14148 . . . . Lancaster
LU 14156 . . . . New York
LU 14158 . . . . Olean
LU 14162 . . . Saratoga Springs
LU 14164 . . . . Sidney
LU 14165 . . . . Canastota
LU 14166 Utica Typographical
  Union . . . . Ilion
LU 14169 Buffalo
  Mailers . . . . Grand Island
LU 14170 New York Mailers
  Union . . . . New York
LU 14177 . . . . Derby
LU 31017 . . . . Rochester
LU 31026 . . . . Buffalo
LU 31034 . . . . Albany
LU 31129 . . . . . New Hartford
LU 31129 . . . . . New Hartford
LU 31180 . . . . Kingston
LU 31222 Wire Service . New York
LU 51011 . . . . New York
LU 51016 NABET Local
  16 . . . . New York
LU 51021 NABET Local 21 . Scotia
LU 51022 . . . . Rochester
LU 51024 . . . . Watertown
LU 51025 . . . . . . West Seneca
LU 51026 . . . . . Johnson City
LU 51211 NABET Local
  211 . . . . Syracuse
LU 81019 . . . . . . Jamestown
LU 81045 . . . . Falconer
LU 81076 . . . . Jamaica
LU 81102 . . . Long Island City
LU 81300 . . . . Syracuse
LU 81304 . . . North Tonawanda
LU 81313 . . . . . . Painted Post
LU 81319 . . . . . East Syracuse
LU 81320 . . . . Liverpool
LU 81321 . . . . Syracuse
LU 81323 . . . . Rochester
LU 81326 . . . . Lancaster
LU 81331 . . . . . . North Chili
LU 81336 . . . . . . Springville
LU 81337 . . . . Rochester
LU 81340 . . . . Cuba
LU 81347 . . . . Depew
LU 81348 . . . . Angola
LU 81353 . . . . . . Springville
LU 81361 . . . . Lancaster
LU 81380 . . . . Waterford
LU 81383 . . . . Rochester
LU 81384 . . . . . . Cheektowaga
LU 81386 . . . . Irving
LU 81388 . . . . . . Cheektowaga
LU 81408 . . . . . . Schenectady
LU 81444 . . . . . . Lake Success
LU 81468 Brushworkers
  Union . . . . Rensselaer
STC Connecticut . . . . Portchester

Commuter Rail Employees
LDIV Local Division 1 . . Patterson
LDIV Local/Division 113 . Brewster
LDIV Local/Division 9 . . . Brewster
LDIV 37 . . . . New York
NHQ Employees . . . . . New York

Education
SA New York Educators
  Association . . . . Albany

Electrical Workers
LU 3 . . . . Flushing
LU 25 Long Island
  Local . . . . Hauppauge
LU 41 . . . . Orchard Park
LU 43 . . . . Syracuse
LU 83 . . . . Binghamton
LU 86 . . . . Rochester
LU 97 Oswego . . . . . Syracuse
LU 106 . . . . Jamestown
LU 139 . . . . Elmira
LU 236 . . . . Schenectady
LU 237 . . . . Niagara Falls
LU 241 . . . . Ithaca
LU 249 . . . . Dundee
LU 320 . . . . Pinebush
LU 325 . . . . Binghamton
LU 363 . . . . New City
LU 503 . . . . Nanuet
LU 544 . . . . Bath
LU 589 . . . . Hicksville
LU 770 . . . . Slingerlands
LU 817 . . . . Tuckahoe
LU 859 . . . . Bronx
LU 910 . . . . Watertown
LU 966 . . . . Lockport
LU 1049 . . . . Hauppauge
LU 1143 . . . . . . Old Chatham
LU 1189 . . . . Fulton
LU 1212 . . . . New York
LU 1249 . . . . . East Syracuse
LU 1381 . . . . Hicksville
LU 1430 . . . North White Plains
LU 1573 . . . . Yonkers
LU 1631 . . . . Peekskill
LU 1632 . . . . Elmira
LU 1799 . . . . Saratoga Springs
LU 1813 . . . . Lancaster
LU 1833 . . . . Elmira
LU 1922 . . . . Westbury
LU 1968 . . . . . . Middle Town
LU 2084 . . . . Syracuse
LU 2154 . . . . . . Orchard Park
LU 2176 . . . . Champlain
LU 2180 . . . . Randolph
LU 2199 . . . . . . Orchard Park
LU 2213 . . . . Syracuse
LU 2230 . . . . Coram
LU 2374 . . . . Jamestown
SC T-3 AT&T . . . . . New City
SC U-7 New York State Electric &
  Gas . . . . Hornell

Electrical, Radio and Machine Workers
LU 203 . . . . . . Mechanicville
LU 210 . . . . Beacon
LU 227 . . . . . . Elizabethtown
LU 319 . . . . North Tonawanda
LU 329 . . . . Elmira
LU 332 . . . . Hudson Falls
LU 334 . . . . Rochester
LU 335 . . . . North Tonawanda

Electronic Workers
LU 301 . . . . . . Schenectady
LU 303 . . . . Albany

LU 381-B Family Service of
  Rochester Inc. . . . . . Rochester
LU 463 . . . . Jamaica
LU 475 . . . . Pelham
LU 485 . . . . Brooklyn
LU 509 . . . . Rochester
LU 1581 . . . . . . West Seneca
LU 22485 . . . . Leroy
LU 23981 . . . . . . Schenectady

Elevator Constructors
LU 1 . . . . Whitestone
LU 14 . . . . Buffalo
LU 27 . . . . Penfield
LU 35 . . . . Albany
LU 62 . . . . Syracuse
LU 138 . . . . Verbank

Federal Employees
LU 346 . . . . Castle Point
LU 387 . . . . Northport
LU 1505 . . . . Hyde Park
LU 2109 . . . . Watervliet

Fire Fighters
LU 7-F. . . . Cornwall-on-Hudson
LU 105-F . . . . . . Adams Center
LU 214-F 914 T A G . East Amherst
SA Professional Fire Fighters
  Association, New York . . Albany

Flint Glass Workers
LU 20 . . . . Port Jervis
LU 135 . . . . Corning
LU 500 . . . . Elmira
LU 522 . . . . Port Jerus
LU 1000 . . . . Corning
LU 1013 . . . . Bath
LU 1026 . . . . Canton
LU 1029 . . . . Unadilla

Food and Commercial Workers
LU 1 Amalgamated Meat Cutters &
  Butcher . . . . Utica
LU 1-D . . . . Brooklyn
LU 2-D . . . . Brooklyn
LU 18-D . . . . Brooklyn
LU 61-C . . . . Catskill
LU 76-C . . . North Tonawanda
LU 94 . . . . Buffalo
LU 95-C . . . . . . Morrisonville
LU 143-C . . . . . . Pearl River
LU 192-C . . . . Auburn
LU 251-C . . . . Norwich
LU 293-C . . . . . Harpursville
LU 342-050 . . . . . . Mineola
LU 348-S . . . . . Forest Hills
LU 350-I . . . . Verona
LU 359 Seafood-Smoked
  Fish-Cannery Workers . New York
LU 500 . . . . . . White Plains
LU 621 . . . . Brooklyn
LU 888 . . . . . . Mount Vernon
LU 1138-T . . . . . . Watervliet
LU 1500 . . . . . Queens Village

Glass, Molders, Pottery and Plastics Workers
LU 27 . . . . Fulton
LU 76-A . . . . Buffalo
LU 77 . . . . Clifton Park
LU 80-B . . . . Canastota
LU 104 . . . . . Elmira Heights
LU 180 . . . . . Elmira Heights
LU 368 . . . . Utica
LU 381-A . . . . Meridian

Government Employees
LU . . . . Brooklyn
LU 201 . . . . Rome
LU 400 . . . . Fort Drum
LU 491 VA . . . . Bath
LU 521 USDA . . . . . Endicott
LU 538 USDA . . . Maspeth
LU 913 HUD . . . . . New York
LU 1119 VA . . . . . Montrose
LU 1151 VA . . . . . New York
LU 1168 VA . . . . Bronx
LU 1667 VA . . . . . Brooklyn
LU 1760 HHS . . . . . Jamaica
LU 1843 VA . . . . . Northport
LU 1917 DoJ . . . . New York
LU 1919 VA . . . . Farmingdale
LU 1940 USDA . . . . Greenport
LU 1968 DoT . . . . . Massena
LU 1988 VA . . . . St. Albans
LU 2094 VA . . . . New York
LU 2116 DoT . . . . Kings Point
LU 2203 . . . . New York
LU 2204 DoD . . . . . Brooklyn
LU 2205 USDA . . . . Albany
LU 2245 Castle Point VA
  Hospital . . . . . Castle Point
LU 2367 DoD . . . . West Point
LU 2431 GSA . . . . New York
LU 2440 VA . . . . . Montrose
LU 2546 DoD . . . . Romulus
LU 2567 DoD . . . . Hempstead
LU 2580 DoJ . . . . . Buffalo
LU 2612 DoD . . . . . Rome
LU 2657 VA . . . . . Batavia
LU 2693 DoD . . . Bethpage
LU 2724 DoJ . . . . . Moira
LU 2739 USAR . . . Fort Totten
LU 2747 DoT . . . Staten Island
LU 2828 DoE . . . . New York
LU 2831 USDA, FHA . . . Batavia
LU 2930 ACE . . . . . Buffalo
LU 3134 SBA . . . . New York
LU 3148 DoJ . . . . New York
LU 3252 FTC . . . . New York
LU 3306 VA . . . Canandaigua
LU 3314 VA . . . . . Buffalo
LU 3342 HHS . . . . Amherst
LU 3343 HHS . . . . . Troy
LU 3367 HUD . . . . Buffalo
LU 3369 HHS . . . . Flushing
LU 3432 NPS . . . . New York
LU 3477 CPSC . . . New York
LU 3555 EEOC . . . New York
LU 3613 SBA . . . . Syracuse
LU 3692 CNC, VA . . . Calverton
LU 3732 DoC . . . Kings Point
LU 3740 DoT, U.S.
  Mint . . . . . . West Point
LU 3797 DoE . . . . New York
LU 3827 CFTC . . . New York
LU 3882 DoJ . . . Vermontville
LU 3883 DCAA . . . Bethpage
LU 3911 . . . . . . New York

Government Employees Association
LU 56 . . . . Endicott
LU 02-33 . . . . . Niagara Falls
LU 02-62 . . . . . Evans Mills
LU 02-65 . . . . . Johnson City
LU R2-61 . . . . Castorland

Government Security Officers
LU 119 . . . . Brooklyn

Graphic Communications
LU 1-H Paper Handlers-Sheet
  Straighteners . . . . . New York

LU 1-SE 100SE . . . . . . Merrick
LU 2-N . . . . New York
LU 17-B . . . . Buffalo
LU 26-H . . . . Cheektowaga
LU 27-C . . . . Buffalo
LU 51-23M . . . . New York
LU 76-SE . . . . Orchard Park
LU 119-B 43B Parent
  Division . . . . New York
LU 259-M Albany-Schenectady
  Local . . . . Troy
LU 261-M . . . . Buffalo
LU 284-M . . . . Cicero
LU 406-C . . . . Farmingdale
LU 503-M . . . . Rochester
LU 757-S . . . . Amsterdam
LU 898-M . . . . Binghamton

Guards
LU 37 . . . . Upton
LU 107 . . . . Schenectady

Horseshoers
LU 8 . . . . Elmont
NHQ . . . . Commack

Hotel and Restaurant Employees
DC Production, Service &
  Sales . . . . Brooklyn
LU 4 . . . . Cheektowaga
LU 6 . . . . New York
LU 37 . . . . Richmond Hill
LU 76 . . . . Monticello
LU 100 . . . . New York
LU 150 . . . . Syracuse
LU 300-S . . . . Brooklyn
LU 422-S . . . . Brooklyn
LU 471 . . . . . . Saratoga Springs
LU 517-S . . . . Brooklyn
LU 815-S . . . . Brooklyn
STC New York . . . . . . Syracuse

Independent Unions Federation
LU 2 Building Service Employees &
  Factory Workers . . . Ozone Park

Industrial Trade Unions
LU 1 . . . . Jamaica
LU 1-A . . . . Jamaica
LU 16 . . . . Jamaica
LU 72 . . . . Jamaica
LU 629 . . . . Jamaica
NHQ . . . . Jamaica

Interns and Residents
LU Einstein College of Medicine &
  Logan Hospital . . . . . New York
NHQ . . . . New York

Iron Workers
DC Greater New York and
  Vicinity . . . . Tarrytown
DC Western New York and
  Vicinity . . . . Niagara Falls
LU 6 . . . . West Seneca
LU 9 . . . . Niagara Falls
LU 12 . . . . Albany
LU 33 . . . . Rochester
LU 40 . . . . New York
LU 46 Metallic Lathers'
  Union . . . . New York
LU 60 . . . . Syracuse
LU 197 . . . . . . Long Island City
LU 361 . . . . Ozone Park
LU 417 . . . . Wallkill
LU 440 . . . . Utica
LU 455 . . . . . . Long Island City
LU 464 . . . . Rochester

LU 470 . . . . Jamestown
LU 576 . . . . Buffalo
LU 580 . . . . New York
LU 612 . . . . Pulaski
LU 824 . . . . Gouverneur

Laborers
DC Cement & Concrete
  Workers . . . . Flushing
DC Eastern New York . . Glenmont
DC Mason Tenders of Greater New
  York . . . . New York
DC Pavers & Road
  Builders . . . . Flushing
LU 6-A . . . . Flushing
LU 7 . . . . Binghamton
LU 17 . . . . Newburgh
LU 18-A . . . . Bronx
LU 20 . . . . New York
LU 29 . . . . Flushing
LU 35 . . . . Utica
LU 60 . . . . Hawthorne
LU 66 . . . . Melville
LU 78 . . . . New York
LU 79 . . . . New York
LU 91 . . . . Niagara Falls
LU 103 . . . . Geneva
LU 108 Waste Material Recycling &
  General Industries . . . New York
LU 147 . . . . Bronx
LU 157 . . . . Schenectady
LU 186 . . . . Plattsburgh
LU 190 . . . . Glenmont
LU 210 . . . . Buffalo
LU 214 . . . . Oswego
LU 235 . . . . Elmsford
LU 322 . . . . Massena
LU 433 . . . . Syracuse
LU 435 . . . . Rochester
LU 589 . . . . Ithaca
LU 601 Professional Service &
  Related Employees . New Rochelle
LU 621 . . . . Olean
LU 731 . . . . New York
LU 754 . . . . Spring Valley
LU 1000 . . . . Poughkeepsie
LU 1010 . . . . Flushing
LU 1018 . . . . Flushing
LU 1175 . . . . Howard Beach
LU 1298 . . . . Hempstead
LU 1358 . . . . . . Elmira Heights

Laundry and Dry Cleaning
LU 168 . . . . Buffalo

Letter Carriers
BR 3 . . . . Buffalo
BR 21 George B. Calveric . . Elmira
BR 29 . . . . Troy
BR 36 . . . . New York
BR 41 . . . . Brooklyn
BR 97 . . . . Oneonta
BR 99 . . . . Staten Island
BR 134 . . . . Syracuse
BR 137 . . . . Poughkeepsie
BR 150 . . . . Dunkirk
BR 165 . . . . Jamestown
BR 178 . . . . Watervliet
BR 190 . . . . Oswego
BR 210 . . . . Rochester
BR 294 . . . . College Point
BR 300 . . . . Corning
BR 301 . . . . Geneva
BR 302 1000 Islands
  Region . . . . Watertown
BR 303 . . . . Oswego
BR 315 . . . . Newburgh
BR 333 . . . . Binghamton

BR 356 . . . . Mount Vernon
BR 357 . . . . . . Long Island City
BR 358 . . . . Schenectady
BR 375 . . . . Utica
BR 376 . . . . Port Jervis
BR 387 . . . . Yonkers
BR 562 . . . . Jamaica
BR 661 . . . . . . North Tonawanda
BR 681 Penn Yan, New
  York . . . . Penn Yan
BR 693 . . . . Peekskill
BR 740 Fort Plain, New
  York . . . . Fort Plain
BR 879 . . . . Wellsville
BR 922 Malone, New York . Malone
BR 1009 Lyons, New York . . Lyons
BR 1163 . . . . Gouverneur
BR 1299 Deposit, New
  York . . . . Deposit
BR 1341 . . . . Walton
BR 1825 Warsaw, New
  York . . . . Warsaw
BR 1847 . . . . Massena
BR 1893 Granville, New
  York . . . . Granville
BR 1905 Clyde, New York . . Clyde
BR 1916 Pulaski, New York . Pulaski
BR 1940 Mount Morris, New
  York . . . . Mount Morris
BR 2022 Groton, New York . Groton
BR 2062 . . . . Elmont
BR 2154 Chatham, New
  York . . . . Chatham
BR 2189 . . . . Valley Stream
BR 2281 Hamilton, New
  York . . . . Hamilton
BR 2481 Little Valley, New
  York . . . . Little Valley
BR 2556 Dolgeville, New
  York . . . . Dolgeville
BR 2625 Holley, New York . Holley
BR 2654 Coxsackie, New
  York . . . . Coxsackic
BR 3050 . . . . Sidney
BR 3105 . . . . Phelps
BR 3219 Ravena, New
  York . . . . Ravena
BR 3246 Castleton on Hudson, New
  York . . . Castleton-on-Hudson
BR 3285 . . . . Homer
BR 3289 Delhi, New York . . Delhi
BR 3366 Cazenovia, New
  York . . . . Cazenovia
BR 3573 Wolcott, New
  York . . . . Wolcott
BR 4067 Avon, New York . . . Avon
BR 4580 North Chili, New
  York . . . . North Chili
BR 4747 Honeoye Falls, New
  York . . . . Honeoye Falls
BR 4918 Brookhaven Long Island,
  New York . . . . . . Brookhaven
BR 5151 . . . . Vestal
BR 5229 . . . . New City
BR 5463 Dundee, New
  York . . . . Dundee
BR 5746 Belmont, New
  York . . . . Belmont
BR 5750 Scottsville, New
  York . . . . Scottsville
BR 6000 . . . . Amityville
BR 6077 Minoa, New York . . Minoa
BR 6559 Lakewood, New
  York . . . . Lakewood
D Joseph T. Tinnelly . . Schenectady
D Niagara Frontier . . . Niagara Falls
SA New York . . . . . Poughkeepsie

Locomotive Engineers
DIV 46 . . . . Selkirk
DIV 54 . . . . Port Jervis
DIV 87 . . . . Scotia
DIV 127 . . . . Pelham
DIV 169 . . . . Kirkville
DIV 220 . . . . Hamburg
DIV 227 . . . . Massena
DIV 269 . . . . . North Massapequa
DIV 311 . . . . Binghamton
DIV 382 . . . . North Tonawanda
DIV 421 . . . . Hamburg
DIV 641 . . . . Ithaca
DIV 659 . . . . Amherst
DIV 752 . . . . Scotia
DIV 867 . . . . Watervliet
DIV 895 . . . . Buffalo
GCA Consolidated Rail
  Corporation . . . . Buffalo
GCA Delaware & Hudson &
  Springfield Term. . . . Greenwich
GCA 269 Long Island
  Railroad . . . . Hicksville
SLB New York . . . . . Hamburg

Longshoremen
D Atlantic Coast . . . New York
DIV United Marine . . Staten Island
JC Buffalo . . . . Derby
LU 3 . . . . Floral Park
LU 109 . . . . Buffalo
LU 217-A . . . . Ogdensburg
LU 333 United Marine
  Division . . . . . . Staten Island
LU 342 United Marine
  Division . . . . Shirley
LU 419 . . . . Howard Beach
LU 824 . . . . New York
LU 901 . . . . New York
LU 901 . . . . New York
LU 920 . . . . Staten Island
LU 928 . . . . Buffalo
LU 976 . . . . New York
LU 1286 . . . . Derby
LU 1294 . . . . Albany
LU 1518 . . . . Selkirk
LU 1570-A . . . . Fulton
LU 1730 . . . . Staten Island
LU 1809 . . . . New York
LU 1814 . . . . Brooklyn
LU 1909 . . . . New York
LU 2000-A . . . . Amherst
LU 2007 . . . . Ransonville
LU 2028 . . . . Buffalo
LU 2057 American Radio
  Association . . . . New York
NHQ . . . . New York

Machinists
DLG 58 . . . . Elmira
DLG 65 . . . . Jamestown
LG 75 . . . . Akron
LG 226 . . . . Staten Island
LG 330 . . . . Cheektowaga
LG 340 . . . . Elmhurst
LG 365 . . . . . . Saratoga Springs
LG 434 . . . . Valley Stream
LG 490-DS . . . . Elma
LG 522 . . . . Wynantskill
LG 585 . . . . Buffalo
LG 588 . . . . Palmyra
LG 753 . . . . Peekskill
LG 754 . . . . Bay Shore
LG 761 . . . . Adams
LG 838 . . . . Albany
LG 948 . . . . Walden
LG 1018 . . . . Lynbrook
LG 1071 . . . . Elma

LG 1145 . . . . Westerlo
LG 1180 . . . . Gasport
LG 1278 . . . . Norwich
LG 1322 . . . . Valley Stream
LG 1379 . . . . Nichols
LG 1415 . . . . Baldwinsville
LG 1509 . . . . Utica
LG 1529 . . . . Sidney
LG 1555 . . . . Westfield
LG 1562 . . . . Kingston
LG 1580. . . . . Wellsville
LG 1607 . . . . Ithaca
LG 1665 . . . . Almond
LG 1678 . . . . Clintondale
LG 1691 . . . . Depew
LG 1765 . . . . Painted Post
LG 1787 . . . . Westmoreland
LG 1793 . . . . Oriskany
LG 1838 . . . . Geneva
LG 1839 . . . . Jamestown
LG 1868 . . . . Rochester
LG 1882 . . . . Lindenhurst
LG 1894 . . . . Plainview
LG 2105 . . . . Jamestown
LG 2115 . . . . Tonawanda
LG 2189 . . . . Unionville
LG 2310 . . . . Clinton
LG 2312 . . . . Rochester
LG 2401 . . . . Freedom
LG 2420 . . . . Celoron
LG 2495 . . . . Falconer
LG 2656 . . . . Woodhaven
LG 2671 . . . . Auburn
LG 2741 . . . . Hornell
LG 2759 . . . . Medford
LLG 2001 . . . . Ithaca
STC New York . . . . Sidney

Maintenance of Way Employes
LG 707 . . . . Albion
LG 1356 . . . . Glenmont
LG 1368 . . . . Howes Cave
LG 1466 . . . . Kingston
LG 1632 . . . . Afton
LG 1743 . . . . Poestankill
LG 1934 . . . . . Saratoga Springs
LG 2957 . . . . Goshen
SLG 482 . . . . Fredonia
SLG 704 . . . . Sodus
SLG 866 . . . . Alden
SLG 881 . . . . Fort Plain
SLG 882 . . . . Eagle
SLG 887 . . . . Hornell
SLG 891 . . . . East Syracuse
SLG 895 . . . . Wellsville
SLG 910 . . . . Brownville
SLG 1042 . . . . Red Creek
SLG 1079 . . . . Port Jervis
SLG 1323 . . . . Willsboro
SLG 1716 . . . . Sangerfield
SLG 3068 . . . . . West Babylon

Marine Engineers
D 2-A Transportation & Service
  Employees. . . . . . . Brooklyn

Mine Workers
LU 717 . . . . Ilion

Musical Artists
NHQ . . . . New York

Musicians
LU 14 . . . . Albany
LU 38-398 . . . . Larchmont
LU 51. . . . . Utica
LU 66 . . . . Rochester
LU 78 . . . . Syracuse

LU 85-133 . . . . . . Schenectady
LU 92 . . . . Buffalo
LU 97. . . . . Newfane
LU 106-209 Greater
  Niagara . . . . . North Tonawanda
LU 132 . . . . Pine City
LU 134 . . . . Jamestown
LU 215 . . . . Kingston
LU 238 . . . . . . Wappingers Falls
LU 267-441 . . . . Mexico
LU 380 . . . . Vestal
LU 398 . . . . . . Yorktown Heights
LU 443 . . . . Oneonta
LU 506 . . . . . . Saratoga Springs
LU 802 . . . . New York
LU 809 . . . . Middletown
LU 1000 North American Traveling
  Musicians. . . . . . . New York
NHQ . . . . New York
STCON New York . . . . . Buffalo

National Staff Organization
LU Staff Organization of New York
  Educators . . . . . Williamsville

Needletrades
JB Amalgamated Service & Allied
  Industries. . . . . . . New York
JB Gloves Cities/Hudson
  District . . . . . . Gloversville
JB Greater Northern
  District . . . . Oswego
JB New York . . . . . . New York
JB New York . . . . . . New York
JB New York Apparel & Allied
  Workers . . . . New York
JB Northeast Regional . . New York
JB Pants Makers . . . . New York
JB Rochester . . . . . . Rochester
JB Western. . . . . Buffalo
JC Dress Makers . . . . New York
LU . . . . New York
LU 3-T . . . . Oswego
LU 4 . . . . New York
LU 7 . . . . New York
LU 10 . . . . New York
LU 14 . . . . Rochester
LU 14-A . . . . Rochester
LU 14-B . . . . Rochester
LU 14-W . . . . Blauvelt
LU 23 . . . . New York
LU 23-25 . . . . New York
LU 25 . . . . New York
LU 49 . . . . Buffalo
LU 62-32 . . . . New York
LU 63 . . . . New York
LU 89-22 . . . . New York
LU 92-T. . . . . New York
LU 125-H . . . . New York
LU 126 . . . . New York
LU 155-I . . . . New York
LU 158-A . . . . New York
LU 160 . . . . New York
LU 163 . . . . Gloversville
LU 169-C . . . . New York
LU 178-C . . . . New York
LU 189 . . . . New York
LU 190-A . . . . New York
LU 201. . . . . Buffalo
LU 204 . . . . Rochester
LU 205 . . . . Rochester
LU 207. . . . . Buffalo
LU 215 . . . . Rochester
LU 220 . . . . Rochester
LU 221 . . . . Buffalo
LU 227-A . . . . Rochester
LU 230 . . . . Rochester
LU 231 . . . . Rochester

LU 239-A . . . . New York
LU 245 . . . . Rochester
LU 246 . . . . New York
LU 246-S . . . . New York
LU 250-C . . . . New York
LU 253-C . . . . New York
LU 279 . . . . New York
LU 284 . . . . New York
LU 300-C . . . . New York
LU 324 . . . . New York
LU 330-A . . . . New York
LU 331 . . . . New York
LU 332 . . . . New York
LU 340 . . . . New York
LU 340-A . . . . New York
LU 340-B . . . . New York
LU 355 . . . . New York
LU 368 . . . . Gloversville
LU 381 . . . . Rochester
LU 388 . . . . Rochester
LU 400 . . . . New York
LU 432 . . . . Gloversville
LU 446 . . . . New York
LU 475-A . . . . New York
LU 482-C . . . . Buffalo
LU 500-A . . . . New York
LU 506-A . . . . New York
LU 548-A . . . . New York
LU 563-SW . . . . New York
LU 574-A . . . . New York
LU 646-T . . . . Gloversville
LU 653-T . . . . Oswego
LU 700-A . . . . New York
LU 701-T . . . . Oswego
LU 800-A . . . . New York
LU 800-A . . . . New York
LU 976-T . . . . Gloversville
LU 1067-T . . . . Buffalo
LU 1095-T . . . . Buffalo
LU 1126-T . . . . Buffalo
LU 1139-T . . . . Rensselace
LU 1712-C . . . . Gloversville
LU 1714-T . . . . Gloversville
LU 1748 . . . . Buffalo
LU 1802 . . . . Buffalo
LU 1822 . . . . Oswego
LU 1827 . . . . Oswego
LU 1947 . . . . Oswego
LU 2342 . . . . Ancramdale
LU 2486 . . . . Gloversville
LU 2538 . . . . Rochester
LU 2541 . . . . Rochester
LU 2585 . . . . New York
LU 2607 . . . . Rochester
NHQ . . . . New York

**Newspaper and Mail Deliverers'
Union**
NHQ . . . . Long Island City

NLRB Professional Association
LU 2 . . . . New York
LU 3 . . . . Buffalo
LU 29 . . . . Brooklyn

Novelty and Production Workers
JB 18 . . . . Mineola
LU 3 Production & Maintenance &
  Service . . . . Mineola
LU 223 Toy & Novelty
  Workers . . . . New York
LU 231 Industrial Trades . . Mineola
LU 298 Amalgamated
  Workers . . . . . Valley Stream

Nurses
SA New York State Nurses
  Association . . . . Latham

Nurses, Professional
LU Lockport Memorial Hospital
  Professional Nurses
  Association . . . . . . Lockport
NHQ . . . . Lockport

Office and Professional Employees
LU 51 . . . . New York
LU 153 . . . . New York
LU 180 . . . . Massena
LU 210 . . . . Massapequa
LU 212 . . . . Buffalo

Operating Engineers
C Upstate New York . . . . Syracuse
CONF New York State . . . Albany
LU 14 . . . . Flushing
LU 15 . . . . New York
LU 17 . . . . West Seneca
LU 30 . . . . Richmond Hill
LU 94 . . . . New York
LU 106 . . . . Albany
LU 137 . . . . . . Briarcliff Manor
LU 138 . . . . Farmingdale
LU 295 . . . . Maspeth
LU 409 . . . . Buffalo
LU 463 . . . . Ransonville
LU 545 . . . . Syracuse
LU 832-ABC . . . . . . Rochester

Painters
DC 4 . . . . Cheektowaga
DC 9 . . . . New York
LU 8-28A . . . . New York
LU 18 . . . . New York
LU 19 . . . . New York
LU 20 . . . . East Rockaway
LU 24 . . . . Brooklyn
LU 25 . . . . Hicksville
LU 28 . . . . Kew Gardens
LU 31 . . . . Syracuse
LU 38 . . . . Oswego
LU 43 . . . . Blasdell
LU 65 . . . . Niagara Falls
LU 112 . . . . Amherst
LU 113 District Council
  9 . . . . Poughquac
LU 150 . . . . Rochester
LU 155 . . . . Poughkeepsie
LU 178 . . . . Candor
LU 201 . . . . Albany
LU 466 . . . . Glens Falls
LU 490 . . . . New York
LU 515 . . . . Cheektowaga
LU 660 . . . . Cheektowaga
LU 677 . . . . Rochester
LU 806 . . . . New York
LU 829 . . . . New York
LU 1281 . . . . New York
LU 1422 . . . . New York
LU 1456 . . . . Bronx
LU 1486 Long Island
  Local. . . . . East Islip
LU 1815 . . . . East Islip
LU 1969 . . . . New York
LU 1974 . . . . New York
LU 1990 . . . . Johnson City

**Paper, Allied-Industrial, Chemical
Employees**
DC 2 . . . . Niagara Falls
LU 236. . . . . Buffalo
LU 1296 . . . . New York
LU I-6992 . . . . Buffalo
LU 01-2 . . . . Hudson Falls
LU 01-4 . . . . Corinth
LU 01-5 . . . . Mineville
LU 01-6 . . . . Athol

LU 01-13. . . . . . . Hudson Falls
LU 01-17 . . . . Troy
LU 01-18 . . . . Queensbury
LU 01-28 . . . Castleton-on-Hudson
LU 01-32. . . . . Auburn
LU 01-45 . . . . Deferiet
LU 01-53. . . . . Oneida
LU 01-54 . . . . Oswego
LU 01-58 . . . . . . Niagara Falls
LU 01-107 . . . . Brooklyn
LU 01-129. . . . . . Ran Somville
LU 01-140. . . . . Redford
LU 01-155. . . . . . . Queensbury
LU 01-209 . . . . . . Niagara Falls
LU 01-250. . . . . . . Ransonville
LU 01-254 . . . . Oswego
LU 01-276 . . . . Carthage
LU 01-277 . . . . . . Niagara Falls
LU 01-298 . . . . Lacona
LU 01-318 . . . . Flushing
LU 01-381. . . . . Mineola
LU 01-387 . . . . Keesville
LU 01-389. . . . . . Morrisonville
LU 01-390 . . . . Cohoes
LU 01-420 . . . . Styvesant
LU 01-429 . . . . Ravena
LU 01-431. . . . . Shoreham
LU 01-442 . . . . Utica
LU 01-497 . . . . Ticonderoga
LU 01-503 . . . . Heuvelton
LU 01-544. . . . . Newark
LU 01-607 . . . . Tonawanda
LU 01-620 . . . . Leicester
LU 01-625 . . . . . . Silver Springs
LU 01-649 . . . . Granville
LU 01-687. . . . . . . Gouverneur
LU 01-748. . . . . Alden
LU 01-828 . . . . Geneva
LU 01-909 . . . . Plattsburgh
LU 01-926 . . . . Croghan
LU 01-955 . . . . Bridgeport
LU 01-956 . . . . . . Port Leyden
LU 01-1066 . . . . Pulaski
LU 01-1186. . . . . Tunnel
LU 01-1280 . . . . Verona
LU 01-1294 . . . . Ellenburg Depot
LU 01-1300 Rock City . . Little Falls
LU 01-1370 . . . . . . Amsterdam
LU 01-1392 . . . . . . Cambridge
LU 01-1430 . . . . Syracuse
LU 01-1438 . . . . . . Little Falls
LU 01-1450 . . . . . . Watertown
LU 01-1478 . . . South Glens Falls
LU 01-1479 . . . . Ancram
LU 01-1734 . . . . . . Tonawanda
LU 01-1736. . . . North Tonawanda
LU 01-1799. . . . . . Beaver Falls
LU 01-1888 . . . . Glenfield
LU 01-1988 . . . . Lowville
LU 01-2058 . . . . . . Niagara Falls
LU 01-3516 . . . . . . Grand Island
LU 01-6220 . . . . Lakeview
LU 08-763 . . . . Geneseo

Plant Protection Employees
LU 18. . . . . Syracuse

Plasterers and Cement Masons
LU 9 . . . . . North Tonawanda
LU 111 . . . . . North Tonawanda
LU 519 . . . . Syracuse
LU 530 . . . . Bronx
LU 780 . . . . Flushing
STCON New
York . . . . . North Tonawanda

Plumbing and Pipe Fitting
LU 1 . . . . Howard Beach

LU 7 . . . . Latham
LU 13 . . . . Rochester
LU 21 . . . . Yonkers
LU 22 . . . . Orchard Park
LU 73 . . . . Oswego
LU 112 . . . . Binghamton
LU 128 . . . . Niskayuna
LU 200 . . . . Mineola
LU 267 . . . . Syracuse
LU 373 . . . . Mountainville
LU 638 . . . . . . Long Island City
LU 773 . . . . . . South Glens Falls
SA New York State Pipe
Trades . . . . Latham

Police
LG 1 Federal Protective Service
Committee . . . . . . New York

Postal and Federal Employees
D 8 . . . . New York
LU . . . . Roosevelt
LU 802 . . . . Brooklyn
LU 803 . . . . Buffalo
LU 807 . . . . Jamaica
LU 809 . . . . . . Mount Vernon
LU 813 . . . . New York
LU 814 . . . . New York

Postal Mail Handlers
LU 300 . . . . New York
LU 309. . . . . Buffalo

Postal Workers
LU Capital District Area . . . . Troy
LU Long Island New York
Area . . . . Farmingdale
LU 10 New York Metro
Area . . . . New York
LU 51 Mount
Vernon . . . . . . Mount Vernon
LU 183 Niagara Frontier
Area . . . . Lockport
LU 212 Glens Falls
Area . . . . Glens Falls
LU 215 Rochester Center
Area . . . . Rochester
LU 231 Staten Island
Area . . . . Staten Island
LU 234 Schenectady
Area . . . . Schenectady
LU 251 Brooklyn . . . . Brooklyn
LU 257 Central New York Area
Local . . . . Syracuse
LU 374 Buffalo . . . . Cheektowaga
LU 390 Albany. . . . . . . Albany
LU 522 Southern New York
Area . . . . Ossining
LU 858 Binghamton
Area . . . . Binghamton
LU 865 Greater Corning Painted Post
Area . . . . Corning
LU 1000 Wellsville
Local . . . . Wellsville
LU 1022 Queens Area. . Ozone Park
LU 1091 White Plains . White Plains
LU 1101 South Shore
Area . . . . Far Rockaway
LU 1151 Ithaca . . . . . . Lansing
LU 1241 Long Island
City . . . . . . Long Island City
LU 1249 Rockville
Centre . . . . . Rockville Centre
LU 1820 Utica Area . . . . . Utica
LU 1893 Malone Local . . . Malone
LU 1894 Plattsburgh
Area . . . . Plattsburgh
LU 2255 Elmira . . . . . . Elmira

LU 2286 New York . . . . Bayside
LU 2530 Canton Local. . . . Canton
LU 2577 The Greater Hicksville
Mid-Island . . . . . . Farmingdale
LU 3095 Boonville Local . Boonville
LU 3106 Falconer Local . . Falconer
LU 3150 Rockland & Orange
Area . . . . Monsey
LU 3197 Geneva . . . . . Geneva
LU 3304 Salamanca . . . Salamanca
LU 3526 Jamestown . . . Jamestown
LU 3722 Mid Hudson
Area . . . . Newburgh
LU 4770 Kingston . . . . Kingston
LU 5191 Penn Yan Local . Penn Yan
LU 5242 Port Jervis
Local . . . . Port Jervis
LU 5668 Warwick Local. . Warwick
LU 6510 Hornell Local . . . Hornell
LU 6753 Lakewood
Local . . . . Lakewood
LU 7015 Woodbury . . . Woodbury
LU 7115 Western Nassau New York
Area . . . . Uniondale
SA New York. . . . . . New York

Professional and Technical Engineers
C Northeast. . . . . . Schenectady
LU 57 . . . . Niagara Falls
LU 147 . . . . Schenectady

Railroad Signalmen
GC 95 Metro North. . . . Rhinebeck
LLG 56 Long Island
Railroad . . . . . . Bay Shore
LLG 59 . . . . Callicoon
LLG 75 . . . . Oneonta
LLG 76 . . . . Rhinebeck
LLG 80 . . . . Watervliet
LLG 86 . . . . . . New Hartford
LLG 93 . . . . Wolcott
LLG 147 . . . . Gansevoort
LLG 225 Buffalo . . . . . Buffalo
LLG 230 . . . . Valatie

Retail, Wholesale and Department Store
LU 1-S . . . . New York
LU 3 United Storeworkers
Union. . . . . New York
LU 88 . . . . Brooklyn
LU 139 . . . . Newfane
LU 220 . . . . . . East Williamson
LU 244 . . . . Wolcott
LU 305 . . . . . Hastings-on-Hudson
LU 338 . . . . Rego Park
LU 377 . . . . . . Long Island City
LU 670 . . . . New York
LU 1102 . . . . Westbury
LU 1195 . . . . Lockport
LU 1974. . . . . Fulton
LU 1975 Nestle United Laboratory
Workers Union . . . . . . Fulton
NHQ . . . . New York

Roofers, Waterproofers and Allied Workers
LU 8 . . . . Brooklyn
LU 22 . . . . Rochester
LU 74 . . . . Buffalo
LU 154. . . . . Hauppauge
LU 195 . . . . Cicero
LU 203 . . . . Binghamton
LU 241 . . . . Albany

Rural Letter Carriers
LU Allegany County . . . . Almond

LU Cayuga County . . . Weed Sport
LU Chautauqua County . . Falconer
LU Chemung County. . . . Lowman
LU Chenango County . . . . Greene
LU Clinton-Essex
Counties . . . . Willsboro
LU Columbia County . East Chatman
LU Cortland County . . . Cortland
LU Delaware County . . . Walton
LU Dutchess County . . Dover Plains
LU Onondago County . . . Memphis
LU Otsego County. . . Cooperstown
LU Rensselaer County Unit
04. . . . . Johnsonville
LU Schenectady County . Cobleskill
LU St. Lawrence
County . . . . . . Oswegatchie
LU Sullivan County . . . . Liberty
LU Washington-Saratoga-Warren
Counties . . . . . Saratoga Springs
LU Wayne County . . . . . Lyons
LU 1 Tompkins County . . Freeville
LU 2 Oswego County . . . . Pulaski
LU 3 Steuben County . . . . Bath
LU 5 Oneida County . . . . Clinton
LU 6 Broome County. . Harpursville
LU 7 Monroe County. . . Pittsford
LU 8 Niagara County . . . Newfane
LU 9 Fulton-Montgomery
Counties. . . . . . . Amsterdam
LU 10 Wyoming
County. . . . . . . Gainesville
LU 11 Ontario-Yates
Counties. . . . . . Canandaigua
LU 12 Erie
County . . . North Tonawanda
LU 15 Jefferson
County . . . . Philadelphia
LU 18 Tioga County . . . Apalachin
LU 19 Genesee
County. . . . . . East Bethany
LU 23 Cattaraugus
County . . . . . Great Valley
LU 25 Livingston County . . . Hunt
LU 26 Herkimer County. . Frankfort
LU 30 Ulster County. . . Ulster Park
LU 32 Madison County . Bridgeport
LU 36 Schuyler
County . . . . . . Dover Plains
LU 37 Schoharie
County . . . . . Cherry Valley
LU 38 Franklin County . . Malone
LU 39 Suffolk-Nassau
Counties . . . . . . Sag Harbor
LU 40 Orleans County . . . Albion
LU 42 Greene County. . . Surprise
LU 46 Putnam/Westchester
County . . . . . . Mahopac
LU 49 Lewis County . . . Lowville
LU 53 Orange County . Tuxedo Park
SA New York . . . . Byron

Security Officers
LU 1 . . . . New York

Security Officers, Police and Guards
LU 2 . . . . New York
LU 18 . . . . Brooklyn
LU 55 . . . . Brooklyn
LU 500 . . . . Jamaica
NHQ . . . . Brooklyn

Security, Police and Fire Professionals
LU 514. . . . Annandale-on-Hudson
LU 515 . . . . Poughkeepsie
LU 529. . . . . Olean

LU 531 . . . . . . North Lawrence

Service Employees
C New York State . . . . New York
JB International Leather Goods,
Plastics, Novelty and Service
Union New York . . . . Brooklyn
LU . . . . Mount Vernon
LU International Leather Goods,
Plastics, Novelty and Service
Union . . . . New York
LU 4 International Leather Goods,
Plastics, Novelty and Service
Union . . . . New York
LU 27 Firemen &
Oilers . . . . South Dayton
LU 29 International Leather Goods,
Plastics, Novelty and Service
Union . . . . New York
LU 32-B . . . . New York
LU 51 . . . . Troy
LU 56 Firemen & Oilers . New York
LU 60 International Leather Goods,
Plastics, Novelty and Service
Union . . . . Brooklyn
LU 74 . . . . . . Long Island City
LU 90 Firemen &
Oilers . . . . . North Tonawanda
LU 105 Firemen &
Oilers . . . . . . Lake George
LU 106 Firemen & Oilers . . Corinth
LU 176 . . . . Forest Hills
LU 177 . . . . Brooklyn
LU 200 . . . . Syracuse
LU 234 . . . . Utica
LU 235 . . . . . West Seneca
LU 253 Firemen &
Oilers . . . . Cassadaga
LU 266 Firemen & Oilers . Mayville
LU 276 . . . . Levittown
LU 299 . . . . Bethpage
LU 311 Firemen &
Oilers . . . . . . Staten Island
LU 348 International Leather Goods,
Plastics, Novelty and Service
Union . . . . Fonda
LU 349 Firemen &
Oilers . . . . . . Brownville
LU 363 . . . . Briarwood
LU 520 Firemen &
Oilers . . . . . . Poughkeepsie
LU 693 University College of
Physicians-Surgeons . . New York
LU 721 . . . . New York
LU 723 Bethpage UFSD Cafeteria
Employees . . . . . . Plainview
LU 758 Hotel and Allied
Services. . . . . New York
LU 933 Firemen & Oilers . . Delmar
LU 1199 Drug Hospital & Health
Care Employees Union. New York
LU 1199 Upstate . . . . . Syracuse

Sheet Metal Workers
C Air Conditioning Production
Workers . . . . Syracuse
LU 28 . . . . New York
LU 31 . . . . Buchanan
LU 38. . . . . Brewster
LU 46 . . . . Rochester
LU 58. . . . . Syracuse
LU 71 . . . . Buffalo
LU 83 . . . . Albany
LU 112 . . . . Wellsburg
LU 137. . . . . . . Long Island City
LU 149. . . . . Westbury
LU 398 . . . . Clifton Park
LU 417 . . . . Fultonville

LU 439. . . . . Jamestown
LU 527 . . . . Syracuse
LU 530 . . . . Deer Park

Solidarity of Labor
LU 947 . . . . Bronx
NHQ. . . . . Bronx

**State, County and Municipal
Employees**
DC 37 New York City . . New York
DC 1707 Community & Social
Agency Employees
Union . . . . Buffalo
LU . . . . Harrison
LU . . . . New York
LU 95 Head Start
Employees . . . . New York
LU 107 Federation of Shorthand
Reporters . . . . New York
LU 205 Dare Care Centers
Employees Union . . . New York
LU 215 Social Service
Employees . . . . New York
LU 253 Teaching & Related
Organizations. . . . . New York
LU 374 . . . . New York
LU 375 Civil Service Technical
Guild . . . . New York
LU 389 Home Care
Employees . . . . New York
LU 702-. . . . . Albany
LU 703 . . . . Middletown
LU 704 . . . . Newburgh
LU 706 . . . . Albany
LU 708 . . . . Schenectady
LU 709 . . . . Watkins Glen
LU 710. . . . . Buffalo
LU 712 . . . . West Falls
LU 714 . . . . Albany
LU 715 . . . . Appleton
LU 716 . . . . Burt
LU 728 Schenectady Family Health
Services . . . . Albany
LU 891 CSEA . . . . Buffalo
LU 1000 Civil Service Employees
Association (CSEA) . . . . Albany
LU 1000 CSEA Local 734 Pioneer
Central Tran . . . . . . Delevan
LU 1000 CSEA Local
738. . . . . Hamburg
LU 1000 CSEA LU
737 . . . . Ronkonkoma
LU 1000 CSEA Region III-
Southern . . . . Beacon
LU 1000 CSEA Region IV-
Capital. . . . . Latham
LU 1000 CSEA Region V-
Central . . . . . . East Syracuse
LU 1000 CSEA Region VI-
Western . . . . . . West Seneca
LU 1000 CSEA SLU 315 Health
Research. . . . . Buffalo
LU 1000 CSEA SLU 316 Health
Research. . . . . . West Seneca
LU 1000 CSEA SLU 620 Alfred
Faculty-Students
Association . . . . Arkport
LU 1000 CSEA SLU 621 SUNY
Buffalo Faculty . . . . . Kenmore
LU 1000 CSEA SLU 622 Oswego
Faculty-Students
Association . . . . Mexico
LU 1000 CSEA SLU 624 Brockport
State University . . . . . Albion
LU 1000 CSEA SLU 625 Potsdam
College Food Service . . . Canton

LU 1000 CSEA SLU 627 Fredonia
State University . . . . Fredonia
LU 1000 CSEA SLU 628 Delhi
Technical College . . . Hamden
LU 1000 CSEA SLU 629 Geneseo
Faculty-Students. . . . Leicester
LU 1000 CSEA SLU 630
St. Lawrence
University . . . . Hannawa Falls
LU 1000 CSEA SLU
701 . . . . East Patchogue
LU 1000 CSEA SLU 707
Rensselaer . . . . Albany
LU 1000 CSEA SLU 713 Geneva B.
Scruggs HCF . . . . . . Albany
LU 1000 CSEA SLU 717 Nioga
Library System . . . . . . Olcott
LU 1000 CSEA SLU 733 Amsterdam
Head Start. . . . . . Amsterdam
LU 1000 CSEA SLU 735 Nassau
Library System . . . . . Uniondale
LU 1000 CSEA SLU 888
Columbia-Greene
Medcenter . . . . Catskill
LU 1000 SLU 727 . . . Ogdensburg
LU 1306 . . . . New York
LU 1501 New York Zoological
Society . . . . Monroe
LU 1502 Brooklyn Museum
Employees. . . . . . . Brooklyn
LU 1503 . . . . New York
LU 1559 American Museum of
Natural History. . . . New York
LU 1930 New York Public Library
Guild . . . . New York
LU 2786 Erie County Human Service
Agencies Employees. Lackawanna
LU 3124 . . . . Auburn
LU 3414 Saratoga County
EOC . . . . . . Saratoga Springs
LU 3755 Professional Services
Group . . . . Scotia
LU 3933 Albany Public Library
Employees. . . . . Albany
R 1 CSEA. . . . . Commack
STC 66 New York . . . . Rochester

Steelworkers
LU 4-420-A. . . . . Massena
LU 4-450-A. . . . . Massena
LU 04-135-L . . . . . Cheektowaga
LU 04-151-G. . . . . . . Bolivar
LU 04-222 . . . . Depew
LU 04-593-S . . . . Buffalo
LU 04-740-L. . . . . . . Rochester
LU 04-897-S . . . . . Orchard Park
LU 04-1277-S . . . . Syracuse
LU 04-1498-S . . . . Rochester
LU 04-1750-S . . . . Utica
LU 04-1753-S . . . . Buffalo
LU 04-2603-S . . . . Blasdell
LU 04-2604-S . . . . Blasdell
LU 04-2693-S . . . . . . Forestville
LU 04-2857-S . . . . Lockport
LU 04-2924-S . . . . North Syracuse
LU 04-3298-S . . . . Geneua
LU 04-3482-S . . . . Auburn
LU 04-3609-S . . . . . . Hamburg
LU 04-4146-S . . . . Rochester
LU 04-4447-S . . North Tonawanda
LU 04-4601-S . . . . Olean
LU 04-4783-S . . . . Syracuse
LU 04-4831-S . . . Richfield Springs
LU 04-4867-S . . . . . Amsterdam
LU 04-4979-S . . . . . Gouverneur
LU 04-5335-S . . . . . Ogdensburg
LU 04-5347-S . . . . Syracuse
LU 04-5376-S . . . . . . Hannibal

LU 04-5429-S . . . . Olean
LU 04-6989. . . . . . . Moravia
LU 04-7110-S . . . . . . Waterloo
LU 04-7338-S . . . . . Kerhonkson
LU 04-7474-S. . . . . Cicero
LU 04-8090-S . . . . Hudson
LU 04-8823-S . . . . Buffalo
LU 04-9265-S . . . . Latham
LU 04-9268-S . . . . Syracuse
LU 04-9367-S . . . . . Jamestown
LU 04-9374-S . . . . East Northport
LU 04-9436 . . . . . . Niagara Falls
LU 04-12230-S . . . . . . Sanborn
LU 04-12330-S . . . . Buffalo
LU 04-12460-S . . Beaver Dams
LU 04-12623-S . . . . . Jamesville
LU 04-12770-S . . . . Troy
LU 04-13226-S . . . . . Saugerties
LU 04-13833-S . . . . . . Buffalo
LU 04-14316-S . . . West Seneca
LU 04-14532-S . . . . . Syracuse
LU 04-14698-S . . . . Brooklyn
LU 04-14753-S . . . . Huntington
LU 04-15135-S . . . . . . Argyle
LU 04-15310-S . . . . Pennellville
LU 11-43-U. . . . . . New York
LU 14-15071 . . . . Niagara Falls

Teachers
LU . . . . Ulster Park
LU 2 New York City
Teachers . . . . . . New York
LU 1460 College
Teachers. . . . . . . Brooklyn
LU 2092 Catholic Teachers,
Federation of. . . . Staten Island
LU 2413 Suffolk Center Teachers
Association . . . . . . Hauppauge
LU 3133 Southampton College
Federation of
Teachers. . . . . . . Southampton
LU 3163 Cooper Union Federation
College Teachers. . . . New York
LU 3517 C.W. Post Collegial
Federation . . . . . . Brookville
LU 3552 Teachers, Lexington School
for Deaf . . . . Jackson Heights
LU 3634 Kadimah Teachers
Association . . . . . Williamsville
LU 3721 Cerebral Palsy
Employees . . . . Depew
LU 3739 The Association of Center
Employees . . . . . . Hicksville
LU 3882 United Staff Association of
New York University . New York
LU 3888 Baker Hall United
Teachers. . . . . . Orchard Park
LU 3890 Dowling College
Chapter . . . . Oakdale
LU 3892 Mill Neck Manor
Educational
Association. . . . . . Mill Neck
LU 3918 Teachers, St. Marys School
for Deaf . . . . Buffalo
LU 4064 Hallen Teachers
Association . . . . . New Rochelle
LU 4228 Cornell University Adjunct
Faculty Federation . . . New York
LU 4265 Association for Retarded
Citizens Employees . Niagara Falls
LU 4503 New York Staff Public
Employees Federation
PEF . . . . Albany
LU 6147 Campus Education
Association . . . . . . Lockport
LU 8053 Verona
Federation . . . . . Staten Island

SFED New York State United
  Teachers . . . . Albany
SFED NYSUT Margaretville
  LPNs-Techs. . . . . . Prattsville
SFED NYSUT Margaretville
  Professional Nurses. . . . Arkville

Teamsters
JC 16 . . . . New York
JC 18 . . . . Albany
JC 46. . . . . Cheektowaga
LU 111 . . . . Brooklyn
LU 118 . . . . Rochester
LU 126 . . . . Troy
LU 182 . . . . Utica
LU 202 . . . . Bronx
LU 210 . . . . New York
LU 264 . . . . Cheektowaga
LU 272 . . . . New York
LU 277. . . . . Great Neck
LU 282. . . . . Lake Success
LU 294 . . . . Albany
LU 295 . . . . Valley Stream
LU 317 . . . . Syracuse
LU 338 . . . . Bronxville
LU 375. . . . . Buffalo
LU 445 . . . . Newburgh
LU 449 . . . . Buffalo
LU 456 . . . . Elmsford
LU 522 . . . . Jamaica
LU 529 . . . . Elmira
LU 531 . . . . Yonkers
LU 550 . . . . . New Hyde Park
LU 553 . . . . New York
LU 584 . . . . New York
LU 669 . . . . Albany
LU 687 . . . . Potsdam
LU 693 . . . . Binghamton
LU 707 . . . . Hempstead
LU 791 . . . . Rochester
LU 802. . . . . . . Long Island City
LU 803 . . . . Woodhaven
LU 804 . . . . . Long Island City
LU 805 . . . . New York
LU 807 . . . . . Long Island City
LU 808 . . . . . Long Island City
LU 810 . . . . New York
LU 812 . . . . Scarsdale
LU 813 . . . . . Long Island City
LU 814 . . . . . Long Island City
LU 817 . . . . Lake Success
LU 819 . . . . Maspeth
LU 840 . . . . New York
LU 851 . . . . Valley Stream
LU 854 . . . . Valley Stream
LU 917 . . . . Floral Park
LU 1149. . . . . . . Baldwinsville
LU 1205. . . . . Melville

Television and Radio Artists
LU Buffalo. . . . . Buffalo
LU Dallas-Fort Worth . . New York
LU New York. . . . . . New York
LU Schenectady . . . . Schenectady
LU 210 Fresno . . . . . New York
LU 223 Rochester . . . . Rochester
NHQ . . . . New York

Theatrical Stage Employees
D 10 New York . . . . Ballston Lake
LU East Coast Council . . New York
LU 1 . . . . New York
LU 4 . . . . Brooklyn
LU 9 . . . . Syracuse
LU 10 . . . . Cheektowaga
LU 14 . . . . Albany
LU 25 . . . . Rochester
LU 29 . . . . Schenectady

LU 52 . . . . New York
LU 54 . . . . Johnson City
LU 72-F . . . . . Massapequa Park
LU 90-B . . . . Rochester
LU 121 . . . . Akron
LU 161 . . . . New York
LU 253 . . . . Canandaigua
LU 266 . . . . Jamestown
LU 272 . . . . Dryden
LU 289 . . . . Elmira
LU 306 . . . . New York
LU 311 . . . . . . Washingtonville
LU 324 . . . . Knox
LU 340 . . . . Rockypoint
LU 353 . . . . New York
LU 376 . . . . Syracuse
LU 474. . . . . Rome
LU 499 . . . . Narrowsburg
LU 524 . . . . Diamond Point
LU 592. . . . . Stillwater
LU 640 . . . . Babylon
LU 702 . . . . New York
LU 749 . . . . Ogdensburg
LU 751 . . . . New York
LU 751-B . . . . New York
LU 764 . . . . New York
LU 783 . . . . . South Cheektowaga
LU 788 . . . . Rochester
LU 794 Television Broadcasting
  Studio. . . . . New York
LU 798 . . . . New York
LU 829 . . . . New York
LU 838 . . . . Syracuse
LU 842-M. . . . . Oneonta
LU 858. . . . . Lancaster
LU 936-AE. . . . . Albany
LU 3038 Billposters &
  Billers . . . . Bayside
LU 18032 Theatrical Press Agents &
  Managers . . . . New York
NHQ . . . . New York

Train Dispatchers
SCOM GCA CSXT-East System
  Committee. . . . . Ravena
SCOM Staten Island Rapid Transit
  Railroad . . . . Brooklyn

Transit Union
LDIV 282 . . . . Rochester
LDIV 580. . . . . Syracuse
LDIV 1179 . . . . Jamaica
LDIV 1181 . . . . . . Ozone Park
LDIV 1342 . . . . . . West Seneca
LDIV 1592. . . . . . Glen Aubrey
LDIV 1625. . . . . Buffalo
LU 1636 . . . . North Troy

Transport Workers
LU 100 . . . . New York
LU 101 Utility Division . . Brooklyn
LU 241 . . . . New York
LU 252. . . . . Westbury
LU 264 . . . . New York
LU 501 . . . . College Point
LU 504 . . . . Jamaica
LU 519. . . . . Buffalo
LU 562 . . . . Jamaica
LU 1460 . . . . New York
LU 2001 . . . . Irvington
LU 2020 . . . . Wyoming
NHQ . . . . New York

**Transportation Communications
Union**
D 491 . . . . West Seneca
D 861 Conrail . . . . Rensselaerville

D 1043 Metro North Commuter
  Railroad . . . . Peekskill
D 1475 . . . . Staten Island
LG United Service Workers of
  America . . . . Briarwood
LG 90 . . . . Farmingdale
LG 177 . . . . East Islip
LG 255 United Service
  Workers . . . . Briarwood
LG 339 United Service
  Workers . . . . Briarwood
LG 355 United Service
  Workers . . . . Briarwood
LG 455 United Service
  Workers . . . . Briarwood
LG 643 . . . . West Islip
LG 955 United Service
  Workers . . . . Briarwood
LG 1212 United Service
  Workers . . . . Briarwood
LG 1277 . . . . Merrick
LG 1444 . . . . . Massapequa Park
LG 5041 Conrail . . . . Verplanck
LG 5085 Amtrak . . . . Troy
LG 5086 Amtrak . . . New Windsor
LG 5097 American Rail & Airway
  Supervisors . . . . . Cold Spring
LG 6983 Binghamton . Harpursville
SBA 167 Long Island . . Hicksville

Transportation Union
GCA GO-299 Delaware & Hudson
  Railway. . . . . . Mechanicville
GCA GO-300 Delaware & Hudson
  Railway. . . . . . . Binghamton
GCA GO-340 . . . . . . Warwick
GCA GO-505 Long Island
  Railroad. . . . . Babylon
GCA GO-619 Conrail-PC-ED-
  NYC-E . . . . Syracuse
GCA GO-621 Conrail-PC-ED-
  NYC-E . . . . Cheektowaga
LU . . . . Watervliet
LU 1 . . . . . South Cheektowaga
LU 29 . . . . Levittown
LU 95 . . . . Latham
LU 211 . . . . Binghamton
LU 212 . . . . Alcove
LU 256 . . . . Mechanicville
LU 292 . . . . East Syracuse
LU 318 . . . . Spencer
LU 377. . . . . Buffalo
LU 385 . . . . Schenectady
LU 394 . . . . Kinderhook
LU 645 . . . . Babylon
LU 722 . . . . . East Farmingdale
LU 982. . . . . Auburn
LU 1007 . . . . Hastings
LU 1393 . . . . West Seneca
LU 1491 . . . . Port Jervis
LU 1582 . . . . Latham
LU 1831. . . . . Massapequa Park
LU 1908 . . . . Buffalo
LU 1951 . . . . Cheektowaga
LU 1978. . . . . Deer Park
SLB LO-35 New York. . . . Albany

Treasury Employees
CH 47 . . . . New York
CH 53 . . . . Garden City
CH 57. . . . . Syracuse
CH 58 . . . . East Amherst
CH 61 . . . . Poughkeepsie
CH 79 . . . . Rochester
CH 99 . . . . Holtsville
CH 138 . . . . Champlain
CH 148 . . . . Champlain
CH 153 . . . . Jamaica

CH 154. . . . . Buffalo
CH 181 Toronto
  Preclearance. . . . Niagara Falls
CH 183 . . . . New York
CH 252. . . . . Hempstead
CH 255 . . . . New York
CH 271 Queens/Brooklyn . Brooklyn

University Professors
CH Adelphi University . Garden City
CH Arnold & Marie Schwartz
  College . . . . Brooklyn
CH Bard
  College . . Annandale-on-Hudson
CH College of Insurance . New York
CH D'Youville College . . . Buffalo
CH Hofstra University . . Hempstead
CH Marymount College . Tarrytown
CH St. John's University . . Jamaica
CH Utica College of Syracuse . Utica
JC New York Institute of
  Technology . . . . . . Greenvale

Utility Workers
C Long Island Water
  Workers. . . . . . . Brookhaven
LU 1-2 . . . . New York
LU 355 . . . . Merrick
LU 365 . . . . Valley Stream
LU 366 . . . . Forest Hills
LU 447 . . . . . . Port Washington

Variety Artists
NHQ . . . . New York

Weather Service Employees
BR 01-17. . . . . Albany
BR 01-18 . . . . Upton
BR 01-19 . . . . Rochester
BR 01-32. . . . . . . Johnson City
BR 01-35. . . . . Buffalo
BR 01-58. . . . . Bohemia
BR 01-65 . . . . Ronkonkoma

Westinghouse Salaried Employees
ASSN Buffalo Salaried
  Employees . . . . . Lackawanna

Writers, East
NHQ . . . . New York

**Unaffiliated Labor
Organizations**
318 Restaurant Workers
  Union. . . . . New York
Adelphi Physical Plant Workers
  Labor Union . . . . . Hempstead
Albany County Deputy Sheriff's
  PBA Police Conference of New
  York LU 3973 . . . . . . Albany
Allied International Union Security
  Guards & Special Police . Mineola
Allied Musicians Union of New York
  Westchester Division. . . Yonkers
Alternative Workers Alliance
  Inc. . . . . Long Beach
Amalgamated Lithographers of
  America LU 1 . . . . . New York
Amalgamated Workers of North
  America . . . . . New Rochelle
American Employees International
  Guild. . . . . . Yorktown Heights
American Federation of Railroad
  Police Inc. . . . . Woodbury
American Guild of
  Employees. . . . . . . New City

American Maritime
Officers . . . . Brooklyn
Amex Employees
Association. . . . . . New York
Anti-Defamation League Professional
Staff Association . . . . New York
Asian Employee
Association. . . . . . . New York
Association of Court Security
Officers of New York . Levittown
Association of Professional and
Specialty Workers LU
279 . . . . New York
Attending Physicians Association
City Hospital at
Elmhurst . . . . Elmhurst
Benefit Fund Staff
Association. . . . . . . New York
Braun Union Independent . . Depew
Building Service Employees
Independent LU 1 . . . New York
Campaign & Professional Workers
LU 1 . . . . Albany
Chemical Workers Independent
Union. . . . . Schenectady
City Wholesale Distributors Union
Association . . . . . . Lancaster
Clerical Employees
Association. . . . . . . Syracuse
Collective Negotiations Committee,
New York Chapter, American
Physical Therapy Associa . Albany
Confort Employees
Association . . . Long Island City
Cornell Police Union . . . . . Ithaca
Crafts & Industrial Workers Union,
United LU 91 . . . Roslyn Heights
Culinary Craft
Association. . . . . . Hyde Park
Defender Employees Union LU
383 . . . . Rochester
Detectives Association Suffolk
County . . . . . . West Sayville
Diversified Employees Union LU
4 . . . . Hauppauge
Doctors Council . . . . New York
Draftsmen's Association of
Syracuse . . . . Phoenix
Ellison Bronze Employees
Union. . . . . Falconer
Elrae Employees Association
Independent Union . . . . . Alden
Entertainment & Amusement
Employees Association LU
99 . . . . Long Island City
Fabric Labor Committee . New York
Factory & Building Employees
Union LU 187 . . . . . Brooklyn
Faculty Association at St. Johns
University. . . . . Jamaica
Federation of Security Guards LU
621 . . . . New Rochelle
Federation of Shorthand
Reporters . . . . New York
Field Staff
Association . . . . Williamsville
Financial Consultants Guild of
America Inc.. . . . . Huntington
Financial Consultants Guild of
America Inc. Employees Industrial
LU 1 . . . . Huntington
Fordham Law School Bargaining
Committee . . . . . . New York
Frank Siviglia Employees
Association. . . . . . . New York
Fraternal Order Court Security
Officers Western New York
FOSCO . . . . . . West Henrietta

Gary Pontiac Workers
Union . . . . Buffalo
General Union for
International . . . . . New York
Guards & Plant Protection
Employees LU 1 . . . Schenectady
H.W. Wilson Employees
Association . . . . Bronx
Half Hollow Hills Library
Employees Association
Independent . . . . . . Dix Hills
Harper Collins Sales
Association. . . . . . . Flushing
Hassall Employees
Association . . . . . . Westbury
Headquarters Staff Union . . Albany
Health Care Professional
Guild . . . . New Hartford
Hearst International Employees
Association. . . . . . . New York
Henry Viscardi School Faculty
Association . . . West Hempstead
Huntington Hospital Nurses
Association . . . . . Huntington
Hunts Point Police Benevolent
Association . . . . Bronx
HVAC & Plumbing Workers LU
1314 . . . . Niagara Falls
Independent Artists of
America . . . . New York
Independent Guard Union . Brooklyn
Independent Railway Supervisors
Association Grand Lodge
NHQ . . . . Plainview
Independent Railway Supervisors
Long Island Railroad LG
1 . . . . Patchogue
Independent School
Transportation Workers
Association . . . . . Staten Island
Independent Theatrical Employees of
America LU 1 . . . New Hartford
Independent Union Drivers and
Dockworkers of Stroehmanns LU
77 . . . . Tonawanda
Independent Union of Court Security
Officers Northern District of New
York . . . . Syracuse
Independent Union Staff
Employees . . . . Cheektowaga
Industrial Employees
Association . . . Long Island City
International Brotherhood of Security
Guards LU 971 . . . . Commack
International Brotherhood of Trade
Unions . . . . Jamaica
International Brotherhood of Trade
Unions LU 122 . . . East Meadow
International Brotherhood of Trade
Unions LU 363 . . . . . Jamaica
International Brotherhood of Trade
Unions LU 713 . . . Garden City
International Shield of
Labor. . . . . Glendale
International Workers Guild . Elmont
IUISTHE D 6 . . . . . New York
Jewish Committee Staff Organization
America . . . . New York
Kingsbrook Jewish Medical Center
Medical Staff
Association . . . . . . Brooklyn
Lay Faculty Association . . Flushing
League of Employees
Guild . . . . New York
League of International Federated
Employees. . . . . . . Brooklyn
Legal Staff Association. . New York

Local 400 Production
Workers . . . . . . New York
Machinists & Mechanics Independent
Association. . . . . . Watervliet
Magtrol Employees
Association . . . . West Seneca
Marine Technicians Guild Marine
Technicians . . North Massapequa
Models and Showroom Employees
LU 1 . . . . Long Beach
Mount Sinai Hospital Pharmacy
Association. . . . . . New York
Municipal Highway Inspectors LU
1042 . . . . Flushing
National Basketball Coaches
Association. . . . . . New York
National Music Instructors Guild BR
120. . . . . Cold Springs Harbor
National Organization of Industrial
Trade Unions LU
36. . . . . Far Rockaway
National Transportation Supervisors
Association LG 78 . . Mineola
National Union of Associated
Employees . . . . . . Port Jervis
National Union of Security Officers
and Guards . . . . . . Jamaica
National United Brotherhood of
Section 3 Workers LU
1888. . . . . Bronx
Neergaard Employees
Association . . . . . . Brooklyn
New Era Cap Company Inc.
Employees Independent
Union . . . . Buffalo
New Independent Leather Novelty &
Plastic Workers
Union . . . . Amsterdam
New School Security
Guards . . . . New York
New York Archdiocesan High School
Lay Faculty Association . . Bronx
New York Physicians & Dentists
SFED . . . . New York
New York Professional Nurses
Union . . . . New York
New York Professional Nurses Union
National . . . . New York
Niagara Frontier Sheet Metal
Workers Union . . . Niagara Falls
Niagara Hooker Employees
Union . . . . Niagara Falls
Niagara Plant Employees
Union . . . . Niagara Falls
Niagara University Lay Teachers
Association . . . . . Lake View
Organization for Negotiated
Change . . . . Rochester
Organization of Union
Representatives. . . . New York
Petroleum Employees Alliance
Independent. . . . . . Commack
Petroleum Workers Independent of
Albany . . . . Delmar
Pius XII Chester Campus Institution
Unit A LU 725. . . . . Albany
Police and Security Guards
International Union . . . Glendale
Police Benevolent Association
Federal Protective
Service . . . . New York
Presbyterian Hospital Occupational
Therapy Association . . New York
Private, Public & Professional
Employees of America LU
654. . . . . Elmsford

Production & Maintenance
Employees LU
116. . . . . . . Port Washington
Production & Service Employees
International Union Independent
LU 143 . . . . Bronx
Production Industrial Technical
Textile & Professional
Employees. . . . North Massapequa
Production Maintenance & Technical
Service Employees Union . Selden
Professional Association Holy Cross
High School . . . . . . Flushing
Professional Camera Repair
Guild . . . . New York
Professional Service & Healthcare
Employees International
Union . . . . Jamaica
Professional Staff
Association . . . . Albany
Retail Wholesale Warehouse and
Production Employees
International Union . . . Brooklyn
Richmond County Nurses
Association . . . . . Staten Island
Rochester Regional Joint
Board . . . . Rochester
Rochester School Bus Employees
Association . . . . . . Rochester
Rochester Telephone Workers
Association . . . . . . Rochester
Salaried Physicians and Dentists
United . . . . New York
Security Employees Union LU
1034 . . . . Brooklyn
Security Officers Association
University of Rochester . . Webster
Security Personnel Brotherhood L.J.
Overton & Associates . New York
Service Professionals Independent
Union LU 726 . . . West Babylon
Sheriff Officers Association Inc.
Nassau County Jail . East Meadow
Southern California Professional
Engineering Association
NHQ . . . . New York
Special & Superior Officers
Benevolent Association . Babylon
Special Patrolmen Benevolent
Association LU 1 . . . . . Bronx
St. John's Preparatory Teacher
Association . . . . Queens
Staff Union. . . . . Buffalo
Stage Directors & Choreographers
Society . . . . New York
Stage Performers Guild . Huntington
Suffolk County Association of
Municipal Employees,
Inc. . . . . Bohemia
Sun Oil Company Employees
Association Oceanside
District . . . . Lawrence
Teachers Association of the Weekend
School of Japanese Educational
Institute of New York . Shoreham
Teachers Representatives
Union . . . . New York
Travel Agents' Guild . . . New York
United Business Workers of
America . . . . Nanuet
United Commercial & Industrial
Workers Union LU
912. . . . . Great Neck
United Construction Trade and
Industrial Employees. . New York
United Construction Trades &
Industrial Employees International
Union . . . . Glendale

United Federation of Security
  Officers Inc. . . . Briarcliff Manor
United Industrial Workers of
  America LU 806 . . . . . Flushing
United Production Workers LU
  17-18 . . . . Brooklyn

United Service Employees Union LU
  1222 . . . . Ronkonkoma
United States Court Security Officers
  South District-New
  York . . . . New York
United Workers Across America LU
  2000 . . . . Bohemia

Upstate New York Laborers
  Organizing Coalition . . . Albany
Visiting Nurses Professional
  Guild . . . . Woodgate
Warren General Hospital
  Professional Employees
  Association . . . . . Jamestown

Warwick Valley Telephone Company
  Employees' Association . Warwick
Women's National Basketball Players
  Association . . . . . . New York
Workers of America Canada
  International Union LU
  11 . . . . Brooklyn

North Carolina

AFL-CIO Trade and Industrial Departments

Food and Allied Service Trades Department
FASTC Carolinas. . . . . . Concord

Affiliated Labor Organizations

Aeronautical Examiners
LU 2. . . . . New Bern
NHQ. . . . . New Bern

Agricultural Employees
BR 34. . . . . Willow Spring

Air Traffic Controllers
LU AVL. . . . . Fletcher
LU CLT . . . . Charlotte
LU FAY . . . . Fayetteville
LU GSO . . . . Greensboro
LU ILM . . . . Wilmington
LU INT . . . . . . Winston-Salem
LU NKT . . . . Havelock
LU RDU . . . . Raleigh

Asbestos Workers
LU 72 . . . . Hillsborough

Automobile, Aerospace Workers
LU 1597. . . . . . . Belews Creek
LU 2404 . . . . Charlotte
LU 2828 . . . . Charlotte
LU 5285 . . . . Mount Holly

Bakery, Confectionery, Tobacco Workers and Grain Millers
C Fourth Regional . . . . . Concord
LU 176-T . . . . Durham
LU 192-T . . . . Reidsville
LU 229-T . . . . Concord
LU 259-T . . . . Wilson
LU 270-T . . . . Wilson
LU 274-T . . . . Farmville
LU 317-T . . . . Burlington
LU 503 . . . . Harrisburg

Boilermakers
LG 30 . . . . Greensboro
LG 31 . . . . New London
LG 613 . . . . Rocky Point
LG 905 . . . . Wilmington

Carpenters
LU 312 . . . . Lexington
LU 2003 . . . . Garner

Civilian Technicians
CH 96 Old Hickory. . . . . St. Pauls

Communications Workers
C North Carolina Political. . Raleigh
LU 3061 . . . . Burlington
LU 3601 . . . . Asheville
LU 3602 . . . . Burlington
LU 3603 . . . . Charlotte
LU 3605 . . . . Shelby
LU 3606 . . . . Goldsboro
LU 3607 . . . . Greensboro
LU 3608 . . . . Morganton
LU 3609 . . . . Lumberton
LU 3610 . . . . Claremont
LU 3611 . . . . Raleigh

LU 3613 . . . . Salisbury
LU 3615. . . . . . . Wilmington
LU 3616. . . . . Winston-Salem
LU 3617. . . . . Ellerbe
LU 3640. . . . . Winston-Salem
LU 3641 . . . . Charlotte
LU 3650 . . . . Greensboro
LU 3672 . . . . Hickory
LU 3673 . . . . Balsam
LU 3676 . . . . Mount Olive
LU 3680 . . . . Hope Mills
LU 3681 . . . . New Bern
LU 3682 . . . . Henderson
LU 3683 . . . . Marshville
LU 3684 . . . . Tobaccoville
LU 3685 . . . . . . Elizabeth City
LU 3695 . . . . Charlotte
LU 3790 . . . . Raleigh
LU 14341 . . . . . Winston-Salem

Education
ASSN Maxwell Education Association . . . . . Fayetteville
C OEA Pacific Area. . . Fayetteville
LU BEA . . . . Fayetteville
LU Fort Bragg Association of Educators . . . . . . Fayetteville
LU Fort Knox Classified Personnel Association . . . . . Fayetteville
LU OEA Fort Rucker Education Association . . . . . Fayetteville
LU OEA Lejeune Education Association . . . . . Fayetteville

Electrical Workers
LU 238 . . . . Enka
LU 289 . . . . Timberlake
LU 312 . . . . Mooresville
LU 342 . . . . . Winston-Salem
LU 379 . . . . Concord
LU 495 . . . . Wilmington
LU 553 . . . Research Triangle Park
LU 962. . . . . Greensboro
LU 1183 . . . . Plymouth
LU 1537 . . . . Asheboro
LU 1863 . . . . Rockwell
LU 1902 . . . . Charlotte
LU 1912 . . . . Siler City
LU 1923 . . . . Hamlet
LU 2290 . . . . Reidsville

Electrical, Radio and Machine Workers
LU 150 North Carolina Public Service Workers Union. . Durham

Electronic Workers
LU 181. . . . . Charlotte
LU 186. . . . . Charlotte
LU 188. . . . . Durham
LU 265-FW. . . . . . Henderson

Elevator Constructors
LU 80 . . . . Hillsborough
LU 135 . . . . Concord

Federal Employees
LU 1563 . . . . Nebo

Flint Glass Workers
LU 45 . . . . Clemmons
LU 47. . . . . Wilson
LU 55. . . . . Henderson
LU 1025. . . . . . . Wilmington
LU 1028 . . . . Raleigh

Food and Commercial Workers
LU 204 . . . . . Winston-Salem
LU 297-C . . . . Raleigh
LU 298-C . . . . Durham
LU 426-T . . . . Tyner
LU 427-C . . . . Morganton
LU 528-C . . . . Weaverville
LU 954-C . . . . Concord
LU 955-C . . . . Statesville
LU 2598-T . . . . Enka

Glass, Molders, Pottery and Plastics Workers
LU 168 . . . . . . Germantown
LU 179 . . . . Henderson
LU 193 . . . . Wilson
LU 222 . . . . Oxford
LU 256 . . . . Rockingham
LU 420 . . . . Creedmoor

Government Employees
LU . . . . Salisbury
LU 405 . . . . Butner
LU 406 Azalea Station . Wilmington
LU 446 VA . . . . Asheville
LU 1708 DoD . . . . . . Southport
LU 1770 DoD . . . . . Fort Bragg
LU 2065 DoD. . . . . Jacksonville
LU 2325 USDA . . . . Siler City
LU 2345 VA . . . . Durham
LU 2364 DoD. . . . . Spring Lake
LU 2652 DoT, Customs Inspectors Association . . . . . . Raleigh
LU 2923 HHS . . . . . . Durham
LU 3347 EPA. . . . Research Triangle Park
LU 3409 HUD. . . . . Greensboro
LU 3696 DoJ . . . . Butner
LU 3977 FPG, SJAFB . . Goldsboro

Government Employees Association
LU 04-75. . . . . Asheville
LU 05-160. . . . . . Fayetteville
LU 05-188 . . . . . . Goldsboro

Government Security Officers
LU 90 . . . . Huntersville
LU 94 . . . . Wilmington
LU 95 . . . . Wilmington
LU 96 . . . . Asheville

Graphic Communications
LU 318-C . . . . . . Clemmons
LU 465-S . . . . Sedalia

Hotel and Restaurant Employees
LU 36 . . . . Durham

Iron Workers
LU 781 . . . . . . Elizabeth City
LU 812 . . . . Leicester
LU 843. . . . . Greensboro

Laborers
LU 1699 Cherokee Indian Health Services . . . . . Cherokee

Letter Carriers
BR 248 . . . . Asheville
BR 382 . . . . Durham
BR 459 . . . . Raleigh
BR 461 . . . . . Winston-Salem
BR 464 . . . . Wilmington
BR 545 . . . . Charlotte

BR 630. . . . . Greensboro
BR 780. . . . . New Bern
BR 876. . . . . Goldsboro
BR 934. . . . . Salisbury
BR 935. . . . . Statesville
BR 936. . . . . High Point
BR 1044. . . . . Kinston
BR 1127 . . . . . Elizabeth City
BR 1128 . . . . . . Fayetteville
BR 1250. . . . . Hickory
BR 1286 . . . . Henderson
BR 1321. . . . . . Rocky Mount
BR 1510 Oxford, North Carolina . . . . Oxford
BR 1512 . . . . Gastonia
BR 1641 . . . . Wilson
BR 1670 . . . . Lumberton
BR 1719 . . . . Tarboro
BR 1729 . . . . Greenville
BR 1843 . . . . Morganton
BR 1852. . . . . Lenoir
BR 1898 Hamlet, North Carolina . . . . Hamlet
BR 1957 . . . . Lincolnton
BR 2216 Taylorsville, North Carolina. . . . . . Taylorsville
BR 2262 . . . . Burlington
BR 2300 . . . . Laurinburg
BR 2307 . . . . Shelby
BR 2381 . . . . Rockingham
BR 2486 . . . . Newton
BR 2560 . . . . Asheboro
BR 2571 North Wilkesboro, North Carolina . . . . North Wilkesboro
BR 2613 . . . . Chapel Hill
BR 2659 Wadesboro, North Carolina . . . . . . Wadesboro
BR 2669. . . . . Reidsville
BR 2679 Mount Olive, North Carolina . . . . . Mount Olive
BR 2731 . . . . Sanford
BR 2794 . . . . Kannapolis
BR 2872 . . . . Thomasville
BR 2893 Rutherfordton, North Carolina . . . . Rutherfordton
BR 3114 . . . . Havelock
BR 3119 Belhaven, North Carolina . . . . . . Belhaven
BR 3145 . . . . Grover
BR 3155 Williamston, North Carolina . . . . . Williamston
BR 3257 Whiteville, North Carolina . . . . . . Whiteville
BR 3281 Albemarle, North Carolina . . . . . . Albemarle
BR 3331 . . . . . Roanoke Rapids
BR 3561 Carolina Beach, North Carolina. . . . Carolina Beach
BR 3712 . . . . Eden
BR 3813 Forest City, North Carolina . . . . . Forest City
BR 3840 Plymouth, North Carolina . . . . . . Plymouth
BR 3859 Elkin, North Carolina . . . . Elkin
BR 3970 . . . . Parkton
BR 3984. . . . . Richlands
BR 4122 . . . . Roxboro
BR 4141 . . . . Bear Creek
BR 4206 Windsor, North Carolina . . . . Windsor
BR 4243 . . . . Benson
BR 4244 Franklinton, North Carolina. . . . . . Franklinton

BR 4264 Cherryville, North
Carolina . . . . Cherryville
BR 4392 Fairmont, North
Carolina . . . . Fairmont
BR 4460 St. Pauls, North
Carolina . . . . St. Pauls
BR 4563 Ayden, North
Carolina . . . . Ayden
BR 4637 Randleman, North
Carolina . . . . Randleman
BR 4765 Enfield, North
Carolina . . . . Enfield
BR 4883 Mayodan, North
Carolina . . . . Mayodan
BR 4970 . . . . Havelock
BR 5067 Tabor City, North
Carolina . . . . Tabor City
BR 5134 Scotland Neck, North
Carolina . . . . . Scotland Neck
BR 5253 . . . . Carrboro
BR 5322 Maiden, North
Carolina . . . . Maiden
BR 5367 Black Mountain, North
Carolina . . . . . Black Mountain
BR 5425 Franklin, North
Carolina . . . . Franklin
BR 5493 La Grange, North
Carolina . . . . La Grange
BR 5529 Madison, North
Carolina . . . . Madison
BR 5544 Landis, North
Carolina . . . . Landis
BR 5629 Spindale, North
Carolina . . . . Spindale
BR 5646 Red Springs, North
Carolina . . . . . . Red Springs
BR 5647 Murfreesboro, North
Carolina. . . . . . Murfreesboro
BR 5658 Sylva, North
Carolina . . . . Sylva
BR 5673 China Grove, North
Carolina . . . . . . China Grove
BR 5690 Dallas, North
Carolina . . . . Dallas
BR 5771 Wallace, North
Carolina. . . . . Wallace
BR 6081 Snow Hill, North
Carolina. . . . . Snow Hill
BR 6345 Jonesville, North
Carolina. . . . . Jonesville
BR 6369 Stanley, North
Carolina . . . . Stanley
BR 6482 Maxton, North
Carolina . . . . Maxton
BR 6528 Hillsborough, North
Carolina . . . . . Hillsborough
BR 6622 Aberdeen, North
Carolina. . . . . Aberdeen
BR 8009 Asheville, North
Carolina. . . . . Asheville
SA North Carolina . . . . Durham

Locomotive Engineers
DIV 166 . . . . Charlotte
DIV 208. . . . . Kernersville
DIV 267. . . . . Arden
DIV 314. . . . . . . Rocky Mount
DIV 375 . . . . Faith
DIV 435 . . . . Hamlet
DIV 849. . . . . Cary
DIV 932. . . . . Wilmington
SLB North Carolina . . . Asheville

Longshoremen
LU 1426. . . . . Wilmington
LU 1766 . . . . Wilmington
LU 1807 . . . . . . Morehead City
LU 1838 . . . . Southport

LU 1847 . . . . . . Morehead City
LU 1968 . . . . Southport

Machinists
DLG 110. . . . . Havelock
LG 108. . . . . Concord
LG 263. . . . . Kannapolis
LG 641. . . . . Hudson
LG 659. . . . . Charlotte
LG 757. . . . . Durham
LG 1725 . . . . Charlotte
LG 1859. . . . . Havelock
LG 2203 . . . . Elizabeth City
LG 2296 . . . . Havelock
LG 2297 . . . . Havelock
LG 2444 . . . . . . Winston-Salem
LG 2541 . . . . Wilson
LG 2555 . . . . Havelock
LLG W-354
Woodworkers . . . . Powellville
LLG W-369 Woodworkers . Sanford
STC North Carolina . . . . . King

Maintenance of Way Employes
LG 523 . . . . Reidsville
LG 525 . . . . Asheville
LG 537 . . . . Siloam
LG 563 . . . . Ridgeway
LG 1993 . . . . Albemarle
LG 2003 . . . . Dobson
LG 2161 . . . . Wilmington
LG 2369 . . . . Littleton
SLG 524 . . . . Gastonia
SLG 600 . . . . Newport
SLG 2102 . . . . Statesville

Mine Workers
LU 140 . . . . Spruce Pine

Musicians
LU 342 Charlotte . . . . . Charlotte
LU 500 . . . . Cary

National Staff Organization
LU Staff Organization, North
Carolina Association of
Educators . . . . Zebulon

Needletrades
LU 294-T . . . . Eden
LU 385-T . . . . Eden
LU 704-C . . . . Eden
LU 1391 . . . . Eden
LU 1708 . . . . Eden
LU 1867 . . . . Eden
LU 1948-002 . . . . Eden
LU 1948-006 . . . . Eden
LU 1994 . . . . Eden
LU 2535 . . . . Kannapolis
LU 2604 . . . . Kannapolis
LU 2605 . . . . Kannapolis
LU 2639 . . . . Eden

NLRB Professional Association
LU 11 . . . . Winston-Salem

Nurses
SA North Carolina Nurses
Association . . . . Raleigh

Nurses, Practical
NHQ . . . . Garner

Office and Professional Employees
LU 354. . . . . Plymouth

Operating Engineers
LU 415 . . . . Windsor

LU 465 . . . . Durham

Painters
LU 1865 . . . . Thomasville

Paper, Allied-Industrial, Chemical Employees
LU 02-425 . . . . . Roanoke Rapids
LU 02-428. . . . . Harrells
LU 02-429. . . . . Hiddenite
LU 02-507 Smoky
Mountain. . . . . Canton
LU 02-639. . . . . Raleigh
LU 02-738. . . . . . . Riegelwood
LU 02-853. . . . . . . High Point
LU 02-1139 . . . . Wilson
LU 02-1167 . . . . New Bern
LU 02-1268 . . . . . . Rockingham
LU 02-1283 . . . . Seaboard
LU 02-1325 . . . . New Bern
LU 02-1356. . . . . . Williamston
LU 02-1423 . . . . Plymouth
LU 02-1475. . . . . . . Whiteville
LU 02-1481. . . . . . . Whiteville
LU 02-1562. . . . . Advance
LU 02-1730 . . . . Spencer
LU 02-1821 . . . . Charlotte
LU 02-1825. . . . . Roanoke Rapids
LU 02-1870 . . . . Winston-Salem
LU 02-1947 . . . . Newton
LU 02-1971 . . . . Brevard

Plasterers and Cement Masons
LU 477. . . . . Charlotte

Police Associations
LU 105 Y . . . . Chapel Hill
LU 1869 Durham Police Officers
Association . . . . Durham

Postal and Federal Employees
D 3. . . . . Greensboro
LU 303. . . . . Greensboro
LU 311. . . . . Charlotte
LU 315 . . . . Durham
LU 316 . . . . Fayetteville
LU 317 . . . . Goldsboro
LU 318. . . . . Greensboro
LU 324. . . . . Raleigh
LU 335 Greensboro
BMC . . . . Greensboro

Postal Workers
LU 17 Elizabeth City . Elizabeth City
LU 24 Durham Area . . . . Durham
LU 145 Wilmington. . . Wilmington
LU 220 Washington
Local . . . . Washington
LU 277 Asheville . . . . Asheville
LU 375 Charlotte Area. . . Charlotte
LU 523 Winston-
Salem . . . . Winston-Salem
LU 591 Rocky Mount. Rocky Mount
LU 711 Greater Greensboro
Area . . . . Greensboro
LU 781 Gastonia . . . . . Gastonia
LU 984 Fayetteville . . . Fayetteville
LU 1046 Goldsboro . . . Goldsboro
LU 1078 Raleigh Cosmopolitan Area
Local . . . . Raleigh
LU 1125 Statesville. . . . Statesville
LU 1129 Greenville . . . Greenville
LU 1217 Chapel Hill . Chapel Hill
LU 1236 Salisbury. . . . Salisbury
LU 1305 Rockingham . Rockingham
LU 1537 Burlington . . Burlington
LU 1561 Mebane Local . . . Mebane

LU 1562 Lexington
Local . . . . Lexington
LU 1563 Eden . . . . Eden
LU 1564 Thomasville Local . Denton
LU 1615 Oxford Local . . . Oxford
LU 1616 Roanoke
Rapids . . . . . Roanoke Rapids
LU 1618 Wilson Area . . . Wilson
LU 1631 Morehead City
Local . . . . . . Morehead City
LU 1632 Franklin Local . . Franklin
LU 1637 Smithfield
Local . . . . Smithfield
LU 1638 Shelby . . . . . . Shelby
LU 1641 Hamlet Local. . . Hamlet
LU 1665 North Wilkesboro
Local . . . . . North Wilkesboro
LU 1666 Concord Local . . Concord
LU 1768 Whiteville
Local . . . . Whiteville
LU 1772 Edenton Local . . Edenton
LU 1807 Hickory . . . . . Hickory
LU 1808 Morganton
Local . . . . Morganton
LU 1809 Murphy Local . . . Murphy
LU 1810 Newton Local . . . Newton
LU 1901 Reidsville Local. Reidsville
LU 1950 Boone Local . . . Boone
LU 2095 Mount Airy
Local . . . . Mount Airy
LU 2154 Waynesville . Waynesville
LU 2158 Beaufort Local . . Beaufort
LU 2187 Siler City Local . Siler City
LU 2196 Kinston . . . . . Kinston
LU 2197 Plymouth Local . Plymouth
LU 2375 Elkin . . . . Elkin
LU 2376 Lenoir Local . . . Lenoir
LU 2508 Lincolnton
Local . . . . Lincolnton
LU 2788 Asheboro Local . Asheboro
LU 2933 Lauringburg
Local. . . . . Laurinburg
LU 2934 Southern Pines
Local. . . . . . . Southern Pines
LU 2950 Sylva Local . . . Sylva
LU 3268 Hillsborough
Local. . . . . Hillsborough
LU 3284 Jacksonville. . Jacksonville
LU 3424 Lillington Local. Lillington
LU 3483 Nashville Local . Nashville
LU 3553 Mount Olive
Local. . . . . . . Mount Olive
LU 3624 Lawndale . . . Lawndale
LU 3644 Havelock Local . Havelock
LU 3648 Highlands
Local . . . . Highlands
LU 3744 Maiden Local . . Maiden
LU 4560 High Point . . High Point
LU 6184 Kernersville
Local . . . . Kernersville
LU 6578 Weaverville
Local . . . . Weaverville
LU 6645 Arden Local. . . . Arden
LU 6671 Carrboro Local. . Carrboro
LU 7035 Greensboro Bulk Mail
Center . . . . Greensboro
SA North Carolina. . . Hillsborough

Retail, Wholesale and Department Store
LU 1050 . . . . . Roanoke Rapids
LU 1052 . . . . Stokesdale

Rural Letter Carriers
D Rockingham County . . Reidsville
D 1 Alamance County. . . Mebane
D 2 Albemarle . . . . . Nags Head
D 5 Peach Belt . . . . . . Hamlet

D 7 Roanoke Chowan. . . . Ahoskie
D 10 Foothills. . . . . . Statesville
D 11 Smokey Mountain . . Franklin
D 15 Catawba-Lincoln
   Counties . . . . Maiden
D 16 Central North
   Carolina . . . . Sanford
D 20 Cumerland-Hoke
   Counties . . . . . Southern Pines
D 23 Sea Level . . . . . . Garland
D 25 Tri-County
   Association. . . . . . Battleboro
D 28 Five County . . . . Louisburg
D 42 Randolph County . Randleman
D 44 Roanoke . . . . . . Plymouth
D 50 Piedmont . . China Grove
D 52 Tidewater . . . . Jacksonville
LU Alleghany County. . . . . Sparta
LU Ashe County . . . West Jefferson
LU Bushy Mountain . Hamptonville
LU Caswell County . . . Providence
LU Cleveland
   County . . . . . Kings Mountain
LU Durham County . . . . Durham
LU French-Broad
   Counties . . . . Black Mountain
LU Guilford County. . . Gibsonville
LU Mecklenburg
   County. . . . . Kannapolis
LU Orange County . . . Chapel Hill
LU Polk-Rutherford
   Counties. . . . . Hendersonville
LU Tar River. . . . . . Winterville
LU Union County . . . . Waxhaw
LU Wake County . . Fuquay Varina
LU Watauga-Avery Counties. Boone
LU Wayne County . . . Goldsboro
LU 8 Southeastern . . . . Winnabow

LU 9 Burke
   County . . . . Connelly Springs
LU 26 Yadkin River. Winston-Salem
LU 29 Gaston County. . . . . Dallas
LU 32 Harnett County . . Lillington
LU 34 Johnston County . Middlesex
LU 36 McDowell County . . Marion
LU 37 Mitchell County. . Burnsville
LU 41 Person County . . Timberlake
SA North Carolina . . . . Stoneville

**Security, Police and Fire
Professionals**
LU 415 . . . . Charlotte

Service Employees
LU 576 Firemen & Oilers. . Spencer

Sheet Metal Workers
LU 393 . . . . Moyock
LU 449 . . . . Gold Hill

**State, County and Municipal
Employees**
LU 77 Duke University
   Employees . . . . Durham

Steelworkers
LU 08-831-L . . . . Providence
LU 09-303-S. . . . . Badin
LU 09-335-U . . . . . Hazlewood
LU 09-345-L. . . . . . Hazlewood
LU 09-447. . . . . Stoneville
LU 09-959-L . . . . . Fayetteville
LU 09-1133-L . . Kings Mountain
LU 09-1811-S. . . . . Indian Trial
LU 09-7202-S. . . . . . . Franklin
LU 09-8205. . . . . . . Burlington

LU 09-8498-S . . . . Winston-Salem
LU 09-8573-S . . . . Landis
LU 94 . . . . Laurinburg

Teachers
SFED 8031 North
   Carolina. . . . . . . Wilmington

Teamsters
JC 9 . . . . Charlotte
LU 61 . . . . Asheville
LU 71 . . . . Charlotte
LU 391. . . . . Greensboro

Theatrical Stage Employees
LU 278. . . . . Asheville
LU 322. . . . . Charlotte
LU 417. . . . . Raleigh
LU 491 North Carolina Studio
   Mechanics . . . . . . Wilmington
LU 574. . . . . Greensboro
LU 635 . . . . . . Winston-Salem
LU 837 Charlotte Exhibition &
   Display Employees . . . Charlotte
LU 870 . . . . Fayetteville

Transit Union
LDIV 1328 . . . . Angier
LDIV 1493. . . . . Raleigh

Transport Workers
LU 248 . . . . . . Winston-Salem
LU 569. . . . . Raleigh

**Transportation Communications
Union**
D 16 . . . . Ellerbe
D 217 . . . . Rocky Mount

LG 6142 Pee Dee. . . . Rockingham
LG 6205 Spencer . . . . Salisbury
LG 6543 Twin City . . Rocky Mount

Transportation Union
GCA GO-898 Southern
   Railway . . . . Asheville
LU 782. . . . . Candler
LU 783. . . . . Lexington
LU 1011 . . . . Hamiet
LU 1021 . . . . Greensboro
LU 1105. . . . . Wilmington
LU 1106. . . . . . . Rocky Mount
LU 1129 . . . . Raleigh
LU 1166 . . . . Hunterville
LU 1715 . . . . Charlotte
SLB LO-36 North Carolina . Garner

Treasury Employees
CH 50 . . . . Salisbury
CH 203. . . . . Charlotte

Weather Service Employees
BR 01-33 . . . . Raleigh
BR 01-46 . . . . Wilmington
BR 01-52 . . . . Newport

Unaffiliated Labor Organizations

Contech Construction Products Inc.
   Shop Committee . . . . . Raleigh
Federal Education Association Inc.
   Stateside Region . . . Fayetteville
Federation of Union
   Representatives . . . . . Charlotte
National Association of Government
   Inspectors UNIT 6. . . . Havelock
Truck Drivers Association
   Inc. . . . . Greensboro

North Dakota

AFL-CIO Trade and Industrial Departments

Building and Construction Trades Department
BCTC Bismarck-Mandan . . Mandan
BCTC Grand Forks . . . Grand Forks
BCTC Minot . . . . Minot
BCTC North Dakota State . Mandan
BCTC Southeastern North
  Dakota . . . . Fargo

AFL-CIO Directly Affiliated Locals
C Fargo-Moorhead Central
  Labor . . . . Fargo

Affiliated Labor Organizations

Air Traffic Controllers
LU BIS . . . . Bismarck
LU FAR . . . . Fargo
LU GFK . . . . Grand Forks

Automobile, Aerospace Workers
LU 9429 . . . . Bismarck

Bakery, Confectionery, Tobacco Workers and Grain Millers
LU 135-G . . . . Grand Forks
LU 326-G . . . . Pembina
LU 372-G . . . . Cummings
LU 405-G . . . . Wahpeton

Bricklayers
LU 2 . . . . Minot
LU 4 . . . . Bismarck
STCON 99 North Dakota . . . Fargo

Carpenters
LU 1091 . . . . Bismarck
LU 1176 . . . . Fargo

Civilian Technicians
CH 112 Roughrider
  Chapter . . . . Devils Lake

Communications Workers
LU 7301 . . . . Bismarck
LU 7303 . . . . Fargo
LU 7304 . . . . Gilby

Electrical Workers
LU 203 . . . . Devils Lake
LU 239 . . . . Spiritwood
LU 395 . . . . Dickinson
LU 524 . . . . Wahpeton
LU 714 . . . . Minot
LU 971 . . . . Williston
LU 975 . . . . Bismarck
LU 1426 . . . . Grand Forks
LU 1532 . . . . Minot
LU 1570 . . . . Beulah

LU 1593 . . . . Hazen
SC U-13 Montana-Dakota
  Utilities . . . . Bismarck
SC U-27 Williston Basin Interstate
  Pipe . . . . Dickinson

Federal Employees
LU 175 . . . . Belcourt
LU 225 . . . . Fargo

Government Employees
LU 888 . . . . Bismarck
LU 1347 DoD . . . . . Grand Forks
LU 1888 AFGE-North
  Dakota-USDA-RD . . . . Minot
LU 2789 DoJ . . . . Reynolds
LU 2989 DoD . . . . . West Fargo
LU 3413 USDA . . . . . Bismarck
LU 3748 USDA . . . . . . Mandan
LU 3884 VA . . . . Fargo
LU 4046 MAFB . . . . . . Minot

Graphic Communications
LU 192-C . . . . Grand Forks
LU 240-C . . . . Bismarck

Iron Workers
LU 793 . . . . Mandan

Laborers
LU 580 . . . . Bismarck

Letter Carriers
BR 205 . . . . Argusville
BR 517 . . . . Grand Forks
BR 957 . . . . Bismarck
BR 965 . . . . Jamestown
BR 1090 . . . . Valley City
BR 1152 . . . . Minot
BR 1253 . . . . Mandan
BR 1388 . . . . Wahpeton
BR 1463 . . . . Dickinson
BR 1494 . . . . Williston
BR 1657 Devils Lake, North
  Dakota . . . . Devils Lake
BR 2287 Grafton, North
  Dakota . . . . Grafton
BR 3057 Carrington, North
  Dakota . . . . Carrington
BR 3078 Harvey, North
  Dakota . . . . Harvey
BR 3594 Enderlin, North
  Dakota . . . . Enderlin
BR 3922 Oakes, North
  Dakota . . . . Oakes
BR 3989 Rugby, North
  Dakota . . . . Rugby
BR 4806 Langdon, North
  Dakota . . . . Langdon
BR 5675 . . . . Bottineau
BR 6279 New Rockford, North
  Dakota . . . . . New Rockford
SA North Dakota . . . . . Bismarck

Locomotive Engineers
DIV 69 . . . . Grand Forks

DIV 160 . . . . Harvey
DIV 202 . . . . Fargo
DIV 671 Ogema . . . . . . Enderlin
DIV 695 . . . . Minot
DIV 746 . . . . Mandan
GCA Soo Line Railroad . . . Minot
SLB North Dakota . . . . . Bismarck

Machinists
LG 810 . . . . Fargo
LG 2525 . . . . Fargo
LLG W-384 Woodworkers . Pembina

Maintenance of Way Employes
LG 19 . . . . Minot
LG 750 . . . . Williston
LG 1326 . . . . Minot
LG 1334 . . . . Fargo
LG 1498 . . . . Max
LG 1654 . . . . Hannaford
SLG 249 . . . . Fargo
SLG 303 . . . . Jamestown
SLG 306 . . . . Mandan
SLG 1280 . . . . Grand Forks
SLG 1481 . . . . Minot
SLG 1524 . . . . Underwood
SLG 1552 . . . . West Fargo

Mine Workers
LU 1101 . . . . Beulah
LU 8957 . . . . Velva

National Staff Organization
LU Staff Organization, Professional,
  North Dakota Education
  Association . . . . . . Dickinson

Painters
LU 1962 . . . . Bismarck

Paper, Allied-Industrial, Chemical Employees
LU 07-10 . . . . Mandan
LU 07-560 . . . . Gwinner
LU 07-566 . . . . Bismarck
LU 07-663 . . . . Bismarck
LU 07-953 . . . . Jamestown

Plumbing and Pipe Fitting
LU 300 . . . . Mandan
SA North Dakota Pipe Trades . Fargo

Postal Workers
LU 55 Devils Lake . . . Devils Lake
LU 88 Fargo . . . . Fargo
LU 137 Williston . . . . . Williston
LU 139 Grand Forks . . Grand Forks
LU 154 Jamestown . . . Jamestown
LU 157 Minot . . . . Minot
LU 349 Bismarck . . . . . Bismarck
LU 590 Dickinson . . . . Dickinson
SA North Dakota . . . . Devils Lake

Rural Letter Carriers
LU Barnes County . . . . . Dazey
LU Big Four Unit . . . . . . Minot

LU Capital Tri-Counties . . Bismarck
LU Cass-Traill Counties . . . . Page
LU Dunn-Mercer Counties . . Hazen
LU Eddy-Foster
  Counties . . . . Carrington
LU Frontier Five
  Association . . . . Dickinson
LU Griggs-Stelle Counties . Binford
LU Lake Region Four Unit . Brocket
LU McLean County . . . Coleharbor
LU Missouri Slope
  Counties . . . . Bismarck
LU Red River Tri-County
  Association . . . . Fordville
LU Richland County . . . Wyndmere
LU Stutsman County . . . . Ypsilanti
LU 2 Southeast Four
  Counties . . . . Forman
LU 12 Peace Garden Unit . Westhope
LU 15 Central Four Unit . . . Harvey
LU 21 Logan-McIntosh
  Counties . . . . Wishek
LU 29 Northwest Tri Unit . Williston
SA North Dakota . . . . . Bismarck

Security, Police and Fire Professionals
LU 560 . . . . Osnabrock

Service Employees
LU 52 . . . . Minot
LU 618 Firemen & Oilers . . Mandan

Steelworkers
LU 11-901 . . . . Hebron

Teamsters
JC 82 . . . . Fargo
LU 116 . . . . Fargo
LU 123 . . . . Bismarck

Theatrical Stage Employees
LU 510 . . . . Fargo

Transportation Communications Union
LG 6440 Mandan . . . . . Bismarck

Transportation Union
LU 980 . . . . Enderlin
LU 1059 . . . . Minot
LU 1137 . . . . Fargo
LU 1344 . . . . Mandan
SLB LO-37 North Dakota . Bismarck

Treasury Employees
CH 2 . . . . Fargo
CH 157 . . . . Sarles

Weather Service Employees
BR 03-31 . . . . Bismarck
BR 03-53 . . . . Grand Forks
BR 03-90 . . . . Williston

Unaffiliated Labor Organizations
North Dakota Joint Legislative
  Board of Railway Labor FED
  73 . . . . Bismarck

Ohio

AFL-CIO Trade and Industrial Departments

Building and Construction Trades Department
BCTC Akron Tri-County . . . Akron
BCTC Butler County . . . Hamilton
BCTC Cincinnati . . . . . Cincinnati
BCTC Cleveland . . . . . Cleveland
BCTC Columbus . . . . . Columbus
BCTC Coshocton . . . . Cambridge
BCTC Dayton . . . . Dayton
BCTC East Central Ohio. . . Canton
BCTC Lima . . . . Lima
BCTC Muskingum County . . . . Zanesville
BCTC North Central Ohio. . . . . Sandusky
BCTC Northwestern Ohio . . Toledo
BCTC Ohio. . . . . Columbus
BCTC Upper Ohio Valley . . . . Steubenville
BCTC Western Reserve. . . . . . Youngstown

Maritime Trades Department
PC Cleveland . . . . . . Cleveland
PC Toledo . . . . Toledo

AFL-CIO Directly Affiliated Locals
DALU 22543 Olan Mills Production Employees . . . . . South Vienna
DALU 24729 Optical Workers . . . . . . Youngstown

Affiliated Labor Organizations

Air Traffic Controllers
LU CAK. . . . . . . North Canton
LU CLE. . . . . Cleveland
LU CMH . . . . Columbus
LU CVG . . . . Cincinnati
LU DAY . . . . Dayton
LU MFD . . . . Mansfield
LU TOL . . . . Swanton
LU YNG . . . . Vienna
LU ZOB . . . . Oberlin

Asbestos Workers
LU 3. . . . . Cleveland
LU 8. . . . . Cincinnati
LU 44 . . . . Columbus
LU 45. . . . . Waterville
LU 79 . . . . Dayton

Automobile, Aerospace Workers
C Ashtabula Geauga Lake County CAP . . . . Willowick
C Butler Warren Highland County CAP . . . . Fairfield
C Central Ohio Area CAP . Ashland
C Columbia Mahoning & Trumbull CAP . . . . Warren
C Columbus Franklin County CAP. . . . . Columbus
C Cuyahoga Medina CAP. . . . . Cleveland
C Dayton Metropolitan CAP. Dayton
C Defiance Area CAP . . . Defiance
C Fostoria Area CAP . . . . Fostoria

C Greater Cincinnati CAP . . . . West Chester
C Greater Springfield Area CAP . . . . Springfield
C Lima Troy Area CAP . . . . Lima
C Lorain County CAP . . . . Lorain
C Ohio State CAP. . . . . Columbus
C Portage-Summit CAP . . . . Stow
C Southeastern Ohio . . . . Logan
C Stark Wayne CAP . . . . Canton
C Toledo Area CAP . . . . . Toledo
C Tri County Area CAP . . Sandusky
LU 12. . . . . Toledo
LU 14. . . . . Toledo
LU 70 . . . . Bedford
LU 86 . . . . Napoleon
LU 91 . . . . Cleveland
LU 101 . . . . Elyria
LU 105 . . . . Wapakoneta
LU 118 . . . . Norton
LU 122 . . . . Twinsburg
LU 128 . . . . Troy
LU 169 . . . . Kent
LU 211 . . . . Defiance
LU 217 Cuyahoga Heights-Cleveland Local . . . . Cleveland
LU 294 . . . . . . Cuyahoga Falls
LU 336 . . . . Fostoria
LU 393. . . . . Sandusky
LU 402. . . . . Springfield
LU 420 . . . . Bedford
LU 425 . . . . Lorain
LU 486 . . . . Cleveland
LU 493. . . . . Bellevue
LU 497 . . . . Port Clinton
LU 533 . . . . Fostoria
LU 538 . . . . Brook Park
LU 549 . . . . Mansfield
LU 573 . . . . Streetsboro
LU 638 . . . . Defiance
LU 647 . . . . Cincinnati
LU 658 . . . . Springfield
LU 674 . . . . Fairfield
LU 696 . . . . Dayton
LU 775 . . . . Fostoria
LU 785 . . . . Kettering
LU 856 . . . . Akron
LU 863 . . . . Cincinnati
LU 877 . . . . Neapolis
LU 886 . . . . Byesville
LU 888 . . . . Dayton
LU 902 . . . . Springfield
LU 913. . . . . Sandusky
LU 959 . . . . Fremont
LU 962 . . . . Spencerville
LU 969 . . . . Columbus
LU 975 . . . . Lima
LU 996 . . . . Elyria
LU 1005. . . . . Parma
LU 1033. . . . . Forest
LU 1037. . . . . Heath
LU 1040 . . . . Dayton
LU 1050. . . . . Cleveland
LU 1055. . . . . McArthur
LU 1063 . . . . Richmond Heights
LU 1094 . . . . Clinton
LU 1112 . . . . Warren
LU 1120. . . . . Marblehead
LU 1181 . . . . Fayette
LU 1196. . . . . Cleveland
LU 1216 . . . . Sandusky
LU 1219 . . . . Lima
LU 1224 . . . . Piqua
LU 1239. . . . . Wooster
LU 1250 . . . . Brook Park

LU 1327. . . . . Bluffton
LU 1366 . . . . Hamilton
LU 1379 . . . . Norwalk
LU 1435 . . . . Perrysburg
LU 1437 . . . . Kenton
LU 1460. . . . . Cincinnati
LU 1484 . . . . Fostoria
LU 1549. . . . . Logan
LU 1588 . . . . Delaware
LU 1619. . . . . Lodi
LU 1623 . . . . Bellevue
LU 1685 . . . . Gallipolis
LU 1686 . . . . Crooksville
LU 1688 . . . . Fairfield
LU 1714 . . . . Warren
LU 1741 . . . . Wickliffe
LU 1765 . . . . Lima
LU 1790 . . . . Logan
LU 1802 . . . . Mount Gilead
LU 1803. . . . . Carey
LU 1825 . . . . Quaker City
LU 1834. . . . . Ashtabula
LU 1842 . . . . Greenfield
LU 1871 . . . . Antwerp
LU 1876 . . . . Springfield
LU 1889 . . . . . North Baltimore
LU 1892 . . . . Toledo
LU 1932. . . . . Ashland
LU 1935. . . . . Hicksville
LU 1939 . . . . . . Mount Vernon
LU 1957 . . . . Sandusky
LU 1978 Obetz-Columbus Local. . . . . Tariton
LU 2000 . . . . . Sheffield Village
LU 2005 . . . . Westerville
LU 2015 . . . . Cleveland
LU 2021 . . . . Carey
LU 2024 . . . . Byesville
LU 2029. . . . . Cincinnati
LU 2063 . . . . Bellevue
LU 2075 . . . . Lima
LU 2089 . . . . Archbold
LU 2147 . . . . Lima
LU 2192 . . . . Elyria
LU 2219 . . . . Dayton
LU 2262 . . . . Euclid
LU 2269 . . . . Richwood
LU 2279. . . . . Delphos
LU 2308 . . . . Trenton
LU 2331 . . . . Wauseon
LU 2332 . . . . Franklin
LU 2333 . . . . Cleveland
LU 2352 . . . . Milan
LU 2353 Mesa . . . . . Mansfield
LU 2359 Mesa . . . . . Eastlake
LU 2375 . . . . Deshler
LU 2387 . . . . Lebanon
LU 2391 . . . . Minster
LU 2413 . . . . Greenville
LU 2425 . . . . Cridersville
LU 2562 . . . . Cleveland
LU 2901. . . . . Girard
LU 4199. . . . . Salem
LU 4444 Mesa . . . . . . Toledo

Bakery, Confectionery, Tobacco Workers and Grain Millers
LU 19 . . . . Cleveland
LU 33-A. . . . . Akron
LU 39-G . . . . Parma
LU 56 . . . . Cleveland
LU 57 . . . . Columbus
LU 58-G . . . . Toledo
LU 138-G . . . . . . Wapakoneta
LU 180-G . Washington Court House

LU 208-G . . . . Cincinnati
LU 253 . . . . Cincinnati
LU 256-G . . . . Cincinnati
LU 294-G . . . . Fremont
LU 336-G . . . . Delphos
LU 346-G . . . . Marion
LU 382-G . . . . . . Fort Loramie

Boilermakers
C State of Ohio 'Buckeye' Industrial. . . . . Canton
LG National Transient Lodge. . . . . Maumee
LG 2-M. . . . . Maumee
LG 3-M . . . . . . East Cleveland
LG 4-p . . . . Youngstown
LG 5-M . . . . Laura
LG 85. . . . . Rossford
LG 105 . . . . Piketon
LG 106. . . . . Okeana
LG 108-M . . . . Sidney
LG 301-M . . . . Bryan
LG 337-D Cement Workers . . . . Sandusky
LG 357-D Cement Workers . . . . Fairborn
LG 375-D Cement Workers . . . . Oakwood
LG 416-D Cement Workers . Lorain
LG 597-D . . . . Clay Center
LG 744 . . . . Cleveland
LG 900 . . . . Barberton
LG 908 . . . . Wooster
LG 1073. . . . . Cleveland
LG 1086. . . . . Parma
LG 1191 . . . . Canton
LG 1603. . . . . Alliance
LG 1622. . . . . Minerva
LG 1633 . . . . Ironton
LG 1664 . . . . Warrensville
LG 1666 . . . . Kettering
LG 1667 . . . . Marion
LG 1702. . . . . Alliance
LG 1704 . . . . Thompson

Bricklayers
DC Northern Ohio . . . Middleburg Heights
DC 96 Southern Ohio . . . Columbus
LU 1 . . . . Defiance
LU 3 . . . . Toledo
LU 5 . . . . Cleveland
LU 6 . . . . Canton
LU 6 Apprenticeship Fund . . Canton
LU 7 . . . . Akron
LU 7 . . . . Ironton
LU 8 . . . . Youngstown
LU 9 . . . . Bethesda
LU 10. . . . . East Liverpool
LU 14. . . . . Steubenville
LU 15 . . . . Marietta
LU 16 . . . . Mentor
LU 18 . . . . Cincinnati
LU 22 . . . . Dayton
LU 32. . . . . Pomeroy
LU 35. . . . . Lima
LU 36 . . . . Cleveland
LU 39 . . . . . West Portsmouth
LU 40 . . . . Mansfield
LU 43 . . . . Warren
LU 44 . . . . Zanesville
LU 45 . . . . Chillicothe
LU 46 . . . . Fremont
LU 52. . . . . Athens
LU 55 . . . . Columbus

Carpenters

C Ohio & Vicinity Regional
Council . . . . Cleveland
LU 2 . . . . New Vienna
LU 21 . . . . Cleveland
LU 69 . . . . Akron
LU 95 . . . . Mentor
LU 104 . . . . Dayton
LU 113 . . . . Middletown
LU 126 . . . . Cincinnati
LU 171 . . . . Youngstown
LU 186 . . . . Steubenville
LU 200 . . . . Columbus
LU 212 . . . . Cleveland
LU 248 . . . . Rossford
LU 305 . . . . Elyria
LU 356 . . . . Marietta
LU 372 . . . . Lima
LU 437 . . . . Portsmouth
LU 509 . . . . Cleveland
LU 639 . . . . Hartville
LU 650 . . . . Pomeroy
LU 684 . . . . Xenia
LU 698 . . . . Lebanon
LU 712 . . . . Springfield
LU 735 . . . . Mansfield
LU 940 . . . . Sandusky
LU 976 . . . . Marion
LU 1066 . . . . Monroe
LU 1138 . . . . Rossford
LU 1241 Millwright . . . Columbus
LU 1242 . . . . West Salem
LU 1359 . . . . Rossford
LU 1365 . . . . Rossford
LU 1393 . . . . Rossford
LU 1413 . . . . Lima
LU 1519 Millwright & Machinery
Erectors . . . . . South Point
LU 1542 . . . . Fairview Park
LU 1581 . . . . Napoleon
LU 1871 . . . . Cleveland
LU 2077 . . . . Columbus
LU 2239 . . . . Fremont
LU 2380 . . . . Forest Park
LU 2420 . . . . Newark
LU 2506 . . . . Marion
LU 2540 . . . . Wilmington

Catholic School Teachers

LU 3504 . . . . Youngstown

Communications Workers

LU 4300 . . . . Youngstown
LU 4302 . . . . Akron
LU 4309 . . . . Cleveland
LU 4310 . . . . Columbus
LU 4318 . . . . St. Clairsville
LU 4319 . . . . Rossford
LU 4320 . . . . Columbus
LU 4321 . . . . Zanesville
LU 4322 . . . . Dayton
LU 4323 . . . . Fostoria
LU 4325 . . . . Lancaster
LU 4326 . . . . Springfield
LU 4340 . . . . Cleveland
LU 4351 . . . . Cincinnati
LU 4352 . . . . Toledo
LU 4370 . . . . Lorain
LU 4371 . . . . Marion
LU 4372 . . . . Portsmouth
LU 4373 . . . . Tiltonsville
LU 4375 . . . . Athens
LU 4377 . . . . Celina
LU 4378 . . . . Bryan
LU 4379 . . . . Perrysburg
LU 4385 . . . . . New Philadelphia
LU 4386 . . . . Urbana
LU 4390 . . . . Cleveland

LU 4400 . . . . Cincinnati
LU 4401 . . . . Cincinnati
LU 4404 . . . . Vandalia
LU 4470 . . . . Bluffton
LU 4471 . . . . Pataskala
LU 4473 . . . . Bellefontaine
LU 4474 . . . . Smithville
LU 4475 . . . . Warren
LU 4484 . . . . North Royalton
LU 4485 . . . . Elyria
LU 4486 . . . . Kenton
LU 4487 . . . . Newark
LU 4488 . . . . Quaker City
LU 4501 . . . . Columbus
LU 4510 . . . . Portsmouth
LU 4527 . . . . Wintersville
LU 14323 . . . . Pedro
LU 14514 . . . . Akron
LU 14516 . . . . . . South Zanesville
LU 14517 . . . . Canton
LU 14519 . . . . Cincinnati
LU 14522 . . . . Coshocton
LU 14526 . . . . Shadyside
LU 14527 . . . . Navarre
LU 14529 . . . . Niles
LU 14532 . . . . Sandusky
LU 14535 . . . . Toledo
LU 14537 . . . . Lisbon
LU 34001 . . . . Cleveland
LU 34009 . . . . Cincinnati
LU 34011 . . . . Youngstown
LU 34043 Toledo Newspaper
Guild/CWA . . . . Toledo
LU 34157 . . . . Dayton
LU 54042 NABET Local
42 . . . . Massillon
LU 54047 . . . . Youngstown
STC Ohio . . . . Rossford

Education

SA Ohio Education
Association . . . . . . Columbus

Electrical Workers

BD Ohio State Electrical
Utility . . . . Rossford
LU 8 . . . . Rossford
LU 32 . . . . Lima
LU 38 . . . . Cleveland
LU 39 . . . . Cleveland
LU 64 . . . . Youngstown
LU 71 . . . . Galloway
LU 82 . . . . Dayton
LU 129 . . . . Lorain
LU 212 . . . . Cincinnati
LU 245 . . . . Rossford
LU 246 . . . . Steubenville
LU 306 . . . . Akron
LU 392 . . . . Greenville
LU 473 . . . . Harrison
LU 540 . . . . Massillon
LU 573 . . . . Warren
LU 575 . . . . Portsmouth
LU 578 . . . . Chillicothe
LU 648 . . . . Hamilton
LU 673 . . . . Mentor
LU 683 . . . . Columbus
LU 688 . . . . Mansfield
LU 696 . . . . Steubenville
LU 774 . . . . North Bend
LU 912 . . . . Mentor
LU 972 . . . . Reno
LU 986 . . . . Norwalk
LU 998 . . . . Vermilion
LU 1047 . . . . Perrysburg
LU 1076 . . . . Rossford
LU 1105 . . . . Zanesville
LU 1108 . . . . Greenwich

LU 1194 . . . . Milan
LU 1206 . . . . Nashport
LU 1224 . . . . Cincinnati
LU 1266 . . . . Miamisburg
LU 1347 . . . . Cincinnati
LU 1377 . . . . Cleveland
LU 1413 . . . . Oak Harbor
LU 1466 . . . . Columbus
LU 1507 . . . . Hudson
LU 1587 . . . . Pomeroy
LU 1612 . . . . Reynoldsburg
LU 1643 . . . . . . Upper Sandusky
LU 1654 . . . . Ottawa
LU 1691 . . . . Bellefontaine
LU 1740 . . . . Urbana
LU 1825 . . . . Ross
LU 1842 . . . . Goshen
LU 1853 . . . . Newark
LU 1907 . . . . Findlay
LU 1977 . . . . Tipp City
LU 1985 . . . . North Canton
LU 1996 . . . . Warren
LU 2020 . . . . Reynoldsburg
LU 2172 . . . . Bellevue
LU 2258 . . . . Middletown
LU 2287 . . . . Oxford
LU 2303 . . . . Akron
LU 2331 . . . . Circleville
LU 2359 . . . . Carroll
SC TCC-2 Telephone
Coordinating . . . . . . Norwalk

Electrical, Radio and Machine Workers

DC 7 . . . . Yellow Springs
LU 704 . . . . Cincinnati
LU 705 . . . . Niles
LU 707 . . . . Parma
LU 712 Kenyon Maintenance Skilled
Trades . . . . Danville
LU 714 . . . . Sandusky
LU 715 . . . . Edon
LU 731 . . . . Ashtabula
LU 751 . . . . Niles
LU 758 . . . . Jefferson
LU 764 . . . . Xenia
LU 766 . . . . Wapakoneta
LU 767 . . . . Yellow Springs
LU 777 . . . . Medina
LU 792 . . . . Fairborn

Electronic Workers

CONBD General Motors . . Warren
DC 7 . . . . Kettering
LU 670 . . . . Kitts Hill
LU 689 . . . . Dayton
LU 692 . . . . Newcomerstown
LU 704 . . . . Bucyrus
LU 705 . . . . Dover
LU 707 . . . . Cleveland
LU 708 . . . . Mansfield
LU 710 . . . . Jacksontown
LU 713 . . . . Heath
LU 715 . . . . Cleveland
LU 716 . . . . Warren
LU 717 . . . . Warren
LU 719 . . . . Mansfield
LU 722 . . . . Warren
LU 724 . . . . Youngstown
LU 725 . . . . Sidney
LU 726 . . . . Lima
LU 727 . . . . Cortland
LU 729 . . . . Cincinnati
LU 734 . . . . Youngstown
LU 737 . . . . Euclid
LU 742 . . . . Lima
LU 745 . . . . Columbus
LU 749 . . . . Tiffin

LU 750 . . . . Alliance
LU 755 . . . . Dayton
LU 757 . . . . Cincinnati
LU 758 . . . . Bellbrook
LU 765 . . . . Cincinnati
LU 768 . . . . Riverside
LU 771 . . . . Yellow Springs
LU 773 . . . . Cincinnati
LU 774 . . . . Norwood
LU 775 . . . . Dayton
LU 778 . . . . Cleveland
LU 798 . . . . Dayton
LU 801 . . . . Kettering

Elevator Constructors

LU 11 . . . . Cincinnati
LU 17 . . . . Cleveland
LU 37 . . . . Grove City
LU 44 . . . . Toledo
LU 45 . . . . Akron

Farm Labor Committee

NHQ . . . . Toledo

Federal Employees

LU 73 . . . . Bratenahl
LU 75 . . . . Lebanon
LU 2062 National Park
Services . . . . Akron

Fire Fighters

LU 88-F . . . . Fairborn
LU 154-F . . . . Vienna

Flint Glass Workers

LU 4 . . . . Newark
LU 25 . . . . Rockbridge
LU 60 . . . . Lancaster
LU 65 . . . . Toledo
LU 73 . . . . Lancaster
LU 105 . . . . St. Louisville
LU 121 . . . . Zanesville
LU 144 . . . . Lancaster
LU 502 . . . . Cambridge
LU 506 . . . . Lancaster
LU 516 . . . . Blanchester
LU 520 . . . . Zanesville
LU 525 . . . . Newark
LU 540 . . . . Lancaster
LU 561 . . . . Lancaster
LU 575 . . . . Lancaster
LU 576 . . . . Lancaster
LU 577 . . . . Lancaster
LU 578 . . . . Logan
LU 598 . . . . Lancaster
LU 600 . . . . Perrysburg
LU 700 . . . . Toledo
LU 725 . . . . Union City
LU 1017 . . . . Logan
LU 1018 . . . . Greenville
LU 1033 . . . . Hiram
NHQ . . . . Toledo

Food and Commercial Workers

C Chemical Workers Council . . Akron
C Ohio State . . . . Cleveland
LU Textile Workers . . . . Cleveland
LU 1 Textile Workers . . . Cleveland
LU 2-C . . . . Akron
LU 7-A . . . . Cincinnati
LU 17-A . . . . Canton
LU 20-C . . . . . New Philadelphia
LU 32-D . . . . Cincinnati
LU 50-I . . . . Cincinnati
LU 54-I . . . . Reynoldsburg
LU 58-I . . . . Cleveland Heights
LU 59-I . . . . North Ridgeville
LU 60-I . . . . Warren

LU 73-C . . . . Elyria
LU 76 . . . . Silverlake
LU 83 . . . . Portage
LU 181 . . . . Dayton
LU 207-C . . . Cuyahoga Falls
LU 342-C . . . . Loveland
LU 343-C . . . . Caldwell
LU 418-C . . . . Cleveland
LU 419-C . . . . Mogadore
LU 501-C . . . . Blanchester
LU 554-C . . . . . Fairview Park
LU 776-C . . . . Circleville
LU 777-T . . . . Port Clinton
LU 838-C . . . . Willoughby
LU 852-C . . . . Elyria
LU 880 . . . . Cleveland
LU 911 . . . . Holland
LU 1020-C . . . . Akron
LU 1033-C . . . . Akron
LU 1034-C . . . . Akron
LU 1059 . . . . Columbus
LU 1099 . . . . Monroe
RB Ohio . . . . Cincinnati

Glass, Molders, Pottery and Plastics Workers
CONBD Ohio . . . . Malta
LU 7-A . . . . Tiffin
LU 24 . . . . . . East Liverpool
LU 45-B . . . . Columbus
LU 51 . . . . Defiance
LU 59 . . . . Toledo
LU 68-B . . . . Hamilton
LU 73 . . . . Euclid
LU 105 . . . . Nashport
LU 123 . . . . Union City
LU 127 . . . . Fairfield
LU 152 . . . . Bridgeport
LU 159 . . . . Philo
LU 164 . . . . Howard
LU 170 . . . . Cincinnati
LU 172 . . . . Zanesville
LU 178 . . . . Zanesville
LU 191 . . . . . New Lexington
LU 207-A . . . . Roseville
LU 235 . . . . Circleville
LU 241 . . . . . East Palestine
LU 244 . . . . Newark
LU 249 . . . . . New Lexington
LU 274 . . . . . East Liverpool
LU 288 . . . . Pickerington
LU 292 . . . . Zanesville
LU 299 . . . . Youngstown
LU 304 . . . . Carey
LU 306 . . . . . . Reynoldsburg
LU 314 . . . . Nashport
LU 328 . . . . . East Liverpool
LU 333-A . . . . East Liverpool
LU 343 . . . . . . New Bremen
LU 380-A . . . . Minerva
LU 384 . . . . Columbiana
LU 389 . . . . Newark
LU 417 . . . . . East Liverpool
LU 419 . . . . . East Liverpool

Government Employees
C 73 National Field Labor Locals . . . . Cleveland
C 164 Guard-Reserve Technician . . . . . Walbridge
C 214 National AFLC Locals . . . . . Wright-Patterson Air Force Base
C 262 . . . . Cleveland
LU . . . . Cincinnati
LU 31 VAMC . . . . . Brecksville
LU 43 IAEP Local 43 . . . . . Akron
LU 128 GSA . . . . . . Cincinnati

LU 519 USDA . . . . . . Huron
LU 600 . . . . Mason
LU 601 . . . . Dayton
LU 602 . . . . Lima
LU 604 . . . . Cleveland
LU 605 . . . . Cleveland
LU 607 . . . . Elkton
LU 1138 DoD . . . . . . Dayton
LU 1148 DoD . . . . . . Columbus
LU 1631 VA . . . . . Chillicothe
LU 1952 DoD . . . . . . Vienna
LU 2031 VA . . . . . Cincinnati
LU 2083 USDA . . . . Cincinnati
LU 2089 DoL . . . . . Columbus
LU 2182 NASA . . . . Cleveland
LU 2209 VA . . . . . . Dayton
LU 2221 DoD . . . . . . Heath
LU 2660 DoJ . . . . . Cleveland
LU 2823 VA . . . . . Cleveland
LU 2835 USDA . . . . . Sardinia
LU 3283 DoD . . . . . Cleveland
LU 3435 HUD . . . . . Columbus
LU 3448 HHS . . . . . Newark
LU 3701 HUD . . . . . Cleveland
LU 3840 HHS . . . . . Cincinnati
LU 3924 . . . . Chillicothe
LU 3970 Ohio Air and Army National Guard . . . . Walbridge

Government Security Officers
LU 56 . . . . Cleveland
LU 114 . . . . Miamisburg
LU 127 . . . . Dublin

Graphic Communications
DJC Tri-State . . . . East Liverpool
LU 5-N . . . . Parma
LU 26-B . . . . Canton
LU 42-C . . . . Barberton
LU 55-C . . . . Whitehouse
LU 62-C . . . . Brice
LU 147-B . . . . Columbus
LU 205-C . . . . . . Youngstown
LU 235-C . . . . . . Middletown
LU 269-M . . . . Logan
LU 270-M . . . . Ottawa
LU 334-C . . . . . . Greenwich
LU 419-M . . . . Warren
LU 508-M . . . . . . Cincinnati
LU 544-C . . . . Canton
LU 546-M . . . . . . Cleveland
LU 566-M . . . . Fostoria
LU 638-S . . . . . East Liverpool
LU 666-S . . . . Shelby
LU 731-S . . . . Norwalk
LU 774-S . . . . . New Holland

Guards
LU 14 . . . . Harrison

Hotel and Restaurant Employees
LU 10 . . . . Macedonia
LU 12 . . . . Cincinnati
LU 84 . . . . Toledo

Independent Unions Federation
LU 5 Zanesville Armco Independent Organization . . . . . Zanesville
LU 239 United Electro-Medical Workers . . . . . . Reading
LU 611 National Industrial Workers . . . . Lima

Industrial Workers
LU 52 . . . . Defiance
NHQ . . . . Defiance

Iron Workers
DC Southern Ohio & Vicinity . . . . Franklin
LU 17 . . . . Cleveland
LU 44 . . . . Cincinnati
LU 55 . . . . Toledo
LU 172 . . . . Columbus
LU 207 . . . . Youngstown
LU 290 . . . . Dayton
LU 372 . . . . Cincinnati
LU 468 . . . . Cleveland
LU 522 . . . . Cincinnati
LU 550 . . . . Canton
LU 778 . . . . Harrod
LU 820 . . . . Fredericktown

Laborers
DC Ohio . . . . . . Westerville
LU 83 . . . . Portsmouth
LU 125 . . . . Youngstown
LU 134 . . . . . Newcomerstown
LU 141 Industrial & Service Employees . . . . . . Dayton
LU 216 . . . . Springfield
LU 245 . . . . Ashtabula
LU 265 . . . . Cincinnati
LU 310 . . . . Cleveland
LU 329 . . . . Lima
LU 423 . . . . Columbus
LU 480 . . . . Sandusky
LU 496 . . . . Madison
LU 500 . . . . Toledo
LU 513 . . . . Winchester
LU 530 . . . . Zanesville
LU 534 . . . . Middletown
LU 574 . . . . Marion
LU 639 . . . . Marietta
LU 758 . . . . Lorain
LU 809 . . . . Steubenville
LU 860 . . . . Cleveland
LU 894 . . . . Akron
LU 935 . . . . Warren
LU 1015 . . . . Canton
LU 1216 . . . . Mansfield
LU 1311 . . . . South Point
LU 1410 . . . . Dayton

Letter Carriers
BR 40 . . . . Cleveland
BR 43 . . . . Cincinnati
BR 45 . . . . Springfield
BR 63 . . . . Zanesville
BR 66 . . . . St. Clairsville
BR 78 . . . . Columbus
BR 84 Williams County . Alvordton
BR 100 . . . . Toledo
BR 105 . . . . Lima
BR 118 . . . . Mansfield
BR 123 . . . . Piqua
BR 140 . . . . Ironton
BR 143 . . . . Findlay
BR 144 . . . . Sandusky
BR 148 . . . . Akron
BR 154 . . . . Marietta
BR 164 . . . . Steubenville
BR 174 . . . . Norwalk
BR 182 . . . . Dayton
BR 184 . . . . Portsmouth
BR 196 . . . . Elyria
BR 238 . . . . Canton
BR 279 . . . . Fostoria
BR 280 . . . . Marion
BR 281 . . . . Newark
BR 288 Washington Court House, Ohio . . Washington Court House
BR 297 . . . . Alliance
BR 298 . . . . . . Mount Vernon
BR 307 . . . . Urbana

BR 340 . . . . Bremen
BR 385 . . . . Youngstown
BR 413 . . . . Tiffin
BR 426 . . . . Hamilton
BR 452 . . . . Chillicothe
BR 465 . . . . Bellefontaine
BR 470 . . . . Defiance
BR 480 . . . . Wooster
BR 482 . . . . Ashtabula
BR 549 . . . . Painesville
BR 583 . . . . Lorain
BR 634 . . . . Cambridge
BR 647 . . . . Coshocton
BR 648 Van Wert, Ohio . . Van Wert
BR 711 . . . . . New Philadelphia
BR 714 . . . . Bellaire
BR 721 . . . . Ashland
BR 800 . . . . Niles
BR 829 Greenfield, Ohio . Greenfield
BR 897 . . . . Barberton
BR 898 . . . . Dover
BR 997 . . . . Athens
BR 1002 St. Marys, Ohio . St. Marys
BR 1061 . . . . Martins Ferry
BR 1137 Bellevue, Ohio . . Bellevue
BR 1149 . . . . Xenia
BR 1224 Wellston, Ohio . . Wellston
BR 1240 . . . . . . Uhrichsville
BR 1252 Jackson, Ohio . . . Jackson
BR 1354 . . . . Barnesville
BR 1380 Cadiz, Ohio . . . . Cadiz
BR 1387 West Chester, Ohio . . . . . . West Chester
BR 1424 Gallipolis, Ohio . Gallipolis
BR 1460 Upper Sandusky, Ohio . . . . Upper Sandusky
BR 1461 Sebring, Ohio . . Sebring
BR 1571 Logan, Ohio . . . . Logan
BR 1629 . . . . . . Cuyahoga Falls
BR 1634 . . . . Wadsworth
BR 1687 New London, Ohio . . . . . . New London
BR 1716 Mount Gilead, Ohio . . . . . . Mount Gilead
BR 2017 Newcomerstown, Ohio . . . . Newcomerstown
BR 2055 . . . . Bradford
BR 2056 Covington, Ohio . . . . . . Covington
BR 2199 Carey, Ohio . . . . Carey
BR 2201 Leipsic, Ohio . . . Leipsic
BR 2221 . . . . Toronto
BR 2238 Hicksville, Ohio . . . . . . Hicksville
BR 2250 Richwood, Ohio . . . . . . Richwood
BR 2308 Paulding, Ohio . . Paulding
BR 2367 North Baltimore, Ohio . . . . North Baltimore
BR 2537 Caldwell, Ohio . . Caldwell
BR 2575 New Lexington, Ohio . . . . New Lexington
BR 2618 Minerva, Ohio . . Minerva
BR 2644 New Bremen, Ohio . . . . . . New Bremen
BR 2678 Pomeroy, Ohio . . Pomeroy
BR 2754 Middleport, Ohio . . . . . . Middleport
BR 2760 Shadyside, Ohio . . . . . . Shadyside
BR 2763 Byesville, Ohio . Byesville
BR 2969 . . . . . . Mingo Junction
BR 3095 Cardington, Ohio . . . . . . Cardington
BR 3188 Manchester, Ohio . . . . . . Manchester
BR 3422 Spencerville, Ohio . . . . . . Spencerville

BR 3433 Camden, Ohio. . . Camden
BR 3437. . . . . Vermilion
BR 3440 Sabina, Ohio . . . . Sabina
BR 3443 Dunkirk, Ohio. . . Dunkirk
BR 3497 Bluffton, Ohio. . . Bluffton
BR 3595 Carrollton,
Ohio . . . . Carrollton
BR 3688 . . . . Willowick
BR 3823 . . . . Lushing
BR 3948 Cleves, Ohio . . . . Cleves
BR 3999 Fredericktown,
Ohio . . . . . . Fredericktown
BR 4195 . . . . Mentor
BR 4343 Belpre, Ohio . . . . Belpre
BR 4408 . . . . Lucas
BR 4592 Mechanicsburg,
Ohio. . . . . . . Mechanicsburg
BR 4804 . . . . Ravenna
BR 5081 . . . . Jeffersonville
BR 5234 Peebles, Ohio . . . Peebles
BR 5401 Ashville, Ohio . . Ashville
BR 5426 Chesapeake,
Ohio. . . . . Chesapeake
BR 5698 Garrettsville,
Ohio . . . . . . Garrettsville
BR 5699 Baltimore, Ohio . Baltimore
BR 5726 Bremen, Ohio . . . Bremen
BR 5727 Tiltonsville,
Ohio . . . . Tiltonsville
BR 5728 Yorkville, Ohio . Yorkville
BR 5729 Brilliant, Ohio. . . Brilliant
BR 5730 Oak Hill, Ohio . . Oak Hill
BR 5732 West Alexandria,
Ohio . . . . . . West Alexandria
BR 6018 Brewster, Ohio. . Brewster
BR 6071 West Lafayette,
Ohio. . . . . . West Lafayette
BR 6117 Johnstown,
Ohio . . . . Johnstown
BR 6280 . . . . Roseville
BR 6501 West Union,
Ohio. . . . . West Union
BR 6520 Uniontown,
Ohio. . . . . Uniontown
BR 6597 Lakeside Marblehead,
Ohio . . . . Lakeside Marblehead
SA Ohio . . . . Marion
SA West Virginia . . . . South Point

Locomotive Engineers
DIV 3. . . . . Brunswick
DIV 4. . . . . Perrysburg
DIV 34. . . . . Galloway
DIV 36. . . . . . . St. Louisville
DIV 79 . . . . Columbus
DIV 95 . . . . Cincinnati
DIV 234 . . . . Hilliard
DIV 257. . . . . Columbus
DIV 260. . . . . Geneva
DIV 273 . . . . Conneaut
DIV 281 . . . . Lima
DIV 292 . . . . Canton
DIV 306. . . . . Loudonville
DIV 329. . . . . Campbell
DIV 411 . . . . Warren
DIV 447 . . . . Bellevue
DIV 457 . . . . Toledo
DIV 480. . . . . Fairfield
DIV 481. . . . . Marietta
DIV 511 . . . . Portsmouth
DIV 526 . . . . Willard
DIV 565 . . . . Youngstown
DIV 607 . . . . Mentor
DIV 678 . . . . Harrod
DIV 735. . . . . Minerva
DIV 757 . . . . Tallmadge
DIV 876 . . . . Rossford
DIV 894 . . . . Powell

DIV 937 . . . . Millbury
NHQ. . . . . Cleveland
SLB Ohio. . . . . Canton

Longshoremen
C Lake Erie Coal & Ore
Dock. . . . . Oregon
DC Great Lakes . . . . Cleveland
LU 153 . . . . Maumee
LU 1317. . . . . Cleveland
LU 1768. . . . . Oregon
LU 1982 . . . . Toledo
LU 2000. . . . . Cleveland
LU 2052 . . . . Conneaut

Machinists
CONF Northeastern
States . . . . Zanesville
DLG 28 . . . . Zanesville
DLG 34 . . . . Cincinnati
DLG 54 . . . . Cleveland
DLG 57 . . . . Wauseon
LG 10-DS . . . . Parma
LG 22. . . . . Canton
LG 30-DS . . . . Alliance
LG 55 . . . . Columbus
LG 90. . . . . Mount Vernon
LG 105 . . . . Wauseon
LG 162 . . . . Cincinnati
LG 225 . . . . Dayton
LG 233 . . . . Cleveland
LG 244 . . . . Cleveland
LG 427 . . . . Marysville
LG 439 . . . . Cleveland
LG 523 . . . . Spencer
LG 584. . . . . Geneva-on-the-Lake
LG 813 . . . . New London
LG 912. . . . . Monroe
LG 956. . . . . Stryker
LG 986 . . . . Zanesville
LG 1019. . . . . Alliance
LG 1038. . . . . Columbus
LG 1042 . . . . Wauseon
LG 1130. . . . . Cleveland
LG 1151 . . . . Galion
LG 1203 . . . . Kent
LG 1210. . . . . Pemberville
LG 1228 . . . . Warren
LG 1234. . . . . Zanesville
LG 1280 . . . . Newark
LG 1285. . . . . Dover
LG 1297. . . . . Ashland
LG 1320. . . . . Columbus
LG 1329. . . . . Sandusky
LG 1346. . . . . Tiffin
LG 1347. . . . . Bellevue
LG 1349. . . . . Bryan
LG 1356. . . . . Defiance
LG 1363. . . . . Cleveland
LG 1412 . . . . Beach City
LG 1444. . . . . Medina
LG 1471. . . . . Columbus
LG 1539 . . . . Amherst
LG 1552 . . . . Tallmadge
LG 1581. . . . . Wooster
LG 1628. . . . . Zanesville
LG 1711. . . . . Sandusky
LG 1731. . . . . Cleveland
LG 1802 . . . . Wauseon
LG 1825 . . . . . . Sheffield Lake
LG 1849 . . . . Elyria
LG 1901. . . . . Hamilton
LG 2050 . . . . . . West Lafayette
LG 2159 . . . . Clyde
LG 2167 . . . . De Graff
LG 2276 . . . . Urbana
LG 2306. . . . . Columbus
LG 2333 . . . . Fairborn

LG 2334 . . . . Dayton
LG 2339-C Cleveland Inflight
Aircraft Lodge . . . . . Sylvania
LG 2475 . . . . Newcomerstown
LG 2484 . . . . Antwerp
LG 2492 . . . . Edon
LG 2535. . . . . Middletown
LG 2690 . . . . Cambridge
LG 2714 . . . . Marion
LG 2787 . . . . Springfield
LG 2794 . . . . Gambier
LG 2910. . . . . Wooster
STC Ohio . . . . Cleveland

Maintenance of Way Employes
FED Nickel Plate-Wheeling & Lake
Erie . . . . Oregon
LG 424 . . . . Hamilton
LG 532 . . . . Caledonia
LG 535. . . . . Peebles
LG 885 . . . . Cincinnati
LG 1047 . . . . Sardis
LG 1234. . . . . Salem
LG 1595. . . . . Ashland
LG 1650 . . . . Geneva
LG 1900. . . . . Londonville
LG 1978 . . . . Dayton
LG 2307 . . . . Solon
LG 2705 . . . . Defiance
LG 2742 . . . . Portsmouth
LG 3016. . . . . Ashtabula
LG 3064 . . . . Beavercreek
LG 3073 . . . . Steubenville
LG 3080 . . . . Uhrichsville
SF Consolidated Rail . . Port Clinton
SLG 267 . . . . Sycamore
SLG 566 . . . . Lucasville
SLG 580 . . . . Ironton
SLG 698 . . . . Carroll
SLG 741 . . . . The Plains
SLG 838 . . . . Zanesville
SLG 888 . . . . Pioneer
SLG 1037. . . . . Toledo
SLG 1264 . . . . Mansfield
SLG 1315 . . . . Hillsboro
SLG 1376 . . . . Willard
SLG 1377 . . . . . . Columbus Grove
SLG 1396 . . . . Marblehead
SLG 1432. . . . . Ravenna
SLG 1562 . . . . Westerville
SLG 1657 . . . . . . South Euclid
SLG 1664 . . . . Oregon
SLG 1679 . . . . Navarre
SLG 1975. . . . . Greenville
SLG 2624 . . . . Waterville
SLG 3007. . . . . Canfield
SLG 3017. . . . . Greenville
SLG 3018 . . . . Canton
SLG 3027 . . . . Wellsville
SLG 3061 . . . . Gahanna

Mine Workers
LU . . . . Cheshire
D 6 . . . . Shadyside
LU 283. . . . . Cambridge
LU 310 . . . . Cambridge
LU 892 . . . . Langsville
LU 911 . . . . Gallipolis
LU 1188 . . . . Coshocton
LU 1304 . . . . New Athens
LU 1340. . . . . Trimble
LU 1360. . . . . Adena
LU 1366. . . . . Trinway
LU 1447. . . . . . . Powhatan Point
LU 1496. . . . . Scio
LU 1506 . . . . Dillonvale
LU 1604 . . . . Duncan Falls
LU 1785 . . . . Bellaire

LU 1810 . . . . Beallsville
LU 1818. . . . . Dresden
LU 1857 . . . . Chester
LU 2262. . . . . Shadyside
LU 2792 . . . . Barnesville
LU 4994. . . . . . . Gnadenhutten
LU 5400 District 17 . . . Cheshire
LU 5497. . . . . Powhatan Point
LU 6989. . . . . New Lexington
LU 7690. . . . . Cadiz
LU 9695. . . . . . St. Clairsville

Musicians
CONF Tri-State . . . . . Warren
LU 1. . . . . Cincinnati
LU 4. . . . . Cleveland
LU 15-286 . . . . Toledo
LU 24 . . . . . . Cuyahoga Falls
LU 31 . . . . Fairfield
LU 86-242 . . . . . Youngstown
LU 101-473 . . . . Dayton
LU 103 . . . . Columbus
LU 111 Canton . . . . . Canton
LU 118 . . . . Warren
LU 142 . . . . Bridgeport
LU 159 . . . . Mansfield
LU 160. . . . . Springfield
LU 179 . . . . Marietta
LU 320 . . . . Lima
LU 482 . . . . Wheelersburg
LU 657 . . . . Willoughby

National Staff Organization
LU Staff Union, Professional,
Ohio Education
Association . . . . . Westerville
LU Staff Union/NSO, Association,
Ohio. . . . . Hilliard

Needletrades
LU 26-I . . . . Cleveland
LU 52 . . . . Cleveland
LU 171 . . . . Cleveland
LU 209 . . . . Cleveland
LU 296 . . . . Cleveland
LU 298 . . . . Cleveland
LU 367 . . . . Cleveland
LU 590-I . . . . Cleveland

NLRB Professional Association
LU 8 . . . . Cleveland
LU 9. . . . . Cincinnati

Nurses
LU . . . . Coshocton
LU . . . . Youngstown
LU Ohio Nurses
Association . . . . . . Cincinnati
LU Ohio Nurses Association Alliance
LU Unit . . . . Beloit
SA Ohio Nurses
Association . . . . . . Columbus
UNIT East Liverpool City
Hospital . . . . . East Liverpool
UNIT Hillside Nurses
Association . . . . . . Warren
UNIT Hoxworth Blood Center
Registered Nurses . . . . Loveland
UNIT Little Forest Medical Center
Nursing Home . . . . Boardman
UNIT Logan County Hi-Point
23 . . . . Bellefontaine
UNIT Lucas County Health
Department RN . . . . . Toledo
UNIT Ohio Geneva Nurses
Association . . . . . . Geneva
UNIT Ohio Nurses Association Allen
Memorial Hospital . . . . Grafton

UNIT Ohio Nurses Association
Ashtabula General . . . Ashtabula
UNIT Ohio Nurses Association PHN
of CCBH. . . . . North Olmsted
UNIT Ohio Nurses Association PPU
State VC Hospital . . . Lakewood
UNIT Ohio Nurses Public Health
Association . . . . Cleveland
UNIT Ohio Professional Staff Nurses
Association . . . . Akron
UNIT RN Coshocton County
Memorial Hospital . . . Coshocton
UNIT Salem Community Hospital
RN . . . . Salem
UNIT Visiting Nurse Service of
Toledo . . . . Toledo

Office and Professional Employees
LU 17 . . . . Parma
LU 19 . . . . Toledo
LU 98 . . . . Cincinnati
LU 339 . . . . Akron
LU 375 . . . . Cincinnati
LU 422 . . . . Chillicothe
LU 502 . . . . Oberlin
LU 514 . . . . Custar
LU 1313 . . . . Cincinnati
LU 1313 . . . . Oberlin
LU 1794 . . . . Cleveland

Operating Engineers
LU 18 . . . . Cleveland
LU 20 . . . . Cincinnati
LU 603 . . . . Mansfield

Painters
DC 6. . . . . Strongsville
DC 12 . . . . Cincinnati
LU 7 . . . . Toledo
LU 13 . . . . Cincinnati
LU 50 . . . . Cincinnati
LU 128 . . . . Westlake
LU 181 . . . . Cleveland
LU 240 . . . . Lorain
LU 249 . . . . Dayton
LU 308 . . . . Hamersville
LU 356 . . . . Zanesville
LU 372 . . . . Columbus
LU 387 . . . . Cincinnati
LU 406 . . . . Mansfield
LU 438 . . . . Steubenville
LU 473 . . . . North Royalton
LU 476 . . . . Youngstown
LU 555 . . . . Portsmouth
LU 603 . . . . Canton
LU 639 . . . . Strongsville
LU 643 . . . . Trenton
LU 765 . . . . Chesterland
LU 788 . . . . Sandusky
LU 841 . . . . Akron
LU 847 . . . . Columbiana
LU 867 . . . . Strongsville
LU 948 . . . . Toledo
LU 1020 . . . . Lima
LU 1103 . . . . Painesville
LU 1162 . . . . Akron
LU 1275 . . . . Columbus

Paper, Allied-Industrial, Chemical Employees
C Ashland Company
Wide . . . . Louisville
C Clark Oil Nationwide . Venedocia
LU 139 Region VIII. . . . Ashtabula
LU 200 . . . . Cleveland
LU 5-757 . . . . Cincinnati
LU 05-48 . . . . Trenton
LU 05-55 . . . . Franklin

LU 05-60 . . . . Perrysburg
LU 05-78 . . . . Atwater
LU 05-98 . . . . Mainville
LU 05-99 . . . . Goshen
LU 05-108 . . . . Montpelier
LU 05-109 . . . . Kenton
LU 05-112 . . . . Mason
LU 05-115 . . . . Middletown
LU 05-141 . . . . Defiance
LU 05-142 . . . . Willowick
LU 05-150 . . . . Doylestown
LU 05-173 . . . . Rittman
LU 05-211 . . . . Sandusky
LU 05-214 . . . . Middleburg Heights
LU 05-220 . . . . Massilon
LU 05-237 . . . . South Euclid
LU 05-243 . . . . . North Olmsted
LU 05-266 . . . . . . Miamisburg
LU 05-284 . . . . Mantua
LU 05-293 . . . . Troy
LU 05-332 . . . . Oceola
LU 05-334 . . . . Massillon
LU 05-339 . . . . Wooster
LU 05-346 . . . . Toledo
LU 05-363 . . . . Bayview
LU 05-377 . . . . Collins
LU 05-435 . . . . Lorain
LU 05-438 . . . . Brunswick
LU 05-443 . . . . Elyria
LU 05-450 . . . . Canton
LU 05-460 . . . . Malvern
LU 05-498 . . . . Mount Orab
LU 05-499 . . . . Marietta
LU 05-513 . . . . Cleveland
LU 05-524 . . . . Van Wert
LU 05-525 . . . . Sandusky
LU 05-526 . . . . . Mount Blanchard
LU 05-530 . . . . Norwood
LU 05-543 Lord Baltimore
Press . . . . Hamilton
LU 05-587 . . . . . Milford Center
LU 05-592 . . . . Andover
LU 05-598 . . . . Youngstown
LU 05-607 . . . . Tallmadge
LU 05-609 . . . . Cincinnati
LU 05-621 . . . . Atwater
LU 05-622 . . . . . Mayfield Heights
LU 05-624 . . . . Lima
LU 05-626 . . . . Kridersville
LU 05-639 . . . . Coolville
LU 05-643 . . . . Castalia
LU 05-662 . . . . Shreve
LU 05-672 . . . . Aurora
LU 05-673 . . . . Olmsted Falls
LU 05-689 . . . . Piketon
LU 05-701 . . . . Bryan
LU 05-711 . . . . Madison
LU 05-712 . . . . Hicksville
LU 05-716 . . . . Thurston
LU 05-718 . . . . . . New London
LU 05-728 . . . . Eaton
LU 05-730 . . . . Grove City
LU 05-731 . . . . Chillicothe
LU 05-756 . . . . Dalton
LU 05-781 . . . . Middletown
LU 05-799 . . . . Sandusky
LU 05-801 . . . . Orville
LU 05-811 . . . . Andover
LU 05-823 . . . . Franklin
LU 05-826 . . . . Willoughby
LU 05-829 . . . . Milford
LU 05-854 . . . . Ohio City
LU 05-864 . . . . Clarksville
LU 05-887 Congo . . . . Toronto
LU 05-912 . . . . Toledo
LU 05-962 . . . . Vermilion
LU 05-966 . . . . Madison
LU 05-967 . . . . Garfield Heights

LU 05-988 . . . . Chillicothe
LU 05-989 . . . . Cincinnati
LU 05-995. . . . Mingo Junction
LU 05-1070 . . . Washington Court
House
LU 05-1152 . . . . Lancaster
LU 05-1193 . . . . Dayton
LU 05-1195 . . . . Piqua
LU 05-1206 . . . . Franklin
LU 05-1228 . . . . Van Wert
LU 05-1237 . . . . Newark
LU 05-1240 . . . . Zanesville
LU 05-1250 . . . . Bedford Heights
LU 05-1258 . . . . Ravenna
LU 05-1263 . . . . Toledo
LU 05-1270 . . . . Ashtabula
LU 05-1313 . . . . Prospect
LU 05-1377 . . . . Salem
LU 05-1462 . . . . Hamilton
LU 05-1467 . . . . St. Paris
LU 05-1493 . . . . Dayton
LU 05-1494 . . . . Dayton
LU 05-1525 . . . . . Mount Vernon
LU 05-1528 . . . . Beloit
LU 05-1544 . . . . . . Valley View
LU 05-1547 . . . . Coshocton
LU 05-1560 . . . . Ashland
LU 05-1567 . . . . Batavia
LU 05-1571 . . . . Monroe
LU 05-1676 . . . . . . Middletown
LU 05-1738 . . . . Amelia
LU 05-1824 . . . . Avon Lake
LU 05-1838 . . . . Reading
LU 05-1967 . . . . Hamilton
LU 05-1968 . . . . Hamilton
LU 05-1973 . . . . Franklin
LU 05-1974 . . . New Philadelphia
LU 05-1996 . . . . Columbus
LU 05-2001 . . . . Cleveland
LU 05-4200 . . . . . . Middletown
LU 06-1108 . . . . Hicksville
LU 07-490 . . . . Andover
LU 07-634-008 . . . . . . Fremont

Plant Protection
LU 107 Cleveland Plants
Unit . . . . Cleveland
LU 108 Lima Plants Unit . . . Lima
LU 110 Lorain Plants Unit . Amherst
LU 111 Batavia Unit . West Chester
LU 112 Cleveland Casting Plants
Unit . . . . . . Warrensville Heights
LU 115 Ford Motor Company
Unit . . . . Sharonville

Plasterers and Cement Masons
LU 80 . . . . Cleveland
LU 109 . . . . Akron
LU 132 . . Washington Court House
LU 179 . . . . Youngstown
LU 404 . . . . Cleveland
LU 886 . . . . Toledo
STCON
Ohio . . Washington Court House

Plumbing and Pipe Fitting
LU 42 . . . . Norwalk
LU 50 . . . . Toledo
LU 55 . . . . Brooklyn Heights
LU 94 . . . . Canton
LU 95 . . . . Cambridge
LU 120 . . . . Cleveland
LU 162 . . . . Dayton
LU 168 . . . . Marietta
LU 189 . . . . Columbus
LU 219 . . . . Akron
LU 392 . . . . Cincinnati
LU 396 . . . . Boardman

LU 577 . . . . Portsmouth
LU 711 . . . . Columbus
LU 776 . . . . Lima
SA Ohio . . . . Westerville

Postal and Federal Employees
D 6 . . . . Cincinnati
LU 601 . . . . Dayton
LU 603 . . . . Cincinnati
LU 604 . . . . Cleveland
LU 605 . . . . Columbus
LU 611 . . . . Toledo
LU 612 . . . . Cincinnati

Postal Mail Handlers
LU 304 . . . . Cincinnati

Postal Workers
LU Dayton Area . . . . . Dayton
LU 72 Cleveland Area . . Cleveland
LU 120 Akron Area . . . Akron
LU 135 Defiance . . . . . Defiance
LU 164 Greater Cincinnati Ohio
Area . . . . Cincinnati
LU 170 Toledo . . . . Toledo
LU 193 Steubenville . . Steubenville
LU 232 Columbus . . . Columbus
LU 315 Lorain County Area . Elyria
LU 318 Portsmouth . . . Portsmouth
LU 358 Fremont . . . . . Fremont
LU 438 Lima . . . . Lima
LU 443 Youngstown . . Youngstown
LU 524 Canton . . . . . . Canton
LU 534 Sandusky . . . . Sandusky
LU 535 Zanesville . . . . Zanesville
LU 556 Cambridge. . . . Cambridge
LU 603 Newark . . . . . . Newark
LU 872 Willoughby . . Willoughby
LU 903 Mansfield . . . . Mansfield
LU 906 Barberton . . . . Barberton
LU 1180 Ironton . . . . . . Ironton
LU 1204 Lake Geauga Area . Mentor
LU 1268 Marietta . . . . . Marietta
LU 1399 Bryan Local . . . . Bryan
LU 1471 Geneva . . . . . Geneva
LU 1821 Wapakoneta
Local . . . . Wapakoneta
LU 1963 Cuyahoga
Falls . . . . . . Cuyahoga Falls
LU 2360 Mogadore
Local . . . . Mogadore
LU 2548 Ravenna . . . . . Ravenna
LU 2558 South Central Ohio
Area . . . . Chillicothe
LU 2824 Ashtabula . . . . Ashtabula
LU 2836 Gallipolis Local . Gallipolis
LU 2965 Warren . . . . . . Warren
LU 3120 St. Clairsville
Local . . . . St. Clairsville
LU 3291 Fostoria . . . . . Fostoria
LU 3352 Wickliffe . . . . Wickliffe
LU 3812 Martins Ferry . Bridgeport
LU 3913 Kenton Local . . . Kenton
LU 3957 Findlay. . . . . . Findlay
LU 3972 Springfield . . . Springfield
LU 4743 Athens . . . . . . Athens
LU 4764 Hillsboro Local . Hillsboro
LU 5129
Bellefontaine . . . . Bellefontaine
LU 5705 Urbana Local. . . . Urbana
LU 6528 Kent. . . . . Kent
LU 6530 Marion . . . . . . Marion
LU 6531 Tiffin. . . . . . . Tiffin
LU 6691 Tallmadge . . . . . Akron
LU 6691 Belpre Local . . . Coolville
LU 7038 Tri County . . . Cincinnati
LU 7105 Northfield. . . . Northfield
SA Ohio . . . . Dayton

Professional and Technical Engineers

C NASA. . . . . Cleveland
LU 7. . . . . Columbus

Railroad Signalmen

GC 58 Norfolk & Southern
   Railroad . . . . Bellevue
GC 60 United. . . . . . Beavercreek
LLG 10 . . . . Swanton
LLG 35 . . . . Eastlake
LLG 52 . . . . Cincinnati
LLG 64. . . . . Crestline
LLG 94. . . . . Springboro
LLG 109. . . . . Creston
LLG 216. . . . . Fostoria
LLG 231 . . . . Norwalk
LLG 236 . . . . Brunswick
LLG 237 Wheeling & Lake Erie
   Railroad Locomotive . . . Orrville

Retail, Wholesale and Department Store

LU 277 . . . . Rayland
LU 310. . . . . Grove City
LU 379 . . . . Columbus
LU 390 . . . . Cincinnati

Roofers, Waterproofers and Allied Workers

DC Mid-States
   Roofers. . . . . Youngstown
LU 42 . . . . Cincinnati
LU 44 . . . . Cleveland
LU 71. . . . . Youngstown
LU 75 . . . . Dayton
LU 86 . . . . Columbus
LU 88 . . . . North Canton
LU 134 . . . . Toledo

Rural Letter Carriers

D 1. . . . . Chesterland
D 2. . . . . Toronto
D 3. . . . . Cadiz
D 4 . . . . Graysville
D 5. . . . . South Point
D 6. . . . . Baltimore
D 7 . . . . Galion
D 8. . . . . Wellington
D 9. . . . . Sycamore
D 10 . . . . Sedalia
D 10 Hardin County. . . . Ridgeway
D 11 . . . . Winchester
D 12 . . . . Loveland
D 13 . . . . New Bremen
D 14 . . . . Liberty Center
LU Allen County. . . . . . . Cairo
LU Athens-Meigs-Vinton-
   Counties . . . . Albany
LU Brown County . . . . Sardinia
LU Carroll County. . . . Magnolia
LU Clark-Madison
   Counties . . . . . . South Solon
LU Columbiana County . . . Negley
LU Delaware County . . . Delaware
LU Fairfield County . . Pickerington
LU Harrison County . . . Carrollton
LU Highland County . . . Hillsboro
LU Knox County . . . Fredericktown
LU Licking County . . . . . Utica
LU Lorain County . . . . Wellington
LU Medina County . . . . . Medina
LU Mercer County . . Fort Recovery
LU Miami-Montgomery
   Counties. . . . . Laura
LU Monroe County. . . . Graysville
LU Muskingum County . Zanesville
LU Noble County . . . . . Caldwell

LU Ottawa County . . . Oak Harbor
LU Pickaway County. . . . Ashville
LU Portage County . . . . Mogadore
LU Richland County . . . . Shiloh
LU Ross County . . . . Chillicothe
LU Scioto County. . . . Lucasville
LU Seneca County. . . . . . Tiffin
LU Stark County. . . . Uniontown
LU Trumbull County . . . Cortland
LU Tuscarawas County . Millersburg
LU Van Wert County . . Rockford
LU Wayne County . . . . Shreve
LU Wood County . . . . Risingsun
LU 1 Adams County. . . Winchester
LU 3 Ashland County. . Loudonville
LU 4 Ashtabula County . Austinburg
LU 5 Lawrence County . South Point
LU 6 Auglaize County . Wapakoneta
LU 7 Belmont County . . . Maynard
LU 9 Butler County . . . . Trenton
LU 13 Clermont County . Loveland
LU 14 Henry County . . Napoleon
LU 17 Crawford County . . . . Tiro
LU 20 Defiance County . . Defiance
LU 21 Logan County . Bellefontaine
LU 32 Hancock County . . Arlington
LU 39 Jackson County . . . Jackson
LU 40 Jefferson
   County . . . . . . Bloomingdale
LU 48 Mahoning
   County . . . . . . Berlin Center
LU 49 Marion County . . . Marion
LU 56 Morgan
   County . . . . . McConnelsville
LU 73 Shelby County . . . Sidney
LU 689 Preble County. . . . Eaton
SA Ohio . . . . Attica

Security, Police and Fire Professionals

LU 64 . . . . Southington
LU 67. . . . . Canton
LU 122. . . . . London
LU 131 . . . . Huron
LU 134 . . . . Scott
LU 136 . . . . Perrysburg
LU 141 . . . . Mansfield
LU 145 . . . . Elyria
LU 146. . . . . Trenton
LU 166 . . . . Union
LU 167 . . . . Akron

Service Employees

D 925 . . . . Cleveland
DALU 3042 Billposters &
   Billers . . . . Strongsville
JC 25 Ohio . . . . Cleveland
LU . . . . Youngstown
LU 35 Firemen & Oilers . Columbus
LU 47 . . . . Cleveland
LU 85 . . . . Willoughby
LU 304 . . . . . . Sagamore Hills
LU 555 . . . . Cleveland
LU 637 Firemen &
   Oilers . . . . Proctorville
LU 700 Firemen &
   Oilers . . . . North Olmsted
LU 1199 NUHHCE, West
   Virginia/Kentucky/
   Ohio . . . . Columbus

Sheet Metal Workers

C Ohio Valley . . . . Toledo
LU 24 . . . . Dayton
LU 33 . . . . Cleveland
LU 183 . . . . Cincinnati
LU 287 . . . . Columbus
LU 368 . . . . Willowick

State, County and Municipal Employees

C 8 Ohio . . . . Worthington
LU . . . . Westerville
LU 4. . . . . Lorain
LU 4 OAPSE/Chapter
   782 . . . . Chillicothe
LU 4 Ohio Association of Public
   School Employees . . . Columbus
LU 11 Civil Service Employees
   Association . . . . . Westerville
LU 33 Goshen (OAPSE) . . Goshen
LU 101 Dayton Public Service
   Union . . . . Dayton
LU 217 Ohio Council 8. . Cincinnati
LU 282 Cincinnati Zoological
   Employees . . . . . Cincinnati
LU 684 Akron City Hospital
   Employees . . . . Akron
LU 797 . . . . Columbus
LU 1039 Portsmouth City
   Employees. . . . . . Portsmouth
LU 1252 O'Bleness Memorial
   Hospital Employees . . . . Athens
LU 1881 Professional Personnel,
   Association of. . . Shaker Heights
LU 2028 Boardman Community Care
   Center . . . . Youngstown
LU 2288 Hillside Hospital. . Warren
LU 2317 Barberton Citizens Hospital
   Employees . . . . . . Barberton
LU 2804 Trumbull Memorial
   Hospital Employees . . . . Warren
LU 2934 Ohio Valley Hospital
   Association
   Employees . . . . . Steubenville
LU 3098 Lucas County
   Non-Profit Agency
   Employees. . . . . Bowling Green
LU 3357 New York Council
   66 . . . . Copley

Steelworkers

LU 6197 . . . . Racine
LU 8027. . . . . Middletown
LU 9419. . . . . . . Powhatan Point
LU 01-2-L. . . . . Akron
LU 01-5-L. . . . . Akron
LU 01-7-L. . . . . Akron
LU 01-8-L. . . . . Atwater
LU 01-9 . . . . Perrysburg
LU 01-23-S . . . . Groveport
LU 01-24-A. . . . . . . McDonald
LU 01-45 . . . . . New Philadelphia
LU 01-48-U . . . . . . Rocky River
LU 01-50-L . . . . . . Coshocton
LU 01-76-L . . . . Akron
LU 01-77-L . . Warrensville Heights
LU 01-87-G . . . . Toledo
LU 01-87-L . . . . Dayton
LU 01-96 . . . . Akron
LU 01-98-L . . . . . . Newton Falls
LU 01-134-S. . . . . . . McDermott
LU 01-156-U . . . . . West Chester
LU 01-169-S . . . . . . Mansfield
LU 01-185-S . Warrensville Heights
LU 01-188-S . Warrensville Heights
LU 01-192 . . . . Springfield
LU 01-196-L . . . . Ashland
LU 01-200-L. . . . . . St. Marys
LU 01-207-L. . . . . . . Findlay
LU 01-241-L . . . . . Green Camp
LU 01-298-L . . . . . . Ravenna
LU 01-302-L . . . . . . Wooster
LU 01-341-S. . . . . Heath
LU 01-418-L. . . . . . Uniontown
LU 01-424-U. . . . . . Grove City
LU 01-496-L. . . . Newcomerstown

LU 01-505. . . . . New Lexington
LU 01-521. . . . . Dover
LU 01-523-B . . . . . . Leetonia
LU 01-524-L . . . . Shelby
LU 01-538-B. . . . . . Stonecreek
LU 01-550-L . . . . . . Naverre
LU 01-557-L . . . . Geneva
LU 01-563-L . . . . . . Crestline
LU 01-582-L . . . . . . Johnstown
LU 01-601-L . . . . . . Massillon
LU 01-627-L. . . . . . . Findlay
LU 01-667-L. . . . Newcomerstown
LU 01-673-L . . . . . . Bucyrus
LU 01-731-L . . . . . . Deerfield
LU 01-735-S . . . . . . Cleveland
LU 01-820-L . . . . Vinton
LU 01-843-L . . . . . . Marysville
LU 01-861-L . . . . Luckey
LU 01-876-L . . . . Dayton
LU 01-890-L . . . . . West Unity
LU 01-898-L . . . . . Rushsylvania
LU 01-905-L . . . . . . Ashtabula
LU 01-921-B . . . . . . Batavia
LU 01-931-L . . . . . New London
LU 01-982-L . . . . . Wapakoneta
LU 01-1014-L. . . . . . . Akron
LU 01-1020-L. . . . . . Ashtabula
LU 01-1042-L . . . Bowling Green
LU 01-1045-L. . . . . . . Akron
LU 01-1046-S . . . . North Canton
LU 01-1098-S . . . . . Cleveland
LU 01-1104-S . . . . . . Lorain
LU 01-1117-L. . . . . Marblehead
LU 01-1123-L . . . . . . Piqua
LU 01-1123-S . . . . . . Canton
LU 01-1124-S . . . . . Massillon
LU 01-1152-L . . . Bowling Green
LU 01-1157-S . . . . . Cleveland
LU 01-1170-S . . . . . Wadsworth
LU 01-1179-S . . . . . . Elyria
LU 01-1190-S . . . . Steubenville
LU 01-1200-S . . . . . . Canton
LU 01-1211-S . . . . . Yorkville
LU 01-1238-S . . . Martins Ferry
LU 01-1331-S . . . . . Struthers
LU 01-1375-S . . . . . . Warren
LU 01-1538-S . . . . . . Salem
LU 01-1761-S . . . . . Barberton
LU 01-1858-S . . . . . Goshen
LU 01-1915-S . . . . . . Clyde
LU 01-1949 . . . . Marion
LU 01-2116-S . . . . New Boston
LU 01-2155-S . . . . . McDonald
LU 01-2163-S . . . . Lowellville
LU 01-2173-S. . . . . Columbus
LU 01-2211-S. . . . . . Alliance
LU 01-2243-S . . . . . . Warren
LU 01-2265-S . . . North Olmsted
LU 01-2310-S . . . . Youngstown
LU 01-2324-S . . . . . Wellston
LU 01-2332-S . . . . Youngstown
LU 01-2342-S. . . . . Columbus
LU 01-2345-S . . . . . . Canton
LU 01-2354-S. . . . . . Lorain
LU 01-2361-S. . . . . . Alliance
LU 01-2377-S . . . New Middletown
LU 01-2463-S. . . . . . Salem
LU 01-2730-S . . . . . Wooster
LU 01-2737-S . . . . . . Dover
LU 01-2887-S . . . . . Navarre
LU 01-3047-S . . . . . . Poland
LU 01-3057-S . . . . . Ashland
LU 01-3059-S . . . . . Alliance
LU 01-3081-S . . . . . Ashtabula
LU 01-3210-S . . . . . Minster
LU 01-3211-S . . . . . St. Henry
LU 01-3241-S . . . . . Marietta
LU 01-3320-S . . . . . . Dayton

LU 01-3372-S . . . . . Columbiana
LU 01-3404-S . . . . . . Cincinnati
LU 01-3446-S . . . . Navarre
LU 01-3523-S . . . . Cortland
LU 01-3610-S . . . . Columbus
LU 01-3664-S . . . Franklin Furnace
LU 01-3703-S . . . . Toronto
LU 01-3816-S . . . . Salem
LU 01-4372-S . . . . Lebanon
LU 01-4377-S . . . . Coshocton
LU 01-4427-S . . . . Hubbard
LU 01-4545-S . . . . . Englewood
LU 01-4564-S . . . . Girard
LU 01-4708-S . . . . Logan
LU 01-4836-S . . . . . Sarahsville
LU 01-4839-S . . . . . . Coldwater
LU 01-4960-S . . . . . . Hubbard
LU 01-5000-S . Middleburg Heights
LU 01-5025-S . . . . . . Boardman
LU 01-5154-S . . . . . . Campbell
LU 01-5439-S . . . . . Magnolia
LU 01-5644-S . . . . . . Toronto
LU 01-5724-S . . . . . Clarington
LU 01-5760-S . . . . Sardis
LU 01-5962-S . . . . Warren
LU 01-6037-S . . . . Stow
LU 01-6328-S . . . . Russia
LU 01-6413-S . . . . . Deer Park
LU 01-6463-S . . . . Sabina
LU 01-6621-S . . . . Lorain
LU 01-6698-S . . . . . . Jefferson
LU 01-6821-S . . . . . Columbiana
LU 01-6931-S . . . . Xenia
LU 01-6985-S . Warrensville Heights
LU 01-7008-S . . . . . . Ashland
LU 01-7014-S . . . . Fresno
LU 01-7187-S . . . New Straitsville
LU 01-7248-S . . . . . Montpelier
LU 01-7318-S . . . . . . Addyson
LU 01-7334-S . . . . . Austinburg
LU 01-7540-S . . . . . Mansfield
LU 01-7597-S . . . . . Lexington
LU 01-7620-S . . . . . Gettysburg
LU 01-7629-S . . . . . . Lebanon
LU 01-7679-S . . . . . Mansfield
LU 01-7697-S . . . . . . Cincinnati
LU 01-7993-S . . . . . Lancaster
LU 01-8130-S . . . . Negley
LU 01-8316-S . . . . . Whitehouse
LU 01-8530-S . . . . . Mansfield
LU 01-8565-S . . . . Mantua
LU 01-8622-S . . . . . . Columbus
LU 01-8645-S . . . . . Wellsville
LU 01-8772-S . . . . . Litchfield
LU 01-8845-S . . . . Lorain
LU 01-8869-S . . . . West Salem
LU 01-9110-S . . . . Pickerington
LU 01-9126-S . . . . . . Cleveland
LU 01-9130-S . . . . . Crestline
LU 01-9187-S . . . . Canton
LU 01-9306-S . . . . Niles
LU 01-9309-S . . . . Carroll
LU 01-9354 . . . . Windham
LU 01-9401-S . . . . . Struthers
LU 01-9433 . . . . Bucyrus
LU 01-9456 . . . . Trotwood
LU 01-12049-S . . . . . Cincinnati
LU 01-12081 . . . . Sterling
LU 01-12319-S . . . . Stubenville
LU 01-12833-S . . . . . Concord
LU 01-12965-S . . . . . Oakharbor
LU 01-13029-S . . . . . Van Wert
LU 01-13656-S . . . . . . Toronto
LU 01-13983-S . . . . . Yorkville
LU 01-14362-S . . . Maple Heights
LU 01-14734-S . . . . . . Milford
LU 01-14742-S . . . . . Van Wert
LU 01-14765-S . . . . . . Lisbon

LU 01-14919-S . . . . Streetsboro
LU 01-14964-S . . . . Painesville
LU 01-14976-S . . . . . . Belpre
LU 01-15050-S . . . . Carey
LU 01-15259-S . . . . . Columbus
LU 01-15489-S . . . . . Brooklyn
LU 01-15519-S . . . . West Union
LU 08-859-L. . . . . . Rio Grande

Teachers
LU 1960 Professional Guild of
　Ohio . . . . Columbus
LU 3499 Dyke College Federation of
　Teachers . . . . Cleveland
SFED 8033 Ohio . . . . . Columbus

Teamsters
CONF Ohio Conference of
　Teamsters . . . . Canton
JC 26 . . . . Cincinnati
JC 41 . . . . Brook Park
JC 44 . . . . Toledo
LU. . . . . Cincinnati
LU 20 . . . . Toledo
LU 24 . . . . Akron
LU 40 . . . . Mansfield
LU 52 . . . . Brook Park
LU 92 . . . . Canton
LU 100 . . . . Cincinnati
LU 113 . . . . Canton
LU 114 . . . . Cincinnati
LU 244 . . . . Cleveland
LU 284 . . . . Columbus
LU 293 . . . . Independence
LU 336 . . . . Independence
LU 348 . . . . Akron
LU 377 . . . . Youngstown
LU 400 . . . . Cleveland
LU 407 . . . . Cleveland
LU 413 . . . . Columbus
LU 416 . . . . Cleveland
LU 422 . . . . Cleveland
LU 436 . . . . Valley View
LU 473 . . . . Cleveland
LU 507 . . . . Cleveland
LU 510. . . . . Orrville
LU 637 . . . . Zanesville
LU 654 . . . . Springfield
LU 661 . . . . Cincinnati
LU 908 . . . . Lima
LU 957 . . . . Dayton
LU 964 . . . . Brookpark
LU 1135 . . . . Perrysburg
LU 1164 . . . . Cleveland
LU 1199. . . . . Cincinnati
LU 1224 Flight Deck Crew Members
　ABX Air . . . . . . Wilmington
LU 1717 Cincinnati Mailers
　Union . . . . Cincinnati

Television and Radio Artists
LU Cleveland . . . . . . Cleveland
LU Tri State . . . . Cincinnati

Theatrical Stage Employees
LU 5. . . . . Cincinnati
LU 12 . . . . Columbus
LU 24 . . . . Maumee
LU 27 . . . . Cleveland
LU 27-B . . . . Cleveland
LU 48 . . . . Akron
LU 66 . . . . Dayton
LU 70 . . . . Struthers
LU 136 . . . . Cincinnati
LU 148-B . . . . Bedford
LU 160 . . . . Cleveland
LU 209 . . . . Cleveland
LU 349 . . . . Lima

LU 364 . . . . Akron
LU 747 . . . . Groveport
LU 754-B . . . . Amelia
LU 756 . . . . . North Royalton
LU 864 . . . . Cincinnati
LU 883 . . . . . North Olmsted
LU 886 Theatrical
　Wardrobe . . . . Yellow Springs
SA Ohio . . . . Hilliard

Train Dispatchers
NHQ. . . . . Cleveland

Transit Union
LU 627 . . . . Cincinnati
LU 697 . . . . Toledo

Transport Workers
LU 2005 . . . . Columbus
LU 2011 . . . . Perrysburg
LU 2019 . . . . . South Euclid
LU 2022. . . . . Malvern

**Transportation Communications
Union**
D 105 Chesapeake & Ohio System
　Board 146 . . . . Toledo
D 234 Southeastern . . . . Oregon
D 308 Chesapeake & Ohio System
　Board . . . . South Point
D 562 Southeastern System Board
　#96 . . . . Cincinnati
D 610 . . . . Orient
D 725 . . . . South Euclid
D 823 . . . . Circleville
D 866 . . . . Niles
D 1097. . . . . . . New Waterford
LG 6132 Tankers. . . . . . Marion
LG 6546 Bellevue . . . . . Bellevue
LG 6731 Willard . . . . . . Shelby

Transportation Union
GCA GO-297 Cuyahoga Valley
　Railroad . . . . . . Rocky River
GCA GO-348 . . . . . Perrysburg
GCA GO-687 Norfolk Southern
　Corp-Nickel Plate . . . . Bellevue
GCA GO-827 River
　Terminal. . . . . Grafton
GCA GO-867 South Buffalo
　Railway. . . . . Cleveland
LLG GO-247 Yardmasters
　Department. . . . . Poland
LU 2 . . . . Waterville
LU 27 . . . . Medina
LU 138 . . . . Elida
LU 145 . . . . . . Reynoldsburg
LU 225 . . . . Bellevue
LU 284. . . . . Valley City
LU 378 . . . . Rock Creek
LU 404. . . . . Newark
LU 421. . . . . Conneaut
LU 440. . . . . Hamilton
LU 586 . . . . Lorain
LU 601 . . . . Mansfield
LU 693 . . . . Akron
LU 792 . . . . Brunswick
LU 991 . . . . . Mingo Junction
LU 1075 . . . . Toledo
LU 1365 . . . . Poland
LU 1376 . . . . Grove City
LU 1377 . . . . Manchester
LU 1386. . . . . Belpre
LU 1397. . . . . Columbus
LU 1529 . . . . Curtice
LU 1549 . . . . Springfield
LU 1638 . . . . Mentor
LU 1748 . . . . . North Royalton

LU 1816 . . . . Oregon
LU 1928 . . . . Oregon
LU 1962 . . . . Sandusky
NHQ. . . . . Cleveland
SLB LO-38 Ohio . . . . . Columbus

Treasury Employees
CH 9 . . . . Cincinnati
CH 27 . . . . Columbus
CH 37 . . . . Cleveland
CH 44. . . . . Toledo
CH 74 . . . . Akron
CH 75 . . . . Dayton
CH 88 . . . . Cincinnati
CH 100 . . . . Youngstown
CH 155 . . . . . Cleveland Heights
CH 224 Staff Attorneys Office of
　Hearings/Appeals. . . . Cleveland
CH 279 . . . . Cincinnati

University Professors
CH University of Toledo. . . Toledo
CH Wilberforce University Faculty
　Association . . . . . Wilber Force

Utility Workers
JC American Electric Power
　Affiliates . . . . Tiffin
JC Ohio Edison . . . . . Shadyside
LU 111. . . . . Tiffin
LU 116 . . . . Dover
LU 118 . . . . Youngstown
LU 126 . . . . Akron
LU 175 . . . . Dayton
LU 270 . . . . Cleveland
LU 296 . . . . Vinton
LU 308 . . . . Lima
LU 349 . . . . Toledo
LU 350 . . . . . . St. Clairsville
LU 351 . . . . Lorain
LU 397 . . . . Ashtabula
LU 425 . . . . Austintown
LU 427 . . . . Massillon
LU 428 . . . . Mentor
LU 430. . . . . Rutland
LU 434 . . . . Marion
LU 436. . . . . Bellaire
LU 438 . . . . Geneva
LU 457 . . . . Wellsville
LU 463 . . . . Wapakoneta
LU 469 . . . . Sidney
LU 477. . . . . Hillsboro
LU 477-W . . . . Peebles
LU 478. . . . . Cadiz
LU 544 . . . . . . Martins Perry
LU 560 . . . . Salem

Weather Service Employees
BR 01-34 . . . . Cleveland
BR 01-39. . . . . Oberlin
BR 01-61 . . . . . Wilmington
BR 01-66 . . . . . Wilimington

Unaffiliated Labor
Organizations
Accurate Printing Union . Cleveland
AFSCME Council 8 Staff Employees
　Ohio . . . . Austintown
Allied Chemical & Alkali
　Workers. . . . . Barberton
Allied Chemical & Alkali Workers
　LU 1. . . . . Barberton
Armco Employees Independent
　Federation Inc. . . . Middletown
Association of Managed Care
　Pharmacists . . . . . . Galloway

Association of WEWS News
　　Reporters . . . . Cleveland
Association of WEWS Videotape
　　Editors . . . . Cleveland
Bardol Employees Association
　　Inc. . . . . Fairview Park
Bettchers Union
　　Independent . . . . . . Cleveland
Bliss Manufacturing Employees
　　Association. . . . . Youngstown
Building & Construction Workers
　　American Association LU 1. Tiffin
Business and Organizing
　　Representatives Union LU
　　1. . . . . Akron
Carmen Steering
　　Committee . . . . Brewster
Cincinnati Shaper
　　Independent . . . . . . Harrison
Cleveland High School & Academy
　　Lay Teachers Association . Mentor
Columbus Diocesan Education
　　Association. . . . . Dublin
Concrete Vault and Sewage System
　　Installers Union of Valley
　　City . . . . Valley City
Conveyor Workers Association
　　United . . . . Madison
Dupont Systems Unions Independent
　　Fort Hill Bargaining
　　Agency . . . . North Bend
Electrical Construction Workers
　　Union . . . . Lowellville
Employees Organization
　　Independent . . . . Amelia
Fram Employees Independent
　　Union. . . . . Greenville
General Organizers
　　Association . . . . Monroe
Girard Machine Company Union
　　Independent . . . . Mineral Ridge

Globe Industries Employees
　　Independent . . . . Dayton
Grafton Ready Mix Drivers . Grafton
Hancock-Wood Electric Employees
　　Group . . . . . North Baltimore
Hull Coal Builders Supply
　　Employees Association. Vermilion
Independent Supervisor's
　　Union . . . . Oregon
Independent Union LU
　　3027 . . . . Columbus
Independent Union of Metal Carbides
　　Employees . . . . Struthers
International Chemical Workers Staff
　　Union. . . . . Cincinnati
International Union of Labor
　　Organization
　　Employees . . . . . . Columbus
Ivorydale & St. Bernard Employees
　　Representation
　　Association. . . . . . Cincinnati
Latex Employees Union Chemionics
　　Corporation . . . . Munroe Falls
Lewis Engineers & Scientists
　　Association . . . . . . Cleveland
Lima Memorial Professional Nurses
　　Association . . . . . Cridersville
Malco Employees Independent
　　Union . . . . Akron
Marietta Truckers Independent LU
　　1. . . . . Beverly
Masonry Institute of Dayton . Dayton
Metal Workers Alliance
　　Inc. . . . . Minerva
Monarch Electric Blue Collar
　　Union. . . . . Brookpark
National Allied Union Allied
　　Professional Associates LU
　　33 . . . . Columbus
National Association of Security
　　Officers and Guards . . Cleveland

Norwood Police Wage & Benefit
　　Committee. . . . . . . Norwood
Ohio Nurses Employee
　　Association . . . . . . Columbus
Ohio Physicians and Dentists
　　Guild . . . . Youngstown
Ohio Typographical & Mailers
　　Conference . . . . Lisbon
Oil Workers Association Independent
　　LU 1 . . . . Dayton
Oil Workers of Cincinnati
　　Independent . . . . . . Cincinnati
Oil Workers of Ohio Independent LU
　　2 . . . . Lima
Physical Plant Employees
　　Union . . . . Springfield
Piqua Quarries Division-Armco Steel
　　Corporation Employees
　　Association . . . . Piqua
Protection Workers of America,
　　United LU 50 . . . . . . Wooster
Public Employees Representative
　　Union. . . . . Columbus
Representatives & Organizers
　　Union . . . . St. Louisville
Rubber Molders of
　　America. . . . . Highland Heights
School Employees Service Union
　　Independent. . . . . . Columbus
Security, Police, Fire
　　Professional . . . . Piketon
Shell Oil Company Employees
　　Association Drivers
　　Warehousemen &
　　Yardmen . . . . Cleveland
Soft Drink Workers Independent-
　　Coca Cola Bottling
　　Works. . . . . Cincinnati
Springfield Newspapers Editorial
　　Association . . . . . Springfield

St. Mary Education
　　Association . . . . . . Lancaster
Sun Council . . . . Toledo
Sun Oil Company Employees
　　Association Akron Terminal
　　Operating Employees. . . . Akron
Sun Oil Company Employees
　　Association Operating Employees
　　of Cleveland . . . . . . Amherst
Sun Oil Company Employees
　　Association Toledo Operating
　　Employees . . . . Toledo
Sun Oil Company Employees
　　Association Warehouse-
　　Maintenance-Drivers . . Columbus
Transit Employees Union
　　Independent. . . . . . . Bedford
Tremco Employees Association
　　Inc. . . . . Cleveland
Tri State Petroleum Workers Union
　　Inc. . . . . Delplos
Truck Drivers Operating
　　Maintenance Workers
　　United . . . . Cadiz
Union Hospital Nurses
　　Association . . . . Navarre
United Archaeological Field
　　Technicians. . . . . . Middletown
United Building Trades
　　Group . . . . Toledo
United Diversified Labor. . Defiance
Vending Machine Seviceman's
　　Union . . . . Cincinnati
Warehouse Maintenance & Drivers
　　Independent Association . Dayton
Washington Court House
　　Independent Federation
　　Inc. . . . . Middle Town
Wayne Professional Nurses
　　Association. . . . . . Greenville
Wittenberg University Physical Plant
　　Employees. . . . . . . Springfield

Oklahoma

AFL-CIO Trade and Industrial Departments

Building and Construction Trades Department
BCTC Eastern Oklahoma . . . Tulsa
BCTC Western
  Oklahoma . . . . . Oklahoma City

Affiliated Labor Organizations

Air Traffic Controllers
LU ADM . . . . Moore
LU EAC . . . . Wheatland
LU LAW. . . . . Lawton
LU OKC. . . . . . . Oklahoma City
LU RVS . . . . Tulsa
LU TUL . . . . Tulsa

Asbestos Workers
LU 64 . . . . Tulsa
LU 94 . . . . Oklahoma City

Automobile, Aerospace Workers
C Oklahoma CAP . . Broken Arrow
LU 286. . . . . . . Oklahoma City
LU 952. . . . . Tulsa
LU 1558 . . . . McAlester
LU 1895 . . . . . . Broken Arrow
LU 1999 . . . . . . Oklahoma City
LU 2130 . . . . Bethany

Bakery, Confectionery, Tobacco Workers and Grain Millers
LU 65 . . . . Tulsa
LU 117-G. . . . . Shawnee
LU 122-G . . . . Blackwell
LU 142-G . . . . El Reno
LU 173. . . . . . . Oklahoma City
LU 191-G . . . . Hitchcock
LU 338-G. . . . . Harrah
LU 346 . . . . Poteau
LU 356-G . . . . Enid
LU 366-G . . . . Edmond

Boilermakers
LG 114-D Cement Workers. . . Ada
LG 414-D Cement Workers . . Adair
LG 421-D Cement
  Workers . . . . . . Collinsville
LG 465-D Cement
  Workers . . . . Midwest
LG 592 . . . . Tulsa

Bricklayers
LU 5 . . . . Oklahoma City

Carpenters
C Great Plains District
  Council . . . . . Oklahoma City
LU 329. . . . . . . Oklahoma City
LU 415 . . . . Cleves
LU 943 . . . . Tulsa
LU 1686 . . . . Stillwater

Civilian Technicians
CH 1 Oklahoma Army 127 . Norman
CH 126 Oklahoma Air . . . . . Tulsa

Communications Workers
C Oklahoma County. Oklahoma City
LU 1135 . . . . . . Oklahoma City
LU 6007 . . . . Drummond

LU 6009 . . . . Lawton
LU 6012 . . . . Tulsa
LU 6015 . . . . Shawnee
LU 6016 . . . . . Oklahoma City
LU 6050 . . . . . Oklahoma City
LU 14621 . . . . Ardmore
LU 14622 . . . . Enid
LU 14625 . . . . Tulsa

Electrical Workers
LU 444 . . . . Ponca City
LU 547 . . . . Catoosa
LU 584 . . . . Tulsa
LU 976 . . . . Pryor
LU 1002 . . . . Tulsa
LU 1141 . . . . . . Oklahoma City
LU 1599 . . . . . . Oklahoma City
LU 2021 . . . . . . Oklahoma City
SA Oklahoma . . . . Oklahoma City

Electronic Workers
LU 1017. . . . . Midwest City
LU 1027. . . . . . . Oklahoma City

Elevator Constructors
LU 63 . . . . Oklahoma City
LU 83 . . . . Tulsa

Federal Employees
LU 273 . . . . Fort Sill
LU 386 . . . . Tulsa
LU 414 . . . . Tahlequah
LU 1922 . . . . Anadarko
LU 2097 . . . . . Oklahoma City

Fire Fighters
LU 211-F. . . Tinker Air Force Base

Flint Glass Workers
LU . . . . Sapulpa
LU 120 . . . . Muskogee
LU 145 . . . . Henryetta
LU 716 . . . . Sapulpa

Food and Commercial Workers
LU 159-I . . . . . Oklahoma City
LU 521-G . . . . Wagoner

Glass, Molders, Pottery and Plastics Workers
LU 48 . . . . Henryetta
LU 195 . . . . Muskogee
LU 239 . . . . Sapulpa
LU 286 . . . . Mill Creek
LU 325 . . . . Tulsa

Government Employees
C 169 Defense Supply
  Agency . . . . Edmond
LU . . . . Ada
LU 171 DoJ . . . . El Reno
LU 689 USDA . . . . Enid
LU 904. . . . . Lawton
LU 916 DoD . . . Oklahoma City
LU 2250 VA . . . . . Muskogee
LU 2282 DoT . . . . Oklahoma City
LU 2505 HHS . . . . . Crescent
LU 2562 VA . . . . Tulsa
LU 2586 DoD . Altus Air Force Base
LU 2815 DoD. . . . . . McAlester
LU 3053 DoD . . . . Oklahoma City
LU 3138 HUD. . . . Oklahoma City
LU 3141 USDA . . . . . Golden
LU 3266 DoD. . . . . . Sallisaw
LU 3506 HHS . . . . . McAlester

LU 3601 PHS, Indian
  Hospital . . . . Ciaremore
LU 3950 HUD . . . . Tulsa

Government Employees Association
LU 20 Emergency Medical
  Technicians &
  Paramedics . . . . Oklahoma City

Government Security Officers
LU 66 . . . . Tulsa
LU 130. . . . . . . Oklahoma City
LU 201. . . . . . . Oklahoma City

Graphic Communications
LU 226-M . . . . Tulsa
LU 286-C . . . . Enid
LU 562-C . . . . Lawton

Hotel and Restaurant Employees
LU 135. . . . . Tulsa
LU 246. . . . . . . Oklahoma City

Iron Workers
LU 48 . . . . Oklahoma City
LU 584 . . . . Tulsa
LU 620 . . . . Tulsa

Laborers
LU 107 . . . . Tulsa

Letter Carriers
BR 458. . . . . . . Oklahoma City
BR 858 . . . . Enid
BR 883 . . . . Shawnee
BR 973 . . . . Calumet
BR 985 . . . . Ardmore
BR 1042 . . . . Cookson
BR 1053. . . . . Chickasha
BR 1123 . . . . Lawton
BR 1166 . . . . McAlester
BR 1336 Blackwell,
  Oklahoma. . . . . . . Blackwell
BR 1355. . . . . Okmulgee
BR 1358 . . . . Tulsa
BR 1491. . . . . Norman
BR 1551 Mangum,
  Oklahoma . . . . Mangum
BR 1595. . . . . Stillwater
BR 1631 . . . . . . Pauls Valley
BR 1646 Hugo, Oklahoma. . . Hugo
BR 1713 Nowata,
  Oklahoma . . . . Nowata
BR 1725 Clinton, Oklahoma. Clinton
BR 1730 . . . . Ponca City
BR 1958. . . . . Miami
BR 2040 Holdenville,
  Oklahoma. . . . . . Holdenville
BR 2087 Tonkawa,
  Oklahoma . . . . Tonkawa
BR 2173 Woodward,
  Oklahoma . . . . . . Woodward
BR 2337 Sulphur,
  Oklahoma . . . . Sulphur
BR 2385 Walters,
  Oklahoma . . . . Walters
BR 2422 Okemah,
  Oklahoma. . . . . . . Okemah
BR 2460 Newkirk,
  Oklahoma . . . . Newkirk
BR 2588 . . . . Carter
BR 2607 . . . . Canton
BR 2789 Drumright,
  Oklahoma . . . . . . Drumright

BR 2840 Atoka, Oklahoma . . Atoka
BR 2918 Coalgate,
  Oklahoma . . . . Coalgate
BR 2944 Cordell, Oklahoma. Cordell
BR 2988 Kingfisher,
  Oklahoma . . . . . Kingfisher
BR 3237 Heavener,
  Oklahoma . . . . Heavener
BR 3264 Guymon,
  Oklahoma . . . . Guymon
BR 3324 Sayre, Oklahoma . . Sayre
BR 3605 Morris, Oklahoma . Morris
BR 3990 Idabell, Oklahoma . Idabel
BR 4155 Marietta,
  Oklahoma. . . . . Marietta
BR 4242 Lindsay,
  Oklahoma. . . . . . . Lindsay
BR 4353 Madill, Oklahoma . Madill
BR 4667 Skiatook,
  Oklahoma . . . . Skiatook
BR 4702 Dewey, Oklahoma . Dewey
BR 5277 Wetumka,
  Oklahoma. . . . . . . Wetumka
BR 5312 Wilburton,
  Oklahoma. . . . . . . Wilburton
BR 5313 Konawa,
  Oklahoma . . . . Konawa
BR 5315 Hartshorne,
  Oklahoma . . . . . . Hartshorne
BR 5320. . . . . . . Tishomingo
BR 5403 Nardin, Oklahoma . Nardin
BR 5422 Watonga,
  Oklahoma. . . . . . Watonga
BR 5481 Waynoka,
  Oklahoma. . . . . . Waynoka
BR 5873 Antlers, Oklahoma. Antlers
BR 6157 Broken Bow,
  Oklahoma . . . . . Broken Bow
BR 6231 Hennessey,
  Oklahoma. . . . . . Hennessey
BR 6251 Wilson, Oklahoma. Wilson
BR 6262 Davis, Oklahoma . . Davis
BR 6348 Commerce,
  Oklahoma . . . . . Commerce
SA Oklahoma. . . . . . Weatherford

Locomotive Engineers
DIV 141 . . . . . Oklahoma City
DIV 201 . . . . Thackerville
DIV 523 . . . . Chickasha
DIV 569 . . . . Hodgen
DIV 578 . . . . Sapulpa
DIV 604 . . . . . . Tishomingo
DIV 721 . . . . Enid
GCA Kansas City Southern
  Railroad . . . . Poteau
SLB Oklahoma . . . . . Wagoner

Machinists
DLG 171 . . . . Tulsa
LG 457 . . . . Mannford
LG 790 . . . . Tulsa
LG 850 . . . . Midwest City
LG 898 . . . . Enid
LG 1461 . . . . Tulsa
LG 2909 . . . . . . Oklahoma City
STC Oklahoma. . . . . . . Tulsa

Maintenance of Way Employes
LG 1251 . . . . Tulsa
LG 2408 . . . . Noble
SF Frisco . . . . Tulsa
SLG 355 . . . . Checotah
SLG 361 . . . . Nenid
SLG 522 . . . . El Reno

SLG 1025 . . . . South Coffeyville
SLG 1254 . . . . Cache
SLG 1540 . . . . Heavener
SLG 1547 . . . . Kenefic
SLG 2717 . . . . Sallisaw

Mine Workers
LU 1329 . . . . Stiglei
LU 1593 . . . . Adair

Musicians
LU 94 . . . . Tulsa
LU 375-703
  Oklahoma . . . . . Oklahoma City

National Staff Organization
LU Associate Staff
  Organization . . . Oklahoma City
LU Staff Organization, Professional,
  Oklahoma . . . . . Oklahoma City

Office and Professional Employees
LU 330 . . . . Tulsa
LU 381 . . . . Oklahoma City
LU 437 . . . . Ponca City

Operating Engineers
LU 627-ABC . . . . Tulsa
LU 641 . . . . Bartlesville
LU 670 . . . . Ardmore

Painters
LU 807 . . . . Oklahoma City

Paper, Allied-Industrial, Chemical
  Employees
LU 05-162 . . . . Valliant
LU 05-174 . . . . Pryor
LU 05-391 . . . . Barnsdall
LU 05-401 . . . . Bartlesville
LU 05-428 . . . . Colcord
LU 05-432 . . . . Bartlesville
LU 05-467 . . . . Arkoma
LU 05-627 . . . . North Miami
LU 05-654 . . . . Maysville
LU 05-669 . . . . Pryor
LU 05-746 . . . . Muskogee
LU 05-857 . . . . . . Ponca City
LU 05-930 . . . . Pryor
LU 05-959 . . . . Coweta
LU 05-1141 . . . . Pryor
LU 05-1480 . . . . Salina

Plasterers and Cement Masons
LU 809 . . . . Oklahoma City

Plumbing and Pipe Fitting
LU 344 . . . . Oklahoma City
LU 430 . . . . Tulsa
LU 798 . . . . Tulsa
SA Oklahoma State Pipe
  Trades . . . . . . Oklahoma City

Postal and Federal Employees
LU 908 . . . . Oklahoma City

Postal Mail Handlers
LU 324 . . . . Oklahoma City

Postal Workers
LU 7 Muskogee Area . . . Muskogee
LU 14 McAlester . . . . . McAlester
LU 30 Durant . . . . Durant
LU 37 Norman . . . . . . Norman
LU 84 Enid . . . . Enid
LU 86 Oklahoma City
  Area . . . . Oklahoma City
LU 344 . . . . Ada
LU 726 Ponca City
  Local . . . . Ponca City
LU 727 Chickasha . . . . Chickasha
LU 990 Ardmore Area . . . Ardmore
LU 1348 Tulsa . . . . Tulsa
LU 1402 El Reno . . . . . El Reno
LU 1474 Altus . . . . Altas
LU 1499 Clinton . . . . . . Clinton
LU 1565 Shawnee Area . . Shawnee
LU 1931 Lawton Area . . . Lawton
LU 2281 Mangum Local . . Mangum
LU 2900 Woodward . . . Woodward
LU 3973 Stillwater . . . . Stillwater
LU 4002 Poteau . . . . . . Poteau
LU 4791 Elk City . . . . . Elk City
SA Oklahoma . . . . Bixby

Railroad Signalmen
LLG 33 . . . . Moore

Roofers, Waterproofers and Allied
  Workers
LU 143 . . . . Oklahoma City

Rural Letter Carriers
D Northeast Oklahoma . . . Hulbert

D Southeast
  Oklahoma . . . . Oklahoma City
D Southwest Oklahoma . . . Cordell
D 6 Northwest
  Oklahoma . . . . . Cleo Springs
SA Oklahoma . . . . . . Chickasha

Security, Police and Fire
  Professionals
LU 794 . . . . Tecumseh
LU 796 . . . . Savanna

Service Employees
LU 1122 Firemen & Oilers . Manford

Sheet Metal Workers
DC Southwest . . . . Tulsa
LU 124 . . . . Oklahoma City
LU 270 . . . . Tulsa
LU 464 . . . . Ponca City

State, County and Municipal
  Employees
LU 2406 Greater Oklahoma City
  Public Employees . Oklahoma City

Steelworkers
LU 14224 . . . . Dewey
LU 12-157-S . . . . Ardmore
LU 12-985-L . . . . Allen
LU 12-998-L . . . . Oklahoma City
LU 12-2741-S . . . . Sand Springs
LU 12-4430-S . . . . Tulsa
LU 12-4785-S . . . Broken Arrow
LU 12-4800-S . . . . Waukomis
LU 12-4992-3 . . . . Tulsa
LU 12-6157-S . . . . Claremore
LU 12-7570-S . . . . Henryetta
LU 12-8511-S . . . . Pryor
LU 12-9227-S . . . . Tulsa
LU 12-9368 . . . . Tulsa
LU 12-9402 . . . . Morris
LU 12-9405 . . . . . Claremore

Teamsters
LU 516 . . . . Muskogee
LU 523 . . . . Tulsa
LU 886 . . . . Oklahoma City

Theatrical Stage Employees
LU 60-B . . . . . . Oklahoma City
LU 112 . . . . Oklahoma City

LU 354 . . . . Tulsa
LU 387 . . . . Lawton
LU 904 . . . . Tulsa

Transit Union
LDIV 993 . . . . . . Oklahoma City

Transport Workers
LU 514 . . . . Tulsa

Transportation Communications
  Union
D 218 . . . . Oklahoma City
LG 6747 Will Rogers . . . . Tulsa

Transportation Union
LU 770 . . . . Shady Point
LU 794 . . . . Blackwell
LU 894 . . . . . . Sand Springs
LU 1016 . . . . Enid
LU 1042 . . . . Norman
LU 1188 . . . . Goldsby
LU 1289 . . . . . . Sand Springs
SLB LO-39
  Oklahoma . . . . . Midwest City

Treasury Employees
CH 45 . . . . Oklahoma City

Weather Service Employees
BR 02-13 . . . . Tulsa
BR 02-34 . . . . Norman
BR 02-37 . . . . . Oklahoma City
BR 02-78 . . . . Norman
BR 02-83 . . . . Norman

Unaffiliated Labor
Organizations

Exxon Employees Federation Central
  Division Tyler Area . . . . Stigler
Professional Association
  Acronautical Center Employees
  Independent . . . . Oklahoma City
Radiographers of
  America . . . . Okmulgee
Standish Pipe Line Guild Oklahoma
  LU 999 . . . . Cushing
Transport Drivers Employees
  Union . . . . Okmulgee
Vance Instructor
  Association . . . . . . Vance Air
                       Force Base

Oregon

AFL-CIO Trade and Industrial Departments

Building and Construction Trades Department
BCTC Central Oregon . . . . . Bend
BCTC Columbia Pacific . . Portland
BCTC Eugene . . . . . . Springfield
BCTC Oregon State. . . . . Tualatin
BCTC Salem . . . . Tangent
BCTC Southern
    Oregon. . . . . . . Central Point

Metal Trades Department
MTC Portland & Vicinity. . Tualatin

Affiliated Labor Organizations

Air Traffic Controllers
LU EUG . . . . Eugene
LU HIO . . . . Hillsboro
LU MFR . . . . Medford
LU P80 . . . . Portland
LU PDX. . . . . Portland

Asbestos Workers
LU 36 . . . . Portland

Automobile, Aerospace Workers
LU 492 Beaverton-Portland
    Local . . . . Beaverton

Bakery, Confectionery, Tobacco Workers and Grain Millers
LU 63-G . . . . Pendleton
LU 114 . . . . Portland
LU 364 . . . . Portland

Boilermakers
LG 72 . . . . Portland
LG 500 . . . . Portland

Bricklayers
LU 1. . . . . Portland
STCON 99 Washington-
    Oregon . . . . Oortland

Carpenters
DC Western C/Lumber-Production-
    Industrial Workers . . . . Portland
LU 190 . . . . Klamath Falls
LU 247 . . . . Portland
LU 306 . . . . Bend
LU 711 Millwrights & Machine
    Erectors . . . . Clackamas
LU 780 . . . . Astoria
LU 1001 . . . . North Bend
LU 1017 . . . . Portland
LU 1065. . . . . Salem
LU 1094 . . . . Corvallis
LU 1273 . . . . Eugene
LU 1388 . . . . Oregon City
LU 1411 . . . . Salem
LU 2058 . . . . Prineville
LU 2066 . . . . St. Helens
LU 2067 . . . . Central Point
LU 2130 . . . . Hillsboro
LU 2154. . . . . Portland
LU 2197 Western
    Council . . . . . . McMinnville
LU 2416. . . . . Portland
LU 2522. . . . . St. Helens

LU 2554 Plywood & Veneer Workers
    Union . . . . Lebanon
LU 2714 . . . . Monmouth
LU 2750 . . . . Springfied
LU 2780 . . . . Elgin
LU 2784 . . . . Coquille
LU 2791 . . . . Coburg
LU 2835. . . . . Salem
LU 2851 . . . . La Grande
LU 2910 . . . . La Grande
LU 2942 . . . . Albany
LU 2949 . . . . Roseburg
LU 2961. . . . . St. Helens
LU 3091 . . . . Saginaw

Classified School Employees
CH 201 South Umpqua Contract
    Employees . . . . Salem
CH 302 Coos Bay Area Contracted
    School Employees . . . . Salem
NHQ . . . . Springfield
SA Oregon (OSEA) . . . . . Salem

Communications Workers
C Oregon . . . . Portland
LU 7901. . . . . Portland
LU 7904. . . . . Salem
LU 7906 . . . . Springfield
LU 7908 . . . . Medford
LU 7955. . . . . Portland
LU 7970 . . . . Odell
LU 7991 . . . . Gresham
LU 14752 . . . . Eugene
LU 14754 . . . . Coos Bay
LU 37194 . . . . Eugene

Electrical Workers
LU 48 . . . . Portland
LU 125 . . . . Gresham
LU 280 . . . . Tangent
LU 659. . . . . Central Point
LU 799 . . . . Umatella
LU 932 . . . . North Bend

Electronic Workers
LU 869. . . . . Roseburg

Elevator Constructors
LU 23 . . . . Portland

Federal Employees
LU 447 . . . . John Day
LU 454 . . . . Yachats
LU 457 . . . . Eugene
LU 642 . . . . Bly
LU 758 . . . . Portland
LU 1141 . . . . Corvallis
LU 1379 . . . . Winston
LU 1888 . . . . Portland
LU 1968. . . . . Portland
LU 2010 . . . . Medford
LU 2079 Umpqua National
    Forest . . . . Roseburg
LU 2085 . . . . Grants Pass
SFED Oregon . . . . . . Corvallis

Food and Commercial Workers
LU 555 . . . . Tigard

Glass, Molders, Pottery and Plastics Workers
LU 112 . . . . Portland
LU 139-B . . . . Portland

Government Employees
LU 928 DoE . . . . Portland
LU 1042 VA . . . . Roseburg
LU 1089 VA . . . . . . White City
LU 1104 . . . . Albany
LU 1188 USDA . . . . . . Eugene
LU 1417 DoD. . . . . . Hermiston
LU 1911 . . . . Eugene
LU 2157 VA . . . . Portland
LU 2336 DoL . . . . . . Portland
LU 2583 VA . . . . Portland
LU 2986 DoD . . . . . . Portland
LU 3116 DoD . . . . . . Portland
LU 3781 USDA . . . . . Portland
LU 3917 HUD . . . . . . Portland
LU 3979 BOP, FCI,
    Sheridan . . . . Sheridan

Government Security Officers
LU 38 . . . . Portland

Graphic Communications
LU 116-C. . . . . . . Cottage Grove
LU 747-M. . . . . Portland

Hotel and Restaurant Employees
LU 9 . . . . Portland

Iron Workers
LU 29 . . . . Portland
LU 516 . . . . Portland

Laborers
DC Oregon, South Idaho, Wyoming
    & Utah . . . . Portland
LU 121 . . . . Bend
LU 296 . . . . Portland
LU 320 . . . . Portland
LU 1241 . . . . Portland
LU 1400 . . . . Central Point

Letter Carriers
BR 82 . . . . Portland
BR 295. . . . . Seaside
BR 347 . . . . Salem
BR 743 . . . . Baker City
BR 909 . . . . Pendleton
BR 916. . . . . Eugene
BR 954 . . . . The Dalles
BR 959 . . . . Albany
BR 1248 . . . . La Grande
BR 1274 . . . . Corvallis
BR 1349 . . . . Grants Pass
BR 1433 . . . . Medford
BR 1450 . . . . Coos Bay
BR 1518 . . . . Roseburg
BR 1784 Crater Lake
    Brance . . . . . . Klamath Falls
BR 1937 . . . . Bend
BR 2251 Forest Grove,
    Oregon. . . . . . . Forest Grove
BR 2296. . . . . Dallas
BR 2342 . . . . North Bend
BR 2558 Tillamook,
    Oregon. . . . . Tillamook
BR 2855 Monmouth,
    Oregon. . . . . Monmouth
BR 2912 Lebanon, Oregon. Lebanon
BR 3083 . . . . Woodburn
BR 3518 Vernonia,
    Oregon. . . . . Vernonia
BR 3601 Independence,
    Oregon. . . . . . . Independence
BR 3607 Enterprise,
    Oregon . . . . Enterprise

BR 3750 . . . . Ontario
BR 4163 . . . . Newport
BR 4229 Sheridan, Oregon. Sheridan
BR 4416 Reedsport,
    Oregon . . . . Reedsport
BR 4425 Nyssa, Oregon. . . Nyssa
BR 4483 Toledo, Oregon. . . Toledo
BR 4500 John Day,
    Oregon. . . . . John Day
BR 4797 Myrtle Point,
    Oregon. . . . . . . Myrtle Point
BR 5093 Burns, Oregon. . . Burns
BR 5094 Canby, Oregon . . . Canby
BR 5464 Florence, Oregon . Florence
BR 6225 Vale, Oregon . . . . Vale
BR 6418 Lincoln City,
    Oregon. . . . . . . Lincoln City
SA Oregon . . . . Beaverton

Locomotive Engineers
DIV 236 . . . . Portland
DIV 277 . . . . Corbett
DIV 362 . . . . La Grande
DIV 476. . . . . Portland
DIV 842. . . . . Klamath Falls
SLB Oregon. . . . . . . Chiloquin

Longshore and Warehouse
DC Columbia River. . . . Portland
LU 1-08. . . . . Portland
LU 12 . . . . North Bend
LU 28 . . . . Portland
LU 40 . . . . Portland
LU 50 . . . . Astoria
LU 53 . . . . Newport
LU 84 . . . . Medford
LU 92 . . . . Portland

Machinists
DLG 1. . . . . Gladstone
DLG 24 . . . . Portland
LG 12-W . . . . Klamath Falls
LG 63 . . . . Portland
LG 246-W . . . . Springfield
LG 261-W . . . . North Bend
LG 1005. . . . . Portland
LG 1110. . . . . Prineville
LG 1160. . . . . Winston
LG 1179 . . . . Astoria
LG 1311 . . . . Eugene
LG 1333 . . . . Hermiston
LG 1432. . . . . Portland
LG 1468 . . . . Medford
LG 1885. . . . . Portland
LG 2911. . . . . Portland
LLG 450 NFFE . . . . Joseph
LLG 2187 . . . . Winchester
LLG FL-7 . . . . Portland
LLG FL-1966 . . . . . . North Bend
STC Oregon. . . . . Portland

Maintenance of Way Employes
LG 236 . . . . Klamath Falls
LG 1054 . . . . Roseburg
LG 1066 . . . . Molalla
SLG 227 . . . . Westfir
SLG 369 . . . . The Dalles
SLG 799 . . . . Milwaukie
SLG 874 . . . . Cove
SLG 1381 . . . . Nyssa

Musicians
CONF Northwest . . . . . Eugene
LU 99 . . . . Portland
LU 560 . . . . Pendleton

LU 689 . . . . Eugene

National Staff Organization
LU Oregon Education
 Association . . . . Tigard

NLRB Professional Association
LU 36 . . . . Portland

Nurses
SA Oregon Nurses
 Association . . . . Tulatin

Office and Professional Employees
LU 11 . . . . Portland

Operating Engineers
LU 701 . . . . Gladstone

Painters
LU 10 . . . . Portland
LU 724 . . . . Salem
LU 740 . . . . Portland
LU 1236. . . . . Portland
LU 1277 . . . . Springfield

Paper, Allied-Industrial, Chemical Employees
LU 04-1199 . . . . Corvallis
LU 08-1097 . . . . Westport
LU 08-1146. . . . . Halsey
LU 08-1171. . . . . Halsey
LU 08-1189 Halsey. . . . . Halsey
LU 08-1234. . . . . Halsey
LU 08-1689 . . . . St. Helens

Plasterers and Cement Masons
LU 82 . . . . Portland
LU 555 . . . . Portland

Plumbing and Pipe Fitting
LU 290 . . . . Tualatin

Postal Mail Handlers
LU 315 . . . . Portland

Postal Workers
LU 128 Portland . . . . . Portland
LU 342 Medford . . . . . Medford
LU 431 Roseburg . . . . Roseburg
LU 457 Klamath
 Falls. . . . . . . Klamath Falls
LU 475 La Grande . . . . La Grande
LU 499 Grants Pass . . . Grants Pass
LU 555 Bend. . . . . Bend
LU 557 Corvallis. . . . . . Corvallis
LU 604 Salem. . . . . . . Salem
LU 666 Baker . . . . Bend
LU 679 Eugene . . . . . Eugene
LU 720 Hood River
 Local . . . . Hood River
LU 921 Cottage
 Grove . . . . . . Cottage Grove
LU 967 Lakeview Local. . Lakeview
LU 1147 North Bend
 Local . . . . North Bend
LU 3189 Newport Local . . Newport
LU 3806 Seaside Local . . . Seaside

LU 4973 Forest Grove
 Local. . . . . . . Forest Grove
LU 6264 Boring Local . . . . Boring
SA Oregon . . . . Salem

Pulp and Paper Workers
LU. . . . . Portland
LU 1 . . . . St. Helens
LU 3 . . . . Albany
LU 13. . . . . Toledo
LU 60. . . . . Newberg
LU 68. . . . . Oregon City
LU 78. . . . . Portland
LU 89. . . . . Medford
LU 396 . . . . Salem
LU 467 . . . . Dallas
LU 677. . . . . Eugene
LU 1000 . . . . North Bend
NHQ . . . . Portland

Railroad Signalmen
LLG 152 . . . . Eugene
LLG 155 . . . . Hermiston

Roofers, Waterproofers and Allied Workers
LU 49 . . . . Portland
LU 156 . . . . Springfield

Rural Letter Carriers
D 1 Oregon . . . . Banks
D 2 . . . . Eagle Creek
D 3. . . . . Hood River
D 4 . . . . Woodburn
D 5 . . . . Bend
D 6. . . . . Pendleton
D 7 . . . . Winston
D 8. . . . . Eagle Point
SA Oregon . . . . Keizer

Security, Police and Fire Professionals
LU 2 . . . . Cascade Locks

Service Employees
C Oregon Service . . . . . Portland
LU 49 . . . . Portland
LU 503 . . . . Salem
LU 999 Firemen &
 Oilers. . . . . Hermiston

Sheet Metal Workers
LU 16. . . . . Portland
LU 92. . . . . Hermiston

State, County and Municipal Employees
LU 88. . . . . Portland
LU 2479 Morrow Company
 Employees . . . . . . Heppner
LU 2699 Columbia River Mental
 Health. . . . . Portland
LU 2746 . . . . Astoria
LU 3115 Corvallis Environ Research
 Employees . . . . Corvallis

LU 3213 Oregon Community
 Support Inc. Employees
 Salem . . . . Salem
LU 3214 Albertina Kerr-Plane
 County . . . . Thurston
LU 3505 . . . . Coquille
LU 3668 Metro Public Defenders Inc.
 Employee . . . . Portland
LU 3670 Trabajadores Unidos y
 Organization . . . . . Forest Grove
LU 4002. . . . . Portland
LU 4003 . . . . Hillsboro
LU 4004 St. Charles Medical Center
 LPN's . . . . Bend
LU 4005 Council 75 . . . . Ontario
STC 75 Oregon . . . . . . Salem

Steelworkers
LU 11-65-U. . . . . Portland
LU 11-330. . . . . Troutdale
LU 11-504-L . . . . Clackamas
LU 11-5074-S . . . . . . Cayonville
LU 11-6163-S . . . . . . Albany
LU 11-7150-S . . . . . . Albany
LU 11-8378-S . . . . . McMinnville
LU 11-9170-S . . . . . The Dalles
LU 12-8509-S . . . . . . Guthrie

Teachers
LU 3432 Willamette Valley Child
 Care Federation. . . . . Portland
LU 3809 Western States Chiropractic
 Faculty . . . . Portland
LU 4912 Lewis & Clark College
 Support Staff . . . . . . Portland
LU 5017 Oregon Federation of
 Nurses-Kaiser . . . . . Clackamas
SFED Oregon. . . . . . . Portland

Teamsters
JC 37 . . . . Portland
LU 81 . . . . Portland
LU 162 . . . . Portland
LU 206 . . . . Portland
LU 223 Titan Union of United
 Staff . . . . Cove
LU 305 . . . . Portland
LU 324 . . . . Salem
LU 670 . . . . Salem
LU 962. . . . . Central Point

Television and Radio Artists
LU Portland. . . . . Portland

Theatrical Stage Employees
D 1 Montana-Idaho-Oregon-
 Washington-Alaska. . . . Portland
LU 20-B. . . . . Portland
LU 28 . . . . Portland
LU 488 . . . . Portland
LU 675. . . . . Eugene

Transit Union
LDIV 757 . . . . Portland

Transportation Communications Union
D 5501 Oregon . . . . . . Portland
LG . . . . Eugene
LG 6486 McNary. . . . . Hermiston

Transportation Union
LU 283 . . . . Portland
LU 471. . . . . Eugene
LU 473 . . . . La Grande
LU 1238. . . . . Tigard
LU 1573. . . . . . . Klamath Falls
LU 1574. . . . . Portland
LU 1841. . . . . . . Klamath Falls
SLB LO-40 Oregon . . . . . Salem

Treasury Employees
CH 40 . . . . Portland
CH 156 . . . . Portland

Utility Workers
LU 197. . . . . Coos Bay

Weather Service Employees
BR 04-9 . . . . Portland
BR 04-11 . . . . Medford
BR 04-31 . . . . Pendleton

Unaffiliated Labor Organizations
Associated Field
 Representatives. . . . . . Portland
Aviators Group . . . . McMinnville
Contech Construction Products
 Hillsboro Plant Shop
 Committee. . . . . Hillsboro
Foundry & Warehouse Employees of
 Esco. . . . . Aloha
Industrial Chrome Union
 Independent. . . . . . . Portland
Industrial Workers of the World
 Portland Public Service
 Workers. . . . . Portland
National Staff Organization. Portland
Northwest Boot & Shoe Workers LU
 1 . . . . Scappoose
Northwest Paramedic
 Alliance. . . . . Portland
Northwestern Telephone Systems
 Employees Committee . . Lebanon
Oregon Federation of Teachers Staff
 Union United Employees
 Guild . . . . Portland
Pacific Northwest Employees
 Association LU 1. . . . . Dexter
Pacific Northwest Employees
 Association Portland LU
 1 . . . . Hillsboro
Pacific Northwest Employees
 Association Portland LU
 2 . . . . Portland
Pineros y Campesinos Unidos del
 Noroeste Inc. . . . . . . Woodburn
Staff Union, Oregon School
 Employees Association . . . Salem
Towboatmen Union United LU
 1 . . . . Coos Bay
United Shop & Service Employees
 Union. . . . . Portland
Valley Imaging Professionals UNIT
 1 . . . . Albany

Pennsylvania

AFL-CIO Trade and Industrial Departments

Building and Construction Trades Department
BCTC Altoona Area. . . . . Altoona
BCTC Beaver County. . . . Monaca
BCTC Berks County . . . . Reading
BCTC Butler Venango
Counties. . . . . Butler
BCTC Central
Pennsylvania. . . . . Harrisburg
BCTC Delaware
Valley. . . . . . . New Portville
BCTC Erie. . . . . Erie
BCTC Johnstown . . . . Pittsburgh
BCTC Lawrence
County. . . . . . . New Castle
BCTC Lehigh-Northampton-Pike-
Monroe Counties. . . . Allentown
BCTC Mercer County . . Hermitage
BCTC North Central
Pennsylvania. . . . Derrick City
BCTC Northeastern
Pennsylvania . . . Wilkes-Barre
BCTC Pennsylvania
State . . . . Harrisburg
BCTC Philadelphia. . Philadelphia
BCTC Pittsburgh . . . . Pittsburgh
BCTC Scranton. . . . . . Scranton
BCTC Southwestern
Pennsylvania. . . New Kensington

Maritime Trades Department
PC Delaware Valley &
Vicinity. . . . . . . Philadelphia

Metal Trades Department
MTC Philadelphia . . . Philadelphia

AFL-CIO Directly Affiliated Locals
DALU 22 Brewery
Workers . . . . Latrobe
DALU 221 Cereal
Workers . . . . . Mechanicsburg
DALU 1242 Slag Workers . Munhall
LJEB Brewery
Workers . . . . . . Allison Park

Affiliated Labor Organizations

Agricultural Employees
BR 7 . . . . Philadelphia

Air Traffic Controllers
LU ABE . . . . Allentown
LU AGC . . . . Pittsburgh
LU AVP . . . . Scranton
LU Capital City
Local . . . . . New Cumberland
LU ERI . . . . Erie
LU LNS . . . . Lititz
LU MDT . . . . Middletown
LU PHL. . . . . Philadelphia
LU PIT . . . . Pittsburgh
LU PNE. . . . . Philadelphia
LU RDG . . . . Reading

Asbestos Workers
LU 2 . . . . Clinton
LU 14 . . . . Philadelphia

LU 23 . . . . Middletown
LU 38 . . . . Wilkes-Barre

Automobile, Aerospace Workers
C Central Pennsylvania
CAP . . . . Williamsport
C Erie County CAP . . . . . Erie
C Lehigh Valley Pennsylvania
CAP . . . . Allentown
C Southeastern Pennsylvania
CAP . . . . Fort Washington
C Southwestern Pennsylvania
CAP. . . . . Dravosburg
C 121-UAW Pennsylvania State
CAP . . . . . . Fort Washington
LU 56 . . . . Altoona
LU 204. . . . . Greensburg
LU 482. . . . . Trout Run
LU 502 . . . . Levittown
LU 544 . . . . Dravosburg
LU 618. . . . . Erie
LU 644 . . . . Pottstown
LU 677. . . . . Allentown
LU 714. . . . . Erie
LU 739. . . . . Erie
LU 757 . . . . Philadelphia
LU 786 . . . . York
LU 787 . . . . Williamsport
LU 813 . . . . Philadelphia
LU 832. . . . . Erie
LU 929 . . . . Philadelphia
LU 1039 . . . . Hatfield
LU 1059 . . . . Jeannette
LU 1069 . . . . Eddystone
LU 1098. . . . . . . Lehighton
LU 1186 . . . . Erie
LU 1191 . . . . . Perkiomenville
LU 1193. . . . . Eynon
LU 1206. . . . . . . Northampton
LU 1242. . . . . . . Old Forge
LU 1282. . . . . . . Bellefonte
LU 1296 . . . . . . Waynesboro
LU 1311 . . . . Imperial
LU 1396 . . . . . . Cranesville
LU 1443 . . . . Carlisle
LU 1561 . . . . Hazleton
LU 1612 . . . . Fort Washington
LU 1695 . . . . Lansdale
LU 1697 . . . . Erie
LU 1799 . . . . . Pleasant Unity
LU 1872 . . . . York
LU 1968 . . . . . . Abbottstown
LU 2177 . . . . Bensalem
LU 2255 . . . . . . Warminster
LU 2412 . . . . . . Wilkes-Barre
LU 8275. . . . . . . Levittown

Bakery, Confectionery, Tobacco Workers and Grain Millers
C Candy Confectionery and
Pasta . . . . Philadelphia
LU 6 . . . . Philadelphia
LU 12-A. . . . . . . Pittsburgh
LU 102-G . . . . . . Clarksville
LU 177-G . . . . . . Cherry Tree
LU 330-G . . . . Hershey
LU 357-G . . . . Shiremanstown
LU 367-G . . . . . . Philadelphia
LU 374-G . . . . . . Lancaster
LU 386-G . . . . . Elizabethtown
LU 387-G . . . . . . Lancaster
LU 401-G. . . . . . . Muncy
LU 464 . . . . Hershey
LU 492 . . . . Philadelphia
LU 10-175-G. . . . . . Jeannette

Boilermakers
C Pennsylvania Industrial. Pittsburgh
LG 13 . . . . Newportville
LG 19 . . . . Philadelphia
LG 87 . . . . Aston
LG 88 . . . . Boothwyn
LG 92-D Cement
Workers. . . . . . . Milesburg
LG 151. . . . . Erie
LG 154 . . . . Pittsburgh
LG 159 . . . . . West Wyoming
LG 173-D Cement
Workers . . . . Wampum
LG 196 . . . . Athens
LG 282-D Cement
Workers. . . . . . . Wind Gap
LG 295 . . . . Dover
LG 300 . . . . Philadelpha
LG 397 . . . . Stroudsburg
LG 398 . . . . Stroudsburg
LG 508-D Cement
Workers . . . . . . Darlington
LG 596-D . . . . Chester
LG 608 . . . . Hanover
LG 648. . . . . . . Northampton
LG 659 . . . . Warren
LG 677. . . . . . Wilkes-Barre
LG 802 . . . . Crum Lynne
LG 906. . . . . Donora
LG 1032 . . . . . . Havertown
LG 1393 . . . . Gallitzin
LG 1506 . . . North Catasauqua
LG 2000 . . . . . . Philadelphia

Bricklayers
LU 1 . . . . Philadelphia
LU 5 . . . . Harrisburg
LU 9 . . . . Monroeville

Carpenters
C Central Pennsylvania
Region . . . . Scranton
DC Metropolitan
Philadelphia . . . . Philadelphia
DC Western
Pennsylvania . . . . . Pittsburgh
LU 8 . . . . Philadelphia
LU 37. . . . . Philadelphia
LU 76. . . . . Hazleton
LU 81. . . . . Erie
LU 99. . . . . Scranton
LU 122 . . . . Collegeville
LU 142 . . . . Pittsburgh
LU 165 . . . . Pittsburgh
LU 191 . . . . York
LU 211 . . . . Pittsburgh
LU 230 . . . . West Mifflin
LU 261 . . . . Scranton
LU 268 . . . . Sharon
LU 287 . . . . Harrisburg
LU 333 . . . . New Kensington
LU 359 . . . . Philadelphia
LU 454 . . . . Philadelphia
LU 462. . . . . . . Greensburg
LU 465 . . . . Audubon
LU 492 . . . . Laureldale
LU 514. . . . . . Wilkes-Barre
LU 541 . . . . Washington
LU 600 . . . . Bethlehem
LU 616 . . . . Hostontown
LU 682 . . . . Venus
LU 845 . . . . Springfield
LU 900 . . . . Ashville
LU 922 . . . . Baden
LU 947 . . . . Reynoldsville

LU 1010. . . . . . . Markleysburg
LU 1014 . . . . Warren
LU 1050 . . . . Philadelphia
LU 1059 . . . . Frackville
LU 1073 . . . . Philadelphia
LU 1160. . . . . . . Pittsburgh
LU 1233. . . . . . . Pittsburgh
LU 1333 . . . . Clarance
LU 1419 . . . . Johnstown
LU 1462 . . . . Croydon
LU 1595 . . . . . Schwenksville
LU 1759. . . . . . . Pittsburgh
LU 1806 . . . . Red Lion
LU 1823 . . . . Philadelphia
LU 1856 . . . . Philadelphia
LU 1906 . . . . Philadelphia
LU 1936 . . . . Lewistown
LU 2183. . . . . . . Pittsburgh
LU 2187 . . . . Milton
LU 2216 . . . . Red Lion
LU 2235. . . . . . . Pittsburgh
LU 2240. . . . . . . Cherry Tree
LU 2274. . . . . . . Pittsburgh
LU 2515 . . . . Croydon
LU 2539 . . . . Coalport
LU 2786 . . . . Auburn
LU 2799 . . . . Coudersport
LU 2837. . . . . . . Mifflinburg
LU 2900. . . . . . . Sunbury
STC Pennsylvania . . . Pittsburgh

Catholic School Teachers
ASSN Scranton
Diocese . . . . . Wilkes-Barre
LU 1776 . . . . Philadelphia
LU 2400. . . . . . . Pittsburgh
NHQ . . . . Philadelphia

Civilian Technicians
CH . . . . Philadelphia
CH 27 Pittsburgh. . . . . Coraopolis
CH 28 Greater Pittsburgh . . . Mars
CH 35 Central Pennsylvania . Bethel
CH 46 Blue Mountain . . . Lebanon
CH 52 Willow Grove. Willow Grove
CH 53 Flood City . . . . . Tyrone
STC Pennsylvania . . . . . Pottsville

Communications Workers
LU 23 . . . . Wilkes-Barre
LU 452 . . . . . Natrona Heights
LU 607 . . . . Emporium
LU 611 . . . . Indiana
LU 612 . . . . Coudersport
LU 621 . . . . Erie
LU 623 . . . . Munhall
LU 628 . . . . Williamsport
LU 632 . . . . Cheswick
LU 640 . . . . Bridgeville
LU 681 . . . . Corry
LU 8645 IUE . . . . . . Johnstown
LU 13000 . . . . . . Philadelphia
LU 13302 . . . . . . Pittsburgh
LU 13500 AT&T
Division. . . . . . . Pittsburgh
LU 13500 Central
Division. . . . . . . Pittsburgh
LU 13500 Eastern
Division. . . . . . . Pittsburgh
LU 13500 Philadelphia
Division. . . . . . . Pittsburgh
LU 13500 Pittsburgh/Western
Division. . . . . . . Pittsburgh
LU 13500 Statewide
Local . . . . Pittsburgh

LU 13550 . . . . Pittsburgh
LU 13552 . . . . Boothwyn
LU 13570 . . . . Gilbert
LU 13571 . . . . Duryea
LU 13572 . . . Schuylkill Haven
LU 13573 . . . . Westfield
LU 13574 . . . . . Peach Bottom
LU 13585 . . . . Altoona
LU 13590 . . . . . . Chadds Ford
LU 13591 . . . . Pittsburgh
LU 14167 . . . . Sayre
LU 14802 . . . . Altoona
LU 14803 . . . . . . Beaver Falls
LU 14804 Bradford Typographical
  Union . . . . Bradford
LU 14806 . . . . Upper Darby
LU 14807 . . . . . Curwensville
LU 14809 . . . . . Punxsutawney
LU 14810 East Stroudsburg
  Typographical . . East Stroudsburg
LU 14812 . . . . Hunker
LU 14813 . . . . Harrisburg
LU 14814 . . . . Mountain Top
LU 14815 . . . . Johnstown
LU 14816 . . . . Kittanning
LU 14817 . . . . Mountville
LU 14819 . . . . Elizabeth
LU 14821 Monongahela Valley
  Typographical . . . . West Newton
LU 14822 New Castle Typographical
  Union . . . . New Castle
LU 14827 . . . . Dormont
LU 14829 . . . . Ringtown
LU 14830 . . . . West Lawn
LU 14831 . . . . Scranton
LU 14834 . . . Pennsylvania Furnace
LU 14836 . . . . . . Washington
LU 14837 . . . . Swoyersville
LU 14838 . . . . . Jersey Shore
LU 14839 . . . . . East Berlin
LU 14840 . . . . Erie
LU 14842 . . . . Pittsburgh
LU 14845 Printers & Bindery
  Workers Union . . . . . . Easton
LU 38010 . . . . . . Philadelphia
LU 38016 . . . . Harrisburg
LU 38049 Lehigh Valley . Allentown
LU 38061 Newspaper Guild of
  Pittsburgh . . . . Pittsburgh
LU 38120 . . . . Wilkes-Barre
LU 38177 Scranton . . . . . Scranton
LU 38187 . . . . Erie
LU 38216 . . . . Hazleton
LU 38218 . . . . York
LU 58028 . . . . Erie
LU 58213 . . . . Harrisburg
LU 81311 . . . . Sayre
LU 88389 . . . . Wellsboro
LU 88400 . . . . Harrisburg
LU 88502 . . . . St. Marys
LU 88601 . . . . Trafford
LU 88609 . . . . Kane
LU 88630 . . . . Creighton
LU 88643 . . . . Sarver
LU 88651 . . . . . Manns Choice
LU 88666 . . . . Latrobe
LU 88667 . . . . Latrobe

Education

LU Katharine Dean
  Tillotson . . . . Pittsburgh
LU Milton Hershey Education
  Association . . . . Hershey
LU 720 PSEA Polyclinic Medical
  Center . . . . Enola
SA Pennsylvania . . . . . Harrisburg

Electrical Workers

C TCC-6 Telephone
  Coordinating . . . . Warren
C 3-EM Western Electric . Allentown
LU 5 . . . . Pittsburgh
LU 29 . . . . Pittsburgh
LU 56 . . . . Erie
LU 81 General Fund . . . . Scranton
LU 98 . . . . Philadelphia
LU 126 . . . . Collegeville
LU 143 . . . . Harrisburg
LU 163 . . . . Wilkes-Barre
LU 201 . . . . Beaver
LU 229 . . . . York
LU 272 . . . . Midland
LU 375 . . . . Allentown
LU 380 . . . . Collegeville
LU 385 . . . . Grove City
LU 459 . . . . Johnstown
LU 607 . . . . Shamokin
LU 654 . . . . Boothwyn
LU 712 . . . . Beaver
LU 743 . . . . Reading
LU 744 . . . . Philadelphia
LU 777 . . . . Middletown
LU 812 . . . . Williamsport
LU 1024 . . . . Pittsburgh
LU 1096 . . . . Blairsville
LU 1298 . . . . Easton
LU 1319 . . . . Wilkes-Barre
LU 1451 . . . . York
LU 1456 . . . . Allentown
LU 1522 . . . . Allentown
LU 1560 . . . . Allentown
LU 1585 . . . . Meadville
LU 1600 . . . . Trexlertown
LU 1602 . . . . Mount Joy
LU 1633 . . . . Howard
LU 1635 . . . . Johnstown
LU 1637 . . . . Erie
LU 1666 . . . . Lancaster
LU 1671 . . . . Birdsboro
LU 1690 . . . . Duke Center
LU 1841 . . . . Bristol
LU 1898 . . . . Laureldale
LU 1914 . . . . Harwick
LU 1919 . . . . Pittsburgh
LU 1927 . . . . Feasterville
LU 1929 . . . . Waynesburg
LU 1941 . . . . Enola
LU 1944 . . . . Harrisburg
LU 1956 . . . . Pittsburgh
LU 1957 . . . . Chicora
LU 1963 . . . . Youngwood
LU 2005 . . . . Philadelphia
LU 2007 . . . . Altoona
LU 2089 . . . . Meadville
LU 2099 . . . . Huntingdon
LU 2118 . . . . Boyertown
LU 2179 . . . . Sandy Lake
LU 2241 . . . . Pulaski
LU 2244 . . . . Scranton
LU 2269 . . . . Dornsife
LU 2271 . . . . Philadelphia
LU 2273 . . . . Altoona
SC T-1 General Telephone Company
  of Pennsylvania . . . . . . York
SC U-22 U.G.I.
  Corporation . . . . . Mount Joy
SC 7 Railroad . . . . . Philadelphia

Electrical, Radio and Machine Workers

DC 1 . . . . Conshohocken
DC 6 . . . . . . North Huntingdon
LU . . . . Pittsburgh
LU 111 . . . . Allentown

LU 112 Bethleham
  Pennsylvania Drivers &
  Dockworkers . . . . . Allentown
LU 155 . . . . Conshohocken
LU 172 . . . . White Haven
LU 327 . . . . Pittsburgh
LU 506 . . . . Erie
LU 610 . . . . Wilmerding
LU 615 . . . . . North Huntingdon
LU 618 . . . . Erie
LU 622 . . . . . North Huntingdon
LU 623 . . . . . North Huntingdon
LU 625 . . . . . North Huntingdon
LU 626 . . . . . North Huntingdon
LU 645 . . . . . North Huntingdon
LU 683 . . . . Erie
LU 689 . . . . . North Huntingdon
LU 690 . . . . . North Huntingdon
LU 692 . . . . Erie
LU 697 . . . . Erie
NHQ . . . . Pittsburgh

Electronic Workers

LU . . . . North Huntingdon
LU 64-FW . . . . Bechtelsville
LU 101 . . . . St. Marys
LU 119 . . . . Philadelphia
LU 120 . . . . Bensalem
LU 123 . . . . Elkins Park
LU 127 . . . . Old Forge
LU 135 . . . . Lykens
LU 144-B Beer
  Bottlers . . . . Allison Park
LU 177 . . . . . . Mountain Top
LU 329 . . . . Gaines
LU 648 . . . . Sharon

Elevator Constructors

LU 5 . . . . Philadelphia
LU 6 . . . . Pittsburgh
LU 59 . . . . Harrisburg
LU 84 . . . . Kempton

Federal Employees

LU 1429 . . . . . . Chambersburg
LU 1430 . . . . Lester
LU 1442 . . . . . . Chambersburg
LU 1984 . . . . Philadelphia

Fire Fighters

LU 17-I . . . . . . Perkiomenville
LU 61-F . . . . Philadelpha
LU 109-F . . . . Carlisle
LU 170-F . . . . . . Chambersburg
LU 221-F . . . . New Cumberland
LU 246-F . . . . Weatherly

Flint Glass Workers

LU 21 . . . . Butler
LU 36 . . . . Monaca
LU 52 . . . . Pittsburgh
LU 67 . . . . Freedom
LU 71 . . . . Falls Creek
LU 100 . . . . Shippenville
LU 102 . . . . . . Mount Pleasant
LU 103 . . . . Jeannette
LU 117 . . . . Connellsville
LU 142 . . . . Washington
LU 146 . . . . Bentleyville
LU 148 . . . . Erie
LU 150 . . . . Port Allegany
LU 505 . . . . . New Alexandria
LU 512 . . . . Beaver Falls
LU 532 . . . . West Mifflin
LU 535 . . . . Irwin
LU 537 . . . . . Mount Pleasant
LU 544 . . . . Monaca
LU 545 . . . . Murrysville

LU 547 . . . . Mount Morris
LU 555 . . . . Enon Valley
LU 580 . . . . Ellwood
LU 590 . . . . Jeannette
LU 1001 . . . . Wellsboro
LU 1019 . . . . . . Port Allegany
LU 1024 . . . . . . Greencastle
LU 1027 . . . . Blanchard

Food and Commercial Workers

C Insurance Workers Area
  VII . . . . Pittsburgh
DC Northeastern . . . . Wilkes-Barre
LU 13 . . . . Bridgeville
LU 23 . . . . Canonsburg
LU 31-T . . . . . . Wilkes-Barre
LU 35-I . . . . . . Wilkes-Barre
LU 38 . . . . Milton
LU 57-I . . . . Duncansville
LU 86 . . . . Clarks Summit
LU 144-C . . . . Forks Township
LU 162 . . . . York
LU 184 . . . . Wilkes-Barre
LU 195-T . . . . . . Wilkes-Barre
LU 211-C . . . . . . Glassport
LU 241-I . . . . Lancaster
LU 266-A . . . . . Wilkes-Barre
LU 283-G . . . Schuylkill Haven
LU 325 . . . . Pittsburgh
LU 406-T . . . . . Wilkes-Barre
LU 416-C . . . . . . Phoenixville
LU 428-T . . . . . Wilkes-Barre
LU 477-C . . . . . . Slatington
LU 570-C . . . . Pottsville
LU 619-C . . . . . Gilbertsville
LU 724-T . . . . . Wilkes-Barre
LU 725-T . . . Schuylkill Haven
LU 727-T . . . . . Wilkes-Barre
LU 728-T . . . . . Wilkes-Barre
LU 737-T . . . . . Wilkes-Barre
LU 740-T . . . . Stowe
LU 741-T . . . . . Wilkes-Barre
LU 835-T . . . . . Wilkes-Barre
LU 959-C . . . . . Gilbertsville
LU 1031-C . . . . Burgettstown
LU 1116-T . . . . . Wilkes-Barre
LU 1776 . . . . Plymouth Meeting
LU 2552-T . . . . Wilkes-Barre
LU 2635-T . . . . Wilkes-Barre

Glass, Molders, Pottery and Plastics Workers

LU 1 . . . . Philadelphia
LU 2-B . . . . Ellwood City
LU 28 . . . . Brockway
LU 36 . . . . Wrightsville
LU 38-B . . . . Erie
LU 42 . . . . Lawrenceburg
LU 46 . . . . Pittsburgh
LU 54 . . . . Port Allegany
LU 61 . . . . Albion
LU 70-B . . . . Media
LU 75 . . . . Port Allegany
LU 76 . . . . Lower Burrell
LU 90 . . . . Hazleton
LU 97 . . . . Media
LU 99 . . . . Beaver Falls
LU 107 . . . . . South Connellsville
LU 110 . . . . Brockport
LU 120 . . . . Clarion
LU 124 . . . . Connellsville
LU 130 . . . . . . New Enterprise
LU 132 . . . . Pottstown
LU 134 . . . . Lower Burrell
LU 136 . . . . Grindstone
LU 139 . . . . Alverton
LU 149 . . . . Connellsville
LU 188 . . . . . South Connellsville

LU 201-B . . . . . . Chambersburg
LU 237 . . . . Nuremberg
LU 238-B . . . . Gilbertsville
LU 240 . . . . Cumbola
LU 243 . . . . Dallas
LU 246 . . . . Clarion
LU 247 . . . . Brookville
LU 272 . . . . Washington
LU 273 . . . . Valant
LU 275 . . . . Grove City
LU 287 . . . . Lancaster
LU 295 . . . . Macungie
LU 297 . . . . Shippenville
LU 304-B . . . . Mansfield
LU 313 . . . . Friedens
LU 321 . . . . West Newton
LU 326 . . . . Media
LU 337 . . . . Washington
LU 361 . . . . Allentown
LU 365-A . . . New Castle
LU 366-B . . . . Hazleton
LU 376 . . . . Mount Joy
LU 422 . . . . Hazleton
LU 454 . . . . Pottsville
NHQ . . . . Media

Government Employees
C 264 3rd District of Veterans Affairs
  LU . . . . Pittsburgh
LU . . . . Philadelphia
LU 62 DoD . . . . . . Philadelphia
LU 148 DoJ . . . . . . Lewisburg
LU 305 . . . . Philadelphia
LU 306 . . . . Williamsport
LU 307 USP Allenwood. White Deer
LU 674 USDA . . . . Philadelphia
LU 940 VA . . . . . Philadelphia
LU 1018 USDA . . . . Penn Hills
LU 1023 DoI . . . . . Philadelphia
LU 1156 DoD . . . . Mechanicsburg
LU 1331 USDA . . . . Wyndmoor
LU 1627 VA . . . . . Pittsburgh
LU 1647 DoD . . . . . Tobyhanna
LU 1698 DoD . . . . . Philadelphia
LU 1699 VA . . . . Wilkes-Barre
LU 1793 VA . . . . . Philadelphia
LU 1862 VA . . . . Altoona
LU 1902 DoD . . . . Philadelphia
LU 1916 DoI . . . . Library
LU 1927 USDA . . . Tunkhannock
LU 1966 VA . . . . . . Lebanon
LU 2004 DoD . . . New Cumberland
LU 2006 HHS . . . Philadelphia
LU 2012 DoJ . . . . . Essington
LU 2028 VA . . . . Pittsburgh
LU 2032 HUD . . . . Philadelphia
LU 2058 DoI . . . . . Philadelphia
LU 2061 GSA . . . . . Philadelphia
LU 2187 DoD . . . . . Pittsburgh
LU 2304 DoD . . . . . Pittsburgh
LU 2316 DoD . . . . Coraopolis
LU 2450 OPM . . . . . . Boyers
LU 2495 DoD . . . . Oakdale
LU 2502 DoL . . . . . . Ebensburg
LU 2531 USDA . . . Fredericksburg
LU 2541 GSA . . . . Pittsburgh
LU 2764 HUD . . . . Pittsburgh
LU 2809 HHS . . . Wilkes-Barre
LU 2935 USDA . . . . . . Pittston
LU 3020 . . . . Port Carbon
LU 3145 DoI . . . . . Gettysburg
LU 3344 VA . . . . . Pittsburgh
LU 3493 USDA . . . . Erie
LU 3610 HHS . . . . . . Johnston
LU 3617 USDA . . . . Claysburg
LU 3631 EPA Region
  III . . . . Philadelphia
LU 3848 DoL . . . . Pleasant Hills

LU 3860 DoJ . . . . . Lake Ariel
LU 3895 DoE . . . . Philadelphia
LU 3951 DoJ . . . . . . Altoona
LU 3974 BOP, FCI,
  McKean . . . . Bradford
LU 4047 Council of
  Prison . . . . White Deer

**Government Employees
Association**
LU 354 Association of Physicians &
  Surgeons . . . . Coatesville
LU 358 Police
  Officers . Lettekenny Army Depot
LU 03-15 . . . . . Willow Grove
LU 03-32 . . . . Wears
LU 03-35 . . . . . . Coatesville
LU 03-74 . . . . Butler
LU 03-76 . . . . . . Elkins Park
LU 03-120 . . . . . Valley Forge

Government Security Officers
LU 12 . . . . Phoenixville
LU 58 . . . . Philadelphia
LU 73 . . . . Wilkes-Barre
LU 129 . . . . Scranton
LU 139 . . . . Pittsburgh

Graphic Communications
LU 4-C . . . . . . Clifton Heights
LU 9-N . . . . Philadelphia
LU 14-M . . . . . . Philadelphia
LU 16-N . . . . . . Philadelphia
LU 24-M . . . . Pittsburgh
LU 64-C . . . . Pittsburgh
LU 73-C . . . . Erie
LU 79-L . . . . Hollidaysburg
LU 137-C . . . . . . Shavertown
LU 138-B . . . . . . Millersville
LU 160-M . . . . Reading
LU 188-C . . . . Windber
LU 206-B . . . East Stroudsburg
LU 241-M . . . Clarks Summit
LU 329-C . . . . York
LU 330-C . . . . . . Lewis Run
LU 338-C . . . . . . Meadville
LU 350-C . . . East Stroudsburg
LU 493-S . . . . . . Clearfield
LU 497-S . . . . . . New Hope
LU 594-S . . . . . Mount Wolf
LU 726-S . . . . Coal Township
LU 732-C . . . . . . Bloomsburg
LU 735-S . . . . Freeland
LU 756-S . . . . Boyertown

Horseshoers
LU 27 . . . . Perkiomenville

Hotel and Restaurant Employees
LU 57 . . . . Pittsburgh
LU 225 . . . . Meadville
LU 274 . . . . Philadelphia
LU 391 . . . . Allentown
LU 634 School Cafeteria Employees
  Union . . . . Philadelphia
STC Pennsylvania . . . Philadelphia

Independent Unions Federation
ASSN United Independent
  Union . . . . Philadelphia
LU Merck Sharpe & Dohme
  Employees
  Organization . . . . West Point
LU 1 United Independent
  Union . . . . Philadelphia
LU 2 United Independent
  Union . . . . Philadelphia

LU 5 United Independent
  Union . . . . Philadelphia
LU 199 Employees Federation of
  South Penn Oil Company. Cyclone
NHQ . . . . Philadelphia

Iron Workers
DC East Ohio-West
  Pennsylvania-North West
  Virginia . . . . Canonsburg
DC Philadelphia &
  Vicinity . . . . Allentown
LU 3 . . . . Pittsburgh
LU 36 . . . . Whitehall
LU 161 . . . . Philadelphia
LU 348 . . . . Erie
LU 401 . . . . Philadelphia
LU 404 . . . . Harrisburg
LU 405 . . . . Philadelphia
LU 420 . . . . Reading
LU 489 . . . . Avoca
LU 502 . . . . Conshohocken
LU 521 . . . . Olyphant
LU 527 . . . . Pittsburgh
LU 594 . . . . Hellertown
LU 621 . . . . Montrose
LU 642 . . . . Erie
LU 772 . . . . Clearfield
LU 822 . . . . Milton

Laborers
DC Eastern
  Pennsylvania . . . . . Harrisburg
DC Federal Public Service
  Employees . . . . . Philadelphia
DC Metropolitan
  Philadelphia . . . . Philadelphia
DC Western
  Pennsylvania . . . . . Pittsburgh
LU 57 . . . . Philadelphia
LU 130 . . . . Scranton
LU 135 . . . . Norristown
LU 158 . . . . Harrisburg
LU 215 . . . . Wilkes-Barre
LU 286 . . . . Brownsville
LU 323 . . . . Butler
LU 332 . . . . Philadelphia
LU 373 . . . . Pittsburgh
LU 413 . . . . Chester
LU 419 . . . . Somerset
LU 471 . . . . Blandon
LU 603 . . . . Erie
LU 708 . . . . South Williamsport
LU 824 . . . . Bellefonte
LU 833 . . . . New Brighton
LU 910 . . . . Johnstown
LU 952 . . . . Kittanning
LU 964 . . . . New Castle
LU 1012 . . . . Philadelphia
LU 1058 . . . . Pittsburgh
LU 1167 . . . . York
LU 1170 . . . . . . Mechanicsburg
LU 1174 . . . . Allentown
LU 1180 . . . . Harrisburg
LU 1300 Public Service
  Employees . . . . Wilkes-Barre
LU 1305 . . . . Ebensburg
LU 1319 . . . . Chester
LU 1354 . . . . Lock Haven
LU 1451 . . . . Latrobe

Laundry and Dry Cleaning
LU 141 . . . . Pittsburgh
LU 241 . . . . York New Salem
NHQ . . . . Pittsburgh

Letter Carriers
BR 17 . . . . Scranton

BR 22 . . . . New Castle
BR 48 . . . . Butler
BR 50 . . . . Williamsport
BR 84 . . . . Pittsburgh
BR 101 . . . . Altoona
BR 113 . . . . Hermitage
BR 115 . . . . . . Wilkes-Barre
BR 146 Corry, Pennsylvania . Corry
BR 157 Keystone . . . . Philadelphia
BR 162 . . . . Pittston
BR 163 . . . . Carbondale
BR 177 Mahanoy City,
  Pennsylvania . . . . Mahanoy City
BR 253 . . . . Hazleton
BR 254 . . . . Bethlehem
BR 258 . . . . Reading
BR 267 . . . . Meadville
BR 273 . . . . Lancaster
BR 274 . . . . Allentown
BR 277 . . . . Chester
BR 284 . . . . Erie
BR 293 . . . . Bradford
BR 332 . . . . McKeesport
BR 389 . . . . Easton
BR 451 . . . . Johnstown
BR 500 . . . . Harrisburg
BR 509 . . . . York
BR 520 . . . . Uniontown
BR 542 . . . . Norristown
BR 575 Towanda,
  Pennsylvania . . . . . Towanda
BR 691 . . . . Indiana
BR 725 . . . . Holmes
BR 771 Ridgway,
  Pennsylvania . . . . . Ridgway
BR 802 . . . . Clearfield
BR 812 Kane, Pennsylvania . . Kane
BR 871 . . . . Sayre
BR 920 . . . . Southampton
BR 961 Huntingdon,
  Pennsylvania . . . . . Huntingdon
BR 1029 . . . . Tarentum
BR 1045 Honesdale,
  Pennsylvania . . . . . Honesdale
BR 1048 Athens,
  Pennsylvania . . . . . Athens
BR 1118 . . . . Irwin
BR 1124 . . . . . . Mount Pleasant
BR 1133 Wellsboro,
  Pennsylvania . . . . . Wellsboro
BR 1139 . . . . New Kensington
BR 1218 Hollidaysburg,
  Pennsylvania . . . . Hollidaysburg
BR 1330 Montrose,
  Pennsylvania . . . . . Montrose
BR 1379 Susquehanna,
  Pennsylvania . . . . Susquehanna
BR 1384 Meyersdale,
  Pennsylvania . . . . . Meyersdale
BR 1403 Cambridge Springs,
  Pennsylvania . Cambridge Springs
BR 1430 . . . . Donora
BR 1473 . . . . . East Pittsburgh
BR 1495 . . . . . . State College
BR 1500 St. Marys,
  Pennsylvania . . . . . St. Marys
BR 1562 . . . . Olyphant
BR 1645 Smethport,
  Pennsylvania . . . . . Smethport
BR 1796 Mount Union,
  Pennsylvania . . . . Mount Union
BR 1929 . . . . Morton
BR 1964 . . . . Everett
BR 1993 Johnsonburg,
  Pennsylvania . . . . Johnsonburg
BR 2248 Weatherly,
  Pennsylvania . . . . . Weatherly

BR 2249 Hawley,
Pennsylvania . . . . . . Hawley
BR 2258 Houtzdale,
Pennsylvania . . . . Houtzdale
BR 2278 Oxford,
Pennsylvania. . . . . . . Oxford
BR 2397 . . . . Belle Vernon
BR 2531 Mifflinburg,
Pennsylvania . . . . Mifflinburg
BR 2572 . . . . Morrisville
BR 2641 McAdoo,
Pennsylvania . . . . . . McAdoo
BR 2657 Clarion,
Pennsylvania. . . . . . . Clarion
BR 2771 . . . . . . Willow Grove
BR 2873 Mansfield,
Pennsylvania . . . . . Mansfield
BR 3013 . . . . Turtle Creek
BR 3024 Montgomery,
Pennsylvania. . . . Montgomery
BR 3034 Port Allegany,
Pennsylvania . . . Port Allegany
BR 3068 Gallitzin,
Pennsylvania . . . . . Gallitzin
BR 3073 Coaldale,
Pennsylvania . . . . . . Coaldale
BR 3225 Tremont,
Pennsylvania . . . . . . Tremont
BR 3337 White Haven,
Pennsylvania . . . . White Haven
BR 3392 . . . . . . West Newton
BR 3449 Tidioute,
Pennsylvania . . . . . . Tidioute
BR 3466 New Wilmington,
Pennsylvania . . New Wilmington
BR 3487 Milford,
Pennsylvania . . . . . . Milford
BR 4094 Glen Lyon,
Pennsylvania . . . . . Glen Lyon
BR 4104 North Wales,
Pennsylvania . . . . North Wales
BR 4105 Clymer,
Pennsylvania. . . . . . . Clymer
BR 4109 . . . . Burnham
BR 4207 Forest City, Pennsylvania
. . . . Forest City
BR 4317 . . . . Paoli
BR 4452 Coplay,
Pennsylvania. . . . . . . Coplay
BR 4663 Trevorton,
Pennsylvania . . . . . Trevorton
BR 4680 New Bethlehem,
Pennsylvania . . . New Bethlehem
BR 4931 . . . . Langhorne
BR 4973. . . . . Levittown
BR 5095 Central City,
Pennsylvania . . . . Central City
BR 5101 Sykesville,
Pennsylvania . . . . Sykesville
BR 5482 Point Marion,
Pennsylvania . . . . Point Marion
BR 5791 . . . . Horsham
BR 5848 Crooked Creek,
Pennsylvania . . Crooked Creek
BR 5931 Matamoras,
Pennsylvania. . . . . Matamoras
BR 6027 McConnellsburg,
Pennsylvania. . . McConnellsburg
BR 6144 . . . . . . Merion Station
BR 6252 Christiana,
Pennsylvania . . . . . Christiana
BR 6286 Saltsburg,
Pennsylvania . . . . . Saltsburg
BR 6338 Mifflintown,
Pennsylvania . . . Mifflintown
BR 6353 Creighton,
Pennsylvania . . . . . Creighton

BR 6371 Lyndora,
Pennsylvania . . . . . Lyndora
BR 6574 Shrewsbury,
Pennsylvania . . . . Shrewsbury
SA Pennsylvania . . . . Philadelphia

Locomotive Engineers
DIV 52 . . . . York
DIV 71 . . . . Fairless Hills
DIV 74. . . . . Enola
DIV 108. . . . . Sarver
DIV 146. . . . . Mohnton
DIV 235. . . . . . . Philadelphia
DIV 250. . . . . . . Montoursville
DIV 259. . . . . . . Allentown
DIV 263. . . . . . . Shavertown
DIV 276. . . . . . . Stroudsburg
DIV 287. . . . . Altoona
DIV 325. . . . . Apollo
DIV 370. . . . . . . Pittsburgh
DIV 459 . . . . . Mechanicsburg
DIV 483 . . . . Lewisberry
DIV 590 . . . . Aliquippa
DIV 700 . . . . Pittsburgh
DIV 730 . . . . Altoona
DIV 851 . . . . Trevose
DIV 886 . . . . Phoenixville
GCA Septa . . . . . Fairless Hills
SLB Pennsylvania . . . . Pittsburgh

Longshoremen
DC Philadelphia . . . . Philadelphia
LU 1242 . . . . Philadelphia
LU 1242-1 . . . . . . Philadelphia
LU 1291 . . . . Philadelphia
LU 1332 . . . . Philadelphia
LU 1566 . . . . Philadelphia
LU 1913 . . . . Linesville
LU 2064
    Warehousemen. . . . Philadelphia

Machinists
DLG 1 . . . . Philadelphia
DLG 83 . . . . Franklin
DLG 98. . . . . York
LG 52 . . . . Pittsburgh
LG 98 . . . . Philadelphia
LG 101 . . . . North East
LG 159 . . . . Philadelphia
LG 175 . . . . York
LG 243 . . . . Dover
LG 380. . . . . Carbondale
LG 648 . . . . Philadelphia
LG 738 . . . . Millersburg
LG 847 . . . . Tunkhannock
LG 885 . . . . Hyndman
LG 917 . . . . Allentown
LG 928 Garden Spot . . . Mount Joy
LG 938 . . . . Girard
LG 993 . . . . Warren
LG 998 . . . . Marble
LG 1044 . . . . Aliquippa
LG 1048 . . . . Clearfield
LG 1060. . . . . . . Pittsburgh
LG 1070 . . . . . . Mechanicsburg
LG 1092. . . . . Perkasie
LG 1174 . . . . Hadley
LG 1190 . . . . Canton
LG 1211 . . . . Erie
LG 1352. . . . . . . Wycombe
LG 1360 . . . . Pleasant Gap
LG 1400 . . . . Spring Grove
LG 1403 . . . . York
LG 1582. . . . . . . Blairsville
LG 1602 . . . . Wyoming
LG 1639 . . . . Altoona
LG 1644. . . . . Eldred
LG 1653 . . . . Archbald

LG 1671 . . . . Wampum
LG 1676 Conway Lodge
    #1676. . . . . . . Allison Park
LG 1776 . . . . Essington
LG 1778 . . . . Lebanon
LG 1780 . . . . Bethlehem
LG 1799. . . . . . . Christiana
LG 1800 . . . . Gilbert
LG 1830 . . . . Fogelsville
LG 1842. . . . . . . Franklin
LG 1869. . . . . . . Shamokin
LG 1928 . . . . Erie
LG 1931 . . . . Altoona
LG 1968 . . . . Erie
LG 1971 . . . . Dunmore
LG 1976 Potomac Air
    Lodge . . . . . Moon Township
LG 1985 . . . . Red Lion
LG 2032 . . . . Greenville
LG 2058 . . . . . Mechanicsburg
LG 2067 . . . . Athens
LG 2171 . . . . Ebensburg
LG 2200 . . . . Shavertown
LG 2278 . . . . Warren
LG 2304 . . . . Warren
LG 2305 . . . . Scranton
LG 2348 . . . . Duncansville
LG 2367 . . . . Hummelstown
LG 2394 . . . . Danville
LG 2430 . . . . Karns City
LG 2439 . . . . Leeper
LG 2448 . . . . Ridgway
LG 2462 . . . . Scranton
LG 2530 . . . . Waynesboro
LG 2549 . . . . Garland
LG 2779 . . . . Portage
LG 2780 . . . . Corry
LG 2813-PM. . . . . . . Sayre
LG 2905 . . . . Wilkes-Barre
LG 2906 . . . . Lititz
STC Pennsylvania . . . Philadelphia

Maintenance of Way Employes
FED Pennsylvania . . . Philadelphia
LG 400 . . . . Easton
LG 935 . . . . Jim Thorpe
LG 1115 . . . . Sarver
LG 1923 . . . . Frackville
LG 1957 . . . . Harrisburg
LG 1997 . . . . Erie
LG 2779 . . . . Brownsville
LG 3006. . . . . . . Brownsville
LG 3008. . . . . . . Greensburg
LG 3014 . . . . Langhorne
LG 3039 . . . . Coatesville
LG 3047 . . . . Loretto
LG 3062 . . . . Irwin
LG 3072. . . . . . . Sinnemohoning
LG 3084 . . . . Jersey Shore
LG 3099 . . . . Oil City
SD Bessemer & Lake
    Erie . . . . Grove City
SLG 275 . . . . Pittston
SLG 362 . . . . Athens
SLG 737 . . . . Library
SLG 1049 . . . . Connellsville
SLG 1350 . . . . Dickson City
SLG 1551 . . . . Wilkes-Barre
SLG 1556 . . . . Buffalo Mills
SLG 1904 . . . . Meadville
SLG 2775 . . . . New Castle
SLG 2780 . . . . Temple
SLG 2800 . . . . East Lansdowne
SLG 2908 . . . . Morrisville
SLG 3002 . . . . Mifflintown
SLG 3004. . . . . . . Carnegie
SLG 3009 . . . . Duncansville
SLG 3011 . . . . Lititz

SLG 3015 . . . . Pittsburgh
SLG 3019. . . . . . . Scotland
SLG 3020 . . . . Reynoldsville
SLG 3023 . . . . Hyde Park
SLG 3024 . . . . Red Lion
SLG 3030 . . . . Woodland
SLG 3063 . . . . Broomall
SLG 3089 . . . . Aston
SLG 3091 . . . . Millmont
SLG 3094 . . . . Rochester
SLG 3098 . . . . Lemoyne

Mine Workers
D 2 . . . . Lucernemines
LU . . . . Jefferson Hills
LU . . . . Pittsburgh
LU . . . . Shelocta
LU 316 . . . . Uniontown
LU 488 . . . . Homer City
LU 600. . . . . . . Penn Run
LU 616 . . . . Beaverdale
LU 762 . . . . Waynesburg
LU 803 . . . . Beaver Brook
LU 819 . . . . Kittanning
LU 850 . . . . Revloc
LU 860 . . . . Colver
LU 998 . . . . Johnstown
LU 1117 . . . . Mahaffey
LU 1197 . . . . Cokeburg
LU 1248 . . . . . . McClellandtown
LU 1257 . . . . Seward
LU 1269 . . . . Belle Vernon
LU 1318 . . . . Portage
LU 1319 . . . . Uniontown
LU 1368 . . . . St. Benedict
LU 1378 . . . . Avonmore
LU 1386 . . . . Nanty Glo
LU 1488 . . . . Pittsburgh
LU 1520 . . . . Houtzdale
LU 1571 . . . . Tamaqua
LU 1609 . . . . Glen Campbell
LU 1642 . . . . Pottsville
LU 1686 . . . . Schuylkill Haven
LU 1687 . . . . Brave
LU 1742 . . . . Freidens
LU 1875 . . . . Garrett
LU 1901 . . . . Waltersburg
LU 1914 . . . . Canonsburg
LU 1957 . . . . Hooversville
LU 1980 . . . . Uniontown
LU 1994 . . . . Sligo
LU 1998 . . . . Monongahela
LU 2022 . . . . Ohiopyle
LU 2026 . . . . Westland
LU 2193 . . . . Clymer
LU 2200 . . . . Broad Top
LU 2244 . . . . Bentleyville
LU 2258 . . . . Carmichaels
LU 2283 . . . . Rural Valley
LU 2291 . . . . Martin
LU 2300 . . . . Uniontown
LU 2350 . . . . Pittsburgh
LU 2485 . . . . Cokeburg
LU 2486 . . . . . . Northern Cambria
LU 2494 . . . . . . Northern Cambria
LU 2578 . . . . Mar-Lin
LU 2587 . . . . Minersville
LU 2874 . . . . Marianna
LU 3123 . . . . Sligo
LU 3246 . . . . Carrolltown
LU 3333 . . . . Merrittstown
LU 3506 . . . . Russellton
LU 3548 . . . . Blairsville
LU 4004 . . . . Coaldale
LU 4426 . . . . Cheswick
LU 4963 . . . . Wildwood
LU 5229 Scalp Level . . . . Windber
LU 6132 . . . . Ford City

LU 6159 . . . . Bobtown	LU 249 . . . . Dunmore	DC 57 . . . . Carnegie	LU 02-614 Yorktowne . . . . . York
LU 6290 . . . . Nemacolin	LU 295 . . . . Dunmore	LU 6 . . . . Pittsburgh	LU 02-615 . . . . . . Bloomsburg
LU 6310 . . . . Nemacolin	LU 306 . . . . Dunmore	LU 41 . . . . Drums	LU 02-623 . . . . Beaver
LU 6321 . . . . Masontown	LU 330-I . . . . Philadelphia	LU 218 . . . . Scranton	LU 02-629 . . . . Gardners
LU 6330 . . . . Clarksville	LU 352 . . . . Philadelphia	LU 252 . . . . Philadelphia	LU 02-635 . . . . Mount Carmel
LU 6359 . . . . St. Michael	LU 371-T . . . . . . Huntingdon	LU 345 . . . . Collindale	LU 02-657 . . . . . Morrisville
LU 6410 . . . . . . Central City	LU 424 . . . . Johnson	LU 409 . . . . Carnegie	LU 02-667 . . . . . Philadelphia
LU 6461 . . . . Shelocta	LU 445 . . . . Johnstown	LU 411 . . . . Harrisburg	LU 02-670 . . . . Lititz
LU 6754 . . . . . . Washington	LU 1034-T . . . . . Huntingdon	LU 426 . . . . Philadelphia	LU 02-672 . . . . West Wyoming
LU 6816 . . . . Blairsville	LU 1071-T . . . . Altoona	LU 479 . . . . Pittsburgh	LU 02-690 . . Cranberry Township
LU 6986 . . . . Apollo	LU 1700 . . . . Bloomsburg	LU 530 . . . . Carnegie	LU 02-701 . . . . . Johnsonburg
LU 7226 . . . . Hazleton	LU 2304 . . . . Bethlehem	LU 549 . . . . Erie	LU 02-714 . . . . Boothwyn
LU 7891 . . . . Pottsville	LU 2520 . . . . Philadelphia	LU 587 . . . . Philadelphia	LU 02-719 . . . . . . Minersville
LU 7925 . . . . Salix		LU 641 . . . . Conshohocken	LU 02-729 . . . . Easton
LU 8776 . . . . Dilliner	**NLRB Professional Association**	LU 703 . . . . Holland	LU 02-788 . . . . White Haven
LU 8923 . . . . Ridgway	LU 4 . . . . Philadelphia	LU 751 . . . . Monroeville	LU 02-789 . . . . North Versailles
LU 9636 . . . . McDonald	LU 6 . . . . Pittsburgh	LU 921 . . . . Philadelphia	LU 02-807 . . . . . . Pottstown
LU 9873 . . . . Pittsburgh		LU 997 . . . . Ridley Park	LU 02-808 . . . . York
	Nurses	LU 1107 . . . . Horsham	LU 02-839 . . . . . . Gardners
Musicians	LU 701 PNA Berks Visiting	LU 1159 . . . . . . Warminster	LU 02-875 . . . . . Williamsport
LU 17 . . . . Erie	Nurse . . . . . Wyomissing	LU 1269 . . . . Nazareth	LU 02-886 . . . . Jeannette
LU 27 . . . . New Castle	LU 702 PNA Braddock	LU 1309 . . . . . Shoemakersville	LU 02-889 . . . . . Karns City
LU 41 . . . . Johnstown	Hospital . . . . . Monroeville	LU 1955 . . . . Philadelphia	LU 02-892 . . . . Monaca
LU 60-471 . . . . Pittsburgh	LU 703 PNA Braddock	LU 1970 . . . . Philadelphia	LU 02-901 . . . . Linwood
LU 77 . . . . Philadelphia	Hospital . . . . Glassport	LU 2006 . . . . Carnegie	LU 02-902 . . . . Hanover
LU 82-545 . . . . Beaver	LU 706 PNA Centre Company Home		LU 02-940 . . . . . . Downingtown
LU 120 . . . . Scranton	Health Service . . . . Bellefonte	**Paper, Allied-Industrial, Chemical**	LU 02-969 . . . . Hatboro
LU 130 . . . . Archbald	LU 707 PNA-Charles Cole Memorial	**Employees**	LU 02-989 . . . . Carlisle
LU 135 . . . . Wernersville	Hospital . . . . . Condersport	C Delaware Valley Oil . . . Linwood	LU 02-993 . . . North Huntingdon
LU 140 . . . . Wilkes-Barre	LU 708 PNA Clearfield	C Industry . . . . Telford	LU 02-1098 . . . . Mechanicsburg
LU 269 . . . . Harrisburg	Hospital . . . . Clearfield	C Pennsylvania Grade Crude	LU 02-1130 . . Delaware Water Gap
LU 294 . . . . York	LU 709 PSEA Crozer Chester	Regional . . . . Oil City	LU 02-1160 . . . . Latrobe
LU 339 . . . . Export	Medical Center . . Wallingford	DC 1 . . . . Northampton	LU 02-1281 . . . . Erie
LU 341 . . . . Norristown	LU 710 PNA Highlands Hospital &	LU 782-008 . . . . White Haven	LU 02-1303 . . . . Hanover
LU 401-750 . . . . Lebanon	Health Center . . . . Connellsville	LU 859 . . . . Monongahela	LU 02-1318 . . . . Milton
LU 472 . . . . York	LU 711 J.C. Blair Unit of	LU 2-1 . . . . Linwood	LU 02-1338 . . . . Coal Township
LU 515 . . . . Pottsville	Pennsylvania . . . . Huntingdon	LU 2-398 . . . . Yeadon	LU 02-1388 . . . . Tyrone
LU 561 . . . . Allentown	LU 712 PNA . . . . . Philadelphia	LU 02-18 . . . . Wind Gap	LU 02-1419 . . . . . Sinking Spring
LU 577 Bangor-	LU 715 PNA-Hazleton General	LU 02-29 . . . . . . Walnutport	LU 02-1442 . . . . . . Alexandria
Stroudsburg . . . . . Stroudsburg	Hospital . . . . . West Hazleton	LU 02-35 . . . . . . Doylestown	LU 02-1443 . . . . Reading
LU 592 . . . . Perryopolis	LU 717 PNA Pocono	LU 02-54 . . . . Fleetwood	LU 02-1448 . . . . Pittston
LU 596 . . . . Uniontown	Hospital . . . . Henryville	LU 02-68 . . . . . . Philadelphia	LU 02-1531 . . . . . Sugar Loaf
LU 630 . . . . . New Kensington	LU 718 PNA Pottsville Hospital &	LU 02-73 Horse Nail	LU 02-1754 . . . . . . Red Lion
LU 660 . . . . State College	Warne Clinic . . . . Port Carbon	Makers . . . . . New Brighton	LU 02-1811 . . . . York
	LU 719 PNA Pottsville School of	LU 02-74 . . . . Beaver	LU 02-1815 . . . . . . Claysville
National Staff Organization	Nursing . . . . Pottsville	LU 02-100 . . . . . . Wernersville	LU 02-1927 . . . . . Williamsport
LU Pennsylvania State Education	LU 722 PNA Suburban General	LU 02-179 . . . . . Spring Grove	LU 05-843 . . . . . . Waynesburg
Association Staff	Hospital . . . . . . Norristown	LU 02-234 . . . . Chester	LU 08-86 . . . . Telford
Organization . . . Mechanicsburg	LU 725 PNA Wayne County	LU 02-240 . . . . . . Pittsburgh	LU 08-240 . . . . New Kensington
	Memorial Hospital . . Honesdale	LU 02-286 . . . . . Philadelphia	
Needletrades	LU 728 PNA Fulton County Medical	LU 02-296 . . . . . . Pittsburgh	**Plasterers and Cement Masons**
JB Pennsylvania Ohio & South	Center . . . . . McConnellsburg	LU 02-304 . . . . . Center Valley	LU 8 . . . . Philadelphia
Jersey . . . . Philadelphia	LU 729 PNA John F. Kennedy	LU 02-308 . . . . . Williamsburg	LU 31 . . . . Munhall
JB Philadelphia . . . . Philadelphia	Memorial Hospital . . Philadelphia	LU 02-326 . . . . . . Columbia	LU 526 . . . . Pittsburgh
LU 11 . . . . Philadelphia	LU 730 PNA Sun Health Services	LU 02-333 . . . . . Downingtown	LU 592 . . . . . . Philadelphia
LU 15-88 . . . . . . Philadelphia	Inc. . . . . Sunbury	LU 02-348 . . . . Erie	STCON Northeast
LU 33-T . . . . Philadelphia	UNIT Pennsylvania Nurses	LU 02-373 . . . . . . Aliquippa	Conference . . . . . Munhall
LU 45-218 . . . . . . Philadelphia	Association . . . . . Allentown	LU 02-375 . . . . . Philadelphia	STCON Tri-State Conference
LU 75-A . . . . Philadelphia		LU 02-376 . . . . . Northampton	#31 . . . . Munhall
LU 93 . . . . Harrisburg	**Office and Professional Employees**	LU 02-412 . . . . . East Bangor	
LU 108-I . . . . Harrisburg	LU 38 . . . . Philadelphia	LU 02-414 . . . . . . Coatesville	**Plate Printers, Die Stampers and**
LU 109-I . . . . Dunmore	LU 45 . . . . Camp Hill	LU 02-417 . . . . . Sadsburyville	**Engravers**
LU 111 . . . . Allentown	LU 63 . . . . Harrisburg	LU 02-422 . . . . . Roaring Spring	LU 1 . . . . Doylestown
LU 119-D . . . . . . Philadelphia	LU 112 . . . . Frackville	LU 02-441 . . . . . . Lamartine	LU 25 . . . . Springfield
LU 125-128 . . . . . Philadelphia	LU 426 . . . . Levittown	LU 02-448 . . . . Chester	NHQ . . . . Doylestown
LU 126-333 . . . . . Philadelphia	LU 457 . . . . Fredricktown	LU 02-455 . . . . Oil City	
LU 127-332 . . . . . Philadelphia	LU 471 . . . . Hiller	LU 02-456 . . . . . . Gettysburg	**Plumbing and Pipe Fitting**
LU 148-C . . . . . . Philadelphia		LU 02-488 . . . . . . Martinsburg	LU 27 . . . . Coraopolis
LU 170-A . . . . . . Philadelphia	**Operating Engineers**	LU 02-504 . . . . . Roaring Spring	LU 47 . . . . Monaca
LU 170-I . . . . Harrisburg	LU 61 . . . . Philadelphia	LU 02-529 . . . . . . Eighty Four	LU 354 . . . . Youngwood
LU 185 . . . . Dunmore	LU 66 . . . . Monroeville	LU 02-547 . . . . . . Treichlers	LU 420 . . . . . . Philadelphia
LU 190 . . . . Philadelphia	LU 95-95A . . . . . . Pittsburgh	LU 02-548 . . . . . . Souderton	LU 449 . . . . Pittsburgh
LU 196 . . . . Harrisburg	LU 367 Brewery Workers . Scranton	LU 02-554 . . . . . . Fogelsville	LU 520 . . . . . . Harrisburg
LU 197 . . . . Harrisburg	LU 542 . . . . . Fort Washington	LU 02-578 . . . . Easton	LU 524 . . . . Scranton
LU 225-I . . . . Dunmore	LU 835 . . . . Drexel Hill	LU 02-580 . . . . Northumberland	LU 542 Pittsburgh Sprinkle
LU 227-I . . . . Philadelphia		LU 02-583 . . . . Bradford	Fitters . . . . Pittsburgh
LU 234 . . . . Allentown	**Painters**	LU 02-604 . . . . . . Darlington	LU 600 . . . . . . Sinking Spring
LU 243-I . . . . Allentown	DC 21 . . . . Philadelphia	LU 02-607 . . . . . . Smethport	LU 690 . . . . . . Philadelphia

LU 692 . . . . Philadelphia
SA Pennsylvania . . . . Philadelpha

Police
LG 1-F First Federal,
Pennsylvania . . . . . Philadelphia
LG 113 University of Pennsylvania
Police . . . . Philadelphia

Postal and Federal Employees
D 5 . . . . Warrendale
LU 507 . . . . Warrendale
LU 509 . . . . Philadelphia
LU 510 . . . . Pittsburgh

Postal Mail Handlers
LU 308 . . . . Philadelphia
LU 322 . . . . Pittsburgh

Postal Workers
LU 81 Pittsburgh Area . . Pittsburgh
LU 89 Philadelphia . . . Philadelphia
LU 95 Lancaster . . . . . Lancaster
LU 101 Scranton . . . . . Scranton
LU 104 McKeesport . . McKeesport
LU 175 Wilkes-Barre . Wilkes-Barre
LU 188 Pottstown . . . . Pottstown
LU 227 New Castle . . New Castle
LU 268 Lehigh Valley
Area . . . . Lehigh Valley
LU 269 Erie Area . . . . Erie
LU 500 Grove City . . . Grove City
LU 502 Mount Union
Local . . . . Mount Union
LU 776 Altoona . . . . . . Altoona
LU 853 Oil City . . . . . . Oil City
LU 869 Sharon . . . West Middlesex
LU 956 Kittanning . . . . Kittanning
LU 1027 Reading . . . . . Reading
LU 1244 York . . . . York
LU 1411 Farrell Local . . . . Farrell
LU 1566 Keystone Area . Harrisburg
LU 1746 Ridgway Local . . Ridgway
LU 1759 Pottsville . . . . Pottsville
LU 1948 Greensburg . . Greensburg
LU 2007 Williamsport . Williamsport
LU 2013 State
College . . . . . . State College
LU 2018 Sharpsville
Local . . . . Sharpsville
LU 2057 Titusville Local . Titusville
LU 2059 Brookville
Local . . . . Brookville
LU 2061 Du Bois . . . . . Du Bois
LU 2063 Bradford . . . . Bradford
LU 2064 Kane Local . . . . . Kane
LU 2065 St. Marys . . . St. Marys
LU 2137 Sayre Local . . . . Sayre
LU 2146 Greenville
Local . . . . Greenville
LU 2153 Washington . . Washington
LU 2171 Donora . . . . . Donora
LU 2179 Warren . . . . . . Warren
LU 2185 Jim Thorpe . . . Jim Thorpe
LU 2233 Eastern Montgomery
County . . . . . Plymouth Meeting
LU 2776 West
Chester . . . . . . West Chester
LU 2781 Upper Darby . Upper Darby
LU 3193 Perkasie Local . . Perkasie
LU 3285 Hanover . . . . Hanover
LU 3327 Uniontown . . . Uniontown
LU 3411 Carbondale . . . . Eynon
LU 3709 Mahanoy City
Local . . . . Mahanoy City
LU 3712 Archbald Local . Archbald
LU 3800 Tri County . . . . . Media

LU 3851 Philipsburg
Local . . . . Philipsburg
LU 3853 Huntingdon
Local . . . . Huntingdon
LU 4169 Windber Local . . Windber
LU 4285 Langhorne . . . Langhorne
LU 4333 Wellsboro . . . . Wellsboro
LU 4469 Johnstown . . . Johnstown
LU 4498 Jermyn . . . . . . Jermyn
LU 5225 Indiana . . . . . Indiana
LU 6728 Bensalem . . . . Bensalem
LU 7048 Philadelphia Bulk Mail
Center . . . . Philadelphia
LU 7067 Wilkes-Barre
PDC . . . . Wilkes-Barre
SA Pennsylvania . . . . Wilkes-Barre

Professional and Technical
Engineers
C General Electric Locals . . . . Erie
LU 3 . . . . Philadelphia
LU 13 . . . . Philadelphia
LU 96 . . . . Pittsburgh
LU 117 . . . . Sellersville
LU 138 . . . . Erie

Railroad Signalmen
GC 4 Baltimore & Ohio
Railroad . . . . . . Connellsville
GC 62 Amtrak Eastern . . . Lansdale
LLG 1 . . . . Port Royal
LLG 2 . . . . Pittsburgh
LLG 18 . . . . Philadelphia
LLG 26 . . . . . Schuylkill Haven
LLG 40 . . . . . North Huntingdon
LLG 53 . . . . Drexel Hill
LLG 57 . . . . Northampton
LLG 63 . . . . Sunbury
LLG 105 . . . New Cumberland
LLG 106 . . . . Elizabethtown
LLG 134 . . . . Castanea
LLG 150 . . . . Pittsburgh
LLG 193 . . . . Pitcairn

Retail, Wholesale and Department
Store
JB Allegheny Regional . . Pittsburgh
LU 101 . . . . Pittsburgh
LU 1034 . . . . Philadelphia
LU 1718 . . . . Berlin

Roofers, Waterproofers and Allied
Workers
DC Northeast Roofers . . . . . Erie
LU 30 . . . . Philadelphia
LU 37 . . . . Bellevue
LU 210 . . . . Erie

Rural Letter Carriers
LU Allegheny County . . . . . Mars
LU Armstrong County . . . Freeport
LU Beaver County . . New Brighton
LU Bedford County . . . . Bedford
LU Berks County . . . . Boyertown
LU Blair County . . . Hollidaysburg
LU Bradford-Sullivan
Counties . . . . Gillett
LU Bucks County . . . New Hope
LU Butler County . . . . . . Cabot
LU Cambria County . . . . . Patton
LU Centre County . . . . Petersburg
LU Clearfield County . . . Grampian
LU Columbia-Montour
Counties . . . . Danville
LU Cumberland-Dauphin
Counties . . . . Harrisburg
LU Delaware-Chester
Counties . . . . Oxford

LU Elk-Cameron
Counties . . . . Weedville
LU Fayette County . . Markleysburg
LU Franklin-Fulton
Counties . . . . . . Chambersburg
LU Huntingdon
County . . . . . Mapleton Depot
LU Indiana County . . . Homer City
LU Jefferson-Clarion . Reynoldsville
LU Lackawanna
County . . . . Clarks Summit
LU Lancaster County . . . Drumore
LU Lebanon County . . . Myerstown
LU Lehigh-Pocono . . Northampton
LU Luzerne County . . . . . Dallas
LU Lycoming-Clinton
Counties . . . . Hughesville
LU Mercer-Lawrence
Counties . . . . Fredonia
LU Montgomery
County . . . . . . Schwenksville
LU Perry-Juanita-Mifflin
Counties . . . . Port Royal
LU Potter-McKean Counties . Eldred
LU Schuylkill County . . Pine Grove
LU Somerset County . . . . Friedens
LU Susquehanna County . Hallstead
LU Tioga County . . . . . . Ulysses
LU Union-Snyder-Northumberland
Counties . . . . Lewisburg
LU Venango-Crawford
Counties . . . . Linersville
LU Warren-Forest Counties . Warren
LU Washington County . McDonald
LU Wayne-Pike Counties . . Hawley
LU Westmoreland
County . . . . Avonmore
LU Wyoming County . Tunkhannock
LU York County . . . . . Hanover
LU 1 Adams County . . . . Gardners
LU 21 Erie County . . . . Edinboro
LU 24 Greene
County . . . . . Rices Landing
SA Pennsylvania . . . Hollidaysburg

Security Officers, Police and
Guards
LU 1536 . . . . Philadelphia

Security, Police and Fire
Professionals
LU 502 . . . . Baden
LU 506 . . . . Philadelphia

Service Employees
JC 45 . . . . Harrisburg
LU 16 . . . . Pittsburgh
LU 22 Firemen & Oilers . . . . Erie
LU 23 Firemen & Oilers . . . Irvine
LU 36 . . . . Philadelphia
LU 40 Firemen &
Oilers . . . . Philadelphia
LU 69 . . . . Greensburg
LU 75 Firemen & Oilers . Pittsburgh
LU 123 Firemen & Oilers . . Oil City
LU 188 . . . . Pittsburgh
LU 252 . . . . Wynnewood
LU 344 Firemen &
Oilers . . . . Philadelphia
LU 395 . . . . Allentown
LU 473 Firemen &
Oilers . . . . Philadelphia
LU 508 . . . . Pittsburgh
LU 585 . . . . Pittsburgh
LU 612 . . . . Philadelphia
LU 668 . . . . Harrisburg

LU 1199 NUHHCE, Pennsylvania
Health Care
Employees . . . . . State College
LU 1206 Firemen & Oilers . Scranton
LU 1215 Firemen &
Oilers . . . . . . Mechanicsburg
LU 1216 Firemen & Oilers . Altoona
LU 1218 Firemen & Oilers . . Baden
LU 1250 Firemen & Oilers . Altoona

Sheet Metal Workers
LU 12 . . . . Pittsburgh
LU 19 . . . . Philadelphia
LU 44 . . . . Wilkes-Barre
LU 194 . . . . Cheltenham
LU 520 . . . . Harrisburg
LU 525 . . . . Tyrone

State, County and Municipal
Employees
C 13 Pennsylvania Public
Employees . . . . . Harrisburg
D 1199-C Philadelphia Health Care
Employees . . . . . Philadelphia
DC 33 DC . . . . . . Philadelphia
DC 47 Philadelphia Administrative,
Professional & Technical
Association . . . . . Philadelphia
DC 83 Pennsylvania Public
Employees,
Southwestern . . . . . Harrisburg
DC 84 Pennsylvania Public
Employees, Western . . Harrisburg
DC 85 Pennsylvania Public
Employees,
Northwestern . . . . . Harrisburg
DC 86 Pennsylvania Public
Employees, North
Central . . . . Harrisburg
DC 87 Pennsylvania Public
Employees,
Northeastern . . . . . Harrisburg
DC 88 Pennsylvania Public
Employees,
Southeastern . . . . . Harrisburg
DC 89 Pennsylvania Public
Employees, Southern . Harrisburg
DC 90 Pennsylvania Public
Employees, Dauphin
County . . . . Harrisburg
LU 45 Mercy Hospital
Employees . . . . Altoona
LU 54 University of Pennsylvania
Cafeteria Workers . . Philadelphia
LU 285 . . . . Reynoldsville
LU 471 . . . . Berlin
LU 488 . . . . Philadelphia
LU 590 University of Pennsylvania
Employees . . . . . Philadelphia
LU 752 Philadelphia Zoo
Employees . . . . . . Philadelphia
LU 816 Hillview Care Center
Employees . . . . Bellwood
LU 1278 Johnstown Water Works
Employees . . . . . . Johnstown
LU 1723 Temple University
Employees . . . . . Philadelphia
LU 1739 Community & Social
Agency Employees . . Philadelphia
LU 1807 . . . . Carnegie
LU 2309 . . . . Indiana
LU 2482 Ashland Regional Medical
Center . . . . Pottsville
LU 2562 Child Development Center
of Northeast Pennsylvania
Employees . . . . Berwick

LU 2631 Shippensburg Area
Pennsylvania
Employees . . . . . Shippensburg
LU 2665 . . . . Clearfield
LU 3070 Sieman Lakeview Manor
Estates . . . . Somerset
LU 3156 Hospital & Mobile
Emergency Medicine
Employees . . . . Altoona
LU 3397 Faculty Federation of Art
Institute . . . . Philadelphia
LU 3853 . . . . Philipsburg
LU 3950 Central Fill Inc.
Pennsylvania
Employees . . . . . Hummelstown

Steelworkers
LU 448 . . . . Madera
LU 473-G . . . . McKeesport
LU 494 . . . . Bensalem
LU 01-1618-S . . . . Sharon
LU 04-6129-S . . . . . . Newtown
LU 04-7825-S . . . . Chester
LU 04-9404-S. . . . . . Slatington
LU 04-12781-S . . . . Ridley Park
LU 07-198-G . . . . . Leisenring
LU 08-26-L . . . . Springs
LU 10-12-G . . . . Creighton
LU 10-22-L . . . . Jeannette
LU 10-53-G . . . . Charleroi
LU 10-88-S . . . . Bristol
LU 10-112-G . . . . Arnold
LU 10-116-L . . . . . East Butler
LU 10-158 . . . . Kittanning
LU 10-256-L . . . . . Beaver Falls
LU 10-285-L . . . . . . Lancaster
LU 10-336-L . . . . . . Pottstown
LU 10-404-U . . . . . Philadelphia
LU 10-409-G . . . . Butler
LU 10-480-A . . . . . Shenandoah
LU 10-482-A . . . . . . Tamaqua
LU 10-485-A . . . . . . Leighton
LU 10-500-L . . . . Herman
LU 10-603-B . . . . York
LU 10-640 . . . . Philipsburg
LU 10-930-B . . . Shoemakersville
LU 10-1016-S . . . . Sharon
LU 10-1035-S. . . . Willow Street
LU 10-1138-S . . . . . Leechburg
LU 10-1145-S . . . . . Jeannette
LU 10-1165-S . . . . . Coatesville
LU 10-1187-S . . . . . Allenport
LU 10-1196-S . . . . Brackenridge
LU 10-1211-S . . . . . . Aliquippa
LU 10-1212-S. . . . . . . Midland
LU 10-1219-S . . . . . . Braddock
LU 10-1324-S. . . . Lower Burrell
LU 10-1355-S . . . Sharpsville
LU 10-1408-S . . . North Versailles
LU 10-1537-S . . . . . . Latrobe
LU 10-1557-S . . . . . McKeesport
LU 10-1660-S . . . . . Hermitage
LU 10-1688-S . . . . Mechanicsburg
LU 10-1843-S . . . North Versailles
LU 10-1852-S . . . . York
LU 10-1913-S . . . North Braddock
LU 10-1917-S . . . . . Meadville
LU 10-1928-S . . . . Milton
LU 10-1940-S . . . . . Lewistown
LU 10-2227-S . . . . West Mifflin
LU 10-2229-S . . . . . . Oil City
LU 10-2599-S . . . . . Bethlehem
LU 10-2632-S . . . . . Johnstown
LU 10-2635-S . . . . . Johnstown
LU 10-3199-S . . . . Erie
LU 10-3269-S . . . . York
LU 10-3403-S. . . . . Fayette City
LU 10-3657-S . . . . . . Pittsburgh

LU 10-3713-S . . . . . Greenville
LU 10-3733-S. . . . . . . Reading
LU 10-4889-S . . . . Fairless Hills
LU 10-4907-S . . . . Williamsport
LU 10-5032 . . . Moon Township
LU 10-5306-S . . . . . Harrisville
LU 10-5652-S . . . . Wilkes-Barre
LU 10-5852-S. . . . . . Pittsburgh
LU 10-6346-S . . . . Slippery Rock
LU 10-6521-S . . . . Altoona
LU 10-6816-S . . . . . Jeffersonville
LU 10-6996-S . . . . . Wyomissing
LU 10-7139-S . . . . . Washington
LU 10-7274-S . . . . . . Lebanon
LU 10-7312-S . . . . Corry
LU 10-7343-S . . . . . Gettysburg
LU 10-7687-S . . . . York
LU 10-8041-S. . . North Charleroi
LU 10-8042-S. . . . . . . Butler
LU 10-8166-S . . . . . . Brockway
LU 10-8183-S . . West Bridgewater
LU 10-8377-S . . . . . Beaver Falls
LU 10-8567-S . . . . . . Hazleton
LU 10-9305-S . . . . . Beaver Falls
LU 10-9445. . . . . . Allison Park
LU 10-9455. . . . . . Collegeville
LU 10-12050-S . . . . . Pittsburgh
LU 10-12698-S . . . . . Boothwyn
LU 10-13836-S . . . Connellsville
LU 10-13987-S. . . . . . . Beaver
LU 10-14034-S. . . . . Pittsburgh
LU 10-14040-S . . . . . . Eldred
LU 10-14372-S . . . . . . Ashland
LU 10-14693-S . . . . Canonsburg
LU 10-15253-S . . . . Bethlehem
LU 12-9462 . . . . Conshohocken
NHQ . . . . Pittsburgh

Teachers
LU . . . . Philadelphia
LU 2208 Moore College of Art &
Design . . . . Philadelphia
LU 3412 Robert Morris College
Faculty Federation . . . . Freedom
LU 3505 Akiba Hebrew
Academy Faculty
Association . . . . Merion Station
LU 3578 Perelman Jewish Day
School . . . . Jenkintown
LU 3845 Lincoln Technical
Institute. . . . . . . Philadelphia
LU 3942 Western Pennsylvania
School for Blind Child . Pittsburgh
LU 4531 Temple
University . . . . . Philadelphia
LU 4802 . . . . Philadelphia
LU 4973 Woodhaven Federation
of Human Service
Professionals . . . . Philadelphia
LU 8036 Pennsylvania . Philadelphia

Teamsters
CONF Pennsylvania Conference of
Teamsters . . . . . . Harrisburg
JC 40 . . . . Mars
JC 53 . . . . Philadelphia
LU 30 . . . . Jeannette
LU 107 . . . . Philadelphia
LU 110 . . . . Ebensburg
LU 115 . . . . Philadelphia
LU 169 . . . . Elkins Park
LU 205 . . . . White Oak
LU 211 . . . . Pittsburgh
LU 229 . . . . Scranton
LU 249 . . . . Pittsburgh
LU 250 . . . . Pittsburgh
LU 261 . . . . New Castle
LU 273 . . . . McKees Rocks

LU 312 . . . . Chester
LU 341 . . . . Ambridge
LU 384 . . . . Norristown
LU 397 . . . . Erie
LU 401 . . . . Wilkes-Barre
LU 429 . . . . Wyomissing
LU 430 . . . . York
LU 463 . . . . . Fort Washington
LU 470 . . . . Philadelphia
LU 485 . . . . Pittsburgh
LU 491 . . . . Uniontown
LU 500 . . . . Philadelphia
LU 538 . . . . Worthington
LU 585 . . . . Washington
LU 623 . . . . Philadelphia
LU 628 . . . . Philadelphia
LU 636. . . . . . . McKees Rocks
LU 764 . . . . Milton
LU 771 . . . . Lancaster
LU 773 . . . . Allentown
LU 776 . . . . Harrisburg
LU 830 . . . . Philadelphia
LU 837 Industrial Workers
Union. . . . . Philadelphia
LU 926 . . . . Pittsburgh
LU 929 . . . . Philadelphia
LU 1414 . . . . Philadelphia

Television and Radio Artists
LU Philadelphia . . . . Philadelphia
LU Pittsburgh . . . . . . Pittsburgh

Theatrical Stage Employees
D 4 Pennsylvania-Delaware-
Maryland-Virginia-West
Virginia-DC . . . . . Philadelphia
LU 3 . . . . Pittsburgh
LU 8 . . . . Philadelphia
LU 82 . . . . Wyoming
LU 97 . . . . Reading
LU 98 . . . . Harrisburg
LU 113 . . . . Erie
LU 152 . . . . Hazleton
LU 179 . . . . South Williamsport
LU 200 Allentown-
Easton . . . . Allentown
LU 218 . . . . Shenandoah
LU 265 . . . . Everson
LU 283 . . . . York
LU 329 . . . . Dalton
LU 403 . . . . Selinsgrove
LU 451 . . . . New Castle
LU 489 . . . . Pittsburgh
LU 561 . . . . Johnstown
LU 627 . . . . Canonsburg
LU 636 . . . . State College
LU 752 . . . . Philadelphia
LU 787 . . . . Pittsburgh
LU 799 . . . . Ambler
LU 820 . . . . Pittsburgh
LU 862 . . . . Pittsburgh
LU 902 . . . . Johnstown

Train Dispatchers
GCA N & W North. . . . . Carnegie
SCOM Conrail System . . . Hatfield

Transit Union
LDIV 85 . . . . Pittsburgh
LDIV 89 . . . . New Castle
LDIV 801 . . . . Altoona
LDIV 956 . . . . Whitehall
LDIV 1119 . . . . Wilkes-Barre
LDIV 1195 . . . . . . Harrisburg
LDIV 1241 . . . . . . Lancaster
LDIV 1345 . . . . Reading
LDIV 1357 . . . . . . Jeannette
LDIV 1496 . . . . . . Trout Run

LDIV 1552 . . . . . . Pittsburgh
LU . . . . Bethel Park
LU . . . . Latrobe
LU 1603 . . . . Lehigh Valley
LU 1729 . . . . Pittsburgh

Transport Workers
LU 234 . . . . Philadelphia
LU 282 . . . . Levittown
LU 289 . . . . Ridley Park
LU 290 . . . . Philadelphia
LU 545 . . . . Imperial
LU 700 . . . . Philadelphia
LU 2008 . . . . McDonald
LU 2009 Railroad
Division . . . . North Huntingdon
LU 2013 . . . . Broomall
LU 2016 . . . . Enola
LU 2017 . . . . Altoona
LU 2035 . . . . Conway

**Transportation Communications
Union**
D 133 . . . . Pittsburgh
D 518 . . . . Lansdowne
D 612 . . . . Dauphin
D 718 Conrail . . . . Langhorne
D 735 . . . . Irwin
D 747 . . . . Coraopolis
D 821 . . . . Altoona
D 878 . . . . Philadelphia
D 1351 Conrail . . . . Philadelphia
D 1472 . . . . Philadelphia

Transportation Union
GCA GO-342 . . . . . . Nazareth
GCA GO-601 Monongahela
Connecting Railroad . Pittsburgh
GCA GO-769 Conrail-PC-Lines
East-PLE . . . . . Philadelphia
GCA GO-969 Union Railroad-
Pittsburgh . . . . . . Verona
LU 60 . . . . Effort
LU 61 . . . . . . King of Prussia
LU 215. . . . . . . Honey Grove
LU 309 . . . . Ashville
LU 340. . . . . . . Connellsville
LU 386. . . . . Shoemakersville
LU 498 . . . . Nazareth
LU 596 . . . . Cranesville
LU 602 . . . . . . Montoursville
LU 632 . . . . Windber
LU 800 . . . . Bangor
LU 816 . . . . . . Elizabethtown
LU 830 . . . . . . Hummelstown
LU 997 . . . . . . York Springs
LU 1006 . . . . . . Finleyville
LU 1074 . . . . . Lower Burrell
LU 1373 . . . . . . Philadelphia
LU 1374 . . . . . . New Castle
LU 1375 . . . . . . Havertown
LU 1379 . . . . . Belle Vernon
LU 1390 . . . . . Fairless Hills
LU 1418 . . . . Conway
LU 1590 . . . . Beaver
LU 1594 . . . . Prospect Park
LU 1628 . . . . . Monroeville
LU 1666 . . . . . . Monessen
LU 1722 . . . . . . Lancaster
LU 1948 . . . . . New Castle
SLB LO-41
Pennsylvania . . . . Harrisburg

Treasury Employees
CH 22 . . . . Philadelphia
CH 34 . . . . Pittsburgh
CH 71 . . . . Philadelphia
CH 89 . . . . Levittown

CH 90. . . . . Philadelphia
CH 135 . . . . Pittsburgh
CH 232 . . . . Philadelphia

University Professors
CH Delaware Valley College
   Chapter . . . . Doylestown
DIV Pennsylvania . . . . . Leesport

Utility Workers
JC Columbia Gas System . Pittsburgh
LU 102 . . . . Rector
LU 102-B . . . . . . Lower Burrell
LU 102-C . . . . Ridgway
LU 102-D . . . . Greensburg
LU 102-F. . . . . Scottdale
LU 102-H . . . . Washington
LU 102-I . . . . Kittanning
LU 102-J . . . . Fenelton
LU 102-K . . . . Smithton
LU 102-L. . . . . . . Beech Creek
LU 102-M . . . . Uniontown
LU 102-N. . . . . . . Waynesboro
LU 140. . . . . New Castle
LU 180 . . . . Altoona
LU 242 . . . . Punxsutawney
LU 262. . . . . Sweet Valley
LU 285 . . . . Hermitage
LU 287. . . . . Connellsville
LU 332 . . . . Forty Fort
LU 334 . . . . Shamokin
LU 406. . . . . Wilkes-Barre
LU 407 . . . South Williamsport
LU 408 . . . . . . Northumberland
LU 419 . . . . Bedford
LU 435. . . . . Lewistown
LU 437 . . . . Midland
LU 456 . . . . Clairton
LU 475 . . . . Wampum
LU 479 . . . . Pittsburgh
LU 489 . . . . Harrisburg
LU 495 . . . . North Huntingdon
LU 506. . . . . Greensburg
LU 516 . . . . Berwick
LU 529 . . . . Millville
LU 537 . . . . Washington
LU 540 . . . . Baden
LU 554 . . . . Stroudsburg
LU 563. . . . . Sayre

Weather Service Employees
BR 51. . . . . Allentown
BR 01-8 . . . . . . Moon Township
BR 01-56 . . . . . State College
BR 01-86 . . . . . . State College

Westinghouse Salaried Employees
ASSN East Pittsburgh Plaza
   Employees. . . . . East Pittsburgh
NHQ . . . . Pittsburgh

Unaffiliated Labor Organizations

African American Workers
   Union. . . . . Pittsburgh
Armco Butler Independent Salary
   Union . . . . Butler
Associated Services for the Blind
   Employees Group . . Philadelphia
Atlantic Richfield Company Guard
   Union. . . . . Philadelphia
Bakers Independent
   Union . . . . . . King of Prussia
Beaver Salaried Employees
   Association. . . . . Beaver
Berry Metal Employees
   Association . Cranberry Township
Bethlehem Corporation Employees
   Association. . . . . . Bethlehem
Brownsville Nurses
   Association . . . . . Belle Vernon
Butler Armco Independent
   Union . . . . Butler
Butler Armco Plant Protection
   Employees-Armco Steel
   Corporation. . . . . Butler
C.A. Spalding Company Employees'
   Association. . . . . Philadelphia
Carnegie Mellon Campus Police
   Association. . . . . . Pittsburgh
Commercial Kitchen
   Equipment Workers United LU
   1 . . . . Philadelphia
Community Mental Health & Mental
   Retardation Center Employees
   Association. . . . . . . Scranton
Concrete Product Workers
   Union. . . . . Fredonia
D.G. Nicholas Employees
   Association . . . . . Carbondale
Delaware County Prison Employees
   Independent Union . . . Thornton
Dupont Employees Philadelphia
   Works Union. . . . Philadelphia
Emes Rabbinic
   Association . . . . . Mifflintown
Fellow Employees Labor
   Organization . . . . New Castle
Fraternal Association of Professional
   Paramedics LU 1 . . . Pittsburgh
Fraternal Association of Professional
   Paramedics LU 4. . . Turtle Creek

Fraternal Association of Professional
   Paramedics LU 8 . . . . Cheswick
General Partitions Manufacturing
   Corporation Shop Union . . . Erie
Guards & Plant Protection
   Employees LU 3 . . . . . . Erie
Hamilton Watch Workers
   Independent . . . . . . Lancaster
Homer Center Riverside Employees
   Independent. . . . . Homer City
Immco Employees
   Association. . . . . . . Easton
Independent Driver's
   Union. . . . . Middletown
Independent Mixed Drivers
   Union . . . . Bensalem
Industrial Workers of the World
   NHQ . . . . Philadelphia
Jeannette Professional Nurses
   Association . . . . . . Ruffsdale
Keystone Rustproofing Independent
   Union. . . . . Arnold
Lady Ester-Undergarment Workers
   Association. . . . . . . Berwick
Legal Services Plan Professional
   Employees Union DC 33 . . Media
Major League Umpires
   Association. . . . . . Philadelphia
McCauley Truck Drivers Dock &
   Mechanics Union
   Independent . . . New Bethlehem
Melrath Employees Union
   Independent . . . . Philadelphia
National Forge Employees Union
   Independent. . . . . Youngsville
North Western Nurses
   Association . . . . . . Horsham
Norwin School Bus Drivers
   Association . . . . Larimer
Nurses, Pennsylvania State Licensed
   Practical, Independent DIV
   701 . . . . Wyomissing
Oil City Giant Eagle Independent
   Union . . . . Oil City
Optical Workers Association of
   Pennsylvania. . . . . Wyomissing
Penn Iron Employees Union
   Association. . . . . Wyomissing
Pennsylvania Association of Staff
   Nurses and Allied
   Professionals. . . . Conshohocken
Pennsylvania Independent
   Nurses. . . . . Butler
Pennsylvania-New York Pipe Line
   System Association . . Coatesville
Pittsburgh Theatrical Unity
   Council . . . . Pittsburgh

PNI Security Union . King of Prussia
Professional Association of Golf
   Officials. . . . . . Bala Cynwyd
Professional Association, Merit
   Systems Protection
   Board. . . . . Philadelphia
Salesmen's Committee
   Inc. . . . . Willow Grove
Shaw Industries Union
   Independent. . . . . . . Franklin
Sovac Petroleum
   Union . . . . Lincoln University
Staff Representatives
   Union . . . . Pittsburgh
Steel Workers Union of
   Beaver Valley
   Independent . . . . New Brighton
Sun Oil Company Employees
   Association Blawnox District
   Operating Employees. . Pittsburgh
Sun Oil Company Employees
   Association Research &
   Development
   Employees . . . . Marcus Hook
Sun Oil Employees Association Twin
   Oaks. . . . . Aston
Susquehanna Valley Automotive
   Alliance. . . . . Danville
Textile Garment Workers
   Association. . . . . Bloomsburg
Union de Trabajadores de
   Kaolin Kaolin Workers
   Union . . . . . Kennett Square
Union Employees Union LU
   1 . . . . Philadelphia
United Independent Aerosol
   Workers . . . . Somerset
United Independent Union LU
   8 . . . . Philadelphia
United Independent Union LU
   9 . . . . Philadelphia
United Independent Union LU
   10. . . . . Philadelphia
United Independent Union LU
   2A . . . . Philadelphia
United Independent Union LU
   9A . . . . Philadelphia
United States Women's National
   Soccer Team Players
   Association . . . . . Philadelphia
Valley Nurses
   Association . . . . Wilkes-Barre
Westfield Tanning Company
   Employees Association . Westfied
WUSA Players . . . . . . Philadelphia
York Engineering Employees
   Association. . . . . York
Yorkco Salaried Employees
   Association. . . . . York

Puerto Rico

Affiliated Labor Organizations

Agricultural Employees
BR 13. . . . . Toa Baja

Air Traffic Controllers
LU SJU. . . . . San Juan
LU ZSU. . . . . Carolina

Automobile, Aerospace Workers
LU 103 . . . . Canovanas
LU 1850 . . . . Carolina
LU 2286 . . . . Manati
LU 2311 . . . Sabana Seca Toa Baja
LU 2312 Hato Rey Community
 Hospital . . . . San Juan

Civilian Technicians
CH 119 Puerto Rico National
 Guard . . . . Juana Diaz

Communications Workers
LU . . . . Aquadilla
LU 3010 Union Trabajadores de Los
 Com de Puerto Rico. . . Aquadilla
LU 33225 Puerto Rico . . . San Juan

Congreso Uniones Industriales
LU 965 Trabajadores de
 Molinos . . . . Catano
NHQ . . . . Catano

Education
LU Antilles Consolidated Education
 Association. . . . . . . San Juan

Federacion Puertorriqueno
LU De Clinicas y
 Hospitales . . . . Bayamon
LU Guardia Hipodromo el
 Comandante. . . . . . Rio Piedras
LU 957 Union Empleados Auxilio
 Mutuo . . . . Trujillo Alto
NHQ. . . . . Puerto Nuevo

Federal Employees
LU 523 International Institute of
 Tropical Forestry. . . . . Palmer
LU 2158 . . . . San Juan

Fire Fighters
LU 97-F . . . . Caguas

Food and Commercial Workers
LU 481 Association de Peloteros
 Profesionales . . . . . . Carolina
LU 481 Federacion Americana de
 Empleados Publicos . . . San Juan

Government Employees
LU 55 . . . . Mayaguez
LU 1503 GSA Center . . . Toa Alta
LU 2408 VA . . . . San Juan
LU 2598 DoL. . . . . . Trujillo Alto
LU 2608 HHS . . . . Caguas
LU 2614 DoD . . . . Fort Buchanan
LU 2698 DoJ . . . . San Juan
LU 2837 HUD . . . . . . San Juan
LU 2951 SBA . . . . . . San Juan
LU 3408 USDA . . . . . . Caguas
LU 3936 AFB. . . . . . . Carolina
LU L-4052 Council of Prisons Locals
 C-33 . . . . San Juan

Government Security Officers
LU 72. . . . . San Juan

Hotel and Restaurant Employees
LU 610 . . . . San Juan

Laborista de Puerto Rico
NHQ . . . . Mayaguez

Letter Carriers
BR 826 . . . . Mayaguez
BR 869 . . . . San Juan

Longshoremen
DC Puerto Rico. . . . . . San Juan
LU 1575 . . . . San Juan
LU 1740 . . . . San Juan
LU 1856 . . . . Fajardo
LU 1901 Empleados de
 Muelles. . . . . San Juan
LU 1902 . . . . San Juan
LU 1903 . . . . Ponce
LU 1904. . . . . Mayaguez
LU 1965 . . . . Vieques
LU 2012 . . . . Lajas

Machinists
LG 2725 . . . . Rio Grande

Musicians
LU 468 . . . . Santurce
LU 555 . . . . San Juan

Needletrades
DC Puerto Rico. . . . . . Santurce
LU 600 . . . . Santurce
LU 601-I . . . . Santurce

NLRB Professional Association
LU 24. . . . . San Juan

Obreros Unidos
LU 3 Union de la Ponce Candy . Ponce
LU 5. . . . . Ponce
LU 14 De la Industria
 Azucarera . . . . Salinas
NHQ . . . . Salinas

Office and Professional Employees
LU 58 . . . . Caguas
LU 402 . . . . Santurce
LU 506 . . . . San Juan

Postal Mail Handlers
LU 313 . . . . San Juan

Postal Workers
LU 1070 Caribbean . . . . San Juan
LU 5898 Gurabo Local . . . Gurabo

Seafarers
LU Puerto Rico Caribbean & Latin
 America . . . . San Juan

Service Employees
D 1199 Nacional Union de
 Trabajodores . . . . . . San Juan

Sindicato Puertorriqueno
LU Tecnicos y Profesionales
 Hospital . . . . Ponce
LU Trabajadores de la Puerto Rico
 Cement Company. . . . . Ponce
LU Union Enfermeras de Clinica Dr
 Pila . . . . Ponce

LU 841 Trabajadores Agricolas
 Hacienda Providencia . Cabo Rojo
LU 929 Trabajadores de Borinquen
 Biscuits . . . . Yauco
LU 951 Trabajadores Clinicas y
 Hospitales . . . . Penuelas
LU 999 Empleados Clemente
 Santisteban. . . . . . . San Juan
NHQ . . . . Rio Piedras

Steelworkers
LU 04-5954-S. . . . . . . Buzon
LU 04-6873 . . . . Bayamon
LU 04-7797-S . . . . . . San Juan
LU 04-8201-S . . . . . . Hato Rey
LU 04-9058. . . . . . . Santurce
LU 04-9242 . . Canoyanas Sanisidro
LU 04-9314-S . . . . . . Hato Rey
LU 09-6135-S . . . . Trujillo Alto
LU 09-6323-S . . . . . . Penuelas
LU 09-6588-S . . . . . Bayamon
LU 09-6871. . . Calle Pluton Dirado
LU 09-8198-S . . . . . . Ponce

Teamsters
LU 901 . . . . Santurce

Trabajadores de Puerto Rico
LU Empleados de Drogeria y
 Farmacia . . . . . Puerto Nuevo
LU Hospital del Nino de
 Guaynabo . . . . . Puerto Nuevo
LU Union Trabajadores Ready
 Mix . . . . Puerto Nuevo
LU 1964 De la Industria del
 Abono . . . . Ensenada
NHQ . . . . Puerto Nuevo

Trabajadores Industriales de Puerto Rico
NHQ . . . . San Juan

Treasury Employees
CH 188 . . . . San Juan
CH 193 . . . . San Juan

Weather Service Employees
BR 02-30 . . . . Carolina

Unaffiliated Labor Organizations

Abono Super A Independent
 Fertilizer Works Inc. . . . Arguada
Asociacion de Empleados del Fondo de
 Bienestar y Pension I L A. Bayamon
Asociacion Empleados Casinos
 Puerto Rico . . . . . Puerto Nuevo
Cemento Mezclado Union Obreros
 Independent . . . . San Juan
Cemento Union de Operadores y
 Canteros de la Industria . . Yauco
Empleados Supermercados Pueblo
 Inc. . . . . San Juan
Equipo Pesado Construccion y
 Ramas. . . . . Rio Piedras
Federacion del Trabajo de Puerto
 Rico Inc. (Federation of Union
 Locals) . . Reparto Metropolitano
Federacion Trabajadores de Empresa
 Privada (FETEMP) . Puerto Nuevo
Fortex Industries de Empleados
 Union Independiente . . Bayamon
Guardias de Seguridad del Hotel
 Caribe Hilton . . . . Vieques

Hermandad de Empleados Exentos
 No. Docentes. . . . . . San Juan
Hermandad Independiente de
 Empleados Telfonicos-
 HIETEL . . . . San Juan
Los Gladiadores Inc. . . . San Juan
Sindicato de Guardias de Seguridad
 de Puerto Rico. . . . Rio Piedras
Sindicato de Trabajadores de la
 Industria Electronica de Puerto
 Rico . . . . Aquadilla
Sindicato de Uniones
 Autonomas . . . . Ponce
Solaridad General de Trabajadores
 de Puerto Rico y Sus
 Afiliadas . . . . Trujillo Alto
Trabajadores de Estacionamiento
 Independent . . . . . Trujillo Alto
Trabajadores de la Cerveceria India
 Inc. Independent . . . Mayaguez
Trabajadores de Servicios Legales
 Union Independiente. . . San Juan
Trabajadores Industriales y
 Construcciones
 Electricas . . . . Guaynabo
Trabajadores Petroquimicos Union
 Carbide . . . . Ponce
Unidad Laboral de Enfermeras (OS)
 Empleados de la Salud de Puerto
 Rico . . . . . Rio Piedras San Juan
Union de Abogados de Servicios
 Legales de Puerto Rico
 U.A.S.L.P.R. . . . . . . San Juan
Union de Carpinteros de Puerto Rico
 CH 27 . . . . San Juan
Union de Carpinteros de Puerto Rico
 CH 0025 . . . . San Juan
Union de Carpinteros de Puerto Rico
 Inc. . . . . San Juan
Union de Construccion de Concreto
 Mixto y Equipo Pesado de Puerto
 Rico. . . . . Mayaguez
Union de Detectives y Guardias de
 Seguridad . . . . San Juan
Union de Empleados de la
 Bombonera . . . . San Juan
Union de Empleados de la Industria
 Petrolera y Sus
 Derivados . . . . Bayamon
Union de Empleados del Hipodromo
 El Comandante. . . . . . Carolina
Union de Musicos de Puerto
 Rico . . . . Santurce
Union de Trabajadores Area Sur y
 Oeste de Puerto Rico . Guayanilla
Union de Trabajadores Borinquen
 Macaroni . . . . Ponce
Union General de
 Trabajadores . . . . . Rio Piedras
Union Independiente de Abogados de
 la Sociedad Para Asistencia
 Legal . . . . San Juan
Union Independiente de Empleados
 de la Cruz Azul. . . . . Guaynabo
Union Independiente de Trabajadores
 de la Industria de la Sal . Boqueron
Union Independiente de Trabajadores
 de Marriott . . . . . . Rio Piedras
Union Independiente Empleados
 Telefonicos de Puerto Rico
 Inc. . . . . Rio Piedras
Union Nacional de Trabajadores de
 Puerto Rico . . . . . Rio Piedras
Union Trabajadores Industria
 Licorera. . . . . Mercedita

Rhode Island

AFL-CIO Trade and Industrial Departments

Building and Construction Trades Department
BCTC Providence . . . . . Cranston

Affiliated Labor Organizations

Air Traffic Controllers
LU PVD . . . . Mapleville

Bricklayers
LU 1 . . . . Cranston

Carpenters
LU 94. . . . . Warwick

Civilian Technicians
CH 22 Rhode Island . . . . . North Kingstown

Communications Workers
LU 14174. . . . . . . Woonsocket
LU 31041 . . . . Providence
LU 31182. . . . . . . Woonsocket
LU 32185. . . . . Pawtucket

Education
ASSN Rhode Island School of Design Faculty. . . . . Providence
LU 845 Roger Williams University Faculty . . . . Bristol
LU 850 Roger Williams University Physical Plant . . . . . . Bristol
LU 892 Roger Williams College Association Clericals/ Technicians. . . . . Bristol
LU 895 Part Time Faculty Association. . . . . . . Cranston
SA Rhode Island National Education Association. . . . . . . Cranston

Electrical Workers
LU 99. . . . . Cranston
LU 1196. . . . . Pawtucket
LU 1203. . . . . Pawtucket
LU 1274 . . . . Warwick
LU 2323 . . . . Cranston

Elevator Constructors
LU 39. . . . . Greenville

Fire Fighters
LU 100-F . . . . Middletown

Flint Glass Workers
LU 1007 . . . . Cumberland

Food and Commercial Workers
C New England . . . . . Providence
LU 328. . . . . Providence

Government Employees
LU 190 DoD . . . . Newport
LU 2910 USDA . . East Providence

Government Employees Association
LU 01-134 . . . . . . Middletown
LU 01-144. . . . . . . Portsmouth
LU 01-240 . . . . . . Narragansett

Graphic Communications
LU 12-N . . . . Providence

Iron Workers
LU 37. . . . . . East Providence
LU 523 . . . . Johnston

Laborers
DC Rhode Island. . . . . Providence
LU 15. . . . . Westerly
LU 226 Lunch Program & Service Employees. . . . . . Providence
LU 271 . . . . Providence
LU 673 . . . . Newport
LU 1322 . . . . Providence

Letter Carriers
BR 15. . . . . Cranston
BR 54. . . . . Woonsocket
BR 55. . . . . Pawtucket
BR 57. . . . . Portsmouth
BR 2158 . . . . . . West Warwick
BR 3166 . . . . Warwick
BR 3501 Manville, Rhode Island. . . . . Manville
BR 6529 Harrisville, Rhode Island. . . . . Harrisville
SA Rhode Island . . . . . Warwick

Longshoremen
LU 1329 . . . . Providence
LU 1996-1. . . . North Kingstown
LU 2001 . . . . Johnston

Machine Printers and Engravers
NHQ . . . . East Providence

Machinists
LG 129. . . . . Riverside
LG 147 . . . . . . East Providence
LG 587 . . . . Cranston
LG 1017 . . . . Cranston
LG 2363 Human Service Providers. . . . . Cranston
LG 2705 . . . . Westerly

Maintenance of Way Employes
SLG 228 . . . . Pawtucket

Musicians
LU 198 . . . . Cranston
LU 262 . . . . Woonsocket
LU 529 . . . . Middletown

National Staff Organization
LU Staff Organization of Rhode Island, National . . . . Cranston

Nurses, Professional
LU Rhode Island Hospital UNAP, LU 5098 . . . . Providence

Office and Professional Employees
LU 25 . . . . Providence

Operating Engineers
LU 57 . . . . Providence

Painters
LU 195 . . . . Warwick
LU 1044 . . . . Roslindale

Paper, Allied-Industrial, Chemical Employees
LU 01-1407. . . . . Tiverton
LU 01-1410. . . . . . Cumberland

Plasterers and Cement Masons
LU 40. . . . . Cranston

Plumbing and Pipe Fitting
LU 51. . . . . . East Providence
SA New England States Pipe Trades . . . . . East Providence

Postal Workers
LU 387 Providence Area . . . . Providence
LU 391 Newport . . . . . Newport
LU 395 Woonsocket . . Woonsocket
LU 621 Westerly . . . . . Westerly
LU 2039 Wakefield. . . . Wakefield
LU 2318 East Greenwich . . . . East Greenwich
LU 3739 Warwick . . . . Warwick
LU 5615 Barrington . . . Barrington
LU 6363 North Scituate. . . . . . North Scituate

Service Employees
C 10 Rhode Island . . . . Providence
LU 69 International Leather Goods, Plastics, Novelty and Service Union . . . . Coventry
LU 134 . . . . Providence
LU 334 . . . . Woonsocket

Steelworkers
LU 04-1530-S . . . East Providence
LU 04-4543-S . . . . . Smithfield
LU 04-4652-S . . . . . . Johnston
LU 04-14845-S . . . . . . Bristol
LU 04-15509-S . . . . . Riverside
LU 04-16031-S . . . West Warwick

Teachers
LU 1769 Bryant Faculty Federation . . . . Smithfield
LU 4940 North Rhode Island Collaborative Employees . . . North Providence
LU 5022 Nurses & Health Professionals, Visiting . . . . . . Portsmouth
LU 5067 Nurses & Health Professionals, Landmark Federation . . . . Smithfield
LU 5075 Federation of Nurses & Health Professionals . . . Westerly

LU 5082 Nurses & Health Professionals, Memorial Hospital Federation . . . . . . Pawtucket
LU 5090 Visiting Nurses . . . . Providence
SFED Rhode Island . . . Providence

Teamsters
LU 64 . . . . West Warwick
LU 251 . . . . . . East Providence

Theatrical Stage Employees
LU 23 . . . . . . North Providence
LU 424 . . . . Bristol
LU 830 . . . . Coventry

Transit Union
LDIV 174 . . . . . Little Compton
LDIV 1116. . . . . West Warwick

Transport Workers
LU 2054 . . . . Lincoln

Transportation Union
LU 1672 . . . . Westerly

Treasury Employees
CH 54 . . . . Providence

Utility Workers
LU 359 . . . . . . East Providence

Unaffiliated Labor Organizations
Ashton Cable Workers Union LU 533 . . . . Cumberland
Brotherhood of Utility Workers of New England LU 310 . Providence
Brotherhood of Utility Workers of New England NHQ . . Warwick
Independent Union of Awning Material Finishers . . . Pawtucket
My Bread Salesmens Union Independent . . . . Lincoln
Newport Firefighting School . . . . Middletown
Rhode Island Private Correctional Officers Union Independent . . . . Providence
Sealol Shop Union . . . . Warwick
Security & Guard Association of Rhode Island . . . . . . Johnston
Sun Oil Company Operating, Maintenance & Delivery Employees Association of New England. . . . . . East Providence
Terminal Employees Association Inc. . . . . Providence
United Nurses & Allied Professional Greater Woonsocket Visiting Nurses LU 5201 . . . . . Glendale
United Nurses & Allied Professional Northwest LU 5033 . . . Cranston
United Nurses and Allied Professionals. . . . . . Providence
United Nurses and Allied Professionals LU 5110 . . Johnston

South Carolina

AFL-CIO Trade and Industrial Departments

Building and Construction Trades Department

BCTC Charleston . . . . Charleston

Affiliated Labor Organizations

Agricultural Employees
BR 19 . . . . . . North Charleston

Air Traffic Controllers
LU CAE . . . . . . West Columbia
LU CHS . . . . Charleston
LU FLO . . . . Florence
LU GSP . . . . Greer
LU MYR . . . . . . Myrtle Beach

Asbestos Workers
LU 92 . . . . Beech Island

Automobile, Aerospace Workers
LU 4616 . . . . Carlisle
LU 5841 . . . . Winnsboro

Boilermakers
LG 687 . . . . Charleston

Bricklayers
LU 2 . . . . Greenville

Carpenters
LU 1468 . . . . Alcolu
LU 1778 . . . . Columbia
LU 2221 Hampton
   Council . . . . North Charleston
LU 2224 . . . . Vance
LU 3130 . . . . Hampton

Communications Workers
LU 3702 . . . . Anderson
LU 3704 . . . . Hanahan
LU 3706 . . . . . . West Columbia
LU 3708 . . . . Florence
LU 3710 . . . . Greenville
LU 3716 . . . . Spartanburg
LU 3719 . . . . Orangeburg
LU 83276 . . . . Florence
LU 83706 . . . . Landrum

Education
C OEA Germany South East
   Area . . . . Pawleys
LU Hampton, South
   Carolina . . . . Beaufort

Electrical Workers
LU 248 . . . . Georgetown
LU 382 . . . . Florence
LU 398 . . . . . . Mount Pleasant
LU 772 . . . . Lexington
LU 776 . . . . Charleston
LU 1431 . . . . . . Johnsonville
LU 1588 . . . . Trenton
LU 1591 . . . . Conway
LU 1649 . . . . Hampton
LU 1753 . . . . . North Charleston
LU 2277 . . . . Lancaster

Electronic Workers
LU 175 . . . . Sumter
LU 273 . . . . Sumter

Federal Employees
LU 117 . . . . Eastover
LU 460 . . . . Columbia
LU 1214 . . . . Gilbert
LU 1639 . . . . Columbia

Food and Commercial Workers
LU 1800-T . . . . . . Winnsboro
LU 2014-T . . . . . . Newberry

Glass, Molders, Pottery and Plastics Workers
LU 15 . . . . Anderson
LU 291 . . . . Shelby
LU 387 . . . . Spartanburg

Government Employees
C 29 South Carolina State . Columbia
C 179 Fifth D Veteran
   Affairs . . . . Columbia
LU 56 . . . . Fort Jackson
LU 429 DoD . . . . . Parris Island
LU 510 . . . . Edgefield
LU 1869 DoD . . . . . Charleston
LU 1872 DoD . Shaw Air Force Base
LU 1909 DoD . . . . Fort Jackson
LU 1915 VA . . . . . . Columbia
LU 1951 DoD . . . . . . Burton
LU 2176 DoD Clarkshill-
   Hartwell . . . . Starr
LU 2298 DoD . . . . Goose Creek
LU 2510 DoD . . . . . Charleston
LU 2796 DoD . . . . . Beaufort
LU 3509 HHS . . . . . Anderson
LU 3654 . . . . Columbia
LU 3976 BOP, FPC, Estill . . . Estill

Government Employees Association
LU 5-150 RN Union . . . Charleston
LU 05-136 . . . . . . Charleston

Iron Workers
LU 601 . . . . Charleston

Letter Carriers
BR 233 . . . . Columbia
BR 439 . . . . Greenville
BR 628 . . . . Spartanburg
BR 904 . . . . Sumter
BR 1003 . . . . Chester
BR 1145 . . . . . . Greenwood
BR 1212 Chester, South
   Carolina . . . . Chester
BR 1416 . . . . Florence
BR 1569 . . . . Aiken
BR 1590 . . . . . . Bennettsville
BR 1666 . . . . Darlington
BR 1746 . . . . Clinton
BR 1782 . . . . . . Orangeburg
BR 1871 . . . . Anderson
BR 1914 . . . . Laurens
BR 2190 . . . . Gaffney
BR 2344 Walhalla, South
   Carolina . . . . Walhalla
BR 2533 . . . . Lancaster
BR 2553 . . . . Greer
BR 2745 Winnsboro, South
   Carolina . . . . . . Winnsboro
BR 2804 York, South Carolina . York
BR 3082 Inman, South
   Carolina . . . . Inman
BR 3161 Lyman, South
   Carolina . . . . Lyman
BR 3262 . . . . Beaufort

BR 3393 Woodruff, South
   Carolina . . . . Woodruff
BR 3648 Clover, South
   Carolina . . . . Clover
BR 3649 . . . . Conway
BR 3822 Kershaw, South
   Carolina . . . . Kershaw
BR 3902 . . . . . . Summerville
BR 3927 Loris, South
   Carolina . . . . Loris
BR 3996 . . . . Liberty
BR 4119 Whitmire, South
   Carolina . . . . . . Whitmire
BR 4223 Kingstree, South
   Carolina . . . . Kingstree
BR 4401 Honea Path, South
   Carolina . . . . . . Honea Path
BR 4616 . . . . . West Columbia
BR 4645 . . . . . . Myrtle Beach
BR 4974 Saluda, South
   Carolina . . . . Saluda
BR 4975 Pelzer, South
   Carolina . . . . Pelzer
BR 5104 Ruby, South
   Carolina . . . . Ruby
BR 5292 . . . . . . Ware Shoals
BR 5321 Calhoun Falls, South
   Carolina . . . . . Calhoun Falls
BR 5411 . . . . Allendale
BR 5413 St. Matthews, South
   Carolina . . . . . St. Matthews
BR 5423 Travelers Rest South
   Carolina . . . . . Travelers Rest
BR 5486 Branchville, South
   Carolina . . . . . . Branchville
BR 5527 Fountain Inn, South
   Carolina . . . . . Fountain Inn
BR 5823 . . . . . North Augusta
BR 5826 Andrews, South
   Carolina . . . . . . Andrews
BR 5857 McColl, South
   Carolina . . . . McColl
BR 6113 . . . . Islandton
BR 6123 . . . . . . Walterboro
BR 6423 Chesterfield, South
   Carolina . . . . . Chesterfield
BR 6490 Joanna, South
   Carolina . . . . Joanna
BR 6549 Great Falls, South
   Carolina . . . . . Great Falls
SA South Carolina . . . . Hartsville

Locomotive Engineers
DIV 84 . . . . Greer
DIV 85 . . . . Columbia
DIV 265 . . . . Florence
DIV 321 . . . . Ravenel
DIV 498 . . . . Abbeville
DIV 598 . . . . Pickens
DIV 717 . . . . Belvedere

Longshoremen
LU 1422 . . . . Charleston
LU 1422-A . . . . . . Charleston
LU 1751 . . . . . . Georgetown
LU 1771 . . . . . . Charleston

Machinists
LG . . . . Rock Hill
LG 183 . . . . . . North Charleston
LG 1002 . . . . . . Georgetown
LG 1879 . . . . Cayce
LLG W-52 Woodworkers . Kingstree
LLG W-77 Woodworkers . Florence
STC South Carolina . . . Charleston

Maintenance of Way Employes
LG 593 . . . . Hamer
LG 1618 . . . . St. Matthews
SLG 544 . . . . Clinton
SLG 562 . . . . Nichols
SLG 624 . . . . Parksville
SLG 1187 . . . . Greenville
SLG 2042 . . . . Ridgeville

Musicians
LU 502 . . . . Charleston

National Staff Organization
LU Staff Organization, South
   Carolina . . . . . . Myrtle Beach

Needletrades
LU 710-T . . . . Columbia
LU 860-A . . . . Columbia
LU 1093-T . . . . . . Rock Hill
LU 1120 . . . . Columbia
LU 2398 . . . . Columbia

Nurses
SA South Carolina Nurses
   Association . . . . . . Columbia

Office and Professional Employees
LU 233 . . . . Georgetown

Operating Engineers
LU 470 . . . . Aiken

Painters
LU 1756 . . . . . New Ellenton
LU 1946 . . . . . New Ellenton

Paper, Allied-Industrial, Chemical Employees
LU 02-1089 . . . . . . Fort Mill
LU 03-216 . . . . . . St. George
LU 03-357 . . . . . . Georgetown
LU 03-377 . . . . . . Georgetown
LU 03-378 . . . . . . Andrews
LU 03-477 . . . . . . Georgetown
LU 03-478 . . . . . New Ellenton
LU 03-508 . . . . . . Hanahan
LU 03-663 . . . . . . Hanahan
LU 03-674 . . . . . . Florence
LU 03-713 . . . . . . Swansea
LU 03-925 . . . . . . Lancaster
LU 03-1099 . . . . . . Spartanburg
LU 03-1099 . . . . . . Rock Hill
LU 03-1425 . . . . . Little Mountain
LU 03-1435 . . . . . . Charleston
LU 03-1569 . . . . . . Catawba
LU 03-1877 . . . . . . Darlington
LU 03-1879 . . . . . . Florence
LU 03-1924 . . . . . . York

Plumbing and Pipe Fitting
LU 421 . . . . . . North Charleston

Postal and Federal Employees
LU 304 . . . . Quinby
LU 313 . . . . Columbia
LU 319 . . . . Greenville
LU 326 . . . . Sumter

Postal Mail Handlers
LU 334 . . . . Columbia

Postal Workers
LU Spartanburg Area . . Spartanburg
LU 18 Anderson . . . . . Anderson

LU 168 Upper Piedmont
   Area . . . . Greenville
LU 566 Charleston . . . . Charleston
LU 795 Sumter. . . . . . . Sumter
LU 807 Columbia . . . . . Columbia
LU 1429 Marion Local. . . . Marion
LU 1581 Aiken . . . . Aiken
LU 1628 . . . . Gaffney
LU 1649 . . . . Greenville
LU 1776 Walterboro
   Local. . . . . Walterboro
LU 1796 Georgetown
   Local . . . . Georgetown
LU 1798 Bennettsville
   Local. . . . . . . Bennettsville
LU 2003 Conway . . . . . Conway
LU 2214 Lancaster . . . . Lancaster
LU 2225 Greer. . . . . . . Greer
LU 2408 Florence . . . . . Florence
LU 2444 Clemson Local . . Clemson
LU 2755 Myrtle
   Beach . . . . . . Myrtle Beach
LU 2841 Beaufort . . . . Beaufort
LU 5591 Mount
   Pleasant . . . . . Mount Pleasant
LU 7064 North Myrtle Beach
   Local . . . North Myrtle Beach
LU 7076 Hilton Head
   Island . . . . Hilton Head
SA South Carolina . . . . Greenville

Rural Letter Carriers
D 1. . . . . Huger
D 2 . . . . Lexington

D 3 . . . . Westminster
D 4 . . . . Taylors
D 5 . . . . Sharon
D 6 6th District South
   Carolina. . . . . Galivants Ferry
LU Abbeville County . . . Abbeville
LU Allendale-Hampton
   Counties . . . . Gifford
LU Anderson County . . . Anderson
LU Beaufort-Jasper
   Counties . . . . Seabrook
LU Cherokee County . . . . Gaffney
LU Chester-Fairfield
   Counties . . . . . . Winnsboro
LU Darlington-Lee Counties . Lamar
LU Florence County . . . Effingham
LU Greenville County . Fountain Inn
LU Kershaw-Lancaster
   Counties . . . . Kershaw
LU Laurens County . . . . Laurens
LU Lexington-Richland
   Counties . . . . Lexington
LU Newberry County. . Silver Street
LU Pickens County . . . . Greenville
LU Spartanburg County. . . Inman
LU Sumter County . . . . Sumter
SA South Carolina. . . . . . Aiken

Security Officers
LU 97. . . . . Charleston
LU 116 . . . . Aiken

**Security, Police and Fire
Professionals**
LU . . . . Cayce
LU 330 . . . . Aiken

Sheet Metal Workers
LU 399 . . . . Charleston Heights

Steelworkers
LU 09-850-L . . . . Fort Mill
LU 09-863-S . . . . . . Charleston
LU 09-7898-S. . . . . Georgetown
LU 09-8634-S . . . . . Bishopville

Teamsters
LU 28 . . . . Taylors
LU 86 . . . . Aiken
LU 509 . . . . Cayce

Theatrical Stage Employees
D 7 Tennessee-Alabama-Georgia-
   Florida-North Carolina-South
   Carolina-Mississippi-
   L. . . . . Walterboro
LU 320. . . . . Walterboro
LU 333 . . . . Charleston
LU 347 . . . . Cayce
LU 629 . . . . Waterboro
LU 929 . . . . Greenville

Transit Union
LDIV 610. . . . . . . Charleston
LDIV 1337 . . . . Columbia

**Transportation Communications
Union**
D 115 . . . . Florence
D 505 Southeastern System Board
   #9. . . . . Lyman
JPB 200 Finley
   Lines . . . . . . Boiling Springs
LG 6474 Florence . . . . . Florence

Transportation Union
LLG 1971 Yardmasters
   Department . . . . . . Cottageville
LU 407. . . . . Walterboro
LU 793 . . . . . . West Columbia
LU 931 . . . . Travelers Rest
LU 942 . . . . Darlington
LU 970 . . . . Abbeville
LU 1814 . . . . Wellford
SLB LO-45 South
   Carolina. . . . . Mount Pleasant

Treasury Employees
CH 55 . . . . Lexington
CH 166 . . . . Hanahan
CH 276 . . . . Columbia

Weather Service Employees
BR 01-3 . . . . . West Columbia
BR 01-40. . . . . Greer
BR 01-50. . . . . Charleston

Unaffiliated Labor
Organizations

Exxon Employees Association
   Southeast . . . . Rock Hill

South Dakota

AFL-CIO Trade and Industrial Departments

Building and Construction Trades Department
BCTC West River . . . . Rapid City

Affiliated Labor Organizations

Air Traffic Controllers
LU FSD . . . . Sioux Falls

Bakery, Confectionery, Tobacco Workers and Grain Millers
LU 143-G. . . . . Rapid City
LU 304-G . . . . Sioux Falls

Bricklayers
LU 1 . . . . Sioux Falls
LU 2 . . . . Yankton
LU 3 . . . . Aberdeen
LU 4 . . . . Rapid City
LU 5 . . . . Watertown
STCON South Dakota . . . Brandon

Communications Workers
LU 7500 . . . . Sioux Falls
LU 7503. . . . . Mitchell
LU 7504 . . . . Aberdeen
LU 7505 . . . . Rapid City
LU 7506. . . . . Huron

Electrical Workers
LU 423 . . . . Mobridge
LU 426. . . . . Sioux Falls
LU 690 . . . . Mitchell
LU 706. . . . . Aberdeen
LU 754 . . . . Yankton
LU 766 . . . . Huron
LU 1250 . . . . Rapid City
LU 1616 . . . . Rapid City
LU 1688 . . . . Yankton
LU 1959. . . . . Iroquois
SC U-26 Northwestern Public
Service Company. . . . . Mitchell

Electrical, Radio and Machine Workers
LU 1128 . . . . Sioux Falls
LU 1187 . . . . Elk Point

Federal Employees
LU 188 . . . . Rosebud

Food and Commercial Workers
LU 304-A . . . . Sioux Falls
LU 353-C . . . . Belle Fourche
LU 394 . . . . Rapid City

Government Employees
LU 901 USDA . . . . . Sioux Falls
LU 1509 VA . . . . . . Sioux Falls
LU 1539 VA . . . . . . Hot Springs
LU 2228 DoD . . . . . Rapid City
LU 2342 VA. . . . . . Fort Meade
LU 3035 DoD . . . . . Sioux Falls
LU 3185 DoD. . . . . . Yankton
LU 3365 USDA . . . . Rapid City
LU 3807 DoE . . . . . Watertown
LU 4040 BOP, FPC,
Yankton . . . . Yankton

Government Security Officers
LU 140 . . . . Rapid City

Laborers
LU 205 . . . . Rapid City
LU 1050 . . . . Rapid City

Letter Carriers
BR 491 . . . . Sioux Falls
BR 498 . . . . Mitchell
BR 502 . . . . Aberdeen
BR 659 . . . . Yankton
BR 724 Deadwood, South
Dakota . . . . Deadwood
BR 751. . . . . Wolsey
BR 1064 . . . . Pierre
BR 1088 . . . . Arlington
BR 1114 . . . . Watertown
BR 1225 . . . . Rapid City
BR 1308 . . . . Madison
BR 1480 Hot Springs, South
Dakota . . . . Hot Springs
BR 1485 Vermillion, South
Dakota . . . . Vermillion
BR 1673 Redfield, South
Dakota . . . . Redfield
BR 2011 Flandreau, South
Dakota . . . . Flandreau
BR 2205 Canton, South
Dakota . . . . Canton
BR 2762 Milbank, South
Dakota . . . . Milbank
BR 3015 . . . . Mobridge
BR 3124 Belle Fourche, South
Dakota . . . . Belle Fourche
BR 3526 Sisseton, South
Dakota . . . . Sisseton
BR 3597 . . . . Sturgis
BR 3622 Clark, South Dakota . Clark

BR 3630 Chamberlain, South
Dakota . . . . Chamberlain
BR 3737 Gregory, South
Dakota . . . . Gregory
BR 4298 Custer, South
Dakota . . . . Custer
BR 4488 Webster, South
Dakota . . . . Webster
BR 4711 . . . . Spearfish
BR 4976 Dell Rapids, South
Dakota . . . . Dell Rapids
BR 4995 Miller, South
Dakota . . . . Miller
BR 4996 Lemmon, South
Dakota . . . . Lemmon
BR 5160 Winner, South
Dakota . . . . Winner
BR 5209 Beresford, South
Dakota. . . . . Beresford
BR 6174 Gettysburg, South
Dakota . . . . Gettysburg
BR 8001 . . . . Rosholt
SA South Dakota . . . . Aberdeen

Locomotive Engineers
DIV 213 . . . . Hot Springs
DIV 726 . . . . Aberdeen

Machinists
DLG 5 . . . . Watertown
LG 862. . . . . Aberdeen
LG 2357 . . . . Watertown
STC Joint Dakota . . . . Aberdeen

Maintenance of Way Employes
LG 2825 . . . . Aberdeen
SF Chicago &
Northwestern . . . . . Wakonda
SLG 908 . . . . Sioux Falls
SLG 2852 . . . . Custer

National Staff Organization
LU Staff Association Professional,
South Dakota . . . . Sioux Falls
LU Staff Organization, South
Dakota. . . . . Pierre

Paper, Allied-Industrial, Chemical Employees
LU 7-1060. . . . . Gregory
LU 07-738 . . . . Lennox
LU 07-1078 . . . . . Chamberlain
LU 07-1457 . . . . . . Sioux Falls

Postal Mail Handlers
LU 328 . . . . Sioux Falls

Postal Workers
LU Mitchell. . . . . . . Mitchell
LU Sioux Falls Area . . . Sioux Falls
LU 68 Aberdeen. . . . . Aberdeen
LU 144 Watertown. . . . Watertown
LU 160 Huron. . . . . . . Huron
LU 760 Rapid City . . . . Rapid City
LU 934 Winner Local . . . Winner
LU 1235 Mobridge . . . . Mobridge
LU 2787 Pierre . . . . . . Pierre
LU 2874 Spearfish. . . . Spearfish
LU 4113 Vermillion
Local. . . . . Vermillion
LU 7141. . . . . Huron
SA South Dakota . . . . Aberdeen

Rural Letter Carriers
SA South Dakota . . . . Garretson

Service Employees
LU 217 Firemen &
Oilers . . . . Sioux Falls

Steelworkers
LU 11-7044-S . . . . . . Lead
LU 11-7833-S . . . . . Rapid City
LU 11-8188-S . . . . . Whitewood

Teamsters
LU 749. . . . . Sioux Falls

Theatrical Stage Employees
LU 220 . . . . Sioux Falls
LU 731 . . . . Rapid City

Transit Union
LDIV 1356. . . . . . . Sioux Falls

Transportation Union
LU 64 . . . . Huron
LU 233. . . . . Aberdeen
LU 375 . . . . Edgemont
SLB LO-46 South
Dakota . . . . Edgemont

Treasury Employees
CH 8 . . . . Aberdeen

Weather Service Employees
BR 03-30. . . . . Sioux Falls
BR 03-74. . . . . Rapid City
BR 03-93 . . . . Aberdeen

Unaffiliated Labor Organizations
Eros Laborers Number
One . . . . Sioux Falls
Eros Laborers Number
Two . . . . Dell Rapids

Tennessee

AFL-CIO Trade and Industrial Departments

Building and Construction Trades Department
BCTC Chattanooga. . . Chattanooga
BCTC East Tennessee . . Blountville
BCTC Knoxville . . . . . Knoxville
BCTC Memphis . . . . . Memphis
BCTC Nashville . . . . . Nashville

Metal Trades Department
MTC Air Engineering . . Tullahoma
MTC Atomic Trades & Labor . . . . Oak Ridge

AFL-CIO Directly Affiliated Locals
DALU 23444 Guards & Watchmen . . . . . . Chattanooga

Affiliated Labor Organizations

Air Traffic Controllers
LU BNA . . . . Nashville
LU CHA . . . . Chattanooga
LU MEM. . . . . Memphis
LU MQY . . . . Smyrna
LU TRI. . . . . Blountville
LU TYS . . . . Louisville
LU ZME . . . . Memphis

Aircraft Mechanics
LU 38 . . . . Memphis

Asbestos Workers
LU 46 . . . . Harriman
LU 52 . . . . Knoxville
LU 86 . . . . Hermitage
LU 90 . . . . Memphis

Automobile, Aerospace Workers
C Region 8 CAP . . . . . Lebanon
C Tennessee CAP . . . . Cookeville
LU . . . . Spring Hill
LU 342 . . . . Lebanon
LU 737. . . . . Nashville
LU 1086 . . . . Memphis
LU 1407 . . . . Cookeville
LU 1577 . . . . Spring Hill
LU 1617 . . . . Morristown
LU 1621 . . . . . . Lawrenceburg
LU 1676 . . . . Cleveland
LU 1832 . . . . Madison
LU 1853 . . . . Spring Hill
LU 1989 . . . . Memphis
LU 2155 . . . . . . Johnson City
LU 2303 . . . . Antioch
LU 2314 . . . . Vonore
LU 2406 . . . . Memphis
LU 2409 . . . . Cookeville
LU 6519 . . . . Memphis

Bakery, Confectionery, Tobacco Workers and Grain Millers
LU 25. . . . . Chattanooga
LU 149. . . . . Memphis
LU 165-G . . . . Knoxville
LU 252-G . . . . Memphis
LU 352-G . . . . Arlington
LU 358-G . . . . Atoka
LU 390-G . . . . Memphis

Boilermakers
C TVIC . . . . Franklin
DLG 57. . . . . . . Chattanooga
LG 2-S . . . . La Vergne
LG 14. . . . . Soddy Daisy
LG 14-S. . . . . . . Lewisburg
LG 140-D Cement Workers. . . . . Knoxville
LG 234-S . . . . Dickson
LG 251-S. . . . . Bolivar
LG 263. . . . . Memphis
LG 272-S . . . . . . La Vergne
LG 453 . . . . Knoxville
LG 454 . . . . Chattanooga
LG 586 . . . . Copperhill
LG 656 . . . . Chattanooga
LG 679 . . . . Chattanooga
LG 911 . . . . Clinton

Bricklayers
LU 5 Tennessee . . . . . Nashville

Carpenters
DC Tennessee . . . . . . Nashville
LU 50 . . . . Knoxville
LU 74. . . . . Chattanooga
LU 223. . . . . Nashville
LU 345 . . . . Memphis
LU 654 . . . . Chattanooga
LU 1544 . . . . Nashville
LU 2394 . . . . Paris
LU 2509 . . . . Jackson
LU 2825 . . . . . . Ashland City
LU 2919 . . . . Memphis
LU 3100 . . . . Gallatin

Civilian Technicians
CH 103 Volunteer . . . . . Smyrna
CH 110 Army Aviation . . . Jackson
CH 114 Smokey Mountain . . . . Louisville
CH 115 Memphis . . . . Memphis
CH 116 Music City Air . . Nashville

Communications Workers
LU 3802 . . . . Chattanooga
LU 3803 . . . . Columbia
LU 3804 . . . . Jackson
LU 3805 . . . . Knoxville
LU 3806 . . . . Memphis
LU 3808 . . . . Nashville
LU 3871. . . . . . . Bluff City
LU 3879 . . . . Nashville
LU 3890 . . . . Brentwood
LU 14347 . . . . Kingsport
LU 14348 . . . . Memphis
LU 14351 . . . . . . Knoxville
LU 33076 . . . . . . Knoxville
LU 33091 . . . . . . Memphis
LU 83706. . . . . Oneida
LU 8-369 . . . . Celina

Electrical Workers
C 4 Telephone Citizen . . Cookeville
LU 175 . . . . Chattanooga
LU 270 . . . . Oak Ridge
LU 311 . . . . Birchwood
LU 318 . . . . Maryville
LU 365 . . . . Morristown
LU 429. . . . . Nashville
LU 474 . . . . Memphis
LU 760 . . . . Knoxville

Boilermakers
LU 400-G . . . . Rossville
LU 407-G . . . . Memphis

LU 881 . . . . Bartlett
LU 934 . . . . Blountville
LU 1087 . . . . Cookeville
LU 1288 . . . . Memphis
LU 1749. . . . . Camden
LU 1925 . . . . Martin
LU 2080 . . . . . Hendersonville
LU 2113 . . . . Manchester
LU 2143. . . . . Sparta
LU 2335 . . . . Martin

Electronic Workers
LU 703 . . . . . . Murfreesboro
LU 748 . . . . . . Jefferson City
LU 791 . . . . Greeneville
LU 796. . . . . Greeneville

Elevator Constructors
LU 30 . . . . Bartlett
LU 64 . . . . Jacksboro
LU 93 . . . . Nashville

Federal Employees
LU 259. . . . . Memphis
LU 1930 . . . . . . Piney Flats

Fire Fighters
LU 2-I X-10 Industrial Firefighters . . . . Norris
LU 14-F . . . . . . Fayetteville
LU 1346 . . . . Oak Ridge

Food and Commercial Workers
C Textile and Garment . . Hermitage
LU 36-B . . . . Memphis
LU 194-C . . . . Memphis
LU 231-T . . . . Tullahoma
LU 233-T . . . . Springfield
LU 252-C . . . . . . Oak Ridge
LU 272-T . . . . . . Russellville
LU 293-T . . . . . Johnson City
LU 297-T . . . . . . Lenoir City
LU 387-C . . . . Alcoa
LU 397-C . . . . Atoka
LU 491-G . . . . . Andersonville
LU 515 . . . . Memphis
LU 522-G . . . . . White House
LU 663-T. . . . . . Bean Station
LU 700-C . . . . . New Market
LU 701 . . . . . . New Market
LU 715-C . . . . . . Kingston
LU 815-T . . . . . . Morristown
LU 1036-C. . . . . . Maynardville
LU 1529 . . . . Cordova
LU 1995 . . . . Hermitage
LU 2207-T . . . . . . Hermitage

Glass, Molders, Pottery and Plastics Workers
LU 319 . . . . Pikeville

Government Employees
LU 530 HUD . . . . . . Knoxville
LU 850 USDA . . . . . Memphis
LU 1687 VA . . . . Mountain Home
LU 1788 USDA . . . . . Smyrna
LU 1844 VA . . . . Murfreesboro
LU 2172 DoD . . . . . . Memphis
LU 2400 VA . . . . . Nashville
LU 2470 VA . . . . . Nashville
LU 2659 DoD . . . . . Kingsport
LU 3136 USDA . . . . Rogersville
LU 3496 DoL . . . . . Jacksboro
LU 3599 EEOC . . . . . Memphis
LU 3731 DoJ. . . . . . Memphis

LU 3930 VA, Medical Center Staff Nurse Association. . . Collierville
LU 3980 COP . . . . . Ashland City

Government Employees Association
LU 147 . . . . Maryville
LU 05-66. . . . . Memphis

Government Security Officers
LU 25 . . . . Oakdale
LU 26 . . . . Hixson
LU 68 . . . . Memphis

Graphic Communications
LU 118-C . . . . Knoxville
LU 197-M . . . . . . Chattanooga
LU 198-B . . . . Rogersville
LU 231-M . . . . Memphis
LU 290-M. . . . . . Goodlettsville
LU 400-C . . . . Rogersville
LU 513-S . . . . . . Murfreesboro
LU 521-M. . . . . Dickson

Guards
LU 3 . . . . Oak Ridge
LU 46 . . . . . . Estill Springs
LU 100 . . . . Delano
LU 137. . . . . Nashville
RC Tenth . . . . . . Oak Ridge

Hotel and Restaurant Employees
LU 623 . . . . Knoxville
LU 775. . . . . Nashville
LU 847. . . . . Memphis

Iron Workers
DC Tennessee Valley & Vicinity. . . . . . Chattanooga
LU 167. . . . . Memphis
LU 384 . . . . Knoxville
LU 492 . . . . Nashville
LU 526 . . . . Chattanooga
LU 704 . . . . Chattanooga
LU 733 . . . . Nashville

Laborers
DC Tennessee . . . . . . Nashville
LU 386 . . . . Madison
LU 818 . . . . Knoxville
LU 846 . . . . Chattanooga
LU 1441 . . . . Memphis

Laundry and Dry Cleaning
LU 550. . . . . Memphis

Letter Carriers
BR 4 . . . . Nashville
BR 27 . . . . Memphis
BR 62. . . . . Hixson
BR 364 . . . . Clarksville
BR 419 . . . . Knoxville
BR 807 . . . . Bristol
BR 1110 . . . . . . Johnson City
BR 1256. . . . . . . Morristown
BR 1402. . . . . . . Murfreesboro
BR 1710 Humboldt, Tennessee. . . . . . . Humboldt
BR 1819 Franklin, Tennessee. . . . . . . Franklin
BR 1838 Rockwood, Tennessee . . . . . . Rockwood
BR 1853 Shelbyville, Tennessee . . . . . Shelbyville

BR 1879 Etowah,
Tennessee . . . . Etowah
BR 1897 Athens, Tennessee . Athens
BR 1994 Dyersburg,
Tennessee . . . . Dyersburg
BR 1995 . . . . Cleveland
BR 1999 . . . . Kingsport
BR 2332 La Follette,
Tennessee . . . . La Follette
BR 2585 McKenzie,
Tennessee . . . . McKenzie
BR 2684 Sweetwater,
Tennessee . . . . . . Sweetwater
BR 2831 . . . . Elizabethton
BR 2910 Clinton, Tennessee. Clinton
BR 2917 . . . . Erwin
BR 3157 Rogersville,
Tennessee . . . . . . Rogersville
BR 3174 Dresden,
Tennessee . . . . Dresden
BR 3214 Livingston,
Tennessee . . . . . . Livingston
BR 3229 Huntingdon,
Tennessee . . . . . . Huntingdon
BR 3255 Carthage,
Tennessee . . . . . . Carthage
BR 3259 Watertown,
Tennessee . . . . . . Watertown
BR 3339 Greenfield,
Tennessee . . . . . Greenfield
BR 3382 Ripley, Tennessee . Ripley
BR 3408 Kenton, Tennessee. Kenton
BR 3431 Newbern,
Tennessee . . . . Newbern
BR 3503 Loudon,
Tennessee . . . . . . Loudon
BR 3509 Sevierville,
Tennessee . . . . . . Sevierville
BR 3549 Sparta, Tennessee. . Sparta
BR 3552 Jonesboro,
Tennessee . . . . . Jonesborough
BR 3644 Halls, Tennessee . . . Halls
BR 3707 Oneida, Tennessee . Oneida
BR 3718 Bolivar, Tennessee. Bolivar
BR 3800 Portland,
Tennessee . . . . Portland
BR 3869 . . . . Kingston
BR 4070 Bruceton,
Tennessee . . . . . Bruceton
BR 4164 Centerville,
Tennessee . . . . . . Centerville
BR 4209 Smithville,
Tennessee . . . . . . Smithville
BR 4210 Selmer, Tennessee . Selmer
BR 4215 Parsons,
Tennessee . . . . Parsons
BR 4884 Monterey,
Tennessee . . . . . . Monterey
BR 5106 Lancaster,
Tennessee . . . . . . Lancaster
BR 5173 Lookout Mountain,
Tennessee . . . Lookout Mountain
BR 5404 . . . . Clarksville
BR 6164 Madisonville,
Tennessee . . . . . Madisonville
BR 6271 Rockford,
Tennessee . . . . . . Rockford
BR 6435 Woodlawn,
Tennessee . . . . . . Woodlawn
BR 6506 Mountain City,
Tennessee . . . . Mountain City
SA Tennessee . . . . Knoxville

Locomotive Engineers
DIV 21 . . . . Memphis
DIV 41 . . . . Hendersonville
DIV 129 . . . . Goodlettsville
DIV 198 . . . . Ooltewah

DIV 205 . . . . Chattanooga
DIV 239 . . . . Knoxville
DIV 473 . . . . Columbia
DIV 508 . . . . . . South Fulton
DIV 547 . . . . Englewood
DIV 610 . . . . Huntingdon
DIV 672 . . . . Bartlett
DIV 756 . . . . Hermitage
DIV 781 . . . . . . Johnson City
DIV 782 . . . . Riceville
GCA 4-175 Norfolk Southern
Railway . . . . Ooltewah
SLB Kentucky . . . . South Fulton
SLB Tennessee . . . . . Ooltewah

Longshoremen
LU 1671 . . . . Memphis

Machinists
DLG 2 . . . . Memphis
DLG 711 . . . . Nashville
LG 3 . . . . Memphis
LG 56 . . . . Chattanooga
LG 58 . . . . Knoxville
LG 61 . . . . Memphis
LG 154 . . . . . . Murfreesboro
LG 476 . . . . Camden
LG 480 . . . . Oak Ridge
LG 555 . . . . Chattanooga
LG 735 . . . . Nashville
LG 792 . . . . Watertown
LG 798 . . . . Nashville
LG 879 . . . . Nashville
LG 1193 . . . . McKenzie
LG 1296 . . . . Big Rock
LG 1387 . . . . Paris
LG 1441 . . . . Springfield
LG 1443 . . . . Erwin
LG 1450 . . . . Harrison
LG 1458 . . . . . . Chattanooga
LG 1479 Old Hickory . . . Burns
LG 1501 . . . . Decherd
LG 1538 . . . . Erin
LG 1640 . . . . Dover
LG 1647 . . . . Brownsville
LG 1959 . . . . Nashville
LG 2212 . . . . Crossville
LG 2325 . . . . . . Waynesboro
LG 2356 . . . . . Tennessee Ridge
LG 2385 . . . . . . Fayetteville
LG 2419 . . . . Humboldt
LG 2528 . . . . Linden
LG 2544 . . . . . . Lenoir City
LG 2709 . . . . . Oliver Springs
LG 2763 . . . . Memphis
LG 2805-PM . . . . Chattanooga
LLG 1-2545 Machinists . . . Loudon
STC Tennessee . . . . Nashville

Maintenance of Way Employes
LG 514 . . . . Atoka
LG 546 . . . . Evensville
LG 654 . . . . Bolivar
LG 667 . . . . Winchester
LG 670 . . . . Smyrna
LG 676 . . . . Camden
SLG 558 . . . . Unicoi
SLG 567 . . . . . . Sevierville
SLG 725 . . . . . . Lewisburg
SLG 986 . . . . Dickson
SLG 1854 . . . . . . Jacksboro
SLG 2600 . . . . . . Millington

Mine Workers
LU 1070 . . . . Cosby

Musicians
LU 71 . . . . Memphis

LU 80 . . . . Chattanooga
LU 257 . . . . Nashville
LU 546 . . . . Knoxville

National Staff Organization
ASSN Memphis
Education . . . . Memphis
LU Staff Organization of the
Tennessee Educators
Association . . . . . Kingsport

Needletrades
LU 95 . . . . Knoxville
LU 338 . . . . Knoxville
LU 609-A . . . . Knoxville
LU 611-A . . . . Knoxville
LU 906 . . . . Knoxville
LU 963-I . . . . Knoxville
LU 1418 . . . . Knoxville
LU 1742 . . . . Knoxville
LU 1933-A . . . . Knoxville
LU 2102 . . . . Knoxville
LU 2408 . . . . Knoxville
LU 2537 . . . . Knoxville
LU 2548 . . . . Knoxville
LU 2589 . . . . Knoxville
LU 2614 . . . . Knoxville
LU 2633 . . . . Knoxville

NLRB Professional Association
LU 26 . . . . Memphis

Office and Professional Employees
LU 144 . . . . Knoxville
LU 182 . . . . Nashville
LU 367 . . . . Memphis
LU 2001 . . . . Knoxville

Operating Engineers
LU 369 . . . . Memphis
LU 900 . . . . Oak Ridge
LU 912 . . . . Columbia
LU 917 . . . . Chattanooga

Painters
LU 49 . . . . Memphis
LU 226 . . . . Chattanooga
LU 242 . . . . Memphis
LU 437 . . . . Knoxville
LU 456 . . . . Nashville
LU 1805 . . . . Harriman

Paper, Allied-Industrial, Chemical Employees
LU 21 . . . . Chattanooga
LU 5-7 . . . . Waverly
LU 5-714 . . . . Cordova
LU 5-899 . . . . Charleston
LU 5-951 . . . . Johnson City
LU 05-1 . . . . Chattanooga
LU 05-80 . . . . Franklin
LU 05-122 . . . . . . Soddy Daisy
LU 05-212 . . . . Jackson
LU 05-288 . . . . . . Oak Ridge
LU 05-357 . . . . Bartlett
LU 05-362 . . . . . . Chattanooga
LU 05-466 Humboldt Boxmakers
Union . . . . Humboldt
LU 05-590 . . . . Jackson
LU 05-631 . . . . Memphis
LU 05-677 . . . . Erwin
LU 05-722 . . . . Collierville
LU 05-724 . . . . Newport
LU 05-733 . . . . Talbott
LU 05-739 . . . . Athens
LU 05-763 . . . . Memphis
LU 05-771 . . . . Memphis
LU 05-790 . . . . Athens

LU 05-978 . . . . Savannah
LU 05-981 . . . . Sevierville
LU 05-983 . . . . Oak Ridge
LU 05-984 . . . . Memphis
LU 05-985 . . . . Kingston
LU 05-987 . . . . Columbia
LU 05-990 . . . . Rockwood
LU 05-992 . . . . Savannah
LU 05-993 . . . . Savannah
LU 05-1197 . . . . Bruceton
LU 05-1274 . . . . Memphis
LU 05-1276 . . . . Corryton
LU 05-1289 . . . . Memphis
LU 05-1337 . . . . Cleveland
LU 05-1411 . . . . Newport
LU 05-1766 . . . . Memphis
LU 05-1816 . . . . Memphis
LU 50-784 . . . . Smithville
NHQ . . . . Nashville

Plant Protection Employees
LU 402 . . . . Nashville

Plasterers and Cement Masons
LU 78 . . . . Knoxville
LU 647 . . . . Church Hill
LU 909 . . . . Nashville

Plumbing and Pipe Fitting
LU 17 . . . . Memphis
LU 43 . . . . Chattanooga
LU 102 . . . . Knoxville
LU 538 . . . . Johnson City
LU 572 . . . . Nashville
LU 614 . . . . Memphis
LU 702 . . . . Nashville
LU 718 . . . . Lake City
LU 854 . . . . Henderson
SA Tennessee Pipe
Trades . . . . Nashville

Postal and Federal Employees
LU 403 . . . . Chattanooga
LU 406 . . . . Knoxville
LU 407 . . . . Memphis
LU 410 . . . . Nashville

Postal Mail Handlers
LU 329 . . . . Memphis

Postal Workers
LU The Hermitage . . . . Hermitage
LU 5 Nashville . . . . . . Nashville
LU 96 Memphis . . . . . Memphis
LU 192 Chattanooga Area . . Athens
LU 245 Jackson . . . . . Jackson
LU 263 Knoxville . . . . Knoxville
LU 308 Clarksville . . . Clarksville
LU 353 Columbia . . . . Columbia
LU 365 Johnson City . Johnson City
LU 736 Elizabethton . . Elizabethton
LU 752 Trenton Local . . . . Trenton
LU 757 Paris . . . . Paris
LU 974 Murfreesboro . Murfreesboro
LU 977 Cookeville . . . . Cookeville
LU 1113 Fayetteville
Local . . . . Fayetteville
LU 1335 Jefferson City
Local . . . . Jefferson City
LU 1384 Maryville . . . . Maryville
LU 1417 La Follette
Local . . . . La Follette
LU 1469 Lawrenceburg
Local . . . . Lawrenceburg
LU 1540 Gallatin Local . . Gallatin
LU 1574 Clinton Local . . . Clinton
LU 1577 Oneida Local . . . . Oneida
LU 1596 Sparta Local . . . . Sparta

LU 1663 Lewisburg Local . . . . Lewisburg
LU 1728 McMinnville Local. . . . . McMinnville
LU 1778 Huntsville. . . . Huntsville
LU 2335 Lexington Local . . . . Lexington
LU 2369 Sevierville Local . . . . Sevierville
LU 2391 Camden Local . . Camden
LU 2394 Dresden Local . . Dresden
LU 2395 Humboldt Local. Humboldt
LU 2464 Crossville . . . . Crossville
LU 2509 Dickson Local . . Dickson
LU 2689 Martin Local . . . Martin
LU 2692 McKenzie. . . . McKenzie
LU 2932 Savannah . . . . Savannah
LU 3097 Milan Local . . . . Milan
LU 3681 Lafayette Local . Lafayette
LU 3955 Smithville Local . . . . Smithville
LU 4059 Dyersburg . . Dyersburg
LU 4426 Mountain City Local . . . . Mountain City
LU 4660 Shelbyville Local. . . . . Shelbyville
LU 4728 Tiptonville Local. . . . . Tiptonville
LU 5060 Gatlinburg Local . . . . Gatlinburg
LU 6783 Hendersonville . . Hendersonville
SA Tennessee . . . . Jackson

Professional and Technical Engineers
LU 2 Judicial Council 2 . . Memphis

Railroad Signalmen
LLG 67 . . . . Gallatin
LLG 110 . . . . Sweetwater
LLG 158 . . . . Madisonville
LLG 162 . . . . Martin
LLG 198 . . . . Erwin

Retail, Wholesale and Department Store
C Central States . . . . . Knoxville
DC Tennessee . . . . . . Knoxville
LU 150 . . . . Nashville
LU 323 . . . . Knoxville
LU 910 . . . . Memphis

Roofers, Waterproofers and Allied Workers
LU 176 . . . . Nashville

Rural Letter Carriers
LU Bedford County . . . Shelbyville
LU Blount County . . . . . Towsend
LU Campbell County . . La Follette
LU Carter County . . . Johnson City
LU Cheatham County. . . . . . Chapmansboro
LU Chester County . . . . . Finger
LU Claiborne County. . . . Cumberland Gap
LU Clay County . . . . . . Celina
LU Cumberland County . Crossville
LU Davidson County. . . . . . Hendersonville
LU Decatur County . . . . Parsons
LU Dyer County . . . . Dyersburg
LU Fayette County . . . . Oakland
LU Gibson County . . . . Rutherford
LU Greene County . . . Greeneville
LU Hamblen County . . Bean Station

LU Hamilton-Bradley-Polk Counties . . . . Cleveland
LU Hancock County . . Sneedville
LU Hardin County . . . . . Enville
LU Hawkins County . . Rogersville
LU Henderson County . . Lexington
LU Henry County. . . . Big Sandy
LU Hickman County. . . Centerville
LU Jefferson County . . . . Talbott
LU Lauderdale County . . . Ripley
LU Lewis County . . . . Hohenwald
LU Loudon County . . . Lenior City
LU Marion County . . . . . Jasper
LU Marshall County . . . . Belfast
LU Maury County . . . . Lynnville
LU Monroe County . . Tellico Plains
LU Montgomery County . Clarksville
LU Morgan County . . . Wartburg
LU Putnam County. . . Cookeville
LU Rhea County . . . . . Dayton
LU Roane County . . . Kingston
LU Robertson County . Cross Plains
LU Scott County . . . . . Oneida
LU Stewart-Houston Counties . Erin
LU Sumner County . . . . Gallatin
LU Union County . . . . Luttrell
LU Washington County . . . Gray
LU Wilson County . . Mount Juliet
LU 1 Anderson County . . . . . Andersonville
LU 9 Carroll County . . Huntingdon
LU 15 Cocke County . . Parrottsville
LU 16 Coffee-Grundy Counties. . . . . . . Manchester
LU 22 Dickson County . . Bon Aqua
LU 25 Fentress County . Jamestown
LU 26 Franklin-Moore Counties . . . . . Estill Springs
LU 29 Grainger County. . Washburn
LU 47 Knox County. . . Knoxville
LU 52 Lincoln County . Fayetteville
LU 54 Macon County . . Byrdstown
LU 55 Madison County . . Jackson
LU 60 McNairy County . . . . . Morris Chapel
LU 61 Meigs County. . . Ten Mile
LU 69 Pickett . . . . . Byrdstown
LU 75 Rutherford County . . Smyrna
LU 78 Sevier County . . Knoxville
LU 79 Shelby County . . Memphis
LU 82 Sullivan County . Kingsport
LU 84 Tipton County . . Brighton
LU 88-89 Warren & Van Buren Counties . . . . . . Woodbury
LU 91 Wayne County . . Collinwood
LU 92 Weakley County. . Dresden
SA Tennessee . . . . . . Bethpage

Security, Police and Fire Professionals
LU 102 . . . . Alcoa
LU 109 . . . . Oak Ridge
LU 403 . . . . Spring Hill

Service Employees
C 4 Tennessee State . . . . Nashville
LU 166 . . . . Oak Ridge
LU 177 Firemen & Oilers. Knoxville
LU 205 . . . . Nashville
LU 784 Firemen & Oilers . Memphis
LU 1160 Firemen & Oilers . . . . Nashville

Sheet Metal Workers
LU 4 . . . . Memphis
LU 5 . . . . Knoxville
LU 177 . . . . Nashville
LU 192 . . . . Blaine

LU 211 . . . . Franklin
LU 267 . . . . Chattanooga
LU 424 . . . . Woodbury
LU 483 . . . . Morrison
LU 555 . . . . Knoxville

State, County and Municipal Employees
LU 1733 Memphis Public Employees Union . . . . Memphis

Steelworkers
LU 3006 . . . . Dyer
LU 9457 . . . . Milan
LU 09-90-G . . . . Knoxville
LU 09-109-S . . . . . . Kingsport
LU 09-117-S . . . . . . Knoxville
LU 09-122-S . . . . Gray
LU 09-194-L . . . . . . Palmyra
LU 09-224 . . . . Camden
LU 09-234-A . . . . . Greeneville
LU 09-244 . . . . Waverly
LU 09-299 . . . . Kingsport
LU 09-309-S . . . . Alcoa
LU 09-440-G . . . . Jackson
LU 09-456-G . . . . . Church Hill
LU 09-496 . . . . Kingsport
LU 09-507-G . . . . . Greeneville
LU 09-634 . . . . . Soddy Daisy
LU 09-641-L . . . . Pulaski
LU 09-672-L . . . . Grand Junction
LU 09-811-L . . . . . . Crossville
LU 09-878-L . . . . . . Union City
LU 09-1002-L . . . . . . Newport
LU 09-1008-L . . . . Obion
LU 09-1055-L . . . . . La Vergne
LU 09-1155-L . . . . . . Morrison
LU 09-2360-L . . . . . . Memphis
LU 09-3115-S . . . . . . Harrison
LU 09-3508-S . . . . Chattanooga
LU 09-4586-S . . . . . Bluff City
LU 09-4802-S . . . . . La Vergne
LU 09-4928-S . . . . Chattanooga
LU 09-5431-S . . . . . . Knoxville
LU 09-5887-S . . . . . . Nashville
LU 09-5945-S . . . . Erwin
LU 09-6638-S . . . . . Philadelphia
LU 09-6817-S . . . . . . Decherd
LU 09-6884-S . . . . . Greeneville
LU 09-7198-S . . . . . . Del Rio
LU 09-7509-S . . . . . Lewisburg
LU 09-7557-S . . . . . Winchester
LU 09-7573-S . . . . . . Savannah
LU 09-7655-S . . . . . Collierville
LU 09-7739-S . . . . Johnson City
LU 09-7894-S . . . . Bristol
LU 09-8413-S . . . . . . Lebanon
LU 09-8681-S . . . . . Greenback
LU 09-8915-S . . . . . . McKenzie
LU 09-9137-S . . . . . Manchester
LU 09-9147-S . . . . . Harriman
LU 09-9410 . . . . Oakdale
LU 09-9426-S . . . . . . Nashville
LU 09-12943-S . . . . . Kingsport
LU 09-14597-S . . . . . . Oneida
LU 09-15120-S . . . . Chattanooga

Teachers
SFED Tennessee . . . . . . Jellico

Teamsters
LU 217 . . . . Jackson
LU 327 . . . . Nashville
LU 480 . . . . Nashville
LU 515 . . . . Chattanooga
LU 519 . . . . Knoxville
LU 549 . . . . Blountville
LU 667 . . . . Memphis

LU 984 . . . . Memphis
LU 1196 . . . . Memphis

Television and Radio Artists
LU Nashville. . . . . . . Nashville

Theatrical Stage Employees
LU 46 . . . . Nashville
LU 69 . . . . Memphis
LU 140 . . . . Chattanooga
LU 197 . . . . Knoxville
LU 492 . . . . Nashville
LU 851 . . . . Maryville
LU 894 . . . . Seymour
LU 915 . . . . Hermitage

Tool Craftsmen
LU 20 . . . . Lenoir City

Transit Union
LDIV 713 . . . . Memphis
LDIV 1164 . . . . Knoxville
LDIV 1212 . . . . . Chattanooga
LDIV 1235 . . . . . . Nashville
LDIV 1285 . . . . Jackson

Transport Workers
LU 590 . . . . Nashville

Transportation Communications Union
D 22 . . . . Knoxville
D 24 Southeastern . . . Chattanooga
D 228 . . . . Nolensville
LG 6047 Marble City . . . Knoxville
LG 6477 Clinchfield . . Elizabethton
LG 6673 Nashville . . . . . Smyrna

Transportation Union
GCA G6-346 . . . . Whitwell
GCA GO-433 Illinois Central Gulf Railroad . . . . . . Memphis
LU 338 . . . . Soddy
LU 339 . . . . Jackson
LU 459 . . . . Hixson
LU 750 . . . . New Market
LU 753 . . . . Munford
LU 974 . . . . Antioch
LU 1162 . . . . Erwin
LU 1301 . . . . Morristown
LU 1308 . . . . McKenzie
LU 1314 . . . . Athens
LU 1345 . . . . Etowak
LU 1346 . . . . . . Chapel Hill
LU 1420 . . . . Collierville
LU 1525 . . . . . . South Fulton
SLB LO-47 Tennessee. . . Nashville

Treasury Employees
CH 39 . . . . Nashville
CH 98 . . . . Memphis
CH 270 . . . . Nashville
CH 277 . . . . Cordova

Weather Service Employees
BR 02-2 . . . . Memphis
BR 02-43 . . . . Old Hickory
BR 02-55 . . . . Memphis
BR 02-82 . . . . . Morristown

Unaffiliated Labor Organizations
C12 Aviation Inc. MKL-Air Traffic Control Tower. . . . . Jackson
Drivers Warehousemen Maintenance Workers LU 1 . . . . . Nashville
Fedex Pilots Association. . Memphis

| Old Hickory Clerk & Technical Workers Union. . . . Old Hickory | Old Hickory Rayon Employees Council. . . . . . . Old Hickory | Trades and Labor Council for Annual of TVA. . . . . . . Chattanooga | USWA . . . . Nashville |

Texas

AFL-CIO Trade and Industrial Departments

Building and Construction Trades Department
BCTC Arkansas-Louisiana-
  Texas . . . . Longview
BCTC Central Texas . . . . . Austin
BCTC Dallas . . . . Dallas
BCTC El Paso . . . . El Paso
BCTC Houston . . . . Houston
BCTC Sabine Area. . . . Pasadena
BCTC San Antonio. . . San Antonio
BCTC Texas Panhandle . . Amarillo
BCTC Texas State . . . . . Austin
NHQ South Texas. . . . . Harlingen

Maritime Trades Department
PC West Gulf . . . . Houston

Metal Trades Department
MTC Amarillo & Vicinity . Amarillo
MTC Freeport . . . . . Lake Jackson
MTC Galveston . . . . . La Marque
MTC Houston. . . . . . . Houston
MTC Texas City . . . . . Texas City

Other Councils and Committees
C Ellis County Labor . . . . . Ennis
C San Antonio . . . . . San Antonio

Affiliated Labor Organizations

Agricultural Employees
BR 4 . . . . Lyford
BR 5 . . . . Laredo
BR 10. . . . . San Juan
BR 15 . . . . El Paso
BR 21. . . . . Houston
BR 27. . . . . Eagle Pass
BR 42 . . Dallas-Fort Worth Airport
BR 53. . . . . Floresville

Air Traffic Controllers
LU . . . . San Angelo
LU ABI . . . . Abilene
LU ACT . . . . Waco
LU ADS . . . . Addison
LU AFW . . . . Fort Worth
LU AMA . . . . Amarillo
LU AUS. . . . . Austin
LU BPT . . . . Beaumont
LU BRO . . . . Brownsville
LU CRP . . . . Corpus Christi
LU D-10 . Dallas-Fort Worth Airport
LU DAL. . . . . Dallas
LU DFW. Dallas-Fort Worth Airport
LU DWH . . . . Tomball
LU ELP . . . . El Paso
LU ESW . . . . Fort Worth
LU FTW . . . . Fort Worth
LU GGG . . . . Longview
LU HOU . . . . Houston
LU HRL. . . . . Harlingen
LU I-90-ASW. . . . . . . Houston
LU IAH . . . . Houston
LU LBB . . . . Lubbok
LU MAF . . . . Midland
LU MFE . . . . McAllen
LU SAT. . . . . San Antonio
LU TKI . . . . McKinney
LU ZFW . . . . Fort Worth
LU ZHU . . . . Houston

Asbestos Workers
LU 21 . . . . Dallas
LU 22 . . . . Pasadena
LU 66. . . . . Lubbock
LU 87. . . . . San Antonio
LU 102 . . . . Clute
LU 111 . . . . Pasadena

Automobile, Aerospace Workers
C Texas State CAP . . . . . Dallas
LU 119 . . . . Cedar Hill
LU 129. . . . . Fort Worth
LU 218 . . . . Hurst
LU 276. . . . . Grand Prairie
LU 317 . . . . Hurst
LU 514 . . . . Cedar Hill
LU 816 . . . . Fort Worth
LU 848. . . . . Grand Prairie
LU 864 . . . . Houston
LU 870 . . . . Cedar Hill
LU 967 . . . . Greenville
LU 2157 . . . . Wichita Falls
LU 2346 . . . . Cedar Hill
LU 2360 . . . . Cedar Hill

Bakery, Confectionery, Tobacco Workers and Grain Millers
LU 64-G. . . . . Savoy
LU 111 . . . . Dallas
LU 163 . . . . Houston
LU 237-G . . . . Denison
LU 257-G . . . . Kenedy
LU 321-G. . . . . Hereford
LU 356 . . . . El Paso
LU 442 . . . . Dallas

Boilermakers
LG 55 . . . . Houston
LG 69-D Cement Workers . . Waco
LG 74 . . . . Houston
LG 78-D Cement Workers . Quanah
LG 132 . . . . La Marque
LG 437-D Cement Workers . Palmer
LG 476-D Cement Workers . Odessa
LG 531 . . . . Amarillo
LG 546-D Cement
  Workers. . . . . . . Beaumont
LG 577-D Cement
  Workers . . . . . . Texarkana
LG 587 . . . . Orange
LG 682. . . . . Lake Jackson
LG 5200 . . . . Wichita Falls

Bricklayers
LU 1 Texas Louisiana New
  Mexico . . . . Austin

Carpenters
DC Texas . . . . Arlington
LU 14. . . . . San Antonio
LU 429. . . . . Arlington
LU 502. . . . . Port Arthur
LU 526 . . . . Texas City
LU 551 . . . . Houston
LU 665 . . . . Amarillo
LU 724 . . . . Houston
LU 1266. . . . . Austin
LU 1421 . . . . Arlington
LU 1751 . . . . San Marcos
LU 2104 . . . . Mesquite
LU 2218 . . . . El Paso
LU 2232. . . . . Houston
LU 2440 . . . . Wimmberly
LU 2713 . . . . Joaquin
LU 2743 . . . . San Antonio

LU 2848. . . . . Dallas
STC Texas. . . . . Arlington

Civilian Technicians
CH 100 Texas Lone Star . . . Austin

Communications Workers
LU 780 . . . . San Antonio
LU 782 . . . . Tyler
LU 1123 . . . . San Antonio
LU 1129-FW . . . . . San Antonio
LU 3263 Manufacturing President's
  Council . . . . Mesquite
LU 6110 . . . . Laredo
LU 6113 . . . . Greenville
LU 6118 . . . . Longview
LU 6127 . . . . Midland
LU 6128 . . . . Amarillo
LU 6132. . . . . Austin
LU 6137 . . . . Corpus Christi
LU 6139 . . . . Beaumont
LU 6143 . . . . San Antonio
LU 6150 . . . . Dallas
LU 6151 . . . . Dallas
LU 6171 . . . . Krum
LU 6174 . . . . Killeen
LU 6178 . . . . Dallas
LU 6182 . . . . San Antonio
LU 6186. . . . . Austin
LU 6200 . . . . Graham
LU 6201 . . . . Fort Worth
LU 6202 . . . . Abilene
LU 6203 . . . . Lubbock
LU 6206 . . . . Temple
LU 6210 . . . . McKinney
LU 6214 . . . . Tyler
LU 6215 . . . . Dallas
LU 6218 . . . . Lufkin
LU 6222 . . . . Houston
LU 6225 . . . . Waco
LU 6228 . . . . Texas City
LU 6229 . . . . Harlingen
LU 6260 . . . . Mesquite
LU 6290 . . . . Dallas
LU 6733 . . . . El Paso
LU 14628 . . . . Austin
LU 14630 . . . . El Paso
LU 14631 Forth Worth . Fort Worth
LU 14635 . . . . Waco
LU 14642 . . . . Waco
LU 86787 . . . . Richardson

Education
SA Texas Teachers
  Association . . . . Austin

Electrical Workers
LU 20 . . . . Dallas
LU 60. . . . . San Antonio
LU 66 . . . . Pasadena
LU 69 . . . . Dallas
LU 72 . . . . Waco
LU 278 . . . . Corpus Christi
LU 301 . . . . Nash
LU 324 . . . . Longview
LU 390. . . . . Port Arthur
LU 418. . . . . Academy
LU 479 . . . . Beaumont
LU 520 . . . . Austin
LU 527 . . . . Galveston
LU 583 . . . . El Paso
LU 602 . . . . Amarillo
LU 681 . . . . Wichita Falls
LU 716 . . . . Houston
LU 726 . . . . El Paso

LU 738 . . . . White Oak
LU 898 . . . . San Angelo
LU 942. . . . . Arlington
LU 960. . . . . El Paso
LU 1146 . . . . Amarillo
LU 1151 . . . . Tyler
LU 1548. . . . . San Marcos
LU 1645 . . . . Lufkin
LU 1794 . . . . Paris
LU 1814. . . . . Houston
LU 1911 . . . . San Antonio
LU 2078 . . . . Rockdale
LU 2155. . . . . Bonham
LU 2286. . . . . Beaumont
LU 2337. . . . . Tatum

Electronic Workers
LU 788 . . . . Dallas
LU 1000 . . . . San Antonio
LU 1029 . . . . Corpus Christi

Elevator Constructors
LU 21 . . . . Grand Prairie
LU 31 . . . . Houston
LU 81 . . . . San Antonio
LU 133 . . . . Austin

Federal Employees
LU 378. . . . . El Paso
LU 513 . . . . Carrollton
LU 516 . . . . Austin
LU 797 . . . . Corpus Christi
LU 1138 . . . . Amarillo
LU 1481 . . . . El Paso

Fire Fighters
LU 89-F. . . . . San Antonio
LU 341 . . . . Houston
LU 1117-I . . . . Canyon

Flint Glass Workers
LU . . . . Baytown
LU 37 . . . . Crawford

Food and Commercial Workers
C Insurance Workers Area
  XIV. . . . . Joshva
C Region 5 . . . . Grapevine
LU 3-C . . . . Grand Saline
LU 14-I. . . . . Mesquite
LU 130-C. . . . . Marshall
LU 408 . . . . Houston
LU 455 . . . . Houston
LU 513-T. . . . . Sherman
LU 514-T . . . . San Angelo
LU 526-C . . . . Texarkana
LU 540 . . . . Dallas
LU 557-C . . . . Groves
LU 680-C . . . . Houston
LU 780-C . . . . Bryan
LU 900-C . . . . Baytown
LU 1000 . . . . Dallas

Glass, Molders, Pottery and Plastics Workers
LU 57 . . . . Bryan
LU 58. . . . . Tyler
LU 125 . . . . Waxahachie
LU 201 . . . . Waxahachie
LU 209 . . . . Hondo
LU 216 . . . . Cleburne
LU 220 . . . . Waco
LU 230 . . . . Palestine
LU 259 . . . . Waco
LU 283 . . . . Houston

LU 284 . . . . Longview
LU 404 . . . . Amarillo
LU 429 . . . . Lufkin

Government Employees
C 83 National Border Patrol . Laredo
C 141 Texas Air National Guard
   Locals . . . . Santa Fe
C 216 National EEOC Locals. Dallas
C 227 VA, Tenth District . . . Waco
C 235 AFGE/AAFES . . . . . Dallas
LU 10 ID . . . . Boerne
LU 33 . . . . Galveston
LU 83 DoJ . . . . El Paso
LU 571 . . . . College Station
LU 681 USDA . . . . Bedford
LU 756 USDA . . . . Houston
LU 779 . . Sheppard Air Force Base
LU 1003 EPA Employees Region
   6. . . . . Dallas
LU 1004 . . . . . Fort Sam Houston
LU 1006 . . . . Fort Worth
LU 1010. . . . . Nederland
LU 1017 . . . . Silsbee
LU 1029 Red River Army Depot
   Firefighters . . . . . . Texarkana
LU 1030. . . . . Houston
LU 1038 . . . . Amarillo
LU 1055 . . . . Boerne
LU 1210 DoJ. . . . . El Paso
LU 1298 DoJ. . . . . . . Fort Worth
LU 1361 USAF . . . . . Fort Worth
LU 1364 DoD . . . . . . Fort Worth
LU 1367 DoD . . . . . Lackland Air
   Force Base
LU 1617 DoD . . . . . San Antonio
LU 1633 VA . . . . Houston
LU 1637 DoJ . . . . Seagoville
LU 1656 DoJ . . . . . San Antonio
LU 1731 DoD . . . . Sheppard Air
   Force Base
LU 1735 DoD. . . . . . . Kingsville
LU 1745. . . . . Austin
LU 1749 DoD . . . . Del Rio
LU 1757 DoD . . . . . San Antonio
LU 1816 DoD . . . . . San Angelo
LU 1822 VA. . . . . Waco
LU 1840 DoD . . . . . Randolph Air
   Force Base
LU 1903 USDA . . . . . Gonzales
LU 1920 DoD . . . . Killeen
LU 1929 DoJ. . . . . El Paso
LU 1934 VA . . . . Big Spring
LU 1944 DoJ . . . . Hidalgo
LU 2109 VA . . . . Temple
LU 2128 DoD . . . . . . Fort Worth
LU 2139 DoL . . . . Dallas
LU 2142 DoD . . . . Corpus Christi
LU 2160 VA . . . . Marlin
LU 2258 HEW . . . San Antonio
LU 2281 VA . . . . Kerrville
LU 2284 NASA . . . . . . Houston
LU 2356 DoD . Dyess Air Force Base
LU 2366 DoJ. . . . . Del Rio
LU 2413 DoC. . . . . Nederland
LU 2427 DoD . . . . . . Fort Worth
LU 2437 VA . . . . Dallas
LU 2455 DoJ . . . . Laredo
LU 2459 DoJ . . . . . . Texarkana
LU 2466 USDA . . . . . . Lufkin
LU 2488 GSA . . . . . Fort Worth
LU 2509 Marfa . . . . Marfa
LU 2516 VA . . . . El Paso
LU 2571 VA. . . . . Waco
LU 2727 HHS. . . . . . . Dallas
LU 2732 DoD . . . . Jasper
LU 2759 USDA . . . . . El Paso
LU 2771 USDA . . . . . . Plainview

LU 2836 VA . . . . Bonham
LU 2911 DoD . . . . San Antonio
LU 2921 DoD. . . . . . . Dallas
LU 2959 SBA . . . . . Fort Worth
LU 3000 DoD . . . . . Fort Worth
LU 3027 DoD . . . . Lackland Air
   Force Base
LU 3060 IBWC. . . . Brownsville
LU 3097 DoD. . . . . . . Houston
LU 3106 USDA . . . . . . Zapata
LU 3165 GSA . . . . . . El Paso
LU 3184 HHS. . . . . . Houston
LU 3307 DoJ . . . . . Harlingen
LU 3320 HUD . . . . San Antonio
LU 3332 DoJ . . . . Baytown
LU 3377 National Immigration
   Naturalization. . . . . Dallas
LU 3388 SSA. . . . . . McAllen
LU 3511 VA . . . . . San Antonio
LU 3519 CPSC . . . . . . Dallas
LU 3523 USDA . . . . . Amarillo
LU 3566 USDA . . . . . . Lufkin
LU 3637 EEOC . . . . . Dallas
LU 3769 USDA. . . . . . Houston
LU 3809 DoJ . . . . . Big Spring
LU 3828 BOP, FCI,
   Bastrop . . . . Bastrop
LU 3839 USDA . . . . Fort Worth
LU 3885 USDA. . . . . Weslaco
LU 3897 DoE Regional Office
   VI. . . . . Dallas
LU 3921 FDA . . . . . . Tyler
LU 3941 USDA, Food
   Inspectors . . . . Mount Pleasant
LU 3961 . . . . San Antonio
LU 3966 DoJ, USA,
   Houston. . . . . Houston
LU 3978 FPC . . . . Bryan
LU 4032 VA, Hospital Professional
   Unit. . . . . San Antonio
LU 4042 . . . . Waco
LU 4044 FPC, FCI. . . Three Rivers

**Government Employees
   Association**
LU 14-22 . . . . Fort Bliss
LU 14-52 . . . . Hooks
LU 14-89 . . . . El Paso
LU 14-151 . . . . Texarkana

Government Security Officers
LU 48 . . . . Arlington
LU 78. . . . . Desoto
LU 85. . . . . Round Rock
LU 86. . . . . Texarkana
LU 108 . . . . . . Corpus Christi
LU 203 . . . . Fort Worth

Graphic Communications
DJC South Western . . . . . Ennis
LU 71-M . . . . Houston
LU 88-C . . . . Waco
LU 139-C . . . . El Paso
LU 167-C . . . . Longview
LU 342. . . . . Arlington
LU 367-M . . . . Dallas
LU 439-S. . . . . Ennis
LU 525-S . . . . Dallas
LU 528-M. . . . . Austin
LU 737-S . . . . . . San Antonio

Guards
LU 38. . . . . Amarillo
LU 50. . . . . Dekalb
LU 80. . . . . Karnack
LU 124 . . . . Hooks
NHQ . . . . Amarillo
RC Eighth . . . . Avery

Hotel and Restaurant Employees
LU 251. . . . . Hurst
LU 353. . . . . Euless
LU 441 . . . . Amarillo

Iron Workers
DC Texas . . . . Georgetown
LU 66. . . . . San Antonio
LU 84 . . . . Houston
LU 125 . . . . Nederland
LU 135 . . . . Texas City
LU 263. . . . . Arlington
LU 482 . . . . Austin
LU 536 . . . . Farmers Branch

Laborers
DC Texas . . . . McKinney
LU 28 . . . . . Fort Sam Houston
LU 80 . . . . Houston
LU 350 . . . . Mauriceville
LU 648. . . . . Arlington
LU 1095 . . . . San Antonio
LU 1168 . . . . . . Wichita Falls

Letter Carriers
BR 23 . . . . Galveston
BR 132 . . . . Dallas
BR 181 . . . . Austin
BR 226 . . . . Fort Worth
BR 251 . . . . Denison
BR 283 . . . . Houston
BR 354 . . . . Laredo
BR 404 . . . . Waco
BR 421 . . . . San Antonio
BR 493 . . . . Tyler
BR 501 . . . . Paris
BR 505 . . . . El Paso
BR 643 . . . . Temple
BR 697 . . . . Weatherford
BR 698 . . . . Greenville
BR 699 . . . . Palestine
BR 752 . . . . Cleburne
BR 842 . . . . Beaumont
BR 890 Terrell, Texas . . . Terrell
BR 950. . . . . Abilene
BR 1032. . . . . Bonham
BR 1037 . . . . Amarillo
BR 1179 . . . . Groves
BR 1203 . . . . San Angelo
BR 1221. . . . . Victoria
BR 1227 T.T. Morris . . Burkburnett
BR 1259 . . . . . . Corpus Christi
BR 1367 . . . . Denton
BR 1389 . . . . Brownwood
BR 1456. . . . . . . Brownsville
BR 1487 Alpine, Texas. . . Alpine
BR 1550 . . . . Brenham
BR 1558. . . . . Taylor
BR 1568 Belton, Texas. . . Belton
BR 1660 Yoakum, Texas. . Yoakum
BR 1757 . . . . Bryan
BR 1872 . . . . Vernon
BR 1891 . . . . Big Spring
BR 1903 Ranger, Texas . . . Ranger
BR 1936 . . . . Cameron
BR 1966 Cisco, Texas. . . . Cisco
BR 2036 Clarksville,
   Texas. . . . . Clarksville
BR 2085 . . . . Plainview
BR 2130 . . . . McAllen
BR 2271 . . . . Mexia
BR 2279 . . . . Lufkin
BR 2309 . . . . Arlington
BR 2501 Crockett, Texas. . Crockett
BR 2511 . . . . Del Rio
BR 2562 . . . . Mercedes
BR 2589 . . . . Lubbock
BR 2623 Mineola, Texas . . Mineola

BR 2712 Gilmer, Texas . . . Gilmer
BR 2805 . . . . . . New Braunfels
BR 2977 Childress, Texas . Childress
BR 2983 . . . . Harlingen
BR 3028 . . . . Kerrville
BR 3053 Lamesa, Texas. . . Lamesa
BR 3094 . . . . Pampa
BR 3096 Dalhart, Texas . . . Dalhart
BR 3147 . . . . Uvalde
BR 3177 Slaton, Texas . . . Slaton
BR 3185 Whitesboro,
   Texas . . . . Whitesboro
BR 3271 Commerce,
   Texas. . . . . Commerce
BR 3291 . . . . Weslaco
BR 3296 Luling, Texas. . . . Luling
BR 3303 . . . . Perryton
BR 3305 Elgin, Texas . . . . Elgin
BR 3307 Eastland, Texas . . Eastland
BR 3309 . . . . Ladonia
BR 3318 Navasota, Texas . Navasota
BR 3467 Caldwell, Texas . Caldwell
BR 3709 . . . . Hearne
BR 3764 West, Texas . . . . West
BR 3792 . . . . Midland
BR 3843 . . . . Bay City
BR 3844 . . . . Borger
BR 3867 . . . . Pasadena
BR 3888 Brady, Texas . . . . Brady
BR 3964 . . . . Odessa
BR 3993 . . . . Garland
BR 4100 . . . . Stephenville
BR 4101 Dublin, Texas . . Dublin
BR 4115 Jasper, Texas . . . Jasper
BR 4168 Raymondville,
   Texas . . . . . . Raymondville
BR 4217 . . . . Killeen
BR 4240 . . . . Irving
BR 4245. . . . . Monahans
BR 4257 Center, Texas. . . Center
BR 4263 La Grange,
   Texas. . . . . La Grange
BR 4274 . . . . Lubbock
BR 4326 . . . . Kermit
BR 4357 Smithville,
   Texas. . . . . Smithville
BR 4504 Wellington,
   Texas. . . . . Wellington
BR 4511 Hondo, Texas. . . . Hondo
BR 4531 Junction, Texas . . Junction
BR 4549 Hamilton, Texas . Hamilton
BR 4561 Nocona, Texas. . . Nocona
BR 4723 . . . . . . Lake Jackson
BR 4728 Schulenburg,
   Texas. . . . . . . Schulenburg
BR 4783 Edna, Texas . . . . Edna
BR 4784 . . . . Richardson
BR 4809 . . . . Andrews
BR 4908 Deleon, Texas . . . Deleon
BR 4909 Columbus,
   Texas. . . . . Columbus
BR 4977 Seminole, Texas . Seminole
BR 4979 Teague, Texas . . . Teague
BR 5109 Memphis, Texas . Memphis
BR 5111 West Columbia,
   Texas . . . . . . West Columbia
BR 5112 . . . . Wills Point
BR 5210 Bellville, Texas. . Bellville
BR 5351 Post, Texas . . . . Post
BR 5397 Azle, Texas. . . . . Azle
BR 5414 Seymour, Texas . Seymour
BR 5435 Jacksboro,
   Texas. . . . . Jacksboro
BR 5445 Atlanta, Texas . . Atlanta
BR 5487 Granbury, Texas . Granbury
BR 5593 Rockdale, Texas . Rockdale
BR 5695 . . . . . . College Station
BR 5734 . . . . . . Copperas Cove

BR 5827 Weimar, Texas . . Weimar
BR 5938. . . . . Bedford
BR 6045 Fort Stockton,
  Texas . . . . Fort Stockton
BR 6083 Morton, Texas . . . Morton
BR 6272 Denver City,
  Texas . . . . Denver City
BR 6421 Llano, Texas. . . . Llano
BR 6474 Madisonville,
  Texas . . . . Madisonville
BR 6479 Ferris, Texas. . . . Ferris
BR 6570 Abernathy,
  Texas . . . . Abernathy
SA Texas . . . . Laredo

Locomotive Engineers
DIV. . . . . Laredo
DIV 22 . . . . El Paso
DIV 62 . . . . . . Deer Park
DIV 139. . . . . . . Spring
DIV 172 . . . . Fort Worth
DIV 177. . . . . . Sherman
DIV 187 . . . . . Mansfield
DIV 192 . . . . . . El Paso
DIV 194. . . . . . . Spring
DIV 197 . . . San Antonio
DIV 206 . . . . . . Temple
DIV 212 . . . . . . Abilene
DIV 242 . . . . . . Ennis
DIV 249. . . . . La Porte
DIV 264 . . . . . . El Paso
DIV 299 D.H. Nichols . . Amarillo
DIV 307 . . . . San Antonio
DIV 350. . . . . Kingsville
DIV 366. . . . . Missouri City
DIV 475. . . . . Smithville
DIV 500 . . . . Fort Worth
DIV 530 . . . . Commerce
DIV 566 . . . . Brackettville
DIV 573. . . . Caddo Mills
DIV 574 . . . . . Amarillo
DIV 588 . . . . . Amarillo
DIV 592 . . . . . Dalhart
DIV 612 . . . . . . Vidor
DIV 620 . . . . . Cleburne
DIV 636. . . . . Beaumont
DIV 703 . . . . . Mexia
DIV 736 . . . . Wichita Falls
DIV 775 City of Roses . . . Victoria
DIV 776. . . . . Santa Fe
DIV 834 . . . . . Mineola
DIV 857 . . . . Whitehouse
DIV 863 . . . . . Abilene
DIV 871 . . . . . Lubbock
DIV 910 . . . . . Nome
DIV 918 . . . . Corpus Christi
DIV 944 . . . . Fort Worth
GCA Union Pacific Railroad-
  Southern Region . . . San Antonio
GCA 177 Southern Pacific
  Transportation Company . El Paso
SLB Texas . . . . . Mineola

Longshoremen
C Central Dock & Marine. Galveston
C Houston Dock & Marine . Pasadena
C Sabine Dock & Marine . Beaumont
D South Atlantic & Gulf
  Coast . . . . Galveston
LU 20 . . . . Galveston
LU 21 . . . . Beaumont
LU 22 . . . . Orange
LU 24 . . . . Houston
LU 25 . . . . Beaumont
LU 26. . . . . Corpus Christi
LU 28 . . . . . . Pasadena
LU 29 . . . . . Brownsville
LU 30 . . . . Freeport

LU 31 . . . . Houston
LU 440. . . . . . Port Arthur
LU 1316. . . . . . Beaumont
LU 1347 . . . . Corpus Christi
LU 1351. . . . . . Houston
LU 1395. . . . . Brownsville
LU 1428. . . . . Galveston
LU 1438 . . . . . Pasadena
LU 1453. . . . . Galveston
LU 1494. . . . . Galveston
LU 1504. . . . . Galveston
LU 1530. . . . . . Houston
LU 1544 Clerk-Checkers. Brownsville
LU 1646 . . . . . . Orange
LU 1665. . . . . Galveston
LU 1692. . . . Corpus Christi
LU 1817. . . . . . Freeport
LU 1924. . . . . Port Neches
LU 2014 . . . . Corpus Christi
LU 2022. . . . . . Houston

Machinists
DLG 37. . . . . . Houston
DLG 776. . . . . Fort Worth
LG . . . . Fort Worth
LG 6. . . . . . League City
LG 12 . . . . . . La Porte
LG 15 . . . . . Fort Worth
LG 36 . . . . . Fort Worth
LG 128 . . . . . Angleton
LG 392 . . . . . . El Paso
LG 517. . . . . Sugar Land
LG 526 . . . . . Fort Worth
LG 643. . . . . . Lott
LG 776-A . . . . Fort Worth
LG 776-B . . . . Fort Worth
LG 776-C . . . . Fort Worth
LG 791 . . . . . Fort Worth
LG 823 . . . . . Lumberton
LG 969 . . . . . . Houston
LG 975 . . . . . Fort Worth
LG 1051 . . . . . Baytown
LG 1243. . . . . . Hooks
LG 1255 Panhandle . . . . Borger
LG 1537. . . . . Houston
LG 1591. . . . . Fort Worth
LG 1727 . . . . West Columbia
LG 1786 . . . . . Pearland
LG 1792. . . . Port Neches
LG 1808 . . . . . . Wells
LG 1923 . . . . White Oak
LG 1999 . . . . . Lufkin
LG 2049 . . . . Fort Worth
LG 2082 . . . . Fort Worth
LG 2121 . . . . Fort Worth
LG 2198. . . . . Houston
LG 2208 . . . . . Bedford
LG 2210 . . . . Universal City
LG 2251 . . . . Fort Worth
LG 2317 . . . . Fort Worth
LG 2340 . . . . Fort Worth
LG 2427 . . . . Fort Worth
LG 2483 . . . . Fort Worth
LG 2513 . . . . Fort Worth
LG 2576 . . . . . Tyler
LG 2641 . . . . Henderson
LG 2768 . . . . Fort Worth
LG 2771 . . . . Wichita Falls
LLG H-2339 Woodworkers. Houston
LLG W-2916
  Woodworkers . . . . Fort Worth
LLG FL-2189 NFFE . . . . Hooks
STC Texas . . . . Fort Worth

Maintenance of Way Employes
FED Southern Pacific
  Atlantic . . . . Houston
LG 526. . . . . Childress

LG 644 . . . . Luling
LG 675. . . . . . . Clyde
LG 949 . . . . . League City
LG 1058 . . . . . . Waller
LG 1099 . . . . . Pottsboro
LG 1252. . . . . Beaumont
LG 1407 . . . . . Tenaha
LG 1732 . . . . . Saginaw
LG 2409 . . . . . Aledo
LG 2410 . . . . . Rockdale
LG 2413 . . . . . Amarillo
LG 2710 . . . . . Odessa
LG 2754 . . . . . San Benito
SF Missouri Pacific . . Longview
SLG 44 . . . . . . Del Rio
SLG 115 . . . . . El Paso
SLG 203 . . . . . . Mexia
SLG 366 . . . . San Antonio
SLG 732 . . . . . Amarillo
SLG 927 . . . Sulphur Springs
SLG 1011 . . . . Highlands
SLG 1021 . . . . . Odem
SLG 1082 . . . Wichita Falls
SLG 1338 . . . . . Waller
SLG 1405 . . . . . Houston
SLG 1507 . . . . . Humble
SLG 1563. . . . . Laredo
SLG 1571 . . . . Normanna
SLG 1634. . . . . Laredo
SLG 1715 . . . . Beaumont
SLG 1862 . . . . . El Paso
SLG 2286 . . . . Benbrook
SLG 2411 . . . . . Silsbee
SLG 2421 . . . . . Sealy
SLG 2762 . . . . . Flint

Musicians
LU 23 . . . . . San Antonio
LU 65-699 . . . . . Houston
LU 72 . . . . . . Arlington
LU 74 . . . . . Galveston
LU 433 . . . . . . Austin
LU 466 . . . . . El Paso
LU 644 . . . . Corpus Christi
STCON Texas . . . . Arlington

National Staff Organization
LU Staff Association,
  Professional, Texas Teachers
  Association . . . . . . Plano
LU Staff Organization,
  Association, Texas Teachers
  Association . . . . . Austin

Needletrades
JB Arkansas . . . . . Dallas
JB Southwest Regional . . . Dallas
LU. . . . . Dallas
LU 50-004. . . . . Dallas
LU 128-H . . . . . Dallas
LU 129-H . . . . . Dallas
LU 211-A . . . . . Dallas
LU 931-A . . . . . Dallas
LU 1022-C . . . . . Dallas
LU 1129-C . . . . . Dallas
LU 1131 . . . . . Dallas
LU 1157. . . . . . Dallas
LU 1162. . . . . . Dallas
LU 1414-D . . . . . Dallas
LU 2368 . . . . . Dallas
LU 2623 . . . . . Dallas
LU 2629 . . . . . Dallas
LU 2630. . . . . . Dallas
LU 2631. . . . . . Dallas
LU 2632. . . . . . Dallas
LU 2645 . . . . . Dallas
LU 2667. . . . . . Dallas
LU 2672. . . . . . Dallas

LU 2673. . . . . . Dallas
LU 2680. . . . . . Dallas
LU 2681. . . . . . Dallas
LU 2700. . . . . . Dallas

NLRB Professional Association
LU 16 . . . . . . Fort Worth

Nurses
SA Texas Nurses Association . Austin

Office and Professional Employees
LU 27 . . . . Galveston
LU 66. . . . . . . Groves
LU 129 . . . . . . Pasadena
LU 277 . . . . . Fort Worth
LU 298 . . . . . . Austin
LU 306 . . . . . . Amarillo

Operating Engineers
LU 178 . . . . . Fort Worth
LU 340 . . . . . Amarillo
LU 347 . . . . . Texas City
LU 351 . . . . . . Borger
LU 450 . . . . . . Houston
LU 560 . . . . . Pleasanton
LU 564. . . . . Lake Jackson

Painters
LU 53 . . . . Dallas
LU 756 . . . . . . Dallas
LU 1008. . . . . . Houston
LU 2348 Professional & Clerical
  Workers . . . . . Burleson

Paper, Allied-Industrial, Chemical Employees
C International Paper Union . Naples
C Mobile Oil Company
  Wide . . . . Beaumont
C Standard Oil of
  Indiana-Nationwide . . Texas City
C TML . . . . Orange
LU 424-4 . . . . . Cleburne
LU 489 . . . . . . Dumas
LU 04-23 . . . . . Port Arthur
LU 04-74 . . . . . Rotan
LU 04-100 . . . . . Corsicana
LU 04-153 . . . . . Ingleside
LU 04-165 . . . . . Orange
LU 04-202 . . . . . Tyler
LU 04-208 . . . . . Arlington
LU 04-211 . . . . . Denton
LU 04-227 . . . . . Pasadena
LU 04-228 . . . . . Port Neches
LU 04-243 . . . . . Beaumont
LU 04-314 . . . . . Edinburg
LU 04-316 . . . . . Aransas Pass
LU 04-367 . . . . . Pasadena
LU 04-391 . . . . . Kirbyville
LU 04-411 . . . . . Lufkin
LU 04-463 . . . . . Rio Vista
LU 04-487 . . . . . Dumas
LU 04-759 . . . . . Dallas
LU 04-771 . . . . . Fort Worth
LU 04-780 . . . . . Joshua
LU 04-801 . . . . . Evadale
LU 04-825 . . . . . Evadale
LU 04-836 . . . . . Orange
LU 04-895 . . . . . Dallas
LU 04-1068 . . . . . Crosby
LU 04-1147 . . . . . Tyler
LU 04-1148 . . . . . Queen City
LU 04-1149 . . . . . Atlanta
LU 04-1398 . . . . . Mauriceville
LU 04-1401 . . . . . Lufkin
LU 04-1706 . . . . . Burleson
LU 04-1710 . . . . . Dallas

LU 04-1856 . . . . Dallas
LU 04-6000 . . . . Pasadena
LU 08-1199 . . . . McGregor

Plant Protection
LU 299 . . . . Dallas

Plasterers and Cement Masons
LU 79 . . . . Houston
LU 681 . . . . Houston
LU 783 . . . . Austin
STCON Texas . . . . Austin

Plumbing and Pipe Fitting
LU 68 . . . . Houston
LU 100 . . . . Garland
LU 142 . . . . San Antonio
LU 146 . . . . Fort Worth
LU 195 . . . . Beaumont
LU 196 . . . . Amarillo
LU 211 . . . . Houston
LU 231 . . . . El Paso
LU 237 . . . . Texarkana
LU 286 . . . . Austin
LU 389 . . . . Wichita Falls
LU 390 . . . . Lake Jackson
LU 529 . . . . Waco
LU 629 . . . . Lubbock
LU 654 . . . . Abilene
LU 823 . . . . Harlingen
SA Texas . . . . . . Harlingen

Postal and Federal Employees
LU 103 . . . . Beaumont
LU 104 . . . . Dallas
LU 105 . . . . Fort Worth
LU 106 . . . . Galveston
LU 107 . . . . Houston
LU 109 . . . . Lubbock
LU 111 Orange . . . . . . Orange
LU 113 . . . . San Antonio

Postal Mail Handlers
LU 311 . . . . Dallas

Postal Workers
LU 87 Paris . . . . Paris
LU 98 Fort Worth . . . . Fort Worth
LU 114 Amarillo . . . . . Amarillo
LU 180 El Paso . . . . . . El Paso
LU 185 Houston . . . . . Houston
LU 195 San Antonio . . San Antonio
LU 246 Bowie Local . . . . Bowie
LU 299 Austin Area . . . . Austin
LU 469 Beaumont Sectional Center
 Area . . . . Beaumont
LU 471 Eagle Pass . . . Eagle Pass
LU 578 Texarkana . . . . Texarkana
LU 652 Vernon . . . . . . Vernon
LU 732 Dallas Area . . . . . Dallas
LU 739 Waco . . . . Waco
LU 741 Denison . . . . . . Denison
LU 742 Sherman . . . . . Sherman
LU 754 Wichita Falls . Wichita Falls
LU 779 Corpus Christi
 Area . . . . Corpus Christi
LU 787 Galveston . . . . Galveston
LU 800 Del Rio . . . . . . Del Rio
LU 802 Uvalde . . . . . . Uvalde
LU 811 Arlington . . . . Arlington
LU 812 Denton . . . . . . Denton
LU 826 Greater East Texas
 Area . . . . Longview
LU 827 Abilene . . . . . . Abilene
LU 952 Lubbock Area . . Lubbock
LU 1045 Temple . . . . . Temple
LU 1093 Brownsville . . Brownsville
LU 1108 Mercedes Local . Mercedes

LU 1354 Borger . . . . . . Borger
LU 1437 Pampa . . . . . . Pampa
LU 1453 Plainview . . . Plainview
LU 1477 Tyler . . . . Tyler
LU 1485 Pecos Local . . . . Pecos
LU 1573 Hereford Local . . Hereford
LU 1589 Richmond . . . Richmond
LU 1624 Dalhart Local . . Dalhart
LU 1696 Midland . . . . . Midland
LU 1726 Comanche Local . Comanche
LU 1783 Graham Local . . Graham
LU 1784 Angleton . . . . Angleton
LU 1849 Liberty Local . . . Liberty
LU 1866 Beeville . . . . . Beeville
LU 1867 Kingsville . . . Kingsville
LU 1868 San Angelo . . San Angelo
LU 1870 Edinburg Local . Edinburg
LU 1871 Mission . . . . . Mission
LU 1882 Athens . . . . . . Athens
LU 1933 Freeport Local . . Freeport
LU 1971 Jasper . . . . . . Jasper
LU 2030 Kilgore . . . . . Kilgore
LU 2066 Canyon . . . . . Canyon
LU 2143 Yoakum . . . . Yoakum
LU 2248 Laredo . . . . . Laredo
LU 2260 Conroe . . . . . Conroe
LU 2421 Harlingen . . . Harlingen
LU 2476 College
 Station . . . . . College Station
LU 2518 McKinney
 Local . . . . McKinney
LU 2622 Lockhart Local . . Lockhart
LU 2633 Palestine . . . Palestine
LU 2640 Llano Local . . . . Llano
LU 2806 Bay City Local . Bay City
LU 2808 El Campo Local . El Campo
LU 2822 Winnsboro
 Local . . . . Winnsboro
LU 2869 Alpine Local . . . Alpine
LU 2944 Center Local . . . Center
LU 2945 Lufkin Area . . . . Lufkin
LU 2952 Gilmer Local . . . Gilmer
LU 3219 Odessa . . . . . Odessa
LU 3231 Mineral Wells
 Local . . . . . . Mineral Wells
LU 3288 Gainesville . . . Gainesville
LU 3347 Lamesa Local . . Lamesa
LU 3419 Sonora Local . . . Sonora
LU 3607 Greenville . . . Greenville
LU 3608 Daingerfield
 Local . . . . Daingerfield
LU 4084 Pasadena . . . Pasadena
LU 4126 Bonham . . . . . Bonham
LU 4138 Brenham Local . . Brenham
LU 4171 Victoria . . . . . Victoria
LU 4326 McAllen . . . . . McAllen
LU 4478 Nacogdoches . Nacogdoches
LU 4962 Killeen . . . . . Killeen
LU 5173 Kerrville . . . . Kerrville
LU 5300 Weslaco Local . . Weslaco
LU 5845 Belton Local . . . Belton
LU 5896 Hillsboro Local . Hillsboro
LU 6192 Brazoria Local . . Brazoria
LU 6197 Rosenburg Local . . Wallis
LU 6551 Bryan . . . . . . Bryan
LU 6552 Cisco Local . . . . Cisco
LU 6553 Cuero Local . . . Cuero
LU 6557 Mount Pleasant
 Local . . . . . Mount Pleasant
LU 6558 San Benito
 Local . . . . San Benito
LU 6707 Clarksville
 Local . . . . Clarksville
LU 6768 Plano . . . . Plano
SA Texas . . . . Beaumont

Railroad Signalmen
LLG 116 . . . . Troy

LLG 121 . . . . Temple
LLG 133 . . . . . . Wichita Falls
LLG 141 . . . . . . Weatherford
LLG 161 . . . . Amarillo
LLG 182 . . . . El Paso
LLG 185 . . . . . Elysian Fields
LLG 206 . . . . Houston

Roofers, Waterproofers and Allied Workers
LU 76 . . . . Fort Worth
LU 116 . . . . Fort Worth
LU 123 . . . . Fort Worth
LU 141 . . . . Fort Worth
LU 174 . . . . Fort Worth

Rural Letter Carriers
LU Alamo Association . San Antonio
LU Angelina County . . . . Diboll
LU Bell-Milam-Falls
 Counties . . . . Rogers
LU Burleson-Lee
 Counties . . . . . . Dime Box
LU Coastal Bend . . . . Victoria
LU Concho Valley . . . San Angelo
LU Denton County . . . . Denton
LU Eastland-Stephens
 Counties . . . . Cisco
LU Erath-Hood-Somervell-Palo Pinto
 County . . . . Granbury
LU Fayette County . . . . La Grange
LU Grayson-Fannin Counties . Savoy
LU Gulf Coast . . . . . . Wharton
LU Hamilton-Coryell
 Counties . . . . . . Lampasas
LU Hill County . . . . . Malone
LU Hopkins-Wood-Franklin-Camp
 Counties . . . Sulphur Springs
LU Johnson County . . . Burleson
LU Kaufman County . . . . Forney
LU Lamar-Delta
 Association . . . . . Arthur City
LU Lavaca-Dewitt
 Counties . . . . Yoakum
LU McLennan County . . . . Waco
LU Nacogdoches
 County . . . . Nacogdoches
LU Palo Duro Association . . Canyon
LU Panhandle Association . Childress
LU Parker County . . . Weatherford
LU Sam Houston
 Association . . . . . Cleveland
LU Shelby-San Augustine-Sabine
 Counties . . . . Center
LU South Plains
 Association . . . . . Hale Center
LU Southeast Texas
 Association . . . . Vidor
LU Tarrant-Dallas
 Counties . . . . . . Richardson
LU West Texas . . . . . Levelland
LU Wise County . . . . . . Chico
LU 2 Anderson-Henderson
 Counties . . . . Palestine
LU 4 Austin County . . . Hempstead
LU 9 Bosque County . . . . Clifton
LU 10 Brazos Valley . . . Hermleigh
LU 13 Bi-Stone
 Association . . . . . . Fairfield
LU 14 Cherokee
 County . . . . . . Jacksonville
LU 17 Collin-Rockwall
 Counties . . . . . . McKinney
LU 28 El Paso Association . El Paso
LU 31 Foard-Hardeman-Wilbarger
 Counties . . . . Quanah
LU 36 Gregg-Rusk-Smith
 Association . . . . . . Henderson

LU 39 Harris-Fort Bend-Waller
 Counties . . . . Houston
LU 40 Harrison-Marion-Panola
 Counties . . . . Karnack
LU 44 Houston County . . Kennaro
LU 45 Hunt-Rains Counties . Emory
LU 54 Lower Rio Grande
 Valley . . . . Edinburg
LU 62 Navarro County . . . Kerens
LU 66 Northeast Texas
 Association . . . . . . Naples
LU 69 Robertson-Brazos
 Counties . . . . College Station
LU 71 South Texas
 Association . . . . . . Sinton
LU 75 Southwest Texas
 Association . . . . . . Odessa
LU 77 Taylor-Callahan
 Counties . . . . Abilene
LU 78 Capitol Area . . . . . Austin
LU 79 Tyler-Jasper-Newton-Hardin
 Counties . . . . Jasper
LU 80 Upshur County . . . . Diana
LU 81 Van Zandt
 County . . . . . . Murchison
LU 83 Washington
 County . . . . . . Chappell Hill
SA Texas . . . . . . Georgetown

Security, Police and Fire Professionals
LU 256 . . . . Fort Worth
LU 258 . . . . Lone Star
LU 262 . . . . . . Wichita Falls
LU 263 . . . . . . Grand Prairie
LU 267 . . . . Austin
LU 269 . . . . Bastrop
LU 299 . . . . Garland
LU 300 . . . . Texas City
LU 723 . . . . Fort Worth
LU 725 . . . . El Paso
LU 727 . . . . Brownsville
LU 728 . . . . Bay City

Service Employees
LU 713 Firemen & Oilers . . El Paso
LU 1016 Firemen & Oilers . Houston
LU 1045 Firemen &
 Oilers . . . . Carrollton
LU 1088 Firemen & Oilers . . Rogers

Sheet Metal Workers
LU 54 . . . . Houston
LU 67 . . . . San Antonio
LU 68 . . . . Euless
LU 121 . . . . Joshua
LU 337 . . . . Tyler
LU 440 . . . . Houston

Steelworkers
LU . . . . Cedar Hill
LU . . . . Corpus Christi
LU 671 . . . . Larue
LU 7681 . . . . Houston
LU 9380 . . . . Ennis
LU 12-166-S . . . . . . Kilgore
LU 12-173-S . . . . . Blackwell
LU 12-201-A . . . . . . Houston
LU 12-235-A . . . . Corpus Christi
LU 12-312-L . . . . Waco
LU 12-422-S . . . . . . Dallas
LU 12-430-S . . . . . . Fort Worth
LU 12-626-B . . . Mineral Wells
LU 12-746-L . . . . Tyler
LU 12-1027-L . . . . Corsicana
LU 12-1124-L . . . . . Odessa
LU 12-1157-L . . . . . . Tyler
LU 12-1822-S . . . . . Rosebud

LU 12-2083-S. . . . . . . Houston
LU 12-4134-S. . . . . . Lone Star
LU 12-4370-S. . . . Point Comfort
LU 12-4654-S. . . . Daingerfield
LU 12-4895-S. . . . . . . Rockdale
LU 12-5022-S. . . Corpus Christi
LU 12-5613-S. . . . . . . Amarillo
LU 12-5754-S. . . . . Wallis
LU 12-6352-S. . . . . El Paso
LU 12-6580-S. . . . Grand Prairie
LU 12-6635-S. . . . . . . Houston
LU 12-7242-S. . . . . Groesbeck
LU 12-7982-S. . . . . Waco
LU 12-8586-S. . . . . China
LU 12-8618-S. . . . . Sadler
LU 12-8923-S. . . . . . Shepherd
LU 12-9448 . . . . . . Queen City

Teachers
SFED Texas. . . . . Austin

Teamsters
JC 58 . . . . Houston
JC 80 . . . . Dallas
LU 19 . . . . Grapevine
LU 577 . . . . Amarillo
LU 657 . . . . San Antonio
LU 745 . . . . Dallas
LU 747 Professional Flight Deck
  Crewmember . . . . . Houston
LU 767 . . . . Forest Hill
LU 919 . . . . Houston
LU 968 . . . . Houston
LU 988 . . . . Houston
LU 997 . . . . Fort Worth
LU 1110 . . . . . . San Antonio

Television and Radio Artists
LU Houston. . . . . . . Houston

Texas Unions
LU 900 Aircraft
  Workers . . . . Fort Worth
NHQ . . . . Fort Worth

Theatrical Stage Employees
D 6 Texas . . . . Dallas
LU 51 . . . . Houston
LU 53-F . . . . San Antonio
LU 76 . . . . San Antonio
LU 126 . . . . Fort Worth
LU 127 . . . . Dallas
LU 153 . . . . El Paso
LU 183 . . . . Port Neches
LU 184-B Front House/
  Ushers . . . . Houston
LU 205 . . . . Austin
LU 249 . . . . Dallas
LU 330 . . . . Weatherford
LU 331 . . . . Killeen
LU 378 . . . . Wichita Falls
LU 484 . . . . Austin
LU 604 . . . . Corpus Christi
LU 803 . . . . Dallas
LU 865 . . . . Odessa
LU 896 . . . . Houston
LU 903 . . . . Lubbock

Train Dispatchers
SCOM Burlington Northern
  Railroad. . . . . Paradise

Transit Union
LDIV 1031 . . . . Beaumont
LDIV 1091 . . . . Austin
LDIV 1338 . . . . Dallas
LDIV 1549 . . . . Austin
LDIV 1635 . . . . Dallas

Transport Workers
LU 276. . . . . Waco
LU 513 Air Transport
  Division. . . . . Southlake
LU 541 . . . . Euless
LU 542 . . . . Euless
LU 555 Southwest Airlines Ramp
  Operations . . . . Dallas
LU 556 Texas . . . . Dallas
LU 565 . . . . Bedford
LU 567 . . . . Fort Worth
LU 575 DFW/LAX . . . . . Dallas
LU 576 . . . . Grapevine

Transportation Communications Union
D 654 . . . . Katy
D 901 . . . . Vidor
D 5509 . . . . El Paso
D 5515 . . . . San Antonio
JPB 320 Missouri
  Pacific . . . . San Antonio
LG 67 . . . . Palestine
LG 75 . . . . Fort Worth
LG 84. . . . . Laredo
LG 317 . . . . Laredo
LG 805 . . . . Fort Worth
LG 886 . . . . Somerville
LG 5060 Missouri Pacific . Palestine
LG 5511 Houston . . . . . Cypress
LG 6005 Pecos Valley . . Amarillo
LG 6023 Fort Worth . . . Burleson
LG 6077 . . . . San Antonio
LG 6452 San Jacinto . Friendswood
LG 6495 Sycamore . . . . Elkhart
LG 6793 Bird Creek . . . . Temple
LG 6824 Four States . . Texarkana
SBA 500 American Rail & Airway
  Supervisors . . . . . . Rockport
SBA 555 Western Railway
  Supervisors . . . . . . Pinehurst

Transportation Union
GCA GO-343 . . . . . . Texarkana
GCA GO-393 Atchison Topeka Santa
  Fe-W-N &S . . . . . . Temple
GCA GO-457 Kansas City Southern
  Railway . . . . Rockwall
GCA GO-460 Kansas City Southern
  Railway . . . . Greenville
GCA GO-577 . . . . Spring
GCA GO-803 Port Terminal Railroad
  Association. . . . . . Kingwood
GCA GO-895 Southern Pacific
  Transportation Company-Eastern
  Line. . . . . Spring
GCA GO-927 Missouri Pacific
  Railroad . . . . . . Fort Worth
LU 9 . . . . Ransom Canyon
LU 18 . . . . El Paso
LU 20 . . . . Beaumont
LU 243 . . . . Keller
LU 293 . . . . Houston
LU 331 . . . . Temple
LU 439 . . . . Longview
LU 489 . . . . La Vernia
LU 508 . . . . Smithville
LU 513 . . . . Gainesville
LU 524 . . . . Conroe
LU 564 . . . . Arlington
LU 569 . . . . Ennis
LU 594 . . . . Mineola
LU 733 . . . . Hooks
LU 756 . . . . Helotes
LU 773 . . . . Friendswood
LU 818 . . . . Saginaw
LU 821 . . . . Del Rio
LU 823 . . . . Big Spring

LU 857 . . . . San Antonio
LU 878 . . . . Richardson
LU 923 . . . . Dalhart
LU 937 . . . . Duncanville
LU 940. . . . . . . Wichita Falls
LU 949. . . . . Whitesboro
LU 953 . . . . Victoria
LU 965 . . . . Terrell
LU 1092 . . . . Teague
LU 1205 . . . . Nursery
LU 1313 . . . . Amarillo
LU 1458 . . . . Klein
LU 1524 . . . . Houston
LU 1571 . . . . El Paso
LU 1593 . . . . Brownwood
LU 1697 . . . . Lubbock
LU 1886 . . . . Tomball
LU 1892 . . . . Houston
LU 1904 . . . . Katy
LU 1918 . . . . El Paso
LU 1957 . . . . Silsbee
LU 1974 . . . . Hurst
SLB LO-48 Texas . . . . . Austin

Treasury Employees
CH 46 . . . . Dallas
CH 52 . . . . Austin
CH 72 . . . . Austin
CH 140 . . . . Dallas
CH 143 . . . . El Paso
CH 145 . . . . Laredo
CH 149 . . . . Pharr
CH 160 . . . . Brownsville
CH 163 . . . . Houston
CH 178 . . . . Eagle Pass
CH 179 . . . . Roma
CH 180 . . . . Del Rio
CH 219 . . . . Dallas
CH 222 . . . . Houston
CH 247 . . . . Austin
CH 260 . . . . Dallas
CH 265 . . . . Dallas

Weather Service Employees
BR 20 . . . . Abilene
BR 02-3 . . . . Brownsville
BR 02-4 . . . . Lubbock
BR 02-8 . . . . Amarillo
BR 02-14 . . . . . New Braunfels
BR 02-16 . . . . Fort Worth
BR 02-22 . . . . Midland
BR 02-27 . . . . . . San Angelo
BR 02-33 . . . . Dickinson
BR 02-63 . . . . . Corpus Christi
BR 02-67 . . . . Fort Worth
BR 02-70 . . . . Houston
BR 02-74 . . . . Houston
BR 02-80 . . . . Fort Worth

Unaffiliated Labor Organizations

Allied Pilots Association (Domicile)
  Chicago (ORD) . . . . Fort Worth
Allied Pilots Association (Domicile)
  Dallas (DFW) . . . . . Fort Worth
Allied Pilots Association (Domicile)
  Los Angeles (LAX) . . Fort Worth
Allied Pilots Association (Domicile)
  Miami (MIA) . . . . . Fort Worth
Allied Pilots Association (Domicile)
  New York (LGA) . . . Fort Worth
Allied Pilots Association (Domicile)
  San Francisco (SFO) . Fort Worth
Allied Pilots Association (Domicile)
  St. Louis (STL) . . . . Fort Worth
Allied Pilots Association Domicile
  (Boston) (BOS) . . . Fort Worth

Allied Pilots Association Washington
  DC (DCA) Domicile . Fort Worth
Allied Pilots Staff Employees
  Association APSEA . . Fort Worth
Association of Union
  Representatives. . . . . Houston
Bell Production Engineering
  Association. . . . . Hurst
Champlin Corpus Christie
  Refinery Employees
  Federation . . . . Corpus Christi
Currency & Security Handlers
  Association. . . . . . . Houston
Exxon Employees Association
  Western Division. . . . . Seguin
Exxon Employees Federation General
  Services Department . . . Houston
Exxon Employees Federation South
  Texas Division . . . . Kingsville
Exxon Pipe Line Employees West
  Texas Area. . . . . . . Odessa
Exxon Radio Officers
  Association. . . . . . . Houston
Exxon Seamens
  Association. . . . . . . Baytown
Exxon Southwestern Employees
  Federation Southwestern
  Division . . . . Lubbock
Flight Attendants Professional
  Association . . . . Euless
Fort Hood Barbers
  Association . . . . Killeen
Guards of the United States
  Associated . . . . . . Texas City
Gulf Coast Industrial Workers
  Union . . . . Baytown
Ingleside Association of Maintenance
  Personnel . . . . Robstown
Machinist Independent
  Union . . . . Fort Worth
Oryx Energy Company Employees
  Association . . . . Cotulla
Petrolcum Employees
  Associated . . . . Hull
Phillips Pipe Line Company
  Employees Chocolate Bayou
  District . . . . La Porte
Phillips Pipe Line Company
  Employees Federation West
  Texas-Borger District . . . Borger
Phillips Pipeline Employees Union
  LU 66. . . . . Goldsmith
Pilots Association Allied. Fort Worth
Radio & Television Broadcast
  Group. . . . . Houston
Schulenberg Plant Shop
  Committee . . . . . . La Grange
Shell Pipe Line Employees
  Federation Independent-West
  Texas Division . . . . . Kermit
Southwest Airlines Employee
  Association . . . . Dallas
Southwest Airlines Pilots
  Association . . . . Dallas
Sun Pipe Line Employees
  Association Texas
  Area. . . . . Longview
Sunoco Terminals Independent
  Association. . . . . . Nederland
Technical Control Union . Nederland
Texas Employees Federation of
  Exxon Pipe Line UNIT 2. La Porte
Third Coast Employee's Association
  Union. . . . . Austin
United Workers Union . Brownsville

Utah

AFL-CIO Trade and Industrial Departments

Building and Construction Trades Department
BCTC Utah . . . . . Salt Lake City

Affiliated Labor Organizations

Air Traffic Controllers
LU S-56 . . . . Salt Lake City
LU SLC . . . . Salt Lake City
LU ZLC . . . . Salt Lake City

Asbestos Workers
LU 69 . . . . Salt Lake City

Bakery, Confectionery, Tobacco Workers and Grain Millers
LU 19-G . . . . . . West Jordan
LU 393 . . . . Salt Lake City
LU 401 . . . . Salt Lake City

Boilermakers
LG 182 . . . . Murray
LG 374-D Cement
  Workers . . . . . . West Jordan

Bricklayers
LU 1 . . . . Salt Lake City

Carpenters
LU 184 . . . . West Jordan
LU 1498 . . . . Provo

Communications Workers
LU 7704 . . . . . . Salt Lake City
LU 7705 . . . . Ogden
LU 14759 . . . . . Salt Lake City

Electrical Workers
LU 57 . . . . Salt Lake City
LU 354 . . . . Salt Lake City
LU 650 . . . . South Jordan
LU 1619 . . . . Delta

Elevator Constructors
LU 38 . . . . Salt Lake City

Federal Employees
LU 125 . . . . Ogden
LU 1724 . . . . Highland
LU 1933 . . . . Cedar City
LU 2118 . . . . Brigham City

Glass, Molders, Pottery and Plastics Workers
LU 231-B . . . . . West Valley City

Government Employees
LU 1592 DoD . . Hill Air Force Base
LU 2118 DCMC
  Thiokol . . . . . . Brigham City
LU 2185 DoD . . . . Tooele
LU 2199 VA . . . . West Valley City
LU 3052 USDA . . . . Logan
LU 3251 HHS . . . . Salt Lake City

Government Employees Association
LU 14-9 . . . . Dugway

Graphic Communications
LU 511-M . . . . . Salt Lake City
LU 541-S . . . . . . Salt Lake City

Iron Workers
LU 27 . . . . Salt Lake City

Laborers
LU 295 . . . . . . Salt Lake City

Letter Carriers
BR 68 . . . . Roy
BR 111 . . . . Salt Lake City
BR 887 . . . . Provo
BR 970 . . . . Logan
BR 1765 Kanab, Utah . . . . Kanab
BR 2112 . . . . . . Brigham City
BR 2171 . . . . East Carbon
BR 2339 Spanish Fork,
  Utah . . . . Spanish Fork
BR 2376 Payson, Utah . . . . Payson
BR 2609 American Fork,
  Utah . . . . American Fork
BR 2821 Springville,
  Utah . . . . Springville
BR 2863 Richfield, Utah . . Richfield
BR 3143 Manti, Utah . . . . Manti
BR 3252 Nephi, Utah . . . . Nephi
BR 3574 . . . . Cedar City
BR 3928 . . . . Clearfield
BR 3931 Tremonton,
  Utah . . . . Tremonton
BR 3932 . . . . Vernal
BR 4012 Heber City,
  Utah . . . . Heber City
BR 4032 Helper, Utah . . . Helper
BR 4043 . . . . St. George
BR 4235 . . . . Orem
BR 4506 . . . . Layton
BR 4789 . . . . Roosevelt
BR 5360 . . . . . . Pleasant Grove
BR 5964 Moab, Utah . . . . Moab
BR 6308 Smithfield,
  Utah . . . . Smithfield
BR 6475 Dugway, Utah . . Dugway
SA Utah . . . . Ogden

Locomotive Engineers
DIV 51 . . . . Ogden
DIV 55 . . . . Roy
DIV 136 . . . . . . Salt Lake City
DIV 222 . . . . . . West Bountiful
DIV 349 . . . . Orem
DIV 374 . . . . Morgan
DIV 681 . . . . Milford
DIV 713 . . . . . . Salt Lake City
DIV 846 . . . . North Ogden
DIV 888 . . . . Price
SLB Utah State . . . . Salt Lake City

Machinists
LG 568 . . . . Salt Lake City
LG 1287 Air
  Transport . . . . West Valley City
LG 1497 . . . . . . Salt Lake City
LG 1976 . . . . Cedar City
STC Utah . . . . . . Salt Lake City

Maintenance of Way Employes
LG 588 . . . . La Crosse
LG 968 . . . . Spanish Fork
LG 1227 . . . . Midvale
LG 1709 . . . . Price
SLG 1348 . . . . Ogden

Mine Workers
D 22 . . . . Price
LU 1206 . . . . Wellington
LU 1261 . . . . Ferron
LU 1681 . . . . Helper
LU 1769 . . . . Huntington
LU 1902 . . . . Wellington
LU 2011 . . . . Helper
LU 2176 . . . . Orangeville
LU 6363 . . . . Ferron
LU 6788 . . . . Helper
LU 8622 . . . . Helper
LU 9958 . . . . Sunnyside

Musicians
LU 104 . . . . . . Salt Lake City

National Staff Organization
LU Staff Organization, Professional,
  Utah . . . . Murray

Office and Professional Employees
LU 286 . . . . Midvale

Painters
LU 77 . . . . Salt Lake City
LU 755 . . . . Erda

Paper, Allied-Industrial, Chemical Employees
LU 8593 . . . . West Jordan
LU 8-182 . . . . Cedar City
LU 08-286 . . . . Roy
LU 08-578 . . . . . . Woods Cross
LU 08-904 . . . . Delta
LU 08-931 . . . . West Valley City

Plasterers and Cement Masons
LU 568 . . . . . . Salt Lake City

Plumbing and Pipe Fitting
LU 19 . . . . Salt Lake City
LU 57 . . . . Salt Lake City
LU 348 . . . . Ogden
SA Utah . . . . . . Salt Lake City

Postal Mail Handlers
LU 332 . . . . . West Valley City

Postal Workers
LU . . . . Orem
LU 6 Salt Lake City . Salt Lake City
LU 75 Utah Area . . . . . Ogden
LU 1568 Price . . . . . . Price
LU 1934 Vernal . . . . . Vernal
LU 2350 St. George . . . St. George
LU 2513 Tooele Local . . . Tooele
LU 5192 Orem Local . . . . Orem
SA Utah . . . . . . Salt Lake City

Railroad Signalmen
LLG 24 . . . . West Jordan

Roofers, Waterproofers and Allied Workers
LU 91 . . . . Salt Lake City

Rural Letter Carriers
SA Utah . . . . . . South Jordan

Service Employees
LU 651 Firemen &
  Oilers . . . . . . Salt Lake City

Sheet Metal Workers
LU 312 . . . . . . Salt Lake City

Steelworkers
LU 948 . . . . Nephi
LU 4261 . . . . Vernal
LU 12-392-S . . . . Magna
LU 12-485-S . . . . Kearns
LU 12-876-S . . . . . . Wendover
LU 12-1654-S . . . . . . Payson
LU 12-2701-S . . . . Orem
LU 12-2932-S . . . . Spanish Fork
LU 12-3318-S . . . . American Fork
LU 12-4265-S . . . . . . Payson
LU 12-6162-S . . . . Ogden
LU 12-7889-S . . . West Jordan
LU 12-8319 . . . . . . Grantsville

Teamsters
LU 222 . . . . Salt Lake City

Theatrical Stage Employees
LU 99 . . . . Salt Lake City

Transportation Communications Union
D 1223 Union Pacific-Eastern Lines
  SD 106 . . . . . . Salt Lake City
D 5517 . . . . Sandy
LG 5019 Union Pacific . Salt Lake City
LG 6542 Ensign . . . . . . Ogden

Transportation Union
LU 166 . . . . Salt Lake City
LU 238 . . . . Ogden
LU 1038 . . . . . . Salt Lake City
LU 1294 . . . . Minersville
LU 1366 . . . . Layton
LU 1554 . . . . Ogden
SLB LO-49 Utah . . . Salt Lake City

Treasury Employees
CH 17 . . . . Salt Lake City
CH 67 . . . . Ogden

Weather Service Employees
BR 04-39 . . . . . Salt Lake City
BR 04-71 . . . . . Salt Lake City
BR 04-78 . . . . . Salt Lake City

Unaffiliated Labor Organizations

Ballet West Dancers
  Association . . . . . Salt Lake City
Concrete Handlers Drivers &
  Operators Independent Union . Roy
International Association of United
  Workers Union . . . . Bountiful
International Association of United
  Workers Union LU
  1-02 . . . . Huntington
Moon Lake Employees
  Association . . . . . . Roosevelt

Vermont

Affiliated Labor Organizations

Air Traffic Controllers
LU BTV . . . . . . South Burlington

Boilermakers
LG 449-D Cement Workers . Chester

Civilian Technicians
CH 66 Green
   Mountain . . . . South Burlington

Communications Workers
LU 81170 . . . . Brandon
LU 81248 . . . . Burlington

Education
SA Vermont-National Education
   Association . . . . . Montpelier

Electrical Workers
LU 300 . . . . . . South Burlington
LU 2326 . . . . . . Essex Junction

Electrical, Radio and Machine Workers
LU . . . . Barre
LU 218 . . . . Springfield
LU 221 . . . . Burlington
LU 225 . . . . Rutland
LU 234 . . . . . . St. Johnsbury
LU 267 . . . . Burlington
LU 295 . . . . Bennington

Government Employees
LU 2076 DoJ . . . . . . St. Albans
LU 2604 VA . . . . South Royalton

Government Employees Association
LU 01-175 . . . . Colchester

Government Security Officers
LU . . . . Vernon
LU 75 . . . . Rutland

Graphic Communications
LU 109-B . . . . Brattleboro
LU 745-C . . . . Woodbury

Laborers
LU 522 . . . . Burlington

Letter Carriers
BR 37 . . . . Brattleboro
BR 252 . . . . Bennington
BR 495 . . . . Rutland
BR 521 . . . . . . Essex Junction
BR 617 . . . . Middlesex
BR 837 . . . . St. Johnsbury
BR 1365 Newport,
   Vermont . . . . Newport
BR 1828 . . . White River Junction
BR 2244 . . . . Northfield
BR 2245 Woodstock,
   Vermont . . . . . . Woodstock
BR 3133 Fair Haven,
   Vermont . . . . Fair Haven
BR 3490 Brandon,
   Vermont . . . . Brandon
SA Vermont . . . . . . Burlington

Machinists
LG 1829 . . . . Newport
LG 2704 . . . . Starksboro

Maintenance of Way Employes
LG 356 . . . . Newport

Musicians
LU 351 . . . . Burlington

National Staff Organization
LU 3 Vermont Staff
   Organization . . . . . Montpelier

Nurses
LU 5109 Copley
   Hospital . . . . Morrisville

Paper, Allied-Industrial, Chemical Employees
LU 01-41 . . . . Gilman
LU 01-340 . . . . St. Albans
LU 01-345 . . . . St. Albans
LU 01-944 . . . . Brattleboro
LU 01-1594 . . . . . . Brattleboro
LU 01-1862 . . . . . Bellows Falls
LU 08-296 Granite Cutters
   Association . . . . Barre

Plant Protection Employees
LU 20 . . . . Burlington

Plumbing and Pipe Fitting
LU 693 . . . . . . South Burlington

Postal Workers
LU 520 White River
   Junction . . . White River Junction
LU 570 Burlington . . . Burlington
LU 759 Montpelier
   Vermont . . . . . . Montpelier
LU 765 Barre . . . . Barre
LU 2677 St. Albans . . . St. Albans
LU 2778 Bellows
   Falls . . . . Bellows Falls
LU 3173 Rutland . . . . . Rutland
LU 3178 Bennington . . Bennington
LU 3184 Springfield
   Local . . . . Springfield
LU 3535 Brattleboro . . Brattleboro
LU 4000 Lydonville
   Local . . . . Lydonville
LU 6322 Manchester
   Center . . . . Manchester Center
SA Vermont . . White River Junction

Rural Letter Carriers
LU Crittenden-Grand Isle
   Counties . . . . Huntington
LU Orleans-Essex . . . . Newport
LU Ruthland County . . . Rutland
LU Washington-Orange
   Counties . . . . . Williamstown
LU Windham-Windson
   Counties . . . . . South Royalton
LU 3 Caledonia-Essex
   Counties . . . . Groton
LU 6 Lamoille County . . St. Albans
SA Vermont . . . . . Williamstown

State, County and Municipal Employees
LU 1674 Vermont Community
   Health Care Centers
   Employees . . . . . . Burlington

Steelworkers
LU 4-4-S . . . . Barre
LU 04-5518-S . . . . Lyndon Center

Teachers
LU 5064 Nurses, Brattleboro
   Federation of . . . . Brattleboro

Teamsters
LU 597 . . . . South Barre

Theatrical Stage Employees
LU 919 . . . . Burlington

Treasury Employees
CH 19 . . . . Burlington
CH 142 . . . . Swanton

Weather Service Employees
BR 01-7 . . . . Burlington

Unaffiliated Labor Organizations

Brattleboro Retreat United Nurses &
Allied Professionals LU
   5086 . . . . Brattleboro

Virgin Islands

Affiliated Labor Organizations

Agricultural Employees
BR . . . . Kingshill

Air Traffic Controllers
LU STT . . . . St. Thomas

Government Security Officers
LU 60 . . . . St. Thomas

Hotel and Restaurant Employees
LU 611 . . . . St. Croix

Letter Carriers
BR 6413 . . . . Christiansted

Postal Workers
LU 6176 Virgin Island
   Area . . . . St. Thomas

Steelworkers
LU 09-7701-S . . . . . . St. Croix
LU 09-8248-S . . . . . . St. Croix
LU 09-8249-S . . . . . St. Thomas
LU 09-8526-S . . . . Christiansted
LU 09-8545-S . . . . . . Kingshill

LU 09-8677-S . Camalie St. Thomas
LU 09-8713-S . . . . . St. Thomas

Treasury Employees
CH 200. . . . . Christiansted

Unaffiliated Labor Organizations

WAPA Employees Association
   Water & Power
   Authority . . . . . . St. Thomas

Virginia

AFL-CIO Trade and Industrial Departments

Building and Construction Trades Department
BCTC Hampton Roads . . . Norfolk
BCTC North Carolina . . . Roanoke
BCTC Richmond . . . . . Richmond
BCTC Southwestern
  Virginia . . . . Roanoke
BCTC Virginia State . . . Richmond

Maritime Trades Department
PC Hampton Roads . . . . Norfolk

Metal Trades Department
MTC Tidewater Virginia Federal
  Employees. . . . . . Portsmouth

Affiliated Labor Organizations

Agricultural Employees
BR 32 . . . . Norfolk

Air Line Employees
LC 87 Florida Gulf . . . . Herndon

Air Traffic Controllers
LU DCC . . . . Herndon
LU HEF . . . . Manassas
LU ORF . . . . Virginia Beach
LU PHF . . . . . . Newport News
LU RIC . . . Richmond International
  Airport
LU ROA . . . . Roanoke
LU ZDC . . . . Leesburg

Asbestos Workers
LU 9. . . . . Chesapeake
LU 85. . . . . West Point
LU 129. . . . . Colonial Heights

Automobile, Aerospace Workers
LU 26 Distributive Workers . Suffolk
LU 149. . . . . Winchester
LU 919. . . . . Norfolk
LU 1748. . . . . Winchester
LU 2069. . . . . Dublin
LU 2123. . . . . . Fredericksburg
LU 2389. . . . . Covington
LU 2807. . . . . Lebanon
LU 2999 . . . . Starsburg

Bakery, Confectionery, Tobacco Workers and Grain Millers
LU 203-T . . . . Richmond
LU 233 . . . . Danville
LU 255-T . . . . Blackston
LU 309-T . . . . . . Chesterfield
LU 314-T . . . . Danville
LU 321-T . . . . . Mechanicsville
LU 348-T . . . . Danville
LU 358 . . . . Richmond
LU 359-T . . . . Colonial Heights

Boilermakers
LG 45 . . . . Richmond
LG 57 . . . . Chesapeake
LG 191-D Cement
  Workers. . . . . . . Chesapeake
LG 314-D Cement
  Workers. . . . . Roanoke
LG 538 . . . . Roanoke

LG 684 . . . . Chesapeake
LG 1999. . . . . Chesapeake

Carpenters
C East Coast Industrial. . . . Marion
LU 319 . . . . Roanoke
LU 388. . . . . Richmond
LU 613. . . . . Norfolk
LU 1078 . . . . Spotsylvania
LU 1402. . . . . Richmond
LU 1665 . . . . Alexandria
LU 2033 . . . . Front Royal
LU 2316. . . . . Boykins
LU 2488 . . . . Berryville
LU 2514. . . . . Chesapeake
LU 3199 . . . . Marion
LU 8222 . . . . Cana

Civilian Technicians
CH 49 Old Dominion . . . Richmond
CH 59 Robert C. Atkinson
  Memorial . . . . Midlothian
CH 102 Southside Virginia . . Crewe
NHQ . . . . Woodbridge

Communications Workers
C Virginia State. . . . . Richmond
LU 2201. . . . . Richmond
LU 2202. . . . . . . Virginia Beach
LU 2203 . . . . Lynchburg
LU 2204 . . . . Roanoke
LU 2205 . . . . . . Newport News
LU 2206 . . . . Melfa
LU 2222 . . . . Annandale
LU 2252. . . . . Richmond
LU 2272 . . . . Winchester
LU 2275 . . . . Woodbridge
LU 2277. . . . . Martinsville
LU 14208 . . . . Norfolk

DuPont Workers
LU United Workers Inc. Waynesboro
NHQ . . . . Waynesboro

Electrical Workers
LU 50 . . . . Richmond
LU 80 . . . . Norfolk
LU 121 . . . . Stephens City
LU 464 . . . . Covington
LU 637 . . . . Roanoke
LU 666 . . . . Richmond
LU 734. . . . . Portsmouth
LU 813 . . . . Roanoke
LU 1142 . . . . Norfolk
LU 1181 . . . . . . Charlottesville
LU 1340 . . . . . . Newport News
LU 1434. . . . . Chesterfield
LU 1737 . . . . Manassas
LU 2173 Lynchburg . . . Concord
LU 2240 . . . . Windsor

Electrical, Radio and Machine Workers
LU 123 . . . . Verona
LU 124. . . . . Fishersville

Electronic Workers
LU 160 . . . . Christiansburg
LU 161 . . . . Salem
LU 162 . . . . Roanoke
LU 173 . . . . Verona
LU 174. . . . . Stanley

Elevator Constructors
LU 51 . . . . Richmond

LU 52 . . . . Norfolk

Federal Employees
C GSA Locals . . . West Springfield
LU 1028 . . . . Norfolk
LU 1309 . . . . Herndon
LU 1332 . . . . Alexandria
LU 1627 . . . . Springfield
LU 1642 . . . . Arlington
LU 1817. . . . . Goodview
LU 1861 . . . . . . Christiansburg
LU 1887 . . . . Alexandria
LU 1957 . . . . Reston
LU 1993 . . . . Springfield

Fire Fighters
LU 13 Norfolk Naval Base . Norfolk
LU 25-F . . . . Portsmouth
LU 287-F Fort Lee Fire &
  Emergency Services . . . Fort Lee
LU 3217 Metro Washington
  Airports . . . . Arlington

Flint Glass Workers
LU 64 . . . . Williamsburg
LU 78 . . . . Danville
LU 1014 . . . . Danville
LU 1022 . . . . Blacksburg

Food and Commercial Workers
LU 94-C. . . . . Shenandoah
LU 591-C . . . . . . Prince George
LU 845-C . . . . Brookneal
LU 851-C . . . . . . Spring Grove

Glass, Molders, Pottery and Plastics Workers
LU 33. . . . . West Point

Government Employees
C 4 VA, Fourth District . . . Salem
C 53 National VA . . . . . Salem
C 210 U.S. Marshals Service Locals,
  International . . . . Alexandria
C 215 National SSA-BHA
  Locals . . . . Falls Church
LU 2 Army Pentagon-
  DoD . . . . Arlington
LU 22 ID . . . . Norfolk
LU 53 DoD . . . . Norfolk
LU 65 ID Retirees. . . . . . Hayes
LU 1052. . . . . Fort Belvior
LU 1052. . . . . Fort Belvoir
LU 1178 DoD . . . . Fort Lee
LU 1356 USDA . . . . Glen Allen
LU 1402 . . . . Arlington
LU 1643 DoD . . . . . Fort Eustis
LU 1739 VA . . . . Salem
LU 1754 FEMA . . . . Winchester
LU 1786 DoD . . . . . . Quantico
LU 1924 DoJ . . . . Arlington
LU 1992. . . . . Richmond
LU 2047 DoD. . . . . . . Richmond
LU 2052 DoJ . . . . . . Petersburg
LU 2096 DoD . . . . . . Dahlgren
LU 2100 USDA. . . . . . Elkton
LU 2117 DoD . . . . . Fort Monroe
LU 2145 VA . . . . . . Richmond
LU 2328 DoVA, MC . . . Hampton
LU 2449 DLA . . . . . . Lorton
LU 2755 NASA . . . Wallops Island
LU 2785 DoJ . . . . . . Arlington
LU 2817 USDA . . . . . Smithfield
LU 2902 DoD . . . Bowling Green
LU 3316 DoL. . . . . . Lebanon

LU 3380 HUD . . . . . . Richmond
LU 3403 NSF . . . . . Arlington
LU 3525 DoJ. . . . . . Falls Church
LU 3615 SSA . . . . Falls Church
LU 4015 DoD . . . . . Portsmouth

Government Employees Association
LU . . . . Hampton
LU 27 . . . . Fort Lee
LU 49 Service Employees. Arlington
LU 55 . . . . Fort Lee
LU 123 . . . . Virginia Beach
LU 03-118 Service Employees
  Intern. . . . . Alexandria
LU 04-1 . . . . Lackey
LU 04-2 . . . . . Newport News
LU 04-6 . . . . . . Fort Eustis
LU 04-11 . . . . Fort Monroe
LU 04-12 . . . . Fort Monroe
LU 04-17. . . . . . . Hampton
LU 04-19 . . . . . Portsmouth
LU 04-26 . . Langley Air Force Base
LU 04-45 . . . . Norfolk
LU 04-47. . . . . . Fort Eustis
LU 04-68 . . . . . Williamsburg
LU 04-69. . . . . . . Hampton
LU 04-86 . . . . . . Alexandria
LU 04-106 . Langley Air Force Base
LU 04-109 . . . . . Portsmouth
LU 04-114 . . . . . . Hampton
LU 04-124 . . . . Virginia Beach

Government Security Officers
LU 84 . . . . Chesterfield
LU 88 . . . . Roanoke

Graphic Communications
LU 40-N . . . . Richmond
LU 210-C . . . . Vinton
LU 538-C . . . . . . Woodbridge
LU 642-S . . . . Grottoes
LU 670-C . . . . Richmond
LU 788-S J.W. Ferguson . Richmond

Iron Workers
DC Mid Atlantic States . . . Fairfax
LU 28 . . . . Richmond
LU 79 . . . . Norfolk
LU 228 . . . . Chesapeake
LU 486 . . . . McLean
LU 697 . . . . Roanoke
LU 753 . . . . Bristol

Laborers
DC Virginia & North
  Carolina. . . . . . Williamsburg
LU 307 . . . . Norfolk
LU 388 . . . . Norfolk
LU 404 Industrial & Commercial
  Employees . . . . Williamsburg
LU 572 . . . . Williamsburg
LU 649. . . . . Portsmouth
LU 980 . . . . Roanoke
LU 1046 . . . . . . Williamsburg
LU 1225 . . . . Sterling

Laundry and Dry Cleaning
LU 212 . . . . Petersburg

Letter Carriers
BR 247 Tidewater . . . . Hampton
BR 325 . . . . Evington
BR 326 . . . . Petersburg
BR 456 Norfolk Branch 456 . Norfolk

BR 496 . . . . Richmond
BR 513 . . . . Staunton
BR 518 . . . . Charlottesville
BR 524 . . . . Roanoke
BR 567 Cavalier . . . . . Alexandria
BR 595 . . . . Danville
BR 609 . . . . Newport News
BR 685 . . . . Fredericksburg
BR 694 . . . . Winchester
BR 1112 . . . . . . Virginia Beach
BR 1185 Bedford, Virginia . Bedford
BR 1605 . . . . Salem
BR 1793 Pulaski, Virginia . . Pulaski
BR 2091 Franklin, Virginia . Franklin
BR 2153 . . . . Hopewell
BR 2280 . . . . Martinsville
BR 2500 Cape Charles,
    Virginia . . . . . Cape Charles
BR 2727 . . . . Front Royal
BR 2819 . . . . . . Virginia Beach
BR 3005 Wytheville,
    Virginia . . . . Wytheville
BR 3138 Crewe, Virginia . . . Crewe
BR 3170 . . . . South Boston
BR 3376 Woodstock,
    Virginia . . . . Woodstock
BR 3379 Strasburg,
    Virginia . . . . Strasburg
BR 3387 Norton, Virginia . . Norton
BR 3508 Big Stone Gap,
    Virginia . . . . . Big Stone Gap
BR 3520 . . . . Annandale
BR 3621 Galax, Virginia . . . Galax
BR 3686 . . . . Radford
BR 3864 Emporia,
    Virginia . . . . Emporia
BR 3882 Onancock,
    Virginia . . . . Onancock
BR 4053 Bluefield,
    Virginia . . . . Bluefield
BR 4276 . . . . Blacksburg
BR 4292 . . . . Christiansburg
BR 4575 Tazewell,
    Virginia . . . . Tazewell
BR 4576 Pennington Gap,
    Virginia . . . . . Pennington Gap
BR 4577 Rocky Mount,
    Virginia . . . . . Rocky Mount
BR 4581 Altavista,
    Virginia . . . . Altavista
BR 4582 Appalachia,
    Virginia . . . . Appalachia
BR 4654 South Hill,
    Virginia . . . . South Hill
BR 4798 NALC . . . . . Springfield
BR 4989 Chincoteague,
    Virginia . . . . . Chincoteague
BR 4990 Chase City,
    Virginia . . . . . . Chase City
BR 4991 Lawrenceville,
    Virginia . . . . . Lawrenceville
BR 5282 Spencer, Virginia . Spencer
BR 5447 Smithfield,
    Virginia . . . . Smithfield
BR 5457 . . . . Richlands
BR 5661 Orange, Virginia . . Orange
BR 5825 Collinsville,
    Virginia . . . . . . Collinsville
BR 5917 Narrows,
    Virginia . . . . Narrows
BR 5920 Colonial Beach,
    Virginia . . . . . Colonial Beach
BR 5921 . . . . Woodbridge
BR 6009 Pearisburg,
    Virginia . . . . Pearisburg
BR 6066 . . . . Chesapeake
BR 6434 Ridgeway,
    Virginia . . . . Ridgeway

SA Virginia . . . . . Newport News

Locomotive Engineers
DIV 14 . . . . Spotsylvania
DIV 26 . . . . Richmond
DIV 37 . . . . Coeburn
DIV 38 . . . . Hot Springs
DIV 143 . . . . Culpeper
DIV 167 . . . . . . Big Stone Gap
DIV 217 . . . . Elkton
DIV 291 . . . . Victoria
DIV 301 . . . . Salem
DIV 456 . . . . Portsmouth
DIV 532 . . . . . . Highland Springs
DIV 561 . . . . Montpelier
GCA Norfolk & Western
    Railway . . . . Stanley
SLB Virginia . . . . . Purcellville

Longshoremen
DC Hampton Roads &
    Vicinity . . . . Norfolk
LU 846 . . . . Newport News
LU 862 . . . . Newport News
LU 970 . . . . Norfolk
LU 1248 . . . . Norfolk
LU 1458 . . . . Norfolk
LU 1624 . . . . Norfolk
LU 1736 . . . . Newport News
LU 1784 . . . . Hampton
LU 1819 . . . . Norfolk
LU 1963 . . . . Chesapeake
LU 1970 . . . . . . Virginia Beach
LU 2060 . . . . Norfolk

Machinists
DLG 74 . . . . Norfolk
LG . . . . Alexandria
LG 10 . . . . Richmond
LG 97 . . . . Virginia Beach
LG 165 . . . . Blue Ridge
LG 680 . . . . . . Virginia Beach
LG 696 . . . . Powhatan
LG 1486 . . . . Catharpin
LG 1747 . . . . Herndon
LG 1759 . . . . Herndon
LG 2461 . . . . . . Newport News
LG 2531 . . . . Hampton
LG 2552 . . . . . Temperanceville
LG 2708 . . . . Norfolk
LG 2829-PM . . . . . Newport News
LG 2914 . . . . Norfolk
LLG W-216
    Woodworkers . . . Mechanicsville
LLG W-331 Woodworkers . Emporia
LLG W-391 Woodworkers . . . Ivor
LLG W-2533 Woodworkers . . Floyd
STC Virginia . . . . . . Hampton

Maintenance of Way Employes
LG 75 . . . . Eagle Rock
LG 367 . . . . Newport News
LG 568 . . . . Dublin
LG 571 . . . . Bluefield
LG 577 . . . . Stanley
LG 598 . . . . Crewe
LG 2925 . . . . Midlothian
SLG 153 . . . . Scottsville
SLG 338 . . . . . . Fredericksburg
SLG 572 . . . . Farmville
SLG 586 . . . . Gate City
SLG 594 . . . . . . Virginia Beach
SLG 599 . . . . Salem
SLG 995 . . . . Chesapeake

Mine Workers
LU 218 . . . . Martinsville
LU 325 . . . . Lebanon

LU 1055 . . . . Appalachia
LU 1256 . . . . Abingdon
LU 1259 . . . . Lebanon
LU 1374 . . . . Grundy
LU 1405 . . . . . . Big Stone Gap
LU 1470 . . . . Castlewood
LU 1509 . . . . Lebanon
LU 1594 . . . . Jewell Ridge
LU 1607 . . . . Appalachia
LU 1640 . . . . Honaker
LU 1671 . . . . Oakwood
LU 1760 . . . . Swords Creek
LU 1976 . . . . . . Big Stone Gap
LU 2158 . . . . Appalachia
LU 2232 . . . . Grundy
LU 2274 . . . . Coeburn
LU 2322 . . . . Cedar Bluff
LU 2354 . . . . Clintwood
LU 2490 . . . . Clintwood
LU 2888 . . . . Abingdon
LU 5997 . . . . Bluefield
LU 6167 . . . . . . Jewell Valley
LU 6229 . . . . Wise
LU 6354 . . . . Norton
LU 6375 . . . . Gate City
LU 6633 . . . . Bandy
LU 6843 . . . . Mavisdale
LU 7025 . . . . Grundy
LU 7170 . . . . Haysi
LU 7276 . . . . Wise
LU 7327 . . . . Rosedale
LU 7528 . . . . Clintwood
LU 7950 . . . . Coeburn
LU 8017 . . . . Roanoke
LU 8181 . . . . Appalachia
LU 8761 . . . . . Pennington Gap
LU 9127 . . . . Keokee
LU 9967 . . . . Wise
NHQ . . . . Fairfax

Musicians
LU 123 . . . . Richmond
LU 125 . . . . Norfolk
LU 165 . . . . Roanoke

National Staff Organization
LU Virginia Professional Staff
    Association . . . . Norfolk

Needletrades
LU 1398 . . . . . . Harrisonburg
LU 2024 . . . . Narrows

Operating Engineers
LU 147 . . . . Norfolk

Painters
LU 474 . . . . Portsmouth
LU 890 . . . . Woodbridge
LU 891 . . . . Roanoke
LU 1018 . . . . Richmond
LU 1100 . . . . Norfolk
LU 1846 . . . . . . Virginia Beach

Paper, Allied-Industrial, Chemical Employees
LU 2-486 . . . . Richmond
LU 02-2 . . . . Radford
LU 02-10 . . . . Hayes
LU 02-294 . . . . . . Chesapeake
LU 02-403 . . . . Culpeper
LU 02-410 . . . . . . Covington
LU 02-467 . . . . . . West Point
LU 02-490 . . . . . . Covington
LU 02-495 . . . . Radford
LU 02-496 . . . . Selma
LU 02-505 . . . . Franklin
LU 02-515 . . . . . . Troutville

LU 02-543 . . . . . . Chesapeake
LU 02-573 . . . . Verona
LU 02-621 . . . . . . Wakefield
LU 02-664 . . . . Chester
LU 02-666 . . . . . . Charles City
LU 02-675 . . . . . . Covington
LU 02-694 . . . . . Chesterfield
LU 02-695 . . . . Critz
LU 02-699 . . . . . . Richmond
LU 02-747 . . . . Providence Forge
LU 02-843 . . . . Hardy
LU 02-884 . . . . . . Covington
LU 02-986 . . . . . . Wytheville
LU 02-1013 . Natural Bridge Station
LU 02-1014 . . . . . . Lynchburg
LU 02-1153 . . . . . . Hopewell
LU 02-1372 . . . . . . Jarratt
LU 02-1374 . . . . . . Vesuvius
LU 02-1389 . . . . . . Covington
LU 02-1408 . . . . . . Richmond
LU 02-1488 . . . . . . Franklin
LU 02-1550 . . . . . . Crozier
LU 02-1553 . . . . . . Richmond
LU 02-1666 . . . . Newport News
LU 02-1692 . . . . . . Richmond
LU 02-1831 . . . . . . Richmond
LU 02-1853 . . . . . . Ridgeway
LU 02-1895 . . . . Madison Heights
LU 02-1898 . . . . . . Chester
LU 02-1941 . . . . . . Petersburg

Pilots, Air Line
LEC 1 Northwest Airlines . Herndon
LEC 2 Trans World
    Airlines . . . . Herndon
LEC 5 United Airlines . . . Herndon
LEC 10 Ryan . . . . . . Herndon
LEC 11 United Airlines . . Herndon
LEC 12 United Airlines . . Herndon
LEC 13 Northwest
    Airlines . . . . Herndon
LEC 16 Delta Airlines . . Herndon
LEC 17 DHL . . . . . . Herndon
LEC 18 Spirit . . . . . . Herndon
LEC 19 Spirit . . . . . . Herndon
LEC 20 Northwest
    Airlines . . . . Herndon
LEC 23 Polar Air Cargo . . Herndon
LEC 25 Champion Air . . . Herndon
LEC 27 United Airlines . . Herndon
LEC 28 Piedmont Airlines . Herndon
LEC 29 Piedmont Airlines . Herndon
LEC 30 Midwest Express . Herndon
LEC 32 USAirways . . . . Herndon
LEC 33 United Airlines . . Herndon
LEC 34 United Airlines . . Herndon
LEC 35 Piedmont Airlines . Herndon
LEC 36 Pan American . . Herndon
LEC 37 Comair . . . . . Herndon
LEC 38 Trans States . . . Herndon
LEC 39 Trans States . . . Herndon
LEC 40 CCAir . . . . . . Herndon
LEC 41 USAirways . . . . Herndon
LEC 44 Delta Airlines . . . Herndon
LEC 45 Comair . . . . . Herndon
LEC 46 Ryan Airlines . . . Herndon
LEC 47 Delta Airlines . . Herndon
LEC 48 Delta . . . . . . Herndon
LEC 50 Air Wisconsin . . Herndon
LEC 52 United Airlines . . Herndon
LEC 53 Air Wisconsin . . Herndon
LEC 55 Northwest
    Airlines . . . . Herndon
LEC 57 United Airlines . . Herndon
LEC 60 Skyway Local . . . Herndon
LEC 61 PSA . . . . Herndon
LEC 62 America West . . . Herndon
LEC 63 Alaska Airlines . . Herndon

LEC 64 Alaska Airlines . . Herndon
LEC 65 Hawaiian Airlines . Herndon
LEC 66 Delta Airlines . . . Herndon
LEC 67 Alaska Airlines . . Herndon
LEC 68 Jetstream PSA . . . Herndon
LEC 69 PSA . . . . Herndon
LEC 70 PSA . . . . Herndon
LEC 71 Delta . . . . Herndon
LEC 72 Atlas Air . . . . . Herndon
LEC 74 Northwest
  Airlines . . . . Herndon
LEC 75 Ross Aviation . . . Herndon
LEC 78 Allegheny . . . . . Herndon
LEC 80 Aloha Airlines . . . Herndon
LEC 81 Delta Airlines . . . Herndon
LEC 83 American Eagle . . Herndon
LEC 84 Mesa . . . . Herndon
LEC 85 Mesa . . . . Herndon
LEC 86 Mesa . . . . Herndon
LEC 88 Mesa . . . . Herndon
LEC 89 Mesa . . . . Herndon
LEC 90 USAirways . . . . Herndon
LEC 91 Allegheny . . . . . Herndon
LEC 92 Allegheny . . . . . Herndon
LEC 93 United Airlines . . Herndon
LEC 94 USAirways . . . . Herndon
LEC 95 Allegheny
  Airlines . . . . Herndon
LEC 96 American Trans
  Air . . . . Herndon
LEC 97 American Trans
  Air . . . . Herndon
LEC 98 American Trans
  Air . . . . Herndon
LEC 102 Hawaiian
  Airlines . . . . Herndon
LEC 105 American Eagle . Herndon
LEC 106 Mesaba Airlines . Herndon
LEC 107 Mesaba Airlines . Herndon
LEC 108 Delta Airlines . . Herndon
LEC 109 Spirit . . . . . . Herndon
LEC 112 Atlantic Southeast
  Airlines . . . . Herndon
LEC 113 Atlantic Southeast
  Airlines . . . . Herndon
LEC 115 Mesa . . . . . . Herndon
LEC 121 American Eagle . Herndon
LEC 126 American Eagle . Herndon
LEC 130 Express Airlines . Herndon
LEC 131 American Eagle . Herndon
LEC 133 American Eagle . Herndon
LEC 135 U.S. Airways . . Herndon
LEC 138 USAirways . . . Herndon
LEC 141 Atlantic Coast . . Herndon
LEC 142 Atlantic Coast . . Herndon
LEC 146 Aloha Island Air . Herndon
LEC 150 United Airlines . . Herndon
LEC 155 American Eagle . Herndon
LEC 170 Continental . . . Herndon
LEC 171 Continental
  Express . . . . Herndon
LEC 172 Continental
  Express . . . . Herndon
LEC 173 Continental . . . Herndon
LEC 175 Continental
  Express . . . . Herndon
LEC 176 Continental
  Express . . . . Herndon
LEC 177 Continental
  Express . . . . Herndon
LEC 178 Continental
  Instructors . . . . . . Herndon
LEC 179 Continental Express
  Instructors . . . . . . Herndon
MEC Air Wisconsin . . . Herndon
MEC Alaska Airlines . . . Herndon
MEC Allegheny . . . . . Herndon
MEC Aloha Airlines . . . Herndon

MEC Aloha Island Air . . . Herndon
MEC America West . . . . Herndon
MEC American Eagle . . . Herndon
MEC American Trans Air . Herndon
MEC Atlantic Coast . . . . Herndon
MEC Atlantic Southeast . . Herndon
MEC Atlas Air . . . . . . Herndon
MEC CCAir . . . . Herndon
MEC Champion Air . . . . Herndon
MEC Comair . . . . Herndon
MEC Continental . . . . . Herndon
MEC Delta Airlines . . . . Herndon
MEC DHL . . . . Herndon
MEC Emery Worldwide . . Herndon
MEC Express Airlines I . . Herndon
MEC Flying Tiger Airlines. Herndon
MEC Hawaiian Airlines . . Herndon
MEC Markair. . . . . . . Herndon
MEC Mesa . . . . Herndon
MEC Mesaba Airlines . . . Herndon
MEC Midway Airlines . . . Herndon
MEC Midwest Express . . . Herndon
MEC Northwest Airlines. . Herndon
MEC Pan American . . . . Herndon
MEC Piedmont Airlines . . Herndon
MEC Polar Air Cargo . . . Herndon
MEC PSA. . . . . Herndon
MEC Reeve Aleutian
  Airways . . . . Herndon
MEC Republic Airlines. . . Herndon
MEC Ross Aviation . . . . Herndon
MEC Ryan . . . . Herndon
MEC Skyway Master. . . . Herndon
MEC Spirit . . . . Herndon
MEC Sun Country . . . . Herndon
MEC Trans States . . . . . Herndon
MEC Trans World Airlines. Herndon
MEC U.S. Airways Shuttle. Herndon
MEC United Airlines . . . . Herndon
MEC USAirways. . . . . Herndon
NHQ . . . . Herndon

Plant Protection

LU 757 National. . . . . . Norfolk

Plumbing and Pipe Fitting

LU 10 . . . . Richmond
LU 110. . . . . Norfolk
LU 272. . . . . Virginia Beach
LU 376. . . . . Norfolk
LU 477. . . . . Portsmouth
LU 491 . . . . Roanoke
LU 540 . . . . Newport News
LU 851 . . . . Disputanta
SA Virginia State Pipe
  Trades . . . . Richmond

Police Associations

LU 34 Policemens Benevolent
  Association . . . . Virginia Beach
NHQ . . . . Alexandria

Postal and Federal Employees

D 2 . . . . Richmond
LU 208 . . . . Richmond
LU 210 Northern Virginia . Stafford

Postal Mail Handlers

LU 305 . . . . Richmond

Postal Workers

LU 171 Portsmouth . . . Portsmouth
LU 199 Richmond . . . . Richmond
LU 262 Norfolk . . . . . . Norfolk
LU 482 Roanoke . . . . . Roanoke
LU 559
  Fredericksburg . . Fredericksburg
LU 713 Petersburg . . . . Petersburg

LU 823 Wytheville
  Local. . . . . Wytheville
LU 830 Cape Charles
  Local. . . . . Cape Charles
LU 834 Culpeper. . . . . Culpeper
LU 862 Hopewell . . . . Hopewell
LU 867 Clifton Forge
  Local . . . . Clifton Forge
LU 875 Orange Local . . . Orange
LU 883 Marion Local . . . Marion
LU 1040 Danville. . . . . Danville
LU 1376 Suffolk . . . . . . Suffolk
LU 1383 Emporia Local . . Emporia
LU 1490 Ashland Local . . Ashland
LU 1491 Chatham Local . . Chatham
LU 1492 Salem . . . . Salem
LU 1493 Blacksburg. . . Blacksburg
LU 1495 Harrisonburg. Harrisonburg
LU 1496 Luray . . . . . . Luray
LU 1518 Virginia
  Beach . . . . . . Virginia Beach
LU 1602 Lynchburg . . . Lynchburg
LU 1604 Galax Local . . . . Galax
LU 1606 Coeburn . . . . . Coeburn
LU 1608 Saltville Local . . Saltville
LU 1609 Pulaski Local. . . Pulaski
LU 1610 Martinsville
  Area. . . . . Martinsville
LU 1611 Radford . . . . . Radford
LU 1614 Bassett Local. . . Bassett
LU 1657
  Charlottesville . . . Charlottesville
LU 2023 Winchester. . . Winchester
LU 2024 Front Royal . . Front Royal
LU 2193 Bristol . . . . . Bristol
LU 2245 Covington
  Local . . . . Covington
LU 2299
  Christiansburg . . . Christiansburg
LU 3484 Gate City Local . Gate City
LU 4759 Chester Local . . . Chester
LU 6324 Woodbridge . Woodbridge
LU 6600 Chesapeake . . Chesapeake
LU 6638 Mechanicsville
  Local . . . . . Mechanicsville
LU 6726 Peninsula Facility
  Area . . . . Hampton
LU 6803 The Northern Virginia
  Area . . . . Annandale
LU 7152 Battlefield. . . . Stafford
LU 7163 Southwest Virginia
  Area . . . . Cedar Bluff
SA Virginia . . . . . . Chesapeake

Professional and Technical Engineers

LU 1 . . . . Portsmouth
LU 10 . . . . Portsmouth

Railroad Signalmen

LLG 77 . . . . Covington
LLG 138 . . . . . . Fredericksburg
LLG 148 . . . . Chesterfield

Rural Letter Carriers

LU Albemarle-Greene-Nelson
  Counties . . . . . Stuarts Draft
LU Amelia-Powhattan
  Counties . . . . Amelia
LU Amherst-Appomattox-Campbell
  Counties . . . . Lynchburg
LU Augusta-Highland
  Counties . . . . Staunton
LU Bedford County. . . . Bedford
LU Clarke-Frederick-Warren
  Counties . . . . . Stephens City
LU Fairfax-Prince William-Loudoun
  Counties . . . . Vienna

LU Fairystone Park County
  Association . . . . Rocky Mount
LU Halifax County. . . . Virgilina
LU Mecklenburg
  County . . . . . Lawrenceville
LU Mount Rogers . . . . . Fries
LU New River Valley-Tri-County
  Association . . . . Christiansburg
LU Piedmont . . . . . . Richmond
LU Pittsylvania County. . . Danville
LU Richmond-Henrico-Chesterfield
  Association . . . . . Richmond
LU Rockbridge
  County . . . . . Rockbridge Baths
LU Rockingham County . Broadway
LU Southampton County . Newsoms
LU Southside Virginia . . . . Rice
LU Tidewater
  Association . . . . Virginia Beach
LU Washington-Scott
  Counties. . . . . . . Abingdon
LU 8 Fredericksburg. Fredericksburg
LU 12 Rappahannock County . Reva
LU 13 Dinwiddie-Prince George
  Counties . . . . . . Sutherland
LU 21 Colonial Area
  Association . . . Providence Forge
LU 29 Roanoke-Craig
  Counties . . . . Goodview
LU 32 Shenandoah
  County. . . . . Strasburg
LU 36 Sussex-Surry Counties . Surry
LU 37 Tazewell
  County . . . . . . Pounding Mill
LU 41 Accomack-Northampton
  Counties . . . Chincoteague Island
LU 42 Bristol . . . . . . Abingdon
NHQ . . . . Alexandria
SA Virginia. . . . . . . Windsor

Security, Police and Fire Professionals

LU 452. . . . . Portsmouth

Service Employees

LU 117. . . . . . . Newport News
LU 176 Firemen & Oilers . Franklin
LU 513 Firemen & Oilers . . Vinton
LU 524 International Leather Goods,
  Plastics, Novelty and Service
  Union. . . . . Petersburg
LU 741 Firemen & Oilers . . Vinton
LU 744 Firemen & Oilers . Suffolk
SC 6 Firemen & Oilers . . . Vinton

Sheet Metal Workers

LU 52 . . . . Vinton
LU 363. . . . . Springfield

State, County and Municipal Employees

LU 1509 . . . . Woodbridge
LU 2027 Action Employees
  Union . . . . Alexandria

Steelworkers

LU 8-1305. . . . . Saltville
LU 08-240-L . . . . Bedford
LU 08-400-A . . . . Chester
LU 08-440-A . . . . . . Petersburg
LU 08-1023-L . . . . Salem
LU 08-2864-S . . Madison Heights
LU 08-2969-S . . . . . . Radford
LU 08-5886-S . . . . . . Damascus
LU 08-6891-S . . . . . Meadowview
LU 08-8270-S . . . . . . Lynchburg
LU 08-8544-S. . . . . . . Honaker
LU 08-8888-S . . . Newport News

LU 08-9336-S . . . . . . Newbern
LU 08-9428 . . . . Chatham
LU 08-12103-S . . . . . Hopewell
LU 08-12276-S . . . . . Newsoms
LU 08-13061-S . . Colonial Heights
LU 08-14187-S . . . . . . Franklin
LU 08-14287-S . . . . . Manassas
LU 08-14440-S . . . . Elliston
LU 08-14459-S . . . . . . Worton
LU 08-14842-S . . . Sugar Grove
LU 08-15094-S . . . . Chilhowie
LU 08-15126-S . . . . Stony Creek

Teamsters
JC 83 . . . . Richmond
LU 22 . . . . Collinsville
LU 29 . . . . Waynesboro
LU 95 . . . . Williamsburg
LU 101 . . . . Hopewell
LU 171 . . . . Roanoke
LU 322 . . . . Richmond
LU 592 . . . . Richmond
LU 822 . . . . Norfolk

Theatrical Stage Employees
LU 55 . . . . Roanoke
LU 87 . . . . Sandston
LU 264 . . . . Hampton
LU 370 . . . . Richmond
LU 699 . . . . Bristol

Transit Union
CONBD Virginia . . Virginia Beach
JCONF ATU . . . . Virginia Beach
LDIV 1220 . . . . Richmond
LU 1177 . . . . Norfolk

Transport Workers
LU 510 . . . . Alexandria

Transportation Communications Union
D 304 Chesapeake & Ohio System
 Board 146 . . . . Richmond
D 500 Southeastern System Board
 96 . . . . Virginia Beach
D 537 Southeastern System Board
 96 . . . . Roanoke
D 619 Southeastern System Board
 96 . . . . Bluefield
D 1153 . . . . Castlewood
FED 622 Western Regional-General
 Chairmen . . . . Suffolk
LG 1090 . . . . Roanoke
LG 6061 Roanoke . . . . . . Salem
LG 6185 Salt Water . Newport News
LG 6465 Pocahontas. Virginia Beach
SBA 96 Southeastern . . . . Suffolk

Transportation Union
GCA GO-679 Norfolk & Western
 Railway . . . . Roanoke
GCA GO-680 Norfolk & Western
 Railway . . . . Roanoke
GCA GO-681 Norfolk & Western
 Railway . . . . Roanoke
LU 48 . . . . Norfolk
LU 363 . . . . Pembroke
LU 623 . . . . Millboro
LU 655 . . . . Falls Mills
LU 662 . . . . Richmond
LU 706 . . . . Roanoke
LU 769 . . . . Manassas

LU 854 . . . . Portsmouth
LU 924 . . . . Petersburg
LU 971 . . . . Victoria
LU 1522 . . . . Lorton
LU 1601 . . . . Duffield
LU 1933 . . . . Ashland
SLB LO-10 District of
 Columbia . . . . Gainsville
SLB LO-51 Virginia . . . . . Vinton

Treasury Employees
CH 48 . . . . Richmond
CH 128 . . . . Newington
CH 130 . . . . Falmouth
CH 136 . . . . Norfolk
CH 226 . . . . Alexandria
CH 243 . . . . Arlington
CH 245 Trademark
 Society . . . . Arlington

Utility Workers
LU 102-P Madison Luray Front
 Royal . . . . Madison

Weather Service Employees
BR 01-1 . . . . Sterling
BR 01-38 . . . . Blacksburg
BR 01-64 . . . . Leesburg
BR 01-87 . . . . Wakefield
BR 06-1 . . . . . . Wallops Island

Unaffiliated Labor Organizations

Amthill Rayon Workers,
 Inc. . . . . Hopewell

Exxon Industrial Employees
 Delaware-Maryland-
 DC . . . . Fredericksburg
Exxon Oil Workers Union of
 Virginia . . . . Richmond
Government Workers National
 Association Independent . Norfolk
Martinsville Dupont Employees
 Union . . . . Collinsville
Motor Carrier Workers Union
 Inc. . . . . Staunton
National Association of Independent
 Labor . . . . Virginia Beach
National Aviation Staff Specialist
 Association . . . . Sterling
Patent Office Professional
 Association . . . . Arlington
Richmond Newspapers Professional
 Association . . . . . . Richmond
Socony Mobil Boatmens
 Union . . . . Port Haywood
Solidarity U.S.A . . . . Woodbridge
Telephone Workers Association
 Independent Waynesboro-
 Covington-Clifton
 Forge . . . . Waynesboro
Transparent Film Workers
 Inc. . . . . Richmond
Union of ALPA Professional &
 Administrative Employees UNIT
 1 . . . . Herndon
Union of ALPA Professional &
 Administrative Employees UNIT
 2 . . . . Herndon
United Defense Workers of America
 LU 1 . . . . Marion

Washington

AFL-CIO Trade and Industrial Departments

Building and Construction Trades Department
BCTC Central Washington . . Pasco
BCTC Longview-Kelso . . Longview
BCTC Northeastern Washington & Northern Idaho . . . . . Spokane
BCTC Northwest Washington . . . . . Bellingham
BCTC Olympia . . . . . . Olympia
BCTC Olympic Peninsula . Silverdale
BCTC Pendleton . . . . . Kennewick
BCTC Pierce County . . . . Tacoma
BCTC Seattle . . . . Seattle
BCTC Washington . . . . . Olympia

Maritime Trades Department
PC Puget Sound District . . . Seattle

Metal Trades Department
MTC Bremerton . . . . . Bremerton
MTC Hanford Atomic . . . Richland
MTC Omaha . . . . Seattle
MTC Puget Sound . . . . . Seattle

Other Councils and Committees
C Aluminum Trades . . . . . . East Wenatchee
C Longview Federated Aluminum . . . . Longview

AFL-CIO Directly Affiliated Locals
C Columbia Basin Irrigation . Seattle

Affiliated Labor Organizations

Agricultural Employees
BR . . . . Blaine
BR 31 . . . . Seattle

Air Traffic Controllers
LU BFI . . . . Seattle
LU ENM . . . . Renton
LU GEG . . . . Spokane
LU MWH . . . . Moses Lake
LU PAE . . . . Everett
LU PSC . . . . Pasco
LU S46 . . . . Seattle
LU SEA . . . . Seattle
LU ZSE . . . . Auburn

Aircraft Mechanics
LU 14 . . . . Seatac

Asbestos Workers
LU 7 . . . . Renton
LU 62 . . . . Silverdale
LU 82 . . . . Spokane
LU 120 . . . . Benton City

Bakery, Confectionery, Tobacco Workers and Grain Millers
C Western . . . . Spokane
C -G Pacific . . . . Spokane
LU 9 . . . . Seattle
LU 74 . . . . Spokane
LU 98-G . . . . Spokane

Boilermakers
LG 37-D Cement Workers . . . . . Port Orchard
LG 104 . . . . Seattle
LG 242 . . . . Spokane
LG 290 . . . . Bremerton
LG 502 . . . . Puyallup

Bricklayers
LU 1 Washington . . . . . . Seattle
LU 3 . . . . Spokane

Carpenters
DC Pacific Northwest Regional . . . . Seatac
LU . . . . Shelton
LU 98 . . . . Spokane
LU 131 . . . . Seattle
LU 204 . . . . Renton
LU 317 . . . . Aberdeen
LU 360 . . . . Olympia
LU 456 . . . . Renton
LU 470 . . . . Tacoma
LU 562 . . . . Everett
LU 756 . . . . Bellingham
LU 770 . . . . Yakima
LU 1136 . . . . Kettle Falls
LU 1144 . . . . Seattle
LU 1148 . . . . Olympia
LU 1184 . . . . Seattle
LU 1303 . . . . . . Port Angeles
LU 1532 . . . . . Mount Vernon
LU 1597 . . . . Bremerton
LU 1699 . . . . Pasco
LU 1707 . . . . Longview
LU 1715 . . . . Vancouver
LU 1797 . . . . Renton
LU 1845 . . . . Snoqualmie
LU 1849 . . . . Pasco
LU 2054 . . . . Shelton
LU 2127 . . . . Centralia
LU 2205 . . . . Wenatchee
LU 2317 . . . . . . Port Orchard
LU 2382 . . . . Spokane
LU 2396 . . . . Tacoma
LU 2403 . . . . Richland
LU 2594 . . . . Kettle Falls
LU 2633 . . . . Tacoma
LU 2659 Lumber & Sawmill Workers . . . . Roslyn
LU 2667 . . . . Bellingham
LU 2739 . . . . Yakima
LU 2761 . . . . McCleary
LU 2767 . . . . Morton
LU 3099 . . . . Aberdeen

Civilian Technicians
CH 107 Evergreen Chapter . Fairchild Air Force Base
CH 108 Ranier . . . . . . Tillicum

Communications Workers
C Washington-North Idaho . Spokane
LU 1002 . . . . Pacific
LU 7800 . . . . Seattle
LU 7803 . . . . Renton
LU 7804 . . . . Tacoma
LU 7810 . . . . Olympia
LU 7812 . . . . Vancouver
LU 7814 . . . . . . Walla Walla
LU 7816 . . . . Yakima
LU 7817 . . . . . . Medical Lake
LU 7818 . . . . Spokane
LU 7990 . . . . Spokane
LU 14710 . . . . Clarkston

LU 14760 . . . . Aberdeen
LU 14764 . . . . Yakima
LU 14766 . . . . Spokane
LU 37082 Pacific Northwest . Seattle
LU 37083 Washington Alliance of Technology Workers . . . . Seattle

Electrical Workers
C Pacific Coast Marine . . . . Seattle
LU 46 . . . . Seattle
LU 73 . . . . Spokane
LU 76 . . . . Tacoma
LU 77 . . . . Seattle
LU 89 . . . . Everett
LU 112 . . . . Kennewick
LU 191 . . . . Everett
LU 483 . . . . Tacoma
LU 574 . . . . Bremerton
LU 970 . . . . Longview
LU 984 . . . . Richland
LU 1769 . . . . . . Federal Way
LU 1782 . . . . . . Battleground

Elevator Constructors
LU 19 . . . . Seattle

Federal Employees
LU 34 . . . . Mount Vernon
LU 1156 . . . . Colville
LU 1174 . . . . Twisp
LU 1641 . . . . Spokane
LU 2014 . . . . Hoodsport

Fire Fighters
LU 24-I Hanford Industrial Fire Fighters . . . . . . Richland
LU 282-F . . . . Keyport
LU 283-F . . . . Fort Lewis

Flint Glass Workers
LU 61 . . . . Vancouver
LU 68 . . . . Renton

Food and Commercial Workers
DC 17 Oregon & Washington . . . . . . Bellevue
LU 44 . . . . Mount Vernon
LU 49 . . . . Spokane
LU 81 . . . . Auburn
LU 110-C . . . . Tacoma
LU 121-C . . . . Bellingham
LU 141 . . . . Federal Way
LU 367 . . . . Lakewood
LU 381 . . . . Silverdale
LU 747-C . . . . Kalama
LU 1001 . . . . Bellevue
LU 1105 . . . . Seattle
LU 1182 Financial Institution Employees . . . . . . Yakima
LU 1439 . . . . Spokane

Glass, Molders, Pottery and Plastics Workers
LU 50 . . . . Seattle
LU 87 . . . . Seattle
LU 289 . . . . Deer Park

Government Employees
C 249 VA, Eleventh District . . . . Tacoma
LU 40 HHS . . . . . . Federal Way
LU 48 DoD . . . . Bremerton
LU 498 VA . . . . Tacoma
LU 1102 Federal Detention Center . . . . Seattle

LU 1108 . . . . Spokane
LU 1170 HHS . . . . Seattle
LU 1176 USDA . . . . . . Yakima
LU 1196 USDA . . . Mount Vernon
LU 1501 DoD . . . . McChord Air Force Base
LU 1502 DoD . . . . . . Tillicum
LU 1504 DoD . . . . Fort Lewis
LU 1589 . . . . Vancouver
LU 2600 GSA . . . . . . Auburn
LU 2913 DoJ . . . . . . Custer
LU 3196 SBA . . . . . . Seattle
LU 3197 VA . . . . Seattle
LU 3294 HUD . . . . . . Seattle
LU 3593 DoD . . . . Fort Lewis

Government Security Officers
LU 65 . . . . Carson
LU 71 . . . . Seattle
LU 133 . . . . Richland
LU 134 . . . . Spokane

Graphic Communications
LU 182-C . . . . Olympia
LU 262-C . . . . Aberdeen
LU 367-C . . . . Bremerton
LU 767-M . . . . Kent

Guards
LU 21 . . . . Richland
RC First . . . . Richland

Hotel and Restaurant Employees
LU 8 . . . . Seattle
LU 360 . . . . Seattle
LU 791 . . . . Aberdeen

Inlandboatmen
NHQ . . . . Seattle

Iron Workers
DC Pacific Northwest . . . . Tacoma
LU 14 . . . . Spokane
LU 86 . . . . Tukwilla
LU 506 . . . . Tukwilla

Laborers
DC Washington & Northern Idaho . . . . Mill Creek
LU 238 . . . . Spokane
LU 242 . . . . Seattle
LU 252 . . . . Tacoma
LU 276 . . . . Bellingham
LU 292 . . . . Everett
LU 335 . . . . Vancouver
LU 348 . . . . Pasco
LU 440 . . . . Seattle
LU 614 . . . . Yakima
LU 791 . . . . Longview
LU 901 . . . . . . Mount Vernon
LU 1239 . . . . Seattle

Letter Carriers
BR 79 . . . . Seattle
BR 130 . . . . Tacoma
BR 351 . . . . Olympia
BR 442 . . . . Bellingham
BR 450 . . . . Bellingham
BR 736 . . . . Walla Walla
BR 791 . . . . Everett
BR 852 . . . . Yakima
BR 853 . . . . Aberdeen
BR 1104 . . . . Vancouver
BR 1266 . . . . Centralia
BR 1296 . . . . Pullman

BR 1302 Hoquiam,
  Washington . . . . . . Hoquiam
BR 1350 . . . . Wenatchee
BR 1414 . . . . Bremerton
BR 1484 . . . . Puyallup
BR 1515 . . . . . Port Townsend
BR 1527. . . . . Anacortes
BR 1528 . . . . Pasco
BR 1606 Raymond,
  Washington . . . . Raymond
BR 1906 . . . . Port Angeles
BR 1947 Clarkston,
  Washington . . . . . Clarkston
BR 2030 Sedro Woolley,
  Washington . . . Sedro Woolley
BR 2038 . . . . Kent
BR 2103 . . . . Kelso
BR 2214 . . . . Longview
BR 2503 . . . . Enumclaw
BR 2914 Dayton,
  Washington . . . . Dayton
BR 2935 Montesano,
  Washington . . . . . Montesano
BR 2948 Cle Elum,
  Washington . . . . . . Cle Elum
BR 3008 . . . . Camas
BR 3127 Sumner,
  Washington . . . . Sumner
BR 3320 Leavenworth,
  Washington . . . . Leavenworth
BR 3877 . . . . . . West Richland
BR 4118 Prosser,
  Washington . . . . Prosser
BR 4132 Lynden,
  Washington . . . . Lynden
BR 4213 Ephrata,
  Washington . . . . Ephrata
BR 4232 Grandview,
  Washington . . . . . Grandview
BR 4498 Coulee Dam,
  Washington . . . . Coulee Dam
BR 4513 Cashmere,
  Washington . . . . . Cashmere
BR 4573. . . . . Moses Lake
BR 4771 Ritzville,
  Washington. . . . . . Ritzville
BR 5194 . . . . Oak Harbor
BR 5262 . . . . Othello
BR 5479 Castle Rock,
  Washington. . . . . Castle Rock
BR 5705 Washougal,
  Washington . . . . . Washougal
BR 6008 . . . . Quincy
SA Washington . . Bainbridge Island

Locomotive Engineers
DIV 58 . . . . Lyle
DIV 60 . . . . Anderson Island
DIV 104. . . . . Spokane
DIV 238 . . . . Tacoma
DIV 402 . . . . Kennewick
DIV 518 . . . . Edmonds
DIV 758 . . . . Vancouver
DIV 892 . . . . Renton
SLB Washington State . . Newcastle

Longshore and Warehouse
DC Puget Sound . . . . . . Seattle
LU 1-04 . . . . Vancouver
LU 1-24 . . . . Hoquiam
LU 7 . . . . Bellingham
LU 9 . . . . Seattle
LU 19 . . . . Seattle
LU 21 . . . . Longview
LU 21 Kalama Grainhandlers
  Division . . . . Kalama
LU 21 Peavey Grain
  Division . . . . Kalama

LU 23 . . . . Tacoma
LU 25 . . . . Anacortes
LU 27 . . . . Port Angeles
LU 32. . . . . Everett
LU 47 . . . . Olympia
LU 51 . . . . Allyn
LU 52 . . . . Seattle
LU 98 Ship and Dock Foremen of
  Washington . . . . . Des Moines
LU 200 . . . . . . Black Diamond

Machinists
DLG 160 . . . . Seattle
DLG 751 . . . . Seattle
LG . . . . Sequim
LG 2 Woodworkers . . . . Aberdeen
LG 79 . . . . Seattle
LG 86 . . . . Spokane
LG 130 . . . . Seattle
LG 130-W Woodworkers . Raymond
LG 157-W . . . . Enumclaw
LG 239 . . . . Seattle
LG 282 . . . . Bremerton
LG 289 . . . . Lynnwood
LG 297 . . . . Tacoma
LG 536-W . . . . Longview
LG 591 . . . . Puyallup
LG 637 . . . . Spokane
LG 695 . . . . Olympia
LG 751-A . . . . Seattle
LG 751-C . . . . Seattle
LG 751-E . . . . Seattle
LG 751-F . . . . Seattle
LG 1040 . . . . Federal Way
LG 1103 . . . . Seattle
LG 1123 . . . . Wenatchee
LG 1350 . . . . Kelso
LG 1351 . . . . Seattle
LG 1374 . . . . Vancouver
LG 1951 . . . . Richland
LG 2202 . . . . Kent
LG 2379 . . . . Ferndale
LLG FL-271 . . . . . . Walla Walla
LLG FL-1373 . . . . . Trout Lake
LLG FL-1974 . . . . . Vancouver
LLG FL-1998 NFFE . . . . Seattle
STC Washington . . . . . Seattle

Maintenance of Way Employes
LG 159. . . . . Kennewick
LG 325 . . . . Spokane
LG 389 . . . . Tacoma
LG 757 . . . . Vancouver
LG 1453 . . . . Wenatchee
LG 1763 . . . . Battle Ground
SLG 104 . . . . Opportunity
SLG 309 . . . . Elma
SLG 683. . . . . Colville
SLG 1218 . . . . Tukwila
SLG 1426 . . . . Arlington

Mine Workers
LU 807 . . . . Shenandoah

Musicians
LU 76 . . . . Seattle
LU 105 . . . . Spokane
LU 461 . . . . . . Mount Vernon

National Staff Organization
LU Staff Organization, Washington
  Education Association . . . . Kent

NLRB Professional Association
LU 19 . . . . Seattle

Nurses
SA Washington State Nurses
  Association . . . . Seattle

Office and Professional Employees
LU. . . . . Spanaway
LU 8 . . . . Seattle
LU 23 . . . . Tacoma

Operating Engineers
LU 280 . . . . Richland
LU 286. . . . . Auburn
LU 302 . . . . Bothell
LU 370 . . . . Spokane
LU 612 . . . . Tacoma

Painters
DC 5 . . . . Seattle
LU 64 . . . . Tacoma
LU 78 . . . . Longview
LU 188 . . . . Renton
LU 269 . . . . Spokane
LU 300 . . . . Olympia
LU 339 . . . . Mount Vernon
LU 360 . . . . Vancouver
LU 427. . . . . Pasco
LU 526 . . . . Woodinville
LU 612 . . . . Othello
LU 743 . . . . Olympia
LU 995. . . . . Yakima
LU 1094 . . . . Seattle
LU 1208 . . . . Belfair
LU 1238. . . . . Tukwila
LU 1726 . . . . Spokane
LU 1789. . . . . Benton City
LU 1982 . . . . Renton

**Paper, Allied-Industrial, Chemical
  Employees**
C Kimberly Clark . . Camano Island
LU 08-167. . . . . Spangle
LU 08-171 . . . . Vancouver
LU 08-175 . . . . . Port Townsend
LU 08-237. . . . . Tacoma
LU 08-279. . . . . Tacoma
LU 08-369. . . . . Richland
LU 08-562. . . . . Spokane
LU 08-586. . . . . Tacoma
LU 08-590. . . . . Ferndale
LU 08-591. . . . . . . Anacortes
LU 08-592. . . . . Fife
LU 08-600. . . . . . . Vancouver
LU 08-784. . . . . . . Wenatchee
LU 08-847. . . . . Tacoma
LU 08-990. . . . . . . Kennewick
LU 08-1103 . . . . Sumner

Plasterers and Cement Masons
LU 72 . . . . Spokane
LU 77. . . . . Seattle
LU 478. . . . . Pasco
LU 528 . . . . Seattle
STCON Northwest
  Conference . . . . Spokane

Plumbing and Pipe Fitting
DC Northwest. . . . . . . Spokane
LU . . . . Everett
LU 32. . . . . Renton
LU 44 . . . . Spokane
LU 82 . . . . Lacey
LU 265 . . . . Everett
LU 598 . . . . Pasco
LU 699 . . . . Seattle
SA Washington. . . . . . . Everett

Police
C National Labor Council . . Auburn

Postal and Federal Employees
LU 1012. . . . . Lacey

Postal Mail Handlers
LU 316 . . . . Seattle

Postal Workers
LU 28 Greater Seattle Area. . Burien
LU 36 Walla Walla. . . Walla Walla
LU 298 Puget Sound Area . Tacoma
LU 338 Inland Empire
  Area . . . . Spokane
LU 484 Everett. . . . . . . Everett
LU 709 Bellingham . . Bellingham
LU 751 Wenatchee. . . . Wenatchee
LU 763 Yakima
  Washington . . . . Yakima
LU 838 Toppenish Local . Toppenish
LU 905 Pullman. . . . . . Pullman
LU 962 Centralia. . . . . Centralia
LU 1686 Kent. . . . . Kent
LU 2293 Tri Cities Area. . . . Pasco
LU 2354 Olympia . . . . Olympia
LU 2568 Auburn. . . . . . Auburn
LU 2779 Camas Local . . . . Camas
LU 3171 Kirkland . . . . Kirkland
LU 3302 Shelton. . . . . Shelton
LU 3463 Vancouver . . . Vancouver
LU 3474 Ellensburg
  Local . . . . Ellensburg
LU 3734 Renton . . . . . Renton
LU 4996 Washougal
  Local. . . . . Washougal
LU 5086 Enumclaw . . . Enumclaw
LU 5213 Bellevue . . . . . Bellevue
LU 6110 Sequim Local . . . Sequim
LU 6231 Stanwood . . . . Stanwood
LU 7042 Seattle Bulk
  Mail . . . . Federal Way
LU 7160 Green River Valley. . Kent
SA Washington . . . . . . Colville

**Professional and Technical
  Engineers**
LU 6 . . . . Bremerton
LU 8 . . . . Seattle
LU 12. . . . . Bremerton
LU 89 . . . . Grand Coulee
LU 2001 SPEEA . . . . . Seattle

Pulp and Paper Workers
LU 5 . . . . Camas
LU 28 . . . . Sumner
LU 69 . . . . Kennewick
LU 153 . . . . Longview
LU 155 . . . . Port Angeles
LU 183 . . . . Camano Island
LU 194 . . . . Beilingham
LU 211 . . . . Cosmopolis
LU 225 . . . . Woodland
LU 293 . . . . Ridgefield
LU 309 . . . . Bellingham
LU 580 . . . . Longview
LU 633 . . . . Longview
LU 644 . . . . Everett
LU 680 . . . . Castle Rock
LU 817 . . . . Bothell
LU 913 . . . . Hoquiam

Railroad Signalmen
LLG 188 . . . . Pasco

**Roofers, Waterproofers and Allied
  Workers**
DC Northwest Roofers . . . . Seattle
LU 54 . . . . Seattle
LU 153 . . . . Tacoma
LU 189 . . . . Spokane

Rural Letter Carriers
LU Chelan-Douglas Counties . Entiat
LU Clallam-Jefferson
   Counties . . . . Sequim
LU Garfield-Columbia-Walla Walla
   Counties . . . . Waitsburg
LU Kitsap County . . . Port Orchard
LU Lincoln-Grant-Adams
   Counties . . . . . Moses Lake
LU Lower Columbia
   County . . . . . . Castle Rock
LU Mutual County . . . . Lakewood
LU Northeast
   Washington . . . . . . Chewelah
LU Okanogan County. . . . . Omak
LU Skagit-San Juan
   Counties . . . . Anacortes
LU Snohomish-King-Island
   Counties . . . . Vashon
LU Spokane County . . . Spokane
LU Whatcom County . . Bellingham
LU Whitman-Asotin
   Counties . . . . Endicott
LU Yakima Valley . . . . . Zillah
SA Washington . . . . . . Spokane

Security, Police and Fire
Professionals
LU . . . . Kennewick
LU 5 . . . . Seattle
LU 9 . . . . Everett

Service Employees
C 14 Northwestern States. . . Seattle
LU 6 . . . . Seattle
LU 6 Staff Union . . . . . . Seattle
LU 51 International Leather Goods,
   Plastics, Novelty and Service
   Union. . . . . Seattle
LU 193 Firemen & Oilers . . Seattle
LU 202 . . . . Spokane
LU 276 Firemen & Oilers . Spokane
LU 395 Firemen & Oilers . Spokane
LU 398 Firemen & Oilers . Spokane
LU 634 Firemen & Oilers . Spokane
LU 690 Firemen & Oilers . Spokane
LU 714 Firemen & Oilers . Spokane
LU 764 Firemen & Oilers . . Seattle
LU 801 Firemen &
   Oilers. . . . . Vancouver
LU 920 Firemen & Oilers . Spokane

LU 925 . . . . Seattle
LU 1184 Firemen & Oilers . Tacoma
LU 1199-NW NUHHCE, District
   1199-Northwest . . . . . Renton
SC 15 Firemen & Oilers . . Spokane

Sheet Metal Workers
DC Northwest . . . . Lacey
LU 66 . . . . Kirkland
LU 492 . . . . Kent

State, County and Municipal
Employees
LU 2 Washington State
   Council. . . . . Everett
LU 780 Spokane City School Bus
   Drivers . . . . Spokane

Steelworkers
LU 11-305-A . . . . . . Longview
LU 11-310-A . . . . East Wenatchee
LU 11-315-A . . . . East Wenatchee
LU 11-329-S . . . . Spokane
LU 11-338-S . . . . Spokane
LU 11-532-B . . . . Kent
LU 11-556 . . . . Spokane
LU 11-7945-S . . . . Fife
LU 11-8147-S . . . . . Goldendale
LU 11-9041-S . . . . . . Auburn
LU 11-9241-S . . . . . . Silverdale

Teachers
SFED Washington . . . . Tukwila

Teamsters
JC 28 . . . . Seattle
LU 38 . . . . Everett
LU 58 . . . . Vancouver
LU 66 . . . . Seattle
LU 117 . . . . Seattle
LU 174 . . . . Seattle
LU 227 . . . . Seattle
LU 231 . . . . Bellingham
LU 252 . . . . Centralia
LU 313 . . . . Tacoma
LU 378 . . . . Olympia
LU 524 . . . . Yakima
LU 556 . . . . Walla Walla
LU 589 . . . . Port Angeles
LU 599 . . . . Tacoma
LU 690 . . . . Spokane

LU 760. . . . . Yakima
LU 763 . . . . Seattle
LU 839. . . . . Pasco

Television and Radio Artists
LU Seattle . . . . Seattle

Theatrical Stage Employees
LU 15 . . . . Seattle
LU 93 . . . . Spokane
LU 887 . . . . Seattle

Transit Union
LDIV 1384 . . . . Olympia
LDIV 1576 . . . . Everett
LDIV 1599 . . . . . . Tri Cities
LU 587 . . . . Seattle
LU 758 . . . . Tacoma

Transportation Communications
Union
D 419 Union Pacific-Eastern Lines
   SB 106 . . . . Vancouver
D 2505 . . . . Seattle
LG 34 . . . . Colbert
LG 1380 . . . . Brush Prairie
LG 6294 Sagebrush . . . . . Pasco
LG 6697 . . . . Auburn
LG 6748 Van-Port . . . . Vancouver

Transportation Union
GCA GO-341 . . . . . Vancouver
GCA GO-386 Burlington Northern
   Railroad . . . . Vancouver
LU 117 . . . . Vancouver
LU 161 . . . . Covington
LU 324 . . . . Sumner
LU 426 . . . . Cheney
LU 556 . . . . Sumner
LU 845 . . . . Auburn
LU 855 . . . . Veradale
LU 977 . . . . Pasco
LU 1348 . . . . Seattle
LU 1468 . . . . Walla Walla
LU 1505 . . . . . . Nine Mile Falls
LU 1637 . . . . Vancouver
LU 1713 . . . . Marysville
LU 1977 . . . . Kent
SLB LO-54 Washington . Longview

Treasury Employees
CH 30 . . . . Seattle
CH 139 . . . . Kent
CH 164 . . . . Blaine
CH 215 . . . . Bothell

Weather Service Employees
BR 04-1 . . . . Seattle
BR 04-3 . . . . Spokane
BR 08-9 . . . . Seattle

Unaffiliated Labor
Organizations
1199 Northwest Staff Union . Renton
Air Cushion Workers Union . Seattle
Atlantic Maritime Employees
   Independent . . . . . Bellingham
Boeing Pilots
   Association . . . . . Gig Harbor
Columbia Basin Trades
   Council . . . . . . Kennewick
Deep Sea Fishermens Union Pacific
   Coast District. . . . . . Seattle
Demil Trades Council . . Kennewick
Fairchild Federal Employees
   Union . . Fairchild Air Force Base
Fellow Associates Involved in
   Representation. . . . . . . Yelm
Industrial Workers of the World
   Puget Sound G M B . . . . Seattle
International Guild of
   Symphony . . . . Seattle
Medical Engineers Association of
   Spokane . . . . Spokane
Northwest Mechanical Services
   Union LU 77 . . . . Kent
Ownership Union . . . Brush Prairie
Portland Pattern Maker's
   Association . . . . . Battle Ground
Public School Employees . . Auburn
Public School Employees,
   Washington CH 522 . . Vancouver
Spokane Editorial Society . Spokane
Symphony Opera & Ballet
   Musicians Seattle Players
   Organization . . . . . . Seattle
Symphony Opera and Ballet
   Musicians Pacific Northwest Ballet
   Players Organization . . . . Seattle
Washington Farm Workers
   Union . . . . Granger
Washington Federation of State
   Employees Staff Union . Olympia
Washington Legal Workers . Everett

West Virginia

AFL-CIO Trade and Industrial Departments

Building and Construction Trades Department
BCTC Kanawha County . Charleston
BCTC North Central West
  Virginia . . . . Clarksburg
BCTC Parkersburg-
  Marietta . . . . Parkersburg
BCTC West Virginia
  State . . . . Charleston

Affiliated Labor Organizations

Air Traffic Controllers
LU CKB . . . . Bridgeport
LU CRW . . . . Charleston
LU HTS . . . . Ceredo

Asbestos Workers
LU 80 . . . . Winfield

Automobile, Aerospace Workers
LU 3399 . . . . Dunbar

Bakery, Confectionery, Tobacco Workers and Grain Millers
LU 2-T . . . . Wheeling

Boilermakers
LG 208-D Cement
  Workers . . . . Martinsburg
LG 249 . . . . Milton
LG 271-D Cement
  Workers . . . . Martinsburg
LG 667 . . . . Winfield
LG 1610 . . . . Triadelphia

Bricklayers
DC West Virginia . . . . . Fairmont
LU 1 . . . . Valley Grove
LU 5 . . . . Fairmont
LU 6 . . . . Fairmont
LU 9 . . . . Fairmont
LU 11 . . . . Wellsburg
LU 15 . . . . Fairmont

Carpenters
LU 3 . . . . Wheeling
LU 302 . . . . Huntington
LU 476 . . . . Shinnston
LU 604 . . . . Morgantown
LU 899 . . . . Parkersburg
LU 1159 . . . . Point Pleasant
LU 1207 . . . . Charleston
LU 1755 . . . . Parkersburg
LU 1911 . . . . Beckley
LU 2101 . . . . Moorefield
LU 2528 . . . . Rainelle

Civilian Technicians
CH 89 Mountaineer . . . . . Nitro
CH 90 Mountain
  State . . . . Point Pleasant
CH 91 Shenandoah . . . Martinsburg

Communications Workers
C West Virginia State . . Clarksburg
LU 620 . . . . Poca
LU 2001 . . . . Charleston
LU 2002 . . . . Omar
LU 2003 . . . . Parkersburg

LU 2004 . . . . Fairview
LU 2006 . . . . Wheeling
LU 2007 . . . . Beckley
LU 2009 . . . . Huntington
LU 2010 . . . . Weston
LU 2011 . . . . Clarksburg
LU 2276 . . . . Bluefield
LU 14210 . . . . Charleston
LU 14211 . . . . Clarksburg
LU 14212 . . . . Fairmont
LU 14214 Morgantown
  Typographical Union . . . Idamay
LU 14215 . . . . Parkersburg
LU 14217 . . . . Wheeling
LU 52027 . . . . Huntington
LU 52212 . . . . . . Beech Bottom

Electrical Workers
LU 141 . . . . Wheeling
LU 317 . . . . Huntington
LU 466 . . . . Charleston
LU 549 . . . . Milton
LU 596 . . . . Clarksburg
LU 736 . . . . Princeton
LU 968 . . . . Parkersburg
LU 978 . . . . Cross Lanes
LU 1653 . . . . Fort Ashby
LU 1935 . . . . Clarksburg
LU 2035 . . . . Kearneysville
LU 2357 . . . . Clarksburg

Electrical, Radio and Machine Workers
LU 611 . . . . Newell

Electronic Workers
LU 625 . . . . Fairmont
LU 627 . . . . Fairmont
LU 647 . . . . Bluefield

Elevator Constructors
LU 48 . . . . Charleston

Flint Glass Workers
LU 22 . . . . Vienna
LU 26 . . . . Westover
LU 53 . . . . Wheeling
LU 508 . . . . Parkersburg
LU 542 . . . . Osage
LU 567 . . . . Lost Creek
LU 570 . . . . Parkersburg
LU 1023 . . . . Martinsburg

Food and Commercial Workers
LU 45-C . . . . Middlebourne
LU 566-C . . . . Moundsville
LU 698-C . . . . New Martinsville
LU 864-C . . . . Moundsville
LU 888-C . . . . . New Martinsville
LU 967-C . . . . Moundsville

Glass, Molders, Pottery and Plastics Workers
LU 16-A . . . . Chester
LU 305 . . . . Normantown

Government Employees
LU . . . . Martinsburg
LU 407 National Park Service
  Virginia and West
  Virginia . . . . Glen Jean
LU 644 DoL . . . . Wheeling
LU 1494 DoJ . . . . Alderson
LU 1995 DoE . . . . Morgantown
LU 2198 VA . . . . Beckley

LU 2344 VA . . . . . . Huntington
LU 2384 VA . . . . . . Clarksburg
LU 2441 DoJ . . . . . Morgantown
LU 3181 DoL . . . . Madison
LU 3430 HHS . . . . Morgantown
LU 3729 DoD . . . . . Huntington

Government Employees Association
LU 04-78 . . . . Martinsburg
LU 04-88 . . . . Valley Bend

Government Security Officers
LU 87 . . . . Clarksburg
LU 92 . . . . Charleston
LU 92 Amalgamated . . . . Kenova

Graphic Communications
LU 53-C . . . . Huntington
LU 95-C . . . . Salem
LU 360-C . . . . Flat Top
LU 392-C . . . . Morgantown
LU 443-C Fairmont Printing
  Pressmen . . . . Fairmont

Hotel and Restaurant Employees
LU 863 . . . . White Sulphur Springs

Iron Workers
LU 301 . . . . Charleston
LU 549 . . . . Wheeling
LU 787 . . . . Parkersburg

Laborers
DC Charleston . . . . . Charleston
LU 379 . . . . Morgantown
LU 453 . . . . Beckley
LU 543 . . . . Huntington
LU 814 . . . . Morgantown
LU 984 . . . . Clarksburg
LU 1085 . . . . Parkersburg
LU 1149 . . . . Wheeling
LU 1182 . . . White Sulphur Springs
LU 1304 . . . . Lewisburg
LU 1353 . . . . Charleston

Letter Carriers
BR 359 . . . . Huntington
BR 481 . . . . Parkersburg
BR 531 . . . . Charleston
BR 783 . . . . Morgantown
BR 817 . . . . Clarksburg
BR 880 . . . . Bluefield
BR 893 . . . . Moundsville
BR 910 . . . . Fairmont
BR 1183 . . . . Elkins
BR 1475 . . . . Martinsburg
BR 1854 New Martinsville, West
  Virginia . . . . . New Martinsville
BR 2042 Mannington, West
  Virginia . . . . Mannington
BR 2237 Chester, West
  Virginia . . . . Chester
BR 2420 . . . . Oak Hill
BR 2936 Marlinton, West
  Virginia . . . . Marlinton
BR 3087 Point Pleasant, West
  Virginia . . . . . Point Pleasant
BR 3535 . . . . Williamstown
BR 3677 . . . . Weirton
BR 4228 Glenville, West
  Virginia . . . . Glenville
BR 4303 Berkeley Springs, West
  Virginia . . . . Berkeley Springs
BR 4458 . . . . Clarksburg

BR 4980 Paden City, West
  Virginia . . . . Paden City
BR 5283 Man, West Virginia . . Man
BR 5599 Milton, West
  Virginia . . . . Milton
BR 5677 Webster Springs, West
  Virgin . . . . . Webster Springs
BR 5679 Mount Hope, West
  Virginia . . . . . . Mount Hope
BR 5792 Parsons, West
  Virginia . . . . Parsons

Locomotive Engineers
DIV 50 . . . . Ridgeley
DIV 101 . . . . Hinton
DIV 124 . . . . Bluefield
DIV 190 . . . . Huntington
DIV 255 Mingo Jet Ohio . Follansbee
DIV 284 . . . . Grafton
DIV 401 . . . . Williamson
DIV 448 . . . . Bluefield
DIV 477 . . . . Parkersburg
DIV 714 . . . . Dunbar
DIV 751 . . . . Exchange
SLB West Virginia . . . . Princeton

Machinists
DLG 20 . . . . Nitro
LG 87-S . . . . Halltown
LG 104 . . . . Huntington
LG 598 . . . . . South Charleston
LG 656 . . . . Benwood
LG 818 . . . . Clarksburg
LG 1027 . . . . Clarksburg
LG 1370 . . . . Milton
LG 1798-FL . . . . . . Martinsburg
LG 2077 . . . . Parkersburg
LG 2798 . . . . . . Barboursville
STC West Virginia . . . . . Nitro

Maintenance of Way Employes
LG 61 . . . . Fairmont
LG 499 . . . . Mason
LG 551 . . . . Bluefield
LG 1509 . . . . Pennsboro
LG 1550 . . . . Elkins
SLG 76 . . . . Leon
SLG 112 . . . . Salt Rock
SLG 130 . . . . Danese
SLG 139 . . . . Danese
SLG 613 . . . . Delbarton
SLG 710 . . . . Martinsburg
SLG 1029 . . . . Arthurdale
SLG 1064 . . . . Belington
SLG 1300 . . . . Sutton
SLG 1450 . . . . Gormania

Mine Workers
D 17 . . . . Charleston
D 31 . . . . Fairmont
LU 93 . . . . Pond Creek
LU 340 . . . . Montgomery
LU 633 . . . . Hewett
LU 750 . . . . Oak Hill
LU 781 . . . . Oceana
LU 1058 . . . . Westover
LU 1110 . . . . Moundsville
LU 1123 . . . . Beckley
LU 1160 . . . . Oceana
LU 1289 . . . . Newburg
LU 1302 . . . . Amherstdale
LU 1330 . . . . Daniels
LU 1335 . . . . Rainelle
LU 1352 . . . . Nettie
LU 1444 . . . . Gormania

LU 1466 . . . . Craigsville
LU 1473 . . . . Wheeling
LU 1498 . . . . Freeman
LU 1501 . . . . Shinnston
LU 1503 . . . . Madison
LU 1570 . . . . Rivesville
LU 1582 . . . . Kenova
LU 1597 . . . . Mannington
LU 1638 . . . . Moundsville
LU 1643 . . . . Fairmont
LU 1648 . . . . Worthington
LU 1698 . . . . Rupert
LU 1702 . . . . Maidsville
LU 1713 . . . . Herndon
LU 1716 District 17 . . . . Oak Hill
LU 1717 . . . . Morgantown
LU 1751 . . . . Accoville
LU 1766 . . . . St. Albans
LU 1852 . . . . Bradshaw
LU 1886 . . . . Hartford
LU 1938 . . . . Buckhannon
LU 1949 . . . . Bridgeport
LU 1961 . . . . Beckley
LU 1971 . . . . Man
LU 2059 . . . . Summersville
LU 2236 . . . . Chesapeake
LU 2286 . . . . Sod
LU 2542 . . . . Seth
LU 2903 . . . . Ridgeview
LU 2935 . . . . Hamlin
LU 3029 . . . . Charleston
LU 3196 . . . . Shinnston
LU 4047 . . . . Grant Town
LU 4172 . . . . Buckhannon
LU 4285 . . . . Triadelphia
LU 4921 District 17 . . . . Scarbro
LU 5396 . . . . Letart
LU 5770 . . . . Scarbro
LU 5817 . . . . Monaville
LU 5850 . . . . Accoville
LU 5921 . . . . Barnabus
LU 5958 . . . . Omar
LU 6025 . . . . Princeton
LU 6026 . . . . Welch
LU 6029 . . . . Thorpe
LU 6033 . . . . Bluefield
LU 6046 . . . . Lochgelly
LU 6105 . . . . Midway
LU 6196 . . . . Northfork
LU 6207 . . . . Nallen
LU 6243 . . . . Jodie
LU 6362 . . . . Wheeling
LU 6426 . . . . Eskdale
LU 6608 . . . . Dorothy
LU 6869 . . . . Amigo
LU 7086 . . . . Beckley
LU 7555 . . . . Verner
LU 7604 . . . . Matheny
LU 7626 . . . . St. Albans
LU 7635 . . . . Gary
LU 7692 . . . . Pineville
LU 8190 . . . . Craigsville
LU 8783 . . . . Bradshaw
LU 8840 . . . . Red Jacket
LU 8843 . . . . Cannelton
LU 9108 . . . . Rainelle
LU 9177 . . . . Bolt
LU 9462 . . . . Williamson
LU 9735 . . . . Madison
LU 9781 . . . . Beckley
LU 9909 . . . . Fairview

Musicians
LU 136 . . . . Charleston
LU 259 . . . . Parkersburg
LU 362-691 . . . . . . Huntington
LU 492 . . . . Moundsville
LU 580 . . . . Clarksburg

National Staff Organization
LU Staff Union, United, West
  Virginia . . . . Charleston

Needletrades
LU 2392 . . . . Summersville

Nurses
LU 201 RN Collective Bargaining
  Unit Association . . . Glen White
LU 202 Man ARH
  Unit . . . . Amherstdale
LU 203 West Virginia . Martinsburg
LU 205 West Virginia . . . Hinton
SA West Virginia Nurses
  Association . . . . . . Charleston

Operating Engineers
LU 132 . . . . Charleston

Painters
DC 53 . . . . Charleston
LU 91 . . . . Wheeling
LU 804 . . . . Clarksburg
LU 813 . . . . Huntington
LU 947 . . . . Ridgeley
LU 970 . . . . Charleston
LU 1144 . . . . Parkersburg
LU 1195 . . . . Charleston

Paper, Allied-Industrial, Chemical Employees
DC 3 . . . . Mount Clare
LU 276 . . . . Mount Clare
LU 02-225 . . . . . . Bruceton Mills
LU 02-1449 . . . . . . Peterstown
LU 05-89 . . . . Boomer
LU 05-180 . . . . . . Huntington
LU 05-295 . . . . . . Shinnston
LU 05-628 . . . . . . Charleston
LU 05-721 . . . . Kenova
LU 05-753 . . . . . . Moatsville
LU 05-957 . . . . . . Morgantown
LU 05-973 . . . . . . Ridgeley
LU 05-997 . . . . . . Ravenswood
LU 05-1673 . . . . . Beech Bottom
LU 05-2971 . . . . . . Wellsburg

Plasterers and Cement Masons
LU 39 . . . . Middlebourne
LU 887 . . . . Charleston

Plumbing and Pipe Fitting
LU 83 . . . . Wheeling
LU 152 . . . . Morgantown
LU 521 . . . . Huntington
LU 565 . . . . Parkersburg
LU 625 . . . . Charleston
SA West Virginia . . . Morgantown

Postal and Federal Employees
LU 203 . . . . Charleston

Postal Workers
LU 99 Elkins Local . . . . . Elkins
LU 133 Charleston . . . Charleston
LU 1350 Fairmont . . . . Fairmont
LU 1488 Kyowva Area . Huntington
LU 1509 Beckley . . . . Beckley
LU 1580 Cecil F. Romine
  Area . . . . . . Parkersburg
LU 1734 Morgantown . Morgantown
LU 2669 Buckhannon
  Local . . . . . . Buckhannon
LU 3264 Clarksburg . . Clarksburg
LU 3339 Keyser Local . . . Keyser
LU 4134 Bluefield Area . Bluefield
LU 4343 Weirton . . . . . Weirton

LU 4571 Wheeling . . . Wheeling
LU 4755 Martinsburg . . Martinsburg
LU 5448 Petersburg . . . Petersburg
SA West Virginia . . . Clarksburg

Railroad Signalmen
GC 16 Northeast-Chesapeake & Ohio
  Railroad . . . . . . Lewisburg
LLG 89 . . . . Oak Hill
LLG 136 . . . . Lewisburg

Retail, Wholesale and Department Store
LU 21 . . . . Barboursville
LU 550 . . . . Fairmont

Roofers, Waterproofers and Allied Workers
LU 34 . . . . Ridgeley
LU 185 . . . . Glendenin
LU 188 . . . . Wheeling
LU 242 . . . . Parkersburg

Rural Letter Carriers
D 1 Buckwheat
  Association . . . . . . Princeton
D 2 Central West
  Virginia . . . . . . Walkersville
D 3 West Virginia . . . Martinsburg
D 5 Southwestern West
  Virginia . . . . . . Huntington
D 6 West Virginia . New Martinsville
LU 4 West Central . . . . . Walker
LU 7 Black Diamond . . . Princeton
SA West Virginia . . . . Princeton

Security, Police and Fire Professionals
LU 65 . . . . Middlebourne
LU 400 . . . . Keyser
LU 418 . . . . Huntington

Service Employees
LU 101 . . . . . New Cumberland
LU 553 . . . . Ranson

Sheet Metal Workers
LU 171 . . . . Mount Clare
LU 187 . . . . Princeton
LU 339 . . . . Ridgeley

Steelworkers
LU 8-22-G . . . . Vienna
LU 01-4195-S . . . . . . Colliers
LU 01-14200-S . . . . Williamstown
LU 08-1-S . . . . Fairmont
LU 08-37-S . . . . . . Huntington
LU 08-40-S . . . . . . Huntington
LU 08-162-s . . . . . . Buckhannon
LU 08-477-S . . . . . Buckhannon
LU 08-516-S . . . . . Harrisville
LU 08-518 . . . . . . Clarksburg
LU 08-604 . . . . . . Buckhannon
LU 08-644-L . . . . . . Henderson
LU 08-874-L . . . . . . Richwood
LU 08-1017-L . . . . . Petersburg
LU 08-1280-S . . . . . Follansbee
LU 08-1651-S . . . . . Parkersburg
LU 08-1652-S . . . . . Huntington
LU 08-2383-S . . . . . Parkersburg
LU 08-4842-S . . . . . . Weirton
LU 08-5171-S . . . . . Huntington
LU 08-5668-S . . . . . Ravenswood
LU 08-5712-S . . . . . Redhouse
LU 08-7047-S . . . . . Prichard
LU 08-8360-S . . . . . . Augusta
LU 08-8621-S . . . . Nitro
LU 08-8851-S . . . . . McMechen

LU 08-8984-S . . . . . . Jane Lew
LU 08-9191-S . . . . . . Wellsburg
LU 08-9281-S . . . . Rock
LU 08-12315-S . . . . . . Colliers
LU 08-12424-S . . . . . . Alderson
LU 08-12610-S . . . Scott Depot
LU 08-12625-S . . South Charleston
LU 08-12757-S . . . . . . Nitro
LU 08-12922-S . . . . . Follansbee
LU 08-13252-S . . . . . Belmont
LU 08-14310-S . . . . . Beckley
LU 08-14400-S . . . . Williamson
LU 08-14505-S . . . . West Logan
LU 08-14614-S . . South Charleston
LU 08-14811-S . . . . Point Pleasant
LU 08-15229-S . . . . Wellsburg
LU 08-15293-S . . . . Richwood

Teamsters
LU 175 . . . . Charleston
LU 505 . . . . Huntington
LU 697 . . . . Wheeling

Theatrical Stage Employees
LU 64 . . . . Wheeling
LU 271 . . . . Charleston
LU 369 . . . . Huntington
LU 578 . . . . Morgantown

Transit Union
LDIV 103 . . . . Wheeling
LDIV 812 . . . . . . Clarksburg

Transportation Communications Union
D 403 . . . . Shepherdstown
LG 5056 Arasa Division . . . Ona
LG 6454 Williamson . . . Delbarton

Transportation Union
GCA GO-201 Chesapeake & Ohio
  Railway . . . . Kenova
LU 118 . . . . Hinton
LU 430 . . . . Keyser
LU 504 . . . . Moundsville
LU 605 . . . . Fairmont
LU 860 . . . . Ripley
LU 915 . . . . Poca
LU 1172 . . . . Lindside
LU 1327 . . . . Branchland
SLB LO-55 West Virginia . . Grafton

Treasury Employees
CH 64 . . . . Bridgeport
CH 82 . . . . Kearneysville
CH 190 . . . . Parkersburg

Utility Workers
LU 102-O Martinsburg . Martinsburg
LU 264 . . . . Wheeling
LU 420 . . . . Moundsville
LU 468 . . . . Moundsville
LU 492 . . . . Wheeling
LU 496 . . . . Wellsburg

Weather Service Employees
BR 01-16 . . . . Charleston

Unaffiliated Labor Organizations
Appalred Staff Employees
  Union . . . . Charleston
Chemical Employees
  Association . . . . Belle
Craig Motor Service Company
  Automotive Parts & Service
  Workers . . . . Flat Top

Exxon Employees Association of
West Virginia . . . . . Charleston
Greenbrier Security
Union. . . . . Sinks Grove
Mechanics Union Independent LU
1 . . . . Wheeling

Nurse Anesthetists Association of
West Virginia Association of Nurse
Anesthetists, Inc.. . . . . Charleston
Steelworkers Union
Independent. . . . . . . Weirton

Swanson Plating Employees
Association . . . . . . Princeton
Swanson Plating Workers
Independent Union . Morgantown

Weirton Steel Corporation Guard
Union Inc.. . . . . Weirton
West Virginia Professional Staff
Union. . . . . Charleston

Wisconsin

AFL-CIO Trade and Industrial Departments

Building and Construction Trades Department
BCTC Central Wisconsin River Valley . . . . Wausau
BCTC Eau Claire . . . . . Eau Claire
BCTC Kenosha . . . . . . Kenosha
BCTC La Crosse . . . . La Crosse
BCTC Milwaukee . . . . Milwaukee
BCTC Northeast Wisconsin . . . . Appleton
BCTC Northern . . . . . . Superior
BCTC South Central Wisconsin . . . . Madison
BCTC Southern Wisconsin . . . . . . Janesville

Other Councils and Committees
JC Badger Ordnance Works . . . . . North Freedom

AFL-CIO Directly Affiliated Locals
DALU 3049 Billposters & Billers . . . . . . Milwaukee
DALU 19806 Smith Steel Workers . . . . . . Milwaukee
DALU 24111 Newspaper Editors . . . . . Random Lake

Affiliated Labor Organizations

Air Traffic Controllers
LU CWA . . . . Mosinee
LU ENW . . . . Kenosha
LU GRB . . . . Green Bay
LU MKE . . . . Milwaukee
LU MSN . . . . Madison

Asbestos Workers
LU 19 . . . . Milwaukee

Automobile, Aerospace Workers
C Fox River Valley Area CAP . . . . Oshkosh
C Janesville Madison Area CAP . . . . Janesville
C Milwaukee Metropolitan Area CAP . . . . Oak Creek
C Racine Kenosha Area CAP . . . . Kenosha
C Rockford Area . . . . . . Beloit
C Sheboygan Area CAP . Sheboygan
LU 9 . . . . West Allis
LU 46 . . . . Beloit
LU 72 . . . . Kenosha
LU 75 . . . . Milwaukee
LU 77 . . . . Beloit
LU 82 . . . . Racine
LU 95 . . . . Janesville
LU 108 . . . . St. Cloud
LU 115 . . . . Milwaukee
LU 173 . . . . Kenosha
LU 180 . . . . Racine
LU 291 . . . . Oshkosh
LU 391 . . . . Racine
LU 407 . . . . Milwaukee
LU 413 . . . . Marinette
LU 438 . . . . Oak Creek
LU 443 . . . . Sun Prairie

LU 459 . . . . Sheboygad
LU 469 . . . . Milwaukee
LU 553 . . . . Racine
LU 557 . . . . Racine
LU 578 . . . . Oshkosh
LU 627 . . . . Racine
LU 633 . . . . . . Trempealeau
LU 646 . . . . . . Fond du Lac
LU 833 . . . . Sheboygan
LU 1076 . . . . . . Sheboygan
LU 1092 West Allis-Milwaukee . . . . . West Allis
LU 1102 . . . . . . Green Bay
LU 1108 . . . . Omro
LU 1291 . . . . . . Plymouth
LU 1329 . . . . Madison
LU 1332 . . . . . . Sheboygan
LU 1472 . . . . . . Sheboygan
LU 1548 . . . . . . Saukville
LU 1866 . . . . . . Oak Creek
LU 2020 . . . . . Stevens Point
LU 2132 . . . . . . Fond du Lac
LU 2376 . . . . . . Plymouth

Bakery, Confectionery, Tobacco Workers and Grain Millers
C Third Region . . . . . West Allis
LU 118-G . . . . Superior
LU 149-G . . . . Amery
LU 180 . . . . . . Stevens Point
LU 205 . . . . West Allis
LU 244 . . . . Milwaukee
LU 340 . . . . Appleton

Boilermakers
LG 10-M . . . . Milwaukee
LG 45-M . . . . . . Union Grove
LG 94-M . . . . Delavan
LG 107 . . . . Waukesha
LG 117 . . . . Superior
LG 177 . . . . Green Bay
LG 443 . . . . Manitowoc
LG 449 . . . . . . Sturgeon Bay
LG 487 . . . . Algoma
LG 696 . . . . Marinette
LG 697 . . . . Pittsville
LG 1162 . . . . Menomonee Falls
LG 1509 . . . . Cudahy
LG 1652 . . . . Pleasant Prairie
LG 1703 . . . . Racine

Bricklayers
DC Wisconsin . . . . . New Berlin
LU 1 . . . . West Salem
LU 2 . . . . Iron River
LU 3 . . . . Green Bay
LU 4 . . . . Kenosha
LU 5 . . . . Germantown
LU 6 . . . . Merrill
LU 7 . . . . Janesville
LU 8 . . . . New Berlin
LU 9 Fox River Valley . . Menasha
LU 11 Wisconsin . . . Sheboygan
LU 13 . . . . Madison
LU 19 . . . . Eau Claire
LU 21 . . . . Waterloo
LU 34 . . . . Reedsburg
LU 74 . . . . New Berlin

Carpenters
C Northern Wisconsin Regional . . . . . . Kaukauna
DC Midwestern Industrial . Oshkosh
DC Milwaukee & Southern Wisconsin . . . . . . Pewaukee

LU 3 Midwestern District Promotional Committee . . . . . . Kaukauna
LU 161 . . . . Kenosha
LU 264 . . . . Pewaukee
LU 310 . . . . Westboro
LU 314 . . . . Madison
LU 344 . . . . Pewaukee
LU 646 . . . . St. Germain
LU 731 . . . . . . Sheboygan
LU 804 . . . . . Stevens Point
LU 955 . . . . Appleton
LU 1025 . . . . . . Medford
LU 1053 . . . . . . Cedarburg
LU 1056 Millwright . New Franken
LU 1074 . . . . . . Eau Claire
LU 1143 . . . . . . La Crosse
LU 1146 . . . . . . Green Bay
LU 1349 . . . . . . Two Rivers
LU 1363 . . . . . . Oshkosh
LU 1435 . . . . . . Conrath
LU 1488 . . . . Merrill
LU 1521 . . . . . . Algoma
LU 1533 . . . . . Two Rivers
LU 1594 . . . . . . Wausau
LU 1733 . . . . . . Stratford
LU 1801 . . . . . . Ladysmith
LU 2190 . . . . . . Madison
LU 2283 . . . . . . Fredonia
LU 2337 . . . . . . Milwaukee
LU 2344 . . . . Merrill
LU 2794 . . . . . . Antigo
LU 2832 . . . . . . Oshkosh
LU 2958 . . . . . Auburndale
LU 2979 . . . . Merrill
LU 3157 . . . . . . Wausau
STC Wisconsin . . . . Madison

Civilian Technicians
CH 26 Wisconsin . . . . . Viroqua
CH 80 Mad City . . . . Marshall
CH 81 Badger State . . . Milwaukee

Communications Workers
C Wisconsin Political . . Milwaukee
LU 4603 . . . . . . Milwaukee
LU 4611 . . . . . . Kenosha
LU 4620 . . . . . . Green Bay
LU 4621 . . . . . . Appleton
LU 4622 . . . . Ripon
LU 4630 . . . . . . Madison
LU 4640 . . . . . . Eau Claire
LU 4641 . . . . . . Beldenville
LU 4642 . . . . . . Auburndale
LU 4670 . . . . . . Nekoosa
LU 4671 . . . . . . Sun Prairie
LU 4672 . . . . . . Wausau
LU 4674 . . . . . . Rice Lake
LU 4675 . . . . . . Mishicot
LU 4690 . . . . . . Milwaukee
LU 4802 . . . . . . Hales Corner
LU 14547 . . . . . . Kenosha
LU 14550 . . . . . Sheboygan
LU 14551 Superior Printing Publishing Media . . . . Superior
LU 34051 Milwaukee . . Milwaukee
LU 34159 . . . . . . Kenosha
LU 34179 . . . . . Sheboygan

Electrical Workers
LU 14 . . . . Fall Creek
LU 127 . . . . Kenosha
LU 158 . . . . Green Bay
LU 159 . . . . Madison
LU 388 . . . . . Stevens Point
LU 430 . . . . Racine

LU 494 . . . . Milwaukee
LU 577 . . . . Appleton
LU 663 . . . . . South Milwaukee
LU 715 . . . . Milwaukee
LU 890 . . . . Janesville
LU 953 . . . . Eau Claire
LU 965 . . . . Madison
LU 1060 . . . . . . Sheboygan
LU 1147 . . . . Wisconsin Rapids
LU 1559 . . . . . . Superior
LU 1791 . . . . . . Wausau
LU 2150 . . . . . . Waukesha
LU 2221 . . . . . . Florence
LU 2285 . . . . . . Kenosha
LU 2304 . . . . . . Madison
LU 2373 . . . . . . Oshkosh
SC EM-5 General Electric . Big Bend
STCON Wisconsin . . Stevens Point

Electrical, Radio and Machine Workers
LU 1107 . . . . Necedah
LU 1111 . . . . . . Milwaukee
LU 1112 . . . . . . Oak Creek
LU 1121 . . . . . . Onalaska
LU 1125 . . . . . . Milwaukee
LU 1135 . . . . . . Milwaukee
LU 1161 . . . . . . Sparta
LU 1172 . . . . . . Cudahy

Electronic Workers
LU 800-FW . . . . . Sheboygan
LU 801-FW . . . . . Janesville
LU 1038 . . . . . . Cadahy
LU 1101 . . . . . . Milwaukee
LU 1161 . . . . . . Menasha
LU 84846 . . . . . New Berlin

Elevator Constructors
LU 15 . . . . New Berlin
LU 132 . . . . . . Cottage Grove

Federal Employees
LU 3 . . . . Milwaukee
LU 276 . . . . Madison
LU 1441 . . . . . Fountain City
LU 1920 . . . . . . Greendale
LU 2137 Blackwell Job Corporation . . . . . Wabeno
LU 2165 . . . . . . Hayward

Flint Glass Workers
LU 114 . . . . . . Burlington

Food and Commercial Workers
C 4 Great Lakes . . Beaver Dam
DC Midwestern . . . . Appleton
LU 1-I . . . . . South Milwaukee
LU 73-A . . . . . . Milwaukee
LU 78-T . . . . . . Appleton
LU 147-T . . . . . Sheboygan
LU 215-T . . . . . . Casco
LU 236-T . . . . . Two Rivers
LU 245 . . . . . . Green Bay
LU 268 . . . . . Chippewa Falls
LU 349-C . . . . Rio
LU 538 . . . . . . Madison
LU 625-T . . . . . Sheboygan
LU 665-T . . . . . Manitowoc
LU 688 . . . . Merrill
LU 717 . . . . Chili
LU 1444 . . . . . . Milwaukee

Glass, Molders, Pottery and Plastics Workers
CONF Wisconsin . . . . . Cudahy
LU 6-B . . . . Cudahy
LU 14-B . . . . Jackson
LU 113-B . . . . . Richland Center
LU 121-B . . . . Neenah
LU 125-B . . . . . South Milwaukee
LU 185. . . . . Jackson
LU 226 . . . . Salem
LU 261 . . . . Cedar Grove
LU 271 . . . . De Pere
LU 301. . . . . Manitowoc
LU 437 . . . . Onalaska

Government Employees
C 33 Prison Locals . . . . Danbury
LU 648 DoL . . . . Portage
LU 666 USDA . . . . . St. Francis
LU 675 USDA. . . . . Whitewater
LU 1732 VA . . . . Madison
LU 1882 VA . . . . . Fort McCoy
LU 2144 DoD . . . . . Milwaukee
LU 2490 USDA . . . New Franken
LU 2722 USDA . . . . Green Bay
LU 2882 DoL. . . . . . Green Bay
LU 3289 USDA . . . . . . Dallas
LU 3495 DoJ . . . . Oxford

Government Security Officers
LU . . . . Muskego

Graphic Communications
LU 7-C . . . . West Allis
LU 23-N . . . . Wauwatosa
LU 77-P Fox Valley . . . . Neenah
LU 254-M . . . . Racine
LU 309-C . . . . Waterloo
LU 370-C . . . . Schofield
LU 577-M . . . . . Milwaukee
LU 585-S . . . . . . Rhinelander

Guards
LU 10 . . . . Portage

Hotel and Restaurant Employees
LU 122 . . . . Milwaukee
LU 315 . . . . . Wisconsin Rapids
LU 361 . . . . River Falls
LU 414 . . . . Oshkosh
LU 479 . . . . La Crosse
LU 517 . . . . Osseo

Independent Unions Federation
LU 175 Larsen Company Employees
   Independent Union. . . Green Bay

Iron Workers
LU 8 . . . . Milwaukee
LU 383 . . . . Madison
LU 665 . . . . Stoughton
LU 811 . . . . Wausau
LU 825 . . . . La Crosse

Laborers
DC Wisconsin . . . . . . Madison
LU 113 . . . . Milwaukee
LU 140 . . . . La Crosse
LU 237 . . . . Kenosha
LU 317 . . . . Eau Claire
LU 392 . . . . Waukesha
LU 464 . . . . Madison
LU 539 . . . . Green Bay
LU 931 . . . . Appleton
LU 1050 . . . . Superior
LU 1086 . . . . . . Fond du Lac
LU 1359 . . . . Wausau
LU 1407 . . . . . Wisconsin Rapids

LU 1440 . . . . Janesville

Laundry and Dry Cleaning
LU 228 . . . . Eau Claire
LU 229 . . . . Madison
LU 3008 . . . . Milwaukee

Letter Carriers
BR 2 . . . . Milwaukee
BR 59 . . . . La Crosse
BR 102 . . . . Sheboygan
BR 125 . . . . Fond du Lac
BR 173 . . . . Oshkosh
BR 215 . . . . Wausau
BR 242 Ashland Area
   Local . . . . Ashland
BR 337 . . . . Superior
BR 346 . . . . Marinette
BR 381 . . . . Stevens Point
BR 397 . . . . Waukesha
BR 436 . . . . Racine
BR 490 . . . . Manitowoc
BR 507 . . . . Madison
BR 572 . . . . Janesville
BR 574 . . . . Kenosha
BR 619 . . . . Green Bay
BR 649 . . . . Watertown
BR 700 . . . . Neenah
BR 715 . . . . Beloit
BR 728 . . . . Eau Claire
BR 729 . . . . Fort Atkinson
BR 778 . . . . Irma
BR 822 . . . . Appleton
BR 944 . . . . Beaver Dam
BR 978 . . . . Marshfield
BR 983 . . . . Antigo
BR 1033 Menomonie,
   Wisconsin. . . . . Menomonie
BR 1083 . . . . Wisconsin Rapids
BR 1144. . . . . Berlin
BR 1181 . . . . Monroe
BR 1208 Ripon, Wisconsin . . Ripon
BR 1222 Port Washington,
   Wisconsin . . . Port Washington
BR 1233 Sparta, Wisconsin. . Sparta
BR 1241 Oconto, Wisconsin. Oconto
BR 1267 Oconomowoc,
   Wisconsin. . . . . Oconomowoc
BR 1272 Platteville,
   Wisconsin. . . . . . . Platteville
BR 1298 Waupaca,
   Wisconsin. . . . . Waupaca
BR 1345 . . . . Two Rivers
BR 1370 Plymouth,
   Wisconsin. . . . . . . Plymouth
BR 1613 Hudson,
   Wisconsin. . . . . . . Hudson
BR 1662 Rice Lake,
   Wisconsin. . . . . . Rice Lake
BR 1890 Clintonville,
   Wisconsin. . . . . . Clintonville
BR 1949 Columbus,
   Wisconsin. . . . . . . Columbus
BR 2025 Prairie du Chien,
   Wisconsin . . Prairie du Chien
BR 2186 Mayville,
   Wisconsin . . . . Mayville
BR 2284 Spooner,
   Wisconsin. . . . . . . Spooner
BR 2285 Hurley, Wisconsin . Hurley
BR 2316 Medford,
   Wisconsin . . . . Medford
BR 2454 Durand,
   Wisconsin. . . . . Durand
BR 2478 Horicon,
   Wisconsin. . . . . . . Horicon
BR 2491 Mineral Point,
   Wisconsin. . . . . Mineral Point

BR 2504 Arcadia,
   Wisconsin. . . . . . . Arcadia
BR 2516 Black River Falls,
   Wisconsin. . . . . Black River
BR 2544 Park Falls,
   Wisconsin. . . . . . Park Falls
BR 2565 Viroqua,
   Wisconsin. . . . . . . Viroqua
BR 2576 River Falls,
   Wisconsin . . . . . River Falls
BR 2594 Chilton,
   Wisconsin. . . . . . . Chilton
BR 2674 Phillips,
   Wisconsin. . . . . . . Phillips
BR 2884 Darlington,
   Wisconsin. . . . . Darlington
BR 2965 New Holstein,
   Wisconsin. . . . New Holstein
BR 2972 Tomah, Wisconsin . Tomah
BR 3002 Stanley,
   Wisconsin. . . . . . . Stanley
BR 3035 . . . . Sturgeon Bay
BR 3100 Niagara,
   Wisconsin. . . . . . . Niagara
BR 3231. . . . . Lodi
BR 3647 Boscobel,
   Wisconsin. . . . . . Boscobel
BR 3683 Kewaunee,
   Wisconsin. . . . . . Kewaunee
BR 3740 Oconto Falls,
   Wisconsin. . . . Oconto Falls
BR 3806 Algoma,
   Wisconsin. . . . . . . Algoma
BR 4123 Bloomer,
   Wisconsin. . . . . . . Bloomer
BR 4124 Barron, Wisconsin . Barron
BR 4225 Little Chute,
   Wisconsin. . . . . Little Chute
BR 4329 Westby,
   Wisconsin. . . . . . . Westby
BR 4630 Brillion,
   Wisconsin. . . . . . . Brillion
BR 4668 New Richmond,
   Wisconsin. . . . New Richmond
BR 4811 . . . . Brookfield
BR 4852 Nekoosa,
   Wisconsin. . . . . . . Nekoosa
BR 4880 Peshtigo,
   Wisconsin. . . . . . . Peshtigo
BR 5123 Arlington,
   Wisconsin. . . . . . . Arlington
BR 5125 Fennimore,
   Wisconsin. . . . . . Fennimore
BR 5129 Pewaukee,
   Wisconsin. . . . . . Pewaukee
BR 5354 Prescott,
   Wisconsin. . . . . . . Prescott
BR 5371 Crandon,
   Wisconsin . . . . . . Crandon
BR 5372 Brodhead,
   Wisconsin. . . . . . Brodhead
BR 5436 Camp Douglas,
   Wisconsin . . . . Camp Douglas
BR 5787 Port Edwards,
   Wisconsin. . . . . Port Edwards
BR 5871 . . . . Mosinee
BR 5940 . . . . Mukwonago
BR 5941 Waterford,
   Wisconsin. . . . . . Waterford
BR 5942 Delafield,
   Wisconsin. . . . . . . Delafield
BR 6216 Amery, Wisconsin . Amery
BR 6217 Randolph,
   Wisconsin. . . . . . Randolph
BR 6292 Oregon,
   Wisconsin. . . . . . . Oregon
BR 6342 Prairie du Sac,
   Wisconsin. . . . . Prairie du Sac

BR 6352 Cuba City,
   Wisconsin. . . . . . Cuba City
SA Wisconsin. . . . . . Madison

Locomotive Engineers
DIV 13 . . . . La Crosse
DIV 66 . . . . Oak Creek
DIV 119 . . . . Janesville
DIV 173 . . . . Fond du Lac
DIV 174 . . . . Stevens Point
DIV 175 . . . . Neenah
DIV 176 . . . . Friendship
DIV 188. . . . . Superior
DIV 209 . . . . Green Bay
DIV 241 . . . . Eau Claire
DIV 253. . . . . Baraboo
DIV 405 . . . . West Berlin
DIV 882 A.C.
   Blainey . . . . South Milwaukee
SLB Wisconsin . . . . Oak Creek

Longshoremen
LU 815 . . . . Milwaukee
LU 1000 . . . . Superior
LU 1014 . . . . Green Bay
LU 1037 . . . . Superior
LU 1295 . . . . West Allis

Machinists
DLG 3 Woodworkers . . . Schofield
DLG 10 . . . . Milwaukee
DLG 66 . . . . La Crosse
DLG 121 . . . . Sun Prairie
DLG 150 . . . . . . New Holstein
LG 21 . . . . La Crosse
LG 34 . . . . Kenosha
LG 66 . . . . Milwaukee
LG 78 . . . . Milwaukee
LG 140-DS . . . . South Milwaukee
LG 173 . . . . Eau Claire
LG 343 . . . . South Range
LG 419 . . . . Milwaukee
LG 437 . . . . Racine
LG 510 . . . . West Allis
LG 516 . . . . Two Rivers
LG 621 . . . . Ashland
LG 655 . . . . . Wisconsin Rapids
LG 747 . . . . Appleton
LG 873 . . . . Horicon
LG 908 . . . . St. Francis
LG 957 . . . . Marshall
LG 1061 Cream City. . . Milwaukee
LG 1115 . . . . La Crosse
LG 1212 . . . . Sun Prairie
LG 1217. . . . . . New Richmond
LG 1259 . . . . . . New Holstein
LG 1266 . . . . Janesville
LG 1326 . . . . West Bend
LG 1367 . . . . . . Fort Atkinson
LG 1377. . . . . Waukesha
LG 1406 . . . . New Glarus
LG 1430 . . . . Sheboygan
LG 1438 . . . . Merill
LG 1493 . . . . Burlington
LG 1516 . . . . Cambria
LG 1543 . . . . . Wisconsin Rapids
LG 1564 . . . . Watertown
LG 1668 . . . . Milwaukee
LG 1713 . . . . Tomahawk
LG 1771 . . . . Bangor
LG 1798 . . . . Green Bay
LG 1845 . . . . Brookfield
LG 1855 . . . . Sherwood
LG 1862 . . . . Cudahy
LG 1904 . . . . Muskego
LG 1916. . . . . Waukesha
LG 1947 . . . . Fond du Lac
LG 2052 . . . . Mayville

LG 2053 . . . . Mayville
LG 2054 . . . . Watertown
LG 2073 . . . . Little Chute
LG 2110 . . . . Cudahy
LG 2180 . . . . . Wisconsin Dells
LG 2185 . . . . Chilton
LG 2191 . . . . La Crosse
LG 2269 . . . . Loganville
LG 2362 . . . . Merrill
LG 2560 . . . . Sussex
LG 2575 . . . . . New Loundon
LLG W-67
  Woodworkers . . . . . Abbotsford
LLG W-110 Woodworkers. Stratford
LLG W-223
  Woodworkers . . . . . White Lake
LLG W-335
  Woodworkers . . . . . South Range
LLG W-401 Woodworkers . Phillips
STC Wisconsin . . . . . Milwaukee

Maintenance of Way Employes

LG 298 . . . . Rice Lake
LG 320 . . . . Superior
LG 509 . . . . Holmen
LG 1841 . . . . Jefferson
LG 1965 . . . . Onalaska
LG 2643 . . . . Madison
LG 2857 . . . . Twin Lakes
SLG 99 . . . . Racine
SLG 239 . . . . Eau Claire
SLG 410 . . . . West Allis
SLG 425 . . . . Green Bay
SLG 472 . . . . Superior
SLG 893 . . . . Merrill
SLG 1034. . . . . . Cottage Grove
SLG 1125. . . . . . . Friendship
SLG 1380. . . . . . . Rothschild

Musicians

LU 8 . . . . Greenfield
LU 42 Racine. . . . . Racine
LU 166 . . . . Madison
LU 193 . . . . Waukesha
LU 205 . . . . Green Bay
LU 469 . . . . Watertown
STCON Wisconsin . . . . . Madison

NLRB Professional Association

LU 30 . . . . Milwaukee

Nurses

LSC Bay Area Medical Center,
  Professionals . . . . . Marinette
SA Wisconsin Nurses
  Association . . . . . . Madison

Office and Professional Employees

LU 9 . . . . Milwaukee
LU 35 . . . . Butler
LU 39 . . . . Madison
LU 74. . . . . Mondovi
LU 95 . . . . . Wisconsin Rapids

Operating Engineers

LU 139 . . . . Pewaukee
LU 305 . . . . Superior
LU 310 . . . . Green Bay
LU 317 . . . . Milwaukee

Painters

LU 108 . . . . Racine
LU 579 . . . . Eagle
LU 770 . . . . New Berlin
LU 781 . . . . New Berlin
LU 802 . . . . Sun Prairie
LU 934 . . . . Kenosha
LU 941 . . . . Madison

LU 1204 . . . . Milwaukee
LU 1355 Glaziers Architectural
  Metal . . . . Janesville

Paper, Allied-Industrial, Chemical Employees

DC Region Ten . . . . . Eau Claire
DC 3 . . . . Campbellsport
LU 7-69 . . . . . West Milwaukee
LU 7-666 . . . . Wausau
LU 01-1279 . . . . Kimberly
LU 07-15. . . . . Tomahawk
LU 07-16. . . . . Appleton
LU 07-18. . . . . Milwaukee
LU 07-20. . . . . Hilbert
LU 07-42 . . . . . Chippewa Falls
LU 07-47 . . . . Green Bay
LU 07-53 Brewers &
  Maltsters . . . . Jefferson
LU 07-59 . . . . Vesper
LU 07-86 . . . . Marinette
LU 07-94 . . . . . Wisconsin Rapids
LU 07-101 . . . . Wausaukee
LU 07-111 . . . . Elkhorn
LU 07-116 . . . . Mosinee
LU 07-131 . . . . Adams
LU 07-144 . . . . . Combined Locks
LU 07-145 . . . . . Campbellsport
LU 07-148 . . . . Neenah
LU 07-150 . . . . Tomah
LU 07-169 . . . . Oshkosh
LU 07-187 . . . . . Wisconsin Rapids
LU 07-200 . . . . Milwaukee
LU 07-201 . . . . Neenah
LU 07-204 . . . . Green Bay
LU 07-209 . . . . West Allis
LU 07-213 . . . . De Pere
LU 07-221 . . . . Mosinee
LU 07-224 . . . . Mosinee
LU 07-227 . . . . Peshtigo
LU 07-231 . . . . Burlington
LU 07-232 . . . . Milwaukee
LU 07-248 . . . . Tomahawk
LU 07-273 . . . . Appleton
LU 07-287 . . . . Conrath
LU 07-291 . . . . Green Bay
LU 07-295 . . . . Brookfield
LU 07-316 . . . . Mosinee
LU 07-319 . . . . Rothschild
LU 07-324 . . . . Appleton
LU 07-327 . . . . De Pere
LU 07-331 . . . . Holmen
LU 07-342 . . . . Watertown
LU 07-345 . . . . Two Rivers
LU 07-356 . . . . Milwaukee
LU 07-359 . . . . . Stevens Point
LU 07-364 . . . . Milwaukee
LU 07-366 . . . . Berlin
LU 07-368 . . . . Two Rivers
LU 07-369 . . . . West Bend
LU 07-370 . . . . . Stevens Point
LU 07-379 . . . . Berlin
LU 07-380 . . . . Sauk City
LU 07-415 . . . . Mishicot
LU 07-432 . . . . Oshkosh
LU 07-445 . . . . Fifield
LU 07-460 . . . . Tomahawk
LU 07-465 . . . . Appleton
LU 07-469 . . . . Appleton
LU 07-475 . . . . Brillion
LU 07-482 . . . . Appleton
LU 07-484 . . . . Neenah
LU 07-535 . . . . Antigo
LU 07-550 . . . . Waupaca
LU 07-579 . . . . Lomira
LU 07-588 . . . . Manawa
LU 07-597 . . . . De Pere
LU 07-598 . . . . Lomira

LU 07-614 . . . . Pine River
LU 07-631 . . . . Wausau
LU 07-681 . . . . Mequon
LU 07-695 . . . . Menomonee Falls
LU 07-696 . . . . Marshfield
LU 07-727 . . . . Menasha
LU 07-736 . . . . Pulaski
LU 07-748 . . . . Winneconne
LU 07-765 . . . . Milwaukee
LU 07-779 . . . . Richfield
LU 07-790 . . . . Clintonville
LU 07-803 . . . . Dorchester
LU 07-812 . . . . Neenah
LU 07-815 . . . . Marion
LU 07-849 . . . . Kewaskum
LU 07-851 . . . . Portage
LU 07-852 . . . . Waukesha
LU 07-857 . . . . Kimberly
LU 07-865 . . . . West Bend
LU 07-877 . . . . Milwaukee
LU 07-888 . . . . Appleton
LU 07-889 . . . . Clintonville
LU 07-902 . . . . West Bend
LU 07-932 . . . . Menasha
LU 07-945 . . . . . Fond du Lac
LU 07-995 . . . . Shiocton
LU 07-1004 . . . . Marinette
LU 07-1096 . . . . Green Bay
LU 07-1166 . . . . Niagara
LU 07-1170 . . . . . New London
LU 07-1202 . . . . Madison
LU 07-1203 . . . . De Pere
LU 07-1207 . . . . Stoughton
LU 07-1225 . . . . Peshtigo
LU 07-1260 . . . . Merrill
LU 07-1306 . . . . . Stevens Point
LU 07-1316 . . . . Shawano
LU 07-1319 . . . . . New Franken
LU 07-1321 . . . . Green Bay
LU 07-1324 . . . . Menasha
LU 07-1381 . . . . Wausau
LU 07-1477 . . . . Appleton
LU 07-1517 . . . . De Pere
LU 07-1670 . . . . Appleton
LU 07-1778 . . . . Rhinelander
LU 07-1822 . . . . Fremont
LU 07-1970 . . . . . New London
LU 07-1980 . . . . Appleton
LU 07-7152 . . . . Hartford
LU 70-322 . . . . Milwaukee

Plasterers and Cement Masons

LU 599. . . . . Wauwatosa

Plumbing and Pipe Fitting

DC 4 Milwaukee Pipe
  Trades . . . . Milwaukee
LU 75 . . . . Milwaukee
LU 118 . . . . Kenosha
LU 183 . . . . Milwaukee
LU 400 Fox River Valley . Greenbay
LU 434 . . . . Mosinee
LU 601 . . . . Milwaukee
SA Wisconsin Pipe
  Trades . . . . Milwaukee

Postal and Federal Employees

LU 708 . . . . Milwaukee

Postal Workers

LU 3 Milwaukee . . . . . Milwaukee
LU 90 Appleton . . . . . Appleton
LU 102 Eau Claire Area . Eau Claire
LU 178 Oshkosh . . . . . Oshkosh
LU 241 Madison Area . . . Madison
LU 360 La Crosse . . . . . La Crosse
LU 577 Sheboygan. . . . Sheboygan
LU 778 Racine . . . . . . Racine

LU 840 Kenosha . . . . . Kenosha
LU 878 West Bend. . . . West Bend
LU 1030 Manitowoc. . . Manitowoc
LU 1041 Ashland . . . . . Ashland
LU 1304 Twin City Area . Marinette
LU 1847 Fond du Lac . Fond du Lac
LU 2100 Plymouth Local . Plymouth
LU 2218 Sturgeon Bay
  Local . . . . Sturgeon Bay
LU 2247 Northeastern
  Area . . . . Green Bay
LU 2496 Watertown . . . Watertown
LU 3452 Port Washington
  Local. . . . . . . Port Washington
LU 4532 Wausau . . . . . Wausau
LU 4763 Spooner . . . . . . Spooner
LU 5341 Whitewater
  Local . . . . Whitewater
LU 6196 Portage. . . . . . Portage
SA Wisconsin. . . . . . . Madison

Professional and Technical Engineers

LU 92 . . . . Cudahy

Railroad Signalmen

LLG 9 . . . . West Bend
LLG 39 . . . . Randolph
LLG 227 . . . . Doylestown

Roofers, Waterproofers and Allied Workers

LU 65 . . . . Milwaukee

Rural Letter Carriers

D West Central . . . . . Eau Claire
LU Adams-Marquette
  Counties . . . . Montello
LU Barron-Washburn
  County . . . . Rice Lake
LU Calumet-Manitowoc-Sheboygan
  Counties. . . . . . Two Rivers
LU Chippewa-Eau Claire
  Counties. . . . . Chippewa Falls
LU Clark County. . . . . . Withee
LU Columbia
  County . . . . . Wisconsin Dells
LU Dodge County . . . . . Neosho
LU Door-Kewaunee
  Counties. . . . . . . Luxemburg
LU Fond du Lac-Green Lake
  Counties. . . . . . Campbellsport
LU Forest-Tri-County
  Association. . . . . . Rhinelander
LU Grant County. . . . . Lone Rock
LU Jefferson County. . . . Waterloo
LU Juneau County . . . New Lisbon
LU La Crosse County . . . Onalaska
LU Lake Superior. . . . . Iron River
LU Milwaukee-Waukesha
  Counties . . . . . . Oconomowoc
LU Monroe County
  Association. . . . . . . Tomah
LU Oconto County . . . . . Suring
LU Outagmie County . . . Seymour
LU Ozaukee County . . . Saukville
LU Polk County . . . . . Centuria
LU Price-Taylor Counties . . Gilman
LU Racine-Kenosha
  Counties . . . . Bristol
LU Rock-Walworth
  Counties . . . . . Lake Geneva
LU Rusk County . . . . . Sheldon
LU Sawyer County . . . Springbrook
LU St. Croix County. . . River Falls
LU Trempealeau-Buffalo County
  Association . . . . . . Eleva
LU Vernon County. . . . . . Viola

LU Washington County . . . Colgate
LU Waupaca County . . . . Marion
LU Waushara County . . Redgranite
LU 4 Brown County . . . Denmark
LU 10 Crawford County . . Eastman
LU 11 Dane County . Cottage Grove
LU 15 Dunn County . . . . Colfax
LU 22 Jackson County . . . Hixton
LU 27 Green-Lafayette
  Counties . . . . Monroe
LU 28 Lincoln-Langlade
  Counties . . . . Tomahawk
LU 30 Marathon County . . Edgar
LU 31 Marinette County . . Pound
LU 38 Pierce-Pepin
  Counties . . . . Nelson
LU 47 Sauk-Richland . . . Baraboo
LU 49 McHenry
  County . . . . . Lake Geneva
LU 49 Shawano County . . . Pulaski
LU 61 Winnebago County . . . Omro
LU 62 Wood-Portage
  Counties . . . . Rosholt
SA 51 Wisconsin . . . . Eau Claire

**Security, Police and Fire
Professionals**
LU 555 . . . . Oak Creek
LU 556 . . . . Kenosha
LU 557 . . . . Genoa
LU 558 . . . . Two Rivers
LU 563 . . . . Park Falls

Service Employees
JC 4 . . . . Milwaukee
LU 150 . . . . Milwaukee
LU 152 . . . . Racine
LU 168 . . . . Racine
LU 1199-W District 1199-W,
  SEIU . . . . Madison

Sheet Metal Workers
LU 18 . . . . Milwaukee
LU 565 . . . . Madison

**State, County and Municipal
Employees**
C 40 Wisconsin State . . . . Madison
DC 48 Milwaukee
  Wisconsin . . . . . . Milwaukee
LU 216 Ashland City and County
  Employees . . . . . . Marengo
LU 255 The Wisconsin Childcare
  Union . . . . Madison
LU 366 Milwaukee, Wisconsin,
  Sewerage Commission
  Employees . . . . . Oak Creek
LU 412 Madison Area Rehabilitation
  Center . . . . . . Fitchburg
LU 524 . . . . Beloit
LU 524-B Beluit Jelco Bus
  Drivers . . . . Beloit
LU 526 Milwaukee Public Museum
  Employees . . . . . . Milwaukee
LU 727-D American Lutheran
  Homes, Inc. . . . . . Menomonie
LU 913 Park Lawn
  Employees . . . . . . Manitowoc
LU 1146 Middle River Health Care
  Center . . . . . . South Range
LU 1155 Memorial Medical
  Center . . . . Ashland

LU 1205 Clara Barton
  Brigade . . . . Green Bay
LU 1440 . . . . Milwaukee
LU 1558 Badger Regional Blood
  Center Employees . . . . Madison
LU 1760 Superior Memorial
  Hospital . . . . Superlor
LU 1760-A . . . . Superior
LU 1954 Rehabilitation & Social
  Service Workers . . . . Milwaukee
LU 2236 Heyde Health
  System . . . . . Chippewa Falls
LU 2276 Wyalusing Academy Child
  Care Worker . . . Prairie du Chien
LU 2418 Jefferson County
  Institutions Employees . Jefferson
LU 2425 Spooner Community
  Memorial Hospital
  Employees . . . . . . Minong
LU 2717-A Family Heritage Nursing
  Home Employees . . . . Merrillan
LU 3152 Pepin Manor Care Center
  Employees . . . . . . Pepin
LU 3305 Bay Area Medical
  Center . . . . . . Marinette
LU 3382 Dental Associates, Ltd.,
  Employees . . . . . New Berlin
LU 3635 Chequamegon Bay Area
  Nursing Employees . . . . Ashland
LU 3635-A . . . . Washburn
LU 3902 Homme Home Employees
  Union . . . . Birnamwood

Steelworkers
LU 02-14-L . . . . La Crosse
LU 02-29-U . . . . Cudahy
LU 02-29-U . . . . Cudahy
LU 02-125-A . . . . . . Manitowoc
LU 02-133-U . . . . . . Sheboygan
LU 02-146-S . . . . . . Niagara
LU 02-175-U . . . . . . Kewaunee
LU 02-333-U . . . . Stevens Point
LU 02-460-L . . . . Chippewa Falls
LU 02-642-U . . . . New London
LU 02-741-L . . . . . . Menomonie
LU 02-892-L . . . . . . Burlington
LU 02-904-L . . . . . Sun Prairie
LU 02-1114-S . . West Milwaukee
LU 02-1173-S . . . . . . Cudahy
LU 02-1327-S . . . . . . Ripon
LU 02-1343-S . . South Milwaukee
LU 02-1527-S . . . . West Allis
LU 02-1533-S . . . . . . Beloit
LU 02-1569-S . . . . . St. Francis
LU 02-1610-S . . . . . Milwaukee
LU 02-2138-S . . . . . Eau Claire
LU 02-3168-S . . . . . . Niagara
LU 02-3205-S . . . . . Oak Creek
LU 02-3245-S . . . . . . Beloit
LU 02-3740-S . . . . . . Pewaukee
LU 02-4547-S . . . . . Oak Creek
LU 02-4845-S . . . . . Waukesha
LU 02-4846-S . . . . . Watertown
LU 02-6050-S . . . . . . Suring
LU 02-6499-S . . . . . Manitowoc
LU 02-6763-S . . South Milwaukee
LU 02-7076-S . . . . . East Troy
LU 02-7875-S . . . . . Milwaukee
LU 02-8114-S . . . . . Hustisford
LU 02-8149-S . . . . . Fredonia
LU 02-9040-S . . Menomonee Falls
LU 02-9184-S . . . . . . Shiocton

LU 02-9435 . . . . Beloit
LU 02-12005-S . . . . . . Racine
LU 32-9408 . . . . . . Rhinelander

Teachers
LU 5012 Nurses & Health
  Professionals . . . . . Burlington
LU 5032 Veterans Administration
  Staff Nurses Council . Milwaukee
LU 5034 Eagle River Memorial
  Hospital Professional
  Nurses . . . . . . Land O'Lakes
LU 5040 Federation of Nurses &
  Health Professionals . Turtle Lake
SFED Nurses & Health
  Professionals, Wisconsin
  Federation of . . . . . West Allis

Teamsters
CONF Dairy Conference-USA and
  Canada . . . . Green Bay
JC 39 . . . . Milwaukee
LU 23 Milwaukee Mailers
  Union . . . . Milwaukee
LU 43 . . . . Racine
LU 75 . . . . Green Bay
LU 200 . . . . Milwaukee
LU 344 . . . . Milwaukee
LU 563 . . . . Appleton
LU 579 . . . . Janesville
LU 662 . . . . Eau Claire
LU 695 . . . . Madison

Theatrical Stage Employees
LU 18 . . . . Milwaukee
LU 32 . . . . Superior
LU 141 . . . . La Crosse
LU 164 . . . . . . South Milwaukee
LU 251 . . . . Madison
LU 470 . . . . Oshkosh
LU 777 . . . . Milwaukee

Tool Craftsmen
LU 2 . . . . Racine
NHQ . . . . Racine

Transit Union
LDIV 998 . . . . Milwaukee

**Transportation Communications
Union**
LG 415 . . . . Superior
LG 6595 Madison . . . . . Horicon

Transportation Union
GCA GO-225 Chicago &
  Northwestern Trans
  Company . . . . . . Milwaukee
GCA GO-987 Wisconsin
  Central . . . . . . New London
LLG GO-256 Yardmasters
  Department . . . . . Prescott
LU 311 . . . . Onalaska
LU 312 . . . . Friendship
LU 322 . . . . Hubertus
LU 581 . . . . Marinette
LU 582 . . . . Milladore
LU 583 . . . . Oshkosh
LU 590 . . . . Portage
LU 832 . . . . Foxboro
LU 1175 . . . . . Lake Nebagomon
LU 1293 . . . . Eau Claire

LU 1382 . . . . Hartland
SLB LO-56 Wisconsin . . . Madison

Treasury Employees
CH 1 . . . . Milwaukee

Weather Service Employees
BR 03-9 . . . . Dousman
BR 03-10 . . . . Green Bay
BR 03-64 . . . . La Crosse

Unaffiliated Labor
Organizations
Atlas Workers Association Green Bay
Bank Employees Union Firststar
  Bank . . . . Milwaukee
Business Agent Association LU
  662 . . . . Altoona
Council Employees Union . Madison
Employees Association of B & T
  Mail Services, Inc. . . Mukwonago
Frigo Cheese Corporation Lena
  Independent LU 101 . Oconto Falls
Independent Employees Union
  of Hillshire Farm Company
  Inc. . . . . New London
Independent Loomis Security
  Employees Union . . . West Allis
Independent Pattern Makers Union of
  Neenah Wisconsin . . . . Marion
Kenosha School Bus Drivers
  Union . . . . Kenosha
Kimberly-Clark Atlas
  Union . . . . . . New London
Lake Superior Professional Nurses
  Association . . . . . Ashland
Lakehead Pipe Line Company
  Inc. Employees
  Representative . . . . . Superior
National Union of Labor
  Investigators . . . . . Milwaukee
North Central Area Labor
  Council . . . . Tomahawk
Northland College Faculty
  Senate . . . . Ashland
Office Employees Carpenters
  Independent . . . . Altoona
Packerland Packing Company
  Inc. Drivers Union
  Independent . . . . . Pulaski
Paper Mill Workers
  Independent . . . . . . Kimberly
Postal Supervisors, National
  Association LU 549 . . . . Berlin
Professional Football Referees
  Association . . . . . Shore Wood
Progressive Organization of
  Workers . . . . Milwaukee
Staff Representatives Union
  (AFSCME) DC 48 . . . Milwaukee
Technical Engineers
  Association . . . . . . Wauwatosa
Tosca Limited Employees
  Union . . . . Green Bay
United Business Representatives
  Union . . . . Monona
United Staff Union . . . . . Onalaska
Western States Envelope Company
  Employees Association . . Butler
Wisconsin Council 40 Field Staff
  Union . . . . Madison

Wyoming

AFL-CIO Trade and Industrial Departments

Building and Construction Trades Department
BCTC Wyoming . . . Rock Springs

Affiliated Labor Organizations

Air Traffic Controllers
LU CPR. . . . . Casper

Bakery, Confectionery, Tobacco Workers and Grain Millers
LU 279-G. . . . . Worland
LU 280-G. . . . . Torrington

Boilermakers
LG 495-D Cement Workers . Lovell

Bricklayers
LU 1. . . . . Cheyenne
LU 2 . . . . Big Horn
LU 3 . . . . Casper
STCON 99 Wyoming . . . Cheyenne

Carpenters
LU 469 . . . . Cheyenne
LU 1564 . . . . Casper
LU 1620 . . . . Rock Springs

Civilian Technicians
CH 113 Wyoming Air. . . Cheyenne

Communications Workers
LU 7601 . . . . Cheyenne

Electrical Workers
C Wyoming State. . . . . . Casper
LU 322 . . . . Casper
LU 415 . . . . Cheyenne
LU 612 . . . . Wheatland
LU 646 . . . . Sheridan
LU 775 . . . . Rawlins
LU 1759 . . . . Casper

Federal Employees
LU 369 . . . . Fort Washakie
LU 2159 . . . . Casper

Government Employees
LU 1014 VA . . . . Cheyenne

LU 1219 VA . . . . Sheridan
LU 2354 DoD . . . . . . Cheyenne

Government Employees Association
LU 14-82. . . . . Guernsey

Iron Workers
LU 454 . . . . Casper
LU 830 . . . . Mills

Laborers
LU 1271 . . . . Cheyenne

Letter Carriers
BR 463 . . . . Laramie
BR 555 . . . . Carpenter
BR 1006 . . . . Sheridan
BR 1372 . . . . . . Rock Springs
BR 1548 . . . . Gillette
BR 1681 . . . . Casper
BR 2177 . . . . Evanston
BR 2580 Douglas, Wyoming . . . . Douglas
BR 2779 Rawlins, Wyoming . . . . Rawlins
BR 2929 Kemmerer, Wyoming. . . . . . . Kemmerer
BR 3139 . . . . Cody
BR 3670 . . . . Torrington
BR 4387 . . . . Wheatland
BR 4456 Thermopolis, Wyoming . . . . . Thermopolis
BR 4482 Powell, Wyoming . Powell
BR 5384 Worland, Wyoming. . . . . Worland
BR 5923 . . . . Riverton
BR 6116 Lovell, Wyoming . . Lovell
BR 6175. . . . . Green River
BR 6587 Greybull, Wyoming. . . . . Greybull
SA Wyoming. . . . . Casper

Locomotive Engineers
DIV 31 . . . . Douglas
DIV 44 . . . . Cheyenne
DIV 93 . . . . Cheyenne
DIV 94 . . . . Gillette
DIV 103 . . . . Cheyenne
DIV 115 . . . . Cheyenne
DIV 142. . . . . Rawlins
DIV 207 . . . . Casper
DIV 245 . . . . Green River
DIV 624 . . . . Sheridan

DIV 869 . . . . Basin
SLB Wyoming. . . . . Gillette

Machinists
LG 1290-FL . . . . Jackson

Maintenance of Way Employes
LG 1074 . . . . Dayton
SD Union Pacific Railroad. . Lyman
SLG 686. . . . . Laramie
SLG 918 . . . . Evanston
SLG 1071. . . . . Lusk
SLG 1142 . . . . Douglas
SLG 1292. . . . . Worland

Mine Workers
LU 1192 Office of Allied Workers . . . . Sheridan
LU 1307 . . . . Diamondville
LU 1316. . . . . . . Diamondville
LU 1972 . . . . Sheridan
LU 2055 . . . . Sheridan
LU 3010 Office of Allied Workers . . . . Frontier
LU 4893 Office of Allied Workers . . . . Rock Springs
LU 7404 . . . . Rock Springs

National Staff Organization
LU Staff Organization, Wyoming Education Association . Cheyenne

Paper, Allied-Industrial, Chemical Employees
LU 02-656 . . . . Shell
LU 08-574. . . . . Cheyenne
LU 08-952 . . . . Powell

Plumbing and Pipe Fitting
LU 192 . . . . Cheyenne

Postal Mail Handlers
LU 319 . . . . Cheyenne

Postal Workers
LU 580 Casper . . . . Casper
LU 769 Cheyenne. . . . . Cheyenne
LU 848 Lander Local . . . . Lander
LU 1317 Rock Springs . . . . . Rock Springs
LU 1762 Rawlins . . . . . Rawlins
LU 2204 Laramie . . . . . Laramie
LU 2338 Worland Area . . Worland
LU 2340 Sheridan . . . . Sheridan

LU 2463 Gillette. . . . . . Gillette
LU 2564 Wheatland . . Wheatland
LU 2621 Cody . . . . Cody
LU 3781 Jackson . . . . . Jackson
LU 7135 Evanston . . . . Evanston
SA Wyoming. . . . . Casper

Rural Letter Carriers
LU Laramie . . . . Laramie
SA Wyoming. . . . . Cody

Steelworkers
LU 11-8499-S. . . . . Green River
LU 11-8810-S . . . . . Worland
LU 11-13214-S . . . . Rock Springs
LU 11-13531-S. . . . . Kemmerer
LU 11-15184-S . . . . Rock Springs
LU 11-15320-S . . . . Rock Springs

Theatrical Stage Employees
LU 426 . . . . Casper

Transportation Communications Union
LG 223 . . . . Cheyenne

Transportation Union
LU 28 . . . . Cheyenne
LU 446 . . . . Cheyenne
LU 465 . . . . Gillette
LU 866 . . . . Rawlins
LU 951 . . . . Sheridan
LU 1279 . . . . Greybull
LU 1280 . . . . Casper
LU 1857. . . . . Green River
SLB LO-57 Wyoming . . . Rawlins

Treasury Employees
CH 31 . . . . Cheyenne

Utility Workers
LU 127 . . . . Casper

Weather Service Employees
BR 43. . . . . Casper
BR 03-5 . . . . Cheyenne
BR 03-20 . . . . Riverton

Unaffiliated Labor Organizations
Western Energy Workers Union . . . . Rock Springs

Foreign

Affiliated Labor Organizations

Air Traffic Controllers
LU KWA . . . . . Marshall Islands

Education
ASSN Teacher Education Association Korea . . South Korea
LU OEA American Education Association Okinawa . . . . Japan
LU OEA North East Asia Teachers Association . . . . Japan

Federal Employees
LU 1363 . . . . South Korea

Government Employees
LU 3712 ID . . . . Italy

Hockey Players
NHQ . . . . Canada

Teachers
LU 1495 Naples Federation of Teachers . . . . Italy
LU 1619 Vincenza Federation . Italy
LU 1628 Izmir Federation of Teachers . . . . Turkey
LU 1862 Rota Chapter Overseas . . . . Spain

Appendix A. BLS Union Membership and Earnings Data, 2001 and 2002

Table 1. Union affiliation of employed wage and salary workers by selected characteristics

(Numbers in thousands)

Characteristic	2001						2002					
	Total employed	Members of unions[1]		Represented by unions[2]			Total employed	Members of unions[1]		Represented by unions[2]		
		Total	Percent of employed	Total	Percent of employed			Total	Percent of employed	Total	Percent of employed	
SEX AND AGE												
Total, 16 years and over	122,482	16,387	13.4	18,114	14.8		122,007	16,107	13.2	17,771	14.6	
16 to 24 years	19,698	1,015	5.2	1,184	6.0		19,258	985	5.1	1,132	5.9	
25 years and over	102,784	15,372	15.0	16,930	16.5		102,748	15,122	14.7	16,639	16.2	
25 to 34 years	28,809	3,264	11.3	3,659	12.7		28,251	3,164	11.2	3,540	12.5	
35 to 44 years	31,962	4,733	14.8	5,191	16.2		31,296	4,442	14.2	4,876	15.6	
45 to 54 years	26,909	5,068	18.8	5,543	20.6		27,086	5,011	18.5	5,470	20.2	
55 to 64 years	12,032	2,063	17.1	2,265	18.8		12,982	2,257	17.4	2,469	19.0	
65 years and over	3,072	243	7.9	272	8.9		3,133	247	7.9	284	9.1	
Men, 16 years and over	63,756	9,578	15.0	10,410	16.3		63,383	9,335	14.7	10,135	16.0	
16 to 24 years	10,137	607	6.0	704	6.9		9,862	610	6.2	691	7.0	
25 years and over	53,619	8,971	16.7	9,706	18.1		53,521	8,724	16.3	9,444	17.6	
25 to 34 years	15,627	1,983	12.7	2,169	13.9		15,297	1,878	12.3	2,075	13.6	
35 to 44 years	16,657	2,821	16.9	3,028	18.2		16,390	2,632	16.1	2,821	17.2	
45 to 54 years	13,561	2,840	20.9	3,070	22.6		13,611	2,793	20.5	3,006	22.1	
55 to 64 years	6,168	1,195	19.4	1,292	20.9		6,593	1,285	19.5	1,386	21.0	
65 years and over	1,605	131	8.1	148	9.2		1,630	136	8.3	156	9.5	
Women, 16 years and over	58,726	6,809	11.6	7,704	13.1		58,624	6,772	11.6	7,636	13.0	
16 to 24 years	9,561	409	4.3	480	5.0		9,397	375	4.0	441	4.7	
25 years and over	49,166	6,400	13.0	7,224	14.7		49,227	6,398	13.0	7,195	14.6	
25 to 34 years	13,181	1,281	9.7	1,490	11.3		12,954	1,285	9.9	1,465	11.3	
35 to 44 years	15,305	1,912	12.5	2,163	14.1		14,906	1,810	12.1	2,055	13.8	
45 to 54 years	13,349	2,227	16.7	2,474	18.5		13,474	2,218	16.5	2,464	18.3	
55 to 64 years	5,864	868	14.8	973	16.6		6,390	972	15.2	1,083	17.0	
65 years and over	1,467	113	7.7	124	8.5		1,503	112	7.4	128	8.5	
RACE, HISPANIC ORIGIN, AND SEX												
White, 16 years and over	101,546	13,209	13.0	14,574	14.4		101,081	12,929	12.8	14,227	14.1	
Men	53,731	7,909	14.7	8,585	16.0		53,304	7,699	14.4	8,334	15.6	
Women	47,815	5,300	11.1	5,989	12.5		47,776	5,230	10.9	5,893	12.3	
Black, 16 years and over	14,261	2,409	16.9	2,668	18.7		14,127	2,383	16.9	2,648	18.7	
Men	6,488	1,221	18.8	1,330	20.5		6,499	1,184	18.2	1,297	20.0	
Women	7,773	1,188	15.3	1,338	17.2		7,628	1,198	15.7	1,351	17.7	
Hispanic origin, 16 years and over	15,174	1,679	11.1	1,876	12.4		15,522	1,637	10.5	1,822	11.7	
Men	8,997	1,032	11.5	1,136	12.6		9,130	1,012	11.1	1,113	12.2	
Women	6,177	647	10.5	740	12.0		6,392	625	9.8	709	11.1	
FULL- OR PART-TIME STATUS[3]												
Full-time workers	101,187	14,921	14.7	16,445	16.3		100,201	14,591	14.6	16,077	16.0	
Part-time workers	21,057	1,437	6.8	1,637	7.8		21,573	1,484	6.9	1,658	7.7	

[1] Data refer to members of a labor union or an employee association similar to a union.
[2] Data refer to members of a labor union or an employee association similar to a union as well as workers who report no union affiliation but whose jobs are covered by a union or an employee association contract.
[3] The distinction between full- and part-time workers is based on hours usually worked. Beginning in 1994, these data will not sum to totals because full- or part-time status on the principal job is not identifiable for a small number of multiple jobholders.

NOTE: Data for 2001 have been revised to reflect the introduction of Census 2000-based population controls. In addition, data on "represented by unions" incorporate a minor change to the allocation procedure for that item. The change in procedure had a small effect on the estimates. Data refer to the sole or principal job of full- and part-time workers. Excluded are all self-employed workers regardless of whether or not their businesses are incorporated. Detail for the above race and Hispanic-origin groups will not sum to totals because data for the "other races" group are not presented and Hispanics are included in both the white and black population groups.

Source: U.S. Department of Labor, Bureau of Labor Statistics, "Labor Force Statistics from the Current Population Survey," available at www.bls.gov/news.release/union2.t01.htm

Table 2. Median weekly earnings of full-time wage and salary workers by union affiliation and selected characteristics

Characteristic	2001				2002			
	Total	Members of unions[1]	Repre-sented by unions[2]	Non-union	Total	Members of unions[1]	Repre-sented by unions[2]	Non-union
SEX AND AGE								
Total, 16 years and over	$595	$717	$711	$573	$609	$740	$734	$587
16 to 24 years.................................	375	471	473	368	381	497	494	374
25 years and over............................	629	732	727	610	647	753	748	623
25 to 34 years.................................	576	654	645	559	591	682	670	577
35 to 44 years.................................	655	742	736	634	669	759	753	647
45 to 54 years.................................	691	775	773	661	707	789	787	675
55 to 64 years.................................	641	745	744	614	673	787	784	639
65 years and over............................	472	607	604	441	502	592	594	484
Men, 16 years and over	668	764	759	642	680	780	776	652
16 to 24 years.................................	390	481	485	384	392	498	494	385
25 years and over............................	718	779	777	700	732	797	793	713
25 to 34 years.................................	616	697	688	605	627	722	710	614
35 to 44 years.................................	752	798	793	741	759	810	806	747
45 to 54 years.................................	797	811	811	788	808	831	831	796
55 to 64 years.................................	767	800	807	749	799	836	838	779
65 years and over............................	550	693	709	522	583	610	616	576
Women, 16 years and over..................	511	643	638	493	530	667	662	510
16 to 24 years.................................	353	456	455	348	366	495	494	361
25 years and over............................	541	655	651	518	570	679	674	542
25 to 34 years.................................	513	600	597	502	531	624	619	517
35 to 44 years.................................	544	641	639	522	573	669	666	548
45 to 54 years.................................	587	720	715	553	603	730	726	581
55 to 64 years.................................	539	656	658	512	574	706	705	542
65 years and over............................	372	494	483	359	428	550	551	414
RACE, HISPANIC ORIGIN, AND SEX								
White, 16 years and over	610	739	734	589	624	763	757	602
Men..	688	782	779	663	702	804	801	674
Women	521	666	660	503	549	695	688	521
Black, 16 years and over	486	604	598	462	498	615	610	477
Men..	517	651	637	497	523	651	640	502
Women	452	563	563	424	474	588	588	445
Hispanic origin, 16 years and over.......	413	575	572	398	423	623	617	408
Men..	433	606	605	413	449	666	656	422
Women	385	500	499	371	396	558	569	381

[1] Data refer to members of a labor union or an employee association similar to a union.
[2] Data refer to members of a labor union or an employee association similar to a union as well as workers who report no union affiliation but whose jobs are covered by a union or an employee association contract.
NOTE: Data for 2001 have been revised to reflect the introduction of Census 2000-based population controls. In addition, data on "represented by unions" incorporate a minor change to the allocation procedure for that item. The change in procedure had a small effect on the estimates. Data refer to the sole or principal job of full- and part-time workers. Excluded are all self-employed workers regardless of whether or not their businesses are incorporated. Detail for the above race and Hispanic-origin groups will not sum to totals because data for the "other races" group are not presented and Hispanics are included in both the white and black population groups.

Table 3. Union affiliation of employed wage and salary workers by occupation and industry

(Numbers in thousands)

Characteristic	2001					2002				
	Total em-ployed	Members of unions[1]		Represented by unions[2]		Total em-ployed	Members of unions[1]		Represented by unions[2]	
		Total	Percent of em-ployed	Total	Percent of em-ployed		Total	Percent of em-ployed	Total	Percent of em-ployed
OCCUPATION										
Managerial and professional specialty ..	36,660	4,665	12.7	5,417	14.8	36,969	4,788	13.0	5,534	15.0
Executive, administrative, and managerial	17,075	945	5.5	1,148	6.7	17,296	1,005	5.8	1,223	7.1
Professional specialty	19,585	3,720	19.0	4,269	21.8	19,674	3,783	19.2	4,310	21.9
Technical, sales, and administrative support	36,335	3,208	8.8	3,632	10.0	35,767	3,175	8.9	3,552	9.9
Technicians and related support.......	4,448	474	10.7	537	12.1	4,349	469	10.8	524	12.0
Sales occupations............................	13,749	480	3.5	549	4.0	13,810	496	3.6	559	4.0
Administrative support, including clerical..	18,138	2,253	12.4	2,545	14.0	17,607	2,210	12.5	2,469	14.0
Service occupations............................	17,434	2,296	13.2	2,504	14.4	17,898	2,249	12.6	2,473	13.8
Protective service	2,482	936	37.7	1,004	40.5	2,584	957	37.0	1,021	39.5
Service, except protective service	14,952	1,360	9.1	1,500	10.0	15,314	1,293	8.4	1,452	9.5
Precision production, craft, and repair...	12,886	2,740	21.3	2,874	22.3	12,413	2,570	20.7	2,686	21.6
Operators, fabricators, and laborers	17,250	3,394	19.7	3,590	20.8	16,901	3,235	19.1	3,422	20.3
Machine operators, assemblers, and inspectors	6,676	1,338	20.0	1,413	21.2	6,269	1,184	18.9	1,244	19.8
Transportation and material moving occupations..	5,226	1,215	23.2	1,292	24.7	5,294	1,163	22.0	1,241	23.4
Handlers, equipment cleaners, helpers, and laborers	5,347	841	15.7	885	16.6	5,338	888	16.6	938	17.6
Farming, forestry, and fishing	1,917	83	4.3	98	5.1	2,058	89	4.3	104	5.1
INDUSTRY										
Private wage and salary workers	103,142	9,201	8.9	10,028	9.7	102,419	8,756	8.5	9,548	9.3
Agriculture...	1,725	27	1.6	36	2.1	1,819	42	2.3	48	2.6
Nonagricultural industries	101,417	9,174	9.0	9,993	9.9	100,598	8,714	8.7	9,501	9.4
Mining..	531	66	12.4	70	13.1	458	39	8.5	46	10.0
Construction	7,054	1,275	18.1	1,321	18.7	6,883	1,184	17.2	1,228	17.8
Manufacturing...............................	18,501	2,697	14.6	2,861	15.5	17,324	2,484	14.3	2,621	15.1
Durable goods............................	11,252	1,690	15.0	1,787	15.9	10,344	1,612	15.6	1,687	16.3
Nondurable goods	7,249	1,008	13.9	1,073	14.8	6,979	872	12.5	935	13.4
Transportation and public utilities ..	7,502	1,752	23.4	1,851	24.7	7,432	1,712	23.0	1,810	24.3
Transportation	4,501	1,077	23.9	1,140	25.3	4,524	1,078	23.8	1,133	25.0
Communications and public utilities	3,001	675	22.5	711	23.7	2,908	634	21.8	677	23.3
Wholesale and retail trade.............	25,354	1,182	4.7	1,298	5.1	25,475	1,134	4.5	1,256	4.9
Wholesale trade	4,615	254	5.5	273	5.9	4,514	220	4.9	238	5.3
Retail trade.................................	20,740	928	4.5	1,025	4.9	20,961	914	4.4	1,018	4.9
Finance, insurance, and real estate ..	7,742	156	2.0	217	2.8	7,849	151	1.9	196	2.5
Services..	34,733	2,046	5.9	2,376	6.8	35,178	2,011	5.7	2,344	6.7
Government workers..........................	19,340	7,186	37.2	8,086	41.8	19,588	7,351	37.5	8,223	42.0
Federal...	3,324	1,046	31.5	1,221	36.8	3,296	1,063	32.3	1,244	37.7
State	5,729	1,737	30.3	1,980	34.6	5,706	1,758	30.8	2,005	35.1
Local	10,287	4,403	42.8	4,885	47.5	10,585	4,530	42.8	4,974	47.0

[1] Data refer to members of a labor union or an employee association similar to a union.
[2] Data refer to members of a labor union or an employee association similar to a union as well as workers who report no union affiliation but whose jobs are covered by a union or an employee association contract.

NOTE: Data for 2001 have been revised to reflect the introduction of Census 2000-based population controls. In addition, data on "represented by unions" incorporate a minor change to the allocation procedure for that item. The change in procedure had a small effect on the estimates. Data refer to the sole or principal job of full- and part-time workers. Excluded are all self-employed workers regardless of whether or not their businesses are incorporated.

Table 4. Median weekly earnings of full-time wage and salary workers by union affiliation, occupation, and industry

Occupation and industry	2001				2002			
	Total	Members of unions[1]	Repre-sented by unions[2]	Non-union	Total	Members of unions[1]	Repre-sented by unions[2]	Non-union
OCCUPATION								
Managerial and professional specialty ..	$859	$865	$860	$859	$884	$890	$884	$884
Executive, administrative, and managerial...	865	869	881	863	890	892	903	889
Professional specialty	854	864	855	854	879	889	880	879
Technical, sales, and administrative support..	521	614	606	513	550	633	625	536
Technicians and related support.......	673	731	737	663	694	775	762	682
Sales occupations..............................	574	557	554	575	601	572	570	601
Administrative support, including clerical...	486	598	588	472	503	613	609	490
Service occupations.............................	377	553	546	351	384	595	585	358
Protective service	628	807	794	518	647	820	811	519
Service, except protective service	345	426	423	333	352	448	445	341
Precision production, craft, and repair...	624	821	815	588	629	821	814	590
Operators, fabricators, and laborers	464	618	611	424	482	635	627	445
Machine operators, assemblers, and inspectors	454	585	579	419	474	616	608	440
Transportation and material moving occupations......................................	572	722	714	520	579	728	716	525
Handlers, equipment cleaners, helpers, and laborers	387	529	522	368	400	555	549	381
Farming, forestry, and fishing	351	588	580	342	363	548	524	357
INDUSTRY								
Private wage and salary workers	578	682	674	563	591	701	691	581
Agriculture...	368	(3)	(3)	367	372	(3)	(3)	371
Nonagricultural industries	582	683	675	569	595	702	692	585
Mining...	791	815	815	784	822	(3)	(3)	825
Construction	605	865	853	562	599	845	836	559
Manufacturing...................................	610	642	638	604	624	654	653	619
Durable goods...........................	631	674	668	622	647	675	673	640
Nondurable goods......................	580	604	602	573	595	613	614	591
Transportation and public utilities..	704	796	791	668	707	810	805	664
Transportation	643	781	775	609	642	782	778	605
Communications and public utilities.......................................	793	816	813	781	810	857	850	785
Wholesale and retail trade..............	466	539	525	462	480	552	540	477
Wholesale trade	622	653	659	620	626	664	659	623
Retail trade.................................	420	494	486	417	434	505	497	430
Finance, insurance, and real estate..	655	587	598	657	676	598	601	681
Services..	579	598	597	578	596	650	645	593
Government workers............................	684	753	748	620	708	770	767	640
Federal..	771	761	767	775	795	780	788	809
State	650	718	712	610	675	738	735	631
Local	667	764	755	580	688	782	773	597

[1] Data refer to members of a labor union or an employee association similar to a union.
[2] Data refer to members of a labor union or an employee association similar to a union as well as workers who report no union affiliation but whose jobs are covered by a union or an employee association contract.
[3] Data not shown where BLS base is less than 50,000.

NOTE: Data for 2001 have been revised to reflect the introduction of Census 2000-based population controls. In addition, data on "represented by unions" incorporate a minor change to the allocation procedure for that item. The change in procedure had a small effect on the estimates. Data refer to the sole or principal job of full- and part-time workers. Excluded are all self-employed workers regardless of whether or not their businesses are incorporated.

Appendix B. BLS Union Membership Data by State, 2001 and 2002

Union affiliation of employed wage and salary workers by state

(Numbers in thousands)

State	2001					2002				
	Total employed	Members of unions[1]		Represented by unions[2]		Total employed	Members of unions[1]		Represented by unions[2]	
		Total	Percent of employed	Total	Percent of employed		Total	Percent of employed	Total	Percent of employed
Alabama	1,803	169	9.4	194	10.7	1,761	157	8.9	185	10.5
Alaska	268	58	21.7	66	24.7	262	64	24.3	70	26.7
Arizona	2,174	127	5.9	141	6.5	2,184	120	5.5	144	6.6
Arkansas	1,036	65	6.3	80	7.8	1,064	63	5.9	73	6.8
California	14,219	2,299	16.2	2,526	17.8	13,983	2,454	17.5	2,639	18.9
Colorado	1,990	173	8.7	203	10.2	1,999	157	7.8	180	9.0
Connecticut	1,555	246	15.8	260	16.7	1,534	257	16.7	273	17.8
Delaware	375	46	12.1	50	13.3	369	41	11.1	45	12.1
District of Columbia	262	42	16.2	54	20.6	260	36	13.8	46	17.8
Florida	6,760	425	6.3	572	8.5	6,697	380	5.7	507	7.6
Georgia	3,652	259	7.1	301	8.2	3,643	218	6.0	256	7.0
Hawaii	522	123	23.7	136	26.0	492	120	24.4	125	25.4
Idaho	551	41	7.5	48	8.7	547	39	7.1	48	8.9
Illinois	5,613	1,016	18.1	1,083	19.3	5,450	1,066	19.6	1,122	20.6
Indiana	2,761	395	14.3	424	15.4	2,826	376	13.3	411	14.5
Iowa	1,365	175	12.8	209	15.3	1,395	155	11.1	190	13.6
Kansas	1,200	111	9.3	139	11.6	1,217	99	8.2	120	9.9
Kentucky	1,665	189	11.3	208	12.5	1,639	164	10.0	184	11.2
Louisiana	1,729	131	7.6	175	10.1	1,649	134	8.1	170	10.3
Maine	569	73	12.9	83	14.6	582	75	12.9	88	15.1
Maryland	2,426	335	13.8	408	16.8	2,460	346	14.1	415	16.9
Massachusetts	2,940	433	14.7	468	15.9	3,003	428	14.2	469	15.6
Michigan	4,488	975	21.7	1,016	22.6	4,335	914	21.1	953	22.0
Minnesota	2,432	428	17.6	445	18.3	2,503	439	17.6	457	18.3
Mississippi	1,099	61	5.5	99	9.0	1,052	69	6.6	84	8.0
Missouri	2,570	365	14.2	395	15.4	2,514	332	13.2	366	14.5
Montana	362	48	13.2	54	15.0	362	51	14.1	56	15.5
Nebraska	789	61	7.7	86	10.9	793	63	7.9	88	11.1
Nevada	954	162	17.0	175	18.4	971	147	15.2	162	16.7
New Hampshire	609	61	10.0	70	11.4	613	60	9.7	69	11.2
New Jersey	3,833	746	19.5	798	20.8	3,870	749	19.4	799	20.6
New Mexico	721	57	7.8	68	9.4	723	48	6.6	63	8.7
New York	7,802	2,063	26.4	2,152	27.6	7,844	1,987	25.3	2,088	26.6
North Carolina	3,521	129	3.7	151	4.3	3,427	111	3.2	138	4.0
North Dakota	293	22	7.5	25	8.6	291	24	8.1	28	9.8
Ohio	5,135	909	17.7	982	19.1	5,123	858	16.7	918	17.9
Oklahoma	1,391	117	8.4	130	9.3	1,421	127	8.9	150	10.6
Oregon	1,463	229	15.6	247	16.9	1,460	227	15.5	242	16.6
Pennsylvania	5,366	910	17.0	984	18.3	5,452	847	15.5	907	16.6
Rhode Island	466	83	17.8	86	18.5	471	81	17.2	84	17.9
South Carolina	1,623	73	4.5	91	5.6	1,643	81	4.9	101	6.1
South Dakota	339	20	6.0	26	7.6	350	19	5.6	24	6.9
Tennessee	2,421	185	7.6	211	8.7	2,466	222	9.0	258	10.5
Texas	8,872	489	5.5	591	6.7	8,818	451	5.1	571	6.5
Utah	971	66	6.8	75	7.8	973	60	6.2	73	7.5
Vermont	283	31	10.8	35	12.3	289	27	9.5	32	11.0
Virginia	3,233	163	5.0	209	6.5	3,208	189	5.9	249	7.8
Washington	2,487	460	18.5	498	20.0	2,553	471	18.4	512	20.0
West Virginia	719	105	14.6	115	16.0	693	92	13.3	97	14.0
Wisconsin	2,587	420	16.2	448	17.3	2,554	398	15.6	420	16.4
Wyoming	221	20	8.9	25	11.1	219	17	7.8	22	9.8

[1] Data refer to members of a labor union or an employee association similar to a union.

[2] Data refer to members of a labor union or an employee association similar to a union as well as workers who report no union affiliation but whose jobs are covered by a union or an employee association contract.

NOTE: Data for 2001 have been revised to reflect the introduction of Census 2000-based population controls. In addition, data on "represented by unions" incorporate a minor change to the allocation procedure for that item. The change in procedure had a small effect on the estimates. Data refer to the sole or principal job of full- and part-time workers. Excluded are all self-employed workers regardless of whether or not their businesses are incorporated.

Source: U.S. Department of Labor, Bureau of Labor Statistics, Current Population Survey, available at www.bls.gov/news.release/union2.nr0.htm

Appendix C. AFL-CIO Membership Data

Membership Report

Schedule No. 1
American Federation of Labor and Congress of Industrial Organizations Membership—
National and International Unions and Directly Affiliated Local Unions

The following table shows the average two-year membership of the AFL-CIO for each two-year convention period. The totals do not include the membership numbers related to affiliates' associate members, for which the affiliates pay a reduced monthly per capita tax. The totals are expressed in thousands of members.

Period	Membership
1955	12,622
1956-57	13,020
1958-59	12,779
1960-61	12,553
1962-63	12,496
1964-65	12,919
1966-67	13,781
1968-69	13,005
1970-71	13,177
1972-73	13,407
1974-75	14,070
1976-77	13,542
1978-79	13,621
1980-81	13,602
1982-83	13,758
1984-85	13,109
1986-87	12,702
1988-89	13,556
1990-91	13,933
1992-93	13,299
1994-95	13,007
1996-97	12,905
1998-99	12,952
2000-01	13,164

Source: AFL-CIO

Schedule No. 2
American Federation of Labor and Congress of Industrial Organizations Membership—
National and International Union Affiliates

The average annual membership figures in this report were computed by taking the total number of regular members on whom per capita tax payments were made to the AFL-CIO for the 12 months ended in June of each year, and dividing that total by the number of months for which payments were made.

Membership reported at conventions and used as the basis for the determination of voting strength at conventions is determined by the average membership reported by affiliates during the 24 months ending in the June just prior to the convention.

Associate member payments are not included in the figures below, nor in computing average membership for the purposes of determining voting strength at conventions.

The figures below incorporate all mergers that have occurred since the convention held in 1999.

Organizations	FYE 6/30/99	FYE 6/30/00	FYE 6/30/01
Actors and Artistes	69,000	69,000	69,000
Air Line Pilots	40,915	43,633	46,048
Air Traffic Controllers	11,503	12,315	13,398
Asbestos Workers	12,000	12,000	15,557
Automobile, Aerospace & Agricultural Implement Workers	741,706	742,409	731,396
Bakery, Confectionery, Tobacco Workers and Grain Millers	104,875	108,250	103,939
Boilermakers	39,728	39,540	39,452
Bricklayers	62,275	63,784	62,275
Communications Workers	625,967	627,080	625,192
Electrical Workers	658,647	663,602	676,611
Elevator Constructors	20,712	21,869	23,093
Engineers, Operating	289,083	281,167	280,000
Farm Workers	16,000	16,000	16,000
Fire Fighters	171,500	175,000	193,750
Flight Attendants	38,757	40,671	42,657
Food and Commercial Workers	1,122,521	1,140,884	1,129,688
Glass, Molders, Pottery, Plastics and Allied Workers	60,667	57,466	53,684
Glass Workers, American Flint	17,616	17,726	18,267
Government Employees	181,317	191,260	196,902
Graphic Communications	86,024	88,772	71,351
Horseshoers	76	75	75
Hotel Employees & Restaurant Employees	229,726	234,509	240,938
Iron Workers	83,054	86,294	90,546
Laborers	299,080	301,591	310,468
Laundry and Dry Cleaning	11,082	8,146	7,903
Letter Carriers	210,000	210,000	210,000
Locomotive Engineers	23,083	25,050	26,000
Longshoremen	61,849	61,601	61,997
Longshore and Warehouse	36,821	37,766	35,373
Machinists and Aerospace Workers	456,030	458,008	446,078
Maintenance of Way Employes	29,307	29,645	29,239
Marine Engineers	29,507	28,055	28,248
Mine Workers	75,250	75,250	70,125
Musicians	22,688	18,267	12,300
Needletrades, Industrial and Textile Employees	205,000	208,232	206,801
Novelty and Production Workers	18,112	16,989	17,420

Organizations	FYE 6/30/99	FYE 6/30/00	FYE 6/30/01
Nurses, United American*	0	0	100,000
Office and Professional Employees	90,635	95,760	106,134
Painters and Allied Trades	97,103	102,044	101,617
Paper, Allied-Industrial, Chemical and Energy Workers	289,969	262,816	283,916
Plasterers and Cement Masons	29,070	29,500	29,500
Plate Printers, Die Stampers and Engravers	200	200	200
Plumbing and Pipe Fitting	219,800	219,800	219,800
Police Associations	31,141	37,184	38,174
Postal Workers	280,956	275,915	266,002
Professional Athletes	1,700	1,700	1,700
Professional and Technical Engineers	24,818	31,743	36,421
Radio Association	243	130	125
Roofers, Waterproofers and Allied Workers	20,907	21,443	20,888
School Administrators	12,300	12,300	12,450
School Employees Association, California**	0	0	129,000
Seafarers	77,250	80,250	80,250
Service Employees	1,143,932	1,261,276	1,281,770
Sheet Metal Workers	93,000	93,000	93,000
Signalmen, Railroad	9,735	9,499	9,319
Stage Employees and Moving Picture Technicians	49,100	55,788	57,150
State, County and Municipal Employees	1,247,051	1,249,306	1,265,894
Steelworkers	468,313	450,436	438,908
Teachers	786,921	822,191	893,453
Teamsters	1,231,144	1,226,300	1,217,880
Train Dispatchers	2,100	2,100	2,100
Transit Union	103,942	108,117	112,142
Transport Workers	75,000	75,000	88,750
Transportation Communications	70,953	90,725	92,300
Utility Workers	43,088	39,511	38,902
Writers	3,600	3,600	3,800
Total	**12,665,449**	**12,869,540**	**13,223,316**

* United American Nurses affiliated 7/1/01.

** California School Employees Association affiliated 8/1/01.

Schedule No. 3
American Federation of Labor and Congress of Industrial Organizations Membership—
National and International Union Affiliates

The following table shows the average per capita membership of current affiliates reported to the AFL-CIO for the year 1955; the two-year periods ending in 1965, 1975 and 1985; and the two-year periods ending June 30, 1995, 1997, 1999 and 2001. The totals are expressed in thousands of members.

Organizations	1955	1965	1975	1985	1995	1997	1999	2001
Actors and Artistes of America, Associated	34	61	76	100	80	69	69	69
Air Line Pilots Association	9	18	47	33	35	37	40	45
Air Traffic Controllers Association, National							o 7	13
Asbestos Workers, International Association of Heat and Frost Insulators and	9	12	13	12	12	12	12	14
Automobile, Aerospace & Agricultural Implement Workers of America International Union, United	1260	1150	c	974	751	766	745	737
Bakery, Confectionery and Tobacco Workers International Union				115	96	95	p	p
Bakery, Confectionery, Tobacco Workers and Grain Millers International Union							p 110	106
Boilermakers, Iron Ship Builders, Blacksmiths, Forgers and Helpers, International Brotherhood of	151	108	123	110	42	43	40	39
Bricklayers and Allied Craftsworkers, International Union of	120	120	143	95	84	71	62	63
Communications Workers of America	249	288	476	524	478	480	508	u 626
Electronic, Electrical, Salaried, Machine and Furniture Workers, AFL-CIO, International Union of					135	130	119	u
Electrical Workers, International Brotherhood of	460	616	856	791	679	657	656	670
Elevator Constructors, International Union of	10	12	13	20	20	20	20	22
Engineers, International Union of Operating	200	270	300	330	298	295	291	281
Farm Workers of America, AFL-CIO, United		d 14		12	16	16	16	16
Fire Fighters, International Association of	72	87	123	142	151	155	166	184
Flight Attendants, Association of				f 17	31	34	38	42
Food and Commercial Workers International Union, United				989	983	986	1101	1135
Glass, Molders, Pottery, Plastics and Allied Workers International Union				72	69	66	63	56
Glass Workers Union, American Flint	28	31	35	24	20	18	18	18
Government Employees, American Federation of	47	132	255	199	153	167	179	194
Grain Millers, American Federation of	33	25	29	30	20	21	p	p
Graphic Communications International Union				141	94	93	87	80
Health and Human Service Employees Union, National						n 57	n	n
Horseshoers of United States and Canada, International Union of Journeymen	1	1	1	1	1	1	1	1
Hotel Employees & Restaurant Employees International Union	300	300	421	327	241	223	228	238
Iron Workers, International Association of Bridge, Structural, Ornamental and Reinforcing	133	132	160	140	82	80	81	88
Laborers' International Union of North America		403	475	383	352	298	298	306
Laundry and Dry Cleaning International Union, AFL-CIO		a 22	20	15	11	11	11	8
Letter Carriers, National Association of	100	130	151	186	210	210	210	210
Locomotive Engineers, Brotherhood of					i 19	19	21	26
Longshoremen's Association, AFL-CIO, International		50	60	65	61	61	61	62
Longshore and Warehouse Union, International					j 36	j 32	35	37
Machinists and Aerospace Workers, International Association of	627	663	780	520	448	411	446	452
Maintenance of Way Employes, Brotherhood of	159	77	71	61	31	29	29	29
Marine Engineers' Beneficial Association					27	27	26	28
Maritime Union, National					21	21	q 13	q
Mine Workers of America, United					k 75	75	75	73
Musicians of the United States and Canada, American Federation of	250	225	215	67	35	33	25	15
Needletrades, Industrial and Textile Employees, Union of						235	210	208
Newspaper Guild, The	21	23	26	24	20	22	r	r
Novelty and Production Workers, International Union of Allied					23	20	19	18	17
Nurses, United American								v 100

Organizations	1955	1965	1975	1985	1995	1997	1999	2001
Office and Professional Employees International Union	44	52	74	90	86	82	90	101
Oil, Chemical and Atomic Workers International Union	160	140	145	108	83	81	s	s
Painters and Allied Trades of the United States and Canada, International Union of	182	160	160	133	95	80	92	102
Paper, Allied-Industrial, Chemical and Energy Workers International Union							s 293	273
Paperworkers International Union, United			275	232	233	230	s	s
Plasterers' and Cement Masons' International Association of the United States and Canada, Operative	60	68	55	46	29	28	29	29
Plate Printers, Die Stampers and Engravers Union of North America, International	1	1	1	1	1	1	1	1
Plumbing and Pipe Fitting Industry of the United States and Canada, United Association of Journeymen and Apprentices of the	200	217	228	226	220	220	220	220
Police Associations, International Union of				g 14	26	25	27	38
Postal Workers Union, AFL-CIO, American			249	232	261	277	279	271
Professional Athletes, Federation of				h 2	2	2	2	2
Professional and Technical Engineers, International Federation of			14	19	22	23	25	34
Radio Association, American	2	2	1	1	1	1	1	1
Retail, Wholesale and Department Store Union	97	114	118	106	76	72	t	t
Roofers, Waterproofers and Allied Workers, United Union of				26	21	20	21	21
School Administrators, American Federation of			e 7	9	11	11	12	12
School Employees Association, California								w 129
Seafarers International Union of North America	42	80	80	80	80	80	79	80
Service Employees International Union, AFL-CIO			480	688	1027	1037	1104	1272
Sheet Metal Workers International Association	50	100	120	108	106	96	93	93
Signalmen, Brotherhood of Railroad	15	11	10	11	10	10	10	9
Stage Employees and Moving Picture Technicians, Artists and Allied Crafts of the United States and Canada, International Alliance of Theatrical	46	50	50	50	51	48	48	56
State, County and Municipal Employees, American Federation of	99	237	647	997	1183	1242	1242	1258
Steelworkers of America, United	980	876	1062	572	403	503	479	445
Teachers, American Federation of	40	97	396	470	613	682	759	858
Teamsters, International Brotherhood of					l 1285	1276	1238	1222
Train Dispatchers Department, American		b 3	3	3	2	2	2	2
Transit Union, Amalgamated		98	90	94	95	97	102	110
Transport Workers Union of America	80	80	95	85	75	75	75	82
Transportation Communications International Union					58	64	67	92
Utility Workers Union of America	53	50	52	52	46	46	42	39
Writers Guild of America, East, Inc.					m 3	3	4	4

a   Charter granted 5/12/58.
b   Charter granted 1/29/57.
c   Disaffiliated 7/1/68. Reaffiliated 7/1/81.
d   Charter granted 2/21/72.
e   Charter granted to School Administrators and Supervisors Organizing Committee 2/22/71; chartered under present title 2/21/76.
f   Charter granted 2/23/84.
g   Charter granted 2/19/79.
h   Charter granted 11/14/79.
i   Charter granted 4/1/89.
j   Charter granted 8/22/88. Exonerated from per capita taxes for calendar year 1995.
k   Affiliated 10/1/89.
l   International Brotherhood of Teamsters, Chauffeurs, Warehousemen and Helpers affiliated 11/1/87.
m   Affiliated 8/19/89.
n   National Health and Human Service Employees Union affiliated 2/20/96, then merged with Service Employees International Union effective 4/1/98.
o   Charter granted 3/20/98.
p   Bakery, Confectionery and Tobacco Workers International Union merged with American Federation of Grain Millers to form Bakery, Confectionery, Tobacco Workers and Grain Millers International Union effective 1/1/99.
q   National Maritime Union affiliated with Marine Engineers' Beneficial Association effective 3/27/98; disaffiliated from MEBA and affiliated with Seafarers International Union of North America effective 1/1/99. Average membership reported for the two-year period ended 6/99 does not include NMU members for which payment was received from MEBA during the nine-month period of NMU's affiliation with MEBA. NMU fully merged with Seafarers International Union of North America effective 3/16/01.
r   The Newspaper Guild merged with Communications Workers of America effective 7/1/97.
s   United Paperworkers International Union merged with Oil, Chemical and Atomic Workers International Union to form Paper, Allied-Industrial, Chemical and Energy Workers International Union effective 1/4/99.
t   Retail, Wholesale and Department Store Union merger with United Food and Commercial Workers International Union completed 10/1/98.
u   International Union of Electronic, Electrical, Salaried, Machine and Furniture Workers merged with Communications Workers of America effective 10/1/00.
v   United American Nurses affiliated 7/1/01.
w   California School Employees Association affiliated 8/1/01.

Schedule No. 4
American Federation of Labor and Congress of Industrial Organizations

The following table shows the average per capita membership paid to the AFL-CIO by former affiliates for the year 1955 and subsequent two-year periods ending in 1965, 1975, 1985 and 1995. The totals are expressed in thousands of members.

Organizations	1955	1965	1975	1985	1995	
Agricultural Workers Organizing Committee AFL-CIO		2				Charter granted to Farm Workers Organizing Committee 8/23/66, bringing together Agricultural Workers Organizing Committee, AFL-CIO and Independent National Farm Workers Association.
Agricultural Workers Union, National	4					Merged into Amalgamated Meat Cutters and Butcher Workmen, 8/16/60.
Air Line Dispatchers Association	1	1	1			Dissolved, 4/1/77.
Aluminum Workers International Union	20	22	27			Merged to form Aluminum, Brick and Clay Workers, 7/23/81.
Aluminum, Brick and Clay Workers International Union						Merged to form Aluminum, Brick and Glass Workers, 9/1/82.
Aluminum, Brick and Glass Workers, International Union of				49	37	Merged with United Steelworkers of America, 12/17/96.
Automobile Workers of America, International Union, United	73					Title changed to Allied Industrial Workers of America, 5/1/56.
Bakery and Confectionery Workers International Union, American		75				Merged to form Bakery and Confectionery Workers International Union of America, 12/4/69.
Bakery and Confectionery Workers International Union of America	136		123			Expelled by convention 12/12/57. Merged with American Bakery and Confectionery Workers 12/4/69 to form Bakery and Confectionery Workers International Union of America; then merged to form Bakery, Confectionery and Tobacco Workers, 8/17/78.
Barbers and Beauty Culturists Union of America	3					Reaffiliated with Barbers, Hairdressers and Cosmetologists', 5/1/56.
Barbers, Hairdressers and Cosmetologists' International Union of America, The Journeymen	65	73	42			Merged with United Food and Commercial Workers, 9/1/80.
Bill Posters, Billers and Distributors of the United States and Canada, International Alliance of	2	1				Charter surrendered 10/31/71.
Bookbinders, International Brotherhood of	51	57				Merged to form Graphic Arts International Union, 9/4/72.
Boot Shoe Workers' Union	40	40	34			Merged with Retail Clerks, 9/1/77.
Brewery, Flour, Cereal, Soft Drink and Distillery Workers, International Union of, United	45	42				Certificate of affiliation revoked, AFL-CIO convention, 10/19/73.
Brick and Clay Workers of America, The United	23	21	16			Merged to form Aluminum, Brick and Clay Workers, 7/23/81.
Broadcast Employees and Technicians, National Association of	4	4	5	5		Merged with Communications Workers of America, 1/1/94.
Broom and Whisk Makers Union, International	1					Disbanded, 8/22/63.
Building Service Employees International Union	205	305				Title changed to Service Employees International Union, 2/19/68.
Cement, Lime and Gypsum Workers International Union, United	35	30	29			Merged with Boilermakers, Iron Ship Builders, Blacksmiths, Forgers and Helpers, 4/1/84.
Chemical Workers Union, International	79	70	58	40	34	Merged with United Food and Commercial Workers International Union, 7/1/96.

Organizations	1955	1965	1975	1985	1995	
Cigarmakers' International Union of America	9	4	2			Merged with Retail, Wholesale and Department Store Union, 8/6/74.
Clerks, National Federation of Post Office	97					Merged with National Postal Transport Association 12/6/61 to become United Federation of Postal Clerks.
Clothing and Textile Workers Union, Amalgamated				228	129	Merged with International Ladies' Garment Workers Union to form Union of Needletrades, Industrial and Textile Employees, 7/1/95.
Clothing Workers of America, Amalgamated	210	288	232			Merged to form Amalgamated Clothing and Textile Workers Union, 6/2/76.
Commercial Telegraphers Union, The	29	22				Title changed to Telegraph Workers, 2/19/68.
Coopers International Union of North America	3	2	2	1		Merged with Glass, Molders, Pottery, Plastics and Allied Workers International Union, 9/1/92.
Distillery, Rectifying, Wine and Allied Workers International Union of America	26	24	18			Title changed to Distillery, Wine and Allied Workers International Union, 2/27/78.
Distillery, Wine and Allied Workers International Union, AFL-CIO/CLC				14	8	Merged with United Food and Commercial Workers International Union, 10/4/95.
Dolls, Toys, Playthings, Novelties and Allied Products of the United States and Canada, AFL-CIO, International Union of	14	22	30			Title changed to Novelty Production Workers, 2/27/78.
Electrical, Radio and Machine Workers, International Union of	271	265	255			Title changed to Electronic, Electrical, Technical, Salaried and Machine Workers, AFL-CIO, International Union of, 7/83.
Electronic, Electrical, Technical, Salaried and Machine Workers, AFL-CIO, International Union of						Title changed to Electronic, Electrical, Salaried, Machine and Furniture Workers, AFL-CIO, International Union, 1/1/87.
Engravers and Marking Device Workers Union, International Metal	1					Merged into International Association of Machinists, 9/1/56.
Firemen and Oilers, International Brotherhood of	57	44	40	25		Merged with Service Employees International Union, 2/1/95.
Furniture Workers of America, United	34	32	28	21		Merged to form Electronic, Electrical, Salaried, Machine and Furniture Workers, AFL-CIO, International Union, 1/1/87.
Garment Workers of America, United	40	35	32	28		Merged with United Food and Commercial Workers International Union, 12/1/94.
Garment Workers Union, International Ladies'	383	363	363	210	123	Merged with Amalgamated Clothing and Textile Workers Union to form Needletrades, Industrial and Textile Employees, 7/1/95.
Glass and Ceramic Workers of North America, United	41	33	28			Merged to form Aluminum, Brick and Glass Workers, 9/1/82.
Glass Bottle Blowers' Association of the United States and Canada	47	65	75			Merged to form Glass, Pottery, Plastics and Allied Workers, 9/1/82.
Glass Cutters League of America, Window	2	1	1			Merged with Glass Bottle Blowers, 8/1/75.
Glove Workers Union of America, International	3					Merged into Amalgamated Clothing Workers, 12/6/61.
Government and Civic Employees Organizing Committee	27					Merged into State, County and Municipal Employees, 8/1/56.
Granite Cutters International Association of America, The	4	3	1			Merged with Tile, Marble, Terrazzo, Finishers and Shopmen, 5/23/83 (Retroactive to 1/7/80).
Graphic Arts International Union			93			Merged to form Graphic Communications International Union, 7/1/83.

Organizations	1955	1965	1975	1985	1995	
Hatters, Cap and Millinery Workers International Union, United	32	32	15			Merged into Amalgamated Clothing and Textile Workers Union, 12/7/82.
Hod Carriers, Building and Common Laborers Union of America, International	372					Title changed to Laborers' International Union, 9/20/65.
Hosiery Workers, American Federation of	15	5				Merged with Textile Workers Union of America, 4/28/65.
Hospital and Health Care Employees, National Union of				23		Charter granted 10/1/84; merged with Service Employees International Union and American Federation of State, County and Municipal Employees, 6/1/89.
Industrial Workers of America, International Union, Allied		71	93	63		Merged with United Paperworkers International, 1/1/94.
Insurance Agents International Union		13				Merged into Insurance Workers International Union, 5/18/59.
Insurance Workers of America		9				Merged into Insurance Workers International Union, 5/18/59.
Insurance Workers International Union, AFL-CIO		21	22			Merged with United Food and Commercial Workers International Union, 10/1/83.
Jewelry Workers Union, International	20	14	10			Merged with Service Employees International Union, 7/1/80.
Lathers, International Union of Wood, Wire and Metal	16	16	12			Merged with United Brotherhood of Carpenters and Joiners, 8/16/79.
Leather Goods, Plastics and Novelty Workers Union, International	30	34	39	21	5	Merged with Service Employees International Union, 5/1/96.
Leather Workers International Union of North America	2	5	2	1		Suspended in accordance with Article XV, Section 5, of the AFL-CIO Constitution.
Lithographers and Photoengravers International Union			30*			*Affiliated for only part of period although membership shown is average for 24-month period. Merged to form Graphic Arts International Union, 9/24/72.
Lithographers of America, Amalgamated	28					Disaffiliated, 8/21/58.
Locomotive Firemen and Enginemen, Brotherhood of		41				Merged into United Transportation Union, 12/16/68.
Longshoremen, International Brotherhood of	8					Merged into Longshoremen's Association, 11/17/59.
Marble, Slate and Stone Polishers, Rubbers and Sawyers, Tile & Marble Setters Helpers and Terrazzo Helpers, International Association of	6	8	8			Title changed to Tile, Marble, Terrazzo, Finishers and Shopmen, 2/20/76.
Marine Engineers' Beneficial Association, National	9	9	20	22		At its 2/95 meeting, the AFL-CIO Executive Council agreed that henceforth the National Marine Engineers' Beneficial Association would become two separate entities: the Marine Engineers' Beneficial Association and the National Maritime Union.
Marine and Shipbuilding Workers of America, Industrial Union of	27	22	22	17		Merged into International Association of Machinists and Aerospace Workers, 10/17/88.
Maritime Union of America, National	37	45	35	17		Merged with National Marine Engineers' Beneficial Association, 3/29/88.
Masters, Mates and Pilots, International Organization of	9	9				Merged with Longshoremen's Association, 5/12/71.
Master Mechanics and Foremen of Navy Yards and Naval Stations, National Association of	1					Withdrew, 4/1/64.
Mechanics Educational Society of America	49	37	23	5	3	Merged with United Automobile, Aerospace & Agricultural Implement Workers International Union, 1/1/97.

Organizations	1955	1965	1975	1985	1995	
Meat Cutters and Butcher Workmen of North America, Amalgamated	263	330	450			Merged to form United Food and Commercial Workers International Union, 8/8/79.
Metal Polishers, Buffers, Platers and Allied Workers International Union	15	11	9	5	3	Merged with International Brotherhood of Boilermakers, Iron Ship Builders, Blacksmiths, Forgers and Helpers, 12/1/96.
Molders and Allied Workers Union, AFL-CIO, International	67	50	50	32		Merged with Glass, Molders, Pottery, Plastics and Allied Workers International Union, 5/1/88.
Packinghouse, Food and Allied Workers, United	118	71				Merged with Meat Cutters and Butcher Workmen, 7/9/68.
Paper Makers, International Brotherhood of	60					Merged into Papermakers and Paperworkers, 3/6/57.
Paper Workers of America, United	40					Merged into Papermakers and Paperworkers, 3/6/57.
Papermakers and Paperworkers, United		121				Merged to form United Paperworkers International Union, 8/9/72.
Pattern Makers League of North America	11	10	10	8		Merged with International Association of Machinists and Aerospace Workers, 10/1/91.
Photo Engravers Union of North America, International	16					Merged into Lithographers and Photoengravers, 9/7/64.
Porters, Brotherhood of Sleeping Car	10	5	1			Merged with Brotherhood of Railway, Airline and Steamship Clerks, Freight Handlers, Express and Station Employees, 4/1/78.
Post Office and General Service Maintenance Employees, National Association						Merged to form American Postal Workers Union, 7/1/71.
Post Office Mail Handlers, Watchmen, Messengers and Group Leaders, National Association of	1	1				Merged with Laborers, 4/20/68.
Post Office Motor Vehicle Employees, National Federation of		5				Merged to form American Postal Workers Union, 7/1/71.
Postal Transport Association, National	22					Merged with National Federation of Post Office Clerks, 12/6/61 to become United Federation of Postal Clerks.
Postal Clerks, United Federation of		117				Merged to form American Postal Workers Union, 7/1/71.
Pottery and Allied Workers, International Brotherhood of	23	19	17			Affiliated with Seafarers, 6/21/76; merged to form Glass, Pottery, Plastics and Allied Workers, 9/1/82.
Printing and Graphic Communications Union, International			105			Merged to form Graphic Communications International Union, 7/1/83.
Printing Pressmen's and Assistants' Union of North America, International	87	100				Merged to form Printing and Graphic Communications Union, 10/17/73.
Pulp, Sulphite and Paper Mill Workers of the United States and Canada, International Brotherhood of	154	135				Merged to form United Paperworkers International Union, 8/9/72
Radio and Television Directors Guild	1					Disaffiliated, 1/1/60.
Railroad Telegraphers, The Order of	30					Title changed to Transportation-Communication Employees Union, 2/25/65.
Railroad Trainmen, Brotherhood of		98				Merged into United Transportation Union, 12/16/68.
Railway Carmen of the United States and Canada, Brotherhood of	116	84	56	33		Merged with Brotherhood of Railway, Airline and Steamship Clerks, Freight Handlers, Express and Station Employees, 8/6/86.

Organizations	1955	1965	1975	1985	1995	
Railway, Airline and Steamship Clerks, Freight Handlers, Express and Station Employees, Brotherhood of	264	186	160	102		Title Changed to Transportation Communications Union, 9/1/87.
Railway Patrolmen's International Union	3	2				Merged with Brotherhood of Railway, Airline and Steamship Clerks, Freight Handlers, Express and Station Employees, 1/1/69.
Railway Supervisors Association, American		6	6			Merged with Brotherhood of Railway, Airline and Steamship Clerks, Freight Handlers, Express and Station Employees, 8/6/80.
Retail Clerks International Union	259	410	602			Merged to form United Food and Commercial Workers, 8/8/79.
Roofers, Damp and Waterproof Workers Association, United Slate, Tile and Composition	18	22	27			Title changed to Roofers, Waterproofers and Allied Workers, 8/7/78.
Rubber, Cork, Linoleum and Plastics Workers of America, United	163	153	173	106	79	Merged with International Brotherhood of Boilermakers, Iron Ship Builders, Blacksmiths, Forgers and Helpers, 12/1/96.
Shoe Workers of America, United	51	45	25			Merged with Amalgamated Clothing and Textile Workers Union, 3/5/79.
Siderographers, International Association of	1	1	1	1		Merged with International Association of Machinists and Aerospace Workers, 9/15/92.
Special Delivery Messengers, The National Association of	2	1				Merged to form American Postal Workers Union, 7/1/71.
Stereotypers', Electrotypers' and Platemakers' Union, International	12	11				Merged to form Printing and Graphic Communications Union, 10/17/73.
Stone and Allied Products Workers of America, United	11	11				Merged with Steelworkers, 11/1/72.
Stonecutters Association of North America, Journeymen	2	2				Merged with Laborers' International Union, 2/19/68.
Stove, Furnace and Allied Appliance Workers International Union of North America	10	9	3	3		Merged with International Brotherhood of Boilermakers, Iron Ship Builders, Blacksmiths, Forgers and Helpers, 10/1/94.
Street and Electric Railway Employees of America, Amalgamated Association of	139					Title changed to Amalgamated Transit Union, 2/5/61.
Switchmen's Union of North America	11	9				Merged into United Transportation Union, 12/16/68.
Technical Engineers, American Federation of	10	11				Title changed to Professional and Technical Engineers, 5/73.
Telegraph Workers, United			12	9		Merged into Communications Workers of America, 10/17/86.
Textile Workers of America, United	49	36	36	23	15	Merged with United Food and Commercial Workers, International Union, 11/1/95.
Textile Workers Union of America	203	123	105			Merged to form Amalgamated Clothing and Textile Workers Union, 6/2/76.
Tile, Marble, Terrazzo, Finishes, Shop Workers and Granite Cutters International Union				7		Merged into United Brotherhood of Carpenters and Joiners, 11/10/88.
Tobacco Workers International Union	27	24	26			Merged to form Bakery, Confectionery and Tobacco Workers, 8/17/78.
Transport Service Employees of America, United	3	3				Merged with Brotherhood of Railway, Airline and Steamship Clerks, Freight Handlers, Express and Station Employees, 10/1/72.

Organizations	1955	1965	1975	1985	1995	
Transportation-Communication Employees Union		29				Merged with Brotherhood of Railway, Airline and Steamship Clerks, Freight Handlers, Express and Station Employees, 2/21/69.
Typographic Union, International	78	87	73	38		Merged with Communications Workers of America, 1/1/87.
Upholsterers' International Union of North America	51	50	50	31		Merged with Steelworkers, 10/8/85.
Wallpaper Craftsmen and Workers of North America, United	1					Merged with Pulp, Sulphite and Paper Mill Workers, 4/28/58.
Weavers Protective Association, American Wire	1					Merged with Papermakers and Paperworkers, 2/16/58.
Woodworkers of America International	91	49	52	34		Merged with International Association of Machinists and Aerospace Workers, 5/1/94.
Yardmasters of America, Railroad	4	4	4	3		Merged with United Transportation Union, 10/1/85.

Appendix D. Reports Required Under the LMRDA and the CSRA

Union Reports

Form Number and Name	Report Required to be Filed by	Signatures Required	When Due
Form LM-1 (initial) Labor Organization Information Report	Each union subject to the LMRDA or CSRA	President and secretary or corresponding principal officers of the reporting union	Within 90 days after the union becomes subject to the LMRDA or CSRA
Form LM-1 (amended) Labor Organization Information Report	Each reporting union (except Federal employee unions) which made changes in practices and procedures listed in Item 18 of Form LM-1 which are not contained in the union's constitution and bylaws	President and treasurer or corresponding principal officers of the reporting union	With union's Form LM-2, LM-3, or LM-4 within 90 days after the end of the union's fiscal year during which the changes were made
Form LM-2* Labor Organization Annual Report	Each reporting union with total annual receipts of $200,000 or more and by the parent union for subordinate unions under trusteeship	President and treasurer or corresponding principal officers of the reporting union or, if under trusteeship at time of filing, by the president and treasurer or corresponding principal officers of the parent union, and trustees of the subordinate union	Within 90 days after the end of the union's fiscal year or, if the union loses its reporting identity through dissolution, merger, consolidation, or otherwise, within 30 days after date of termination
Form LM-3* Labor Organization Annual Report	Each reporting union with total annual receipts of less than $200,000 may use the simplified Form LM-3 if not in trusteeship	President and treasurer or corresponding principal officers of the reporting union	Within 90 days after the end of the union's fiscal year or, if the union loses its reporting identity through dissolution, merger, consolidation, or otherwise, within 30 days after date of termination
Form LM-4* Labor Organization Annual Report	Each reporting union with total annual receipts of less than $10,000 may use the abbreviated Form LM-4 if not in trusteeship	President and treasurer or corresponding principal officers of the reporting union	Within 90 days after the end of the union's fiscal year or, if the union loses its reporting identity through dissolution, merger, consolidation, or otherwise, within 30 days after date of termination

Source: U.S. Department of Labor. *Ed. Note: Copies of reports for the years 2000 and later may be viewed at http://www.union-reports.dol.gov.

Union Trusteeship Reports

Form Number and Name	Report Required to be Filed by	Signatures Required	When Due
Form LM-15 (initial) Trusteeship Report (including Statement of Assets and Liabilities)	Each parent union which imposes a trusteeship over a subordinate union	President and treasurer or corresponding principal officers of the parent union, and trustees of the subordinate union	Within 30 days after imposing the trusteeship
Form LM-15 (semiannual) Trusteeship Report (excluding Statement of Assets and Liabilities)	Each parent union which continues a trusteeship over a subordinate union for 6 months or more	President and treasurer or corresponding principal officers of the parent union, and trustees of the subordinate union	Within 30 days after the end of each 6-month period during the trusteeship
Form LM-15A Report on Selection of Delegates and Officers	Each parent union which imposes a trusteeship over a subordinate union if during the trusteeship the parent union held any convention or other policy-determining body to which the subordinate union sent delegates or would have sent delegates if not in trusteeship, or the parent union conducted an election of officers	President and treasurer or corresponding principal officers of the parent union, and trustees of the subordinate union	As required, with Form LM-15 within 30 days after the imposition of the trusteeship or end of each 6-month period, or with Form LM-16 within 90 days after the end of the trusteeship or the subordinate union's loss of reporting identity through dissolution, merger, consolidation, or otherwise
Form LM-16 Terminal Trusteeship Report	Each parent union which ends a trusteeship over a subordinate union or if the union in trusteeship loses its reporting identity	President and treasurer or corresponding principal officers of the parent union, and trustees of the subordinate union	Within 90 days after the end of the trusteeship or the subordinate union's loss of reporting identity through dissolution, merger, consolidation, or otherwise

Other Reports

Form Number and Name	Report Required to be Filed by	Signatures Required	When Due
Form LM-10 Employer Report	Each employer which engages in certain specified financial dealings with its employees, unions, union officers, or labor relations consultants or which makes expenditures for certain objects relating to employees' or unions' activities	President and treasurer or corresponding principal officers of the reporting employer	Within 90 days after the end of the employer's fiscal year
Form LM-20 Agreement and Activities Report	Each person who enters into an agreement or arrangement with an employer to persuade employees about exercising their rights to organize and bargain collectively, or to obtain information about employee or union activity in connection with a labor dispute involving the employer	President and treasurer or corresponding principal officers of the consultant firm or, if self-employed, the individual required to file the report	Within 30 days after entering into such agreement or arrangement
Form LM-21 Receipts and Disbursements Report	Each person who enters into an agreement or arrangement with an employer to persuade employees about exercising their rights to organize and bargain collectively, or to obtain information about employee or union activity in connection with a labor dispute involving the employer	President and treasurer or corresponding principal officers of the consultant firm or, if self-employed, the individual required to file the report	Within 90 days after the end of the consultant's fiscal year
Form LM-30 Labor Organization Officer and Employee Report	Each union officer (including trustees of subordinate unions under trusteeship) and employee (other than employees performing exclusively clerical or custodial services), if the officer/employee, or the office/employee's spouse, or minor child directly or indirectly had certain economic interests during past fiscal year	Union officers and employees required to file such reports	Within 90 days after the end of the union officer's or employee's fiscal year
Form S-1 Surety Company Annual Report	Each surety company having a bond in force insuring a welfare or pension plan covered by ERISA, or insuring any union or trust in which a union covered by the LMRDA is interested	President and treasurer or corresponding principal officers of the surety company	Within 150 days after the end of the surety company's fiscal year

Abbreviations Index

Labor Organizations Index

Officers and Key Staff Index

Web Sites Index